AZ SUPER SCALE
GREAT BRITAIN
NORTHERN IRELAND

Journey Route Planning maps

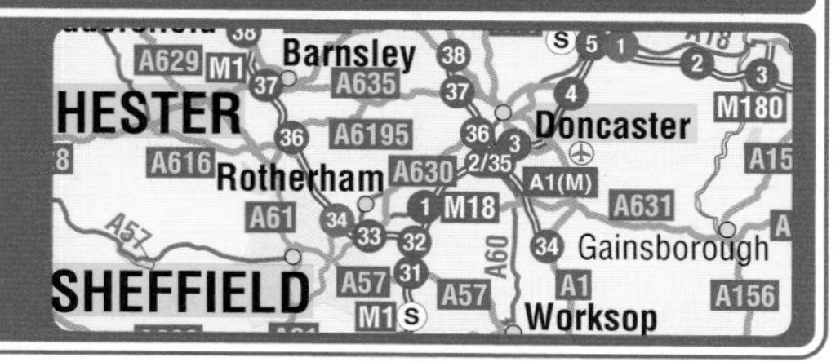

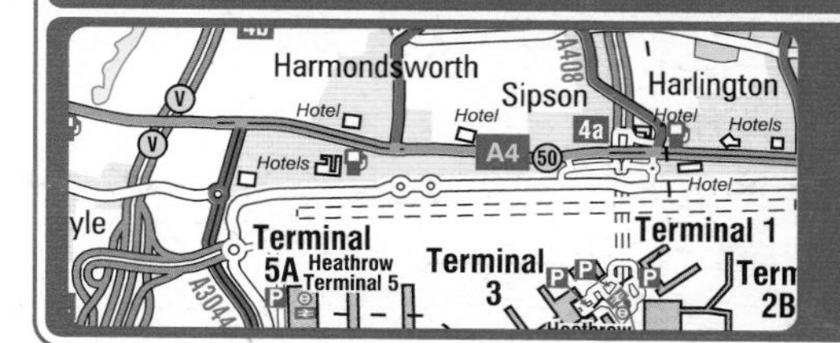

Britain & Northern Ireland Road maps

Detailed Main Route maps

City and Town centre maps

Sea Port & Channel Tunnel plans

Airport plans

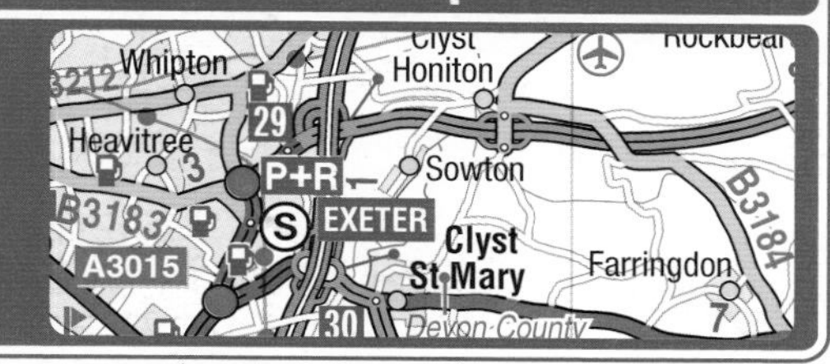

Over 32,000 Index References

Including cities, towns, villages, hamlets and locations..................206-238

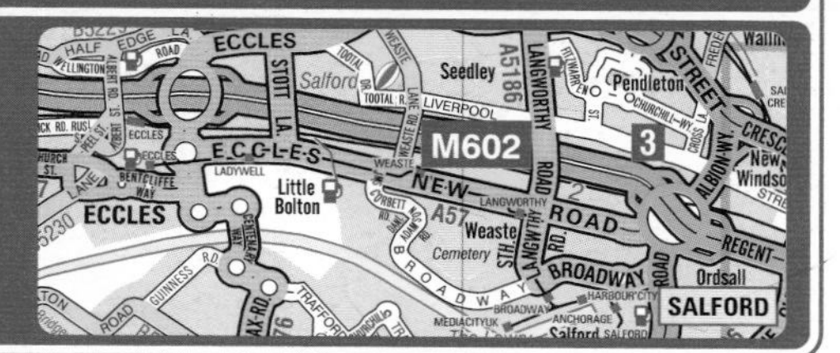

Index to Places of Interest

Full postcodes to easily locate popular places of interest on your SatNav 239-242

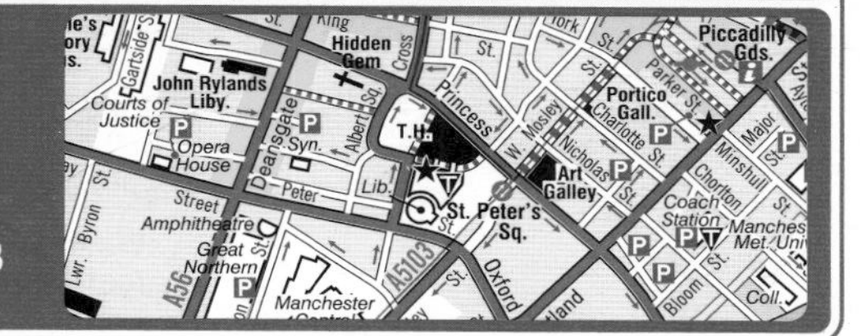

Motorway Junctions

Junction	M1	
2	Northbound	No exit, access from A1 only
	Southbound	No access, exit to A1 only
4	Northbound	No exit, access from A41 only
	Southbound	No access, exit to A41 only
6a	Northbound	No exit, access from M25 only
	Southbound	No access, exit to M25 only

Details of motorway junctions with limited interchange..................243

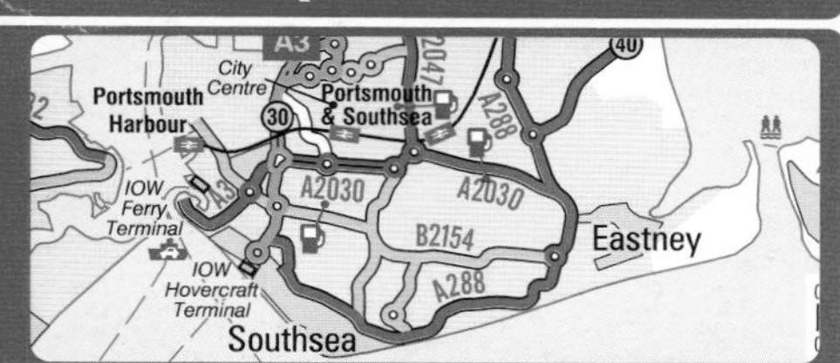

Safety Camera Information

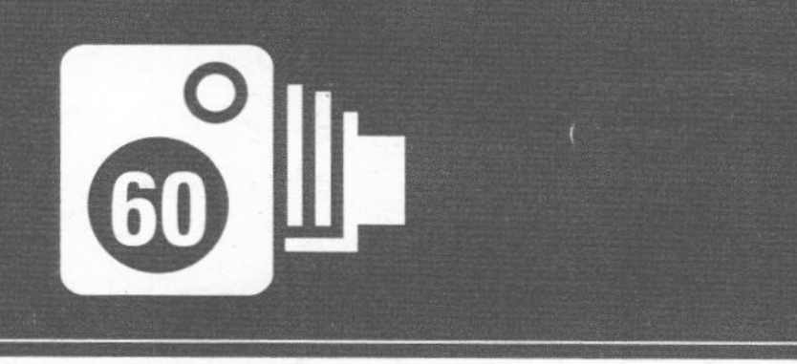

Details of Safety Camera symbols used on the maps, and the responsible use of Camera information ....Inside back cover

EDITION 27 2018
Copyright © Geographers' A-Z Map Company Ltd.

registered trade marks of Geographers' A-Z Map Company Ltd

www./az.co.uk

Contains Ordnance Survey data © Crown copyright and database right 2017

Northern Ireland: This is Based upon Crown Copyright and is reproduced with the permission of Land & Property Services under delegated authority from the Controller of Her Majesty's Stationery Office, © Crown copyright and database right 2017 PMLPA No 100508. The inclusion of parts or all of the Republic of Ireland is by permission of the Government of Ireland who retain copyright in the data used. © Ordnance Survey Ireland and Government of Ireland.

Land & Property Services
Paper Map Licensed Partner
ORDNANCE SURVEY OF NORTHERN IRELAND

This is a registered Trade Mark of Department of Finance and Personnel.

Safety Camera & Fuel Station Databases copyright 2017, © PocketGPSWorld.com. PocketGPSWorld.com's CamerAlert is a self-contained speed and red light camera warning system for SatNavs and Android or Apple iOS smartphones or tablets. Visit www.cameralert.com to download.

Base Relief by Geo-Innovations, © www.geoinnovations.co.uk

The Shopmobility logo is a registered symbol of The National Federation of Shopmobility

The representation on the maps of a road, track or footpath is no evidence of the existence of a right of way.

Every possible care has been taken to ensure that, to the best of our knowledge, the information contained in this atlas is accurate at the date of publication. However, we cannot warrant that our work is entirely error free and whilst we would be grateful to learn of any inaccuracies, we do not accept responsibility for loss or damage resulting from reliance on information contained within this publication.

No reproduction by any method whatsoever of any part of this publication is permitted without the prior consent of the copyright owners.

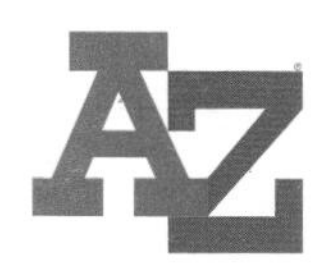

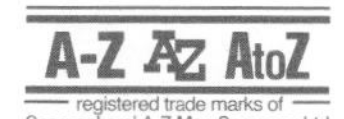

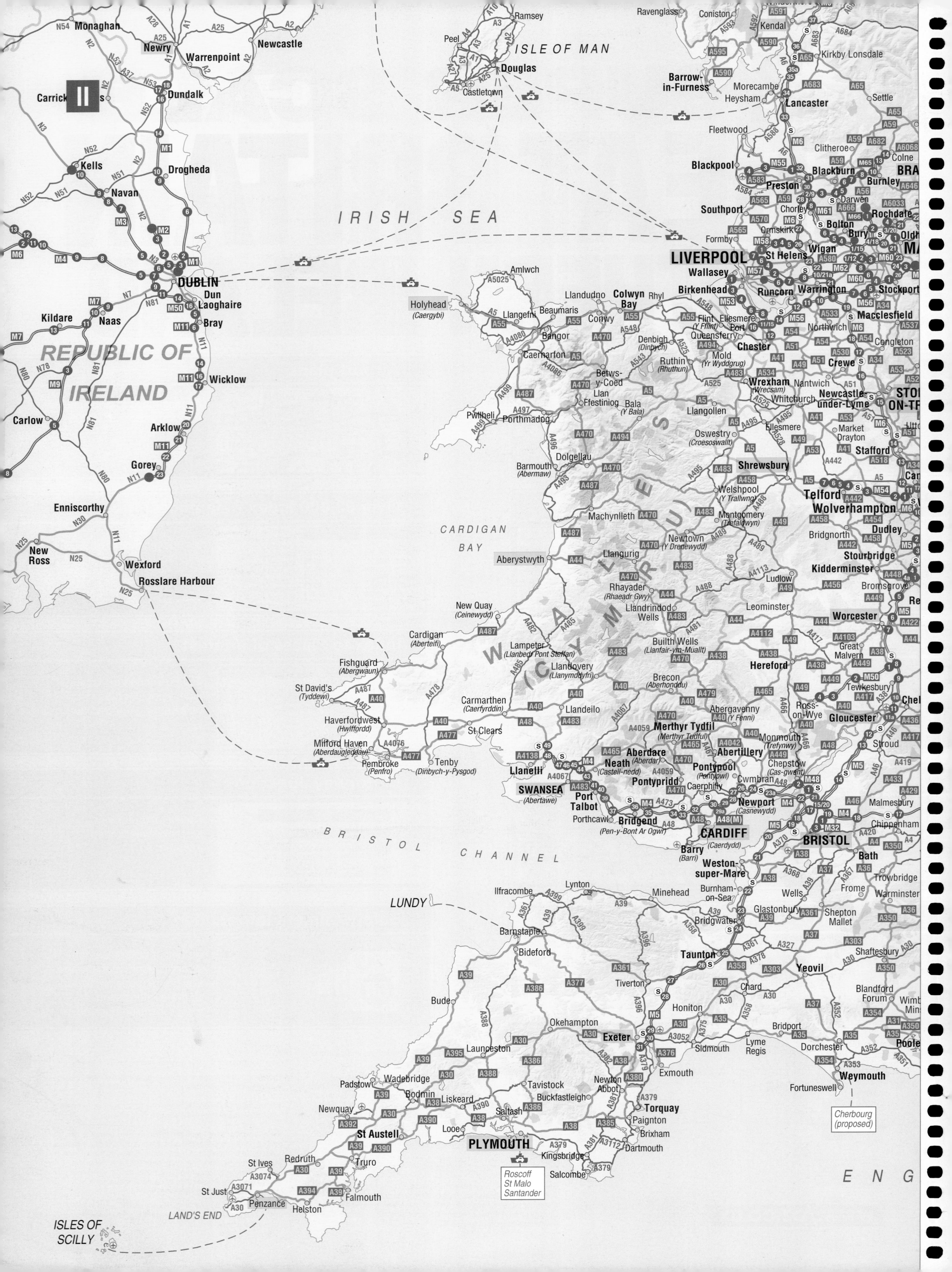

II
Monaghan
Newry
Warrenpoint
Newcastle
Dundalk
Kells
Navan
Drogheda
DUBLIN
Dun Laoghaire
Bray
Kildare
Naas
REPUBLIC OF IRELAND
Wicklow
Carlow
Arklow
Gorey
Enniscorthy
New Ross
Wexford
Rosslare Harbour
Ramsey
Peel
ISLE OF MAN
Douglas
Castletown
IRISH SEA
Ravenglass
Coniston
Kendal
Kirkby Lonsdale
Barrow-in-Furness
Morecambe
Heysham
Lancaster
Settle
Fleetwood
Clitheroe
Colne
Blackpool
Blackburn
Burnley
Preston
Darwen
Southport
Chorley
Rochdale
Bolton
Ormskirk
Bury
Formby
St Helens
Wigan
LIVERPOOL
Wallasey
Birkenhead
Runcorn
Warrington
Stockport
Amlwch
Holyhead
(Caergybi)
Llangefni
Beaumaris
Llandudno
Colwyn Bay
Rhyl
Conwy
Bangor
Flint
(Y Fflint)
Ellesmere Port
Macclesfield
Denbigh
(Dinbych)
Queensferry
Northwich
Chester
Congleton
Caernarfon
Ruthin
(Rhuthun)
Mold
(Yr Wyddgrug)
Crewe
Betws-y-Coed
Wrexham
(Wrecsam)
Nantwich
Llan Ffestiniog
Bala
(Y Bala)
Llangollen
Whitchurch
Newcastle-under-Lyme
Pwllheli
Porthmadog
Ellesmere
Market Drayton
Oswestry
(Croesoswallt)
Stafford
Dolgellau
Barmouth
(Abermaw)
Shrewsbury
Telford
Welshpool
(Y Trallwng)
Wolverhampton
Machynlleth
Montgomery
(Trefaldwyn)
Dudley
Bridgnorth
CARDIGAN BAY
Newtown
(Y Drenewydd)
Aberystwyth
Llangurig
Stourbridge
Kidderminster
Ludlow
Bromsgrove
Rhayader
(Rhaeadr Gwy)
Llandrindod Wells
Leominster
Worcester
New Quay
(Ceinewydd)
Cardigan
(Aberteifi)
Lampeter
(Llanbedr Pont Steffan)
Builth Wells
(Llanfair-ym-Muallt)
Great Malvern
WALES
(CYMRU)
Fishguard
(Abergwaun)
Llandovery
(Llanymddyfri)
Hereford
St David's
(Tyddewi)
Brecon
(Aberhonddu)
Tewkesbury
Carmarthen
(Caerfyrddin)
Llandeilo
Abergavenny
(Y Fenni)
Ross-on-Wye
Gloucester
Haverfordwest
(Hwlffordd)
Merthyr Tydfil
(Merthyr Tudful)
St Clears
Monmouth
(Trefynwy)
Stroud
Milford Haven
(Aberdaugleddau)
Aberdare
(Aberdar)
Abertillery
Pembroke
(Penfro)
Tenby
(Dinbych-y-Pysgod)
Neath
(Castell-nedd)
Pontypool
(Pontypwl)
Chepstow
(Cas-gwent)
Llanelli
Cwmbran
Pontypridd
Caerphilly
SWANSEA
(Abertawe)
Port Talbot
Newport
(Casnewydd)
Malmesbury
Porthcawl
Bridgend
(Pen-y-Bont Ar Ogwr)
CARDIFF
(Caerdydd)
Chippenham
BRISTOL
BRISTOL CHANNEL
Barry
(Barri)
Bath
Weston-super-Mare
Trowbridge
Lynton
Ilfracombe
Minehead
Wells
Frome
Warminster
LUNDY
Burnham-on-Sea
Glastonbury
Shepton Mallet
Bridgwater
Barnstaple
Bideford
Taunton
Shaftesbury
Yeovil
Tiverton
Chard
Blandford Forum
Bude
Honiton
Okehampton
Bridport
Exeter
Lyme Regis
Sidmouth
Dorchester
Poole
Launceston
Exmouth
Weymouth
Padstow
Wadebridge
Newton Abbot
Tavistock
Fortuneswell
Bodmin
Liskeard
Buckfastleigh
Cherbourg
(proposed)
Newquay
Torquay
Saltash
Paignton
St Austell
Looe
Brixham
PLYMOUTH
Dartmouth
Redruth
Kingsbridge
St Ives
Truro
Roscoff
St Malo
Santander
Salcombe
ENG
St Just
Falmouth
Penzance
Helston
LAND'S END
ISLES OF SCILLY

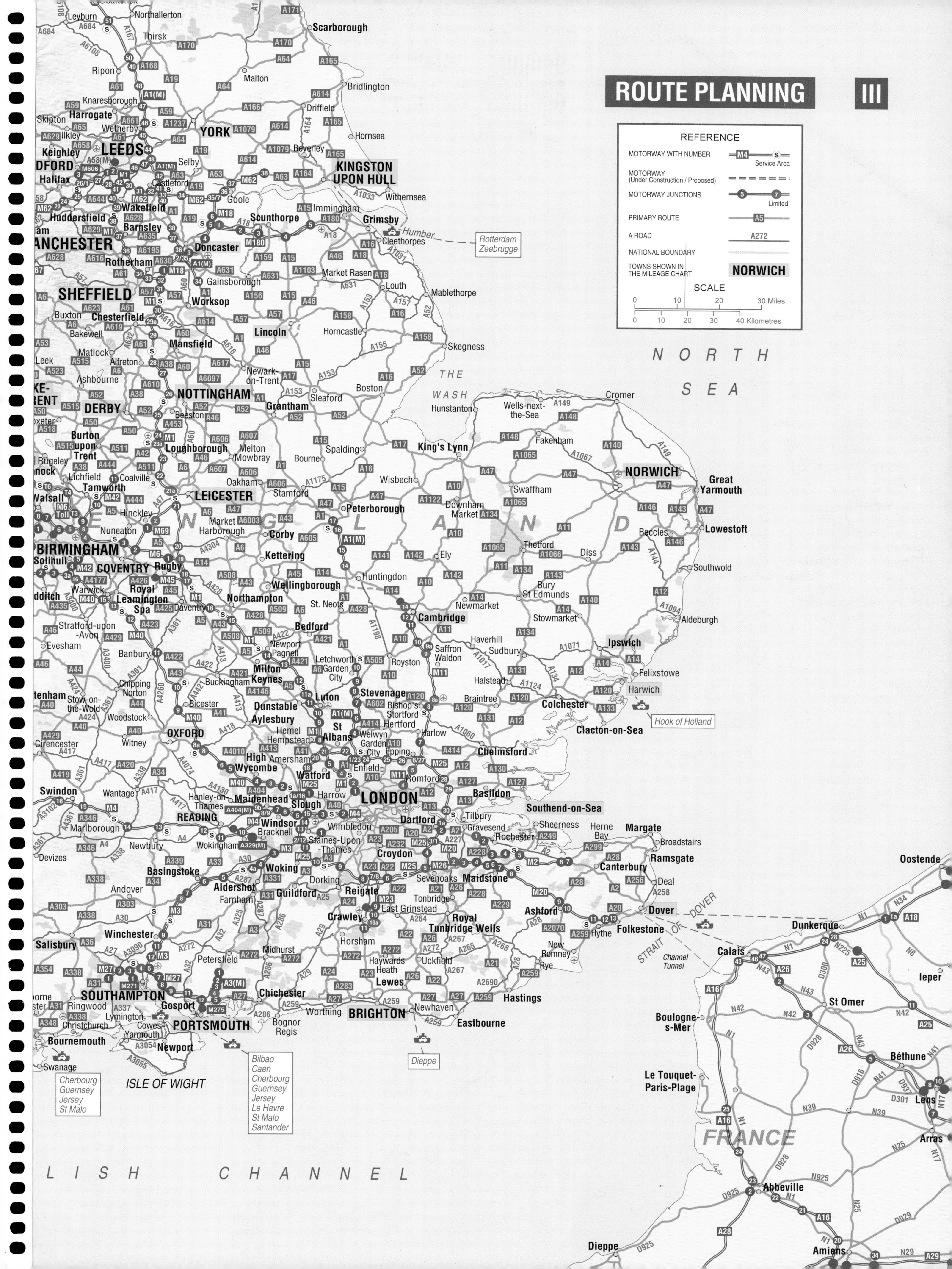

REFERENCE

MOTORWAY WITH NUMBER	M4 — s / Service Area
MOTORWAY (Under Construction / Proposed)	-----
MOTORWAY JUNCTIONS	5 — 7 / Limited
PRIMARY ROUTE	A5
A ROAD	A272
NATIONAL BOUNDARY	
TOWNS SHOWN IN THE MILEAGE CHART	NORWICH

SCALE

0   10   20   30 Miles
0   10   20   30   40 Kilometres

N O R T H   S E A

E N G L A N D

THE WASH

Humber

Rotterdam Zeebrugge

Hook of Holland

Dieppe

Cherbourg
Guernsey
Jersey
St Malo

Bilbao
Caen
Cherbourg
Guernsey
Jersey
Le Havre
St Malo
Santander

ISLE OF WIGHT

LISH   C H A N N E L

STRAIT OF DOVER

Channel Tunnel

FRANCE

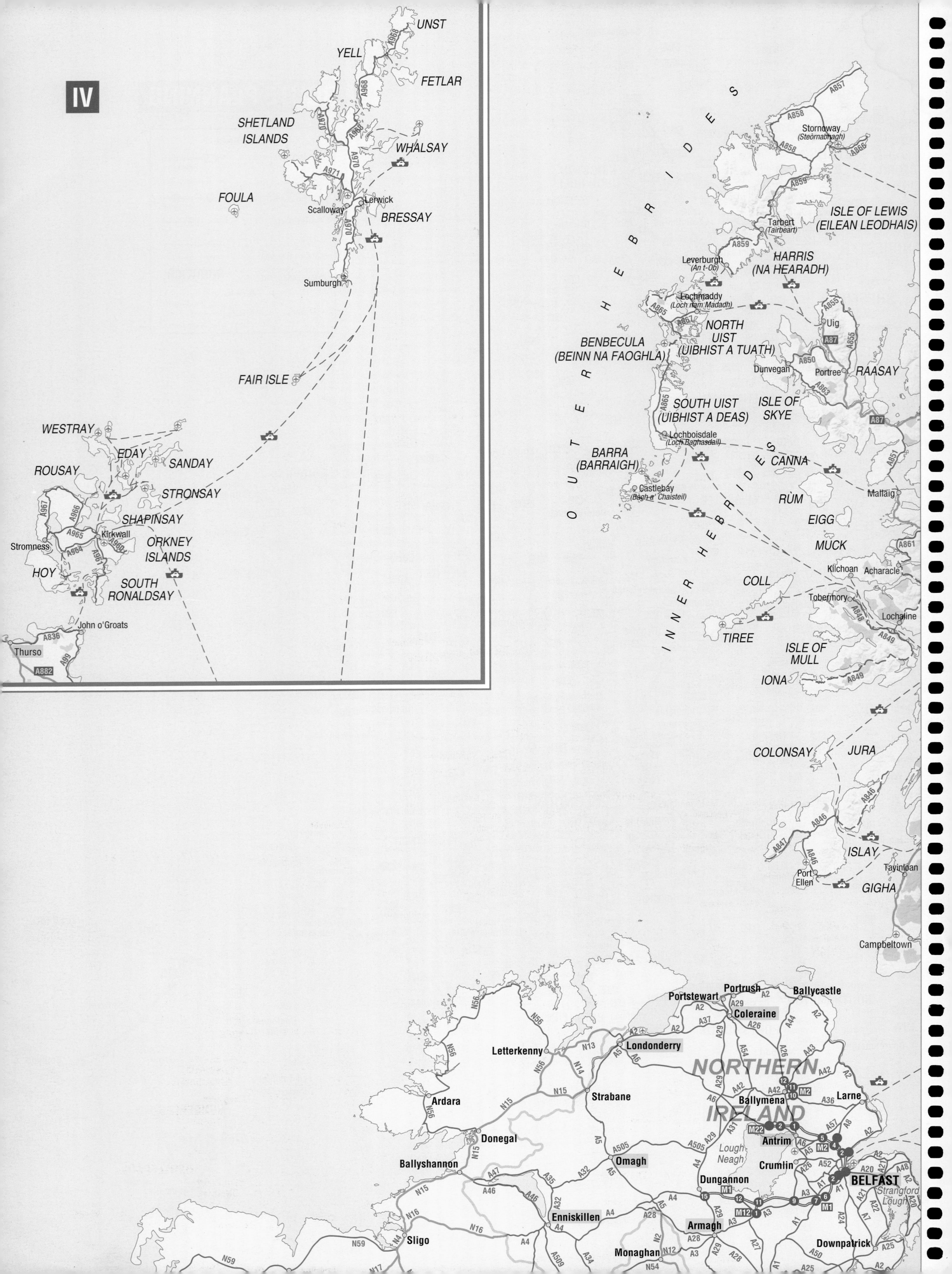

IV

UNST
YELL
FETLAR
SHETLAND
ISLANDS
WHALSAY
FOULA
Scalloway
Lerwick
BRESSAY
Sumburgh

FAIR ISLE

WESTRAY
EDAY
ROUSAY
SANDAY
STRONSAY
SHAPINSAY
Kirkwall
ORKNEY
Stromness
ISLANDS
HOY
SOUTH
RONALDSAY
John o'Groats
Thurso

ISLE OF LEWIS
(EILEAN LEODHAIS)
Stornoway
(Steòrnabhagh)
Tarbert
(Tairbeart)
HARRIS
(NA HEARADH)
Leverburgh
(An t-Ob)
Lochmaddy
(Loch nam Madadh)
Uig
NORTH
UIST
(UIBHIST A TUATH)
BENBECULA
(BEINN NA FAOGHLA)
Dunvegan
Portree
RAASAY
SOUTH UIST
(UIBHIST A DEAS)
ISLE OF
SKYE
Lochboisdale
(Loch Baghasdail)
BARRA
(BARRAIGH)
CANNA
Castlebay
(Bàgh a' Chaisteil)
RÙM
Mallaig
EIGG
MUCK
Kilchoan
Acharacle
COLL
Tobermory
Lochaline
TIREE
ISLE OF
MULL
IONA

O U T E R   H E B R I D E S

I N N E R   H E B R I D E S

COLONSAY
JURA

ISLAY
Tayinloan
Port
Ellen
GIGHA

Campbeltown

Portrush
Portstewart
Ballycastle
Coleraine
Letterkenny
Londonderry
NORTHERN
Ardara
Strabane
Ballymena
Larne
IRELAND
Donegal
Antrim
Ballyshannon
Lough
Neagh
Crumlin
Omagh
Dungannon
BELFAST
Enniskillen
Armagh
Strangford
Lough
Sligo
Monaghan
Downpatrick

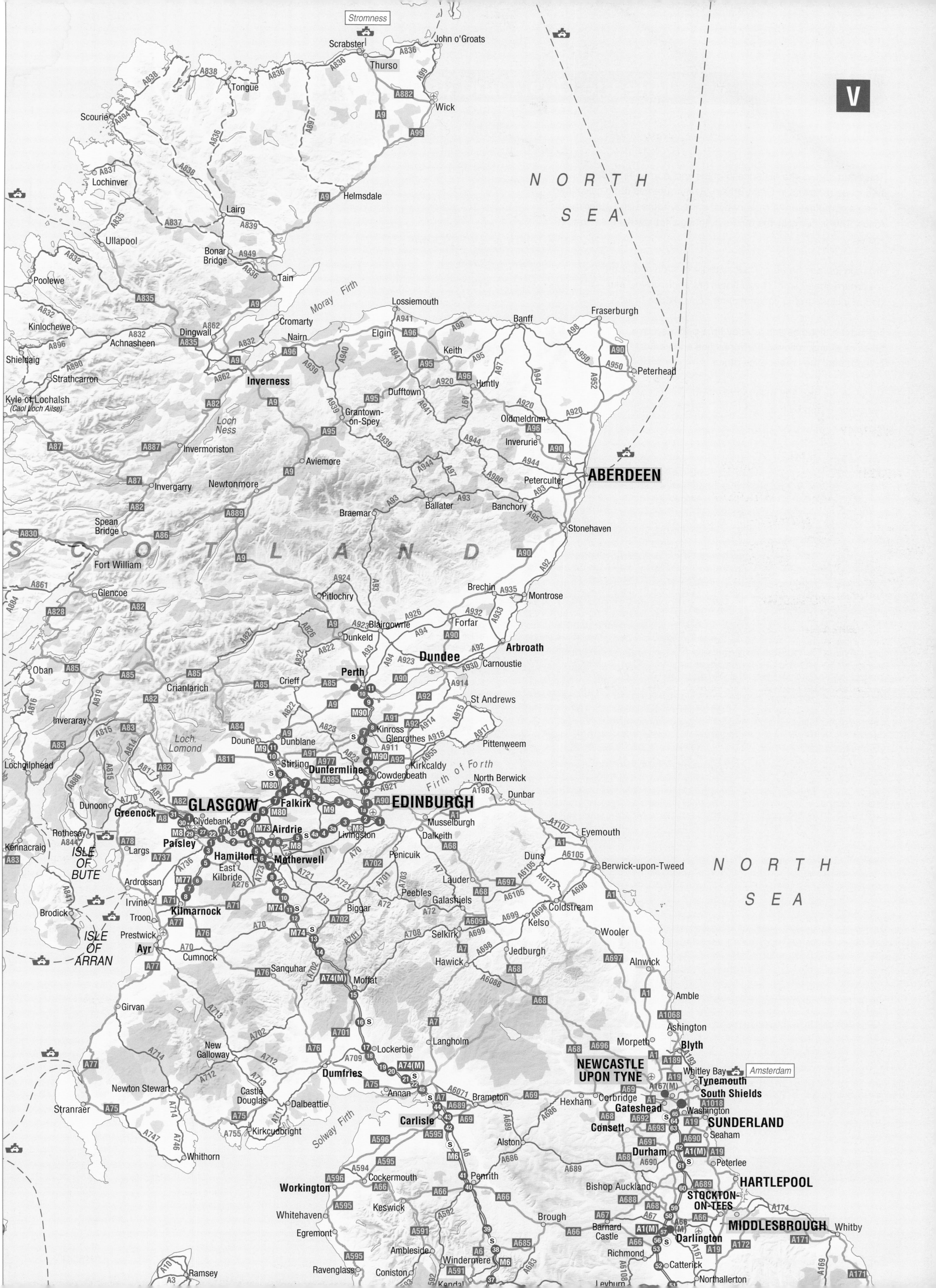

NORTH SEA

NORTH SEA

SCOTLAND

Stromness
Scrabster
Thurso
John o'Groats
Tongue
Wick
Scourie
Helmsdale
Lochinver
Lairg
Ullapool
Bonar Bridge
Tain
Poolewe
Cromarty
Lossiemouth
Fraserburgh
Kinlochewe
Dingwall
Nairn
Elgin
Keith
Banff
Peterhead
Shieldaig
Achnasheen
Inverness
Dufftown
Huntly
Oldmeldrum
Strathcarron
Inverurie
Kyle of Lochalsh
(Caol Loch Ailse)
Loch Ness
Grantown-on-Spey
Invermoriston
Peterculter
ABERDEEN
Aviemore
Invergarry
Newtonmore
Ballater
Banchory
Spean Bridge
Braemar
Stonehaven
Fort William
Glencoe
Brechin
Montrose
Pitlochry
Dunkeld
Blairgowrie
Forfar
Oban
Crieff
Dundee
Arbroath
Carnoustie
Crianlarich
Perth
St Andrews
Inveraray
Kinross
Glenrothes
Pittenweem
Doune
Dunblane
Loch Lomond
Stirling
Kirkcaldy
Lochgilphead
Dunfermline
Cowdenbeath
North Berwick
Falkirk
EDINBURGH
Firth of Forth
GLASGOW
Airdrie
Musselburgh
Dunbar
Greenock
Clydebank
Livingston
Dalkeith
Eyemouth
Rothesay
Paisley
Berwick-upon-Tweed
Kennacraig
Largs
Hamilton
Motherwell
Penicuik
Duns
ISLE OF BUTE
East Kilbride
Peebles
Lauder
Ardrossan
Galashiels
Coldstream
Irvine
Kilmarnock
Biggar
Selkirk
Kelso
Troon
Wooler
Brodick
Prestwick
ISLE OF ARRAN
Ayr
Cumnock
Jedburgh
Hawick
Alnwick
Girvan
Sanquhar
Moffat
Amble
Ashington
New Galloway
Morpeth
Blyth
Newton Stewart
Lockerbie
Langholm
NEWCASTLE UPON TYNE
Whitley Bay
Amsterdam
Stranraer
Dumfries
Annan
Brampton
Tynemouth
South Shields
Castle Douglas
Hexham
Corbridge
Gateshead
SUNDERLAND
Whithorn
Kirkcudbright
Carlisle
Alston
Consett
Durham
Seaham
Workington
Cockermouth
Penrith
Bishop Auckland
HARTLEPOOL
Peterlee
Whitehaven
Keswick
Brough
STOCKTON-ON-TEES
Egremont
Barnard Castle
Darlington
MIDDLESBROUGH
Whitby
Ravenglass
Ambleside
Windermere
Richmond
Catterick
Coniston
Kendal
Leyburn
Northallerton
Ramsey

Mileage Chart and Journey Times

This chart shows the distance in miles and journey time between two cities or towns in Great Britain. Each route has been calculated using a combination of motorways, primary routes and other major roads. This is normally the quickest, though not always the shortest route.

Average journey times are calculated whilst driving at the maximum speed limit. These times are approximate and do not include traffic congestion or convenience breaks.

To find the distance and journey time between two cities or towns, follow a horizontal line and vertical column until they meet each other.

For example, the 285 mile journey from London to Penzance is approximately 4 hours and 59 minutes.

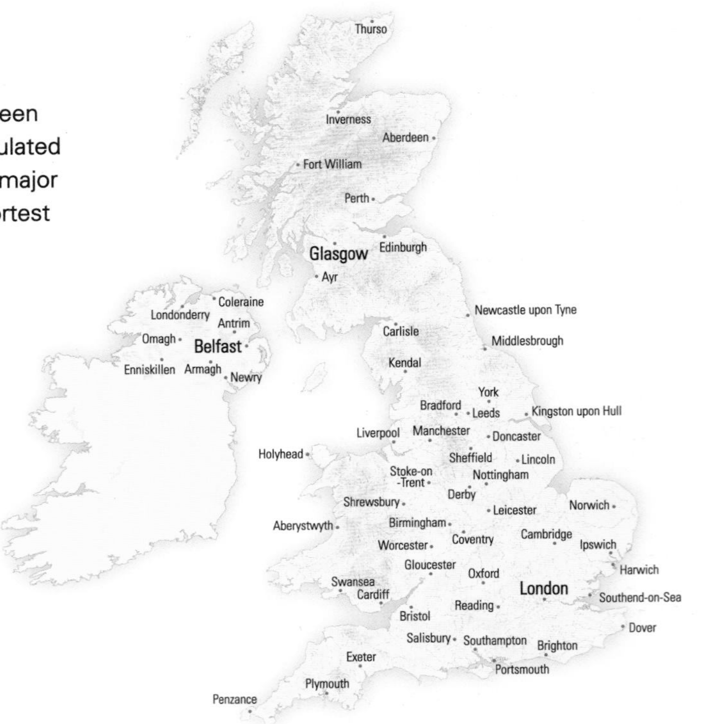

Northern Ireland

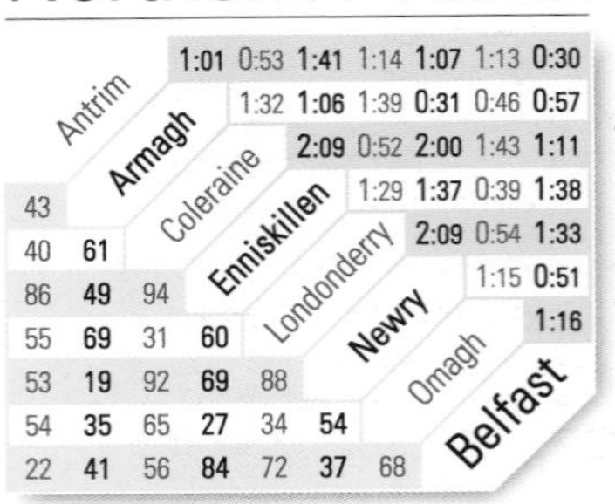

Journey times (above the diagonal) / Distance in miles (below the diagonal)

	Antrim	Armagh	Coleraine	Enniskillen	Londonderry	Newry	Omagh	Belfast
Antrim		1:01	0:53	1:41	1:14	1:07	1:13	0:30
Armagh	43		1:32	1:06	1:39	0:31	0:46	0:57
Coleraine	40	61		2:09	0:52	2:00	1:43	1:11
Enniskillen	86	49	94		1:29	1:37	0:39	1:38
Londonderry	55	69	31	60		2:09	0:54	1:33
Newry	53	19	92	69	88		1:15	0:51
Omagh	54	35	65	27	34	54		1:16
Belfast	22	41	56	84	72	37	68	

Distance in miles

Belfast to London = 440m / 9:46h (excluding ferry)
Belfast to Glasgow = 104m / 4:46h (excluding ferry)

Britain

Journey times (above the diagonal) / Distance in miles (below the diagonal)

	Aberdeen	Aberystwyth	Ayr	Birmingham	Bradford	Brighton	Bristol	Cambridge	Cardiff	Carlisle	Coventry	Derby	Doncaster	Dover	Edinburgh	Exeter	Fort William	Glasgow	Gloucester	Harwich	Holyhead	Inverness	Ipswich	Kendal	Kingston upon Hull	Leeds	Leicester	Lincoln	Liverpool	Manchester	Middlesbrough	Newcastle upon Tyne	Norwich	Nottingham	Oxford	Penzance	Perth	Plymouth	Portsmouth	Reading	Salisbury	Sheffield	Shrewsbury	Southampton	Southend-on-Sea	Stoke-on-Trent	Swansea	Thurso	Worcester	York	London
Aberdeen		8:21	3:31	7:13	6:28	9:56	8:26	8:15	8:55	4:08	7:27	7:09	6:25	10:16	2:39	9:38	3:38	2:50	7:55	9:32	7:41	2:30	9:08	4:55	6:51	6:16	7:40	7:07	6:13	6:01	5:16	4:39	9:18	7:14	8:18	11:22	1:48	10:16	9:33	8:57	9:21	6:42	7:07	9:25	9:22	6:28	9:31	4:52	7:35	6:07	9:03
Aberystwyth	471		6:34	2:34	3:27	5:21	2:44	4:00	2:29	4:24	2:52	2:56	3:45	5:41	6:20	3:51	8:13	5:53	2:34	5:17	2:29	8:39	4:53	3:40	4:20	3:29	3:18	4:11	2:39	2:54	4:34	5:07	5:03	3:17	3:43	5:35	6:41	4:29	4:27	3:50	4:01	3:41	1:47	4:18	4:56	2:48	1:48	11:00	2:19	4:00	4:28
Ayr	181	324		5:28	4:28	8:11	6:42	6:31	7:10	2:24	5:43	5:25	4:41	8:32	1:48	7:54	3:03	0:48	6:11	7:48	5:56	3:51	7:24	3:10	5:06	4:32	5:55	5:22	4:29	4:16	3:56	3:28	7:34	5:29	6:34	9:37	1:53	8:31	7:49	7:13	7:37	4:57	5:23	7:40	7:37	4:43	7:46	6:12	5:50	4:22	7:16
Birmingham	423	114	272		2:15	3:04	1:41	1:43	2:09	3:16	0:36	1:01	1:40	3:25	5:12	2:53	7:05	4:45	1:10	3:01	2:59	7:31	2:37	2:32	2:21	2:05	1:01	1:55	1:49	1:46	2:55	3:28	2:46	1:08	1:27	4:36	5:33	3:30	2:42	2:06	2:39	1:36	0:59	2:33	2:39	1:02	2:44	9:52	0:49	2:21	2:11
Bradford	377	159	196	124		4:30	3:34	2:43	4:03	2:17	2:19	1:34	0:53	4:37	4:17	4:46	6:06	3:46	3:03	4:01	2:49	6:31	3:37	1:32	1:18	0:28	2:02	1:35	1:22	0:57	1:32	2:06	3:46	1:37	3:05	6:29	4:33	5:24	4:20	3:44	4:18	1:00	2:15	4:12	3:50	1:36	4:38	8:52	2:42	0:59	3:32
Brighton	596	258	441	169	263		2:49	2:09	3:26	6:00	2:42	3:15	3:53	1:53	7:53	3:41	9:49	7:29	2:47	2:19	5:39	10:14	2:20	5:15	4:35	4:19	2:57	3:43	4:32	4:29	5:08	5:42	3:05	3:21	1:58	5:24	8:16	4:18	1:14	1:39	1:54	3:49	3:45	1:35	1:41	3:45	4:01	12:35	3:07	4:35	1:27
Bristol	505	122	375	88	215	129		3:02	0:56	4:31	1:44	2:21	2:59	3:18	6:27	1:37	8:20	6:00	0:47	3:27	4:13	8:45	3:28	3:46	3:41	3:25	2:17	3:11	3:03	3:01	4:15	4:48	3:58	2:28	1:30	3:20	6:48	2:14	2:03	1:26	1:37	2:56	2:14	1:54	2:58	2:17	1:30	11:07	1:07	3:41	2:07
Cambridge	487	198	366	102	156	117	167		3:28	4:20	1:30	1:52	2:03	2:06	6:04	4:11	8:09	5:49	2:29	1:28	4:20	8:35	1:04	3:56	2:37	2:34	1:25	1:47	3:12	3:10	3:19	3:52	1:13	1:41	1:55	5:54	6:37	4:49	2:34	1:51	2:47	2:15	2:26	2:35	1:19	2:26	4:03	10:56	2:08	2:45	1:17
Cardiff	525	106	377	106	233	168	42	201		4:58	2:15	2:48	3:27	3:54	6:54	2:02	8:47	6:27	1:16	4:03	4:23	9:13	4:03	4:14	4:09	3:53	2:46	3:39	3:31	3:28	4:42	5:16	4:31	2:55	2:05	3:46	7:15	2:40	2:38	2:01	2:12	3:23	2:24	2:29	3:33	2:44	0:53	11:34	1:35	4:09	2:43
Carlisle	229	232	89	183	107	345	286	256	288		3:30	3:12	2:28	6:19	2:08	5:41	4:01	1:41	3:58	5:35	3:44	4:27	5:11	0:58	2:54	2:19	3:43	3:10	2:16	2:04	1:44	1:15	5:21	3:17	4:21	7:25	2:29	6:19	5:36	5:00	5:24	2:45	3:10	5:28	5:25	2:31	5:34	6:48	3:38	2:10	5:07
Coventry	442	134	297	18	124	157	102	84	129	200		1:03	1:41	3:05	5:29	2:55	7:22	5:02	1:12	2:49	3:13	7:48	2:21	2:49	2:23	2:06	0:45	1:39	2:06	2:03	2:56	3:30	2:31	1:09	1:04	4:38	5:50	3:32	2:19	1:43	2:17	1:37	1:18	2:11	2:20	1:19	2:49	10:09	0:56	2:22	1:53
Derby	418	137	269	41	88	188	134	99	159	180	43		0:57	3:33	4:58	3:31	7:02	4:42	1:48	3:09	2:52	7:27	2:45	2:28	1:39	1:23	0:49	1:24	1:45	1:42	2:13	2:46	2:55	0:33	1:51	5:14	5:29	4:08	3:06	2:30	3:04	0:54	1:21	2:58	2:48	0:53	3:22	9:49	1:27	1:39	2:19
Doncaster	371	192	239	95	40	232	184	117	210	150	94	57		3:58	4:13	4:12	6:19	3:59	2:30	3:21	3:17	6:44	2:57	2:16	0:56	0:43	1:27	0:55	1:48	1:25	1:28	2:02	3:07	1:02	2:30	5:56	4:46	4:50	3:45	3:09	3:43	0:30	2:13	3:36	3:11	1:44	4:04	9:05	2:09	0:54	2:57
Dover	620	315	477	195	284	81	194	118	233	393	180	208	244		7:56	4:14	10:08	7:48	3:16	2:16	5:59	10:34	2:17	5:35	4:29	4:26	3:14	3:40	4:52	4:49	5:11	5:45	3:02	3:34	2:27	5:57	8:36	4:51	2:23	2:08	2:50	4:06	4:05	2:38	1:37	4:05	4:29	12:55	3:36	4:38	1:34
Edinburgh	126	340	75	284	198	466	377	326	379	91	303	266	212	444		7:38	3:01	1:05	5:55	7:20	5:41	3:02	6:56	2:55	4:38	4:04	5:26	4:54	4:13	4:00	3:00	2:23	7:06	5:01	6:18	9:21	1:02	8:16	7:33	6:57	7:21	4:29	5:07	7:25	7:09	4:28	7:30	5:24	5:34	3:54	6:57
Exeter	581	199	425	161	282	170	75	323	107	336	166	213	257	244	439		9:31	7:11	1:58	4:36	5:24	9:56	4:37	4:57	4:52	4:36	3:28	4:22	4:14	4:12	5:26	5:59	5:07	3:39	2:46	1:54	7:59	0:53	2:38	2:43	1:55	4:07	3:25	2:27	4:02	3:28	2:37	12:18	2:18	4:52	3:16
Fort William	159	430	136	391	305	568	478	456	486	198	415	387	345	591	131	549		2:26	7:49	9:26	7:35	1:32	9:02	4:49	6:44	6:10	7:34	7:00	6:07	5:54	5:34	5:06	9:12	7:07	8:12	11:15	2:09	10:10	9:27	8:51	9:15	6:35	7:01	9:19	9:16	6:22	9:24	4:04	7:28	6:01	8:56
Glasgow	146	322	36	291	203	468	378	355	384	96	313	282	245	491	46	449	100		5:28	7:05	5:13	3:08	6:41	2:28	4:23	3:49	5:12	4:39	3:46	3:33	3:13	2:45	6:51	4:46	5:51	8:54	1:10	7:48	7:06	6:30	6:54	4:14	4:40	6:57	6:55	4:01	7:03	5:29	5:07	3:40	6:36
Gloucester	473	109	317	53	171	152	35	132	53	228	59	93	149	189	331	107	435	324		3:25	3:42	8:14	3:22	3:15	3:10	2:54	1:46	2:39	2:32	2:29	3:43	4:17	3:31	1:56	1:11	3:39	6:16	2:33	2:00	1:24	1:42	2:24	1:42	1:52	2:56	1:45	1:49	10:35	0:36	3:10	2:05
Harwich	568	258	411	170	224	130	203	64	234	323	152	167	185	129	397	262	524	419	171		5:38	9:53	0:42	5:13	3:55	3:52	2:43	3:05	4:30	4:28	4:37	5:10	1:32	2:59	2:26	6:20	7:55	5:14	2:49	2:17	3:12	3:33	3:44	3:01	1:09	3:44	4:38	12:14	3:26	4:03	1:42
Holyhead	452	96	315	151	158	330	204	252	209	226	167	156	169	358	316	279	423	323	189	331		7:58	5:16	2:59	3:39	2:49	3:23	3:52	1:53	2:13	3:53	4:26	5:25	3:15	4:06	7:06	6:00	6:00	5:21	4:45	5:05	3:06	2:10	5:12	5:18	2:11	4:33	10:19	3:19	3:19	4:47
Inverness	105	492	198	449	353	620	536	490	558	260	458	421	369	601	157	607	63	162	496	554	481		9:27	5:14	7:10	6:35	7:59	7:26	6:32	6:20	5:41	5:04	9:37	7:33	8:37	11:41	2:10	10:35	9:52	9:16	9:40	7:01	7:26	9:44	9:41	6:47	9:50	2:31	7:54	6:26	9:21
Ipswich	538	268	420	156	210	125	206	54	240	311	138	155	171	127	381	264	510	409	177	21	307	538		4:50	3:31	3:28	2:20	2:41	4:06	4:04	4:13	4:46	1:08	2:35	2:27	6:21	7:31	5:15	2:50	2:18	3:13	3:09	3:20	3:02	1:10	3:20	4:39	11:50	3:02	3:39	1:43
Kendal	280	182	139	151	62	324	235	215	232	50	170	136	99	344	141	307	248	146	200	279	180	310	268		2:44	1:53	3:02	3:00	1:36	1:23	1:38	1:59	5:00	2:54	3:41	6:44	3:13	5:38	4:56	4:20	4:44	2:22	2:30	4:47	4:53	1:50	4:53	7:32	2:57	2:04	4:22
Kingston upon Hull	398	235	255	139	68	243	228	134	239	165	123	94	37	254	230	290	367	255	195	204	218	387	189	127		1:08	2:08	0:58	2:13	1:49	1:54	2:27	3:18	1:43	3:10	6:36	5:12	5:30	4:25	3:49	4:23	1:11	2:53	4:17	3:43	2:25	4:44	9:31	2:49	1:02	3:39
Leeds	359	171	198	119	9	256	209	144	226	111	117	74	32	275	190	279	309	208	167	217	162	345	197	72	60		1:53	1:25	1:23	0:58	1:20	1:53	3:37	1:27	2:55	6:21	4:38	5:15	4:10	3:34	4:08	0:50	2:16	4:02	3:40	1:37	4:29	8:57	2:34	0:46	3:23
Leicester	445	155	294	43	99	163	118	70	140	214	24	30	73	183	282	189	412	312	83	146	182	431	125	166	98	97		1:16	2:17	2:14	2:42	3:15	2:27	0:46	1:32	5:11	6:01	4:05	2:47	2:11	2:45	1:23	1:43	2:39	2:29	1:24	3:20	10:20	1:25	2:08	2:01
Lincoln	411	208	249	87	80	207	170	88	192	178	76	53	41	206	247	241	376	274	135	152	204	402	124	140	46	72	52		2:31	2:02	2:11	2:44	2:20	0:59	2:28	6:07	5:29	5:01	3:43	3:07	3:41	1:07	2:33	3:34	2:54	2:10	4:16	9:48	2:21	1:35	2:51
Liverpool	354	120	199	99	67	267	180	179	169	110	113	90	89	294	201	240	308	213	142	265	95	370	236	75	126	73	110	118		0:48	2:28	3:01	4:16	2:10	2:56	6:00	4:33	4:54	4:11	3:35	3:59	1:52	1:25	4:03	4:09	1:06	3:48	8:53	2:13	1:54	3:39
Manchester	349	128	204	87	37	252	167	159	188	117	99	58	51	273	208	239	315	215	132	230	120	363	211	72	96	42	95	87	34		2:03	2:36	4:12	1:51	2:52	5:55	4:22	4:49	4:07	3:30	3:55	1:14	1:41	3:58	4:04	1:01	4:04	8:41	2:08	1:29	3:37
Middlesbrough	289	233	181	174	69	316	265	196	287	92	175	130	84	316	147	337	279	192	230	266	226	306	253	77	88	64	154	127	134	106		0:55	4:20	2:15	3:43	7:09	3:40	6:03	4:58	4:22	4:56	1:43	3:20	4:50	4:24	2:40	5:17	8:02	3:22	1:05	4:12
Newcastle upon Tyne	252	266	146	209	98	345	300	232	312	58	209	165	115	350	104	369	237	153	263	297	257	263	287	88	130	96	188	153	167	136	40		4:54	2:49	4:17	7:43	3:03	6:37	5:32	4:56	5:30	2:17	3:54	5:24	4:58	3:14	5:51	7:25	3:56	1:43	4:46
Norwich	536	270	348	163	185	174	234	62	256	280	142	146	142	169	351	284	478	378	193	72	289	505	44	249	145	178	112	103	222	177	221	252		2:44	2:58	6:51	7:40	5:45	3:31	2:48	3:43	3:18	3:29	3:32	2:00	3:28	5:06	11:59	3:10	3:48	2:13
Nottingham	416	155	267	54	78	191	140	84	165	188	52	15	48	210	256	218	386	286	108	165	177	410	140	141	92	72	27	37	107	68	128	159	118		1:57	5:23	5:34	4:17	3:12	2:36	3:10	0:57	1:44	3:04	2:49	1:18	3:31	9:53	1:36	1:42	2:25
Oxford	497	151	335	68	167	106	73	92	106	267	57	101	138	142	358	151	465	365	47	134	208	515	128	223	175	162	76	123	168	157	218	253	159	104		4:30	6:40	3:24	1:28	0:45	1:25	2:25	2:08	1:19	1:56	2:09	2:40	10:59	1:31	3:10	1:15
Penzance	688	301	552	269	394	279	184	343	218	463	278	316	369	355	551	109	663	561	217	374	388	715	375	419	412	391	310	359	353	344	449	481	393	323	261		9:43	1:41	4:22	4:27	3:39	5:51	5:09	4:11	5:46	5:12	4:20	14:02	4:02	6:36	4:59
Perth	86	366	85	336	245	509	412	370	422	134	346	309	254	485	43	487	103	59	362	439	360	113	424	184	273	233	326	290	244	254	191	148	394	299	404	598		8:37	7:54	7:18	7:42	5:03	5:28	7:46	7:43	4:49	7:52	4:30	5:55	4:28	7:24
Plymouth	619	232	461	203	325	206	111	274	159	372	209	254	300	286	485	43	592	490	150	305	322	648	305	348	326	323	231	284	299	281	379	412	327	255	193	75	529		3:16	3:20	2:32	4:44	4:02	3:04	4:39	4:05	3:14	12:55	2:55	5:29	3:54
Portsmouth	579	231	440	147	274	50	95	132	138	357	132	184	231	137	448	127	555	455	114	161	303	603	158	308	268	245	166	209	254	237	315	360	200	191	83	235	486	170		1:18	0:52	3:39	3:23	0:32	2:11	3:23	3:13	12:13	2:20	4:25	1:39
Reading	538	180	399	103	213	79	77	90	112	309	90	138	184	115	402	141	506	406	75	129	264	554	126	263	209	207	113	168	193	197	264	295	152	129	25	251	445	184	60		1:22	3:01	2:45	1:09	1:46	2:45	2:37	11:35	1:44	3:47	0:56
Salisbury	538	178	383	121	245	82	53	140	101	312	113	159	207	158	400	91	510	408	73	177	262	569	177	265	251	230	132	187	213	208	287	318	200	162	65	201	443	132	43	57		3:37	3:09	0:40	2:37	3:12	2:47	12:02	2:02	4:22	1:52
Sheffield	390	173	235	79	40	225	163	121	193	154	75	35	21	268	230	245	352	250	139	185	164	387	176	102	66	33	68	46	74	40	102	133	144	37	137	361	273	293	228	160	203		2:08	3:32	3:22	1:40	3:59	9:22	2:04	1:11	2:53
Shrewsbury	419	73	260	47	100	216	116	140	107	171	64	67	114	249	262	175	369	267	77	215	104	424	195	125	163	102	79	123	59	67	166	203	196	86	105	286	309	218	195	147	150	85		3:16	3:22	1:04	2:45	9:46	1:23	2:46	2:53
Southampton	564	213	401	128	235	64	75	129	122	330	114	167	201	150	433	106	528	426	98	157	287	590	162	276	249	230	136	189	235	215	288	320	190	162	66	217	476	149	20	47	23	206	175		2:26	3:15	3:05	12:05	2:12	4:16	1:40
Southend-on-Sea	549	258	431	152	220	85	177	64	211	342	129	168	185	89	395	226	548	438	152	57	303	549	57	283	200	213	139	156	255	225	262	299	99	160	105	337	439	269	117	98	132	197	173	126		3:21	4:09	12:02	3:03	3:51	1:07
Stoke-on-Trent	381	108	243	47	75	217	127	137	140	150	64	36	74	236	241	202	348	248	95	201	122	410	179	121	117	78	55	87	56	36	142	173	171	55	118	311	287	241	201	147	168	50	35	183	199		3:18	9:08	1:23	2:09	2:53
Swansea	529	76	368	124	220	209	80	236	41	279	150	184	244	264	370	154	477	375	91	279	172	578	279	249	262	229	174	226	168	187	293	323	286	178	144	266	446	196	175	147	136	202	124	159	245	159		12:11	2:10	4:44	3:18
Thurso	212	584	304	557	461	728	644	589	640	352	552	529	475	706	262	715	169	268	604	657	589	108	654	402	492	453	544	510	463	471	410	367	613	519	621	823	220	758	709	662	664	506	523	682	659	502	631		10:15	8:47	11:43
Worcester	448	96	309	29	135	162	62	119	73	220	46	68	124	197	306	136	418	311	28	168	151	480	174	169	166	146	72	118	108	101	203	229	180	85	57	244	350	177	146	95	101	103	49	124	150	65	97	572		2:49	2:24
York	345	193	201	129	34	269	227	151	237	116	129	84	33	269	187	289	314	214	181	232	185	344	200	81	38	24	108	76	96	65	48	83	176	84	174	400	230	331	257	217	244	54	132	244	214	114	268	450	164		3:39
London	537	228	440	118	203	53	118	61	151	309	97	129	171	76	403	179	511	404	116	86	277	562	82	263	214	195	103	155	211	209	251	283	117	128	59	285	451	216	84	41	92	166	161	82	43	161	187	669	136	211	

Distance in miles

Scale to Map Pages 4-169

1:158,400 = 2.5 miles to 1 inch (2.54 cm) / 1.6 km to 1 cm

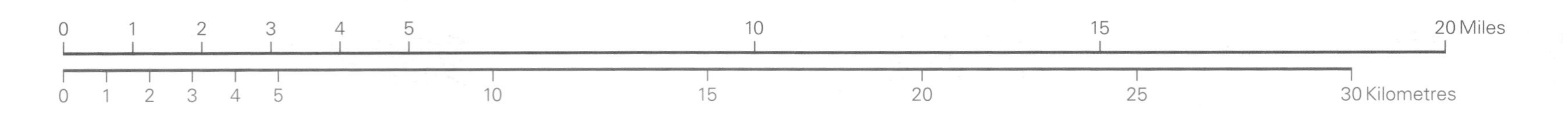

Reference

Motorway
Autoroute
Autobahn
`M1`

Motorway Under Construction
Autoroute en construction
Autobahn im Bau

Motorway Proposed
Autoroute prévue
Geplante Autobahn

Motorway Junctions with Numbers
Unlimited Interchange **4**
Limited Interchange **5**

Autoroute échangeur numéroté
Echangeur complet
Echangeur partiel

Autobahnanschlußstelle mit Nummer
Unbeschränkter Fahrtrichtungswechsel
Beschränkter Fahrtrichtungswechsel

Motorway Service Area (with fuel station)
with access from one carriageway only

Aire de services d'autoroute (avec station service)
accessible d'un seul côté
Rastplatz oder Raststätte (mit tankstelle)
Einbahn

Major Road Service Area (with fuel station) with 24 hour facilities
Primary Route (S)   Class A Road (S)
Aire de services sur route prioritaire (avec station service) Ouverte 24h sur 24
Route à grande circulation   Route de type A
Raststätte (mit tankstelle) Durchgehend geöffnet
Hauptverkehrsstraße   A- Straße

Major Road Junctions   Detailed **4**
Jonctions grands routiers   Détaillé
Hauptverkehrsstraße Kreuzungen   Ausführlich
                            Other Autre Andere

Truckstop (selection of)
Sélection d'aire pour poids lourds
Auswahl von Fernfahrerrastplatz
(T)

Primary Route
Route à grande circulation
Hauptverkehrsstraße
`A41`

Primary Route Junction with Number
Echangeur numéroté
Hauptverkehrsstraßenkreuzung mit Nummer
5

Primary Route Destination
Route prioritaire, direction
Hauptverkehrsstraße Richtung
DOVER

Dual Carriageways (A & B roads)
Route à double chaussées séparées (route A & B)
Zweispurige Schnellstraße (A- und B- Straßen)

Class A Road
Route de type A
A-Straße
`A129`

Class B Road
Route de type B
B-Straße
`B177`

Narrow Major Road (passing places)
Route prioritaire étroite (possibilité de dépassement)
Schmale Hauptverkehrsstraße (mit Überholmöglichkeit)

Major Roads Under Construction
Route prioritaire en construction
Hauptverkehrsstaße im Bau

Major Roads Proposed
Route prioritaire prévue
Geplante Hauptverkehrsstaße

Safety Cameras with Speed Limits
Single Camera   (30)
Multiple Cameras located along road   (50)
Single & Multiple Variable Speed Cameras (V) (V)

Radars de contrôle de vitesse
Radar simple
Radars multiples situés le long de la route
Radars simples et multiples de contrôle de vitesse variable

Sicherheitskameras mit Tempolimit
Einzelne Kamera
Mehrere Kameras entlang der Straße
Einzelne und mehrere Kameras für variables Tempolimit

Fuel Station
Station service
Tankstelle

Gradient 1:7 (14%) **& steeper**
(descent in direction of arrow)
Pente égale ou supérieure à 14% (dans le sens de la descente)
14% Steigung und steiler (in Pfeilrichtung)

Toll *Toll*
Barrière de péage
Gebührenpflichtig

Dart Charge (C)
www.gov.uk/pay-dartford-crossing-charge

Park & Ride **P+R**
Parking avec Service Navette
Parken und Reisen

Mileage between markers 8
Distence en miles entre les flèches
Strecke zwischen Markierungen in Meilen

Airport ⊕
Aéroport
Flughafen

Airfield +
Terrain d'aviation
Flugplatz

Heliport Ⓗ
Héliport
Hubschrauberlandeplatz

Ferry
(vehicular, sea) (véhicules, mer) (auto, meer)
(vehicular, river) (véhicules, rivière) (auto, fluß)
(foot only) (piétons) (nur für Personen)

Railway and Station
Voie ferrée et gare
Eisenbahnlinie und Bahnhof

Level Crossing and Tunnel
Passage à niveau et tunnel
Bahnübergang und Tunnel

River or Canal
Rivière ou canal
Fluß oder Kanal

County or Unitary Authority Boundary
Limite de comté ou de division administrative
Grafschafts- oder Verwaltungsbezirksgrenze

National Boundary
Frontière nationale
Landesgrenze

Built-up Area
Agglomération
Geschlossene Ortschaft

Town, Village or Hamlet
Ville, Village ou hameau
Stadt, Dorf oder Weiler

Wooded Area
Zone boisée
Waldgebiet

Spot Height in Feet · 813
Altitude (en pieds)
Höhe in Fuß

Relief above 400' (122m)
Relief par estompage au-dessus de 400' (122m)
Reliefschattierung über 400' (122m)

National Grid Reference (kilometres) ¹00
Coordonnées géographiques nationales (Kilomètres)
Nationale geographische Koordinaten (Kilometer)

Page Continuation
Suite à la page indiquée
Seitenfortsetzung
48

Area covered by Main Route map **MAIN ROUTE 180**
Repartition des cartes des principaux axes routiers
Von Karten mit Hauptverkehrsstrecken

Area covered by Town Plan **PAGE 194**
Ville ayant un plan à la page indiquée
Von Karten mit Stadtplänen erfaßter Bereich

Tourist Information

Abbey, Church, Friary, Priory ✝
Abbaye, église, monastère, prieuré
Abtei, Kirche, Mönchskloster, Kloster

Animal Collection
Ménagerie
Tiersammlung

Aquarium
Aquarium
Aquarium

Arboretum, Botanical Garden
Jardin Botanique
Botanischer Garten

Aviary, Bird Garden
Volière
Voliere

Battle Site and Date 1066
Champ de bataille et date
Schlachtfeld und Datum

Blue Flag Beach
Plage Pavillon Bleu
Blaue Flagge Strand

Bridge
Pont
Brücke

Castle (open to public)
Château (ouvert au public)
Schloß / Burg (für die Öffentlichkeit zugänglich)

Castle with Garden (open to public)
Château avec parc (ouvert au public)
Schloß mit Garten (für die Öffentlichkeit zugänglich)

Cathedral ✝
Cathédrale
Kathedrale

Cidermaker
Cidrerie (fabrication)
Apfelwein Hersteller

Country Park
Parc régional
Landschaftspark

Distillery
Distillerie
Brennerei

Farm Park, Open Farm
Park Animalier
Bauernhof Park

Fortress, Hill Fort ※
Château Fort
Festung

Garden (open to public) �֎
Jardin (ouvert au public)
Garten (für die Öffentlichkeit zugänglich)

Golf Course ⚑
Terrain de golf
Golfplatz

Historic Building (open to public) 🏛
Monument historique (ouvert au public)
Historisches Gebäude (für die Öffentlichkeit zugänglich)

Historic Building with Garden (open to public) 🏛
Monument historique avec jardin (ouvert au public)
Historisches Gebäude mit Garten (für die Öffentlichkeit zugänglich)

Horse Racecourse
Hippodrome
Pferderennbahn

Industrial Monument ☼
Monument Industrielle
Industriedenkmal

Leisure Park, Leisure Pool
Parc d'Attraction, Loisirs Piscine
Freizeitpark, Freizeit pool

Lighthouse ♟
Phare
Leuchtturm

Mine, Cave
Mine, Grotte
Bergwerk, Höhle

Monument ♟
Monument
Denkmal

Motor Racing Circuit
Circuit Automobile
Automobilrennbahn

Museum, Art Gallery Ⓜ
Musée
Museum, Galerie

National Park
Parc national
Nationalpark

National Trust Property
National Trust Property
National Trust- Eigentum

Nature Reserve or Bird Sanctuary
Réserve naturelle botanique ou ornithologique
Natur- oder Vogelschutzgebiet

Nature Trail or Forest Walk
Chemin forestier, piste verte
Naturpfad oder Waldweg

Picnic Site
Lieu pour pique-nique
Picknickplatz

Place of Interest *Craft Centre* •
Site, curiosité
Sehenswürdigkeit

Prehistoric Monument
Monument Préhistorique
Prähistorische Denkmal

Railway, Steam or Narrow Gauge
Chemin de fer, à vapeur ou à voie étroite
Eisenbahn, Dampf- oder Schmalspurbahn

Roman Remains
Vestiges Romains
Römischen Ruinen

Theme Park
Centre de loisirs
Vergnügungspark

Tourist Information Centre ℹ
Office de Tourisme
Touristeninformationen

Viewpoint (360 degrees) (180 degrees)
Vue panoramique (360 degrés) (180 degrés)
Aussichtspunkt (360 Grade) (180 Grade)

Vineyard
Vignoble
Weinberg

Visitor Information Centre Ⓥ
Centre d'information touristique
Besucherzentrum

Wildlife Park
Réserve de faune
Wildpark

Windmill
Moulin à vent
Windmühle

Zoo or Safari Park
Parc ou réserve zoologique
Zoo oder Safari-Park

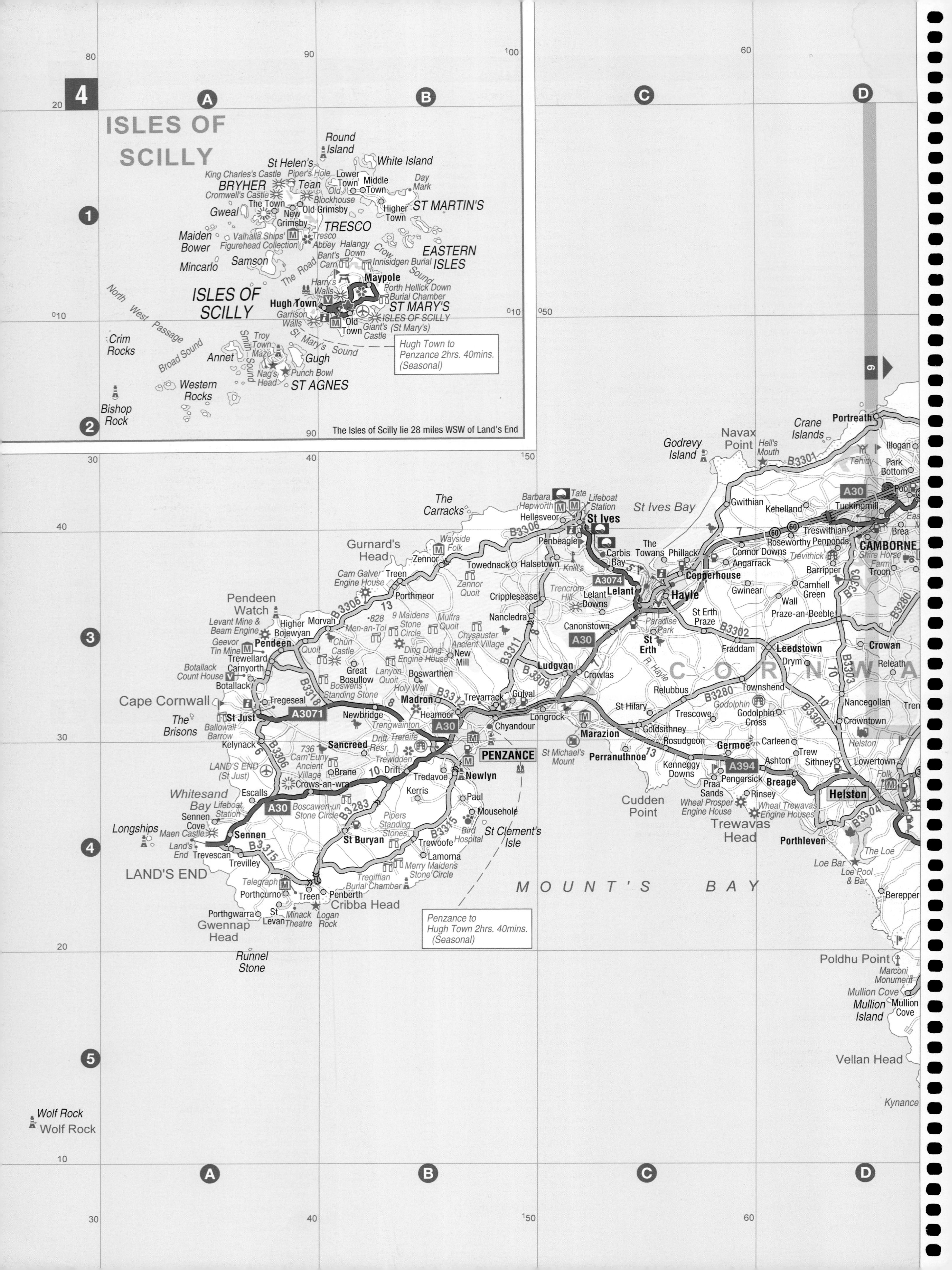

4

ISLES OF SCILLY

80 · 90 · 100 · 60

20

A · **B** · **C** · **D**

Round Island
St Helen's
White Island
King Charles's Castle
Piper's Hole
Lower Town · Middle Town
BRYHER · Tean · Old Town
Day Mark
Cromwell's Castle · Blockhouse
The Town · Old Grimsby
Gweal · New Grimsby · Higher Town
ST MARTIN'S
TRESCO
Maiden Bower
Valhalla Ships' Figurehead Collection
Tresco Abbey
Halangy Down
EASTERN ISLES
Mincarlo · Samson · Bant's Carn · Innisidgen Burial Chamber
Crow Sound
Maypole
Harry's Walls · Porth Hellick Down Burial Chamber
ISLES OF SCILLY
Hugh Town
ST MARY'S
Garrison Walls · Old Town · **ISLES OF SCILLY (St Mary's)**
Giant's Castle
010 · 010 · 050

Crim Rocks
North West Passage
Troy Town Maze
Annet · Smith Sound · Nag's Head · Gugh · Punch Bowl
Broad Sound · **ST AGNES**
The Road
St Mary's Sound

Hugh Town to Penzance 2hrs. 40mins. (Seasonal)

Western Rocks
Bishop Rock

2

The Isles of Scilly lie 28 miles WSW of Land's End

30 · 40 · 150

6

Portreath
Navax Point
Crane Islands
Godrevy Island
Hell's Mouth
B3301
Illogan · Tehidy · Park Bottom
A30
Gwithian · Kehelland · Tuckingmill
Pool
The Carracks
Barbara Hepworth Tate Lifeboat Station
St Ives Bay
Treswithian · **CAMBORNE** · East...
Brea
Gurnard's Head
Wayside Folk
St Ives
Roseworthy Penponds
7 · 60
Shire Horse Farm
Zennor · Penbeagle
Carbis Bay
The Towans · Phillack
Connor Downs · Angarrack · Trevithick
Barripper · Troon
Carn Galver Engine House · Treen
Porthmeor
Halsetown
Knill's
Copperhouse
Gwinear · Carnhell Green · Wall · Praze-an-Beeble
Pendeen Watch
Towednack
Zennor Quoit
Trencrom Hill
A3074
Hayle
St Erth Praze
Levant Mine & Beam Engine
Higher Bojewyan · Morvah
·828
9 Maidens Men-an-Tol Stone Circle
Mulfra Quoit
Cripplesease
Lelant Downs · **Lelant**
St Erth
Paradise Park
B3302 · **Leedstown** · **Crowan**
Geevor Tin Mine
Pendeen
Chûn Castle Quoit
Ding Dong Engine House
Chysauster Ancient Village
Nancledra
A30
Fraddam · Drym
Releath
Trewellard Carnyorth
Great Bosullow
Lanyon Quoit
New Mill
B3311
Canonstown
St Erth
Relubbus · Townshend
B3303
Botallack Count House
Boswens Standing Stone
Boswarthen
Holy Well
Ludgvan
Crowlas
B3280 · Godolphin
Nancegollan · Tren...
C · O · R · N · W · A
Botallack
Cape Cornwall
Tregeseal
Newbridge
Trengwainton
Madron · Heamoor
Trevarrack
Gulval
B3309
St Hilary
Trescowe · Godolphin Cross
Crowntown
The Brisons
St Just
A3071
Ballowall Barrow
Drift Trereife
Chyandour
Longrock
Marazion
Goldsithney · Rosudgeon
Carleen · Helston
Kelynack
736 Carn Euny Ancient Village
Sancreed
Trewidden · Drift
PENZANCE
St Michael's Mount
Germoe
Trew Sithney
Lowertown
LAND'S END (St Just)
Brane
Tredavoe
Newlyn
Kennegy Downs · Ashton
Helston
Escalls
Crows-an-wra
Kerris · Paul
Cudden Point
Praa Sands · Pengersick
Breage
Whitesand Bay
A30
Boscawen-un Stone Circle
Mousehole
Wheal Prosper Engine House
Helston
Sennen Cove Lifeboat Station
B3283
Pipers Standing Stones
Bird Hospital
St Clement's Isle
Wheal Trewavas Engine Houses
Longships · Maen Castle
Sennen
B3315 · Trewoofe
Lamorna
Trewavas Head
B3304
Land's End · Trevescan · Trevilley
St Buryan
Merry Maidens Stone Circle
Porthleven
The Loe
LAND'S END
Telegraph
Tregiffian Burial Chamber
Penberth
MOUNT'S BAY
Loe Bar · Loe Pool & Bar
Porthcurno · Treen
Cribba Head
Porthgwarra · St Levan · Minack Theatre · Logan Rock
Berepper
Gwennap Head
Runnel Stone
Penzance to Hugh Town 2hrs. 40mins. (Seasonal)
Poldhu Point
Marconi Monument
Mullion Cove
Mullion
Mullion Island · Mullion Cove

5

Wolf Rock
Wolf Rock

Vellan Head

Kynance

A · **B** · **C** · **D**

30 · 40 · 150 · 60

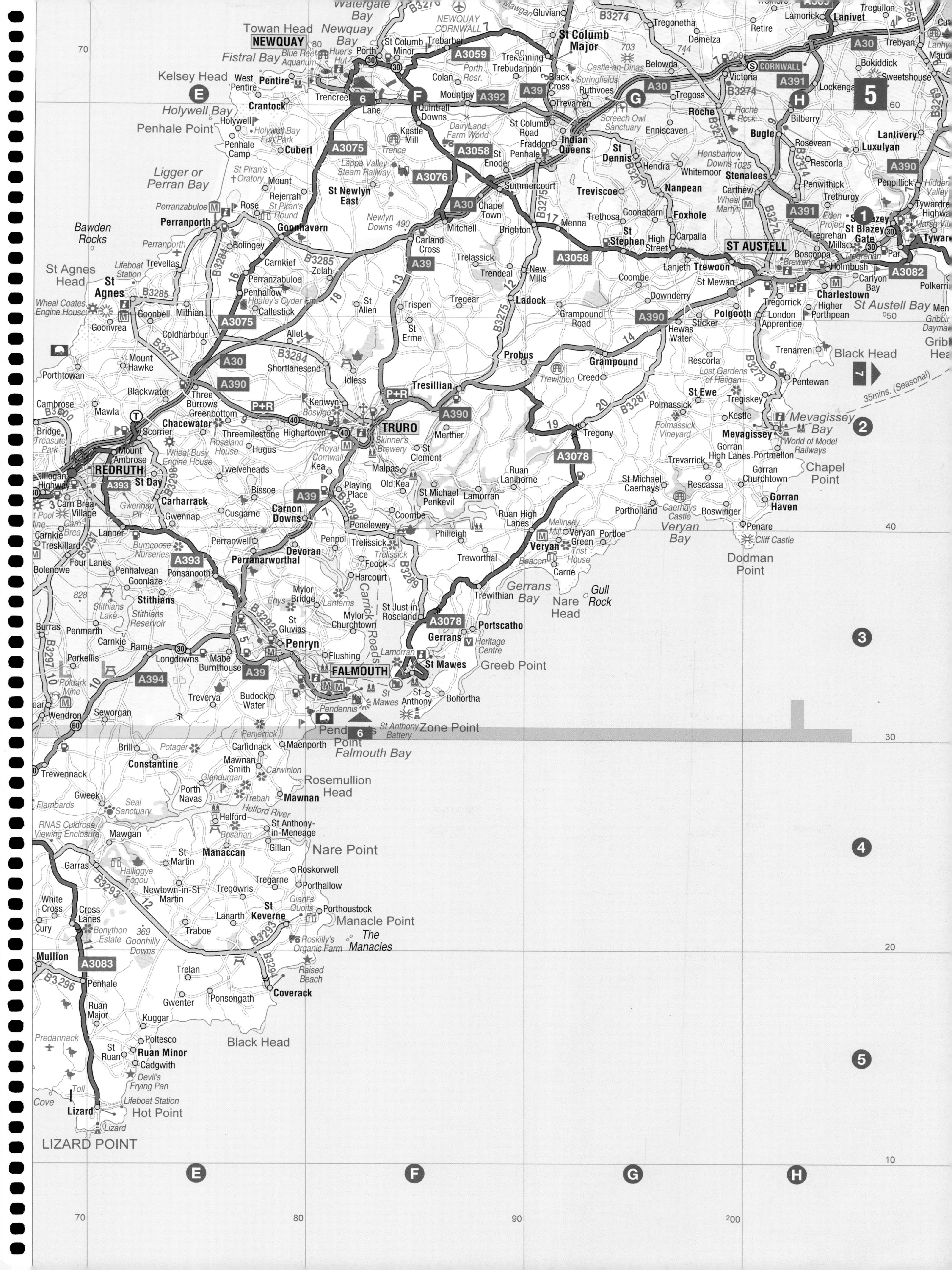

NEWQUAY
Newquay Bay
Towan Head
Fistral Bay
Kelsey Head
West Pentire
Pentire
Crantock
Holywell Bay
Penhale Point
Cubert
Ligger or Perran Bay
Perranporth
Bawden Rocks
St Agnes Head
St Agnes
Goonhavern
St Newlyn East
St Columb Major
St Columb Minor
Indian Queens
Roche
Bugle
Luxulyan
Lanlivery
St Dennis
Nanpean
Foxhole
St Stephen
ST AUSTELL
St Blazey
Par
Charlestown
St Austell Bay
Black Head
Polgooth
Grampound
Probus
Tresillian
TRURO
Chacewater
REDRUTH
St Day
Carharrack
Mevagissey
Mevagissey Bay
Gorran Haven
Chapel Point
Dodman Point
Veryan
Veryan Bay
Tregony
Nare Head
Gull Rock
Gerrans Bay
Portscatho
Gerrans
St Mawes
Greeb Point
Zone Point
FALMOUTH
Penryn
Falmouth Bay
Pendennis Point
Mylor Bridge
Devoran
Perranarworthal
Stithians
Constantine
Mawnan
Rosemullion Head
Nare Point
Manaccan
St Keverne
Manacle Point
The Manacles
Coverack
Black Head
Mullion
Ruan Minor
Lizard
Hot Point
LIZARD POINT
A30
A39
A390
A391
A392
A393
A394
A3058
A3059
A3075
A3076
A3078
A3082
A3083
B3274
B3275
B3284
B3285
B3287
B3289
B3292
B3293
B3294
B3296
B3297
B3298
B3273
B3277
35mins. (Seasonal)
E
F
G
H
1
2
3
4
5
70
80
90
200
60
50
40
30
20
10

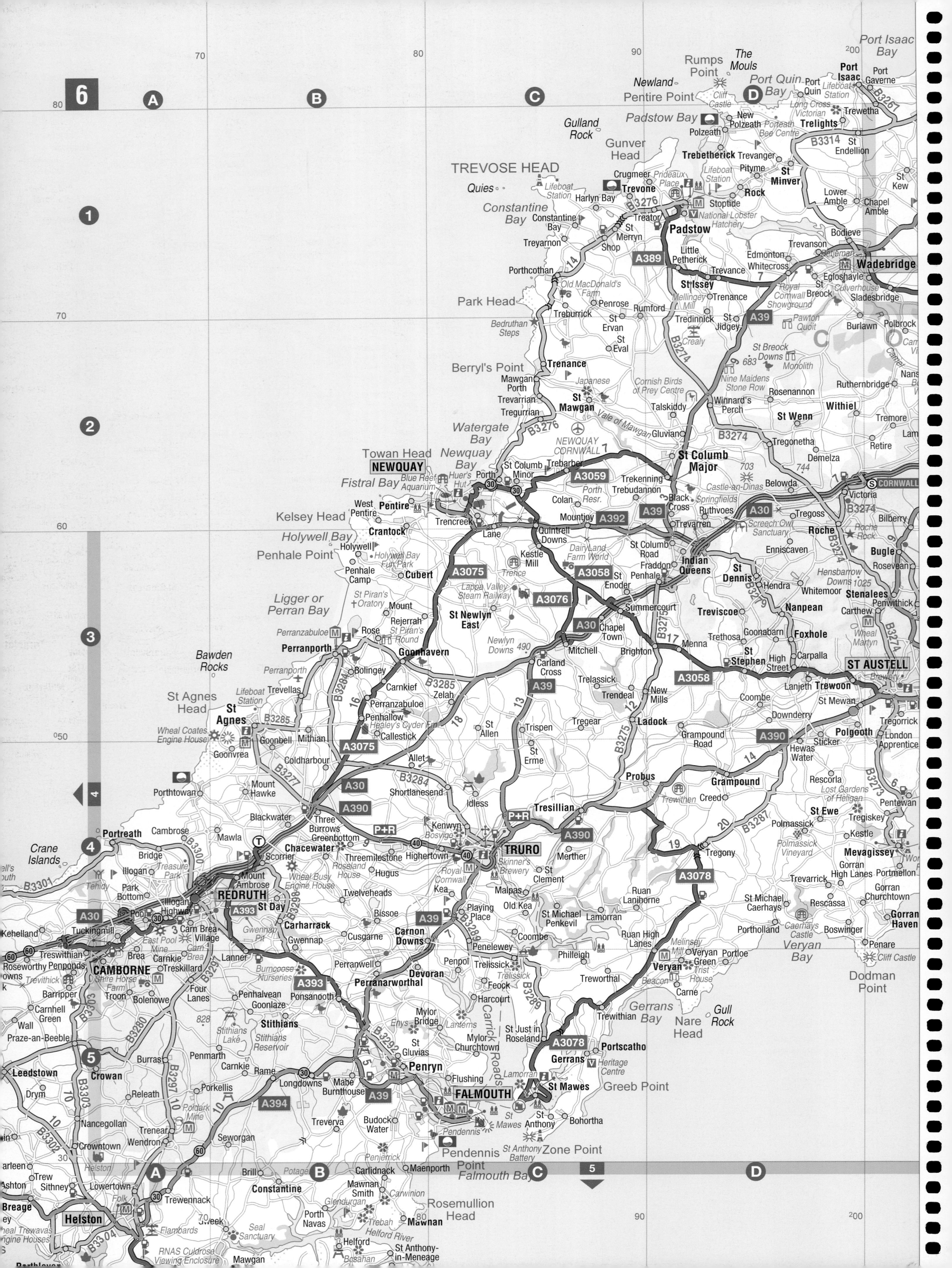

6
A
B
C
D
1
2
3
4
5
70
80
90
200
60
50
Port Isaac Bay
Port Isaac
Port Gaverne
Rumps Point
The Mouls
Newland
Pentire Point
Cliff Castle
Port Quin Bay
Port Quin
Lifeboat Station
Long Cross Victorian Gardens
Trewetha
Trelights
Padstow Bay
New Polzeath
Polzeath
Bee Centre
St Endellion
B3314
B3267
Gulland Rock
Gunver Head
Trebetherick
Trevanger
Pityme
St Minver
TREVOSE HEAD
Crugmeer
Prideaux Place
Lifeboat Station
Quies
Trevone
Harlyn Bay
Rock
Stoptide
Lower Amble
Chapel Amble
St Kew
Constantine Bay
Treator
B3276
National Lobster Hatchery
Padstow
St Merryn
Shop
Treyarnon
A389
Little Petherick
Edmonton
Whitecross
Trevanson
Bodieve
Wadebridge
Porthcothan
Trevance
St Issey
Egloshayle
St Breock
Royal Cornwall Showground
Sladesbridge
Old MacDonald's Farm
Penrose
Rumford
Park Head
Mellingey Mill
Trenance
Tredinnick
St Jidgey
A39
Pawton Quoit
Burlawn
Polbrock
Treburrick
St Ervan
St Eval
Bedruthan Steps
B3274
Crealy
St Breock Downs
Monolith
Berryl's Point
Trenance
Nine Maidens Stone Row
Mawgan Porth
Japanese Garden
Cornish Birds of Prey Centre
Rosenannon
Ruthernbridge
Trevarrian
St Mawgan
Talskiddy
Winnard's Perch
Withiel
Tregurrian
Vale of Mawgan
Gluvian
St Wenn
Tremore
Watergate Bay
NEWQUAY CORNWALL
Tregonetha
Retire
Demelza
Town Head
Newquay Bay
NEWQUAY
St Columb Major
Trebarber
St Columb Minor
Porth
A3059
Blue Reef Aquarium
Huer's Hut
Fistral Bay
Trekenning
Trebudannon
Castle-an-Dinas
Belowda
Victoria
Colan
Porth Resr.
Black Cross
Springfields
Ruthvoes
West Pentire
Pentire
Kelsey Head
Mountjoy
A392
A39
A30
Tregoss
Trevarren
Bilberry
Trencreek
Crantock
Quintrell Downs
Screech Owl Sanctuary
Roche
Roche Rock
Holywell Bay
Holywell
Lane
St Columb Road
Holywell Bay Fun Park
Dairyland Farm World
Enniscaven
Bugle
Penhale Point
Kestle Mill
Trerice
Indian Queens
Fraddon
Penhale Camp
Cubert
A3075
A3058
St Enoder
Penhale
St Dennis
Rosevean
Hensbarrow Downs
Hendra
Whitemoor
Stenalees
Penwithick
Lappa Valley Steam Railway
A3076
St Piran's Oratory
Mount
Summercourt
Ligger or Perran Bay
Rejerrah
St Newlyn East
Chapel Town
Treviscoe
Nanpean
Carthew
Wheal Martyn
Perranzabuloe
Rose
St Piran's Round
Goonhavern
A30
Mitchell
Brighton
Menna
Trethosa
Goonabarn
Foxhole
Perranporth
Newlyn Downs
Carland Cross
St Stephen
High Street
Carpalla
ST AUSTELL
Bawden Rocks
Bolingey
Carnkief
B3285
Zelah
A39
Trelassick
A3058
New Mills
Lanjeth
Trewoon
St Agnes Head
Trevellas
Lifeboat Station
Trendeal
Coombe
St Mewan
St Agnes
Perranzabuloe
Penhallow
Healey's Cyder Farm
Callestick
St Allen
Trispen
Tregear
Ladock
Downderry
Tregorrick
Wheal Coates Engine House
Goonbell
Mithian
A3075
Grampound Road
A390
Polgooth
London Apprentice
Goonvrea
Coldharbour
St Erme
Sticker
Hewas Water
B3277
Allet
B3275
Mount Hawke
Probus
Grampound
Resrcolla
Porthtowan
A30
B3284
Shortlanesend
Lost Gardens of Heligan
Pentewan
Idless
Creed
Trewithen
Blackwater
A390
Tresillian
St Ewe
Three Burrows
P+R
B3287
Polmassick
Tregiskey
Kestle
Portreath
Cambrose
Mawla
Chacewater
Kenwyn
Bosvigo
A390
Crane Islands
Greenbottom
TRURO
Polmassick Vineyard
Mevagissey
Bridge
Scorrier
Threemilestone
Highertown
Merther
Tregony
Illogan
Treasure Park
Mount Ambrose
Roseland House
Hugus
Skinner's Brewery
St Clement
A3078
Gorran High Lanes
Portmellon
B3301
Tehidy
Park Bottom
REDRUTH
Wheal Busy Engine House
Royal Cornwall Hospital
Kea
Trevarrick
Gorran Churchtown
Illogan Highway
St Day
Twelveheads
Malpas
Ruan Lanihorne
St Michael Caerhays
Rescassa
A30
Pool
A393
B3298
Old Kea
Tuckingmill
Cam Brea Village
Carharrack
Bissoe
Playing Place
St Michael Penkevil
Lamorran
Portholland
Caerhays Castle
Boswinger
Gorran Haven
Kehelland
East Pool Mine
Gwennap Pit
A39
Gwennap
Cusgarne
Carnon Downs
B3289
Coombe
Ruan High Lanes
Veryan Bay
Penare
Treswithian
Brea
Carnkie
Carn Brea
Penelewey
Melinsey Mill
Veryan Green
Portloe
Cliff Castle
Roseworthy
Penponds
CAMBORNE
Treskillard
Lanner
Perranwell
Penpol
Trelissick
Philleigh
Veryan
Trist House
Dodman Point
Trevithick
Shire Horse Farm
B3297
Burncoose Nurseries
Devoran
Trelissick
Treworthal
Barripper
Troon
Bolenowe
Four Lanes
A393
Perranarworthal
Feock
Beacon
Carne
Carnhell Green
B3303
Penhalvean
Goonlaze
Ponsanooth
Harcourt
Gerrans Bay
Gull Rock
Wall
828
Stithians
Mylor Bridge
Lanterns
Trewithian
Nare Head
Praze-an-Beeble
B3280
Stithians Lake
Stithians Reservoir
Enys
St Gluvias
Mylor Churchtown
Carrick Roads
St Just in Roseland
A3078
Portscatho
Burras
Penmarth
B3292
Gerrans
Heritage Centre
Leedstown
Crowan
Carnkie
Rame
Penryn
Flushing
Lamorran
St Mawes
Drym
Releath
Porkellis
Longdowns
Mabe Burnthouse
A39
FALMOUTH
Greeb Point
A394
Poldark Mine
Treverva
Budock Water
St Mawes
St Anthony
Bohortha
Nancegollan
B3302
Trenear
Wendron
Seworgan
Pendennis
Crowntown
Penjerrick
Pendennis Point
St Anthony Battery
Zone Point
Helston
Potager
Brill
Carlidnack
Maenporth
Falmouth Bay
Trew
Sithney
Lowertown
Constantine
Mawnan Smith
Carwinion
Breage
Folk Museum
Trewennack
Glendurgan
Rosemullion Head
Helston
Gweek
Seal Sanctuary
Porth Navas
Trebah
Mawnan
Flambards
Helford River
B3304
RNAS Culdrose Viewing Enclosure
Helford
Bosahan
St Anthony-in-Meneage
Mawgan

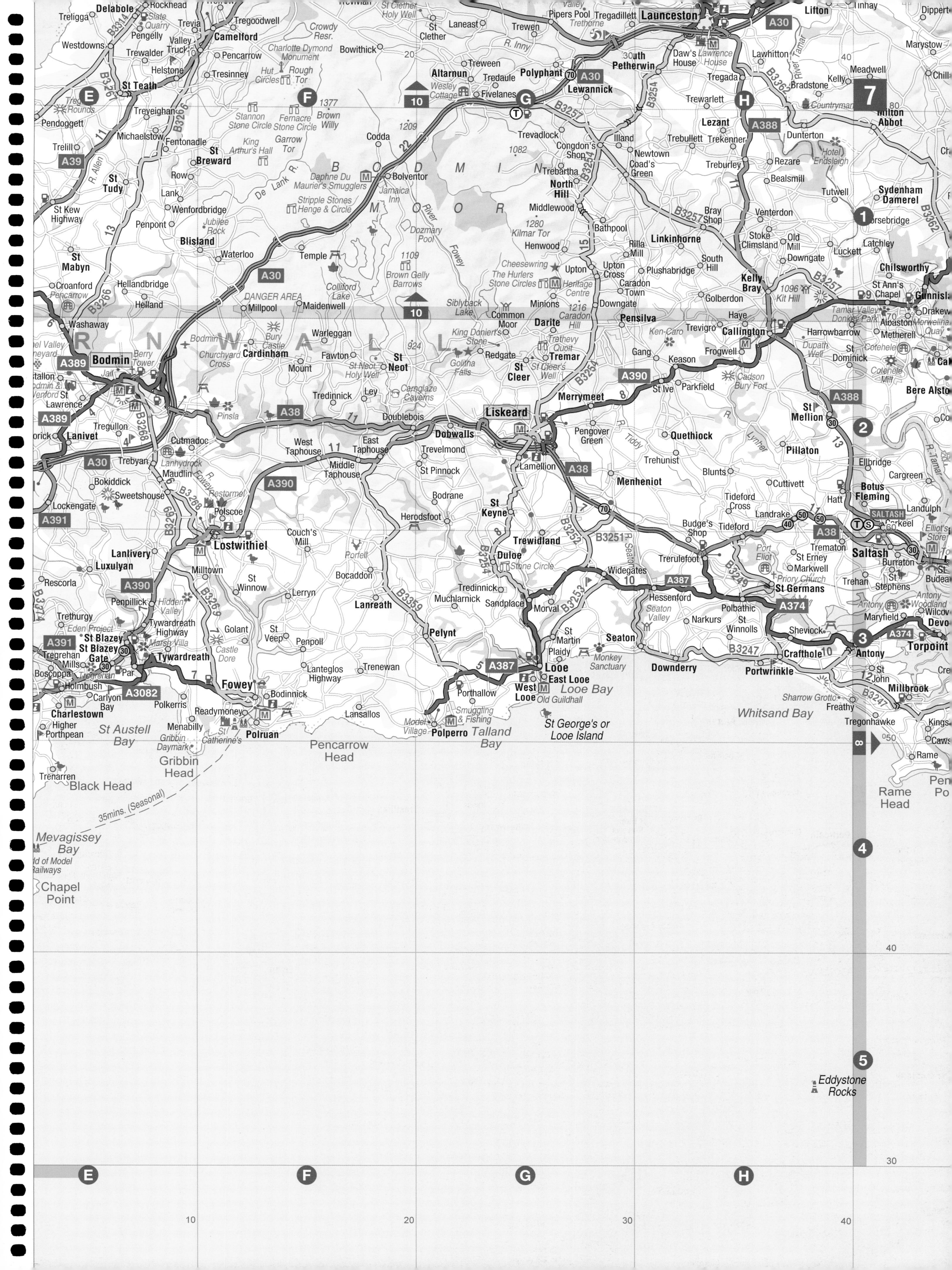

Delabole
Rockhead
Treligga
Slate Quarry
Pengelly
Trevia
Tregoodwell
Crowdy Resr.
St Clether Holy Well
St Clether
Laneast
Trewen
Pipers Pool
Tregadillett
Trethorne
Launceston
A30
Lifton
Tinhay
Dippert
Westdowns
Valley Truckle
Camelford
Charlotte Dymond Monument
Bowithick
20
R. Inny
Marystow
Trewalder
Pencarrow
Hut Circles
Rough Tor
Treween
South Petherwin
Daw's House
Lawrence House
Lawhitton
40
Meadwell
Helstone
Tresinney
Altarnun
Tredaule
Polyphant
A30
Lewannick
Tregada
B3362
Bradstone
Kelly
Chill
St Teath
E
F
Wesley Cottage
Fivelanes
G
H
Trewarlett
7
B3267
Treveighan
Stannon Stone Circle
Fernacre Stone Circle
1377 Brown Willy
10
B3257
Countryman
80
Milton Abbot
Tregeare Rounds
Pendoggett
B3266
1209
Trevadlock
Congdon's Shop
Illand
Lezant
Trebullett
Trekenner
A388
Dunterton
Michaelstow
Fentonadle
King Arthur's Hall
Garrow Tor
Codda
1082
Newtown
Trelill
St Breward
B
O
D
M
I
N
Trebartha
Coad's Green
Treburley
Rezare
Hotel Endsleigh
A39
Bolventor
Daphne Du Maurier's Smugglers
Jamaica Inn
North Hill
B3254
Bealsmill
Row
St Tudy
Lank
De Lank R.
R. Allen
Stripple Stones Henge & Circle
Tutwell
Sydenham Damerel
St Kew Highway
Wenfordbridge
M
O
O
R
Middlewood
B3257
Bray Shop
Venterdon
Penpont
Jubilee Rock
River Fowey
1280 Kilmar Tor
Bathpool
Horsebridge
1
13
Blisland
Dozmary Pool
Rilla Mill
Linkinhorne
Stoke Climsland
Old Mill
Luckett
Latchley
Henwood
St Mabyn
Waterloo
Temple
1109 Brown Gelly Barrows
Cheesewring
Upton
Upton Cross
Plushabridge
South Hill
Downgate
Chilsworthy
Croanford
Pencarrow
Hellandbridge
A30
Colliford Lake
The Hurlers Stone Circles
Heritage Centre
Caradon Town
Kelly Bray
1096 Kit Hill
B3257
St Ann's Chapel
Gunnislake
Helland
DANGER AREA
Millpool
Maidenwell
Siblyback Lake
Minions
1216 Caradon Hill
Downgate
Golberdon
B3266
10
Common Moor
Haye
Tamar Valley Donkey Park
Albaston
Drakewalls
Morwellham Quay
Washaway
Bury Castle
Warleggan
Darite
Pensilva
Callington
Metherell
R
N
W
A
L
L
Bodmin Moor
King Doniert's Stone
Trethevy Quoit
Ken-Caro
Trevigro
Harrowbarrow
Cotehele
Bodmin
Berry Tower
Churchyard Cross
Cardinham
Fawton
924
Redgate
Tremar
Gang
Frogwell
Dupath Well
St Dominick
A389
Jail
Mount
St Neot
St Neot Holy Well
Golitha Falls
St Cleer
St Cleer's Well
Keason
A390
Cadson Bury Fort
Cotehele Mill
Lanhydrock
Tredinnick
Ley
Carnglaze Caverns
Merrymeet
St Ive
Parkfield
A388
Bere Alston
A389
Pinsla
A38
Doublebois
Liskeard
St Mellion
2
Lanivet
Tregullon
B3268
Cutmadoc
West Taphouse
East Taphouse
Dobwalls
Pengover Green
R. Tiddy
Quethiock
R. Lynher
Pillaton
A30
Trebyan
Lanhydrock
Maudlin
R. Fowey
Trevelmond
Middle Taphouse
Lamellion
A38
Trehunist
Blunts
Ellbridge
Cargreen
R. Tamar
Bokiddick
Sweetshouse
A390
St Pinnock
Menheniot
Cuttivett
Botus Fleming
Lockengate
Restormel
Bodrane
St Keyne
Tideford Cross
Hatt
Landulph
A391
Polscoe
B3268
Herodsford
Landrake
SALTASH
Notter
Elliot's Store
Lanlivery
Luxulyan
Lostwithiel
Couch's Mill
Porfell
Trewidland
B3252
B3251
R. Seaton
Budge's Shop
Tideford
A38
Trematon
Saltash
Burraton
Rescorla
A390
Milltown
St Winnow
Bocaddon
Duloe
Stone Circle
B3254
Widegates
Trerulefoot
Port Eliot
St Erney
Markwell
Priory Church
St Germans
Trehan
St Stephens
Penpillick
Hidden Valley
Lerryn
Lanreath
B3359
Tredinnick
Muchlarnick
Sandplace
Morval
B3253
A387
Hessenford
Seaton Valley
Narkurs
Polbathic
St Winnolls
A374
Antony Woodland
Trethurgy
Eden Project
Tywardreath Highway
Marsh Villa
B3269
Golant
St Veep
Penpoll
Pelynt
St Martin
Seaton
Sheviock
Maryfield
Wilcove
Devonport
A391
St Blazey
St Blazey Gate
Tregrehan Mills
Tywardreath
Castle Dore
Plaidy
Monkey Sanctuary
B3247
Crafthole
3
A374
Antony
Torpoint
Boscoppa
Par
7
Fowey
Lanteglos Highway
Trenewan
A387
Looe
East Looe
Downderry
Portwrinkle
St John
Millbrook
Holmbush
Carlyon Bay
Bodinnick
Porthallow
West Looe
Old Guildhall
Looe Bay
Sharrow Grotto
Freathy
A3082
Polkerris
Charlestown
Readymoney
Lansallos
Smuggling & Fishing
Whitsand Bay
B3247
Higher Porthpean
St Austell Bay
Menabilly
Gribbin Daymark
St Catherine's
Polruan
Model Village
Polperro
Talland Bay
St George's or Looe Island
Tregonhawke
Kingsand
Cawsand
Pencarrow Head
Gribbin Head
8
Rame
Trenarren
Black Head
Rame Head
Penlee Point
35mins. (Seasonal)
Mevagissey Bay
World of Model Railways
Chapel Point
4
40
5
Eddystone Rocks
30
E
F
G
H
10
20
30
40

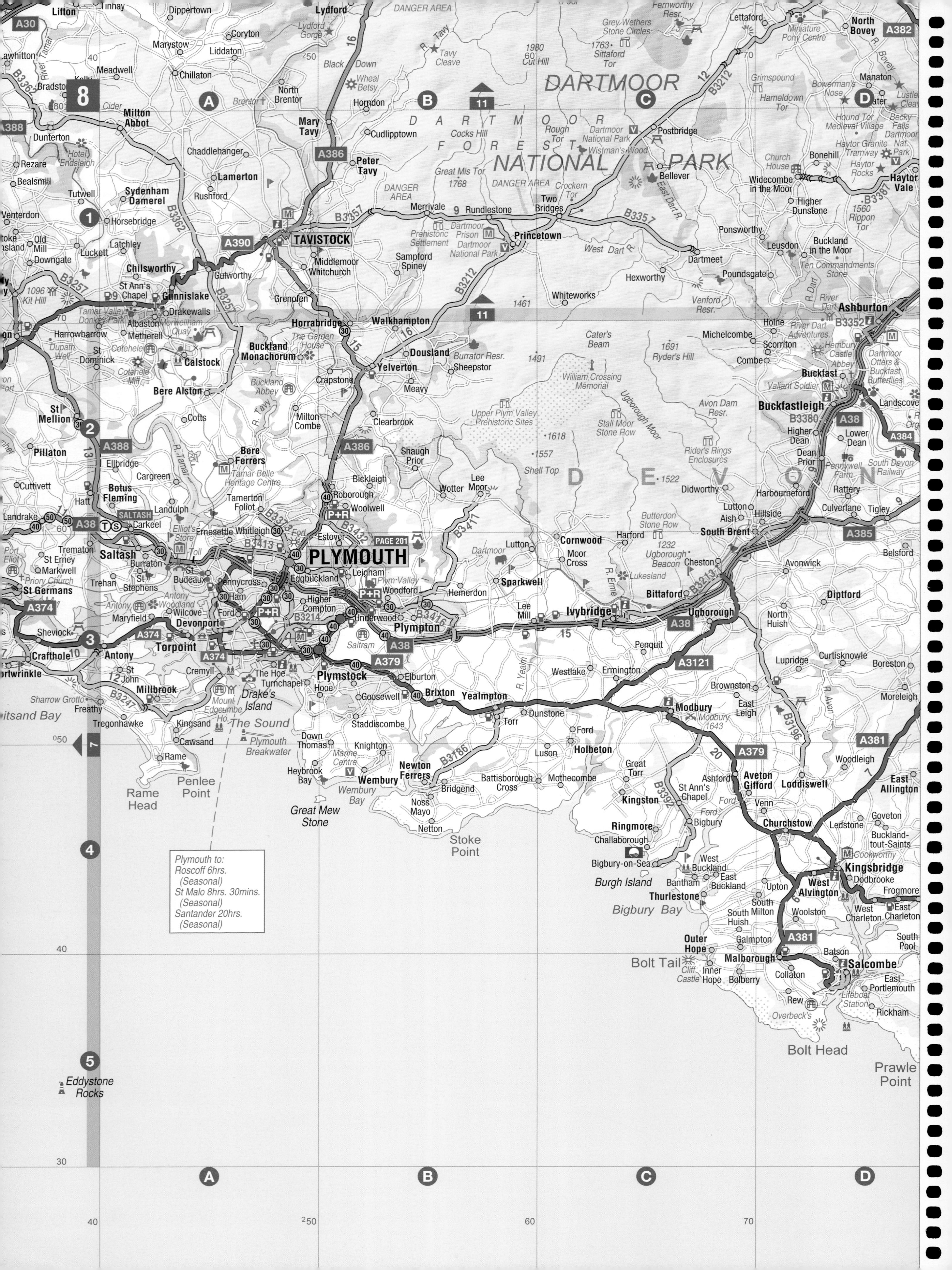

8
DARTMOOR
DARTMOOR FOREST
NATIONAL PARK
DEVON
PLYMOUTH
TAVISTOCK
Princetown
Ivybridge
Plympton
Plymstock
Saltash
Torpoint
Kingsbridge
Salcombe
Ashburton
Buckfastleigh
South Brent
Modbury
Yelverton
Horrabridge
Gunnislake
Calstock
Bere Alston
Yealmpton
Newton Ferrers
Bigbury-on-Sea
Burgh Island
Bigbury Bay
Bolt Tail
Bolt Head
Prawle Point
Rame Head
Penlee Point
Great Mew Stone
Stoke Point
The Sound
Eddystone Rocks
PAGE 201
Plymouth to:
Roscoff 6hrs.
(Seasonal)
St Malo 8hrs. 30mins.
(Seasonal)
Santander 20hrs.
(Seasonal)
A38
A386
A390
A374
A379
A381
A385
A3121
A388
A382
A384

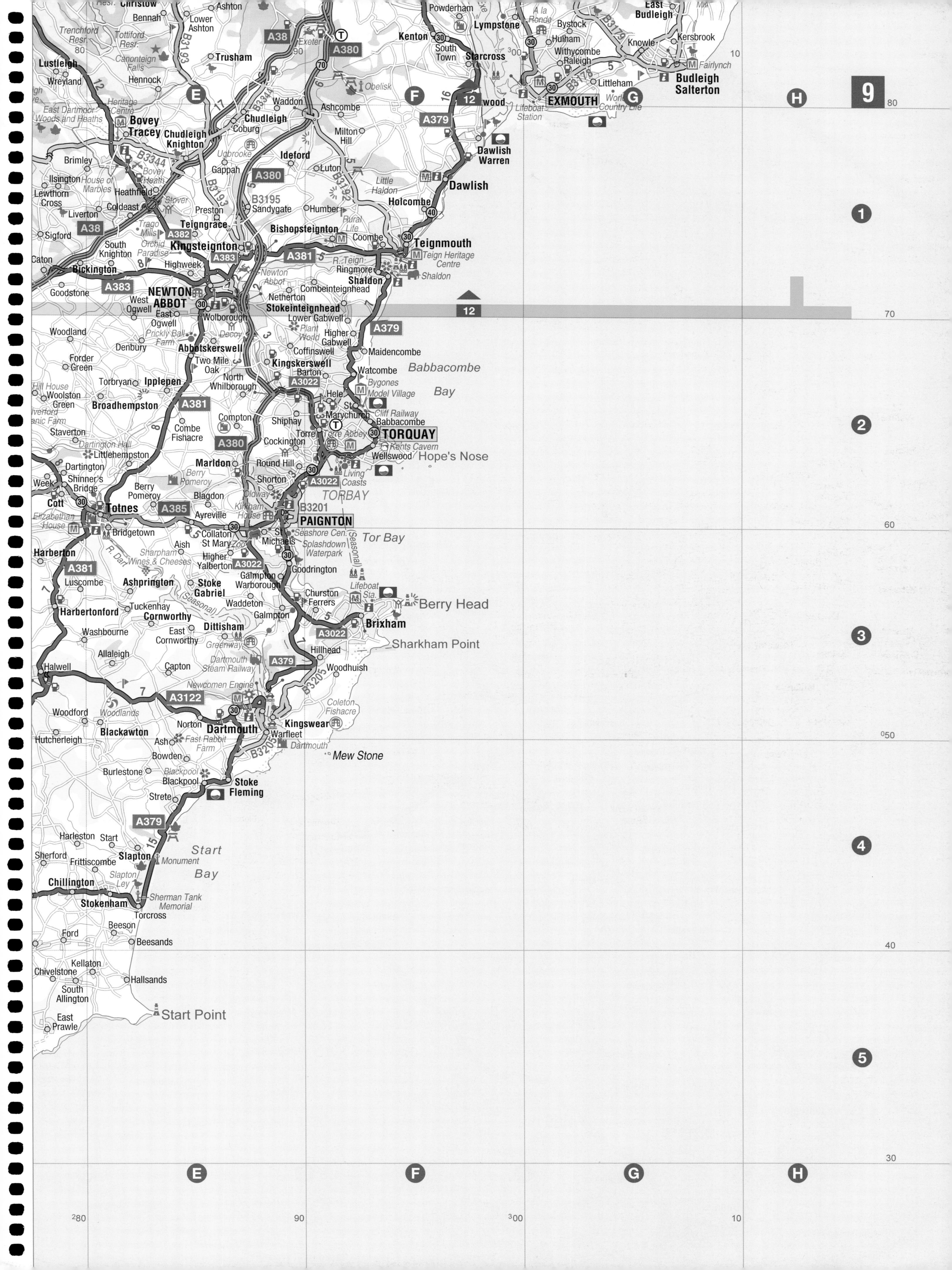
9
Christow
Bennah
Ashton
Lower Ashton
Trenchford Resr.
Tottiford Resr.
Canonteign Falls
Hennock
Trusham
Lustleigh
Wreyland
East Dartmoor Woods and Heaths
Heritage Centre
Bovey Tracey
Chudleigh Knighton
Chudleigh
Coburg
Waddon
Ashcombe
Milton Hill
Obelisk
Exeter
Powderham
Kenton
South Town
Starcross
Lympstone
A la Ronde
Bystock
Hulham
Withycombe Raleigh
East Budleigh
Knowle
Kersbrook
Fairlynch
Budleigh Salterton
Littleham
EXMOUTH
Lifeboat Station
World Country Life
Dawlish Warren
Dawlish
Holcombe
Little Haldon
Luton
Ideford
Ugbrooke
Gappah
Brimley
Ilsington
House of Marbles
Bovey Heath
Lewthorn Cross
Heathfield
Stover
Coldeast
Liverton
Sigford
Trago Mills
Preston
Teigngrace
B3195
Sandygate
Humber
Bishopsteignton
Rural Life
Coombe
Teignmouth
Teign Heritage Centre
South Knighton
Orchid Paradise
Kingsteignton
Caton
Bickington
Highweek
R. Teign
Ringmore
Shaldon
Newton Abbot
Combeinteignhead
Netherton
Goodstone
West Ogwell
NEWTON ABBOT
East Ogwell
Wolborough
Stokeinteignhead
Lower Gabwell
Higher Gabwell
Plant World
Woodland
Denbury
Prickly Ball Farm
Decoy
Abbotskerswell
Coffinswell
Maidencombe
Forder Green
Two Mile Oak
Kingskerswell
Watcombe
Babbacombe Bay
Barton
Bygones
Model Village
Torbryan
Ipplepen
North Whilborough
Hele
Hill House
Woolston Green
Broadhempston
St Marychurch
Cliff Railway
Babbacombe
Compton
Shiphay
Torre
Torre Abbey
TORQUAY
Staverton
Combe Fishacre
Cockington
Kents Cavern
Dartington Hall
Littlehempston
Wellswood
Hope's Nose
Dartington
Marldon
Round Hill
Berry Pomeroy
Shinner's Bridge
Shorton
Living Coasts
Week
Berry Pomeroy
Blagdon
TORBAY
Oldway
Cott
Totnes
Ayreville
Kirkham House
B3201
PAIGNTON
Elizabethan House
Bridgetown
Collaton St Mary
Zoo
St Michaels
Seashore Cen.
Splashdown Waterpark
Tor Bay
Aish
Harberton
Sharpham Wines & Cheeses
Higher Yalberton
Goodrington
R. Dart
Galmpton Warborough
Luscombe
Ashprington
Stoke Gabriel
Lifeboat Sta.
Churston Ferrers
Berry Head
Tuckenhay
Waddeton
Harbertonford
Cornworthy
Galmpton
Brixham
Washbourne
East Cornworthy
Dittisham
Sharkham Point
Greenway
Allaleigh
Hillhead
Dartmouth Steam Railway
Halwell
Capton
Woodhuish
Newcomen Engine
Coleton Fishacre
Woodford
Woodlands
Norton
Kingswear
Hutcherleigh
Blackawton
Dartmouth
Warfleet
Ash
Fast Rabbit Farm
Mew Stone
Bowden
Burlestone
Blackpool
Stoke Fleming
Strete
Harleston
Start
Start Bay
Sherford
Frittiscombe
Slapton
Monument
Slapton Ley
Chillington
Sherman Tank Memorial
Stokenham
Torcross
Beeson
Ford
Beesands
Kellaton
Chivelstone
Hallsands
South Allington
Start Point
East Prawle
A38
A380
A379
A381
A382
A383
A385
A3022
A3122
B3193
B3344
B3192
B3178
B3179
B3205
12
E
F
G
H
1
2
3
4
5
80
70
60
50
40
30
280
90
300
10

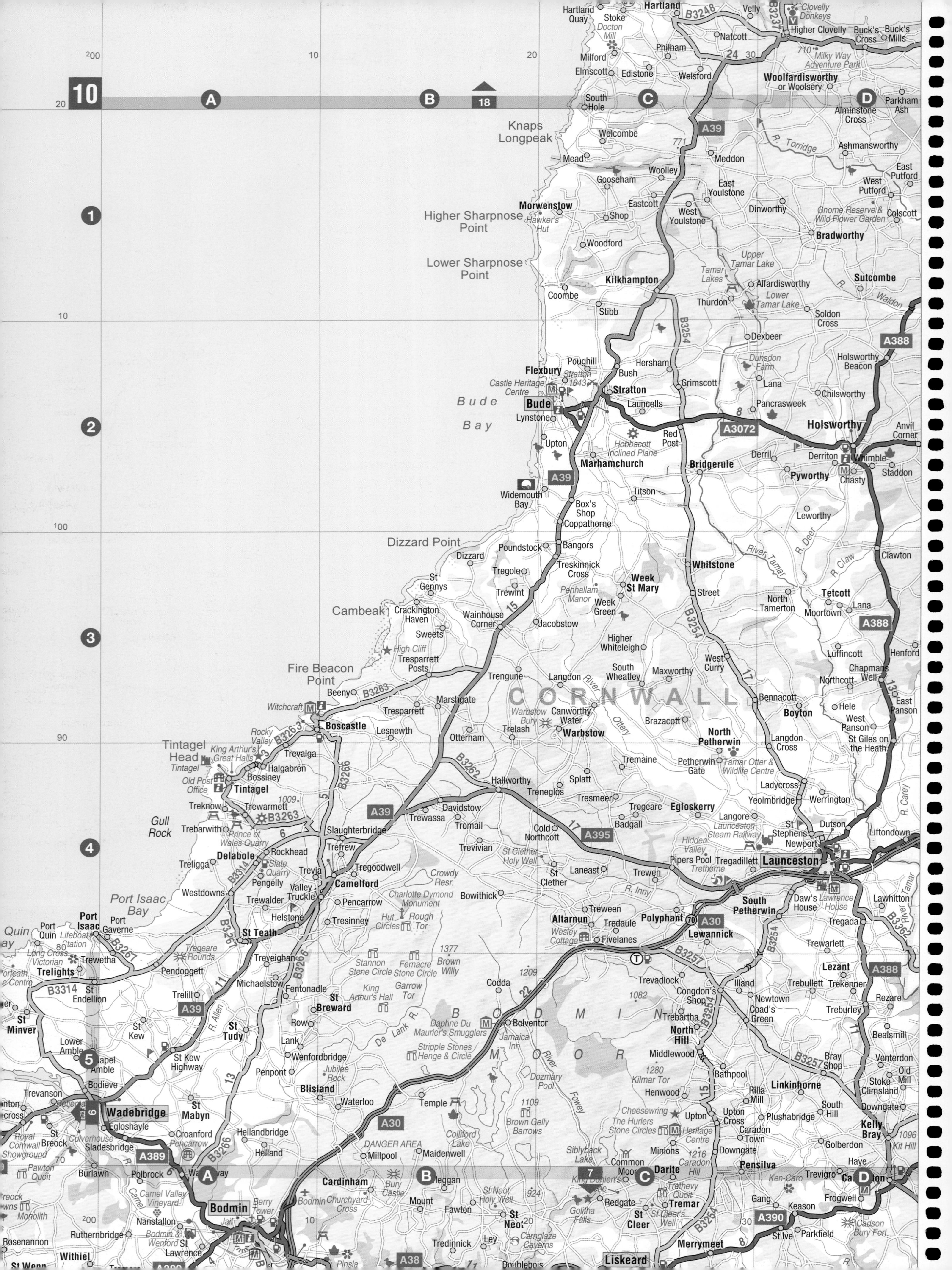

10
A
B
18
C
D
Hartland Quay
Stoke
Docton Mill
Hartland
B3248
Velly
Clovelly Donkeys
Higher Clovelly
Buck's Cross
Buck's Mills
Natcott
Philham
Milford
Elmscott
Edistone
Welsford
Milky Way Adventure Park
Woolfardisworthy or Woolsery
South Hole
Alminstone Cross
Parkham Ash
Knaps Longpeak
Welcombe
A39
R. Torridge
Ashmansworthy
Mead
Meddon
Gooseham
Woolley
East Youlstone
East Putford
West Putford
Morwenstow
Hawker's Hut
Eastcott
Shop
West Youlstone
Dinworthy
Gnome Reserve & Wild Flower Garden
Colscott
Higher Sharpnose Point
Woodford
Bradworthy
Lower Sharpnose Point
Upper Tamar Lake
Tamar Lakes
Kilkhampton
Alfardisworthy
Sutcombe
Coombe
Thurdon
Lower Tamar Lake
Soldon Cross
Stibb
B3254
Dexbeer
A388
Flexbury
Poughill
Hersham
Dunsdon Farm
Holsworthy Beacon
Castle Heritage Centre
Stratton 1643
Bush
Grimscott
Lana
Chilsworthy
Bude
Stratton
Launcells
Pancrasweek
Bude Bay
Lynstone
Red Post
A3072
Holsworthy
Anvil Corner
Upton
Hobbacott Inclined Plane
Derril
Derriton
Whimble
Marhamchurch
Bridgerule
Pyworthy
Chasty
Staddon
Widemouth Bay
Titson
Box's Shop
Lewtorthy
Coppathorne
Dizzard Point
Poundstock
Bangors
R. Deer
Dizzard
River Tamar
Clawton
Tregole
Treskinnick Cross
Whitstone
R. Claw
St Gennys
Trewint
Week St Mary
Penhallam Manor
Street
Tetcott
Cambeak
Crackington Haven
Wainhouse Corner
Week Green
North Tamerton
Moortown
Lana
Sweets
Jacobstow
High Cliff
Higher Whiteleigh
Luffincott
Henford
Tresparrett Posts
West Curry
Chapmans Well
Fire Beacon Point
Trengune
Langdon
South Wheatley
Maxworthy
Northcott
Beeny
B3263
CORNWALL
Bennacott
East Panson
Witchcraft
Marshgate
Hele
Trelash
Boyton
Tresparrett
Warbstow Bury
Canworthy Water
Brazacott
West Panson
Boscastle
Lesnewth
Warbstow
Otterham
Ottery
North Petherwin
Langdon Cross
St Giles on the Heath
Rocky Valley
Tintagel Head
King Arthur's Great Halls
Trevalga
Halgabron
Bossiney
Tintagel
Old Post Office
Tremaine
Petherwin Gate
Tamar Otter & Wildlife Centre
Hallworthy
Splatt
Ladycross
B3262
Treneglos
Tresmeer
Yeolmbridge
Werrington
R. Carey
Treknow
Trewarmett
B3266
Tregeare
Egloskerry
Gull Rock
Trebarwith
Prince of Wales Quarry
Davidstow
Trewassa
Tremail
Badgall
Langore
Launceston Steam Railway
St Stephens
Dutson
Liftondown
Slaughterbridge
Cold Northcott
A395
Newport
Rockhead
Trefrew
Trevivian
St Clether Holy Well
Hidden Valley
Treligga
Delabole
Slate Quarry
Tregoodwell
Laneast
St Clether
Pipers Pool
Tregadillett
Trethorne
Launceston
Pengelly
Trevia
Crowdy Resr.
Trewen
Westdowns
Valley Truckle
Camelford
R. Inny
Daw's House
Lawrence House
Lawhitton
Port Isaac Bay
Trewalder
Charlotte Dymond Monument
Bowithick
Treween
South Petherwin
Pencarrow
Helstone
Hut Circles
Rough Tor
Altarnun
Polyphant
A30
Port Isaac
Port Gaverne
Tresinney
Wesley Cottage
Tredaule
Lewannick
Tregada
Quin
Lifeboat Station
St Teath
Fivelanes
B3362
Long Cross Victorian
Trewetha
Tregeare Rounds
Stannon Stone Circle
Fernacre Stone Circle
Brown Willy
B3257
Trewarlett
Trelights
Pendoggett
Treveighan
Trevadlock
Lezant
A388
B3314
St Endellion
Michaelstow
Fentonadle
King Arthur's Hall
Garrow Tor
Codda
Congdon's Shop
Illand
Trebullett
Trekenner
Trelill
Newtown
Rezare
St Breward
BODMIN
Coad's Green
Treburley
St Minver
R. Allen
St Kew
St Tudy
Row
De Lank R.
Daphne Du Maurier's Smugglers
Bolventor
Jamaica Inn
MOOR
Trebartha
North Hill
Bealsmill
Lower Amble
Lank
Stripple Stones Henge & Circle
Middlewood
Venterdon
Chapel Amble
St Kew Highway
Wenfordbridge
River Fowey
Dozmary Pool
Kilmar Tor
Bray Shop
Penpont
Jubilee Rock
Bathpool
Stoke Climsland
Old Mill
Bodieve
Blisland
Henwood
Rilla Mill
Linkinhorne
Trevanson
Wadebridge
St Mabyn
Waterloo
Temple
Cheesewring
Upton
South Hill
Downgate
Egloshayle
Brown Gelly Barrows
The Hurlers Stone Circles
Upton Cross
Plushabridge
Kelly Bray
Royal Cornwall Showground
St Breock
Colverhouse
Croanford
Pencarrow
Hellandbridge
Colliford Lake
Heritage Centre
Caradon Town
Golberdon
Kit Hill
Sladesbridge
A389
Helland
DANGER AREA
Millpool
Maidenwell
Siblyback Lake
Minions
Caradon Hill
Downgate
Pawton Quoit
Burlawn
Polbrock
Washaway
Common Moor
Darite
Pensilva
Trevigro
Haye
Callington
Cardinham
Bury Castle
Meggan
St Neot Holy Well
King Doniert's Stone
Trethevy Quoit
Ken-Caro
Frogwell
Camel Valley Vineyard
Bodmin
Berry Tower
Bodmin Churchyard Cross
Mount
Redgate
Tremar
Gang
Keason
Monolith
Nanstallon
Fawton
St Neot
Golitha Falls
St Cleer
St Cleer's Well
A390
Cadson Bury Fort
Rutherbridge
Bodmin & Wenford
Carnglaze Caverns
St Ive
Parkfield
Rosenannon
St Lawrence
Tredinnick
Ley
Merrymeet
Withiel
St Wenn
Pinsla
A38
Doublebois
Liskeard

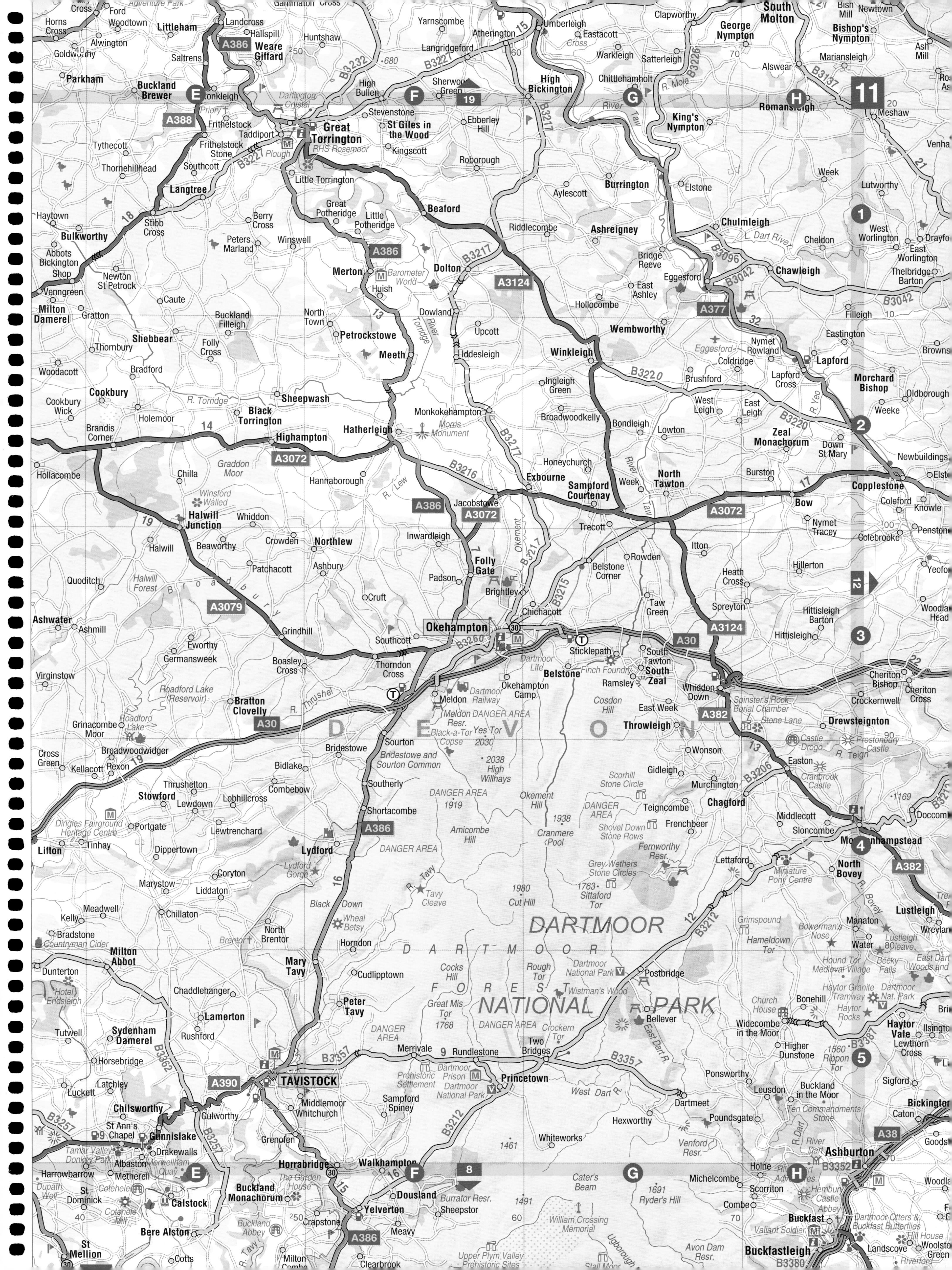

11
12
19
8
E
F
G
H
1
2
3
4
5
Littleham
Landcross
Hallspill
Weare Giffard
A386
Huntshaw
Yarnscombe
Langridgeford
Atherington
Umberleigh
Eastacott
Warkleigh
Satterleigh
George Nympton
South Molton
Bishop's Nympton
Alswear
Mariansleigh
Horns Cross
Ford
Woodtown
Alwington
Goldworthy
Saltrens
Parkham
Buckland Brewer
Monkleigh
High Bullen
Sherwood Green
High Bickington
Chittlehamholt
Romansleigh
Meshaw
King's Nympton
Frithelstock
Taddiport
Great Torrington
Stevenstone
St Giles in the Wood
Kingscott
Ebberley Hill
Roborough
RHS Rosemoor
Tythecott
Frithelstock Stone
Thornehillhead
Southcott
Langtree
Little Torrington
Great Potheridge
Little Potheridge
Beaford
Aylescott
Burrington
Elstone
Week
Lutworthy
Haytown
Bulkworthy
Stibb Cross
Berry Cross
Peters Marland
Winswell
Riddlecombe
Ashreigney
Chulmleigh
West Worlington
East Worlington
Cheldon
Abbots Bickington
Newton St Petrock
Shop
Merton
Barometer World
Huish
Dolton
Bridge Reeve
East Ashley
Eggesford
Chawleigh
Thelbridge Barton
Venngreen
Milton Damerel
Gratton
Caute
Buckland Filleigh
North Town
Petrockstowe
Dowland
Upcott
Hollocombe
Wembworthy
Filleigh
Eastington
Shebbear
Thornbury
Folly Cross
Meeth
Iddesleigh
Winkleigh
Nymet Rowland
Coldridge
Lapford
Lapford Cross
Morchard Bishop
Oldborough
Woodacott
Bradford
Cookbury
Cookbury Wick
Holemoor
Sheepwash
Black Torrington
Monkokehampton
Ingleigh Green
Broadwoodkelly
Brushford
West Leigh
East Leigh
Bondleigh
Lowton
Weeke
Brandis Corner
Highampton
Hatherleigh
Morris Monument
Zeal Monachorum
Down St Mary
Newbuildings
Hollacombe
Chilla
Graddon Moor
Hannaborough
Honeychurch
Exbourne
Sampford Courtenay
North Tawton
Burston
Copplestone
Winsford Walled
Halwill Junction
Whiddon
Jacobstowe
Bow
Coleford
Knowle
Trecott
Nymet Tracey
Colebrooke
Halwill
Beaworthy
Crowden
Northlew
Inwardleigh
Itton
Patchacott
Ashbury
Folly Gate
Belstone Corner
Rowden
Hillerton
Quoditch
Halwill Forest
Padson
Heath Cross
Brightley
Taw Green
Spreyton
Cruft
Chichacott
Hittisleigh Barton
Ashwater
Ashmill
Grindhill
Okehampton
Hittisleigh
Eworthy
Southcott
Sticklepath
South Tawton
South Zeal
Germansweek
Boasley Cross
Thorndon Cross
Dartmoor Life
Belstone
Finch Foundry
Ramsley
Whiddon Down
Cheriton Bishop
Cheriton Cross
Virginstow
Roadford Lake (Reservoir)
Bratton Clovelly
Meldon
Dartmoor Railway
Okehampton Camp
Cosdon Hill
East Week
Spinster's Rock Burial Chamber
Crockernwell
Stone Lane
Drewsteignton
Grinacombe Moor
Roadford Lake
Meldon Resr.
DANGER AREA
Black-a-Tor Copse
Yes Tor 2030
Throwleigh
Castle Drogo
Prestonbury Castle
Cross Green
Broadwoodwidger
Bridestowe
Sourton
Bridestowe and Sourton Common
2038 High Willhays
Wonson
Easton
Kellacott
Rexon
Bidlake
Scorhill Stone Circle
Gidleigh
Murchington
Cranbrook Castle
Thrushelton
Combebow
Southerly
Stowford
Lewdown
Lobhillcross
Okement Hill
Teigncombe
Chagford
Dingles Fairground Heritage Centre
Portgate
Shortacombe
1919
1938
Shovel Down Stone Rows
Frenchbeer
Middlecott
Sloncombe
Lewtrenchard
Amicombe Hill
Cranmere Pool
Moretonhampstead
Lifton
Tinhay
Dippertown
Lydford
Fernworthy Resr.
North Bovey
Lydford Gorge
Grey Wethers Stone Circles
Lettaford
Miniature Pony Centre
A382
Marystow
Coryton
Liddaton
Tavy Cleave
1763 Sittaford Tor
1980 Cut Hill
Black Down
Wheal Betsy
Lustleigh
Meadwell
Chillaton
Kelly
Bradstone
Countryman Cider
North Brentor
Brentor
Horndon
DARTMOOR
Grimspound
Hameldown Tor
Manaton
Bowerman's Nose
Water
Lustleigh Cleave
Wreyland
Milton Abbot
Mary Tavy
DARTMOOR FOREST
Cocks Hill
Rough Tor
Dartmoor National Park
Postbridge
Hound Tor Medieval Village
Becky Falls
East Dart Woods and
Dunterton
Hotel Endsleigh
Cudlipptown
Chaddlehanger
Peter Tavy
Great Mis Tor 1768
NATIONAL PARK
Wistman's Wood
Haytor Granite Tramway
Haytor Rocks
Dartmoor Nat. Park
Bonehill
Church House
Bellever
Widecombe in the Moor
Haytor Vale
Ilsington
Lewthorn Cross
Tutwell
Sydenham Damerel
Lamerton
Rushford
DANGER AREA
Crockern Tor
Higher Dunstone
1560 Rippon Tor
East Dart R.
Horsebridge
Merrivale
Rundlestone
Two Bridges
Prehistoric Settlement
Dartmoor Prison
Dartmoor National Park
Princetown
West Dart R.
Ponsworthy
Leusdon
Buckland in the Moor
Sigford
Luckett
Latchley
TAVISTOCK
A390
Middlemoor
Whitchurch
Sampford Spiney
Dartmeet
Ten Commandments Stone
Poundsgate
Hexworthy
Bickington
Caton
Chilsworthy
Gulworthy
St Ann's Chapel
Gunnislake
Tamar Valley Donkey Park
Drakewalls
Albaston
Metherell
Grenofen
1461
Whiteworks
Venford Resr.
River Dart
A38
Ashburton
Harrowbarrow
Dupath Well
St Dominick
Cotehele House
Cotehele Mill
Calstock
Buckland Monachorum
The Garden House
Horrabridge
Walkhampton
Dousland
Burrator Resr.
Sheepstor
1491
Cater's Beam
1691 Ryder's Hill
Michelcombe
Holne
Scorriton
Hembury Castle
Combe
Buckfast Abbey
Buckfast
Bere Alston
Buckland Abbey
Crapstone
Yelverton
Meavy
William Crossing Memorial
Dartmoor Otters & Buckfast Butterflies
Valiant Soldier
Hill House
Landscove
St Mellion
Cotts
Milton Combe
Clearbrook
A386
Upper Plym Valley Prehistoric Sites
Ugborough
Avon Dam Resr.
Buckfastleigh
B3380
DEVON
A30
A3072
A3079
A3124
A377
A388
B3227
B3232
B3217
B3220
B3216
B3215
B3260
B3042
B3096
B3137
B3226
B3206
B3212
B3357
B3362
B3257
B3387
B3352
R. Torridge
R. Lew
R. Thrushel
R. Taw
R. Mole
R. Tavy
R. Teign
R. Yeo
R. Okement
L. Dart River

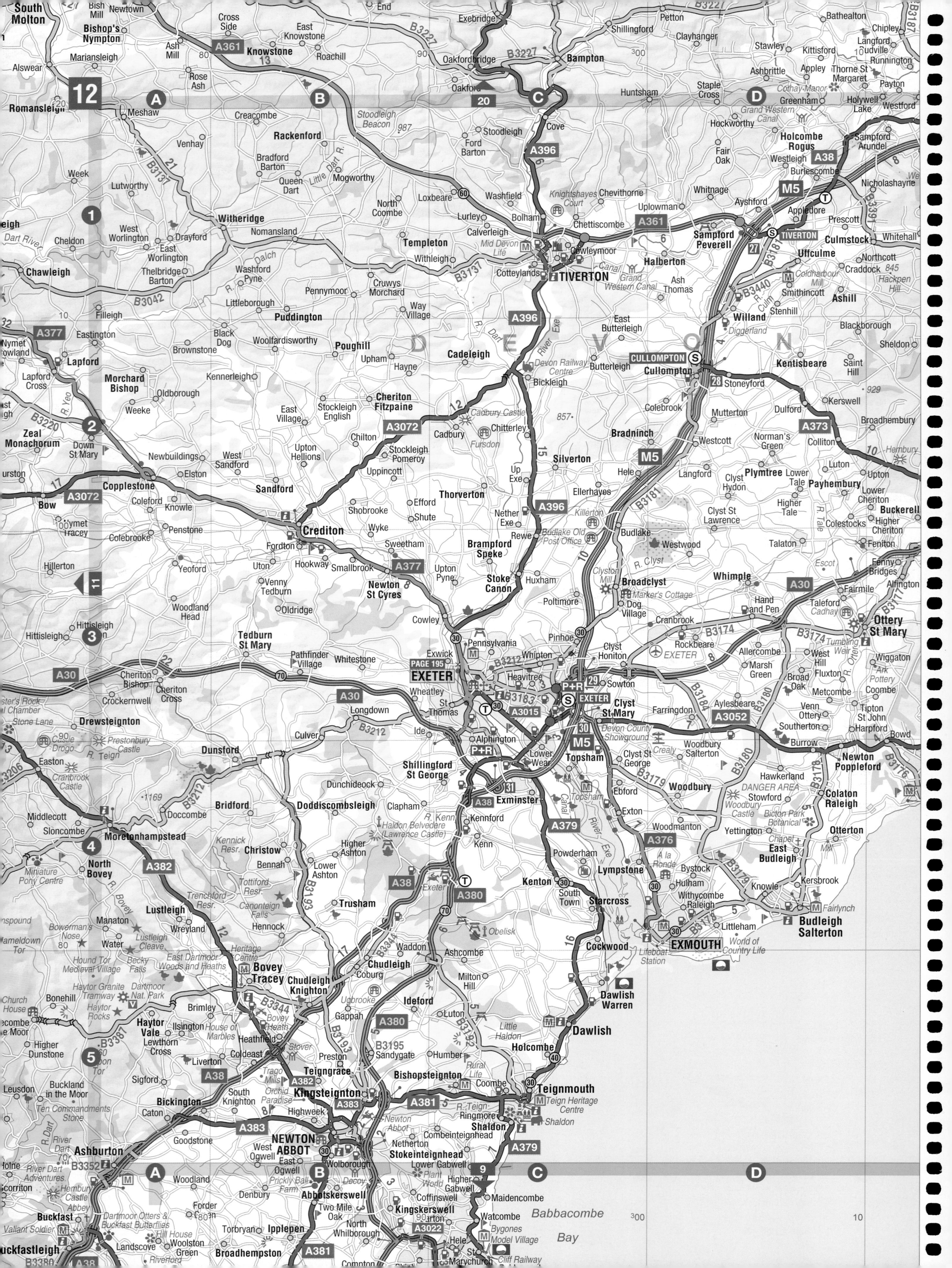

12
A
B
C
D
20
South Molton
Bishop's Nympton
Mariansleigh
Alswear
Romansleigh
Meshaw
Cross Side
Ash Mill
Rose Ash
A361
Knowstone
East Knowstone
Roachill
B3227
Oakfordbridge
Oakford
Exebridge
Bampton
Shillingford
Petton
Clayhanger
Huntsham
Staple Cross
Stawley
Kittisford
Langford Budville
Runnington
Ashbrittle
Appley
Thorne St Margaret
Cothay Manor
Greenham
Payton
Holywell Lake
Westford
Bathealton
Chipley
Creacombe
Rackenford
Stoodleigh Beacon
Stoodleigh
Ford Barton
Cove
A396
Hockworthy
Grand Western Canal
Fair Oak
Holcombe Rogus
Westleigh
Burlescombe
Sampford Arundel
A38
M5
Nicholashayne
Venhay
Bradford Barton
Queen Dart
Little Dart R.
Mogworthy
Week
Lutworthy
B3131
North Coombe
Loxbeare
Washfield
Knightshayes Court
Chevithorne
Whitnage
Uplowman
Ayshford
Appledore
Prescott
Culmstock
Whitehall
Witheridge
Nomansland
West Worlington
Drayford
East Worlington
Thelbridge Barton
Cheldon
Dart River
Chawleigh
Templeton
Withleigh
Lurley
Calverleigh
Bolham
Mid Devon Life
Chettiscombe
Cowleymoor
A361
Sampford Peverell
TIVERTON
Uffculme
Northcott
Craddock
Hackpen Hill
Coldharbour Mill
Smithincott
Ashill
Halberton
Ash Thomas
Grand Western Canal
Cotteylands
TIVERTON
B3137
Washford Pyne
R. Dalch
Pennymoor
Cruwys Morchard
Way Village
Littleborough
Puddington
B3042
Fillegih
B3440
Willand
Stenhill
Diggerland
Blackborough
Sheldon
A377
Eastington
Nymet Rowland
Lapford
Lapford Cross
Brownstone
Black Dog
Woolfardisworthy
Poughill
Upham
Hayne
Cadeleigh
DEVON
River Exe
Devon Railway Centre
Bickleigh
Butterleigh
East Butterleigh
CULLOMPTON
Cullompton
Stoneyford
Kentisbeare
Saint Hill
Kerswell
Morchard Bishop
Kennerleigh
Oldborough
Weeke
Zeal Monachorum
Down St Mary
B3220
Stockleigh English
East Village
Cheriton Fitzpaine
Cadbury Castle
Cadbury
Chitterley
Fursdon
A3072
Colebrook
Mutterton
Dulford
Broadhembury
Bradninch
Westcott
Norman's Green
A373
Colliton
Hembury
Newbuildings
Elston
West Sandford
Upton Hellions
Chilton
Stockleigh Pomeroy
Uppincott
Silverton
Up Exe
M5
Hele
Langford
Clyst Hydon
Plymtree
Lower Tale
Payhembury
Upton
Lower Cheriton
Copplestone
Bow
Coleford
Knowle
Sandford
Shobrooke
Efford
Shute
Thorverton
Ellerhayes
Nether Exe
Killerton
B3181
Higher Tale
Clyst St Lawrence
Buckerell
Higher Cheriton
Colestocks
Nymet Tracey
Colebrooke
Penstone
Crediton
Wyke
Sweetham
Brampford Speke
Rewe
Budlake Old Post Office
Budlake
Westwood
Talaton
Feniton
Fordton
Hookway
Smallbrook
A377
Uton
Hillerton
Yeoford
Venny Tedburn
Upton Pyne
Stoke Canon
Huxham
R. Clyst
Clyst Mill
Broadclyst
Marker's Cottage
Whimple
Escot
Fenny Bridges
A30
Fairmile
Alfington
Newton St Cyres
Oldridge
Woodland Head
Cowley
Poltimore
Dog Village
Hand and Pen
Taleford
Cadhay
Cranbrook
Ottery St Mary
Hittisleigh
Hittisleigh Barton
Tedburn St Mary
Pathfinder Village
Whitestone
Pennsylvania
Pinhoe
Clyst Honiton
Rockbeare
B3174
EXETER
Allercombe
West Hill
Tumbling Weir
Wiggaton
Exwick
Whipton
PAGE 195
EXETER
Heavitree
B3212
Sowton
Marsh Green
Fluxton
Ark Pottery
A30
Cheriton Bishop
Cheriton Cross
Crockernwell
Wheatley
St Thomas
B3183
P+R
A3015
Clyst St Mary
Farringdon
B3184
Aylesbeare
B3180
A3052
Broad Oak
Metcombe
Coombe
Venn Ottery
Tipton St John
Southerton
Harpford
Bowd
Drewsteignton
Castle Drogo
Prestonbury Castle
Longdown
Culver
B3212
Ide
Alphington
Devon County Showground
Crealy
Woodbury Salterton
Burrow
Newton Poppleford
Spinster's Rock
Stone Lane
Dunsford
R. Teign
Easton
Cranbrook Castle
B3206
Shillingford St George
Lower Wear
Topsham
M5
Clyst St George
B3179
Hawkerland
B3178
Colaton Raleigh
Dunchideock
Exminster
Topsham
Ebford
Woodbury
DANGER AREA
Stowford
Woodbury Castle
Bicton Park Botanical Gardens
B3176
Middlecott
Sloncombe
Doccombe
Bridford
B3212
Doddiscombsleigh
Clapham
R. Kenn
Kennford
A38
Haldon Belvedere (Lawrence Castle)
Exton
Woodmanton
Yettington
Otterton
Moretonhampstead
Kennick Resr.
Christow
Bennah
Higher Ashton
Lower Ashton
Kenn
A379
Powderham
A376
A la Ronde
Lympstone
Chapel
East Budleigh
North Bovey
Miniature Pony Centre
A382
Tottiford Resr.
Trenchford Resr.
Canonteign Falls
B3193
A38
Exeter Racecourse
A380
Kenton
South Town
Starcross
Bystock
Hulham
Withycombe Raleigh
Knowle
Kersbrook
Fairlynch
Budleigh Salterton
Lustleigh
Manaton
Wreyland
Hennock
Trusham
Obelisk
Littleham
EXMOUTH
World of Country Life
Bowerman's Nose
Hameldown Tor
Water
Lustleigh Cleave
Becky Falls
Hound Tor Medieval Village
East Dartmoor Woods and Heaths
Heritage Centre
Bovey Tracey
Chudleigh Knighton
Chudleigh
Coburg
B3344
Waddon
Ashcombe
Cockwood
Lifeboat Station
Milton Hill
Dawlish Warren
Haytor Granite Tramway
Dartmoor Nat. Park
Haytor Rocks
Church House
Bonehill
Brimley
Ugbrooke
Ideford
A380
Luton
B3192
Little Haldon
Dawlish
Widecombe in the Moor
Haytor Vale
Ilsington
House of Marbles
Lewthorn Cross
Heathfield
Bovey Heath
Gappah
B3195
Sandygate
Humber
Holcombe
Higher Dunstone
B3387
Liverton
Coldeast
Stover
Preston
Teigngrace
Bishopsteignton
Rural Life
Coombe
Teignmouth
Teign Heritage Centre
Leusdon
Buckland in the Moor
Sigford
A38
Trago Mills
A382
Orchid Paradise
South Knighton
Kingsteignton
A383
A381
R. Teign
Ringmore
Shaldon
Ten Commandments Stone
Bickington
Caton
Highweek
Newton Abbot
A383
Goodstone
NEWTON ABBOT
Netherton
Combeinteignhead
Stokeinteignhead
A379
R. Dart
River Dart Adventures
Ashburton
B3352
West Ogwell
East Ogwell
Wolborough
Lower Gabwell
Higher Gabwell
9
Hembury Castle
Woodland
Prickly Ball Farm
Decoy
Abbotskerswell
Plant World
Coffinswell
Maidencombe
Denbury
Forder Green
Two Mile Oak
Kingskerswell
Babbacombe Bay
Watcombe
Buckfast
Buckfast Abbey
Dartmoor Otters & Buckfast Butterflies
Valiant Soldier
Hill House
Torbryan
Ipplepen
North Whilborough
A3022
Bygones Model Village
Buckfastleigh
Landscove
Woolston Green
Broadhempston
A381
Compton
Hele
Marychurch
Cliff Railway
B3380
A38
Riverford
Page 11

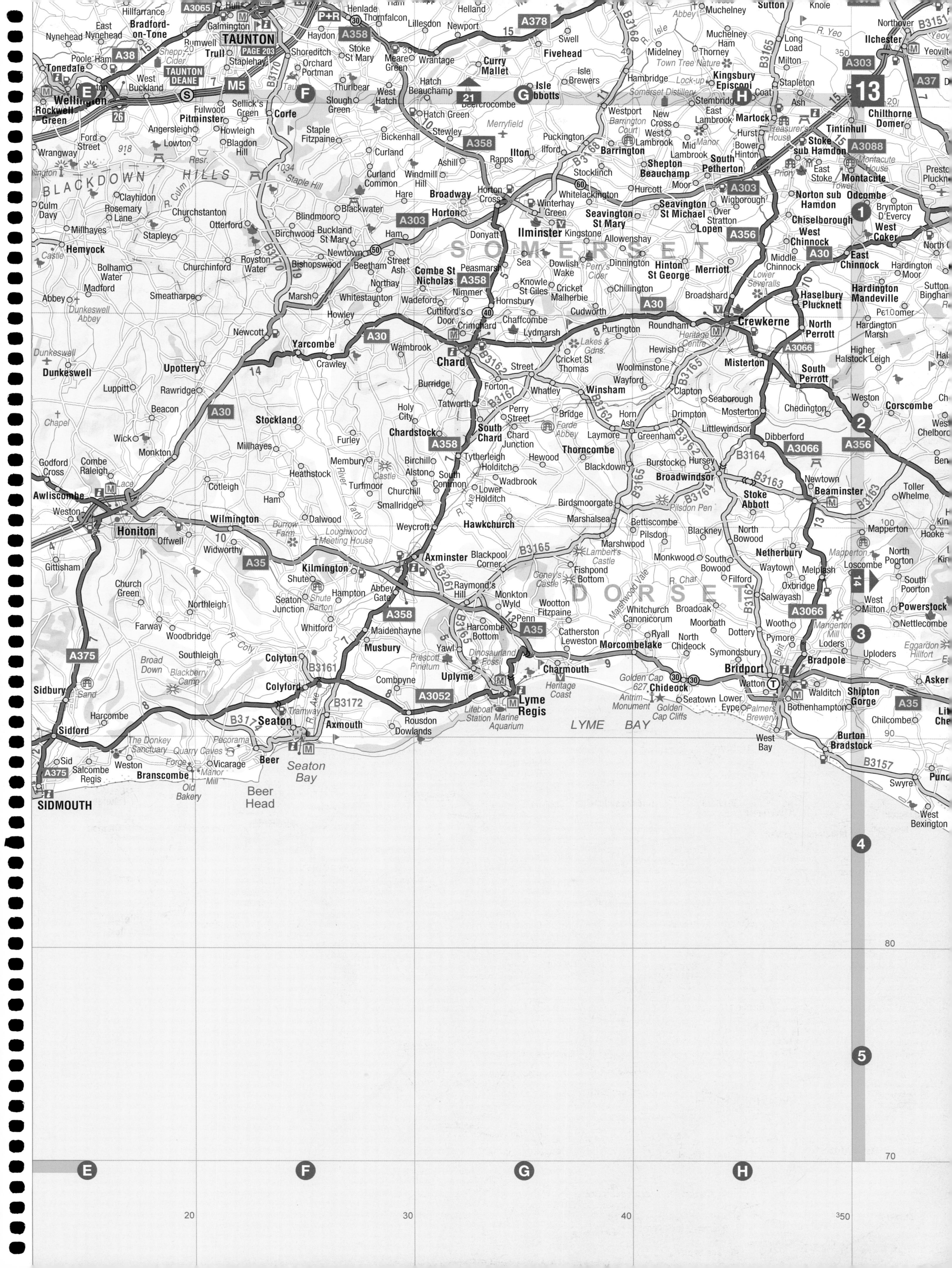

Hillfarrance
A3065
Henlade
Thornfalcon
Helland
Muchelney
Sutton
Knole
East Nynehead
Bradford-on-Tone
Nynehead
Galmington
TAUNTON
PAGE 203
Haydon
P+R
A358
Lillesdon
Newport
A378
Swell
Muchelney Ham
Long Load
Northover
B3151
Ilchester
Yeovilton
Poole
Ham
A38
Rumwell
Trull
Staplehay
Shoreditch
Orchard Portman
Stoke St Mary
Meare Green
Wrantage
Curry Mallet
Fivehead
Midelney
Thorney
Town Tree Nature
Milton
A303
Tonedale
TAUNTON DEANE
West Buckland
M5
Thurlbear
West Hatch
Hatch Beauchamp
Isle Brewers
Hambridge
Lock-up
Kingsbury Episcopi
Stapleton
A37
Wellington
Rockwell Green
Fulwood
Sellick's Green
Pitminster
Corfe
Slough Green
Beercrocombe
Isle Abbotts
Somerset Distillery
Stembridge
Coat
Ash
13
Westport
Barrington Court
New Cross
East Lambrook
Martock
Chilthorne Domer
Tintinhull
Angersleigh
Howleigh
Staple Fitzpaine
Hatch Green
Merryfield
Puckington
West Lambrook
Mid Lambrook
Manor
Hurst
Treasurer's House
Stoke sub Hamdon
A3088
Ford Street
Lowton
Blagdon Hill
Bickenhall
Stewley
A358
Ilton
Ilford
Barrington
Shepton Beauchamp
South Petherton
Bower Hinton
Montacute House
Wrangway
918
Curland
Ashill
Rapps
B3168
Stocklinch
Priory
East Stoke
Montacute
BLACKDOWN HILLS
Resr.
1034
Staple Hill
Curland Common
Windmill Hill
Horton Cross
Whitelackington
Hurcott
Moor
A303
Wigborough
Norton sub Hamdon
Odcombe
Culm Davy
Clayhidon
Rosemary Lane
R. Culm
Churchstanton
Blindmoor
Blackwater
Hare
Broadway
Winterhay Green
Seavington St Mary
Seavington St Michael
Over Stratton
Brympton D'Evercy
Millhayes
Otterford
Birchwood
Buckland St Mary
A303
Horton
Ilminster
Kingstone
Lopen
Chiselborough
West Chinnock
West Coker
Stapley
Ham
Donyatt
SOMERSET
Allowenshay
A356
Hemyock
Castle
Newtown
Dinnington
Middle Chinnock
A30
East Chinnock
Bolham Water
Churchinford
Royston Water
Bishopswood
Beetham
Street Ash
Combe St Nicholas
Peasmarsh
Sea
Dowlish Wake
Perry's Cider
Hinton St George
Merriott
Hardington Moor
Madford
Northay
A358
Knowle St Giles
Cricket Malherbie
Chillington
Lower Severalls
Hardington Mandeville
Abbey
Dunkeswell Abbey
Smeatharpe
Marsh
Whitestaunton
Wadeford
Nimmer
Hornsbury
Broadshard
Haselbury Plucknett
Howley
Cuttiford's Door
Chaffcombe
Cudworth
A30
Pendomer
Crimchard
Lydmarsh
Purtington
Roundham
Crewkerne
North Perrott
Hardington Marsh
Newcott
Yarcombe
A30
Wambrook
Chard
Lakes & Gdns.
Heritage Centre
Hewish
A3066
Dunkeswell
Crawley
Cricket St Thomas
Street
Woolminstone
Misterton
South Perrott
Higher Halstock Leigh
Upottery
Wayford
Luppitt
Rawridge
Burridge
Forton
Whatley
Winsham
Clapton
Seaborough
Weston
Corscombe
Beacon
Holy City
Tatworth
Perry Street
Bridge
Mosterton
Chedington
Chapel
A30
Stockland
South Chard
Chard Junction
Forde Abbey
Horn Ash
Drimpton
Littlewindsor
Wick
Furley
Chardstock
A358
Laymore
Greenham
Dibberford
A356
Monkton
Millhayes
Membury
Birchill
Tytherleigh
Holditch
Hewood
Thorncombe
Blackdown
Burstock
Hursey
B3164
A3066
Godford Cross
Combe Raleigh
Heathstock
Castle
Alston
South Common
Wadbrook
Broadwindsor
B3163
Newtown
Beaminster
Toller Whelme
Awliscombe
Cotleigh
Turfmoor
Churchill
Lower Holditch
Birdsmoorgate
B3164
Pilsdon Pen
Stoke Abbott
Weston
Ham
Smallridge
Marshalsea
Bettiscombe
North Bowood
Mapperton
Honiton
Offwell
Wilmington
Dalwood
Burrow Farm
Weycroft
Hawkchurch
Pilsdon
Blackney
Netherbury
Gittisham
Widworthy
Loughwood Meeting House
Axminster
Blackpool Corner
B3165
Marshwood
Lambert's Castle
Monkwood
South Bowood
Waytown
Melplash
Loscombe
North Poorton
A35
Kilmington
Fishpond Bottom
Coney's Castle
Marshwood Vale
R. Char
Filford
Oxbridge
South Poorton
Church Green
Shute
Abbey Gate
Raymond's Hill
Monkton Wyld
DORSET
Salwayash
West Milton
Powerstock
Northleigh
Seaton Junction
Shute Barton
Hampton
A358
Wootton Fitzpaine
Whitchurch Canonicorum
Broadoak
A3066
Nettlecombe
Farway
Woodbridge
Whitford
Maidenhayne
Harcombe Bottom
Penn
Catherston Leweston
Ryall
Moorbath
Wooth
Dottery
Mangerton Mill
Loders
Uploders
Eggardon Hillfort
A375
Southleigh
R. Coly
Musbury
Prescott Pinetum
Yawl
Dinosaurland Fossil
A35
Morcombelake
North Chideock
Pymore
Broad Down
Blackberry Camp
Colyton
B3161
Uplyme
Charmouth
Symondsbury
Bridport
Bradpole
Sidbury
Sand
Colyford
Combpyne
A3052
Heritage Coast
Golden Cap 627
Chideock
Watton
Walditch
Shipton Gorge
Askerswell
Harcombe
B3172
Tramway
Lyme Regis
Lifeboat Station
Marine Aquarium
Antrim Monument
Golden Cap Cliffs
Seatown
Lower Eype
Palmers Brewery
A35
Sidford
Seaton
Axmouth
Rousdon
Dowlands
LYME BAY
West Bay
Chilcombe
Burton Bradstock
The Donkey Sanctuary
Pecorama
Quarry Caves
Sid
Salcombe Regis
Weston
Forge
Vicarage
Beer
Seaton Bay
B3157
Swyre
A375
Branscombe
Manor Mill
Old Bakery
Beer Head
SIDMOUTH
West Bexington
E
F
G
H
1
2
3
4
5
14
20
30
40
350
70
80
90
100

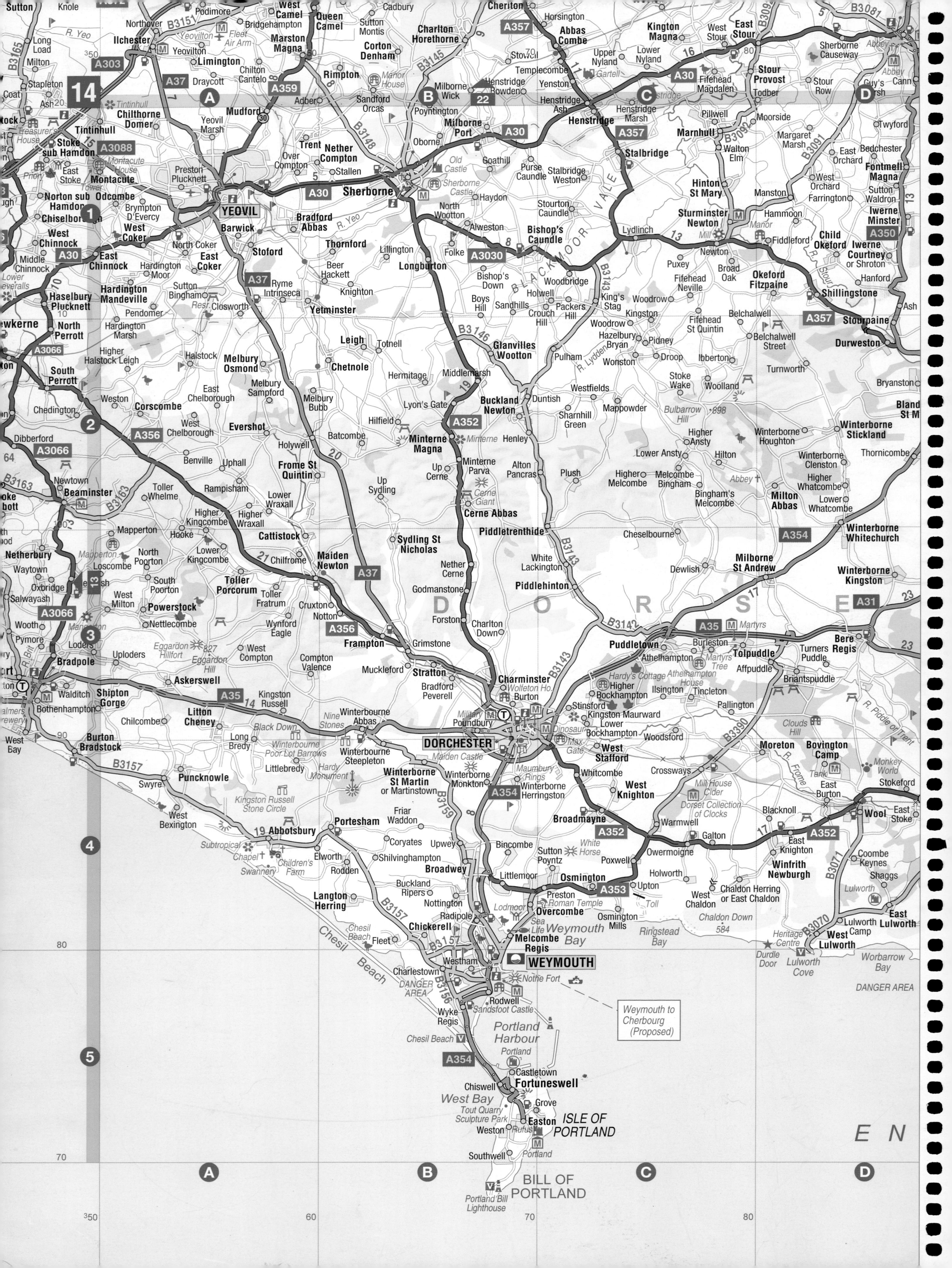

14
A
B
C
D
1
2
3
4
5
13
22
Sutton
Knole
Podimore
West Camel
Queen Camel
Cadbury
Cheriton
Horsington
Kington Magna
West Stour
East Stour
B3081
Northover
B3151
Bridgehampton
Sutton Montis
Charlton Horethorne
A357
Abbas Combe
Long Load
R. Yeo
Ilchester
Yeovilton
Fleet Air Arm
Marston Magna
Corton Denham
Upper Nyland
Lower Nyland
Sherborne Causeway
Milton
A303
Limington
Rimpton
B3145
Stowell
Templecombe
Stour Provost
Abbey
Stapleton
A37
Draycott
Chilton Cantelo
A359
Manor House
Henstridge Bowden
Milborne Wick
Yenston
A30
Fifehead Magdalen
Stour Row
Guy's Marsh
Cann
Coat
Ash
Tintinhull
Adber
Sandford Orcas
Poyntington
Henstridge Ash
Henstridge Marsh
Todber
Chilthorne Domer
Mudford
Henstridge
Pillwell
Moorside
Twyford
Tintinhull
Yeovil Marsh
Milborne Port
A357
Marnhull
Treasurer's House
Stoke sub Hamdon
A3088
Trent
Nether Compton
B3148
Oborne
Walton Elm
Margaret Marsh
East Orchard
Bedchester
Montacute House
Over Compton
Old Castle
Goathill
Purse Caundle
Stalbridge
Fontmell Magna
Priory
East Stoke
Montacute
Preston Plucknett
Stallen
Stalbridge Weston
Hinton St Mary
West Orchard
Sutton Waldron
Tower
Sherborne Castle
Sherborne
Farrington
Norton sub Hamdon
Odcombe
YEOVIL
Haydon
Stourton Caundle
Manston
Chiselborough
Brympton D'Evercy
North Wootton
Bishop's Caundle
Sturminster Newton
Hammoon
Iwerne Minster
West Chinnock
West Coker
Bradford Abbas
R. Yeo
Alweston
BLACKMOOR VALE
Lydlinch
Manor
A350
Middle Chinnock
Barwick
North Coker
East Coker
Stoford
Thornford
Lillington
Folke
A3030
Mill
Fiddleford
Child Okeford
Iwerne Courtney or Shroton
East Chinnock
Hardington Moor
Longburton
Newton
Puxey
Broad Oak
Lower Severalls
Beer Hackett
Bishop's Down
Woodbridge
Fifehead Neville
Okeford Fitzpaine
Hanford
Haselbury Plucknett
Hardington Mandeville
Sutton Bingham
A37
Ryme Intrinseca
Knighton
Boys Hill
Holwell
King's Stag
Woodrow
Shillingstone
Closworth
Yetminster
Sandhills
Crouch Hill
Packers Hill
Kingston
Belchalwell
Ash
Pendomer
Woodrow
Fifehead St Quintin
A357
Stourpaine
Crewkerne
North Perrott
Hardington Marsh
Hazelbury Bryan
Pidney
Belchalwell Street
Durweston
A3066
Higher Halstock Leigh
Halstock
Leigh
Totnell
B3146
Glanvilles Wootton
Pulham
R. Lydden
Droop
Ibberton
Melbury Osmond
Chetnole
Wonston
Turnworth
South Perrott
Hermitage
Middlemarsh
Stoke Wake
Westfields
Woolland
Bryanston
Weston
East Chelborough
Melbury Sampford
Melbury Bubb
Buckland Newton
Duntish
Mappowder
Blandford St Mary
Chedington
Corscombe
Lyon's Gate
Sharnhill Green
Bulbarrow Hill
898
West Chelborough
Hilfield
A352
Winterborne Stickland
A356
Evershot
Batcombe
Higher Ansty
Winterborne Houghton
Dibberford
Minterne Magna
Minterne
Henley
A3066
Holywell
Lower Ansty
Hilton
Winterborne Clenston
Thornicombe
Benville
Uphall
Frome St Quintin
20
Minterne Parva
Alton Pancras
Plush
Higher Melcombe
Melcombe Bingham
Abbey
Higher Whatcombe
Newtown
B3163
Toller Whelme
Rampisham
Up Cerne
Up Sydling
Cerne Giant
Beaminster
Lower Wraxall
Bingham's Melcombe
Milton Abbas
Lower Whatcombe
Higher Kingcombe
Higher Wraxall
Cerne Abbas
Mapperton
Hooke
Piddletrenthide
Cattistock
Sydling St Nicholas
Cheselbourne
Winterborne Whitechurch
Netherbury
Lower Kingcombe
A354
Mapperton
North Poorton
Chilfrome
Maiden Newton
B3143
Waytown
Loscombe
White Lackington
Dewlish
Milborne St Andrew
Winterborne Kingston
Oxbridge
South Poorton
Toller Porcorum
A37
Nether Cerne
West Milton
Toller Fratrum
Piddlehinton
Salwayash
Godmanstone
D O R S E
Powerstock
Cruxton
A31
A3066
Notton
Nettlecombe
Forston
Charlton Down
Wooth
Wynford Eagle
B3142
A35
Martyrs
Pymore
A356
Bere Regis
Loders
Eggardon Hillfort
827
West Compton
Frampton
Grimstone
Puddletown
Burleston
Eggardon Hill
Compton Valence
Athelhampton
Martyrs Tree
Tolpuddle
Turners Puddle
Uploders
Affpuddle
Bradpole
Muckleford
Stratton
Hardy's Cottage
Athelhampton House
Askerswell
Bradford Peverell
Charminster
Wolfeton Ho.
Higher Bockhampton
Briantspuddle
Walditch
Shipton Gorge
A35
Kingston Russell
Burton
Ilsington
Tincleton
Bothenhampton
Nine Stones
Winterbourne Abbas
Military
Poundbury
Stinsford
Kingston Maurward
Pallington
Chilcombe
Litton Cheney
Black Down
Lower Bockhampton
Clouds Hill
West Bay
Long Bredy
Winterbourne Poor Lot Barrows
DORCHESTER
Dinosaur
Max Gate
Woodsford
B3390
R. Piddle or Trent
Burton Bradstock
Winterbourne Steepleton
Maiden Castle
West Stafford
Moreton
Bovington Camp
B3157
Littlebredy
Hardy Monument
Winterborne St Martin or Martinstown
Winterborne Monkton
Maumbury Rings
Crossways
R. Frome
Tank
Monkey World
Swyre
Puncknowle
Whitcombe
Winterborne Herringston
West Knighton
Mill House Cider
Stokeford
Kingston Russell Stone Circle
A354
Dorset Collection of Clocks
East Burton
West Bexington
Friar Waddon
Broadmayne
Blacknoll
Wool
East Stoke
Abbotsbury
Portesham
Warmwell
A352
Galton
East Knighton
A352
Subtropical
Chapel
Coryates
Upwey
Bincombe
White Horse
Sutton Poyntz
Owermoigne
Coombe Keynes
Children's Farm
Elworth
Shilvinghampton
Poxwell
Winfrith Newburgh
Swannery
Rodden
Broadwey
Osmington
Holworth
Shaggs
B3071
Buckland Ripers
Littlemoor
Upton
Chaldon Herring or East Chaldon
Lulworth
Langton Herring
Preston
Roman Temple
A353
West Chaldon
Nottington
Lodmoor
Overcombe
Toll
B3157
Radipole
Osmington Mills
Chaldon Down
584
East Lulworth
Chickerell
Sea Life
Weymouth Bay
Ringstead Bay
B3070
Lulworth Camp
Chesil Beach
Fleet
Melcombe Regis
Heritage Centre
West Lulworth
B3157
Westham
WEYMOUTH
Durdle Door
Lulworth Cove
Worbarrow Bay
Chesil Beach
Charlestown
Nothe Fort
DANGER AREA
DANGER AREA
B3156
Rodwell
Sandsfoot Castle
Weymouth to Cherbourg (Proposed)
Wyke Regis
Portland Harbour
Chesil Beach
Portland
A354
Castletown
Chiswell
Fortuneswell
West Bay
Grove
Tout Quarry Sculpture Park
Easton
ISLE OF PORTLAND
Weston
Rufus
E N
Southwell
Portland
BILL OF PORTLAND
Portland Bill Lighthouse
350
60
70
80
70
80

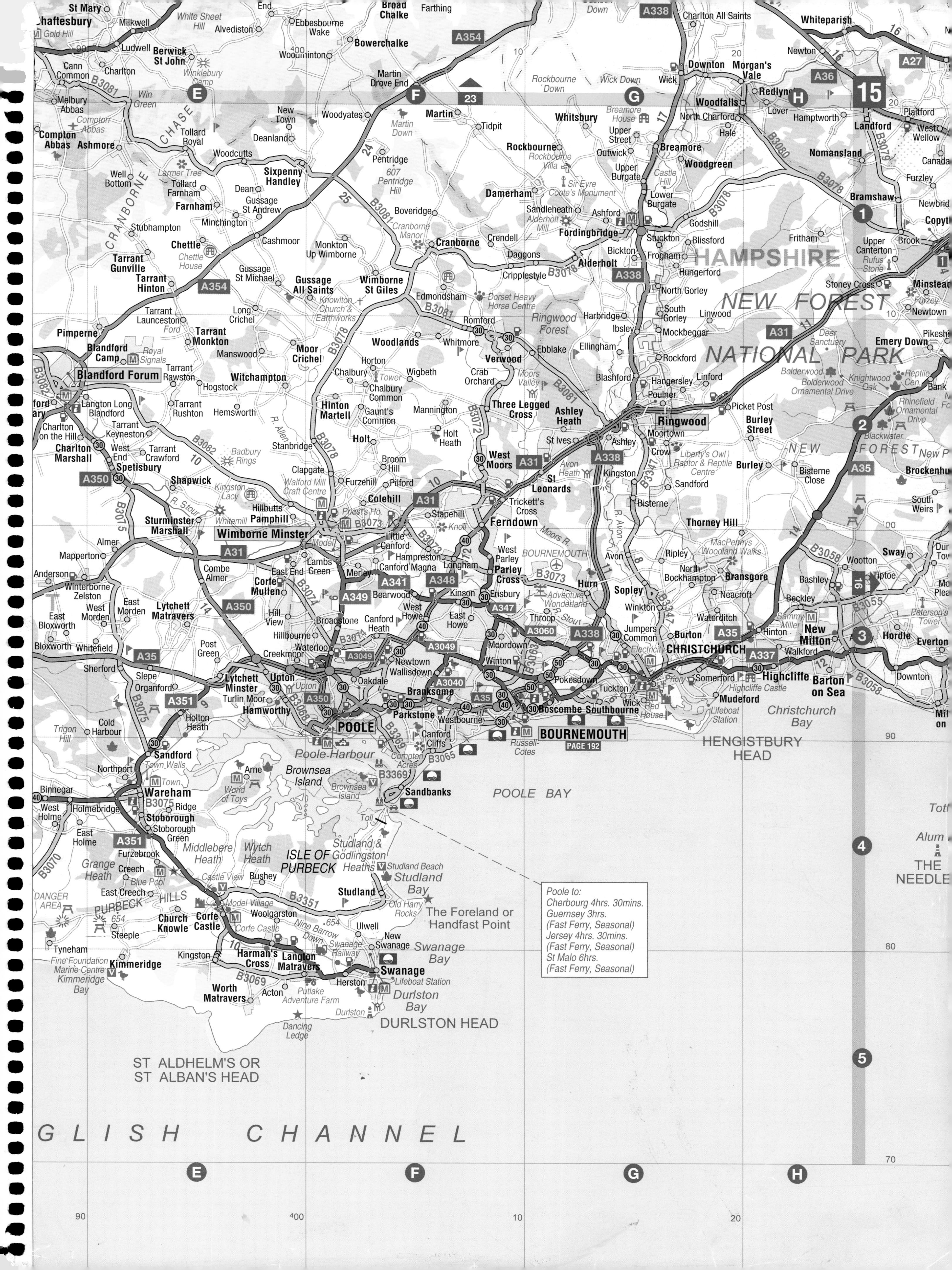
15
16
23
HAMPSHIRE
NEW FOREST
NATIONAL PARK
ENGLISH CHANNEL
POOLE BAY
Poole Harbour
Brownsea Island
ISLE OF PURBECK
Christchurch Bay
Swanage Bay
Studland Bay
Durlston Bay
HENGISTBURY HEAD
DURLSTON HEAD
ST ALDHELM'S OR ST ALBAN'S HEAD
The Foreland or Handfast Point
THE NEEDLES
PURBECK HILLS
CRANBORNE CHASE
Poole to:
Cherbourg 4hrs. 30mins.
Guernsey 3hrs.
(Fast Ferry, Seasonal)
Jersey 4hrs. 30mins.
(Fast Ferry, Seasonal)
St Malo 6hrs.
(Fast Ferry, Seasonal)
BOURNEMOUTH
PAGE 192
POOLE
CHRISTCHURCH
Ringwood
Blandford Forum
Wimborne Minster
Wareham
Swanage
Shaftesbury
Fordingbridge
Verwood
Ferndown
Three Legged Cross
West Moors
St Leonards
Corfe Castle
Sandbanks
Highcliffe
New Milton
Barton on Sea
Mudeford
Boscombe
Southbourne
Branksome
Parkstone
Hamworthy
Upton
Lytchett Minster
Sturminster Marshall
Cranborne
Alderholt
Downton
Whiteparish
Landford
Bramshaw
Burley
Sway
A31
A35
A338
A348
A349
A350
A351
A354
A36
A27
A337
A341
A347
A3049
A3060
A3040
B3078
B3081
B3082
B3073
B3074
B3075
B3065
B3369
B3351
B3069
B3070
B3347
B3055
B3058
B3080
B3079
B3072
B3068
B3063
B3064
E
F
G
H
1
2
3
4
5
70
80
90
400
10
20

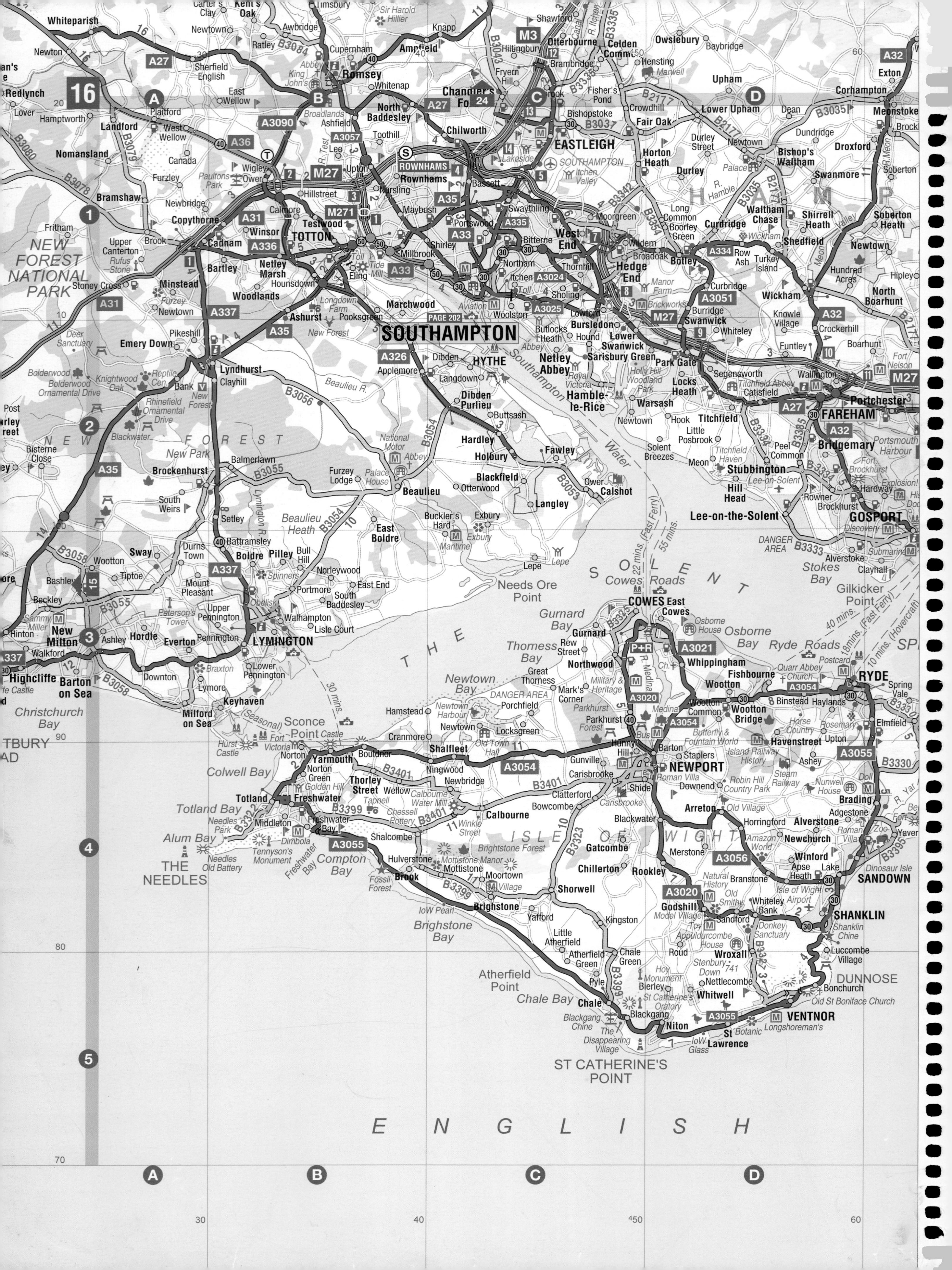
16
Whiteparish
Newton
Redlynch
Lover
Hamptworth
Landford
Plaitford
West Wellow
East Wellow
Nomansland
Canada
Furzley
Bramshaw
Newbridge
Copythorne
Fritham
Brook
Cadnam
Upper Canterton
NEW FOREST NATIONAL PARK
Stoney Cross
Minstead
Furzey
Newtown
Bartley
Woodlands
Netley Marsh
Hounsdown
Totton
Testwood
Winsor
Calmore
Ower
Wigley
Paultons Park
Romsey
Awbridge
Timsbury
Kent's Oak
Carter's Clay
Newtown
Ratley
Sherfield English
Cupernham
Ampfield
Knapp
Sir Harold Hillier
Whitenap
North Baddesley
Chandler's Ford
Broadlands
Ashfield
Toothill
Chilworth
Lee
Upton
Nursling
ROWNHAMS
Rownhams
Hillstreet
Maybush
Shirley
Millbrook
Eling
Tide Mill
Marchwood
Ashurst
Pooksgreen
Longdown Farm
New Forest
SOUTHAMPTON
PAGE 202
Woolston
Itchen
Sholing
Northam
Bitterne
Portswood
Swaythling
Bassett
EASTLEIGH
Bishopstoke
Otterbourne
Colden Common
Shawford
Hiltingbury
Fryern Hill
Brambridge
Hensting
Marwell
Owslebury
Baybridge
Fisher's Pond
Crowdhill
Fair Oak
Horton Heath
Upham
Lower Upham
Durley
Durley Street
Dean
Newtown
Bishop's Waltham
Dundridge
Droxford
Corhampton
Meonstoke
Exton
Soberton
Swanmore
Soberton Heath
Shirrell Heath
Waltham Chase
Curdridge
Boorley Green
Long Common
Moorgreen
West End
Hedge End
Botley
Row Ash
Turkey Island
Shedfield
Wickham
Newtown
Hundred Acres
Hipley
North Boarhunt
Knowle Village
Crockerhill
Boarhunt
Funtley
Fort Nelson
Curbridge
Burridge
Swanwick
Whiteley
Lower Swanwick
Bursledon
Lowford
Butlocks Heath
Hound
Netley Abbey
Sarisbury Green
Park Gate
Locks Heath
Segensworth
Titchfield Abbey
Catisfield
Wallington
Portchester
FAREHAM
Hamble-le-Rice
Warsash
Newtown
Hook
Titchfield
Little Posbrook
Solent Breezes
Meon
Stubbington
Peel Common
Bridgemary
Portsmouth Harbour
Hill Head
Lee-on-the-Solent
Rowner
Brockhurst
Hardway
GOSPORT
Alverstoke
Stokes Bay
Clayhall
Gilkicker Point
Hythe
Dibden
Applemore
Langdown
Dibden Purlieu
Buttsash
Hardley
Holbury
Fawley
Blackfield
Langley
Calshot
Southampton Water
Lyndhurst
Clayhill
Emery Down
Pikeshill
Bank
Bolderwood
Knightwood Oak
Rhinefield Ornamental Drive
Blackwater
NEW FOREST
New Park
Balmerlawn
Brockenhurst
South Weirs
Bisterne Close
Beaulieu
Beaulieu Heath
Furzey Lodge
Palace House
National Motor
East Boldre
Otterwood
Buckler's Hard
Exbury
Lepe
Setley
Battramsley
Boldre
Pilley
Bull Hill
Norleywood
East End
Portmore
South Baddesley
Sway
Durns Town
Wootton
Tiptoe
Bashley
Mount Pleasant
Upper Pennington
Beckley
Hinton
New Milton
Ashley
Hordle
Everton
Pennington
LYMINGTON
Walhampton
Lisle Court
Walkford
Highcliffe
Barton on Sea
Downton
Lower Pennington
Braxton
Eymore
Keyhaven
Milford on Sea
Christchurch Bay
Hurst Castle
Needs Ore Point
THE SOLENT
Cowes Roads
COWES
East Cowes
Osborne House
Osborne Bay
Ryde Roads
Gurnard Bay
Gurnard
Thorness Bay
Rew Street
Northwood
Whippingham
Fishbourne
Quarr Abbey
RYDE
Spring Vale
Wootton
Binstead
Haylands
Wootton Bridge
Elmfield
Great Thorness
Mark's Corner
Newtown Bay
Newtown
Porchfield
Parkhurst Forest
Parkhurst
Hamstead
Locksgreen
Cranmore
Shalfleet
Hunny Hill
NEWPORT
Barton
Staplers
Havenstreet
Upton
Ashey
Sconce Point
Fort Victoria
Norton
Yarmouth
Bouldnor
Ningwood
Gunville
Carisbrooke
Shide
Downend
Robin Hill Country Park
Nunwell House
Brading
Colwell Bay
Norton Green
Thorley Street
Wellow
Newbridge
Calbourne
Clatterford
Bowcombe
Totland
Freshwater
Arreton
Adgestone
Totland Bay
Middleton
Freshwater Bay
Alum Bay
THE NEEDLES
Needles Old Battery
Tennyson's Monument
Compton Bay
Shalcombe
Brook
Hulverstone
Mottistone
Moortown
ISLE OF WIGHT
Brighstone Forest
Gatcombe
Blackwater
Horringford
Alverstone
Newchurch
Merstone
Winford
Apse Heath
Lake
SANDOWN
Chillerton
Rookley
Shorwell
Brighstone
Yafford
Kingston
Godshill
Sandford
Whiteley Bank
SHANKLIN
Shanklin Chine
Brighstone Bay
Little Atherfield
Atherfield Green
Chale Green
Roud
Wroxall
Luccombe Village
DUNNOSE
Bonchurch
Atherfield Point
Chale Bay
Chale
Pyle
Bierley
Nettlecombe
Whitwell
Blackgang
Niton
St Lawrence
VENTNOR
Old St Boniface Church
St Catherine's Oratory
ST CATHERINE'S POINT
ENGLISH
A27
A36
A3090
M27
M271
A31
A336
A35
A33
A335
A3024
A3025
A326
A337
M3
B3335
B3354
A334
A3051
A32
A3054
A3020
A3021
A3055
A3056
B3401
B3399
B3055
B3056
B3054
B3053
B3058
B3330
B3395
B3333
B3385
B3334
B3035
B2177
B3037
B3043
B3084
B3079
B3080
B3078
B3057
B3342
B3323
B3322
B3327
22 mins. (Fast Ferry)
55 mins.
40 mins.
18mins. (Fast Ferry)
10 mins. (Hovercraft)
30 mins.
DANGER AREA
A
B
C
D
1
2
3
4
5
30
40
450
60
70
80
90
10
20

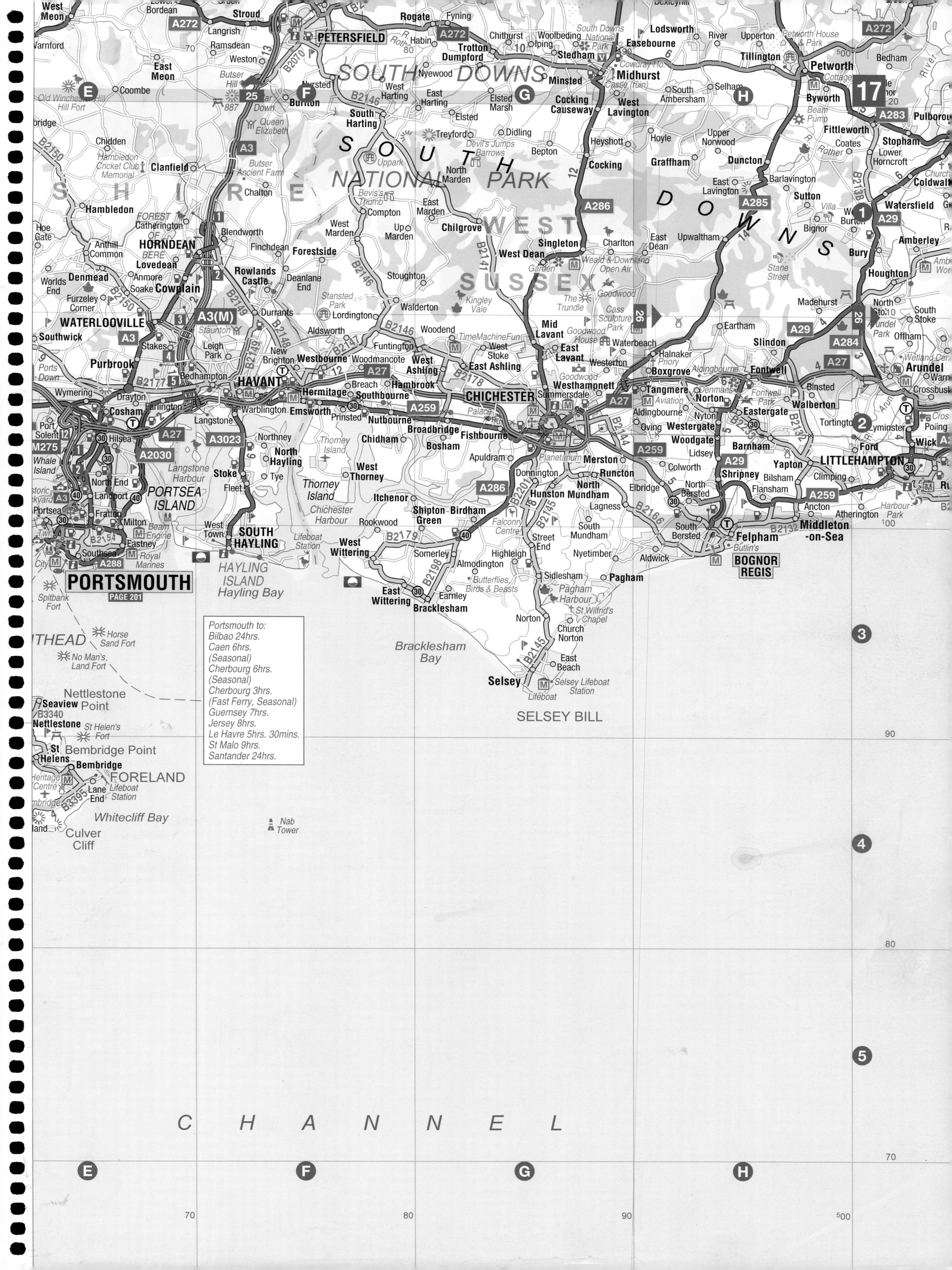
West Meon
Bordean
Stroud
A272
Langrish
Ramsdean
Weston
PETERSFIELD
Rogate
Fyning
Habin
A272
Trotton
Dumpford
Chithurst
Woolbeding
Iping
South Downs National Park
Stedham
Lodsworth
Easebourne
River
Upperton
Petworth House & Park
A272
Tillington
Petworth
Bedham
East Meon
Butser Hill
Nursted
SOUTH DOWNS
Nyewood
Minsted
Midhurst
Cowdray Ho. Castle (ruin)
South Ambersham
Selham
Byworth
17
Coombe
Old Winchester Hill Fort
Buriton
West Harting
East Harting
Elsted
Elsted Marsh
Cocking Causeway
West Lavington
Beam Pump
A283
Pulborough
War Down
Queen Elizabeth
South Harting
Elsted
Treyford
Didling
Devil's Jumps Barrows
Bepton
Heyshott
Hoyle
Upper Norwood
Fittleworth
Coates
Stopham
Lower Horncroft
A3
Chidden
Hambledon Cricket Club Memorial
Clanfield
Butser Ancient Farm
Uppark
SOUTH
NATIONAL PARK
North Marden
Cocking
Graffham
Duncton
Barlavington
East Lavington
Sutton
Coldwaltham
Chalton
Bevis's Thumb
SHIRE
Hambledon
FOREST OF BERE
Catherington
Compton
East Marden
A286
A285
DOWNS
Waterfield
Villa
Bignor
West Burton
A29
Hoe Gate
Blendworth
HORNDEAN
Anthill Common
Finchdean
Forestside
West Marden
Up Marden
Chilgrove
WEST
Singleton
Charlton
East Dean
Upwaltham
Amberley
Bury
Lovedean
Denmead
Worlds End
Rowlands Castle
Deanlane End
Stoughton
B2141
West Dean Garden
Weald & Downland Open Air
Stane Street
Houghton
Furzeley Corner
Anmore
Soake
Cowplain
Stansted Park
B2146
SUSSEX
Goodwood
The Trundle
Kingley Vale
Madehurst
North Stoke
South Stoke
WATERLOOVILLE
A3(M)
Staunton
Durrants
Lordington
Walderton
Mid Lavant
Cass Sculpture Park
26
Eartham
Slindon
A29
Arundel Park
Offham
Southwick
A3
Stakes
Leigh Park
Aldsworth
Woodend
TimeMachineFun
Goodwood House
Waterbeach
Halnaker Priory
A284
Purbrook
New Brighton
B2147
Funtington
West Stoke
East Lavant
Westerton
Boxgrove
Aldingbourne
Fontwell
Arundel
Ports Down
Bedhampton
HAVANT
Westbourne
Woodmancote
A27
West Ashling
East Ashling
Goodwood
Westhampnett
Tangmere
Denmans
Binsted
Wymering
Drayton
Hermitage
Breach
Hambrook
Southbourne
CHICHESTER
Summersdale
A27
Aviation
Norton
Fontwell Park
Walberton
Crossbush
Cosham
Farlington
Warblington
Emsworth
A259
Aldingbourne
Nyton
Eastergate
Port Solent
Langstone
Printed
Nutbourne
Broadbridge
Palace
Oving
Westergate
Tortington
Lyminster
Poling
M275
Hilsea
A27
A3023
Northney
Thorney Island
Chidham
Bosham
Fishbourne
A259
Woodgate
Barnham
Ford
Wick
A2030
North Hayling
Apuldram
Planetarium
Merston
Colworth
Lidsey
Yapton
LITTLEHAMPTON
Whale Island
Langstone Harbour
Stoke
Tye
West Thorney
Donnington
Runcton
A29
Shripney
Bilsham
Climping
North End
PORTSEA ISLAND
Fleet
Thorney Island
A286
North Mundham
Hunston
Elbridge
North Bersted
Flansham
A259
Landport
Fratton
Itchenor
Chichester Harbour
Lagness
Ancton
Atherington
Harbour Park
Portsea
Milton
Beam Engine
West Town
SOUTH HAYLING
Rookwood
Shipton Green
Birdham
Falconry Centre
South Mundham
South Bersted
Felpham
Middleton-on-Sea
Eastney
Southsea
Royal Marines
Lifeboat Station
West Wittering
B2179
Somerley
Street End
Nyetimber
Aldwick
Butlin's
BOGNOR REGIS
A288
HAYLING ISLAND
Hayling Bay
Almodington
Highleigh
Sidlesham
Pagham
PORTSMOUTH
PAGE 201
Spitbank Fort
East Wittering
Bracklesham
Earnley
B2198
Butterflies, Birds & Beasts
Pagham Harbour
St Wilfrid's Chapel
Norton
Church Norton
Horse Sand Fort
No Man's Land Fort
Bracklesham Bay
East Beach
Selsey
Selsey Lifeboat Station
Lifeboat
SELSEY BILL
Portsmouth to:
Bilbao 24hrs.
Caen 6hrs. (Seasonal)
Cherbourg 6hrs. (Seasonal)
Cherbourg 3hrs. (Fast Ferry, Seasonal)
Guernsey 7hrs.
Jersey 8hrs.
Le Havre 5hrs. 30mins.
St Malo 9hrs.
Santander 24hrs.
Nettlestone Point
Seaview
B3340
Nettlestone
St Helen's Fort
St Helens
Bembridge Point
Bembridge
Heritage Centre
FORELAND
Lifeboat Station
Lane End
B3395
Whitecliff Bay
Nab Tower
Culver Cliff
CHANNEL
E
F
G
H
1
2
3
4
5
70
80
90
500

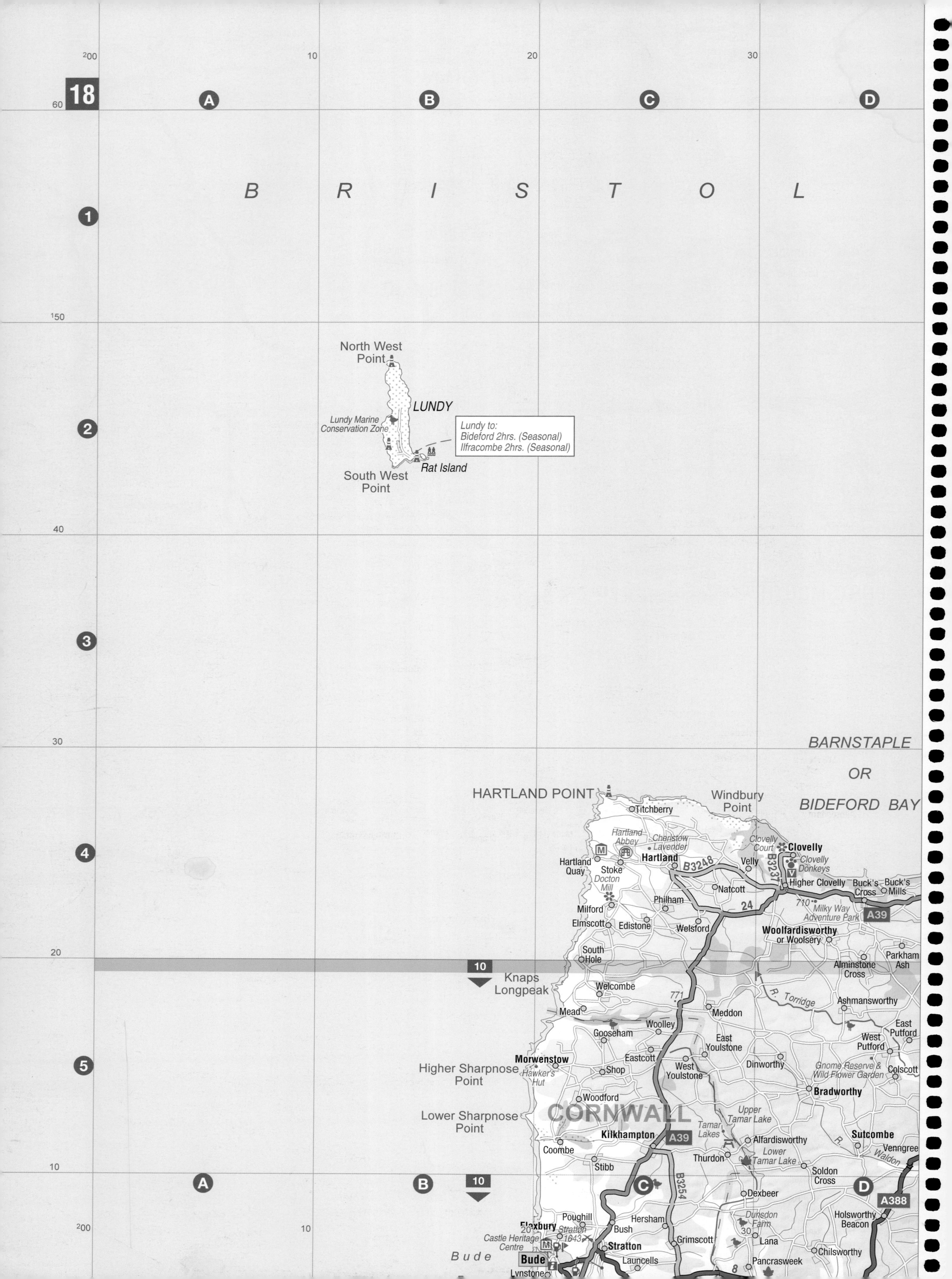

200   10   20   30

60

Ⓐ   Ⓑ   Ⓒ   Ⓓ

B R I S T O L

①

150

North West
Point

LUNDY

②

Lundy Marine
Conservation Zone

Lundy to:
Bideford 2hrs. (Seasonal)
Ilfracombe 2hrs. (Seasonal)

Rat Island

South West
Point

40

③

30

BARNSTAPLE

OR

BIDEFORD BAY

HARTLAND POINT   Windbury
Point

○Titchberry

Hartland   *Cheristow*   Clovelly
Abbey   *Lavender*   Court   Clovelly

④   Hartland   Ⓜ   Hartland   B3248   Velly   Clovelly
Quay   Stoke   Donkeys
Docton   Natcott   Higher Clovelly   Buck's   Buck's
Mill   Cross   Mills

Milford   Philham   24   Milky Way
Elmscott○   Edistone   Adventure Park   A39
Welsford   Woolfardisworthy
or Woolsery   Parkham
South   Alminstone   Ash
Hole   Cross

20   10   Knaps   R. Torridge   Ashmansworthy
Longpeak   Welcombe   771
Meddon   East
Mead   Woolley   Putford   West
Gooseham   East   Dinworthy   Putford
Youlstone   Gnome Reserve &   Colscott
⑤   Higher Sharpnose   Morwenstow   Eastcott   West   Wild Flower Garden
Point   Hawker's   Shop   Youlstone   **Bradworthy**
Hut   Woodford

Lower Sharpnose   *CORNWALL*   Upper
Point   Tamar   Tamar Lake   **Sutcombe**
Kilkhampton   A39   Lakes   Alfardisworthy   Venngree
Coombe   Lower   R.   Waldon
Thurdon   Tamar Lake   Soldon
Stibb   Cross
10   B3254   Dexbeer   Holsworthy
Ⓐ   Ⓑ   10   Ⓒ   Dunsdon   Ⓓ   Beacon
Farm   A388
200   Poughill   Hersham
Flexbury   Stratton   Bush   Lana
Castle Heritage   1643   Grimscott   Pancrasweek   Chilsworthy
Centre   **Stratton**   30
Bude   Launcells
Bude   Lynstone   8

10

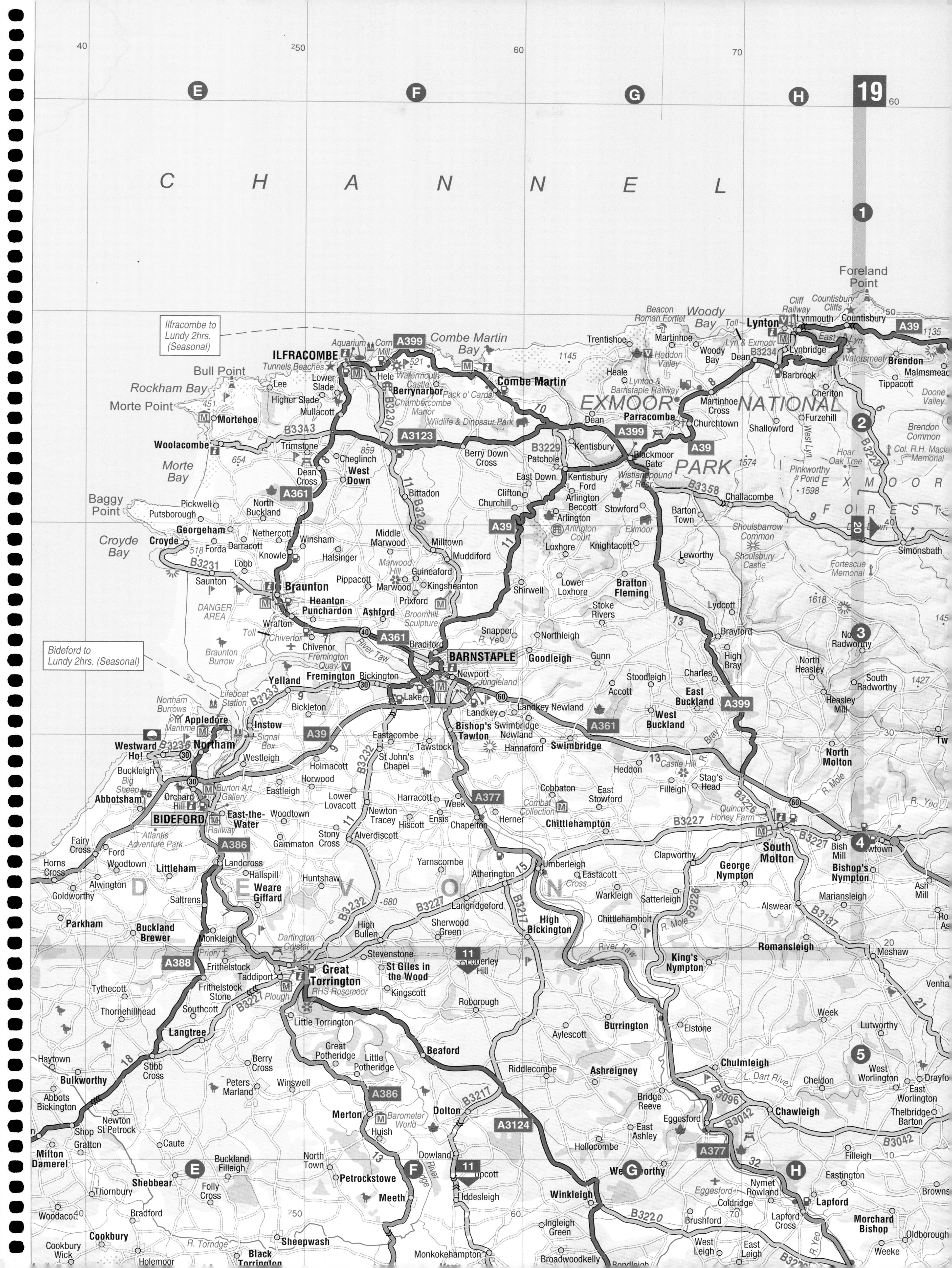

19
E
F
G
H
40
250
60
70
C H A N N E L
Foreland Point
Countisbury Cliffs
Cliff Railway
Beacon Roman Fortlet
Woody Bay
Lynton
Lynmouth
Countisbury
A39
Trentishoe
Martinhoe
Heddon Valley
Woody Bay
Toll
Lyn & Exmoor
Dean
B3234
Lynbridge
East Lyn
Watersmeet
Brendon
Malmsmead
Tippacott
Barbrook
Cheriton
Doone Valley
Ilfracombe to Lundy 2hrs. (Seasonal)
ILFRACOMBE
Tunnels Beaches
Aquarium
Combe Mill
A399
Combe Martin Bay
Combe Martin
Bull Point
Rockham Bay
Lee
Lower Slade
Hele
Watermouth Castle
Berrynarbor
Pack o' Cards
Morte Point
Mortehoe
Higher Slade
Chambercombe Manor
Mullacott
Wildlife & Dinosaur Park
B3230
EXMOOR NATIONAL PARK
Heale
Lynton & Barnstaple Railway
Martinhoe Cross
Parracombe
Churchtown
Furzehill
Shallowford
West Lyn
Brendon Common
B3223
Col. R.H. Maclean Memorial
Woolacombe
B3343
Trimstone
A3123
Berry Down Cross
Dean
Kentisbury
A399
Blackmoor Gate
A39
Hoar Oak Tree
Morte Bay
Cheglinch
B3229
Patchole
Pinkworthy Pond
EXMOOR FOREST
Dean Cross
West Down
East Down
Kentisbury Ford
Wistlandpound Resr.
B3358
Challacombe
Baggy Point
A361
Bittadon
Clifton
Churchill
Arlington Beccott
Stowford
Barton Town
Pickwell
North Buckland
Putsborough
Arlington
Arlington Court
Exmoor Zoo
Shoulsbarrow Common
Georgeham
Nethercott
Middle Marwood
Croyde Bay
Croyde
Darracott
Winsham
Milltown
Loxhore
Knightacott
Leworthy
Shoulsbury Castle
Simonsbath
Forda
Knowle
Halsinger
Muddiford
B3231
Lobb
Marwood Hill
Guineaford
Fortescue Memorial
Saunton
Braunton
Pippacott
Marwood
Kingsheanton
Shirwell
Lower Loxhore
Bratton Fleming
Heanton Punchardon
Prixford
DANGER AREA
Ashford
Broomhill Sculpture
Stoke Rivers
Lydcott
Wrafton
Toll
Chivenor
A361
Snapper
R. Yeo
Northleigh
Brayford
North Radworthy
Bideford to Lundy 2hrs. (Seasonal)
Braunton Burrow
Fremington Quay
River Taw
Bradiford
BARNSTAPLE
Goodleigh
Gunn
High Bray
North Heasley
South Radworthy
Yelland
Fremington
Bickington
Newport
Jungleland
Stoodleigh
Charles
East Buckland
Heasley Mill
Northam Burrows
Lifeboat Station
B3233
Bickleton
Lake
Accott
Landkey
Landkey Newland
A399
Appledore
Instow
Signal Box
A361
West Buckland
Westward Ho!
Northam
A39
Eastacombe
Bishop's Tawton
Swimbridge Newland
Hannaford
Swimbridge
North Molton
B3236
Westleigh
St John's Chapel
Tawstock
Buckleigh
Big Sheep
Holmacott
B3232
Heddon
Castle Hill
Filleigh
Stag's Head
Abbotsham
Orchard Hill
Burton Art Gallery
Horwood
Eastleigh
Lower Lovacott
Harracott
Week
A377
Cobbaton
Combat Collection
East Stowford
B3226
Quince Honey Farm
R. Mole
R. Yeo
BIDEFORD
East-the-Water
Woodtown
Newton Tracey
Hiscott
Ensis
Chapelton
Herner
Chittlehampton
B3227
South Molton
Bish Mill
Fairy Cross
Ford
Atlantis Adventure Park
Railway
A386
Gammaton
Stony Cross
Alverdiscott
B3227
Bishop's Nympton
Horns Cross
Woodtown
Landcross
Yarnscombe
Umberleigh
Clapworthy
George Nympton
Alwington
Littleham
Hallspill
Huntshaw
Atherington
Eastacott Cross
Ash Mill
Goldworthy
Weare Giffard
Warkleigh
Satterleigh
Mariansleigh
D E V O N
Saltrens
B3232
680
B3227
Langridgeford
B3217
Alswear
Parkham
Buckland Brewer
Sherwood Green
High Bickington
Chittlehamholt
B3137
Monkleigh
High Bullen
Dartington Crystal
Romansleigh
Meshaw
Priory
Stevenstone
River Taw
A388
Frithelstock
Taddiport
Great Torrington
St Giles in the Wood
Eburley Hill
King's Nympton
Venhay
Tythecott
Frithelstock Stone
Plough
RHS Rosemoor
Kingscott
Thornehillhead
Southcott
B3227
Roborough
Little Torrington
Week
Lutworthy
Langtree
Burrington
Elstone
Aylescott
Haytown
Great Potheridge
Little Potheridge
Beaford
Berry Cross
Stibb Cross
Riddlecombe
Ashreigney
Chulmleigh
West Worlington
Bulkworthy
Peters Marland
Winswell
L. Dart River
Cheldon
East Worlington
Abbots Bickington
A386
Bridge Reeve
B3096
Merton
Barometer World
Dolton
B3217
Eggesford
Chawleigh
Thelbridge Barton
Newton St Petrock
Huish
A3124
B3042
East Ashley
Shop
Gratton
A377
Filleigh
Milton Damerel
Caute
Buckland Filleigh
North Town
Dowland
Hollocombe
B3042
Petrockstowe
Upcott
Wembworthy
Eastington
Shebbear
Folly Cross
Nymet Rowland
Thornbury
Meeth
Iddesleigh
Winkleigh
Eggesford
Coldridge
Lapford
Woodacott
Bradford
B3220
Ingleigh Green
Brushford
Lapford Cross
Morchard Bishop
Cookbury
Sheepwash
R. Torridge
Monkokehampton
West Leigh
East Leigh
Weeke
Oldborough
Cookbury Wick
Holemoor
Black Torrington
Broadwoodkelly
Bondleigh

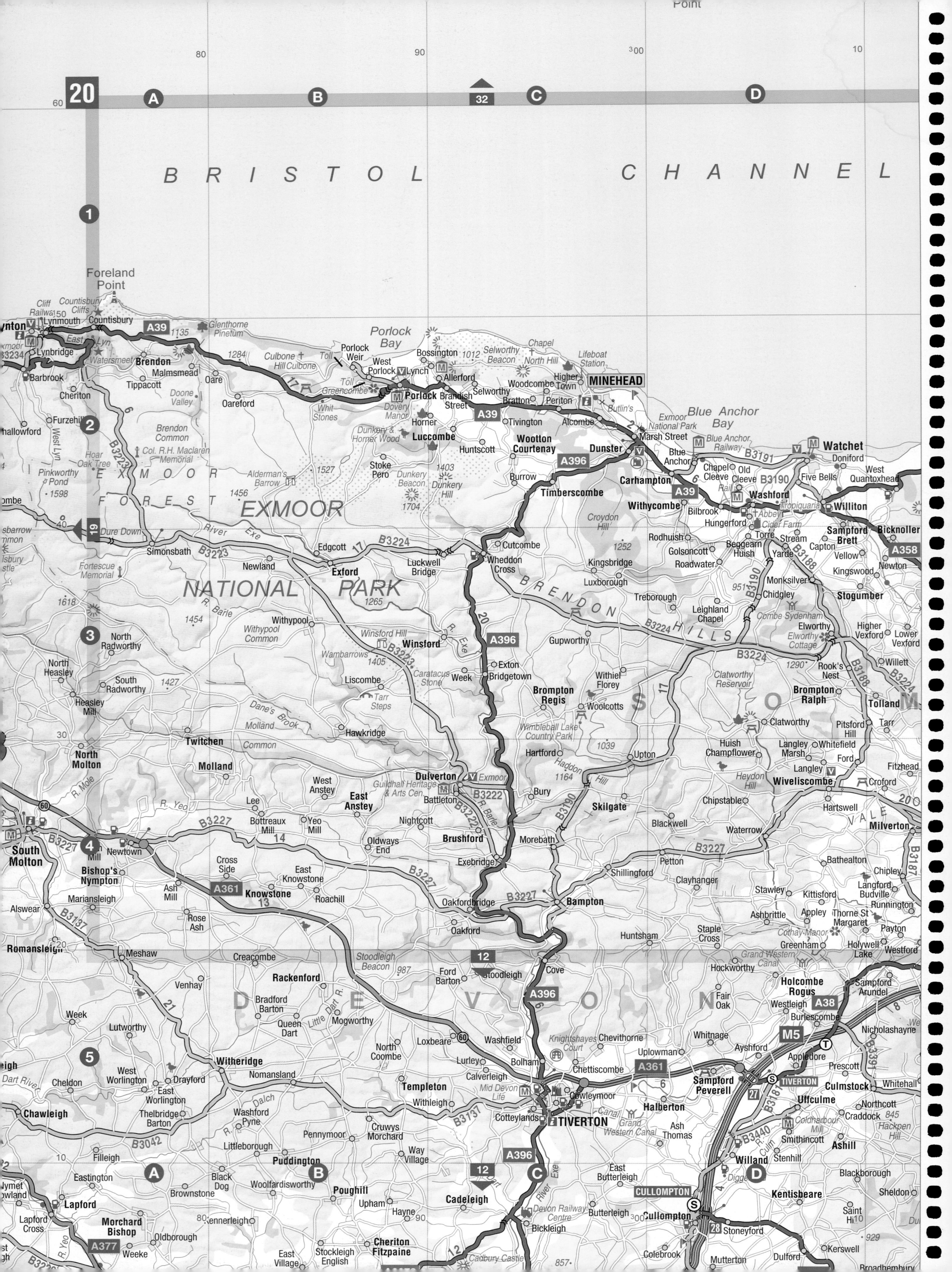

20
A
B
32
C
D
80
90
300
10
60
BRISTOL CHANNEL
1
2
3
4
5
Foreland Point
Countisbury Cliffs
Cliff Railway
Lynmouth
Countisbury
Lynton
A39
Glenthorne Pinetum
Lynbridge
East Lyn
Watersmeet
Brendon
Malmsmead
Oare
Barbrook
Tippacott
Cheriton
Doone Valley
Oareford
Culbone Hill
Culbone
Toll
Porlock Weir
West Porlock
Lynch
Porlock Bay
Bossington
Selworthy Beacon
Chapel
North Hill
Lifeboat Station
Higher Town
MINEHEAD
Greencombe
Porlock
Allerford
Brandish Street
Selworthy
Woodcombe
Bratton
Periton
Alcombe
Butlin's
Whit Stones
Dovery Manor
Horner
Tivington
Wootton Courtenay
Exmoor National Park
Blue Anchor Bay
Dunkery & Horner Wood
Luccombe
Huntscott
Dunster
Marsh Street
Blue Anchor Railway
Blue Anchor
Watchet
Doniford
Furzehill
Challowfield
West Lyn
Brendon Common
Col. R.H. Maclaren Memorial
Hoar Oak Tree
Pinkworthy Pond
EXMOOR FOREST
Alderman's Barrow
Stoke Pero
Dunkery Beacon
Dunkery Hill
A396
Burrow
Timberscombe
Carhampton
Chapel Cleeve
Old Cleeve
B3190
Five Bells
West Quantoxhead
B3191
Washford
Withycombe
Bilbrook
Abbey
Tropiquaria
Williton
Hungerford
Cider Farm
Croydon Hill
Rodhuish
Torre
Stream
Sampford Brett
Bicknoller
EXMOOR
Dure Down
Simonsbath
River Exe
B3223
Edgcott
B3224
Cutcombe
Wheddon Cross
Golsoncott
Roadwater
Beggearn Huish
Yarde
Capton
Vellow
A358
Fortescue Memorial
Newland
Exford
Luckwell Bridge
Kingsbridge
Luxborough
B3188
Kingswood
Newton
NATIONAL PARK
R. Barle
BRENDON HILLS
Treborough
Monksilver
Chidgley
Stogumber
Leighland Chapel
Combe Sydenham
Elworthy
Elworthy Cottage
Higher Vexford
Lower Vexford
North Radworthy
Withypool
Withypool Common
Winsford Hill
Winsford
R. Exe
Wambarrows
Gupworthy
B3224
Willett
North Heasley
South Radworthy
Heasley Mill
Liscombe
Caratacus Stone
Exton
Bridgetown
Week
Withiel Florey
Clatworthy Reservoir
Rook's Nest
Brompton Regis
Woolcotts
Brompton Ralph
Tolland
Tarr Steps
Dane's Brook
Molland Common
Hawkridge
Wimbleball Lake Country Park
Clatworthy
Pitsford Hill
Tarr
Twitchen
Hartford
Haddon Hill
Upton
Huish Champflower
Langley Marsh
Whitefield
Ford
Fitzhead
North Molton
Molland
Dulverton
Exmoor
Guildhall Heritage & Arts Cen.
Battleton
Heydon Hill
Langley
Wiveliscombe
Croford
West Anstey
East Anstey
B3222
Bury
Chipstable
Hartswell
R. Mole
R. Yeo
Lee
Skilgate
Bottreaux Mill
Yeo Mill
Nightcott
Blackwell
Waterrow
VALE
Milverton
South Molton
B3227
Newtown
Oldways End
Brushford
Morebath
Bish Mill
Bishop's Nympton
Cross Side
East Knowstone
Exebridge
Petton
Bathealton
Chipley
Langford Budville
Mariansleigh
Ash Mill
A361
Knowstone
Roachill
Oakfordbridge
Bampton
Shillingford
Clayhanger
Stawley
Kittisford
Runnington
Alswear
B3137
Rose Ash
Oakford
Ashbrittle
Appley
Thorne St Margaret
Payton
Romansleigh
Meshaw
Creacombe
Stoodleigh Beacon
12
Huntsham
Staple Cross
Cothay Manor
Greenham
Holywell Lake
Westford
Cove
Grand Western Canal
Hockworthy
Rackenford
Ford Barton
Stoodleigh
Venhay
Holcombe Rogus
Sampford Arundel
DEVON
Bradford Barton
Little Dart R.
Fair Oak
Westleigh
A38
Burlescombe
Week
Queen Dart
Mogworthy
Lutworthy
Loxbeare
Washfield
Knightshayes Court
Chevithorne
Whitnage
Ayshford
M5
Nicholashayne
B3391
North Coombe
Lurley
Bolham
Uplowman
Appledore
Prescott
West Worlington
Drayford
Witheridge
Nomansland
Calverleigh
Chettiscombe
A361
Sampford Peverell
TIVERTON
Whitehall
Cheldon
Dart River
East Worlington
Templeton
Mid Devon Life
Cowleymoor
Halberton
27
Culmstock
Withleigh
B3181
Uffculme
Chawleigh
Thelbridge Barton
Washford Pyne
R. Dalch
B3737
Cotteylands
Grand Western Canal
Ash Thomas
Coldharbour Mill
Northcott
Craddock
Hackpen Hill
Pennymoor
Cruwys Morchard
B3440
Smithincott
B3042
Littleborough
Way Village
Stenhill
Ashill
Filleigh
Puddington
A396
Willand
Eastington
Black Dog
East Butterleigh
Blackborough
Woolfardisworthy
Digges
Lapford
Brownstone
Poughill
Cadeleigh
River Exe
CULLOMPTON
Kentisbeare
Sheldon
Upham
Hayne
Devon Railway Centre
Butterleigh
Cullompton
Saint Hill
Lapford Cross
Morchard Bishop
Kennerleigh
Bickleigh
28
Stoneyford
Oldborough
Cheriton Fitzpaine
A377
Weeke
Stockleigh English
East Village
Cadbury Castle
Colebrook
Mutterton
Dulford
Kerswell
Broadhembury

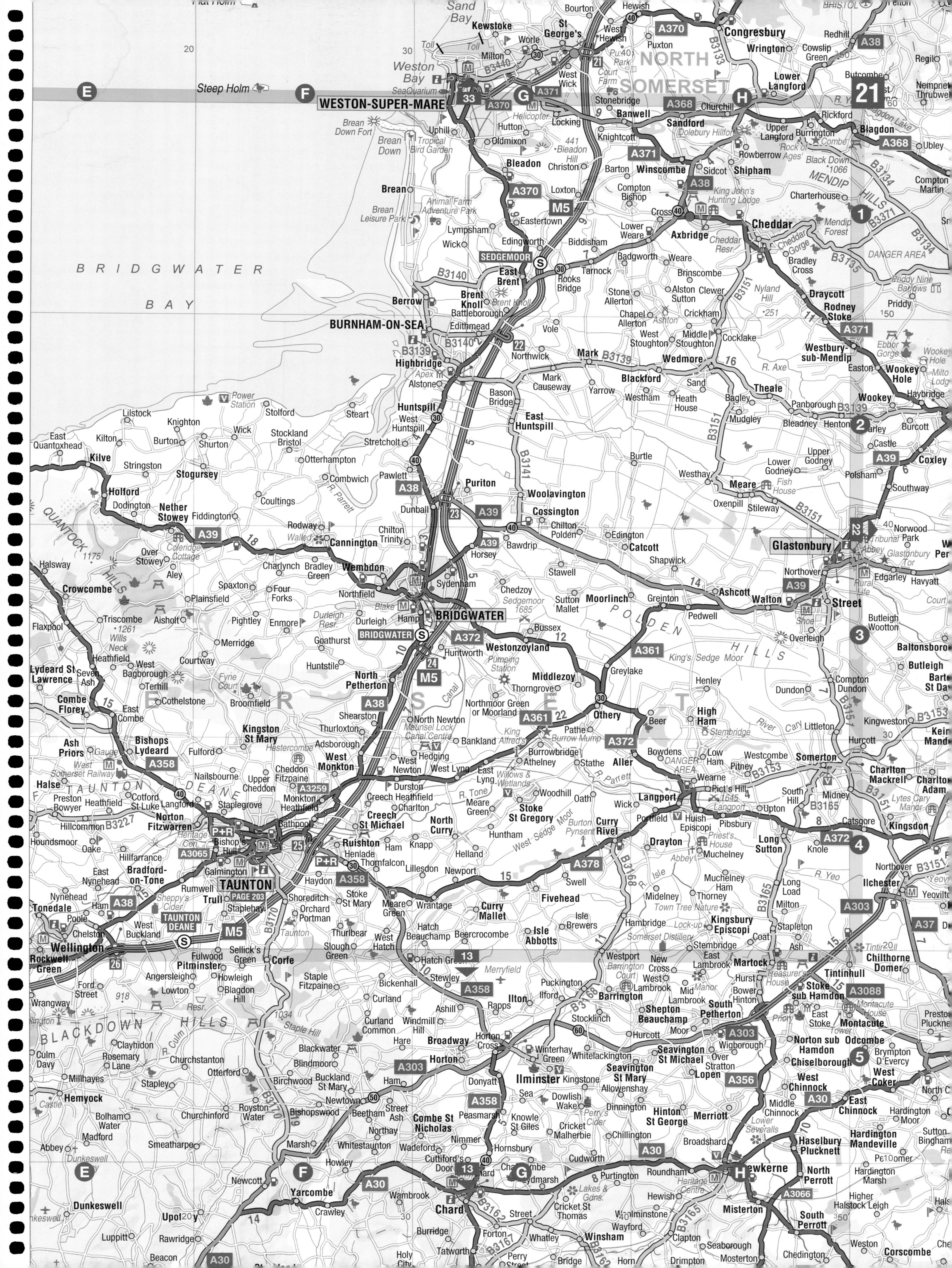

Steep Holm
WESTON-SUPER-MARE
Sand Bay
Kewstoke
St George's
Worle
Milton
Weston Bay
SeaQuarium
Hewish
West Hewish
Bourton
A370
Congresbury
Puxton
NORTH
SOMERSET
Wrington
Redhill
Cowslip Green
A38
Regil
Lower Langford
Butcombe
21
Nempnett Thrubwell
West Wick
Court Farm
Stonebridge
Banwell
A368
Churchill
Sandford
Rickford
Blagdon
Blagdon Lake
Ubley
Uphill
Brean Down Fort
Hutton
Locking
Knightcott
Upper Langford
Burrington
Brean Down
Tropical Bird Garden
Oldmixon
441 Bleadon Hill
A371
Rowberrow
Black Down 1066
Bleadon
Christon
Barton
Winscombe
Sidcot
Shipham
MENDIP
Compton Martin
Brean
A370
Loxton
Compton Bishop
A38
King John's Hunting Lodge
Charterhouse
HILLS
B3134
B3371
M5
Cross
Cheddar
Mendip Forest
Animal Farm Adventure Park
Brean Leisure Park
Eastertown
Lympsham
Edingworth
Biddisham
Lower Weare
Axbridge
Cheddar Resr.
Cheddar Gorge
Bradley Cross
DANGER AREA
B3135
Wick
SEDGEMOOR
Badgworth
Weare
Brinscombe
BRIDGWATER
BAY
B3140
East Brent
Tarnock
Rooks Bridge
Stone Allerton
Alston Sutton
Clewer
Nyland Hill
Draycott
Priddy Nine Barrows
Priddy
Berrow
Brent Knoll
Battleborough
Chapel Allerton
Ashton
Crickham
Rodney Stoke
BURNHAM-ON-SEA
Edithmead
Vole
West Stoughton
Middle Stoughton
Cocklake
A371
B3139
B3140
22
Northwick
Mark
B3139
Wedmore
16
Westbury-sub-Mendip
Ebbor Gorge
Wookey Hole
Highbridge
Apex
Alstone
Mark Causeway
Blackford
R. Axe
Easton
Bason Bridge
Sand
Yarrow
Westham
Heath House
Theale
Wookey
Haybridge
Power Station
Stolford
Lilstock
Knighton
Wick
Stockland Bristol
Steart
Huntspill
West Huntspill
East Huntspill
B3151
Bagley
Mudgley
Panborough
B3139
Bleadney
Henton
Burcott
East Quantoxhead
Kilton
Burton
Shurton
Stretcholt
Castle
Kilve
Stringston
Otterhampton
Burtle
Upper Godney
Lower Godney
A39
Coxley
Polsham
Stogursey
Combwich
Pawlett
Puriton
B3141
Westhay
Meare
Fish House
Southway
Holford
R. Parrett
A38
Woolavington
Oxenpill
Stileway
B3151
Dodington
Nether Stowey
Fiddington
Coultings
Dunball
Cossington
QUANTOCK
Rodway
Walled Garden
Cannington
Chilton Trinity
23
A39
Chilton Polden
Edington
Norwood Park
A39
18
Horsey
Bawdrip
Catcott
Tribunal
Glastonbury
Glastonbury Tor
Abbey
Over Stowey
Coleridge Cottage
1175
Halsway
HILLS
Aley
Charlynch
Bradley Green
Wembdon
Stawell
Shapwick
Northover
Edgarley
Havyatt
Crowcombe
Spaxton
Four Forks
Sydenham
Chedzoy
Sedgemoor 1685
Sutton Mallet
Moorlinch
14
Ashcott
Walton
A39
Plainsfield
Northfield
Greinton
Pedwell
Street
Triscombe
1261 Wills Neck
Aisholt
Pightley
Enmore
Durleigh Resr.
Durleigh
Blake
Hamp
BRIDGWATER
POLDEN
Shoe
Butleigh Wootton
Flaxpool
Merridge
Goathurst
BRIDGWATER
A372
Bussex
12
Overleigh
Westonzoyland
A361
King's Sedge Moor
HILLS
Baltonsborough
Heathfield
Courtway
Huntworth
Pumping Station
Greylake
Lydeard St Lawrence
Seven Ash
West Bagborough
Huntstile
M5
24
North Petherton
Middlezoy
Henley
Butleigh
Compton Dundon
Terhill
Fyne Court
Thorngrove
Dundon
Combe Florey
Cothelstone
Broomfield
Canal
Shearston
A38
Northmoor Green or Moorland
Othery
High Ham
15
East Combe
Kingston St Mary
Thurloxton
North Newton
Maunsel Lock Canal Centre
King Alfred's
A361
22
Beer
Kingweston
B3153
Ash Priors
Bishops Lydeard
Gauge
Hestercombe
Adsborough
Bankland
Pathe
Burrow Mump
Stembridge
River Cary
Littleton
Hurcott
A358
West Somerset Railway
Fulford
West Monkton
Hedging
West Newton
West Lyng
Burrowbridge
Athelney
A372
Bowdens
Low Ham
DANGER AREA
Westcombe
Somerton
Halse
TAUNTON
Nailsbourne
Cheddon Fitzpaine
East Lyng
Willows & Wetlands
Stathe
Aller
Pitney
Wearne
B3153
Charlton Mackrell
Charlton Adam
Preston Bowyer
Heathfield
Cotford St Luke
DEANE
Langford
Upper Cheddon
A3259
Durston
Creech Heathfield
R. Tone
Meare Green
Woodhill
Oath
Langport
Pict's Hill 1645
South Hill
Midney
Lytes Cary Manor
Norton Fitzwarren
Staplegrove
Monkton Heathfield
Charlton
Stoke St Gregory
Wick
Huish Episcopi
Langport
Upton
B3165
Hillcommon
B3227
Bathpool
Creech St Michael
North Curry
Burton Pynsent
Curry Rivel
Portfield
Pibsbury
Catsgore
Kingsdon
Houndsmoor
Oake
Heritage Cen.
Bishop's Hull
25
Ruishton
Henlade
Ham
Knapp
Huntham
West Sedge Moor
Drayton
Priest's House
Long Sutton
A372
Knole
Hillfarrance
A3065
Thornfalcon
Lillesdon
Helland
Abbey
Muchelney
East Nynehead
Bradford-on-Tone
Galmington
TAUNTON
PAGE 203
Haydon
A358
Newport
15
A378
B3168
Swell
R. Isle
Muchelney Ham
Long Load
R. Yeo
Northover
B3151
Ilchester
Yeovilton
Nynehead
Rumwell
Trull
Shoreditch
Stoke St Mary
Wrantage
Fivehead
Midelney
Thorney
Town Tree Nature
Milton
A303
Tonedale
Ham
A38
Sheppy's Cider
Staplehay
Orchard Portman
Meare Green
Curry Mallet
Isle Brewers
Kingsbury Episcopi
B3165
Stapleton
A37
Poole
TAUNTON DEANE
Chelston
West Buckland
M5
7
B3170
Taunton
Thurlbear
West Hatch
Hatch Beauchamp
Beercrocombe
Isle Abbotts
Hambridge
Lock-up
Somerset Distillery
Coat
Ash
Wellington
26
Rockwell Green
Fulwood
Pitminster
Sellick's Green
Corfe
Slough Green
Hatch Green
13
Merryfield
Westport
Barrington Court
New Cross
Stembridge
East Lambrook
Martock
Tintinhull
Chilthorne Domer
Angersleigh
Howleigh
Lowton
Blagdon Hill
Staple Fitzpaine
Bickenhall
Stewley
A358
Ilton
Puckington
Ilford
B3168
Barrington
West Lambrook
Mid Lambrook
Treasurer's House
Hurst
Bower Hinton
Stoke sub Hamdon
A3088
Ford Street
918
Resr.
Curland
Rapps
Ashill
Stocklinch
Shepton Beauchamp
South Petherton
Montacute House
Wrangway
BLACKDOWN
HILLS
1034
Staple Hill
Curland Common
Windmill Hill
Hurcott
Moor
East Stoke
Montacute
Preston Plucknett
Clayhidon
R. Culm
Hare
Broadway
Horton Cross
60
A303
Wigborough
Norton sub Hamdon
Odcombe
Culm Davy
Rosemary Lane
Churchstanton
Blackwater
Winterhay Green
Whitelackington
Seavington St Michael
Over Stratton
Brympton D'Evercy
Otterford
Blindmoor
Buckland St Mary
A303
Horton
Ilminster
Kingstone
Seavington St Mary
Lopen
Chiselborough
West Coker
Millhayes
Stapley
Birchwood
Ham
Donyatt
Allowenshay
A356
West Chinnock
North Coker
Hemyock
Castle
Royston Water
Newtown
50
Street Ash
A358
Sea
Dowlish Wake
Perry's Cider
Dinnington
Middle Chinnock
A30
East Chinnock
Bolham Water
Churchinford
Bishopswood
Beetham
Combe St Nicholas
Peasmarsh
Knowle St Giles
Cricket Malherbie
Hinton St George
Merriott
Lower Severalls
Hardington Moor
Madford
B3170
Northay
Chillington
Haselbury Plucknett
Hardington Mandeville
Sutton Bingham
Abbey
Dunkeswell Abbey
Smeatharpe
Marsh
Whitestaunton
Wadeford
Nimmer
Hornsbury
Cudworth
A30
Broadshard
Pendomer
Howley
Cuttiford's Door
13
Chaffcombe
Crewkerne
North Perrott
Hardington Marsh
Newcott
Yarcombe
A30
Chard
Tatworth
Perry Street
Lakes & Gdns.
Purtington
Roundham
Heritage Centre
A3066
Higher Halstock Leigh
Dunkeswell
Wambrook
Crawley
B3162
Street
Cricket St Thomas
Hewish
Winsham
Misterton
South Perrott
Upottery
Luppitt
Rawridge
Burridge
Forton
B3167
Whatley
Wayford
B3165
Clapton
Seaborough
Weston
Corscombe
Beacon
A30
Holy City
Perry Street
Bridge
Horn
Drimpton
Mosterton
Chedington

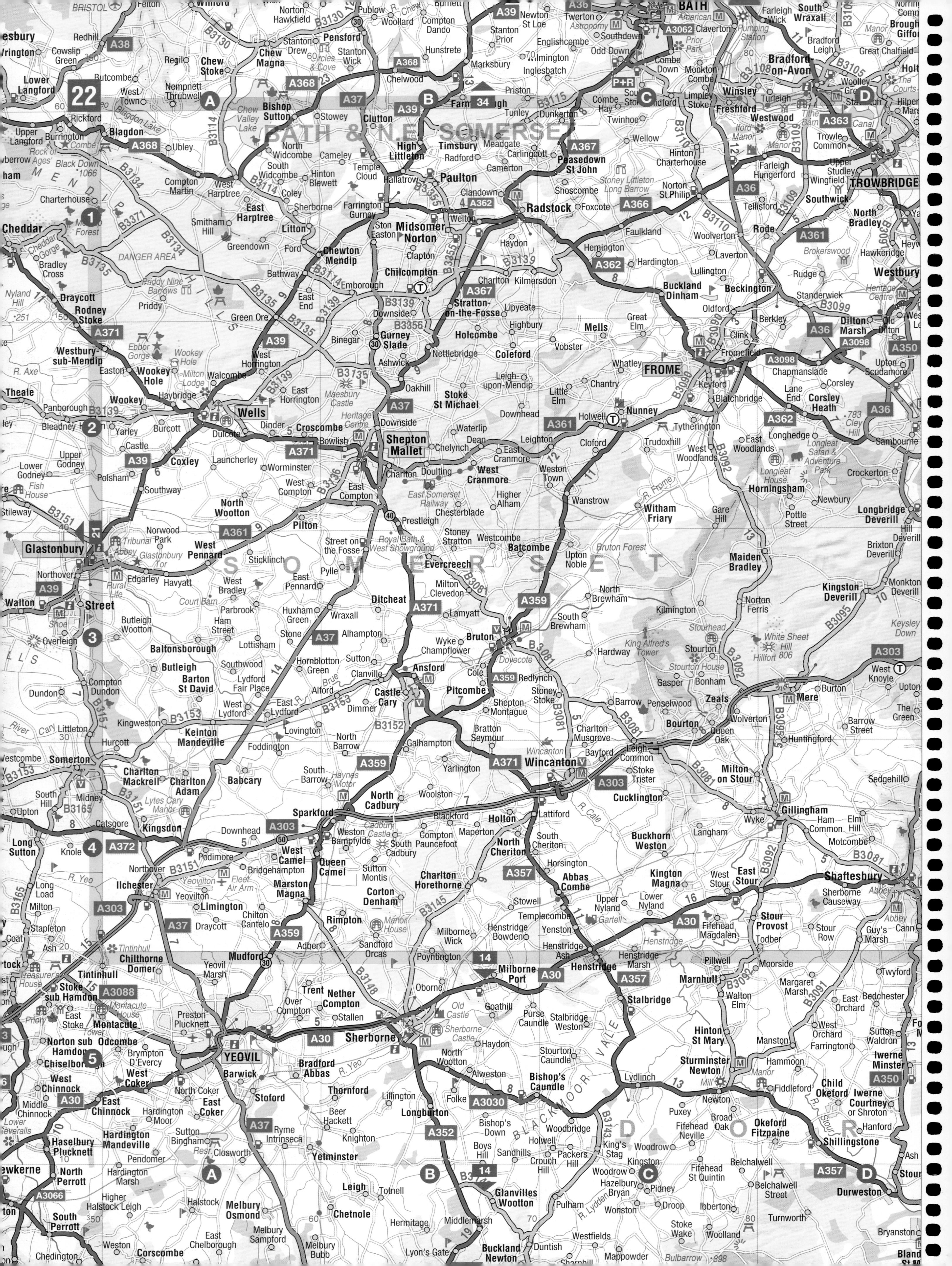
22
34
14
A
B
C
D
1
2
3
4
5
BATH & N.E. SOMERSET
SOMERSET
DORSET
BLACKMOOR VALE
MENDIP HILLS
BRISTOL
BATH
Felton
Winford
Norton Hawkfield
Publow
Woollard
Compton Dando
Burnett
Newton St Loe
Stanton Prior
Twerton
Southdown
Englishcombe
Odd Down
Claverton
Combe Down
Monkton Combe
Farleigh Wick
South Wraxall
Bradford Leigh
Great Chalfield
Broughton Gifford
Bradford-on-Avon
Holt
Woolley Green
Staverton
Hilperton Marsh
Redhill
Cowslip Green
Wrington
Regil
Chew Stoke
Chew Magna
Stanton Drew
Pensford
Stanton Wick
Hunstrete
Marksbury
Wilmington
Inglesbatch
Lower Langford
Butcombe
Nempnett Thrubwell
West Town
Chelwood
Priston
Farmborough
Tunley
Dunkerton
Combe Hay
South Stoke
Midford
Limpley Stoke
Winsley
Freshford
Turleigh
Westwood
Iford Manor
Rickford
Blagdon
Blagdon Lake
Chew Valley Lake
Bishop Sutton
Stowey
Clutton
High Littleton
Timsbury
Meadgate
Carlingcott
Peasedown St John
Wellow
Twinhoe
Hinton Charterhouse
Farleigh Hungerford
Trowle Common
Upper Studley
Wingfield
TROWBRIDGE
Upper Langford
Burrington
Burrington Combe
Ubley
North Widcombe
Cameley
Temple Cloud
Radford
Camerton
Rock of Ages
Black Down 1066
South Widcombe
Hinton Blewett
Hallatrow
Paulton
Stoney Littleton Long Barrow
Norton St Philip
Tellisford
Southwick
Compton Martin
West Harptree
Coley
Clandown
Radstock
Shoscombe
Foxcote
Charterhouse
East Harptree
Sherborne
Farrington Gurney
Welton
North Bradley
Cheddar
Mendip Forest
Smitham Hill
Litton
Ston Easton
Midsomer Norton
Haydon
Faulkland
Rode
Woolverton
Hemington
Laverton
Brokerswood
Hawkeridge
Cheddar Gorge
Greendown
Ford
Chewton Mendip
Clapton
Hardington
Lullington
Westbury
Bradley Cross
Danger Area
Bathway
Chilcompton
Charlton
Kilmersdon
Buckland Dinham
Beckington
Rudge
Heritage Centre
Priddy Nine Barrows
Emborough
Stratton-on-the-Fosse
Lipyeate
Standerwick
Nyland Hill
Draycott
Rodney Stoke
Priddy
East End
Downside
Great Elm
Mells
Oldford
Berkley
Dilton Marsh
Old Dilton
Green Ore
Holcombe
Highbury
Clink
Fromefield
Binegar
Gurney Slade
Vobster
Ebbor Gorge
Wookey Hole
Westbury-sub-Mendip
West Horrington
Ashwick
Nettlebridge
Coleford
Whatley
FROME
Chapmanslade
Upton Scudamore
Corsley
R. Axe
Easton
Wookey Hole
Milton Lodge
Walcombe
Leigh-upon-Mendip
Chantry
Keyford
Oakhill
Stoke St Michael
Little Elm
Blatchbridge
Lane End
Corsley Heath
Theale
Wookey
Haybridge
East Horrington
Maesbury Castle
Downhead
Nunney
Holwell
Tytherington
Panborough
Wells
Bleadney
Yarley
Burcott
Dinder
Croscombe
Downside
Shepton Mallet
Waterlip
Dean
Leighton
Cloford
Trudoxhill
East Woodlands
Longhedge
Longleat Safari & Adventure Park
Cley Hill
Sambourne
Castle
Dulcote
Bowlish
Chelynch
East Cranmore
West Woodlands
Coxley
Launcherley
Doulting
West Cranmore
Weston Town
Longleat House
Crockerton
Lower Godney
Upper Godney
Polsham
Worminster
West Compton
East Compton
East Somerset Railway
Higher Alham
Horningsham
Newbury
Fish House
Southway
North Wootton
Chesterblade
Wanstrow
R. Frome
Witham Friary
Gare Hill
Pottle Street
Longbridge Deverill
Stileway
Prestleigh
Pilton
Stoney Stratton
Westcombe
Batcombe
Bruton Forest
Hill Deverill
Glastonbury
Tribunal
Norwood Park
West Pennard
Glastonbury Abbey
Glastonbury Tor
Sticklinch
Street on the Fosse
Royal Bath & West Showground
Upton Noble
Brixton Deverill
Maiden Bradley
Northover
Edgarley
Havyatt
Rural Life
East Pennard
Pylle
Evercreech
Kingston Deverill
Monkton Deverill
West Bradley
Milton Clevedon
North Brewham
Walton
Street
Shoe
Court Barn
Parbrook
Huxham Green
Wraxall
Ditcheat
Lamyatt
Kilmington
Norton Ferris
Keysley Down
Butleigh Wootton
Ham Street
Stone
Alhampton
South Brewham
Stourhead
White Sheet Hill
Overleigh
Lottisham
Bruton
Wyke Champflower
Hardway
King Alfred's Tower
Stourton
Hillfort 806
Baltonsborough
Hornblotton Green
Sutton
Butleigh
Southwood
Ansford
Clanville
Cole
Dovecote
Redlynch
Stourton House
Gasper
Bonham
West Knoyle
Compton Dundon
Barton St David
Lydford Fair Place
Alford
Castle Cary
Pitcombe
Stoney Stoke
Zeals
Mere
Burton
Dundon
West Lydford
East Lydford
Dimmer
Shepton Montague
Barrow
Penselwood
Wolverton
Upton
The Green
River Cary
Littleton
Kingweston
Keinton Mandeville
Lovington
Bratton Seymour
Charlton Musgrove
Bourton
Queen Oak
Barrow Street
Hurcott
North Barrow
Galhampton
Wincanton
Bayford
Huntingford
Westcombe
Somerton
Foddington
Leigh Common
Charlton Mackrell
Charlton Adam
Babcary
South Barrow
Haynes Motor Museum
Yarlington
Stoke Trister
Milton on Stour
Sedgehill
South Hill
Midney
Lytes Cary Manor
North Cadbury
Woolston
Cucklington
Upton
Kingsdon
Sparkford
Blackford
Holton
Lattiford
Gillingham
Catsgore
Downhead
Weston Bampfylde
Cadbury Castle
Compton Pauncefoot
Maperton
South Cheriton
Buckhorn Weston
Langham
Wyke
Ham Common
Elm Hill
Long Sutton
Knole
Podimore
West Camel
South Cadbury
North Cheriton
Motcombe
Long Load
Northover
Bridgehampton
Queen Camel
Sutton Montis
Charlton Horethorne
Horsington
Kington Magna
West Stour
East Stour
Shaftesbury
R. Yeo
Yeovilton
Fleet Air Arm
Ilchester
Yeovilton
Marston Magna
Corton Denham
Abbas Combe
Upper Nyland
Lower Nyland
Sherborne Causeway
Milton
Limington
Stowell
Templecombe
Gartell
Stour Provost
Stour Row
Guy's Marsh
Cann
Stapleton
Draycott
Chilton Cantelo
Rimpton
Manor House
Milborne Wick
Henstridge Bowden
Yenston
Fifehead Magdalen
Todber
Tintinhull
Ash
Sandford Orcas
Henstridge Ash
Henstridge
Coat
Adber
Poyntington
Henstridge Marsh
Pillwell
Moorside
Chilthorne Domer
Mudford
Yeovil Marsh
Milborne Port
Marnhull
Twyford
Tintinhull
Stoke sub Hamdon
Treasurer's House
Trent
Nether Compton
Oborne
Stalbridge
Walton Elm
Margaret Marsh
East Orchard
Bedchester
Montacute
Montacute House
Over Compton
Old Castle
Goathill
Purse Caundle
Stalbridge Weston
East Stoke
Preston Plucknett
Stallen
Sherborne
Sherborne Castle
West Orchard
Sutton Waldron
Norton sub Hamdon
Odcombe
Brympton D'Evercy
YEOVIL
Haydon
Hinton St Mary
Manston
Farrington
Iwerne Minster
Chiselborough
Bradford Abbas
North Wootton
Stourton Caundle
Sturminster Newton
Hammoon
West Chinnock
West Coker
Barwick
Alweston
Bishop's Caundle
Lydlinch
Fiddleford
Child Okeford
Middle Chinnock
East Chinnock
North Coker
East Coker
Stoford
Thornford
Folke
Newton
Iwerne Courtney or Shroton
Lower Severalls
Hardington Moor
Lillington
Longburton
Puxey
Broad Oak
Okeford Fitzpaine
Hanford
Haselbury Plucknett
Hardington Mandeville
Sutton Bingham
Ryme Intrinseca
Beer Hackett
Bishop's Down
Woodbridge
Fifehead Neville
Shillingstone
Pendomer
Closworth
Knighton
Holwell
King's Stag
Woodrow
Crewkerne
North Perrott
Hardington Marsh
Yetminster
Boys Hill
Sandhills
Crouch Hill
Packers Hill
Kingston
Belchalwell
Fifehead St Quintin
Ash
Stourpaine
Leigh
Totnell
Glanvilles Wootton
Woodrow
Hazelbury Bryan
Pidney
Belchalwell Street
Durweston
Higher Halstock Leigh
Halstock
Melbury Osmond
Chetnole
Pulham
R. Lydden
Wonston
Droop
Ibberton
South Perrott
Hermitage
Middlemarsh
Turnworth
Melbury Sampford
Westfields
Stoke Wake
Woolland
Bryanston
Weston
Corscombe
East Chelborough
Melbury Bubb
Lyon's Gate
Buckland Newton
Duntish
Mappowder
Bulbarrow 898
Blandford St Mary
Chedington
A39
A36
A38
A368
A37
A367
A362
A366
A361
A371
A3098
A350
A359
A303
A372
A3088
A30
A357
A3030
A352
A3066
B3130
B3114
B3134
B3371
B3135
B3139
B3356
B3355
B3115
B3108
B3110
B3109
B3105
B3099
B3090
B3092
B3081
B3095
B3136
B3151
B3153
B3152
B3165
B3145
B3148
B3091
B3143
B3097
P+R

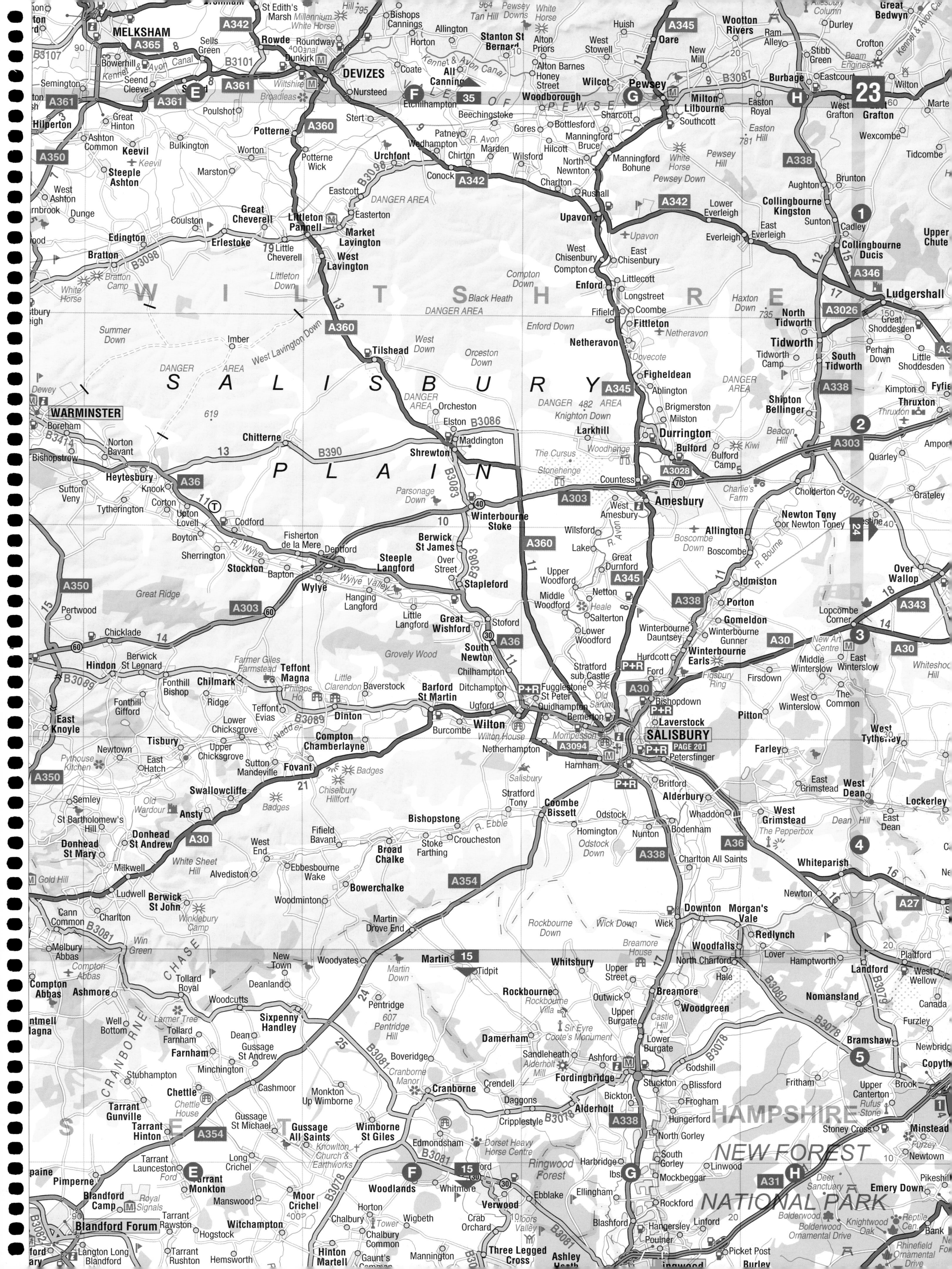

MELKSHAM
A365
A342
A361
A360
A350
A345
A346
A338
A3026
A303
A3028
A36
A30
A3094
A354
A343
A27
A31
B3107
B3101
B3098
B3087
B390
B3086
B3083
B3084
B3089
B3081
B3078
B3080
B3079
B3082
B3414
St Edith's Marsh
Millennium White Horse
Rowde
Roundway
Dunkirk
Sells Green
Bowerhill
Kennet & Avon Canal
Seend Cleeve
Semington
Hilperton
Great Hinton
Poulshot
DEVIZES
Wiltshire
Broadleas
Nursteed
Bishops Cannings
Horton
Allington
Coate
All Cannings
Etchilhampton
Stanton St Bernard
Tan Hill
Pewsey Downs
Alton Priors
Alton Barnes
Honey Street
West Stowell
Huish
Oare
Wilcot
Woodborough
VALE OF PEWSEY
Pewsey
Sharcott
Wootton Rivers
New Mill
Milton Lilbourne
Southcott
Easton Royal
Easton Hill
Burbage
Eastcourt
Ram Alley
Stibb Green
Crofton
Beam Engines
Durley
Great Bedwyn
Wilton
West Grafton
East Grafton
Marten
Wexcombe
Tidcombe
Potterne
Stert
Patney
Wedhampton
Beechingstoke
Gores
Bottlesford
Manningford Bruce
Hilcott
Chirton
Marden
R. Avon
Wilsford
North Newnton
Manningford Bohune
White Horse
Pewsey Hill
Pewsey Down
Worton
Bulkington
Ashton Common
Keevil
Steeple Ashton
Marston
Potterne Wick
Urchfont
Conock
Eastcott
DANGER AREA
Charlton
Rushall
Upavon
Lower Everleigh
Everleigh
East Everleigh
Collingbourne Kingston
Sunton
Aughton
Brunton
Cadley
Collingbourne Ducis
Upper Chute
Ludgershall
West Ashton
Dunge
Coulston
Great Cheverell
Littleton Pannell
Easterton
Market Lavington
West Lavington
Little Cheverell
Erlestoke
Edington
Bratton
Bratton Camp
White Horse
Littleton Down
West Chisenbury
East Chisenbury
Compton
Compton Down
Enford
Littlecott
Longstreet
Coombe
Fifield
Fittleton
Netheravon
Haxton Down
North Tidworth
Tidworth
Great Shoddesden
Perham Down
Little Shoddesden
South Tidworth
Tidworth Camp
W I L T S H I R E
Black Heath
Summer Down
Imber
West Lavington Down
Tilshead
West Down
Orcheston Down
Enford Down
Dovecote
Fighelden
Ablington
Shipton Bellinger
Kimpton
Thruxton
Fyfield
S A L I S B U R Y
P L A I N
Dewey
WARMINSTER
Boreham
619
Orcheston
Elston
Maddington
Shrewton
Chitterne
482
Knighton Down
Larkhill
Brigmerston
Milston
Durrington
Bulford
Bulford Camp
Kiwi
Beacon Hill
Amport
Quarley
Norton Bavant
Bishopstrow
Heytesbury
Knook
Sutton Veny
Tytherington
Corton
Upton Lovell
Codford
Boyton
Sherrington
Stockton
Bapton
Fisherton de la Mere
Deptford
Wylye
Wylye Valley
Parsonage Down
Winterbourne Stoke
The Cursus
Stonehenge
Woodhenge
Countess
Amesbury
West Amesbury
Charlie's Farm
Cholderton
Grateley
Newton Tony or Newton Toney
Allington
Boscombe Down
Boscombe
R. Bourne
Idmiston
Over Wallop
Berwick St James
Over Street
Steeple Langford
Stapleford
Hanging Langford
Little Langford
Great Wishford
Stoford
Wilsford
Lake
Great Durnford
Upper Woodford
Middle Woodford
Netton
Heale
Salterton
Lower Woodford
Porton
Gomeldon
Winterbourne Dauntsey
Winterbourne Gunner
Lopcombe Corner
Great Ridge
Pertwood
Chicklade
Hindon
Berwick St Leonard
Farmer Giles Farmstead
Teffont Magna
Little Clarendon
Grovely Wood
South Newton
Chilhampton
Hurdcott
Ford
Winterbourne Earls
Figsbury Ring
Firsdown
Middle Winterslow
East Winterslow
New Art Centre
Whiteshoot Hill
Fonthill Bishop
Chilmark
Fonthill Gifford
Ridge
Teffont Evias
Dinton
Philipps House
Baverstock
Barford St Martin
Ditchampton
Ugford
Wilton
Burcombe
Wilton House
Fugglestone St Peter
Quidhampton
Old Sarum
Stratford sub Castle
Bemerton
Bishopdown
Laverstock
SALISBURY
PAGE 201
Petersfinger
West Winterslow
The Common
Pitton
East Knoyle
Lower Chicksgrove
Tisbury
Upper Chicksgrove
R. Nadder
Compton Chamberlayne
Mompesson
Netherhampton
Harnham
Farley
West Tytherley
Newtown
Pythouse Kitchen
East Hatch
Sutton Mandeville
Fovant
Badges
Chiselbury Hillfort
Salisbury
Stratford Tony
Coombe Bissett
Britford
Alderbury
East Grimstead
West Dean
Lockerley
Semley
Old Wardour
Swallowcliffe
Ansty
St Bartholomew's Hill
Donhead St Andrew
Donhead St Mary
White Sheet Hill
West End
Fifield Bavant
Bishopstone
R. Ebble
Stoke Farthing
Croucheston
Broad Chalke
Odstock
Homington
Odstock Down
Nunton
Bodenham
Whaddon
West Grimstead
The Pepperbox
Dean Hill
East Dean
Milkwell
Gold Hill
Alvediston
Ebbesbourne Wake
Charlton All Saints
Whiteparish
Ludwell
Berwick St John
Winkelbury Camp
Woodminton
Bowerchalke
Newton
Cann Common
Charlton
Martin Drove End
Rockbourne Down
Wick Down
Wick
Downton
Morgan's Vale
Redlynch
Melbury Abbas
Win Green
CHASE
Breamore House
Woodfalls
Lover
Plaitford
Compton Abbas
Tollard Royal
New Town
Woodyates
Martin
Martin Down
Tidpit
Whitsbury
Upper Street
North Charford
Hale
Hamptworth
Landford
West Wellow
Ashmore
Deanland
Pentridge
Rockbourne
Rockbourne Villa
Outwick
Breamore
Woodgreen
Nomansland
Canada
Fontmell Magna
Well Bottom
Larmer Tree
Tollard Farnham
Woodcutts
Sixpenny Handley
607
Pentridge Hill
Sir Eyre Coote's Monument
Upper Burgate
Castle Hill
Lower Burgate
Furzley
Farnham
Dean
Gussage St Andrew
Damerham
Bramshaw
Newbridge
CRANBORNE
Minchington
Boveridge
Cranborne Manor
Sandleheath
Alderholt Mill
Ashford
Fordingbridge
Godshill
Copythorne
Stubhampton
Chettle
Chettle House
Cashmoor
Monkton Up Wimborne
Cranborne
Crendell
Daggons
Stuckton
Blissford
Frogham
Fritham
Upper Canterton
Rufus Stone
Brook
Tarrant Gunville
Tarrant Hinton
Gussage St Michael
Gussage All Saints
Wimborne St Giles
Cripplestyle
Alderholt
Bickton
Hungerford
HAMPSHIRE
Stoney Cross
Minstead
Furzey
Newtown
Tarrant Launceston
Long Crichel
Knowlton Church & Earthworks
Edmondsham
Dorset Heavy Horse Centre
Ringwood Forest
Harbridge
North Gorley
South Gorley
NEW FOREST
NATIONAL PARK
Linwood
Pimperne
Tarrant Monkton
Moor Crichel
Woodlands
Whitmore
Verwood
Ebblake
Ellingham
Ibsley
Mockbeggar
Deer Sanctuary
Emery Down
Pikeshill
Blandford Camp
Royal Signals
Manswood
Horton
Chalbury
Tower
Wigbeth
Crab Orchard
Moors Valley
Blashford
Rockford
Linford
Bolderwood
Bolderwood Ornamental Drive
Knightwood Oak
Reptile Centre
Bank
Blandford Forum
Tarrant Rawston
Hogstock
Witchampton
Chalbury Common
Hinton Martell
Gaunt's Common
Mannington
Three Legged Cross
Ashley Heath
Hangersley
Poulner
Picket Post
Burley
Rhinefield Ornamental Drive
Langton Long Blandford
Tarrant Rushton
Hemsworth
Ringwood
23
24
35
15

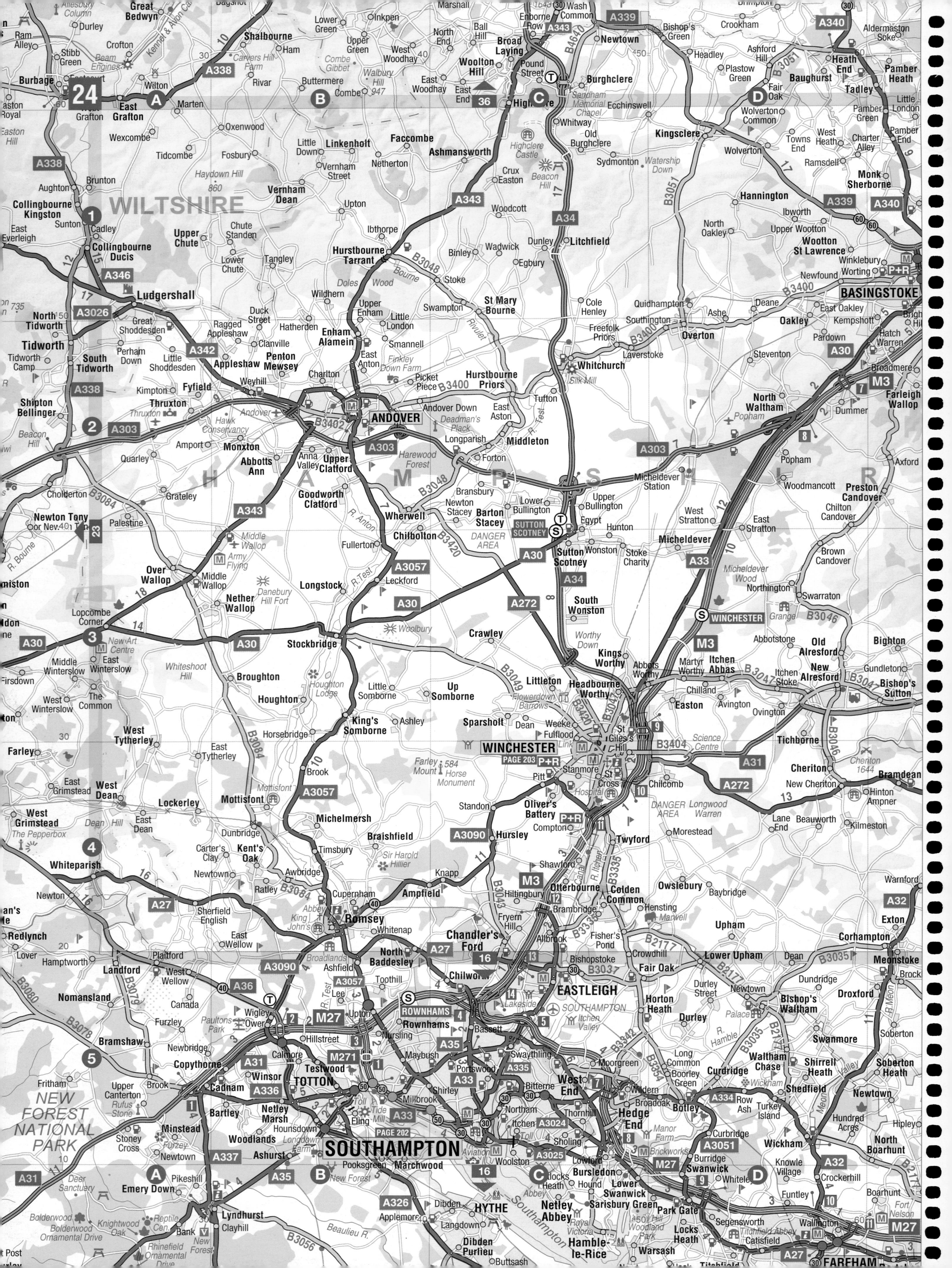

24
Great Bedwyn
Durley
Ram Alley
Stibb Green
Burbage
Crofton
Shalbourne
Ham
Wilton
Marten
East Grafton
Grafton
A338
Rivar
Lower Green
Inkpen
Upper Green
West Woodhay
Combe
Buttermere
Walbury Hill 947
East Woodhay
East End
36
North End
Ball Hill
Broad Laying
Woolton Hill
Pound Street
Highclere
Enborne Row
Wash Common
A343
A339
Newtown
Burghclere
Bishop's Green
Crookham
Headley
Ashford Hill
Plastow Green
Fair Oak
Baughurst
Heath End
Tadley
Pamber Heath
Aldermaston Soke
A340
Little London
Pamber Green
Pamber End
Wolverton Common
Ecchinswell
Whitway
Old Burghclere
Sandham Memorial Chapel
Highclere Castle
Kingsclere
Towns End
West Heath
Charter Alley
Wolverton
Ramsdell
Sydmonton
Watership Down
Beacon Hill
Monk Sherborne
Oxenwood
Wexcombe
Tidcombe
Fosbury
Little Down
Linkenholt
Faccombe
Ashmansworth
Vernham Street
Netherton
Crux Easton
Haydown Hill 860
Vernham Dean
WILTSHIRE
Brunton
Aughton
Collingbourne Kingston
Sunton
Cadley
East Everleigh
Collingbourne Ducis
A346
Upper Chute
Chute Standen
Lower Chute
Tangley
Upton
Ibthorpe
Hurstbourne Tarrant
A343
Woodcott
A34
Dunley
Litchfield
Binley
Wadwick
Egbury
Hannington
A339
A340
North Oakley
Upper Wootton
Ibworth
Wootton St Lawrence
Winklebury
Worting
Newfound
BASINGSTOKE
Ludgershall
A3026
North Tidworth
Tidworth
Tidworth Camp
South Tidworth
Great Shoddesden
Ragged Appleshaw
Perham Down
Little Shoddesden
A342
Appleshaw
Duck Street
Hatherden
Clanville
Penton Mewsey
Wildhern
Upper Enham
Enham Alamein
Little London
Smannell
East Anton
Charlton
Doles Wood
Stoke
Swampton
St Mary Bourne
Cole Henley
Freefolk Priors
Quidhampton
Southington
Overton
Ashe
Deane
Oakley
East Oakley
Kempshott
Hatch Warren
Pardown
Steventon
Laverstoke
Whitchurch
Silk Mill
A30
Broadmere
M3
Farleigh Wallop
Dummer
Shipton Bellinger
Kimpton
Fyfield
Thruxton
Weyhill
Andover
ANDOVER
Finkley Down Farm
Picket Piece
B3400
Hurstbourne Priors
Tufton
Andover Down
Deadman's Plack
East Aston
Longparish
Middleton
Forton
Harewood Forest
A303
North Waltham
Popham
A303
Axford
Preston Candover
Chilton Candover
Woodmancott
Beacon Hill
Hawk Conservancy
Amport
Monxton
Abbotts Ann
Anna Valley
Upper Clatford
Quarley
Cholderton
Grateley
Goodworth Clatford
Bransbury
Newton Stacey
Barton Stacey
Lower Bullington
Upper Bullington
Micheldever Station
Newton Tony
Palestine
A343
Wherwell
Chilbolton
SUTTON SCOTNEY
DANGER AREA
Egypt
Hunton
West Stratton
East Stratton
Micheldever
Brown Candover
Middle Wallop
Army Flying
Over Wallop
Fullerton
A3057
A30
Sutton Scotney
Wonston
Stoke Charity
A33
Micheldever Wood
Northington
Swarraton
Grange
B3046
Lopcombe Corner
Middle Wallop
Nether Wallop
Danebury Hill Fort
Longstock
Leckford
A30
A272
South Wonston
A34
WINCHESTER
New Art Centre
A30
Stockbridge
Woolbury
Crawley
Worthy Down
Kings Worthy
Abbots Worthy
Martyr Worthy
Itchen Abbas
M3
Abbotstone
Old Alresford
Bighton
Middle Winterslow
East Winterslow
Whiteshoot Hill
Broughton
Houghton Lodge
Little Somborne
Up Somborne
Littleton
Headbourne Worthy
Chilland
Itchen Stoke
New Alresford
Gundleton
Bishop's Sutton
Easton
Avington
Ovington
Firsdown
West Winterslow
The Common
Houghton
King's Somborne
Ashley
Sparsholt
Flowerdown Barrows
Weeke
Fulflood
St Giles's Hill
Science Centre
Tichborne
West Tytherley
Horsebridge
WINCHESTER
PAGE 203
P+R
B3404
A31
Cheriton
Cheriton 1644
Bramdean
Farley
East Tytherley
Farley Mount
584 Horse Monument
Brook
Pitt
Stanmore
St Cross
Chilcomb
A272
New Cheriton
Hinton Ampner
East Grimstead
West Dean
Mottisfont
Lockerley
Mottisfont
A3057
Standon
Oliver's Battery
P+R
DANGER AREA
Longwood Warren
Lane End
Beauworth
Kilmeston
West Grimstead
The Pepperbox
Dean Hill
East Dean
Dunbridge
Michelmersh
Braishfield
A3090
Hursley
Compton
Twyford
Morestead
Carter's Clay
Kent's Oak
Timsbury
Sir Harold Hillier
Shawford
Whiteparish
Newtown
Awbridge
Knapp
M3
Hiltingbury
Otterbourne
Colden Common
Owslebury
Baybridge
Warnford
Newton
Ratley
Cupernham
Ampfield
Brambridge
Hensting
Marwell
A27
Sherfield English
Abbey
King John's
Romsey
Whitenap
Fryern Hill
Fisher's Pond
Upham
A32
Exton
Redlynch
East Wellow
Chandler's Ford
Allbrook
Corhampton
Lover
Hamptworth
Plaitford
Broadlands
Ashfield
North Baddesley
A27
16
Bishopstoke
Crowdhill
Lower Upham
Dean
Meonstoke
Landford
West Wellow
A3090
A3057
Toothill
Chilworth
Fair Oak
Durley Street
Dundridge
Brock
A36
Lee
ROWNHAMS
EASTLEIGH
Lakeside
SOUTHAMPTON
Itchen Valley
Horton Heath
Newtown
Bishop's Waltham
Droxford
Nomansland
Canada
Wigley
Ower
Paultons Park
M27
Upton
Rownhams
Nursling
Bassett
Durley
Palace
Furzley
Bramshaw
Hillstreet
A35
Swaythling
B3342
Hamble
Swanmore
Soberton
Newbridge
Copythorne
A31
Winsor
Calmore
Testwood
M271
Maybush
Portswood
A335
Moorgreen
Long Common
Curdridge
Waltham Chase
Shirrell Heath
Soberton Heath
Fritham
Upper Canterton
Brook
Cadnam
A336
TOTTON
Shirley
A33
Bitterne
West End
Wildern
Boorley Green
Wickham
Shedfield
NEW FOREST NATIONAL PARK
Rufus Stone
Bartley
Netley Marsh
Millbrook
Eling
Tide Mill
Hounsdown
Northam
Itchen
A3024
Thornhill
Broadoak
Hedge End
Botley
A334
Row Ash
Turkey Island
Newtown
Minstead
Stoney Cross
Furzey
Newtown
Woodlands
Longdown
Ashurst
A337
PAGE 202
SOUTHAMPTON
Pooksgreen
Marchwood
Aviation
Woolston
A3025
Sholing
Manor Farm
Brickworks
A3051
Curbridge
Hundred Acres
Hipley
North Boarhunt
Lowford
Bursledon
Hound
M27
Burridge
Swanwick
Knowle Village
A32
A31
Deer Sanctuary
Pikeshill
Emery Down
A35
New Forest
A326
Dibden
HYTHE
Southampton
Netley Abbey
Old Netley
Netley
Lower Swanwick
Sarisbury Green
Park Gate
Whiteley
Crockerhill
Funtley
Boarhunt
Fort Nelson
Bolderwood
Bolderwood Ornamental Drive
Knightwood Oak
Reptile Cen.
Lyndhurst
Bank
New Forest
Clayhill
Applemore
Langdown
Royal Victoria
Woodland Park
Locks Heath
Segensworth
Titchfield Abbey
Catisfield
Wallington
M27
Rhinefield Ornamental Drive
Beaulieu R.
B3056
Dibden Purlieu
Buttsash
Hamble-le-Rice
Warsash
Titchfield
A27
FAREHAM
Post

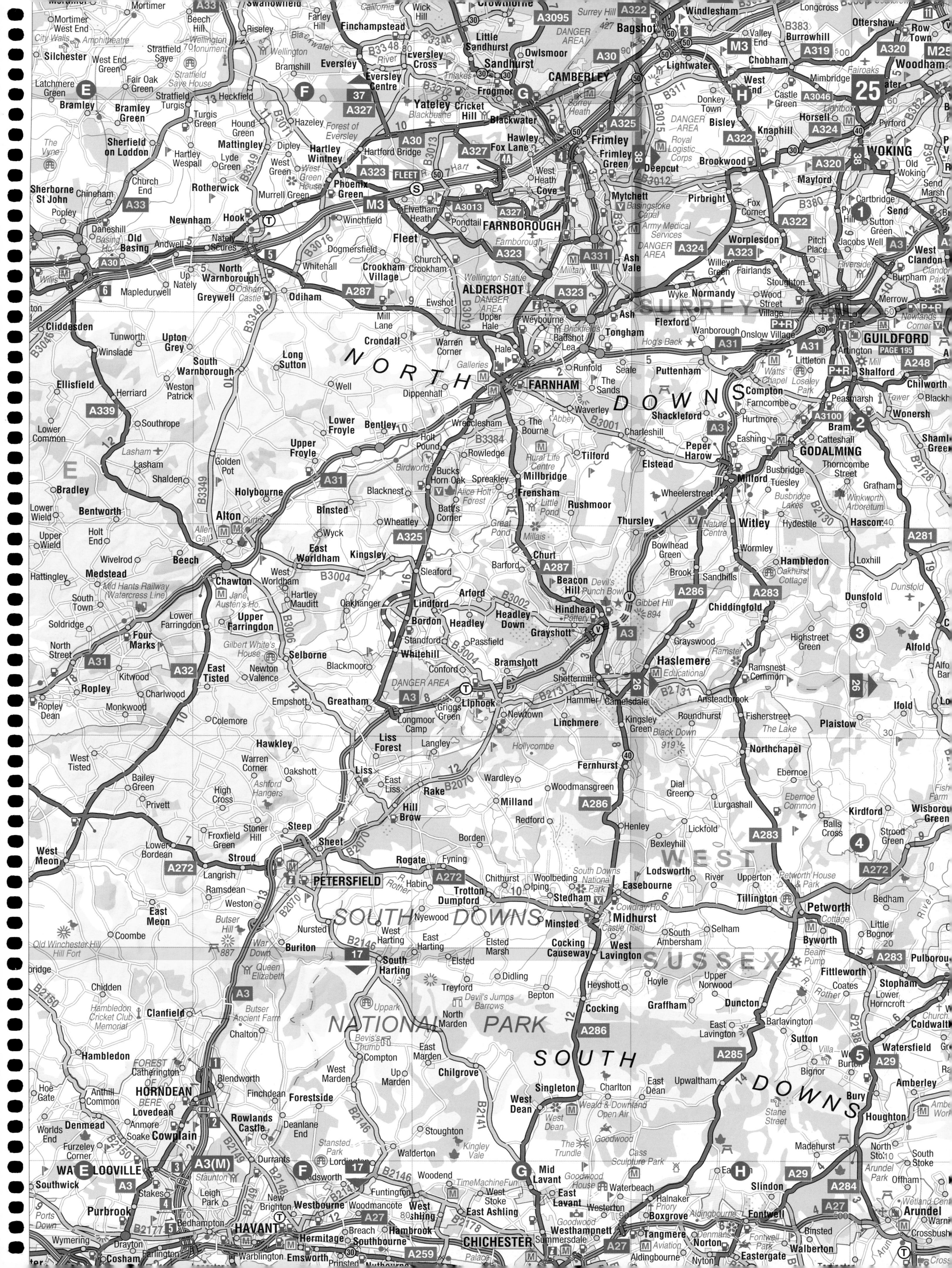
Mortimer
Mortimer West End
Silchester
Stratfield Saye
Wellington Monument
Riseley
Farley Hill
Finchampstead
Wick Hill
Crowthorne
Little Sandhurst
Sandhurst
Owlsmoor
A3095
Bagshot
Windlesham
Longcross
Ottershaw
Row Town
Latchmere Green
West End Green
Fair Oak Green
Bramshill
Eversley
Eversley Cross
Eversley Centre
Camberley
Lightwater
Chobham
Burrowhill
Valley End
Woodham
A320
A319
M3
M25
Bramley
Bramley Green
Stratfield Turgis
Heckfield
Hazeley
Yateley
Cricket Hill
Blackwater
Frogmore
Frimley
Deepcut
West End
Castle Green
Donkey Town
Bisley
Knaphill
Horsell
Pyrford
Woking
Old Woking
Sherfield on Loddon
Hartley Wespall
Mattingley
Lyde Green
Dipley
Hartley Wintney
West Green
Hartford Bridge
Hawley
Fox Lane
Frimley Green
Brookwood
Mayford
Send Marsh
Sherborne St John
Chineham
Church End
Rotherwick
Phoenix Green
Fleet
Murrell Green
Elvetham Heath
Cove
Mytchett
Pirbright
Fox Corner
Cartbridge
Send
Sutton Green
Popley
Newnham
Hook
Winchfield
Farnborough
Ash Vale
Worplesdon
Pitch Place
Jacobs Well
Daneshill
Old Basing
Andwell
Nately Scures
North Warnborough
Up Nately
Dogmersfield
Church Crookham
Crookham Village
Aldershot
Wellington Statue
Willey Green
Fairlands
Stoughton
West Clandon
Burpham
Merrow
Mapledurwell
Greywell
Odiham
Whitehall
Ewshot
Normandy
Wyke
Wood Street Village
Surrey
Guildford
Cliddesden
Tunworth
Upton Grey
Mill Lane
Crondall
Warren Corner
Upper Hale
Weybourne
Ash
Tongham
Flexford
Wanborough
Onslow Village
Winslade
Long Sutton
South Warnborough
Hale
Badshot Lea
Hog's Back
Artington
Littleton
Shalford
Chilworth
North Downs
Ellisfield
Herriard
Weston Patrick
Well
Dippenhall
Farnham
Runfold
The Sands
Seale
Puttenham
Compton
Farncombe
Peasmarsh
Wonersh
A339
Southrope
Lower Froyle
Bentley
Wrecclesham
The Bourne
Waverley Abbey
Shackleford
Charleshill
Hurtmore
Eashing
Godalming
Lower Common
Upper Froyle
Holt Pound
Rowledge
Rural Life Centre
Tilford
Elstead
Peper Harow
Catteshall
Busbridge
Thorncombe Street
Lasham
Golden Pot
Shalden
Birdworld
Bucks Horn Oak
Alice Holt Forest
Spreakley
Millbridge
Frensham
Frensham Little Pond
Milford
Tuesley
Grafham
Winkworth Arboretum
Bradley
Holybourne
Blacknest
Rushmoor
Wheelerstreet
Bentworth
Alton
Binsted
Batt's Corner
Thursley
Witley
Hydestile
Hascombe
Lower Wield
Upper Wield
Holt End
Wheatley
Great Pond
Millais
Nature Centre
Wyck
Churt
Bowlhead Green
Wormley
Hambledon
Loxhill
Wivelrod
Beech
East Worldham
Kingsley
Sleaford
Barford
Brook
Sandhills
Oakhurst Cottage
Hattingley
Medstead
Chawton
West Worldham
Beacon Hill
Devil's Punch Bowl
Gibbet Hill
Dunsfold
Mid Hants Railway (Watercress Line)
South Town
Jane Austen's Ho.
Hartley Mauditt
Oakhanger
Lindford
Arford
Headley Down
Hindhead
Chiddingfold
Soldridge
Lower Farringdon
Upper Farringdon
Bordon
Headley
Grayshott
Grayswood
Highstreet Green
Alfold
North Street
Four Marks
Gilbert White's House
Selborne
Standford
Passfield
Whitehill
Ramster
Newton Valence
Blackmoor
Conford
Bramshott
Shottermill
Haslemere
Ramsnest Common
Kitwood
Ropley
East Tisted
Danger Area
Liphook
Hammer
Camelsdale
Anstead Brook
Charlwood
Ropley Dean
Empshott
Greatham
Griggs Green
Newtown
Linchmere
Kingsley Green
Roundhurst
Fisherstreet
Plaistow
Ifold
Monkwood
Colemore
Longmoor Camp
Black Down
The Lake
Hawkley
Liss Forest
Langley
Hollycombe
Northchapel
West Tisted
Warren Corner
Oakshott
Liss
East Liss
Fernhurst
Ebernoe
Bailey Green
Privett
High Cross
Ashford Hangers
Rake
Wardley
Woodmansgreen
Dial Green
Lurgashall
Ebernoe Common
Kirdford
Wisborough Green
Hill Brow
Milland
Redford
Henley
Lickfold
Balls Cross
Strood Green
West Meon
Lower Bordean
Froxfield Green
Stoner Hill
Steep
Sheet
Borden
Bexleyhill
West
Stroud
Langrish
Petersfield
Rogate
Fyning
Chithurst
Woolbeding
Lodsworth
River
Upperton
Petworth House & Park
Ramsdean
Habin
Trotton
Dumpford
Iping
South Downs National Park
Stedham
Easebourne
Tillington
Petworth
Bedham
Weston
East Meon
Butser Hill
Nursted
Nyewood
South Downs
Minsted
Midhurst
Cowdray Ho.
Selham
South Ambersham
Byworth
Little Bognor
Coombe
Old Winchester Hill Hill Fort
War Down
Buriton
West Harting
East Harting
Elsted
Elsted Marsh
Cocking Causeway
West Lavington
Sussex
Beam Pump
Fittleworth
Pulborough
Queen Elizabeth
South Harting
Didling
Heyshott
Hoyle
Upper Norwood
Coates
Stopham
Chidden
Treyford
Devil's Jumps Barrows
Bepton
Cocking
Graffham
Duncton
Lower Horncroft
Hambledon Cricket Club Memorial
Clanfield
Butser Ancient Farm
Uppark
North Marden
National Park
Barlavington
Coldwaltham
Chalton
Bevis's Thumb
East Lavington
Sutton
Hambledon
Forest of Bere
Catherington
Compton
East Marden
South Downs
Villa
Bignor
Watersfield
Up Marden
Chilgrove
West Marden
Singleton
Charlton
East Dean
Upwaltham
Amberley
Hoe Gate
Anthill Common
Horndean
Blendworth
Finchdean
Forestside
West Dean
Weald & Downland Open Air
Stane Street
Bury
Houghton
Lovedean
Rowlands Castle
Deanlane End
Worlds End
Denmead
Anmore
Soake
Cowplain
Stoughton
Kingley Vale
Goodwood
The Trundle
Madehurst
North Stoke
South Stoke
Furzeley Corner
Stansted Park
Walderton
Cass Sculpture Park
Waterlooville
Durrants
Lordington
Mid Lavant
Eartham
Arundel Park
Offham
Southwick
Staunton
Woodend
TimeMachineFun
Goodwood House
Waterbeach
Slindon
Stakes
Leigh Park
Aldsworth
Funtington
West Stoke
East Lavant
Halnaker
Purbrook
New Brighton
Westbourne
Woodmancote
West Ashling
East Ashling
Westerton
Boxgrove
Fontwell
Arundel
Ports Down
Bedhampton
Havant
Hermitage
Hambrook
Breach
Southbourne
Westhampnett
Tangmere
Norton
Denmans
Binsted
Walberton
Crossbush
Wymering
Drayton
Cosham
Farlington
Warblington
Emsworth
Chichester
Summersdale
Aldingbourne
Nyton
Eastergate
Aviation
A3
A3(M)
A27
A29
A31
A32
A272
A283
A285
A286
A287
A325
A323
A324
A331
A30
A33
A259
A284
A281
A248
A3100
M3
Page 195

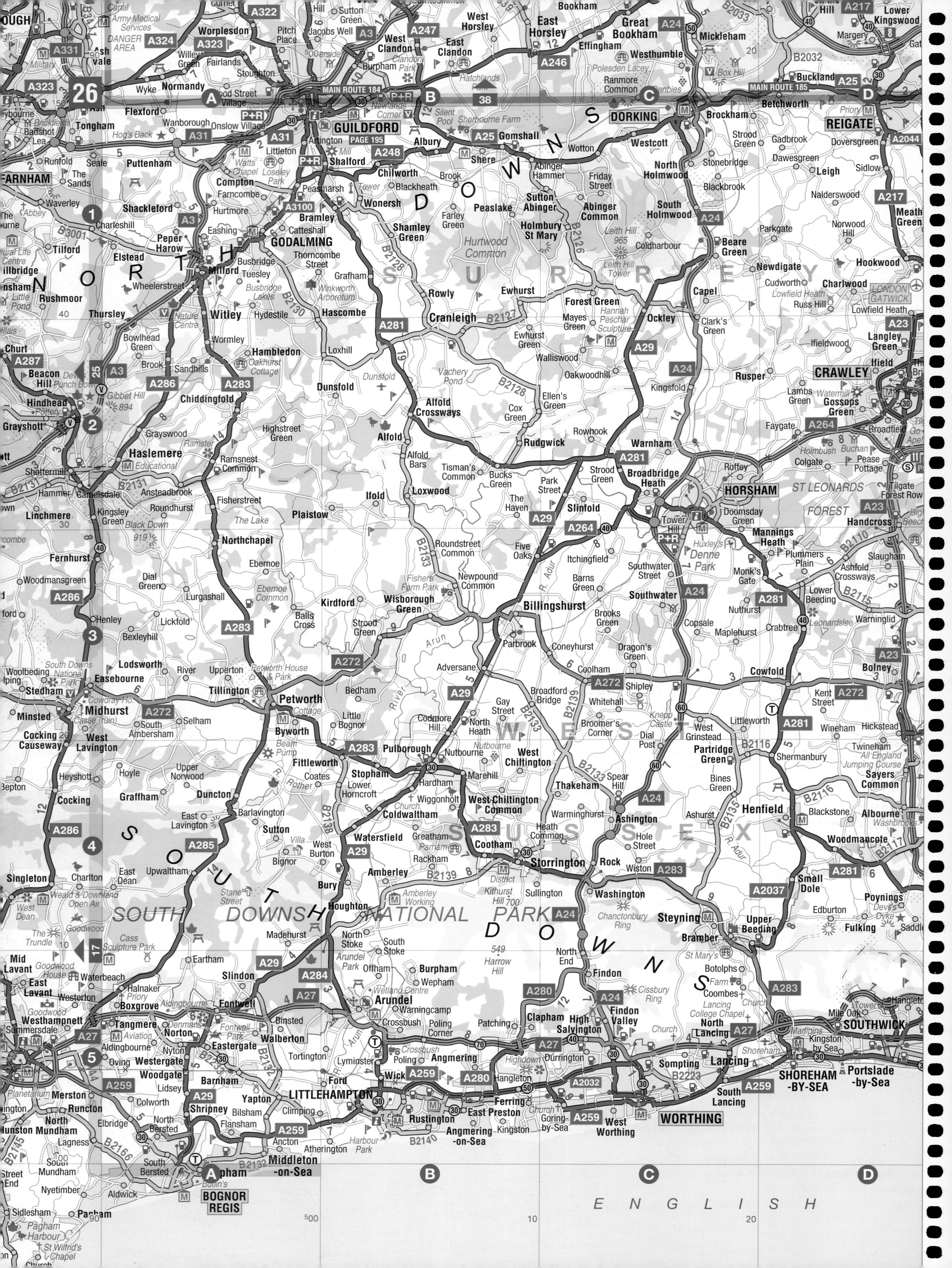

26
A322
A323
A324
A331
A247
A24
A217
A25
A246
A31
A3
A3100
A248
A281
A29
A264
A283
A286
A287
A272
A285
A284
A27
A280
A259
A2032
A2037
A23
A2044
A44
MAIN ROUTE 184
MAIN ROUTE 185
GUILDFORD
PAGE 195
DORKING
REIGATE
GODALMING
CRAWLEY
HORSHAM
WORTHING
LITTLEHAMPTON
SHOREHAM -BY-SEA
SOUTHWICK
BOGNOR REGIS
FARNHAM
Worplesdon
Normandy
Wanborough
Tongham
Puttenham
Compton
Farncombe
Shalford
Chilworth
Wonersh
Bramley
Albury
Shere
Gomshall
West Clandon
East Clandon
Burpham
West Horsley
East Horsley
Great Bookham
Effingham
Westhumble
Mickleham
Box Hill
Buckland
Betchworth
Brockham
Westcott
Wotton
Abinger Hammer
Peaslake
Holmbury St Mary
Abinger Common
Sutton Abinger
North Holmwood
South Holmwood
Beare Green
Capel
Newdigate
Charlwood
LONDON GATWICK
Ockley
Forest Green
Ewhurst
Cranleigh
Rowly
Shamley Green
Milford
Witley
Elstead
Hambledon
Chiddingfold
Haslemere
Hindhead
Grayshott
Liphook
Dunsfold
Alfold
Alfold Crossways
Rudgwick
Warnham
Broadbridge Heath
Slinfold
Rusper
Faygate
Colgate
Handcross
Mannings Heath
Southwater
Billingshurst
Wisborough Green
Kirdford
Loxwood
Northchapel
Fernhurst
Midhurst
Easebourne
Petworth
Tillington
Pulborough
Fittleworth
Storrington
Washington
Ashington
West Chiltington
Steyning
Bramber
Upper Beeding
Henfield
Cowfold
Partridge Green
Findon
Findon Valley
Sompting
Lancing
Worthing
Angmering
Rustington
East Preston
Ferring
Goring-by-Sea
Arundel
Amberley
Bury
Houghton
Slindon
Fontwell
Walberton
Tangmere
Westhampnett
Boxgrove
Barnham
Yapton
Middleton -on-Sea
Felpham
Cocking
Singleton
Lavant
Sutton
Duncton
Graffham
Portslade -by-Sea
Kingston by Sea
Small Dole
Poynings
Fulking
Edburton
Albourne
Bolney
Warninglid
Lower Beeding
Nuthurst
ST LEONARDS FOREST
N O R T H D O W N S
S U R R E Y
W E S T S U S S E X
S O U T H D O W N S
SOUTH DOWNS NATIONAL PARK
E N G L I S H
A
B
C
D
1
2
3
4
5

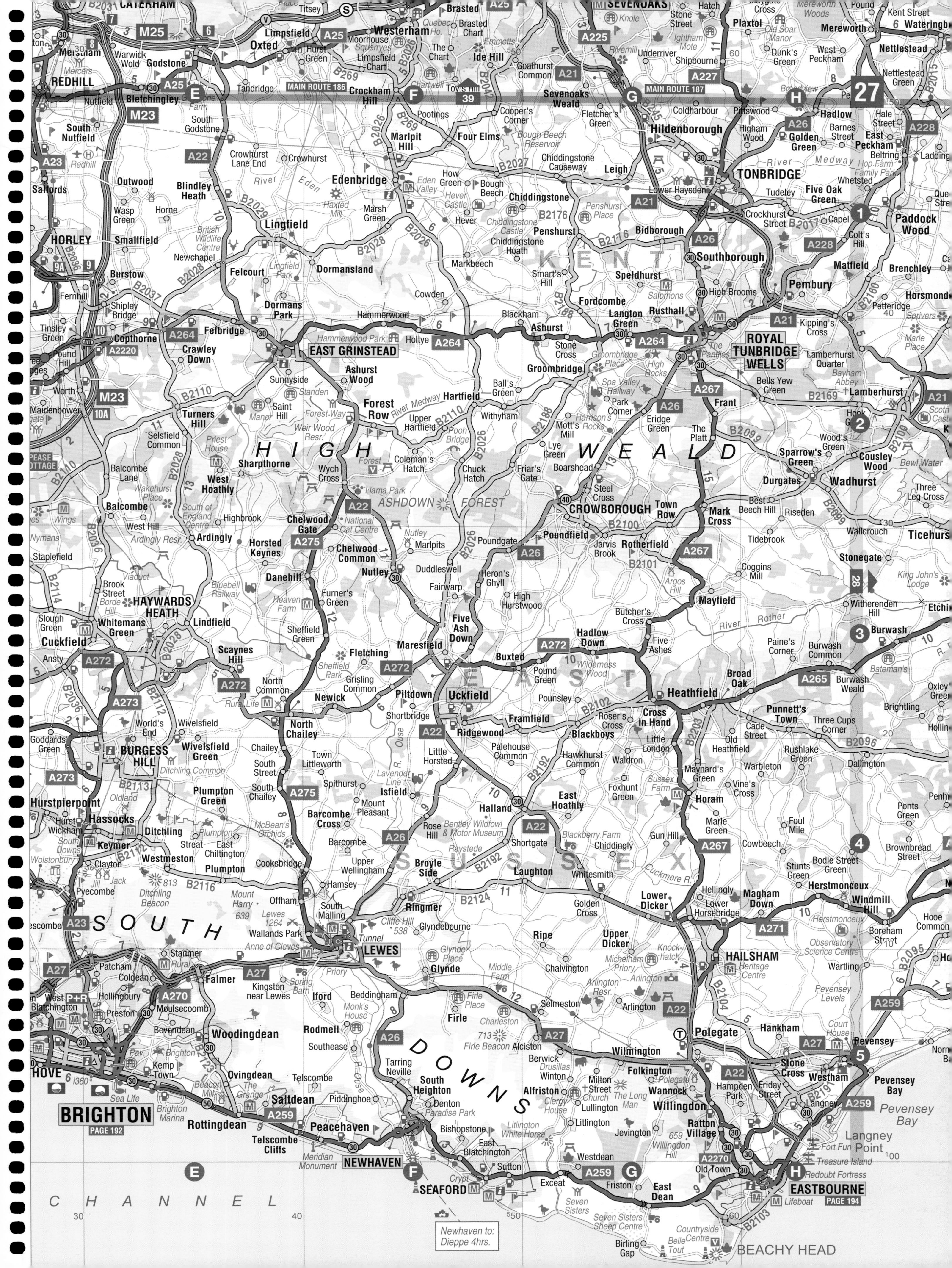

CATERHAM
Titsey
Brasted
A25
SEVENOAKS
Knole
Hatch
Stone Street
Plaxtol
Kent Street
Wateringbury
M25
Limpsfield
Westerham
Brasted Chart
A225
Ightham Mote
Mereworth
Nettlestead
Merstham
Warwick Wold
Oxted
Hurst Green
Moorhouse
Limpsfield Chart
The Chart
Ide Hill
Emmetts
Underriver
Shipbourne
Dunk's Green
West Peckham
Godstone
Goathurst Common
A21
A227
Nettlestead Green
REDHILL
A25
Tandridge
MAIN ROUTE 186
Crockham Hill
Chartwell
Toy's Hill
39
Sevenoaks Weald
MAIN ROUTE 187
27
Nutfield
Bletchingley
Pootings
Cooper's Corner
Fletcher's Green
Coldharbour
Pittswood
Hadlow
Hale Street
M23
South Godstone
Marlpit Hill
Four Elms
Bough Beech Reservoir
Hildenborough
Higham Wood
A26
Golden Green
Barnes Street
East Peckham
A228
South Nutfield
Beltring
Laddingford
A22
Crowhurst Lane End
Crowhurst
Chiddingstone Causeway
Leigh
Medway
Hop Farm Family Park
A23
Redhill
Eden
Edenbridge
Eden Valley
How Green
Bough Beech
B2027
TONBRIDGE
Whetsted
Salfords
Outwood
Blindley Heath
River Eden
Hever Castle
Chiddingstone
Lower Haysden
Tudeley
Five Oak Green
Haxted Mill
Marsh Green
Penshurst Place
A21
Crockhurst Street
B2017
Capel
Paddock Wood
Wasp Green
Horne
British Wildlife Centre
Lingfield
Hever
Chiddingstone Castle
B2176
Penshurst
Bidborough
HORLEY
Smallfield
B2028
B2026
Chiddingstone Hoath
KENT
A26
Colt's Hill
A228
Newchapel
Lingfield Park
Dormansland
Markbeech
Southborough
Matfield
Brenchley
Burstow
Felcourt
Smart's Hill
Speldhurst
Salomons
Pembury
Fernhill
B2037
Cowden
Fordcombe
High Brooms
Horsmonden
Shipley Bridge
Dormans Park
Hammerwood
Blackham
Langton Green
Rusthall
A21
Kipping's Cross
Petteridge
Sprivers
Tinsley Green
Copthorne
Felbridge
Hammerwood Park
Holtye
A264
Ashurst
A264
ROYAL TUNBRIDGE WELLS
Marle Place
Pound Hill
A2220
A264
Crawley Down
EAST GRINSTEAD
Stone Cross
Groombridge Place
High Rocks
The Pantiles
Lamberhurst Quarter
Ashurst Wood
Groombridge
Bayham Abbey
Worth
Sunnyside
Spa Valley Railway
A267
Bells Yew Green
Lamberhurst
M23
Maidenbower
10A
B2110
Standen
Forest Row
Saint Hill
River Medway
Hartfield
Ball's Green
Park Corner
A26
Frant
B2169
A21
Turners Hill
Manor
Forest Way
Upper Hartfield
B2110
Withyham
Harrison's Rocks
Eridge Green
Hook Green
Scotney Castle
Selsfield Common
Weir Wood Resr.
Pooh Bridge
B2188
Mott's Mill
The Platt
B2099
Wood's Green
Priest House
HIGH
WEALD
Lye Green
Sparrow's Green
Cousley Wood
Bewl Water
Balcombe Lane
B2028
Sharpthorne
Wych Cross
Forest
Coleman's Hatch
Chuck Hatch
Friar's Gate
Boarshead
Durgates
Wadhurst
Wakehurst Place
West Hoathly
Llama Park
Steel Cross
Three Leg Cross
Balcombe
ASHDOWN
FOREST
CROWBOROUGH
Town Row
Mark Cross
Best Beech Hill
Riseden
Wings
South of England Centre
Highbrook
A22
Chelwood Gate
National Cat Centre
B2100
Wallcrouch
Ticehurst
Nymans
West Hill
Ardingly Resr.
Ardingly
Horsted Keynes
A275
Nutley
Marlpits
Poundgate
A26
Poundfield
Jarvis Brook
Rotherfield
A267
Tidebrook
Staplefield
Chelwood Common
B2026
B2101
Stonegate
Danehill
Nutley
Duddleswell
Heron's Ghyll
Coggins Mill
Argos Hill
King John's Lodge
B2114
Brook Street
Viaduct
Bluebell Railway
Heaven Farm
Furner's Green
Fairwarp
High Hurstwood
Mayfield
Witherenden Hill
Etchingham
Borde Hill
HAYWARDS HEATH
Slough Green
Whitemans Green
Lindfield
Sheffield Green
Five Ash Down
Butcher's Cross
River Rother
Cuckfield
Scaynes Hill
Fletching
Maresfield
Hadlow Down
Five Ashes
Burwash
Paine's Corner
Burwash Common
Ansty
A272
Sheffield Park
A272
Buxted
A272
Wilderness Wood
Pound Green
EAST
Broad Oak
Bateman's
A265
Burwash Weald
Oxley's Green
North Common
Grisling Common
Piltdown
Uckfield
Pounsley
Heathfield
Brightling
B2036
A273
A272
B2112
Rural Life
Newick
Shortbridge
Framfield
B2102
Roser's Cross
Cross in Hand
Punnett's Town
Three Cups Corner
Hollingrove
World's End
Wivelsfield
North Chailey
A22
Ridgewood
Blackboys
Cade Street
Little London
Old Heathfield
B2096
Goddards' Green
BURGESS HILL
Wivelsfield Green
Chailey
Town Littleworth
Little Horsted
Palehouse Common
Hawkhurst Common
Waldron
Rushlake Green
Dallington
A273
Ditchling Common
South Street
Spithurst
Lavender Line
B2192
Maynard's Green
Warbleton
B2113
Oldland
South Chailey
A275
Isfield
Sussex Farm
Vine's Cross
Hurstpierpoint
Plumpton Green
Mount Pleasant
Halland
East Hoathly
Foxhunt Green
Horam
Penhurst
Hassocks
Hurst Wickham
Ditchling
McBean's Orchids
Barcombe Cross
Rose Hill
Bentley Wildfowl & Motor Museum
A22
Foul Mile
Ponts Green
Keymer
Plumpton
Streat
East Chiltington
Barcombe
A26
Raystede
Shortgate
Blackberry Farm
Chiddingly
Gun Hill
Marle Green
Cowbeech
Brownbread Street
Wolstonbury
Clayton
Westmeston
Plumpton
Cooksbridge
Upper Wellingham
Broyle Side
B2192
SUSSEX
A267
Bodle Street Green
Stunts Green
Pyecombe
Jack and Jill
Ditchling Beacon
813
B2116
Mount Harry 639
Hamsey
Laughton
Whitesmith
Cuckmere R.
Hellingly
Herstmonceux
Magham Down
Offham
Lewes 1264
South Malling
Ringmer
B2124
Golden Cross
Lower Dicker
Lower Horsebridge
Windmill Hill
A23
SOUTH
Wallands Park
Cliffe Hill 538
Glyndebourne
A271
Herstmonceux
Hooe Common
Boreham Street
Stanmer
Anne of Cleves
Tunnel
LEWES
Glynde Place
Ripe
Upper Dicker
Knockhatch
HAILSHAM
Observatory Science Centre
Hooe
A27
Patcham
Coldean
A27
Falmer
Priory
Glynde
Middle Farm
Chalvington
Michelham Priory
Heritage Centre
Wartling
A270
Kingston near Lewes
Iford
Beddingham
Arlington Resr.
Arlington
B2095
West Blatchington
P+R
Hollingbury
Preston
Moulsecoomb
Monk's House
Firle Place
Charleston
Selmeston
A22
Pevensey Levels
A259
Bevendean
Woodingdean
Rodmell
Southease
A26
Firle
713
Firle Beacon
Alciston
A27
Polegate
Hankham
Court House
A27
Pevensey
Norman's Bay
HOVE
Kemp Town
Pav.
Brighton
B2123
Ovingdean
The Grange
Telscombe
DOWNS
Tarring Neville
South Heighton
Berwick
Drusillas
Wilmington
Folkington
A22
Stone Cross
Westham
Pevensey Bay
Sea Life
BRIGHTON
PAGE 192
Brighton Marina
Rottingdean
Saltdean
A259
Piddinghoe
Denton
Paradise Park
Alfriston
Milton Street
Clergy House
Lullington
The Long Man
Wannock
Willingdon
Hampden Park
Friday Street
Langney
A259
Pevensey Bay
Telscombe Cliffs
Peacehaven
Bishopstone
East Blatchington
Litlington
White Horse
Litlington
Jevington
659 Willingdon Hill
Ratton Village
Langney Point
Fort Fun
Treasure Island
Meridian Monument
NEWHAVEN
Crypt
Sutton
Westdean
A259
A2270
Old Town
Redoubt Fortress
SEAFORD
Exceat
Friston
East Dean
EASTBOURNE
PAGE 194
Lifeboat
CHANNEL
Seven Sisters
Seven Sisters Sheep Centre
Countryside Centre
Belle Tout
B2103
Newhaven to: Dieppe 4hrs.
Birling Gap
BEACHY HEAD

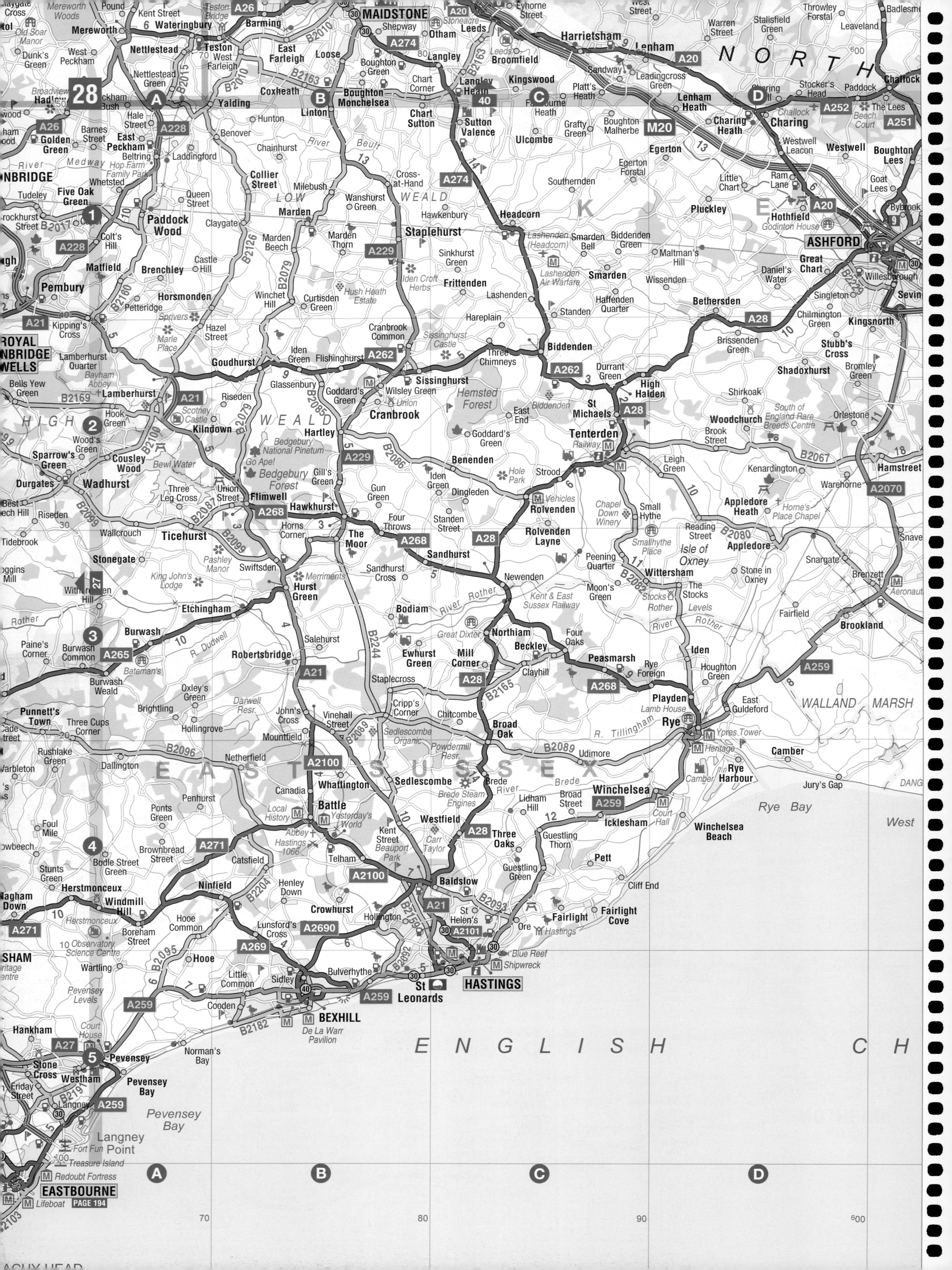

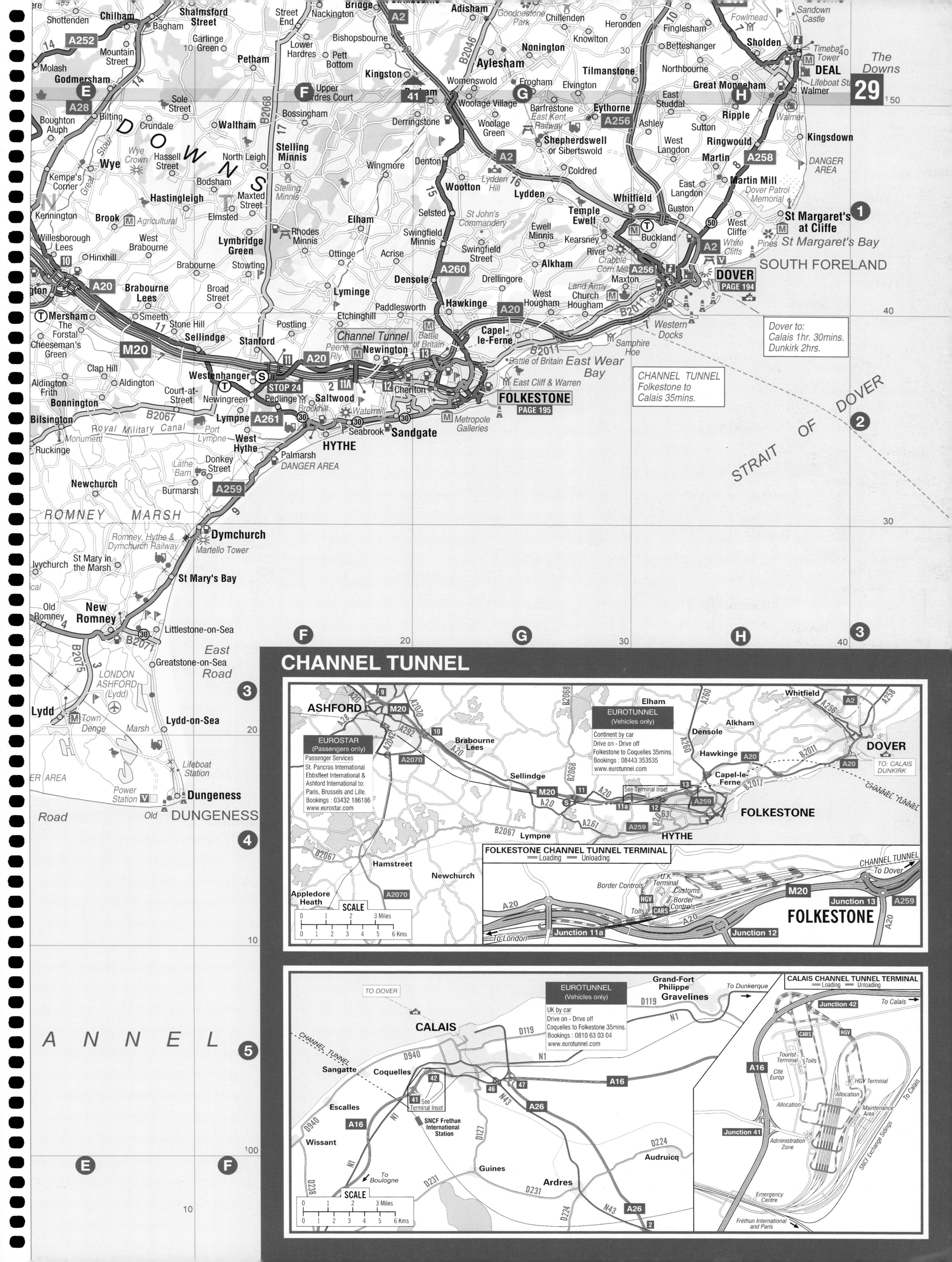
29
CHANNEL TUNNEL
Chilham
Shalmsford Street
Bagham
Shottenden
A252
Molash
Mountain Street
Garlinge Green
Petham
Godmersham
Street End
Nackington
Lower Hardres
Bishopsbourne
Pett Bottom
Kingston
Upper Hardres Court
Bossingham
Adisham
Goodnestone Park
Chillenden
Knowlton
Heronden
Finglesham
Fowlmead
Sandown Castle
Betteshanger
Sholden
Timeball Tower
DEAL
The Downs
Nonington
Aylesham
Tilmanstone
Northbourne
Womenswold
Frogham
Elvington
Great Mongeham
Walmer
Lifeboat Sta
Woolage Village
Barfrestone
East Kent Railway
Eythorne
East Studdal
Ripple
Sutton
Kingsdown
Woolage Green
Shepherdswell or Sibertswold
Ashley
West Langdon
Ringwould
Martin
Derringstone
Denton
Coldred
A258
DANGER AREA
Martin Mill
Dover Patrol Memorial
East Langdon
Guston
Whitfield
Lydden Hill
Lydden
Wootton
Temple Ewell
St Margaret's at Cliffe
St Margaret's Bay
West Cliffe
White Cliffs
Pines
SOUTH FORELAND
Buckland
Kearsney
River
Crabble Corn Mill
Ewell Minnis
Alkham
Maxton
DOVER
PAGE 194
Land Army
Church Hougham
West Hougham
Western Docks
Samphire Hoe
Dover to: Calais 1hr. 30mins. Dunkirk 2hrs.
CHANNEL TUNNEL Folkestone to Calais 35mins.
STRAIT OF DOVER
Boughton Aluph
Bilting
Crundale
Waltham
DOWNS
Stelling Minnis
Wye
Wye Crown
Hassell Street
North Leigh
Kempe's Corner
Bodsham
Wingmore
Hastingleigh
Maxted Street
Elmsted
Kennington
Brook
Agricultural
Rhodes Minnis
Elham
Selsted
St John's Commandery
Swingfield Minnis
Swingfield Street
Willesborough Lees
West Brabourne
Lymbridge Green
Ottinge
Acrise
Hinxhill
Brabourne
Stowting
Densole
Drellingore
Brabourne Lees
Broad Street
Lyminge
Paddlesworth
Hawkinge
Mersham
Smeeth
Etchinghill
The Forstal
Stone Hill
Postling
Channel Tunnel
Capel-le-Ferne
Cheeseman's Green
Sellindge
Stanford
Battle of Britain
Peene Rly.
Newington
M20
A20
A260
A256
A2
B2011
East Wear Bay
Battle of Britain
Clap Hill
Aldington Frith
Aldington
Westenhanger
Court-at-Street
Newingreen
STOP 24
Pedlinge
Saltwood
Cheriton
East Cliff & Warren
FOLKESTONE
PAGE 195
Bonnington
Brockhill
Watermill
Metropole Galleries
Bilsington
B2067
Royal Military Canal
Lympne
A261
Port Lympne
West Hythe
Seabrook
Sandgate
Monument
Ruckinge
HYTHE
Palmarsh
DANGER AREA
Lathe Barn
Donkey Street
Newchurch
Burmarsh
A259
ROMNEY MARSH
Dymchurch
Romney, Hythe & Dymchurch Railway
Martello Tower
Ivychurch
St Mary in the Marsh
St Mary's Bay
Old Romney
New Romney
Littlestone-on-Sea
B2071
B2075
East Road
Greatstone-on-Sea
LONDON ASHFORD (Lydd)
Lydd
Town
Denge
Marsh
Lydd-on-Sea
Lifeboat Station
Power Station
Dungeness
Old
DUNGENESS
Road
ANNEL
ASHFORD
Elham
Whitfield
EUROTUNNEL (Vehicles only)
Continent by car
Drive on - Drive off
Folkestone to Coquelles 35mins.
Bookings : 08443 353535
www.eurotunnel.com
EUROSTAR (Passengers only)
Passenger Services
St. Pancras International
Ebbsfleet International &
Ashford International to:
Paris, Brussels and Lille.
Bookings : 03432 186186
www.eurostar.com
Brabourne Lees
Densole
Alkham
Hawkinge
DOVER
TO: CALAIS DUNKIRK
Sellindge
Capel-le-Ferne
See Terminal Inset
FOLKESTONE
Lympne
HYTHE
FOLKESTONE CHANNEL TUNNEL TERMINAL
Loading
Unloading
Hamstreet
Newchurch
Appledore Heath
SCALE
3 Miles
6 Kms
Border Controls
U.K. Terminal
Customs
Border Controls
HGV
Tolls
CARS
Junction 13
Junction 12
Junction 11a
To London
To Dover
CHANNEL TUNNEL
TO DOVER
EUROTUNNEL (Vehicles only)
UK by car
Drive on - Drive off
Coquelles to Folkestone 35mins.
Bookings : 0810 63 03 04
www.eurotunnel.com
Grand-Fort Philippe
Gravelines
To Dunkerque
CALAIS
CALAIS CHANNEL TUNNEL TERMINAL
Loading
Unloading
Junction 42
To Calais
Sangatte
Coquelles
Escalles
Wissant
SNCF Frethun International Station
See Terminal Inset
Guines
Audruicq
Ardres
To Boulogne
SCALE
3 Miles
6 Kms
Tourist Terminal
Tolls
Cité Europ
HGV Terminal
Allocation
Maintenance Area
Junction 41
Administration Zone
SNCF Exchange Sidings
Emergency Centre
Fréthun International and Paris

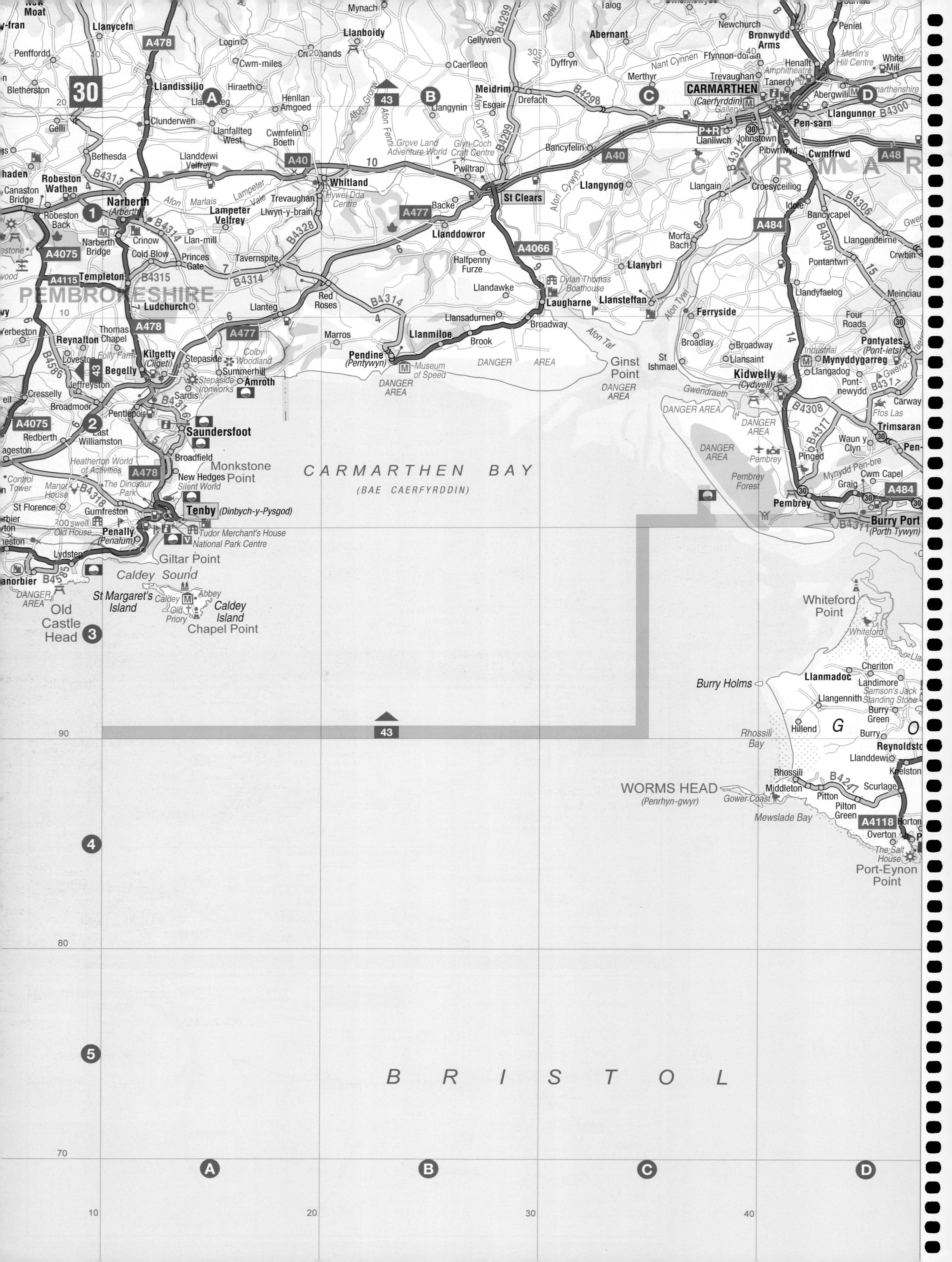
30
PEMBROKESHIRE
CARMARTHEN
(Caerfyrddin)
CARMARTHEN BAY
(BAE CAERFYRDDIN)
BRISTOL
Narberth
(Arberth)
Whitland
St Clears
Laugharne
Llansteffan
Kidwelly
(Cydweli)
Pembrey
Burry Port
(Porth Tywyn)
Tenby
(Dinbych-y-Pysgod)
Saundersfoot
Kilgetty
(Cilgeti)
Pendine
(Pentywyn)
Llanmiloe
Caldey Island
St Margaret's Island
Old Castle Head
Giltar Point
Caldey Sound
Chapel Point
Monkstone Point
Ginst Point
Whiteford Point
Burry Holms
WORMS HEAD
(Penrhyn-gwyr)
Rhossili Bay
Port-Eynon Point
Mewslade Bay
Rhossili
Llanmadoc
Reynoldston
A40
A477
A478
A4066
A484
A48
A4075
A4115
A4118
43
A
B
C
D
1
2
3
4
5
10
20
30
40
70
80
90

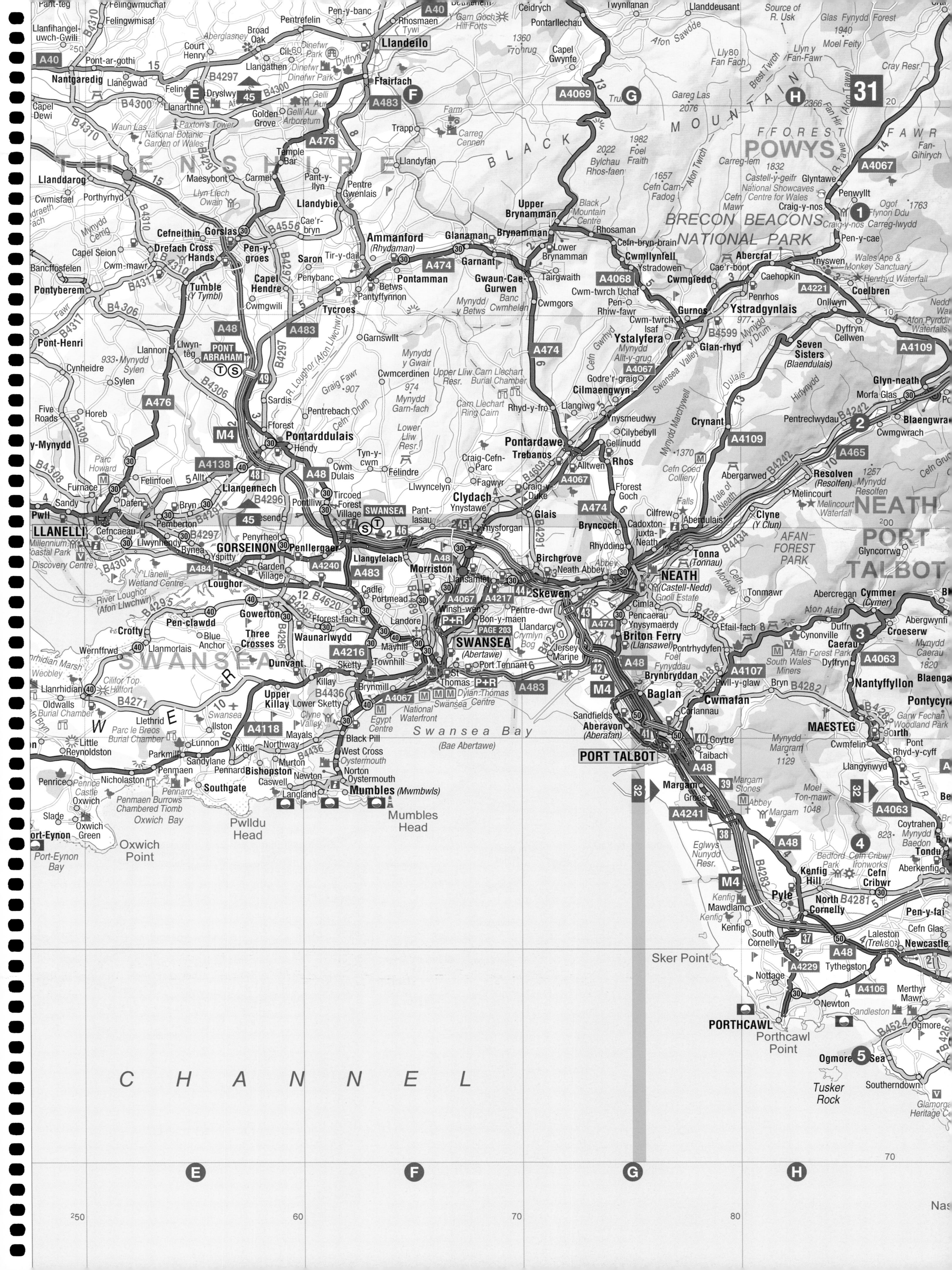

Felingwmisaf
Llanfihangel-uwch-Gwili
Pentrefelin
Pen-y-banc
A40
Rhosmaen
Llandeilo
Broad Oak
Court Henry
Pont-ar-gothi
Nantgaredig
Llanegwad
Cilsan
Dinefwr Park
Llangathen
Ffairfach
Drysllwyn
Llanarthne
B4297
B4300
A483
Golden Grove
Gelli Aur Arboretum
Capel Dewi
National Botanic Garden of Wales
Paxton's Tower
Trapp
Carreg Cennen
A476
Temple Bar
Llandyfan
BLACK MOUNTAIN
Llanddarog
Maesybont
Carmel
Pant-y-llyn
Pentre Gwenlais
Cwmisfael
Porthyrhyd
Llyn Llech Owain
Llandybie
Cefneithin
Gorslas
Drefach
Cross Hands
Pen-y-groes
Cae'r-bryn
Ammanford (Rhydaman)
Capel Seion
Cwm-mawr
Saron
Tir-y-dail
Glanaman
Brynamman
Upper Brynamman
Lower Brynamman
Pontamman
Garnant
Gwaun-Cae-Gurwen
Tairgwaith
Capel Hendre
Penybanc
Betws
Pantyffynnon
Cwmgors
Pontyberem
Tumble (Y Tymbl)
Cwmgwili
Tycroes
A474
A48
Pont-Henri
Garnswllt
Llannon
Llwyn-têg
PONT ABRAHAM
Mynydd y Gwair
Cwmcerdinen
Mynydd Sylen
Sylen
Cynheidre
Upper Lliw Resr.
Carn Llechart Burial Chamber
Sardis
Pentrebach
Mynydd Garn-fach
Five Roads
Horeb
A476
M4
Fforest
Pontarddulais
Hendy
Lower Lliw Resr.
Pontardawe
Trebanos
Craig-Cefn-Parc
Tyn-y-cwm
Cwm Dulais
Felindre
Parc Howard
A4138
Allt
Felinfoel
Llangennech
Furnace
Sandy
Pwll
LLANELLI
Dafen
Bryn
Pemberton
Tircoed Forest Village
Pontlliw
SWANSEA
Pant-lasau
Llwyncelyn
Clydach
Ynystawe
Ynysforgan
Fagwyr
Glais
Millennium Coastal Park
Discovery Centre
Cefncaeau
Llwynhendy
Bynea
GORSEINON
Penllergaer
Penyrheol
Ysbytty
Llangyfelach
Morriston
Birchgrove
Llansamlet
Skewen
Neath Abbey
NEATH (Castell-Nedd)
Llanelli Wetland Centre
Loughor
Garden Village
A4240
A484
River Loughor (Afon Llwchwr)
Gowerton
Pen-clawdd
Crofty
Three Crosses
Waunarlwydd
Cadle
Portmead
Fforest-fach
Landore
Winsh-wen
Bon-y-maen
Llandarcy
Pentre-dwr
Crymlyn Bog
Jersey Marine
Blue Anchor
Llanmorlais
Wernffrwd
Llanrhidian Marsh
SWANSEA (Abertawe)
Mayhill
Townhill
Dunvant
Sketty
Killay
Upper Killay
Lower Skettty
Port Tennant
St Thomas
Dylan Thomas Centre
National Waterfront
Egypt Centre
Swansea Bay (Bae Abertawe)
Weobley
Cilifor Top Hillfort
Llanrhidian
Oldwalls
Burial Chamber
Llethrid
Parc le Breos Burial Chamber
Ilston
Clyne Valley
Mayals
Black Pill
West Cross
Oystermouth
Norton
Little Reynoldston
Lunnon
Parkmill
Kittle
Northway
Murton
Bishopston
Penmaen
Sandylane
Pennard
Newton
Caswell
Langland
Mumbles (Mwmbwls)
Mumbles Head
Penrice
Penrice Castle
Nicholaston
Southgate
Oxwich
Penmaen Burrows Chambered Tomb
Oxwich Bay
Pwlldu Head
Slade
Oxwich Green
Port-Eynon
Port-Eynon Bay
Oxwich Point
CHANNEL
Ceidrych
Pontarllechau
Twynllanan
Llanddeusant
Source of R. Usk
Capel Gwynfe
Afon Sawdde
A4069
Glas Fynydd Forest
Moel Feity
Cray Resr.
Fan Fach
Fan-Fawr
Gareg Las
Brest Twrch
Fan Hir
POWYS
FFOREST FAWR
Fan-Gihirych
Foel Fraith
Bylchau Rhos-faen
Cefn Carn-Fadog
Carreg-lem
Castell-y-geifr
National Showcaves Centre for Wales
Glyntawe
Penwyllt
Craig-y-nos
A4067
Ogof Ffynnon Ddu
Carreg-lwydd
BRECON BEACONS NATIONAL PARK
Black Mountain Centre
Rhosaman
Cefn-bryn-brain
Cwmllynfell
Ystradowen
Abercraf
Cae'r-bont
Pen-y-cae
Ynyswen
Wales Ape & Monkey Sanctuary
Henrhyd Waterfall
Coelbren
Caehopkin
A4068
Cwm-twrch Uchaf
Pen-Rhiw-fawr
Cwmgiedd
Penrhos
Gurnos
Ystradgynlais
A4221
Onllwyn
Cwm-twrch Isaf
Ystalyfera
Glan-rhyd
Dyffryn Cellwen
Seven Sisters (Blaendulais)
A4109
Godre'r-graig
Cilmaengwyn
Swansea Valley
Glyn-neath
Morfa Glas
Llangiwg
Rhyd-y-fro
Ynysmeudwy
Cilybebyll
Gellinudd
Crynant
Pentreclwydau
Blaengwrach
Cwmgwrach
Alltwen
Rhos
Cefn Coed Colliery
Abergarwed
Resolven (Resolfen)
Mynydd Resolfen
Melincourt
Melincourt Waterfall
Fforest Goch
Craig-y-Duke
Vale of Neath
Bryncoch
Cilfrew
Aberdulais
Clyne (Y Clun)
NEATH PORT TALBOT
Cadoxton-juxta-Neath
Rhydding
Tonna (Tonnau)
AFAN FOREST PARK
Glyncorrwg
Tonmawr
Abercregan
Cymmer (Cymer)
Cimla
Gnoll Estate
Pencaerau
Ynysmaerdy
Briton Ferry (Llansawel)
Pontrhydyfen
Efail-fach
Afon Afan
Duffryn
Cynonville
Croeserw
Abergwynfi
Caerau
Afan Forest Park
South Wales Miners
Dyffryn
A4063
Nantyffyllon
Brynbryddan
A4107
Pwll-y-glaw
Bryn
Baglan
Cwmafan
Corlannau
Sandfields
Aberavon (Aberafan)
PORT TALBOT
Goytre
Taibach
MAESTEG
Cwmfelin
Garw Fechan Woodland Park
Pontycymer
Rhyd-y-cyff
Mynydd Margam
Llangynwyd
Margam
Margam Stones
Groes
A4241
Moel Ton-mawr
Coytrahen
Mynydd Baedon
Eglwys Nunydd Resr.
Bedford Park
Cefn Cribwr Ironworks
Kenfig Hill
Cefn Cribwr
Aberkenfig
Pyle
North Cornelly
Kenfig
Mawdlam
South Cornelly
Laleston
Newcastle
Sker Point
Nottage
Tythegston
Merthyr Mawr
Newton
Candleston
PORTHCAWL
Porthcawl Point
Ogmore
Ogmore-by-Sea
Tusker Rock
Southerndown
Glamorgan Heritage Coast
31
32

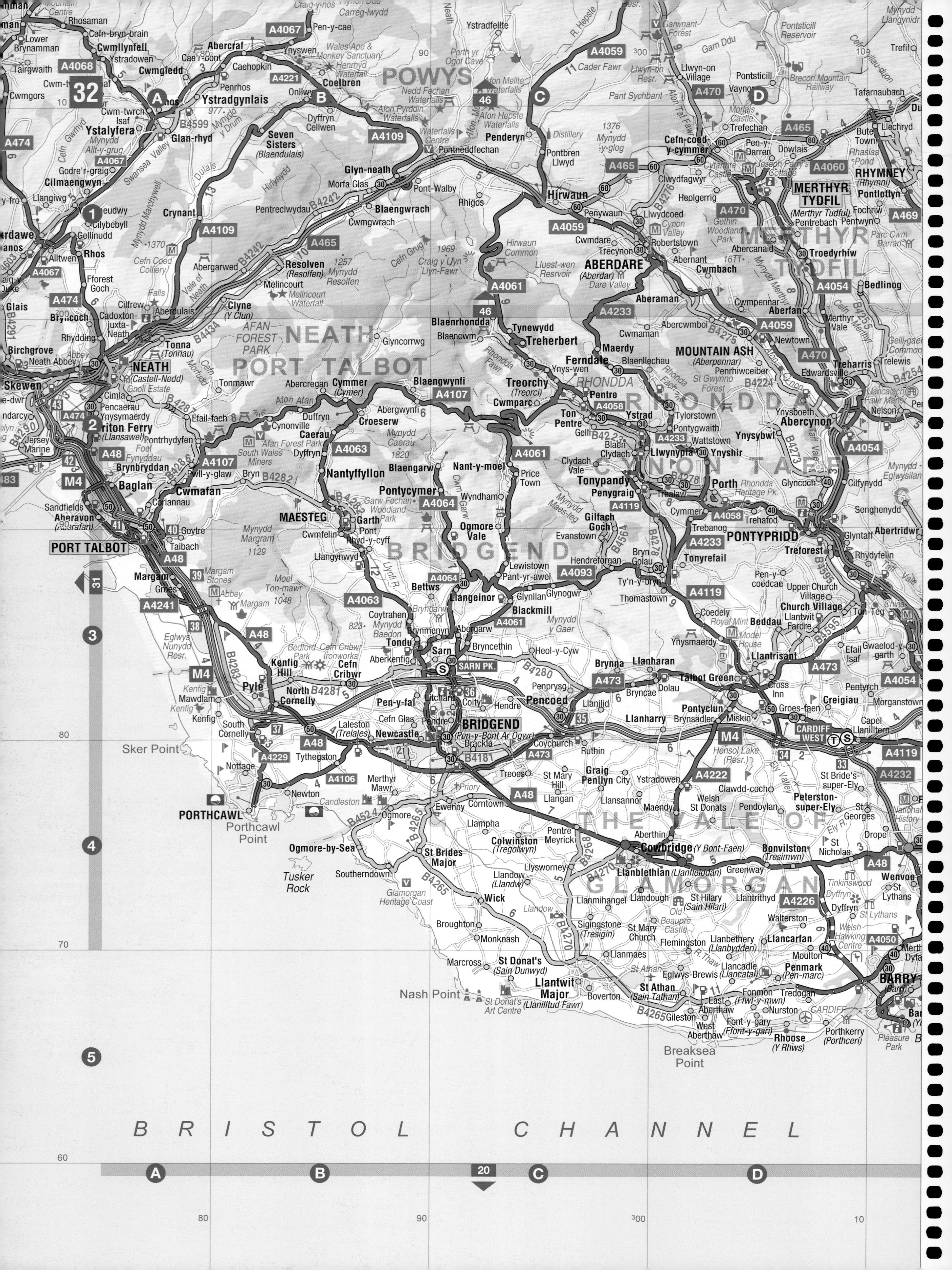

32
POWYS
NEATH
PORT TALBOT
BRIDGEND
RHONDDA
CYNON TAFF
MERTHYR TYDFIL
THE VALE OF GLAMORGAN
BRISTOL CHANNEL
Rhosaman
Cefn-bryn-brain
Lower Brynamman
Cwmllynfell
Ystradowen
Tairgwaith
Cwmgiedd
Cwmgors
Ystradgynlais
Abercraf
Caehopkin
Penrhos
Coelbren
Onllwyn
Pen-y-cae
Ynyswen
Wales Ape & Monkey Sanctuary
Henrhyd Waterfall
Carreg-lwydd
Ystradfellte
Porth yr Ogof Cave
Nedd Fechan Waterfalls
Afon Pyrddin Waterfalls
Afon Mellte Waterfalls
Afon Hepste Waterfalls
Waterfalls Centre
Pontneddfechan
Penderyn
Distillery
Pontbren Llwyd
Cader Fawr
Garwnant Forest
Llwyn-on Resr.
Llwyn-on Village
Pontsticill Reservoir
Pontsticill
Vaynor
Brecon Mountain Railway
Pant Sychbant
Garn Ddu
Morlais Castle
Trefechan
Cefn-coed-y-cymmer
Pen-y-Darren
Dowlais
Cyfarthfa Castle
Joseph Parry's Cottage
Tafarnaubach
Trefil
Llechryd
Bute Town
Rhaslas Pond
RHYMNEY (Rhymni)
Pontlottyn
Fochriw
Pentwyn
Pentrebach
MERTHYR TYDFIL (Merthyr Tudful)
Troedyrhiw
Abercanaid
Gethin Woodland Park
Heolgerrig
Clwydfagwyr
Bedlinog
Parc Cwm Darran
Cwm-twrch Isaf
Ystalyfera
Mynydd Allt-y-grug
Godre'r-graig
Cilmaengwyn
Glan-rhyd
Swansea Valley
Mynydd y Drum
Dyffryn Cellwen
Seven Sisters (Blaendulais)
Glyn-neath
Morfa Glas
Pont-Walby
Rhigos
Hirwaun
Penywaun
Llwydcoed
Cynon Valley
Robertstown
Abernant
Cwmbach
Cwmdare
Trecynon
ABERDARE (Aberdar)
Dare Valley
Hirwaun Common
Lluest-wen Resrvoir
Craig y Llyn
Llyn-Fawr
Aberaman
Abercwmboi
Cwmaman
MOUNTAIN ASH (Aberpennar)
Penrhiwceiber
Cwmpennar
Aberfan
Merthyr Vale
Newtown
Treharris
Trelewis
Edwardsville
Gelli-gaer Common
Llancaiach Fawr Manor
Nelson
Ynysboeth
Abercynon
Ynysybwl
Cilfynydd
Glyncoch
Senghenydd
Abertridwr
Pentreclwydau
Blaengwrach
Cwmgwrach
Resolven (Resolfen)
Mynydd Resolfen
Melincourt
Melincourt Waterfall
Abergarwed
Vale of Neath
Clyne (Y Clun)
Aberdulais
Cilfrew
Cadoxton-juxta-Neath
Rhydding
Crynant
Cilybebyll
Gellinudd
Alltwen
Rhos
Fforest Goch
Bryncoch
Birchgrove
Neath Abbey
Skewen
NEATH (Castell-Nedd)
Gnoll Estate
Tonna (Tonnau)
Tonmawr
AFAN FOREST PARK
Glyncorrwg
Blaenrhondda
Blaencwm
Tynewydd
Treherbert
Ferndale
Maerdy
Blaenllechau
Ynys-wen
Treorchy (Treorci)
Cwmparc
Pentre
Ton Pentre
Gelli
Ystrad
Tylorstown
Pontygwaith
Wattstown
Llwynypia
Ynyshir
Blaen Clydach
Clydach Vale
Tonypandy
Penygraig
Trealaw
Porth
Rhondda Heritage Pk.
Cymmer
Trehafod
PONTYPRIDD
Trebanog
Treforest
Glyntaff
Rhydyfelin
Taff Vale
Tonyrefail
Gilfach Goch
Evanstown
Hendreforgan
Bryn Golau
Ty'n-y-bryn
Thomastown
Pen-y-coedcae
Upper Church Village
Church Village
Llantwit Fardre
Beddau
Ton-Teg
Efail Isaf
Gwaelod-y-garth
Coedely
Royal Mint
Model House
Ynysmaerdy
Llantrisant
Talbot Green
Cross Inn
Groes-faen
Creigiau
Pentyrch
Morganstown
Capel Llanilltern
Miskin
CARDIFF WEST
Abercregan
Cymmer (Cymer)
Afon Afan
Blaengwynfi
Abergwynfi
Croeserw
Duffryn
Caerau
Mynydd Caerau
Cynonville
Afan Forest Park
South Wales Miners
Efail-fach
Pencaerau
Cimla
Ynysmaerdy
Briton Ferry (Llansawel)
Jersey Marine
Pontrhydyfen
Foel Fynyddau
Brynbryddan
Pwll-y-glaw
Bryn
Cwmafan
Corlannau
Baglan
Sandfields
Aberavon (Aberafan)
PORT TALBOT
Goytre
Taibach
Mynydd Margam
Margam
Groes
Margam Stones
Abbey
Moel Ton-mawr
Nantyffyllon
Blaengarw
Nant-y-moel
Price Town
Wyndham
Pontycymer
Garw Fechan Woodland Park
MAESTEG
Garth
Cwmfelin
Pont Rhyd-y-cyff
Llangynwyd
Ogmore Vale
Lewistown
Pant-yr-awel
Glynllan
Glynogwr
Blackmill
Bettws
Llangeinor
Llynfi R.
Coytrahen
Mynydd Baedon
Brynmenyn
Abergarw
Tondu
Aberkenfig
Sarn
SARN PK.
Bryncethin
Heol-y-Cyw
Mynydd y Gaer
Brynna
Llanharan
Bryncae
Dolau
Pontyclun
Brynsadler
Llanharry
Penprysg
Pencoed
Llanilid
Hendre
Coity
Litchard
Pendre
BRIDGEND (Pen-y-Bont Ar Ogwr)
Brackla
Coychurch
Ruthin
Pen-y-fai
Cefn Glas
Laleston (Trelales)
Newcastle
Cefn Cribwr
Cefn Cribwr Ironworks
Bedford Park
Kenfig Hill
North Cornelly
Pyle
Kenfig
Mawdlam
Eglwys Nunydd Resr.
South Cornelly
Sker Point
Nottage
Tythegston
Merthyr Mawr
Newton
Candleston
PORTHCAWL
Porthcawl Point
Ogmore
Ewenny
Priory
Corntown
Treoes
St Mary Hill
Llangan
Graig Penllyn
City
Ystradowen
Llansannor
Hensol Lake (Resr.)
Ely Valley
Clawdd-coch
Welsh St Donats
Maendy
Pendoylan
Peterston-super-Ely
St Bride's-super-Ely
St Georges
Drope
St Nicholas
Bonvilston (Tresimwn)
Aberthin
Cowbridge (Y Bont-Faen)
Llanblethian (Llanfleiddan)
Greenway
Wenvoe
St Lythans
Tinkinswood
Dyffryn
Welsh Hawking Centre
Walterston
Llancarfan
Llantrithyd
St Hilary (Sain Hilari)
Old Beaupre Castle
Llandough
Llanmihangel
Llysworney
Pentre Meyrick
Colwinston (Tregolwyn)
Llampha
St Brides Major
Ogmore-by-Sea
Southerndown
Tusker Rock
Glamorgan Heritage Coast
Wick
Llandow (Llandw)
Broughton
Monknash
Sigingstone (Tresigin)
St Mary Church
Flemingston
Llanbethery (Llanbydderi)
Moulton
Penmark (Pen-marc)
Llancadle (Llancatal)
Eglwys-Brewis
Llanmaes
Marcross
St Donat's (Sain Dunwyd)
Nash Point
St Donat's Art Centre
Llantwit Major (Llanilltud Fawr)
Boverton
St Athan (Sain Tathan)
East Aberthaw
Gileston
West Aberthaw
Fonmon (Ffwl-y-mwn)
Font-y-gary (Ffont-y-gari)
Nurston
Tredogan
Rhoose (Y Rhws)
Porthkerry (Porthceri)
Breaksea Point
CARDIFF
BARRY (Barri)
Pleasure Park
A4067
A4068
A474
A4221
A4109
A4059
A470
A465
A4060
A469
A4054
A4233
A4061
A4107
A4058
A4063
A4064
A4119
A4093
A4241
A48
A473
A4229
A4106
A4222
A4226
A4232
A4050
A4107
M4
B4599
B4242
B4434
B4282
B4287
B4283
B4281
B4280
B4181
B4524
B4265
B4270
B4268
B4564
B4278
B4273
B4275
B4255
B4254
B4595
B4291
B4290
46
31
20
A
B
C
D
1
2
3
4
5
80
90
300
10
70
60

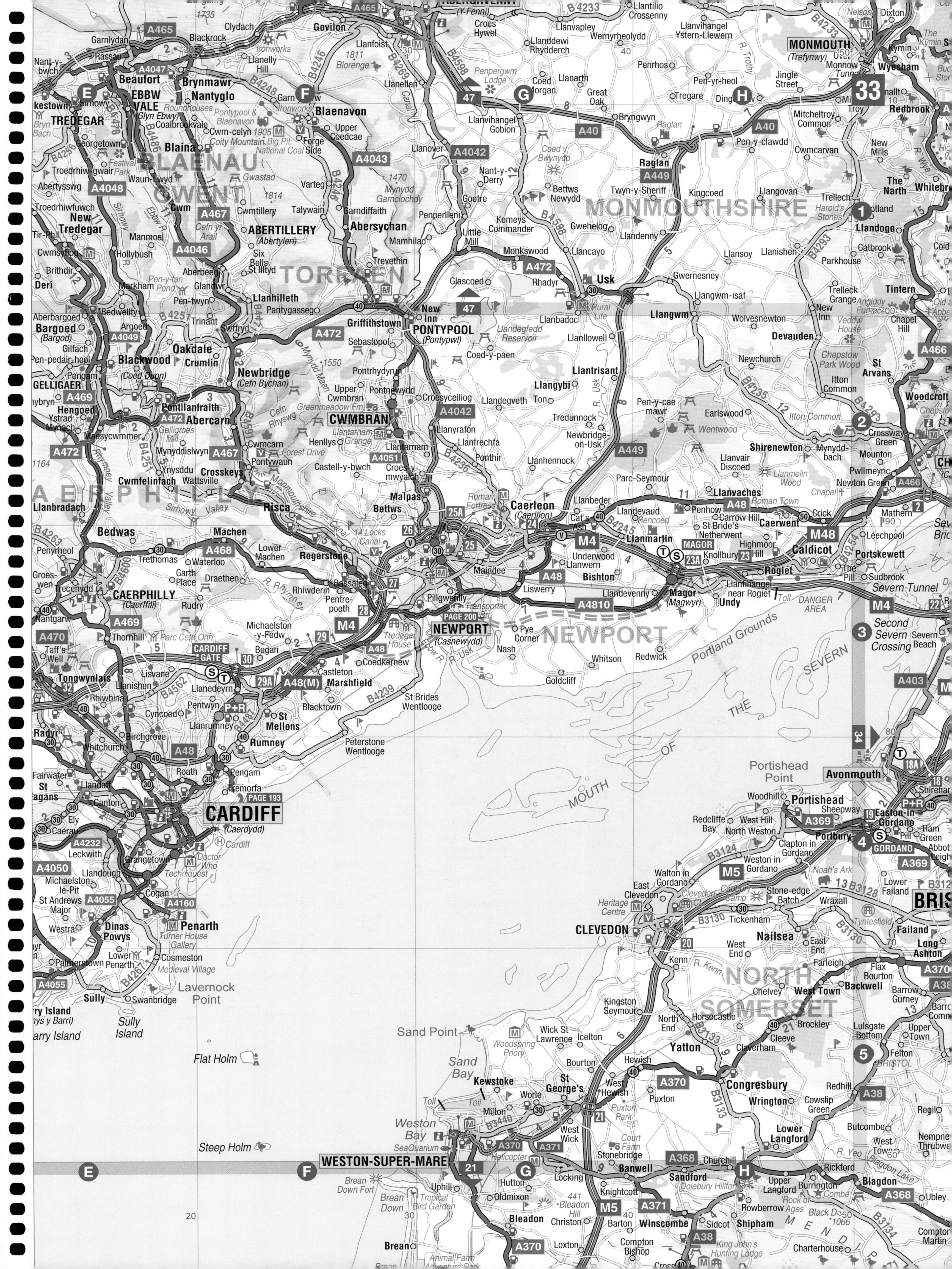

ABERGAVENNY (Y Fenni)
Llantilio Crossenny
Dixton
MONMOUTH (Trefynwy)
Wyesham
33
Redbrook
Clydach
Govilon
Llanfoist
Blorenge
Garnlydan
Blackrock
Llanelly Hill
Beaufort
Brynmawr
Nantyglo
EBBW VALE (Glyn Ebwy)
TREDEGAR
Blaenavon
Pontypool & Blaenavon Railway
Coalbrookvale
Cwm-celyn
Big Pit: National Coal Museum
Forge Side
Upper Coedcae
Blaina
Georgetown
BLAENAU GWENT
Llanover
Llanvihangel Gobion
Llanvapley
Llanddewi Rhydderch
Wernyrheolydd
Llanvihangel Ystern-Llewern
Penrhos
Llanarth
Great Oak
Coed Morgan
Pen-yr-heol
Tregare
Dingestow
Jingle Street
Mitcheltroy Common
Troy
Bryngwyn
Raglan
Pen-y-clawdd
Cwmcarvan
New Mills
The Narth
Whitebrook
Troedrhiw-gwair
Abertysswg
Waun-Lwyd
Gwastad
Varteg
Garndiffaith
Nant-y-Derry
Goetre
Bettws Newydd
Twyn-y-Sheriff
Kingcoed
Llangovan
Trellech
MONMOUTHSHIRE
Llandogo
New Tredegar
Cwm
Cwmtillery
Talywain
Abersychan
Penperlleni
Kemeys Commander
Gwehelog
Llandenny
Manmoel
Hollybush
ABERTILLERY (Abertyleri)
Mamhilad
Little Mill
Monkswood
Llancayo
Llansoy
Llanishen
Catbrook
Parkhouse
Six Bells
St Illtyd
Trevethin
TORFAEN
Glascoed
Rhadyr
Usk
Gwernesney
Tintern
Deri
Markham
Aberbeeg
Glandwr
Pen-twyn
Llanhilleth
Pantygasseg
New Inn
PONTYPOOL (Pontypŵl)
Llanbadoc
Llangwm
Llangwm-isaf
Wolvesnewton
Devauden
Trelleck Grange
New Inn
Chapel Hill
Aberbargoed
Bargoed (Bargod)
Gilfach
Pen-pedair-heol
GELLIGAER
Bedwellty
Argoed
Trinant
Swffryd
Griffithstown
Sebastopol
Llandegfedd Reservoir
Llanllowell
Oakdale
Crumlin
Blackwood (Coed Duon)
Pengam
Newbridge (Cefn Bychan)
Coed-y-paen
Llantrisant
Newchurch
St Arvans
Chepstow Park Wood
Itton Common
Hengoed
Ystrad Mynach
Pontllanfraith
Abercarn
Upper Cwmbran
Pontnewydd
CWMBRAN
Croesyceiliog
Llandegveth
Llangybi
Tredunnock
Pen-y-cae mawr
Earlswood
Wentwood
Woodcroft
Maesycwmmer
Mynyddislwyn
Cwmcarn
Pontywaun
Henllys
Llantarnam
Llanyrafon
Llanfrechfa
Newbridge-on-Usk
Shirenewton
Mynydd-bach
Crossway Green
Mounton
Cwmfelinfach
Ynysddu
Wattsville
Crosskeys
Castell-y-bwch
Croes-y-mwyalch
Ponthir
Llanhennock
Llanvair Discoed
Pwllmeyric
Newton Green
CAERPHILLY
Llanbradach
Risca
Malpas
Bettws
Caerleon (Caerllion)
Parc-Seymour
Llanvaches
Penhow
Llanbeder
Llandevaud
Cat's Ash
Carrow Hill
St Bride's Netherwent
Caerwent
Crick
Mathern
Bedwas
Machen
Lower Machen
Rogerstone
Llanmartin
MAGOR
Highmoor Hill
Caldicot
Leechpool
Portskewett
Penyrheol
Trethomas
Waterloo
Garth Place
Draethen
Bassaleg
Maindee
Underwood
Llanwern
Bishton
Knollbury
Rogiet
The Pill
Sudbrook
Groes-wen
Tredenydd
CAERPHILLY (Caerffili)
Rudry
Rhiwderin
Pentre-poeth
Pillgwenlly
Liswerry
Llandevenny
Magor (Magwyr)
Llanfihangel near Rogiet
Undy
Severn Tunnel
Nantgarw
Thornhill
Michaelston-y-Fedw
NEWPORT (Casnewydd)
Pye Corner
NEWPORT
Second Severn Crossing
Severn Beach
Taff's Well
Tongwynlais
CARDIFF GATE
Lisvane
Llanishen
Began
Castleton
Coedkernew
Marshfield
Nash
Whitson
Redwick
Portland Grounds
Goldcliff
Rhiwbina
Llanedeyrn
Pentwyn
Cyncoed
St Mellons
Llanrumney
Blacktown
St Brides Wentlooge
Peterstone Wentlooge
THE SEVERN
MOUTH OF
Radyr
Birchgrove
Whitchurch
Rumney
Roath
Pengam
Tremorfa
Fairwater
Llandaff
St Fagans
Canton
CARDIFF (Caerdydd)
Ely
Caerau
Leckwith
Grangetown
Llandough
Michaelston-le-Pit
St Andrews Major
Cogan
Westra
Dinas Powys
Penarth
Palmerstown
Lower Penarth
Cosmeston Medieval Village
Sully
Swanbridge
Lavernock Point
Sully Island
Barry Island
Flat Holm
Steep Holm
Portishead Point
Avonmouth
Portishead
Woodhill
Sheepway
Redcliffe Bay
West Hill
North Weston
Easton-in-Gordano
Portbury
Clapton in Gordano
Weston in Gordano
Walton in Gordano
East Clevedon
Lower Failand
BRISTOL
Stone-edge Batch
Wraxall
CLEVEDON
Tickenham
Nailsea
Failand
Long Ashton
West End
East End
Kenn
Farleigh
Flax Bourton
Backwell
NORTH SOMERSET
Chelvey
West Town
Barrow Gurney
Kingston Seymour
North End
Horsecastle
Brockley
Lulsgate Bottom
Upper Town
Sand Point
Wick St Lawrence
Icelton
Yatton
Cleeve
Claverham
Felton
Sand Bay
Kewstoke
Bourton
Hewish
Worle
West Hewish
Puxton
Congresbury
Redhill
Wrington
Cowslip Green
Milton
St George's
Weston Bay
WESTON-SUPER-MARE
West Wick
Stonebridge
Lower Langford
Butcombe
West Town
Nempnett Thrubwell
Banwell
Churchill
Sandford
Rickford
Upper Langford
Burrington
Blagdon
Ubley
Uphill
Hutton
Locking
Knightcott
Oldmixon
Brean Down
Bleadon
Christon
Barton
Winscombe
Sidcot
Shipham
Rowberrow
Black Down
Compton Bishop
Charterhouse
Compton Martin
Brean
Loxton
A465
A4047
A467
A4046
A4048
A4043
A4042
A40
A449
A472
A4049
A469
A472
A466
A468
A4051
M4
A48
A4810
M48
A470
A48(M)
A4232
A4050
A4055
A4160
A4055
A403
A369
M5
A370
A38
A371
A368
PAGE 193
PAGE 200

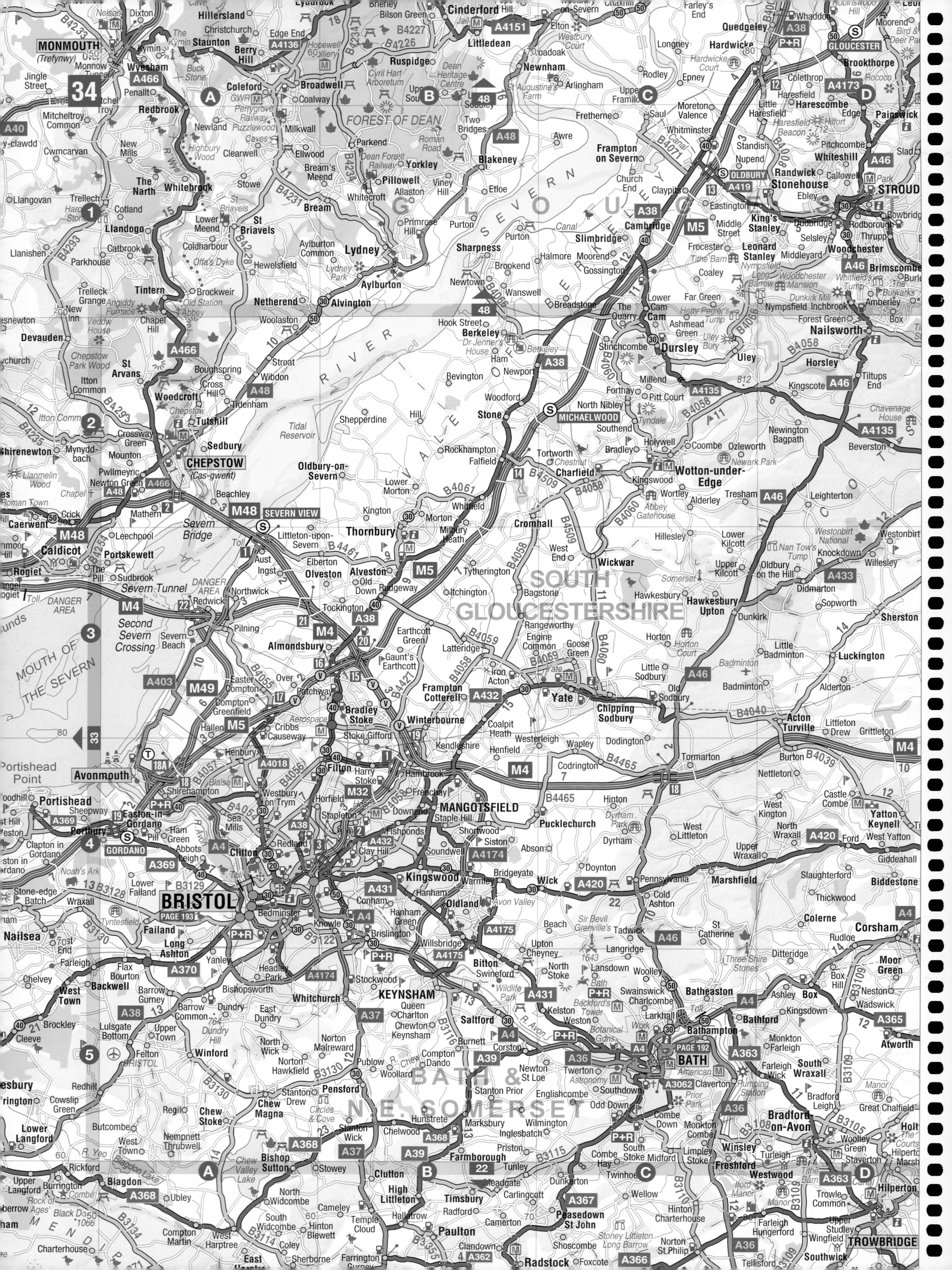

34
33
MONMOUTH
(Trefynwy)
Wyesham
Kymin
Staunton
Hillersland
Christchurch
Berry Hill
Coleford
Broadwell
Ruspidge
Cinderford
Littledean
Bilson Green
Edge End
Cyril Hart Arboretum
Dean Heritage Centre
FOREST OF DEAN
Parkend
Yorkley
Pillowell
Bream
Whitecroft
Lydney
Aylburton
Alvington
Woolaston
Netherend
St Briavels
Hewelsfield
Brockweir
Tintern
Chapel Hill
Llandogo
Trellech
Redbrook
Newland
Clearwell
Milkwall
Ellwood
Penallt
Mitcheltroy Common
Jingle Street
Cwmcarvan
Whitebrook
The North
Devauden
St Arvans
Itton Common
Woodcroft
Tidenham
Tutshill
Sedbury
CHEPSTOW
(Cas-gwent)
Mounton
Pwllmeyric
Mathern
Crick
Caerwent
Caldicot
Portskewett
Sudbrook
Rogiet
Severn Tunnel
Second Severn Crossing
MOUTH OF THE SEVERN
Severn Bridge
Beachley
SEVERN VIEW
Aust
Elberton
Olveston
Alveston
Thornbury
Littleton-upon-Severn
Oldbury-on-Severn
Kington
Morton
Tytherington
Rudgeway
Tockington
Almondsbury
Pilning
Severn Beach
Redwick
Northwick
Easter Compton
Compton Greenfield
Hallen
Cribbs Causeway
Patchway
Bradley Stoke
Stoke Gifford
Winterbourne
Frampton Cotterell
Iron Acton
Yate
Chipping Sodbury
Old Sodbury
Wickwar
Cromhall
Charfield
Wotton-under-Edge
Kingswood
Tortworth
Falfield
Stone
Berkeley
Newport
Sharpness
Purton
Slimbridge
Cambridge
Frampton on Severn
Saul
Whitminster
Moreton Valence
Fretherne
Arlingham
Newnham
Blakeney
Awre
Dursley
Cam
Uley
Stinchcombe
North Nibley
MICHAELWOOD
Nailsworth
Horsley
STROUD
Stonehouse
King's Stanley
Leonard Stanley
Woodchester
Brimscombe
Amberley
Painswick
Edge
Harescombe
Brookthorpe
Quedgeley
Hardwicke
GLOUCESTER
OLDBURY
Kingscote
Tiltups End
Beverston
Leighterton
Westonbirt
Knockdown
Hillesley
Hawkesbury Upton
Sopworth
Sherston
Luckington
Badminton
Acton Turville
Tormarton
Dodington
Codrington
Pucklechurch
Wick
Marshfield
Cold Ashton
SOUTH GLOUCESTERSHIRE
Westerleigh
Coalpit Heath
Kendleshire
Henfield
MANGOTSFIELD
Staple Hill
Downend
Frenchay
Hambrook
Filton
Horfield
Henbury
Shirehampton
Avonmouth
Portishead
Portishead Point
Easton-in-Gordano
Portbury
Pill
GORDANO
Clifton
BRISTOL
PAGE 193
Bedminster
Knowle
Brislington
Kingswood
Hanham
Oldland
Bitton
Willsbridge
Keynsham
KEYNSHAM
Saltford
Whitchurch
Long Ashton
Failand
Nailsea
Backwell
West Town
Flax Bourton
Barrow Gurney
Winford
Felton
Chew Stoke
Chew Magna
Pensford
Stanton Drew
Bishop Sutton
Blagdon
Burrington
Ubley
Compton Martin
West Harptree
Clutton
High Littleton
Timsbury
Paulton
Farmborough
Marksbury
Camerton
Peasedown St John
Radstock
BATH
PAGE 192
BATH & N.E. SOMERSET
Batheaston
Bathampton
Bathford
Box
Corsham
Colerne
Biddestone
Batheaston
Lansdown
Weston
Twerton
Newton St Loe
Combe Down
Monkton Combe
Freshford
Winsley
Bradford-on-Avon
Westwood
Hilperton
TROWBRIDGE
Southwick
Norton St Philip
Wellow
Dunkerton
Atworth
South Wraxall
Yatton Keynell
Castle Combe
Grittleton
Nettleton
M4
M5
M48
M49
M32
A38
A46
A48
A4135
A432
A4174
A420
A4
A36
A37
A39
A368
A369
A370
A403
A466
A4151
A4136
A4173
A419
A363
A365
A367
A366
A362
A3062
A4018
A4175
A431
A433

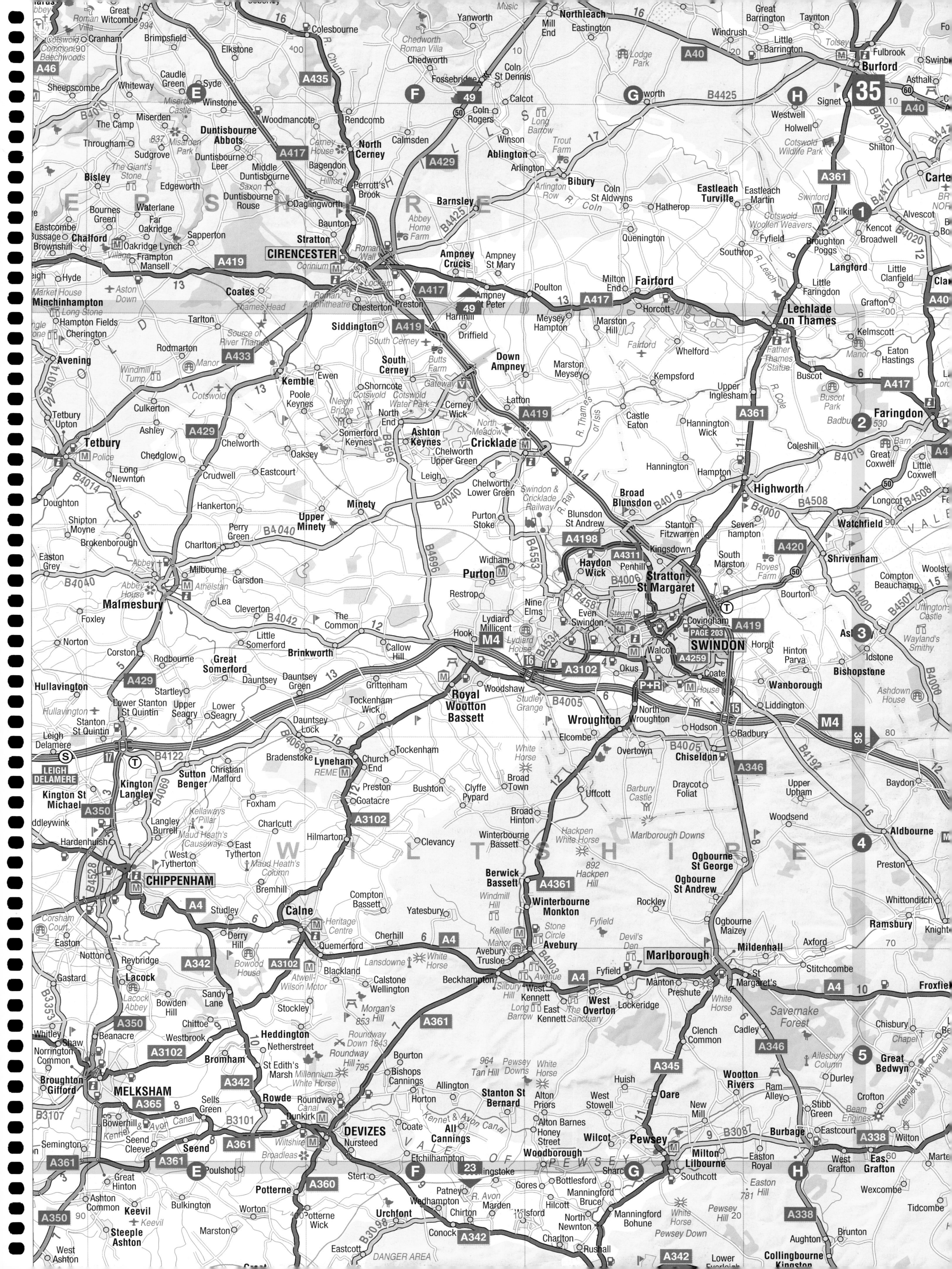

Great Witcombe
Cranham
Brimpsfield
Elkstone
Colesbourne
Yanworth
Chedworth Roman Villa
Chedworth
Northleach
Mill End
Eastington
Great Barrington
Taynton
Windrush
Little Barrington
Fulbrook
Burford
Asthall
Signet
35
A40
A46
A435
Caudle Green
Syde
Sheepscombe
Whiteway
Winstone
Miserden
The Camp
Duntisbourne Abbots
Woodmancote
Rendcomb
North Cerney
Calmsden
Fossebridge
Coln St Dennis
Calcot
Coln Rogers
Winson
Long Barrow
Ablington
Arlington
Bibury
Trout Farm
Westwell
Holwell
Cotswold Wildlife Park
Shilton
B4425
B4020
Throughamn
Sudgrove
Duntisbourne Leer
Middle Duntisbourne
Bagendon
A417
A429
Bisley
Edgeworth
Duntisbourne Rouse
Daglingworth
Perrott's Brook
Barnsley
Coln St Aldwyns
Hatherop
Eastleach Turville
Eastleach Martin
A361
Carterton
Filkins
Kencot
Broadwell
Alvescot
Bournes Green
Waterlane
Far Oakridge
Eastcombe
Bussage
Chalford
Brownshill
Oakridge Lynch
Sapperton
Frampton Mansell
Baunton
Stratton
CIRENCESTER
Abbey Home Farm
Ampney Crucis
Ampney St Mary
Quenington
Southrop
Cotswold Woollen Weavers
Fyfield
Broughton Poggs
Langford
Little Clanfield
A419
Hyde
Aston Down
Minchinhampton
Coates
Poulton
Milton End
Fairford
Little Faringdon
Grafton
Lechlade on Thames
Ampney St Peter
Chesterton
Preston
Harnhill
Driffield
Meysey Hampton
Marston Hill
Horcott
Kelmscott
Hampton Fields
Cherington
Tarlton
Siddington
Rodmarton
A433
South Cerney
Whelford
Down Ampney
Marston Meysey
Kempsford
Father Thames Statue
Eaton Hastings
Buscot
Buscot Park
Avening
Kemble
Ewen
Shorncote
Poole Keynes
Cotswold Water Park
North End
Cerney Wick
Latton
Castle Eaton
Upper Inglesham
Hannington Wick
Faringdon
Tetbury Upton
Culkerton
Ashley
Somerford Keynes
Ashton Keynes
Cricklade
Tetbury
Chelworth
Chedglow
Oaksey
Chelworth Upper Green
Long Newnton
Crudwell
Eastcourt
Leigh
Chelworth Lower Green
Hannington
Hampton
Coleshill
Great Coxwell
Little Coxwell
Highworth
Doughton
Hankerton
Minety
Swindon & Cricklade Railway
Broad Blunsdon
Longcot
Shipton Moyne
Brokenborough
Upper Minety
Purton Stoke
Blunsdon St Andrew
Stanton Fitzwarren
Sevenhampton
Watchfield
Perry Green
Charlton
Easton Grey
Widham
Haydon Wick
Penhill
Kingsdown
Stratton St Margaret
South Marston
Roves Farm
Shrivenham
Milbourne
Garsdon
Purton
Compton Beauchamp
Malmesbury
Lea
Restrop
Nine Elms
Bourton
Foxley
Cleverton
The Common
Lydiard Millicent
Even Swindon
Covingham
Uffington Castle
Norton
Little Somerford
Hook
M4
SWINDON
Horpit
Ashbury
Wayland's Smithy
Corston
Brinkworth
Callow Hill
Walcot
Hinton Parva
Idstone
Rodbourne
Great Somerford
Dauntsey
Dauntsey Green
Grittenham
Royal Wootton Bassett
Woodshaw
Okus
Coate
Bishopstone
Hullavington
Startley
Wanborough
Ashdown House
Lower Stanton St Quintin
Upper Seagry
Lower Seagry
Tockenham Wick
Studley Grange
Wroughton
North Wroughton
Liddington
Stanton St Quintin
Dauntsey Lock
Elcombe
Hodson
Badbury
Leigh Delamere
Bradenstoke
Lyneham
Church End
Tockenham
Overtown
Chiseldon
LEIGH DELAMERE
Sutton Benger
Christian Malford
Preston
Goatacre
Bushton
Clyffe Pypard
Broad Town
Uffcott
Draycot Foliat
Upper Upham
Baydon
Kington St Michael
Kington Langley
Foxham
Broad Hinton
Barbury Castle
Woodsend
Langley Burrell
Charlcutt
Hilmarton
A3102
Winterbourne Bassett
Marlborough Downs
Aldbourne
Hardenhuish
West Tytherton
East Tytherton
Clevancy
Hackpen White Horse
Ogbourne St George
Ogbourne St Andrew
W I L T S H I R E
CHIPPENHAM
Bremhill
Compton Bassett
Berwick Bassett
Winterbourne Monkton
Hackpen Hill
Preston
Studley
Calne
Yatesbury
Windmill Hill
Rockley
Whittonditch
Corsham Court
Derry Hill
Quemerford
Cherhill
Avebury
Fyfield
Ogbourne Maizey
Ramsbury
Easton
Notton
Reybridge
Bowood House
Blackland
Calstone Wellington
Lansdowne White Horse
Avebury Trusloe
Beckhampton
Silbury Hill
Marlborough
Mildenhall
Axford
Gastard
Lacock
Lacock Abbey
Atwell-Wilson Motor
Sandy Lane
West Kennett
East Kennett
West Overton
Manton
Preshute
Lockeridge
St Margaret's
Stitchcombe
Froxfield
Bowden Hill
Stockley
Morgan's Hill
The Sanctuary
Savernake Forest
Chittoe
Westbrook
Beanacre
Whitley
Shaw
Norrington Common
Heddington
Netherstreet
Roundway Down 1643
Roundway Hill
Bourton
Clench Common
Cadley
Chisbury
Great Bedwyn
Bromham
St Edith's Marsh
Bishops Cannings
Tan Hill
Pewsey Downs
Huish
Wootton Rivers
Broughton Gifford
MELKSHAM
Sells Green
Rowde
Roundway
Allington
Horton
Stanton St Bernard
Alton Priors
West Stowell
Oare
New Mill
Ram Alley
Crofton
Bowerhill
Seend Cleeve
Dunkirk
DEVIZES
Coate
Alton Barnes
Honey Street
Wilcot
Pewsey
Burbage
Stibb Green
Semington
Seend
Nursteed
All Cannings
Woodborough
Milton Lilbourne
Easton Royal
Eastcourt
Wilton
West Grafton
East Grafton
Poulshot
Etchilhampton
Great Hinton
Potterne
Stert
Patney
Gores
Bottlesford
Manningford Bruce
Southcott
Easton Hill
Wexcombe
Ashton Common
Keevil
Bulkington
Worton
Potterne Wick
Urchfont
Wedhampton
Chirton
Marden
Wilsford
Hilcott
North Newnton
Manningford Bohune
Pewsey Down
Pewsey Hill
Tidcombe
Steeple Ashton
Marston
Conock
Charlton
Rushall
Brunton
Aughton
West Ashton
Eastcott
DANGER AREA
Lower Everleigh
Collingbourne Kingston
A342
A345
A346
A338
A350
A360
A361
A365
A4
A3102
A4361
B4192

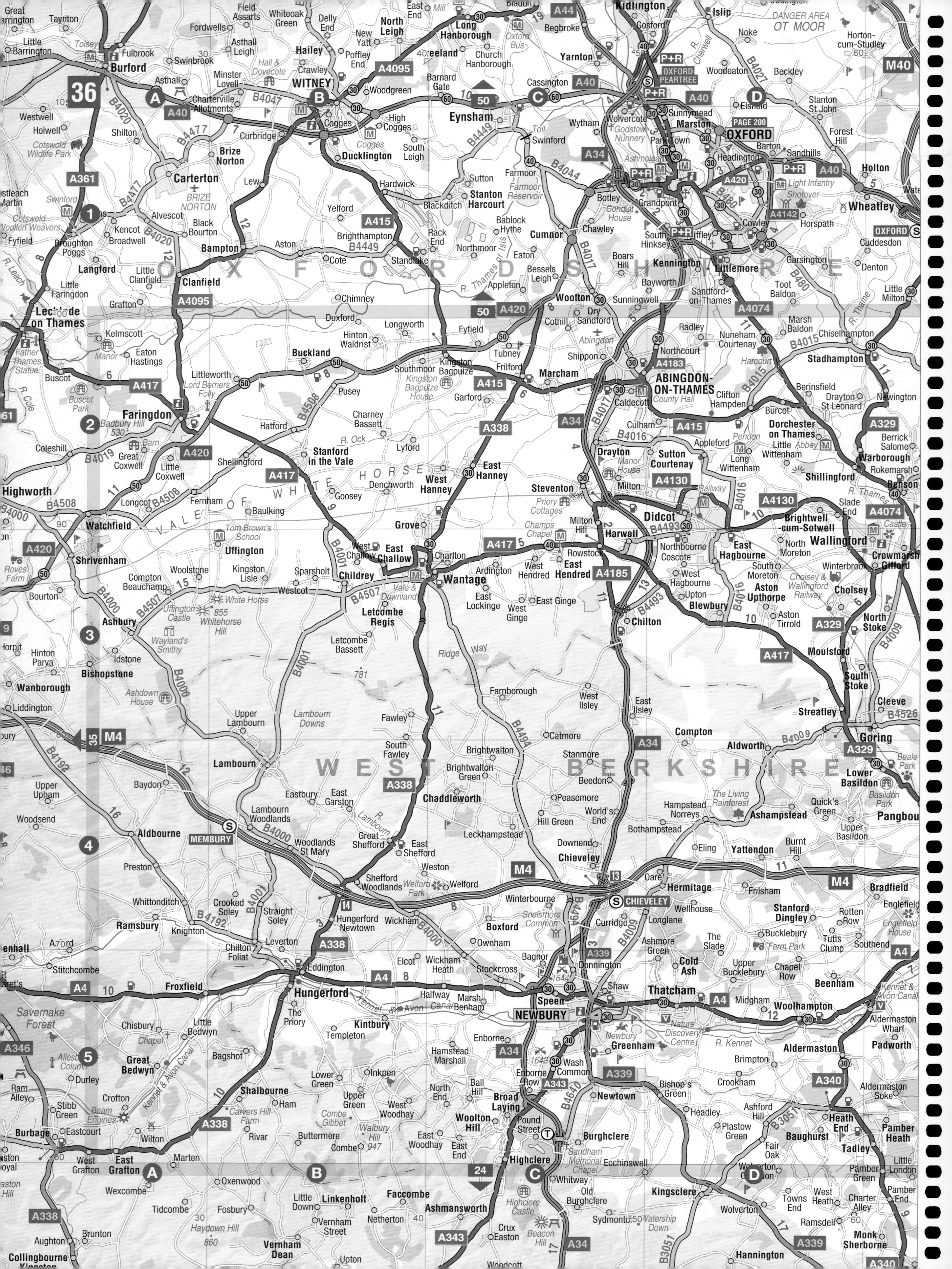

36
Burford
Witney
Eynsham
Kidlington
Islip
OT MOOR
DANGER AREA
Yarnton
Begbroke
Long Hanborough
North Leigh
Hailey
Crawley
Carterton
Brize Norton
BRIZE NORTON
Ducklington
Cogges
Curbridge
Minster Lovell
Asthall
Asthall Leigh
Fulbrook
Swinbrook
Taynton
Great Barrington
Little Barrington
Westwell
Holwell
Shilton
Cotswold Wildlife Park
Charterville Allotments
High Cogges
South Leigh
Woodgreen
Church Hanborough
Freeland
Barnard Gate
Cassington
Wytham
Swinford
Wolvercote
Godstow Nunnery
Marston
Sunnymead
OXFORD
PAGE 200
OXFORD PEARTREE
Elsfield
Beckley
Woodeaton
Noke
Horton-cum-Studley
Stanton St John
Forest Hill
Headington
Barton
Sandhills
Holton
Wheatley
Light Infantry
Shotover
Horspath
Cowley
Iffley
Garsington
Cuddesdon
Denton
Littlemore
Kennington
Sandford-on-Thames
South Hinksey
Grandpont
Botley
Farmoor
Farmoor Reservoir
Cumnor
Chawley
Boars Hill
Bayworth
Wootton
Sunningwell
Bessels Leigh
Appleton
Eaton
Eynsham
Sutton
Stanton Harcourt
Blackditch
Bablock Hythe
Northmoor
Rack End
Standlake
Hardwick
Yelford
Brighthampton
Aston
Cote
Bampton
Black Bourton
Alvescot
Kencot
Broadwell
Broughton Poggs
Filkins
Langford
Little Clanfield
Clanfield
Little Faringdon
Grafton
Lechlade on Thames
Kelmscott
Eaton Hastings
Buscot
Buscot Park
Faringdon
Littleworth
Lord Berners Folly
Chimney
Duxford
Hinton Waldrist
Longworth
Buckland
Fyfield
Tubney
Kingston Bagpuize
Southmoor
Kingston Bagpuize House
Frilford
Marcham
Garford
Pusey
Charney Bassett
Hatford
Stanford in the Vale
Lyford
Shellingford
Great Coxwell
Little Coxwell
Coleshill
Highworth
Longcot
Fernham
Baulking
Goosey
Denchworth
West Hanney
East Hanney
Grove
Wantage
Charlton
Ardington
West Hendred
East Hendred
Rowstock
Milton Hill
Steventon
Harwell
Milton
Didcot
Drayton
Sutton Courtenay
Culham
Appleford
Long Wittenham
Little Wittenham
ABINGDON-ON-THAMES
Caldecott
Northcourt
Radley
Nuneham Courtenay
Clifton Hampden
Burcot
Dorchester on Thames
Berinsfield
Drayton St Leonard
Newington
Stadhampton
Chiselhampton
Marsh Baldon
Toot Baldon
Little Milton
Berrick Salome
Warborough
Rokemarsh
Shillingford
Benson
Brightwell-cum-Sotwell
Wallingford
Crowmarsh Gifford
North Moreton
South Moreton
Cholsey
Aston Upthorpe
Aston Tirrold
Blewbury
Upton
West Hagbourne
East Hagbourne
Northbourne
Coscote
Chilton
North Stoke
Moulsford
South Stoke
Cleeve
Streatley
Goring
Compton
Aldworth
East Ilsley
West Ilsley
Farnborough
Catmore
Brightwalton
Brightwalton Green
Stanmore
Beedon
Peasemore
World's End
Hill Green
Leckhampstead
Chaddleworth
South Fawley
Fawley
Letcombe Regis
Letcombe Bassett
Childrey
Sparsholt
West Challow
East Challow
Kingston Lisle
Uffington
Tom Brown's School
Woolstone
Compton Beauchamp
Uffington Castle
White Horse
Whitehorse Hill
Wayland's Smithy
Ashbury
Bourton
Shrivenham
Watchfield
Idstone
Bishopstone
Hinton Parva
Wanborough
Liddington
Ashdown House
Upper Lambourn
Lambourn Downs
Lambourn
Eastbury
East Garston
Lambourn Woodlands
Woodlands St Mary
Great Shefford
East Shefford
Baydon
Upper Upham
Aldbourne
Woodsend
MEMBURY
Preston
Whittonditch
Ramsbury
Crooked Soley
Straight Soley
Knighton
Chilton Foliat
Leverton
Hungerford Newtown
Shefford Woodlands
Weston
Welford
Welford Park
Wickham
Boxford
Winterbourne
Snelsmore Common
Ownham
Chieveley
Downend
CHIEVELEY
Curridge
Longlane
Hermitage
Frilsham
Yattendon
Burnt Hill
Eling
Hampstead Norreys
Bothampstead
Ashampstead
Quick's Green
Upper Basildon
Lower Basildon
Basildon Park
Pangbourne
Bradfield
Stanford Dingley
Bucklebury
Rotten Row
Englefield
Tutts Clump
Southend
Chapel Row
Upper Bucklebury
Cold Ash
Ashmore Green
The Slade
Beenham
Woolhampton
Midgham
Thatcham
Donnington
Bagnor
Shaw
Speen
NEWBURY
Stockcross
Wickham Heath
Elcot
Eddington
Hungerford
Froxfield
Stitchcombe
The Priory
Halfway
Marsh Benham
Kintbury
Templeton
Enborne
Hamstead Marshall
Greenham
Wash Common
Enborne Row
Newtown
Crookham
Brimpton
Aldermaston
Aldermaston Wharf
Padworth
Aldermaston Soke
Heath End
Baughurst
Tadley
Pamber Heath
Pamber Green
Little London
Ashford Hill
Headley
Plastow Green
Fair Oak
Bishop's Green
Burghclere
Sandham Memorial Chapel
Ecchinswell
Old Burghclere
Highclere
Highclere Castle
Whitway
Pound Street
Woolton Hill
Broad Laying
North End
Ball Hill
East End
East Woodhay
West Woodhay
Inkpen
Lower Green
Upper Green
Combe Gibbet
Walbury Hill
Buttermere
Combe
Rivar
Ham
Shalbourne
Carvers Hill Farm
Bagshot
Little Bedwyn
Great Bedwyn
Chisbury
Savernake Forest
Durley
Crofton
Crofton Beam Engines
Wilton
Marten
East Grafton
West Grafton
Burbage
Eastcourt
Stibb Green
Ram Alley
Wexcombe
Oxenwood
Tidcombe
Fosbury
Haydown Hill
Vernham Dean
Little Down
Linkenholt
Vernham Street
Faccombe
Netherton
Ashmansworth
Crux Easton
Beacon Hill
Sydmonton
Watership Down
Kingsclere
Wolverton
Hannington
Ramsdell
Monk Sherborne
Charter Alley
West Heath
Towns End
Collingbourne Kingston
Aughton
Brunton
VALE OF WHITE HORSE
OXFORDSHIRE
WEST BERKSHIRE
M4
M40
A40
A34
A338
A417
A420
A415
A4095
A361
A4074
A4130
A4185
A329
A4
A339
A343
A340
A346

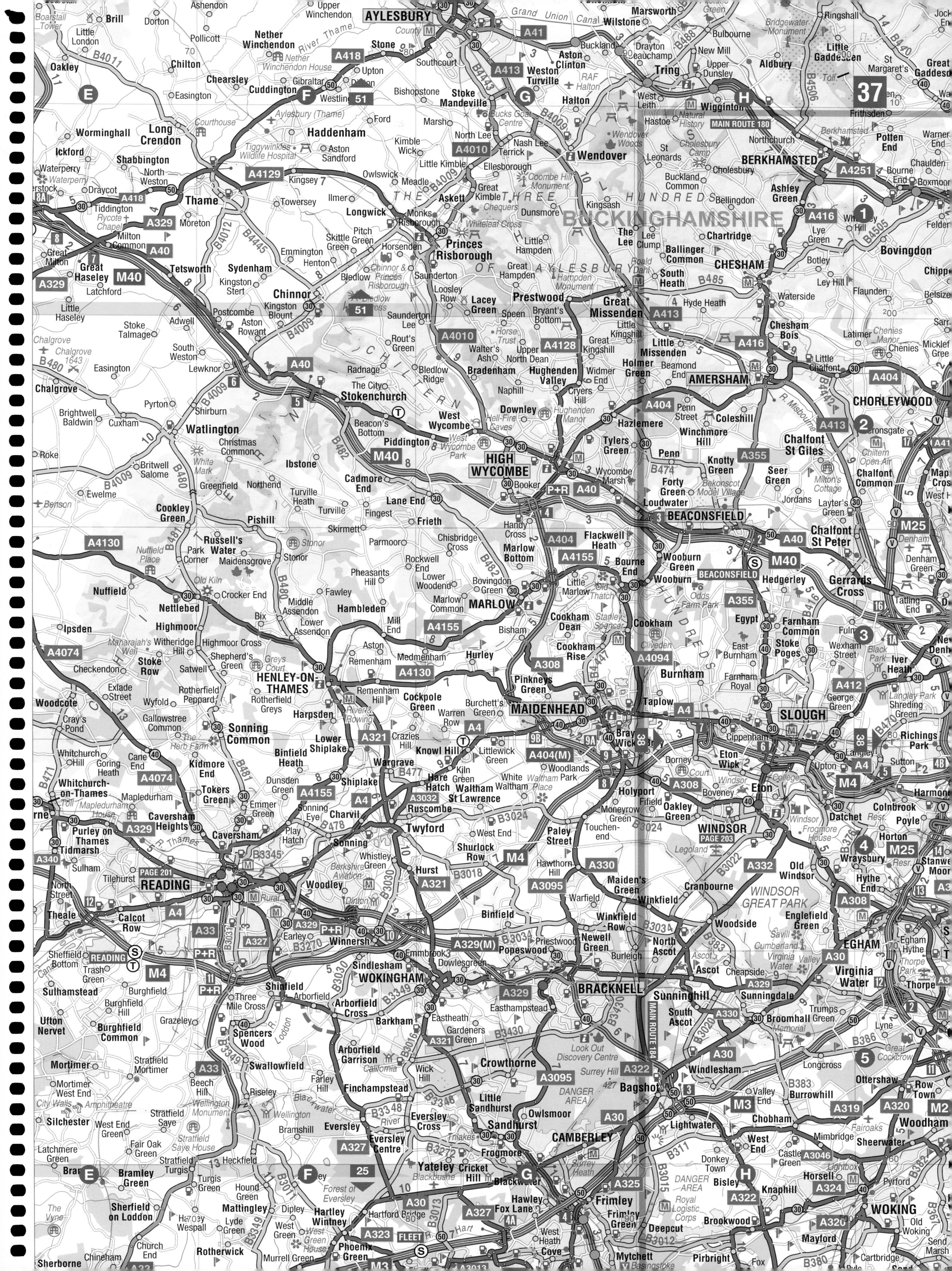

37
38
AYLESBURY
Stone
Haddenham
Thame
Long Crendon
Wendover
Tring
BERKHAMSTED
Princes Risborough
Chinnor
BUCKINGHAMSHIRE
CHESHAM
Great Missenden
Prestwood
AMERSHAM
CHORLEYWOOD
Chalfont St Giles
Chalfont St Peter
BEACONSFIELD
Gerrards Cross
HIGH WYCOMBE
Stokenchurch
Watlington
MARLOW
HENLEY-ON-THAMES
MAIDENHEAD
SLOUGH
Burnham
Cookham
WINDSOR
Eton
EGHAM
Virginia Water
READING
Caversham
Sonning Common
Twyford
WOKINGHAM
BRACKNELL
Ascot
Sunninghill
Crowthorne
Sandhurst
CAMBERLEY
Bagshot
Frimley
Yateley
WOKING
Chobham
Woodley
Windlesham
Thames
Grand Union Canal
M40
M4
M25
M3
A41
A40
A4010
A4155
A4130
A404(M)
A329(M)
A30
A322
MAIN ROUTE 180
MAIN ROUTE 184

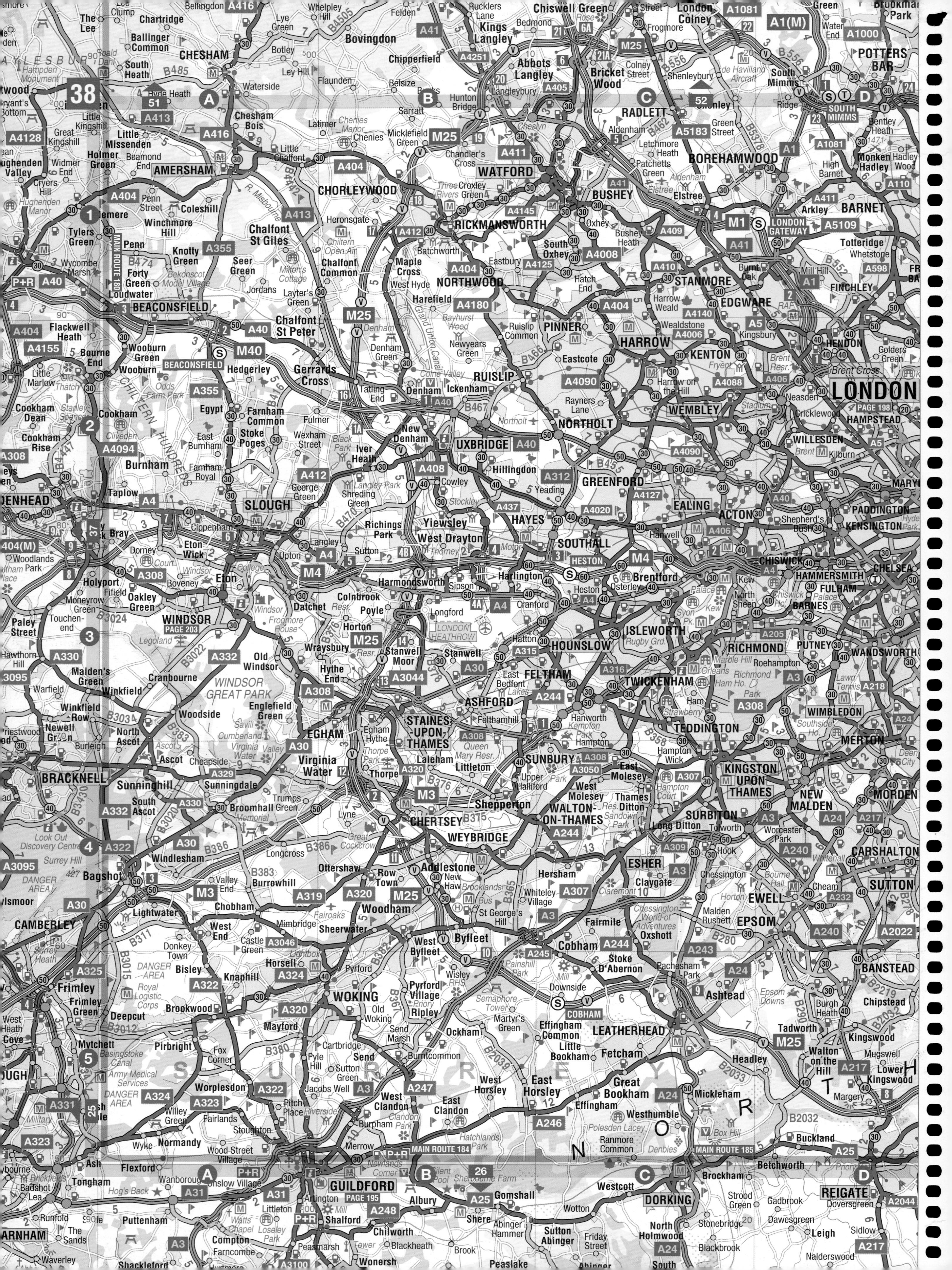

38
CHESHAM
Chartridge
Bovingdon
Chipperfield
Kings Langley
Abbots Langley
Chiswell Green
London Colney
POTTERS BAR
South Mimms
RADLETT
Shenley
BOREHAMWOOD
Elstree
WATFORD
BUSHEY
RICKMANSWORTH
CHORLEYWOOD
AMERSHAM
Chalfont St Giles
Chalfont St Peter
BEACONSFIELD
Gerrards Cross
NORTHWOOD
PINNER
HARROW
STANMORE
EDGWARE
BARNET
FINCHLEY
HENDON
LONDON
PAGE 198
WEMBLEY
RUISLIP
Denham
UXBRIDGE
NORTHOLT
GREENFORD
EALING
ACTON
PADDINGTON
KENSINGTON
HAMPSTEAD
WILLESDEN
SLOUGH
HAYES
SOUTHALL
Yiewsley
West Drayton
Iver Heath
Stoke Poges
Farnham Common
Burnham
Taplow
Cookham
Bourne End
Wooburn Green
Eton
WINDSOR
PAGE 203
Datchet
Colnbrook
Harmondsworth
Harlington
LONDON HEATHROW
HOUNSLOW
ISLEWORTH
Brentford
CHISWICK
HAMMERSMITH
FULHAM
CHELSEA
BARNES
PUTNEY
WANDSWORTH
RICHMOND
TWICKENHAM
FELTHAM
ASHFORD
STAINES-UPON-THAMES
EGHAM
Virginia Water
WINDSOR GREAT PARK
Old Windsor
Wraysbury
Sunninghill
Sunningdale
Ascot
BRACKNELL
Bagshot
CAMBERLEY
Frimley
Lightwater
Windlesham
Chobham
CHERTSEY
WEYBRIDGE
Addlestone
SUNBURY
Shepperton
WALTON-ON-THAMES
TEDDINGTON
KINGSTON UPON THAMES
WIMBLEDON
MERTON
MORDEN
NEW MALDEN
SURBITON
ESHER
EWELL
EPSOM
SUTTON
CARSHALTON
BANSTEAD
Cobham
Oxshott
LEATHERHEAD
Ashtead
WOKING
Byfleet
Ripley
Send
Knaphill
Bisley
Pirbright
Worplesdon
Normandy
GUILDFORD
PAGE 195
Shalford
Chilworth
Gomshall
Shere
Albury
East Horsley
West Horsley
Effingham
Great Bookham
Fetcham
DORKING
Westcott
Brockham
Betchworth
REIGATE
Buckland
Mickleham
Headley
Kingswood
Tadworth
Chipstead
S U R R E Y
N O R T H
MAIN ROUTE 184
MAIN ROUTE 185
MAIN ROUTE 180
M25
M40
M4
M3
M1
A1(M)

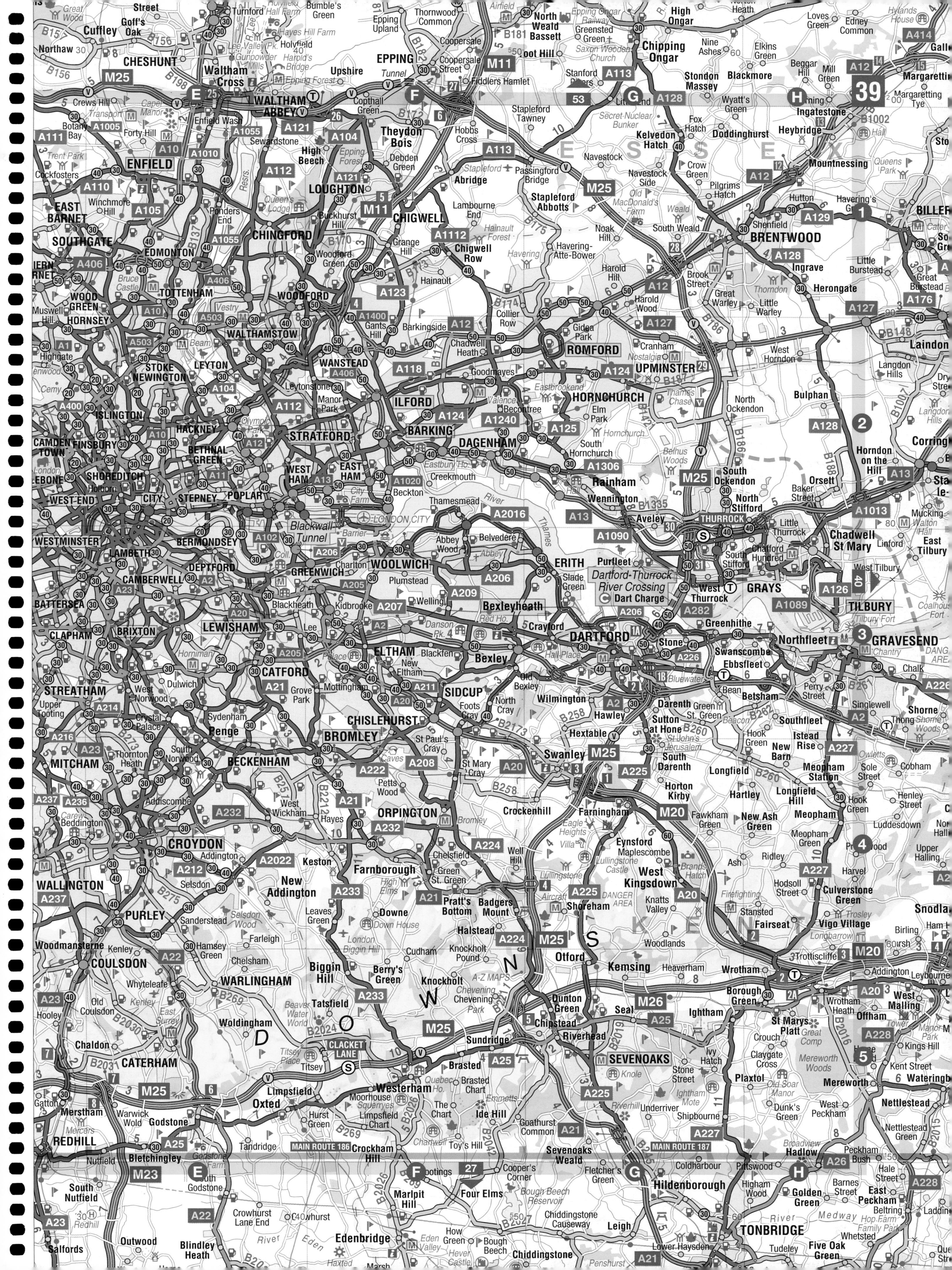

39
E
F
G
H
E S S E X
K E N T
N O R T H D O W N S
Cuffley
Goff's Oak
CHESHUNT
Waltham Cross
WALTHAM ABBEY
Upshire
EPPING
Theydon Bois
High Beech
LOUGHTON
CHIGWELL
Chigwell Row
Abridge
Stapleford Abbotts
Havering-Atte-Bower
Chipping Ongar
High Ongar
North Weald Bassett
Kelvedon Hatch
Navestock
Doddinghurst
Ingatestone
Mountnessing
BRENTWOOD
Ingrave
Herongate
South Weald
Harold Wood
ROMFORD
UPMINSTER
HORNCHURCH
Rainham
DAGENHAM
BARKING
ILFORD
WANSTEAD
WOODFORD
CHINGFORD
WALTHAMSTOW
LEYTON
STRATFORD
ENFIELD
EDMONTON
TOTTENHAM
SOUTHGATE
EAST BARNET
WOOD GREEN
HORNSEY
STOKE NEWINGTON
ISLINGTON
HACKNEY
CAMDEN TOWN
FINSBURY
SHOREDITCH
BETHNAL GREEN
CITY
STEPNEY
POPLAR
WEST HAM
EAST HAM
WEST END
WESTMINSTER
BERMONDSEY
LAMBETH
CAMBERWELL
DEPTFORD
GREENWICH
WOOLWICH
Blackwall Tunnel
LONDON CITY
BATTERSEA
CLAPHAM
BRIXTON
LEWISHAM
CATFORD
ELTHAM
SIDCUP
Bexleyheath
Bexley
Crayford
ERITH
DARTFORD
Dartford-Thurrock River Crossing
Dart Charge
Purfleet
West Thurrock
GRAYS
Chadwell St Mary
TILBURY
Northfleet
GRAVESEND
Swanscombe
Ebbsfleet
Greenhithe
Stone
Bluewater
Betsham
Southfleet
Istead Rise
Longfield
Meopham
Shorne
Cobham
Swanley
Hextable
Farningham
Eynsford
West Kingsdown
Shoreham
Otford
Kemsing
Wrotham
SEVENOAKS
Sevenoaks Weald
Riverhead
Chipstead
Seal
Ightham
Borough Green
West Malling
Hildenborough
TONBRIDGE
Hadlow
Plaxtol
Mereworth
STREATHAM
MITCHAM
CROYDON
WALLINGTON
PURLEY
COULSDON
CATERHAM
WARLINGHAM
REDHILL
Merstham
Godstone
Oxted
Limpsfield
Westerham
Biggin Hill
Tatsfield
Edenbridge
Penge
BECKENHAM
BROMLEY
CHISLEHURST
ORPINGTON
New Addington
Keston
Farnborough
Downe
Halstead
Knockholt
Brasted
Sundridge
Ide Hill
Crockham Hill
MAIN ROUTE 186
MAIN ROUTE 187
CLACKET LANE
THURROCK
M25
M11
M20
M26
M23
A12
A13
A127
A128
A2
A20
A21
A25
A22
A23
Horndon on the Hill
Orsett
Laindon
Billericay
Mucking
East Tilbury
South Ockendon
Aveley
Wennington

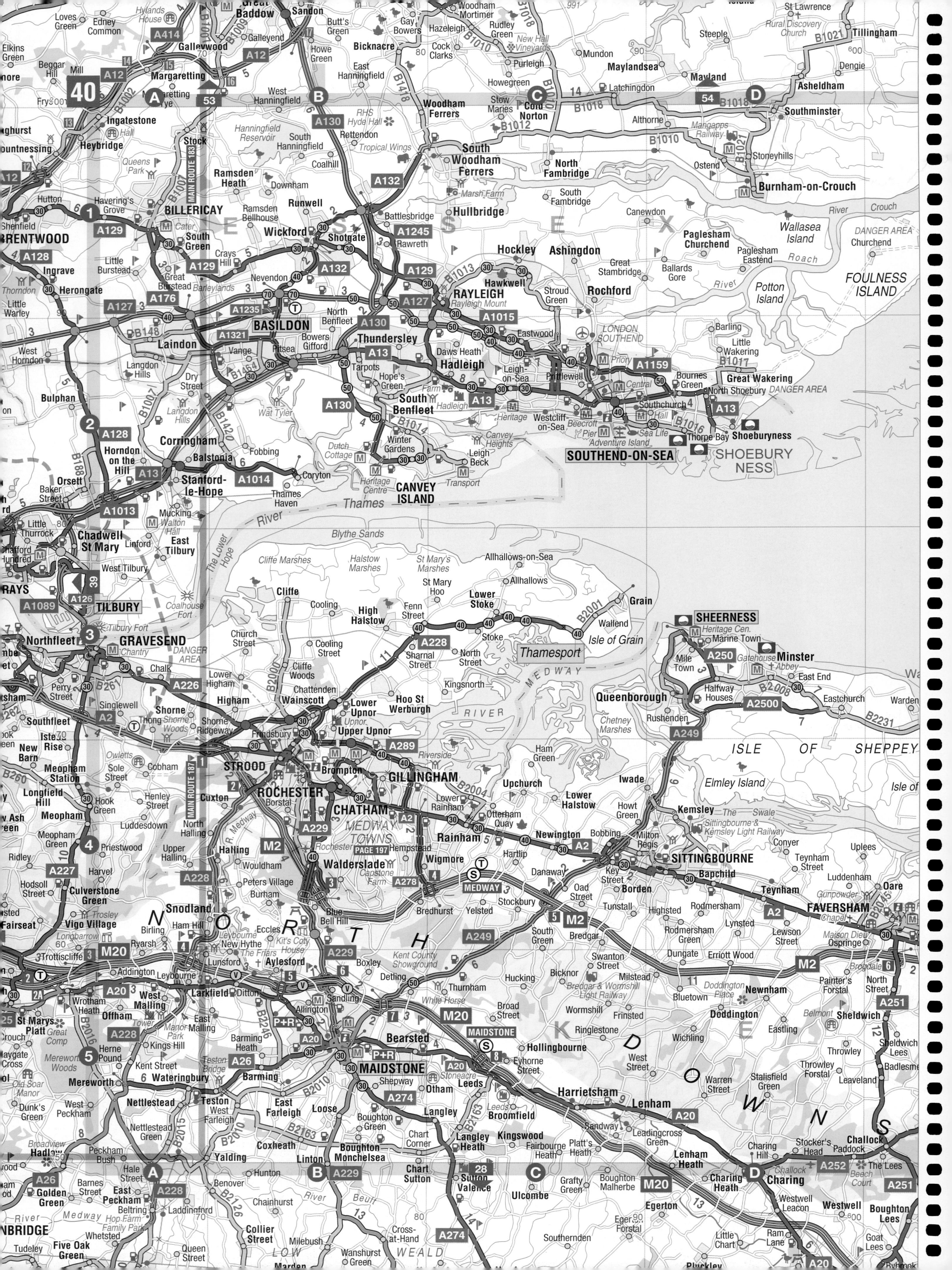
40
Loves Green
Edney Common
Elkins Green
Beggar Hill
Mill Green
Margaretting
Gallevwood
Galleyend
Great Baddow
Sandon
Butt's Green
Howe Green
Gay Bowers
Bicknacre
East Hanningfield
Hazeleigh
Woodham Mortimer
Rudley Green
New Hall Vineyards
Purleigh
Cock Clarks
Howegreen
Mundon
Maylandsea
Steeple
St Lawrence
Rural Discovery Church
Tillingham
Dengie
Mayland
Latchingdon
Asheldham
Southminster
West Hanningfield
Ingatestone
Heybridge
Stock
Hanningfield Reservoir
South Hanningfield
RHS Hyde Hall
Rettendon
Tropical Wings
Woodham Ferrers
Stow Maries
Cold Norton
Althorne
Mangapps Railway
Ostend
Stoneyhills
Burnham-on-Crouch
Queens Park
Ramsden Heath
Downham
Coalhill
South Woodham Ferrers
Marsh Farm
North Fambridge
South Fambridge
Hutton
Havering's Grove
BILLERICAY
Ramsden Bellhouse
Runwell
Battlesbridge
Hullbridge
Canewdon
River Crouch
Wallasea Island
Shenfield
BRENTWOOD
Cater
South Green
Crays Hill
Wickford
Shotgate
Rawreth
Hockley
Ashingdon
Paglesham Churchend
Paglesham Eastend
Roach
Churchend
DANGER AREA
Ingrave
Little Burstead
Great Burstead
Barleylands
Nevendon
Rayleigh
Hawkwell
Stroud Green
Rochford
Great Stambridge
Ballards Gore
Potton Island
FOULNESS ISLAND
Thorndon
Herongate
Little Warley
BASILDON
North Benfleet
Rayleigh Mount
Eastwood
LONDON SOUTHEND
Barling
Little Wakering
Laindon
Vange
Pitsea
Bowers Gifford
Thundersley
Daws Heath
Hadleigh
Leigh-on-Sea
Prittlewell
Priory
Great Wakering
Bournes Green
North Shoebury
West Horndon
Langdon Hills
Dry Street
Tarpots
Hope's Green
South Benfleet
Southchurch
Central
Thorpe Bay
Shoeburyness
Bulphan
Wat Tyler
Heritage
Westcliff-on-Sea
Beecroft
Pier
Adventure Island
Sea Life
Canvey Heights
Leigh Beck
SOUTHEND-ON-SEA
SHOEBURY NESS
Horndon on the Hill
Corringham
Fobbing
Dutch Cottage
Winter Gardens
Balstonia
Orsett
Stanford-le-Hope
Coryton
Heritage Centre
CANVEY ISLAND
Transport
Baker Street
Thames Haven
River Thames
Mucking
Walton Hall
Little Thurrock
Chadwell St Mary
Linford
East Tilbury
Blythe Sands
The Lower Hope
Cliffe Marshes
Halstow Marshes
St Mary's Marshes
Allhallows-on-Sea
Allhallows
West Tilbury
Chafford Hundred
GRAYS
TILBURY
Coalhouse Fort
Tilbury Fort
Cliffe
Cooling
High Halstow
Fenn Street
St Mary Hoo
Lower Stoke
Grain
Wallend
Isle of Grain
SHEERNESS
Heritage Cen.
Marine Town
Northfleet
GRAVESEND
Chantry
Church Street
Cooling Street
Stoke
Thamesport
Mile Town
Minster
Gatehouse
Abbey
East End
Chalk
Lower Higham
Cliffe Woods
Sharnal Street
North Street
Perry Street
Higham
Chattenden
Kingsnorth
MEDWAY
Halfway Houses
Eastchurch
Warden
Singlewell
Shorne
Wainscott
Hoo St Werburgh
Queenborough
Southfleet
Thong
Shorne Woods
Shorne Ridgeway
Lower Upnor
Upnor
Upper Upnor
RIVER
Chetney Marshes
Rushenden
Istead Rise
Frindsbury
Ham Green
ISLE OF SHEPPEY
New Barn
Owletts
Cobham
Meopham Station
Sole Street
STROOD
Riverside
Brompton
GILLINGHAM
Iwade
Elmley Island
Longfield Hill
Henley Street
Cuxton
ROCHESTER
Borstal
CHATHAM
Upchurch
Lower Halstow
Lower Rainham
Otterham Quay
Howt Green
Kemsley
The Swale
Sittingbourne & Kemsley Light Railway
Meopham
Hook Green
Luddesdown
North Halling
MEDWAY TOWNS
Rainham
Newington
Bobbing
Milton Regis
Conyer
Uplees
Meopham Green
Priestwood
Upper Halling
Halling
Rochester
PAGE 197
Hempstead
Hartlip
SITTINGBOURNE
Teynham Street
Ridley
Harvel
Wouldham
Walderslade
Capstone Farm
Wigmore
Danaway
Key Street
Bapchild
Luddenham
Oare
Hodsoll Street
Culverstone Green
Peters Village
Burham
Bredhurst
Yelsted
Oad Street
Borden
Teynham
Gunpowder
FAVERSHAM
Trosley
Snodland
Blue Bell Hill
Stockbury
Tunstall
Highsted
Rodmersham
Fairseat
Vigo Village
Ham Hill
Eccles
Rodmersham Green
Lynsted
Lewson Street
Chapel
Maison Dieu
Ospringe
Longbarrow
Birling
Leybourne
New Hythe
Kit's Coty House
South Green
Bredgar
Ryarsh
The Friars
Aylesford
Kent County Showground
Swanton Street
Dungate
Erriott Wood
Trottiscliffe
Lunsford
Addington
Boxley
Detling
Hucking
Bicknor
Milstead
Bredgar & Wormshill Light Railway
Doddington Place
Newnham
Painter's Forstal
North Street
Brogdale
West Malling
Larkfield
Ditton
Sandling
Allington
Thurnham
White Horse
Broad Street
Bluetown
Doddington
Wrotham Heath
Offham
Tower
East Malling
Manor Park
Wormshill
Frinsted
Ringlestone
Belmont
Sheldwich
St Marys Platt
Great Comp
Barming Heath
Bearsted
MAIDSTONE
Hollingbourne
Wichling
Eastling
Throwley
Kings Hill
Herne Pound
Teston Bridge
Eyhorne Street
West Street
Sheldwich Lees
Merewort Woods
Kent Street
Wateringbury
Barming
Stoneacre
Leeds
Throwley Forstal
Badlesmere
Mereworth
Shepway
Otham
Harrietsham
Warren Street
Stalisfield Green
Leaveland
Oxon Hoath
Old Soar Manor
Nettlestead
Teston
West Farleigh
East Farleigh
Loose
Langley
Leeds Castle
Broomfield
Lenham
Dunk's Green
West Peckham
Boughton Green
Chart Corner
Sandway
Leadingcross Green
NORTH DOWNS
Nettlestead Green
Coxheath
Boughton Monchelsea
Langley Heath
Kingswood
Fairbourne Heath
Platt's Heath
Lenham Heath
Charing Hill
Stocker's Head
Challock
Paddock
Broadview
Hadlow
Peckham Bush
Yalding
Hunton
Linton
Chart Sutton
Sutton Valence
Ulcombe
Grafty Green
Boughton Malherbe
Egerton
Charing Heath
Charing
Challock
The Lees
Beech Court
Hale Street
Barnes Street
East Peckham
Beltring
Hop Farm Family Park
Benover
Laddingford
Chainhurst
River Beult
Westwell Leacon
Westwell
Boughton Lees
Golden Green
Whetsted
Collier Street
Egerton Forstal
Little Chart
Ram Lane
Goat Lees
TONBRIDGE
Tudeley
Five Oak Green
Queen Street
Milebush
Wanshurst Green
Cross-at-Hand
Southernden
LOW WEALD
Marden
Pluckley
MAIN ROUTE 183
MAIN ROUTE 187
ESSEX
KENT
A12
A414
A130
A132
A129
A1245
A128
A176
A127
A1235
A1321
A13
A1015
A1159
A1014
A1013
A1089
A126
A228
A226
A2
A289
A250
A2500
A249
A229
A278
A227
M2
M20
A20
A26
A274
A252
A251
B1002
B1009
B1010
B1012
B1013
B1018
B1021
B1418
B1007
B148
B1464
B1420
B1014
B1016
B1017
B186
B2001
B2000
B2004
B2008
B2231
B2045
B260
B262
B261
B2016
B2015
B2010
B2246
B2163
B2126
B2163

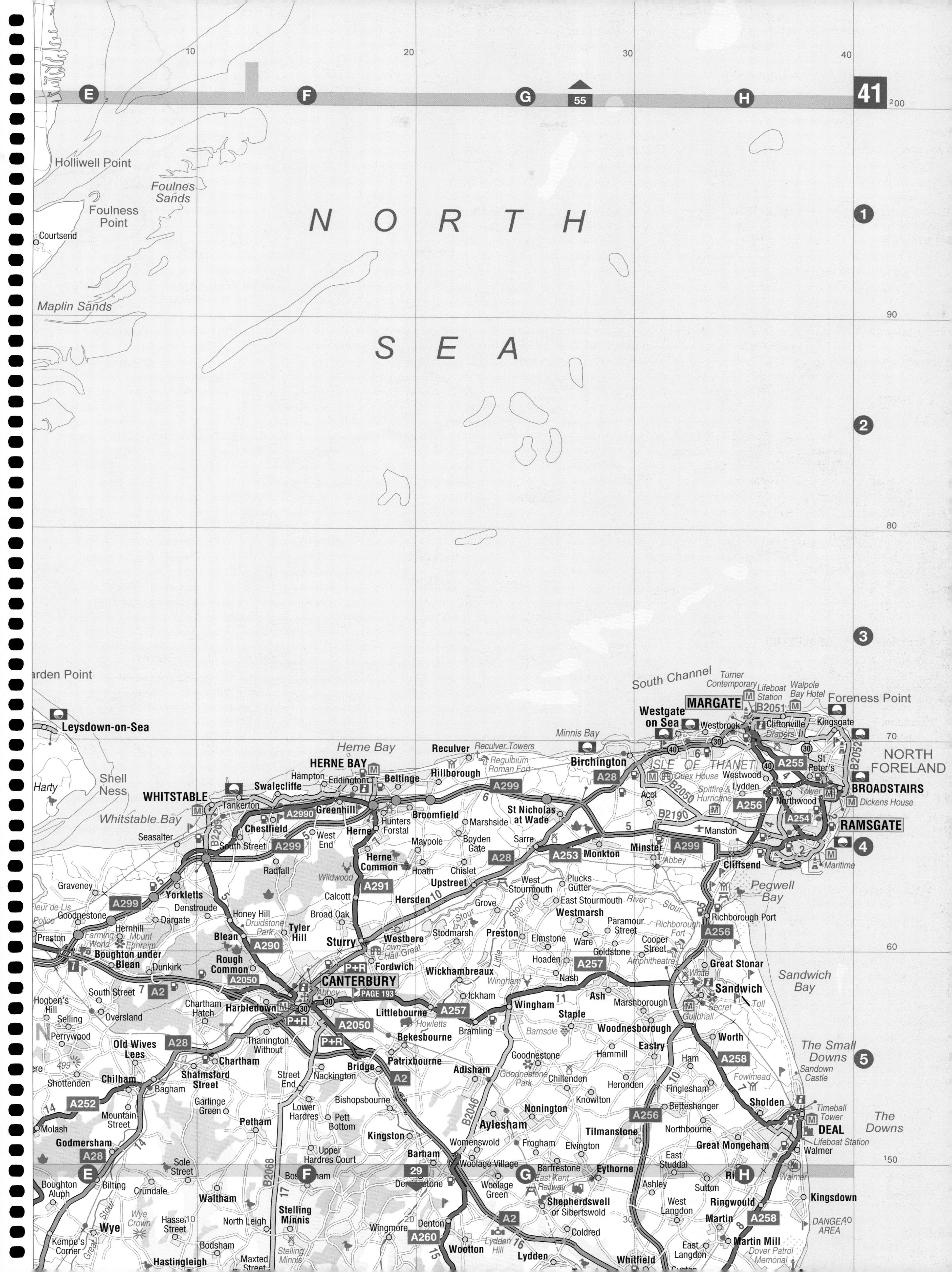

10   20   30   40

NORTH

SEA

Holliwell Point

Foulnes
Sands

Foulness
Point

Courtsend

Maplin Sands

90

80

1

2

3

arden Point

South Channel

Turner
Contemporary   Lifeboat   Walpole
Station   Bay Hotel   Foreness Point

Westgate   Quex House   Westwood
on Sea   Westbrook   Cliftonville   Kingsgate
Drapers

Leysdown-on-Sea   MARGATE   B2051

Herne Bay   Reculver Towers   Minnis Bay   70   NORTH

Shell   Reculver   Regulbium   ISLE OF THANET   St   FORELAND
Ness   HERNE BAY   Hillborough   Roman Fort   Birchington   A28   Peter's

Harty   Hampton   Eddington   Beltinge   A299   Acol   Spitfire &   BROADSTAIRS
Swalecliffe   Greenhill   Lydden   Hurricane   Northwood   Dickens House

WHITSTABLE   Tankerton   Hunters   St Nicholas   B2190   A256   RAMSGATE
Chestfield   West   Forstal   Broomfield   at Wade   Manston   4
Whitstable Bay   A2990   Herne   Marshside   5   Abbey   Maritime
Seasalter   A299   End   Boyden   Sarre   A253   Minster   A299   Cliffsend

South Street   Herne   Maypole   Gate   Monkton   Pegwell
Graveney   Radfall   Common   Hoath   Chislet   A28   Bay

Fleur de Lis   Yorkletts   Wildwood   A291   Upstreet   West   Plucks   Richborough Port
Police   Denstroude   Calcott   Stourmouth   Gutter   River   Stour   A256

Goodnestone   A299   Honey Hill   Druidstone   Broad Oak   Hersden   10   East Stourmouth   Richborough
Preston   Hernhill   Dargate   Park   Tyler   Westbere   Stodmarsh   Grove   Westmarsh   Fort   Great Stonar
Farming   Mount   Hill   Sturry   Great   Preston   Paramour   Sandwich
World   Ephraim   Blean   A290   Fordwich   Elmstone   Ware   Street   Bay
Boughton under   Rough   Town   Hoaden   Goldstone   Cooper   Secret
Blean   Dunkirk   Common   Hall   Wickhambreaux   Nash   Street   Guildhall
South Street   A2050   Ickham   Amphitheatre   A257
Hogben's   7   CANTERBURY   Wingham   Marshborough   White
Hill   A2   Harbledown   PAGE 193   Littlebourne   A257   Ash   Worth   The Small
Selling   Old Wives   A2050   Bekesbourne   Bramling   Staple   Woodnesborough   A258   Downs
Perrywood   Lees   Thanington   Patrixbourne   Adisham   Goodnestone   Hammill   Eastry   Sandown   5
499   A28   Without   Bridge   Park   Chillenden   Ham   Castle
Chartham   Street   Nackington   Heronden   Betteshanger   Fowlmead   The
Chilham   Shalmsford   End   Bishopsbourne   Knowlton   Finglesh1am   A256   Sholden   Downs
Shottenden   Street   Garlinge   Kingston   Womenswold   Northbourne   Timeball
Mountain   Green   Petham   Barham   Aylesham   Frogham   Elvington   DEAL   Tower
Molash   Street   Lower   Pett   Nonington   Great Mongeham   Lifeboat Station
Godmersham   A252   Hardres   Bottom   Tilmanstone   A256   Walmer
Bagham   Upper   Hardres Court   Barfrestone   Eythorne   East   Great   Ringwould
Boughton   Bilting   Crundale   B2068   Woolage Village   Woolage   East Kent   Studdal   A258   Kingsdown
Aluph   Waltham   Bosom   Green   Railway   West   Martin
Wye   Hassell   North Leigh   Stelling   Denton   Shepherdswell   Langdon
Wye   Street   Bodsham   Minnis   Wingmore   A2   or Sibertswold   Ashley   Sutton   Martin Mill
Kempe's   Crown   Stelling   A260   Coldred   Lydden   A258   DANGE
Corner   Maxted   Minnis   Wootton   Hill   East   AREA
Hastingleigh   Street   Lydden   Langdon   Dover Patrol
Denton   Whitfield   Memorial

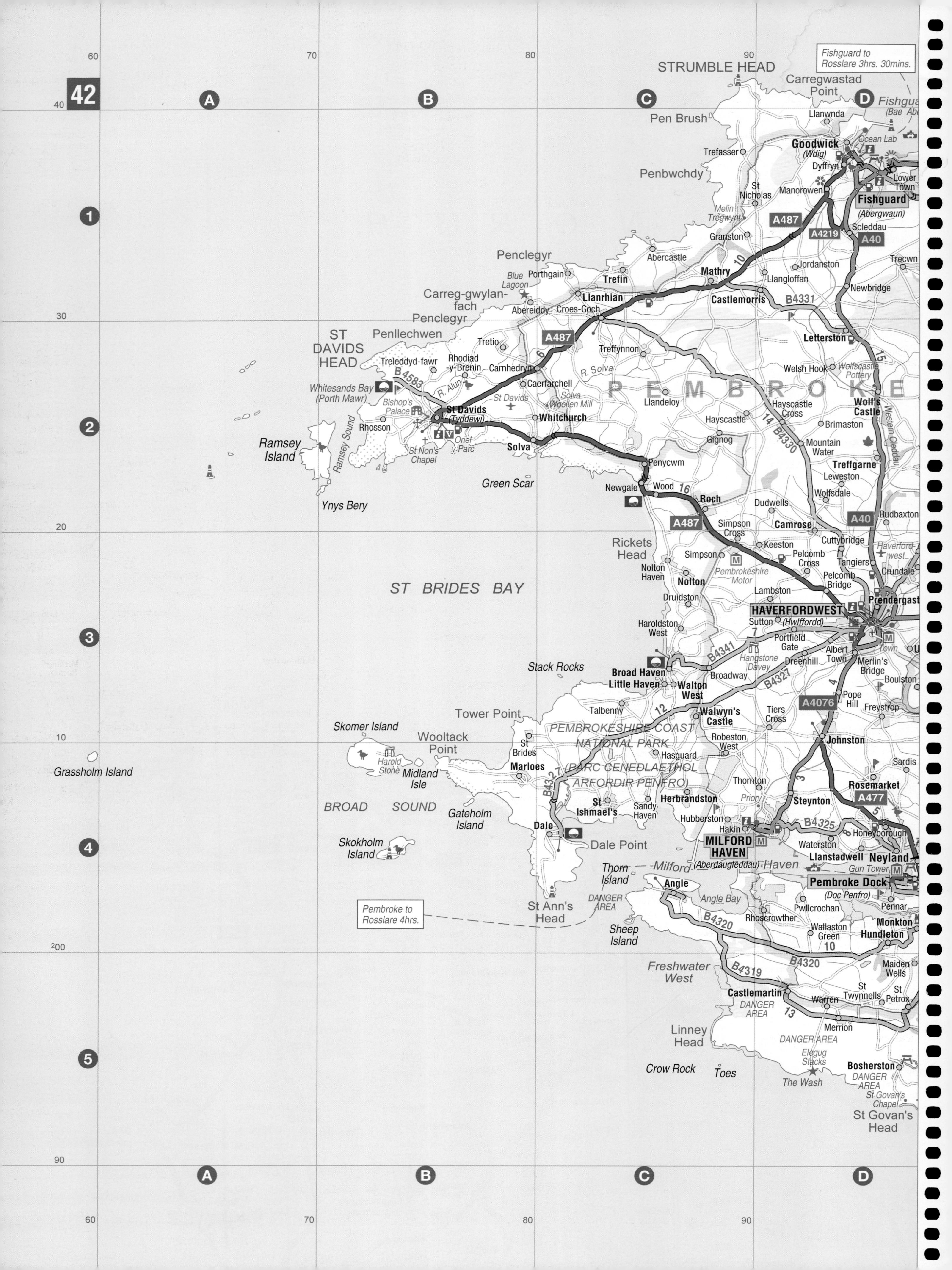
STRUMBLE HEAD
Fishguard to Rosslare 3hrs. 30mins.
Carregwastad Point
Pen Brush
Llanwnda
Goodwick (Wdig)
Dyffryn
Trefasser
Penbwchdy
St Nicholas
Manorowen
Fishguard (Abergwaun)
Lower Town
Ocean Lab
Melin Tregwynt
Granston
A487
A4219
Scleddau
A40
Penclegyr
Abercastle
Jordanston
Trecwn
Blue Lagoon
Porthgain
Trefin
Mathry
Llangloffan
Newbridge
Carreg-gwylan-fach
Llanrhian
Castlemorris
B4331
Abereiddy
Croes-Goch
Penclegyr
Letterston
ST DAVIDS HEAD
Penllechwen
Tretio
Treffynnon
Treleddyd-fawr
Rhodiad -y-Brenin
Carnhedryn
R. Solva
Welsh Hook
Wolfscastle Pottery
Caerfarchell
PEMBROKE
Whitesands Bay (Porth Mawr)
B4583
R. Alun
St Davids
Solva Woollen Mill
Llandeloy
Hayscastle Cross
Wolf's Castle
Bishop's Palace
St Davids (Tyddewi)
Whitchurch
Hayscastle
Brimaston
Rhosson
Western Cleddau
Ramsey Island
Ramsey Sound
St Non's Chapel
Oriel y Parc
Solva
Gignog
B4330
Mountain Water
Treffgarne
Penycwm
Lewston
Green Scar
Newgale
Wood
Roch
Wolfsdale
Ynys Bery
Dudwells
Rudbaxton
A487
Simpson Cross
Camrose
A40
Cuttybridge
Rickets Head
Keeston
Haverfordwest
Simpson
Pelcomb Cross
Tangiers
Nolton Haven
Nolton
Pembrokeshire Motor
Pelcomb Bridge
Crundale
ST BRIDES BAY
Lambston
Druidston
Prendergast
HAVERFORDWEST (Hwlffordd)
Sutton
Haroldston West
Portfield Gate
B4341
Hangstone Davey
Albert Town
Dreenhill
Merlin's Bridge
Stack Rocks
Broad Haven
Broadway
B4327
Boulston
Little Haven
Walton West
A4076
Pope Hill
Freystrop
Talbenny
Walwyn's Castle
Tiers Cross
Tower Point
PEMBROKESHIRE COAST NATIONAL PARK (PARC CENEDLAETHOL ARFORDIR PENFRO)
Skomer Island
Wooltack Point
St Brides
Robeston West
Johnston
Hasguard
Sardis
Grassholm Island
Harold Stone
Midland Isle
Marloes
Thornton
Rosemarket
B4327
St Ishmael's
Herbrandston
Priory
Steynton
A477
BROAD SOUND
Gateholm Island
Sandy Haven
Hubberston
B4325
Honeyborough
Dale
Hakin
MILFORD HAVEN (Aberdaugleddau)
Waterston
Skokholm Island
Dale Point
Llanstadwell
Neyland
Thorn Island
Milford Haven
Gun Tower
Angle
Pembroke Dock (Doc Penfro)
Angle Bay
DANGER AREA
Pwllcrochan
Pennar
Pembroke to Rosslare 4hrs.
St Ann's Head
Rhoscrowther
B4320
Wallaston Green
Monkton
Sheep Island
Hundleton
B4320
Maiden Wells
Freshwater West
B4319
Castlemartin
St Twynnells
St Petrox
DANGER AREA
Warren
Merrion
Linney Head
DANGER AREA
Elegug Stacks
Bosherston
Crow Rock
Toes
The Wash
DANGER AREA
St Govan's Chapel
St Govan's Head

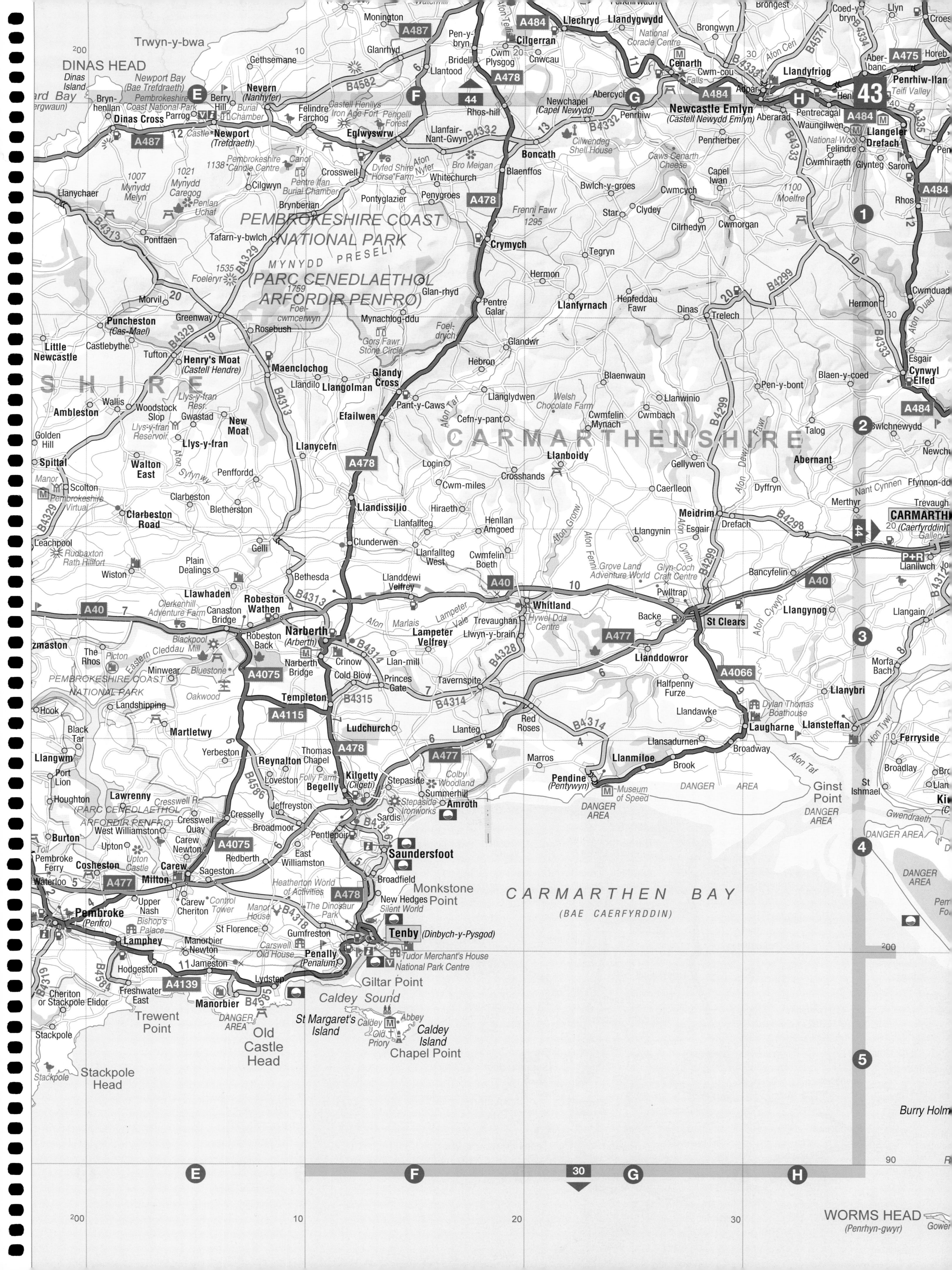DINAS HEAD
Dinas Island
Trwyn-y-bwa
Newport Bay (Bae Trefdraeth)
Pembrokeshire Coast National Park
Monington
Glanrhyd
Gethsemane
Bryn-henllan
Dinas Cross
Berry Hill
Nevern (Nanhyfer)
Burial Chamber
Parrog
Newport (Trefdraeth)
Castle
Felindre Farchog
Castell Henllys Iron Age Fort
Pengelli Forest
Eglwyswrw
Pen-y-bryn
Bridell
Llantood
Cwm Plysgog
Cilgerran
Cnwcau
Llechryd
Llandygwydd
National Coracle Centre
Brongest
Brongwyn
Coed-y-bryn
Llyn
Croes
Cenarth
Falls
Cwm-cou
Adpar
Llandyfriog
Aber-banc
Penrhiw-llan
Teifi Valley
Henllan
Newchapel (Capel Newydd)
Abercych
Penrhiw
Newcastle Emlyn (Castell Newydd Emlyn)
Aberarad
Pentrecagal
Waungilwen
National Wool Museum
Felindre
Llangeler
Drefach
Rhos-hill
Llanfair-Nant-Gwyn
Boncath
Cilwendeg Shell House
Penrherber
Caws Cenarth Cheese
Cwmhiraeth
Glynteg
Saron
Ty Canol
Pembrokeshire Candle Centre
Crosswell
Dyfed Shire Horse Farm
Afon Nyfer
Whitechurch
Bro Meigan
Blaenffos
Capel Iwan
Cwmcych
1100 Moelfre
Rhos
Llanychaer
1007 Mynydd Melyn
1021 Mynydd Caregog
1138
Penlan Uchaf
Cilgwyn
Pentre Ifan Burial Chamber
Brynberian
Pontyglazier
Penygroes
Bwlch-y-groes
Clydey
Star
Frenni Fawr 1295
Cilrhedyn
Cwmorgan
Pontfaen
Tafarn-y-bwlch
PEMBROKESHIRE COAST NATIONAL PARK
MYNYDD PRESELI
(PARC CENEDLAETHOL ARFORDIR PENFRO)
Crymych
Tegryn
1535 Foeleryr
1759 Foel-cwmcerwyn
Glan-rhyd
Hermon
Morvil
Pentre Galar
Llanfyrnach
Henfeddau Fawr
Dinas
Trelech
Cwmduad
Puncheston (Cas-Mael)
Greenway
Rosebush
Mynachlog-ddu
Foel-drych
Gors Fawr Stone Circle
Glandwr
Little Newcastle
Castlebythe
Tufton
Henry's Moat (Castell Hendre)
Maenclochog
Llandilo
Llangolman
Glandy Cross
Hebron
Blaenwaun
Esgair
Cynwyl Elfed
Blaen-y-coed
Pen-y-bont
Llanwinio
SHIRE
Wallis
Ambleston
Woodstock Slop
Llys-y-fran Resr.
Gwastad
New Moat
Llys-y-fran Reservoir
Llys-y-fran
Efailwen
Pant-y-Caws
Llanglydwen
Welsh Chocolate Farm
Cefn-y-pant
Cwmfelin Mynach
Cwmbach
Talog
Bwlchnewydd
Golden Hill
Spittal
Walton East
Afon Syfynwy
Penffordd
Llanycefn
CARMARTHENSHIRE
Llanboidy
Login
Crosshands
Cwm-miles
Gellywen
Abernant
Newchurch
Caerlleon
Dyffryn
Nant Cynnen
Ffynnon-ddrain
Merthyr
Trevaughan
CARMARTHEN (Caerfyrddin)
Manor
Scolton
Pembrokeshire Virtual
Clarbeston
Bletherston
Clarbeston Road
Llandissilio
Hiraeth
Llanfallteg
Henllan Amgoed
Afon Gronw
Afon Fenni
Llangynin
Meidrim
Esgair
Drefach
Leachpool
Rudbaxton Rath Hillfort
Gelli
Clunderwen
Llanfallteg West
Cwmfelin Boeth
Grove Land Adventure World
Glyn-Coch Craft Centre
Bancyfelin
Llanllwch
Wiston
Plain Dealings
Bethesda
Llanddewi Velfrey
Whitland
Pwlltrap
Llawhaden
Robeston Wathen
Canaston Bridge
Clerkenhill Adventure Farm
Narberth (Arberth)
Afon Marlais
Lampeter Vale
Lampeter Velfrey
Trevaughan
Hywel Dda Centre
Llwyn-y-brain
Backe
St Clears
Afon Cywyn
Llangynog
Llangain
Blackpool Mill
Robeston Back
Eastern Cleddau
Picton
The Rhos
Minwear
Bluestone
Narberth Bridge
Crinow
Cold Blow
Llan-mill
Princes Gate
Taverspite
Llanddowror
Halfpenny Furze
Llanybri
Morfa Bach
PEMBROKESHIRE COAST NATIONAL PARK
Oakwood
Landshipping
Templeton
Hook
Martletwy
Black Tar
Ludchurch
Llanteg
Red Roses
Llandawke
Dylan Thomas Boathouse
Laugharne
Llansteffan
Afon Tywi
Ferryside
Llangwm
Yerbeston
Reynalton
Thomas Chapel
Loveston
Folly Farm
Kilgetty (Cilgeti)
Begelly
Stepaside
Colby Woodland
Marros
Llanmiloe
Llansadurnen
Broadway
Brook
Afon Taf
Pendine (Pentywyn)
Museum of Speed
DANGER AREA
Ginst Point
St Ishmael
Broadlay
Port Lion
Houghton
Lawrenny
Cresswell
(PARC CENEDLAETHOL ARFORDIR PENFRO)
West Williamston
Cresswell Quay
Cresselly
Jeffreyston
Summerhill
Stepaside Ironworks
Amroth
Sardis
Broadmoor
Pentlepoir
Gwendraeth
Burton
Upton
Carew Newton
Upton Castle
East Williamston
Saundersfoot
Toll
Pembroke Ferry
Cosheston
Carew
Redberth
Sageston
Milton
Waterloo
Heatherton World of Activities
Broadfield
Monkstone Point
New Hedges
Silent World
CARMARTHEN BAY
(BAE CAERFYRDDIN)
Pembroke (Penfro)
Upper Nash
Carew Cheriton
Control Tower
Manor House
The Dinosaur Park
Bishop's Palace
St Florence
Gumfreston
Tenby (Dinbych-y-Pysgod)
Lamphey
Manorbier Newton
Carswell Old House
Penally (Penalun)
Tudor Merchant's House
National Park Centre
Hodgeston
Jameston
Lydstep
Giltar Point
Caldey Sound
Cheriton or Stackpole Elidor
Freshwater East
Manorbier
Trewent Point
Old Castle Head
St Margaret's Island
Caldey Abbey
Old Priory
Caldey Island
Chapel Point
Stackpole
Stackpole Head
Burry Holms
WORMS HEAD (Penrhyn-gwyr)
Gower
A487
A484
A478
A475
B4582
B4332
B4333
B4571
B4334
B4335
B4313
B4329
B4299
B4298
B4312
A40
A477
A4066
A4075
A4115
B4314
B4315
B4328
B4316
B4318
B4585
B4584
B4319
B4586
A4139
44
43
30
E
F
G
H
1
2
3
4
5
200
10
20
30
90

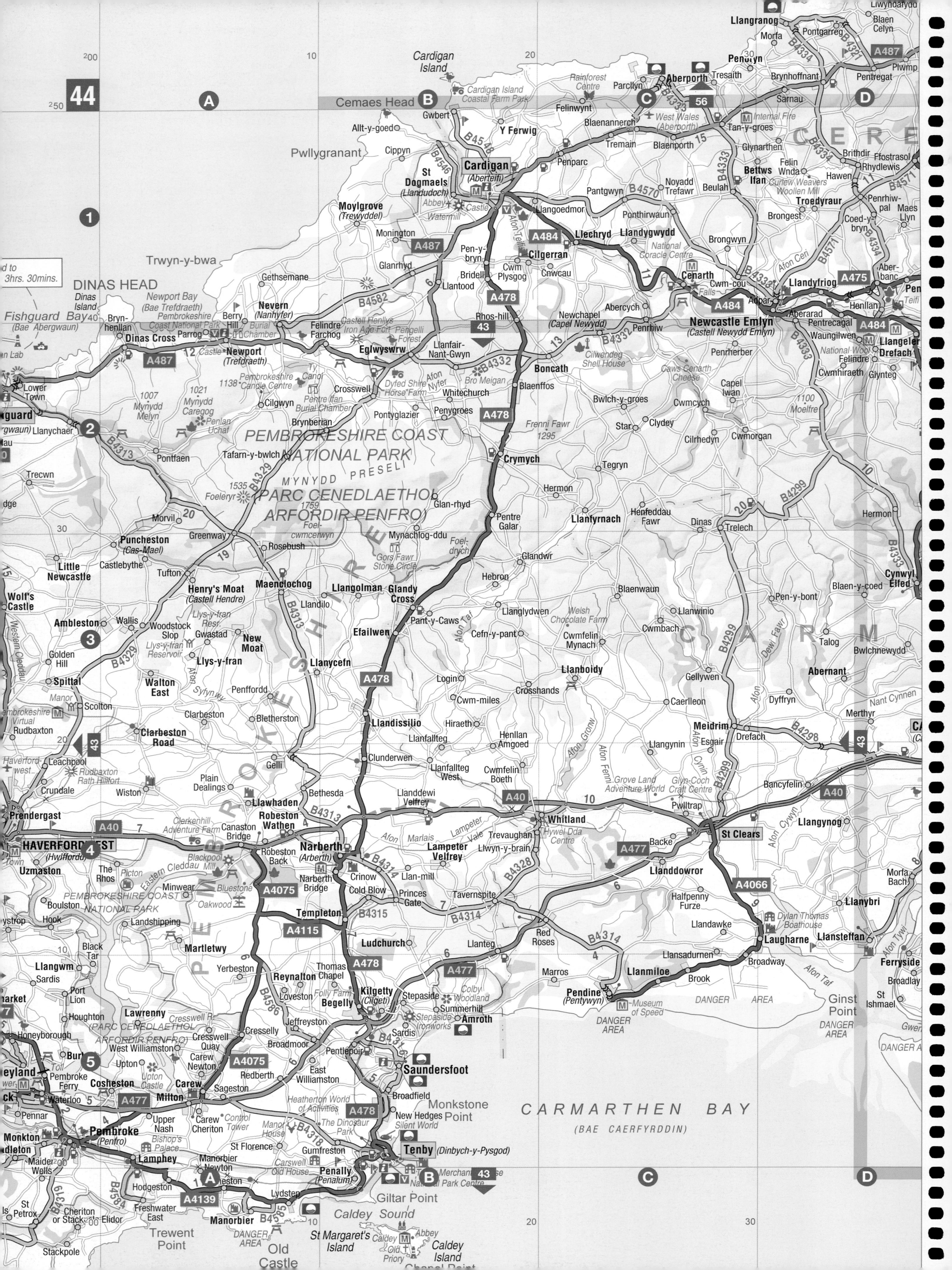

44
Cardigan Island
Cemaes Head
Cardigan Island Coastal Farm Park
Aberporth
Llangranog
Penbryn
Tresaith
Parcllyn
Felinwynt
Rainforest Centre
West Wales (Aberporth)
Blaenannerch
Gwbert
Y Ferwig
Allt-y-goed
Cippyn
Pwllygranant
Cardigan (Aberteifi)
St Dogmaels (Llandudoch)
Moylgrove (Trewyddel)
Monington
Penparc
Tremain
Blaenporth
Tan-y-groes
Glynarthen
Sarnau
Brynhoffnant
Pentregat
Plwmp
Blaen Celyn
Pontgarreg
Morfa
Bettws Ifan
Beulah
Felin Wnda
Curlew Weavers Woollen Mill
Troedyraur
Brongest
Brithdir
Ffostrasol
Rhydlewis
Hawen
Penrhiw-pal
Maes Llyn
Coed-y-bryn
Aber-banc
Pantgwyn
Noyadd Trefawr
Llangoedmor
Ponthirwaun
Llechryd
Llandygwydd
National Coracle Centre
Brongwyn
Cilgerran
Cwm Plysgog
Cnwcau
Pen-y-bryn
Bridell
Llantood
Cenarth
Cwm-cou
Adpar
Llandyfriog
Henllan
Newcastle Emlyn (Castell Newydd Emlyn)
Aberarad
Pentrecagal
Waungilwen
Llangeler
Drefach
Felindre
Cwmhiraeth
Glynteg
National Wool Museum
Penrherber
Caws Cenarth Cheese
Capel Iwan
Moelfre
Abercych
Newchapel (Capel Newydd)
Penrhiw
Cilwendeg Shell House
Boncath
Rhos-hill
Blaenffos
Trwyn-y-bwa
DINAS HEAD
Dinas Island
Newport Bay (Bae Trefdraeth)
Fishguard Bay (Bae Abergwaun)
Pembrokeshire Coast National Park
Gethsemane
Glanrhyd
Nevern (Nanhyfer)
Berry Hill
Bryn-henllan
Dinas Cross
Parrog
Newport (Trefdraeth)
Felindre Farchog
Castell Henllys Iron Age Fort
Pengelli Forest
Eglwyswrw
Llanfair-Nant-Gwyn
Bro Meigan
Lower Town
Llanychaer
Pembrokeshire Candle Centre
Mynydd Carregog
Mynydd Melyn
Penlan Uchaf
Cilgwyn
Pentre Ifan Burial Chamber
Crosswell
Dyfed Shire Horse Farm
Afon Nyfer
Whitechurch
Penygroes
Pontyglazier
Brynberian
Bwlch-y-groes
Cwmcych
Star
Clydey
Cilrhedyn
Cwmorgan
Frenni Fawr
Crymych
Tegryn
PEMBROKESHIRE COAST NATIONAL PARK
MYNYDD PRESELI
(PARC CENEDLAETHOL ARFORDIR PENFRO)
Tafarn-y-bwlch
Pontfaen
Trecwn
Foeleryr
Glan-rhyd
Foel-cwmcerwyn
Mynachlog-ddu
Foel-drych
Gors Fawr Stone Circle
Hermon
Pentre Galar
Llanfyrnach
Henfeddau Fawr
Dinas
Trelech
Hermon
Morvil
Greenway
Puncheston (Cas-Mael)
Little Newcastle
Castlebythe
Rosebush
Tufton
Henry's Moat (Castell Hendre)
Maenclochog
Llandilo
Llangolman
Glandy Cross
Glandwr
Hebron
Blaenwaun
Cynwyl Elfed
Blaen-y-coed
Pen-y-bont
Llanwinio
Wolf's Castle
Ambleston
Wallis
Woodstock Slop
Gwastad
Llys-y-fran Reservoir
Llys-y-fran
New Moat
Pant-y-Caws
Llanglydwen
Welsh Chocolate Farm
Cwmbach
Efailwen
Cefn-y-pant
Cwmfelin Mynach
Talog
Bwlchnewydd
Golden Hill
Spittal
Walton East
Penffordd
Llanycefn
Login
Llanboidy
Gellywen
Abernant
Scolton Manor
Pembrokeshire Virtual
Rudbaxton
Clarbeston
Bletherston
Cwm-miles
Crosshands
Caerlleon
Dyffryn
Merthyr
Nant Cynnen
Clarbeston Road
Llandissilio
Hiraeth
Llanfallteg
Henllan Amgoed
Llangynin
Meidrim
Esgair
Drefach
Haverfordwest
Leachpool
Rudbaxton Rath Hillfort
Crundale
Wiston
Plain Dealings
Gelli
Clunderwen
Llanfallteg West
Cwmfelin Boeth
Grove Land Adventure World
Glyn-Coch Craft Centre
Bancyfelin
Prendergast
Clerkenhill Adventure Farm
Llawhaden
Robeston Wathen
Bethesda
Llanddewi Velfrey
Whitland
Hywel Dda Centre
Pwlltrap
St Clears
Llangynog
HAVERFORDWEST (Hwlffordd)
Canaston Bridge
Robeston Back
Narberth (Arberth)
Marlais
Lampeter Velfrey
Lampeter Vale
Trevaughan
Llwyn-y-brain
Backe
Llanddowror
Uzmaston
The Rhos
Picton
Eastern Cleddau
Blackpool Mill
Minwear
Bluestone
Oakwood
Narberth Bridge
Crinow
Llan-mill
Cold Blow
Princes Gate
Tavernspite
Halfpenny Furze
Morfa Bach
Llanybri
Boulston
Hook
Landshipping
Templeton
Red Roses
Dylan Thomas Boathouse
Llandawke
Laugharne
Llansteffan
Black Tar
Martletwy
Ludchurch
Llanteg
Llansadurnen
Broadway
Ferryside
Llangwm
Sardis
Yerbeston
Reynalton
Thomas Chapel
Marros
Llanmiloe
Brook
Broadlay
Port Lion
Loveston
Folly Farm
Kilgetty (Cilgeti)
Begelly
Stepaside
Colby Woodland
Summerhill
Amroth
Pendine (Pentywyn)
Museum of Speed
DANGER AREA
Ginst Point
St Ishmael
Houghton
Lawrenny
Cresswell
Jeffreyston
Stepaside Ironworks
Honeyborough
Cresselly
Cresswell Quay
West Williamston
Broadmoor
Sardis
Pentlepoir
Burton
Upton
Carew Newton
Saundersfoot
Neyland
Pembroke Ferry
Cosheston
Upton Castle
Carew
Redberth
East Williamston
Sageston
Waterloo
Milton
Heatherton World of Activities
Broadfield
Monkstone Point
Pennar
Pembroke (Penfro)
Upper Nash
Carew Cheriton
Control Tower
Manor House
The Dinosaur Park
New Hedges
Silent World
CARMARTHEN BAY
(BAE CAERFYRDDIN)
Monkton
Bishop's Palace
St Florence
Gumfreston
Tenby (Dinbych-y-Pysgod)
Maiden Wells
Lamphey
Manorbier Newton
Carswell Old House
Penally (Penalum)
Merchant's House
National Park Centre
Hodgeston
Jameston
Lydstep
Giltar Point
St Petrox
Cheriton or Stackpole Elidor
Freshwater East
Manorbier
Caldey Sound
Trewent Point
Stackpole
Old Castle
St Margaret's Island
Caldey Island
Abbey
Old Priory
Chapel Point
43
56

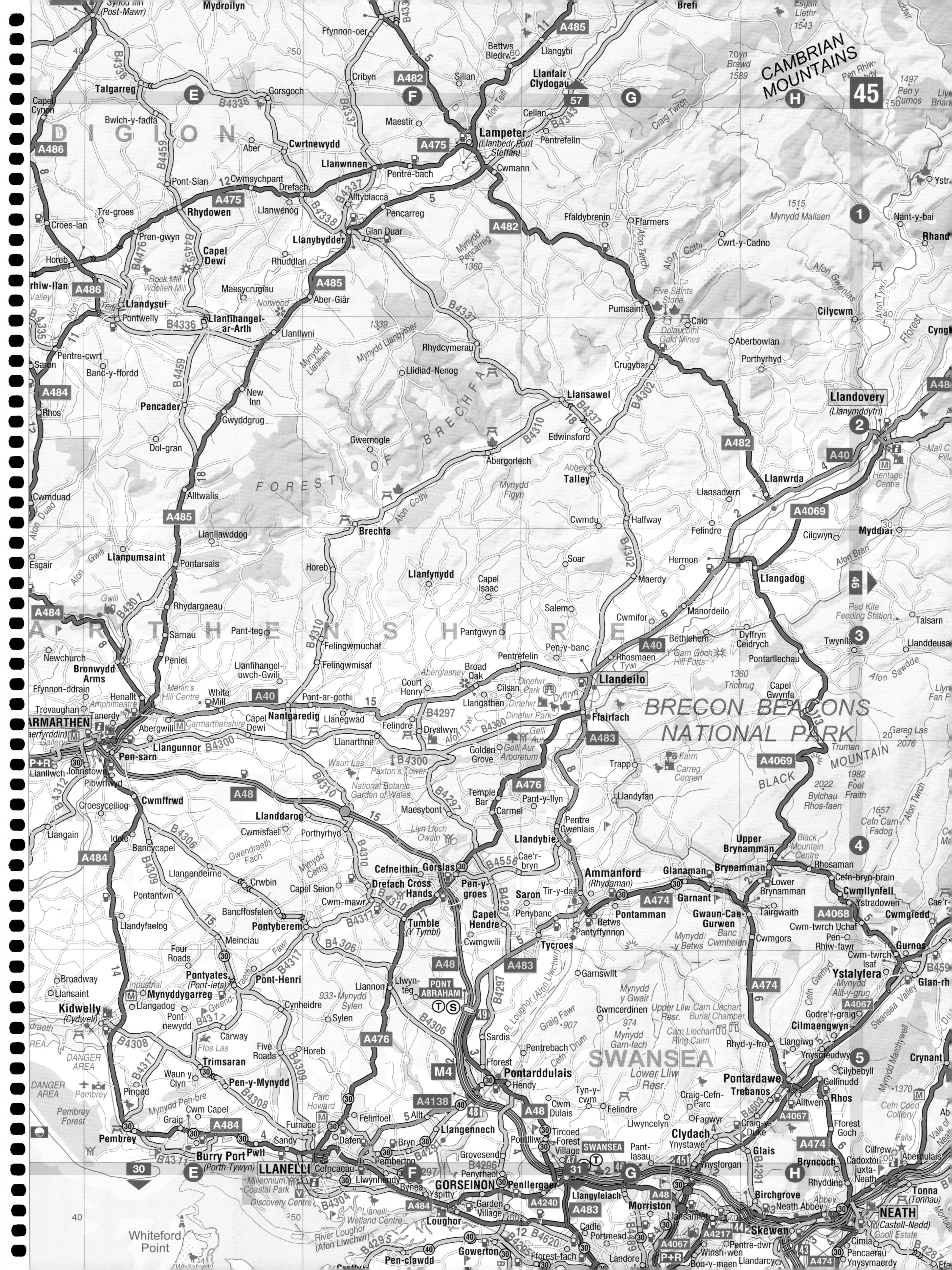

45
46
30
CAMBRIAN MOUNTAINS
BRECON BEACONS NATIONAL PARK
BLACK MOUNTAIN
FOREST OF BRECHFA
SWANSEA
Lampeter (Llanbedr Pont Steffan)
Llandeilo
Llandovery (Llanymddyfri)
Llangadog
Ammanford (Rhydaman)
Llanelli
Gorseinon
Pontarddulais
Pontardawe
Neath (Castell-Nedd)
Skewen
Morriston
Loughor
Gowerton
Burry Port (Porth Tywyn)
Pwll
Pembrey
Kidwelly (Cydweli)
Carmarthen
Nantgaredig
Brechfa
Llansawel
Talley
Pumsaint
Llanwrda
Brynamman
Ystalyfera
Llandysul
Llanybydder
Cwrtnewydd
Talgarreg
Rhydowen
Cross Hands
Tumble (Y Tymbl)
Pontyberem
Trimsaran
Llangennech
Clydach
Glais
Ystradgynlais
Gurnos
A40
A48
A474
A476
A482
A483
A484
A485
A486
A475
A4069
A4067
A4068
A4138
A4240
A4217
M4

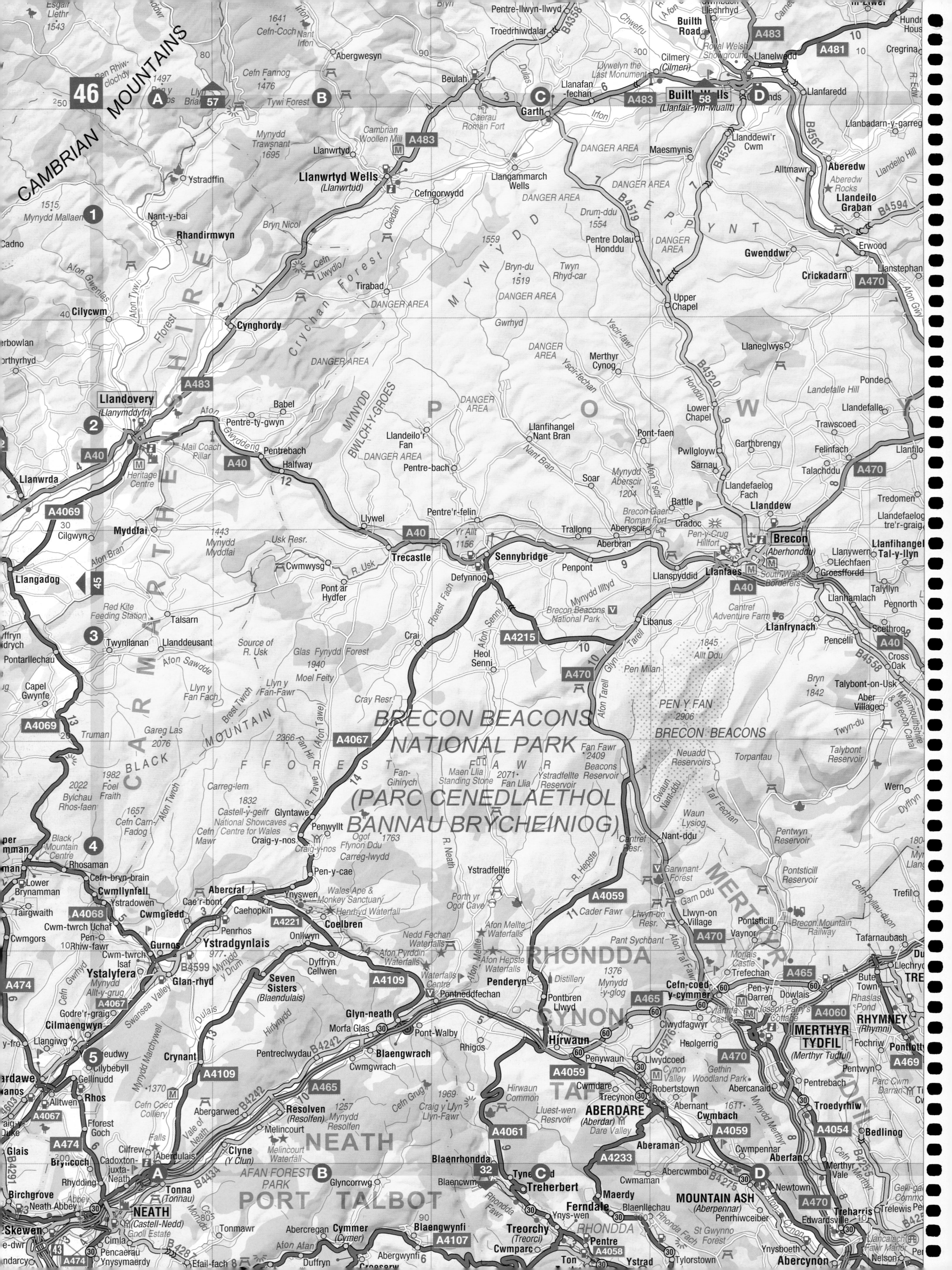

46
CAMBRIAN MOUNTAINS
57
58
45
32
Llanwrtyd Wells
(Llanwrtud)
Builth Wells
(Llanfair-ym-Muallt)
Builth Road
Royal Welsh Showground
Cilmeri
(Cilmeri)
Llywelyn the Last Monument
Llanelwedd
Llanfareddd
Llanafan-fechan
Garth
Beulah
Abergwesyn
Tywi Forest
Cefn Fannog
1476
Pen y Garn
Llyn Brianne
Cefn-Coch
Nant Irfon
Ystradffin
Mynydd Trawsnant
1695
Cambrian Woollen Mill
Caerau Roman Fort
Llangammarch Wells
Cefngorwydd
Maesmynis
Llanddewi'r Cwm
Alltmawr
Aberedw
Aberedw Rocks
Llandeilo Graban
Erwood
Llanstephan
Gwenddwr
Crickadarn
Upper Chapel
Lower Chapel
Llaneglwys
Merthyr Cynog
Drum-ddu
1554
Pentre Dolau Honddu
Bryn-du
1519
Twyn Rhyd-car
DANGER AREA
MYNYDD EPPYNT
Tirabad
Cefn Llwydlo Forest
Crychan Forest
Cynghordy
Rhandirmwyn
Nant-y-bai
Mynydd Mallaen
1515
Cilycwm
Llandovery
(Llanymddyfri)
Llanwrda
Myddfai
Cilgwyn
Llangadog
Babel
Pentre-ty-gwyn
Pentrebach
Halfway
Mail Coach Pillar
Heritage Centre
MYNYDD BWLCH-Y-GROES
Llandeilo'r Fan
Pentre-bach
Llanfihangel Nant Bran
Pont-faen
Pwllgloyw
Sarnau
Garthbrengy
Llandefaelog Fach
Llanddew
Battle
Brecon
(Aberhonddu)
Llanfaes
Llanspyddid
Cradoc
Pen-y-Crug Hillfort
Brecon Gaer Roman Fort
Aberyscir
Aberbran
Trallong
Pentre'r-felin
Soar
Mynydd Aberscir
1204
Llywel
Trecastle
Sennybridge
Defynnog
Yr Allt
1156
Penpont
Usk Resr.
Cwmwysg
Pont ar Hydfer
Mynydd Myddfai
1443
Red Kite Feeding Station
Talsarn
Twynllanan
Llanddeusant
Source of R. Usk
Glas Fynydd Forest
Crai
Cray Resr.
Heol Senni
Libanus
Mynydd Illtyd
Brecon Beacons National Park
Llanfrynach
Cantref Adventure Farm
South Wales Borderers
Groesffordd
Llanfihangel Tal-y-llyn
Llanywern
Llechfaen
Talyllyn
Llanhamlach
Pennorth
Pencelli
Scethrog
Cross Oak
Talybont-on-Usk
Aber Village
Bryn
1842
Allt Ddu
1845
Pen Milan
PEN Y FAN
2906
BRECON BEACONS
BRECON BEACONS NATIONAL PARK
(PARC CENEDLAETHOL BANNAU BRYCHEINIOG)
FFOREST FAWR
BLACK MOUNTAIN
CARMARTHENSHIRE
POWYS
Llyn y Fan Fach
Llyn y Fan-Fawr
Moel Feity
1940
Gareg Las
2076
Fan Hir
2366
Foel Fraith
1982
Bylchau Rhos-faen
2022
Cefn Carn-Fadog
1657
Carreg-lem
Castell-y-geifr
1832
Craig-y-nos
National Showcaves Centre for Wales
Glyntawe
Penwyllt
Ogof Ffynon Ddu
1763
Carreg-lwydd
Fan Gihirych
Maen Llia Standing Stone
Fan Llia
2071
Ystradfellte Reservoir
Fan Fawr
2409
Beacons Reservoir
Neuadd Reservoirs
Torpantau
Talybont Reservoir
Wern
Waun Lysiog
Nant-ddu
Cantref Resr.
Pentwyn Reservoir
Pontsticill Reservoir
Garwnant Forest
Llwyn-on Village
Llwyn-on Resr.
Pontsticill
Vaynor
Brecon Mountain Railway
Morlais Castle
Trefechan
Cefn-coed-y-cymmer
Pen-y-Darren
Dowlais
Cyfarthfa Castle
Joseph Parry's Cottage
MERTHYR TYDFIL
(Merthyr Tudful)
RHYMNEY
(Rhymni)
Tafarnaubach
Trefil
Ystradfellte
Porth yr Ogof Cave
Afon Mellte Waterfalls
Afon Hepste Waterfalls
Nedd Fechan Waterfalls
Afon Pyrddin Waterfalls
Waterfalls Centre
Pontneddfechan
Penderyn
Distillery
Pontbren Llwyd
Mynydd y-glog
1376
Cader Fawr
Pant Sychbant
RHONDDA CYNON TAF
Hirwaun
Penywaun
Llwydcoed
Cwmdare
Trecynon
Robertstown
Abernant
Cwmbach
Gethin Woodland Park
ABERDARE
(Aberdar)
Dare Valley
Aberaman
Abercwmboi
Cwmaman
Mountain Ash
(Aberpennar)
Penrhiwceiber
Abercynon
Aberfan
Merthyr Vale
Troedyrhiw
Pentrebach
Abercanaid
Bedlinog
Treharris
Edwardsville
Hirwaun Common
Lluest-wen Reservoir
Craig y Llyn
1969
Llyn-Fawr
Rhigos
Blaenrhondda
Treherbert
Tynewydd
Blaencwm
Treorchy
(Treorci)
Cwmparc
Ynys-wen
Pentre
Ferndale
Maerdy
Blaenllechau
Ystrad
Tylorstown
Glyn-neath
Morfa Glas
Pont-Walby
Blaengwrach
Cwmgwrach
Pentreclwydau
Resolven
(Resolfen)
Mynydd Resolfen
1257
Melincourt
Melincourt Waterfall
NEATH PORT TALBOT
Aberdulais
Clyne
(Y Clun)
Tonna
(Tonnau)
Cilfrew
Cadoxton-juxta-Neath
Rhyddings
Neath Abbey
NEATH
(Castell-Nedd)
Gnoll Estate
Cimla
Pencaerau
Ynysymaerdy
Skewen
Birchgrove
Bryncoch
Glais
Fforest Goch
Abergarwed
Cefn Coed Colliery
Rhos
Alltwen
Gellinudd
Cilybebyll
Pontardawe
Llangiwg
Cilmaengwyn
Godre'r-graig
Ystalyfera
Glan-rhyd
Cwm-twrch Isaf
Gurnos
Ystradgynlais
Penrhos
Caehopkin
Abercraf
Cae'r-bont
Ynyswen
Coelbren
Onllwyn
Dyffryn Cellwen
Seven Sisters
(Blaendulais)
Crynant
Henrhyd Waterfall
Wales Ape & Monkey Sanctuary
Pen-y-cae
Cwmgiedd
Ystradowen
Cwmllynfell
Cefn-bryn-brain
Rhosaman
Lower Brynamman
Tairgwaith
Cwm-twrch Uchaf
Pen-Rhiw-fawr
Cwmgors
Black Mountain Centre
Capel Gwynfe
Pontarllechau
Truman
Glyncorrwg
AFAN FOREST PARK
Cymmer
(Cymer)
Abercregan
Blaengwynfi
Abergwynfi
Duffryn
Tonmawr
Efail-fach
Ton
A483
A481
A470
A40
A4069
A4067
A4215
A4059
A4068
A4221
A4109
A465
A474
A4061
A4233
A4058
A4107
A4054
A4060
A469
A4220
B4358
B4519
B4520
B4567
B4594
B4558
B4599
B4242
B4434
B4276
B4275
B4255
B4291

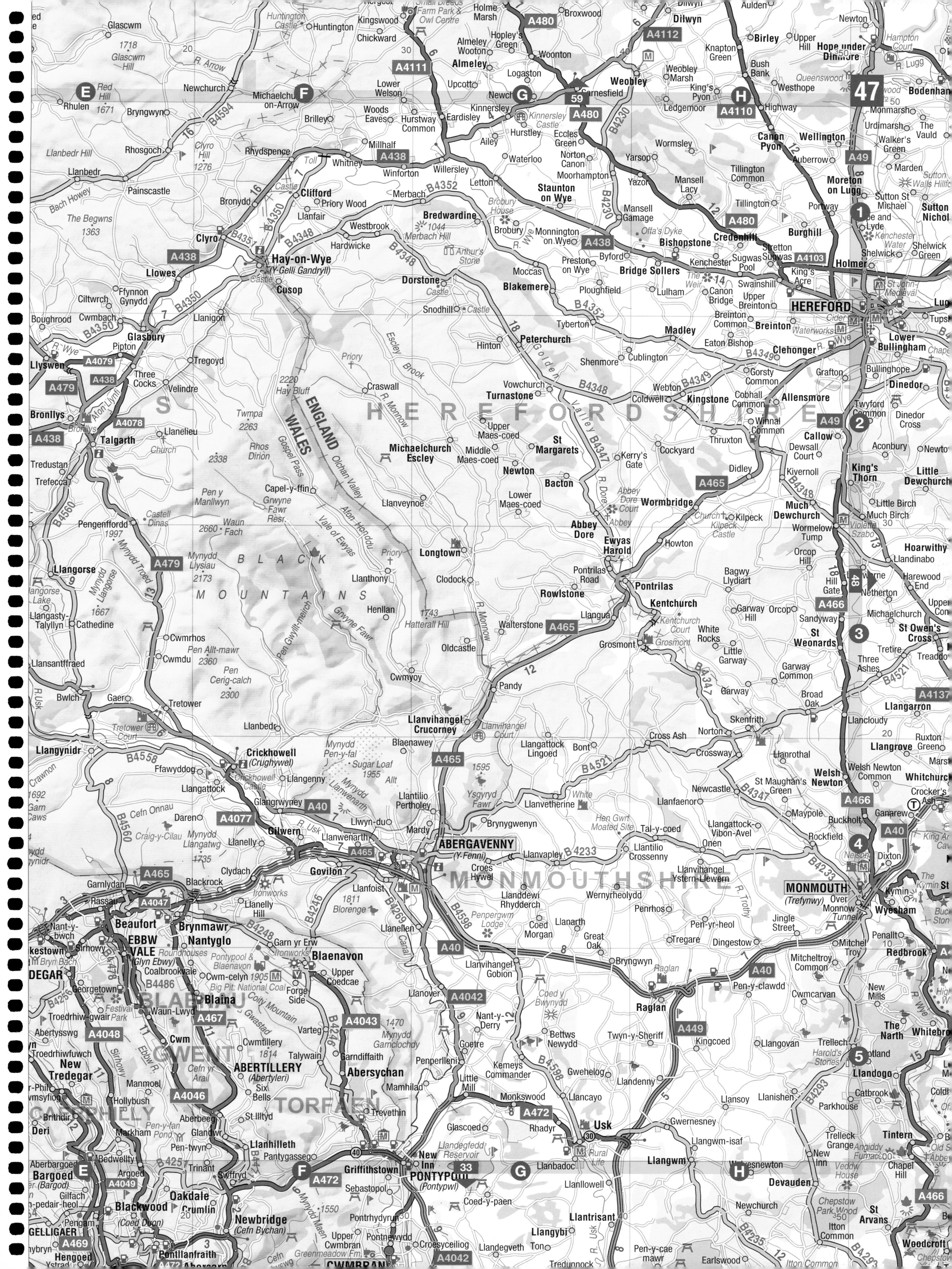
47
HEREFORDSHIRE
ENGLAND
WALES
BLACK MOUNTAINS
MONMOUTHSHIRE
GWENT
TORFAEN
HEREFORD
Hay-on-Wye
(Y Gelli Gandryll)
ABERGAVENNY
(Y Fenni)
MONMOUTH
(Trefynwy)
PONTYPOOL
(Pontypwl)
CWMBRAN
Crickhowell
(Crughywel)
Usk
Raglan
Weobley
Talgarth
Glasbury
Clyro
Clifford
Cusop
Dorstone
Peterchurch
Madley
Kingstone
Callow
King's Thorn
Much Dewchurch
Wormbridge
Ewyas Harold
Pontrilas
Kentchurch
Grosmont
Pandy
Llanvihangel Crucorney
Longtown
Llanthony
Michaelchurch Escley
St Margarets
Bacton
Abbey Dore
Skenfrith
Welsh Newton
St Weonards
Llangarron
Llangrove
Whitchurch
Wyesham
Llandogo
Tintern
Devauden
St Arvans
Llantrisant
Llangybi
Blaenavon
Blaina
Nantyglo
Brynmawr
Beaufort
EBBW VALE
(Glyn Ebwy)
ABERTILLERY
(Abertyleri)
Abersychan
Govilon
Gilwern
Llanfoist
Blackwood
Newbridge
(Cefn Bychan)
Oakdale
Crumlin
Bargoed
New Tredegar
Griffithstown
New Inn
Bredwardine
Staunton on Wye
Credenhill
Bishopstone
Bridge Sollers
Holmer
Burghill
Canon Pyon
Wellington
Moreton on Lugg
Hope under Dinmore
Dilwyn
Almeley
Kinnersley
Eardisley
Whitney
Winforton
Willersley
Llowes
Bronllys
Llangorse
Cathedine
Llangynidr
Bwlch
Tretower
A438
A4079
A479
A4078
A465
A40
A4077
A4047
A4048
A467
A4046
A4043
A4042
A472
A449
A466
A4137
A49
A480
A4103
A4110
A4112
A4111
B4350
B4348
B4352
B4347
B4348
B4521
B4233
B4598
B4293
B4235
B4246
B4248
B4558
B4560
59
33
48
1
2
3
4
5
E
F
G
H

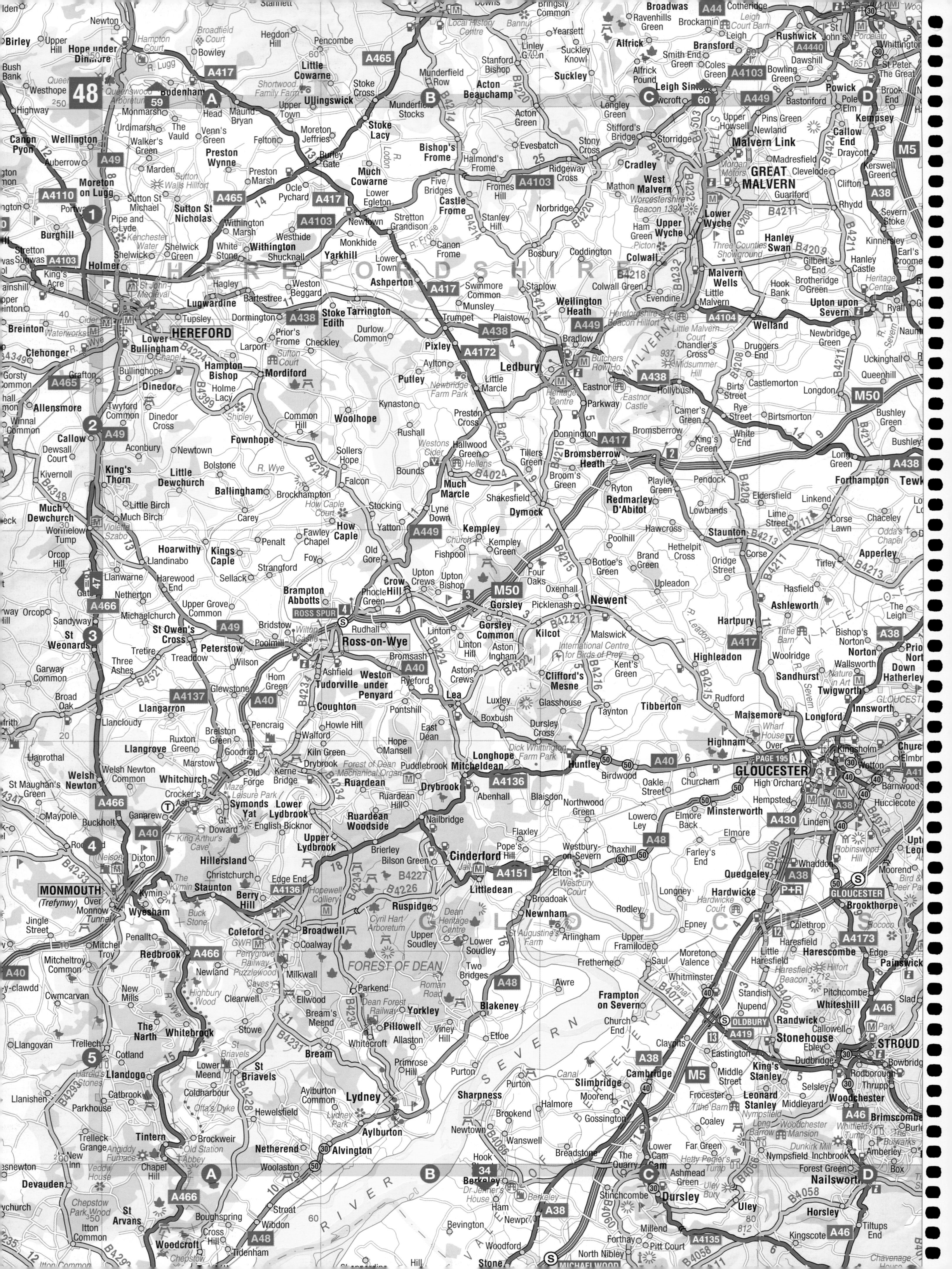

48
HEREFORDSHIRE
HEREFORD
Ledbury
GREAT MALVERN
Malvern Link
Malvern Wells
Upton upon Severn
Ross-on-Wye
MONMOUTH
(Trefynwy)
GLOUCESTER
STROUD
Newent
Cinderford
Coleford
Lydney
Mitcheldean
Dursley
Berkeley
Nailsworth
Stonehouse
FOREST OF DEAN
RIVER SEVERN
M50
M5
A49
A465
A417
A438
A4103
A449
A40
A48
A466
A38
A4136
A4151
A4172
A4110
A4137
A430
A46
A4173
A419
A4135
A4104
59
60
47
34
PAGE 195
ROSS SPUR
OLDBURY
GLOUCESTER
MICHAEL WOOD

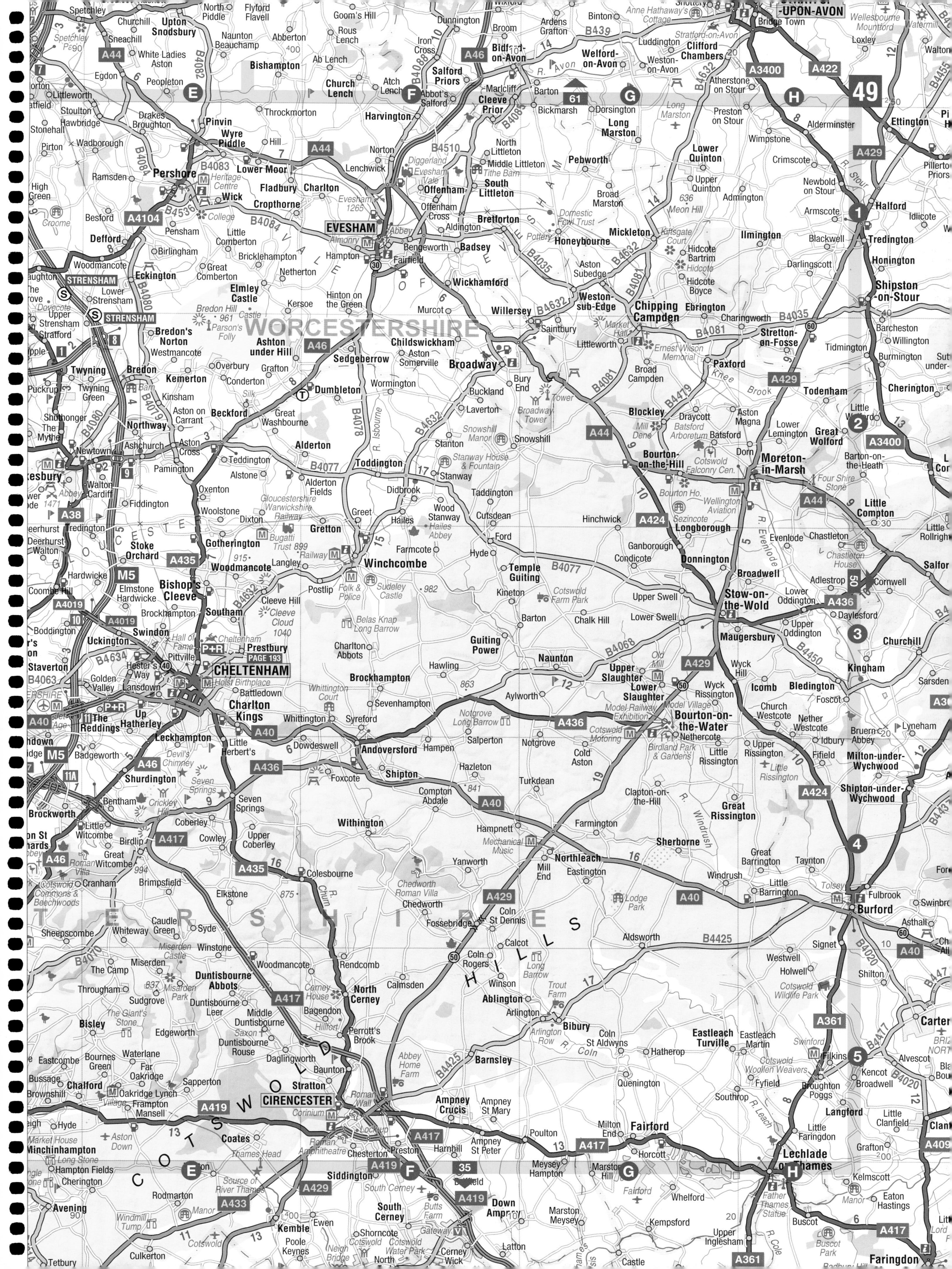

Spetchley
Churchill
Upton Snodsbury
North Piddle
Flyford Flavell
Goom's Hill
Dunnington
Broom
Ardens Grafton
Binton
Anne Hathaway's Cottage
-UPON-AVON
Bridge Town
Wellesbourne Mountford
Loxley
Walton
Sneachill
White Ladies Aston
Naunton Beauchamp
Abberton
Rous Lench
Iron Cross
Bidford-on-Avon
Luddington
Stratford-on-Avon
Clifford Chambers
Weston-on-Avon
Welford-on-Avon
Egdon
Peopleton
Bishampton
Ab Lench
Church Lench
Atch Lench
Salford Priors
Abbot's Salford
Marlcliff
Cleeve Prior
Barton
Bickmarsh
Dorsington
Long Marston
Atherstone on Stour
Preston on Stour
Alderminster
Ettington
A3400
A422
A44
A46
A429
B4082
B4088
B439
B4632
B4085
E
F
G
H
49
61
Littleworth
Stoulton
Hawbridge
Drakes Broughton
Throckmorton
Harvington
Stonehall
Pirton
Wadborough
Pinvin
Wyre Piddle
Hill
Norton
B4510
Diggerland
Evesham Vale
North Littleton
Middle Littleton
Tithe Barn
Pebworth
Lower Quinton
Wimpstone
Crimscote
Upper Quinton
Newbold on Stour
Pillerton Priors
Ramsden
B4084
Pershore
B4083
Heritage Centre
Lower Moor
Lenchwick
Fladbury
Charlton
Offenham
South Littleton
Broad Marston
Admington
High Green
Croome
Besford
A4104
B4536
Wick
College
Cropthorne
Evesham 1265
Offenham Cross
Domestic Fowl Trust
Meon Hill
Armscote
Halford
Idlicote
Defford
Pensham
Little Comberton
B4084
EVESHAM
Almonry
Abbey
Aldington
Bretforton
Pottery
Honeybourne
Mickleton
Kiftsgate Court
Hidcote Bartrim
Ilmington
Blackwell
Tredington
Birlingham
Bricklehampton
Hampton
Bengeworth
Badsey
Fairfield
Aston Subedge
Hidcote Boyce
Darlingscott
Honington
Woodmancote
STRENSHAM
Eckington
Great Comberton
Netherton
VALE OF EVESHAM
Wickhamford
B4035
B4081
Shipston-on-Stour
Lower Strensham
Upper Strensham
Elmley Castle
Kersoe
Hinton on the Green
Murcot
Willersey
Weston-sub-Edge
Chipping Campden
Ebrington
Charingworth
Bredon Hill 961
Parson's Folly
Castle
WORCESTERSHIRE
Saintbury
Market Hall
Stretton-on-Fosse
Barcheston
Willington
Strafford
Bredon's Norton
Westmancote
Ashton under Hill
Childswickham
Aston Somerville
Broadway
Littleworth
Ernest Wilson Memorial
Broad Campden
Paxford
Tidmington
Burmington
Twyning
Twyning Green
Bredon
Kemerton
Overbury
Conderton
Grafton
Sedgeberrow
Wormington
Bury End
Knee Brook
A429
Todenham
Cherington
Puckrup
Kinsham
B4079
B4080
Aston on Carrant
Beckford
Dumbleton
Buckland
Laverton
Broadway Tower
Tower
Blockley
Draycott
Batsford Arboretum
Aston Magna
Little Wolford
Great Wolford
Lower Lemington
Shuthonger
The Mythe
Northway
Great Washbourne
R. Isbourne
B4078
B4632
Snowshill Manor
Snowshill
Stanton
Mill Dene
Batsford
Dorn
A3400
Newtown
Ashchurch
Aston Cross
Teddington
Alderton
Toddington
Stanway House & Fountain
Stanway
Bourton-on-the-Hill
Cotswold Falconry Cen.
Moreton-in-Marsh
Barton-on-the-Heath
Tewkesbury
Abbey
Walton Cardiff
Pamington
Alstone
B4077
Alderton Fields
Didbrook
Taddington
Bourton Ho.
Wellington Aviation
Four Shire Stone
Little Compton
Fiddington
Oxenton
Gloucestershire Warwickshire Railway
Wood Stanway
Hailes Abbey
Cutsdean
Sezincote
Longborough
Deerhurst
Tredington
Woolstone
Dixton
Gretton
Greet
Hailes
Hinchwick
A424
R. Evenlode
Evenlode
Chastleton
Little Rollright
Deerhurst Walton
Stoke Orchard
Gotherington
Bugatti Trust 899
Railway
Farmcote
Ford
Ganborough
Condicote
Donnington
Chastleton House
Hardwicke
M5
Elmstone Hardwicke
A435
Woodmancote
Langley
Winchcombe
Hyde
Temple Guiting
B4077
Broadwell
Adlestrop
Cornwell
Salford
Coombe Hill
A4019
Bishop's Cleeve
Cleeve Hill
Postlip
Folk & Police
Sudeley Castle
982
Kineton
Cotswold Farm Park
Upper Swell
Stow-on-the-Wold
Lower Oddington
A436
Daylesford
Boddington
Brockhampton
Southam
Cleeve Cloud 1040
Belas Knap Long Barrow
Barton
Chalk Hill
Lower Swell
Upper Oddington
Maugersbury
Uckington
Swindon
Hall of Fame
Cheltenham
Pittville
P+R
Prestbury
PAGE 193
Charlton Abbots
Guiting Power
Naunton
B4068
Old Mill
Upper Slaughter
A429
Wyck Hill
B4450
Churchill
Kingham
Staverton
B4634
Hester's Way
CHELTENHAM
Holst Birthplace
Golden Valley
Lansdown
Battledown
Brockhampton
Hawling
863
Aylworth
Lower Slaughter
Wyck Rissington
Icomb
Bledington
Foscot
Sarsden
B4063
Charlton Kings
Whittington Court
Sevenhampton
Model Village
Model Railway Exhibition
Bourton-on-the-Water
Church Westcote
Nether Westcote
Up Hatherley
The Reddings
Leckhampton
Whittington
Syreford
Notgrove Long Barrow
A436
Cotswold Motoring
Nethercote
Bruern Abbey
Lyneham
A40
Little Herbert's
Dowdeswell
Andoversford
Hampen
Salperton
Notgrove
Cold Aston
Birdland Park & Gardens
Upper Rissington
Little Rissington
Idbury
Fifield
Milton-under-Wychwood
Badgeworth
Devil's Chimney
A46
A436
Shipton
Hazleton
Foxcote
Shurdington
Seven Springs
Compton Abdale
841
Turkdean
Clapton-on-the-Hill
R. Windrush
Great Rissington
A424
Shipton-under-Wychwood
Bentham
Crickley Hill
Seven Springs
Brockworth
Little Witcombe
Coberley
Cowley
Withington
Hampnett
Farmington
Mechanical Music
Northleach
Sherborne
Great Barrington
Taynton
Birdlip
A417
Upper Coberley
Yanworth
Mill End
Eastington
Windrush
Little Barrington
Tolsey
Fulbrook
Burford
Swinbrook
Great Witcombe
Roman Villa
994
A435
Colesbourne
Chedworth Roman Villa
Chedworth
A429
Coln St Dennis
Lodge Park
A40
Cranham
Brimpsfield
Elkstone
875
R. Churn
Cotswold Commons & Beechwoods
Caudle Green
Syde
Fossebridge
Calcot
Aldsworth
B4425
Signet
Asthall
Sheepscombe
Whiteway
Winstone
Miserden Castle
Coln Rogers
Long Barrow
Westwell
Holwell
B4020
A40
Miserden
Misarden Park
837
Duntisbourne Abbots
Woodmancote
Rendcomb
Winson
Trout Farm
Shilton
The Camp
Throughham
Sudgrove
Duntisbourne Leer
Middle Duntisbourne
A417
Cerney House
North Cerney
Calmsden
Ablington
Arlington
Bibury
Cotswold Wildlife Park
A361
Carterton
The Giant's Stone
Bisley
Edgeworth
Bagendon
Hillfort
Perrott's Brook
Arlington Row
R. Coln
Coln St Aldwyns
Eastleach Turville
Eastleach Martin
Swinford
Filkins
Alvescot
Waterlane
Far Oakridge
Duntisbourne Rouse
Daglingworth
Abbey Home Farm
B4425
Barnsley
Hatherop
Cotswold Woollen Weavers
Kencot
Broadwell
Eastcombe
Bournes Green
Baunton
Quenington
Fyfield
Broughton Poggs
Bussage
Chalford
Oakridge Lynch
Sapperton
Stratton
Roman Wall
Ampney Crucis
Ampney St Mary
Southrop
R. Leach
Langford
Little Clanfield
Brownshill
Frampton Mansell
A419
CIRENCESTER
Corinium
Lockup
Hyde
Market House
Aston Down
Coates
Roman Amphitheatre
Chesterton
Preston
A417
Harnhill
Ampney St Peter
Poulton
Milton End
Fairford
Horcott
Little Faringdon
Grafton
Minchinhampton
Long Stone
Thames Head
A419
Meysey Hampton
Marston Hill
Lechlade on Thames
A409
Hampton Fields
Cherington
Source of River Thames
Siddington
South Cerney
35
Driffield
Fairford
Whelford
Father Thames Statue
Kelmscott
Eaton Hastings
A429
A433
Rodmarton
Avening
Manor
Windmill Tump
Kemble
Ewen
South Cerney
Butts Farm
A419
Down Ampney
Marston Meysey
Kempsford
Manor
Buscot
A417
Poole Keynes
Shorncote
Cotswold Water Park
Gateway
Cerney Wick
Latton
Upper Inglesham
A361
R. Cole
Buscot Park
Tetbury
Culkerton
Neigh Bridge
North
Castle
Faringdon
COTSWOLD HILLS
GLOUCESTERSHIRE

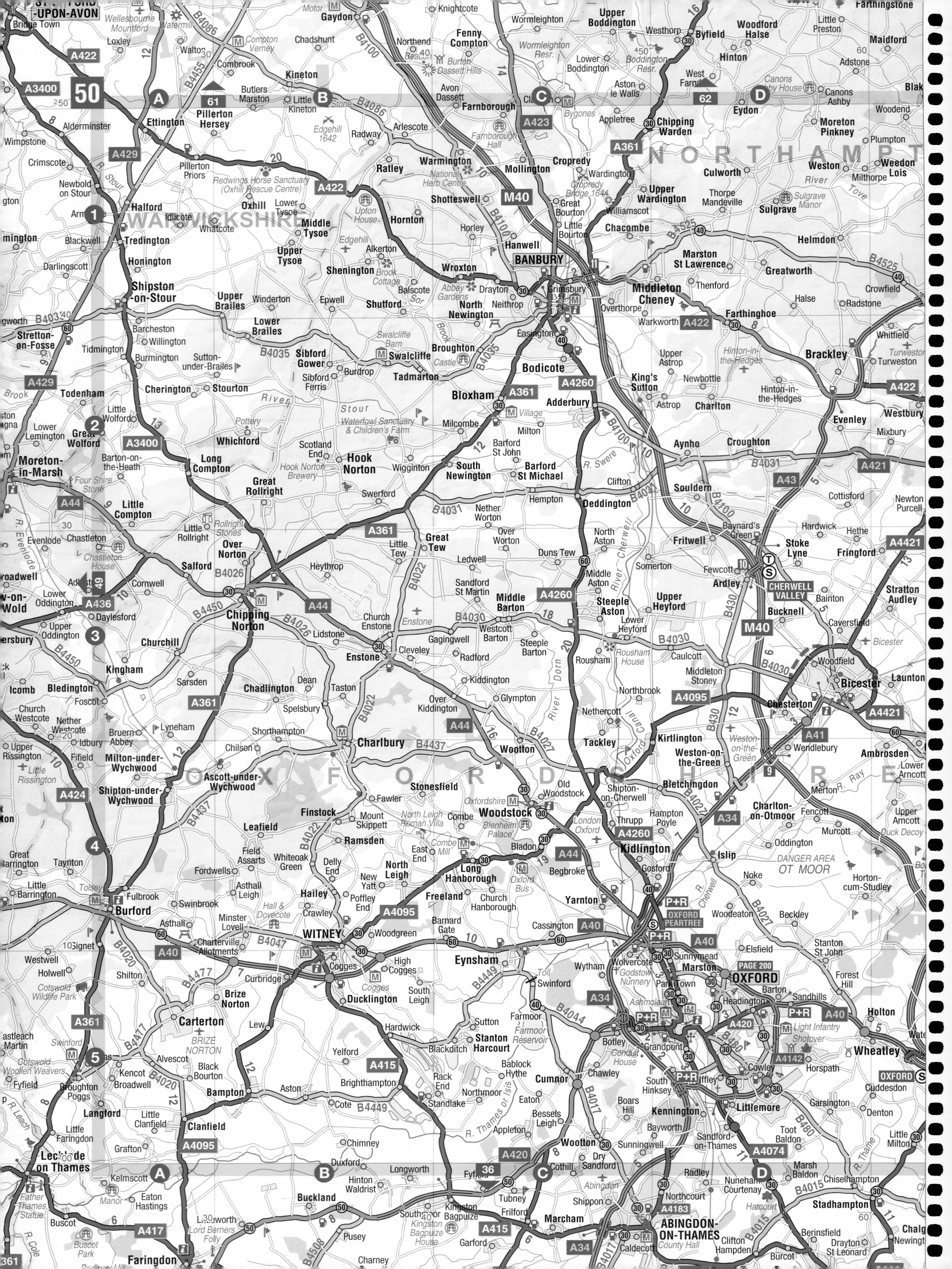

-UPON-AVON
Bridge Town
Wellesbourne Mountford
Gaydon
Knightcote
Wormleighton
Upper Boddington
Byfield
Woodford Halse
Little Preston
Farthingstone
Maidford
Loxley
Walton
Compton Verney
Chadshunt
Northend
Fenny Compton
Wormleighton Resr.
Westhorp
Hinton
Adstone
Combrook
Burton Dassett Hills
Lower Boddington
Boddington Resr.
Kineton
Avon Dassett
Aston le Walls
West Farndon
Canons Ashby House
Canons Ashby
A3400
50
Butlers Marston
Little Kineton
Farnborough
Bygones
Appletree
Chipping Warden
Eydon
Woodend
Alderminster
Ettington
Pillerton Hersey
Edgehill 1642
Radway
Arlescote
Farnborough Hall
A423
A361
Moreton Pinkney
Plumpton
Wimpstone
Crimscote
A429
Pillerton Priors
Ratley
Warmington
National Herb Centre
Mollington
Cropredy
Wardington
Culworth
Weston
Weedon Lois
Milthorpe
NORTHAMPT
Newbold on Stour
Redwings Horse Sanctuary (Oxhill Rescue Centre)
A422
Cropredy Bridge 1644
Upper Wardington
Thorpe Mandeville
Sulgrave Manor
Sulgrave
Halford
Idlicote
Oxhill
Lower Tysoe
Upton House
Hornton
Shotteswell
M40
Great Bourton
Williamscot
Little Bourton
WARWICKSHIRE
Whatcote
Middle Tysoe
Horley
Chacombe
B4525
Helmdon
Blackwell
Tredington
Edgehill
Alkerton
Hanwell
Upper Tysoe
Marston St Lawrence
BANBURY
Honington
Darlingscott
Shenington
Brook Cottage
Wroxton
Greatworth
Shipston-on-Stour
Abbey Gardens
Drayton
Balscote
Grimsbury
Middleton Cheney
Thenford
Crowfield
Upper Brailes
Winderton
Epwell
Shutford
North Newington
Neithrop
Overthorpe
Halse
Radstone
Stretton-on-Fosse
Lower Brailes
Warkworth
Farthinghoe
Barcheston
Willington
Swalcliffe Barn
Easington
Whitfield
Tidmington
Burmington
Sutton-under-Brailes
B4035
Sibford Gower
Swalcliffe
Broughton Castle
Upper Astrop
Hinton-in-the-Hedges
Brackley
Turweston
Sibford Ferris
Burdrop
Tadmarton
Bodicote
A4260
King's Sutton
Newbottle
A429
Todenham
Cherington
Stourton
Bloxham
Adderbury
Astrop
Charlton
Hinton-in-the-Hedges
Little Wolford
Stour
Waterfowl Sanctuary & Children's Farm
Village
Milcombe
Milton
Evenley
Westbury
Lower Lemington
Great Wolford
A3400
Whichford
Scotland End
Hook Norton
Barford St John
Aynho
Croughton
Mixbury
Moreton-in-Marsh
Barton-on-the-Heath
Long Compton
Hook Norton Brewery
Wigginton
South Newington
Barford St Michael
R. Swere
B4031
A421
Four Shire Stone
Great Rollright
Swerford
Clifton
Souldern
A43
Cottisford
Newton Purcell
A44
Little Compton
Hempton
Deddington
Nether Worton
Evenlode
Chastleton
Little Rollright
Rollright Stones
Over Norton
A361
Little Tew
Great Tew
Over Worton
North Aston
Fritwell
Baynard's Green
Hardwick
Hethe
A4421
Chastleton House
Stoke Lyne
Fringford
Salford
B4026
Heythrop
Ledwell
Duns Tew
Somerton
Fewcott
Ardley
CHERWELL VALLEY
Stratton Audley
Adlestrop
Cornwell
Sandford St Martin
Middle Aston
Bainton
Lower Oddington
A436
Chipping Norton
B4450
Church Enstone
Middle Barton
A4260
Steeple Aston
Upper Heyford
Bucknell
Daylesford
Enstone
Westcott Barton
Lower Heyford
Caversfield
Upper Oddington
Churchill
Lidstone
Gagingwell
Steeple Barton
B4030
M40
Bicester
Cleveley
Radford
Rousham
Rousham House
Caulcott
Woodfield
Kingham
Middleton Stoney
Bicester
Launton
Icomb
Bledington
Sarsden
Chadlington
Dean
Taston
Kiddington
Glympton
Northbrook
Foscot
Spelsbury
Over Kiddington
A4095
Chesterton
A4421
Church Westcote
Nether Westcote
Bruern Abbey
Lyneham
Shorthampton
Nethercott
Tackley
Kirtlington
A41
Upper Rissington
Idbury
Fifield
Chilson
Charlbury
B4437
Wootton
Weston-on-the-Green
Wendlebury
Ambrosden
Little Rissington
Milton-under-Wychwood
Ascott-under-Wychwood
OXFORDSHIRE
Old Woodstock
Shipton-on-Cherwell
Bletchingdon
Lower Arncott
A424
Shipton-under-Wychwood
Stonesfield
Fawler
Oxfordshire Museum
Merton
Charlton-on-Otmoor
Fencott
Upper Arncott
Finstock
Mount Skipgett
North Leigh Roman Villa
Combe
Woodstock
Thrupp
Hampton Poyle
Leafield
Blenheim Palace
London Oxford
A4260
Murcott
Duck Decoy
Great Barrington
Taynton
Field Assarts
Ramsden
Combe Mill
Bladon
Kidlington
Oddington
Whiteoak Green
East End
A44
Islip
DANGER AREA OT MOOR
Fordwells
Delly End
North Leigh
Long Hanborough
Begbroke
Gosford
Noke
Horton-cum-Studley
Little Barrington
Tolsey
Fulbrook
Asthall Leigh
New Yatt
Hailey
Poffley End
Freeland
Church Hanborough
Oxford Bus
Yarnton
Burford
Swinbrook
Minster Lovell
Hall & Dovecote
Crawley
A4095
Barnard Gate
Cassington
A40
OXFORD PEARTREE
Woodeaton
Beckley
Asthall
Charterville Allotments
B4047
WITNEY
Woodgreen
P+R
A40
Elsfield
Stanton St John
Signet
Westwell
Holwell
Cotswold Wildlife Park
Shilton
A40
Cogges
High Cogges
Eynsham
Wytham
Toll
Wolvercote
Godstow Nunnery
Sunnymead
Marston
PAGE 200
OXFORD
Forest Hill
Brize Norton
B4477
Curbridge
Cogges
South Leigh
Ducklington
Swinford
Park Town
A34
Ashmolean
Barton
Sandhills
Headington
Holton
A361
Carterton
BRIZE NORTON
Lew
Hardwick
Sutton
Stanton Harcourt
Farmoor
Farmoor Reservoir
B4044
Botley
Grandpont
A420
Light Infantry
Shotover
Wheatley
Eastleach Martin
Swinford
Alvescot
Yelford
Blackditch
Conduit House
A4142
Cotswold Woollen Weavers
Kencot
Broadwell
Black Bourton
A415
Babbock Hythe
Cumnor
Chawley
South Hinksey
Iffley
Cowley
Horspath
OXFORD
Cuddesdon
Fyfield
Broughton Poggs
Bampton
Aston
Brighthampton
Rack End
Northmoor
Standlake
Eaton
B4017
Boars Hill
Kennington
Littlemore
Garsington
Langford
Little Clanfield
Clanfield
Cote
B4449
R. Thames or Isis
Bessels Leigh
Appleton
Bayworth
Sandford-on-Thames
Toot Baldon
Denton
Little Faringdon
Chimney
Wootton
Sunningwell
A4074
Little Milton
Lechlade on Thames
Grafton
A4095
A420
Dry Sandford
Duxford
Longworth
Fyfield
Cothill
Radley
Nuneham Courtenay
Marsh Baldon
Chiselhampton
Kelmscott
Buckland
Hinton Waldrist
Abingdon
Northcourt
A4183
Father Thames Statue
Manor
Eaton Hastings
Kingston Bagpuize
Tubney
Frilford
Shippon
Marcham
ABINGDON-ON-THAMES
Harcourt
Stadhampton
Buscot
Littleworth
Lord Berners Folly
Southmoor
Kingston Bagpuize House
Pusey
A415
A417
A34
County Hall
Clifton Hampden
Berinsfield
Drayton St Leonard
Chalgrove
Newington
Buscot Park
Faringdon
B4508
Charney
Garford
Caldecott
Burcot

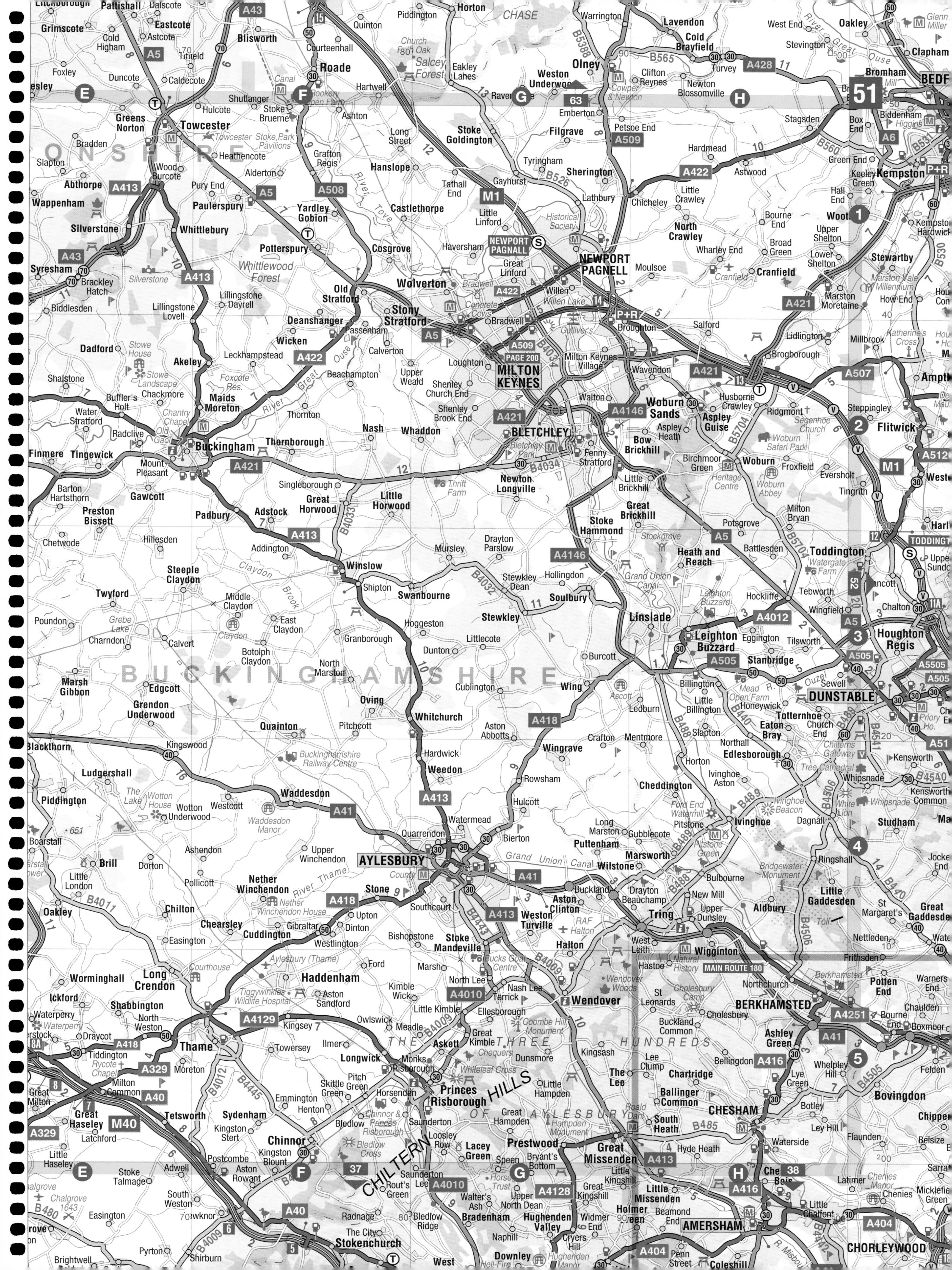

Pattishall
Dalscote
Eastcote
Astcote
Grimscote
Cold Higham
Tiffield
Blisworth
Quinton
Piddington
Horton
CHASE
Warrington
Lavendon
Cold Brayfield
West End
Oakley
Glenn Miller
Stevington
Clapham
River Great Ouse
Courteenhall
Church 80 Oak
Salcey Forest
Eakley Lanes
Roade
Olney
B565
Turvey
A428
Bromham
BEDF
Foxley
Duncote
Caldecote
Canal
Hartwell
Weston Underwood
Clifton Reynes
Newton Blossomville
51
Shutlanger
Stoke Bruerne
Ravenstone
Cowper & Newton
Biddenham
Higgins
Hulcote
Towcester
Greens Norton
Ashton
Long Street
Stoke Goldington
Emberton
Petsoe End
Stagsden
Box End
Filgrave
A509
A6
Bradden
ONSHIRE
Towcester
Stoke Park Pavilions
Heathencote
Grafton Regis
Hanslope
Tyringham
Hardmead
B560
Green End
Slapton
Wood Burcote
Alderton
Sherington
A422
Astwood
Keeley Green
Kempston
P+R
Abthorpe
A413
Pury End
A5
A508
Tathall End
Gayhurst
B526
Little Crawley
Hall End
Wappenham
Paulerspury
Yardley Gobion
River Tove
Castlethorpe
M1
Lathbury
Chicheley
Bourne End
Wootton
Kempston Hardwick
Silverstone
Whittlebury
Little Linford
Historical Society
North Crawley
Upper Shelton
Potterspury
Cosgrove
Haversham
NEWPORT PAGNALL
Broad Green
Wharley End
Lower Shelton
A43
Syresham
Whittlewood Forest
Great Linford
NEWPORT PAGNELL
Moulsoe
Cranfield
Stewartby
B530
Brackley Hatch
Silverstone
A413
Wolverton
Bradwell
Willen
Willen Lake
Marston Vale Millennium
Marston Moreteine
Houghton Conquest
How End
Biddlesden
Lillingstone Dayrell
Lillingstone Lovell
Old Stratford
Stony Stratford
Concrete Cows
A422
A421
P+R
Broughton
Salford
Deanshanger
Passenham
Bradwell
Gulliver's
Lidlington
Millbrook
Katherine's Cross
Dadford
Stowe House
Leckhampstead
Wicken
Calverton
A5
A509
PAGE 200
B4034
Milton Keynes Village
Wavendon
Brogborough
Stowe Landscape
A422
River Great Ouse
Loughton
MILTON KEYNES
A421
A507
Ampthill
Shalstone
Akeley
Foxcote Res.
Beachampton
Upper Weald
Shenley Church End
Walton
Woburn Sands
Husborne Crawley
Ridgmont
Steppingley
Buffler's Holt
Chackmore
Maids Moreton
Shenley Brook End
A4146
Aspley Heath
Aspley Guise
Segenhoe Church
Flitwick
Water Stratford
Chantry Chapel
River Great Ouse
Thornton
Nash
Whaddon
A421
BLETCHLEY
Bow Brickhill
B5704
Woburn Safari Park
Radclive
Old Gaol
Buckingham
Thornborough
Bletchley Park
Fenny Stratford
Birchmoor Green
Woburn
Froxfield
A5120
Finmere
Tingewick
Mount Pleasant
A421
12
Thrift Farm
B4034
Newton Longville
Little Brickhill
Heritage Centre
Woburn Abbey
Eversholt
M1
Westoning
Barton Hartshorn
Gawcott
Singleborough
Little Horwood
Great Horwood
Great Brickhill
Milton Bryan
Tingrith
Preston Bissett
Padbury
Adstock
B4033
Stoke Hammond
Potsgrove
Harlington
Chetwode
Hillesden
A413
Addington
Drayton Parslow
Mursley
A4146
Stockgrove
A5
Battlesden
B5704
Toddington
TODDINGTON
Steeple Claydon
Claydon Brook
Winslow
Shipton
Swanbourne
B4032
Stewkley Dean
Hollingdon
Soulbury
Grand Union Canal
Heath and Reach
Watergate Farm
Upper Sundon
Twyford
Middle Claydon
Leighton Buzzard
Hockliffe
Tebworth
Chalton
Harlington
Poundon
Grebe Lake
Claydon
East Claydon
Hoggeston
Stewkley
Linslade
A4012
Wingfield
A5
Charndon
Calvert
Botolph Claydon
Granborough
Littlecote
Leighton Buzzard
Eggington
Tilsworth
Houghton Regis
BUCKINGHAMSHIRE
North Marston
Dunton
Burcott
A505
Stanbridge
A5505
Marsh Gibbon
Edgcott
Cublington
Wing
Ascott
Billington
Sewell
DUNSTABLE
Grendon Underwood
Oving
Whitchurch
Ledburn
Little Billington
Mead Open Farm
Honeywick
Totternhoe
Priory Ho.
Quainton
Pitchcott
Aston Abbotts
A418
Crafton
Mentmore
B488
Eaton Bray
Church End
Blackthorn
Kingswood
Buckinghamshire Railway Centre
Hardwick
Wingrave
Northall
Edlesborough
Chilterns Gateway
A5
Kensworth
Ludgershall
Weedon
Rowsham
Horton
Cheddington
Ivinghoe Aston
Tree Cathedral
Whipsnade
B4540
Kensworth Common
Piddington
The Lake
Wotton House
Wotton Underwood
Westcott
Waddesdon
A413
Hulcott
Ford End Watermill
Ivinghoe
Ivinghoe Beacon
Whipsnade
White Lion
Dagnall
Studham
Waddesdon Manor
Watermead
Long Marston
Gubblecote
Pitstone
Boarstall
Ashendon
Upper Winchendon
Quarrendon
AYLESBURY
Bierton
Puttenham
Grand Union Canal
Marsworth
Wilstone
Pitstone Green
Bridgewater Monument
Ringshall
Jockey End
Brill
Dorton
County
A41
Buckland
Bulbourne
Little London
Pollicott
Nether Winchendon
River Thame
Stone
Drayton Beauchamp
Aston Clinton
New Mill
Little Gaddesden
Oakley
B4011
Chilton
Nether Winchendon House
A418
Upton
Southcourt
A413
Weston Turville
Tring
Upper Dunsley
Aldbury
St Margaret's
Great Gaddesden
Chearsley
Cuddington
Gibraltar
Dinton
B4443
RAF Halton
Easington
Westlington
Bishopstone
Stoke Mandeville
Halton
West Leith
Wigginton
Nettleden
Frithsden
Courthouse
Aylesbury (Thame)
Ford
Bucks Goat Centre
B4009
Hastoe
Natural History
MAIN ROUTE 180
Berkhamsted
Potten End
Warners End
Long Crendon
Worminghall
Haddenham
Marsh
North Lee
Wendover Woods
Northchurch
Ickford
Tiggywinkles Wildlife Hospital
Aston Sandford
Kimble Wick
A4010
Nash Lee
Terrick
Wendover
St Leonards
Cholesbury Camp
Cholesbury
BERKHAMSTED
A4251
Chaulden
Waterperry
Shabbington
North Weston
A4129
Kingsey
Little Kimble
Ellesborough
Coombe Hill Monument
Buckland Common
Bourne End
Boxmoor
Draycott
A418
Owlswick
Meadle
Great Kimble
THE THREE HUNDREDS
Ashley Green
A41
Tiddington
Rycote Chapel
Thame
Towersey
Ilmer
Askett
Chequers
Dunsmore
Kingsash
Lee Clump
Bellingdon
A416
Whelpley Hill
Felden
A329
Moreton
Longwick
Monks Risborough
Whiteleaf Cross
The Lee
Chartridge
Lye Green
Great Milton
Milton Common
A40
B4012
B4445
Pitch Green
Skittle Green
Horsenden
Princes Risborough
HILLS
Little Hampden
Ballinger Common
B4505
Bovingdon
Great Haseley
M40
Tetsworth
Sydenham
Emmington
Henton
Chinnor & Princes Risborough
Great Hampden
OF AYLESBURY
Road Dam
South Heath
CHESHAM
Botley
Chipperfield
A329
Kingston Stert
Latchford
Bledlow
Bledlow Cross
Saunderton
Hampden Monument
B485
Ley Hill
Flaunden
Belsize
Little Haseley
Chinnor
Kingston Blount
CHILTERN
Loosley Row
Lacey Green
Prestwood
Bryant's Bottom
Great Missenden
Hyde Heath
Waterside
Stoke Talmage
Adwell
Postcombe
Aston Rowant
Speen
A413
Little Kingshill
Cheddington
Chesham Bois
A4010
Saunderton Lee
Rout's Green
Horse Trust
A4128
Great Kingshill
Little Missenden
A416
Latimer
Chenies Manor
Chenies
Mickleﬁeld Green
Sarratt
Chalgrove
South Weston
Lewknor
Easington
A40
Radnage
Bledlow Ridge
Walter's Ash
Bradenham
Upper North Dean
Hughenden Valley
Widmer End
Holmer Green
Beamond End
AMERSHAM
Little Chalfont
A404
B480
The City
Stokenchurch
Naphill
Cryers Hill
Hughenden Manor
Penn Street
A404
Coleshill
CHORLEYWOOD
Brightwell
Pyrton
Shirburn
B4009
West
Downley
Hell-Fire
R. Misbourne
B4442

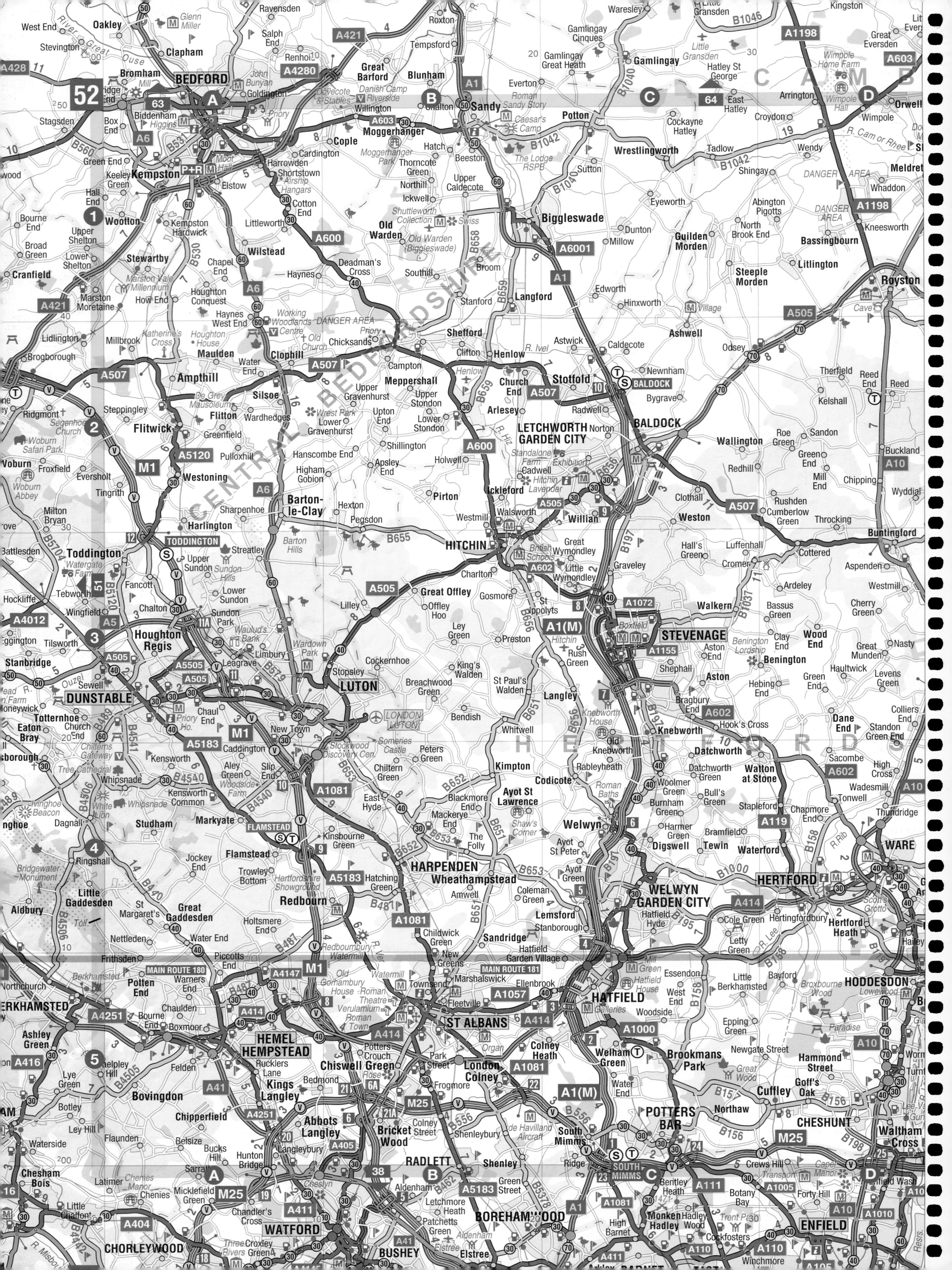

52
BEDFORD
Kempston
Sandy
Biggleswade
Gamlingay
Potton
Wrestlingworth
Royston
Bassingbourn
Ashwell
Baldock
LETCHWORTH GARDEN CITY
HITCHIN
STEVENAGE
LUTON
DUNSTABLE
Houghton Regis
Toddington
Flitwick
Ampthill
Shefford
Stotfold
Arlesey
Barton-le-Clay
HARPENDEN
Wheathampstead
Redbourn
Welwyn
WELWYN GARDEN CITY
HERTFORD
WARE
HODDESDON
HATFIELD
ST ALBANS
HEMEL HEMPSTEAD
Kings Langley
Abbots Langley
WATFORD
RADLETT
BOREHAMWOOD
POTTERS BAR
CHESHUNT
ENFIELD
BUSHEY
CHORLEYWOOD
BERKHAMSTED
Buntingford
Knebworth
Codicote
Kimpton
Markyate
Studham
Chiswell Green
London Colney
Shenley
Elstree
Waltham Cross
CENTRAL BEDFORDSHIRE
HERTFORDSHIRE
CAMB
A1
A1(M)
M1
M25
A6
A507
A505
A600
A10
A414
A5183
A1081
A4251
A41
A602
A1198
A421
A428
A603
A4280
MAIN ROUTE 180
MAIN ROUTE 181
TODDINGTON
BALDOCK
FLAMSTEAD
SOUTH MIMMS
LONDON LUTON

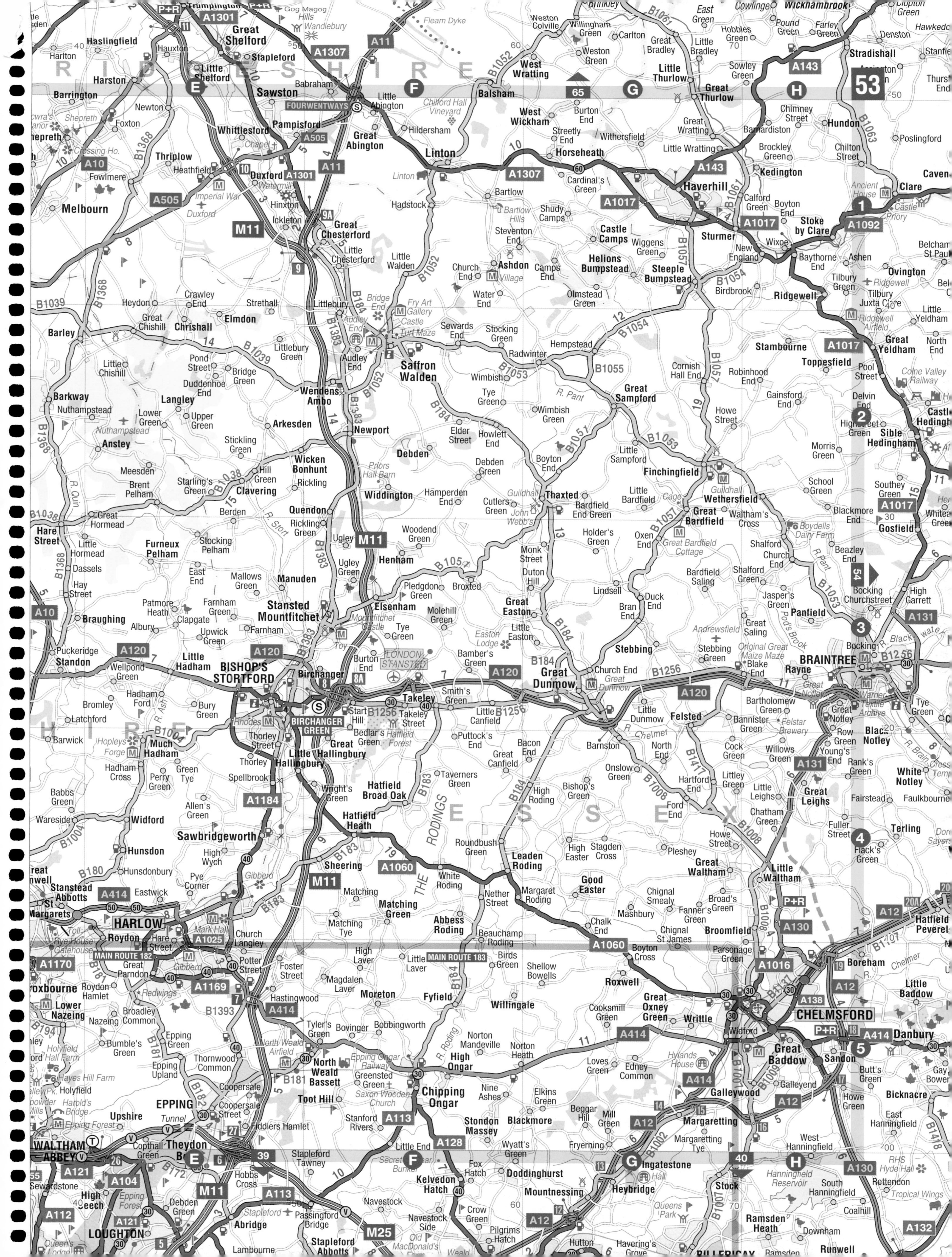

53
Trumpington
Gog Magog Hills
Wandlebury
Fleam Dyke
Weston Colville
Willingham Green
Carlton
Great Bradley
Little Bradley
East Green
Cowlinge
Wickhambrook
Pound Green
Farley Green
Denston
Stradishall
Haslingfield
Harlton
Hauxton
Great Shelford
Little Shelford
Stapleford
A1301
A1307
A11
West Wratting
Weston Green
Little Thurlow
Hobbles Green
Sowley Green
A143
Harston
Barrington
Sawston
Babraham
Little Abington
Balsham
Great Thurlow
Newton
FOURWENTWAYS
Chilford Hall Vineyard
Shepreth
Foxton
Pampisford
Whittlesford
Great Abington
Hildersham
West Wickham
Burton End
Streetly End
Withersfield
Great Wratting
Barnardiston
Chimney Street
Hundon
Poslingford
Thriplow
Heathfield
Duxford
Linton
Horseheath
Little Wratting
Brockley Green
Kedington
Chilton Street
Fowlmere
Melbourn
Imperial War Museum Duxford
Hinxton
Cardinal's Green
Haverhill
Calford Green
Boyton End
Clare
Ickleton
Great Chesterford
Little Chesterford
Hadstock
Bartlow
Shudy Camps
Steventon End
Castle Camps
Wiggens Green
Sturmer
Stoke by Clare
Wixoe
New England
Baythorne End
Ashen
Ovington
M11
A505
A10
A1017
A1092
Little Walden
Church End
Ashdon
Camps End
Helions Bumpstead
Steeple Bumpstead
Birdbrook
Tilbury Green
Ridgewell
Tilbury Juxta Clare
Water End
Olmstead Green
Heydon
Crawley End
Strethall
Elmdon
Littlebury
Great Chishill
Chrishall
Barley
Audley End
Saffron Walden
Sewards End
Stocking Green
Radwinter
Hempstead
Stambourne
Toppesfield
Great Yeldham
Little Yeldham
North End
Littlebury Green
Little Chishill
Pond Street
Bridge Green
Duddenhoe End
Langley
Wendens Ambo
Wimbish
Tye Green
Wimbish Green
Cornish Hall End
Robinhood End
Great Sampford
Gainsford End
Pool Street
Delvin End
Barkway
Nuthampstead
Lower Green
Upper Green
Arkesden
Newport
Elder Street
Howlett End
Debden
Howe Street
Highstreet Green
Sible Hedingham
Castle Hedingham
Anstey
Stickling Green
Wicken Bonhunt
Rickling
Debden Green
Boyton End
Little Sampford
Finchingfield
Morris Green
Meesden
Brent Pelham
Starling's Green
Hill Green
Clavering
Widdington
Hamperden End
Thaxted
Bardfield End Green
Little Bardfield
Wethersfield
School Green
Southey Green
Great Hormead
Hare Street
Little Hormead
Berden
Quendon
Rickling Green
Cutlers Green
Great Bardfield
Waltham's Cross
Blackmore End
Gosfield
Furneux Pelham
Stocking Pelham
Ugley
Woodend Green
Holder's Green
Oxen End
Shalford
Beazley End
Dassels
East End
Ugley Green
Henham
Monk Street
Duton Hill
Shalford Green
Church End
Bardfield Saling
Hay Street
Mallows Green
Manuden
Pledgdon Green
Broxted
Lindsell
Duck End
Jasper's Green
Bocking Churchstreet
High Garrett
Patmore Heath
Farnham Green
Stansted Mountfitchet
Elsenham
Molehill Green
Great Easton
Bran End
Panfield
Braughing
Albury
Clapgate
Upwick Green
Farnham
Tye Green
Little Easton
Great Saling
Puckeridge
Standon
Little Hadham
Bishop's Stortford
Birchanger
Burton End
Bamber's Green
Stebbing
Stebbing Green
Blake End
Bocking
Braintree
Rayne
Wellpond Green
Hadham Ford
Bury Green
Takeley
Smith's Green
Great Dunmow
Church End
Felsted
Bartholomew Green
Great Notley
Tye Green
Bromley
Latchford
Start Hill
Takeley Street
Little Canfield
Little Dunmow
Bannister Green
Black Notley
Barwick
Much Hadham
Thorley Street
Little Hallingbury
Great Hallingbury
Puttock's End
Bacon End
Barnston
North End
Cock Green
Willows Green
Young's End
Rank's Green
White Notley
Hadham Cross
Perry Green
Green Tye
Thorley
Spellbrook
Taverners Green
Great Canfield
Onslow Green
Littley Green
Hartford End
Little Leighs
Great Leighs
Faulkbourne
Babbs Green
Wareside
Allen's Green
Wright's Green
Hatfield Broad Oak
High Roding
Bishop's Green
Ford End
Chatham Green
Fairstead
Widford
Sawbridgeworth
Hatfield Heath
The Rodings
Essex
Fuller Street
Terling
Hunsdon
High Wych
Hunsdonbury
Sheering
Roundbush Green
Leaden Roding
High Easter
Stagden Cross
Pleshey
Howe Street
Great Waltham
Flack's Green
Little Waltham
Stanstead Abbotts
Eastwick
Pye Corner
Matching
White Roding
Nether Street
Margaret Roding
Good Easter
Chignal Smealy
Broad's Green
St Margarets
Harlow
Roydon
Hare Street
Church Langley
Matching Green
Matching Tye
Abbess Roding
Beauchamp Roding
Chalk End
Mashbury
Fanner's Green
Chignal St James
Broomfield
Hatfield Peverel
Great Parndon
Potter Street
Foster Street
High Laver
Little Laver
Birds Green
Shellow Bowells
Boyton Cross
Parsonage Green
Boreham
Roxbourne
Roydon Hamlet
Lower Nazeing
Nazeing
Broadley Common
Magdalen Laver
Hastingwood
Moreton
Fyfield
Willingale
Roxwell
Cooksmill Green
Great Oxney Green
Writtle
Chelmsford
Little Baddow
Danbury
Bumble's Green
Epping Green
Tyler's Green
Bovinger
Bobbingworth
Norton Mandeville
Norton Heath
Widford
Great Baddow
Sandon
Butt's Green
Thornwood Common
Epping Upland
North Weald Bassett
Greensted Green
High Ongar
Loves Green
Edney Common
Galleyend
Holyfield
Coopersale
Coopersale Street
Toot Hill
Chipping Ongar
Nine Ashes
Elkins Green
Beggar Hill
Mill Green
Galleywood
Margaretting
Howe Green
Bicknacre
Epping
Upshire
Fiddlers Hamlet
Stanford Rivers
Stondon Massey
Blackmore
Margaretting Tye
East Hanningfield
Waltham Abbey
Copthall Green
Theydon Bois
Little End
Wyatt's Green
Fryerning
West Hanningfield
Stapleford Tawney
Fox Hatch
Doddinghurst
Ingatestone
Stock
Hanningfield Reservoir
South Hanningfield
Retendon
Sewardstone
Hobbs Cross
Kelvedon Hatch
Mountnessing
Heybridge
High Beech
Debden Green
Abridge
Passingford Bridge
Navestock
Navestock Side
Crow Green
Pilgrims Hatch
Ramsden Heath
Downham
Coalhill
Loughton
Lambourne
Stapleford Abbotts
Hutton
Havering's Grove
Billericay
Ramsden
Runwell
M25
A12
A120
A131
A1060
A414
A1184
A113
A128
A130
A132
A121
A104
A112
A1016
A138
A1025
A1169
A1170
MAIN ROUTE 182
MAIN ROUTE 183

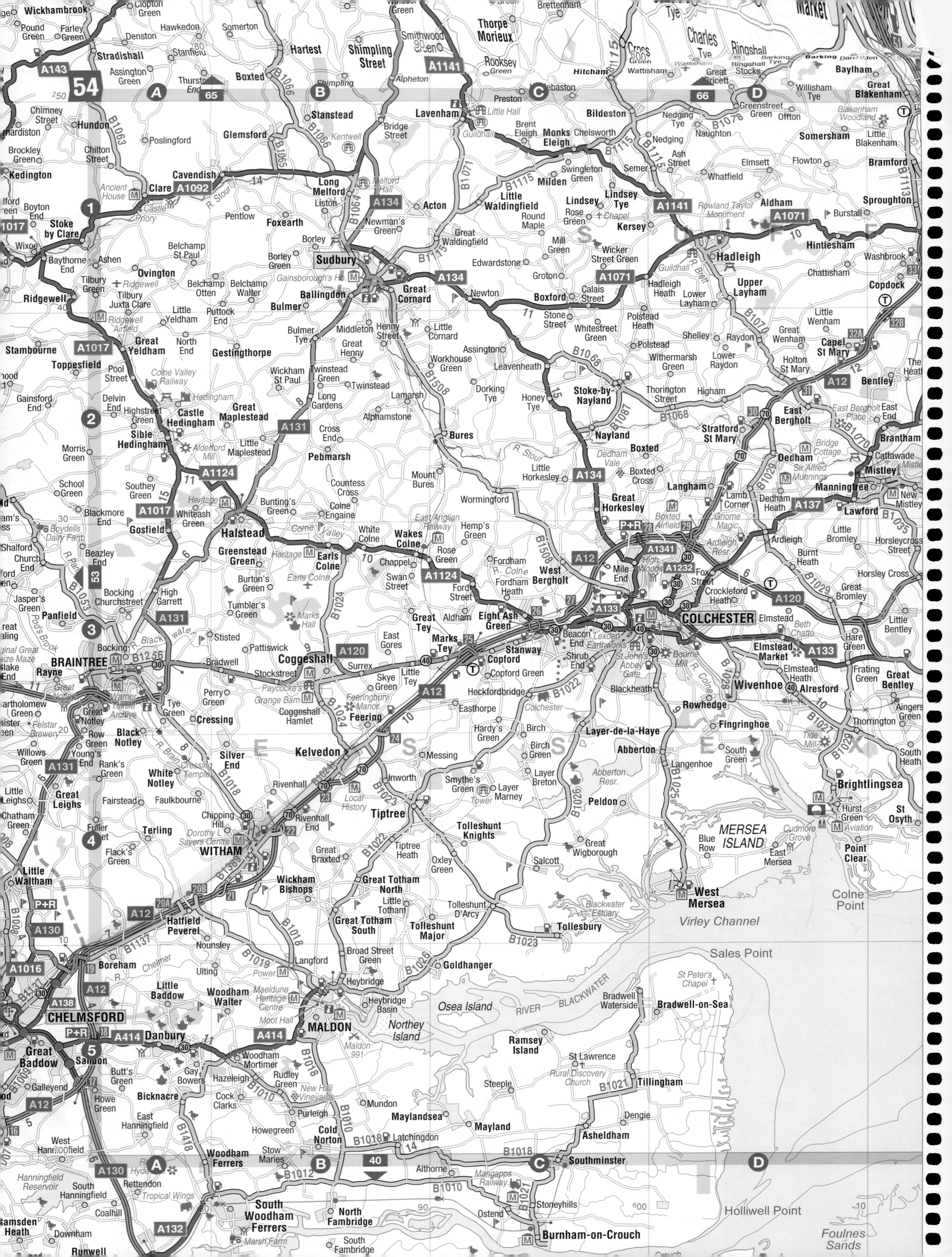

54
A
B
C
D
65
66
40
Wickhambrook
Clopton Green
Pound Green
Farley Green
Denston
Hawkedon
Somerton
Stradishall
Stansfield
Hartest
Shimpling Street
Smithwood Green
Thorpe Morieux
Brettenham
Cross Green
Charles Tye
Ringshall
Barking Tye
Barking
Darmsden
Baylham
Rooksey Green
Hitcham
Wattisham
Great Bricett
Ringshall Stocks
Willisham Tye
Great Blakenham
Assington Green
Thurston End
Boxted
Shimpling
Alpheton
A1141
A143
Preston
Kettlebaston
Chimney Street
Hundon
Stanstead
Lavenham
Little Hall
Brent Eleigh
Monks Eleigh
Chelsworth
Bildeston
Nedging Tye
Greenstreet Green
Offton
Blakenham Woodland
Little Blakenham
Barnardiston
Brockley Green
Chilton Street
Poslingford
Glemsford
Kentwell
Bridge Street
Guildhall
Nedging
Naughton
Somersham
Kedington
Cavendish
Clare
A1092
Ancient House
Castle
Priory
R. Stour
Long Melford
Melford Hall
Liston
A134
Acton
B1071
Swingleton Green
Milden
Semer
Ash Street
Whatfield
Elmsett
Flowton
Bramford
Sproughton
Boyton End
Stoke by Clare
A1017
Pentlow
Foxearth
Newman's Green
Little Waldingfield
Lindsey
Lindsey Tye
Rose Green
Chapel
A1141
Rowland Taylor Monument
Aldham
A1071
Burstall
Round Maple
Kersey
Hintlesham
Wixoe
Baythorne End
Ashen
Belchamp St Paul
Borley
Borley Green
Great Waldingfield
Mill Green
Wicker Street Green
Edwardstone
Hadleigh
Washbrook
Chattisham
Copdock
Ridgewell
Tilbury Green
Ovington
Sudbury
Gainsborough's Ho.
Belchamp Otten
Belchamp Walter
Tilbury Juxta Clare
Ballingdon
Great Cornard
Newton
Groton
Boxford
Calais Street
Hadleigh Heath
Lower Layham
Upper Layham
Bulmer
Little Yeldham
Puttock End
Middleton
Henny Street
Little Cornard
Stone Street
Whitestreet Green
Polstead Heath
Little Wenham
Stambourne
A1017
Great Yeldham
North End
Gestingthorpe
Bulmer Tye
Great Henny
Assington
Polstead
Shelley
Raydon
Great Wenham
Capel St Mary
Toppesfield
Pool Street
Colne Valley Railway
Wickham St Paul
Twinstead Green
Twinstead
Workhouse Green
Leavenheath
B1068
Withermarsh Green
Lower Raydon
Holton St Mary
The Heath
Gainsford End
Delvin End
Hedingham
Long Gardens
Lamarsh
B1508
Dorking Tye
Honey Tye
Stoke-by-Nayland
Thorington Street
Higham
A12
Bentley
Highstreet Green
Castle Hedingham
Great Maplestead
A131
Alphamstone
Nayland
B1087
Stratford St Mary
East Bergholt
East Bergholt Place
East End
Sible Hedingham
Alderford Mill
Little Maplestead
Cross End
Bures
R. Stour
Dedham Vale
Boxted
Dedham
Bridge Cottage
Brantham
Morris Green
Pebmarsh
Little Horkesley
A134
Boxted Cross
Sir Alfred Munnings
Cattawade
Mistley
A1124
Mount Bures
Langham
Lamb Corner
Manningtree
School Green
Southey Green
Countess Cross
Wormingford
Great Horkesley
Dedham Heath
A137
New Mistley
Blackmore End
Heritage
Colne Engaine
Bunting's Green
Whiteash Green
A1017
East Anglian Railway
Hemp's Green
Boxted Airfield
Gnome Magic
Lawford
B1035
Boydells Dairy Farm
Gosfield
Halstead
Colne Valley
White Colne
Wakes Colne
Rose Green
B1508
P+R
A1341
Ardleigh
Ardleigh Resr.
Little Bromley
Horsleycross Street
Shalford Church End
Beazley End
Greenstead Green
Heritage
Earls Colne
Chappel
Fordham
R. Colne
West Bergholt
A12
Mile End
High Woods
A1232
Fox Street
Burnt Heath
Horsley Cross
Bocking Churchstreet
High Garrett
Burton's Green
Earls Colne
Swan Street
A1124
Ford Street
Fordham Heath
Crockleford Heath
A120
Great Bromley
Jasper's Green
Panfield
B1053
Tumbler's Green
Marks Hall
B1024
Great Tey
Aldham
Eight Ash Green
A133
COLCHESTER
Elmstead
Beth Chatto
Little Bentley
A131
Stisted
Black
Bocking
Pattiswick
East Gores
Marks Tey
Stanway
Beacon End
Lexden Earthworks
Elmstead Market
A133
Hare Green
BRAINTREE
Rayne
B1256
Bradwell
Coggeshall
A120
Surrex
Copford
Shrub End
St John's Abbey Gate
Bourne Mill
R. Colne
Frating Green
Great Bentley
Stockstreet
Paycocke's
Skye Green
Little Tey
Copford Green
Elmstead Heath
Wivenhoe
Alresford
Great Notley
Warner Textile Archive
Perry Green
Grange Barn
Coggeshall Hamlet
Feeringbury Manor
A12
Heckfordbridge
B1022
Blackheath
Aingers Green
Bartholomew Green
Felstar Brewery
Tye Green
Cressing
Feering
Easthorpe
Colchester Zoo
Rowhedge
Thorrington
Great Notley
Black Notley
Hardy's Green
Birch
Layer-de-la-Haye
Fingringhoe
Tide Mill
Willows Green
Row Green
Young's End
R. Brain
Silver End
Kelvedon
Messing
Birch Green
Abberton
South Green
B1027
B1029
South Heath
A131
Rank's Green
White Notley
Cressing Temple
Inworth
Smythe's Green
Layer Marney Tower
Layer Breton
Abberton Resr.
Langenhoe
B1025
Brightlingsea
Little Leighs
Great Leighs
Fairstead
Faulkbourne
Rivenhall
Local History
B1023
Peldon
Hurst Green
St Osyth
Chatham Green
Fuller Street
Chipping Hill
Dorothy L Sayers Centre
Rivenhall End
Tiptree
Tolleshunt Knights
MERSEA ISLAND
Cudmore Grove
Aviation
Terling
Flack's Green
WITHAM
Great Braxted
Tiptree Heath
Oxley Green
Great Wigborough
Blue Row
East Mersea
Point Clear
Little Waltham
Wickham Bishops
Great Totham North
Little Totham
Salcott
West Mersea
Colne Point
P+R
A12
Hatfield Peverel
Great Totham South
Tolleshunt D'Arcy
Blackwater Estuary
Virley Channel
A130
Tolleshunt Major
Tollesbury
B1023
Nounsley
B1019
B1018
Broad Street Green
Sales Point
A1016
Boreham
Chelmer
Ulting
Langford
B1026
Goldhanger
St Peter's Chapel
A12
Little Baddow
Power
Maeldune Heritage Centre
Heybridge
Heybridge Basin
Woodham Walter
Osea Island
RIVER BLACKWATER
Bradwell Waterside
Bradwell-on-Sea
A138
CHELMSFORD
Moot Hall
P+R
A414
Danbury
A414
MALDON
Northey Island
Ramsey Island
Great Baddow
Sandon
Woodham Mortimer
Gay Bowers
Rudley Green
B1018
Maldon
St Lawrence
Rural Discovery Church
Butt's Green
Galleyend
Hazeleigh
B1010
New Hall Vineyards
Steeple
B1021
Tillingham
Bicknacre
Cock Clarks
Purleigh
Mundon
A12
Howe Green
East Hanningfield
Maylandsea
Dengie
B1418
Howegreen
Cold Norton
Mayland
Asheldham
West Hanningfield
Woodham Ferrers
Stow Maries
B1018
Latchingdon
B1018
Southminster
A130
Hyde Hall
B1012
Althorne
Mangapps Railway
Hanningfield Reservoir
South Hanningfield
Rettendon
Tropical Wings
B1010
Stoneyhills
Coalhill
South Woodham Ferrers
North Fambridge
Ostend
Holliwell Point
Ramsden Heath
A132
Downham
Marsh Farm
South Fambridge
Burnham-on-Crouch
Foulness Sands
Runwell

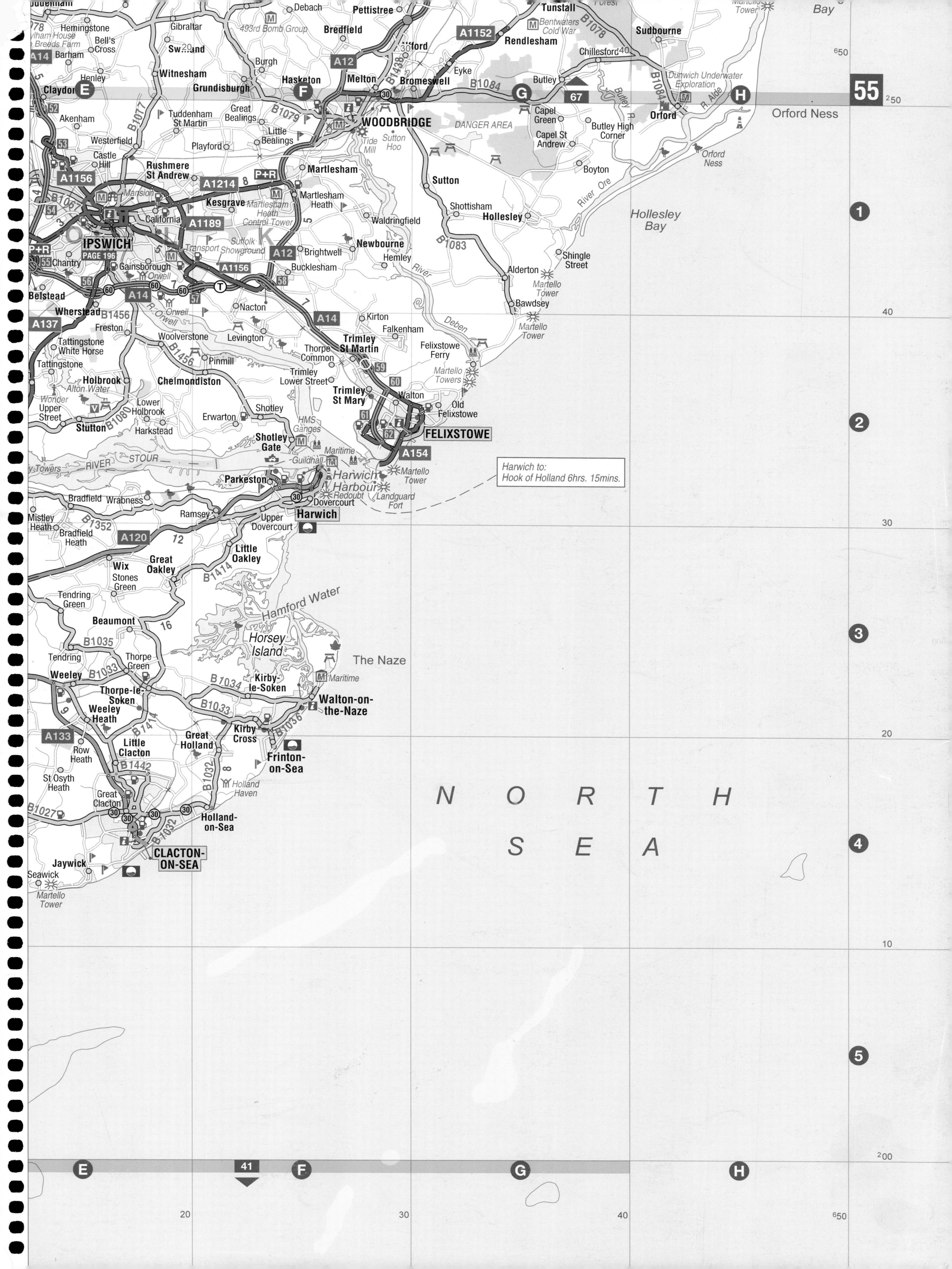

55
Debach
Pettistree
Tunstall
Bay
Hemingstone
Gibraltar
493rd Bomb Group
Bredfield
Bentwaters Cold War
Sudbourne
Bell's Cross
Swilland
A1152
Rendlesham
A14
Barham
Burgh
A12
Ufford
Chillesford
Henley
Witnesham
Grundisburgh
Hasketon
Melton
Eyke
Butley
Dunwich Underwater Exploration
Claydon
E
F
Bromeswell
B1084
G
67
H
Orford Ness
Akenham
Tuddenham St Martin
Great Bealings
B1079
WOODBRIDGE
DANGER AREA
Capel Green
Orford
Butley High Corner
Capel St Andrew
Westerfield
Little Bealings
Tide Mill
Sutton Hoo
Castle Hill
Playford
Orford Ness
Rushmere St Andrew
Martlesham
Boyton
A1156
A1214
P+R
Sutton
River Ore
Kesgrave
Martlesham Heath
Martlesham Heath Control Tower
Shottisham
Hollesley
Hollesley Bay
California
A1189
Waldringfield
IPSWICH
PAGE 196
Suffolk Showground
Transport
Brightwell
Newbourne
B1083
Chantry
Gainsborough
Orwell
A1156
Bucklesham
Hemley
Shingle Street
Alderton
Martello Tower
Belstead
A14
Nacton
Bawdsey
Wherstead
B1456
Orwell
A14
Kirton
A137
Freston
Falkenham
Deben
Woolverstone
Levington
Trimley St Martin
Tattingstone White Horse
Thorpe Common
Felixstowe Ferry
Tattingstone
B1456
Pinmill
Trimley Lower Street
Martello Towers
Holbrook
Chelmondiston
Alton Water
Trimley St Mary
Walton
Wonder
Upper Street
Lower Holbrook
Shotley
Old Felixstowe
Erwarton
Stutton
B1080
Harkstead
HMS Ganges
FELIXSTOWE
Shotley Gate
Maritime
A154
RIVER STOUR
Guildhall
Harwich to:
Hook of Holland 6hrs. 15mins.
Parkeston
Harwich Harbour
Martello Tower
Redoubt
Landguard Fort
Bradfield
Wrabness
Dovercourt
Mistley Heath
Ramsey
Harwich
B1352
Bradfield Heath
Upper Dovercourt
A120
Little Oakley
Wix
Great Oakley
Stones Green
B1414
Tendring Green
Hamford Water
Beaumont
B1035
Horsey Island
Tendring
Thorpe Green
The Naze
Weeley
B1033
Maritime
Thorpe-le-Soken
B1034
Kirby-le-Soken
Walton-on-the-Naze
Weeley Heath
B1033
Kirby Cross
A133
Great Holland
B1036
Row Heath
Little Clacton
Frinton-on-Sea
B1442
St Osyth Heath
B1032
Holland Haven
NORTH SEA
Great Clacton
B1027
Holland-on-Sea
B1032
CLACTON-ON-SEA
Jaywick
Seawick
Martello Tower
1
2
3
4
5
41
E
F
G
H
20
30
40
650
250
200
10

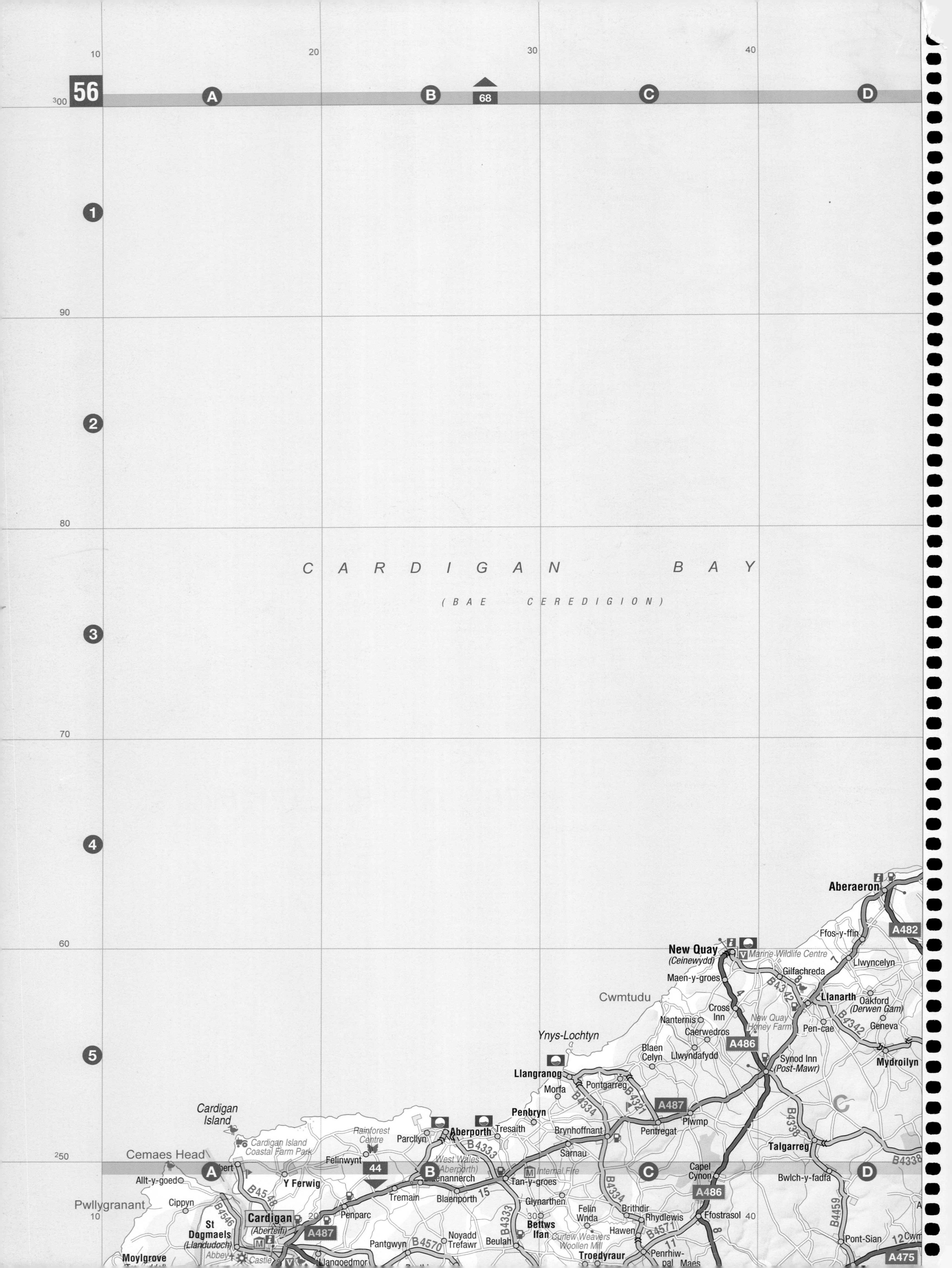

68
44
C A R D I G A N B A Y
(B A E C E R E D I G I O N)
Aberaeron
A482
Ffos-y-ffin
New Quay
(Ceinewydd)
Marine Wildlife Centre
Llwyncelyn
Gilfachreda
Maen-y-groes
Cwmtudu
Llanarth
Oakford
(Derwen Gam)
Cross Inn
Nanternis
New Quay Honey Farm
Pen-cae
Geneva
Caerwedros
Ynys-Lochtyn
A486
Blaen Celyn
Llwyndafydd
Synod Inn
(Post-Mawr)
Mydroilyn
Llangranog
Morfa
Pontgarreg
B4334
B4321
A487
Penbryn
Plwmp
Pentregat
B4338
Cardigan Island
Rainforest Centre
Aberporth
Tresaith
Brynhoffnant
Talgarreg
Cardigan Island Coastal Farm Park
Parcllyn
B4333
Cemaes Head
Felinwynt
West Wales (Aberporth)
Internal Fire
Sarnau
Capel Cynon
Bwlch-y-fadfa
B4338
Allt-y-goed
Y Ferwig
Tan-y-groes
Tremain
Blaenporth
Glynarthen
A486
Pwllygranant
Cippyn
B4548
B4546
Cardigan
(Aberteifi)
Penparc
Felin Wnda
Brithdir
Rhydlewis
Ffostrasol
B4459
St Dogmaels
(Llandudoch)
A487
Noyadd Trefawr
Beulah
Bettws Ifan
Curlew Weavers Woollen Mill
Hawen
B4571
Pont-Sian
Moylgrove
Abbey
Castle
Llangoedmor
Pantgwyn
B4570
Troedyraur
Penrhiw-pal
Maes
A475

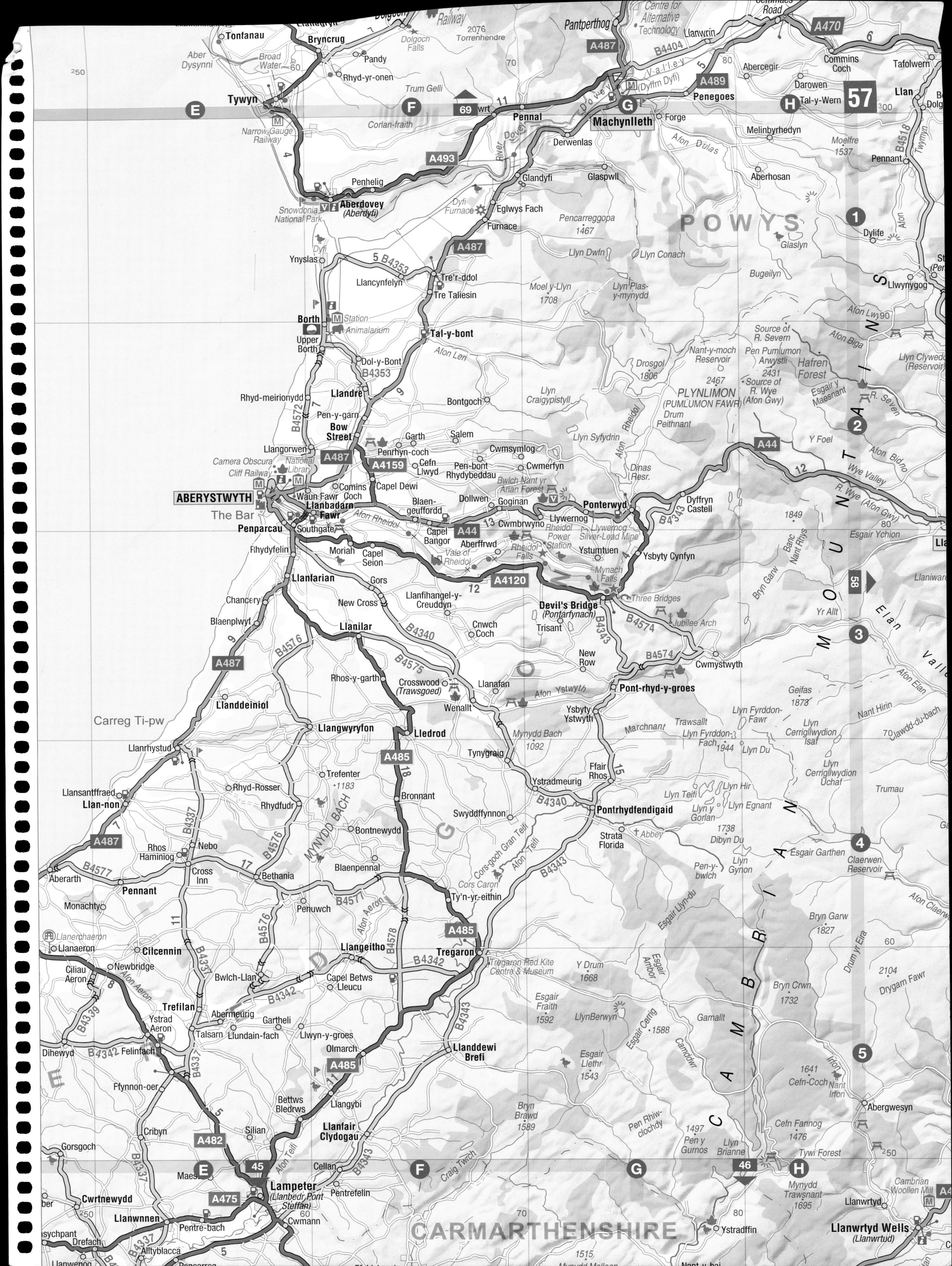

Tonfanau
Bryncrug
Dolgoch Falls
Pandy
Rhyd-yr-onen
Aber Dysynni
Broad Water
Tywyn
Narrow Gauge Railway
Trum Gelli
2076 Torrenhendre
Corlan-fraith
Pantperthog
Centre for Alternative Technology
Llanwrin
A487
B4404
A470
Commins Coch
Tafolwern
Abercegir
Darowen
A489
Penegoes
Tal-y-Wern
57
Llan
(Dyffryn Dyfi)
Machynlleth
Forge
Pennal
69
Derwenlas
Melinbyrhedyn
Moelfre 1537
Pennant
A493
Penhelig
Glandyfi
Glaspwll
Aberhosan
Aberdovey
(Aberdyfi)
Snowdonia National Park
Dyfi Furnace
Eglwys Fach
Furnace
Pencarreggopa 1467
POWYS
Dylife
Glaslyn
A487
Ynyslas
B4353
Llyn Dwfn
Llyn Conach
Tre'r-ddol
Llancynfelyn
Tre Taliesin
Moel y-Llyn 1708
Llyn Plas-y-mynydd
Bugeilyn
Llwynygog
Borth
Station
Animalarium
Upper Borth
Tal-y-bont
Afon Leri
Dol-y-Bont
B4353
Source of R. Severn
Pen Pumlumon Arwystli 2431
Nant-y-moch Reservoir
Drosgol 1806
Hafren Forest
Llyn Clywedog (Reservoir)
Source of R. Wye (Afon Gwy)
Llandre
Rhyd-meirionydd
2467
PLYNLIMON
(PUMLUMON FAWR)
Drum Peithnant
Llyn Craigypistyll
Bontgoch
Pen-y-garn
Bow Street
B4572
Garth
Salem
Llangorwen
Llyn Syfydrin
Afon Rheidol
A44
Y Foel
Camera Obscura
National Library
Cliff Railway
A487
Penrhyn-coch
A4159
Cwmsymlog
Cefn Llwyd
Pen-bont Rhydybeddau
Cwmerfyn
Dinas Resr.
Wye Valley
ABERYSTWYTH
Comins Coch
Capel Dewi
Bwlch Nant yr Arian Forest
Waun Fawr
Llanbadarn Fawr
Dollwen
Goginan
Ponterwyd
Dyffryn Castell
The Bar
Blaen-geuffordd
Afon Rheidol
Llywernog
B4343
1849
Penparcau
Southgate
A44
Capel Bangor
Cwmbrwyno
Rheidol Power Station
Llywernog Silver-Lead Mine
Esgair Ychion
Rhydyfelin
Moriah
Capel Seion
Aberffrwd
Vale of Rheidol
Rheidol Falls
Ystumtuen
Ysbyty Cynfyn
Banc Nant Rhys
Llanfarian
Gors
A4120
Mynach Falls
Bryn Garw
58
Chancery
New Cross
Llanfihangel-y-Creuddyn
Devil's Bridge
(Pontarfynach)
Three Bridges
Yr Allt
Blaenplwyf
Llanilar
B4340
Cnwch Coch
Trisant
B4574
Jubilee Arch
Elan
B4576
A487
B4575
New Row
Cwmystwyth
Rhos-y-garth
Crosswood (Trawsgoed)
Llanafan
Afon Ystwyth
Pont-rhyd-y-groes
Afon Elan
Geifas 1873
Wenallt
Llanddeiniol
Ysbyty Ystwyth
Nant Hirin
Llyn Fyrddon-Fawr
Marchnant
Trawsallt
Llyn Fyrddon-Fach 1944
Llyn Cerrigllwydion Isaf
Carreg Ti-pw
Llangwyryfon
Lledrod
Mynydd Bach 1092
Llyn Du
Llanrhystud
A485
Tynygraig
Llyn Cerrigllwydion Uchaf
Trefenter 1183
Ffair Rhos
Llansantffraed
Rhyd-Rosser
Ystradmeurig
Llyn Hir
Llan-non
Bronnant
Llyn Teifi
Trumau
Rhydfudr
Swyddffynnon
B4340
Pontrhydfendigaid
Llyn y Gorlan
Llyn Egnant
B4337
MYNYDD BACH
Bontnewydd
Strata Florida
Abbey
1738 Dibyn Du
A487
Rhos Haminiog
Nebo
B4576
Cors-goch Gran Teifi
Afon Teifi
Esgair Garthen
Claerwen Reservoir
B4577
Aberarth
Cross Inn
Bethania
Blaenpennal
B4343
Pen-y-bwlch
Llyn Gynon
Pennant
Cors Caron
Ty'n-yr-eithin
B4577
Monachty
Penuwch
Esgair Llyn-du
Afon Claerwen
Bryn Garw 1827
Afon Aeron
B4576
A485
Llanerchaeron
Llanaeron
Cilcennin
Llangeitho
B4578
Tregaron
Tregaron Red Kite Centre & Museum
Drum yr Eira
Y Drum 1668
Esgair Ambor
Ciliau Aeron
Newbridge
Afon Aeron
Bwlch-Llan
B4342
Capel Betws Lleucu
2104
Drygarn Fawr
Bryn Crwn 1732
Esgair Fraith 1592
B4337
B4342
Trefilan
LlynBerwyn
B4343
Gamallt
Ystrad Aeron
Abermeurig
Gartheli
Esgair Cerrig 1588
B4339
Talsarn
Llundain-fach
Llwyn-y-groes
Camddwr
Olmarch
Dihewyd
B4342
Felinfach
Llanddewi Brefi
Esgair Llethr 1543
A485
B4337
Ffynnon-oer
1641 Cefn-Coch
Irfon
Nant Irfon
Bettws Bledrws
Llangybi
Abergwesyn
Bryn Brawd 1589
Pen Rhiw-clochdy
Cribyn
Llanfair Clydogau
1497 Pen y Gurnos
Llyn Brianne
Cefn Fannog 1476
Silian
A482
Gorsgoch
B4337
B4343
Craig Twrch
Tywi Forest
Afon Teifi
45
Cellan
46
Maes
Lampeter
(Llanbedr Pont Steffan)
Mynydd Trawsnant 1695
Cambrian Woollen Mill
Cwrtnewydd
A475
Pentrefelin
Llanwrtyd
Llanwnnen
Pentre-bach
Cwmann
Ystradffin
Llanwrtyd Wells
(Llanwrtud)
CARMARTHENSHIRE
Drefach
Alltyblacca
B4337
CAMBRIAN MOUNTAINS
CEREDIGION

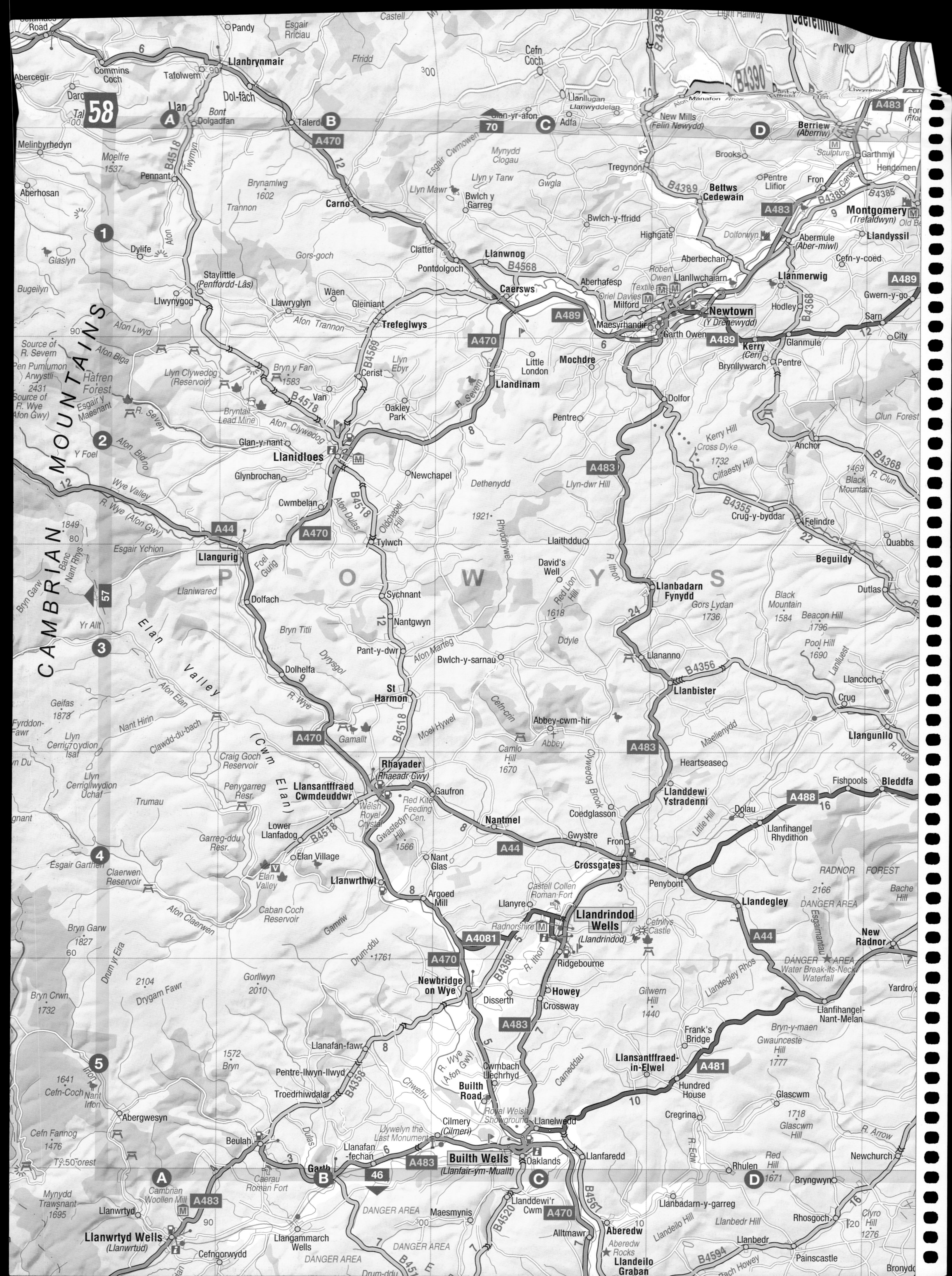

58
70
46
57
A
B
C
D
1
2
3
4
5
CAMBRIAN MOUNTAINS
P O W Y S
Pandy
Esgair Rriciau
Castell
Llanbrynmair
Commins Coch
Abercegir
Tafolwern
Dol-fâch
Cefn Coch
Llanllugan
Llanwyddelan
Ffridd
Llan
Bont Dolgadfan
Talerddig
Glan-yr-afon
Adfa
New Mills (Felin Newydd)
Manafon
Berriew (Aberriw)
Melinbyrhedyn
Moelfre 1537
Pennant
Twymyn
Esgair Cwmowen
Mynydd Clogau
Llyn y Tarw
Gwgla
Tregynon
Brooks
Pentre Llifior
Fron
Garthmyl
Hendomen
Sculpture
Aberhosan
Brynamlwg 1602
Trannon
Llyn Mawr
Bwlch y Garreg
Carno
Bettws Cedewain
Montgomery (Trefaldwyn)
Dylife
Afon
Bwlch-y-ffridd
Highgate
Dolforwyn
Abermule (Aber-miwl)
Llandyssil
Glaslyn
Gors-goch
Clatter
Llanwnog
Pontdolgoch
Aberbechan
Cefn-y-coed
Robert Owen
Llanllwchaiarn
Llanmerwig
Staylittle (Penffordd-Lâs)
Aberhafesp
Textile
Oriel Davies
Bugeilyn
Llwynygog
Waen
Caersws
Milford
Hodley
Gwern-y-go
Llawryglyn
Gleiniant
Newtown (Y Drenewydd)
Maesyrhandir
Garth Owen
Afon Trannon
Trefeglwys
Sarn
Afon Lwyd
Kerry (Ceri)
Glanmule
City
Source of R. Severn
Pen Pumlumon Arwystli 2431
Source of R. Wye Afon Gwy
Afon Biga
Hafren Forest
Llyn Ebyr
Cerist
Bryn y Fan 1583
Llyn Clywedog (Reservoir)
Little London
Mochdre
Bryntail Lead Mine
Brynllywarch
Pentre
Esgair y Maesnant
Van
Llandinam
Dolfor
R. Severn
Oakley Park
Afon Clywedog
Pentre
Clun Forest
Afon Biddno
Glan-y-nant
Kerry Hill
Cross Dyke 1732
Anchor
Y Foel
Llanidloes
Cilfaesty Hill
Glynbrochan
Newchapel
Dethenydd
Llyn-dwr Hill
1469 Black Mountain
R. Clun
Wye Valley
Cwmbelan
Afon Dulas
Oldchapel Hill
1921
Crug-y-byddar
Felindre
R. Wye (Afon Gwy)
1849
Banc Nant Rhys
Llangurig
Foel Gurig
Tylwch
Rhydhywel
Llaithddu
Quabbs
Esgair Ychion
Beguildy
Llaniwared
David's Well
R. Ithon
Llanbadarn Fynydd
Dutlas
Bryn Garw
Dolfach
Sychnant
Red Lion Hill 1618
Gors Lydan 1736
Black Mountain 1584
Beacon Hill 1796
Yr Allt
Elan Valley
Nantgwyn
Bryn Titli
Ddyle
Pool Hill 1690
Pant-y-dwr
Afon Marteg
Bwlch-y-sarnau
Llananno
Llanbister
Llancoch
Dyrysgol
Dolhelfa
Afon Elan
St Harmon
Crug
Geifas 1873
Fyrddon-Fawr
Nant Hirin
Clawdd-du-bach
Moel Hywel
Cefn-crin
Abbey-cwm-hir
Llangunllo
Llyn Cerrig Llwydion Isaf
Gamallt
Camlo Hill 1670
Maelienydd
R. Lugg
Llyn Cerrigllwydion Uchaf
Craig Goch Reservoir
(Cwm Elan)
Rhayader (Rhaeadr Gwy)
Clywedog Brook
Heartsease
Trumau
Pen-ygarreg Resr.
Llansantffraed Cwmdeuddwr
Gaufron
Llanddewi Ystradenni
Fishpools
Bleddfa
Red Kite Feeding Cen.
Welsh Royal Crystal
Nantmel
Coedglasson
Dolau
Lower Llanfadog
Gwastedyn Hill 1566
Gwystre
Fron
Little Hill
Llanfihangel Rhydithon
Garreg-ddu Resr.
Esgair Garthen
Elan Village
Nant Glas
Crossgates
RADNOR FOREST
Claerwen Reservoir
Elan Valley
Llanwrthwl
Castell Collen Roman Fort
Penybont
2166
Bache Hill
Argoed Mill
Llanyre
Llandegley
DANGER AREA
Caban Coch Reservoir
Afon Claerwen
Radnorshire
Llandrindod Wells (Llandrindod)
Cefnllys Castle
Bryn Garw 1827
Gamriw
Drum-ddu 1761
R. Ithon
Ridgebourne
New Radnor
Drum yr Eira
Gorllwyn 2010
Newbridge on Wye
Disserth
Howey
Crossway
Llandegley Rhos
DANGER AREA
Water Break-its-Neck Waterfall
2104
Drygarn Fawr
Gilwern Hill 1440
Yardro
Bryn Crwn 1732
Llanfihangel-Nant-Melan
Frank's Bridge
Bryn-y-maen
Gwaunceste Hill 1777
Llanafan-fawr
R. Wye (Afon Gwy)
Carneddau
Llansantffraed-in-Elwel
1572 Bryn
Cwmbach Llechrhyd
Irfon
1641 Cefn-Coch
Nant Irfon
Pentre-llwyn-llwyd
Chwefru
Builth Road
Hundred House
Glascwm
Troedrhiwdalar
1718 Glascwm Hill
Abergwesyn
Royal Welsh Showground
Llanelwedd
Cregrina
Cefn Fannog 1476
Dulas
Llywelyn the Last Monument
Cilmery (Cilmeri)
R. Arrow
Beulah
R. Edw
Irfon Forest
Llanafan-fechan
Builth Wells (Llanfair-ym-Muallt)
Llanfaredd
Newchurch
Garth
Oakland
Rhulen
Red Hill 1671
Bryngwyn
Caerau Roman Fort
Cambrian Woollen Mill
Mynydd Trawsnant 1695
Llanwrtyd
DANGER AREA
Maesmynis
Llanddewi'r Cwm
Llanbadarn-y-garreg
Llanwrtyd Wells (Llanwrtud)
Llangammarch Wells
Alltmawr
Aberedw
Aberedw Rocks
Llandeilo Hill
Llanbedr Hill
Rhosgoch
Clyro Hill 1276
Cefngorwydd
DANGER AREA
Llandeilo Graban
Llanbedr
Painscastle
Bronydd
A470
A44
A483
A489
A4081
A488
A481
B4518
B4569
B4568
B4358
B4520
B4561
B4389
B4390
B4385
B4386
B4368
B4355
B4356
B4594

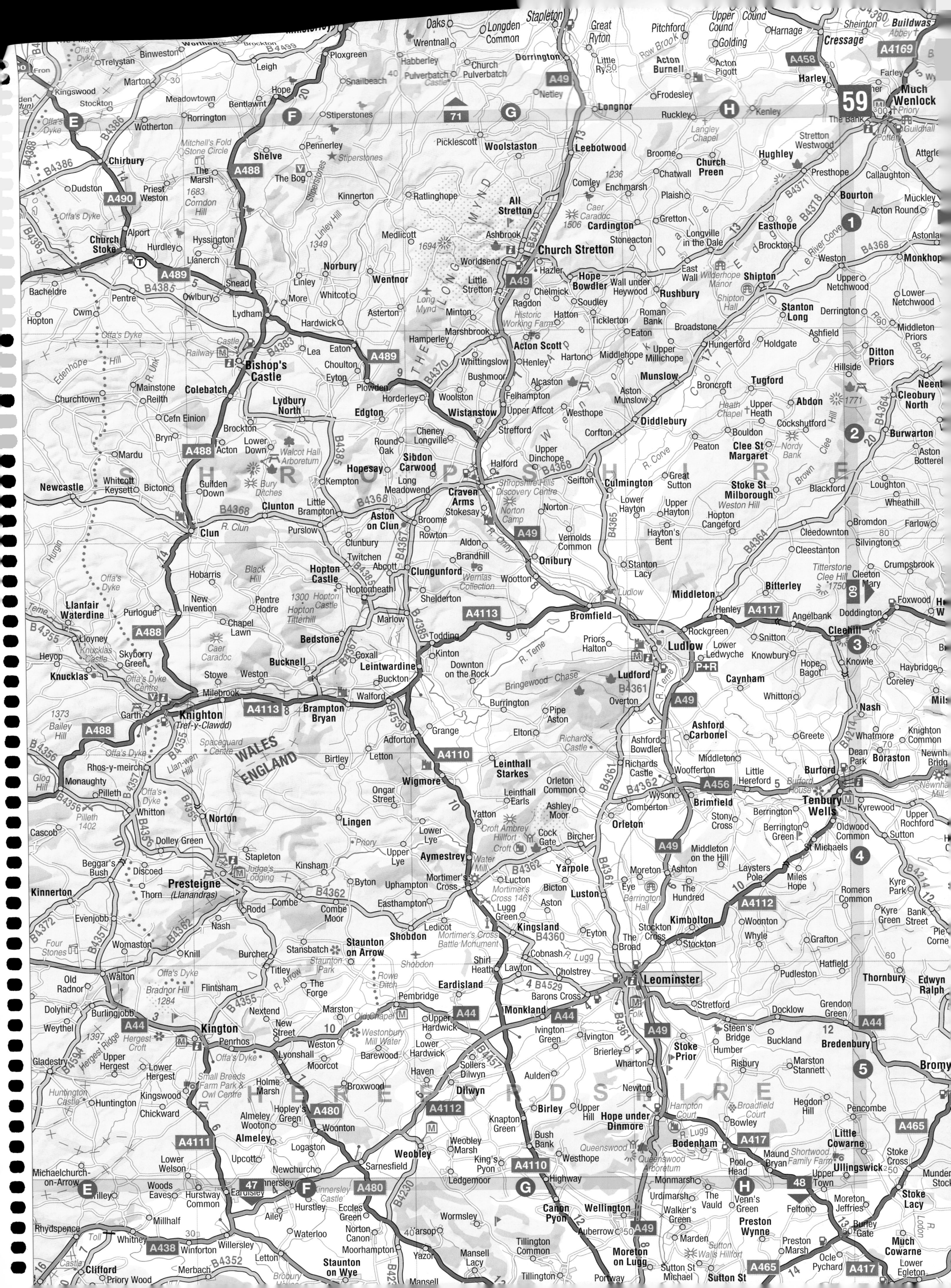

Stapleton
Great Ryton
Pitchford
Upper Cound
Cound
Harnage
Sheinton
Buildwas
Abbey
Cressage
A4169
Oaks
Longden Common
Wrentnall
Dorrington
Row Brook
Golding
Acton Burnell
Acton Pigott
A458
Harley
Farley
Much Wenlock
Priory
Guildhall
Offa's Dyke
Trelystan
Binweston
Worthen
Brockton
B4499
Ploxgreen
Habberley
Pulverbatch Castle
Church Pulverbatch
Little Ryton
Leigh
Snailbeach
A49
Netley
Frodesley
Marton
Kingswood
Stockton
Meadowtown
Bentlawnt
Hope
Longnor
Ruckley
Kenley
59
The Bank
Rorrington
Stiperstones
71
Langley Chapel
Stretton Westwood
Wotherton
B4386
Mitchell's Fold Stone Circle
Pennerley
Pickelscott
Woolstaston
Leebotwood
Broome
Church Preen
Hughley
Attlerley
Chirbury
Shelve
Stiperstones
The Marsh
A488
The Bog
Chatwall
Presthope
Callaughton
Dudston
Priest Weston
Corndon Hill
Kinnerton
Ratlinghope
Comley
Enchmarsh
Plaish
Bourton
Muckley
A490
All Stretton
Caer Caradoc
Gretton
Acton Round
Offa's Dyke
Linley Hill
Medlicott
Ashbrook
Cardington
Longville in the Dale
Easthope
Alport
Hyssington
Church Stoke
Hurdley
Llanerch
Stoneacton
Brockton
Weston
B4368
Monkhopton
Astonlane
Church Stretton
Worldsend
Norbury
Wentnor
Hazler
Hope Bowdler
Wall under Heywood
East Wall
Wilderhope Manor
Shipton
Upper Netchwood
A489
B4385
Shead
Owlbury
Linley
Little Stretton
Chelmick
Rushbury
Lower Netchwood
Bacheldre
Pentre
More
Whitcot
Long Mynd
Ragdon
Soudley
Shipton Hall
Stanton Long
Derrington
Hopton
Cwm
Lydham
Asterton
Minton
Hatton
Ticklerton
Roman Bank
Middleton Priors
Hardwick
Historic Working Farm
Broadstone
Eaton
Offa's Dyke
Marshbrook
Hungerford
Holdgate
Ashfield
Ditton Priors
Castle
Railway
B4383
Lea
Eaton
Hamperley
Acton Scott
Harton
Middlehope
Upper Millichope
Bishop's Castle
Choulton
A489
Whittingslow
Henley
Edenhope Hill
Mainstone
Eyton
Plowden
Bushmoor
Alcaston
Munslow
Broncroft
Tugford
Hillside
Neenton
Churchtown
Reilth
Colebatch
Lydbury North
Horderley
Woolston
Felhampton
Aston Munslow
Heath Chapel
Upper Heath
Abdon
Cleobury North
Cefn Einion
Edgton
Wistanstow
Upper Affcot
Westhope
Diddlebury
Cockshutford
Brockton
Cheney Longville
Strefford
Corfton
Boulton
Burwarton
Bryn
Acton
Lower Down
Round Oak
Sibdon Carwood
Upper Dinchope
Peaton
Clee St Margaret
Nordy Bank
Aston Botterell
Mardu
Walcot Hall Arboretum
Hopesay
Halford
Newcastle
Whitcott Keysett
Bicton
Guilden Down
Bury Ditches
Kempton
Long Meadowend
Craven Arms
Shropshire Hills Discovery Centre
Seifton
Culmington
Great Sutton
Stoke St Milborough
Blackford
Loughton
Wheathill
Clunton
Little Brampton
Aston on Clun
Stokesay
Norton Camp
Lower Hayton
Upper Hayton
Hopton Cangeford
Weston Hill
Norton
Clun
Purslow
Broome
Rowton
A49
Vernolds Common
Hayton's Bent
Bromdon
Farlow
Clunbury
Aldon
Cleedownton
Silvington
Twitchen
Brandhill
Onibury
Cleestanton
Hobarris
Black Hill
Hopton Castle
Abcott
Clungunford
Stanton Lacy
Titterstone Clee Hill
Crumpsbrook
Cleeton St Mary
Offa's Dyke
New Invention
Pentre Hodre
Hoptonheath
Wernlas Collection
Wootton
Ludlow
Bitterley
Llanfair Waterdine
Purlogue
Shelderton
Middleton
Foxwood
Hopton Titterhill
Marlow
A4113
Bromfield
Henley
A4117
Angelbank
Doddington
Chapel Lawn
Rockgreen
Cleehill
Lloyney
A488
Bedstone
Todding
Priors Halton
Snitton
Heyop
Knucklas Castle
Skyborry Green
Caer Caradoc
Bucknell
Coxall
Kinton
Ludlow
Lower Ledwyche
Knowbury
Knowle
Knucklas
Stowe
Weston
Leintwardine
Downton on the Rock
Hope Bagot
Haybridge
Offa's Dyke Centre
Buckton
Bringewood Chase
Ludford
P+R
Caynham
Coreley
Milebrook
Walford
B4361
Knighton
Tref-y-Clawdd
A4113
Brampton Bryan
Burrington
Overton
A49
Whitton
Nash
Garth
Bailey Hill
Pipe Aston
Ashford Carbonel
A488
Adforton
Grange
Elton
Richard's Castle
Greete
Whatmore
Knighton Common
Spaceguard Centre
WALES
ENGLAND
Ashford Bowdler
Dean Park
Boraston
Offa's Dyke
Letton
A4110
Leinthall Starkes
Middleton
Burford
Rhos-y-meirch
Llan-wen Hill
Birtley
Richards Castle
Woofferton
Little Hereford
Glog Hill
Monaughty
Wigmore
Orleton Common
B4362
A456
Burford House
Pilleth
Ongar Street
Leinthall Earls
Wyson
Brimfield
Tenbury Wells
Kyrewood
Offa's Dyke
Ashley Moor
Comberton
Pilleth 1402
Whitton
Norton
Lingen
Yatton
Croft Ambrey Hillfort
Orleton
Stony Cross
Berrington
Upper Rochford
Berrington Green
Oldwood Common
Sutton
Cascob
Dolley Green
Lower Lye
Croft
Cock Gate
Bircher
A49
St Michaels
Priory
Middleton on the Hill
Stapleton
Upper Lye
Aymestrey
Beggar's Bush
Discoed
Judge's Lodging
Kinsham
Water Mill
Yarpole
Laysters Pole
Miles Hope
Moreton
Ashton
Kyre Park
Presteigne
Llanandras
Byton
Uphampton
Mortimer's Cross
Lucton
Mortimer's Cross 1461
Bicton
Eye
Berrington Hall
The Hundred
Romers Common
Kinnerton
Thorn
B4362
Aston
Luston
A4112
Combe
Combe Moor
Easthampton
Lugg Green
Kimbolton
Kyre Green
Bank Street
Rodd
Woonton
Evenjobb
Nash
Ledicot
Kingsland
B4360
Stockton Cross
Eyton
Whyle
Four Stones
Womaston
Shobdon
Mortimer's Cross Battle Monument
The Broad
Stockton
Grafton
Stansbatch
Staunton on Arrow
Cobnash
Knill
Burcher
Shobdon
Shirl Heath
Lugg
Hatfield
Staunton Park
Walton
Offa's Dyke
Titley
Rowe Ditch
Lawton
Cholstrey
Leominster
Pudleston
Thornbury
Edwyn Ralph
Old Radnor
R. Arrow
Bradnor Hill 1284
Flintsham
The Forge
Eardisland
B4529
Barons Cross
Pembridge
Stretford
Docklow
Grendon Green
Dolyhir
Burlingjobb
B4355
Nextend
Marston
Old Chapel
Upper Hardwick
A44
Monkland
A44
A49
Steen's Bridge
A44
Weythel
A44
Kington
New Street
Westonbury Mill Water
Ivington Green
Ivington
Humber
Buckland
Bredenbury
Bromyard
Hergest Ridge
Hergest Croft
Penrhos
Weston
Lower Hardwick
Brierley
Wharton
Stoke Prior
Gladestry
Upper Hergest
Lower Hergest
Offa's Dyke
Lyonshall
Moorcot
Barewood
B4457
Risbury
Marston Stannett
Small Breeds Farm Park & Owl Centre
Holme Marsh
Haven
Sollers Dilwyn
Aulden
Huntington Castle
Kingswood
Broxwood
Dilwyn
Newton
HEREFORDSHIRE
Huntington
Chickward
Almeley Wooton
Hopley's Green
A480
A4112
Birley
Upper Hill
Hope under Dinmore
Hampton Court
Broadfield Court
Bowley
Hegdon Hill
Pencombe
A465
A4111
Almeley
Woonton
Knapton Green
Bush Bank
Queenswood
Bodenham
A417
Little Cowarne
Logaston
Weobley
Weobley Marsh
King's Pyon
Westhope
Queenswood Arboretum
Maund Bryan
Shortwood Family Farm
Ullingswick
Stoke Cross
Lower Welson
Upcott
Newchurch
Sarnesfield
A4110
Pool Head
Munderfield Stocks
Michaelchurch-on-Arrow
Woods Eaves
47
Eardisley
Kinnersley Castle
A480
Ledgemoor
Highway
Monmarsh
48
Upper Town
Tilley
Hurstway Common
Hurstley
Eccles Green
Canon Pyon
Wellington
Urdimarsh
The Vauld
Venn's Green
Felton
Moreton Jeffries
Stoke Lacy
Ailey
Norton Canon
Wormsley
Walker's Green
Preston Wynne
Burley Gate
Millhalf
Rhydspence
Whitney
Winforton
Willersley
Waterloo
Moorhampton
Tarsop
Auberrow
A49
Marden
Sutton Walls Hillfort
Preston Marsh
Much Cowarne
A438
Letton
Staunton on Wye
Yazor
Mansell Lacy
Tillington Common
Moreton on Lugg
Ocle Pychard
Clifford
Priory Wood
Merbach
B4352
Bredwardine
Mansell
Tillington
Portway
Sutton St Michael
Sutton St Nicholas
A465
A417
Lower Egleton

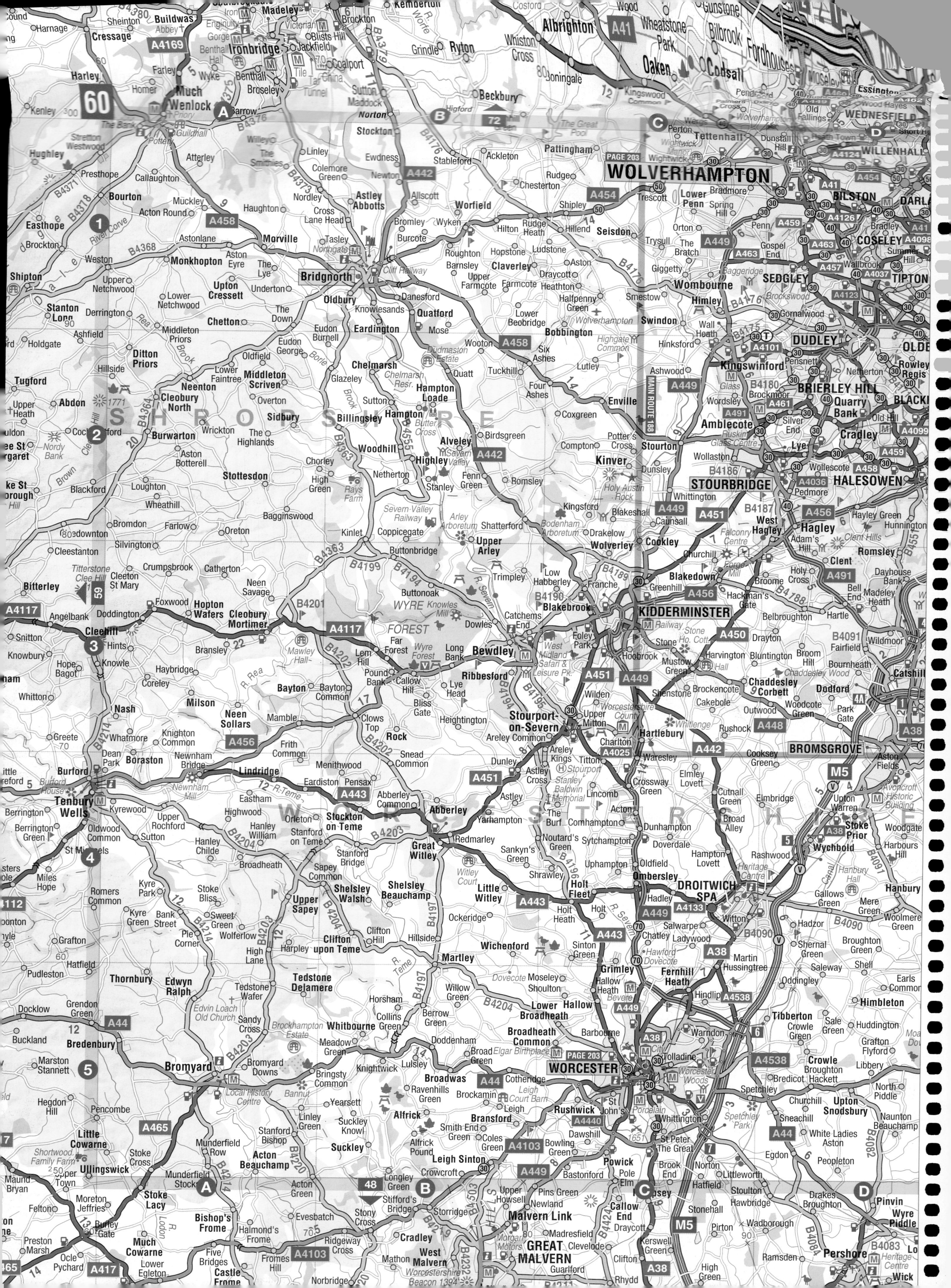

60
Much Wenlock
Buildwas
Cressage
Ironbridge
Madeley
Broseley
Coalport
Harley
Kemberton
Brockton
Ryton
Albrighton
A41
Whiston Cross
Beckbury
72
Codsall
Oaken
Bilbrook
Fordhouses
Perton
Tettenhall
Pattingham
WOLVERHAMPTON
PAGE 203
Wednesfield
Willenhall
Bilston
Coseley
Sedgley
Tipton
Dudley
Trescott
Lower Penn
Wombourne
Himley
Swindon
Kingswinford
Brierley Hill
Quarry Bank
Amblecote
Cradley
Stourbridge
Halesowen
Hagley
West Hagley
Clent
Romsley
Kinver
Stourton
Enville
Cookley
Wolverley
Blakedown
KIDDERMINSTER
Bewdley
Stourport-on-Severn
Hartlebury
Bromsgrove
M5
Droitwich Spa
Ombersley
Holt Fleet
Worcester
PAGE 203
Great Malvern
Malvern Link
Pershore
Upton Snodsbury
Bridgnorth
Oldbury
Quatford
Worfield
Claverley
Morville
Monkhopton
Shipton
Bourton
Easthope
Hughley
Stanton Long
Ditton Priors
Tugford
Abdon
Cleobury North
Burwarton
Neenton
Middleton Scriven
Sidbury
Chelmarsh
Billingsley
Highley
Alveley
Hampton Loade
Kinlet
Stottesdon
Cleehill
Cleobury Mortimer
Hopton Wafers
Bitterley
A4117
Wyre Forest
Bayton
Rock
Tenbury Wells
Burford
Lindridge
Stockton on Teme
Abberley
Great Witley
Shelsley Walsh
Shelsley Beauchamp
Little Witley
Martley
Wichenford
Tedstone Delamere
Whitbourne
Thornbury
Edwyn Ralph
Bredenbury
Bromyard
Little Cowarne
Ullingswick
Stoke Lacy
Bishop's Frome
Much Cowarne
Castle Frome
Cradley
West Malvern
Leigh Sinton
Suckley
Alfrick
Broadwas
Bransford
Rushwick
Powick
Callow End
Kempsey
SHROPSHIRE
WORCESTERSHIRE
A458
A442
A449
A451
A456
A443
A44
A38
A4103
A465
A417

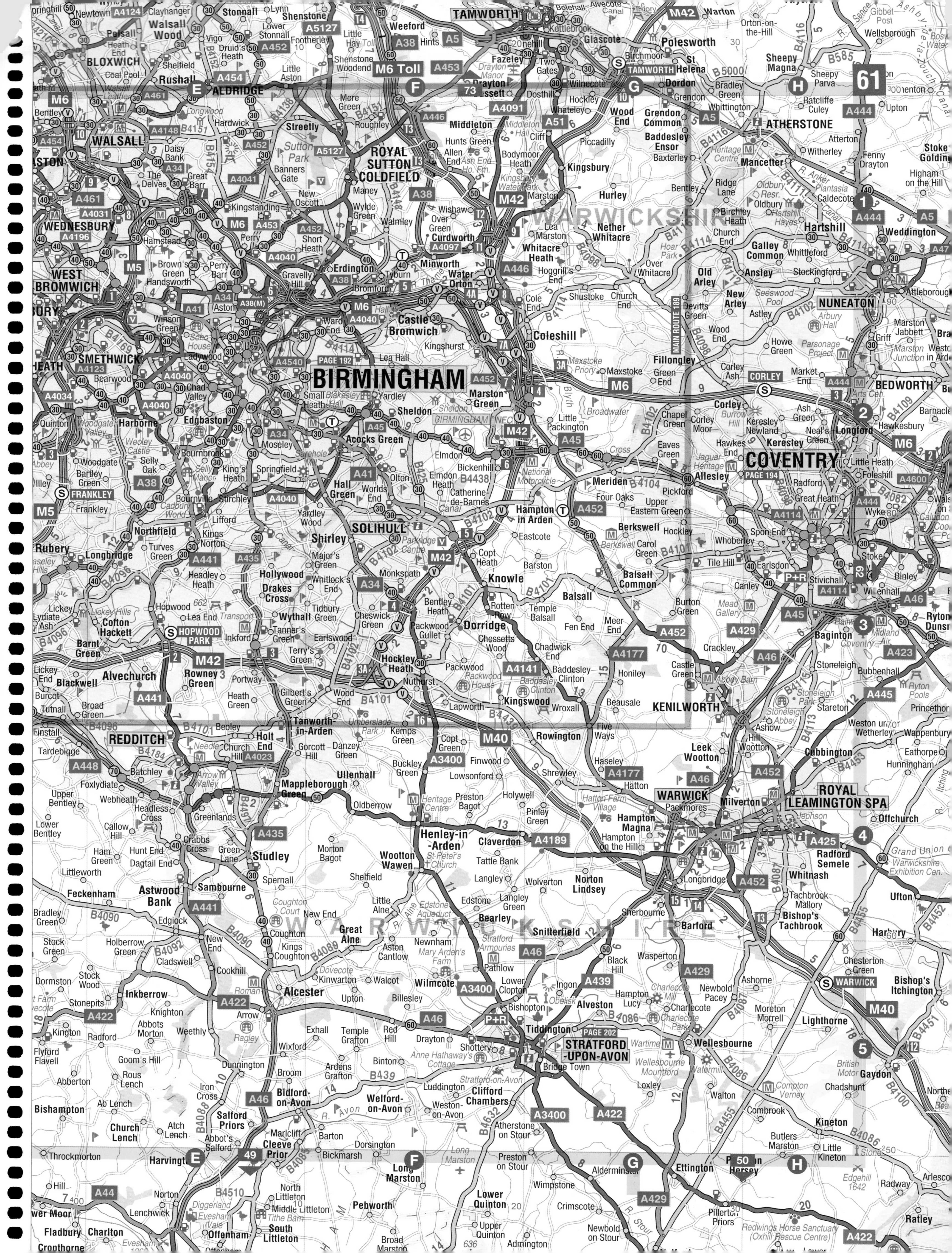

61
TAMWORTH
Polesworth
Shenstone
Weeford
Walsall Wood
BLOXWICH
ALDRIDGE
Rushall
WALSALL
WEDNESBURY
WEST BROMWICH
SMETHWICK
ROYAL SUTTON COLDFIELD
Streetly
Middleton
Kingsbury
WARWICKSHIRE
ATHERSTONE
Mancetter
Hartshill
NUNEATON
BEDWORTH
Erdington
Minworth
Water Orton
Castle Bromwich
Coleshill
BIRMINGHAM
PAGE 192
Harborne
Edgbaston
Moseley
Acocks Green
Sheldon
Marston Green
Meriden
Allesley
COVENTRY
PAGE 194
Fillongley
Corley
Keresley
Longford
Northfield
Rubery
Longbridge
Kings Norton
Shirley
SOLIHULL
Knowle
Dorridge
Balsall Common
Berkswell
Kenilworth
KENILWORTH
Baginton
Stoneleigh
Hollywood
Hockley Heath
Lapworth
Kingswood
Rowington
REDDITCH
Alvechurch
HOPWOOD PARK
FRANKLEY
Tanworth-in-Arden
Ullenhall
Henley-in-Arden
Claverdon
Hatton
WARWICK
ROYAL LEAMINGTON SPA
Whitnash
Radford Semele
Offchurch
Studley
Wootton Wawen
Snitterfield
Barford
Sherbourne
Wellesbourne
Alcester
Wilmcote
STRATFORD -UPON-AVON
PAGE 202
Tiddington
Clifford Chambers
Bidford-on-Avon
Welford-on-Avon
Ettington
Gaydon
Kineton
Long Marston
Pebworth
Harvington
Inkberrow
Feckenham
Astwood Bank
Evesham
Offenham
WARWICK
M40
M42
M6
M6 Toll
M5
A452
A46
A435
A3400
A422
A429

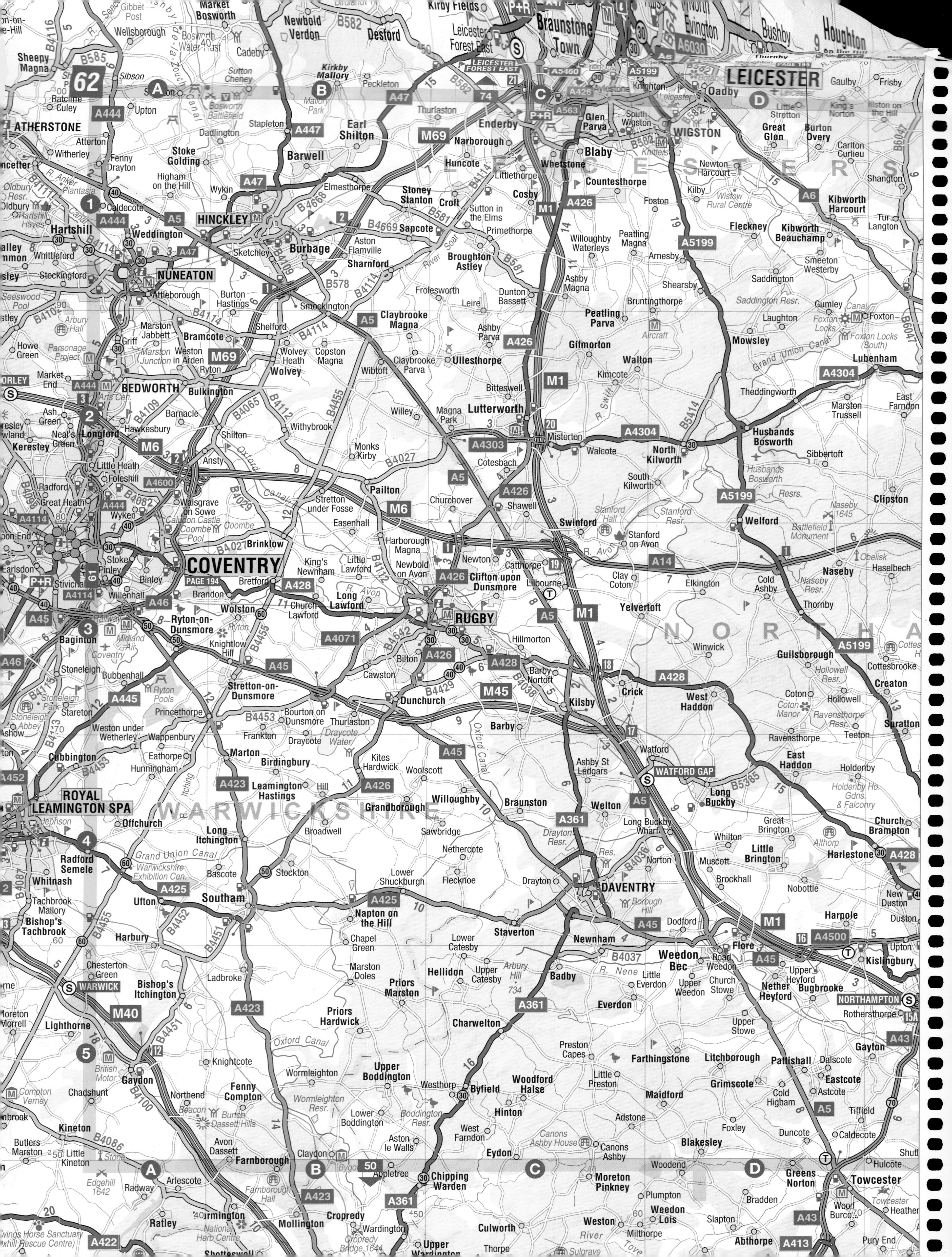

62
Market Bosworth
Newbold Verdon
Desford
Kirby Fields
Braunstone Town
North Evington
Bushby
Houghton on the Hill
Thurnby
Leicester Forest East
LEICESTER FOREST EAST
LEICESTER
Oadby
Wellsborough
Bosworth Water Trust
Cadeby
Sutton Cheney
Sibson
Kirkby Mallory
Peckleton
Sheepy Magna
Ratcliffe Culey
Upton
ATHERSTONE
Atterton
Witherley
Fenny Drayton
Stapleton
Earl Shilton
Thurlaston
Enderby
Narborough
Glen Parva
Aylestone
Knighton
South Wigston
WIGSTON
Gaulby
Frisby
King's Norton
Little Stretton
Great Glen
Burton Overy
Illston on the Hill
Carlton Curlieu
Stoke Golding
Dadlington
Barwell
Huncote
Blaby
Whetstone
Countesthorpe
Newton Harcourt
Higham on the Hill
Wykin
Elmesthorpe
Littlethorpe
Cosby
Foston
Kilby
Wistow Rural Centre
Shangton
Kibworth Harcourt
Kibworth Beauchamp
Tur Langton
Caldecote
HINCKLEY
Stoney Stanton
Croft
Sutton in the Elms
Fleckney
Hartshill
Weddington
Sapcote
Primethorpe
Willoughby Waterleys
Peatling Magna
Arnesby
Smeeton Westerby
Whittleford
Sketchley
Burbage
Aston Flamville
Sharnford
Broughton Astley
NUNEATON
Stockingford
Attleborough
Burton Hastings
Frolesworth
Dunton Bassett
Ashby Magna
Shearsby
Saddington
Saddington Resr.
Leire
Bruntingthorpe
Gumley
Foxton
Foxton Locks
Smockington
Claybrooke Magna
Peatling Parva
Laughton
Marston Jabbett
Bramcote
Shelford
Ashby Parva
Gilmorton
Mowsley
Griff
Weston in Arden
Copston Magna
Wolvey Heath
Wolvey
Claybrooke Parva
Ullesthorpe
Walton
Kimcote
Lubenham
Grand Union Canal
Howe Green
Parsonage Project
Marston Junction
Ryton
Bulkington
Wibtoft
Bitteswell
Theddingworth
Market End
BEDWORTH
Barnacle
Willey
Magna Park
Lutterworth
East Farndon
Marston Trussell
Ash Green
Hawkesbury
Withybrook
Misterton
Husbands Bosworth
Longford
Keresley
Shilton
Ansty
Monks Kirby
Walcote
North Kilworth
Sibbertoft
Cotesbach
South Kilworth
Little Heath
Foleshill
Radford
Great Heath
Wyken
Walsgrave on Sowe
Caludon Castle
Coombe Pool
Stretton under Fosse
Pailton
Churchover
Shawell
Clipston
Easenhall
Swinford
Stanford Hall
Stanford Resr.
Welford
Naseby 1645
Battlefield Monument
Brinklow
Harborough Magna
Stanford on Avon
COVENTRY
PAGE 194
Stoke
Binley
Pinley
King's Newnham
Little Lawford
Newbold on Avon
Newton
Catthorpe
Clay Coton
Elkington
Cold Ashby
Naseby
Haselbech
Bretford
Clifton upon Dunsmore
Lilbourne
Naseby Resr.
Willenhall
Brandon
Long Lawford
Church Lawford
Thornby
Wolston
RUGBY
Yelvertoft
Ryton-on-Dunsmore
Baginton
Knightlow Hill
Hillmorton
Winwick
Guilsborough
Cottesbrooke
Bilton
Stoneleigh
Bubbenhall
Cawston
Barby Nortoft
Hollowell Resr.
Creaton
Stretton-on-Dunsmore
Dunchurch
Crick
West Haddon
Coton
Hollowell
Coton Manor
Ravensthorpe Resr.
Stareton
Princethorpe
Bourton on Dunsmore
Thurlaston
Kilsby
Barby
Spratton
Weston under Wetherley
Wappenbury
Frankton
Draycote
Draycote Water
Ravensthorpe
Teeton
Cubbington
Eathorpe
Marton
Birdingbury
Kites Hardwick
Watford
WATFORD GAP
East Haddon
Holdenby
Hunningham
Woolscott
Ashby St Ledgars
Long Buckby
Holdenby Ho. Gdns. & Falconry
ROYAL LEAMINGTON SPA
Leamington Hastings
Grandborough
Willoughby
Braunston
Welton
Long Buckby Wharf
WARWICKSHIRE
Offchurch
Long Itchington
Broadwell
Sawbridge
Drayton Resr.
Great Brington
Church Brampton
Nethercote
Whilton
Althorp
Little Brington
Harlestone
Radford Semele
Norton
Muscott
Whitnash
Bascote
Stockton
Lower Shuckburgh
Flecknoe
Drayton
DAVENTRY
Brockhall
Nobottle
Southam
Borough Hill
New Duston
Tachbrook Mallory
Ufton
Napton on the Hill
Staverton
Dodford
Harpole
Bishop's Tachbrook
Harbury
Chapel Green
Lower Catesby
Newnham
Flore
Upton
Kislingbury
Weedon Bec
Road Weedon
Chesterton Green
Marston Doles
Hellidon
Upper Catesby
Arbury Hill 734
Little Everdon
Upper Heyford
WARWICK
Bishop's Itchington
Ladbroke
Priors Marston
Badby
Upper Weedon
Church Stowe
Nether Heyford
Bugbrooke
NORTHAMPTON
Priors Hardwick
Everdon
Rothersthorpe
Lighthorne
Charwelton
Upper Stowe
Oxford Canal
Preston Capes
Farthingstone
Litchborough
Pattishall
Dalscote
Gayton
British Motor
Gaydon
Knightcote
Upper Boddington
Little Preston
Chadshunt
Wormleighton
Fenny Compton
Westhorp
Byfield
Woodford Halse
Maidford
Grimscote
Eastcote
Astcote
Cold Higham
Northend
Wormleighton Resr.
Lower Boddington
Boddington Resr.
Hinton
Adstone
Tiffield
Burton Dassett Hills
Kineton
West Farndon
Foxley
Butlers Marston
Little Kineton
Avon Dassett
Aston le Walls
Canons Ashby House
Canons Ashby
Blakesley
Duncote
Caldecote
Farnborough
Claydon
Eydon
Woodend
Edgehill 1642
Radway
Arlescote
Appletree
Chipping Warden
Moreton Pinkney
Greens Norton
Towcester
Farnborough Hall
Plumpton
Bradden
Wood Burcote
Towcester Racecourse
Ratley
Mollington
Cropredy
Weedon Lois
Wardington
Slapton
Weston
Culworth
Milthorpe
Cropredy Bridge 1644
Upper Wardington
Thorpe
Sulgrave
Abthorpe
Pury End
Heather
National Herb Centre

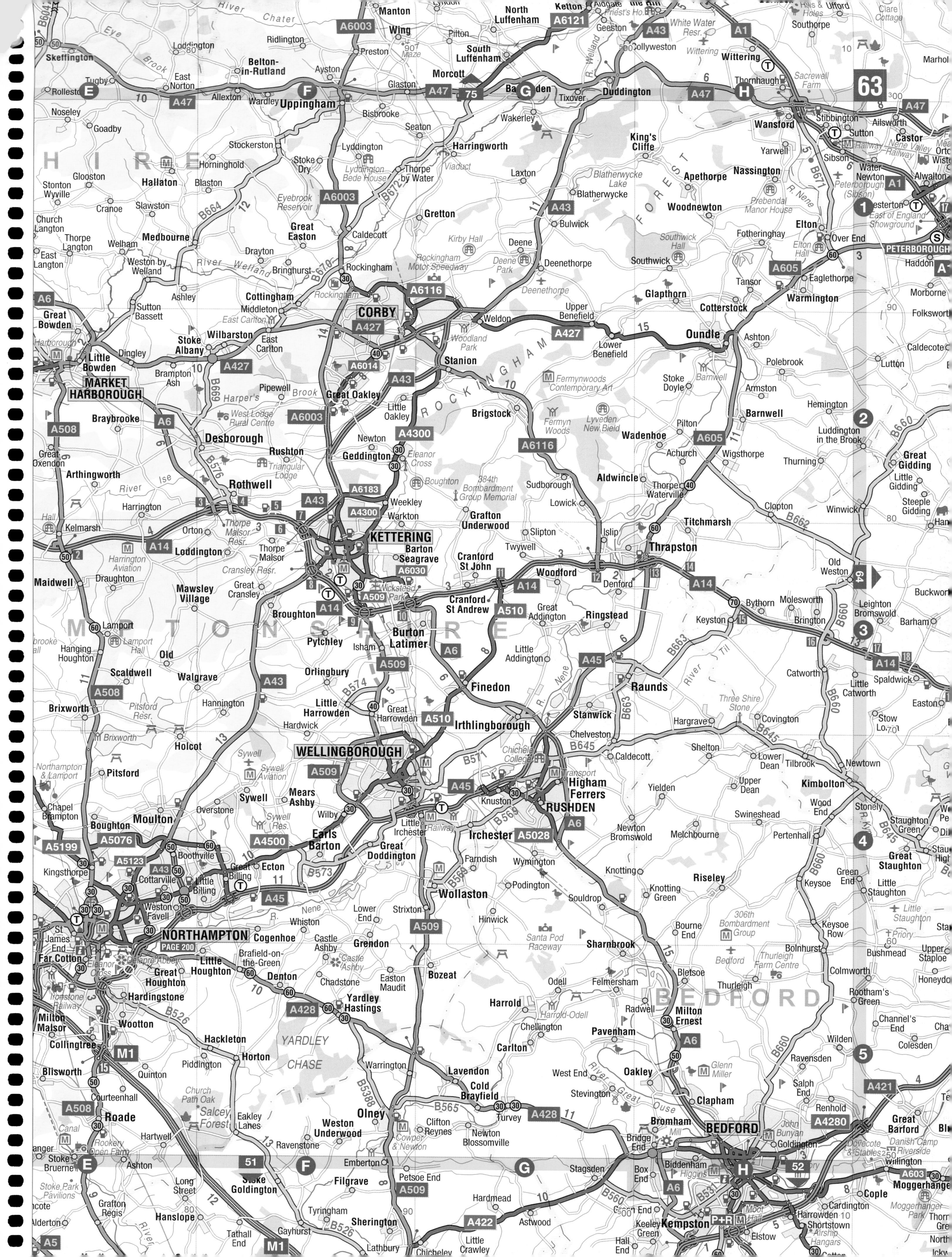

63
64
51
52
Manton
Wing
North Luffenham
Ketton
Aldgate
Geeston
Collyweston
Ufford
Southorpe
Skeffington
Loddington
Ridlington
Preston
Pilton
South Luffenham
White Water Resr.
Wittering
Belton-in-Rutland
Ayston
Morcott
Thornhaugh
Sacrewell Farm
Tugby
East Norton
Glaston
Barrowden
Duddington
Rolleston
Allexton
Wardley
Uppingham
Tixover
Noseley
Bisbrooke
Seaton
Wakerley
Wansford
Stibbington
Ailsworth
Sutton
Castor
Goadby
Stockerston
Lyddington
Harringworth
King's Cliffe
Yarwell
Stoke Dry
Horninghold
Lyddington Bede House
Thorpe by Water
Viaduct
Nassington
Apethorpe
Sibson
Water Newton
Alwalton
Glooston
Hallaton
Blaston
Laxton
Blatherwycke Lake
Blatherwycke
Woodnewton
Prebendal Manor House
Stonton Wyville
Cranoe
Slawston
Eyebrook Reservoir
Gretton
Bulwick
Elton
Orton
Church Langton
Medbourne
Great Easton
Caldecott
Kirby Hall
Deene
Fotheringhay
Over End
East of England Showground
Thorpe Langton
Welham
Drayton
Southwick Hall
Elton Hall
PETERBOROUGH
East Langton
Weston by Welland
River Welland
Bringhurst
Rockingham
Rockingham Motor Speedway
Deene Park
Deenethorpe
Southwick
Haddon
Tansor
Eaglethorpe
Warmington
Morborne
Ashley
Cottingham
Sutton Bassett
Middleton
East Carlton
CORBY
Glapthorn
Cotterstock
Upper Benefield
Great Bowden
Weldon
Folksworth
Oundle
Ashton
Lower Benefield
Woodland Park
Caldecote
Stoke Albany
Wilbarston
Little Bowden
Dingley
MARKET HARBOROUGH
Brampton Ash
Stanion
Polebrook
Lutton
Fermynwoods Contemporary Art
Stoke Doyle
Barnwell
Armston
Pipewell
Brook
Great Oakley
Harper's
West Lodge Rural Centre
Little Oakley
ROCKINGHAM
Brigstock
Hemington
Braybrooke
Fermyn Woods
Lyveden New Bield
Wadenhoe
Pilton
Luddington in the Brook
Desborough
Newton
Geddington
Eleanor Cross
Achurch
Wigsthorpe
Great Gidding
Rushton
Triangular Lodge
Thurning
Little Gidding
Great Oxendon
Arthingworth
Aldwincle
Boughton
384th Bombardment Group Memorial
Sudborough
Thorpe Waterville
Rothwell
River Ise
Weekley
Lowick
Steeple Gidding
Harrington
Warkton
Grafton Underwood
Clopton
Winwick
Hall
Kelmarsh
Orton
Thorpe Malsor Resr.
KETTERING
Slipton
Islip
Titchmarsh
Loddington
Thorpe Malsor
Barton Seagrave
Twywell
Thrapston
Harrington Aviation
Cransley Resr.
Cranford St John
Old Weston
Maidwell
Draughton
Great Cransley
Woodford
Denford
Buckworth
Mawsley Village
Wicksteed Park
Cranford St Andrew
Great Addington
Ringstead
Bythorn
Molesworth
Leighton Bromswold
Broughton
Keyston
Brington
Barham
Lamport
Lamport Hall
Pytchley
Burton Latimer
Isham
Hanging Houghton
Old
Little Addington
Scaldwell
Walgrave
Orlingbury
Finedon
Raunds
Catworth
Little Catworth
Spaldwick
Brixworth
Hannington
Pitsford Resr.
Little Harrowden
Great Harrowden
Irthlingborough
Three Shire Stone
Stanwick
Easton
Hardwick
Hargrave
Covington
Stow Longa
Brixworth
Holcot
WELLINGBOROUGH
Chichele College
Chelveston
Caldecott
Shelton
Lower Dean
Tilbrook
Newtown
Sywell
Sywell Aviation
Pitsford
Northampton & Lamport
Mears Ashby
Overstone
Higham Ferrers
Yielden
Upper Dean
Kimbolton
Chapel Brampton
Wilby
Sywell Res.
Knuston
RUSHDEN
Wood End
Stonely
Boughton
Moulton
Earls Barton
Little Irchester
Irchester
Newton Bromswold
Melchbourne
Swineshead
Pertenhall
Staughton Green
Kingsthorpe
Boothville
Great Doddington
Farndish
Wymington
Great Staughton
Cottarsville
Little Billing
Great Billing
Ecton
Podington
Knotting
Riseley
Green End
Keysoe
Little Staughton
Weston Favell
Whiston
Lower End
Strixton
Wollaston
Souldrop
Knotting Green
306th Bombardment Group
St James End
NORTHAMPTON
PAGE 200
Cogenhoe
Castle Ashby
Grendon
Hinwick
Santa Pod Raceway
Sharnbrook
Bourne End
Keysoe Row
Priory
Far Cotton
Eleanor Cross
Delapre Abbey
Brafield-on-the-Green
Little Houghton
Chadstone
Easton Maudit
Bozeat
Bedford
Thurleigh Farm Centre
Bolnhurst
Bushmead
Upper Staploe
Great Houghton
Denton
Yardley Hastings
Odell
Felmersham
Bletsoe
Thurleigh
Colmworth
Honeydon
Hardingstone
Harrold
Harrold-Odell
Radwell
BEDFORD
Rootham's Green
Milton Malsor
Wootton
Chellington
Milton Ernest
Channel's End
Collingtree
Hackleton
YARDLEY CHASE
Pavenham
Carlton
Horton
Piddington
Quinton
Warrington
Lavendon
Cold Brayfield
West End
Oakley
Glenn Miller
Wilden
Ravensden
Colesden
Blisworth
Courteenhall
Church Path Oak
Salcey Forest
Eakley Lanes
Olney
Weston Underwood
Clifton Reynes
Turvey
Newton Blossomville
Stevington
River Great Ouse
Clapham
Salph End
Renhold
Great Barford
Roade
Hartwell
Ravenstone
Cowper & Newton
Bromham
John Bunyan
Goldington
Danish Camp Riverside
Stoke Bruerne
Rookery Open Farm
Ashton
Emberton
Bridge End
Dovecote & Stables
Willington
Moggerhanger
Stagsden
Biddenham
Higgins
Box End
Petsoe End
Filgrave
Stoke Goldington
Stoke Park Pavilions
Long Street
Hardmead
Cople
Cardington
Moggerhanger Park
Grafton Regis
Hanslope
Tyringham
Sherington
Astwood
Keeley Green
Kempston
Harrowden
Shortstown
Airship Hangars
Elstow
Alderton
Tathall End
Gayhurst
Lathbury
Little Crawley
Hall End
Chicheley
A47
A6003
A6121
A43
A1
A6
A427
A6116
A6014
A4300
A605
A14
A508
A6183
A6030
A509
A510
A45
A5076
A5199
A5123
A4500
A5028
A428
M1
A421
A4280
A603
A422
A5
B664
B672
B670
B669
B576
B671
B662
B660
B663
B645
B574
B571
B569
B573
B526
B565
B5388
B531
B560

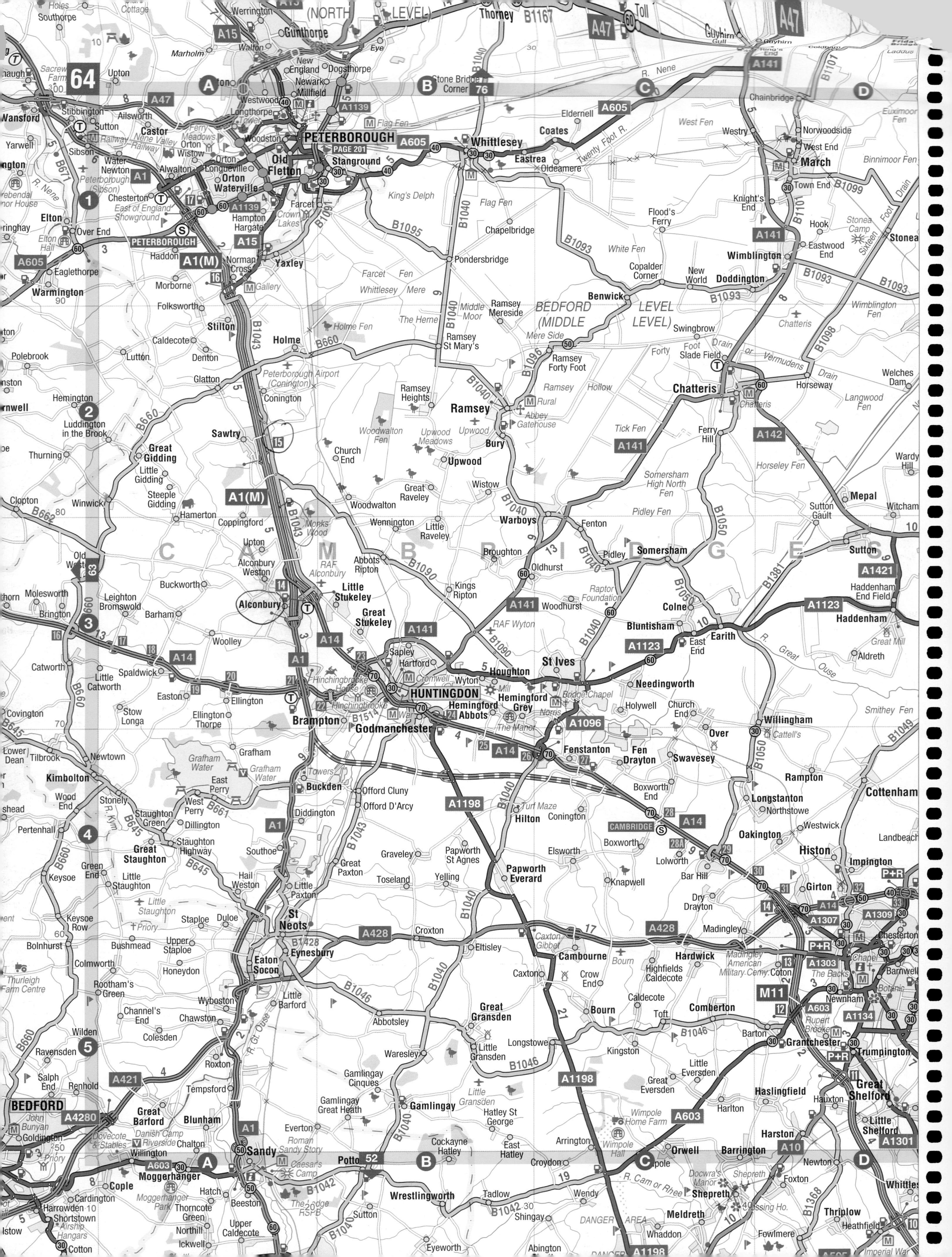

64
Southorpe
Werrington
(NORTH LEVEL)
Thorney
B1167
Toll
A47
Gunthorpe
Guyhirn
A15
Walton
Eye
Marholm
New England
Dogsthorpe
Newark
Millfield
Upton
Stone Bridge Corner
76
R. Nene
Chainbridge
Stibbington
Westwood
A1139
A47
Wansford
Ailsworth
Sutton
Castor
Longthorpe
Flag Fen
Eldernell
A605
West Fen
Westry
Norwoodside
Coates
West End
Yarwell
Nene Valley Railway
Ferry Meadows
Woodston
PETERBOROUGH
PAGE 201
A605
Whittlesey
Twenty Foot R.
March
Sibson
Orton
Wistow
Old Fletton
Stanground
Eastrea
Oldeamere
Binnimoor Fen
Water Newton
Alwalton
Longueville
Orton Waterville
Town End
B1099
Peterborough (Sibson)
A1
King's Delph
Knight's End
R. Nene
Chesterton
East of England Showground
A1139
Hampton Hargate
Farcet
Crown Lakes
Flag Fen
Flood's Ferry
Hook
Stonea Camp
Stonea
Elton
Over End
B1091
B1095
Chapelbridge
A141
Eastwood End
Elton Hall
PETERBOROUGH
A15
B1093
White Fen
Wimblington
Haddon
A1(M)
Norman Cross
Yaxley
Pondersbridge
A605
Eaglethorpe
Copalder Corner
New World
Doddington
B1093
Morborne
Farcet Fen
Whittlesey Mere
Gallery
Benwick
B1093
Warmington
Folksworth
Middle Moor
Ramsey Mereside
BEDFORD (MIDDLE LEVEL)
Wimblington Fen
Stilton
The Herne
Holme Fen
Mere Side
Swingbrow
Chatteris
B1043
Holme
B660
Ramsey St Mary's
Forty Foot
Drain or Vermudens
Caldecote
Denton
Polebrook
Lutton
Ramsey Forty Foot
Glatton
Peterborough Airport (Conington)
Chatteris
Welches Dam
Horseway
Ramsey Heights
Ramsey
Rural
Abbey Gatehouse
Ramsey Hollow
Langwood Fen
Hemington
Conington
Luddington in the Brook
B660
Sawtry
Woodwalton Fen
Upwood Meadows
Upwood
Bury
Tick Fen
Ferry Hill
A142
Thurning
Great Gidding
Church End
Upwood
A141
Little Gidding
Somersham High North Fen
Horseley Fen
Wardy Hill
Steeple Gidding
A1(M)
Great Raveley
Wistow
Clopton
Winwick
Hamerton
Woodwalton
B1040
Pidley Fen
Mepal
Sutton Gault
Witcham
B662
Coppingford
Monks Wood
Wennington
Little Raveley
Warboys
Fenton
B1050
Upton
Broughton
Pidley
Somersham
Sutton
C A M B R I D G E S
Old Weston
63
Alconbury Weston
RAF Alconbury
Abbots Ripton
B1090
Oldhurst
B1040
B1381
A1421
Buckworth
Little Stukeley
Kings Ripton
Raptor Foundation
Haddenham End Field
Molesworth
Leighton Bromswold
Alconbury
A141
Woodhurst
Colne
A1123
Haddenham
Brington
Barham
Great Stukeley
RAF Wyton
Bluntisham
Earith
A14
Woolley
A141
A1123
East End
Great Mill
Aldreth
Catworth
Spaldwick
A14
Sapley
Hartford
Houghton
St Ives
R. Great Ouse
Little Catworth
Hinchingbrooke House
Cromwell
Wyton
Needingworth
Easton
Ellington
HUNTINGDON
Mill
Hemingford Grey
Bridge Chapel
Covington
Stow Longa
Ellington Thorpe
Hinchingbrooke
Hemingford Abbots
Norris
Holywell
Church End
Smithey Fen
Brampton
B1514
Godmanchester
The Manor
A1096
Willingham
Over
B1049
Lower Dean
Tilbrook
Newtown
Grafham
Fenstanton
Fen Drayton
Swavesey
Cattell's
Grafham Water
A14
B1050
Rampton
Kimbolton
East Perry
Towers
Buckden
Offord Cluny
A1198
Boxworth End
Longstanton
Cottenham
Wood End
Stonely
West Perry
Offord D'Arcy
Turf Maze
Northstowe
Staughton Green
Dillington
B661
Diddington
Hilton
Conington
CAMBRIDGE
A14
Westwick
Pertenhall
B645
A1
Oakington
Landbeach
Great Staughton
Staughton Highway
Southoe
B1043
Graveley
Papworth St Agnes
Elsworth
Boxworth
Histon
Keysoe
Green End
Little Staughton
B645
Hail Weston
Great Paxton
Papworth Everard
Lolworth
Impington
Bar Hill
Girton
P+R
Little Paxton
Toseland
Yelling
Knapwell
Dry Drayton
Little Staughton
Keysoe Row
Priory
Staploe
Duloe
St Neots
Croxton
A428
Madingley
A1307
A1309
Chesterton
Bolnhurst
Bushmead
Upper Staploe
B1428
Eynesbury
A428
Eltisley
Caxton Gibbet
Cambourne
Bourn
Hardwick
P+R
A1303
Eaton Socon
Highfields Caldecote
Madingley American Military Cemy.
Coton
The Backs
Barnwell
Colmworth
Honeydon
Caxton
Crow End
M11
Thurleigh Farm Centre
Rootham's Green
B1046
Little Barford
Caldecote
Newnham
Botanic
Wyboston
Great Gransden
Toft
Comberton
A603
A1134
Channel's End
Chawston
Abbotsley
Bourn
Rupert Brooke
B660
Wilden
Colesden
R. Gt. Ouse
Little Gransden
Longstowe
B1046
Barton
Grantchester
Trumpington
Ravensden
Roxton
Waresley
Kingston
P+R
B1046
Little Eversden
A1198
Great Shelford
A421
Tempsford
Gamlingay Cinques
Little Gransden
Great Eversden
Haslingfield
Hauxton
Salph End
Renhold
Gamlingay Great Heath
Gamlingay
Hatley St George
Wimpole Home Farm
A603
Harlton
Little Shelford
BEDFORD
A4280
Great Barford
Blunham
Danish Camp Riverside
Everton
Cockayne Hatley
East Hatley
Arrington
Wimpole Hall
Harston
A1301
John Bunyan
Goldington
Dovecote & Stables
Chalton
A1
Roman Sandy Story
Orwell
Barrington
A10
Willington
Moggerhanger
Sandy
Caesars Camp
Potton
52
Croydon
Newton
Copel
Cardington
Moggerhanger Park
Hatch
B1042
Wrestlingworth
Tadlow
Wendy
R. Cam or Rhee
Docwra's Manor
Shepreth
Foxton
Whittlesford
Harrowden
Thorncote Green
Beeston
The Lodge RSPB
Sutton
B1042
Shingay
DANGER AREA
Meldreth
Thriplow
B1368
Shortstown
Airship Hangars
Northill
Upper Caldecote
Melbourn
Whaddon
Heathfield
Cotton
Ickwell
Eyeworth
Abington
A1198
Fowlmere
Imperial War

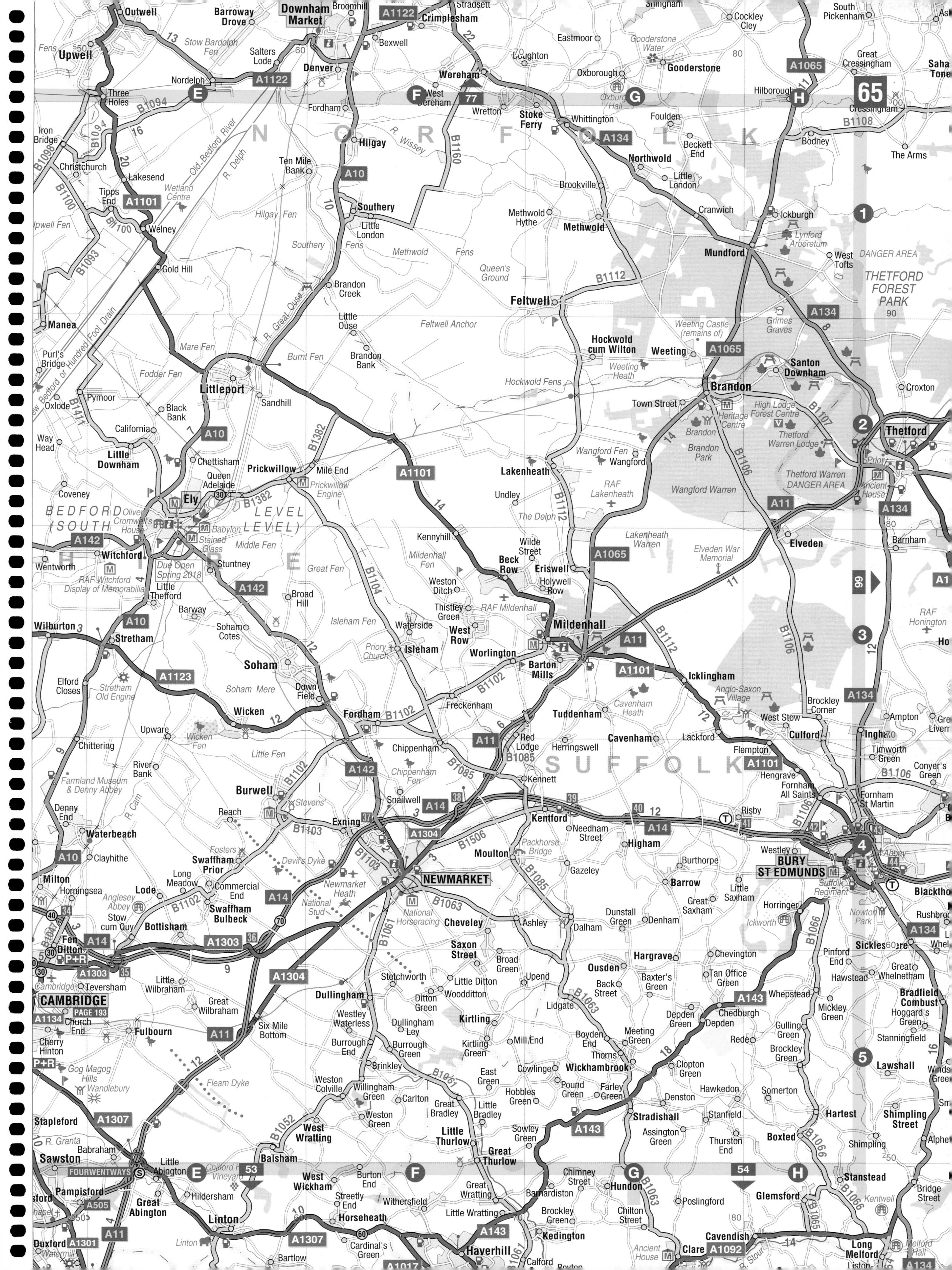
65
Downham Market
Upwell
Outwell
Littleport
Ely
Soham
NEWMARKET
Mildenhall
Brandon
Thetford
BURY ST EDMUNDS
Haverhill
CAMBRIDGE
PAGE 193
Lakenheath
Feltwell
Methwold
Mundford
Wereham
Stoke Ferry
Northwold
Hockwold cum Wilton
Weeting
Elveden
Icklingham
Kentford
Exning
Burwell
Fordham
Isleham
Wicken
Stretham
Witchford
Linton
Sawston
Clare
Cavendish
Long Melford
Wickhambrook
Kedington
NORFOLK
SUFFOLK
THETFORD FOREST PARK
A10
A11
A14
A134
A142
A143
A1065
A1101
A1122
A1303
A1304
A1307
A1092
FOURWENTWAYS

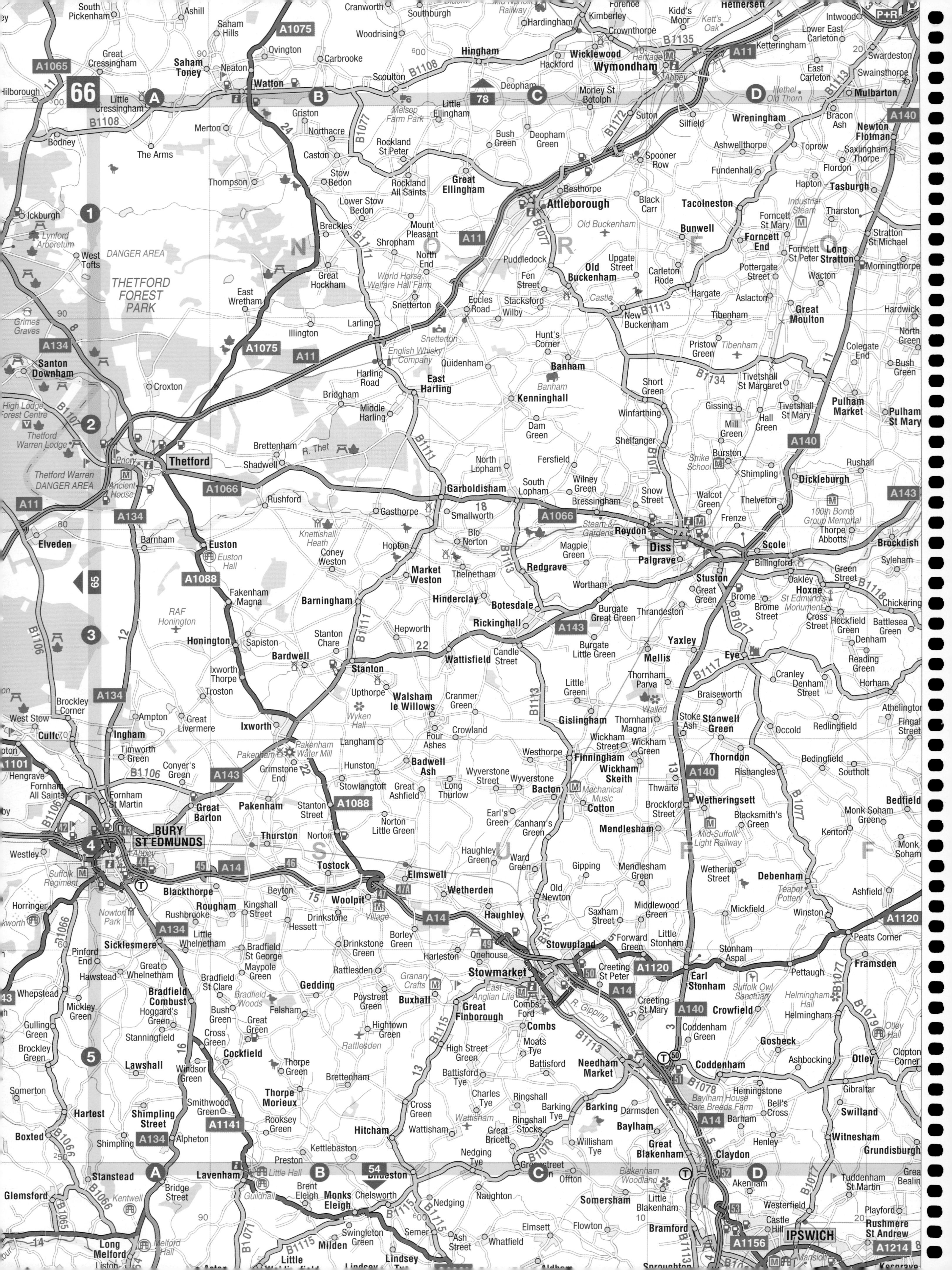

66
78
65
54
A
B
C
D
1
2
3
4
5
N
O
R
F
S
U
South Pickenham
Ashill
Saham Hills
A1075
Cranworth
Southburgh
Hardingham
Kimberley
Crownthorpe
Kidd's Moor
Kett's Oak
Hethersett
Intwood
P+R
Lower East Carleton
Woodrising
Ovington
Carbrooke
Hingham
Hackford
Wicklewood
Wymondham
Heritage
Abbey
B1135
A11
Ketteringham
Swardeston
East Carleton
Swainsthorpe
A1065
Great Cressingham
Saham Toney
Neaton
Watton
Scoulton
B1108
Deopham
Morley St Botolph
Hethel
Old Thorn
Mulbarton
Hilborough
Little Cressingham
Griston
Melsop Farm Park
Little Ellingham
Suton
Silfield
Wreningham
Bracon Ash
Newton Flotman
A140
B1108
Merton
Bodney
Northacre
Caston
Rockland St Peter
Bush Green
Deopham Green
B1172
Spooner Row
Ashwellthorpe
Toprow
Saxlingham Thorpe
The Arms
Thompson
Stow Bedon
Rockland All Saints
Great Ellingham
Besthorpe
Fundenhall
Flordon
Hapton
Tasburgh
Ickburgh
Lynford Arboretum
Lower Stow Bedon
Breckles
Mount Pleasant
Attleborough
Black Carr
Tacolneston
Bunwell
Forncett St Mary
Industrial Steam
Tharston
West Tofts
DANGER AREA
Shropham
North End
A11
Old Buckenham
Forncett End
Forncett St Peter
Long Stratton
Stratton St Michael
Morningthorpe
THETFORD FOREST PARK
East Wretham
Great Hockham
World Horse Welfare Hall Farm
Puddledock
Fen Street
Upgate Street
Old Buckenham
Carleton Rode
Pottergate Street
Wacton
Snetterton
Eccles Road
Stacksford
Wilby
Castle
Hargate
Aslacton
Grimes Graves
New Buckenham
B1113
Tibenham
Great Moulton
Hardwick
Illington
Larling
Snetterton
Hunt's Corner
Pristow Green
Tibenham
North Green
A134
A1075
A11
English Whisky Company
Colegate End
Santon Downham
Quidenham
Banham
Short Green
Tivetshall St Margaret
Bush Green
Harling Road
East Harling
Banham
B1134
Croxton
Bridgham
Kenninghall
Winfarthing
Gissing
Tivetshall St Mary
Pulham Market
Pulham St Mary
High Lodge Forest Centre
Middle Harling
Dam Green
Mill Green
Hall Green
Thetford Warren Lodge
Brettenham
R. Thet
Shelfanger
A140
Priory
Thetford
Shadwell
North Lopham
Fersfield
Burston
Rushall
Thetford Warren DANGER AREA
Ancient House
A1066
Garboldisham
South Lopham
Wilney Green
Strike School
Shimpling
Dickleburgh
A143
Rushford
Snow Street
Bressingham
Walcot Green
Thelveton
A11
A134
Gasthorpe
Smallworth
A1066
Steam & Gardens
Roydon
Frenze
100th Bomb Group Memorial
Elveden
Barnham
Euston
Knettishall Heath
Hopton
Blo' Norton
Diss
Thorpe Abbotts
Scole
Brockdish
Euston Hall
Coney Weston
Magpie Green
Palgrave
Billingford
Syleham
A1088
Market Weston
Thelnetham
Redgrave
Stuston
Oakley
Green Street
B1118
Fakenham Magna
Barningham
Hinderclay
Botesdale
Wortham
Great Green
Brome
Hoxne
St Edmund's Monument
Chickering
RAF Honington
Rickinghall
Burgate Great Green
Thrandeston
Brome Street
Cross Street
Heckfield Green
Battlesea Green
A143
B1106
Honington
Sapiston
Stanton Chare
Hepworth
Burgate Little Green
Yaxley
Denham
Bardwell
22
Wattisfield
Candle Street
Mellis
Eye
Reading Green
Ixworth Thorpe
Stanton
Thornham Parva
B1117
Cranley
Denham Street
Horham
Troston
Upthorpe
Walsham le Willows
Cranmer Green
Little Green
Braiseworth
A134
Brockley Corner
Wyken Hall
Walled
Athelington
West Stow
Ampton
Great Livermere
Ixworth
Crowland
B1113
Gislingham
Thornham Magna
Stoke Ash
Stanwell Green
Occold
Redlingfield
Fingal Street
Culford
Ingham
Four Ashes
Wickham Street
Wickham Green
Timworth Green
Pakenham Water Mill
Langham
Westhorpe
Finningham
Thorndon
Bedingfield
Southolt
A1101
Hengrave
Conyer's Green
B1106
Grimstone End
Hunston
Badwell Ash
Wyverstone Street
Wyverstone
Wickham Skeith
Rishangles
Fornham All Saints
Fornham St Martin
A143
Stowlangtoft
Great Ashfield
Long Thurlow
Bacton
Mechanical Music
Thwaite
Wetheringsett
Bedfield
Great Barton
Pakenham
Stanton Street
A1088
Cotton
Brockford Street
Blacksmith's Green
Monk Soham Green
BURY ST EDMUNDS
Thurston
Norton
Norton Little Green
Earl's Green
Canham's Green
Mendlesham
Mid-Suffolk Light Railway
Kenton
Westley
Abbey
A14
Tostock
Haughley Green
Ward Green
Gipping
Mendlesham Green
Wetherup Street
Monk Soham
Suffolk Regiment
Blackthorpe
Beyton
Elmswell
Debenham
Ashfield
Horringer
Rougham
Kingshall Street
Woolpit
Wetherden
Old Newton
Middlewood Green
Teapot Pottery
Nowton Park
Rushbrooke
Drinkstone
Village
A14
Haughley
Saxham Street
Mickfield
Winston
Hessett
A134
Little Whelnetham
Borley Green
Forward Green
Little Stonham
A1120
B1066
Sicklesmere
Bradfield St George
Drinkstone Green
Harleston
Onehouse
Stowupland
Peats Corner
Pinford End
Great Whelnetham
Maypole Green
Rattlesden
Stowmarket
Creeting St Peter
A1120
Stonham Aspal
Framsden
Hawstead
Bradfield St Clare
Granary Crafts
Earl Stonham
Pettaugh
Whepstead
Bradfield Combust
Bradfield Woods
Gedding
Poystreet Green
Buxhall
East Anglian Life
Great Finborough
A14
Suffolk Owl Sanctuary
Helmingham Hall
Mickley Green
Hoggard's Green
Felsham
Combs Ford
R. Gipping
Creeting St Mary
A140
Crowfield
Helmingham
Bush Green
Great Green
Combs
Coddenham Green
Otley Hall
Gulling Green
Stanningfield
Cross Green
Hightown Green
B1115
Moats Tye
B1113
B1079
Brockley Green
Cockfield
Rattlesden
High Street Green
Gosbeck
Lawshall
Windsor Green
Thorpe Green
Battisford
Needham Market
Coddenham
Ashbocking
Otley
Clopton Corner
Battisford Tye
Somerton
Brettenham
B1078
Hemingstone
Gibraltar
Smithwood Green
Thorpe Morieux
Charles Tye
Ringshall
Baylham House Rare Breeds Farm
Bell's Cross
Hartest
Shimpling Street
Cross Green
Barking
Barking Tye
Darmsden
Swilland
Wattisham
A14
Barham
A1141
Rooksey Green
Ringshall Stocks
Boxted
Hitcham
Wattisham
Baylham
Witnesham
Shimpling
A134
Alpheton
Great Bricett
Willisham Tye
Great Blakenham
Henley
Grundisburgh
B1066
Kettlebaston
B1078
Claydon
Preston
Nedging Tye
Stanstead
Lavenham
Little Hall
Bildeston
Greenstreet Green
Blakenham Woodland
Offton
Akenham
Tuddenham St Martin
Bridge Street
Brent Eleigh
Monks Eleigh
Chelsworth
Glemsford
Kentwell
Guildhall
Nedging
Naughton
Somersham
Little Blakenham
Westerfield
Playford
B1065
B1115
Castle Hill
Rushmere St Andrew
Swingleton Green
Semer
Elmsett
Flowton
Bramford
IPSWICH
Long Melford
Melford Hall
B1115
Milden
Ash Street
Whatfield
A1156
A1214
B1071
Little
Lindsey
Lindsey Tye

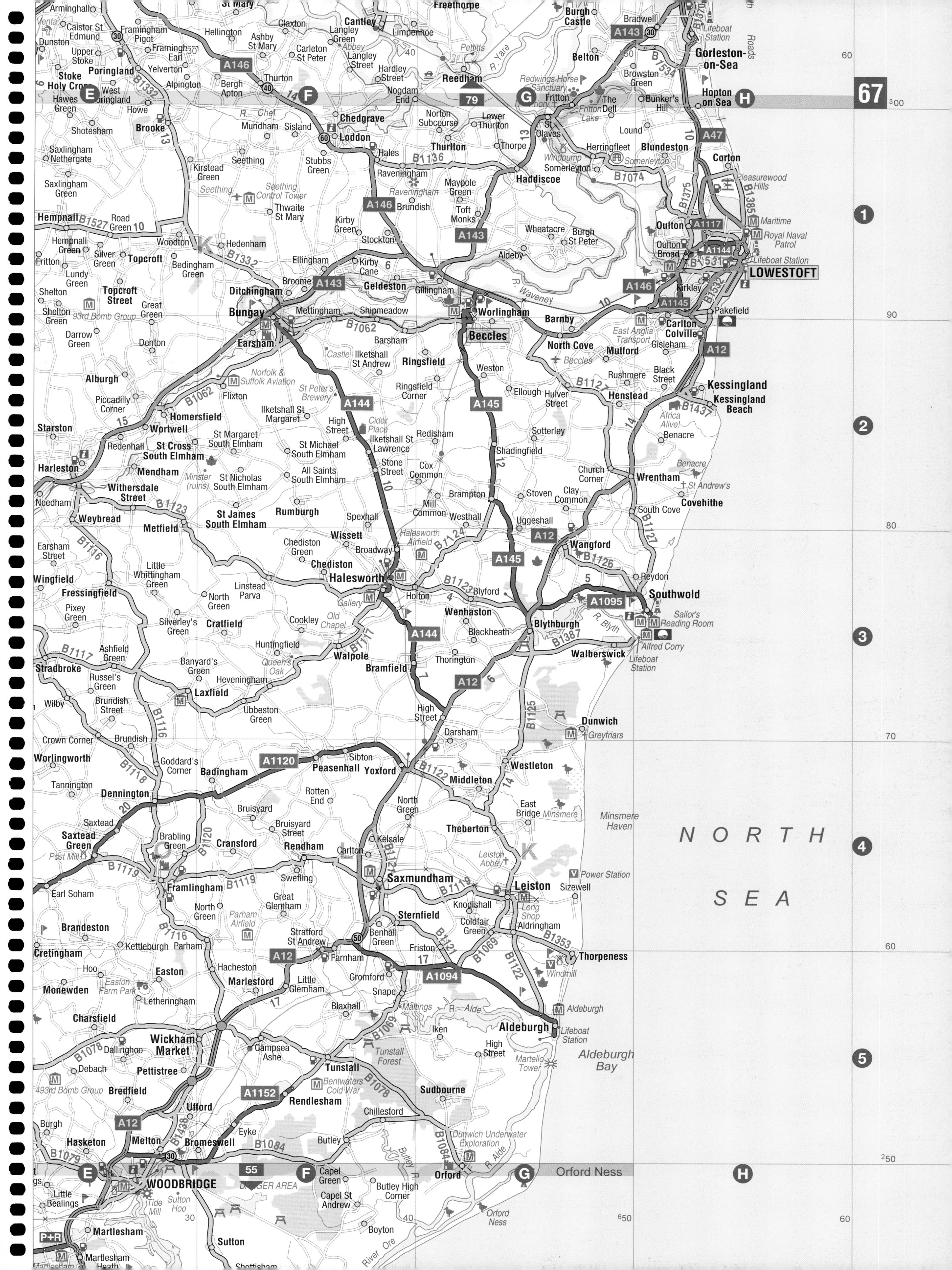

Arminghall
Caistor St Edmund
Framingham Pigot
Hellington
Ashby St Mary
Claxton
Cantley
Limpenhoe
Freethorpe
Burgh Castle
Bradwell
A143
Dunston
Upper Stoke
Framingham Earl
Carleton St Peter
Langley Green
Langley Abbey
Langley Street
Hardley Street
Pettitts
R. Yare
Belton
Gorleston-on-Sea
Lifeboat Station
B1370
Roads
Stoke Holy Cross
Poringland
Yelverton
Alpington
A146
Bergh Apton
Thurton
Reedham
Redwings Horse Sanctuary
Browston Green
B1534
West Poringland
Hawes Green
Howe
Brooke
Nogdam End
79
Fritton
The Dell
Fritton Lake
Bunker's Hill
Hopton on Sea
67
Shotesham
R. Chet
Mundham
Sisland
Chedgrave
Loddon
Norton Subcourse
Lower Thurlton
Thurlton
Thorpe
St Olaves
Lound
Herringfleet
Blundeston
A47
Corton
Saxlingham Nethergate
Kirstead Green
Seething
Stubbs Green
Hales
B1136
Raveningham
Windpump
Somerleyton
Haddiscoe
B1074
Pleasurewood Hills
Saxlingham Green
Seething Control Tower
Thwaite St Mary
A146
Brundish
Maypole Green
Toft Monks
B1375
B1385
Hempnall
B1527
Road Green
Kirby Green
Stockton
A143
Wheatacre
Burgh St Peter
Oulton
A1117
Maritime
Royal Naval Patrol
Hempnall Green
Woodton
Hedenham
B1332
Aldeby
Oulton Broad
A1144
Lifeboat Station
LOWESTOFT
Fritton
Silver Green
Topcroft
Bedingham Green
Ellingham
Kirby Cane
Lundy Green
Broome
Geldeston
Gillingham
R. Waveney
A146
Kirkley
Shelton
Topcroft Street
Ditchingham
A1145
Shelton Green
93rd Bomb Group
Great Green
Bungay
Mettingham
Shipmeadow
Worlingham
Barnby
Pakefield
Darrow Green
Earsham
B1062
Barsham
Beccles
East Anglia Transport
Carlton Colville
Gisleham
Denton
Castle
Ilketshall St Andrew
Ringsfield
North Cove
Beccles
Mutford
A12
Alburgh
Norfolk & Suffolk Aviation
Flixton
St Peter's Brewery
Weston
Rushmere
Black Street
Kessingland
Piccadilly Corner
B1062
Ringsfield Corner
Ellough
Hulver Street
B1127
Henstead
Kessingland Beach
Starston
Homersfield
Wortwell
Ilketshall St Margaret
A144
A145
B1437
Africa Alive!
Benacre
Redenhall
St Cross South Elmham
St Margaret South Elmham
High Street
Cider Place
Ilketshall St Lawrence
Redisham
Sotterley
Harleston
Mendham
St Michael South Elmham
Stone Street
Cox Common
Shadingfield
Benacre
Church Corner
Wrentham
St Andrew's
Withersdale Street
Minster (ruins)
St Nicholas South Elmham
All Saints South Elmham
Brampton
Stoven
Clay Common
Covehithe
Needham
B1123
Mill Common
Westhall
South Cove
Weybread
Metfield
St James South Elmham
Rumburgh
Spexhall
Uggeshall
Halesworth Airfield
B1124
A12
Wangford
B1127
Earsham Street
B1116
Chediston Green
Wissett
Broadway
A145
B1126
Little Whittingham Green
Linstead Parva
Chediston
Halesworth
Reydon
Wingfield
Fressingfield
North Green
Holton
B1123
Blyford
A1095
Southwold
Pixey Green
Gallery
Wenhaston
Sailor's Reading Room
Silverley's Green
Cratfield
Cookley
Old Chapel
Blythburgh
R. Blyth
Blackheath
A144
B1387
Alfred Corry
Ashfield Green
Huntingfield
B1117
Walpole
Walberswick
Lifeboat Station
Stradbroke
B1117
Banyard's Green
Queen's Oak
Bramfield
Thorington
Russel's Green
Heveningham
A12
Laxfield
Wilby
Brundish Street
Ubbeston Green
B1116
High Street
B1125
Dunwich
Greyfriars
Crown Corner
Brundish
Darsham
Worlingworth
Goddard's Corner
Badingham
A1120
Sibton
Peasenhall
Yoxford
B1122
Middleton
Westleton
Tannington
B1118
Rotten End
Dennington
North Green
East Bridge
Minsmere
Minsmere Haven
NORTH SEA
Saxtead
Bruisyard
Bruisyard Street
Theberton
Saxtead Green
Post Mill
Brabling Green
B1120
Cransford
Rendham
Carlton
Kelsale
Leiston Abbey
B1119
B1121
Power Station
Swefling
Saxmundham
Leiston
Sizewell
Earl Soham
Framlingham
B1119
Great Glemham
Knodishall
Long Shop
North Green
Parham Airfield
Sternfield
Aldringham
Brandeston
B1116
Coldfair Green
B1353
Kettleburgh
Parham
Stratford St Andrew
Benhall Green
Friston
B1121
B1069
Thorpeness
Cretingham
A12
Farnham
B1122
Windmill
Hoo
Hacheston
Easton
Easton Farm Park
Marlesford
Gromford
A1094
Monewden
Little Glemham
Snape
Letheringham
Maltings
R. Alde
Aldeburgh
Blaxhall
Charsfield
B1069
Iken
Aldeburgh
Lifeboat Station
Wickham Market
Dallinghoo
B1078
Campsea Ashe
Tunstall Forest
High Street
Aldeburgh Bay
Martello Tower
Debach
Pettistree
Tunstall
493rd Bomb Group
Bredfield
A1152
Bentwaters Cold War
B1078
Sudbourne
Rendlesham
Ufford
Chillesford
Burgh
A12
B1438
Eyke
Dunwich Underwater Exploration
Hasketon
Melton
Bromeswell
B1084
Butley
B1084
B1079
Butley R.
Orford
R. Alde
Orford Ness
55
DANGER AREA
Capel Green
Butley High Corner
WOODBRIDGE
Little Bealings
Tide Mill
Sutton Hoo
Capel St Andrew
Orford Ness
Martlesham
Boyton
P+R
Sutton
River Ore
Martlesham Heath
Shottisham
E
F
G
H
1
2
3
4
5

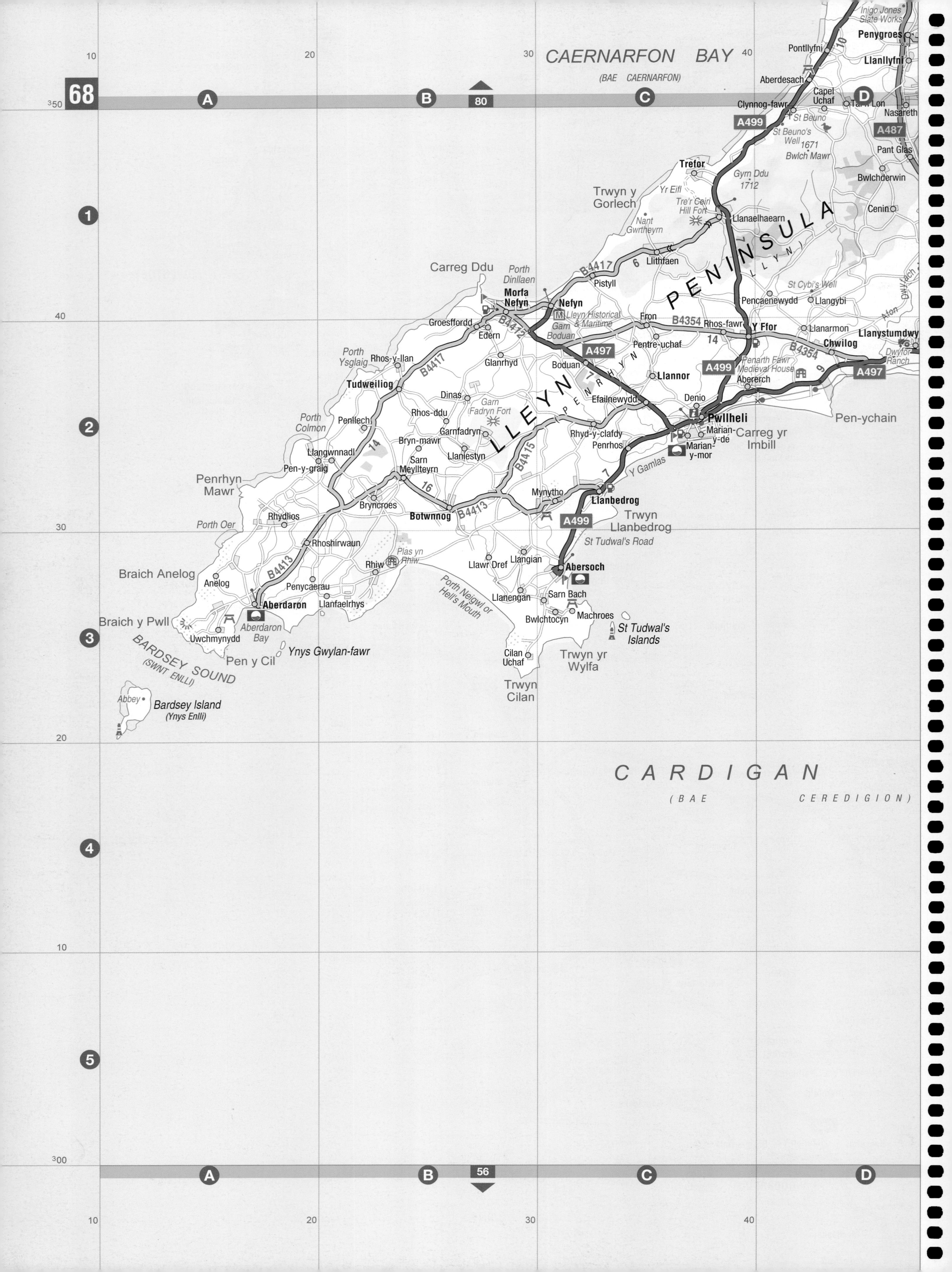

68
CAERNARFON BAY
(BAE CAERNARFON)
80
56
A
B
C
D
1
2
3
4
5
LLEYN PENINSULA
(LLYN)
LLEYN
(PENRHYN)
CARDIGAN
(BAE CEREDIGION)
BARDSEY SOUND
(SWNT ENLLI)
Bardsey Island
(Ynys Enlli)
Abbey
Inigo Jones Slate Works
Penygroes
Pontllyfni
Llanllyfni
Aberdesach
Capel Uchaf
Tai'n Lon
Clynnog-fawr
Nasareth
St Beuno
St Beuno's Well
1671
Bwlch Mawr
Pant Glas
Trefor
Gyrn Ddu
1712
Bwlchderwin
Trwyn y Gorlech
Yr Eifl
Tre'r Ceiri Hill Fort
Llanaelhaearn
Cenin
Nant Gwrtheyrn
Llithfaen
Carreg Ddu
Porth Dinllaen
Pistyll
St Cybi's Well
Morfa Nefyn
Nefyn
Pencaenewydd
Llangybi
Lleyn Historical & Maritime
Garn Boduan
Fron
Rhos-fawr
Y Ffor
Llanarmon
Llanystumdwy
Groesffordd
Edern
Pentre-uchaf
Chwilog
Dwyfor Ranch
Porth Ysgaig
Rhos-y-llan
Boduan
Penarth Fawr Medieval House
Glanrhyd
Llannor
Abererch
Tudweiliog
Dinas
Denio
Pen-ychain
Garn Fadryn Fort
Efailnewydd
Porth Colmon
Penllech
Rhos-ddu
Pwllheli
Garnfadryn
Rhyd-y-clafdy
Marian-y-de
Carreg yr Imbill
Llangwnnadl
Bryn-mawr
Llaniestyn
Penrhos
Marian-y-mor
Pen-y-graig
Sarn Meyllteyrn
Y Gamlas
Penrhyn Mawr
Mynytho
Llanbedrog
Bryncroes
Botwnnog
Trwyn Llanbedrog
Rhydlios
Porth Oer
St Tudwal's Road
Rhoshirwaun
Plas yn Rhiw
Llangian
Rhiw
Llawr Dref
Abersoch
Braich Anelog
Anelog
Penycaerau
Porth Neigwl or Hell's Mouth
Llanengan
Sarn Bach
Aberdaron
Llanfaelrhys
Machroes
Bwlchtocyn
Braich y Pwll
Aberdaron Bay
St Tudwal's Islands
Uwchmynydd
Ynys Gwylan-fawr
Pen y Cil
Cilan Uchaf
Trwyn yr Wylfa
Trwyn Cilan
A499
A487
A497
B4417
B4354
B4412
B4415
B4413
Afon Dwyfach

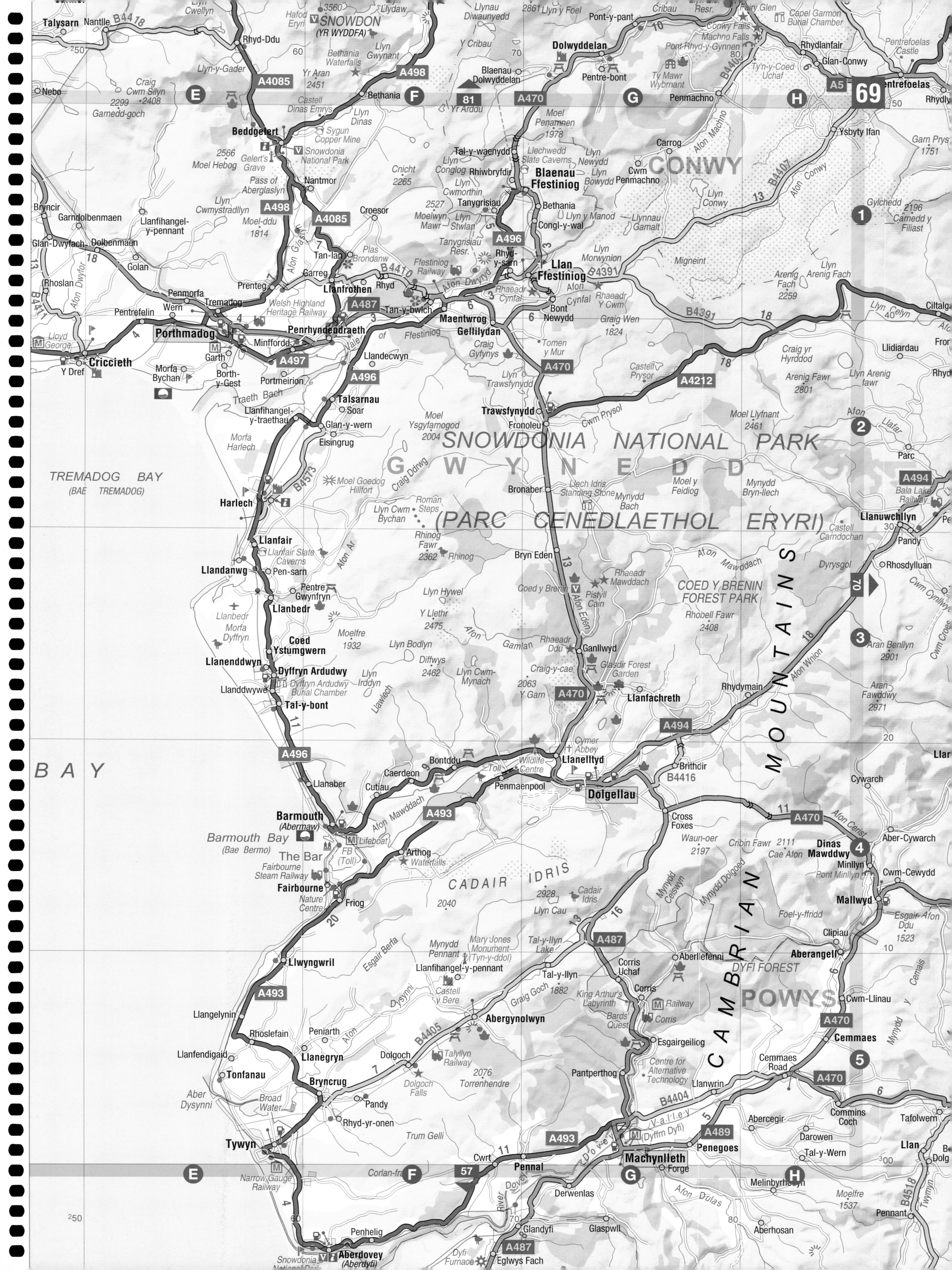

69
70
81
57
E
F
G
H
1
2
3
4
5
SNOWDON (YR WYDDFA)
CONWY
SNOWDONIA NATIONAL PARK
(PARC CENEDLAETHOL ERYRI)
GWYNEDD
CAMBRIAN MOUNTAINS
POWYS
TREMADOG BAY
(BAE TREMADOG)
BAY
Barmouth Bay
(Bae Bermo)
CADAIR IDRIS
COED Y BRENIN FOREST PARK
DYFI FOREST
Talysarn
Nantlle
Rhyd-Ddu
Nebo
Craig Cwm Silyn 2408
2299
Garnedd-goch
Llyn-y-Gader
Bethania
Bethania Waterfalls
Llyn Gwynant
Yr Aran 2451
Castell Dinas Emrys
Llyn Dinas
Sygun Copper Mine
Beddgelert
Gelert's Grave
Snowdonia National Park
Moel Hebog 2566
Pass of Aberglaslyn
Nantmor
Cnicht 2265
Croesor
Llyn Cwmystradllyn
Moel-ddu 1814
Bryncir
Garndolbenmaen
Llanfihangel-y-pennant
Glan-Dwyfach
Dolbenmaen
Golan
Rhoslan
Afon Dwyfor
Afon Glaslyn
Tan-lan
Plas Brondanw
Garreg
Llanfrothen
Rhyd
Prenteg
Penmorfa
Tremadog
Wern
Pentrefelin
Welsh Highland Heritage Railway
Porthmadog
Minffordd
Penrhyndeudraeth
Lloyd George
Criccieth
Y Dref
Garth
Morfa Bychan
Borth-y-Gest
Portmeirion
Traeth Bach
Tan-y-bwlch
Maentwrog
Gellilydan
Vale of Ffestiniog
Llandecwyn
Talsarnau
Soar
Llanfihangel-y-traethau
Glan-y-wern
Eisingrug
Morfa Harlech
Harlech
Moel Goedog Hillfort
Craig Ddrwg
Roman Steps
Llyn Cwm Bychan
Rhinog Fawr 2362
Rhinog
Moel Ysgyfarnogod 2004
Llanfair
Llanfair Slate Caverns
Llandanwg
Pen-sarn
Afon Artro
Pentre Gwynfryn
Llanbedr
Llanbedr Morfa Dyffryn
Coed Ystumgwern
Moelfre 1932
Llyn Hywel
Y Llethr 2475
Llyn Bodlyn
Diffwys 2462
Llyn Cwm-Mynach
Llyn Irddyn
Llanenddwyn
Dyffryn Ardudwy
Dyffryn Ardudwy Burial Chamber
Llanddwywe
Tal-y-bont
Llanaber
Barmouth
(Abermaw)
Caerdeon
Cutiau
Bontddu
Toll
Wildlife Centre
Penmaenpool
Afon Mawddach
Lifeboat
FB (Toll)
The Bar
Fairbourne Steam Railway
Fairbourne
Nature Centre
Friog
Arthog
Arthog Waterfalls
Llwyngwril
Esgair Berfa
Llangelynin
Rhoslefain
Llanfendigaid
Tonfanau
Aber Dysynni
Broad Water
Peniarth
Llanegryn
Bryncrug
Pandy
Rhyd-yr-onen
Tywyn
Narrow Gauge Railway
Corlan-fraith
Penhelig
Aberdovey
(Aberdyfi)
Snowdonia National Park
Dolgoch
Dolgoch Falls
Talyllyn Railway
Torrenhendre 2076
Trum Gelli
Abergynolwyn
Castell y Bere
Llanfihangel-y-pennant
Mynydd Pennant
Mary Jones Monument (Tyn-y-ddol)
Craig Goch
Tal-y-llyn 1882
Tal-y-llyn Lake
Llyn Cau
2928
Cadair Idris
2040
Corris Uchaf
Corris
Railway
King Arthur's Labyrinth
Bards' Quest
Esgairgeiliog
Centre for Alternative Technology
Pantperthog
Llanwrin
Aberllefenni
Mynydd Celwyn
Mynydd Dolgoed
Dolgellau
Llanelltyd
Cymer Abbey
Brithdir
Cross Foxes
Waun-oer 2197
Cribin Fawr 2111
Cae Afon
Dinas Mawddwy
Minllyn
Pont Minllyn
Mallwyd
Foel-y-ffridd
Clipiau
Aberangell
Cwm-Llinau
Cemmaes
Cemmaes Road
Commins Coch
Abercegir
Darowen
Tal-y-Wern
Tafolwern
Llan
Melinbyrhedyn
Moelfre 1537
Pennant
Aberhosan
Machynlleth
Forge
Penegoes
Dyffryn Dyfi
Dovey Valley
Pennal
Cwrt
Derwenlas
Glandyfi
Glaspwll
Afon Dulas
River Dovey
Dyfi Furnace
Eglwys Fach
Llanfachreth
Ganllwyd
Rhaeadr Ddu
Gamlan
Craig-y-cae
2063 Y Garn
Glasdir Forest Garden
Coed y Brenin
Pistyll Cain
Rhaeadr Mawddach
Afon Eden
Bryn Eden
Bronaber
Llech Idris Standing Stone
Mynydd Bach
Moel y Feidiog
Mynydd Bryn-llech
Rhobell Fawr 2408
Dyrysgol
Rhydymain
Afon Wnion
Aran Benllyn 2901
Aran Fawddwy 2971
Cywarch
Aber-Cywarch
Cwm-Cewydd
Esgair Afon Ddu 1523
Afon Cerist
Llanuwchllyn
Castell Carndochan
Pandy
Rhosdylluan
Cwm Cynllwyd
Bala Lake Railway
Parc
Afon Llafar
Moel Llyfnant 2461
Arenig Fawr 2801
Llyn Arenig fawr
Craig yr Hyrddod
Llidiardau
Castell Prysor
Cwm Prysol
Trawsfynydd
Fronoleu
Llyn Trawsfynydd
Craig Gyfynys
Tomen y Mur
Bont Newydd
Cynfal
Rhaeadr Cynfal
Rhaeadr Y Cwm
Graig Wen 1824
Llan Ffestiniog
Rhyd-y-sarn
Tanygrisiau Resr.
Ffestiniog Railway
Afon Dwyryd
Moelwyn Mawr 2527
Llyn Stwlan
Tanygrisiau
Llyn Cwmorthin
Llyn Conglog
Rhiwbryfdir
Tal-y-waenydd
Llechwedd Slate Caverns
Blaenau Ffestiniog
Bethania
Congl-y-wal
Llyn y Manod
Llynnau Gamallt
Llyn Morwynion
Moel Penamnen 1978
Llyn Newydd
Llyn Bowydd
Cwm Penmachno
Carrog
Afon Machno
Llyn Conwy
Migneint
Arenig Fach 2259
Llyn Arenig Fach
Llyn Celyn
Ciltalgarth
Frongoch
Gylchedd 2196
Carnedd y Filiast
Garn Prys 1751
Ysbyty Ifan
Afon Conwy
Pentrefoelas
Pentrefoelas Castle
Rhydlanfair
Glan-Conwy
Ty'n-y-Coed Uchaf
Ty Mawr Wybrnant
Penmachno
Pont Rhyd-y-Gynnen
Machno Falls
Conwy Falls
Fairy Glen
Capel Garmon Burial Chamber
Pentre-bont
Dolwyddelan
Blaenau Dolwyddelan
Yr Arddu
Y Cribau
Llynau Diwaunyedd
2861 Llyn y Foel
Pont-y-pant
Cribau
Llydaw
Hafod Eryri
3560
Llyn Cwellyn
A4085
A498
A470
A5
A496
A487
A497
A4212
A494
A493
A489
B4418
B4410
B4391
B4406
B4407
B4573
B4405
B4404
B4416
B4411
B4518

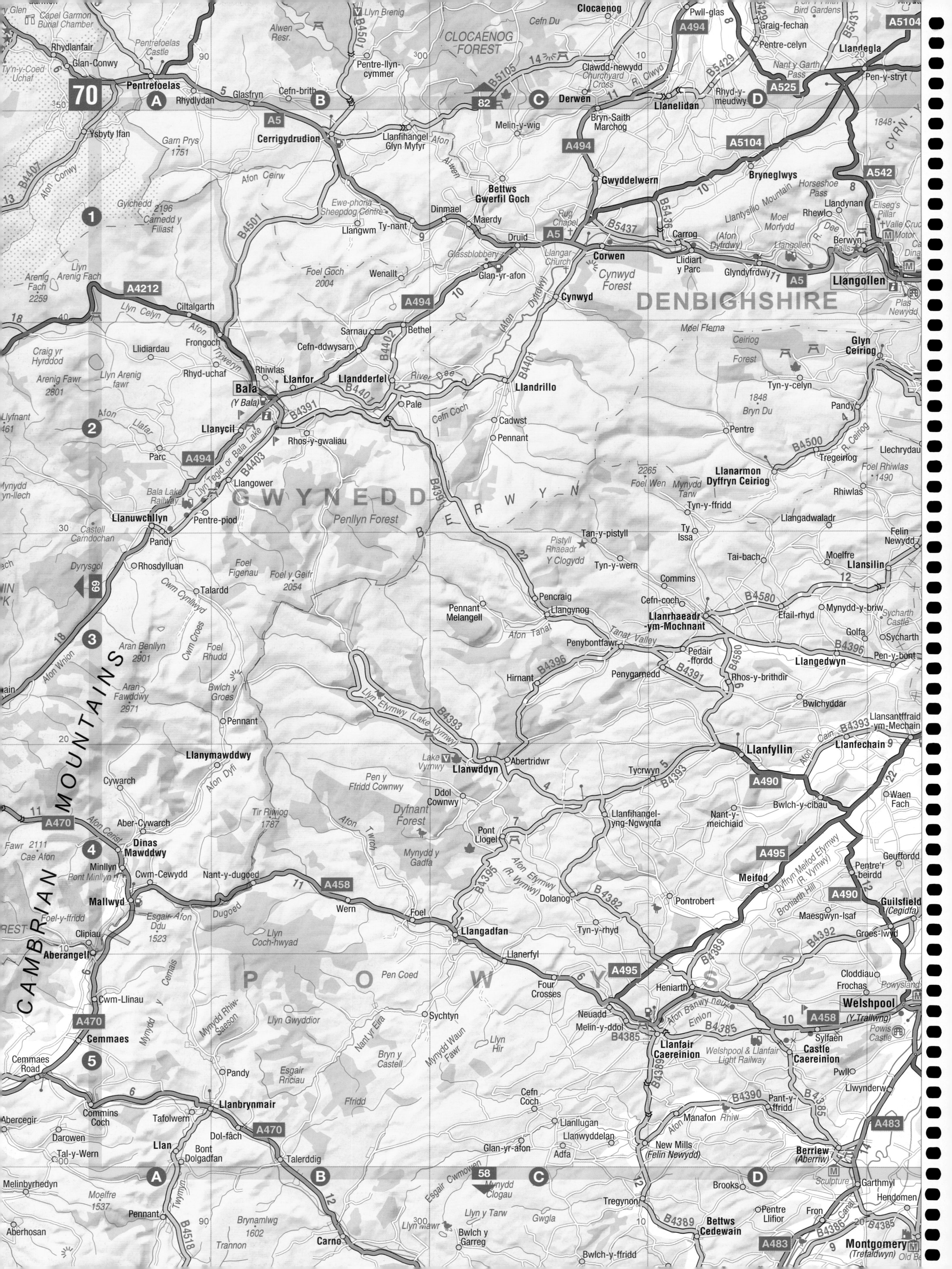

70
69
82
58
A
B
C
D
1
2
3
4
5
DENBIGHSHIRE
GWYNEDD
POWYS
BERWYN
CAMBRIAN MOUNTAINS
CLOCAENOG FOREST
Glen
Capel Garmon Burial Chamber
Rhydlanfair
Glan-Conwy
Ty'n-y-Coed Uchaf
Pentrefoelas Castle
Pentrefoelas
Rhydlydan
Glasfryn
Cefn-brith
Alwen Resr.
Llyn Brenig
Pentre-llyn-cymmer
Clocaenog
Cefn Du
Clawdd-newydd
Churchyard Cross
R. Clwyd
Derwen
Pwll-glas
Llanelidan
Rhyd-y-meudwy
Graig-fechan
Pentre-celyn
Nant y Garth Pass
Llandegla
Pen-y-stryt
Bird Gardens
Ysbyty Ifan
Garn Prys 1751
Cerrigydrudion
Llanfihangel Glyn Myfyr
Afon Alwen
Melin-y-wig
Bryn-Saith Marchog
Gwyddelwern
Bryneglwys
Horseshoe Pass
Llandynan
Eliseg's Pillar
Valle Crucis
Rhewl
Afon Conwy
Afon Ceirw
Bettws Gwerfil Goch
Llantysilio Mountain
Moel Morfydd
Gylchedd 2196
Carnedd y Filiast
Ewe-phoria Sheepdog Centre
Llangwm
Ty-nant
Dinmael
Maerdy
Rug Chapel
Druid
Carrog
Llangollen
Berwyn
Horseshoe Falls
Motor Museum
Glassblobbery
Llangar Church
Corwen
Llidiart y Parc
Glyndyfrdwy
Llangollen
Afon Dyfrdwy
Cynwyd Forest
Foel Goch 2004
Wenallt
Glan-yr-afon
Plas Newydd
Llyn Arenig Fach
Arenig Fach 2259
Ciltalgarth
Llyn Celyn
Cynwyd
Sarnau
Bethel
Frongoch
Moel Fferna
Ceiriog Forest
Glyn Ceiriog
Craig yr Hyrddod
Llidiardau
Cefn-ddwysarn
Afon Tryweryn
Arenig Fawr 2801
Llyn Arenig fawr
Rhyd-uchaf
Rhiwlas
Llanfor
Llandderfel
River Dee
Llandrillo
Tyn-y-celyn
Bala
(Y Bala)
Pale
Cefn Coch
1848
Bryn Du
Pandy
Llyfnant 461
Llanycil
Llafar
Rhos-y-gwaliau
Cadwst
Pennant
Pentre
R. Ceiriog
Llechrydau
Parc
Llyn Tegid or Bala Lake
Llangower
Tregeiriog
Foel Rhiwlas 1490
2265 Foel Wen
Mynydd Tarw
Llanarmon Dyffryn Ceiriog
Rhiwlas
Mynydd Tyn-y-llech
Bala Lake Railway
Llanuwchllyn
Pentre-piod
Penllyn Forest
Tyn-y-ffridd
Llangadwaladr
Castell Carndochan
Pandy
Ty Issa
Pistyll Rhaeadr
Y Clogydd
Tan-y-pistyll
Felin Newydd
Tai-bach
Moelfre
Llansilin
Dyrysgol
Rhosdylluan
Foel Figenau
Foel y Geifr 2054
Tyn-y-wern
Commins
Cwm Cynllwyd
Talardd
Pencraig
Cefn-coch
Llangynog
Pennant Melangell
Mynydd-y-briw
Efail-rhyd
Sycharth Castle
Llanrhaeadr-ym-Mochnant
Afon Tanat
Tanat Valley
Golfa
Sycharth
Penybontfawr
Pedair-ffordd
Pen-y-bont
Llangedwyn
Aran Benllyn 2901
Cwm Croes
Foel Rhudd
Afon Wnion
Hirnant
Penygarnedd
Rhos-y-brithdir
Aran Fawddwy 2971
Bwlch y Groes
Bwlchyddar
Llyn Efyrnwy (Lake Vyrnwy)
Pennant
Llansantffraid-ym-Mechain
Llanfechain
Llanymawddwy
Lake Vyrnwy
Llanwddyn
Abertridwr
Llanfyllin
Cywarch
Afon Dyfi
Pen y Ffridd Cownwy
Tycrwyn
Waen Fach
Ddol Cownwy
Bwlch-y-cibau
Llanfihangel-yng-Ngwynfa
Nant-y-meichiaid
Tir Rhiwiog 1787
Dyfnant Forest
Afon Twrch
Pont Llogel
Aber-Cywarch
Afon Cerist
Fawr 2111
Cae Afon
Dinas Mawddwy
Minllyn
Pont Minllyn
Mynydd y Gadfa
Afon Efyrnwy (R. Vyrnwy)
Geuffordd
Pentre'r beirdd
Meifod
Dyffryn Meifod Efyrnwy (R. Vyrnwy)
Cwm-Cewydd
Nant-y-dugoed
Dolanog
Broniarth Hill
Mallwyd
Dugoed
Wern
Foel
Pontrobert
Guilsfield (Cegidfa)
Maesgwyn-Isaf
Foel-y-ffridd
Esgair Afon Ddu 1523
Llyn Coch-hwyad
Llangadfan
Tyn-y-rhyd
Groes-lwyd
Clipiau
Aberangell
Llanerfyl
Cemais
Pen Coed
Four Crosses
Heniarth
Cloddiau
Frochas
Powysland Museum
Welshpool (Y Trallwng)
Cwm-Llinau
Mynydd Rhiw-Saeson
Llyn Gwyddior
Nant yr Eira
Sychtyn
Neuadd
Melin-y-ddol
Afon Banwy neu Einion
Llanfair Caereinion
Welshpool & Llanfair Light Railway
Castle Caereinion
Sylfaen
Powis Castle
Cemmaes
Mynydd Waun Fawr
Llyn Hir
Cemmaes Road
Bryn y Castell
Esgair Rhiciau
Pandy
Pwll
Llwynderw
Abercegir
Commins Coch
Llanbrynmair
Ffridd
Cefn Coch
Llanllugan
Llanwyddelan
Manafon
Afon Rhiw
Pant-y-ffridd
Tafolwern
Darowen
Dol-fâch
Llan
Bont Dolgadfan
Talerddig
Glan-yr-afon
Adfa
New Mills (Felin Newydd)
Berriew (Aberriw)
Tal-y-Wern
Esgair Cwmowen
Sculpture
Garthmyl
Melinbyrhedyn
Moelfre 1537
Mynydd Clogau
Brooks
Hendomen
Pennant
Twymyn
Tregynon
Pentre Llifior
Fron
Aberhosan
Brynamlwg 1602
Llyn y Tarw
Gwgla
Llyn Mawr
Bwlch y Garreg
Bettws Cedewain
Trannon
Carno
Bwlch-y-ffridd
Montgomery (Trefaldwyn)
Canal
A5
A5104
A494
A525
A542
A4212
A458
A470
A495
A490
A483
B4501
B5105
B5429
B5431
B5436
B5437
B4407
B4402
B4401
B4391
B4403
B4500
B4580
B4396
B4393
B4395
B4382
B4389
B4390
B4385
B4392
B4386
B4518

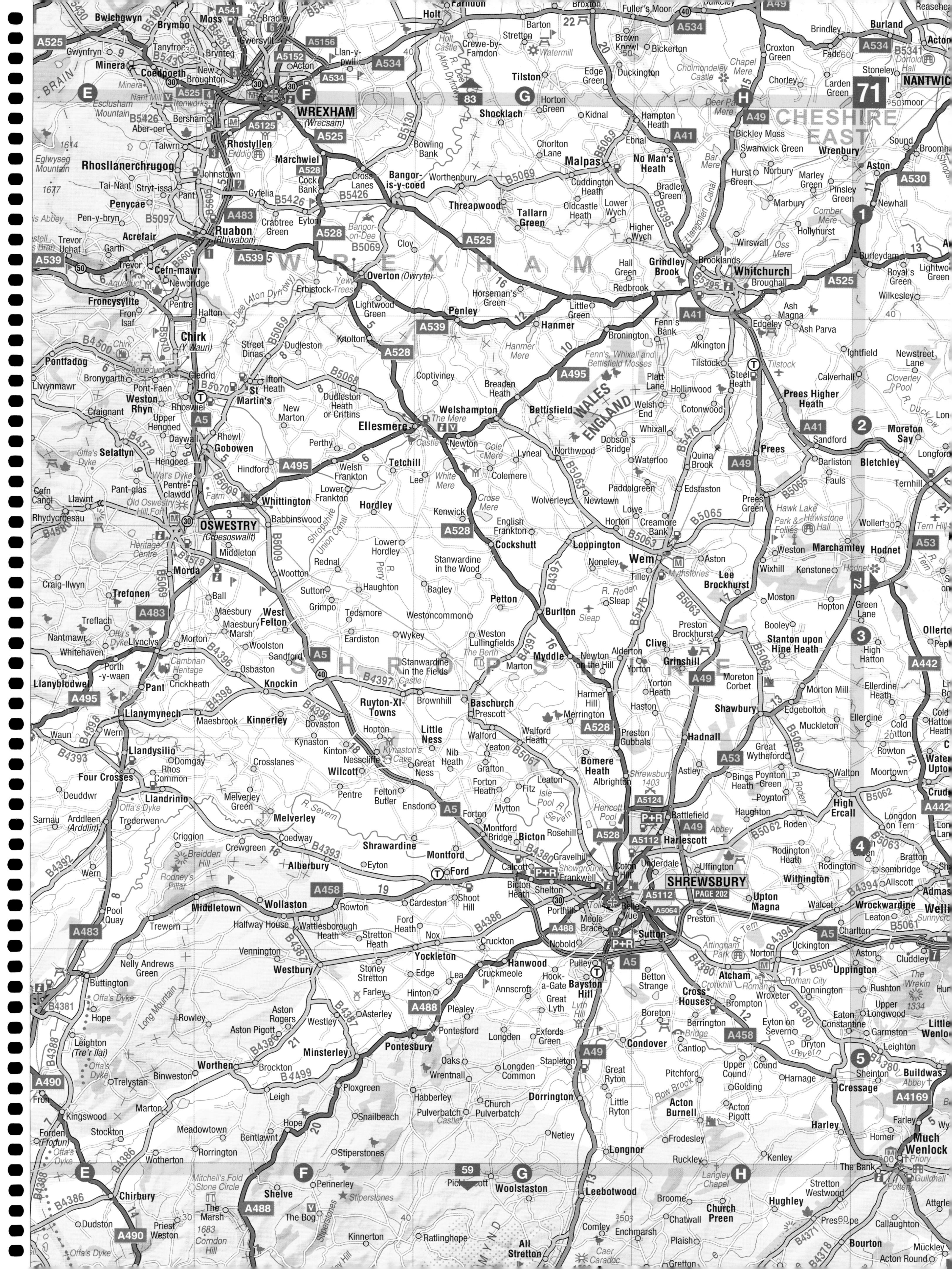

Bwlchgwyn
Brymbo
Moss
A541
Bradley
Gwersyllt
Holt
Farndon
Barton
Stretton
Broxton
Fuller's Moor
A534
A49
Reaseheath
Burland
Acton
Brindley
A525
Gwynfryn
Minera
Coedpoeth
Tanyfron
Brynteg
New Broughton
A5156
A5152
Acton
Llan-y-pwll
A534
Holt Castle
Crewe-by-Farndon
R. Dee (Afon Dyfrdwy)
Watermill
Brown Knowl
Bickerton
Duckington
Edge Green
Tilston
Chapel Mere
Croxton Green
Chorley
Faddiley
Larden Green
Stoneley Green
A534
B5341
Dorfold Hall
NANTWICH
71
E
F
G
H
Esclusham Mountain
Nant Mill
Ironworks
WREXHAM
(Wrecsam)
A525
Bersham
Aber-oer
83
Shocklach
Horton Green
Kidnal
Hampton Heath
Deer Park Mere
A49
CHESHIRE EAST
Bickley Moss
Swanwick Green
Wrenbury
Sound
Broomhall
Aston
A530
Eglwyseg Mountain
Rhosllanerchrugog
Talwrn
Rhostyllen
Erddig
Marchwiel
B5130
Bowling Bank
Chorlton Lane
Malpas
Ebnal
No Man's Heath
A41
Bar Mere
Hurst Green
Norbury
Marley Green
Pinsley Green
Newhall
Tai-Nant
Stryt-issa
Johnstown
Gyfelia
Pant
A528
Cock Bank
Cross Lanes
Bangor-is-y-coed
Worthenbury
B5069
Cuddington Heath
Bradley Green
Marbury
Comber Mere
Penycae
B5426
Crabtree Green
Eyton
Threapwood
Tallarn Green
Oldcastle Heath
Lower Wych
Higher Wych
B5395
Llangollen Canal
Pen-y-bryn
B5097
A483
Ruabon
(Rhiwabon)
Bangor-on-Dee
Hollyhurst
Trevor Uchaf
Acrefair
Garth
A528
Cloy
A525
Wirswall
Oss Mere
Burleydam
A539
Trevor
Cefn-mawr
Newbridge
Aqueduct
A539
WREXHAM
B5069
Overton (Owrytn)
Yew Trees
Erbistock
Horseman's Green
Hall Green
Grindley Brook
Redbrook
Brooklands
Whitchurch
Broughall
A525
Royal's Green
Lightwood Green
Wilkesley
Froncysyllte
Fron Isaf
Pentre
Halton
Lightwood Green
Penley
Little Green
Hanmer
Ash Magna
Ash Parva
Edgeley
A41
Chirk
(Y Waun)
Street Dinas
Dudleston
Knolton
A539
A528
Fenn's Bank
Bronington
Alkington
Ightfield
Newstreet Lane
Pontfadog
Bronygarth
B5070
B5069
B5068
Coptiviney
Hanmer Mere
Fenn's, Whixall and Bettisfield Mosses
Tilstock
Calverhall
Cloverley Pool
Llwynmawr
Pont-Faen
Gledrid
Rhoswiel
St Martin's
Ifton Heath
Dudleston Heath or Criftins
Breaden Heath
A495
Platt Lane
Hollinwood
Steel Heath
Prees Higher Heath
Weston Rhyn
Craignant
Upper Hengoed
A5
New Marton
Ellesmere
Welshampton
The Mere
Bettisfield
WALES
ENGLAND
Welsh End
Cotonwood
A41
Sandford
Moreton Say
Selattyn
Daywall
Rhewl
Gobowen
Hengoed
Offa's Dyke
Perthy
Castle
Newton
Cole Mere
Lyneal
Northwood
Dobson's Bridge
Whixall
Quina Brook
Waterloo
Prees
A49
Darliston
Bletchley
Longford
Hindford
A495
Welsh Frankton
Tetchill
Lee
White Mere
Colemere
Paddolgreen
Edstaston
Fauls
Ternhill
Cefn Canol
Llawnt
Pant-glas
Wat's Dyke
Pentre-clawdd
Lower Frankton
Hordley
Whittington
Old Oswestry Hill Fort
Kenwick
Crose Mere
Wolverley
Newtown
Prees Green
B5065
Rhydycroesau
OSWESTRY
(Croesoswallt)
Babbinswood
Shropshire Union Canal
English Frankton
Lowe
Horton
Creamore Bank
Hawk Lake
Hawkstone Park & Follies
Hawkstone Hall
Wollerton
Heritage Centre
Middleton
Lower Hordley
A528
Cockshutt
Loppington
Noneley
Wem
Aston
Marchamley
Hodnet
A53
Morda
Rednal
Stanwardine in the Wood
Mythstories
Lee Brockhurst
Wixhill
Kenstone
Craig-llwyn
Trefonen
Wootton
Sutton
Haughton
Bagley
Petton
Tilley
Weston
Moston
Ball
Grimpo
R. Roden
Sleap
Hopton
Green Lane
A483
Maesbury
West Felton
Tedsmore
Westoncommon
Burlton
Maesbury Marsh
Eardiston
Wykey
Weston Lullingfields
Preston Brockhurst
Booley
Stanton upon Hine Heath
Treflach
Nantmawr
Llynclys
Morton
Woolston
The Berth
Myddle
Alderton
Clive
High Hatton
A442
Whitehaven
Sandford
A5
Stanwardine in the Fields
Marton
Newton on the Hill
Yorton
Grinshill
Moreton Corbet
Porth-y-waen
Osbaston
SHROPSHIRE
Llanyblodwel
Pant
Crickheath
Knockin
B4397
Castle
Ruyton-XI-Towns
Brownhill
Baschurch
Prescott
Harmer Hill
Yorton Heath
Haston
A49
Morton Mill
Ellerdine Heath
A495
B4398
Llanymynech
Maesbrook
Kinnerley
Dovaston
Merrington
A528
Shawbury
Edgebolton
Ellerdine
Waun
Wern
Kynaston
Hopton
Little Ness
Walford
Walford Heath
Preston Gubbals
Hadnall
Muckleton
Llandysilio
Domgay
Kinton
Nesscliffe
Kynaston's Cave
Nib Heath
Great Ness
Yeaton
Bomere Heath
Great Wytheford
Rowton
B4393
Rhos Common
Crosslanes
Wilcott
Grafton
Albrighton
Astley
A53
Walton
Moortown
Four Crosses
Shrewsbury 1403
Bings Heath
Poynton Green
Poynton
Deuddwr
Llandrinio
Melverley Green
Pentre
Felton Butler
Forton Heath
Fitz
Leaton
Isle Pool
A5124
High Ercall
B5062
Sarnau
Arddleen (Ardd-lîn)
Offa's Dyke
Trederwen
Melverley
R. Severn
Ensdon
A5
Forton
Mytton
Hencott Pool
P+R
Battlefield
Haughton
Longdon on Tern
Criggion
Coedway
Montford Bridge
Bicton
A528
A49
Abbey
B5062
Roden
Breidden Hill
Crewgreen
B4393
Shrawardine
Montford
Rosehill
A5112
Harlescott
Rodington Heath
Rodington
Rodney's Pillar
Alberbury
Eyton
Ford
Calcott
Gravelhill
Showground
Frankwell
Coton Hill
Underdale
Uffington
SHREWSBURY
PAGE 202
Withington
Isombridge
Allscott
Wern
A458
Cardeston
Shoot Hill
Bicton Heath
Shelton
Porthill
Belle Vue
A5112
A5064
Upton Magna
Walcot
Wrockwardine
Leaton
Wellington
Pool Quay
Middletown
Wollaston
Rowton
B4386
Meole Brace
Preston
Charlton
A483
Trewern
Halfway House
Wattlesborough Heath
Stretton Heath
Ford Heath
Nox
Cruckton
A488
Nobold
Sutton
P+R
Attingham Park
Uckington
Norton
Aston
Cluddley
Vennington
Yockleton
Hanwood
Pulley
Bayston Hill
A5
Betton Strange
Atcham
Cronkhill
Roman City
Uppington
Nelly Andrews Green
Buttington
Westbury
Stoney Stretton
Edge
Lea
Cruckmeole
Hook-a-Gate
Annscroft
Cross Houses
Wroxeter
Donnington
Rushton
The Wrekin
Offa's Dyke
Long Mountain
Farley
Hinton
A488
Great Lyth
Lyth Hill
Brompton
Upper Longwood
B4381
Hope
Rowley
Aston Rogers
Westley
Asterley
Plealey
Boreton
Berrington
Eaton Constantine
Aston Pigott
Pontesford
Longden
Exfords Green
Condover
A458
Eyton on Severn
Garmston
Leighton
(Tre'r Llai)
Offa's Dyke
B4388
Worthen
Minsterley
Pontesbury
Oaks
Stapleton
A49
Cantlop
Drayton
Leighton
Binweston
Brockton
B4499
Wrentnall
Longden Common
Great Ryton
Pitchford
Upper Cound
Cound
Harnage
Sheinton
Buildwas Abbey
A490
Trelystan
Ploxgreen
Leigh
Habberley
Church Pulverbatch
Dorrington
Little Ryton
Golding
Acton Burnell
Acton Pigott
Cressage
A4169
Kingswood
Marton
Pulverbatch Castle
Row Brook
Forden (Ffordun)
Stockton
Meadowtown
Hope
Snailbeach
Harley
Farley
Bentlawnt
Netley
Frodesley
Homer
Much Wenlock
Rorrington
Stiperstones
Longnor
Wotherton
Ruckley
Kenley
The Bank
Priory
59
Pennerley
Mitchell's Fold Stone Circle
Pickle Scott
Woolstaston
Leebotwood
Langley Chapel
Chirbury
B4386
Shelve
Stiperstones
Broome
Stretton Westwood
Guildhall
The Marsh
A488
The Bog
Hughley
Church Preen
Chatwall
Atterley
Priest Weston
Corndon Hill
Dudston
A490
Kinnerton
Ratlinghope
Comley
Enchmarsh
Presthope
Callaughton
B4371
Bourton
Offa's Dyke
All Stretton
Caer Caradoc
Plaish
Gretton
Muckley
Acton Round

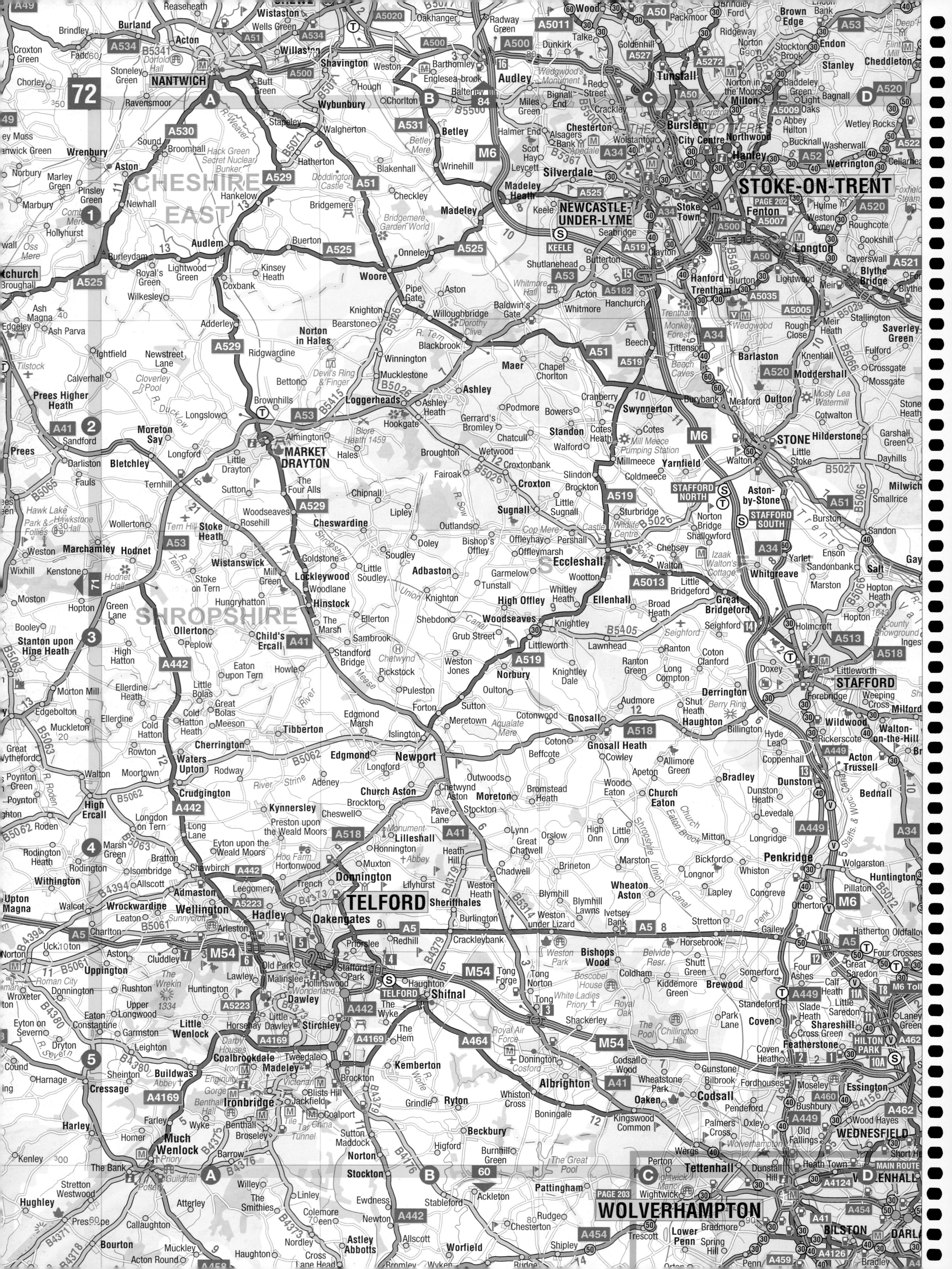

72
NANTWICH
Acton
Burland
Brindley
Wistaston
Willaston
Shavington
Weston
Wybunbury
Hough
Chorlton
Audley
Talke
Tunstall
Burslem
Packmoor
Brown Edge
Endon
Stanley
Cheddleton
Milton
Bagnall
Wetley Rocks
Werrington
Hanley
Northwood
City Centre
Stoke-on-Trent
STOKE-ON-TRENT
PAGE 202
Fenton
Longton
Stoke Town
NEWCASTLE-UNDER-LYME
Silverdale
Chesterton
Madeley Heath
Madeley
Keele
KEELE
Betley
Wrinehill
Walgherton
Hatherton
Blakenhall
Checkley
Bridgemere
Bridgemere Garden World
Doddington Castle
CHESHIRE EAST
Wrenbury
Aston
Sound
Broomhall
Hack Green Secret Nuclear Bunker
Hankelow
Newhall
Audlem
Buerton
Onneley
Woore
Pipe Gate
Knighton
Bearstone
Norton in Hales
Willoughbridge
Dorothy Clive
Baldwin's Gate
Whitmore
Butterton
Clayton
Trentham
Hanford
Blurton
Lightwood
Meir
Blythe Bridge
Caverswall
Barlaston
Beech
Tittensor
Moddershall
Oulton
Meaford
STONE
Hilderstone
Little Stoke
Walton
Aston-by-Stone
STAFFORD NORTH
STAFFORD SOUTH
Sandon
Salt
Hopton
STAFFORD
Weeping Cross
Milford
Wildwood
Walton-on-the-Hill
Acton Trussell
Dunston
Bednall
Penkridge
Huntington
Pillaton
Otherton
Gailey
Hatherton
Four Ashes
Calf Heath
Slade Heath
Shareshill
Featherstone
HILTON PARK
Essington
Coven
Standeford
Brewood
Somerford
Kiddemore Green
Codsall
Bilbrook
Oaken
Pendeford
Fordhouses
Moseley
Bushbury
Wednesfield
Wolverhampton
WOLVERHAMPTON
PAGE 203
Tettenhall
Perton
Wightwick
Lower Penn
Bilston
Pattingham
Ackleton
Stableford
Worfield
Rudge
Chesterton
Trescott
Ryton
Grindle
Beckbury
Kemberton
Albrighton
Donington
Boningale
Whiston Cross
Shifnal
TELFORD
The Wyke
The Hem
Tong
Tong Norton
Tong Forge
Weston Park
Bishops Wood
Shackerley
Wheaton Aston
Lapley
Stretton
Blymhill
Weston under Lizard
Sheriffhales
Donnington
Oakengates
Hadley
Wellington
Priorslee
Dawley
Little Dawley
Stirchley
Madeley
Ironbridge
Coalbrookdale
Little Wenlock
Broseley
Much Wenlock
Jackfield
Coalport
Sutton Maddock
Norton
Stockton
Beckbury
Harley
Cressage
Sheinton
Buildwas
Leighton
Garmston
Eaton Constantine
Wroxeter
Uppington
Aston
Cluddley
Admaston
Allscott
Leegomery
Shawbirch
Bratton
Isombridge
Rodington
Withington
Upton Magna
Walcot
Wrockwardine
High Ercall
Crudgington
Waters Upton
Rodway
Cherrington
Tibberton
Edgmond
Newport
Longford
Church Aston
Chetwynd Aston
Moreton
Lilleshall
Kynnersley
Preston upon the Weald Moors
Eyton upon the Weald Moors
Muxton
Honnington
Edgmond Marsh
Forton
Sutton
Meretown
Aqualate Mere
Gnosall
Gnosall Heath
Coton
Beffcote
Cowley
Apeton
Allimore Green
Bradley
Church Eaton
Wood Eaton
Haughton
Derrington
Billington
Shut Heath
Norbury
Oulton
Knightley
Knightley Dale
Woodseaves
High Offley
Ellenhall
Eccleshall
Wootton
Seighford
Great Bridgeford
Little Bridgeford
Whitgreave
Yarnfield
Millmeece
Coldmeece
Swynnerton
Cotes
Cotes Heath
Standon
Bowers
Walford
Croxton
Sugnall
Slindon
Chatcull
Broughton
Wetwood
Croxtonbank
Fairoak
Ashley
Ashley Heath
Loggerheads
Hookgate
Mucklestone
Winnington
Maer
Chapel Chorlton
Cranberry
MARKET DRAYTON
Almington
Little Drayton
Sutton
The Four Alls
Hales
Cheswardine
Chipnall
Lipley
Soudley
Adbaston
Goldstone
Lockleywood
Woodlane
Hinstock
Ellerton
Sambrook
Child's Ercall
Standford Bridge
Pickstock
Puleston
Howle
Stoke Heath
Wistanswick
Stoke on Tern
Hodnet
Marchamley
Weston
Hopton
Moston
Ollerton
Peplow
High Hatton
Eaton upon Tern
Ellerdine Heath
Great Bolas
Little Bolas
Cold Hatton
Cold Hatton Heath
Meeson
Rowton
Moortown
SHROPSHIRE
Bletchley
Moreton Say
Longford
Ternhill
Prees
Prees Higher Heath
Sandford
Darliston
Fauls
Calverhall
Ightfield
Adderley
Coxbank
Wilkesley
Ash Magna
Ash Parva
Burleydam
Royal's Green
Lightwood Green
Pinsley Green
Marbury
Norbury
Hollyhurst
Chorley
Ravensmoor
Stoneley Green
M6
M54
A5
A41
A442
A449
A518
A519
A525
A529
A53
A51
A34
A50
A500
A520

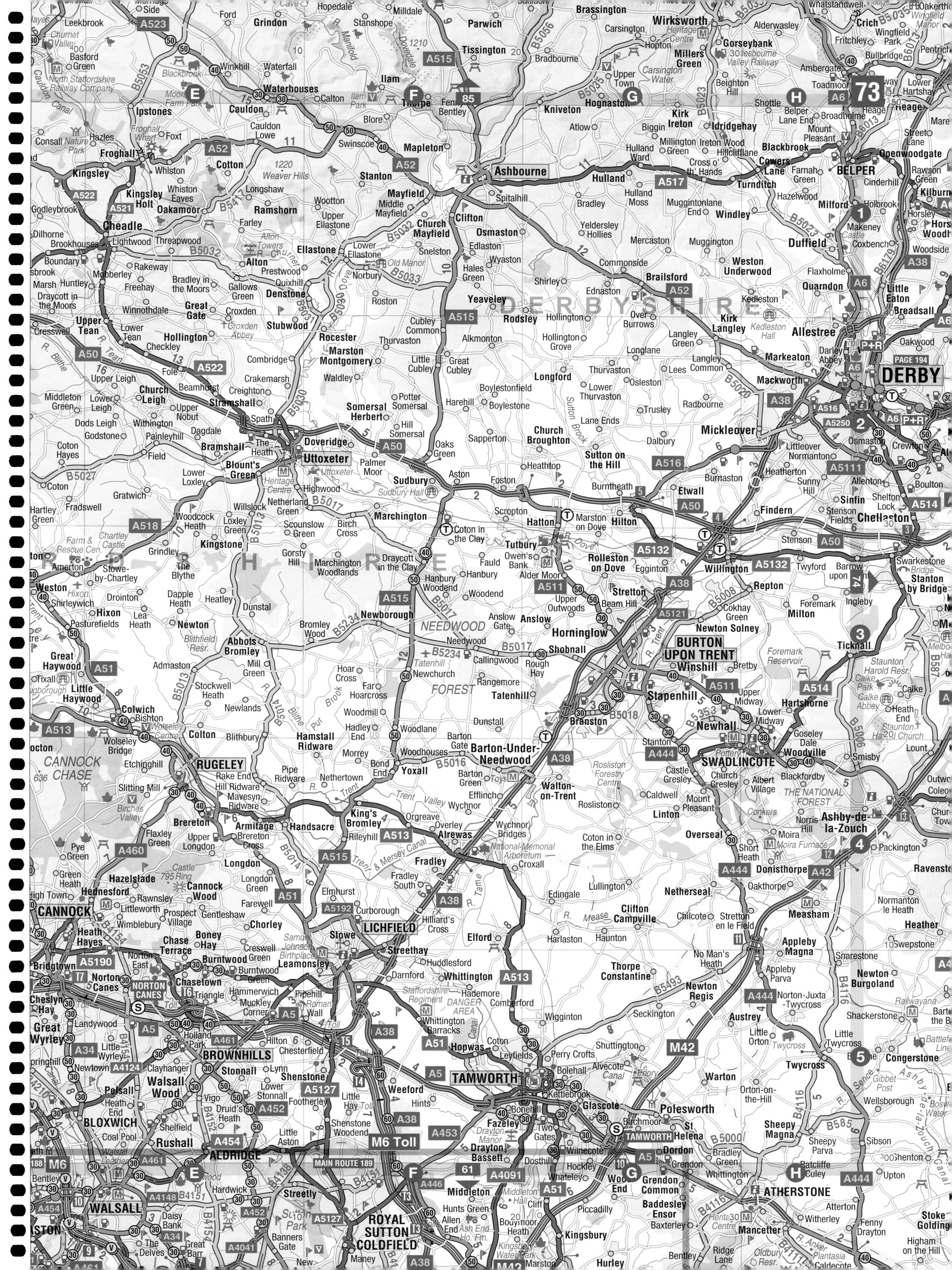

73
Leekbrook
Grindon
Hopedale
Milldale
Parwich
Brassington
Wirksworth
Carsington
Alderwasley
Crich
A523
Ford
Stanshope
Tissington
Hopton
Gorseybank
Wingfield Park
Fritchley
Basford Green
Winkhill
Waterfall
A515
Bradbourne
Millers Green
Bullbridge
Pentrich
North Staffordshire Railway Company
Ilam
Upper Town
Carsington Water
Ambergate
Waterhouses
Calton
Thorpe
Fenny Bentley
Kniveton
Hognaston
Beighton Hill
Shottle
Belper Lane End
Toadmoor
Heage
Lower Hartshay
Ipstones
Cauldon
Blore
Atlow
Biggin
Kirk Ireton
Idridgehay
Broadholme
Cauldon Lowe
Mount Pleasant
Consall
Hazles
Foxt
Swinscoe
Mapleton
Hulland Ward
Millington Green
Ireton Wood
Hillcliff Lane
Blackbrook
Openwoodgate
Froghall
A52
Cross o' th' Hands
Cowers Lane
Farnah Green
BELPER
Kingsley
Whiston
Cotton
Weaver Hills
Stanton
Ashbourne
Hulland
A517
Turnditch
Cinderhill
Kingsley Holt
Whiston Eaves
Longshaw
Mayfield
Middle Mayfield
Spitalhill
Bradley
Hulland Moss
Muggintonlane End
Windley
Hazelwood
Milford
Holbrook
Godleybrook
Oakamoor
Ramshorn
Wootton
Clifton
A522
A521
Cheadle
Farley
Upper Ellastone
Church Mayfield
Osmaston
Yeldersley Hollies
Mercaston
Mugginton
Makeney
Duffield
Coxbench
Dilhorne
Brookhouses
Lightwood
Threapwood
Alton Towers
Ellastone
Lower Ellastone
Snelston
Edlaston
Wyaston
Commonside
Weston Underwood
Woodside
Boundary
Alton
Prestwood
Old Manor
Norbury
Hales Green
Brailsford
Flaxholme
Marsh
Huntley
Rakeway
Freehay
Bradley in the Moors
Gallows Green
Quixhill
Shirley
Ednaston
Quarndon
Little Eaton
Draycott in the Moors
Winnothdale
Great Gate
Denstone
Roston
Yeaveley
DERBYSHIRE
Kedleston
Breadsall
Croxden
Stubwood
Rodsley
Hollington
Over Burrows
Kirk Langley
Kedleston Hall
Allestree
Upper Tean
Lower Tean
Hollington
Croxden Abbey
Rocester
Cubley Common
Thurvaston
Alkmonton
Hollington Grove
Langley Green
Markeaton
Darley Abbey
Oakwood
Cresswell
Checkley
Marston Montgomery
Little Cubley
Great Cubley
Longlane
Langley Common
Mackworth
P+R
PAGE 194
DERBY
A50
A522
Cambridge
Fole
Longford
Thurvaston
Lees
Osleston
Upper Leigh
Church Leigh
Beamhurst
Crakemarsh
Creighton
Waldley
Potter Somersal
Boylestonfield
Lower Thurvaston
Middleton Green
Lower Leigh
Stramshall
Spath
Somersal Herbert
Harehill
Boylestone
Trusley
Radbourne
A38
A516
A5250
Dods Leigh
Withington
Upper Nobut
Dagdale
Hill Somersal
Lane Ends
Mickleover
Godstone
Painleyhill
Bramshall
The Heath
Doveridge
Sapperton
Church Broughton
Dalbury
Littleover
Osmaston
Crewton
Coton Hayes
Field
Blount's Green
Uttoxeter
Palmer Moor
Oaks Green
Sutton on the Hill
Normanton
Heatherton
Sunny Hill
A5111
Allenton
Lower Loxley
Highwood
Sudbury
Aston
Foston
Heathtop
Burnaston
Etwall
Boulton
Coton
Gratwich
Sudbury Hall
Burntheath
Sinfin
Shelton Lock
A514
Hartley Green
Fradswell
Netherland Green
B5017
Willslock
Marchington
Scropton
Marston on Dove
Hilton
Findern
Stenson Fields
Chellaston
A518
Woodcock Heath
Loxley Green
Scounslow Green
Birch Cross
Coton in the Clay
Hatton
Stenson
A50
Farm & Rescue Cen.
Chartley Castle
Kingstone
Tutbury
Owen's Bank
Fauld
Rolleston on Dove
A5132
Swarkestone
Amerton
Grindley
Gorsty Hill
Marchington Woodlands
Draycott in the Clay
Hanbury
Egginton
Willington
Twyford
Barrow upon Trent
Stanton by Bridge
Stowe-by-Chartley
The Blythe
Hanbury Woodend
Alder Moor
A511
Stretton
Repton
Ingleby
Weston
Hixon
Drointon
Dapple Heath
Woodend
Upper Outwoods
Beam Hill
Foremark
Shirleywich
Hixon
Heatley
Lea Heath
Dunstal
A515
A5121
Cokhay Green
Milton
Pasturefields
Newton
Bromley Wood
Newborough
NEEDWOOD
Anslow Gate
Anslow
Horninglow
Newton Solney
Blithfield Resr.
Abbots Bromley
Needwood
Tatenhill
Shobnall
BURTON UPON TRENT
Ticknall
Great Haywood
A51
Admaston
Callingwood
Rough Hay
Winshill
Bretby
Foremark Reservoir
Staunton Harold Resr.
Mill Green
Hoar Cross
Newchurch
Rangemore
A511
Upper Midway
A514
Calke
Little Haywood
Stockwell Heath
Far Hoarcross
FOREST
Tatenhill
Stapenhill
Calke Park
Calke Abbey
Colwich
Bishton
Newlands
Woodmill
Dunstall
Branston
Lower Midway
Hartshorne
Heath End
A513
Colton
Wolseley Bridge
Blithbury
Hamstall Ridware
Hadley End
Woodlane
Barton Gate
Newhall
Goseley Dale
Staunton Harold Church
CANNOCK CHASE
Etchinghill
RUGELEY
Pipe Ridware
Morrey
Woodhouses
Barton-Under-Needwood
Stanton
A444
SWADLINCOTE
Woodville
Smisby
Lount
Rake End
Hill Ridware
Bond End
Yoxall
Nethertown
Barton Green
Castle Gresley
Church Gresley
Albert Village
Blackfordby
Slitting Mill
Mavesyn Ridware
Walton-on-Trent
Rosliston Forestry Centre
Caldwell
Rosliston
THE NATIONAL FOREST
Birches Valley
Efflinch
Wychnor
Mount Pleasant
Linton
Ashby-de-la-Zouch
Brereton
Armitage
Handsacre
King's Bromley
Orgreave
Alrewas
Wychnor Bridges
Conkers
Norris Hill
Moira
Overseal
Pye Green
A460
Flaxley Green
Upper Longdon
Brereton Cross
Rileyhill
A513
National Memorial Arboretum
Coton in the Elms
Moira Furnace
Packington
Longdon
A515
Trent & Mersey Canal
Fradley
Croxall
Short Heath
Donisthorpe
Ravenstone
Green Heath
Hazelslade
Castle Ring
Cannock Wood
Longdon Green
Fradley South
Edingale
Lullington
A444
A42
Hednesford
Rawnsley
Elmhurst
A38
Netherseal
Oakthorpe
Normanton le Heath
CANNOCK
Littleworth
Prospect Village
Gentleshaw
Farewell
A51
A5192
Curborough
Clifton Campville
Chilcote
Stretton en le Field
Measham
Heather
Heath Hayes
Wimblebury
Chorley
Hilliard's Cross
Mease
Harlaston
Haunton
Appleby Magna
Swepstone
Chase Terrace
Boney Hay
Samuel Johnson Birthplace
Stowe
LICHFIELD
Elford
No Man's Heath
Snarestone
Bridgtown
A5190
Norton East
Burntwood
Creswell Green
Streethay
Thorpe Constantine
Appleby Parva
Newton Burgoland
Norton Canes
NORTON CANES
Chasetown
Burntwood Green
Leamonsley
Huddlesford
Darnford
Whittington
A513
B5493
Newton Regis
Norton-Juxta-Twycross
Cheslyn Hay
Triangle
Hammerwich
Pipehill
Staffordshire Regiment
Hademore
DANGER AREA
Comberford
A444
Shackerstone
Great Wyrley
Landywood
Muckley Corner
A5
Roman Wall
Whittington Barracks
Wigginton
Seckington
Austrey
Little Orton
Little Twycross
A34
Holland Park
A461
Hilton
Chesterfield
A38
A51
Hopwas
Coton
Leyfields
Perry Crofts
Shuttington
Twycross
Congerstone
Little Wyrley
BROWNHILLS
M42
Newtown
A4124
Clayhanger
Stonnall
Lynn
Shenstone
A5
TAMWORTH
Bolehall
Alvecote
Warton
Orton-on-the-Hill
Walsall Wood
A5127
Weeford
Kettlebrook
Glascote
Polesworth
Gibbet Post
Pelsall
Lower Stonnall
Footherley
Little Hay
Hints
Wellsborough
Heath End
Vigo
Druid's Heath
A452
A38
Bonehill
Birchmoor
St Helena
Sheepy Magna
BLOXWICH
Shelfield
Shenstone Woodend
Fazeley
Two Gates
B5000
Coal Pool
Rushall
A454
Little Aston
M6 Toll
A453
Drayton Manor
TAMWORTH
Sheepy Parva
Sibson
ALDRIDGE
Drayton Bassett
Wilnecote
Dordon
Bradley Green
Shenton
M6
A461
MAIN ROUTE 189
Dosthill
Hockley
Grendon
Whittington
Ratcliffe Culey
Upton
A444
Bentley
A4148
B4151
Hardwick
A446
61
Middleton
A4091
Whateley
Wood End
Grendon Common
ATHERSTONE
WALSALL
Streetly
Middleton Hall
Cliff
A51
Baddesley Ensor
Atterton
A454
Daisy Bank
A452
A5127
ROYAL SUTTON COLDFIELD
Hunts Green
Allen End
Ash End Ho. Fm.
Piccadilly
Baxterley
Mancetter
Witherley
Fenny Drayton
Stoke Golding
A34
Sutton Park
Bodymoor Heath
Kingsbury
Heritage Centre
Higham on the Hill
The Delves
Great Barr
A4041
Banners Gate
Kingsbury Water Park
Ridge Lane
Oldbury Resr.
Bentley
Plantasia
Caldecote
Maney
A38
New
M42
Marston
Hurley

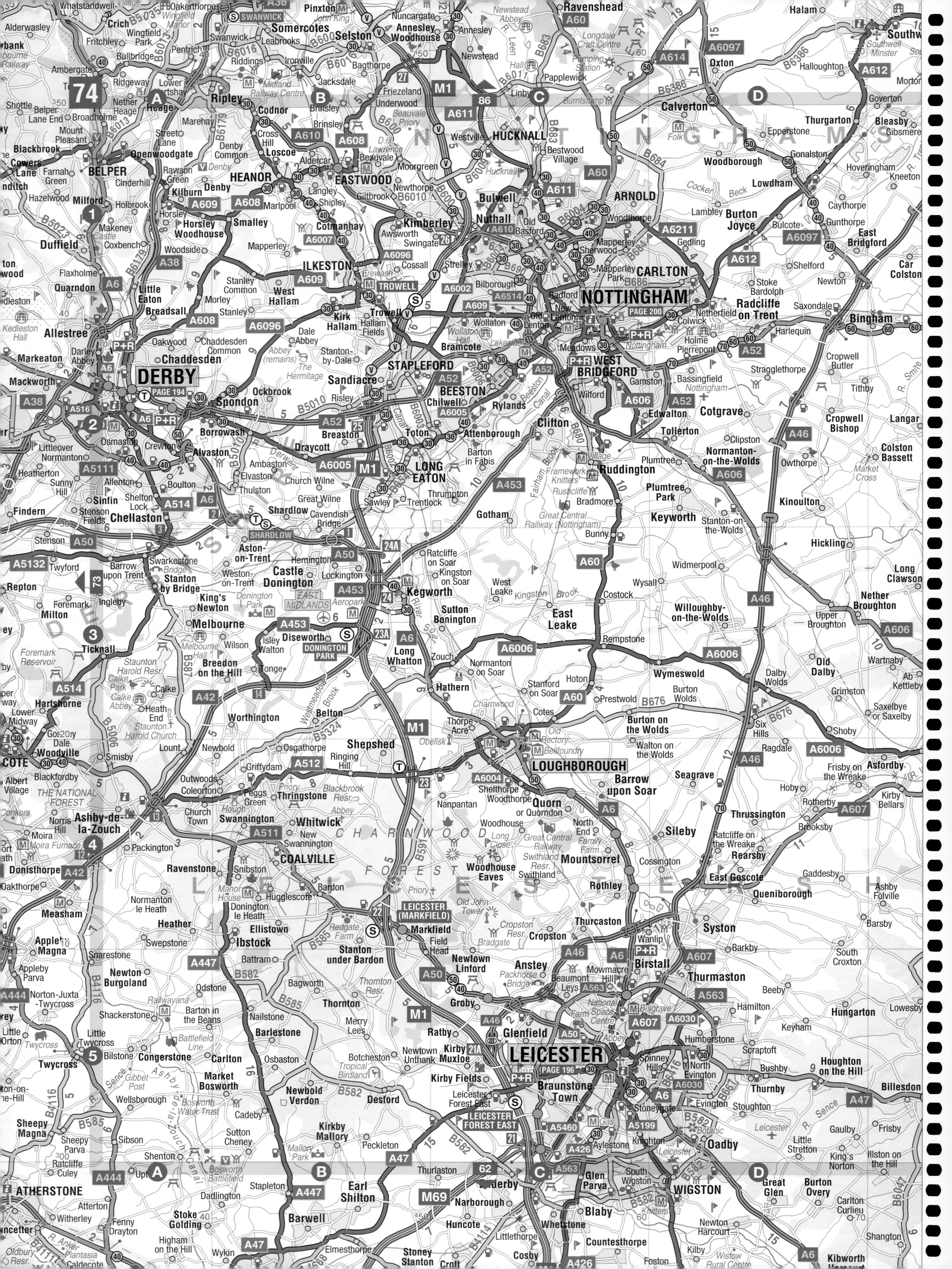

74
73
A
B
C
D
NOTTINGHAM
PAGE 200
DERBY
PAGE 194
LEICESTER
PAGE 196
LOUGHBOROUGH
COALVILLE
HUCKNALL
ARNOLD
CARLTON
BELPER
HEANOR
EASTWOOD
ILKESTON
STAPLEFORD
BEESTON
WEST BRIDGFORD
LONG EATON
WIGSTON
ATHERSTONE
Ripley
Alfreton
Somercotes
Selston
Kimberley
Bulwell
Nuthall
Radcliffe on Trent
Bingham
Cotgrave
Ruddington
Keyworth
Clifton
Kegworth
Castle Donington
Melbourne
Ashby-de-la-Zouch
Shepshed
Quorn
Mountsorrel
Sileby
Syston
Birstall
Thurmaston
Oadby
Braunstone Town
Glenfield
Kirby Muxloe
Ratby
Groby
Anstey
Earl Shilton
Barwell
Market Bosworth
Ibstock
Whitwick
Swadlincote
Chellaston
Spondon
Borrowash
Duffield
Allestree
Chaddesden
Burton Joyce
Calverton
East Leake
Hathern
Barrow upon Soar
Rothley
Sandiacre
Trowell
Kirk Hallam
Breaston
Draycott
Kibworth
Great Glen
Blaby
Whetstone
Countesthorpe
Enderby
Narborough
Desford
Newbold Verdon
Stoney Stanton
Stoke Golding
Twycross
Measham
Castle Donington
Breedon on the Hill
DONINGTON PARK
EAST MIDLANDS Aeroport
LEICESTER (MARKFIELD)
LEICESTER FOREST EAST
SHARDLOW
SWANWICK
TROWELL
CHARNWOOD FOREST
THE NATIONAL FOREST
NOTTINGHAMSHIRE
LEICESTERSHIRE
DERBYSHIRE
M1
M69
A6
A38
A50
A52
A60
A42
A46
A47
A444
A447
A453
A511
A512
A514
A563
A606
A607
A608
A609
A610
A611
A612
A614
A5111
A5132
A6005
A6006
A6096
A6097
A6211
A6514
A5460
A5199
A6030
A4304
A6004
A6007
A6002
P+R

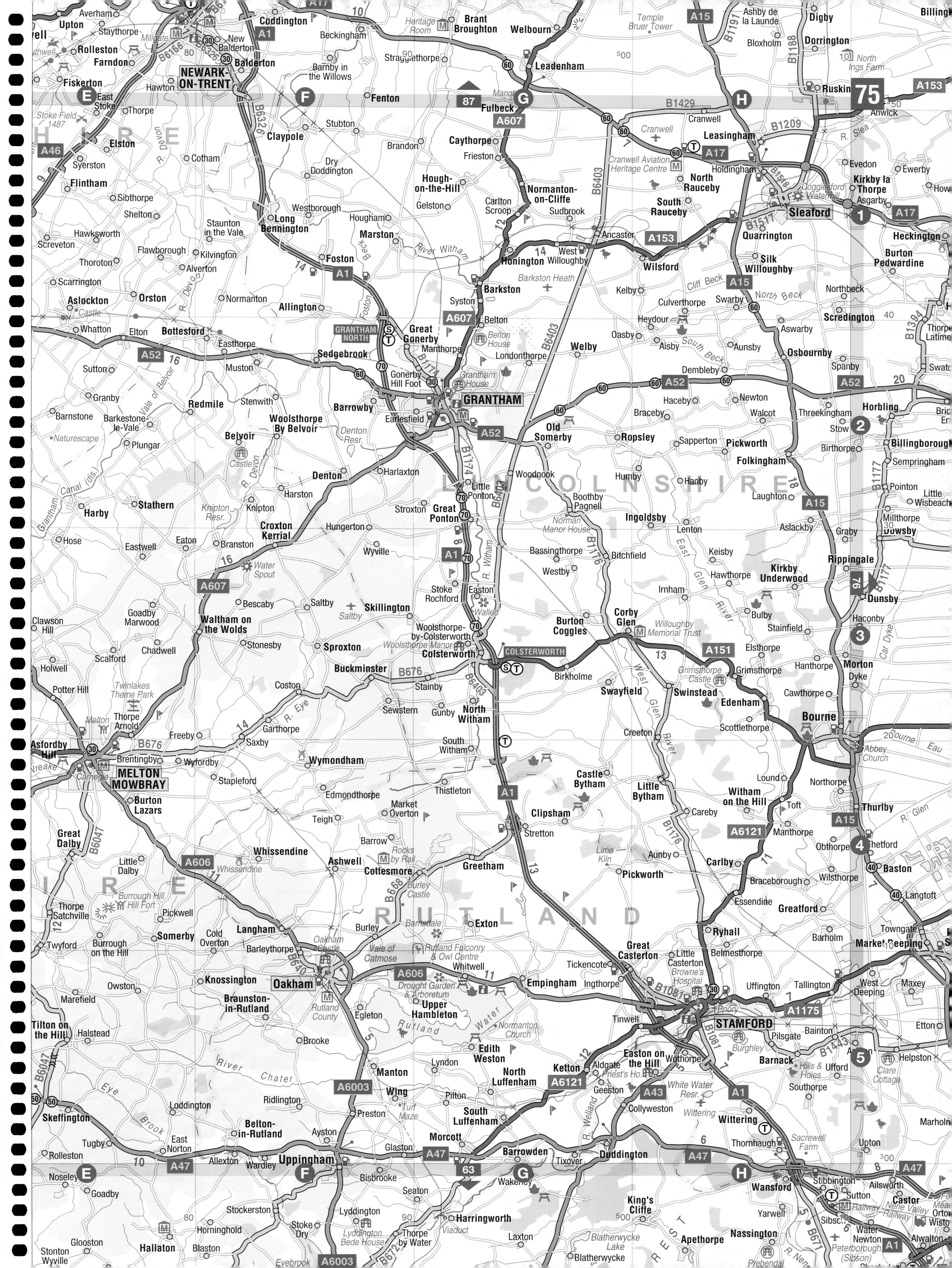

75
Averham
Upton
Staythorpe
Rolleston
Farndon
Fiskerton
East Stoke
Thorpe
Stoke Field 1487
Elston
Syerston
Flintham
Sibthorpe
Shelton
Hawksworth
Screveton
Thoroton
Scarrington
Aslockton
Orston
Whatton
Elton
Bottesford
Easthorpe
Sutton
Granby
Barnstone
Barkestone-le-Vale
Naturescape
Plungar
Redmile
Stenwith
Muston
Sedgebrook
Woolsthorpe By Belvoir
Belvoir
Castle
Denton
Denton Resr.
Harlaxton
Harston
Knipton
Knipton Resr.
Stathern
Harby
Hose
Eastwell
Eaton
Branston
Croxton Kerrial
Hungerton
Wyville
Water Spout
Goadby Marwood
Bescaby
Waltham on the Wolds
Saltby
Skillington
Clawson Hill
Holwell
Scalford
Chadwell
Stonesby
Sproxton
Buckminster
Potter Hill
Twinlakes Theme Park
Coston
Thorpe Arnold
Melton
Freeby
Garthorpe
Saxby
Asfordby Hill
Brentingby
Wyfordby
MELTON MOWBRAY
Burton Lazars
Stapleford
Wymondham
Edmondthorpe
Great Dalby
Little Dalby
Whissendine
Teigh
Market Overton
Barrow
Ashwell
Rocks by Rail
Cottesmore
Burley Castle
Thorpe Satchville
Burrough Hill Hill Fort
Pickwell
Somerby
Cold Overton
Langham
Barleythorpe
Oakham Castle
Twyford
Burrough on the Hill
Knossington
Oakham
Owston
Marefield
Braunston-in-Rutland
Rutland County
Egleton
Tilton on the Hill
Halstead
Brooke
Manton
Wing
Ridlington
Preston
Loddington
Skeffington
Belton-in-Rutland
East Norton
Tugby
Rolleston
Allexton
Wardley
Uppingham
Ayston
Glaston
Noseley
Goadby
Bisbrooke
Seaton
Stockerston
Horninghold
Lyddington
Lyddington Bede House
Stoke Dry
Glooston
Hallaton
Blaston
Stonton Wyville
Evebrook
Thorpe by Water
Harringworth
Viaduct
Laxton
Coddington
Beckingham
NEWARK-ON-TRENT
New Balderton
Balderton
Hawton
Barnby in the Willows
Stragglethorpe
Fenton
Stubton
Claypole
Cotham
Dry Doddington
Brandon
Westborough
Long Bennington
Staunton in the Vale
Flawborough
Kilvington
Alverton
Foston
Normanton
Allington
Hougham
Marston
River Witham
Great Gonerby
Manthorpe
Gonerby Hill Foot
GRANTHAM NORTH
GRANTHAM
Barrowby
Earlesfield
Heritage Room
Brant Broughton
Welbourn
Leadenham
Manor
Fulbeck
Caythorpe
Frieston
Hough-on-the-Hill
Gelston
Carlton Scroop
Normanton-on-Cliffe
Sudbrook
Honington
West Willoughby
Barkston
Barkston Heath
Syston
Belton
Belton House
Londonthorpe
Grantham House
Little Ponton
Stroxton
Great Ponton
Stoke Rochford
Easton
Walled
Woolsthorpe-by-Colsterworth
Woolsthorpe Manor
Colsterworth
COLSTERWORTH
Stainby
Sewstern
Gunby
North Witham
South Witham
Thistleton
Clipsham
Stretton
Greetham
Exton
Barnsdale
Vale of Catmose
Rutland Falconry & Owl Centre
Whitwell
Drought Garden & Arboretum
Upper Hambleton
Rutland Water
Normanton Church
Edith Weston
Lyndon
North Luffenham
Pilton
South Luffenham
Morcott
Barrowden
Wakerley
Tixover
Turf Maze
RUTLAND
LINCOLNSHIRE
Temple Bruer Tower
Ashby de la Launde
Bloxholm
Digby
Dorrington
North Ings Farm
Ruskin
Anwick
Cranwell
Cranwell Aviation Heritage Centre
Leasingham
Holdingham
North Rauceby
South Rauceby
Cogglesford Watermill
Sleaford
Evedon
Ewerby
Kirkby la Thorpe
Asgarby
Quarrington
Heckington
Ancaster
Wilsford
Silk Willoughby
Burton Pedwardine
Kelby
Culverthorpe
Swarby
Northbeck
Heydour
Oasby
Aisby
Aswarby
Scredington
Aunsby
Osbournby
Spanby
Dembleby
Welby
Haceby
Newton
Braceby
Walcot
Threekingham
Horbling
Stow
Birthorpe
Billingborough
Sempringham
Old Somerby
Ropsley
Sapperton
Pickworth
Folkingham
Woodnook
Humby
Hanby
Boothby Pagnell
Laughton
Pointon
Little Wisbeach
Millthorpe
Dowsby
Ingoldsby
Lenton
Norman Manor House
Aslackby
Graby
Bassingthorpe
Bitchfield
Keisby
Rippingale
Westby
Hawthorpe
Kirkby Underwood
Irnham
Dunsby
Corby Glen
Burton Coggles
Willoughby Memorial Trust
Bulby
Stainfield
Haconby
Elsthorpe
Grimsthorpe Castle
Grimsthorpe
Hanthorpe
Morton
Dyke
Birkholme
Swayfield
Swinstead
Edenham
Cawthorpe
Bourne
Scottlethorpe
Creeton
Abbey Church
Bourne Eau
Lound
Northorpe
Castle Bytham
Little Bytham
Witham on the Hill
Toft
Thurlby
Careby
Manthorpe
Obthorpe
Thetford
Lime Kiln
Aunby
Carlby
Baston
Pickworth
Braceborough
Wilsthorpe
Langtoft
Essendine
Greatford
Ryhall
Towngate
Barholm
Market Deeping
Great Casterton
Belmesthorpe
Tickencote
Little Casterton
Browne's Hospital
Empingham
Ingthorpe
Uffington
Tallington
West Deeping
Maxey
Tinwell
Priory
STAMFORD
Etton
Pilsgate
Bainton
Easton on the Hill
Wothorpe
Burghley
Barnack
Helpston
Ketton
Aldgate
Priest's Ho.
Hills & Holes
Ufford
Clare Cottage
Geeston
White Water Resr.
Southorpe
Collyweston
Wittering
Wittering
Marholm
Thornhaugh
Sacrewell Farm
Upton
Duddington
Wansford
Stibbington
Ailsworth
Sutton
Castor
Nene Valley Railway
Yarwell
King's Cliffe
Nassington
Apethorpe
Blatherwycke Lake
Blatherwycke
Water Newton
Peterborough (Sibson)
Alwalton
Prebendal

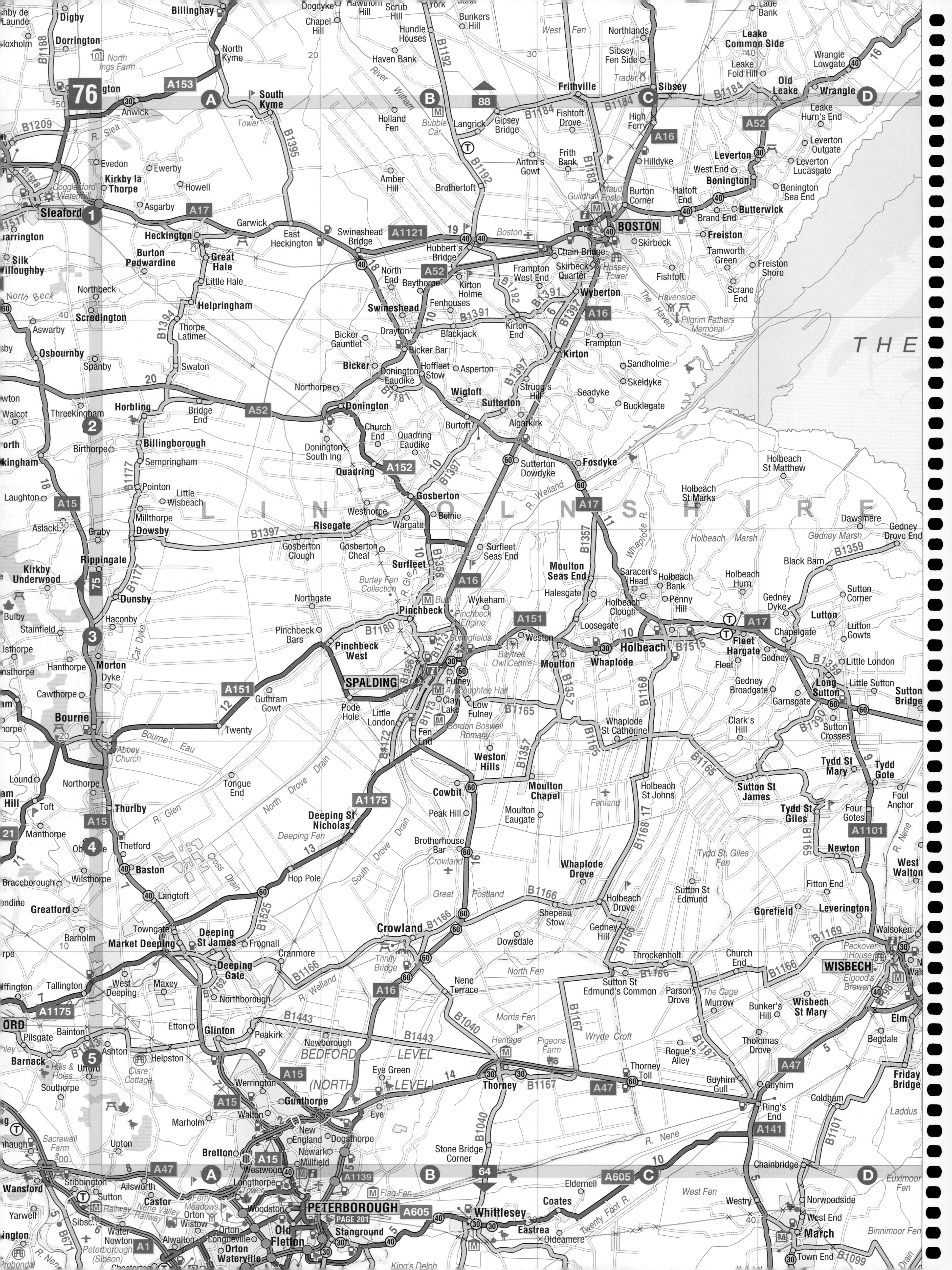

Digby
Billinghay
Dogdyke
Chapel Hill
Scrub Hill
York
Bunkers Hill
Lade Bank
Dorrington
Hundle Houses
West Fen
Northlands
Leake Common Side
North Ings Farm
North Kyme
Haven Bank
Sibsey Fen Side
Leake Fold Hill
Wrangle Lowgate
B1188
B1192
76
A153
A
South Kyme
B
88
Frithville
C
Sibsey
B1184
Old Leake
Wrangle
D
Anwick
Tower
Holland Fen
Bubble Car
Langrick
Gipsey Bridge
Fishtoft Drove
High Ferry
Leake Hurn's End
B1209
B1395
A16
A52
R. Slea
Evedon
Ewerby
Anton's Gowt
Frith Bank
Hilldyke
Leverton
Leverton Outgate
Kirkby la Thorpe
Howell
Amber Hill
Brothertoft
B1183
West End
Leverton Lucasgate
Cogglesford Watermill
Asgarby
Burton Corner
Haltoft End
Benington
Benington Sea End
Sleaford
A17
Butterwick
Brand End
Garwick
BOSTON
Freiston
Heckington
East Heckington
Swineshead Bridge
A1121
Hubbert's Bridge
Boston
Skirbeck
Burton Pedwardine
Great Hale
Chain Bridge
Tamworth Green
Silk Willoughby
Little Hale
North End
A52
Frampton West End
Skirbeck Quarter
Hussey Tower
Fishtoft
Freiston Shore
Baythorpe
Kirton Holme
Northbeck
B1192
Wyberton
Scrane End
North Beck
Helpringham
Fenhouses
B1391
The Haven
Havenside
Scredington
Swineshead
Pilgrim Fathers Memorial
B1394
Drayton
Blackjack
Kirton End
B1397
A16
Aswarby
Thorpe Latimer
Bicker Gauntlet
Frampton
THE
Osbournby
Bicker Bar
Kirton
Spanby
Swaton
Bicker
Hoffleet Stow
Asperton
Sandholme
Donington Eaudike
Skeldyke
Northorpe
B1181
Struggs Hill
Seadyke
Horbling
Bridge End
A52
Donington
Wigtoft
Sutterton
Bucklegate
Threekingham
Church End
Burtoft
Algarkirk
Billingborough
Quadring Eaudike
Birthorpe
Donington South Ing
Fosdyke
Sempringham
Quadring
A152
Sutterton Dowdyke
Holbeach St Matthew
Pointon
Gosberton
R. Welland
Holbeach St Marks
Laughton
Little Wisbeach
A15
Millthorpe
Westhorpe
Belnie
A17
LINCOLNSHIRE
Dawsmere
Aslackby
Graby
Risegate
Wargate
Gedney Drove End
Dowsby
B1397
Gosberton Clough
Gosberton Cheal
Surfleet
Surfleet Seas End
B1357
Whaplode R.
Holbeach Marsh
Gedney Marsh
Rippingale
B1356
Moulton Seas End
Saracen's Head
Holbeach Bank
B1359
Black Barn
Kirkby Underwood
B1177
Burtey Fen Collection
R. Glen
A16
Holbeach Hurn
Sutton Corner
Dunsby
Northgate
Bulb
Wykeham
Halesgate
Penny Hill
Gedney Dyke
Lutton
Bulby
Haconby
Pinchbeck
Pinchbeck Engine
Holbeach Clough
Loosegate
A151
A17
Lutton Gowts
Stainfield
Pinchbeck Bars
B1180
Springfields
Weston
Holbeach
B1515
Fleet Hargate
Chapelgate
Pinchbeck West
Baytree Owl Centre
Moulton
Whaplode
Gedney
Little London
Hanthorpe
Morton
Dyke
Car Dyke
SPALDING
Fulney
Ayscoughfee Hall
Fleet
B1359
Long Sutton
Little Sutton
Sutton Bridge
Cawthorpe
A151
Guthram Gowt
Pode Hole
Clay Lake
Low Fulney
B1165
B1168
Gedney Broadgate
Garnsgate
Bourne
Little London
B1173
Whaplode St Catherine
Clark's Hill
Sutton Crosses
B1390
Twenty
Gordon Boswell Romany
Bourne Eau
Abbey Church
Fen End
B1172
Weston Hills
B1165
Tydd St Mary
Tydd Gote
Lound
Tongue End
North Drove Drain
Cowbit
Moulton Chapel
Holbeach St Johns
Sutton St James
Foul Anchor
Northorpe
A1175
Peak Hill
Moulton Eaugate
Fenland
Tydd St Giles
Four Gotes
Toft
Thurlby
R. Glen
Deeping St Nicholas
B1168
A1101
A15
Deeping Fen
South Drove Drain
Brotherhouse Bar
Crowland
Tydd St. Giles Fen
Newton
R. Nene
Manthorpe
Thetford
West Walton
Baston
Cross Drain
Whaplode Drove
Braceborough
Wilsthorpe
Hop Pole
Great
Postland
Sutton St Edmund
Fitton End
Langtoft
B1166
Holbeach Drove
Gorefield
Leverington
Greatford
B1525
Shepeau Stow
Townsgate
Crowland
B1166
Gedney Hill
Walsoken
Barholm
Deeping St James
Frognall
Dowsdale
B1169
Market Deeping
Cranmore
Throckenholt
Church End
Peckover House
WISBECH
Deeping Gate
Trinity Bridge
B1166
North Fen
B1166
Elgood's Brewery
Tallington
West Deeping
Maxey
Sutton St Edmund's Common
Parson Drove
The Cage
Murrow
A16
Nene Terrace
B1162
R. Welland
Bunker's Hill
Wisbech St Mary
Northborough
B1167
A1175
Morris Fen
Elm
Etton
B1040
Wryde Croft
Begdale
Bainton
Glinton
B1443
Heritage
Pigeons Farm
Pilsgate
Ashton
Peakirk
Newborough
B1443
Rogue's Alley
Tholomas Drove
Barnack
Helpston
BEDFORD LEVEL
B1187
Ufford
Clare Cottage
A15
Eye Green
14
Thorney Toll
Guyhirn Gull
A47
Friday Bridge
Southorpe
Werrington
(NORTH LEVEL)
Thorney
B1167
A47
Guyhirn
A15
Gunthorpe
Coldham
Marholm
Walton
Eye
B1040
Ring's End
Laddus
Sacrewell Farm
New England
Dogsthorpe
A141
Upton
Newark
Millfield
R. Nene
B1101
Bretton
Stone Bridge Corner
A15
Chainbridge
A47
Westwood
64
A605
A
B
C
D
Wansford
Stibbington
Ailsworth
Longthorpe
A1139
Flag Fen
Eldernell
West Fen
Euximoor Fen
Sutton
Castor
Ferry Meadows
PETERBOROUGH
PAGE 201
A605
Coates
Westry
Norwoodside
Yarwell
Nene Valley Railway
Orton Wistow
Woodston
Whittlesey
Twenty Foot R.
West End
B671
Water Newton
Orton Longueville
Old Fletton
Stanground
Eastrea
March
Binnimoor Fen
Peterborough (Sibson)
Alwalton
A1
Orton Waterville
Oldeamere
Town End
B1099
King's Delph

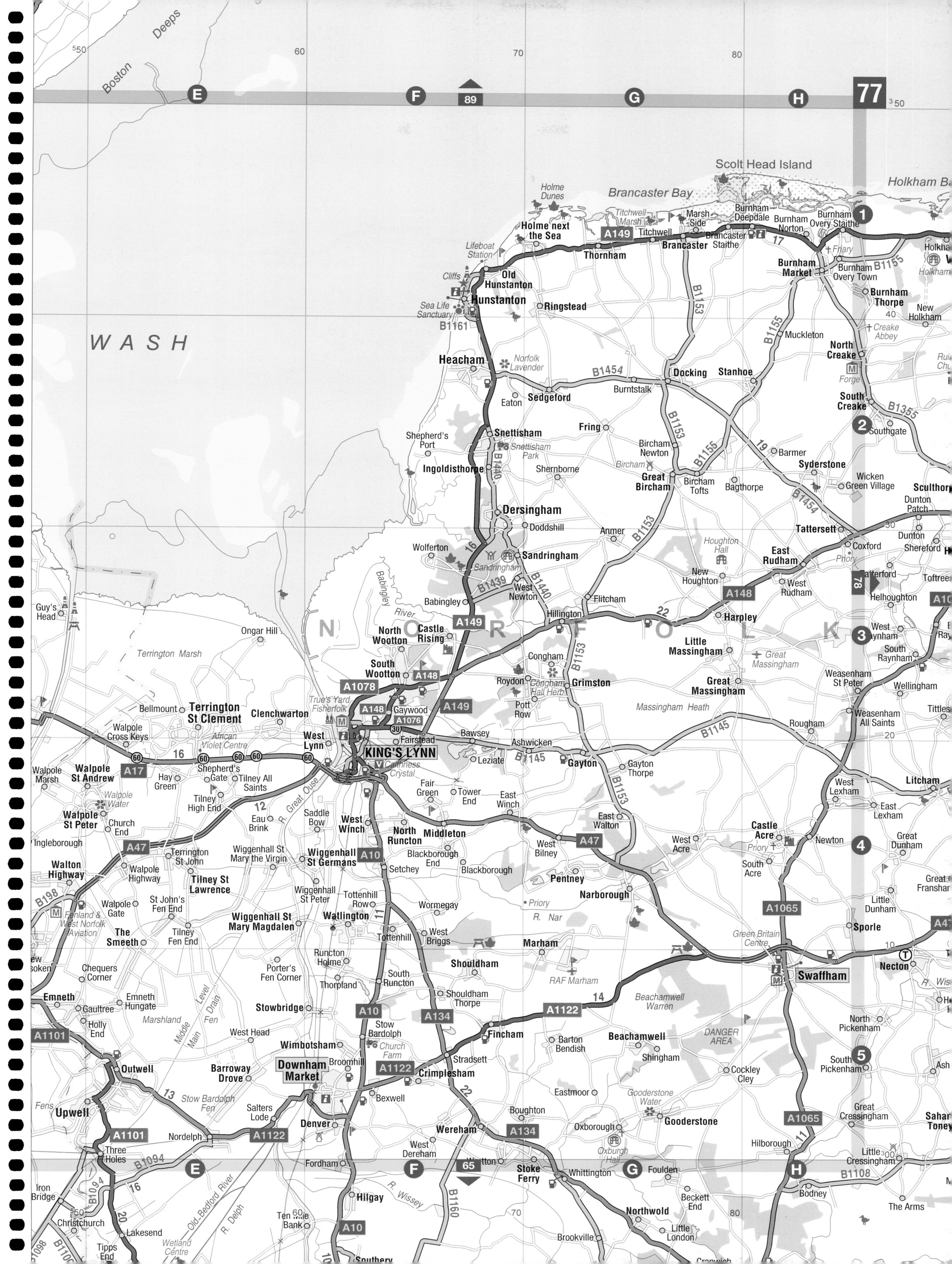

77
Boston
Deeps
WASH
89
65
E
F
G
H
1
2
3
4
5
78
Scolt Head Island
Brancaster Bay
Holkham Bay
Holme Dunes
Titchwell Marsh
Holme next the Sea
Titchwell
Marsh Side
Brancaster
Brancaster Staithe
Burnham Deepdale
Burnham Norton
Burnham Overy Staithe
Burnham Market
Burnham Overy Town
Burnham Thorpe
New Holkham
Friary
Thornham
Lifeboat Station
Cliffs
Old Hunstanton
Hunstanton
Sea Life Sanctuary
Ringstead
Heacham
Norfolk Lavender
Sedgeford
Eaton
Docking
Stanhoe
Burntstalk
Muckleton
North Creake
Creake Abbey
Forge
South Creake
Southgate
Snettisham
Snettisham Park
Shepherd's Port
Ingoldisthorpe
Shernborne
Fring
Bircham Newton
Bircham
Great Bircham
Bircham Tofts
Bagthorpe
Barmer
Syderstone
Wicken Green Village
Sculthorpe
Dunton Patch
Dersingham
Doddshill
Anmer
Tattersett
Coxford
Priory
Dunton
Shereford
Wolferton
Sandringham
Houghton Hall
New Houghton
East Rudham
West Rudham
Tatterford
Toftrees
Helhoughton
Babingley
Babingley River
West Newton
Flitcham
Hillington
Harpley
North Wootton
Castle Rising
NORFOLK
Little Massingham
Great Massingham
South Raynham
West Raynham
Congham
Roydon
Grimston
Pott Row
Massingham Heath
Weasenham St Peter
Weasenham All Saints
Wellingham
South Wootton
Gaywood
Fairstead
Bawsey
Ashwicken
Leziate
Gayton
Gayton Thorpe
Rougham
Guy's Head
Ongar Hill
Terrington Marsh
Terrington St Clement
Clenchwarton
True's Yard Fisherfolk
West Lynn
KING'S LYNN
Caithness Crystal
Bellmount
Walpole Cross Keys
African Violet Centre
Walpole Marsh
Walpole St Andrew
Hay Green
Shepherd's Gate
Tilney All Saints
Tilney High End
Walpole Water
Walpole St Peter
Church End
Eau Brink
R. Great Ouse
Saddle Bow
West Winch
Fair Green
Tower End
East Winch
North Runcton
Middleton
East Walton
West Bilney
West Lexham
East Lexham
Litcham
Castle Acre
West Acre
South Acre
Newton
Great Dunham
Ingleborough
Terrington St John
Wiggenhall St Mary the Virgin
Wiggenhall St Germans
Blackborough End
Blackborough
Setchey
Pentney
Narborough
Priory
R. Nar
Walton Highway
Walpole Highway
Tilney St Lawrence
Wiggenhall St Peter
Tottenhill Row
Wormegay
Walpole Gate
St John's Fen End
Fenland & West Norfolk Aviation
Wiggenhall St Mary Magdalen
Watlington
Tottenhill
West Briggs
Marham
RAF Marham
Green Britain Centre
Sporle
Little Dunham
Great Fransham
The Smeeth
Tilney Fen End
Runcton Holme
Shouldham
Swaffham
Necton
Chequers Corner
Porter's Fen Corner
South Runcton
Thorpland
Shouldham Thorpe
Emneth
Emneth Hungate
Gaultree
Holly End
Marshland
Middle Level Main Drain
Fen
Stowbridge
Beachamwell Warren
North Pickenham
West Head
Stow Bardolph
Church Farm
Wimbotsham
Fincham
Barton Bendish
Beachamwell
Shingham
DANGER AREA
South Pickenham
Outwell
Barroway Drove
Downham Market
Broomhill
Crimplesham
Stradsett
Cockley Cley
Bexwell
Eastmoor
Gooderstone Water
Gooderstone
Great Cressingham
Upwell
Fens
Stow Bardolph Fen
Salters Lode
Denver
Boughton
Wereham
Oxborough
Oxburgh Hall
Hilborough
Little Cressingham
Nordelph
Three Holes
West Dereham
Wretton
Stoke Ferry
Whittington
Foulden
Iron Bridge
Fordham
Beckett End
Bodney
The Arms
Christchurch
Hilgay
R. Wissey
Ten Mile Bank
Old Bedford River
R. Delph
Northwold
Little London
Lakesend
Wetland Centre
Tipps End
Brookville
Southery
A149
A148
A1078
A1076
A10
A17
A47
A134
A1122
A1065
A1101
B1161
B1153
B1155
B1454
B1355
B1440
B1439
B1145
B1094
B198
B1108
B1160

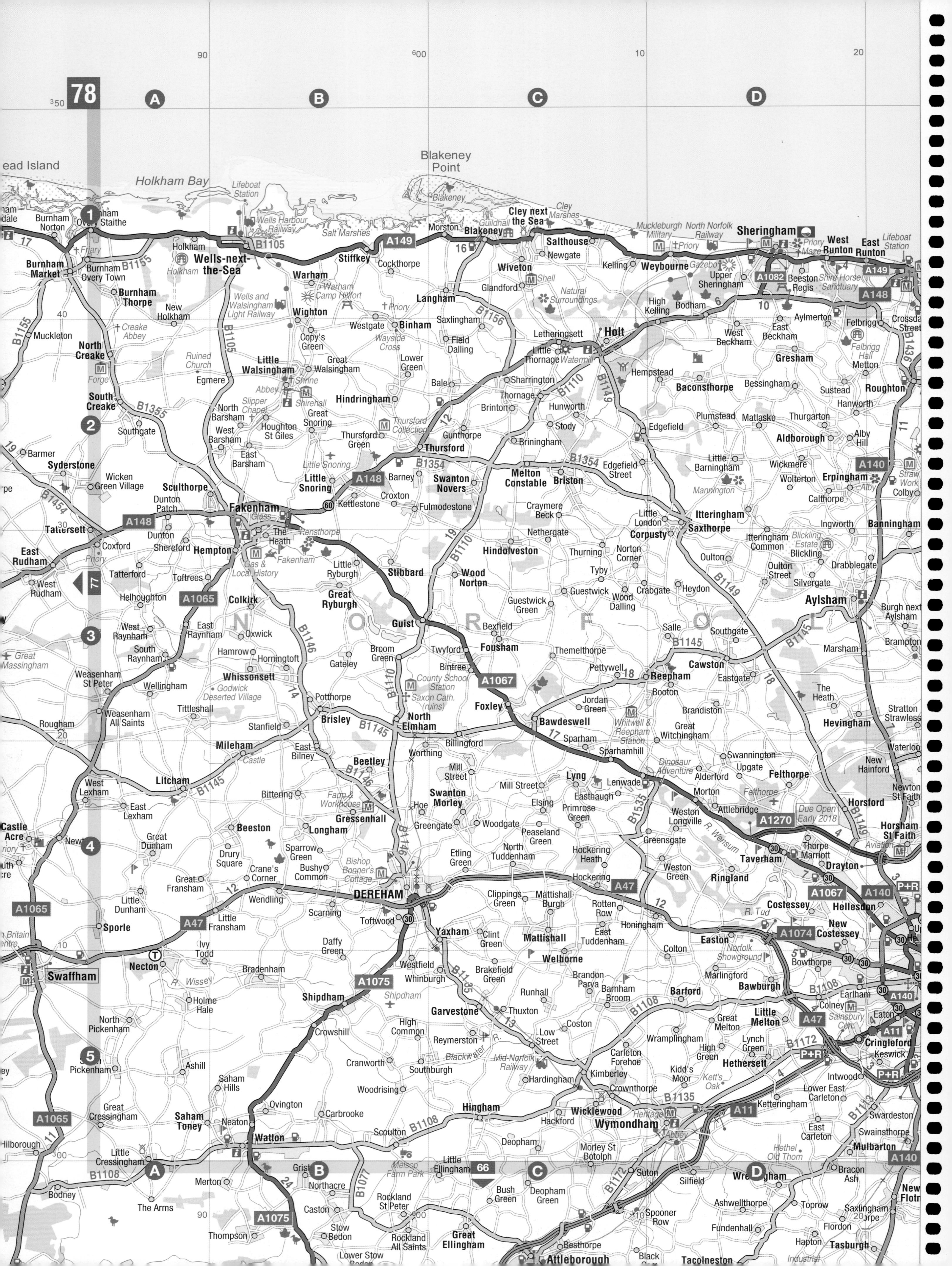

78
90
600
10
20
350
A
B
C
D
ead Island
Holkham Bay
Lifeboat Station
Blakeney Point
Blakeney
Cley next the Sea
Cley Marshes
Burnham Norton
Burnham Overy Staithe
Burnham Market
Burnham Overy Town
Friary
Holkham
Wells-next-the-Sea
Wells Harbour Railway
Salt Marshes
B1105
A149
B1155
Stiffkey
Cockthorpe
Morston
Guildhall
Salthouse
Newgate
Kelling
Weybourne
Muckleburgh Military
North Norfolk Railway
Sheringham
Priory
West Runton
East Runton
Lifeboat Station
Gazebo
Upper Sheringham
Beeston Regis
Shire Horse Sanctuary
A1082
A148
Wiveton
Glandford
Shell
Natural Surroundings
Langham
Warham
Warham Camp Hillfort
Wells and Walsingham Light Railway
Wighton
Priory
Westgate
Binham
Saxlingham
Field Dalling
B1156
High Kelling
Bodham
Aylmerton
Felbrigg
Crossdale Street
Burnham Thorpe
New Holkham
Creake Abbey
Muckleton
North Creake
Forge
Ruined Church
Egmere
Copy's Green
Wayside Cross
Little Walsingham
Great Walsingham
Shrine
Abbey
Shirehall
Lower Green
Letheringsett
Little Thornage
Watermill
Holt
West Beckham
East Beckham
Gresham
Felbrigg Hall
Metton
Hempstead
Sharrington
Thornage
Bale
Hindringham
Slipper Chapel
North Barsham
West Barsham
East Barsham
Houghton St Giles
Great Snoring
Thursford Collection
Thursford Green
Thursford
South Creake
B1355
Southgate
Brinton
Hunworth
Stody
Gunthorpe
Briningham
B1110
B1149
Baconsthorpe
Bessingham
Sustead
Roughton
Hanworth
Edgefield
Plumstead
Matlaske
Thurgarton
Alby Hill
Aldborough
Barmer
Syderstone
Wicken Green Village
Sculthorpe
Dunton Patch
Fakenham
Little Snoring
Little Snoring
A148
Barney
B1354
Swanton Novers
Croxton
Kettlestone
Fulmodestone
Melton Constable
Briston
Edgefield Street
Little Barningham
Wickmere
Wolterton
Mannington
Erpingham
Calthorpe
Colby
Straw Work
Alby
A140
B1454
Tattersett
Coxford
Dunton
Shereford
Hempton
Glass
The Heath
Pensthorpe
Gas & Local History
Fakenham
Craymere Beck
Little London
Corpusty
Saxthorpe
Itteringham
Itteringham Common
Blickling Estate
Blickling
Ingworth
Banningham
East Rudham
West Rudham
Priory
Tatterford
Toftrees
Little Ryburgh
Stibbard
Wood Norton
Hindolveston
Nethergate
Thurning
Norton Corner
Tyby
Oulton
Oulton Street
Drabblegate
Silvergate
Aylsham
Burgh next Aylsham
Helhoughton
A1065
Colkirk
Great Ryburgh
Guist
Guestwick
Guestwick Green
Wood Dalling
Crabgate
Heydon
West Raynham
East Raynham
Oxwick
Bexfield
Fousham
Salle
Southgate
Great Massingham
South Raynham
Hamrow
Horningtoft
Broom Green
Gateley
Twyford
Themelthorpe
B1145
Cawston
Marsham
Brampton
Weasenham St Peter
Wellingham
Whissonsett
Godwick Deserted Village
Bintree
County School Station
Saxon Cath. (ruins)
A1067
Pettywell
Reepham
Booton
Eastgate
The Heath
Weasenham All Saints
Tittleshall
Potthorpe
Brisley
North Elmham
Foxley
Jordan Green
Bawdeswell
Whitwell & Reepham Station
Brandiston
Great Witchingham
Stratton Strawless
Hevingham
Rougham
Stanfield
Billingford
Sparham
Sparhamhill
Mileham
Castle
East Bilney
Beetley
Worthing
Mill Street
Dinosaur Adventure
Swannington
Upgate
Alderford
Felthorpe
Waterloo
New Hainford
West Lexham
Litcham
Bittering
Farm & Workhouse
Swanton Morley
Mill Street
Lyng
Lenwade
Eashaugh
Elsing
Primrose Green
Morton
Attlebridge
Weston Longville
Due Open Early 2018
A1270
Horsford
Newton St Faith
East Lexham
Castle Acre
Beeston
Gressenhall
Longham
Hoe
Greengate
Woodgate
Peaseland Green
Greensgate
R. Wensum
Thorpe Marriott
Horsham St Faith
Aviation
Great Dunham
Drury Square
Sparrow Green
Bushy Common
Bishop Bonner's Cottage
Etling Green
North Tuddenham
Hockering Heath
Weston Green
Taverham
Drayton
Ringland
Great Fransham
Crane's Corner
Hockering
A47
Little Dunham
Wendling
DEREHAM
Scarning
Clippings Green
Mattishall Burgh
Rotten Row
Honingham
A1067
Costessey
Hellesdon
A140
P+R
A1065
Little Fransham
Toftwood
Yaxham
Clint Green
Mattishall
East Tuddenham
Easton
R. Tud
New Costessey
Sporle
Ivy Todd
Daffy Green
A1074
Swaffham
Necton
Bradenham
Westfield
Whinburgh
Welborne
Colton
Norfolk Showground
Bowthorpe
R. Wissey
A1075
B1135
Brakefield Green
Brandon Parva
Barnham Broom
Barford
Marlingford
Bawburgh
Earlham
Holme Hale
Shipdham
Shipdham
Garvestone
Runhall
Thuxton
B1108
Colney
Sainsbury Centre
North Pickenham
Crowshill
High Common
Reymerston
Low Street
Coston
Great Melton
Little Melton
Eaton
Cringleford
Keswick
Wramplingham
High Green
Lynch Green
B1172
South Pickenham
Ashill
Cranworth
Blackwater R.
Southburgh
Mid-Norfolk Railway
Carleton Forehoe
Kimberley
Kidd's Moor
Kett's Oak
Hethersett
Intwood
Saham Hills
Woodrising
Hardingham
Crownthorpe
Lower East Carleton
Ketteringham
Great Cressingham
Ovington
Carbrooke
Hingham
Wicklewood
Heritage
Abbey
Wymondham
A11
Swardeston
Saham Toney
Neaton
Scoulton
B1108
Hackford
East Carleton
Swainsthorpe
Hilborough
Watton
Deopham
Morley St Botolph
Hethel
Old Thorn
Mulbarton
Little Cressingham
Griston
Little Ellingham
66
Bracon Ash
A140
B1108
Merton
Northacre
Melsop Farm Park
Suton
Silfield
Wreningham
Bodney
The Arms
Caston
Rockland St Peter
Bush Green
Deopham Green
Ashwellthorpe
Toprow
Newton Flotman
Thompson
A1075
Stow Bedon
Rockland All Saints
Great Ellingham
Spooner Row
Fundenhall
Flordon
Saxlingham Thorpe
Hapton
Tasburgh
Lower Stow Bedon
Besthorpe
Attleborough
Black
Tacolneston
Industrial
N O R F O L K
77
1
2
3
4
5

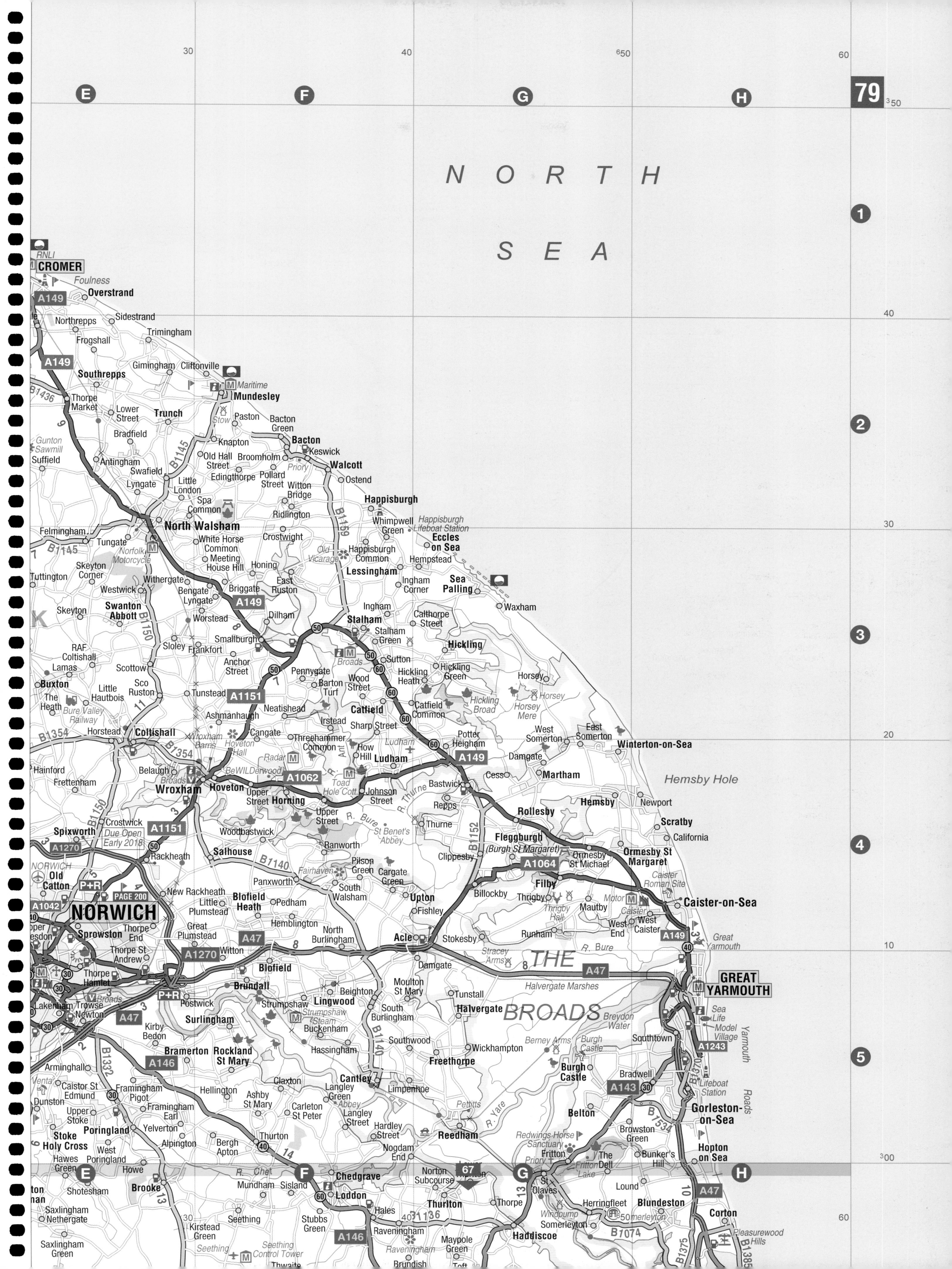
NORTH SEA
CROMER
RNLI
Foulness
Overstrand
Northrepps
Sidestrand
Trimingham
Frogshall
Southrepps
Gimingham
Cliftonville
Maritime
Mundesley
Thorpe Market
Lower Street
Trunch
Paston
Stow
Bacton Green
Bacton
Keswick
Walcott
Ostend
Bradfield
Knapton
Gunton Sawmill
Suffield
Antingham
Old Hall Street
Broomholm
Priory
Swafield
Little London
Edingthorpe
Pollard Street
Witton Bridge
Lyngate
Happisburgh
Spa Common
North Walsham
Ridlington
Whimpwell Green
Happisburgh Lifeboat Station
Felmingham
Tungate
White Horse Common
Crostwight
Eccles on Sea
Norfolk Motorcycle
Meeting House Hill
Old Vicarage
Happisburgh Common
Hempstead
Skeyton Corner
Honing
Lessingham
Tuttington
Withergate
East Ruston
Ingham Corner
Sea Palling
Westwick
Bengate
Lyngate
Briggate
Waxham
Skeyton
Swanton Abbott
Dilham
Ingham
Worstead
Stalham
Calthorpe Street
Stalham Green
Smallburgh
Hickling
RAF Coltishall
Sloley
Frankfort
Sutton
Lamas
Anchor Street
Broads
Hickling Green
Scottow
Pennygate
Hickling Heath
Horsey
Buxton
Little Hautbois
Sco Ruston
Barton Turf
Wood Street
The Heath
Bure Valley Railway
Tunstead
Neatishead
Catfield
Catfield Common
Hickling Broad
Horsey Mere
Irstead
Ashmanhaugh
Sharp Street
West Somerton
East Somerton
Horstead
Coltishall
Cangate
Threehammer Common
Potter Heigham
Winterton-on-Sea
Wroxham Barns
Hoveton Hall
How Hill
Ludham
Damgate
Hainford
Belaugh
Radar
BeWILDerwood
Cess
Martham
Hemsby Hole
Frettenham
Broads
Hoveton
Wroxham
Upper Street
Toad Hole Cott.
Johnson Street
Bastwick
Hemsby
Newport
Horning
R. Thurne
Repps
Rollesby
Scratby
California
Crostwick
Spixworth
Due Open Early 2018
Woodbastwick
Upper Street
Thurne
St Benet's Abbey
R. Bure
Fleggburgh (Burgh St Margaret)
Ormesby St Margaret
Ormesby St Michael
Rackheath
Salhouse
Ranworth
Clippesby
NORWICH
Old Catton
Fairhaven
Pilson Green
Cargate Green
Filby
Caister Roman Site
PAGE 200
New Rackheath
Panxworth
South Walsham
Upton
Billockby
Thrigby
Motor
Caister-on-Sea
Blofield Heath
Pedham
Little Plumstead
Fishley
Thrigby Hall
Mautby
West Caister
Sprowston
Thorpe End
Great Plumstead
Hemblington
North Burlingham
Acle
Stokesby
Runham
West End
Great Yarmouth
Thorpe St Andrew
Witton
Stracey Arms
THE
R. Bure
Blofield
Damgate
Thorpe Hamlet
Brundall
Beighton
Moulton St Mary
Tunstall
Halvergate Marshes
GREAT YARMOUTH
Lakenham
Trowse Newton
Broads
Postwick
Strumpshaw
Lingwood
South Burlingham
Halvergate
BROADS
Breydon Water
Sea Life
Model Village
Surlingham
Strumpshaw Steam
Buckenham
Kirby Bedon
Southwood
Berney Arms
Burgh Castle
Southtown
Yarmouth Roads
Hassingham
Wickhampton
Bramerton
Rockland St Mary
Freethorpe
Burgh Castle
Arminghall
Cantley
Limpenhoe
Bradwell
Caistor St Edmund
Framingham Pigot
Hellington
Claxton
Langley Green
Abbey
Lifeboat Station
Dunston
Ashby St Mary
Carleton St Peter
Pettits
R. Yare
Gorleston-on-Sea
Framingham Earl
Langley Street
Belton
Upper Stoke
Poringland
Yelverton
Hardley Street
Reedham
Browston Green
Stoke Holy Cross
West Poringland
Alpington
Bergh Apton
Thurton
Redwings Horse Sanctuary
Fritton
Priory
Nogdam End
The Dell
Fritton Lake
Bunker's Hill
Hopton on Sea
Hawes Green
Howe
R. Chet
Chedgrave
Norton Subcourse
St Olaves
Lound
Shotesham
Brooke
Mundham
Sisland
Loddon
Thurlton
Thorpe
Herringfleet
Blundeston
Corton
Saxlingham Nethergate
Seething
Stubbs Green
Hales
Raveningham
Windpump
Somerleyton
Kirstead Green
Haddiscoe
Maypole Green
Pleasurewood Hills
Saxlingham Green
Seething
Seething Control Tower
Raveningham
Brundish
Thwaite
Toft
A149
A1151
A1062
A1270
A1042
A47
A1064
A146
A143
A1243
B1436
B1145
B1159
B1150
B1354
B1140
B1152
B1332
B1370
B1534
B1136
B1074
B1375
B1385
67
E
F
G
H
1
2
3
4
5
30
40
50
60
350
300

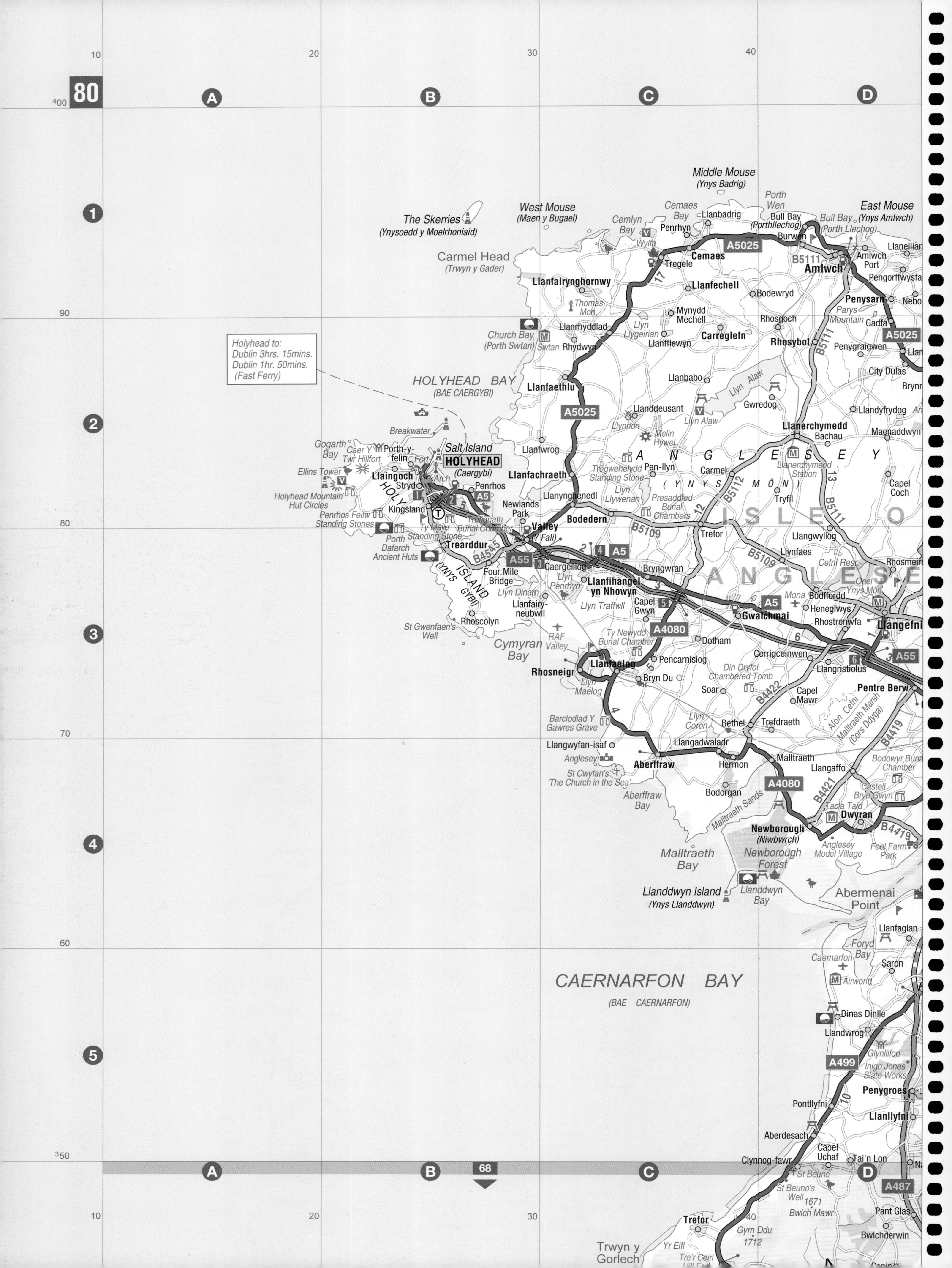

10   20   30   40

400

A   B   C   D

1

Middle Mouse
(Ynys Badrig)

West Mouse
(Maen y Bugael)

The Skerries
(Ynysoedd y Moelrhoniaid)

Cemaes
Bay

Porth
Wen

East Mouse
(Ynys Amlwch)

Bull Bay
(Porthllechog)

Bull Bay
(Porth Llechog)

Cemlyn
Bay

Penrhyn

Llanbadrig

Burwen

Llaneilian

A5025

Wylfa

B5111

Amlwch

Carmel Head
(Trwyn y Gader)

Tregele

Llanfechell

Amlwch
Port

Pengorffwysfa

Llanfairynghornwy

Bodewryd

Penysarn

Nebo

90

Thomas
Mon

Mynydd
Mechell

Rhosgoch

Parys
Mountain

Gadfa

Llanrhyddlad

Church Bay
(Porth Swtan)

Swtan   Rhydwyn

Llanfflewyn

Carreglefn

Rhosybol

Penygraigwen

A5025

City Dulas

Llan

Llyn
Llygeirian

Llanbabo

Brynr

Llanddeusant

Gwredog

Llandyfrydog

HOLYHEAD BAY
(BAE CAERGYBI)

Llanfaethlu

Llyn Alaw

Llanerchymedd

Magnaddwyn

A5025

Llyn Alaw

Bachau

Holyhead to:
Dublin 3hrs. 15mins.
Dublin 1hr. 50mins.
(Fast Ferry)

Llynnon

Melin
Hywel

A N G L E S E Y

Pen-llyn

Carmel

Llanerchymedd
Station

Capel
Coch

B5112

Breakwater

Gogarth
Bay

Caer Y
Twr Hillfort

Porth-y-
felin

Salt Island

HOLYHEAD
(Caergybi)

Llanfwrog

Tregwehelydd
Standing Stone

Presaddfed
Burial
Chambers

I S L E O

13

2

Ellins Tower

Laingoch
Strydd

Fort

Arch

Penrhos

Llanfachraeth

Llanynghenedl

Tryfil

Llyn
Llywenan

B5109

Trefor

Llangwyllog

Rhosmeir

80

Holyhead Mountain
Hut Circles

Kingsland

A5

Newlands
Park

Bodedern

B5109

Llynfaes

Cefni Resr

A N G L E S E

Penrhos Feilw
Standing Stones

Ty Mawr
Standing Stone

Burial Chamber

Valley
(Y Fali)

Trearddur

B4545

A55

Four Mile
Bridge

Caergeiliog

'Llyn
Penrhyn

4

Llanfihangel
yn Nhowyn

A5

Bryngwran

Mona

A5

Bodffordd

Heneglwys

Oriel
Ynys Mon

Llangefni

3

St Gwenfaen's
Well

Rhoscolyn

Cymyran
Bay

Llanfairy-
neubwll

Llyn Dinam

Llyn Traffwll

RAF
Valley

Capel
Gwyn

Ty Newydd
Burial Chamber

Dotham

A4080

Pencarnisiog

Cerrigceinwen

Din Dryfol
Chambered Tomb

Rhostrenwfa

Llangristiolus

A5

A55

Pentre Berw

70

Rhosneigr

Llanfaelog

Bryn Du

Soar

B4422

Capel
Mawr

Afon Cefni
Malltraeth Marsh
(Cors Ddyga)

B4419

Llyn
Maelog

Barclodiad Y
Gawres Grave

Llyn
Coron

Bethel

Trefdraeth

Bodowyr Burial
Chamber

Llangwyfan-isaf

Anglesey

St Cwyfan's
'The Church in the Sea'

Llangadwaladr

Hermon

Malltraeth

Llangaffo

B4421

Castell
Bryn Gwyn

Aberffraw

Bodorgan

A4080

Tacla Taid

Dwyran

B4419

Aberffraw
Bay

Malltraeth Sands

Newborough
(Niwbwrch)

Foel Farm
Park

4

Malltraeth
Bay

Newborough
Forest

Anglesey
Model Village

Abermenai
Point

Llanddwyn Island
(Ynys Llanddwyn)

Llanddwyn
Bay

Llanfaglan

60

Foryd
Bay

CAERNARFON BAY
(BAE   CAERNARFON)

Caernarfon
Bay

Saron

Airworld

Dinas Dinlle

Llandwrog

5

A499

Glynllifon

Inigo Jones
Slate Works

Penygroes

350

Pontllyfni

Llanllyfni

Aberdesach

A   B   C   D

10   20   30

68

Capel
Uchaf

Tai'n Lon

A487

St Beuno

St Beuno's
Well
1671

Bwlch Mawr

Trefor

Gyrn Ddu
1712

Pant Glas

Trwyn y
Gorlech

Yr Eifl

Bwlchderwin

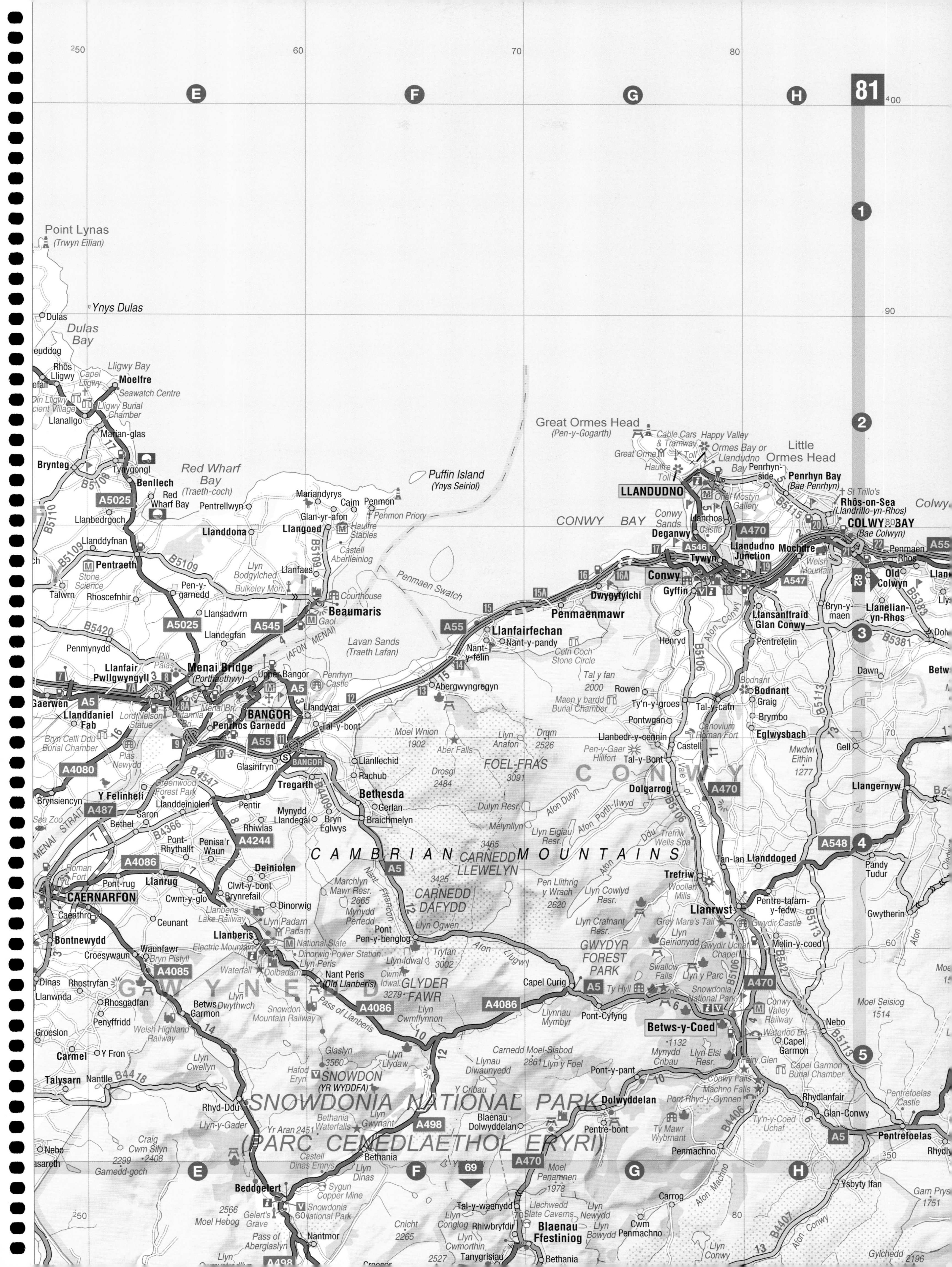
Point Lynas
(Trwyn Eilian)
Ynys Dulas
Dulas Bay
Moelfre
Red Wharf Bay
(Traeth-coch)
Puffin Island
(Ynys Seiriol)
Great Ormes Head
(Pen-y-Gogarth)
Little Ormes Head
LLANDUDNO
Penrhyn Bay
(Bae Penrhyn)
Rhôs-on-Sea
(Llandrillo-yn-Rhos)
COLWYN BAY
(Bae Colwyn)
CONWY BAY
Conwy
Deganwy
Llandudno Junction
Penmaenmawr
Llanfairfechan
Beaumaris
Lavan Sands
(Traeth Lafan)
Menai Bridge
(Porthaethwy)
BANGOR
Llanfair Pwllgwyngyll
Bethesda
CAERNARFON
Llanberis
CAMBRIAN MOUNTAINS
CARNEDD LLEWELYN
CARNEDD DAFYDD
GLYDER FAWR
SNOWDON
(YR WYDDFA)
SNOWDONIA NATIONAL PARK
(PARC CENEDLAETHOL ERYRI)
GWYNEDD
CONWY
GWYDYR FOREST PARK
Llanrwst
Betws-y-Coed
Capel Curig
Dolwyddelan
Beddgelert
Blaenau Ffestiniog
Pentrefoelas
Llangernyw
Eglwysbach
Dolgarrog
Trefriw
69

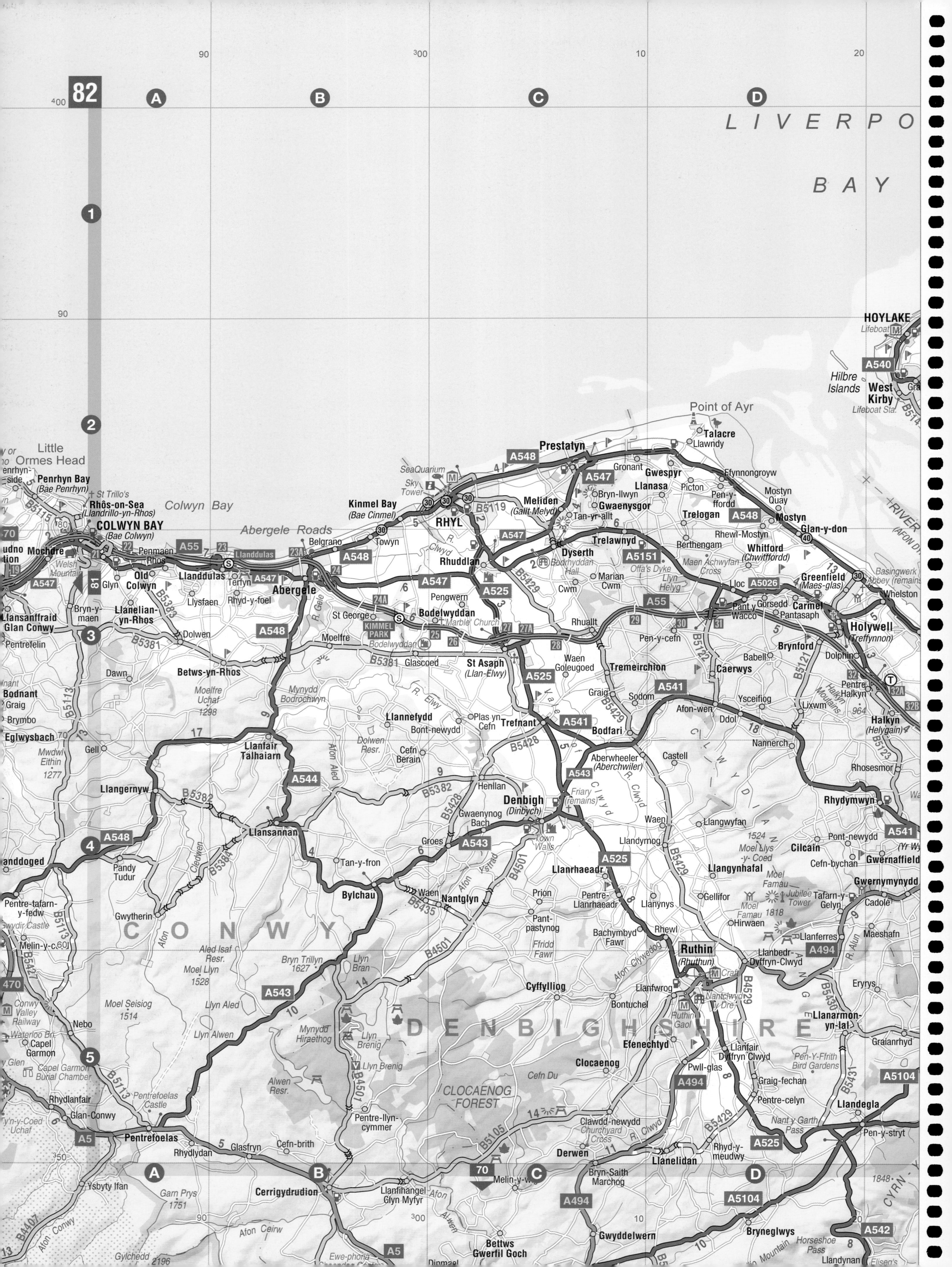
LIVERPOOL BAY
HOYLAKE
West Kirby
Hilbre Islands
Point of Ayr
Talacre
Prestatyn
RHYL
Kinmel Bay
Towyn
Abergele
COLWYN BAY
Rhôs-on-Sea
Penrhyn Bay
Little Ormes Head
Colwyn Bay
Abergele Roads
Llanddulas
Old Colwyn
Rhuddlan
Dyserth
Meliden
Gronant
Gwespyr
Llanasa
Mostyn
Whitford
Greenfield
Holywell
St Asaph
Trefnant
Denbigh
Bodfari
Llangernyw
Llansannan
Llanfair Talhaiarn
Betws-yn-Rhos
Bylchau
Nantglyn
Ruthin
Llanrhaeadr
Cyffylliog
Efenechtyd
Clocaenog
Derwen
Llanelidan
Llandegla
Cilcain
Rhydymwyn
Halkyn
Pentrefoelas
Cerrigydrudion
Gwyddelwern
Bryneglwys
CONWY
DENBIGHSHIRE
CLOCAENOG FOREST
Llyn Brenig
Alwen Resr.
A55
A548
A547
A525
A541
A543
A544
A494
A5104
A5
A5151
A5026
A540
A542

70
81

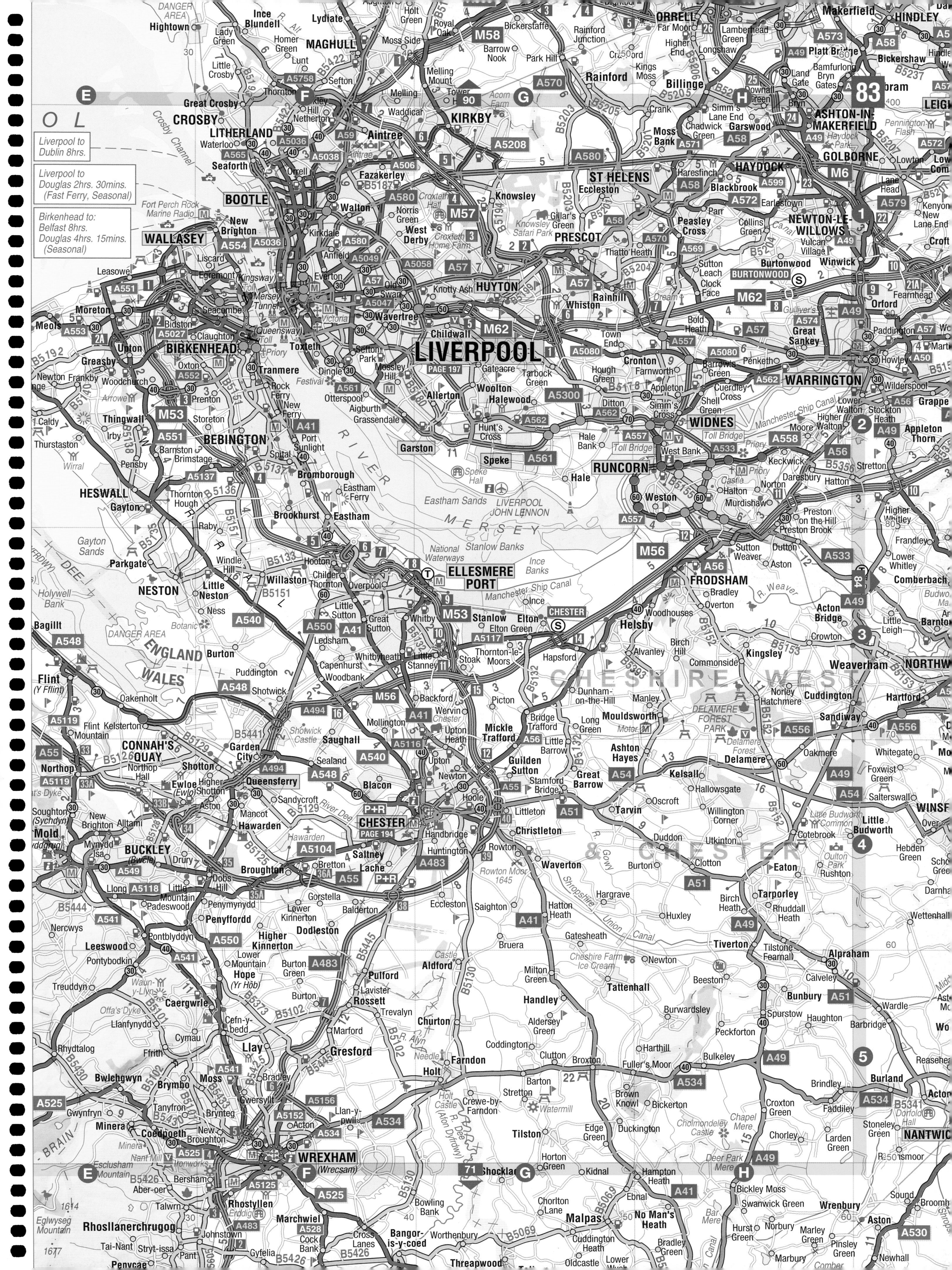

83
E
F
G
H
Liverpool to Dublin 8hrs.
Liverpool to Douglas 2hrs. 30mins. (Fast Ferry, Seasonal)
Birkenhead to: Belfast 8hrs. Douglas 4hrs. 15mins. (Seasonal)
LIVERPOOL
PAGE 197
CHESTER
PAGE 194
Hightown
Ince Blundell
Lydiate
MAGHULL
Holt Green
Royal Oak
Bickerstaffe
Rainford Junction
ORRELL
Far Moor
Lamberhead Green
Makerfield
HINDLEY
Lady Green
Homer Green
Little Crosby
Lunt
Moss Side
Melling Mount
Barrow Nook
Park Hill
Crawford
Kings Moss
Higher End
Longshaw
Platt Bridge
Bickershaw
Sefton
Thornton
Melling
Tower Hill
Rainford
Billinge
Land Gate
Bamfurlong
Bryn Gates
Great Crosby
CROSBY
LITHERLAND
Waterloo
Seaforth
Aintree
Waddicar
KIRKBY
Crank
Simm's Lane End
Chadwick Green
Garswood
ASHTON-IN-MAKERFIELD
Moss Bank
Haydock Park
GOLBORNE
Lowton
Orrell
Fazakerley
Knowsley
ST HELENS
Eccleston
Haresfinch
HAYDOCK
Blackbrook
Lane Head
BOOTLE
Walton
Norris Green
West Derby
Croxteth Hall
Knowsley Safari Park
Gillar's Green
PRESCOT
Peasley Cross
Parr
Collins Green
Earlestown
NEWTON-LE-WILLOWS
Vulcan Village
Kenyon
Fort Perch Rock Marine Radio
New Brighton
WALLASEY
Liscard
Egremont
Kirkdale
Anfield
Everton
Croxteth Home Farm
Thatto Heath
Sutton Leach
Clock Face
Burtonwood
BURTONWOOD
Winwick
Croft
Leasowe
Moreton
Meols
Seacombe
Bidston
Claughton
BIRKENHEAD
Mersey Tunnel
Queensway Toll
Old Swan
Wavertree
Knotty Ash
HUYTON
Whiston
Rainhill
Bold Heath
Orford
Fearnhead
Great Sankey
Paddington
Upton
Greasby
Oxton
Toxteth
Sefton Park
Childwall
Town End
Cronton
Farnworth
Penketh
Howley
Newton
Frankby
Woodchurch
Tranmere
Rock Ferry
Dingle
Mossley Hill
Gateacre
Tarbock Green
Hough Green
Barrow's Green
Cuerdley Cross
WARRINGTON
Wilderspool
Arrowe
Prenton
New Ferry
Festival
Otterspool
Allerton
Woolton
Halewood
Ditton
Appleton
Caldy
Thingwall
Irby
Storeton
Aigburth
Grassendale
Hunt's Cross
Simm's Cross
Shell Green
WIDNES
Higher Walton
Stockton Heath
Appleton Thorn
Thurstaston
Barnston
Brimstage
BEBINGTON
Port Sunlight
Garston
Speke
Hale Bank
West Bank
Moore
Wirral
Pensby
Spital
Bromborough
RIVER MERSEY
Speke Hall
Hale
RUNCORN
Kekwick
Daresbury
Stretton
Hatton
HESWALL
Thornton Hough
Eastham Ferry
LIVERPOOL JOHN LENNON
Weston
Halton
Norton
Murdishaw
Gayton
Raby
Brookhurst
Eastham
Eastham Sands
Preston on the Hill
Preston Brook
Higher Whitley
Gayton Sands
Parkgate
Windle Hill
Willaston
Hooton
Childer Thornton
Overpool
National Waterways
Stanlow Banks
Ince Banks
ELLESMERE PORT
Sutton Weaver
Dutton
Aston
Frandley
Lower Whitley
Comberbach
DEE
Holywell Bank
NESTON
Little Neston
Ness
Botanic
Little Sutton
Great Sutton
Whitby
Manchester Ship Canal
Ince
Stanlow
Elton
Elton Green
FRODSHAM
Bradley
Overton
R. Weaver
Acton Bridge
Little Leigh
Bagillt
DANGER AREA
ENGLAND
WALES
Burton
Ledsham
Whitbyheath
Little Stanney
Stoak
Thornton-le-Moors
Hapsford
Helsby
Woodhouses
Alvanley
Birch Hill
Commonside
Kingsley
Crowton
Weaverham
NORTHWICH
Flint
(Y Fflint)
Puddington
Capenhurst
Woodbank
Shotwick
CHESHIRE WEST & CHESTER
Dunham-on-the-Hill
Manley
Norley
Hatchmere
Cuddington
Hartford
Oakenholt
Backford
Picton
Wervin
Mollington
Bridge Trafford
Long Green
Mouldsworth
DELAMERE FOREST PARK
Sandiway
Flint Mountain
Kelsterton
CONNAH'S QUAY
Garden City
Shotwick Castle
Saughall
Upton Heath
Mickle Trafford
Little Barrow
Ashton Hayes
Delamere Forest
Delamere
Whitegate
Northop
Northop Hall
Shotton
Sealand
Guilden Sutton
Kelsall
Oakmere
Foxwist Green
Ewloe
(Ewlo)
Higher Shotton
Queensferry
Blacon
Newton
Stamford Bridge
Great Barrow
Hallowsgate
Salterswall
Soughton
(Sychdyn)
New Brighton
Alltami
Aston
Mancot
Sandycroft
River Dee
Hoole
Littleton
Tarvin
Oscroft
Willington Corner
WINSFORD
Little Budworth
Mold
(Yr Wyddgrug)
Hawarden
Handbridge
Christleton
Duddon
Utkinton
Cotebrook
Mynydd Isa
BUCKLEY
(Bwcle)
Drury
Saltney
Huntington
Rowton
Burton
Clotton
Oulton Park
Eaton
Rushton
Hebden Green
Bretton
Lache
Waverton
Rowton Moor 1645
Llong
Little Mountain
Broughton
Dobs Hill
Padeswood
Penymynydd
Gorstella
Lower Kinnerton
Balderton
Eccleston
Saighton
Hatton Heath
Hargrave
Huxley
Tarporley
Birch Heath
Rhuddall Heath
Nercwys
Penyffordd
Higher Kinnerton
Dodleston
Shropshire Union Canal
Gatesheath
Tiverton
Tilstone Fearnall
Alpraham
Leeswood
Pontybodkin
Pontblyddyn
Lower Mountain
Hope
(Yr Hôb)
Burton Green
Castle Aldford
Bruera
Milton Green
Cheshire Farm Ice Cream
Beeston
Calveley
Treuddyn
Waun-y-Llyn
Caergwrle
Pulford
Lavister
Rossett
Tattenhall
Bunbury
Handley
Aldersey Green
Burwardsley
Spurstow
Haughton
Wardle
Barbridge
Offa's Dyke
Llanfynydd
Cefn-y-bedd
Marford
Trevalyn
Churton
Coddington
Peckforton
Rhydtalog
Cymau
Ffrith
Llay
Gresford
Needle
Farndon
Clutton
Broxton
Harthill
Bulkeley
Fuller's Moor
Reaseheath
Bwlchgwyn
Brymbo
Moss
Bradley
Holt
Barton
Stretton
Watermill
Brown Knowl
Bickerton
Croxton Green
Faddiley
Brindley
Burland
Acton
Gwynfryn
Tanyfron
Gwersyllt
Brynteg
Minera
Coedpoeth
New Broughton
Acton
Llan-y-pwll
Holt Castle
Crewe-by-Farndon
R. Dee
(Afon Dyfrdwy)
Tilston
Edge Green
Duckington
Cholmondeley Castle
Chapel Mere
Chorley
Stoneley Green
Larden Green
NANTWICH
Nant Mill
Esclusham Mountain
Bersham
WREXHAM
(Wrecsam)
Shocklach
Horton Green
Kidnal
Hampton Heath
Deer Park Mere
Ravensmoor
Aber-oer
Talwrn
Rhostyllen
Erddig
Marchwiel
Bowling Bank
Chorlton Lane
Malpas
Ebnal
No Man's Heath
Bar Mere
Bickley Moss
Swanwick Green
Wrenbury
Sound
Broomhall
Eglwyseg Mountain
Rhosllanerchrugog
Johnstown
Tai-Nant
Stryt-issa
Penycae
Gyfelia
Cross Lanes
Cock Bank
Bangor-is-y-coed
Worthenbury
Cuddington Heath
Oldcastle
Lower Wych
Threapwood
Bradley Green
Hurst Green
Norbury
Marley Green
Pinsley Green
Marbury
Aston
Newhall
Combermere
M58
M57
M62
M53
M56
M6
90
71
A5758
A59
A5036
A565
A5038
A506
A5208
A570
A580
A58
A573
A49
A599
A572
A579
A554
A5049
A5058
A57
A5047
A569
A551
A553
A5027
A552
A5080
A574
A561
A5300
A562
A557
A533
A558
A56
A41
A5137
A550
A5117
A540
A548
A5119
A494
A5116
A55
A54
A51
A556
A5104
A483
A5118
A549
A541
A525
A5156
A5152
A534
A5125
A528
A530
B5422
B5197
B5187
B5203
B5201
B5205
B5206
B5207
B5237
B5204
B5194
B5199
B5180
B5178
B5192
B5140
B5136
B5133
B5151
B5138
B5135
B5132
B5152
B5153
B5393
B5356
B5355
B5129
B5125
B5126
B5444
B5373
B5102
B5101
B5430
B5433
B5425
B5445
B5130
B5069
B5426
B5341

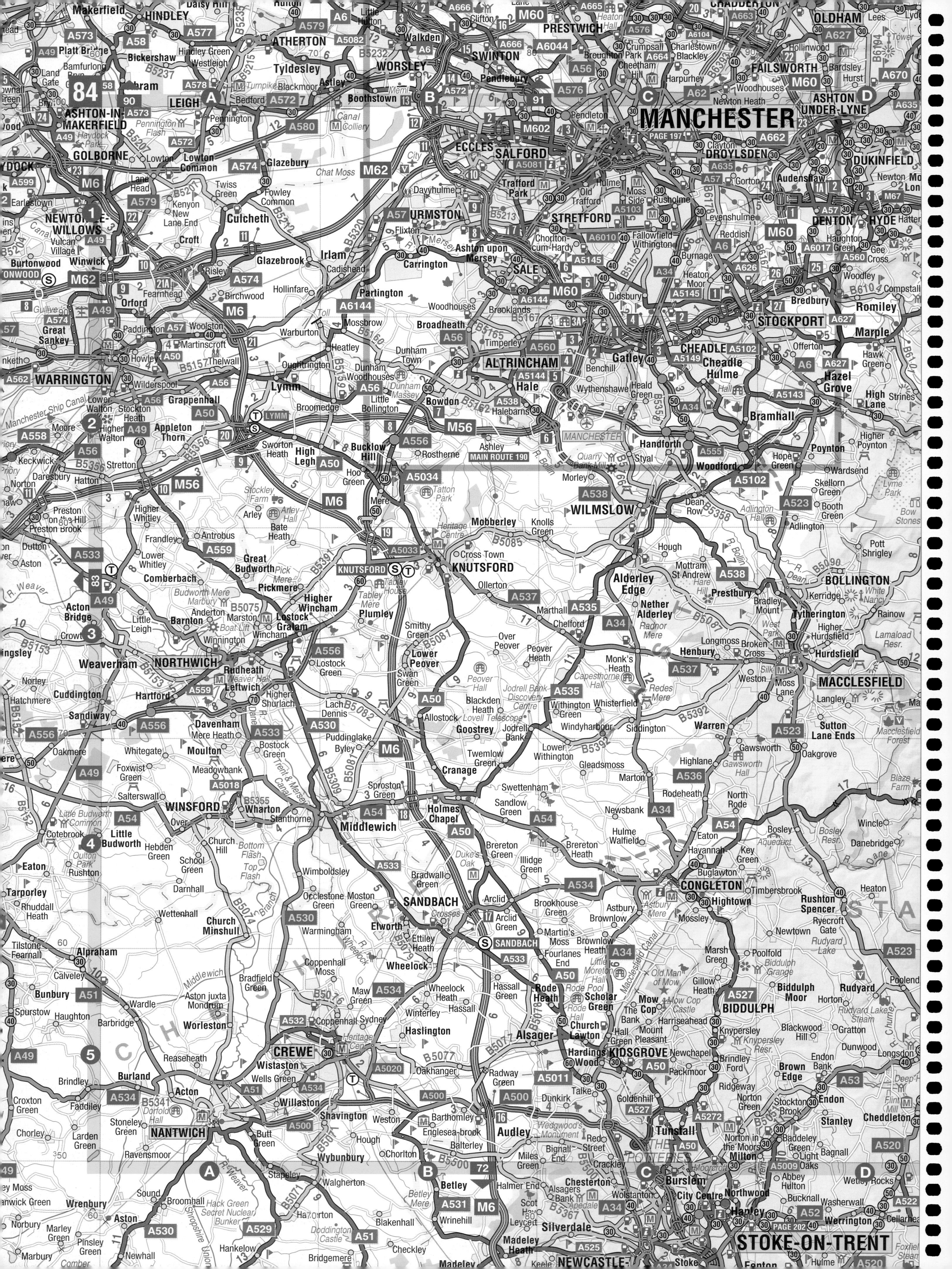

84
88
MANCHESTER
PAGE 197
STOKE-ON-TRENT
PAGE 202
Makerfield
HINDLEY
ATHERTON
Little Hulton
Walkden
Clifton
PRESTWICH
OLDHAM
Lees
Platt Bridge
Bickershaw
Hindley Green
Westleigh
Tyldesley
Astley
WORSLEY
SWINTON
Pendlebury
Crumpsall
Charlestown
Blackley
Broughton Park
Cheetham Hill
Harpurhey
FAILSWORTH
Hollinwood
Bardsley
Hurst
ASHTON-IN-MAKERFIELD
LEIGH
Bedford
Pennington
Boothstown
Pennington Flash
Haydock Park
GOLBORNE
Lowton
Lowton Common
Glazebury
Chat Moss
ECCLES
SALFORD
Pendleton
Clayton
DROYLSDEN
ASHTON UNDER-LYNE
DUKINFIELD
Audenshaw
Newton Heath
Woodhouses
Trafford Park
Davyhulme
Old Trafford
Hulme
Moss Side
Rusholme
Gorton
Levenshulme
DENTON
HYDE
Twiss Green
Kenyon
New Lane End
Culcheth
Fowley Common
Croft
Glazebrook
Irlam
Cadishead
URMSTON
Flixton
Carrington
Ashton upon Mersey
STRETFORD
Chorlton-cum-Hardy
Fallowfield
Withington
Reddish
Burnage
Heaton Moor
Haughton Green
Gee Cross
Woodley
Bredbury
Romiley
Compstall
NEWTON-LE-WILLOWS
Earlestown
Vulcan Village
Winwick
Burtonwood
Risley
Fearnhead
Birchwood
Hollinfare
Partington
Woodhouses
SALE
Brooklands
Didsbury
STOCKPORT
Orford
Great Sankey
Paddington
Woolston
Martinscroft
Warburton
Mossbrow
Broadheath
Timperley
ALTRINCHAM
Gatley
CHEADLE
Cheadle Hulme
Offerton
Marple
WARRINGTON
Howley
Thelwall
Heatley
Oughtrington
Dunham Town
Dunham Woodhouses
Dunham Massey
Benchill
Wythenshawe
Heald Green
Hazel Grove
Hawk Green
Wilderspool
Grappenhall
Lymm
Little Bollington
Bowdon
Hale
Halebarns
Bramhall
High Lane
Strines
Manchester Ship Canal
Lower Walton
Stockton Heath
Moore
Higher Walton
Appleton Thorn
Broomedge
MANCHESTER
Handforth
Poynton
Higher Poynton
Keckwick
Stretton
Sworton Heath
High Legh
Bucklow Hill
Rostherne
Ashley
MAIN ROUTE 190
Quarry Bank Mill
Styal
Woodford
Hope Green
Wardsend
Daresbury
Hatton
Hoo Green
Morley
Skellorn Green
Lyme Park
Norton
Preston on the Hill
Preston Brook
Stockley Farm
Arley
Arley Hall
Higher Whitley
Mere
Tatton Park
WILMSLOW
Dean Row
Adlington Hall
Booth Green
Adlington
Bow Stones
Dutton
Aston
Frandley
Antrobus
Bate Heath
Heritage Centre
Mobberley
Knolls Green
Hough
Pott Shrigley
Lower Whitley
Great Budworth
Pick Mere
Cross Town
KNUTSFORD
Mottram St Andrew
Comberbach
Pickmere
Ollerton
Alderley Edge
Prestbury
BOLLINGTON
White Nancy
Kerridge
Budworth Mere
Marbury
Tabley House
Tabley Mere
Nether Alderley
Bradley Mount
Acton Bridge
Anderton
Marston
Higher Wincham
Plumley
Marthall
Chelford
Radnor Mere
West Park
Tytherington
Rainow
Little Leigh
Barnton
Lostock Gralam
Wincham
Boat Lift
Smithy Green
Over Peover
Longmoss
Broken Cross
Higher Hurdsfield
Lamaload Resr.
Crowton
Winnington
Lower Peover
Peover Heath
Monk's Heath
Henbury
Hurdsfield
Weaverham
NORTHWICH
Rudheath
Lostock Green
Capesthorne Hall
Silk
Weston
Moss Lane
MACCLESFIELD
Norley
Swan Green
Peover Hall
Jodrell Bank Discovery Centre
Redes Mere
Langley
Hatchmere
Cuddington
Hartford
Leftwich
Higher Shurlach
Blackden Heath
Lovell Telescope
Withington Green
Whisterfield
Sandiway
Davenham
Lach Dennis
Allostock
Goostrey
Jodrell Bank
Windyharbour
Siddington
Warren
Sutton Lane Ends
Macclesfield Forest
Mere Heath
Bostock Green
Puddinglake
Byley
Lower Withington
Oakgrove
Oakmere
Whitegate
Moulton
Twemlow Green
Gawsworth
Gawsworth Hall
Foxwist Green
Meadowbank
Cranage
Gleadsmoss
Highlane
Marton
Trent & Mersey Canal
Salterswall
Sproston Green
Swettenham
Rodeheath
North Rode
Blaze Farm
Little Budworth Common
WINSFORD
Wharton
Stanthorne
Middlewich
Holmes Chapel
Sandlow Green
Newsbank
Over
Hulme Walfield
Eaton
Bosley
Wincle
Cotebrook
Little Budworth
Hebden Green
Church Hill
Bottom Flash
Brereton Green
Brereton Heath
Havannah
Key Green
Bosley Resr.
Danebridge
Oulton Park
Rushton
School Green
Top Flash
Duke's Oak
Illidge Green
Buglawton
Wimboldsley
Bradwall Green
CONGLETON
Timbersbrook
Tarporley
Darnhall
Occlestone Green
Moston Green
SANDBACH
Arclid
Brookhouse Green
Astbury
Hightown
Rushton Spencer
Heaton
Rhuddall Heath
Wettenhall
Church Minshull
Warmingham
Elworth
Crosses
Arclid Green
Brownlow
Mossley
Ryecroft Gate
Tilstone Fearnall
Alpraham
Ettiley Heath
Martin's Moss
Brownlow Heath
Newtown
Rudyard Lake
Calveley
Coppenhall Moss
Wheelock
Fourlanes End
Little Moreton Hall
Marsh Green
Poolfold
Biddulph Grange
Poolend
Bradfield Green
Old Man of Mow
Gillow Heath
Bunbury
Middlewich
Aston juxta Mondrum
Maw Green
Wheelock Heath
Hassall Green
Rode Heath
Rode Pool
Scholar Green
Mow Cop
Mow Cop Castle
BIDDULPH
Biddulph Moor
Rudyard
Spurstow
Haughton
Wardle
Hassall
The Cop
Bank
Harriseahead
Horton
Rudyard Lake Steam
Barbridge
Worleston
Coppenhall
Sydney
Winterley
Rode Hall
Church Lawton
Hall Green
Mount Pleasant
Knypersley
Blackwood Hill
Gratton
Haslington
Alsager
Knypersley Resr.
Dunwood
Reaseheath
CREWE
Heritage Centre
Hardings Wood
KIDSGROVE
Newchapel
Brindley Ford
Endon Bank
Longsdon
Brindley
Burland
Wistaston
Wells Green
Oakhanger
Radway Green
Packmoor
Brown Edge
Acton
Talke
Ridgeway
Deep Hayes
Croxton Green
Faddiley
Willaston
Dunkirk
Goldenhill
Norton Green
Stockton Brook
Endon
Flint Mill
Dorfold Hall
Shavington
Weston
Barthomley
Englesea-brook
Audley
Wedgwood's Monument
Tunstall
Stanley
Cheddleton
Chorley
Stoneley Green
NANTWICH
Butt Green
Hough
Balterley
Red Street
Norton in the Moors
Baddeley Green
Light Oaks
Bagnall
Larden Green
Ravensmoor
Wybunbury
Chorlton
Miles Green
Bignall End
Crackley
THE POTTERIES
Milton
Stapeley
Walgherton
Betley
Halmer End
Chesterton
Burslem
Moorcroft
Abbey Hulton
Wetley Rocks
Sound
Broomhall
Hack Green Secret Nuclear Bunker
Betley Mere
Scot Hay
Alsagers Bank
Wolstanton
City Centre
Northwood
Bucknall
Washerwall
Wrenbury
Aston
Shropshire Union
Hatherton
Wrinehill
Apedale
Hanley
Werrington
Cellarhead
Norbury
Marley Green
Doddington Castle
Blakenhall
Leycett
Silverdale
Pinsley Green
Hankelow
Checkley
Madeley Heath
Marbury
Newhall
Bridgemere
Madeley
Keele
NEWCASTLE-
Stoke
Fenton
Hulme
Foxfield Steam
CHESHIRE
STAFFS
R. Weaver
R. Mersey
R. Bollin
R. Dean
R. Dane
R. Wheelock
Canal
Macclesfield Canal
Trent & Mersey Canal
LYMM
KNUTSFORD
SANDBACH
M6
M56
M60
M62
M602
M67
A49
A50
A556
A34
A523
A54
A530
A533
A534
A500
A51
A529
A530
A531
A525
A527
A537
A538
A535
A536
A559
A5018
A5020
A5034
A5033
B5075
B5077
B5081
B5082
B5309
B5355
B5392
B5470
A B C D
1 2 3 4 5

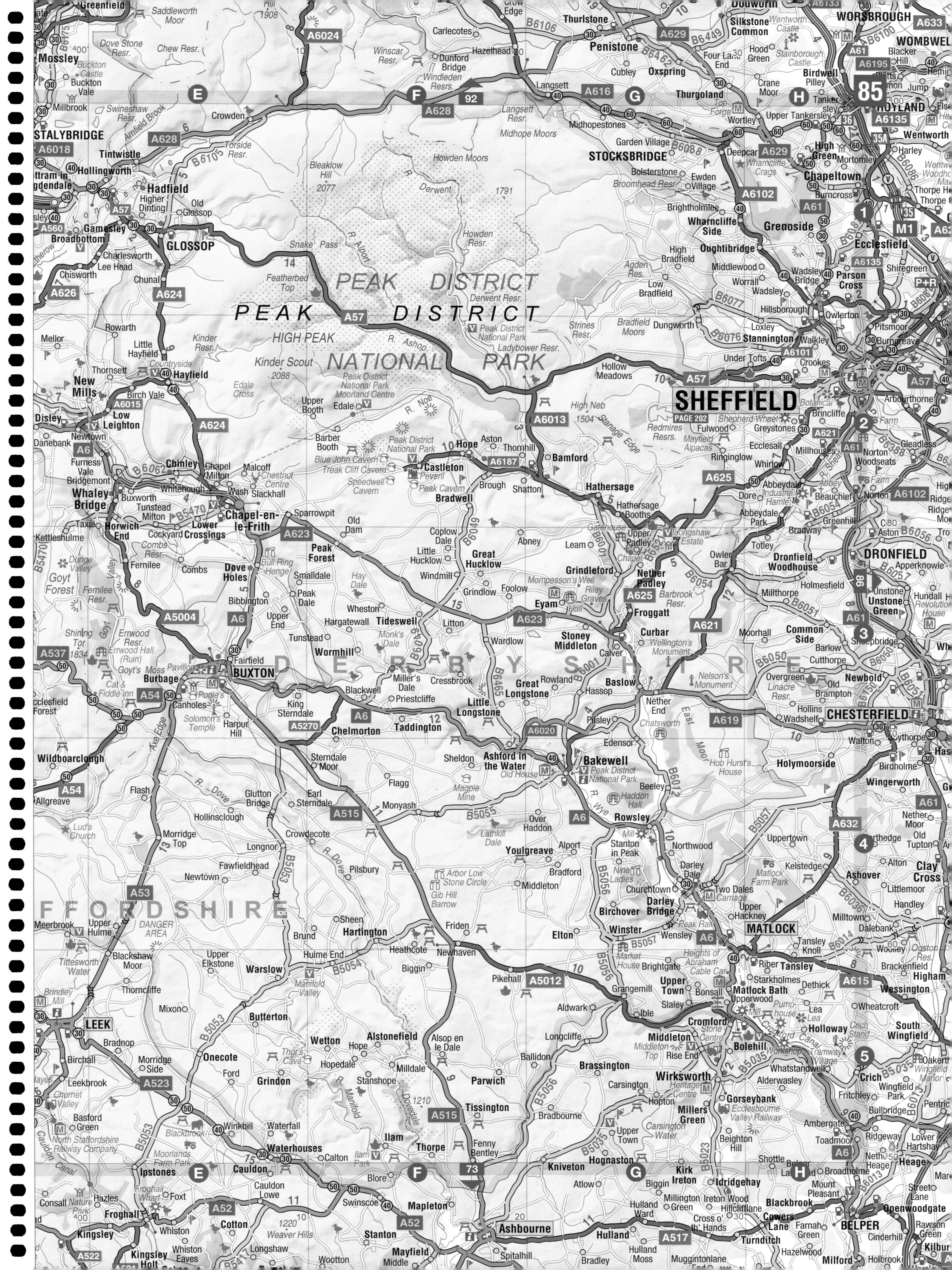

PEAK DISTRICT
PEAK DISTRICT NATIONAL PARK
DERBYSHIRE
FFORDSHIRE
SHEFFIELD
PAGE 202
Greenfield
Saddleworth Moor
Mossley
Dove Stone Resr.
Chew Resr.
Buckton Castle
Buckton Vale
Millbrook
STALYBRIDGE
Swineshaw Resr.
Tintwistle
Hollingworth
Hadfield
Torside Resr.
Crowden
Dunford Bridge
Windleden Resrs.
Winscar Resr.
Carlecotes
Hazelhead
Thurlstone
Penistone
Langsett
Langsett Resr.
Midhope Moors
Midhopestones
Silkstone Common
Wentworth Castle
Stainborough Castle
Oxspring
Cubley
Four Lane End
Hood Green
Thurgoland
Crane Moor
Birdwell
Pilley
WORSBROUGH
WOMBWELL
HOYLAND
Tankersley
Upper Tankersley
Wortley
Garden Village
STOCKSBRIDGE
Deepcar
Wharncliffe Crags
High Green
Mortomley
Chapeltown
Harley
Wentworth
Thorpe Hesley
Burncross
Bolsterstone
Ewden Village
Broomhead Resr.
Howden Moors
Bleaklow Hill
Derwent
Howden Resr.
Old Glossop
GLOSSOP
Gamesley
Broadbottom
Charlesworth
Lee Head
Chunal
Chisworth
Snake Pass
Featherbed Top
Derwent Resr.
Ladybower Resr.
Agden Res.
Low Bradfield
High Bradfield
Bradfield Moors
Dungworth
Strines Resr.
Brightholmlee
Wharncliffe Side
Oughtibridge
Middlewood
Grenoside
Ecclesfield
Shiregreen
Parson Cross
Wadsley Bridge
Wadsley
Worrall
Hillsborough
Owlerton
Pitsmoor
Burngreave
Loxley
Stannington
Walkley
Crookes
Under Tofts
Hollow Meadows
Rowarth
Mellor
Little Hayfield
Kinder Resr.
Kinder Scout
Hayfield
Thornsett
New Mills
Birch Vale
Low Leighton
Disley
Newtown
Danebank
Furness Vale
Bridgemont
Whaley Bridge
Chinley
Chapel Milton
Edale Cross
Upper Booth
Edale
Peak District National Park Moorland Centre
Barber Booth
Peak District National Park
Blue John Cavern
Treak Cliff Cavern
Speedwell Cavern
Castleton
Peveril
Peak Cavern
Hope
Aston
Thornhill
Bamford
Brough
Shatton
Bradwell
High Neb
Stanage Edge
Redmires Resrs.
Fulwood
Mayfield Alpacas
Ringinglow
Shepherd Wheel
Greystones
Botanical
Brincliffe
Ecclesall
Millhouses
Whirlow
Norton
Norton Woodseats
Gleadless
Arbourthorne
Abbeydale
Abbeydale Industrial Hamlet
Beauchief
Dore
Abbeydale Park
Bradway
Greenhill
Totley
Hathersage
Hathersage Booths
Upper Padley
Longshaw Estate
Leam
Abney
Owler Bar
Dronfield Woodhouse
DRONFIELD
Apperknowle
Holmesfield
Millthorpe
Unstone
Unstone Green
Malcoff
Chestnut Centre
Wash
Slackhall
Whitehough
Buxworth
Tunstead Milton
Chapel-en-le-Frith
Lower Crossings
Horwich End
Taxal
Cockyard
Combs Resr.
Kettleshulme
Dunge Valley
Goyt Forest
Fernilee
Fernilee Resr.
Combs
Sparrowpit
Old Dam
Coplow Dale
Little Hucklow
Great Hucklow
Windmill
Grindlow
Foolow
Peak Forest
Dove Holes
Bull Ring Henge
Smalldale
Hay Dale
Peak Dale
Bibbington
Upper End
Wheston
Hargatewall
Tideswell
Litton
Eyam
Mompesson's Well
Riley Graves
Grindleford
Nether Padley
Barbrook Resr.
Froggatt
Curbar
Calver
Stoney Middleton
Wardlow
Tunstead
Wormhill
Monk's Dale
Shining Tor
Errwood Resr.
Errwood Hall (Ruin)
Goyt's Moss
Fairfield
BUXTON
Burbage
Cat & Fiddle Inn
Poole's
Canholes
Solomon's Temple
Harpur Hill
King Sterndale
Blackwell
Miller's Dale
Priestcliffe
Cressbrook
Great Longstone
Little Longstone
Rowland
Hassop
Baslow
Wellington's Monument
Nelson's Monument
Moorhall
Common Side
Barlow
Cutthorpe
Sheepbridge
Overgreen
Linacre Resr.
Old Brampton
Newbold
Hollins
Wadshelf
CHESTERFIELD
Walton
Holymoorside
Birdholme
Wingerworth
Macclesfield Forest
Wildboarclough
Allgreave
Flash
Axe Edge
Chelmorton
Taddington
Sterndale Moor
Sheldon
Ashford in the Water
Bakewell
Peak District National Park
Old House
Pilsley
Edensor
Chatsworth
Nether End
Hob Hurst's House
Beeley
Haddon Hall
Rowsley
Glutton Bridge
Earl Sterndale
Flagg
Magpie Mine
Monyash
Over Haddon
Lathkill Dale
Youlgreave
Alport
Stanton in Peak
Northwood
Uppertown
Nether Moor
Old Tupton
Alton
Clay Cross
Kelstedge
Ashover
Littlemoor
Handley
Milltown
Dalebank
Hollinsclough
Morridge Top
Lud's Church
Crowdecote
Longnor
Fawfieldhead
Newtown
Pilsbury
Arbor Low Stone Circle
Gib Hill Barrow
Middleton
Bradford
Nine Ladies
Darley Dale
Matlock Farm Park
Churchtown
Two Dales
Carriage
Darley Bridge
Birchover
Upper Hackney
Winster
Wensley
Peak Rail
MATLOCK
Tansley Knoll
Ogston Res.
Woolley
Tansley
Brackenfield
Higham
Meerbrook
Upper Hulme
DANGER AREA
Blackshaw Moor
Tittesworth Water
Sheen
Hartington
Brund
Friden
Heathcote
Newhaven
Elton
Upper Elkstone
Warslow
Hulme End
Manifold Valley
Biggin
Pikehall
Market House
Brightgate
Heights of Abraham Cable Car
Riber
Starkholmes
Dethick
Wessington
Upper Town
Bonsall
Matlock Bath
Upperwood
Lea
Wheatcroft
Grangemill
Ible
Slaley
Aldwark
Brindley Mill
Thorncliffe
Mixon
LEEK
Butterton
Cromford
Cromford Canal
Holloway
Crich Stand
South Wingfield
Middleton
Middleton Top
Rise End
Stone Centre
Bolehill
Workshop
Tramway
Whatstandwell
Crich
Wingfield Manor
Oakerthorpe
Bradnop
Wetton
Alstonefield
Hope
Alsop en le Dale
Longcliffe
Ballidon
Brassington
Wirksworth
Heritage Centre
Alderwasley
Wingfield Park
Fritchley
Birchall
Morridge Side
Onecote
Thor's Cave
Hopedale
Milldale
Leekbrook
Churnet Valley
Ford
Grindon
Stanshope
Parwich
Carsington
Hopton
Gorseybank
Ecclesbourne Valley Railway
Bullbridge
Pentrich
Dovedale
Manifold
Tissington
Bradbourne
Carsington Water
Millers Green
Ambergate
Basford Green
Winkhill
Waterfall
Blackbrook
Upper Town
Beighton Hill
Toadmoor
Ridgeway
Lower Hartshay
North Staffordshire Railway Company
Moorlands Farm Park
Waterhouses
Calton
Ilam
Ilam Park
Thorpe
Fenny Bentley
Shottle
Nether Heage
Caldon Canal
Ipstones
Cauldon
Blore
Kniveton
Hognaston
Kirk Ireton
Idridgehay
Broadholme
Heage
Froghall Wharf
Cauldon Lowe
Atlow
Biggin
Ireton Wood
Mount Pleasant
Street Lane
Consall Nature Park
Hazles
Foxt
Froghall
Swinscoe
Mapleton
Hulland Ward
Millington Green
Hillcliffe Lane
Blackbrook
Openwoodgate
Cowers Lane
Cross o' th' Hands
Farnah Green
BELPER
Whiston
Cotton
Weaver Hills
Stanton
Ashbourne
Hulland
Turnditch
Cinderhill
Rawson Green
Kingsley
Longshaw
Whiston Eaves
Kingsley Holt
Wootton
Mayfield
Middle
Spitalhill
Hulland Moss
Bradley
Mugginton Lane End
Hazelwood
Milford
Holbrook
Kilburn

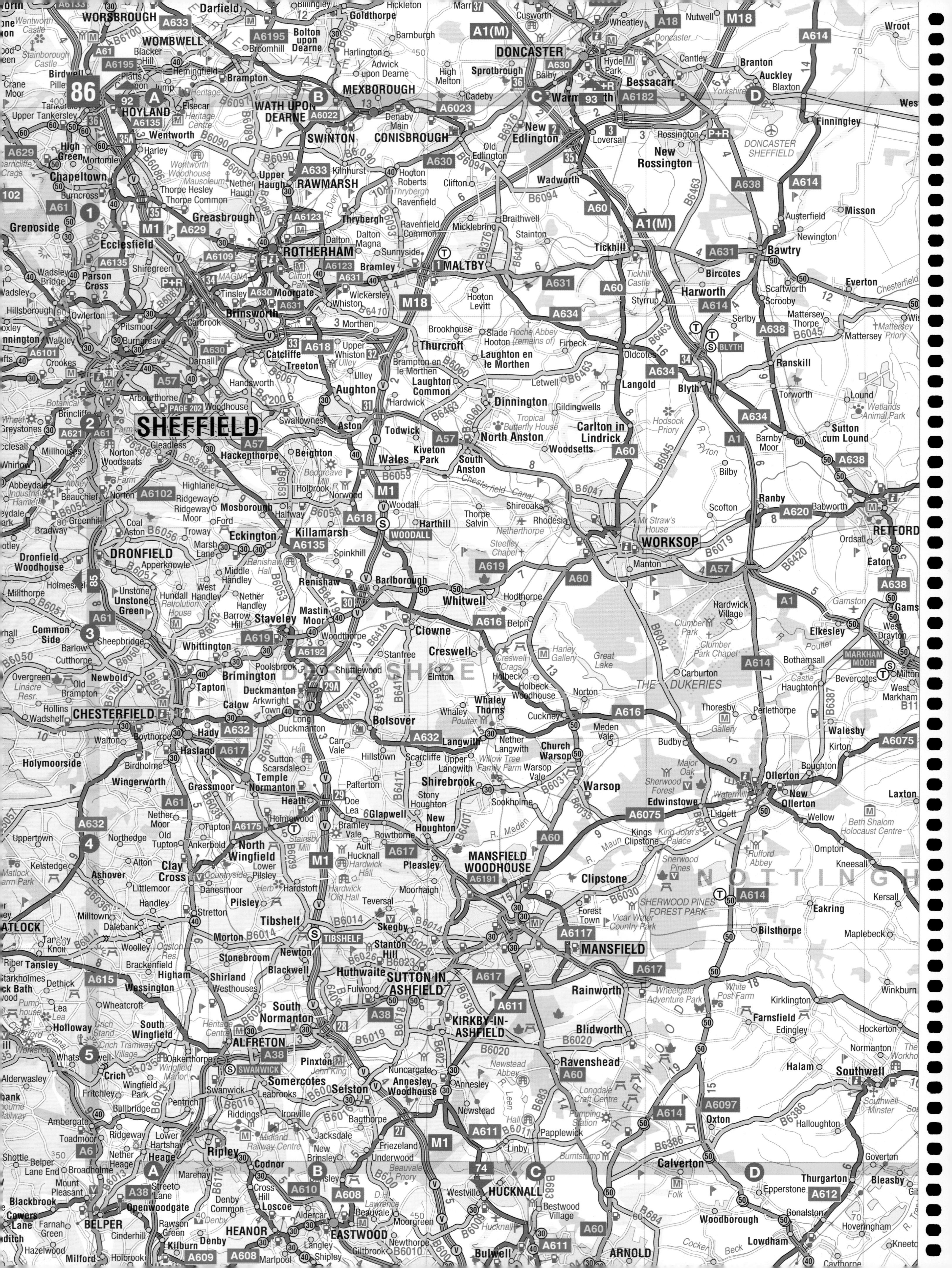

86
92
93
WORSBROUGH
WOMBWELL
Darfield
HOYLAND
Chapeltown
Grenoside
Ecclesfield
Wentworth
Greasbrough
Rawmarsh
ROTHERHAM
MEXBOROUGH
WATH UPON DEARNE
SWINTON
CONISBROUGH
Goldthorpe
Bolton upon Dearne
DONCASTER
Sprotbrough
Bessacarr
Cantley
Warmsworth
New Edlington
Old Edlington
Rossington
New Rossington
DONCASTER SHEFFIELD
Finningley
Wroot
Misson
Austerfield
Bawtry
Tickhill
MALTBY
Bramley
Wickersley
Brinsworth
Tinsley
Moorgate
Catcliffe
Treeton
Thurcroft
Dinnington
Laughton en le Morthen
Langold
Blyth
Harworth
Bircotes
Carlton in Lindrick
North Anston
South Anston
Kiveton Park
Wales
Todwick
Aughton
Aston
Swallownest
Beighton
SHEFFIELD
Hackenthorpe
Mosborough
Eckington
Killamarsh
Renishaw
DRONFIELD
Dronfield Woodhouse
Unstone
Staveley
Barlborough
Clowne
Whitwell
Creswell
WORKSOP
Manton
RETFORD
Ranby
Babworth
Elkesley
Sutton cum Lound
Barnby Moor
Everton
Mattersey
Ranskill
Torworth
Lound
CHESTERFIELD
Brimington
Whittington
Old Whittington
Hasland
Bolsover
Wingerworth
Grassmoor
Clay Cross
North Wingfield
Pilsley
Tibshelf
Shirebrook
Warsop
Church Warsop
MANSFIELD WOODHOUSE
MANSFIELD
Clipstone
Edwinstowe
Ollerton
New Ollerton
Forest Town
Rainworth
Blidworth
Ravenshead
SUTTON IN ASHFIELD
KIRKBY-IN-ASHFIELD
Huthwaite
South Normanton
ALFRETON
Somercotes
Selston
Ripley
Codnor
Heanor
EASTWOOD
HUCKNALL
BELPER
Bulwell
ARNOLD
Calverton
Woodborough
Lowdham
Southwell
Farnsfield
Bilsthorpe
Eakring
Laxton
Tuxford
ATLOCK
Crich
Holloway
Wessington
Higham
Shirland
Stonebroom
Denby
DERBYSHIRE
THE DUKERIES
NOTTINGH
SHERWOOD PINES FOREST PARK
PAGE 202
M1
M18
A1(M)
A1
A57
A60
A61
A614
A616
A617
A619
A631
A634
A638

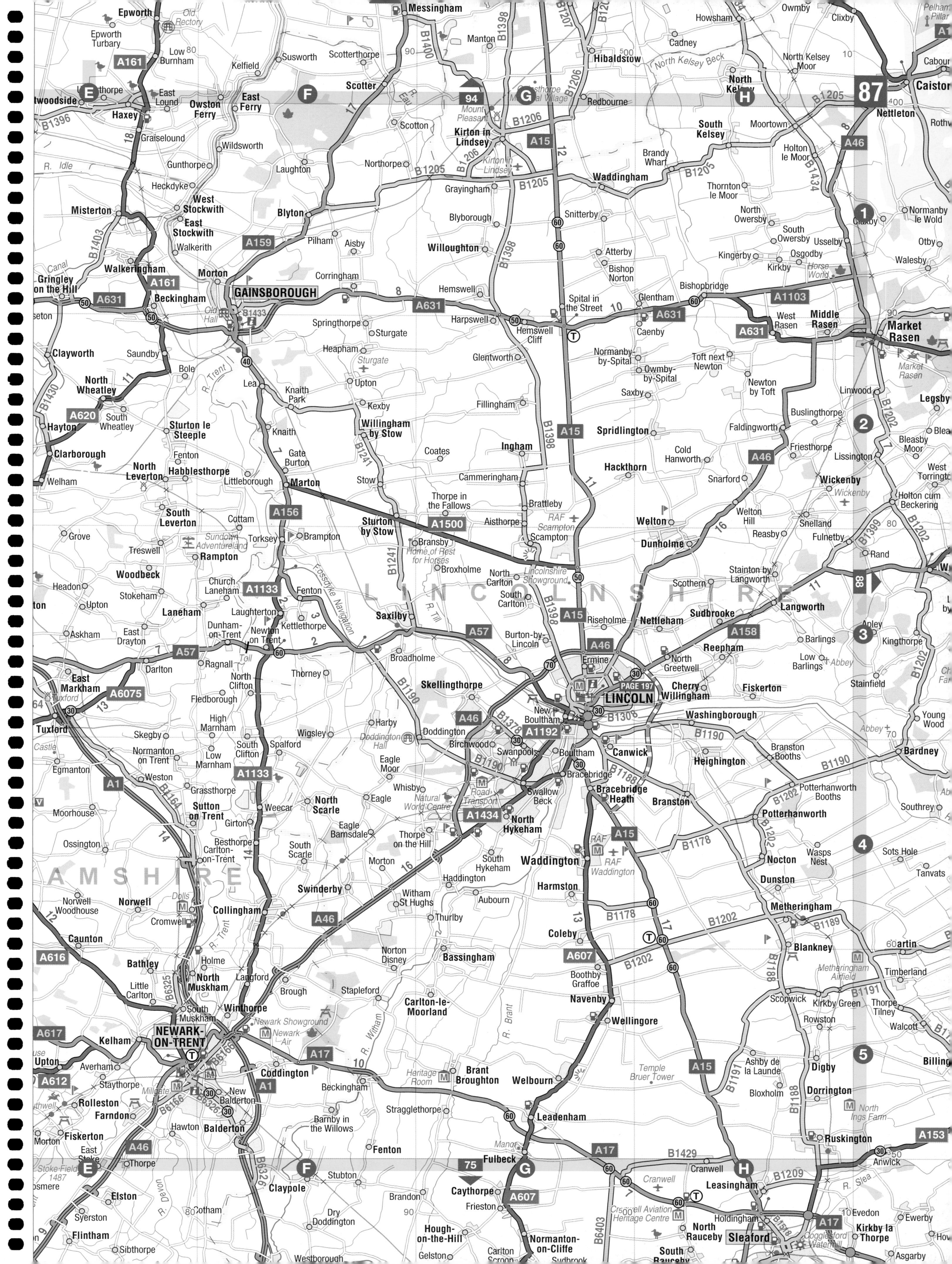

87
88
94
75
LINCOLNSHIRE
PAGE 197
Epworth
Epworth Turbary
Old Rectory
Low Burnham
Kelfield
Susworth
Scotterthorpe
Messingham
Manton
Hibaldstow
Cadney
Howsham
Owmby
Clixby
North Kelsey Moor
North Kelsey Beck
North Kelsey
Caistor
Nettleton
Redbourne
Kirton in Lindsey
Mount Pleasant
Scotter
Scotton
East Lound
Owston Ferry
East Ferry
Haxey
Graiseloud
Wildsworth
Gunthorpe
Laughton
Northorpe
Grayingham
Waddingham
South Kelsey
Moortown
Holton le Moor
Brandy Wharf
Thornton le Moor
North Owersby
South Owersby
Usselby
Normanby le Wold
Claxby
Otby
Walesby
Osgodby
Kingerby
Kirkby
Horse World
Heckdyke
West Stockwith
East Stockwith
Walkerith
Misterton
Blyton
Pilham
Aisby
Blyborough
Willoughton
Snitterby
Atterby
Bishop Norton
Bishopbridge
Glentham
Caenby
Spital in the Street
Hemswell
Hemswell Cliff
Harpswell
Gringley on the Hill
Walkeringham
Morton
GAINSBOROUGH
Corringham
Beckingham
Old Hall
Springthorpe
Sturgate
Heapham
Glentworth
Normanby-by-Spital
Owmby-by-Spital
Toft next Newton
Newton by Toft
West Rasen
Middle Rasen
Market Rasen
Linwood
Legsby
Clayworth
Saundby
Bole
Lea
Knaith Park
Upton
Kexby
Willingham by Stow
Fillingham
Saxby
Spridlington
Faldingworth
Buslingthorpe
Friesthorpe
Lissington
Bleasby Moor
North Wheatley
South Wheatley
Hayton
Clarborough
Sturton le Steeple
Fenton
North Leverton
Habblesthorpe
Littleborough
Welham
Knaith
Gate Burton
Marton
Coates
Ingham
Cold Hanworth
Hackthorn
Snarford
Wickenby
West Torrington
Holton cum Beckering
Stow
Cammeringham
Thorpe in the Fallows
Brattleby
Welton
Welton Hill
Snelland
Reasby
Fulnetby
Rand
South Leverton
Cottam
Sturton by Stow
Aisthorpe
RAF Scampton
Scampton
Dunholme
Grove
Treswell
Sundown Adventureland
Torksey
Brampton
Bransby
Home of Rest for Horses
Broxholme
Rampton
Woodbeck
North Carlton
Lincolnshire Showground
South Carlton
Sothern
Stainton by Langworth
Langworth
Headon
Church Laneham
Fenton
Fossdyke Navigation
R. Till
Upton
Stokeham
Laneham
Laughterton
Kettlethorpe
Saxilby
Riseholme
Nettleham
Sudbrooke
Apley
Kingthorpe
Barlings
Askham
East Drayton
Dunham-on-Trent
Newton on Trent
Burton-by-Lincoln
Reepham
Low Barlings
Abbey
Darlton
Ragnall
Toll
Thorney
Broadholme
Ermine
North Greetwell
Stainfield
East Markham
Tuxford
North Clifton
Fledborough
Skellingthorpe
LINCOLN
Cherry Willingham
Fiskerton
High Marnham
Skegby
Harby
Doddington Hall
Doddington
New Boultham
Washingborough
Young Wood
Castle
Normanton on Trent
Low Marnham
South Clifton
Spalford
Wigsley
Birchwood
Swanpool
Boultham
Canwick
Heighington
Branston Booths
Bardney
Egmanton
Weston
Grassthorpe
Eagle Moor
Whisby
Bracebridge
Bracebridge Heath
Branston
Potterhanworth Booths
Southrey
Moorhouse
Sutton on Trent
Girton
Weecar
North Scarle
Eagle
Natural World Centre
Road Transport
Swallow Beck
North Hykeham
Potterhanworth
Ossington
Besthorpe
Carlton-on-Trent
South Scarle
Eagle Barnsdale
Thorpe on the Hill
RAF Waddington
Nocton
Wasps Nest
Sots Hole
Tanvats
Morton
South Hykeham
Waddington
Haddington
Dunston
Harmston
Norwell Woodhouse
Norwell
Dolls
Cromwell
Collingham
Swinderby
Witham St Hughs
Aubourn
Thurlby
Metheringham
Caunton
Coleby
Blankney
Bathley
Holme
North Muskham
Norton Disney
Bassingham
Boothby Graffoe
Navenby
Metheringham Airfield
Timberland
Little Carlton
Langford
Brough
Stapleford
Carlton-le-Moorland
Scopwick
Kirkby Green
Thorpe Tilney
Walcott
South Muskham
Winthorpe
Newark Showground
Newark Air
Wellingore
Rowston
Kelham
NEWARK-ON-TRENT
Coddington
Brant Broughton
Heritage Room
Welbourn
Temple Bruer Tower
Ashby de la Laundé
Digby
Billinghay
Upton
Averham
Staythorpe
Beckingham
Bloxholm
Dorrington
Rolleston
Farndon
New Balderton
Stragglethorpe
Leadenham
North Ings Farm
Barnby in the Willows
Hawton
Balderton
Fiskerton
Ruskington
Morton
East Stoke
Fenton
Manor
Fulbeck
Cranwell
Anwick
Stoke Field 1487
Thorpe
Stubton
Claypole
Caythorpe
Cranwell
Leasingham
Evedon
Ewerby
Elston
Brandon
Frieston
Cranwell Aviation Heritage Centre
Holdingham
Syerston
Cotham
Dry Doddington
North Rauceby
Sleaford
Kirkby la Thorpe
Cogglesford Watermill
Flintham
Sibthorpe
Hough-on-the-Hill
Normanton-on-Cliffe
South Rauceby
Westborough
Gelston
Carlton Scroop
Sudbrook
Asgarby
R. Idle
R. Trent
R. Witham
R. Brant
R. Devon
R. Slea
A161
A631
A159
A620
A156
A1500
A1133
A57
A6075
A1
A46
A1192
A1434
A15
A158
A1103
A616
A617
A612
A17
A607
A153
B1396
B1403
B1430
B1433
B1241
B1398
B1400
B1206
B1205
B1434
B1202
B1399
B1190
B1378
B1308
B1188
B1178
B1189
B1191
B1164
B6325
B6166
B6326
B1429
B1209
B1518
B6403
B1207

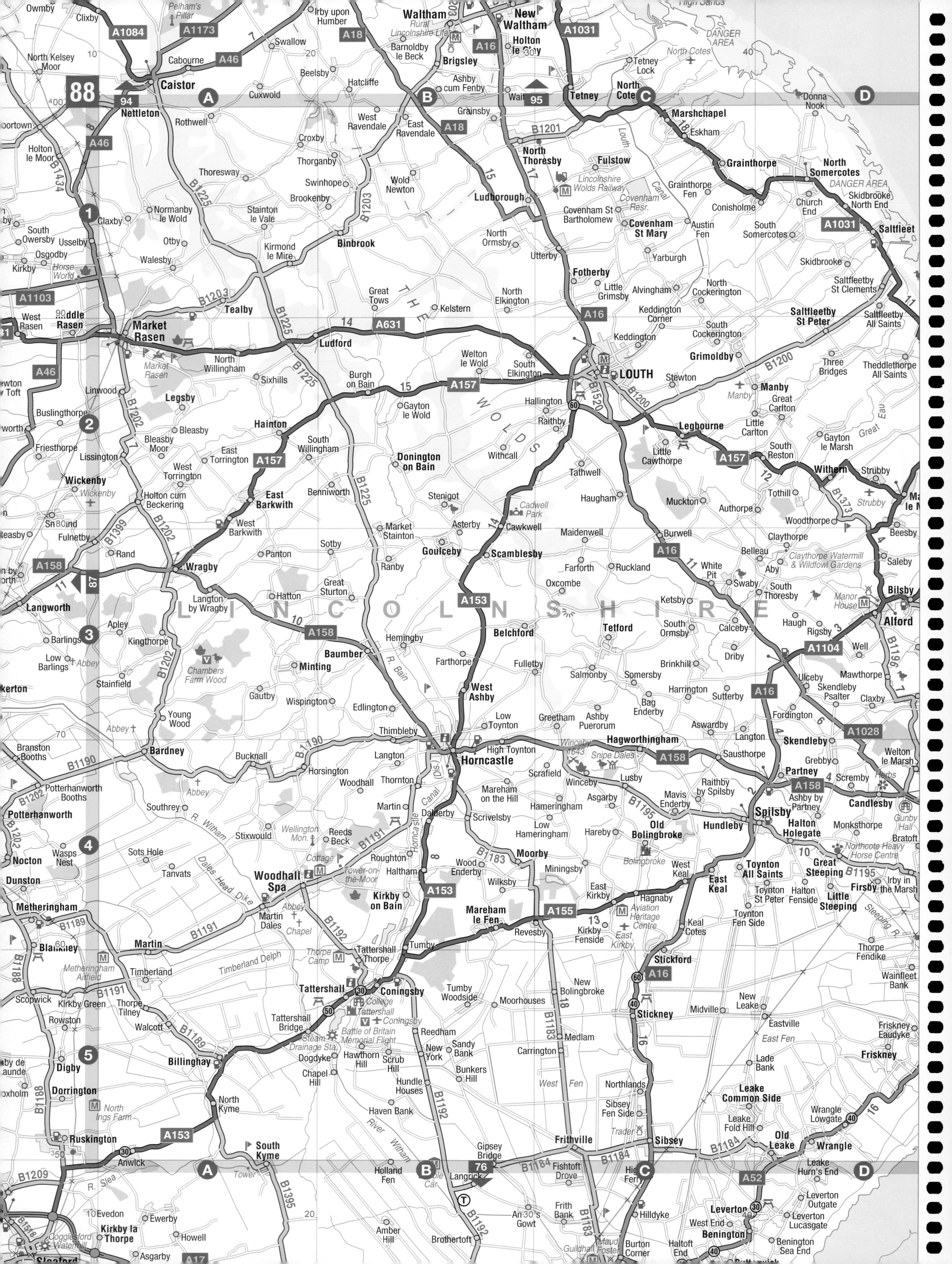

88
94
95
87
76
A
B
C
D
LINCOLNSHIRE
THE WOLDS
Owmby
Clixby
Pelham's Pillar
A1084
A1173
Irby upon Humber
Waltham
Rural Lincolnshire Life
New Waltham
A1031
A18
A16
Holton le Clay
DANGER AREA
Swallow
North Kelsey Moor
Cabourne
A46
Barnoldby le Beck
Brigsley
North Cotes
Tetney Lock
Beelsby
Caistor
Hatcliffe
Ashby cum Fenby
Cuxwold
Tetney
North Cote
Donna Nook
Nettleton
Grainsby
Marshchapel
West Ravendale
East Ravendale
Rothwell
B1201
Eskham
Holton le Moor
Croxby
North Thoresby
Fulstow
Grainthorpe
North Somercotes
Thorganby
Lincolnshire Wolds Railway
Thoresway
Swinhope
Wold Newton
Ludborough
Grainthorpe Fen
DANGER AREA
B1434
B1225
Brookenby
B1203
Covenham Resr.
Conisholme
Church End
Skidbrooke North End
Normanby le Wold
Stainton le Vale
Covenham St Bartholomew
Covenham St Mary
Austin Fen
South Somercotes
Saltfleet
A1031
South Owersby
Claxby
Usselby
Otby
Binbrook
North Ormsby
Osgodby
Kirmond le Mire
Utterby
Yarburgh
Skidbrooke
Walesby
Kirkby
Horse World
Fotherby
Saltfleetby St Clements
Little Grimsby
Alvingham
North Cockerington
A1103
B1203
Great Tows
North Elkington
Tealby
Kelstern
Keddington Corner
Saltfleetby St Peter
Saltfleetby All Saints
West Rasen
Middle Rasen
Market Rasen
A631
South Cockerington
Keddington
Ludford
Grimoldby
North Willingham
Welton le Wold
South Elkington
B1200
Three Bridges
Theddlethorpe All Saints
A46
Newton by Toft
Sixhills
Burgh on Bain
A157
LOUTH
Stewton
Manby
Great Carlton
Linwood
Legsby
B1202
Gayton le Wold
Hallington
B1520
Raithby
Little Carlton
Buslingthorpe
Bleasby
Hainton
South Willingham
Legbourne
Gayton le Marsh
Great Eau
Friesthorpe
Bleasby Moor
East Torrington
A157
Donington on Bain
Withcall
Little Cawthorpe
South Reston
Lissington
West Torrington
Tathwell
Withern
Strubby
Wickenby
Benniworth
B1225
Stenigot
Haugham
Muckton
Tothill
Authorpe
B1373
Holton cum Beckering
East Barkwith
Cadwell Park
Woodthorpe
Snarford
West Barkwith
Market Stainton
Asterby
Cawkwell
Maidenwell
Burwell
Claythorpe
Beesby
Fulnetby
B1399
Rand
Panton
Sotby
Goulceby
Scamblesby
A16
Belleau
Claythorpe Watermill & Wildfowl Gardens
Saleby
A158
Wragby
Ranby
Farforth
Ruckland
White Pit
Aby
Great Sturton
Oxcombe
Swaby
South Thoresby
Bilsby
Langworth
Langton by Wragby
Hatton
A153
Ketsby
Manor House
Alford
Apley
A158
Belchford
Tetford
South Ormsby
Calceby
Haugh
Rigsby
Barlings
Kingthorpe
Hemingby
A1104
Well
Low Barlings
Abbey
Baumber
Driby
Minting
Farthorpe
Fulletby
Brinkhill
B1196
Chambers Farm Wood
Salmonby
Somersby
Mawthorpe
Stainfield
West Ashby
Ulceby
Skendleby Psalter
Harrington
Gautby
Wispington
Sutterby
Claxby
Edlington
Bag Enderby
Young Wood
Low Toynton
Greetham
Ashby Puerorum
Aswardby
Fordington
Abbey
Thimbleby
Langton
A1028
Branston Booths
Bardney
B1190
Hagworthingham
Winceby 1643
Snipe Dales
A158
Sausthorpe
Skendleby
Welton le Marsh
Bucknall
Langton
Horncastle
High Toynton
Gredby
Horsington
Scrafield
Partney
Scremby
Woodhall
Thornton
Mareham on the Hill
Winceby
Lusby
Raithby by Spilsby
A158
Potterhanworth Booths
Mavis Enderby
Ashby by Partney
Candlesby
B1202
Abbey
Asgarby
B1195
Gunby Hall
Potterhanworth
Southrey
Martin
Dalderby
Hameringham
Spilsby
Hundleby
Halton Holegate
Monksthorpe
Scrivelsby
Low Hameringham
Old Bolingbroke
R. Witham
Stixwould
Wellington Mon.
Reeds Beck
Bratoft
Nocton
Wasps Nest
Sots Hole
Moorby
Hareby
Northcote Heavy Horse Centre
B1191
Cottage
Roughton
B1183
Bolingbroke
West Keal
Great Steeping
Dunston
Tanvats
Dales Head Dike
Tower-on-the-Moor
Haltham
Wood Enderby
Miningsby
Toynton All Saints
East Keal
B1195
Irby in the Marsh
Woodhall Spa
Wilksby
East Kirkby
Firsby
Metheringham
Toynton St Peter
Halton Fenside
Little Steeping
Abbey
Kirkby on Bain
A153
Hagnaby
B1189
Martin Dales
Chapel
Mareham le Fen
A155
Aviation Heritage Centre
Steeping R.
B1192
Revesby
Kirkby Fenside
Keal Cotes
Toynton Fen Side
Blankney
Martin
Thorpe Camp
Tattershall Thorpe
Tumby
East Kirkby
Thorpe Fendike
B1188
Metheringham Airfield
Timberland
Timberland Delph
Stickford
A16
Wainfleet Bank
Tattershall
Coningsby
Tumby Woodside
New Bolingbroke
Scopwick
Kirkby Green
B1191
Thorpe Tilney
College
Tattershall
Coningsby
Moorhouses
B1183
Stickney
Midville
New Leake
Rowston
Walcott
Tattershall Bridge
Steam Drainage Sta.
Battle of Britain Memorial Flight
Reedham
Medlam
Eastville
Friskney Eaudyke
B1189
New York
Sandy Bank
East Fen
Digby
Billinghay
Dogdyke
Hawthorn Hill
Scrub Hill
Bunkers Hill
Carrington
Lade Bank
Friskney
Ashby de la Launde
Chapel Hill
Hundle Houses
West Fen
Northlands
Dorrington
North Kyme
North Ings Farm
Haven Bank
B1192
Sibsey Fen Side
Leake Common Side
B1188
Ruskington
A153
River Witham
Trader
Wrangle Lowgate
Leake Fold Hill
Frithville
Sibsey
B1184
Old Leake
Wrangle
Anwick
South Kyme
Gipsey Bridge
Fishtoft Drove
B1184
Leake Hurn's End
B1209
R. Slea
Tower
B1395
Holland Fen
Langrick
Hilldyke
A52
Leverton Outgate
Evedon
Kirkby la Thorpe
Ewerby
Howell
Amber Hill
Brothertoft
Anton's Gowt
Frith Bank
B1183
Burton Corner
Leverton
West End
Benington
Leverton Lucasgate
Benington Sea End
Haltoft End
Cogglesford Watermill
Asgarby
A17
Sleaford

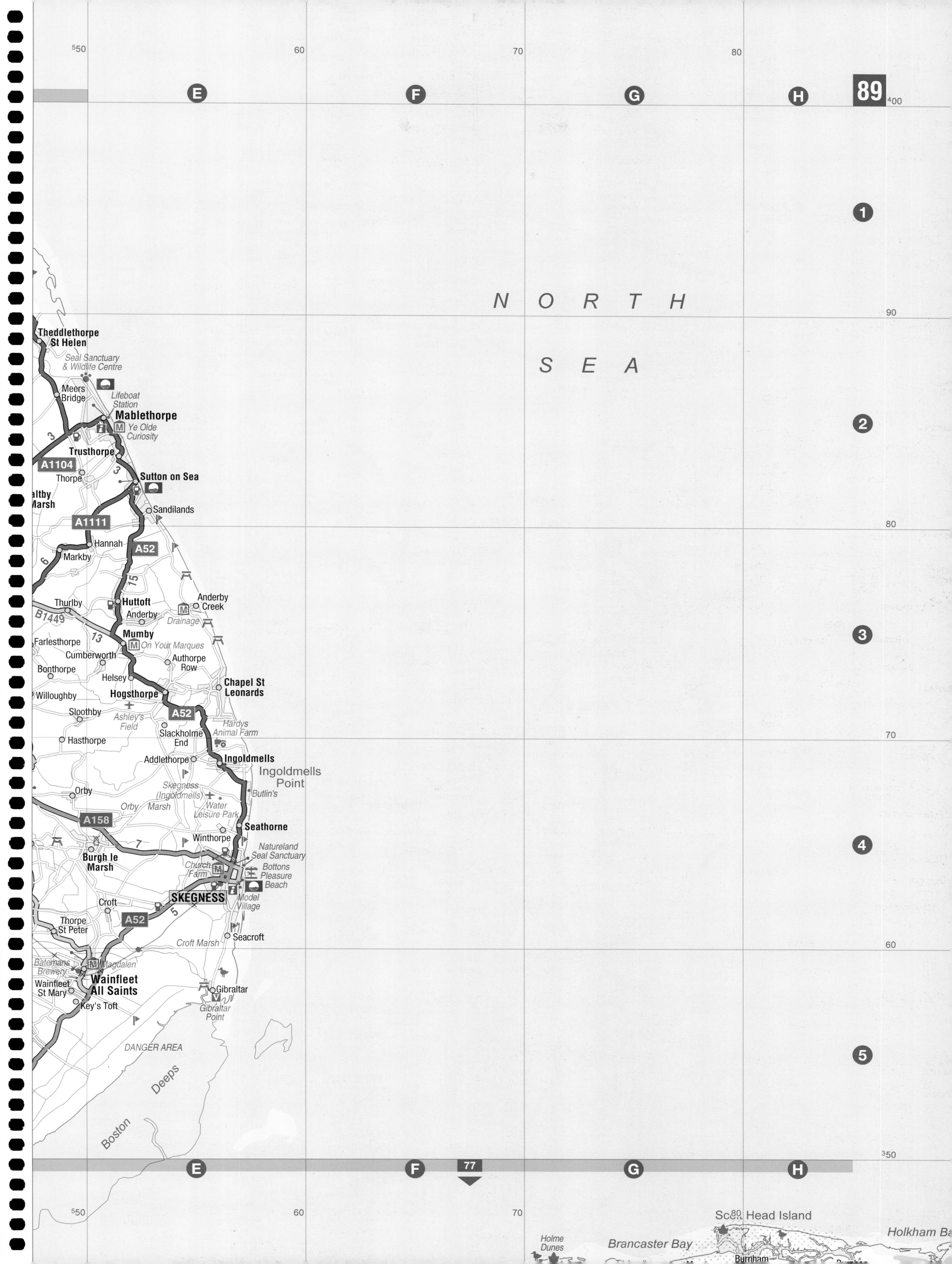

1

N O R T H

S E A

90

Theddlethorpe
St Helen

*Seal Sanctuary
& Wildlife Centre*

Meers
Bridge

*Lifeboat
Station*

Mablethorpe

2

Ⓜ *Ye Olde
Curiosity*

Trusthorpe

A1104

Thorpe

Sutton on Sea

 altby
Marsh

Sandilands

A1111

Hannah

Markby   A52

80

6

15

Thurlby   **Huttoft**   Anderby
Creek

Anderby   Ⓜ *Drainage*

Farlesthorpe

B1449   13   **Mumby**

3

Cumberworth   Ⓜ *On Your Marques*

Authorpe
Row

Bonthorpe

Helsey

Willoughby   **Hogsthorpe**   **Chapel St
Leonards**

Sloothby   *Ashley's
Field*   A52

Hasthorpe   Slackholme
End   *Hardys
Animal Farm*

70

Addlethorpe   **Ingoldmells**

*Ingoldmells
Point*

Orby   *Skegness
(Ingoldmells)*   *Butlin's*

*Orby
Marsh*   *Water
Leisure Park*

A158   **Seathorne**

7   Winthorpe

4

*Natureland
Seal Sanctuary*

**Burgh le
Marsh**   *Church
Farm*   Ⓜ   *Bottons
Pleasure
Beach*

Croft   **SKEGNESS**   *Model
Village*

Thorpe
St Peter   A52   5

60

Croft Marsh   Seacroft

*Batemans
Brewery*   Ⓜ *Magdalen*

Wainfleet
St Mary   **Wainfleet
All Saints**   Gibraltar

Key's Toft   *Gibraltar
Point*

DANGER AREA   5

Deeps

350

Boston

Sc Head Island

*Holme
Dunes*   *Brancaster Bay*   *Holkham Ba*

Burnham

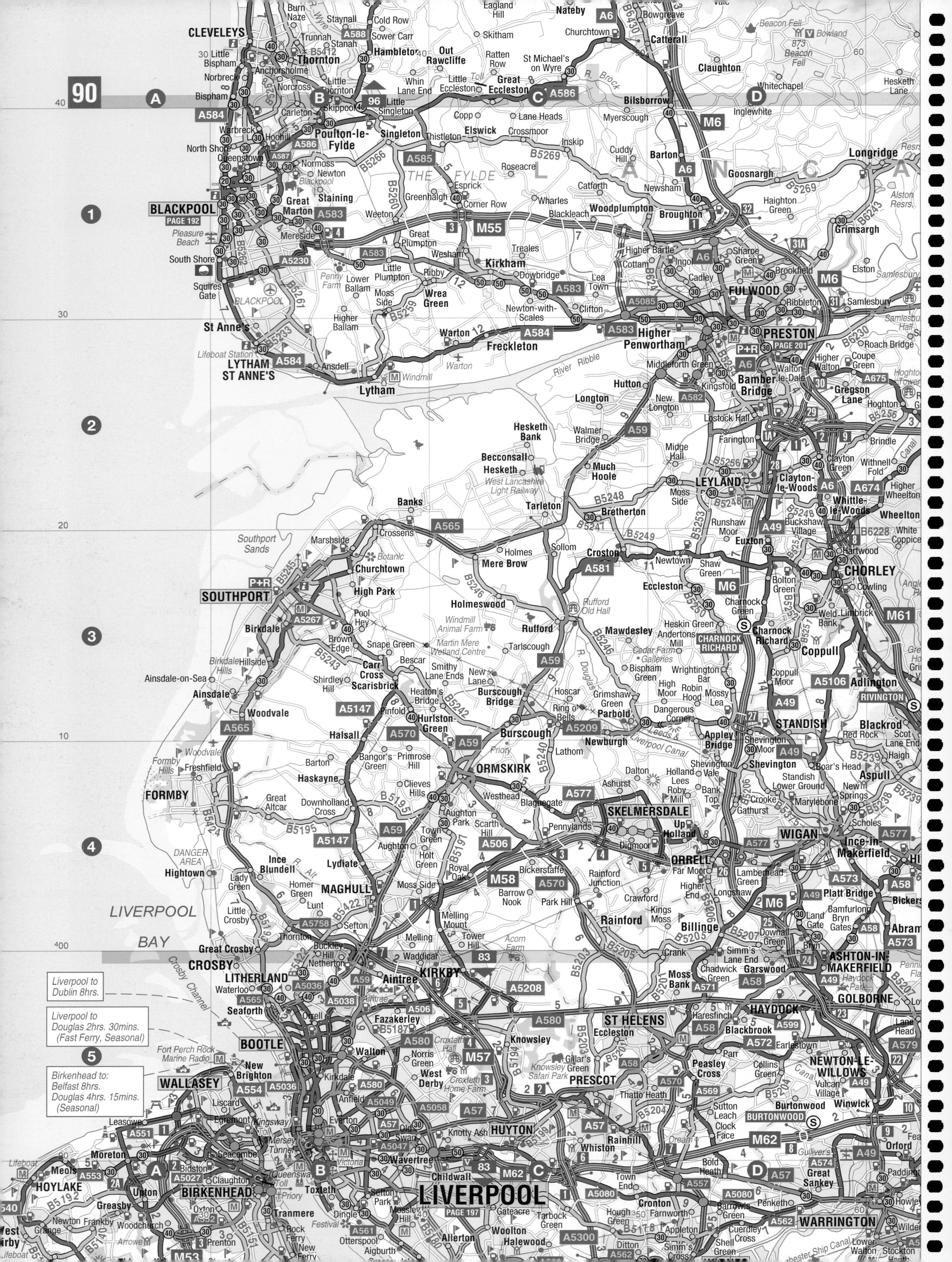

90
A
B
C
D
1
2
3
4
5
CLEVELEYS
Thornton
Poulton-le-Fylde
Singleton
BLACKPOOL
PAGE 192
Pleasure Beach
South Shore
Squires Gate
St Anne's
LYTHAM ST ANNE'S
Lytham
Warton
Freckleton
Kirkham
THE FYLDE
Garstang
Catterall
Bilsborrow
Longridge
Goosnargh
Broughton
FULWOOD
PRESTON
PAGE 201
Higher Penwortham
Bamber Bridge
River Ribble
Hutton
Longton
Hesketh Bank
Much Hoole
LEYLAND
Tarleton
Banks
Southport Sands
SOUTHPORT
Churchtown
Birkdale
Ainsdale
Woodvale
Croston
Eccleston
CHORLEY
Coppull
Rufford
Burscough
Scarisbrick
Parbold
STANDISH
Adlington
Blackrod
Aspull
WIGAN
FORMBY
ORMSKIRK
SKELMERSDALE
ORRELL
Rainford
Billinge
Maghull
Lydiate
Ince Blundell
Hightown
LIVERPOOL BAY
Crosby Channel
CROSBY
LITHERLAND
Aintree
KIRKBY
ASHTON-IN-MAKERFIELD
HAYDOCK
GOLBORNE
ST HELENS
NEWTON-LE-WILLOWS
PRESCOT
HUYTON
Knowsley
Bootle
BOOTLE
WALLASEY
New Brighton
BIRKENHEAD
HOYLAKE
Meols
Moreton
LIVERPOOL
PAGE 197
Walton
Everton
Wavertree
Childwall
Woolton
Halewood
Widnes
WARRINGTON
Great Sankey
M6
M55
M58
M57
M62
M61
M53
Liverpool to Dublin 8hrs.
Liverpool to Douglas 2hrs. 30mins. (Fast Ferry, Seasonal)
Birkenhead to: Belfast 8hrs. Douglas 4hrs. 15mins. (Seasonal)

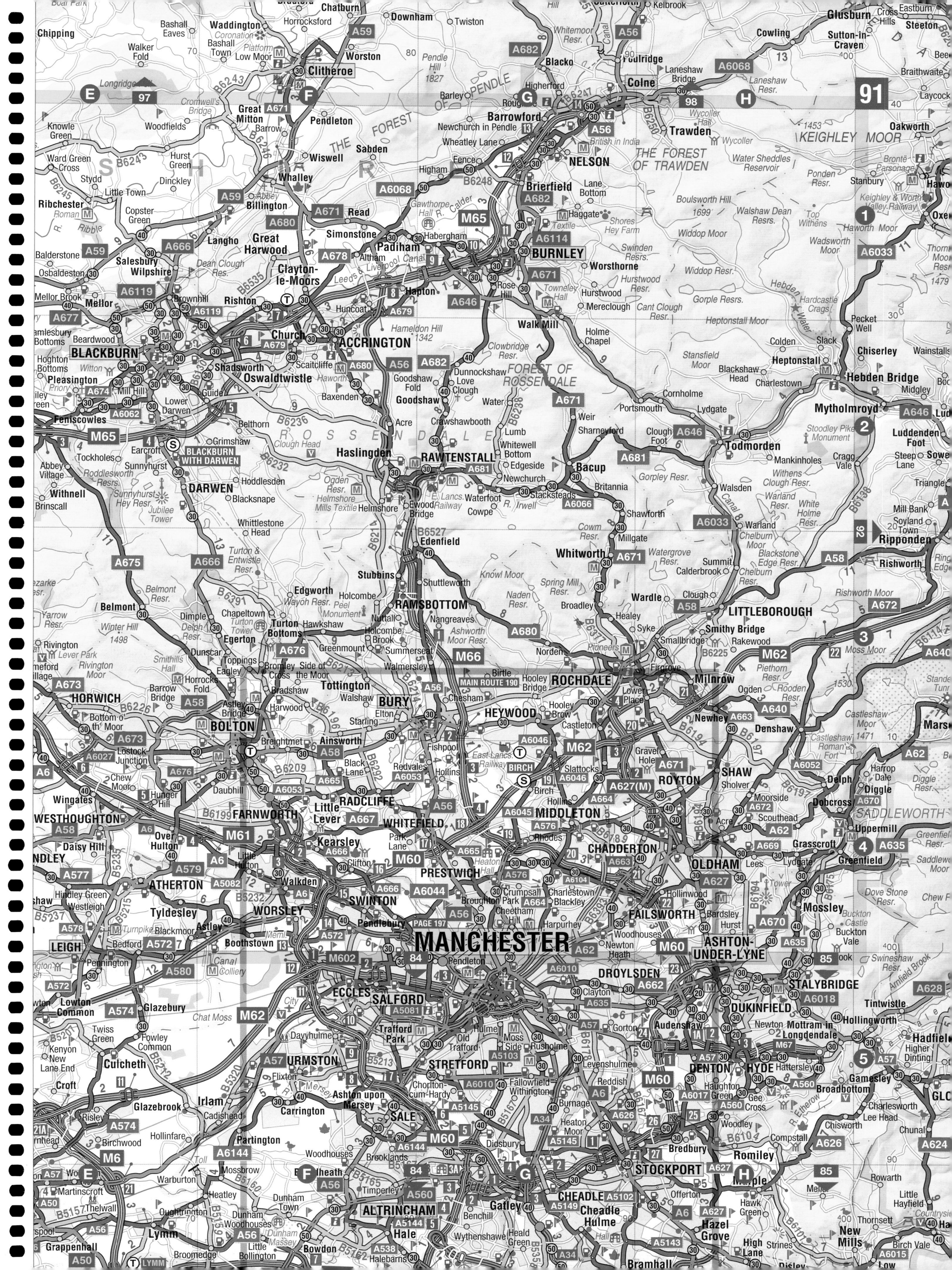
91
MANCHESTER
BLACKBURN
BURNLEY
ACCRINGTON
ROCHDALE
BOLTON
BURY
OLDHAM
STOCKPORT
SALFORD
ALTRINCHAM
RAMSBOTTOM
LITTLEBOROUGH
Clitheroe
Colne
NELSON
Brierfield
Padiham
Haslingden
RAWTENSTALL
Bacup
Todmorden
Hebden Bridge
Mytholmroyd
Ripponden
DARWEN
HORWICH
HEYWOOD
MIDDLETON
ROYTON
SHAW
CHADDERTON
FAILSWORTH
ASHTON-UNDER-LYNE
STALYBRIDGE
DUKINFIELD
DENTON
HYDE
ECCLES
URMSTON
STRETFORD
SALE
LEIGH
ATHERTON
Tyldesley
WORSLEY
SWINTON
FARNWORTH
RADCLIFFE
WHITEFIELD
PRESTWICH
WESTHOUGHTON
Tottington
Whitworth
Oswaldtwistle
Great Harwood
Clayton-le-Moors
THE FOREST OF PENDLE
THE FOREST OF TRAWDEN
FOREST OF ROSSENDALE
ROSSENDALE
KEIGHLEY MOOR
SADDLEWORTH
M65
M66
M62
M60
M61
M602
M6
M67
A627(M)
PAGE 197
MAIN ROUTE 190

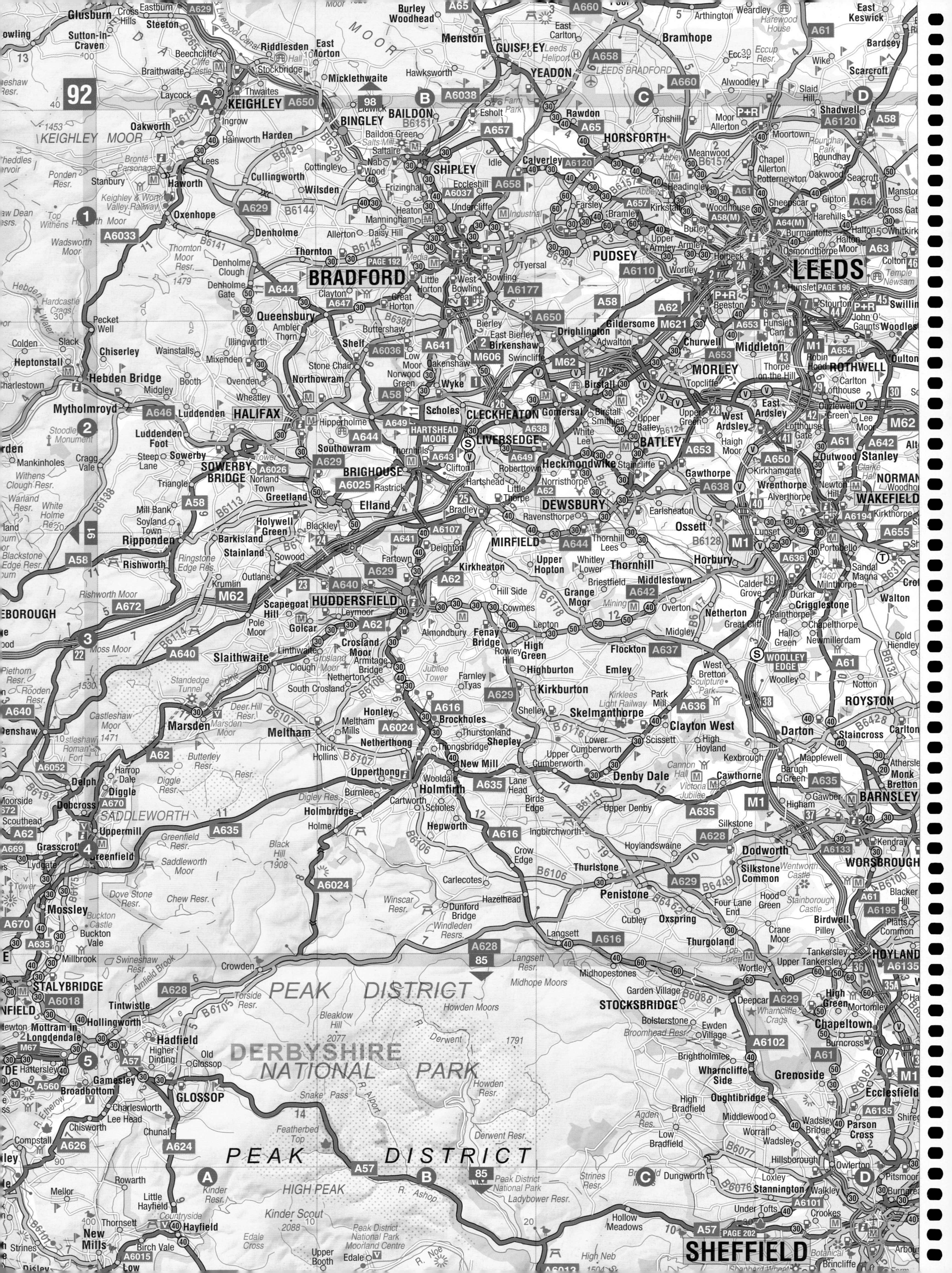

92
98
85
91
PAGE 192
PAGE 196
PAGE 202
Glusburn
Cross Hills
Eastburn
Steeton
Sutton-in-Craven
Riddlesden
East Morton
Burley Woodhead
Menston
GUISELEY
YEADON
East Carlton
Arthington
Weardley
Harewood House
East Keswick
Bramhope
Bardsey
Leeds Heliport
LEEDS BRADFORD
Eccup Resr.
Alwoodley
Wike
Scarcroft
Slaid Hill
Shadwell
Beechcliffe
Braithwaite
Stockbridge
Micklethwaite
Hawksworth
Laycock
Thwaites
KEIGHLEY
Bingley
BAILDON
Esholt
Rawdon
Tinshill
Moor Allerton
Moortown
Roundhay
Ingrow
Oakworth
Keighley Moor
Hainworth
Harden
Baildon Green
Saltaire
Salts Mill
Horsforth
Meanwood
Chapel Allerton
Bronte Parsonage
Lees
Ponden Resr.
Stanbury
Haworth
Cullingworth
Cottingley
Nab Wood
Shipley
Idle
Calverley
Keighley & Worth Valley Railway
Wilsden
Frizinghall
Eccleshill
Undercliffe
Farsley
Kirkstall
Headingley
Potternewton
Oakwood
Seacroft
Top Withens
Oxenhope
Heaton
Bramley
Woodhouse
Gipton
Manston
Harehills
Cross Gates
Manningham
Daisy Hill
Allerton
Denholme
Upper Armley
Burley
Burmantofts
Halton
Whitkirk
Wadsworth Moor
Thornton Moor Resr.
Thornton
BRADFORD
PUDSEY
Tyersal
Holbeck
Osmondthorpe
LEEDS
Colton
Temple Newsam
Denholme Clough
Wortley
Little Horton
West Bowling
Bowling
Hunslet
Hebden Water
Hardcastle Crags
Denholme Gate
Clayton
Great Horton
Beeston
Stourton
Swillington
Pecket Well
Queensbury
Ambler Thorn
Buttershaw
Bierley
East Bierley
Birkenshaw
Drighlington
Gildersome
Adwalton
Churwell
Middleton
Rothwell
Oulton
John O' Gaunts
Woodlesford
Colden
Slack
Heptonstall
Chiserley
Wainstalls
Illingworth
Mixenden
Shelf
Stone Chair
Low Moor
Oakenshaw
Norwood Green
Swincliffe
MORLEY
Thorpe on the Hill
Robin Hood
Carlton
Lofthouse
Charlestown
Hebden Bridge
Booth
Midgley
Ovenden
Northowram
Wyke
Birstall
Topcliffe
Mytholmroyd
Luddenden
HALIFAX
Wheatley
Hipperholme
Scholes
CLECKHEATON
Gomersal
Birstall Smithies
Upper Batley
Upper Green
East Ardsley
West Ardsley
Outwood
Lofthouse Gate
Lee Moor
Stoodley Monument
Luddenden Foot
HARTSHEAD MOOR
LIVERSEDGE
White Lee
BATLEY
Haigh Moor
Stanley
Mankinholes
Cragg Vale
Steep Lane
Sowerby
SOWERBY BRIDGE
Southowram
Thornhills
Clifton
Heckmondwike
Staincliffe
Gawthorpe
Kirkhamgate
Clarke Hall
NORMANTON
Withens Clough Resr.
Norland Town
BRIGHOUSE
Rastrick
Roberttown
Hartshead
Little Thorpe
Norristhorpe
Wrenthorpe
Newton Hill
Alverthorpe
WAKEFIELD
Warland Resr.
White Holme Res.
Triangle
Greetland
Elland
Bradley
DEWSBURY
Earlsheaton
Kirkthorpe
Mill Bank
Soyland Town
Holywell Green
Blackley
Ravensthorpe
Ossett
Ripponden
Barkisland
Stainland
Deighton
MIRFIELD
Thornhill Lees
Horbury
Lupset
Portobello
Sandal Magna
Blackstone Edge Resr.
Rishworth
Ringstone Edge Res.
Sowood
Fartown
Kirkheaton
Upper Hopton
Whitley Lower
Thornhill
Calder Grove
Milnthorpe
Walton
Krumlin
Outlane
Briestfield
Middlestown
Grange Moor
Durkar
Rishworth Moor
Scapegoat Hill
HUDDERSFIELD
Hill Side
Cowmes
Overton
Netherton
Crigglestone
Painthorpe
Chapelthorpe
Pole Moor
Golcar
Leymoor
Almondbury
Fenay Bridge
Lepton
Great Cliff
Hall Green
Newmillerdam
Cold Hiendley
Crosland Moor
High Green
Rowley Hill
Flockton
Midgley
Moss Moor
Slaithwaite
Linthwaite
Armitage Bridge
Clough
Netherton
South Crosland
Jubilee Tower
Farnley Tyas
Highburton
Emley
West Bretton
Sculpture Park
WOOLLEY EDGE
Woolley
Notton
Standedge Tunnel
Deer Hill Resr.
Honley
Kirkburton
Kirklees Light Railway
Park Mill
Marsden
Meltham
Meltham Mills
Brockholes
Thurstonland
Shelley
Skelmanthorpe
Clayton West
Darton
Staincross
ROYSTON
Carlton
Castleshaw Moor
Marsden Moor
Netherthong
Thongsbridge
Lower Cumberworth
Scissett
High Hoyland
Kexbrough
Mapplewell
Butterley Resr.
Thick Hollins
Upperthong
New Mill
Upper Cumberworth
Cannon Hall
Cawthorne
Barugh Green
Athersley
Monk Bretton
Harrop Dale
Diggle
Diggle Resr.
Wooldale
Holmfirth
Lane Head
Denby Dale
Victoria Jubilee
Higham
Gawber
BARNSLEY
Delph
Dobcross
SADDLEWORTH
Digley Res.
Burnlee
Cartworth
Scholes
Birds Edge
Upper Denby
Silkstone
Uppermill
Greenfield Resr.
Holmbridge
Holme
Hepworth
Ingbirchworth
Hoylandswaine
Grasscroft
Greenfield
Black Hill
Saddleworth Moor
Crow Edge
Thurlstone
Dodworth
Kendray
WORSBROUGH
Lydgate
Silkstone Common
Wentworth Castle
Dove Stone Resr.
Chew Resr.
Carlecotes
Penistone
Hood Green
Blacker Hill
Mossley
Buckton Castle
Winscar Resr.
Dunford Bridge
Hazlehead
Four Lane End
Stainborough Castle
Buckton Vale
Windleden Resrs.
Cubley
Oxspring
Crane Moor
Birdwell
Pilley
Platts Common
Thurgoland
Langsett
Millbrook
Swineshaw Resr.
Crowden
Langsett Resr.
Midhope Moors
Midhopestones
Wortley
Upper Tankersley
Tankersley
HOYLAND
STALYBRIDGE
Arnfield Brook
Torside Resr.
PEAK DISTRICT
Garden Village
Deepcar
Wharncliffe Crags
High Green
Mortomley
Tintwistle
Howden Moors
STOCKSBRIDGE
Hollingworth
Bleaklow Hill
Derwent
Bolsterstone
Ewden Village
Broomhead Resr.
Chapeltown
Mottram in Longdendale
Hadfield
Burncross
Higher Dinting
Old Glossop
DERBYSHIRE NATIONAL PARK
Brightholmlee
Hattersley
Gamesley
Wharncliffe Side
Grenoside
Broadbottom
GLOSSOP
Snake Pass
Howden Resr.
High Bradfield
Oughtibridge
Ecclesfield
Charlesworth
Lee Head
Featherbed Top
Agden Res.
Middlewood
Parson Cross
Chisworth
Chunal
Derwent Resr.
Low Bradfield
Worrall
Wadsley Bridge
Compstall
Wadsley
Hillsborough
Owlerton
PEAK DISTRICT
Rowarth
Kinder Resr.
HIGH PEAK
Peak District National Park
Strines Resr.
Dungworth
Loxley
Pitsmoor
Mellor
Little Hayfield
R. Ashop
Ladybower Resr.
Stannington
Walkley
Burngreave
Under Tofts
Crookes
Thornsett
Countryside
Hayfield
Kinder Scout
Hollow Meadows
New Mills
Birch Vale
Edale Cross
Peak District National Park Moorland Centre
Upper Booth
Edale
R. Noe
High Neb
SHEFFIELD
Botanical
Arbourthorne
Brincliffe
Strines
Disley
Low

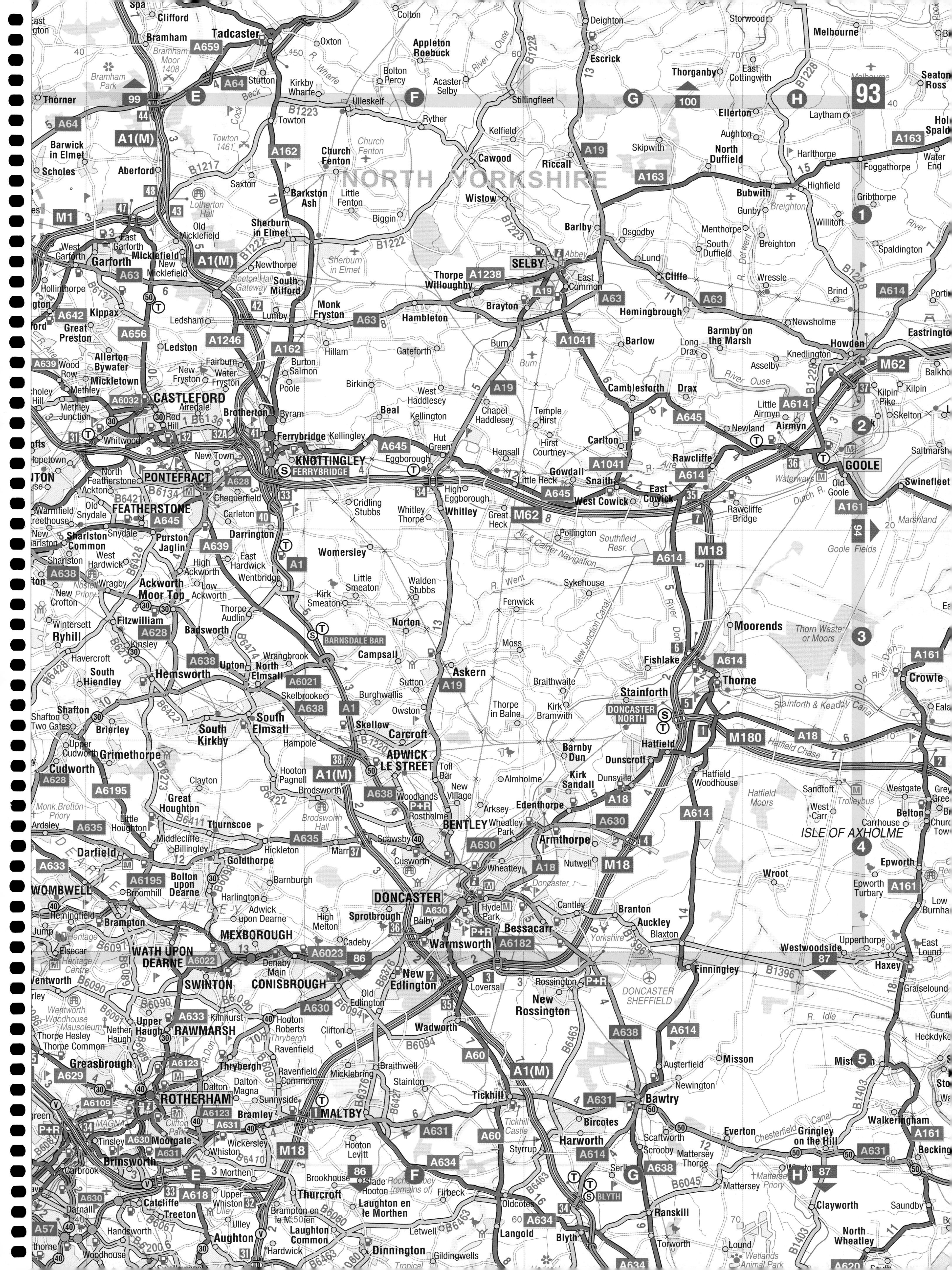
NORTH YORKSHIRE
Clifford
Tadcaster
Bramham
A659
Oxton
Colton
Appleton Roebuck
Deighton
Escrick
Storwood
Melbourne
Bramham Park
A64
Stutton
Kirkby Wharfe
Bolton Percy
Acaster Selby
River Ouse
Thorganby
East Cottingham
Seaton Ross
Thorner
99
E
Ulleskelf
F
Stillingfleet
G
100
H
Ellerton
Laytham
B1223
Towton
Ryther
Kelfield
Aughton
A64
A1(M)
Towton 1461
A162
Church Fenton
Cawood
Riccall
A19
Skipwith
North Duffield
Harlthorpe
A163
Foggathorpe
Barwick in Elmet
Scholes
Aberford
B1217
Saxton
Barkston Ash
Little Fenton
Wistow
Bubwith
Highfield
Gribthorpe
Lotherton Hall
Old Micklefield
Sherburn in Elmet
Biggin
Barlby
Osgodby
Gunby
Breighton
Menthorpe
Willitoft
M1
Garforth
East Garforth
Micklefield
New Micklefield
A1(M)
Newthorpe
B1222
Selby
Abbey
Lund
South Duffield
Breighton
Spaldington
A63
Hollinthorpe
Steeton Hall Gateway
South Milford
Thorpe Willoughby
A1238
East Common
Cliffe
Wressle
Brind
A614
Kippax
Lumby
Monk Fryston
Brayton
A63
Hemingbrough
Newsholme
Great Preston
A642
A656
Ledsham
Hambleton
Barlow
Long Drax
Barmby on the Marsh
Howden
Eastrington
Ledston
A1246
A162
Hillam
Gateforth
Burn
A1041
Knedlington
Asselby
M62
Allerton Bywater
Fairburn
Burton Salmon
River Ouse
Wood Row
Mickletown
New Fryston
Water Fryston
Poole
Birkin
West Haddlesey
Camblesforth
Drax
Kilpin Pike
Kilpin
Methley
Castleford
Airedale
Brotherton
Byram
Beal
Kellington
Chapel Haddlesey
Temple Hirst
A645
Little Airmyn
Airmyn
Skelton
Methley Junction
Red Hill
B6136
Ferrybridge
Kellingley
Hut Green
Hensall
Hirst Courtney
Carlton
Newland
Whitwood
Knottingley
Ferrybridge
Eggborough
A1041
Rawcliffe
Goole
Saltmarsh
Hopetown
New Town
Pontefract
A628
Gowdall
Little Heck
Snaith
East Cowick
Waterways
Old Goole
Swinefleet
North Featherstone
Ackton
B6134
Chequerfield
High Eggborough
West Cowick
Rawcliffe Bridge
Dutch R.
A161
Featherstone
Old Snydale
B6421
Cridling Stubbs
Whitley Thorpe
Whitley
Great Heck
M62
Carleton
Warmfield
A645
Darrington
Pollington
Southfield Resr.
Marshland
Snydale
Sharlston Common
Purston Jaglin
A639
Air & Calder Navigation
A614
M18
Goole Fields
Sharlston
West Hardwick
High Ackworth
East Hardwick
Womersley
A638
Wragby
Ackworth Moor Top
Wentbridge
A1
Little Smeaton
Walden Stubbs
R. Went
Sykehouse
New Crofton
Low Ackworth
Kirk Smeaton
Fenwick
Thorpe Audlin
Norton
Moorends
Thorn Waste or Moors
Wintersett
Ryhill
Fitzwilliam
A628
Badsworth
Barnsdale Bar
New Junction Canal
Moss
River Don
Kinsley
Havercroft
A638
Upton
Wrangbrook
North Elmsall
Campsall
Askern
Fishlake
A614
Thorne
A161
Crowle
South Hiendley
Hemsworth
A6021
Sutton
A19
Braithwaite
Stainforth
Old River Don
Skelbrooke
Burghwallis
Thorpe in Balne
Kirk Bramwith
Doncaster North
Stainforth & Keadby Canal
Shafton
Brierley
South Kirkby
South Elmsall
A638
A1
Owston
Skellow
Carcroft
Hampole
B1220
Adwick le Street
Toll Bar
Barnby Dun
Hatfield
M180
A18
Hatfield Chase
Shafton Two Gates
Upper Cudworth
Grimethorpe
Cudworth
A628
Clayton
Hooton Pagnell
A1(M)
Brodsworth
Woodlands
Rostholme
New Village
Almholme
Kirk Sandall
Dunscroft
Dunsville
Hatfield Woodhouse
Sandtoft
Westgate
A6195
Great Houghton
B6422
Brodsworth Hall
A638
P+R
Arksey
Edenthorpe
A18
Hatfield Moors
Trolleybus
West Carr
Carrhouse
Belton
Monk Bretton Priory
Little Houghton
B6411
Thurnscoe
Bentley
Wheatley Park
A630
Isle of Axholme
Ardsley
A635
Middlecliffe
Billingley
A635
Hickleton
Scawsby
Marr
Armthorpe
Darfield
Goldthorpe
Cusworth
A630
Wheatley
A18
Nutwell
M18
Epworth
A633
A6195
Bolton upon Dearne
Barnburgh
Wroot
Epworth Turbary
A161
Wombwell
Broomhill
Harlington
Adwick upon Dearne
Doncaster
A630
Hyde Park
Cantley
Branton
Auckley
Blaxton
Low Burnham
Hemingfield
Brampton
High Melton
Sprotbrough
Balby
Bessacarr
P+R
Dearne Valley
Elsecar Heritage Centre
Wath upon Dearne
Mexborough
Cadeby
Warmsworth
A6182
Yorkshire Wildlife Park
Westwoodside
Upperthorpe
East Lound
A6022
Denaby Main
A6023
86
New Edlington
Loversall
Finningley
B1396
87
Haxey
Wentworth
Swinton
Conisbrough
Old Edlington
Rossington
P+R
Doncaster Sheffield
Graiseland
New Rossington
Wentworth Woodhouse Mausoleum
A630
Upper Haugh
Nether Haugh
A633
Rawmarsh
Kilnhurst
Hooton Roberts
Thrybergh
Clifton
Wadworth
A638
A614
R. Idle
Thorpe Hesley
Thorpe Common
Ravenfield
B6094
A60
Misson
Misterton
Heckdyke
Greasbrough
A6123
Thrybergh
Ravenfield Common
Micklebring
Braithwell
A1(M)
Austerfield
A629
Dalton
Dalton Magna
Stainton
Newington
A6109
Rotherham
Sunnyside
Maltby
Tickhill
A631
Bawtry
Walkeringham
Magna
A6123
A631
Bramley
A631
Bircotes
Everton
Gringley on the Hill
A161
P+R
Tinsley
Moorgate
Wickersley
Hooton Levitt
Tickhill Castle
A60
Harworth
Scaftworth
Scrooby
Mattersey Thorpe
Chesterfield Canal
A631
Beckingham
Brinsworth
Whiston
M18
Styrrup
A614
A638
Carbrook
Morthen
86
A634
F
Serlby
G
Mattersey
Mattersey Priory
H
87
Catcliffe
A618
Upper Whiston
Brookhouse
Slade Hooton
Roche Abbey (remains of)
Firbeck
Blyth
B6045
Clayworth
Saundby
A630
Darnall
Treeton
Ulley
Thurcroft
Laughton en le Morthen
Oldcotes
A634
Ranskill
A57
Handsworth
Aughton
Brampton en le Morthen
Laughton Common
Letwell
Langold
Blyth
North Wheatley
Woodhouse
Hardwick
Dinnington
Gildingwells
Torworth
Lound
Wetlands Animal Park
A634
A620

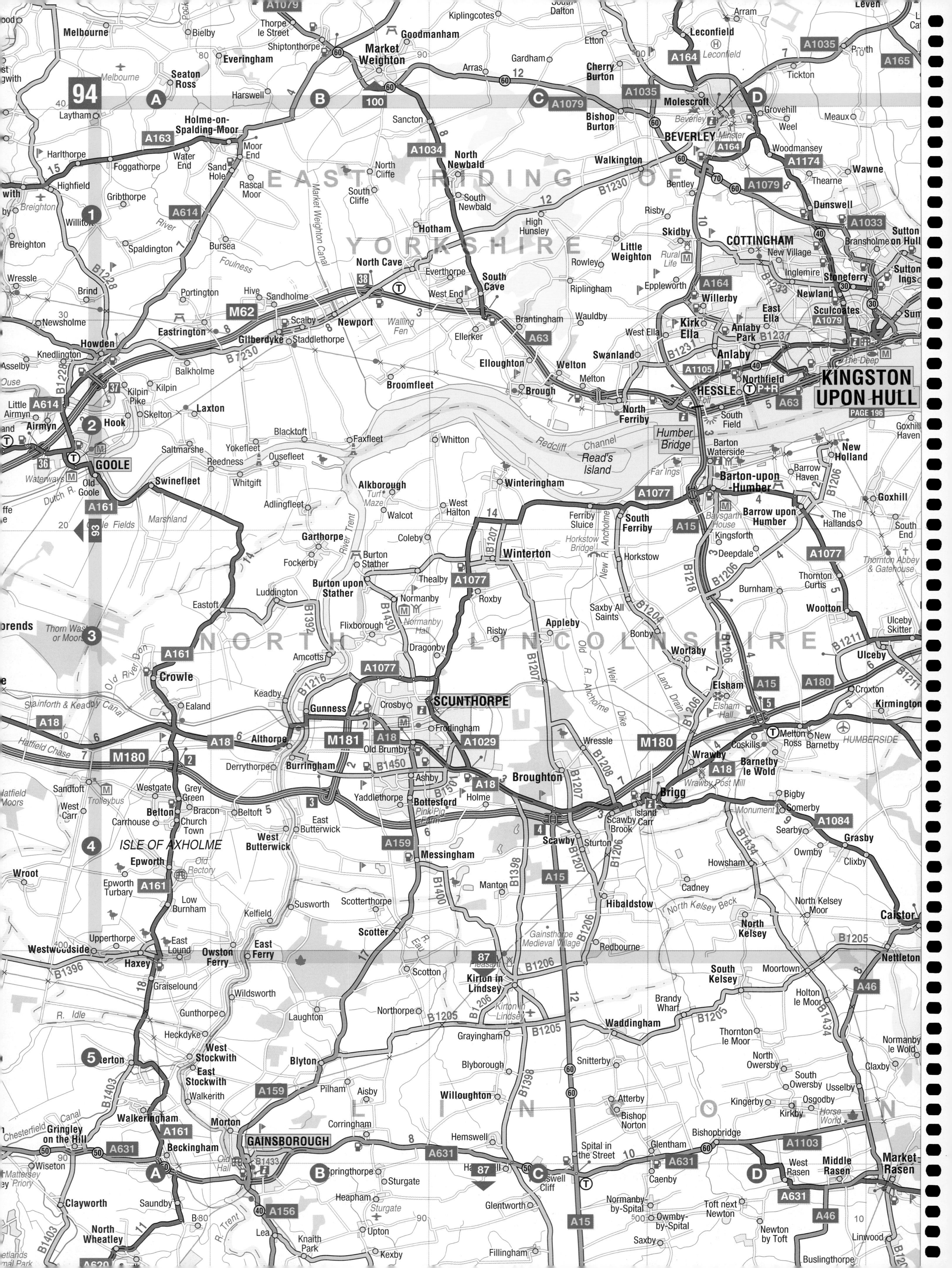

94
100
93
87
Melbourne
Bielby
Thorpe le Street
Shiptonthorpe
Goodmanham
Market Weighton
Kiplingcotes
Dalton
Etton
Leconfield
Arram
Seaton Ross
Everingham
Harswell
Arras
Gardham
Cherry Burton
Molescroft
Bishop Burton
BEVERLEY
Tickton
Grovehill
Weel
Meaux
Laytham
Holme-on-Spalding-Moor
Sancton
Harlthorpe
Foggathorpe
Water End
Sand Hole
Moor End
North Newbald
North Cliffe
South Cliffe
South Newbald
Walkington
Woodmansey
Wawne
Thearne
Highfield
Gribthorpe
Rascal Moor
EAST RIDING OF YORKSHIRE
Market Weighton Canal
Bentley
Risby
Dunswell
Breighton
Willitoft
Spaldington
Bursea
River Foulness
Hotham
High Hunsley
Skidby
COTTINGHAM
New Village
Little Weighton
Rural Life
Bransholme
Sutton on Hull
Wressle
Brind
Portington
Hive
Sandholme
North Cave
Everthorpe
South Cave
West End
Rowley
Riplingham
Eppleworth
Willerby
Inglemire
Stoneferry
Newland
Sculcoates
Sutton Ings
Newsholme
Eastrington
Gilberdyke
Scalby
Staddlethorpe
Newport
Walling Fen
Brantingham
Wauldby
Ellerker
East Ella
West Ella
Kirk Ella
Anlaby Park
Anlaby
Howden
Knedlington
Asselby
Balkholme
Kilpin
Kilpin Pike
Skelton
Laxton
Broomfleet
Elloughton
Welton
Swanland
Melton
Brough
Northfield
HESSLE
KINGSTON UPON HULL
PAGE 196
The Deep
South Field
North Ferriby
Little Airmyn
Airmyn
Hook
GOOLE
Old Goole
Blacktoft
Saltmarshe
Yokefleet
Reedness
Ousefleet
Faxfleet
Whitton
Redcliff Channel
Read's Island
Humber Bridge
Barton Waterside
Far Ings
Barton-upon-Humber
Barrow Haven
New Holland
Goxhill Haven
Swinefleet
Whitgift
Dutch R.
Adlingfleet
Alkborough
Turf Maze
Walcot
West Halton
Winteringham
South Ferriby
Ferriby Sluice
Barrow upon Humber
Goxhill
The Hallands
South End
Marshland
Garthorpe
Fockerby
River Trent
Burton Stather
Coleby
Winterton
Horkstow Bridge
Horkstow
New R. Ancholme
Baysgarth House
Kingsforth
Deepdale
Thornton Abbey & Gatehouse
Thornton Curtis
Luddington
Burton upon Stather
Thealby
Normanby
Normanby Hall
Roxby
Saxby All Saints
Burnham
Wootton
Eastoft
Thorn Waste or Moors
Flixborough
Dragonby
Risby
Appleby
Bonby
Worlaby
Ulceby Skitter
Ulceby
NORTH LINCOLNSHIRE
Amcotts
Old River Don
Crowle
Keadby
Gunness
Crosby
SCUNTHORPE
Frodingham
Old R. Ancholme
Weir Dike
Land Drain
Elsham
Elsham Hall
Croxton
Kirmington
Stainforth & Keadby Canal
Ealand
Althorpe
Old Brumby
Wressle
Melton Ross
New Barnetby
HUMBERSIDE
Hatfield Chase
Derrythorpe
Burringham
Broughton
Wrawby
Barnetby le Wold
Wrawby Post Mill
Sandtoft
Trolleybus
Westgate
Grey Green
Ashby
Yaddlethorpe
Bottesford
Holme
Brigg
Monument
Bigby
Somerby
Hatfield Moors
West Carr
Belton
Bracon
Church Town
Beltoft
Carrhouse
East Butterwick
Pink Pig Farm
Scawby Brook
Island Carr
Searby
Grasby
ISLE OF AXHOLME
West Butterwick
Messingham
Scawby
Sturton
Owmby
Clixby
Howsham
Wroot
Epworth
Old Rectory
Epworth Turbary
Manton
Cadney
Low Burnham
Kelfield
Susworth
Scotterthorpe
Hibaldstow
North Kelsey Beck
North Kelsey Moor
Caistor
North Kelsey
Upperthorpe
East Lound
Westwoodside
Haxey
Owston Ferry
East Ferry
Scotter
R. Eau
Gainsthorpe Medieval Village
Redbourne
Nettleton
Scotton
Kirton in Lindsey
South Kelsey
Moortown
Holton le Moor
Graiselound
Wildsworth
Gunthorpe
R. Idle
Laughton
Northorpe
Brandy Wharf
Waddingham
Heckdyke
Grayingham
Thornton le Moor
Normanby le Wold
West Stockwith
East Stockwith
Walkerith
Blyton
Blyborough
Snitterby
North Owersby
South Owersby
Claxby
Usselby
Pilham
Aisby
Willoughton
Atterby
Bishop Norton
Kingerby
Osgodby
Kirkby
Horse World
Chesterfield Canal
Gringley on the Hill
Walkeringham
Morton
Beckingham
GAINSBOROUGH
Corringham
Hemswell
Spital in the Street
Glentham
Bishopbridge
Middle Rasen
West Rasen
Market Rasen
Wiseton
Mattersey Priory
Springthorpe
Sturgate
Caenby
Clayworth
Saundby
Heapham
Glentworth
Normanby-by-Spital
Owmby-by-Spital
Toft next Newton
Newton by Toft
Linwood
North Wheatley
R. Trent
Lea
Knaith Park
Upton
Kexby
Fillingham
Saxby
Buslingthorpe
M62
M180
M181
A1079
A163
A614
A1034
A1035
A164
A165
A1174
A1033
A63
A1105
B1230
B1228
B1231
B1233
A161
A1077
A15
A18
A1029
A180
A159
A631
A156
A1084
A46
A1103
B1206
B1207
B1218
B1204
B1211
B1216
B1392
B1430
B1450
B1501
B1208
B1398
B1400
B1434
B1205
B1396
B1403
B1433

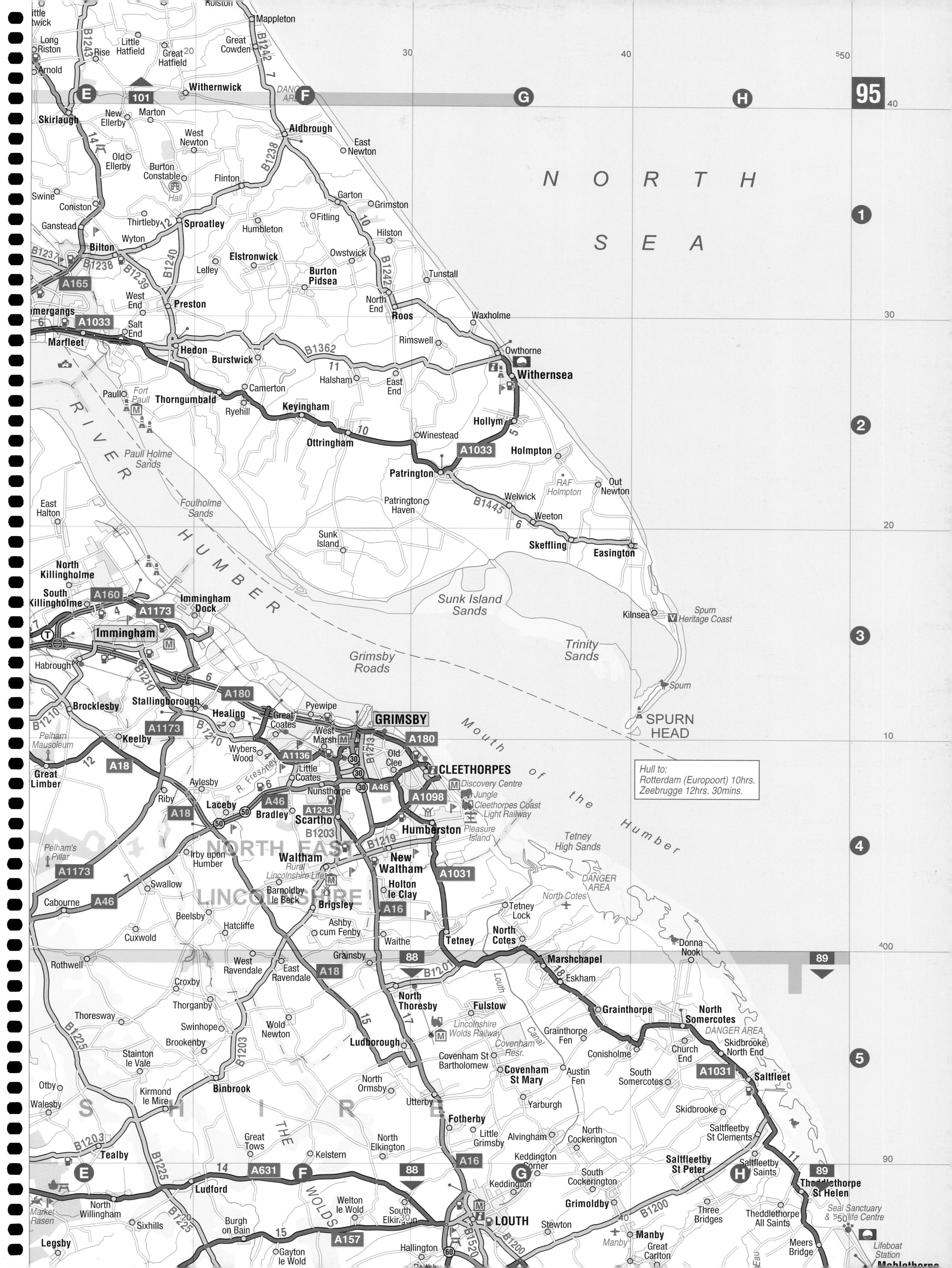

95
NORTH SEA
RIVER HUMBER
Mouth of the Humber
Hull to:
Rotterdam (Europoort) 10hrs.
Zeebrugge 12hrs. 30mins.
NORTH EAST LINCOLNSHIRE
SHIRE
THE WOLDS
GRIMSBY
CLEETHORPES
Immingham
LOUTH
Withernsea
Hedon
Patrington
Keyingham
Ottringham
Aldbrough
Skirlaugh
Withernwick
Mappleton
Roos
Hollym
Holmpton
Easington
Kilnsea
SPURN HEAD
Spurn Heritage Coast
Sunk Island Sands
Trinity Sands
Grimsby Roads
Tetney High Sands
Paull Holme Sands
Foulholme Sands
Humberston
Scartho
Waltham
New Waltham
Holton le Clay
Tetney
North Cotes
Marshchapel
Grainthorpe
North Somercotes
Saltfleet
Theddlethorpe St Helen
Manby
Binbrook
Tealby
Ludford
Market Rasen
Ludborough
North Thoresby
Fulstow
Covenham St Mary
Fotherby
Keelby
Stallingborough
Healing
Laceby
Bradley
Brigsley
Great Limber
Brocklesby
Habrough
North Killingholme
South Killingholme
Immingham Dock
Marfleet
Thorngumbald
Burstwick
Preston
Sproatley
Bilton
Elstronwick
Burton Pidsea
Pleasure Island
Discovery Centre
Jungle
Cleethorpes Coast Light Railway
Lincolnshire Wolds Railway
Rural Lincolnshire Life
Seal Sanctuary & Wildlife Centre
Lifeboat Station
RAF Holmpton
DANGER AREA
A1033
A165
A160
A1173
A180
A18
A46
A1136
A1243
A1098
A1031
A16
A631
A157
B1242
B1362
B1445
B1210
B1203
B1225
B1200
B1201
88
89
101

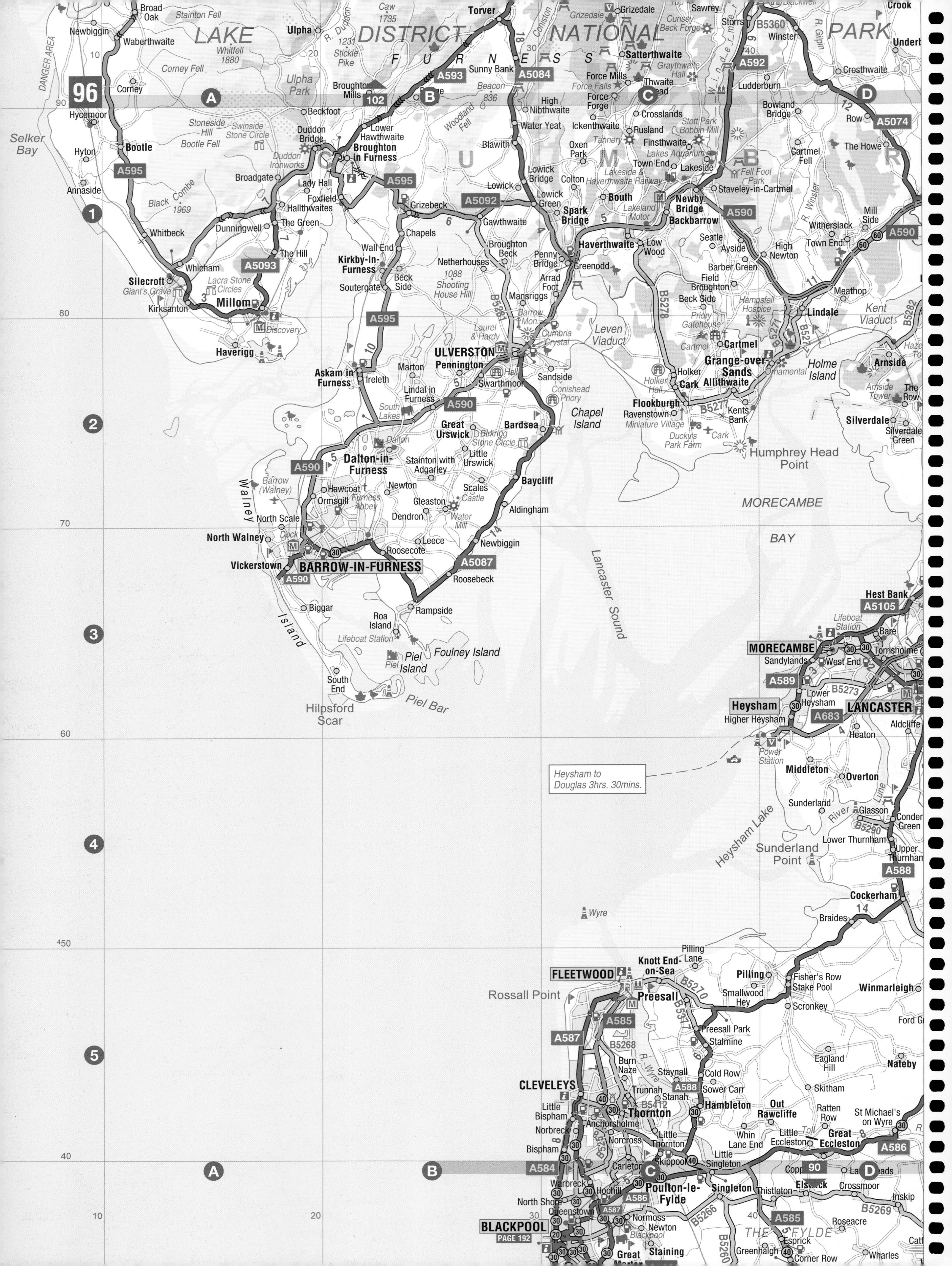

96
LAKE DISTRICT NATIONAL PARK
FURNESS
CUMBRIA
MORECAMBE BAY
BARROW-IN-FURNESS
ULVERSTON
Dalton-in-Furness
Millom
Kirkby-in-Furness
Askam in Furness
Broughton in Furness
Grange-over-Sands
MORECAMBE
Heysham
LANCASTER
FLEETWOOD
CLEVELEYS
BLACKPOOL
PAGE 192
Poulton-le-Fylde
Thornton
Preesall
Knott End-on-Sea
Walney Island
Piel Island
Foulney Island
Lancaster Sound
Chapel Island
Humphrey Head Point
Heysham Lake
Sunderland Point
Rossall Point
Selker Bay
Heysham to Douglas 3hrs. 30mins.
THE FYLDE
A595
A5093
A590
A5087
A5092
A593
A5084
A592
A5074
A5105
A589
A683
A588
A585
A587
A584
A586
B5278
B5277
B5270
B5268
B5269
B5266
Hilpsford Scar
Piel Bar

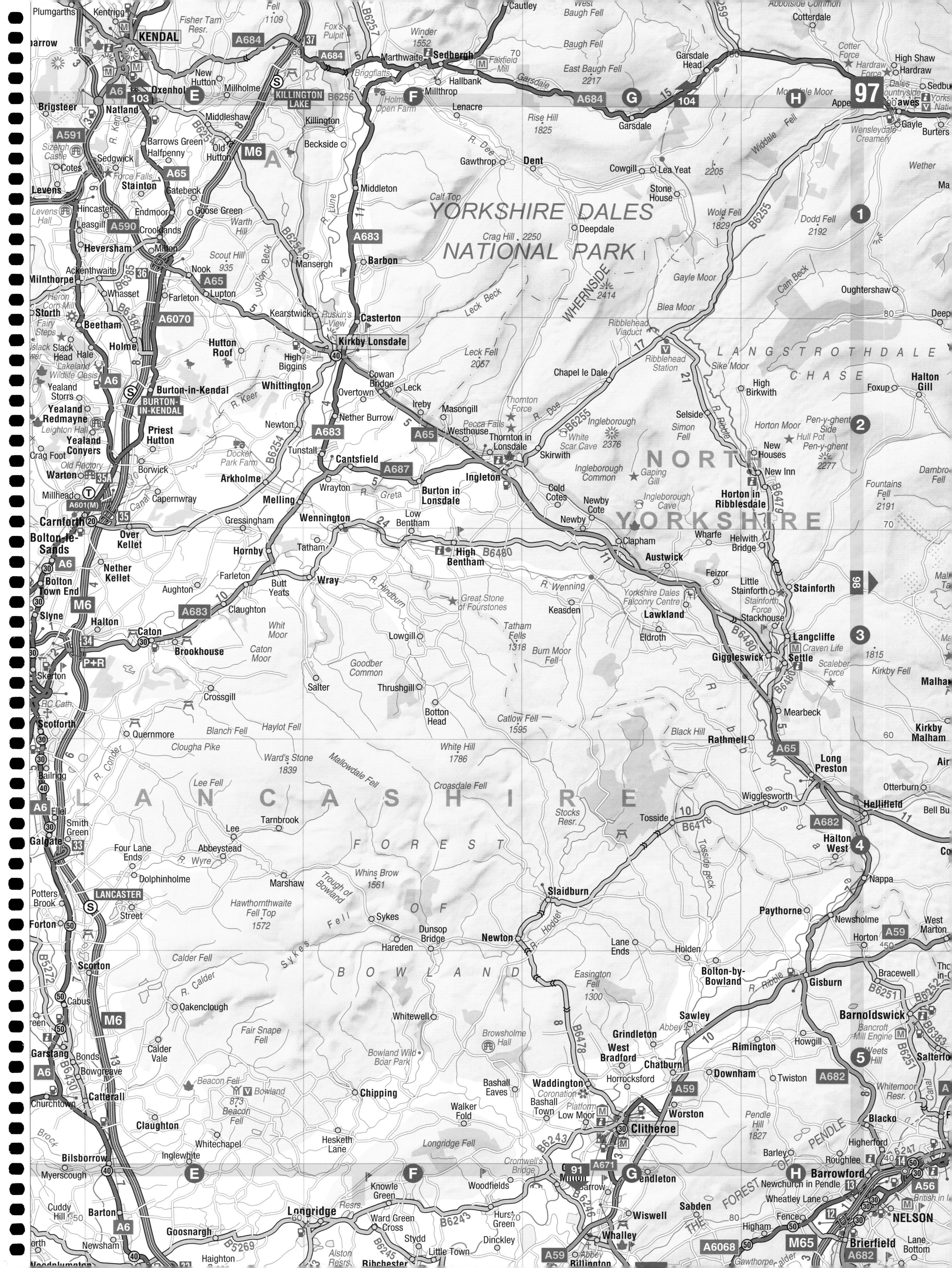
KENDAL
Plumgarths
Kentrigg
Fisher Tarn Resr.
A684
37
A684
Sedbergh
Marthwaite
Winder 1552
Fox's Pulpit
B6257
Cautley
Baugh Fell
Garsdale Head
Cotterdale
Cotter Force
Hardraw Force
High Shaw
Hardraw
97
Oxenholme
Millholme
New Hutton
KILLINGTON LAKE
Hallbank
Millthrop
Fairfield Mill
Briggflatts
Holme Open Farm
B6256
East Baugh Fell 2217
A684
Garsdale
104
Moorcock Moor
Appersett
Hawes
Gayle
Burtersett
Wensleydale Creamery
Dales Countryside Museum
Brigsteer
Natland
103
A6
A591
Sizergh Castle
Cotes
Sedgwick
Force Falls
Stainton
Middleshaw
Killington
Lenacre
Rise Hill 1825
Beckside
Barrows Green
Halfpenny
Old Hutton
M6
A65
B6254
R. Kent
R. Dee
Gawthrop
Dent
Cowgill
Lea Yeat
Stone House
2205
Widdale Fell
Wether Fell
Levens
Levens Hall
Hincaster
Leasgill
A590
Heversham
Endmoor
Gatebeck
Goose Green
Crooklands
Milton
Warth Hill
Middleton
Calf Top
YORKSHIRE DALES
NATIONAL PARK
Crag Hill 2250
Deepdale
Wold Fell 1829
B6255
Dodd Fell 2192
1
A683
Mansergh
Barbon
R. Lune
Scout Hill 935
Lupton Beck
Ackenthwaite
Milnthorpe
Heron Corn Mill
Whasset
B6385
36
Nook
A65
Lupton
Farleton
A6070
B6384
Storth
Fairy Steps
Beetham
Hale
Holme
Slack Head
Lakeland Wildlife Oasis
Kearstwick
Ruskin's View
Casterton
Kirkby Lonsdale
Hutton Roof
High Biggins
Leck Beck
WHERNSIDE 2414
Gayle Moor
Blea Moor
Cam Beck
Oughtershaw
Ribblehead Viaduct
Ribblehead Station
Leck Fell 2057
LANGSTROTHDALE
CHASE
Sike Moor
Chapel le Dale
High Birkwith
Foxup
Halton Gill
Yealand Storrs
Yealand Redmayne
Leighton Hall
Yealand Conyers
Burton-in-Kendal
BURTON-IN-KENDAL
Priest Hutton
Whittington
Cowan Bridge
Leck
Overtown
Ireby
Nether Burrow
Masongill
Thornton Force
Pecca Falls
Westhouse
Thornton in Lonsdale
R. Doe
B6255
Ingleborough 2376
White Scar Cave
Selside
Simon Fell
R. Ribble
Horton Moor
Pen-y-ghent Side
Pen-y-ghent 2277
Hull Pot
2
Crag Foot
Old Rectory
Warton
35A
Millhead
Carnforth
A601(M)
35
20
Borwick
Docker Park Farm
Newton
Tunstall
A683
Cantsfield
A687
A65
Skirwith
Ingleton
Ingleborough Common
Gaping Gill
NORTH
YORKSHIRE
New Houses
New Inn
Horton in Ribblesdale
B6479
Fountains Fell 2191
Darnbrook Fell
Arkholme
Capernwray
Melling
Wrayton
R. Greta
Burton in Lonsdale
Low Bentham
Cold Cotes
Newby Cote
Ingleborough Cave
Newby
Clapham
Wharfe
Helwith Bridge
Bolton-le-Sands
A6
Over Kellet
Gressingham
Hornby
Wennington
Tatham
24
High Bentham
B6480
Austwick
Nether Kellet
Bolton Town End
Farleton
Butt Yeats
Wray
R. Hindburn
R. Wenning
Feizor
Little Stainforth
Stainforth
98
Aughton
M6
Slyne
Halton
34
Caton
Brookhouse
Claughton
A683
Whit Moor
Caton Moor
Great Stone of Fourstones
Tatham Fells 1318
Keasden
Yorkshire Dales Falconry Centre
Lawkland
Eldroth
Stainforth Force
Stackhouse
Langcliffe
Craven Life
3
1815
Lowgill
Burn Moor Fell
Giggleswick
Settle
B6480
Scaleber Force
Kirkby Fell
Skerton
P+R
Goodber Common
Salter
Thrushgill
Crossgill
Botton Head
Scotforth
Quernmore
Blanch Fell
Haylot Fell
Catlow Fell 1595
Black Hill
Mearbeck
Rathmell
A65
Kirkby Malham
Clougha Pike
Ward's Stone 1839
Mallowdale Fell
White Hill 1786
Long Preston
Bailrigg
R. Conder
Lee Fell
Crossdale Fell
Otterburn
LANCASHIRE
Stocks Resr.
Tosside
B6478
Wigglesworth
Hellifield
A682
Ellel
Smith Green
Lee
Tarnbrook
Galgate
33
Four Lane Ends
Abbeystead
R. Wyre
FOREST
Tosside Beck
Halton West
4
Dolphinholme
Marshaw
Trough of Bowland
Whins Brow 1561
Nappa
Slaidburn
Potters Brook
LANCASTER
Hawthornthwaite Fell Top 1572
Street
Sykes
Dunsop Bridge
OF
Paythorne
Newsholme
Forton
Fell
R. Hodder
Newton
Lane Ends
Horton
A59
West Marton
Hareden
Sykes
Holden
B5272
Scorton
Calder Fell
BOWLAND
Easington Fell 1300
Bolton-by-Bowland
Gisburn
Bracewell
R. Ribble
B6251
R. Calder
Cabus
Oakenclough
M6
Whitewell
Sawley
Barnoldswick
Bancroft Mill Engine
Fair Snape Fell
Browsholme Hall
B6478
Grindleton
Abbey
Rimington
Howgill
Garstang
Bonds
Calder Vale
Bowland Wild Boar Park
West Bradford
Chatburn
Downham
Twiston
Weets Hill
5
A6
Bowgreave
B6430
A682
Salterforth
Beacon Fell
Bowland
873 Beacon Fell
Chipping
Bashall Eaves
Waddington
Horrocksford
A59
Whitemoor Resr.
Churchtown
Catterall
Coronation Platform
Bashall Town
Low Moor
Walker Fold
Worston
Pendle Hill 1827
Blacko
Claughton
Hesketh Lane
Clitheroe
FOREST OF PENDLE
Higherford
Bilsborrow
Whitechapel
Inglewhite
Longridge Fell
B6243
Barley
Roughlee
E
F
G
H
Myerscough
Cromwell's Bridge
91
A671
Pendleton
Barrowford
Newchurch in Pendle
A56
Knowle Green
Woodfields
Mitton
Barrow
B6246
Wheatley Lane
Cuddy Hill
Barton
Longridge
Resrs.
Ward Green Cross
B6243
Hurst Green
Wiswell
Sabden
THE FOREST
Fence
NELSON
A6
Goosnargh
B5269
Stydd
Dinckley
Whalley
Higham
M65
Newsham
B6245
Little Town
A59
Abbey
A6068
Brierfield
Lane Bottom
Haighton
Alston Resrs.
Ribchester
Billington
Gawthorpe
A682

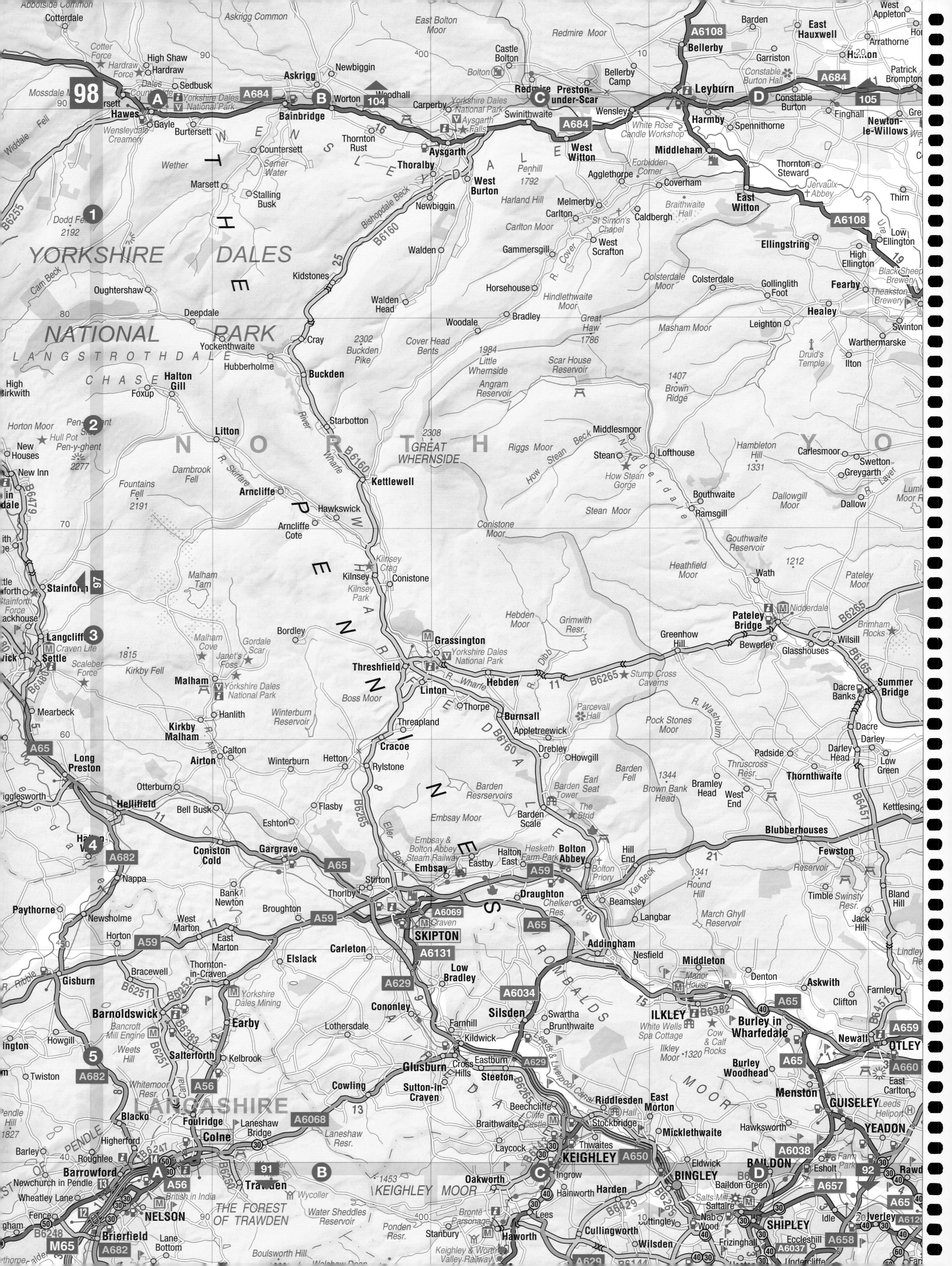
98
104
105
91
92
YORKSHIRE DALES NATIONAL PARK
NORTH YORKSHIRE
LANCASHIRE
THE PENNINES
WENSLEYDALE
LANGSTROTHDALE CHASE
NIDDERDALE
RUMBALDS MOOR
AIREDALE
KEIGHLEY MOOR
THE FOREST OF TRAWDEN
Hawes
Askrigg
Bainbridge
Aysgarth
Leyburn
Middleham
Kettlewell
Grassington
Pateley Bridge
Malham
Settle
Skipton
Keighley
Ilkley
Otley
Bingley
Shipley
Colne
Nelson
Barnoldswick
Gisburn
Hellifield
Long Preston
Great Whernside
Yeadon
Guiseley
Burley in Wharfedale
Addingham
Silsden
Haworth
Bolton Abbey
Masham Moor
Buckden Pike
Penhill

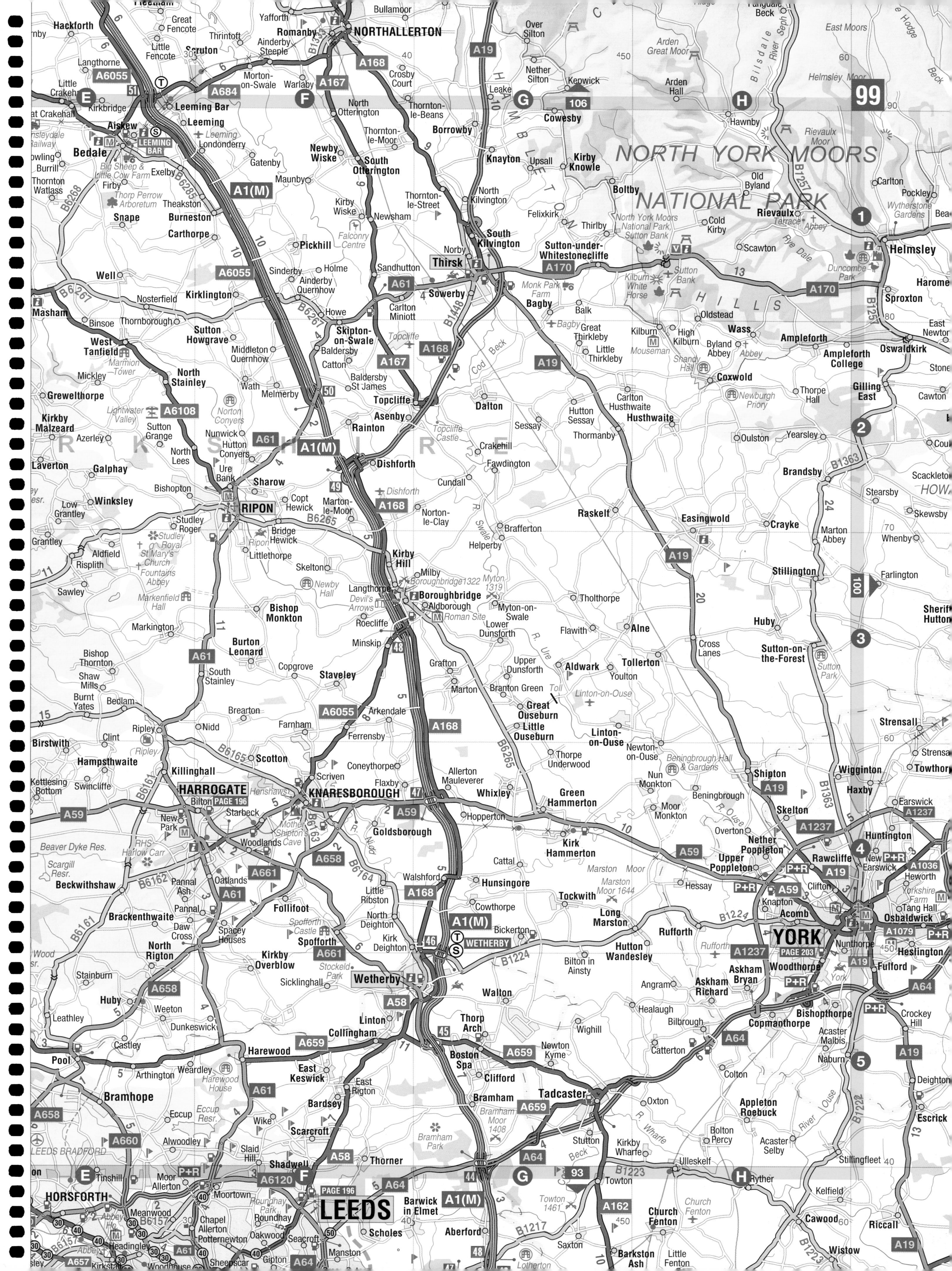
NORTHALLERTON
Hackforth
Great Fencote
Little Fencote
Scruton
Thrintoft
Yafforth
Romanby
Ainderby Steeple
Morton-on-Swale
Warlaby
Bullamoor
Crosby Court
Over Silton
Nether Silton
Kepwick
Arden Great Moor
Arden Hall
Bilsdale
River Seph
East Moors
Helmsley Moor
Langthorne
Little Crakehall
Crakehall
Kirkbridge
Aiskew
Bedale
Leeming Bar
Leeming
Londonderry
Gatenby
Exelby
Burrill
Thornton Watlass
Firby
Thorp Perrow Arboretum
Theakston
Snape
Burneston
Carthorpe
Big Sheep & Little Cow Farm
North Otterington
Thornton-le-Beans
Thornton-le-Moor
Newby Wiske
South Otterington
Maunby
Kirby Wiske
Newsham
Thornton-le-Street
Borrowby
Knayton
Upsall
Kirby Knowle
Cowesby
Leake
Hawnby
Rievaulx Moor
Rievaulx
NORTH YORK MOORS
NATIONAL PARK
Old Byland
Boltby
Felixkirk
Thirlby
North Kilvington
South Kilvington
Sutton-under-Whitestonecliffe
North York Moors National Park, Sutton Bank
Sutton Bank
Cold Kirby
Scawton
Rye Dale
Carlton
Pockley
Wytherstone Gardens
Helmsley
Duncombe Park
Harome
Sproxton
Pickhill
Falconry Centre
Sinderby
Holme
Ainderby Quernhow
Sandhutton
Norby
Thirsk
Sowerby
Carlton Miniott
Monk Park Farm
Bagby
Balk
Kilburn White Horse
Kilburn
High Kilburn
Mouseman
Oldstead
Wass
Byland Abbey
Shandy Hall
Coxwold
Ampleforth
Ampleforth College
Gilling East
Oswaldkirk
East Newton
Stonegrave
Cawton
Well
Masham
Nosterfield
Kirklington
Binsoe
Thornborough
Howe
Skipton-on-Swale
Baldersby
Catton
Topcliffe
Great Thirkleby
Little Thirkleby
Cod Beck
West Tanfield
Marmion Tower
Sutton Howgrave
Middleton Quernhow
North Stainley
Mickley
Grewelthorpe
Wath
Melmerby
Baldersby St James
Asenby
Rainton
Dalton
Hutton Sessay
Sessay
Carlton Husthwaite
Husthwaite
Newburgh Priory
Thorpe Hall
Kirkby Malzeard
Lightwater Valley
Norton Conyers
Nunwick
Hutton Conyers
Sutton Grange
Azerley
North Lees
Topcliffe Castle
Crakehill
Thormanby
Oulston
Yearsley
Laverton
Galphay
Ure Bank
Dishforth
Fawdington
Cundall
Brandsby
Stearsby
Scackleton
Sharow
Bishopton
RIPON
Copt Hewick
Marton-le-Moor
Norton-le-Clay
Raskelf
Easingwold
Crayke
Skewsby
Low Grantley
Winksley
Studley Roger
Studley Royal
Bridge Hewick
Brafferton
Helperby
Marton Abbey
Whenby
Grantley
Aldfield
Risplith
St Mary's Church
Fountains Abbey
Littlethorpe
Skelton
Kirby Hill
Milby
Boroughbridge 1322
Myton 1319
Stillington
Farlington
Sawley
Markenfield Hall
Newby Hall
Langthorpe
Devil's Arrows
Boroughbridge
Aldborough
Roman Site
Myton-on-Swale
Tholthorpe
Bishop Monkton
Roecliffe
Lower Dunsforth
Flawith
Alne
Huby
Sheriff Hutton
Markington
Burton Leonard
Minskip
Cross Lanes
Sutton-on-the-Forest
Sutton Park
Bishop Thornton
Shaw Mills
Copgrove
Staveley
Grafton
Upper Dunsforth
Aldwark
Tollerton
Youlton
South Stainley
Marton
Branton Green
Toll
Linton-on-Ouse
Burnt Yates
Bedlam
Brearton
Arkendale
Great Ouseburn
Little Ouseburn
Strensall
Ripley
Nidd
Farnham
Ferrensby
Linton-on-Ouse
Newton-on-Ouse
Birstwith
Clint
Scotton
Thorpe Underwood
Beningbrough Hall & Gardens
Shipton
Hampsthwaite
Killinghall
Coneythorpe
Allerton Mauleverer
Nun Monkton
Wigginton
Towthorpe
Kettlesing Bottom
Swincliffe
HARROGATE
PAGE 196
Bilton
Henshaws
Scriven
KNARESBOROUGH
Flaxby
Whixley
Green Hammerton
Beningbrough
Haxby
Earswick
New Park
Starbeck
Mother Shipton's Cave
Goldsborough
Hopperton
Moor Monkton
R. Ouse
Skelton
Nether Poppleton
Overton
Huntington
Beaver Dyke Res.
RHS Harlow Carr
Woodlands
R. Nidd
Kirk Hammerton
Upper Poppleton
Rawcliffe
New Earswick
Heworth
Scargill Resr.
Beckwithshaw
Pannal Ash
Oatlands
Cattal
Marston Moor
Marston Moor 1644
Hessay
Clifton
Walshford
Hunsingore
Little Ribston
Pannal
Follifoot
Tockwith
Knapton
Acomb
Yorkshire Farm
Brackenthwaite
Spofforth Castle
Spofforth
North Deighton
Cowthorpe
Long Marston
Rufforth
Tang Hall
Osbaldwick
Daw Cross
Spacey Houses
Kirk Deighton
WETHERBY
Bickerton
YORK
PAGE 203
Nunthorpe
North Rigton
Kirkby Overblow
Stockeld Park
Hutton Wandesley
Heslington
Wetherby
Bilton in Ainsty
Askham Bryan
Askham Richard
Woodthorpe
Fulford
Stainburn
Sicklinghall
Angram
Huby
Weeton
Walton
Healaugh
Bishopthorpe
Crockey Hill
Leathley
Dunkeswick
Linton
Thorp Arch
Wighill
Bilbrough
Copmanthorpe
Castley
Collingham
Acaster Malbis
Pool
Harewood
Boston Spa
Newton Kyme
Catterton
Naburn
Arthington
Weardley
Harewood House
East Keswick
Clifford
Colton
Deighton
Bramhope
East Rigton
Bramham
Tadcaster
Oxton
Appleton Roebuck
Escrick
Eccup
Eccup Resr.
Bardsey
Bramham Moor 1408
R. Wharfe
River Ouse
Wike
Scarcroft
Bramham Park
Stutton
Kirkby Wharfe
Bolton Percy
Acaster Selby
Alwoodley
LEEDS BRADFORD
Slaid Hill
Shadwell
Thorner
Ulleskelf
Stillingfleet
Tinshill
Moor Allerton
Towton
Ryther
Kelfield
HORSFORTH
Moortown
Roundhay Park
Roundhay
LEEDS
Barwick in Elmet
Towton 1461
Church Fenton
Cawood
Riccall
Meanwood
Chapel Allerton
Potternewton
Oakwood
Seacroft
Scholes
Aberford
Saxton
Barkston Ash
Little Fenton
Wistow
Headingley
Sheepscar
Gipton
Manston
Lotherton
A1(M)
A6055
A684
A167
A168
A19
A61
A6108
A170
A59
A658
A661
A1237
A1036
A1079
A64
A659
A58
A660
A6120
A162
A657
B1448
B6267
B6265
B6165
B6161
B6162
B6163
B6164
B1224
B1363
B1257
B1222
B1223
B1217
B6157
B6268
B6285
P+R
PAGE 196
99
100
106
93
HAMBLETON HILLS
YORKSHIRE
HOWARDIAN

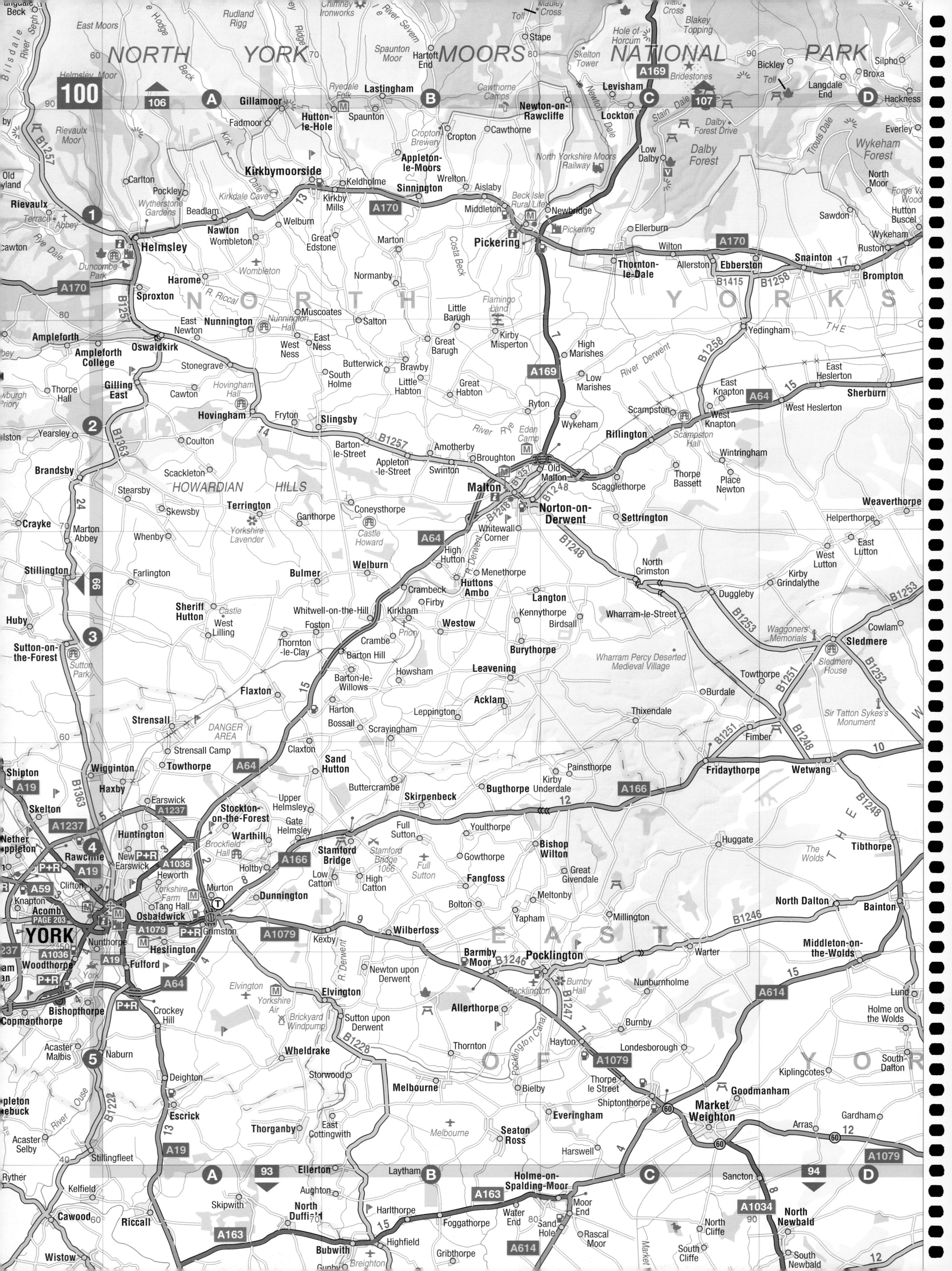

100
NORTH YORK MOORS NATIONAL PARK
106
107
A
B
C
D
Helmsley Moor
East Moors
Rudland Rigg
Chimney Ironworks
River Severn
Spaunton Moor
Hartoft End
Stape
Hole of Horcum
Skelton Tower
Blakey Topping
Bridestones
Bickley
Langdale End
Broxa
Silpho
Hackness
Gillamoor
Fadmoor
Hutton-le-Hole
Ryedale Folk
Lastingham
Spaunton
Cawthorne Camps
Newton-on-Rawcliffe
Levisham
Lockton
A169
Stain Dale
Dalby Forest Drive
Dalby Forest
Cropton Brewery
Cropton
Cawthorne
North Yorkshire Moors Railway
Low Dalby
Everley
Wykeham Forest
Trouts Dale
North Moor
Rievaulx Moor
B1257
Old Byland
Rievaulx
Rievaulx Terrace
Rievaulx Abbey
Carlton
Pockley
Wytherstone Gardens
Kirkdale Cave
Kirkbymoorside
Keldholme
Kirkby Mills
Appleton-le-Moors
Sinnington
Wrelton
Aislaby
Middleton
Beck Isle Rural Life
Newbridge
Pickering
Ellerburn
Sawdon
Hutton Buscel
Wykeham
Ruston
Beadlam
Nawton
Wombleton
Welburn
Great Edstone
Marton
Costa Beck
A170
Helmsley
Duncombe Park
Rye Dale
Harome
Sproxton
Normanby
Thornton-le-Dale
Wilton
Allerston
Ebberston
Snainton
Brompton
B1415
B1258
Ampleforth
Ampleforth College
Oswaldkirk
East Newton
Nunnington
Nunnington Hall
Muscoates
Salton
R. Riccal
West Ness
East Ness
Little Barugh
Great Barugh
Flamingo Land
Kirby Misperton
High Marishes
Low Marishes
River Derwent
Yedingham
East Heslerton
East Knapton
A64
Sherburn
West Heslerton
Scampston
West Knapton
Stonegrave
Gilling East
Thorpe Hall
Cawton
Hovingham Hall
Hovingham
Butterwick
South Holme
Brawby
Little Habton
Great Habton
Ryton
Wykeham
Rillington
Yearsley
Coulton
Fryton
Slingsby
River Rye
Eden Camp
Scampston Hall
Wintringham
Brandsby
B1363
Scackleton
HOWARDIAN HILLS
Barton-le-Street
B1257
Appleton-le-Street
Amotherby
Swinton
Broughton
Malton
Old Malton
Scagglethorpe
Thorpe Bassett
Place Newton
Stearsby
Skewsby
Terrington
Yorkshire Lavender
Ganthorpe
Coneysthorpe
Castle Howard
Norton-on-Derwent
Settrington
B1248
Weaverthorpe
Helperthorpe
East Lutton
West Lutton
Crayke
Marton Abbey
Whenby
Whitewall Corner
High Hutton
Stillington
Farlington
Bulmer
Welburn
Menethorpe
Huttons Ambo
Crambeck
North Grimston
Kirby Grindalythe
Duggleby
B1253
Sheriff Hutton
Castle
West Lilling
Whitwell-on-the-Hill
Firby
Kirkham
Westow
Langton
Kennythorpe
Birdsall
Wharram-le-Street
Huby
Sutton-on-the-Forest
Sutton Park
Foston
Thornton-le-Clay
Crambe
Barton Hill
Priory
Burythorpe
Waggoners' Memorials
Sledmere
Sledmere House
Cowlam
B1252
Wharram Percy Deserted Medieval Village
Flaxton
Barton-le-Willows
Howsham
Leavening
Towthorpe
Burdale
B1251
Strensall
DANGER AREA
Harton
Bossall
Scrayingham
Leppington
Acklam
Thixendale
Sir Tatton Sykes's Monument
Strensall Camp
Claxton
Sand Hutton
Fimber
Shipton
A19
Wigginton
Towthorpe
Paînsthorpe
Fridaythorpe
Wetwang
Haxby
Buttercrambe
Kirby Underdale
A166
Skelton
Earswick
A1237
Stockton-on-the-Forest
Upper Helmsley
Gate Helmsley
Skirpenbeck
Bugthorpe
Nether Poppleton
Huntington
Warthill
Full Sutton
Youlthorpe
Bishop Wilton
Huggate
Tibthorpe
The Wolds
Rawcliffe
New Earswick
A1036
Brockfield Hall
Holtby
Stamford Bridge
Stamford Bridge 1066
Gowthorpe
Great Givendale
P+R
Clifton
Heworth
Low Catton
High Catton
Full Sutton
Fangfoss
A59
Knapton
Acomb
Murton
Yorkshire Farm
Dunnington
Meltonby
North Dalton
Bainton
Tang Hall
Osbaldwick
Bolton
Yapham
Millington
B1246
PAGE 203
YORK
A1079
Grimston
Wilberfoss
Kexby
Nunthorpe
Heslington
Fulford
Woodthorpe
EAST
Barmby Moor
Pocklington
Warter
Middleton-on-the-Wolds
R. Derwent
Newton upon Derwent
Burnby Hall
Nunburnholme
A614
Lund
Elvington
Yorkshire Air
Bishopthorpe
Copmanthorpe
Crockey Hill
Brickyard Windpump
Sutton upon Derwent
Allerthorpe
Pocklington Canal
B1247
Holme on the Wolds
Burnby
Acaster Malbis
Naburn
Wheldrake
B1228
Thornton
Hayton
Londesborough
South Dalton
Deighton
Storwood
Melbourne
Bielby
Thorpe le Street
Kiplingcotes
Goodmanham
Appleton Roebuck
River Ouse
Escrick
B1222
Thorganby
East Cottingwith
Melbourne
Seaton Ross
Everingham
Shiptonthorpe
Market Weighton
Gardham
Arras
Acaster Selby
Stillingfleet
Harswell
Ryther
Ellerton
Laytham
Holme-on-Spalding-Moor
Sancton
93
94
Kelfield
Aughton
A163
A1034
Skipwith
North Duffield
Harlthorpe
Water End
Moor End
North Newbald
Cawood
Riccall
Foggathorpe
Sand Hole
Rascal Moor
North Cliffe
Highfield
A614
Wistow
Bubwith
Gribthorpe
South Cliffe
South Newbald
Breighton

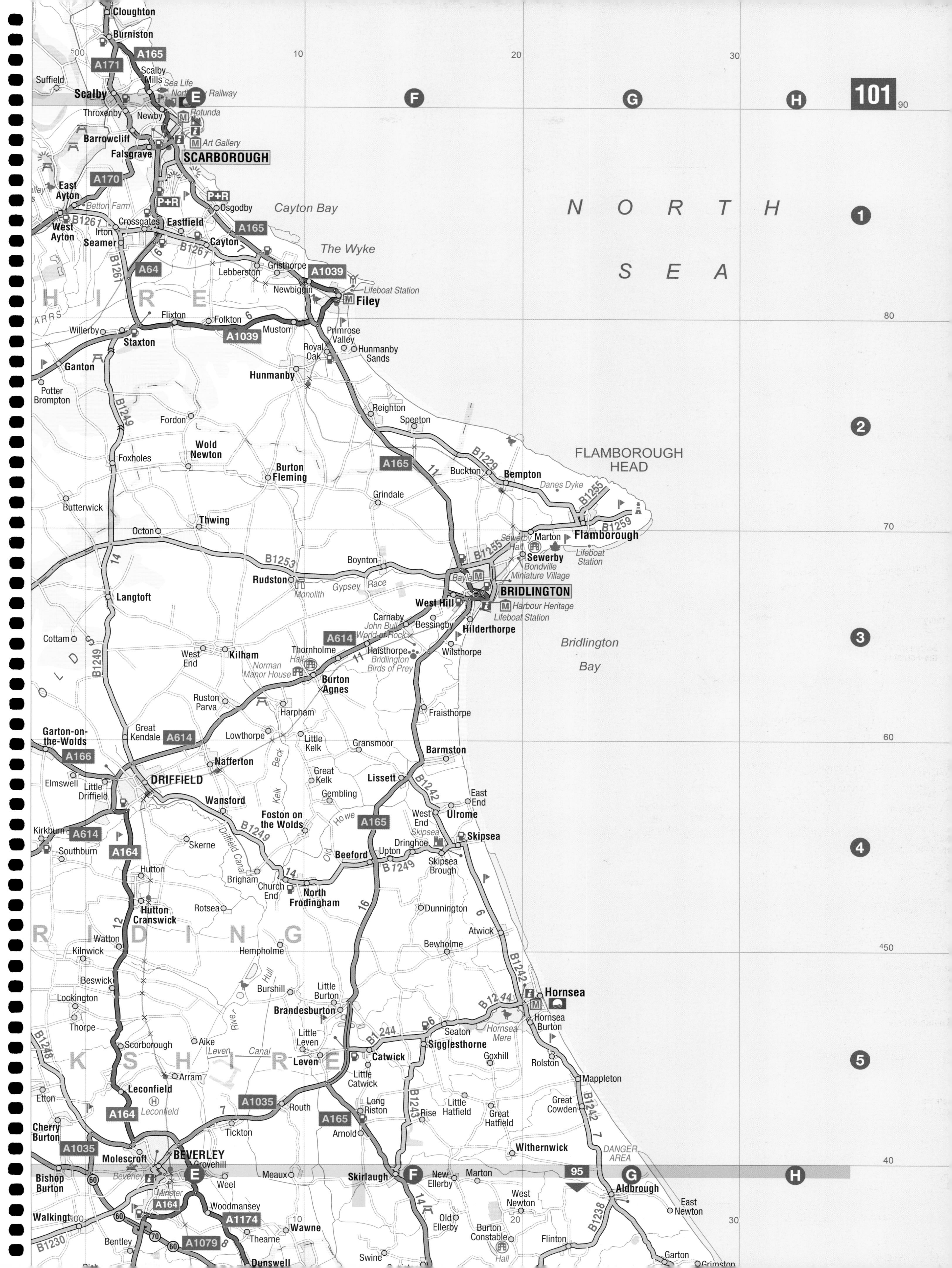
NORTH SEA
Cayton Bay
The Wyke
FLAMBOROUGH HEAD
Bridlington Bay
Cloughton
Burniston
Suffield
Scalby
Scalby Mills
Sea Life
North Bay Railway
Throxenby
Newby
Rotunda
Barrowcliff
Art Gallery
Falsgrave
SCARBOROUGH
East Ayton
Betton Farm
West Ayton
Irton
Seamer
Crossgates
Eastfield
Osgodby
Cayton
Lebberston
Gristhorpe
Newbiggin
Lifeboat Station
Filey
Flixton
Folkton
Muston
Willerby
Staxton
Primrose Valley
Royal Oak
Hunmanby Sands
Ganton
Hunmanby
Potter Brompton
Reighton
Speeton
Fordon
Wold Newton
Foxholes
Burton Fleming
Buckton
Bempton
Danes Dyke
Grindale
Butterwick
Thwing
Octon
Flamborough
Sewerby Hall
Marton
Sewerby
Bondville Miniature Village
Lifeboat Station
Boynton
Rudston
Monolith
Gypsey Race
Bayle
BRIDLINGTON
Langtoft
West Hill
Harbour Heritage
Lifeboat Station
Carnaby
John Bull World of Rock
Bessingby
Hilderthorpe
Cottam
West End
Kilham
Thornholme
Haisthorpe
Bridlington Birds of Prey
Wilsthorpe
Norman Manor House
Burton Agnes
Ruston Parva
Harpham
Fraisthorpe
Great Kendale
Lowthorpe
Little Kelk
Gransmoor
Barmston
Garton-on-the-Wolds
Nafferton
Beck
Great Kelk
Lissett
Elmswell
Little Driffield
DRIFFIELD
Gembling
East End
Wansford
Kelk
Foston on the Wolds
Howe
West End
Ulrome
Skipsea
Kirkburn
Skerne
Driffield Canal
Dringhoe
Southburn
Old
Beeford
Upton
Skipsea Brough
Hutton
Brigham
Church End
North Frodingham
Rotsea
Dunnington
Hutton Cranswick
Atwick
Watton
Bewholme
Kilnwick
Hempholme
Beswick
Hull
Burshill
Little Burton
Hornsea
Lockington
Brandesburton
River
Hornsea Burton
Thorpe
Seaton
Hornsea Mere
Scorborough
Aike
Little Leven
Sigglesthorne
Leven Canal
Leven
Catwick
Goxhill
Rolston
Arram
Little Catwick
Mappleton
Leconfield
Etton
Long Riston
Little Hatfield
Great Cowden
Routh
Rise
Great Hatfield
Cherry Burton
Tickton
Arnold
Withernwick
Molescroft
BEVERLEY
Grovehill
DANGER AREA
Bishop Burton
Beverley
Weel
Meaux
Skirlaugh
New Ellerby
Marton
Aldbrough
Minster
West Newton
Walkington
Woodmansey
Old Ellerby
East Newton
Wawne
Burton Constable
Thearne
Bentley
Flinton
Hall
Swine
Garton
Dunswell
Grimston
H I R E
R I D I N G
K S H I R E
W O L D S
A165
A171
A170
A64
A1039
A614
A166
A164
A1035
A1174
A1079
B1261
B1249
B1229
B1255
B1259
B1253
B1242
B1244
B1243
B1238
B1248
B1230
P+R
E F G H
1 2 3 4 5
10 20 30
90 80 70 60 450 40
95

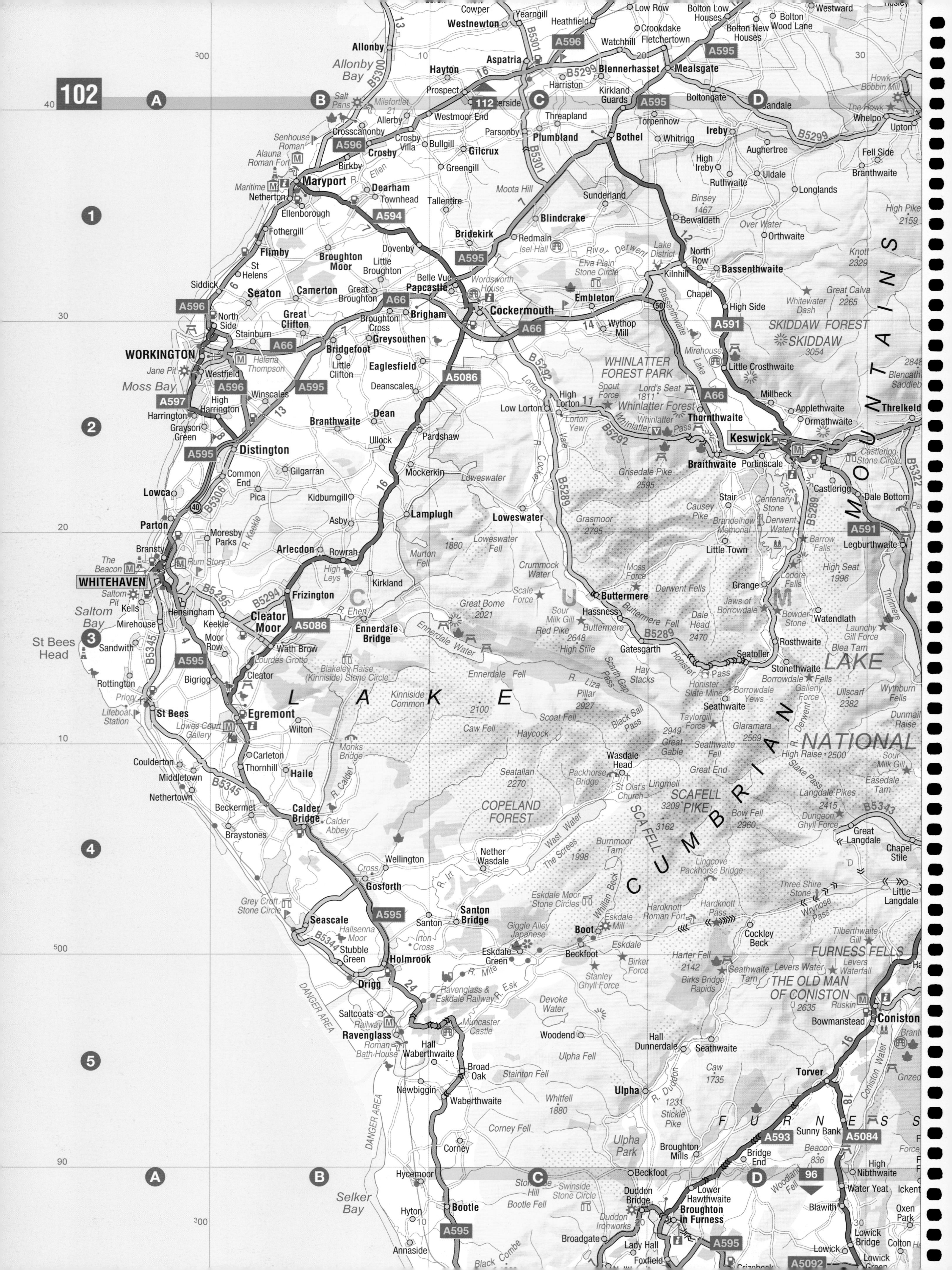
Cowper
Westnewton
Yearngill
Heathfield
Low Row
Bolton Low Houses
Bolton
Westward
Crookdake
Bolton New Houses
Wood Lane
Allonby
Allonby Bay
Watchhill
Fletchertown
A596
A595
Hayton
Aspatria
Blennerhasset
Mealsgate
Prospect
Harriston
Kirkland Guards
Boltongate
Howk
Bobbin Mill
Salt Pans
Milefortlet 21
112
A
B
C
D
Sandale
The Howk
Whelpo
Upton
Allerby
Westmoor End
Threapland
Torpenhow
Crosscanonby
Parsonby
Plumbland
Bothel
Whitrigg
Ireby
Senhouse Roman
Crosby Villa
Bullgill
Crosby
Gilcrux
Aughertree
Fell Side
Alauna Roman Fort
Birkby
Greengill
High Ireby
Uldale
Branthwaite
Maritime
Maryport
Dearham
Ruthwaite
Longlands
Netherton
Townhead
Tallentire
Moota Hill
Sunderland
Binsey 1467
High Pike 2159
Ellenborough
A594
Blindcrake
Bewaldeth
Over Water
Orthwaite
Fothergill
Bridekirk
Redmain
Isel Hall
River Derwent
Lake District
Flimby
Dovenby
North Row
Knott 2329
Broughton Moor
Little Broughton
A595
Elva Plain Stone Circle
Bassenthwaite
St Helens
Belle Vue
Kilnhill
Siddick
Seaton
Camerton
Great Broughton
Papcastle
Wordsworth House
Embleton
Chapel
Great Calva 2265
Whitewater Dash
A596
A66
Cockermouth
Wythop Mill
High Side
North Side
Great Clifton
Broughton Cross
Brigham
A66
A591
SKIDDAW FOREST
SKIDDAW 3054
Stainburn
Greysouthen
Bassenthwaite Lake
WORKINGTON
A66
Bridgefoot
Mirehouse
Jane Pit
Helena Thompson
Little Clifton
Eaglesfield
WHINLATTER FOREST PARK
Little Crosthwaite
Westfield
Moss Bay
A596
A595
A5086
B5292
Spout Force
Lord's Seat 1811
Blencathra Saddleback
A597
High Harrington
Winscales
Deanscales
High Lorton
Whinlatter Forest
A66
Millbeck
Harrington
Low Lorton
Thornthwaite
Applethwaite
Threlkeld
Grayson Green
Branthwaite
Dean
Lorton Vale
Whinlatter Pass
Ormathwaite
Keswick
Distington
Ullock
Pardshaw
B5292
Castlerigg Stone Circle
A595
Braithwaite
Portinscale
Gilgarran
Mockerkin
Loweswater
Common End
Grisedale Pike 2595
Lowca
Pica
Kidburngill
Castlerigg
Dale Bottom
Stair
Centenary Stone
B5289
B5306
Causey Pike
Lamplugh
Loweswater
Parton
Asby
Grasmoor 2795
Brandelhow Memorial
Derwent Water
A591
Moresby Parks
R. Keekle
Loweswater Fell
Barrow Falls
Legburthwaite
Bransty
Arlecdon
Rowrah
1880
Murton Fell
Little Town
The Beacon
Rum Story
High Leys
Crummock Water
Moss Force
Lodore Falls
High Seat 1996
WHITEHAVEN
Kirkland
Grange
Thirlmere
Saltom Pit
B5295
B5294
Frizington
Scale Force
Buttermere
Derwent Fells
Jaws of Borrowdale
Saltom Bay
Kells
Hensingham
R. Ehen
Great Borne 2021
Sour Milk Gill
Hassness
Dale Head 2470
Bowder Stone
Watendlath
Mirehouse
Keekle
Cleator Moor
A5086
Ennerdale Bridge
Ennerdale Water
Red Pike 2648
Buttermere Fell
B5289
Launchy Gill Force
St Bees Head
Sandwith
Moor Row
Wath Brow
High Stile
Gatesgarth
Rosthwaite
Blea Tarn
B5345
A595
Lourdes Grotto
Scarth Gap Pass
Honister Pass
Seatoller
Stonethwaite
LAKE
Bigrigg
Cleator
Blakeley Raise (Kinniside) Stone Circle
Ennerdale Fell
R. Liza
Hay Stacks
Borrowdale
Rottington
Priory
Kinniside Common
Pillar 2927
Honister Slate Mine
Borrowdale Yews
Galleny Force
Ullscarf 2382
Wythburn Fells
Lifeboat Station
St Bees
Egremont
L
A
K
E
2100
Scoat Fell
Black Sail Pass
Seathwaite
Taylorgill Force
Dunmail Raise
Lowes Court Gallery
Wilton
Caw Fell
Haycock
2949
Great Gable
Glaramara 2569
NATIONAL
Carleton
Monks Bridge
Wasdale Head
Seathwaite Fell
High Raise 2500
Sour Milk Gill
Couldert
Thornhill
Haile
Seatallan 2270
Packhorse Bridge
Great End
Stake Pass
Easedale Tarn
Middletown
R. Calder
St Olaf's Church
Lingmell
SCAFELL PIKE 3209
Langdale Pikes 2415
Nethertown
B5345
COPELAND FOREST
3162
Bow Fell 2960
Dungeon Ghyll Force
B5343
Beckermet
Calder Bridge
Calder Abbey
Wast Water
SCA FELL
Great Langdale
Braystones
Burnmoor Tarn
The Screes 1998
Chapel Stile
Nether Wasdale
Wellington
Lingcove Packhorse Bridge
Cross
Gosforth
R. Irt
CUMBRIAN
Three Shire Stone
Little Langdale
Grey Croft Stone Circle
Eskdale Moor Stone Circles
Whillan Beck
Hardknott Roman Fort
Hardknott Pass
Wrynose Pass
Seascale
A595
Santon
Santon Bridge
Giggle Alley Japanese
Boot
Eskdale Mill
Cockley Beck
Tilberthwaite Gill
Hallsenna Moor
Irton Cross
B5344
Stubble Green
Holmrook
Eskdale Green
Beckfoot
Eskdale
Birker Force
Harter Fell 2142
Seathwaite Tarn
Levers Water
FURNESS FELLS
Levers Waterfall
R. Mite
Stanley Ghyll Force
Birks Bridge Rapids
THE OLD MAN OF CONISTON 2635
Drigg
Ravenglass & Eskdale Railway
R. Esk
DANGER AREA
Devoke Water
Ruskin
Saltcoats
Railway
Muncaster Castle
Bowmanstead
Coniston
Ravenglass
Woodend
Hall Dunnerdale
Seathwaite
Roman Bath House
Hall Waberthwaite
Ulpha Fell
Broad Oak
Stainton Fell
Caw 1735
Torver
Coniston Water
Newbiggin
Waberthwaite
Ulpha
R. Duddon
Whitfell 1880
1231 Stickle Pike
F
U
R
N
E
S
S
DANGER AREA
Corney Fell
A593
Sunny Bank
A5084
Corney
Ulpha Park
Broughton Mills
Bridge End
Beacon 836
High Nibthwaite
Beckfoot
Woodland Fell
96
Hycemoor
Stoneside Hill
Swinside Stone Circle
Duddon Bridge
Lower Hawthwaite
Water Yeat
Selker Bay
Bootle Fell
Broughton in Furness
Blawith
Hyton
Bootle
Duddon Ironworks
Oxen Park
A595
Broadgate
Lowick Bridge
Colton
Annaside
Lady Hall
A595
Lowick
Black Combe
Foxfield
A5092
Lowick Green
1
2
3
4
5
40
30
20
10
500
90
300

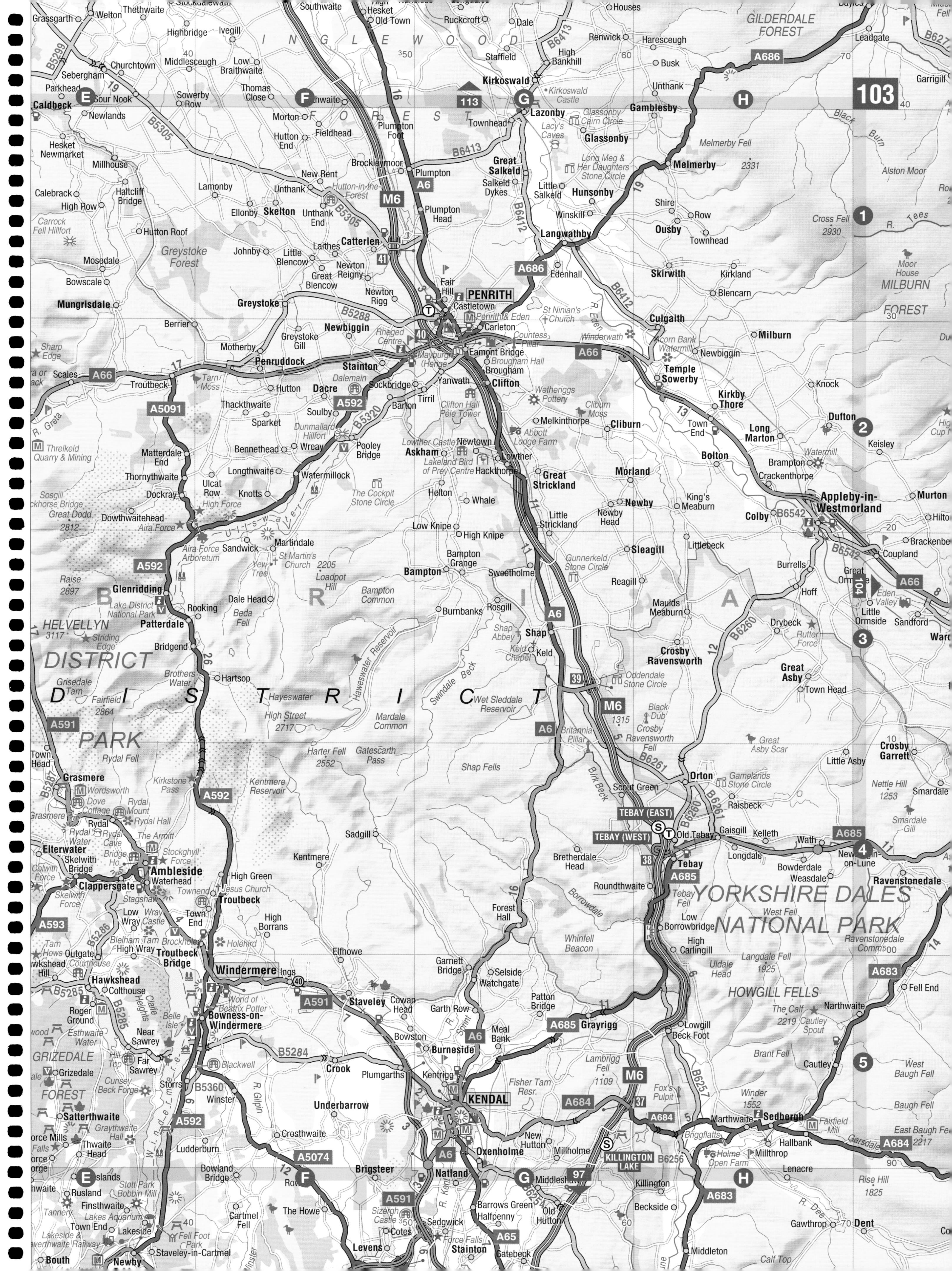

103
104
113
97
E
F
G
H
1
2
3
4
5
INGLEWOOD FOREST
GILDERDALE FOREST
MILBURN FOREST
LAKE DISTRICT NATIONAL PARK
YORKSHIRE DALES NATIONAL PARK
HOWGILL FELLS
GRIZEDALE FOREST
Grassgarth
Welton
Thethwaite
Southwaite
Hesket
Old Town
Ruckcroft
Dale
Houses
Highbridge
Ivegill
Renwick
Haresceugh
Leadgate
Churchtown
Middlesceugh
Low Braithwaite
Staffield
High Bankhill
Busk
Garrigill
Sebergham
Parkhead
Caldbeck
Sour Nook
Thomas Close
Sowerby Row
Kirkoswald
Kirkoswald Castle
Unthank
Gamblesby
Newlands
Morton
Plumpton Foot
Townhead
Lazonby
Glassonby Cairn Circle
Lacy's Caves
Glassonby
Melmerby Fell
Hesket Newmarket
Hutton End
Fieldhead
Millhouse
Brockleymoor
Plumpton
Great Salkeld
Long Meg & Her Daughters Stone Circle
Melmerby
Alston Moor
New Rent
Calebrack
Haltcliff Bridge
Lamonby
Unthank
Hutton-in-the-Forest
Salkeld Dykes
Little Salkeld
Hunsonby
High Row
Carrock Fell Hillfort
Ellonby
Skelton
Unthank End
Plumpton Head
Winskill
Shire
Row
Ousby
Townhead
Cross Fell 2930
R. Tees
Hutton Roof
Catterlen
Langwathby
Mosedale
Greystoke Forest
Johnby
Little Blencow
Laithes
Newton Reigny
Great Blencow
Edenhall
Skirwith
Kirkland
Moor House
Bowscale
Fair Hill
PENRITH
Newton Rigg
Blencarn
Mungrisdale
Greystoke
Castletown
Penrith & Eden
St Ninian's Church
Culgaith
Berrier
Newbiggin
Carleton
Countess Pillar
Winderwath
Acorn Bank Watermill
Milburn
Greystoke Gill
Rheged Centre
Motherby
Mayburgh (Henge)
Eamont Bridge
Brougham Hall
Newbiggin
Sharp Edge
Scales
Penruddock
Stainton
Brougham
Temple Sowerby
Troutbeck
Tarn Moss
Hutton
Dacre
Dalemain
Sockbridge
Yanwath
Clifton
Knock
Kirkby Thore
Thackthwaite
Soulby
Tirril
Barton
Clifton Hall Pele Tower
Wetheriggs Pottery
Cliburn Moss
Sparket
Dunmallard Hillfort
Melkinthorpe
Cliburn
Town End
Long Marton
Dufton
R. Greta
Threlkeld Quarry & Mining
Matterdale End
Bennethead
Wreay
Pooley Bridge
Lowther Castle
Newtown
Abbott Lodge Farm
Bolton
Keisley
Askham
Lakeland Bird of Prey Centre
Lowther
Watermill
Brampton
Longthwaite
Watermillock
Hackthorpe
Great Strickland
Morland
Crackenthorpe
Thornythwaite
Ulcat Row
Knotts
The Cockpit Stone Circle
Helton
Whale
Newby
King's Meaburn
Appleby-in-Westmorland
Murton
Dockray
High Force
Newby Head
Sosgill Bridge
Great Dodd 2812
Dowthwaitehead
Aira Force
Little Strickland
Colby
Ullswater
Low Knipe
High Knipe
Littlebeck
Brackenber
Aira Force Arboretum
Sandwick
Martindale
St Martin's Church
Yew Tree
Loadpot Hill 2205
Bampton Grange
Sleagill
Burrells
Coupland
Raise 2897
Bampton
Sweetholme
Gunnerkeld Stone Circle
Reagill
Great Ormside
Glenridding
Lake District National Park
Dale Head
Bampton Common
Rosgill
Hoff
Eden Valley
Rooking
Beda Fell
Burnbanks
Mauld's Meaburn
Little Ormside
Sandford
HELVELLYN 3117
Patterdale
Striding Edge
Shap Abbey
Shap
Drybeck
Rutter Force
Keld Chapel
Keld
Haweswater Reservoir
Crosby Ravensworth
Bridgend
Great Asby
Brothers Water
Hartsop
Oddendale Stone Circle
Town Head
Grisedale Tarn
Swindale Beck
Fairfield 2864
Hayeswater
Wet Sleddale Reservoir
Black Dub
High Street 2717
Mardale Common
Crosby Ravensworth Fell
Britannia Pillar
Great Asby Scar
Crosby Garrett
Harter Fell 2552
Gatescarth Pass
Shap Fells
Rydal Fell
Kirkstone Pass
Kentmere Reservoir
Birk Beck
Scout Green
Orton
Gamelands Stone Circle
Little Asby
Nettle Hill 1253
Smardale
Grasmere
Wordsworth
Dove Cottage
Rydal Mount
Rydal Hall
Raisbeck
Smardale Gill
Rydal
Rydal Cave
The Armitt
Sadgill
TEBAY (EAST)
TEBAY (WEST)
Old Tebay
Gaisgill
Kelleth
Wath
Newbiggin-on-Lune
Elterwater
Skelwith Bridge
Bridge Ho.
Stockghyll Force
Kentmere
Bretherdale Head
Tebay
Longdale
Bowderdale
Ambleside
Colwith Force
Waterhead
High Green
Weasdale
Ravenstonedale
Clappersgate
Stagshaw
Townend
Jesus Church
Troutbeck
Roundthwaite
Skelwith Force
Low Wray
Wray Castle
Town End
Borrowdale
Tebay Fell
West Fell
Forest Hall
High Borrans
Low Borrowbridge
Blelham Tarn
Brockhole
Holehird
Whinfell Beacon
Ravenstonedale Common
Tarn Hows
Outgate
High Wray
Troutbeck Bridge
Elfhowe
High Carlingill
Langdale Fell 1925
Hawkshead Hill
Hawkshead Courthouse
Uldale Head
Hawkshead
Windermere
Ings
Garnett Bridge
Selside
Fell End
Colthouse
Watchgate
Patton Bridge
Roger Ground
Claife Heights
World of Beatrix Potter
Staveley
Cowan Head
Garth Row
Northwaite
The Calf 2219
Cautley Spout
Belle Isle
Bowness-on-Windermere
Grayrigg
Esthwaite Water
Near Sawrey
Bowston
Meal Bank
Lowgill
Beck Foot
Burneside
Brant Fell
Cautley
Far Sawrey
B5284
Crook
Lambrigg Fell 1109
West Baugh Fell
Hill Top
Blackwell
Plumgarths
Kentrigg
Fisher Tarn Resr.
Grizedale
Cunsey Beck Forge
Storrs
Winster
R. Gilpin
Fox's Pulpit
Winder 1552
Satterthwaite
Underbarrow
KENDAL
Baugh Fell
Graythwaite Hall
Marthwaite
Sedbergh
Fairfield Mill
East Baugh Fell 2217
Force Mills
Crosthwaite
Briggflatts
Hallbank
Garsdale
Force Falls
Thwaite Head
Lindale
Ludderburn
New Hutton
Millholme
KILLINGTON LAKE
Holme Open Farm
Millthrop
Bowland Bridge
Oxenholme
Brigsteer
Natland
Middleshaw
Lenacre
Rusland
Stott Park Bobbin Mill
Row
Killington
Rise Hill 1825
Finsthwaite
Sizergh Castle
Barrows Green
Halfpenny
Old Hutton
Tannery
Lakes Aquarium
Cartmel Fell
The Howe
Beckside
R. Dee
Town End
Lakeside
Cotes
Sedgwick
Gawthrop
Dent
Lakeside & Haverthwaite Railway
Fell Foot Park
Levens
Stainton
Gatebeck
Middleton
Staveley-in-Cartmel
Calf Top
Newby Bridge
Booth
M6
A6
A66
A686
A592
A5091
A591
A593
A685
A684
A683
A5074
A65
B5299
B5305
B6413
B6412
B5288
B5320
B6542
B6260
B6261
B5287
B5286
B5285
B5360
B6257
B6256
B6254

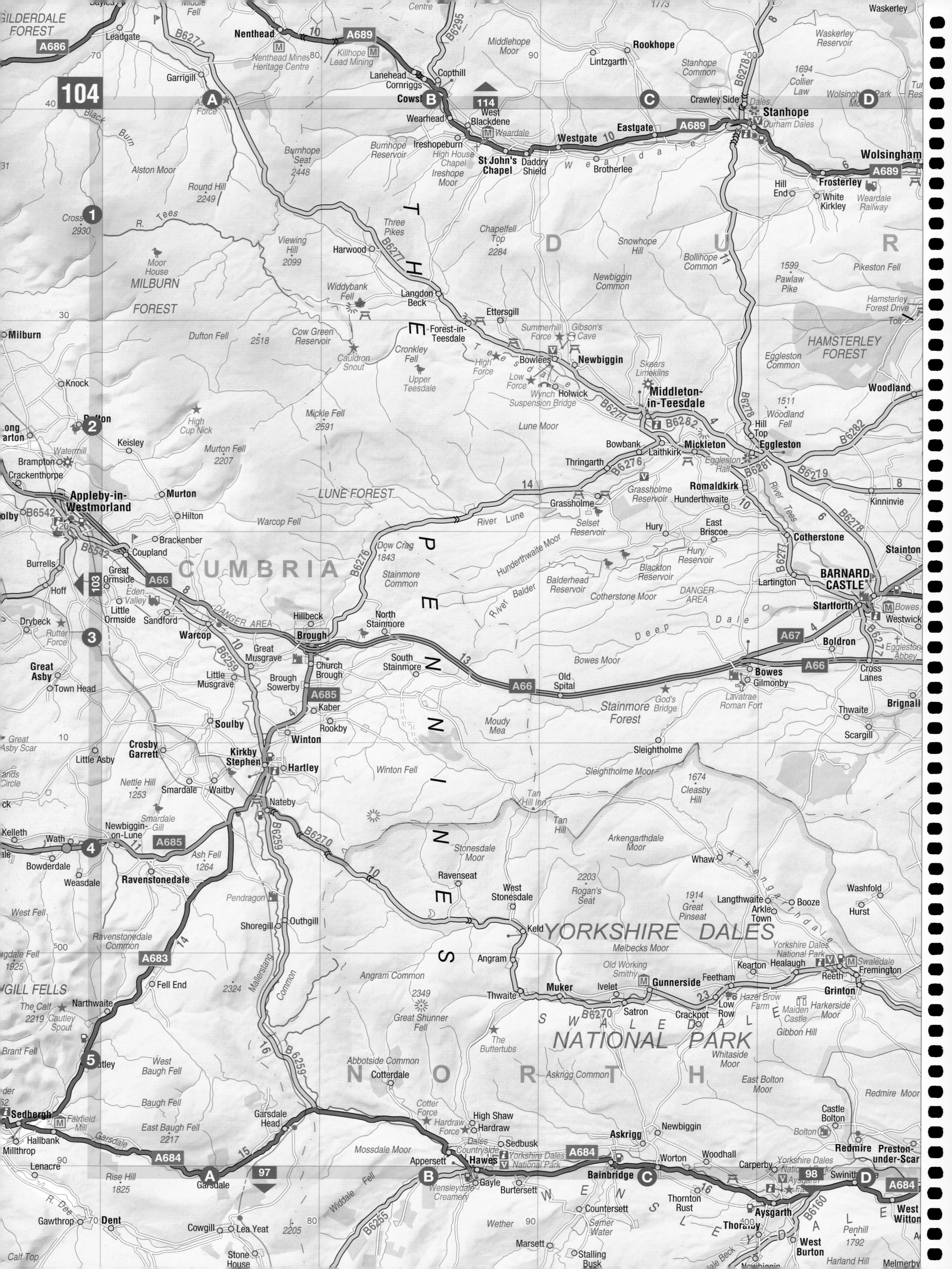
104
114
103
97
98
GILDERDALE FOREST
A686
Leadgate
Nenthead
Nenthead Mines Heritage Centre
Killhope Lead Mining
A689
B6277
B6295
Middlehope Moor
Rookhope
Lintzgarth
Stanhope Common
Waskerley
Waskerley Reservoir
Collier Law
Wolsingham Park Moor
Garrigill
Lanehead
Cornriggs
Copthill
Cowshill
West Blackdene
Wearhead
Weardale
Eastgate
Westgate
Crawley Side
Stanhope
Durham Dales
Wolsingham
Frosterley
Hill End
White Kirkley
Weardale Railway
Ireshopeburn
High House Chapel
Ireshope Moor
Burnhope Reservoir
Burnhope Seat
2448
St John's Chapel
Daddry Shield
Brotherlee
Alston Moor
Round Hill
2249
Cross Fell
2930
R. Tees
Three Pikes
Viewing Hill
2099
Harwood
Chapelfell Top
2284
Snowhope Hill
Bollihope Common
1599
Pawlaw Pike
Pikeston Fell
Moor House
MILBURN FOREST
Widdybank Fell
Langdon Beck
Newbiggin Common
Hamsterley Forest Drive
HAMSTERLEY FOREST
Ettersgill
Summerhill Force
Gibson's Cave
Eggleston Common
Milburn
Dufton Fell
2518
Cow Green Reservoir
Forest-in-Teesdale
Cronkley Fell
Cauldron Snout
High Force
Bowlees
Newbiggin
Skears Limekilns
Low Force
Wynch Suspension Bridge
Holwick
Middleton-in-Teesdale
Upper Teesdale
Woodland
1511
Woodland Fell
Knock
Dufton
High Cup Nick
Mickle Fell
2591
Lune Moor
Keisley
Watermill
Brampton
Crackenthorpe
Murton Fell
2207
Bowbank
Laithkirk
Mickleton
Hill Top
Eggleston
Eggleston Hall
B6282
B6276
B6281
B6279
Thringarth
Romaldkirk
Hunderthwaite
Grassholme
Grassholme Reservoir
Kinninvie
Appleby-in-Westmorland
Murton
LUNE FOREST
Hilton
B6542
Warcop Fell
River Lune
Selset Reservoir
Hury
East Briscoe
Hury Reservoir
Cotherstone
B6278
Brackenber
Coupland
Burrells
Dow Crag
1843
Hunderthwaite Moor
Blackton Reservoir
Stainton
CUMBRIA
Great Ormside
A66
Hoff
Eden Valley
Stainmore Common
Balderhead Reservoir
Lartington
BARNARD CASTLE
Little Ormside
Sandford
River Balder
Cotherstone Moor
DANGER AREA
Startforth
Bowes Museum
Westwick
Drybeck
Rutter Force
Warcop
Hillbeck
North Stainmore
Deep Dale
A67
Boldron
Brough
Great Musgrave
Church Brough
South Stainmore
Bowes Moor
Egglestone Abbey
Cross Lanes
Great Asby
Town Head
Little Musgrave
B6259
Brough Sowerby
Old Spital
Bowes
Gilmonby
God's Bridge
Lavatrae Roman Fort
Stainmore Forest
Brignall
Thwaite
A685
Kaber
Rookby
Moudy Mea
Scargill
Great Asby Scar
Soulby
Winton
Sleightholme
Crosby Garrett
Little Asby
Kirkby Stephen
Hartley
Winton Fell
Sleightholme Moor
1674
Cleasby Hill
Nettle Hill
1253
Smardale
Waitby
Tan Hill Inn
Nateby
Smardale Gill
Newbiggin-on-Lune
Tan Hill
Arkengarthdale Moor
Kelleth
Wath
Ash Fell
1264
B6270
Stonesdale Moor
Whaw
Arkengarthdale
Bowderdale
Weasdale
Ravenstonedale
Ravenseat
West Stonesdale
2203
Rogan's Seat
Washfold
Pendragon
1914
Great Pinseat
Langthwaite
Arkle Town
Booze
Hurst
West Fell
Shoregill
Outhgill
Keld
YORKSHIRE DALES
Ravenstonedale Common
Melbecks Moor
Yorkshire Dales National Park
A683
Angram
Old Working Smithy
Kearton
Healaugh
Swaledale
Fremington
Reeth
Angram Common
Gunnerside
Feetham
Fell End
2324
Mallerstang Common
2349
Thwaite
Muker
Ivelet
Grinton
Narthwaite
Hazel Brow Farm
Low Row
Harkerside Moor
Maiden Castle
The Calf
2219
Cautley Spout
Great Shunner Fell
Satron
Crackpot
Gibbon Hill
SWALEDALE
NATIONAL PARK
The Buttertubs
Whitaside Moor
Brant Fell
West Baugh Fell
Abbotside Common
Cotterdale
Askrigg Common
East Bolton Moor
Redmire Moor
NORTH
Baugh Fell
Cotter Force
High Shaw
Castle Bolton
Sedbergh
Fairfield Mill
Garsdale Head
Hardraw Force
Hardraw
Askrigg
Newbiggin
Bolton
Hallbank
East Baugh Fell
2217
Dales Countryside Museum
Sedbusk
Woodhall
Redmire
Preston-under-Scar
Millthrop
Garsdale
A684
Mossdale Moor
Appersett
Hawes
Yorkshire Dales National Park
Worton
Carperby
Aysgarth Falls
Swinithwaite
Lenacre
Rise Hill
1825
Gayle
Wensleydale Creamery
Burtersett
Bainbridge
Thornton Rust
WENSLEYDALE
West Witton
R. Dee
Dent
Gawthrop
Cowgill
Lea Yeat
2205
Widdale Fell
B6255
Wether Fell
Countersett
Semer Water
Aysgarth
Thoralby
B6160
West Burton
Penhill
1792
Calf Top
Stone House
Marsett
Stalling Busk
Harland Hill
Melmerby

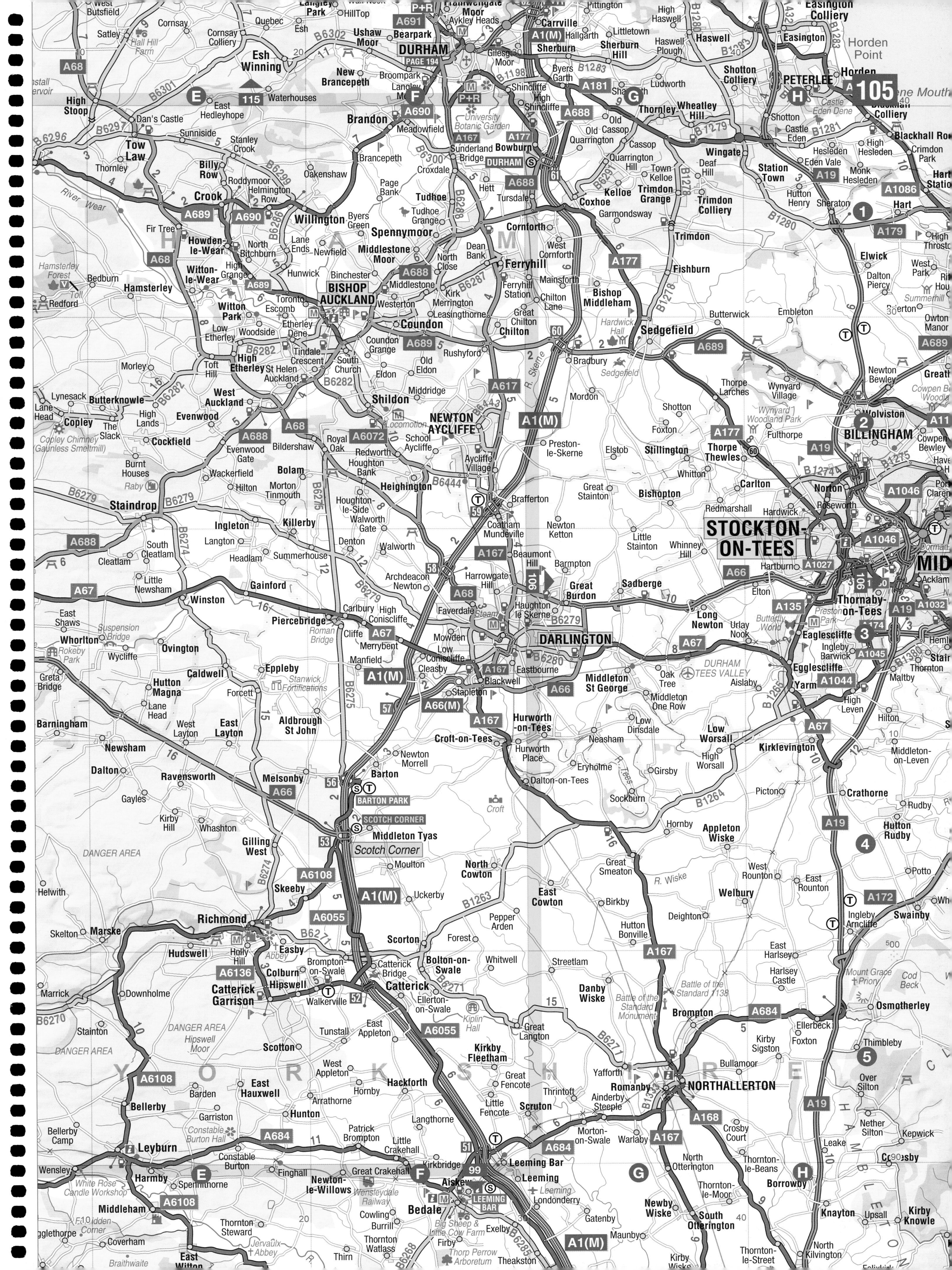

105
DURHAM
PAGE 194
PETERLEE
Easington Colliery
Horden Point
Horden
Esh Winning
Ushaw Moor
Bearpark
Carrville
Sherburn
Sherburn Hill
Haswell
Easington
Shotton Colliery
New Brancepeth
Brandon
Waterhouses
High Stoop
Dan's Castle
Tow Law
Thornley
Stanley Crook
Billy Row
Crook
Brancepeth
Meadowfield
University Botanic Garden
Bowburn
Sunderland Bridge
Croxdale
Old Cassop
Quarrington Hill
Cassop
Wingate
Station Town
Hutton Henry
Sheraton
Hart
Hesleden
Monk Hesleden
Crimdon Park
Blackhall Colliery
Castle Eden
Page Bank
Tudhoe
Tudhoe Grange
Hett
Tursdale
Coxhoe
Kelloe
Trimdon Grange
Trimdon Colliery
Trimdon
Garmondsway
Willington
Spennymoor
Cornforth
West Cornforth
Ferryhill
Ferryhill Station
Chilton
Great Chilton
Fishburn
Bishop Middleham
Sedgefield
Elwick
Dalton Piercy
Embleton
Butterwick
Howden-le-Wear
Witton-le-Wear
Hamsterley
Hamsterley Forest
Bedburn
Redford
Bishop Auckland
Middlestone Moor
Binchester
Escomb
Toronto
Witton Park
Etherley Dene
Woodside
Low Etherley
High Etherley
Toft Hill
Coundon
Coundon Grange
Leasingthorne
Merrington
Westerton
Rushyford
Tindale Crescent
St Helen Auckland
South Church
Eldon
Old Eldon
Shildon
Middridge
Newton Aycliffe
School Aycliffe
Aycliffe Village
Bradbury
Mordon
Preston-le-Skerne
Morley
Lynesack
Butterknowle
Copley
Lane Head
The Slack
West Auckland
Evenwood
Cockfield
Evenwood Gate
High Lands
Copley Chimney (Gaunless Smeltmill)
Burnt Houses
Wackerfield
Raby
Hilton
Bildershaw
Royal Oak
Redworth
Heighington
Bolam
Morton Tinmouth
Houghton Bank
Staindrop
Ingleton
Langton
Killerby
Houghton-le-Side
Walworth Gate
Walworth
Denton
South Cleatlam
Cleatlam
Headlam
Summerhouse
Little Newsham
Gainford
Winston
Archdeacon Newton
Brafferton
Coatham Mundeville
Beaumont Hill
Harrowgate Hill
Barmpton
Great Burdon
Newton Ketton
Great Stainton
Little Stainton
Bishopton
Whinney Hill
Sadberge
Elstob
Stillington
Thorpe Thewles
Whitton
Carlton
Redmarshall
Hardwick
Thorpe Larches
Wynyard Village
Wynyard Woodland Park
Fulthorpe
Newton Bewley
Wolviston
BILLINGHAM
Norton
Roseworth
STOCKTON-ON-TEES
Hartburn
Elton
Thornaby-on-Tees
Preston Park
Long Newton
Urlay Nook
Butterfly World
Eaglescliffe
Ingleby Barwick
Egglescliffe
Yarm
Aislaby
Durham Tees Valley
Oak Tree
Middleton St George
Middleton One Row
Low Dinsdale
Neasham
Low Worsall
High Worsall
Kirklevington
Picton
Crathorne
Rudby
Hutton Rudby
Middleton-on-Leven
Hilton
High Leven
Maltby
Thornton
Potto
East Shaws
Whorlton
Rokeby Park
Suspension Bridge
Wycliffe
Ovington
Piercebridge
Roman Bridge
Carlbury
High Coniscliffe
Cliffe
Merrybent
Manfield
Low Coniscliffe
Cleasby
Mowden
Faverdale
Haughton le Skerne
DARLINGTON
Blackwell
Eastbourne
Stapleton
Hurworth-on-Tees
Hurworth Place
Croft-on-Tees
Eryholme
Dalton-on-Tees
Girsby
Sockburn
Greta Bridge
Caldwell
Eppleby
Stanwick Fortifications
Forcett
Hutton Magna
Lane Head
Barningham
West Layton
East Layton
Aldbrough St John
Newsham
Dalton
Ravensworth
Melsonby
Newton Morrell
Barton
BARTON PARK
SCOTCH CORNER
Middleton Tyas
Scotch Corner
Gayles
Kirby Hill
Whashton
Gilling West
DANGER AREA
Moulton
North Cowton
Uckerby
Great Smeaton
Hornby
Appleton Wiske
West Rounton
East Rounton
R. Wiske
East Cowton
Birkby
Welbury
Deighton
Ingleby Arncliffe
Swainby
Helwith
Skeeby
Richmond
Marske
Skelton
Hudswell
Easby
Holly Hill
Brompton-on-Swale
Colburn
Hipswell
Catterick Garrison
Catterick Bridge
Catterick
Scorton
Forest
Whitwell
Bolton-on-Swale
Ellerton-on-Swale
Pepper Arden
Streetlam
Hutton Bonville
Danby Wiske
Battle of the Standard 1138
Brompton
East Harsley
Harlsey Castle
Mount Grace Priory
Cod Beck
Osmotherley
Ellerbeck
Foxton
Thimbleby
Marrick
Downholme
Walkerville
Stainton
Hipswell Moor
Tunstall
East Appleton
Kiplin Hall
Great Langton
Kirby Fleetham
Kirby Sigston
Over Silton
Scotton
West Appleton
Hornby
Hackforth
Great Fencote
Little Fencote
Yafforth
Thrintoft
Romanby
NORTHALLERTON
Bullamoor
Ainderby Steeple
Scruton
Barden
East Hauxwell
Arrathorne
Hunton
Bellerby
Garriston
Bellerby Camp
Constable Burton Hall
Langthorne
Patrick Brompton
Little Crakehall
Morton-on-Swale
Warlaby
Crosby Court
Nether Silton
Kepwick
Leyburn
Constable Burton
Wensley
Harmby
Spennithorne
Finghall
Newton-le-Willows
Great Crakehall
Kirkbridge
Aiskew
Leeming Bar
Leeming
LEEMING BAR
Londonderry
North Otterington
Thornton-le-Beans
Thornton-le-Moor
Leake
Borrowby
White Rose Candle Workshop
Middleham
Wensleydale Railway
Bedale
Newby Wiske
South Otterington
Knayton
Upsall
Kirby Knowle
Thornton Steward
Cowling
Burrill
Exelby
Gatenby
Maunby
Coverham
Jervaulx Abbey
Thornton Watlass
Firby
Big Sheep & Little Cow Farm
Thorp Perrow Arboretum
Theakston
Thirn
East Witton
Braithwaite
North Kilvington
Thornton-le-Street
Kirby Wiske
A68
A689
A690
A688
A691
A167
A177
A181
A19
A1086
A179
A617
A6072
A1(M)
A66
A66(M)
A67
A135
A1027
A1046
A1045
A1044
A6108
A6055
A6136
A684
A168
A172
A1032
B6300
B6287
B6282
B6279
B6275
B6274
B1263
B1264
B6271
B6270
B1280
B1283
B1278
B6291

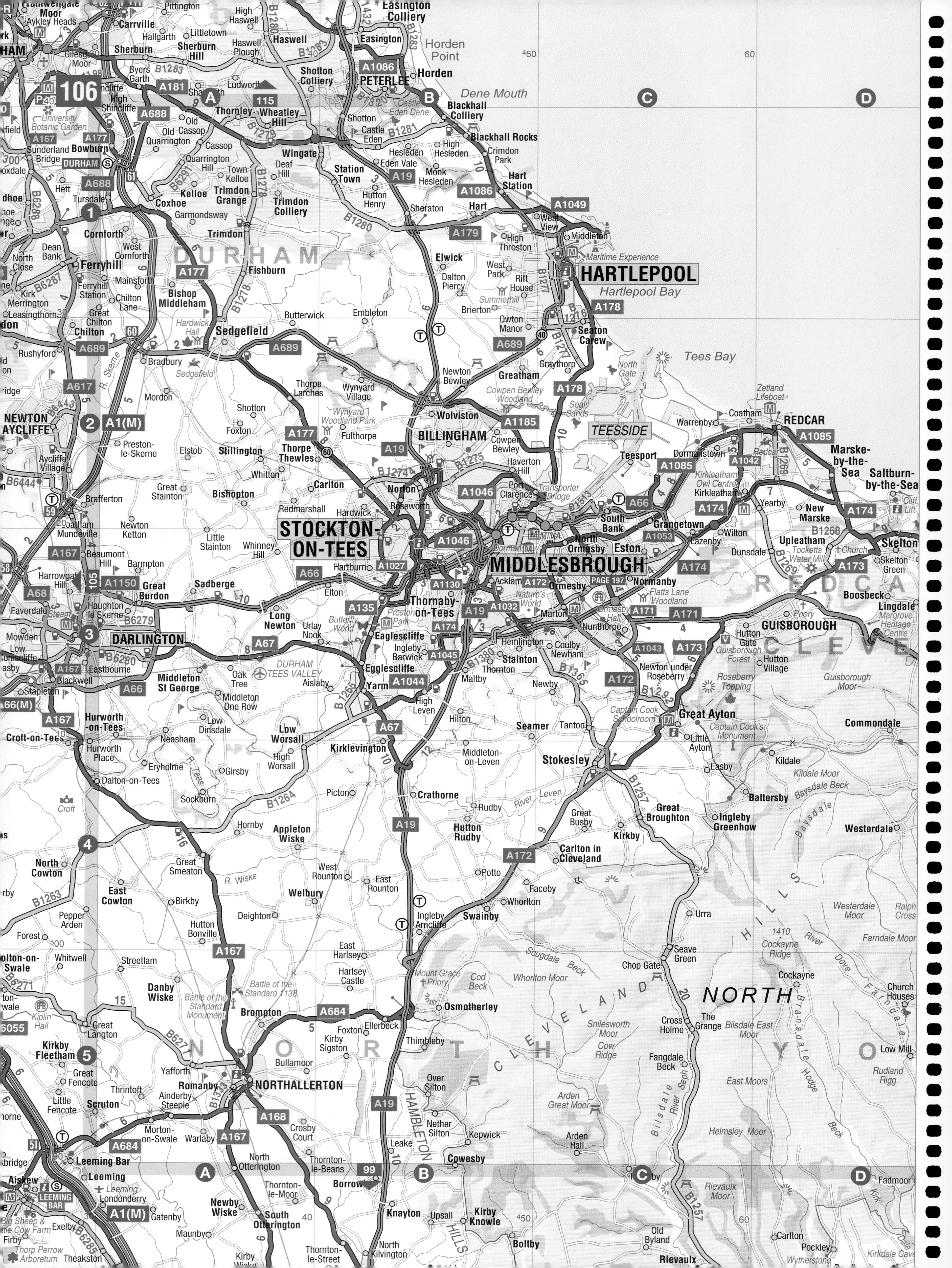
106
115
99
A
B
C
D
450
60
40
Easington Colliery
Horden Point
Dene Mouth
PETERLEE
Horden
Blackhall Colliery
Blackhall Rocks
Crimdon Park
Hart Station
Shotton Colliery
Haswell
Pittington
High Haswell
Carrville
Littletown
Sherburn
Sherburn Hill
Haswell Plough
Ludworth
Shadforth
Thornley
Wheatley Hill
Old Cassop
Cassop
Quarrington Hill
Bowburn
Sunderland Bridge
DURHAM
University Botanic Garden
Coxhoe
Kelloe
Trimdon Grange
Trimdon Colliery
Garmondsway
Trimdon
Wingate
Station Town
Hutton Henry
Sheraton
Hart
Hesleden
High Hesleden
Monk Hesleden
Eden Vale
Castle Eden
Shotton
West View
Middleton
High Throston
Elwick
Dalton Piercy
West Park
Rift House
Summerhill
Brierton
Owton Manor
Seaton Carew
HARTLEPOOL
Hartlepool Bay
Maritime Experience
Tees Bay
North Gare
Graythorp
Greatham
Cowpen Bewley Woodland
Newton Bewley
Seal Sands
TEESSIDE
Zetland Lifeboat
Coatham
REDCAR
Warrenby
Dormanstown
Teesport
Kirkleatham Owl Centre
Kirkleatham
Yearby
Marske-by-the-Sea
Saltburn-by-the-Sea
New Marske
Upleatham
Skelton
Skelton Green
Boosbeck
Lingdale
Margrove Heritage Centre
GUISBOROUGH
Hutton Gate
Guisborough Forest
Hutton Village
Guisborough Moor
Commondale
DURHAM
Cornforth
West Cornforth
Ferryhill
Ferryhill Station
Chilton Lane
Mainsforth
Bishop Middleham
Fishburn
Sedgefield
Hardwick Hall
Great Chilton
Chilton
Rushyford
Bradbury
Mordon
NEWTON AYCLIFFE
Aycliffe Village
Preston-le-Skerne
Elstob
Stillington
Shotton
Foxton
Thorpe Larches
Wynyard Village
Wynyard Woodland Park
Thorpe Thewles
Fulthorpe
Whitton
Butterwick
Embleton
Wolviston
BILLINGHAM
Cowpen Bewley
Haverton Hill
Port Clarence
Transporter Bridge
Norton
Roseworth
Carlton
Redmarshall
Hardwick
Bishopton
Great Stainton
Brafferton
Coatham Mundeville
Newton Ketton
Little Stainton
Whinney Hill
STOCKTON-ON-TEES
MIDDLESBROUGH
PAGE 197
South Bank
Grangetown
Eston
North Ormesby
Normanby
Ormesby
Lazenby
Wilton
Dunsdale
Flatts Lane Woodland
Acklam
Nature's World
Marton
Ormesby Hall
Nunthorpe
Hemlington
Coulby Newham
Stainton
Thornton
Maltby
Newby
Newton under Roseberry
Roseberry Topping
Captain Cook Schoolroom
Great Ayton
Captain Cook's Monument
Little Ayton
Easby
Kildale
Kildale Moor
Baysdale Beck
Battersby
Ingleby Greenhow
Westerdale
Hartburn
Elton
Thornaby-on-Tees
Preston Park
Butterfly World
Eaglescliffe
Ingleby Barwick
Egglescliffe
Yarm
High Leven
Hilton
Seamer
Tanton
Stokesley
Middleton-on-Leven
Aislaby
DURHAM TEES VALLEY
Long Newton
Urlay Nook
Sadberge
Great Burdon
Barmpton
Beaumont Hill
Harrowgate Hill
Haughton le Skerne
Faverdale
Mowden
DARLINGTON
Eastbourne
Blackwell
Stapleton
Middleton St George
Oak Tree
Middleton One Row
Low Dinsdale
Hurworth-on-Tees
Hurworth Place
Croft-on-Tees
Neasham
Eryholme
Girsby
Dalton-on-Tees
Sockburn
Croft
Low Worsall
High Worsall
Kirklevington
Picton
Crathorne
Rudby
River Leven
Hutton Rudby
Great Busby
Kirkby
Great Broughton
Carlton in Cleveland
Hornby
Appleton Wiske
North Cowton
Great Smeaton
R. Wiske
West Rounton
East Rounton
Welbury
Potto
Faceby
Whorlton
Swainby
Ingleby Arncliffe
Urra
East Cowton
Birkby
Pepper Arden
Deighton
Hutton Bonville
Forest
Whitwell
Streetlam
East Harlsey
Harlsey Castle
Mount Grace Priory
Cod Beck
Whorlton Moor
Scugdale Beck
Chop Gate
Seave Green
Cockayne Ridge
Cockayne
Westerdale Moor
Ralph Cross
Farndale Moor
Church Houses
Danby Wiske
Battle of the Standard 1138
Battle of the Standard Monument
Kiplin Hall
Great Langton
Brompton
Foxton
Ellerbeck
Kirby Sigston
Osmotherley
Thimbleby
CLEVELAND
Snilesworth Moor
Cow Ridge
Cross Holme
The Grange
Bilsdale East Moor
NORTH
HILLS
Kirkby Fleetham
Great Fencote
Little Fencote
Yafforth
Thrintoft
Romanby
Ainderby Steeple
NORTHALLERTON
Bullamoor
Over Silton
Nether Silton
Kepwick
Arden Great Moor
Arden Hall
Fangdale Beck
Bilsdale
River Seph
East Moors
Helmsley Moor
Low Mill
Rudland Rigg
Scruton
Morton-on-Swale
Warlaby
Crosby Court
Leake
Cowesby
HAMBLETON
Leeming Bar
Leeming
Londonderry
Aiskew
Gatenby
North Otterington
Thornton-le-Beans
Thornton-le-Moor
Borrowby
Newby Wiske
South Otterington
Knayton
Upsall
Kirby Knowle
Boltby
Maunby
Exelby
Thornton-le-Street
North Kilvington
Thorp Perrow Arboretum
Theakston
Old Byland
Rievaulx
Rievaulx Moor
Carlton
Pockley
Wytherstone
Kirkdale Cave
Fadmoor
A1(M)
A19
A66
A67
A167
A168
A177
A178
A179
A181
A688
A689
A684
A1086
A1049
A1185
A1046
A1027
A1130
A1032
A135
A174
A1045
A1044
A1150
A1085
A1042
A1053
A171
A172
A173
A1043
A617
A68
A66(M)
A6055
B1283
B1280
B1278
B1279
B1320
B1281
B1277
B1274
B1275
B1513
B1380
B1365
B1292
B1264
B1265
B1263
B6275
B6280
B6279
B6287
B6291
B6288
B6443
B6444
B6271
B1257
B1268
B1269
B6285
B1267

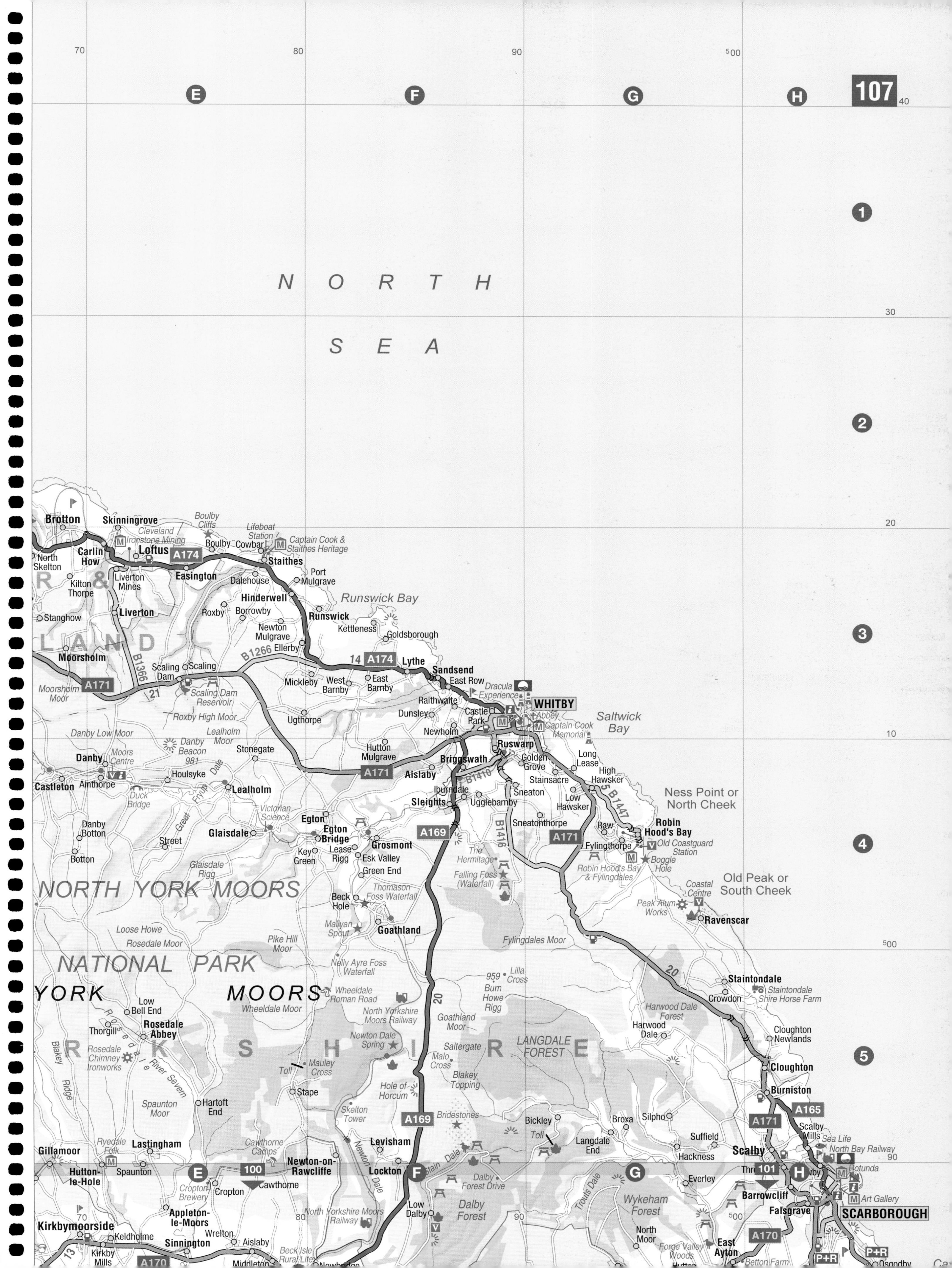

NORTH SEA

Brotton
Skinningrove
Boulby Cliffs
Cleveland Ironstone Mining
Boulby
Cowbar
Lifeboat Station
Captain Cook & Staithes Heritage
North Skelton
Carlin How
Loftus
A174
Staithes
Port Mulgrave
Easington
Dalehouse
Kilton Thorpe
Liverton Mines
Hinderwell
Borrowby
Runswick
Runswick Bay
Stanghow
Liverton
Roxby
Newton Mulgrave
Kettleness
Goldsborough
Moorsholm
B1266
Ellerby
14 A174
Lythe
Sandsend
L A N D
B1366
Scaling
Scaling
Mickleby
West Barnby
East Barnby
East Row
Dracula Experience
WHITBY
Moorsholm
A171
Scaling Dam
Scaling Dam Reservoir
Raithwaite
Dunsley
Castle Park
Abbey
Saltwick Bay
Moorsholm Moor
Roxby High Moor
Ugthorpe
Newholm
Captain Cook Memorial
Danby Low Moor
Lealholm Moor
Hutton Mulgrave
Briggswath
Ruswarp
Long Lease
Danby Beacon 981
Stonegate
A171
Aislaby
Golden Grove
Stainsacre
High Hawsker
Danby
Moors Centre
Houlsyke
B1410
Iburndale
Sneaton
Low Hawsker
Ness Point or North Cheek
Castleton
Ainthorpe
Lealholm
Sleights
Ugglebarnby
B1447
Danby Bottom
Duck Bridge
Victorian Science
Egton
Egton Bridge
Sneatonthorpe
Raw
Robin Hood's Bay
Botton
Glaisdale
Lease Rigg
Grosmont
The Hermitage
Fylingthorpe
Old Coastguard Station
Glaisdale Rigg
Key Green
Esk Valley
Falling Foss (Waterfall)
A171
Boggle Hole
Robin Hood's Bay & Fylingdales
NORTH YORK MOORS
Green End
Thomason Foss Waterfall
Coastal Centre
Loose Howe
Beck Hole
Peak Alum Works
Ravenscar
Rosedale Moor
Mallyan Spout
Goathland
Fylingdales Moor
Old Peak or South Cheek
NATIONAL PARK
Nelly Ayre Foss Waterfall
Pike Hill Moor
YORK
MOORS
Wheeldale Roman Road
Wheeldale Moor
959
Lilla Cross
Burn Howe Rigg
Staintondale
Crowdon
Staintondale Shire Horse Farm
Low Bell End
North Yorkshire Moors Railway
Goathland Moor
Harwood Dale Forest
Cloughton Newlands
Thorgill
Rosedale Abbey
Saltergate
Malo Cross
LANGDALE FOREST
Harwood Dale
R
K
S
H
I
R
E
Newton Dale Spring
Rosedale Chimney Ironworks
Blakey Ridge
River Severn
Toll
Mauley Cross
Blakey Topping
Cloughton
Burniston
Spaunton Moor
Hartoft End
Stape
Hole of Horcum
Bickley
Toll
Langdale End
Suffield
Silpho
A165
Scalby Mills
Sea Life
Gillamoor
Ryedale Folk
Lastingham
Skelton Tower
Bridestones
Broxa
Hackness
Scalby
North Bay Railway
Hutton-le-Hole
Spaunton
E
100
Newton-on-Rawcliffe
Levisham
Lockton
F
Dalby Forest Drive
G
Everley
101
Rotunda
Cropton Brewery
Cawthorne
Cawthorne Camps
Low Dalby
Dalby Forest
Wykeham Forest
Barrowcliff
Art Gallery
Kirkbymoorside
Keldholme
Appleton-le-Moors
Wrelton
Aislaby
North Yorkshire Moors Railway
North Moor
Forge Valley Woods
Falsgrave
SCARBOROUGH
Kirkby Mills
Sinnington
A170
Middleton
Beck Isle Rural Life
Newbridge
East Ayton
Hutton
A170
Betton Farm
P+R
P+R

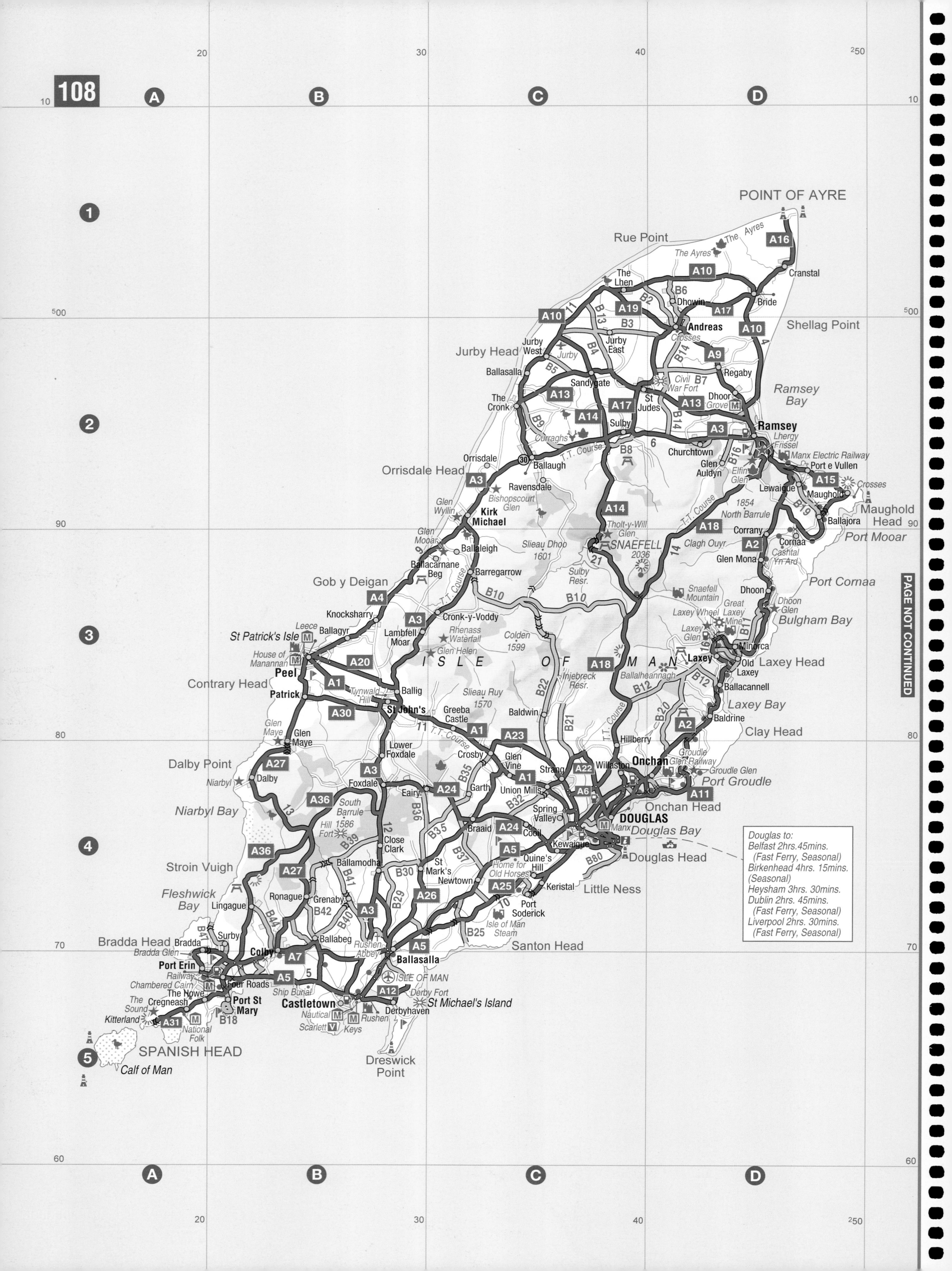

A   B   C   D

20   30   40   250

10   10

POINT OF AYRE

Rue Point

The Ayres

A16

The Ayres

The Lhen

A10   B6   Dhowin   Cranstal

B2   Bride

500   A10   B13   A19   B3   A17   500

A10   11   Jurby West   Jurby East   Andreas   A10   Shellag Point

Jurby Head   Jurby   Crosses   A9

Ballasalla   B4   B5   Civil   B7   Regaby   Ramsey Bay

Sandygate   War Fort   B14

The Cronk   A13   St   A13   Dhoor   Lhergy Frissel

A14   A17   Judes   Grove   M   Ramsey

B9   Sulby   A3   Manx Electric Railway

Orrisdale   Curraghs   B8   Churchtown   Glen   B16   Port e Vullen

90   Orrisdale Head   30   Ballaugh   T.T. Course   6   Auldyn   Elfin   A15   90

A3   Glen   Glen   Crosses

Ravensdale   A14   Maughold

Bishopscourt   Glen   Tholt-y-Will   1854   Lewaigue   B19   Ballajora

Kirk   Glen   Glen   North Barrule   Maughold Head

Michael   A18   Corrany   A2   Cornaa   Port Mooar

Glen   Ballaleigh   SNAEFELL   Clagh Ouyr   Cashtal   Port Cornaa

Mooar   Barregarrow   2036   Glen Mona   Yn Ard

Ballacarnane   Snaefell   Dhoon

Gob y Deigan   Beg   B10   21   Sulby   Mountain   Laxey Wheel   Great   Dhoon   Bulgham Bay

A4   Resr.   Laxey   Glen   Laxey

Knocksharry   B10   Mine   B11

Leece   A3   Cronk-y-Voddy   Colden   Ballaheannagh   Laxey   Minorca   Old Laxey Head

St Patrick's Isle   Ballagyr   Lambfell   Rhenass   1599   Injebreck   A18   Glen   Laxey

M   Moar   Waterfall   ISLE   OF   MAN   B12   Old

House of   A20   Glen Helen   B22   Resr.   B12   Laxey

Mananan   M   Slieau Ruy   B20   Ballacannell

Peel   Ballig   1570   B21   A2   Baldrine

Contrary Head   A1   Tynwald   St John's   Greeba   Baldwin   Laxey Bay

Patrick   Hill   Castle   T.T. Course   Hillberry   Clay Head

80   A30   A1   A23   A1   Groudle   80

Glen   Lower   Crosby   Glen   Strang   A22   Willaston   Groudle Glen Railway

Dalby Point   Maye   Glen   Foxdale   Vine   Onchan   Port Groudle

A27   Maye   A3   Garth   A1   A6   A11

Niarbyl   Dalby   Foxdale   A24   Union Mills   B32   Onchan Head

Niarbyl Bay   A36   South   Eairy   Spring   DOUGLAS   Groudle

Barrule   B35   Valley   M   Manx

A36   Hill 1586   B36   Braaid   A24   Cooil   Douglas Bay

4   Fort   B39   Close   Kewaigue   Douglas Head

Stroin Vuigh   A27   Clark   B35   A5   Quine's

Ballamodha   St   Newtown   B37   Hill   Home for   Little Ness

Fleshwick   Lingague   Ronague   Grenaby   Mark's   B30   Old Horses   Keristal

Bay   B41   B42   B29   A25

Ballabeg   B40   A26   Port   Douglas to:

Surby   B44   A3   Rushen   A5   Soderick   Belfast 2hrs.45mins.

Bradda Head   Bradda   Colby   Ballabeg   Abbey   B25   Isle of Man   (Fast Ferry, Seasonal)

70   Bradda Glen   A7   Ballasalla   Steam   Santon Head   Birkenhead 4hrs. 15mins.   70

Port Erin   Railway   A5   5   A5   (Seasonal)

Chambered Cairn   Four Roads   Ship Burial   Isle of Man   Heysham 3hrs. 30mins.

The Howe   M   Castletown   A12   Derby Fort   Dublin 2hrs. 45mins.

The   Cregneash   Port St   B18   M   Derbyhaven   St Michael's Island   (Fast Ferry, Seasonal)

Sound   A31   Mary   Nautical   M   Rushen   Liverpool 2hrs. 30mins.

Kitterland   National   Scarlett   V   Keys   (Fast Ferry, Seasonal)

5   Folk

SPANISH HEAD   Dreswick

Calf of Man   Point

A   B   C   D

20   30   40   250

PAGE NOT CONTINUED

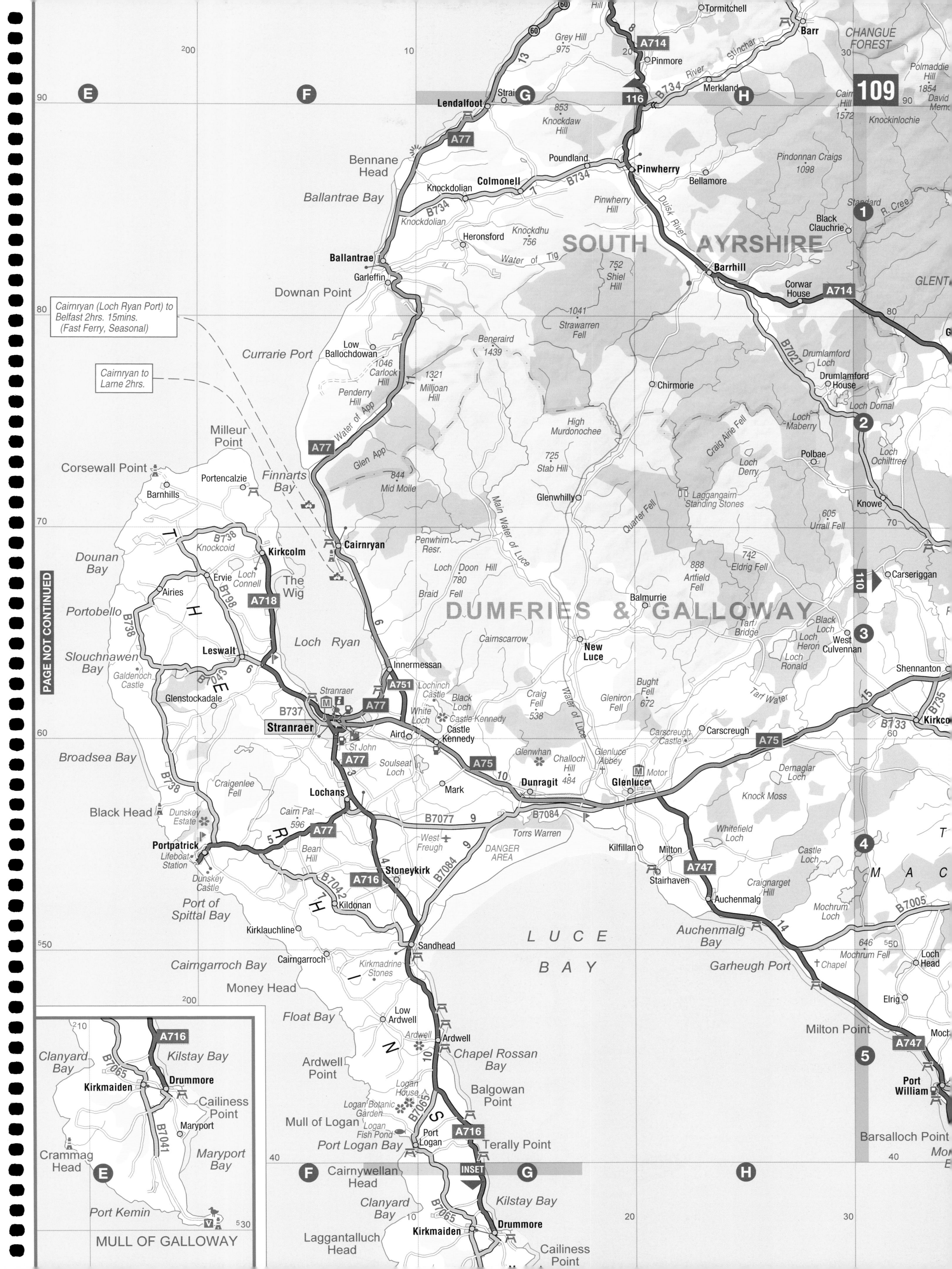

109
110
116
INSET
PAGE NOT CONTINUED
SOUTH AYRSHIRE
DUMFRIES & GALLOWAY
Cairnryan (Loch Ryan Port) to Belfast 2hrs. 15mins. (Fast Ferry, Seasonal)
Cairnryan to Larne 2hrs.
Lendalfoot
Bennane Head
Ballantrae Bay
Colmonell
Knockdolian
Ballantrae
Garleffin
Downan Point
Currarie Port
Low Ballochdowan
Milleur Point
Corsewall Point
Portencalzie
Barnhills
Finnarts Bay
Kirkcolm
Cairnryan
Dounan Bay
Portobello
The Wig
Loch Ryan
Leswalt
Slouchnawen Bay
Glenstockadale
Stranraer
Innermessan
Broadsea Bay
Black Head
Portpatrick
Port of Spittal Bay
Lochans
Stoneykirk
Kildonan
Kirklauchline
Sandhead
Cairngarroch Bay
Money Head
Float Bay
Low Ardwell
Ardwell
Ardwell Point
Chapel Rossan Bay
Balgowan Point
Mull of Logan
Port Logan
Port Logan Bay
Terally Point
Cairnywellan Head
Clanyard Bay
Kilstay Bay
Drummore
Kirkmaiden
Laggantalluch Head
Cailiness Point
LUCE BAY
Pinwherry
Barrhill
Barr
Pinmore
Merkland
Poundland
Chirmorie
Glenwhilly
New Luce
Castle Kennedy
Dunragit
Glenluce
Auchenmalg
Auchenmalg Bay
Garheugh Port
Milton Point
Port William
Barsalloch Point
MULL OF GALLOWAY
Crammag Head
Port Kemin
Maryport
Maryport Bay

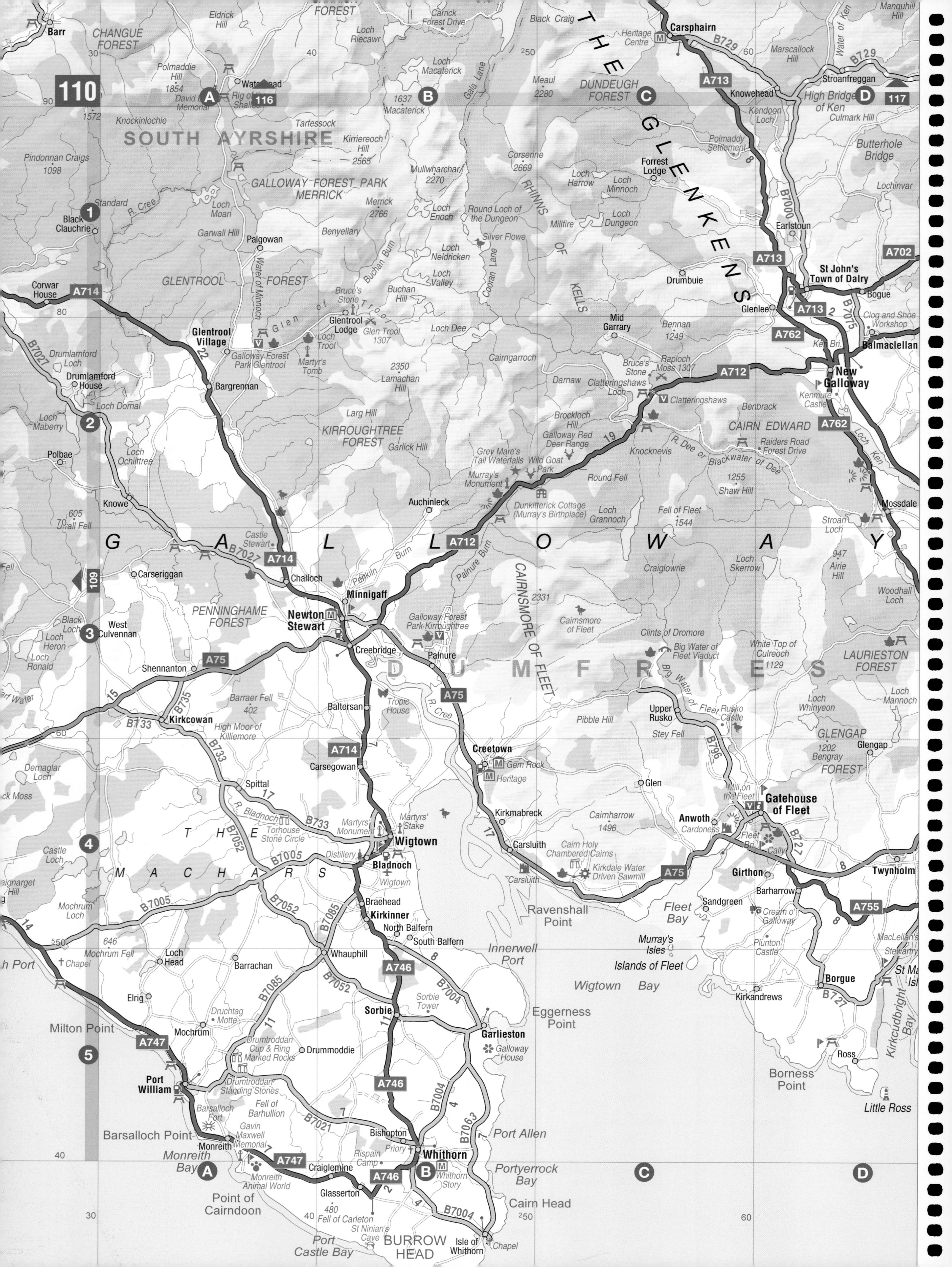
110
116
117
109
SOUTH AYRSHIRE
GALLOWAY FOREST PARK
MERRICK
GLENTROOL FOREST
KIRROUGHTREE FOREST
THE GLENKENS
RHINNS OF KELLS
GALLOWAY
DUMFRIES
CAIRNSMORE OF FLEET
THE MACHARS
CAIRN EDWARD
LAURIESTON FOREST
GLENGAP FOREST
PENNINGHAME FOREST
DUNDEUGH FOREST
CHANGUE FOREST
Barr
Carsphairn
Newton Stewart
Minnigaff
Creebridge
Glentrool Village
Bargrennan
St John's Town of Dalry
New Galloway
Balmaclellan
Creetown
Gatehouse of Fleet
Wigtown
Bladnoch
Kirkinner
Sorbie
Garlieston
Whithorn
Isle of Whithorn
Port William
Monreith
Mochrum
Kirkcowan
Shennanton
Glasserton
Borgue
Twynholm
Kirkandrews
Wigtown Bay
Islands of Fleet
Fleet Bay
Burrow Head
Port Castle Bay
Point of Cairndoon
Barsalloch Point
Milton Point
Monreith Bay
Eggerness Point
Ravenshall Point
Cairn Head
Port Allen
Portyerrock Bay
Borness Point
Little Ross
Kirkcudbright Bay
A714
A712
A713
A762
A702
A75
A746
A747
A755
B7027
B7005
B7052
B7085
B733
B735
B7004
B7063
B7021
B727
B796
B729
B7000
B7075
A
B
C
D
1
2
3
4
5

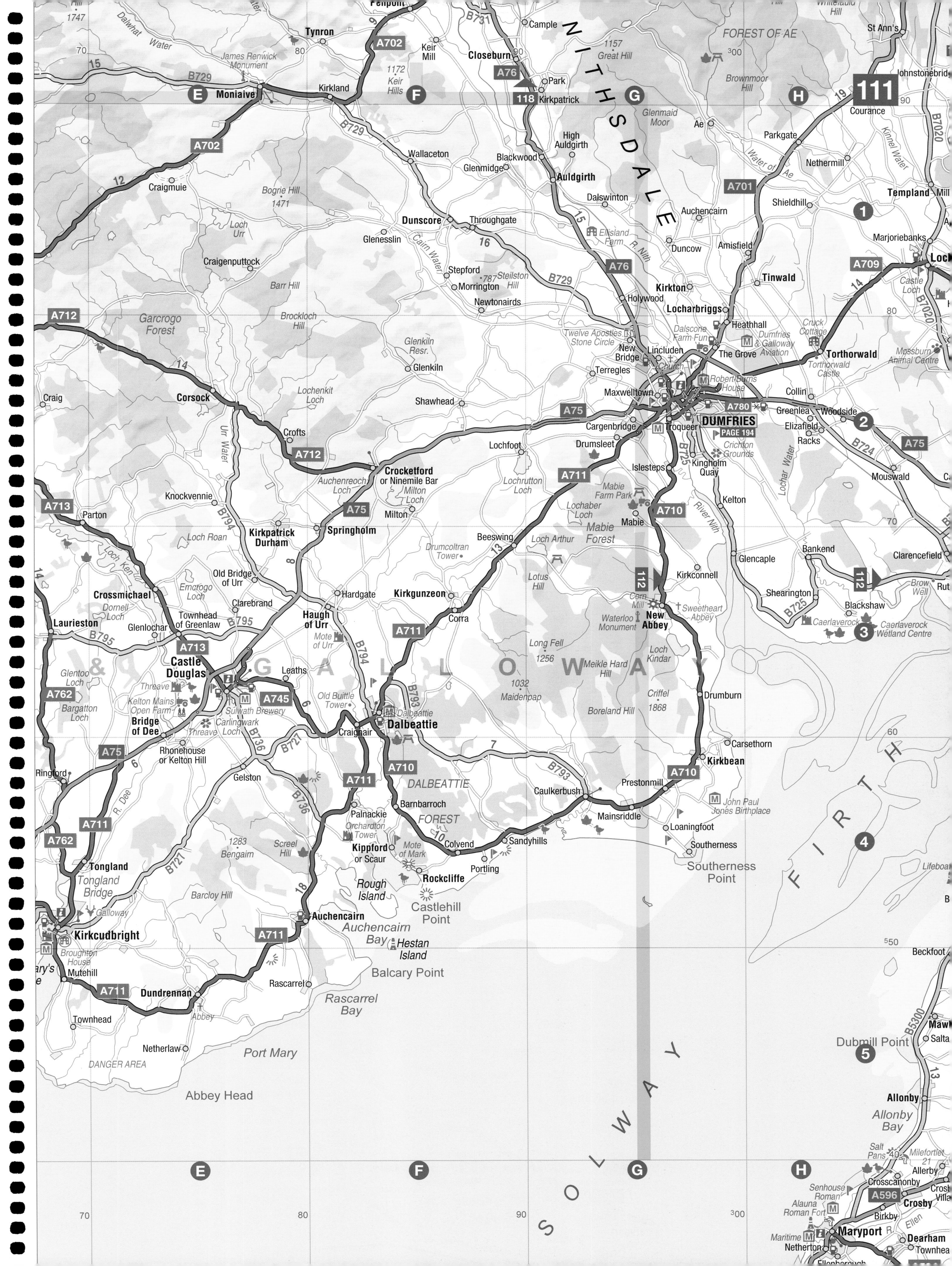

111
NITHSDALE
FOREST OF AE
GALLOWAY
DALBEATTIE FOREST
SOLWAY FIRTH
Tynron
Keir Mill
Closeburn
Cample
Park
Kirkpatrick
1157 Great Hill
St Ann's
Johnstonebridge
Courance
1747
Dalwhat Water
James Renwick Monument
Moniaive
Kirkland
1172 Keir Hills
B729
A702
A76
118
Glenmaid Moor
Ae
Brownmoor Hill
Parkgate
B7020
Kinnel Water
Water of Ae
Nethermill
Templand
Mill
Wallaceton
Blackwood
High Auldgirth
Glenmidge
Auldgirth
Craigmuie
Bogrie Hill 1471
Dalswinton
A701
Shieldhill
Auchencairn
Dunscore
Throughgate
Glenesslin
Loch Urr
Ellisland Farm
R. Nith
Duncow
Amisfield
Marjoriebanks
Cairn Water
Craigenputtock
Stepford
Morrington
787 Steilston Hill
Newtonairds
Barr Hill
B729
Kirkton
Tinwald
A709
Castle Loch
Holywood
Locharbriggs
A712
Garcrogo Forest
Brockloch Hill
Twelve Apostles Stone Circle
Dalscone Farm Fun
Heathhall
Dumfries & Galloway Aviation
Cruck Cottage
Torthorwald
Torthorwald Castle
Mossburn Animal Centre
Glenkiln Resr.
Glenkiln
New Bridge
Lincluden
Church
The Grove
Terregles
Robert Burns House
Craig
Corsock
Lochenkit Loch
Shawhead
Maxwelltown
Collin
A780
DUMFRIES
PAGE 194
Greenlea
Woodside
Elizafield
Racks
A75
Cargenbridge
Troqueer
Crichton Grounds
Urr Water
Crofts
Lochfoot
Drumsleet
B725
Kingholm Quay
B724
A75
Mouswald
Isleesteps
Crocketford or Ninemile Bar
Auchenreoch Loch
Milton Loch
Lochrutton Loch
A711
Mabie Farm Park
Lochar Water
Knockvennie
Milton
Lochaber Loch
Mabie
A710
River Nith
Kelton
A713
Parton
B794
Springholm
Mabie Forest
Beeswing
Loch Arthur
Kirkpatrick Durham
Loch Roan
Drumcoltran Tower
Glencaple
Bankend
Clarencefield
Loch Ken
Old Bridge of Urr
Lotus Hill
112
Kirkconnell
Shearington
Brow Well
Crossmichael
Ernorogo Loch
Hardgate
Kirkgunzeon
Corra
Corn Mill
Sweetheart Abbey
New Abbey
Blackshaw
Dornell Loch
Clarebrand
Waterloo Monument
Caerlaverock
Caerlaverock Wetland Centre
Laurieston
Townhead of Greenlaw
Haugh of Urr
B795
Glenlochar
Mote of Urr
Long Fell 1256
Loch Kindar
Glentoo Loch
Castle Douglas
Leaths
Meikle Hard Hill
1032 Maidenpap
A762
Threave
Kelton Mains Open Farm
A745
Sulwath Brewery
Old Buittle Tower
Dalbeattie
Criffel 1868
Drumburn
Boreland Hill
Bargatton Loch
Bridge of Dee
Carlingwark Loch
Craignair
Rhonehouse or Kelton Hill
B736
B721
B793
Carsethorn
Kirkbean
Ringford
Gelston
Caulkerbush
Prestonmill
R. Dee
Palnackie
Barnbarroch
Mainsriddle
John Paul Jones Birthplace
Loaningfoot
Orchardton Tower
Southerness
1283 Bengairn
Screel Hill
Kippford or Scaur
Mote of Mark
Colvend
Sandyhills
Tongland
Tongland Bridge
B727
Portling
Southerness Point
Rockcliffe
Rough Island
Barcloy Hill
Castlehill Point
Galloway
Kirkcudbright
Auchencairn
Auchencairn Bay
Hestan Island
Broughton House
Mutehill
Balcary Point
Beckfoot
Dundrennan
Rascarrel
Abbey
Rascarrel Bay
Townhead
B5300
Maw
Salta
Netherlaw
Port Mary
DANGER AREA
Dubmill Point
Abbey Head
Allonby
Allonby Bay
Salt Pans
Milefortlet 21
Allerby
Crosscanonby
Senhouse Roman
A596
Crosby
Alauna Roman Fort
Birkby
Maritime
Maryport
Ellen
Netherton
Dearham
Townhead
E
F
G
H
1
2
3
4
5
70
80
90
300
60
50

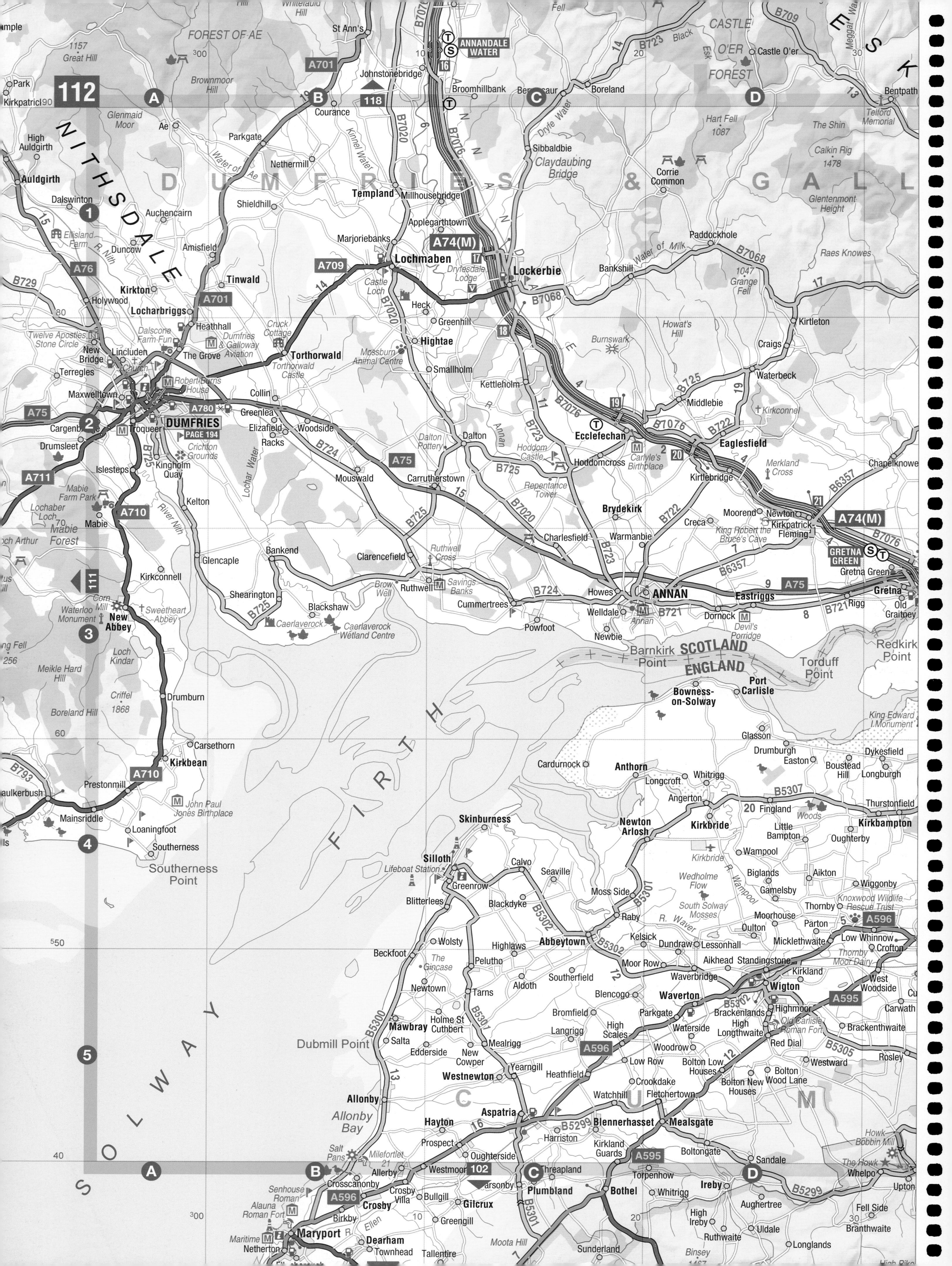

112
A
B
C
D
118
102
111
PAGE 194
FOREST OF AE
Great Hill
Park
Kirkpatrick
Glenmaid Moor
Ae
High Auldgirth
Auldgirth
NITHSDALE
Brownmoor Hill
Parkgate
Nethermill
Water of Ae
Kinnel Water
St Ann's
Johnstonebridge
Courance
A701
ANNANDALE WATER
Broomhillbank
Boreland
CASTLE O'ER FOREST
Castle O'er
Black Esk
B723
B709
Bentpath
Telford Memorial
ESK
Dryfe Water
Sibbaldbie
Claydaubing Bridge
Hart Fell 1087
The Shin
Calkin Rig 1478
Corrie Common
Glentenmont Height
DUMFRIES & GALLOWAY
Templand
Millhousebridge
Shieldhill
Applegarthtown
Marjoriebanks
Dalswinton
Auchencairn
Amisfield
Ellisland Farm
Duncow
R. Nith
A76
A74(M)
Lochmaben
Lockerbie
Dryfesdale Lodge
Paddockhole
Water of Milk
B7068
Raes Knowes
Bankshill
1047 Grange Fell
A709
Castle Loch
B729
Kirkton
Holywood
Tinwald
A701
Locharbriggs
Heathhall
Dalscone Farm Fun
Dumfries & Galloway Aviation
Cruck Cottage
Twelve Apostles Stone Circle
New Bridge
Lincluden
Terregles
The Grove
Torthorwald
Torthorwald Castle
Heck
Greenhill
Hightae
Mossburn Animal Centre
Smallholm
Kettleholm
B7020
Howat's Hill
Burnswark
Kirtleton
Craigs
Waterbeck
B725
Middlebie
Kirkconnel
Maxwelltown
Robert Burns House
Collin
A780
DUMFRIES
A75
Cargenbridge
Troqueer
Greenlea
Elizafield
Woodside
Racks
Drumsleet
Crichton Grounds
Kingholm Quay
B724
Dalton
Dalton Pottery
R. Annan
B723
Hoddom Castle
Ecclefechan
Carlyle's Birthplace
B7076
Eaglesfield
Kirtlebridge
Merkland Cross
Chapelknowe
A711
Isle steps
Mouswald
Carrutherstown
B725
Repentance Tower
Hoddomcross
Mabie Farm Park
Mabie
Mabie Forest
Lochaber Loch
A710
Kelton
River Nith
Lochar Water
Brydekirk
Creca
Moorend
Newton
Kirkpatrick Fleming
King Robert the Bruce's Cave
B6357
GRETNA GREEN
Gretna Green
Charlesfield
Warmanbie
Glencaple
Bankend
Clarencefield
Ruthwell Cross
Kirkconnell
Shearington
Brow Well
Ruthwell
Savings Banks
Cummertrees
Howes
ANNAN
Eastriggs
Gretna
Rigg
Old Graitney
Welldale
B721
Dornock
Devil's Porridge
Corn Mill
Sweetheart Abbey
Waterloo Monument
New Abbey
Blackshaw
Caerlaverock
Caerlaverock Wetland Centre
Powfoot
Newbie
Loch Kindar
Meikle Hard Hill
Criffel 1868
Boreland Hill
Drumburn
Barnkirk Point
SCOTLAND
ENGLAND
Torduff Point
Redkirk Point
Bowness-on-Solway
Port Carlisle
King Edward I Monument
Glasson
Drumburgh
Easton
Dykesfield
Boustead Hill
Longburgh
Carsethorn
Kirkbean
Cardurnock
Anthorn
Whitrigg
Longcroft
Angerton
B5307
Fingland
Thurstonfield
Kirkbampton
Prestonmill
Southerness
Southerness Point
Mainsriddle
Loaningfoot
John Paul Jones Birthplace
B793
Skinburness
Newton Arlosh
Kirkbride
Little Bampton
Oughterby
Wampool
FIRTH
SOLWAY
Silloth
Lifeboat Station
Greenrow
Calvo
Seaville
Wedholme Flow
R. Wampool
Biglands
Aikton
Wiggonby
Gamelsby
Blitterlees
Blackdyke
Moss Side
B5302
South Solway Mosses
Raby
R. Waver
Knoxwood Wildlife Rescue Trust
Thornby
Moorhouse
Parton
Oulton
A596
Kelsick
Dundraw
Lessonhall
Micklethwaite
Low Whinnow
Crofton
Wolsty
Highlaws
Abbeytown
Beckfoot
The Gincase
Pelutho
Moor Row
Aikhead
Standingstone
Thornby Moor Dairy
Waverbridge
Kirkland
West Woodside
Newtown
Tarns
Aldoth
Southerfield
Blencogo
Waverton
Wigton
A595
Carwath
Highmoor
Brackenlands
Mawbray
Holme St Cuthbert
Bromfield
Parkgate
High Longthwaite
Old Carlisle Roman Fort
Brackenthwaite
B5300
B5301
Salta
Dubmill Point
Langrigg
High Scales
Waterside
Red Dial
Edderside
Mealrigg
New Cowper
Woodrow
B5305
Rosley
Westward
Low Row
Bolton Low Houses
Bolton New Houses
Bolton Wood Lane
Yearngill
Westnewton
Heathfield
Crookdake
Allonby
Watchhill
Fletchertown
Allonby Bay
CUMBRIA
Hayton
Aspatria
Blennerhasset
Mealsgate
Prospect
Harriston
B5299
Kirkland Guards
Boltongate
Howk Bobbin Mill
Salt Pans
Milefortlet 21
Oughterside
A595
Sandale
The Howk
Whelpo
Allerby
Westmoor
Threapland
Torpenhow
Ireby
Senhouse Roman Museum
Crosscanonby
Crosby Villa
Parsonby
Plumbland
Bothel
Whitrigg
Aughertree
Upton
Crosby
Bullgill
Gilcrux
Fell Side
Alauna Roman Fort
Birkby
High Ireby
Branthwaite
Maryport
Ellen
Greengill
Uldale
Maritime
Netherton
Dearham
Townhead
Tallentire
Moota Hill
Sunderland
Ruthwaite
Longlands
Binsey

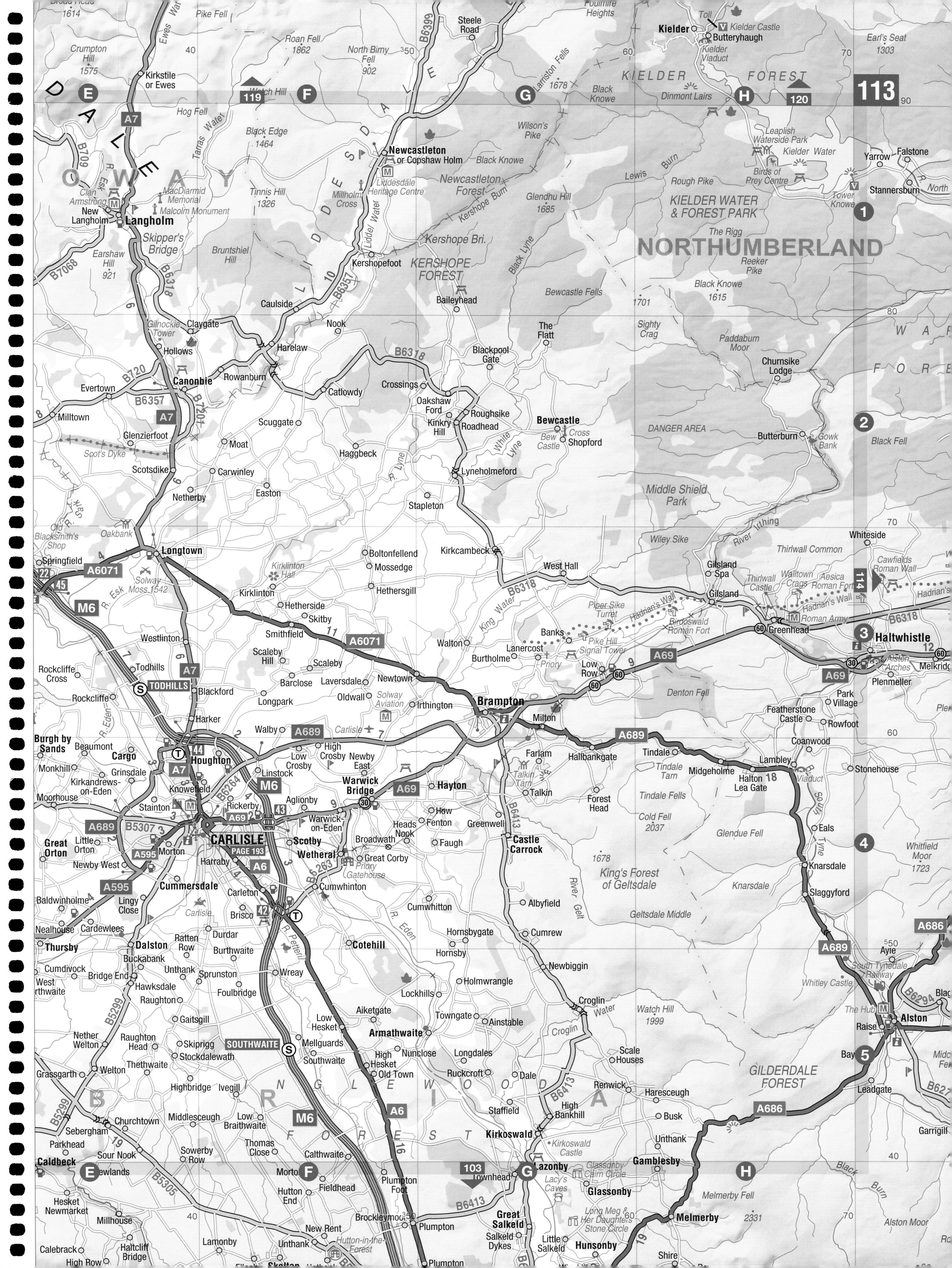
113
NORTHUMBERLAND
KIELDER WATER & FOREST PARK
KIELDER FOREST
CARLISLE
PAGE 193
Brampton
Langholm
Newcastleton or Copshaw Holm
Longtown
Haltwhistle
Alston
Kielder
Bewcastle
Canonbie
Dalston
Wetheral
Armathwaite
Kirkoswald
Lazonby
Great Salkeld
Melmerby
Gilsland
Hadrian's Wall
King's Forest of Geltsdale
Middle Shield Park
KERSHOPE FOREST
Newcastleton Forest
GILDERDALE FOREST
DANGER AREA
M6
A7
A69
A689
A6071
A686
A6
A595
119
120
114
103

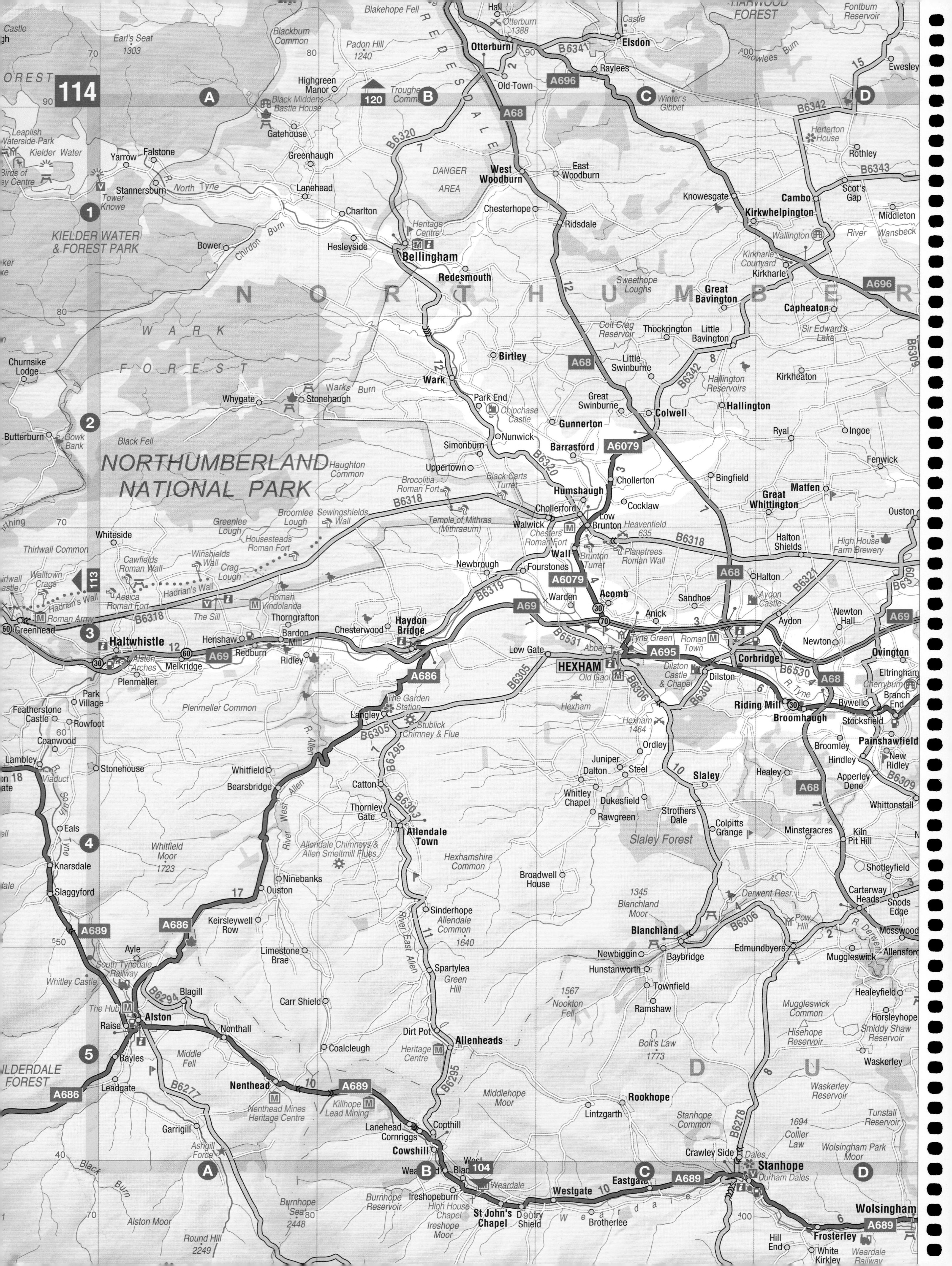

114
120
113
104
NORTHUMBERLAND NATIONAL PARK
KIELDER WATER & FOREST PARK
N O R T H U M B E R
W A R K F O R E S T
Kielder Water
Bellingham
Otterburn
Elsdon
West Woodburn
Kirkwhelpington
Cambo
Great Bavington
Capheaton
Wark
Humshaugh
Chollerton
Colwell
Hallington
Gunnerton
Barrasford
Matfen
Great Whittington
Haltwhistle
Haydon Bridge
HEXHAM
Corbridge
Acomb
Riding Mill
Broomhaugh
Ovington
Painshawfield
Slaley
Allendale Town
Blanchland
Alston
Nenthead
Allenheads
Cowshill
Stanhope
St John's Chapel
Westgate
Eastgate
Wolsingham
Frosterley
Rookhope
Slaley Forest
Derwent Resr.
Hadrian's Wall
A68
A69
A686
A689
A695
A696
A6079
B6318
B6320
B6342
B6305
B6295
B6303
B6306
B6278
B6277
B6294

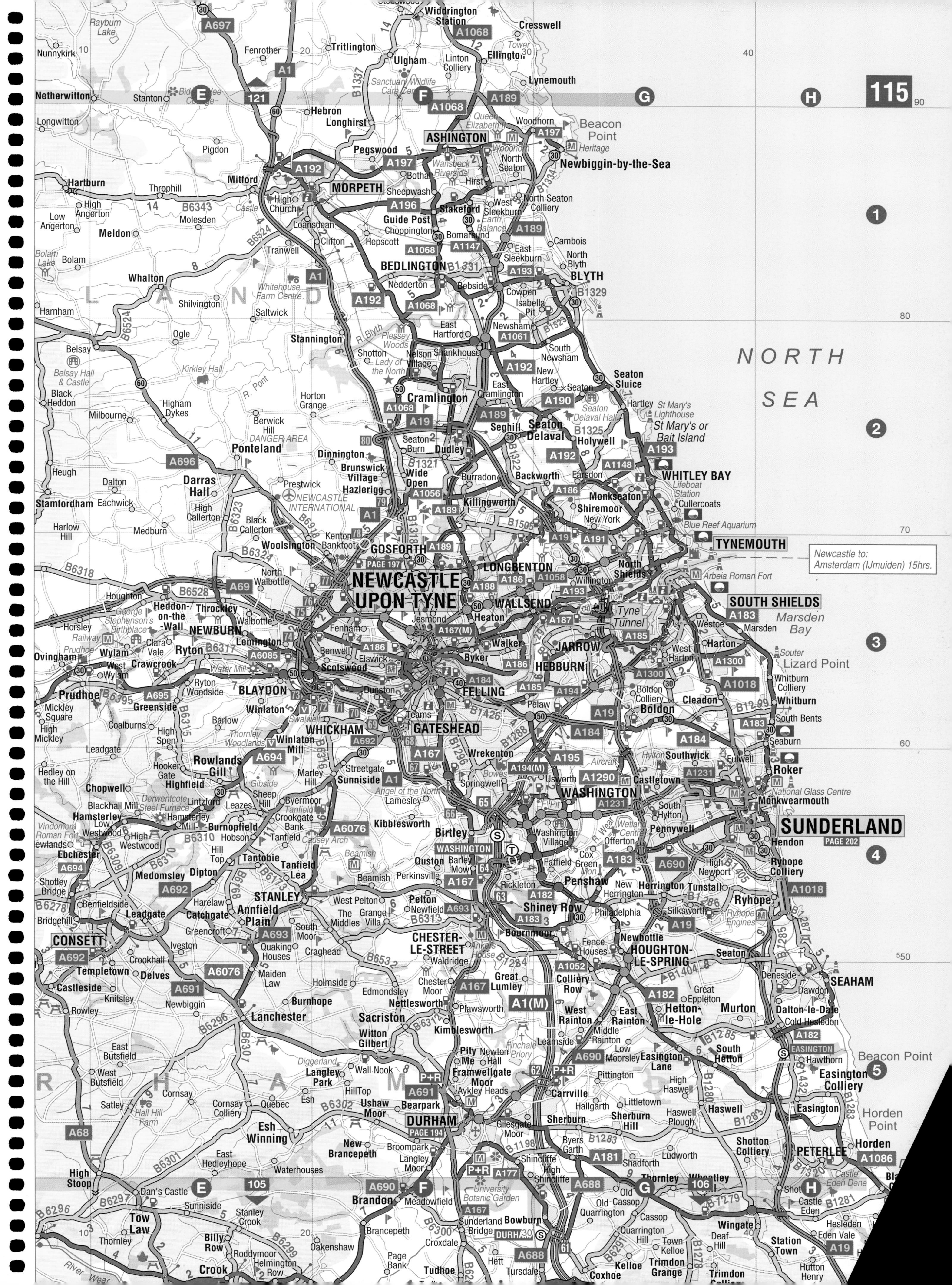
115
NORTH SEA
NEWCASTLE UPON TYNE
PAGE 197
SUNDERLAND
PAGE 202
DURHAM
PAGE 194
GATESHEAD
MORPETH
ASHINGTON
BEDLINGTON
BLYTH
WHITLEY BAY
TYNEMOUTH
SOUTH SHIELDS
WALLSEND
GOSFORTH
JARROW
HEBBURN
FELLING
WHICKHAM
BLAYDON
NEWBURN
WASHINGTON
CHESTER-LE-STREET
HOUGHTON-LE-SPRING
STANLEY
CONSETT
PETERLEE
SEAHAM
EASINGTON
Newcastle to: Amsterdam (IJmuiden) 15hrs.
Cramlington
Ponteland
Darras Hall
Prudhoe
Ryton
Lanchester
Sacriston
Birtley
Boldon
Cleadon
Whitburn
Roker
Ryhope
Murton
Hetton-le-Hole
Shiney Row
Penshaw
Newbiggin-by-the-Sea
Cresswell
Lynemouth
Ellington
Widdrington Station
Ulgham
Longhirst
Pegswood
Stakeford
Seaton Delaval
Holywell
Killingworth
Longbenton
Dudley
Seaton Sluice
St Mary's or Bait Island
Beacon Point
Horden Point
Marsden Bay
Lizard Point
NEWCASTLE INTERNATIONAL
A1
A1(M)
A19
A69
A68
A167
A182
A183
A184
A189
A190
A192
A193
A194(M)
A195
A196
A197
A690
A691
A692
A693
A694
A695
A696
A697
A1018
A1068
A1231
A1290
A1300
A6076
A6085
E
F
G
H
1
2
3
4
5
105
106
121

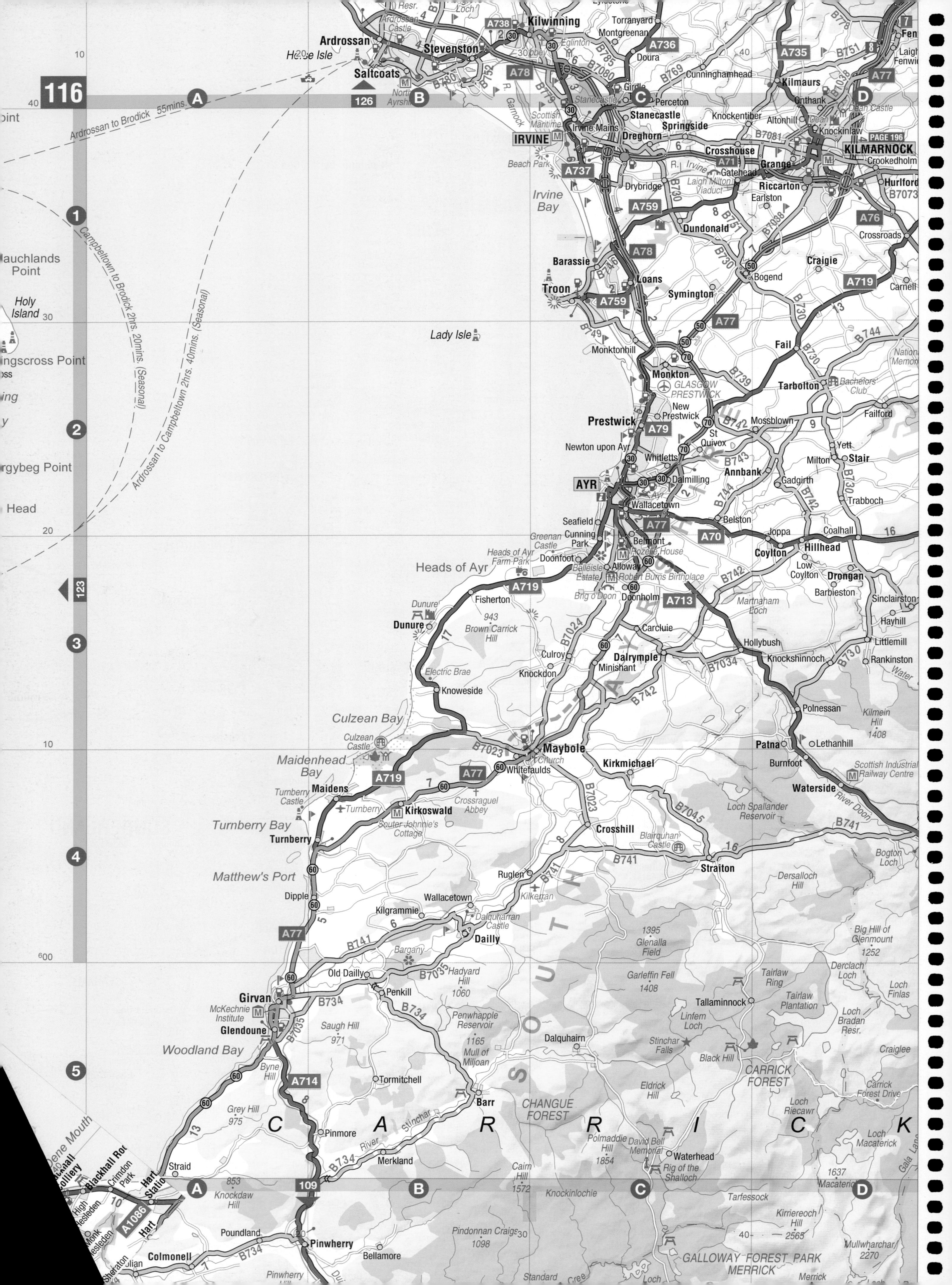
116
126
123
109
Ardrossan
Saltcoats
Stevenston
Kilwinning
Irvine
Troon
Prestwick
Ayr
Maybole
Girvan
Kilmarnock
Dundonald
Symington
Monkton
Tarbolton
Annbank
Coylton
Dalrymple
Kirkmichael
Crosshill
Straiton
Dailly
Kirkoswald
Maidens
Turnberry
Dunure
Barr
Pinwherry
Colmonell
Patna
Waterside
Drongan
Irvine Bay
Heads of Ayr
Culzean Bay
Maidenhead Bay
Turnberry Bay
Woodland Bay
Lady Isle
Holy Island
South Ayrshire
Carrick
Carrick Forest
Galloway Forest Park
Ardrossan to Brodick 55mins.
Campbeltown to Brodick 2hrs. 20mins. (Seasonal)
Ardrossan to Campbeltown 2hrs. 40mins. (Seasonal)

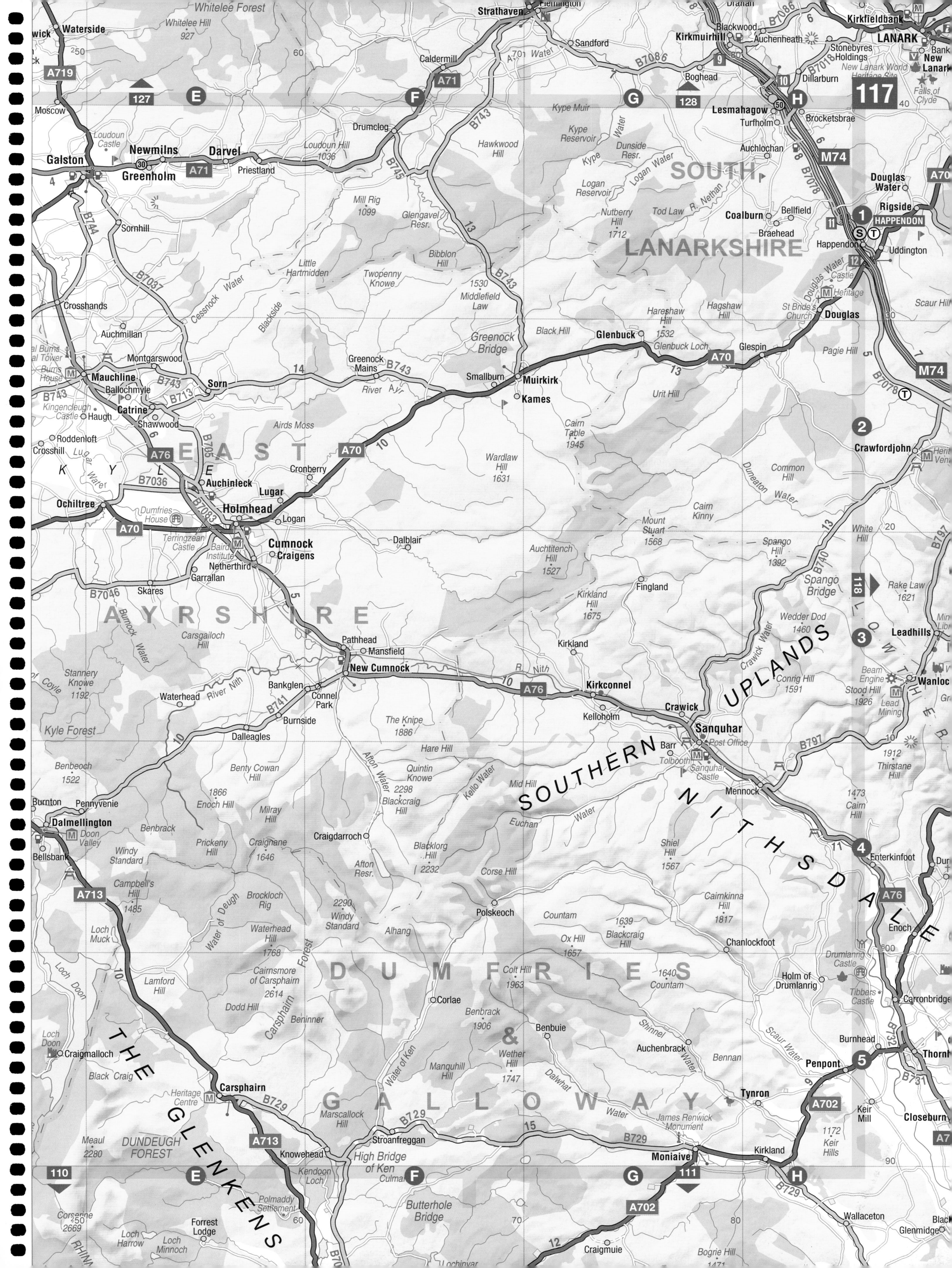

117
Whitelee Forest
Waterside
Whitelee Hill
927
Strathaven
Sandford
Kirkmuirhill
Blackwood
Auchenheath
Kirkfieldbank
LANARK
Stonebyres Holdings
New Lanark
New Lanark World Heritage Site
Falls of Clyde
Dillarburn
Boghead
Caldermill
A719
A71
127
128
E
F
G
H
Moscow
Drumclog
Kype Muir
Kype Reservoir
Lesmahagow
Turfholm
Brocketsbrae
Loudoun Castle
Loudoun Hill
1036
Hawkwood Hill
Dunside Resr.
Auchlochan
M74
Galston
Newmilns
Darvel
Priestland
Greenholm
Logan Reservoir
Logan Water
SOUTH
Douglas Water
Rigside
HAPPENDON
Happendon
Uddington
A70
B744
Sornhill
Mill Rig
1099
Glengavel Resr.
Nutberry Hill
1712
Tod Law
R. Nethan
Coalburn
Bellfield
Braehead
LANARKSHIRE
Bibblon Hill
Little Hartmidden
Twopenny Knowe
B7037
B743
1530
Middlefield Law
Hareshaw Hill
1532
Hagshaw Hill
Douglas Water
Castle
Heritage
St Bride's Church
Douglas
Scaur Hill
Crosshands
Cessnock Water
Blackside
Auchmillan
Greenock Bridge
Black Hill
Glenbuck
Glenbuck Loch
Glespin
Pagie Hill
Burns House
Mauchline
Montgarswood
Greenock Mains
Ballochmyle
B713
Sorn
Smallburn
Muirkirk
Kames
Urit Hill
B7078
Kingencleugh Castle
Haugh
Catrine
River Ayr
Shawwood
Airds Moss
Cairn Table
1945
Roddenloft
Crosshill
EAST
A76
B705
KYLE
Lugar Water
B7036
Auchinleck
Lugar
Cronberry
Wardlaw Hill
1631
Common Hill
Crawfordjohn
Duneaton Water
Ochiltree
Dumfries House
Holmhead
B7083
Logan
Cairn Kinny
Terringzean Castle
Cumnock
Craigens
Dalblair
Mount Stuart
1568
White Hill
Spango Hill
1392
Baird Institute
Netherthird
Auchtitench Hill
1527
B740
Garrallan
Skares
B7046
Fingland
Spango Bridge
118
Rake Law
1621
AYRSHIRE
Kirkland Hill
1675
Wedder Dod
1460
Leadhills
Burnock Water
Carsgailoch Hill
Pathhead
Mansfield
Kirkland
Crawick Water
UPLANDS
LOWTHER
Coyle
Stannery Knowe
1192
New Cumnock
R. Nith
Conrig Hill
1591
Beam Engine
Stood Hill
1926
Wanlock
Lead Mining
Waterhead
River Nith
Bankglen
Connel Park
Kirkconnel
Crawick
Kelloholm
B741
Burnside
The Knipe
1886
Sanquhar
Post Office
Kyle Forest
Dalleagles
Hare Hill
Barr
Tolbooth
Sanquhar Castle
B797
1912
Thirstane Hill
Benbeoch
1522
Benty Cowan Hill
Afton Water
Quintin Knowe
2298
Kello Water
Mid Hill
SOUTHERN
Mennock
1473
Cairn Hill
Burnton
Pennyvenie
1866
Enoch Hill
Blackcraig Hill
Milray Hill
NITHSDALE
Dalmellington
Doon Valley
Benbrack
Euchan Water
Bellsbank
Windy Standard
Prickeny Hill
Craignane
1646
Craigdarroch
Blackorg Hill
2232
Shiel Hill
1567
Enterkinfoot
Afton Resr.
Corse Hill
A713
Campbell's Hill
1485
Water of Deugh
Brockloch Rig
2290
Windy Standard
Polskeoch
Countam
Cairnkinna Hill
1817
Enoch
Loch Muck
Waterhead Hill
1768
Alhang
1639
Blackcraig Hill
Ox Hill
1657
Chanlockfoot
Drumlanrig Castle
Loch Doon
Lamford Hill
Cairnsmore of Carsphairn
2614
Forest
DUMFRIES
Colt Hill
1963
1640
Countam
Holm of Drumlanrig
Tibbers Castle
Carronbridge
Dodd Hill
Corlae
Carsphairn Forest
Beninner
Benbrack
1906
&
Benbuie
Shinnel Water
Scaur Water
Loch Doon
Craigmalloch
THE
Wether Hill
1747
Auchenbrack
Bennan
Burnhead
Penpont
Thornhill
Black Craig
Manquhill Hill
Water of Ken
Dalwhat Water
Tynron
B731
B732
Heritage Centre
Carsphairn
B729
GALLOWAY
James Renwick Monument
A702
Keir Mill
Closeburn
GLENKENS
Marscalloch Hill
Stroanfreggan
1172
Keir Hills
Meaul
2280
DUNDEUGH FOREST
Knowehead
High Bridge of Ken
Moniaive
Kirkland
Kendoon Loch
Culmark
110
111
Polmaddy Settlement
Butterhole Bridge
Corserine
2669
Forrest Lodge
Loch Harrow
Loch Minnoch
Wallaceton
Glenmidge
Craigmuie
Bogrie Hill
Lochinvar

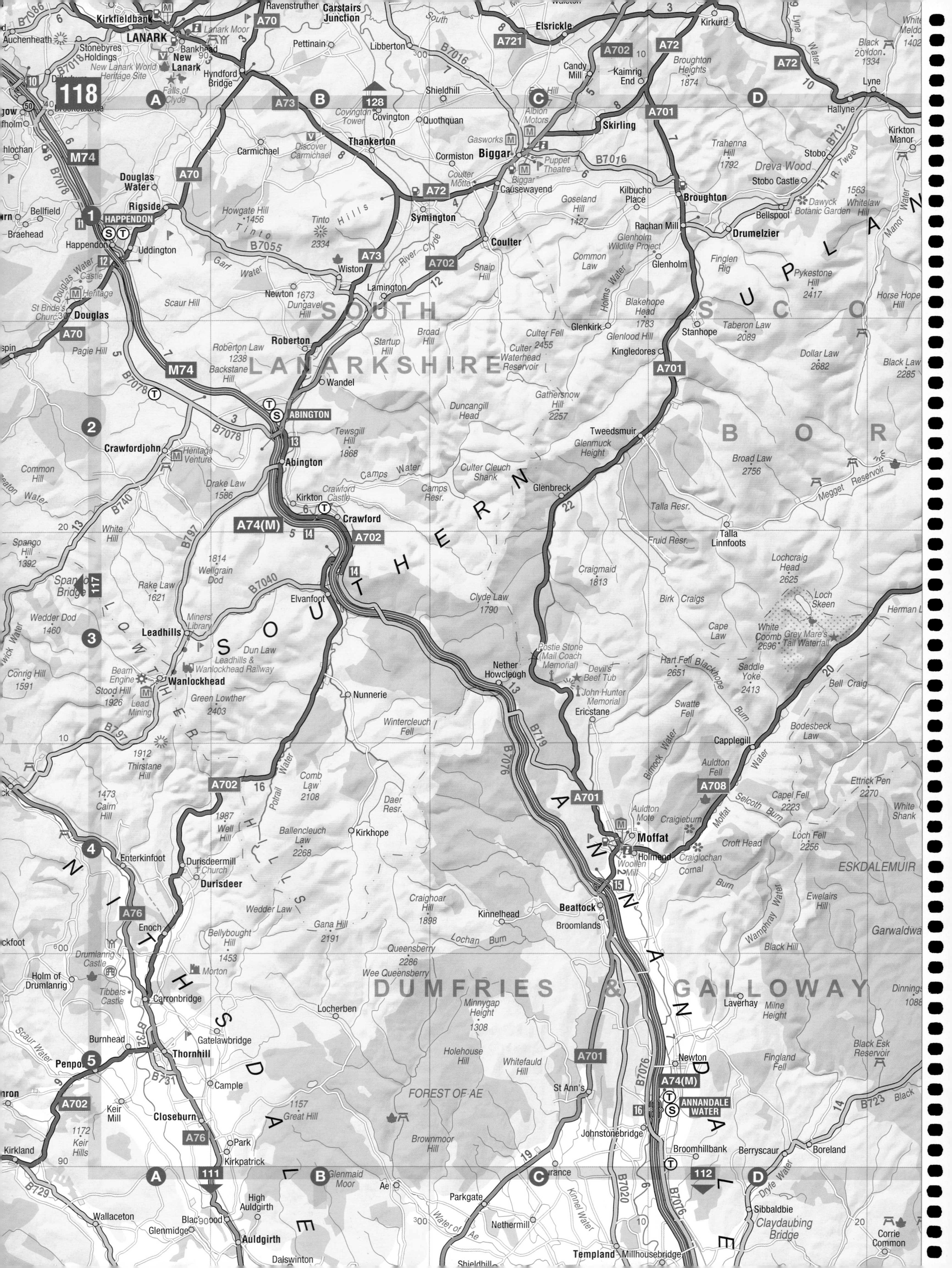
118
LANARK
Kirkfieldbank
Ravenstruther
Carstairs Junction
Auchenheath
Stonebyres Holdings
Lanark Moor
Bankhead
New Lanark
New Lanark World Heritage Site
Falls of Clyde
Hyndford Bridge
Pettinain
Libberton
Elsrickle
Candy Mill
Kaimrig End
Kirkurd
Broughton Heights 1874
Black Meldon 1334
Lyne
Hallyne
Kirkton Manor
A70
A721
A702
A72
A73
A701
B7016
B7086
B7018
128
Covington Tower
Covington
Quothquan
Shieldhill
Albion Motors
Skirling
Thankerton
Discover Carmichael
Carmichael
Gasworks
Biggar
Puppet Theatre
Cormiston
Coulter Motte
Causewayend
Trahenna Hill 1792
Dreva Wood
Stobo
Stobo Castle
Dawyck Botanic Garden
Whitelaw Hill 1563
Manor Water
R. Tweed
B712
M74
Douglas Water
Rigside
Bellfield
Braehead
HAPPENDON
Happendon
Uddington
Howgate Hill 1456
Tinto Hills
Tinto 2334
B7055
Symington
Goseland Hill 1427
Kilbucho Place
Broughton
Bellspool
Rachan Mill
Drumelzier
Coulter
Glenholm Wildlife Project
Glenholm
Common Law
Finglen Rig
Pykestone Hill 2417
River Clyde
Garf Water
Douglas Water
Castle
Heritage
St Bride's Church
Douglas
Scaur Hill
Newton
Dungavel Hill 1673
Wiston
Lamington
Snaip Hill
Holms Water
Blakehope Head 1783
Glenkirk
Glenlood Hill
Stanhope
Taberon Law 2089
Horse Hope Hill
SOUTH LANARKSHIRE
Pagie Hill
Roberton Law 1238
Backstane Hill
Roberton
Startup Hill
Broad Hill
Culter Fell 2455
Culter Waterhead Reservoir
Kingledores
Dollar Law 2682
Black Law 2285
B7078
Wandel
ABINGTON
Tewsgill Hill 1868
Duncangill Head
Gathersnow Hill 2257
Tweedsmuir
Glenmuck Height
Crawfordjohn
Heritage Venture
Common Hill
Drake Law 1586
Abington
Camps Water
Culter Cleuch Shank
Camps Resr.
Glenbreck
Broad Law 2756
Megget Reservoir
Talla Resr.
Talla Linnfoots
Kirkton
Crawford Castle
Crawford
A74(M)
White Hill
Spango Hill 1392
B740
B797
1814 Wellgrain Dod
Fruid Resr.
Craigmaid 1813
Lochcraig Head 2625
Loch Skeen
Spango Bridge
117
Rake Law 1621
B7040
Elvanfoot
Clyde Law 1790
Birk Craigs
Cape Law
White Coomb 2696
Grey Mare's Tail Waterfall
Herman Law
Wedder Dod 1460
Leadhills
Miners' Library
Dun Law
Leadhills & Wanlockhead Railway
Postie Stone (Mail Coach Memorial)
Devil's Beef Tub
John Hunter Memorial
Nether Howcleugh
Hart Fell 2651
Blackhope Burn
Saddle Yoke 2413
Bell Craig
Conrig Hill 1591
Beam Engine
Stood Hill 1926
Wanlockhead
Lead Mining
Green Lowther 2403
Nunnerie
Ericstane
Swatte Fell
Wintercleuch Fell
B7076
B719
Capplegill
Bodesbeck Law
1912 Thirstane Hill
Potrail Water
Comb Law 2108
Daer Resr.
Birnock Water
Auldton Fell
Ettrick Pen 2270
Capel Fell 2223
Selcoth Burn
White Shank
1473 Cairn Hill
1987 Well Hill
Ballencleuch Law 2268
Kirkhope
Auldton Mote
Craigieburn
Moffat
Moffat Water
A708
Croft Head
Loch Fell 2256
Enterkinfoot
Durisdeermill
Church
Durisdeer
Holmend
Woollen Mill
Craiglochan
Cornal
ESKDALEMUIR
A76
Wedder Law
Craighoar Hill 1898
Kinnelhead
Beattock
Broomlands
Wamphray Water
Ewelairs Hill
Enoch
Bellybought Hill 1453
Gana Hill 2191
Lochan Burn
Queensberry 2286
Wee Queensberry
Black Hill
Garwaldwater
Drumlanrig Castle
Holm of Drumlanrig
Morton
Tibbers Castle
Carronbridge
DUMFRIES & GALLOWAY
Minnygap Height 1308
Laverhay
Milne Height
Dinnings 1086
Locherben
NITHSDALE
LOWTHER HILLS
SOUTHERN UPLANDS
BORDERS
ANNANDALE
Scaur Water
Burnhead
Gatelawbridge
B732
Thornhill
Holehouse Hill
Whitefauld Hill
Newton
Fingland Fell
Black Esk Reservoir
Penpont
B731
Cample
A702
St Ann's
FOREST OF AE
ANNANDALE WATER
B723
Black Esk
Keir Mill
Closeburn
1157 Great Hill
1172 Keir Hills
Brownmoor Hill
Johnstonebridge
Park
Kirkpatrick
Broomhillbank
Berryscaur
Boreland
Kirkland
111
Glenmaid Moor
Ae
Courance
B7020
112
B729
Dryfe Water
High Auldgirth
Parkgate
Kinnel Water
Sibbaldbie
Wallaceton
Blackwood
Water of Ae
Claydaubing Bridge
Glenmidge
Nethermill
Corrie Common
Auldgirth
Dalswinton
Shieldhill
Templand
Millhousebridge

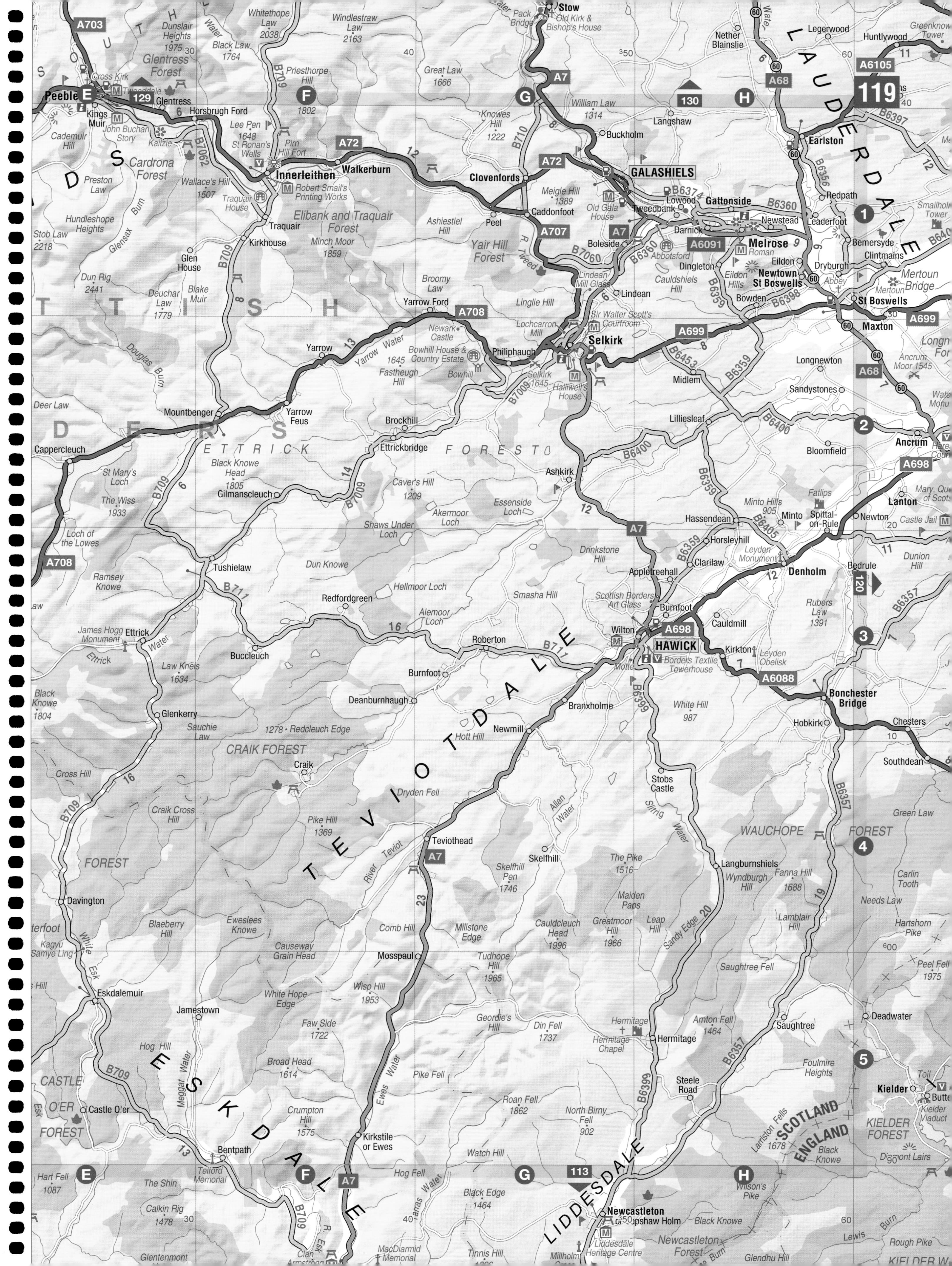

A703
Peebles
Cross Kirk
Glentress
Glentress Forest
Dunslair Heights
1975
Whitehope Law
2038
Windlestraw Law
2163
Black Law
1764
Priesthorpe Hill
1802
Pack Bridge
Stow
Old Kirk & Bishop's House
Nether Blainslie
Legerwood
Huntlywood
Greenknowe Tower
A6105
119
LAUDERDALE
Great Law
1666
A7
130
A68
Kings Muir
Horsbrugh Ford
Cademuir Hill
John Buchan Story
Kailzie
Lee Pen
1648
St Ronan's Wells
Pirn Hill Fort
Knowes Hill
1222
William Law
1314
Langshaw
Buckholm
Earlston
B6397
Cardrona Forest
Preston Law
Wallace's Hill
1507
A72
Innerleithen
Walkerburn
Robert Smail's Printing Works
Traquair House
Traquair
Clovenfords
GALASHIELS
B6356
Redpath
Meigle Hill
1389
Old Gala House
B6374
Lowood
Gattonside
B6360
Tweedbank
Newstead
Leaderfoot
Smailholm Tower
Hundleshope Heights
Elibank and Traquair Forest
Ashiestiel Hill
Peel
Caddonfoot
A707
Darnick
Melrose
Roman
Bemersyde
Clintmains
Stob Law
2218
Glensax
Kirkhouse
Minch Moor
1859
Yair Hill Forest
Boleside
A6091
Abbotsford
Dingleton
Eildon
Newtown St Boswells
Dryburgh Abbey
Mertoun Bridge
Glen House
B7060
Lindean Mill Glass
Eildon Hills
Cauldshiels Hill
Dun Rig
2441
Deuchar Law
1779
Blake Muir
Broomy Law
Linglie Hill
Lindean
B6359
Bowden
B6398
St Boswells
Yarrow Ford
A708
Sir Walter Scott's Courtroom
A699
Maxton
Douglas Burn
Lochcarron Mill
Newark Castle
Bowhill House & Country Estate
Yarrow
Yarrow Water
1645
Fastheugh Hill
Bowhill
Philiphaugh
Selkirk
1645
Halliwell's House
B6453
Midlem
Longnewton
Ancrum Moor 1545
Sandystones
Deer Law
Mountbenger
Yarrow Feus
Brockhill
Lilliesleaf
B6400
Ancrum
Cappercleuch
ETTRICK
Ettrickbridge
FOREST
Bloomfield
A698
Black Knowe Head
1805
St Mary's Loch
Gilmanscleuch
B709
B7009
Caver's Hill
1209
Ashkirk
Essenside Loch
Akermoor Loch
Minto Hills
905
Minto
Fatlips
Spittal-on-Rule
Lanton
Newton
Castle Jail
The Wiss
1933
Loch of the Lowes
Shaws Under Loch
Hassendean
B6405
Horsleyhill
Drinkstone Hill
Leyden Monument
Clarilaw
Denholm
Bedrule
Dunion Hill
A708
Tushielaw
Dun Knowe
Appletreehall
Ramsey Knowe
B711
Hellmoor Loch
Redfordgreen
Smasha Hill
Scottish Borders Art Glass
Burnfoot
Rubers Law
1391
B6357
Alemoor Loch
Cauldmill
James Hogg Monument
Ettrick
Ettrick Water
Buccleuch
Robertson
Wilton
HAWICK
Motte
Borders Textile Towerhouse
Kirkton
Leyden Obelisk
A6088
Law Kneis
1634
Burnfoot
Bonchester Bridge
Black Knowe
1804
Deanburnhaugh
Branxholme
White Hill
987
B6399
Glenkerry
Sauchie Law
1278 • Redcleuch Edge
Newmill
Hott Hill
Hobkirk
Chesters
CRAIK FOREST
Craik
TEVIOTDALE
Southdean
Cross Hill
Dryden Fell
Stobs Castle
Craik Cross Hill
Pike Hill
1369
Allan Water
Slitrig Water
Green Law
WAUCHOPE FOREST
FOREST
Teviothead
River Teviot
Skelfhill
Skelfhill Pen
1746
The Pike
1516
Langburnshiels
Wyndburgh Hill
Fanna Hill
1688
Carlin Tooth
Davington
Maiden Paps
Lamblair Hill
Needs Law
Blaeberry Hill
Eweslees Knowe
Comb Hill
Millstone Edge
Cauldcleuch Head
1996
Greatmoor Hill
1966
Leap Hill
Sandy Edge
Hartshorn Pike
Kagyu Samye Ling
White Esk
Causeway Grain Head
Mosspaul
Tudhope Hill
1965
Saughtree Fell
Peel Fell
1975
Eskdalemuir
Jamestown
White Hope Edge
Wisp Hill
1953
Faw Side
1722
Geordie's Hill
Din Fell
1737
Hermitage
Hermitage Castle
Hermitage Chapel
Arnton Fell
1464
Saughtree
Deadwater
Hog Hill
Meggat Water
ESKDALE
Broad Head
1614
Ewes Water
Pike Fell
B6357
Foulmire Heights
Kielder
Butteryhaugh
Kielder Viaduct
CASTLE O'ER FOREST
Castle O'er
Crumpton Hill
1575
Roan Fell
1862
North Birny Fell
902
Steele Road
Larriston Fells
1678
SCOTLAND
ENGLAND
Black Knowe
KIELDER FOREST
Kirkstile or Ewes
Watch Hill
Bentpath
Telford Memorial
Diamont Lairs
Hart Fell
1087
The Shin
Hog Fell
113
LIDDESDALE
Wilson's Pike
Tarras Water
Black Edge
1464
Calkin Rig
1478
Newcastleton
Copshaw Holm
Black Knowe
Liddesdale Heritage Centre
Newcastleton Forest
Lewis Burn
Rough Pike
Glentenmont
Clan Armstrong
MacDiarmid Memorial
Tinnis Hill
Millholm
Glendhu Hill
KIELDER WATER

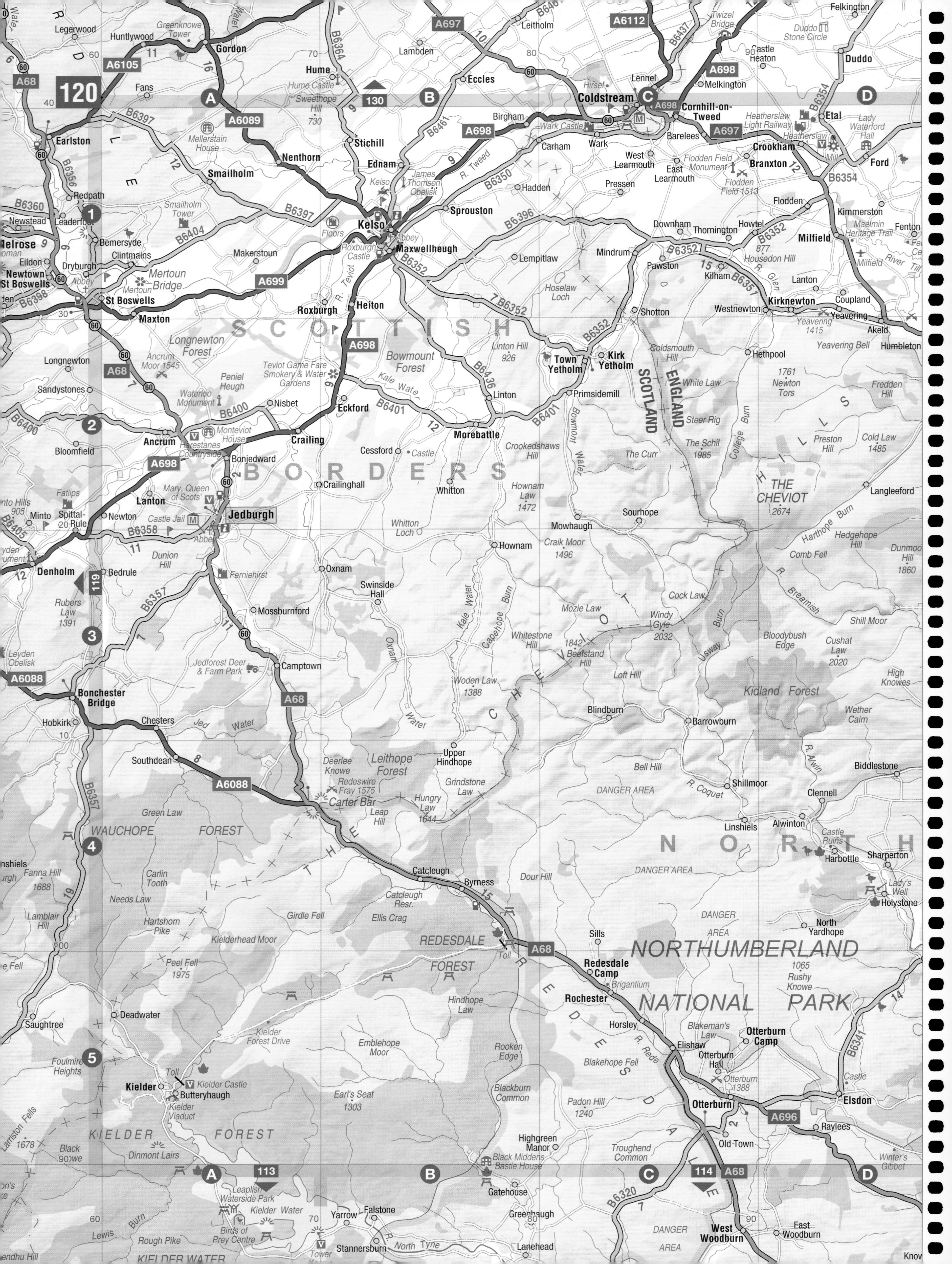

120
130
119
113
114
A B C D
1 2 3 4 5
SCOTTISH
BORDERS
THE CHEVIOT HILLS
SCOTLAND
ENGLAND
NORTHUMBERLAND
NATIONAL PARK
NORTH
REDESDALE
KIELDER FOREST
WAUCHOPE FOREST
Legerwood
Huntlywood
Greenknowe Tower
Gordon
Earlston
Fans
Hume
Hume Castle
Sweethope Hill 730
Lambden
Leitholm
Eccles
Twizel Bridge
Duddo Stone Circle
Castle Heaton
Duddo
Felkington
Lennel
Coldstream
Cornhill-on-Tweed
Melkington
Hirsel
Birgham
Wark Castle
Wark
Carham
Barelees
Heatherslaw Light Railway
Etal
Lady Waterford Hall
Crookham
Ford
Branxton
Flodden Field Monument
Flodden Field 1513
West Learmouth
East Learmouth
Pressen
Hadden
Sprouston
Flodden
Kimmerston
Maelmin Heritage Trail
Fenton
Milfield
Mellerstain House
Nenthorn
Stichill
Ednam
James Thomson Obelisk
Smailholm
Smailholm Tower
Redpath
Leaderfoot
Bemersyde
Melrose
Newstead
Eildon
Dryburgh
Clintmains
Mertoun Bridge
Makerstoun
Floors
Kelso
Abbey
Roxburgh Castle
Maxwellheugh
Newtown St Boswells
St Boswells
Maxton
Roxburgh
Heiton
Downham
Thornington
Howtel
Mindrum
Pawston
Lempitlaw
Housedon Hill
Kilham
Lanton
Kirknewton
Westnewton
Coupland
Yeavering
Yeavering Bell
Akeld
Humbleton
Hoselaw Loch
Shotton
Longnewton Forest
Longnewton
Ancrum Moor 1545
Bowmount Forest
Linton Hill 926
Town Yetholm
Kirk Yetholm
Coldsmouth Hill
Hethpool
Newton Tors
Fredden Hill
Sandystones
Peniel Heugh
Teviot Game Fare Smokery & Water Gardens
Waterloo Monument
Nisbet
Eckford
Kale Water
Linton
Primsidemill
White Law
Steer Rig
Bloomfield
Ancrum
Harestanes Countryside
Monteviot House
Crailing
Morebattle
Cessford
Castle
Crookedshaws Hill
Bowmont Water
The Schil
The Curr
Preston Hill
Cold Law
College Burn
Bonjedward
Crailinghall
Whitton
Hownam Law
THE CHEVIOT
Langleeford
Fatlips
Minto
Spittal-on-Rule
Lanton
Mary, Queen of Scots
Newton
Castle Jail
Jedburgh
Whitton Loch
Mowhaugh
Sourhope
Denholm
Dunion Hill
Bedrule
Hownam
Craik Moor 1496
Hedgehope Hill
Comb Fell
Dunmoor Hill 1860
Harthope Burn
Ferniehirst
Oxnam
Swinside Hall
Rubers Law 1391
Mossburnford
Mozie Law
Cock Law
Windy Gyle 2032
R. Breamish
Shill Moor
Whitestone Hill
Beefstand Hill
Bloodybush Edge
Cushat Law 2020
High Knowes
Leyden Obelisk
Jedforest Deer & Farm Park
Camptown
Woden Law 1388
Capehope Burn
Loft Hill
Kidland Forest
Bonchester Bridge
Hobkirk
Chesters
Jed Water
Blindburn
Barrowburn
Wether Cairn
Southdean
Deerlee Knowe
Leithope Forest
Upper Hindhope
Redeswire Fray 1575
Carter Bar
Grindstone Law
Bell Hill
Biddlestone
Shillmoor
R. Coquet
Clennell
DANGER AREA
Green Law
Leap Hill
Hungry Law 1644
Linshiels
Alwinton
Castle Ruins
Harbottle
Sharperton
Fanna Hill 1688
Carlin Tooth
Catcleugh
Byrness
Dour Hill
Lady's Well
Holystone
Needs Law
Catcleugh Resr.
Ellis Crag
Girdle Fell
Lamblair Hill
Hartshorn Pike
North Yardhope
Kielderhead Moor
Sills
Toll
Peel Fell 1975
Redesdale Camp
Brigantium
Rochester
Hindhope Law
1065 Rushy Knowe
Deadwater
Saughtree
Kielder Forest Drive
Horsley
R. Rede
Blakeman's Law
Otterburn Camp
Emblehope Moor
Rooken Edge
Elishaw
Otterburn Hall
Otterburn 1388
Foulmire Heights
Blakehope Fell
Kielder
Kielder Castle
Butteryhaugh
Kielder Viaduct
Earl's Seat 1303
Blackburn Common
Padon Hill 1240
Otterburn
Elsdon
Castle
Larriston Fells 1678
Black Knowe
Dinmont Lairs
Highgreen Manor
Black Middens Bastle House
Troughend Common
Old Town
Raylees
Winter's Gibbet
Leaplish Waterside Park
Kielder Water
Birds of Prey Centre
Gatehouse
Yarrow
Falstone
Greenhaugh
Lewis Burn
Rough Pike
Tower
Stannersburn
North Tyne
Lanehead
West Woodburn
East Woodburn
KIELDER WATER
A68
A697
A6112
A698
A6105
A6089
A699
A6088
A696
B6364
B6397
B6356
B6360
B6404
B6461
B6350
B6396
B6352
B6351
B6354
B6437
B6436
B6401
B6400
B6358
B6357
B6405
B6341
B6320

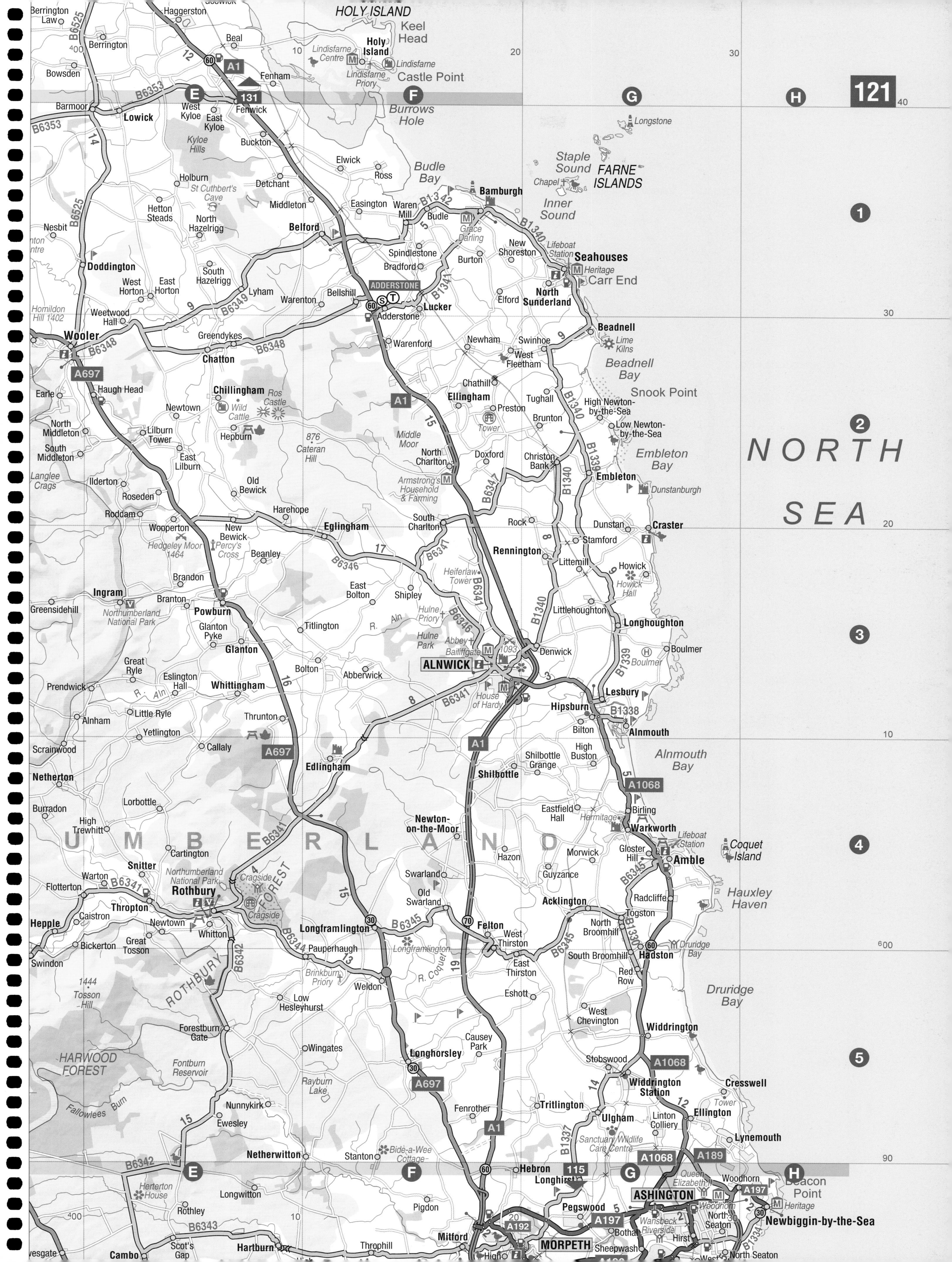

121
HOLY ISLAND
Holy Island
Lindisfarne Castle
Lindisfarne Priory
Castle Point
Keel Head
Burrows Hole
Budle Bay
FARNE ISLANDS
Staple Sound
Inner Sound
Longstone
Bamburgh
Seahouses
Beadnell
Beadnell Bay
Snook Point
Embleton Bay
Embleton
Dunstanburgh
Craster
Howick
Longhoughton
Boulmer
ALNWICK
Lesbury
Alnmouth
Alnmouth Bay
Warkworth
Amble
Coquet Island
Hauxley Haven
Druridge Bay
Widdrington
Cresswell
Ellington
Lynemouth
ASHINGTON
Newbiggin-by-the-Sea
MORPETH
Wooler
Chillingham
Powburn
Rothbury
Longframlington
Felton
Belford
Lowick
Doddington
Chatton
Eglingham
Edlingham
Shilbottle
Acklington
Longhorsley
Netherwitton
HARWOOD FOREST
NORTH SEA
UMBERLAND

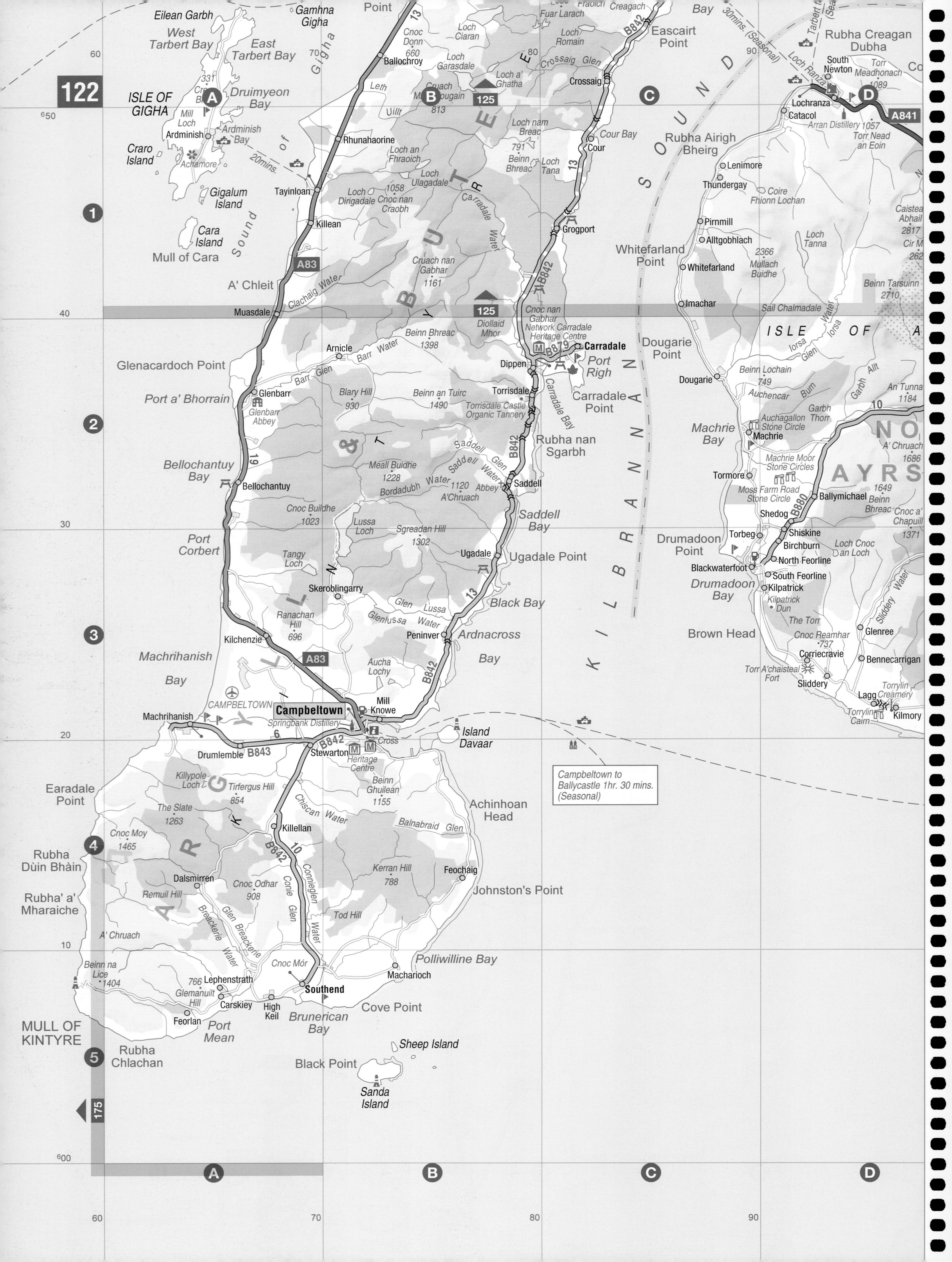

122
ISLE OF GIGHA
Eilean Garbh
West Tarbert Bay
East Tarbert Bay
Gamhna Gigha
Druimyeon Bay
Ardminish
Ardminish Bay
Craro Island
Achamore
Gigalum Island
Cara Island
Mull of Cara
Sound of Gigha
20mins.
Tayinloan
Killean
Rhunahaorine
Ballochroy
A83
A' Chleit
Clachaig Water
Muasdale
Glenacardoch Point
Port a' Bhorrain
Glenbarr
Glenbarr Abbey
Bellochantuy Bay
Bellochantuy
Port Corbert
Machrihanish Bay
Kilchenzie
Machrihanish
Campbeltown
Springbank Distillery
Drumlemble
B843
B842
Stewarton
Heritage Centre
Earadale Point
Killypole Loch
Tirfergus Hill 854
The Slate 1263
Cnoc Moy 1465
Rubha Dùin Bhàin
Rubha' a' Mharaiche
Dalsmirren
Remuil Hill
Cnoc Odhar 908
A' Chruach
Beinn na Lice 1404
Lephenstrath
Glemanuilt Hill 766
Carskiey
Feorlan
Port Mean
MULL OF KINTYRE
Rubha Chlachan
High Keil
Southend
Brunerican Bay
Cnoc Mór
Macharioch
Polliwilline Bay
Cove Point
Sheep Island
Black Point
Sanda Island
Killellan
Chiscan Water
Conieglen Water
Glen Breackerie
Tod Hill
Kerran Hill 788
Feochaig
Johnston's Point
Achinhoan Head
Beinn Ghuilean 1155
Balnabraid Glen
Island Davaar
Cross
Mill Knowe
Campbeltown to Ballycastle 1hr. 30 mins. (Seasonal)
ARGYLL & BUTE
Cnoc Donn 660
Loch Ciaran
Loch Garasdale
Cruach Mhougain 813
Loch a' Ghatha
125
Loch nam Breac
Loch an Fhraoich
Loch Ulagadale
Loch Dirigadale
Cnoc nan Craobh 1058
Carradale Water
Cruach nan Gabhar 1161
Beinn Bhreac 791
Loch Tana
Fuar Larach
Loch Romain
Crossaig Glen
Crossaig
Eascairt Point
B842
Cour Bay
Cour
Grogport
Diollaid Mhor
Cnoc nan Gabhar
Network Carradale Heritage Centre
B879
Carradale
Port Righ
Dippen
Carradale Point
Torrisdale
Torrisdale Castle Organic Tannery
Carradale Bay
Rubha nan Sgarbh
Arnicle
Barr Water
Beinn Bhreac 1398
Barr Glen
Blary Hill 930
Beinn an Tuirc 1490
Meall Buidhe 1228
Saddell Glen
Saddell Water
Saddell Abbey
Saddell
Saddell Bay
Bordadubh Water
A'Chruach 1120
Cnoc Buildhe 1023
Lussa Loch
Sgreadan Hill 1302
Tangy Loch
Ugadale
Ugadale Point
Skeroblingarry
Glen Lussa
Glenlussa Water
Black Bay
Ranachan Hill 696
Peninver
Ardnacross Bay
Aucha Lochy
CAMPBELTOWN
KILBRANNAN SOUND
30mins. (Seasonal)
Bay
Rubha Creagan Dubha
South Newton
Torr Meadhonach 1089
Lochranza
Catacol
Arran Distillery
A841
Torr Nead an Eoin 1057
Rubha Airigh Bheirg
Lenimore
Thundergay
Coire Fhionn Lochan
Pirnmill
Alltgobhlach
Mullach Buidhe 2366
Loch Tanna
Whitefarland Point
Whitefarland
Imachar
Beinn Tarsuinn 2710
Sail Chalmadale
ISLE OF ARRAN
Iorsa Water
Glen Iorsa
Dougarie Point
Dougarie
Beinn Lochain 749
Auchencar Burn
Garbh Thorr
Machrie Bay
Auchagallon Stone Circle
Machrie
Machrie Moor Stone Circles
Tormore
Moss Farm Road Stone Circle
Shedog
B880
Ballymichael
Beinn Bhreac 1649
A' Chruach 1686
NORTH AYRSHIRE
Cnoc a' Chapuill 1371
Drumadoon Point
Torbeg
Shiskine
Birchburn
North Feorline
Blackwaterfoot
South Feorline
Kilpatrick
Drumadoon Bay
Kilpatrick Dun
The Torr
Loch Cnoc an Loch
Sliddery Water
Brown Head
Cnoc Reamhar 737
Glenree
Corriecravie
Torr A'chaisteal Fort
Sliddery
Bennecarrigan
Lagg
Torrylin Creamery
Torrylin Cairn
Kilmory
An Tunna 1184
Garbh Allt
175

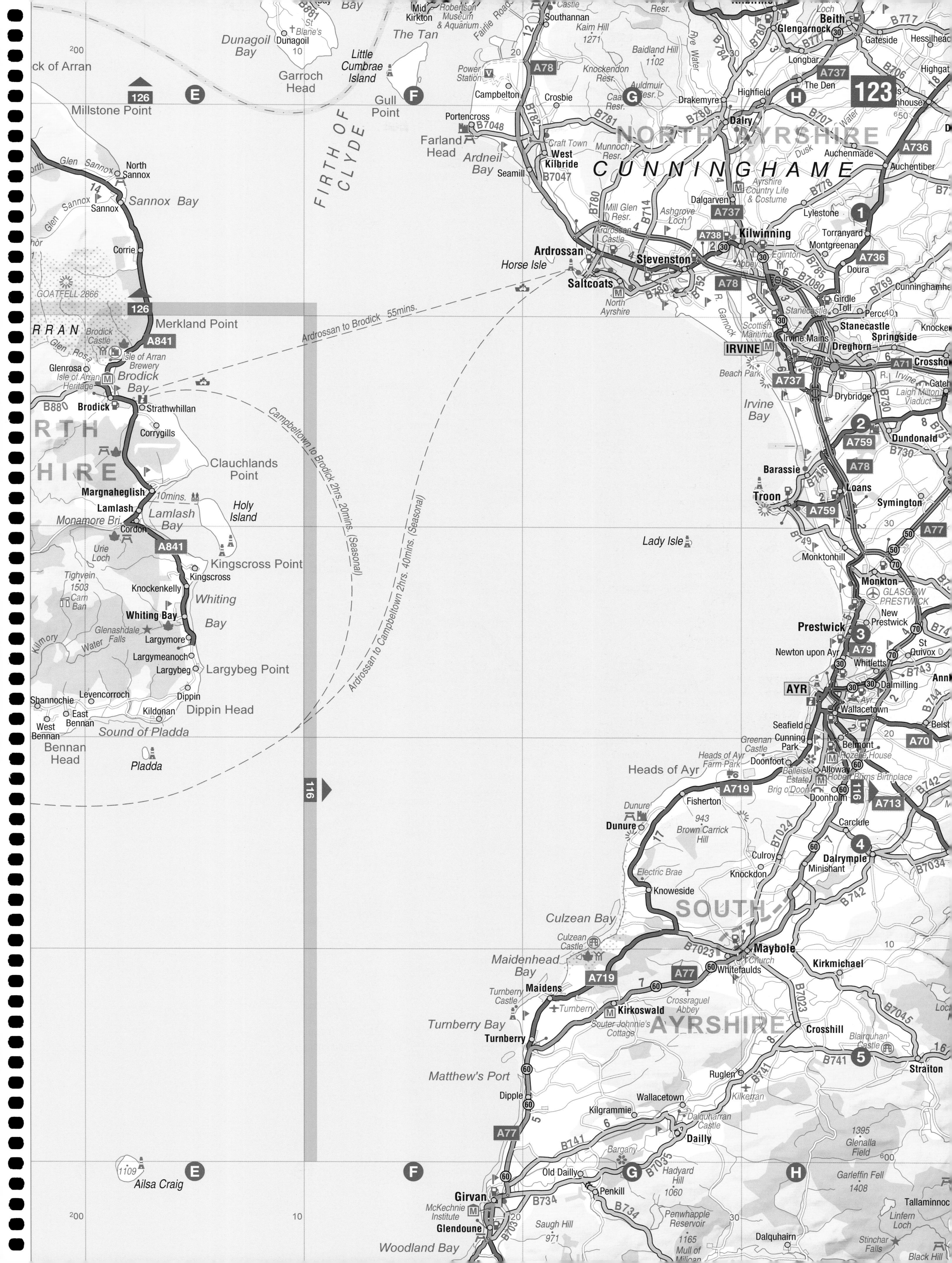

FIRTH OF CLYDE
NORTH AYRSHIRE
CUNNINGHAME
SOUTH AYRSHIRE
Dunagoil Bay
Little Cumbrae Island
The Tan
Garroch Head
Millstone Point
Gull Point
Portencross
Farland Head
Ardneil Bay
Seamill
West Kilbride
Southannan
Beith
Glengarnock
Dalry
Kilwinning
Ardrossan
Horse Isle
Saltcoats
Stevenston
IRVINE
Irvine Bay
Dreghorn
Springside
Stanecastle
Dundonald
Barassie
Troon
Loans
Symington
Lady Isle
Monktonhill
Monkton
GLASGOW PRESTWICK
Prestwick
New Prestwick
Newton upon Ayr
Whitletts
AYR
Wallacetown
Dalmilling
Heads of Ayr
Doonfoot
Alloway
Dunure
Fisherton
Brown Carrick Hill
Culroy
Dalrymple
Minishant
Knoweside
Culzean Bay
Culzean Castle
Maybole
Kirkmichael
Maidenhead Bay
Maidens
Kirkoswald
Crossraguel Abbey
Turnberry Bay
Turnberry
Crosshill
Straiton
Matthew's Port
Dipple
Kilgrammie
Dailly
Old Dailly
Penkill
Girvan
Glendoune
Woodland Bay
Ailsa Craig
North Sannox
Sannox Bay
Sannox
Corrie
GOATFELL 2866
Merkland Point
Brodick Castle
Brodick Bay
Brodick
Strathwhillan
Corrygills
Clauchlands Point
Margnaheglish
Lamlash
Lamlash Bay
Holy Island
Cordon
Kingscross Point
Kingscross
Knockenkelly
Whiting Bay
Largymore
Largymeanoch
Largybeg
Largybeg Point
Dippin
Dippin Head
Kildonan
Sound of Pladda
Pladda
Bennan Head
Ardrossan to Brodick 55mins.
Campbeltown to Brodick 2hrs. 20mins. (Seasonal)
Ardrossan to Campbeltown 2hrs. 40mins. (Seasonal)
A78
A737
A736
A759
A77
A79
A719
A713
A841
123
126
116

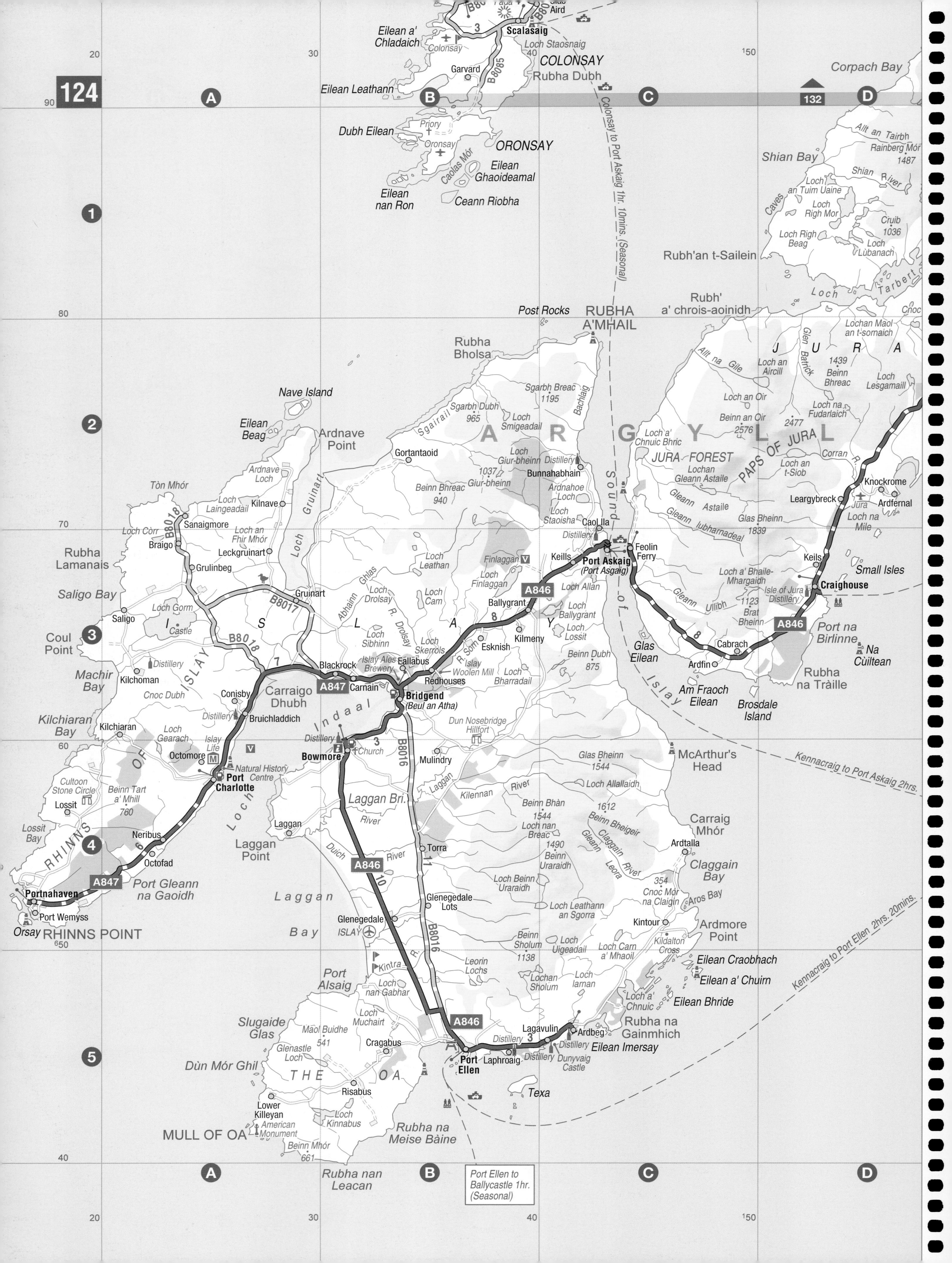

124
132
COLONSAY
Scalasaig
Eilean a' Cladaich
Colonsay
Loch Staosnaig
Garvard
B8085
Rubha Dubh
Eilean Leathann
Dubh Eilean
Priory
Oronsay
ORONSAY
Caolas Mór
Eilean Ghaoideamal
Eilean nan Ron
Ceann Riobha
Corpach Bay
Colonsay to Port Askaig 1hr. 10mins. (Seasonal)
Allt an Tairbh
Rainberg Mór 1487
Shian Bay
Shian River
Loch an Tuim Uaine
Caves
Loch Righ Mor
Loch Righ Beag
Cruib 1036
Loch Lùbanach
Rubh'an t-Sailein
Tarbert
Loch
Rubh' a' chrois-aoinidh
Post Rocks
RUBHA A'MHAIL
Lochan Maol an t-sornaich
Glen Batrick
JURA
Rubha Bholsa
Allt na Gile
Loch an Aircill
1439 Beinn Bhreac
Loch Lesgamaill
Sgarbh Breac 1195
Bachlaig
Loch an Oir
Nave Island
Sgarbh Dubh 965
Loch Smigeadail
Beinn an Oir 2576
2477
Loch na Fudarlaich
Eilean Beag
Ardnave Point
Sgairail
ARGYLL
Loch a' Chnuic Bhric
PAPS OF JURA
JURA FOREST
Corran
Gortantaoid
Loch Giur-bheinn
Distillery
Bunnahabhain
Ardnave Loch
Tòn Mhór
Gruinart
1037 Giur-bheinn
Ardnahoe Loch
Sound of Islay
Lochan Gleann Astaile
Loch an t-Siob
Knockrome
Loch Laingeadail
Kilnave
Beinn Bhreac 940
Gleann Astaile
Leargybreck
Jura
Ardfernal
B8018
Sanaigmore
Loch Staoisha
Caol Ila
Gleann Iubharnadeal
Glas Bheinn 1839
Loch na Mile
Loch Còrr
Braigo
Loch an Fhir Mhór
Loch
Distillery
Rubha Lamanais
Leckgruinart
Loch Leathan
Finlaggan
Keills
Port Askaig (Port Asgaig)
Feolin Ferry
Keills
Small Isles
Grulinbeg
Loch Finlaggan
A846
Loch Allan
Loch a' Bhaile-Mhargaidh
Craighouse
Saligo Bay
Gruinart
Abhainn Ghlas
Loch Drolsay
Loch Cam
Ballygrant
Isle of Jura Distillery
Gleann Ullibh
1123 Brat Bheinn
Loch Gorm
B8017
Loch Ballygrant
Saligo
ISLAY
Castle
R. Drolsay
A846
Port na Birlinne
Coul Point
B8018
Loch Sibhinn
Loch Skerrols
Esknish
Loch Lossit
Kilmeny
Cabrach
Na Cùiltean
Glas Eilean
Beinn Dubh 875
Ardfin
Rubha na Tràille
Machir Bay
Distillery
Kilchoman
Blackrock
Islay Ales Brewery
Eallabus
R. Sorn
Islay Woolen Mill
Redhouses
Loch Bharradail
Am Fraoch Eilean
Brosdale Island
Cnoc Dubh
Carraigo Dhubh
A847
Carnain
Bridgend (Beul an Atha)
Conisby
Distillery
Bruichladdich
Loch Indaal
Kilchiaran Bay
Kilchiaran
Loch Gearach
Islay Life
Distillery
Church
Dun Nosebridge Hillfort
B8016
McArthur's Head
Kennacraig to Port Askaig 2hrs.
RHINNS OF ISLAY
Octomore
Bowmore
Mulindry
Glas Bheinn 1544
Natural History Centre
Port Charlotte
Laggan
Kilennan
River
Loch Allallaidh
Cultoon Stone Circle
Beinn Tart a' Mhill 760
Laggan Bri.
Beinn Bhàn 1544
1612
Lossit
Loch nan Breac
Beinn Bheigeir
Carraig Mhór
Lossit Bay
Laggan
River
Claggain River
1490 Beinn Uraraidh
Gleann Leora
Ardtalla
Neribus
Laggan Point
Torra
Claggain Bay
Octofad
Duich River
A846
Loch Beinn Uraraidh
354 Cnoc Mór na Claigin
Aros Bay
Portnahaven
A847
Port Gleann na Gaoidh
Laggan Bay
Glenegedale Lots
Loch Leathann an Sgorra
Port Wemyss
Glenegedale
ISLAY
B8016
Kintour
Ardmore Point
Orsay
RHINNS POINT
Beinn Sholum 1138
Loch Uigeadail
Loch Carn a' Mhaoil
Kildalton Cross
Leorin Lochs
Eilean Craobhach
Port Alsaig
Kintra
Loch nan Gabhar
Lochan Sholum
Loch Iarnan
Eilean a' Chuirn
Kennacraig to Port Ellen 2hrs. 20mins.
Loch a' Chnuic
Eilean Bhride
Loch Muchairt
A846
Rubha na Gainmhich
Slugaide Glas
Maol Buidhe 541
Lagavulin
Ardbeg
Distillery
Distillery
Eilean Imersay
Glenastle Loch
Cragabus
Port Ellen
Laphroaig
Distillery
Dunyvaig Castle
Dùn Mór Ghil
THE OA
Risabus
Texa
Lower Killeyan
Loch Kinnabus
MULL OF OA
American Monument
Rubha na Meise Bàine
Beinn Mhór 661
Rubha nan Leacan
Port Ellen to Ballycastle 1hr. (Seasonal)
A B C D
1 2 3 4 5
20 30 40 150
90 80 70 60 650 40

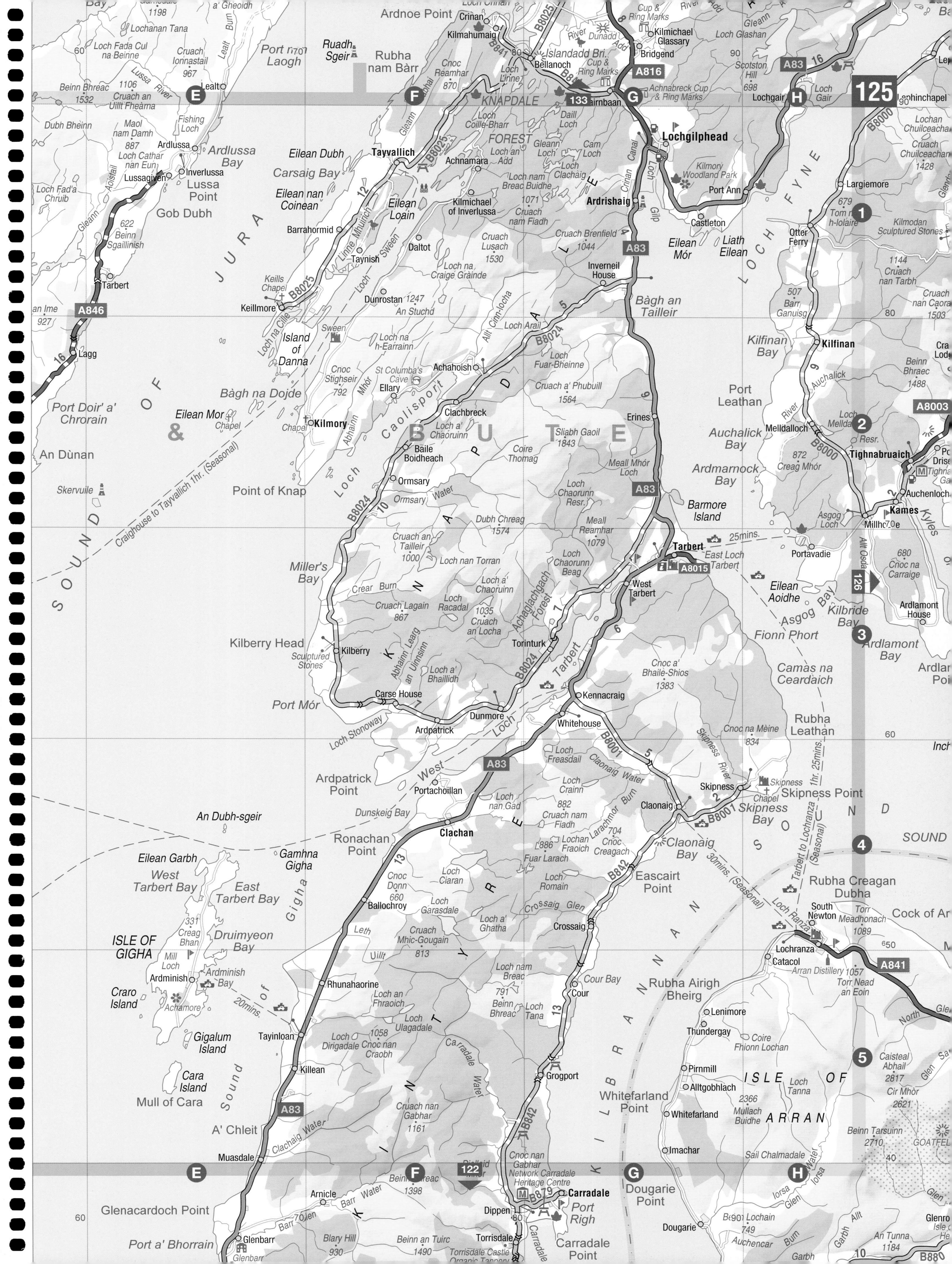

125
Ardnoe Point
Crinan
Kilmahumaig
Bellanoch
Islandadd Bri.
Kilmichael Glassary
Bridgend
Loch Glashan
Lochgair
Cairnbaan
KNAPDALE
FOREST
Lochgilphead
Ardrishaig
Tayvallich
Carsaig Bay
Eilean Dubh
Achnamara
Kilmichael of Inverlussa
Barrahormid
Taynish
Daltot
Keills Chapel
Keillmore
Island of Danna
Dunrostan
Sween
Achahoish
Ellary
Kilmory
Clachbreck
Baile Boidheach
Ormsary
Bàgh na Dojde
Eilean Mor
Chapel
Point of Knap
Skervuile
SOUND OF JURA
Craighouse to Tayvallich 1hr. (Seasonal)
Lealt
Ardlussa
Inverlussa
Lussagiven
Lussa Point
Gob Dubh
Tarbert
Lagg
A846
Port Doir' a' Chrorain
An Dùnan
Miller's Bay
Kilberry Head
Kilberry
Sculptured Stones
Port Mór
Carse House
Ardpatrick
Dunmore
Torinturk
Loch Stonoway
West Loch Tarbert
Ardpatrick Point
Portachoillan
Dunskeig Bay
An Dubh-sgeir
Ronachan Point
Clachan
Eilean Garbh
West Tarbert Bay
East Tarbert Bay
Gamhna Gigha
ISLE OF GIGHA
Ardminish
Ardminish Bay
Achamore
Craro Island
Gigalum Island
Cara Island
Mull of Cara
Sound of Gigha
20mins.
Ballochroy
Rhunahaorine
Tayinloan
Killean
A' Chleit
Muasdale
Glenacardoch Point
Port a' Bhorrain
Glenbarr
Arnicle
Dippen
Torrisdale
Carradale
Port Righ
Carradale Point
Network Carradale Heritage Centre
Dougarie Point
Dougarie
Grogport
Cour
Cour Bay
Crossaig
Eascairt Point
Claonaig
Claonaig Bay
Skipness
Skipness Point
Skipness Bay
Whitehouse
Kennacraig
West Tarbert
Tarbert
East Loch Tarbert
25mins.
Portavadie
Erines
Inverneil House
Bàgh an Tailleir
Barmore Island
Castleton
Port Ann
Eilean Mór
Liath Eilean
LOCH FYNE
Otter Ferry
Largiemore
Kilfinan
Kilfinan Bay
Port Leathan
Auchalick Bay
Ardmarnock Bay
Melldalloch
Tighnabruaich
Kames
Millhouse
Ardlamont House
Kilbride Bay
Asgog Bay
Eilean Aoidhe
Fionn Phort
Ardlamont Bay
Camas na Ceardaich
Rubha Leathan
Tarbert to Lochranza 1hr. 25mins. (Seasonal)
30mins. (Seasonal)
Rubha Creagan Dubha
South Newton
Lochranza
Catacol
Arran Distillery
Cock of Arran
Rubha Airigh Bheirg
Lenimore
Thundergay
Pirnmill
Alltgobhlach
Whitefarland
Whitefarland Point
Imachar
ISLE OF ARRAN
KILBRANNAN SOUND
KINTYRE
KNAPDALE
A83
A816
A8015
B8024
B8025
B8001
B842
B879
B8000
A841
A8003
122
126
133

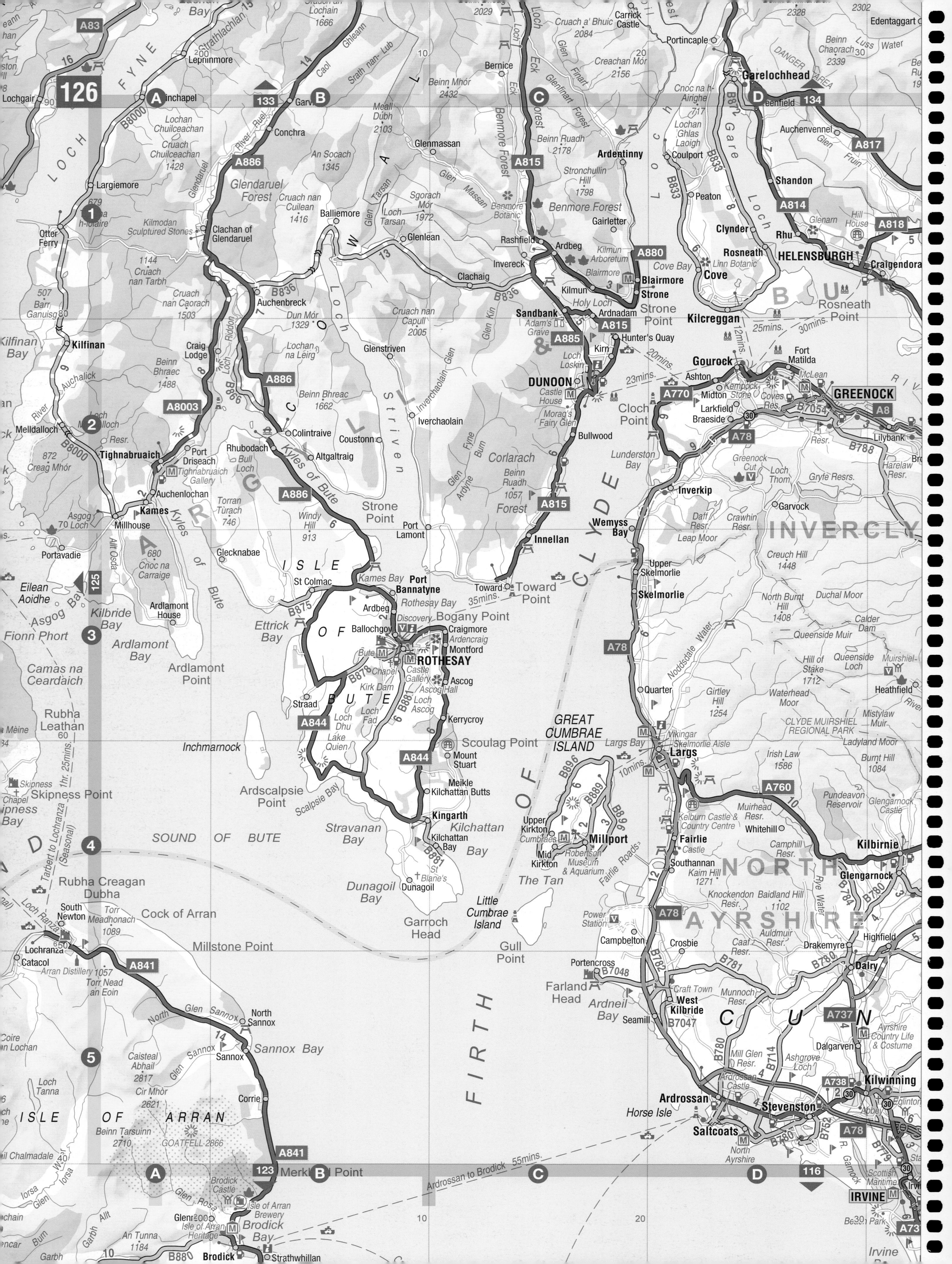
126
133
134
125
123
116
A
B
C
D
1
2
3
4
5
10
20
A83
Loch Fyne
Lochgair
Strathlachlan
Lephinmore
Inchapel
Garvie
Caol Ghleann
Strath nan Lub
Lochan Chuilceachan
Cruach Chuilceachan
1428
Largiemore
Otter Ferry
Loch Riddon
Glendaruel Forest
Cruach nan Cuilean
1416
Kilmodan Sculptured Stones
Clachan of Glendaruel
Conchra
A886
An Socach
1345
Meall Dubh
2103
Glenmassan
Beinn Mhór
2432
Bernice
Loch Eck
Glen Finart
Cruach a' Bhuic
2084
Carrick Castle
Creachan Mór
2156
Portincaple
Garelochhead
Cnoc na h-Airighe
717
Lochan Ghlas Laoigh
Coulport
Beinn Ruadh
2178
Ardentinny
Stronchullin Hill
1798
Benmore Forest
Benmore Botanic
Gairletter
Kilmun Arboretum
Rashfield
Ardbeg
Invereck
Blairmore
Strone
A880
Cove Bay
Cove
Linn Botanic
Kilcreggan
Rosneath
Rosneath Point
Clynder
Rhu
HELENSBURGH
Craigendoran
Shandon
A814
A817
A818
Auchenvennel
Peaton
Glen Fruin
Edentaggart
Beinn Chaorach
2339
Danger Area
Gare Loch
B833
Balliemore
Glen Tarsan
Loch Tarsan
Sgorach Mór
1972
Glenlean
Clachaig
B836
Auchenbreck
Cruach nan Tarbh
1144
Cruach nan Caorach
1503
Dun Mór
1329
Cruach nan Capull
2005
Glen Kin
Holy Loch
Kilmun
Sandbank
Adam's Grave
Ardnadam
Strone Point
A815
A885
Hunter's Quay
Kirn
Loch Loskin
DUNOON
Castle House
Morag's Fairy Glen
Gourock
Fort Matilda
Ashton
McLean
GREENOCK
Kempock Stone
Midton
Larkfield
Braeside
A770
A78
A8
B7054
Lilybank
Cloch Point
Bullwood
Lunderston Bay
Greenock Cut
Loch Thom
Gryfe Resrs.
B788
Harelaw Resr.
Inverkip
Garvock
Daff Resr.
Crawhin Resr.
Leap Moor
INVERCLYDE
Wemyss Bay
Innellan
Corlarach Forest
Beinn Ruadh
1057
Glen Fyne
Ardyne Burn
Kilfinan
Kilfinan Bay
Barr Ganuisg
507
Auchalick
Craig Lodge
Beinn Bhraec
1488
Lochan na Leirg
Glenstriven
Loch Striven
Inverchaolain
Inverchaolain Glen
Beinn Bhreac
1662
Coustonn
A8003
Melldalloch
Loch Melldalloch
B8000
Creag Mhór
872
Tighnabruaich
Tighnabruaich Gallery
Port Driseach
Rhubodach
Bull Loch
Colintraive
Altgaltraig
Kyles of Bute
Auchenlochan
Kames
Millhouse
Torran Turach
746
Windy Hill
913
Strone Point
Port Lamont
Portavadie
Allt Osda
Asgog Loch
Cnoc na Carraige
680
Glecknabae
ISLE OF BUTE
Eilean Aoidhe
Asgog Bay
Kilbride Bay
Fionn Phort
Ardlamont House
Ardlamont Bay
Ardlamont Point
Camas na Ceardaich
St Colmac
Kames Bay
Port Bannatyne
Ardbeg
Rothesay Bay
Discovery
Bogany Point
Ettrick Bay
B875
Ballochgoy
Craigmore
Ardencraig
Montford
ROTHESAY
Bute
Chapel
Castle
Gallery
Ascog
Ascog Hall
Kirk Dam
B878
B881
Loch Ascog
Straad
Loch Fad
Loch Dhu
Lake Quien
A844
Kerrycroy
Scoulag Point
Mount Stuart
Toward
Toward Point
35mins.
Upper Skelmorlie
Skelmorlie
Rubha Leathan
Inchmarnock
Skipness
Skipness Point
Skipness Bay
Ardscalpsie Point
Scalpsie Bay
Meikle Kilchattan Butts
Kingarth
Kilchattan Bay
Stravanan Bay
SOUND OF BUTE
St Blane's
Dunagoil
Dunagoil Bay
Garroch Head
Rubha Creagan Dubha
Cock of Arran
Tarbert to Lochranza (Seasonal)
1hr. 25mins.
Loch Ranza
South Newton
Torr Meadhonach
1089
Lochranza
Catacol
Arran Distillery
Millstone Point
A841
Torr Nead an Eoin
1057
North Glen Sannox
North Sannox
Sannox
Sannox Bay
Glen Sannox
Caisteal Abhail
2817
Cir Mhór
2621
Loch Tanna
Corrie
ISLE OF ARRAN
Beinn Tarsuinn
2710
Goatfell 2866
Brodick Castle
Isle of Arran Brewery
Glen Rosa
Glen Iorsa
Isle of Arran Heritage
Brodick Bay
Brodick
Strathwhillan
An Tunna
1184
Merkland Point
Ardrossan to Brodick 55mins.
B880
GREAT CUMBRAE ISLAND
Largs Bay
Largs
Vikingar
Skelmorlie Aisle
10mins.
B896
B899
Upper Kirkton
Cumbraes
Millport
Mid Kirkton
Robertson Museum & Aquarium
The Tan
Fairlie Roads
Little Cumbrae Island
Gull Point
FIRTH OF CLYDE
Kelburn Castle & Country Centre
Fairlie
Southannan
Kaim Hill
1271
Power Station
Campbelton
Portencross
B7048
Farland Head
Ardneil Bay
Seamill
West Kilbride
B7047
B782
Crosbie
Craft Town
Quarter
Noddsdale Water
Girtley Hill
1254
Creuch Hill
1448
North Burnt Hill
1408
Duchal Moor
Calder Dam
Queenside Muir
Hill of Stake
1712
Queenside Loch
Muirshiel
Heathfield
Waterhead Moor
Mistylaw Muir
CLYDE MUIRSHIEL REGIONAL PARK
Ladyland Moor
Irish Law
1586
Burnt Hill
1084
A760
Pundeavon Reservoir
Glengarnock Castle
Muirhead Resr.
Whitehill
Camphill Resr.
Kilbirnie
NORTH AYRSHIRE
Glengarnock
Knockendon Resr.
Baidland Hill
1102
Rye Water
B784
B780
Auldmuir Resr.
Caaf Resr.
B781
Drakemyre
Highfield
Dalry
Munnoch Resr.
A737
Ayrshire Country Life & Costume
Dalgarven
Mill Glen Resr.
B714
Ashgrove Loch
B780
Ardrossan Castle
Kilwinning
A738
Eglinton
Ardrossan
Horse Isle
Stevenston
Saltcoats
B752
North Ayrshire
A78
B779
Scottish Maritime
IRVINE
A71
Irvine

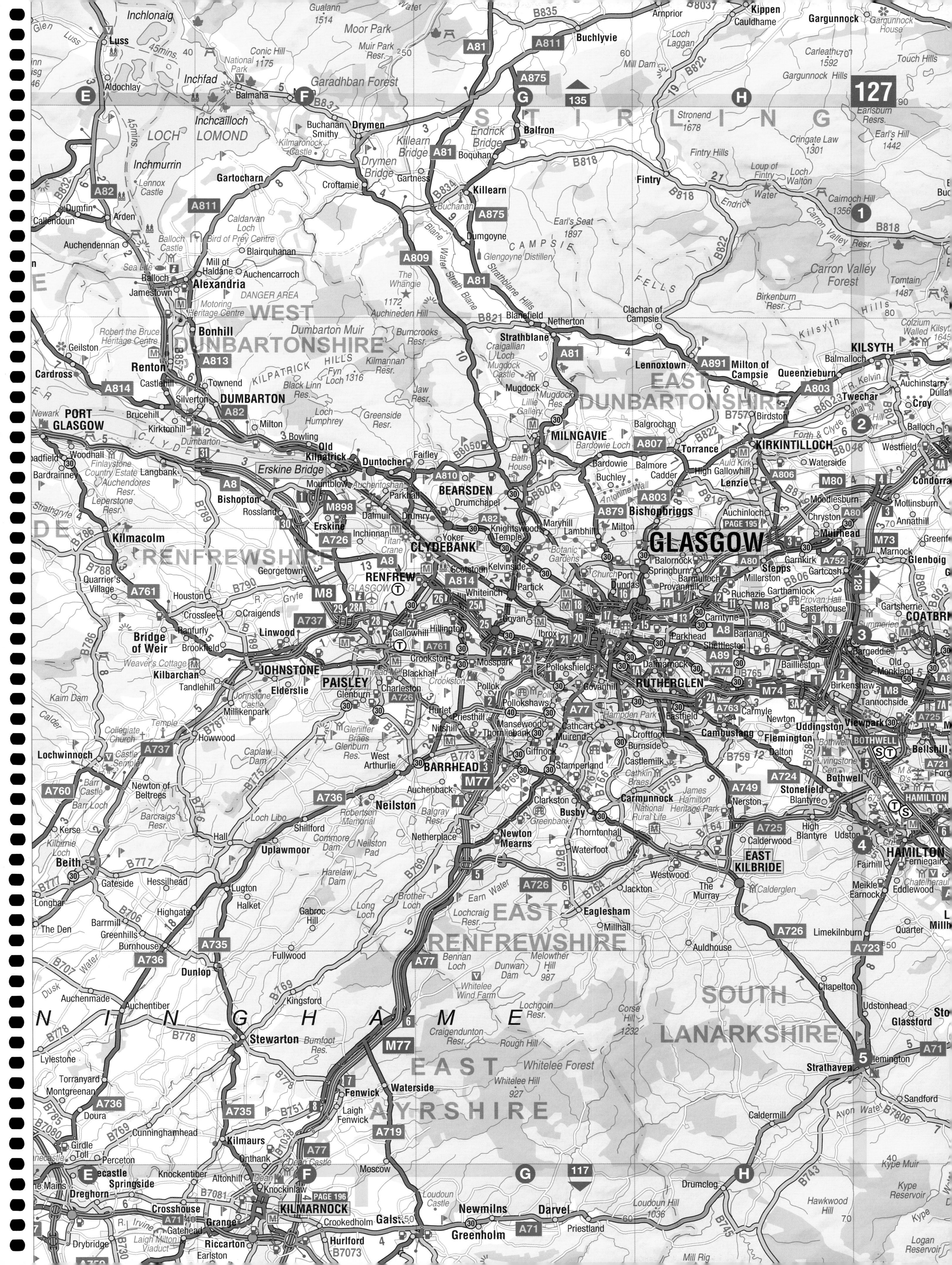

127
135
117
PAGE 195
PAGE 196
STIRLING
WEST DUNBARTONSHIRE
EAST DUNBARTONSHIRE
RENFREWSHIRE
EAST RENFREWSHIRE
SOUTH LANARKSHIRE
EAST AYRSHIRE
LOCH LOMOND
CAMPSIE FELLS
KILPATRICK HILLS
GLASGOW
Luss
Inchlonaig
Inchfad
Balmaha
Inchcailloch
Inchmurrin
Aldochlay
Arden
Dumfin
Callendoun
Auchendennan
Balloch
Jamestown
Alexandria
Bonhill
Renton
Geilston
Cardross
Dumbarton
Port Glasgow
Milton
Bowling
Old Kilpatrick
Duntocher
Faifley
Bearsden
Milngavie
Mugdock
Strathblane
Blanefield
Killearn
Balfron
Drymen
Gartocharn
Croftamie
Buchlyvie
Kippen
Gargunnock
Arnprior
Fintry
Lennoxtown
Milton of Campsie
Kilsyth
Queenzieburn
Twechar
Croy
Kirkintilloch
Lenzie
Torrance
Bishopbriggs
Erskine Bridge
Erskine
Bishopton
Kilmacolm
Clydebank
Renfrew
Paisley
Johnstone
Linwood
Houston
Bridge of Weir
Kilbarchan
Elderslie
Howwood
Lochwinnoch
Beith
Barrhead
Neilston
Uplawmoor
Newton Mearns
Clarkston
Busby
Eaglesham
Rutherglen
Cambuslang
East Kilbride
Uddingston
Bothwell
Hamilton
Blantyre
Coatbridge
Stepps
Muirhead
Chryston
Glenboig
Strathaven
Dunlop
Stewarton
Kilmaurs
Fenwick
Waterside
Kilmarnock
Crosshouse
Riccarton
Hurlford
Galston
Newmilns
Darvel
Greenholm
Priestland
Drumclog
Chapelton
Glassford
Sandford
Caldermill
Whitelee Forest
Carron Valley Forest
Garadhban Forest

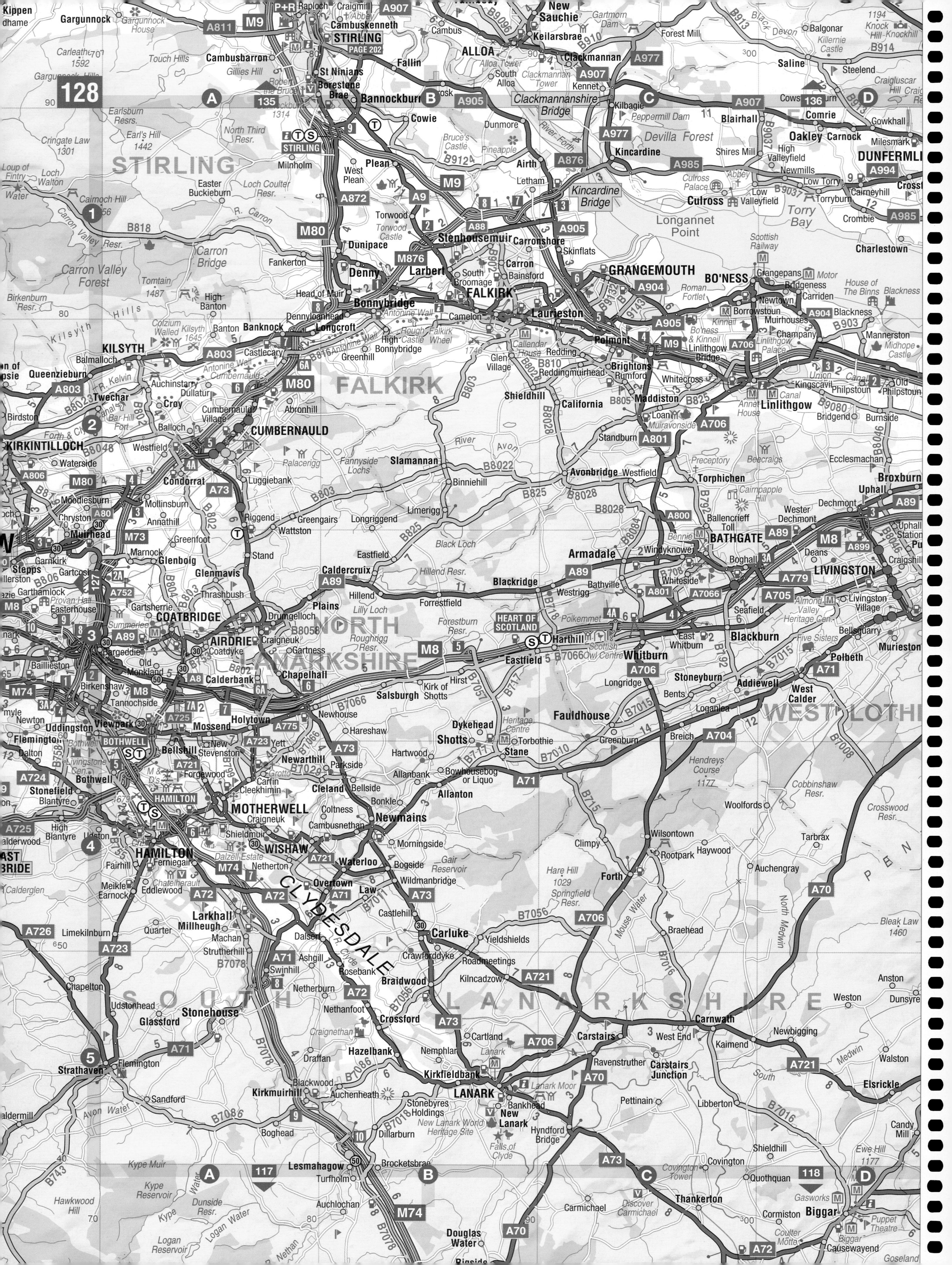

128
Kippen
Gargunnock
Gargunnock House
STIRLING
PAGE 202
Raploch
Craigmill
Cambuskenneth
Cambusbarron
St Ninians
Borestone Brae
Bannockburn
Fallin
Cambus
ALLOA
New Sauchie
Keilarsbrae
Clackmannan
Clackmannan Tower
South Alloa
Kennet
Forest Mill
Balgonar
Saline
Steelend
Knockhill
Clackmannanshire Bridge
Kilbagie
Peppermill Dam
Blairhall
Comrie
Oakley
Carnock
Gowkhall
Milesmark
DUNFERMLINE
Devilla Forest
Kincardine
Shires Mill
High Valleyfield
Newmills
Low Torry
Cairneyhill
Crossford
Culross
Culross Palace
Low Valleyfield
Torryburn
Torry Bay
Crombie
Longannet Point
Charlestown
Kincardine Bridge
Cowie
Plean
West Plean
Airth
Letham
Dunmore
Bruce's Castle
Pineapple
Milnholm
Easter Buckieburn
Loch Coulter Resr.
North Third Resr.
Earlsburn Resrs.
Earl's Hill 1442
Cringate Law 1301
Carleatheran 1592
Touch Hills
Gillies Hill
Loup of Fintry
Loch Walton
Cairnoch Hill
Carron Valley Resr.
Carron Valley Forest
Carron Bridge
Tomtain 1487
Birkenburn Resr.
High Banton
Banton
Banknock
Kilsyth Hills
KILSYTH
Colzium Walled Garden
Torwood
Torwood Castle
Dunipace
Denny
Stenhousemuir
Carronshore
Skinflats
Larbert
South Broomage
Carron
Bainsford
FALKIRK
GRANGEMOUTH
Fankerton
Head of Muir
Bonnybridge
Dennyloanhead
Longcroft
Castlecary
Antonine Wall
Camelon
Falkirk Wheel
Rough Castle
High Bonnybridge
Greenhill
Laurieston
Polmont
BO'NESS
Grangepans
Bridgeness
Carriden
Newtown
Borrowstoun
Muirhouses
Champany
Blackness
House of The Binns
Blackness Castle
Mannerston
Midhope Castle
Kinneil
Linlithgow Bridge
Linlithgow Palace
Callendar House
Glen Village
Redding
Reddingmuirhead
Brightons
Rumford
Whitecross
Kingscavil
Philpstoun
Old Philpstoun
Union Canal
Linlithgow
Annet House
Bridgend
Burnside
Balmalloch
Queenzieburn
Twechar
Auchinstarry
Dullatur
Croy
Bar Hill Fort
Balloch
Cumbernauld Village
CUMBERNAULD
Abronhill
Birdston
KIRKINTILLOCH
Waterside
Westfield
Condorrat
Luggiebank
Palacerigg
Fannyside Lochs
Slamannan
FALKIRK
Shieldhill
California
Maddiston
Loan
Muiravonside
Standburn
River Avon
Avonbridge
Westfield
Preceptory
Beecraigs
Ecclesmachan
Torphichen
Cairnpapple Hill
Broxburn
Uphall
Moodiesburn
Chryston
Muirhead
Mollinsburn
Annathill
Riggend
Greengairs
Wattston
Longriggend
Limerigg
Binniehill
Ballencrieff Toll
Wester Dechmont
Dechmont
Uphall Station
Stepps
Garnkirk
Gartcosh
Marnock
Greenfoot
Glenboig
Glenmavis
Stand
Eastfield
Black Loch
Caldercruix
Hillend Resr.
Hillend
Armadale
Windyknowe
BATHGATE
Boghall
Deans
LIVINGSTON
Craigshill
Garthamlock
Provan Hall
Gartsherrie
Thrashbush
Easterhouse
Summerlee
COATBRIDGE
Drumgelloch
Plains
Lilly Loch
Forrestfield
Blackridge
Westrigg
Bathville
Whiteside
Seafield
Livingston Village
Almond Valley Heritage Cen.
Bargeddie
Baillieston
AIRDRIE
Coatdyke
Craigneuk
Gartness
Roughrigg Resr.
NORTH LANARKSHIRE
Forestburn Resr.
HEART OF SCOTLAND
Polkemmet
Harthill
Scottish Owl Centre
Eastfield
East Whitburn
Blackburn
Five Sisters
Bellsquarry
Murieston
Old Monkland
Calderbank
Chapelhall
Birkenshaw
Tannochside
Kirk of Shotts
Salsburgh
Hirst
Whitburn
Longridge
Stoneyburn
Bents
Addiewell
Polbeth
West Calder
Loganlea
WEST LOTHIAN
Newton
Uddingston
Viewpark
Flemington
BOTHWELL
Dalton
Livingston Cen.
Bothwell
Holytown
Mossend
Bellshill
New Stevenston
Yett
Newhouse
Hareshaw
Dykehead
Heritage Centre
Shotts
Torbothie
Stane
Fauldhouse
Greenburn
Breich
Hendreys Course 1177
Cobbinshaw Resr.
Stonefield
Blantyre
Forgewood
Newarthill
Parkside
Hartwood
Carfin
Cleekhimin
Cleland
Bellside
Allanbank
Bowhousebog or Liquo
Allanton
Woolfords
Crosswood Resr.
HAMILTON
MOTHERWELL
Craigneuk
Coltness
Newmains
Bonkle
High Blantyre
Udston
Shieldmuir
WISHAW
Cambusnethan
Morningside
Wilsontown
Rootpark
Haywood
Tarbrax
Auchengray
Climpy
Fairhill
Ferniegair
Dalzell Estate
Chatelherault
Netherton
Waterloo
Bogside
Gair Reservoir
Hare Hill 1029
Springfield Resr.
Forth
Wildmanbridge
Overtown
Law
Meikle Earnock
Eddlewood
Larkhall
Millheugh
Castlehill
Carluke
Yieldshields
Mouse Water
Braehead
North Medwin
Bleak Law 1460
CLYDESDALE
Limekilnburn
Quarter
Machan
Dalserf
Strutherhill
Ashgill
Swinhill
Rosebank
Crawforddyke
Roadmeetings
Kilncadzow
Braidwood
Chapelton
Netherburn
Udstonhead
Glassford
Stonehouse
Nethanfoot
Crossford
Craignethan Castle
SOUTH LANARKSHIRE
Anston
Weston
Dunsyre
Cartland
Carstairs
West End
Carnwath
Kaimend
Newbigging
Hazelbank
Nemphlar
Draffan
Ravenstruther
Carstairs Junction
Walston
Strathaven
Flemington
Kirkfieldbank
LANARK
Lanark Moor
Elsrickle
Sandford
Avon Water
Blackwood
Auchenheath
Kirkmuirhill
Stonebyres Holdings
New Lanark World Heritage Site
Bankhead
New Lanark
Pettinain
Libberton
Boghead
Dillarburn
Falls of Clyde
Hyndford Bridge
Candy Mill
Shieldhill
Ewe Hill 1177
Kype Muir
Lesmahagow
Brocketsbrae
Turfholm
Covington Tower
Covington
Quothquan
Thankerton
Gasworks
Biggar
Cormiston
Puppet Theatre
Kype Reservoir
Hawkwood Hill
Dunside Resr.
Logan Water
Logan Reservoir
Auchlochan
Carmichael
Discover Carmichael
Douglas Water
Coulter Motte
Causewayend
Goseland
Rigside
135
136
117
118

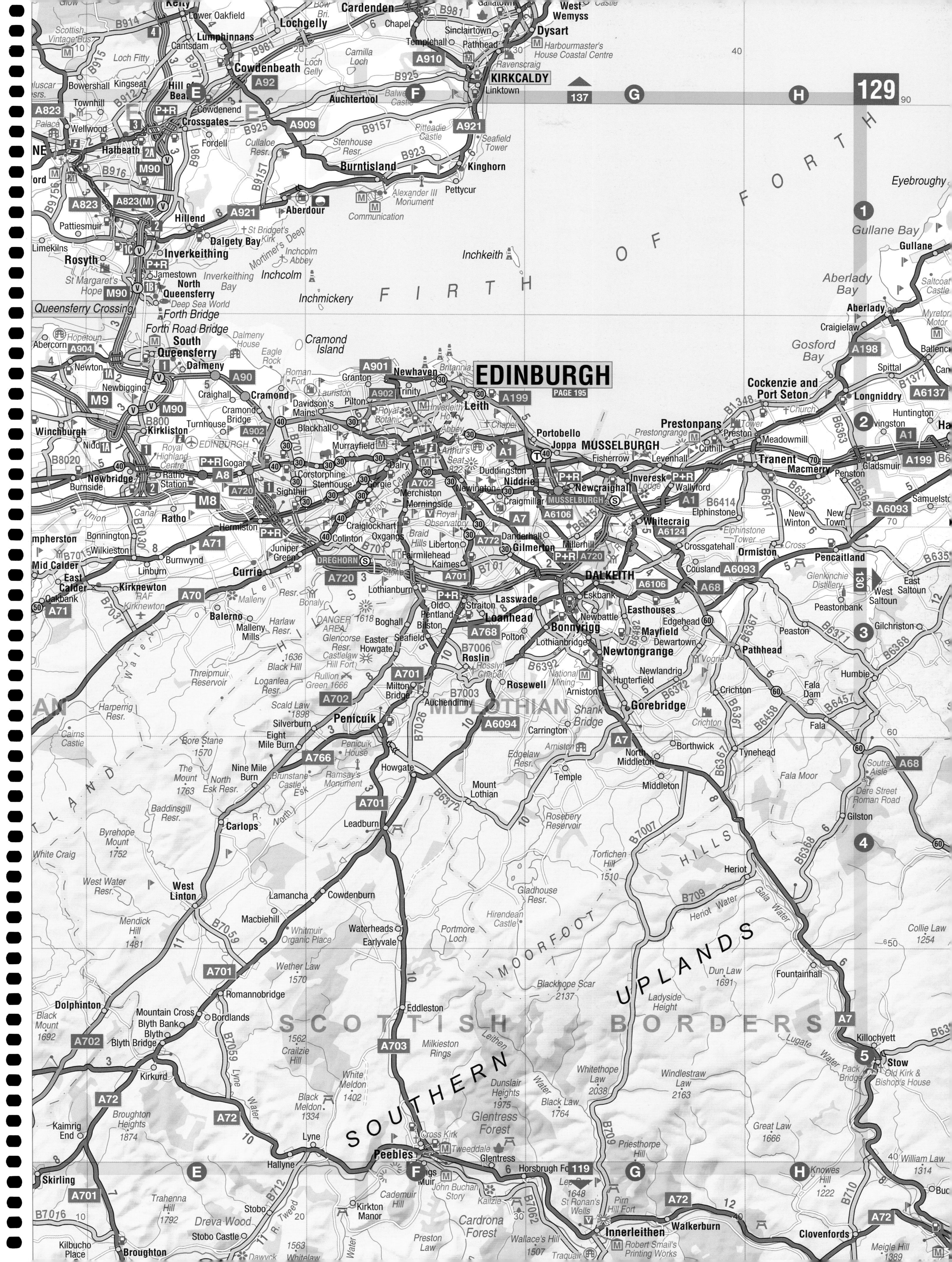

129
EDINBURGH
PAGE 195
FIRTH OF FORTH
Kirkcaldy
Cardenden
Lochgelly
Lumphinnans
Cowdenbeath
Dysart
West Wemyss
Sinclairtown
Pathhead
Templehall
Chapel
Ravenscraig
Harbourmaster's House Coastal Centre
Linktown
Auchtertool
Balwearie Castle
Crossgates
Cowdenend
Halbeath
Wellwood
Townhill
Bowershall
Kingseat
Fordell
Cullaloe Resr.
Stenhouse Resr.
Burntisland
Kinghorn
Pettycur
Seafield Tower
Pitteadie Castle
Alexander III Monument
Communication
Aberdour
Hillend
Dalgety Bay
St Bridget's Kirk
Inchcolm Abbey
Inchcolm
Mortimer's Deep
Inverkeithing
Inverkeithing Bay
Rosyth
Pattiesmuir
Limekilns
St Margaret's Hope
Jamestown
North Queensferry
Deep Sea World
Forth Bridge
Queensferry Crossing
Forth Road Bridge
South Queensferry
Dalmeny
Dalmeny House
Hopetoun
Abercorn
Newton
Inchkeith
Inchmickery
Cramond Island
Eagle Rock
Cramond
Cramond Bridge
Craighall
Newbigging
Winchburgh
Kirkliston
Turnhouse
Nidd
Royal Highland Centre
EDINBURGH
Gogar
Ratho Station
Newbridge
Burnside
Ratho
Hermiston
Bonnington
Wilkieston
Mid Calder
East Calder
Oakbank
Kirknewton
RAF Kirknewton
Linburn
Burnwynd
Currie
Balerno
Malleny Mills
Harlaw Resr.
Threipmuir Reservoir
Harperrig Resr.
Cairns Castle
Bore Stane 1570
The Mount 1763
North Esk Resr.
Baddinsgill Resr.
Byrehope Mount 1752
White Craig
West Water Resr.
West Linton
Mendick Hill 1481
Carlops
Nine Mile Burn
Eight Mile Burn
Silverburn
Penicuik
Penicuik House
Brunstane Castle
Ramsay's Monument
Howgate
Leadburn
Lamancha
Cowdenburn
Macbiehill
Whitmuir Organic Place
Waterheads
Earlyvale
Portmore Loch
Wether Law 1570
Romannobridge
Dolphinton
Black Mount 1692
Mountain Cross
Blyth Bank
Blyth
Blyth Bridge
Bordlands
Eddleston
Milkieston Rings
Crailzie Hill
Kirkurd
Broughton Heights 1874
Kaimrig End
Skirling
White Meldon 1402
Black Meldon 1334
Lyne
Hallyne
Peebles
Cross Kirk
Tweeddale
Glentress
Glentress Forest
Dunslair Heights 1975
Cademuir Hill
John Buchan Story
Kailzie
Kirkton Manor
Trahenna Hill 1792
Stobo
Dreva Wood
Stobo Castle
Kilbucho Place
Broughton
Cardrona Forest
Preston Law
Wallace's Hill 1507
Traquair
Innerleithen
Robert Smail's Printing Works
Pirn Hill Fort
St Ronan's Wells
Lee Pen 1648
Horsbrugh Ford
Walkerburn
Clovenfords
Meigle Hill 1389
Priesthorpe Hill
Whitehope Law 2038
Black Law 1764
Windlestraw Law 2163
Great Law 1666
Knowes Hill 1222
William Law 1314
Blackhope Scar 2137
Ladyside Height
Dun Law 1691
Fountainhall
Collie Law 1254
Killochyett
Stow
Old Kirk & Bishop's House
Pack Bridge
Lugate Water
Gala Water
Heriot
Heriot Water
Torfichen Hill 1510
Gladhouse Resr.
Hirendean Castle
Rosebery Reservoir
Temple
Mount Lothian
Middleton
North Middleton
Borthwick
Gorebridge
Arniston
Newtongrange
Hunterfield
Newlandrig
Crichton
Tynehead
Fala
Fala Dam
Fala Moor
Soutra Aisle
Dere Street Roman Road
Gilston
Humbie
Pathhead
Dewartown
Mayfield
Easthouses
Edgehead
Peaston
Gilchriston
Peastonbank
West Saltoun
East Saltoun
Glenkinchie Distillery
Pencaitland
Ormiston
Cousland
Crossgatehall
Elphinstone Tower
Elphinstone
New Winton
New Town
Samuelston
Penston
Gladsmuir
Macmerry
Tranent
Meadowmill
Cockenzie and Port Seton
Longniddry
Spittal
Gosford Bay
Aberlady
Aberlady Bay
Craigielaw
Saltcoat Castle
Gullane
Gullane Bay
Eyebroughy
Huntington
Prestonpans
Prestongrange
Preston
Cuthill
Musselburgh
Fisherrow
Levenhall
Inveresk
Inveresk Lodge
Wallyford
Newcraighall
Whitecraig
Millerhill
Dalkeith
Eskbank
Newbattle
Bonnyrigg
Lothianbridge
Lasswade
Loanhead
Polton
Straiton
Bilston
Old Pentland
Roslin
Rosslyn Chapel
Rosewell
Auchendinny
Milton Bridge
National Mining
Carrington
Shank Bridge
Portobello
Joppa
Niddrie
Craigmillar
Duddingston
Arthur's Seat 822
Danderhall
Gilmerton
Liberton
Kaimes
Fairmilehead
Oxgangs
Colinton
Craiglockhart
Juniper Green
Morningside
Merchiston
Newington
Dalry
Gorgie
Stenhouse
Corstorphine
Sighthill
Murrayfield
Blackhall
Davidson's Mains
Pilton
Granton
Trinity
Newhaven
Leith
Britannia
Royal Botanic
Inverleith
Holyrood Abbey
Royal Observatory
Braid Hills
Caiy Stone
Lothianburn
Boghall
Seafield
Easter Howgate
Glencorse Resr.
Castlelaw Hill Fort
Rullion Green 1666
Black Hill 1636
Loganlea Resr.
Scald Law 1898
Bonaly
Malleny
DANGER AREA
MIDLOTHIAN
MOORFOOT HILLS
SCOTTISH BORDERS
SOUTHERN UPLANDS
PENTLAND HILLS
DREGHORN
MUSSELBURGH
Scottish Vintage Bus
Loch Fitty
Loch Gelly
Camilla Loch
Palace

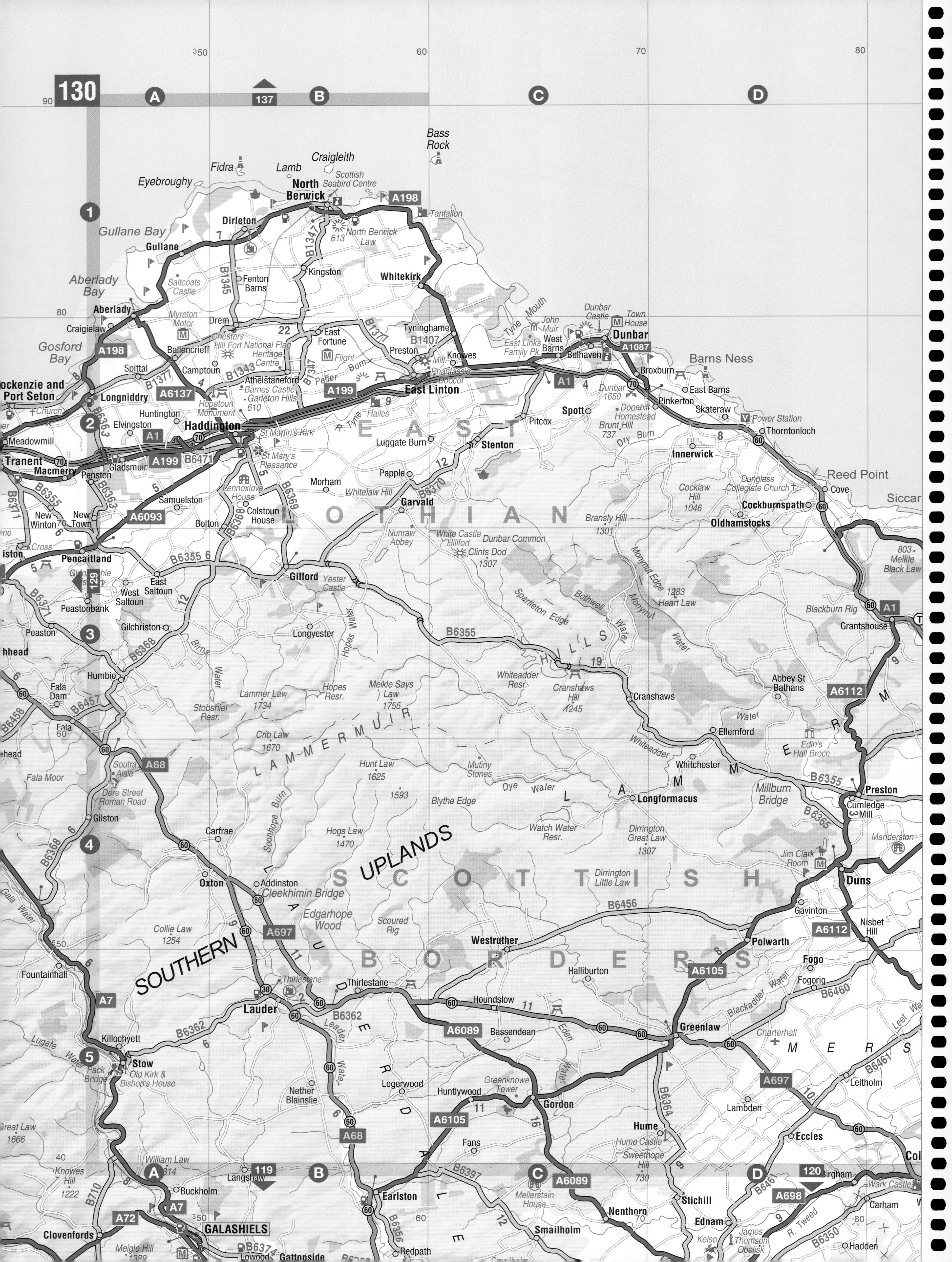

137
119
120
129
Bass Rock
Craigleith
Fidra
Lamb
Eyebroughy
North Berwick
Scottish Seabird Centre
A198
Tantallon
Gullane Bay
Dirleton
Gullane
North Berwick Law
613
B1347
Kingston
Whitekirk
Aberlady Bay
Saltcoats Castle
B1345
Fenton Barns
Aberlady
Craigielaw
Myreton Motor
Drem
Gosford Bay
Chesters Hill Fort
National Flag Heritage Centre
East Fortune
Tyninghame
B1407
Tyne Mouth
John Muir
Dunbar Castle
Town House
Dunbar
A1087
Ballencrieff
Spittal
B1377
Camptoun
B1343
Flight
Preston
Knowes
Mill
Phantassie Doocot
East Links Family Pk.
West Barns
Belhaven
Barns Ness
Broxburn
Cockenzie and Port Seton
Longniddry
A6137
Athelstaneford
Barnes Castle
Garleton Hills
610
B1347
Peffer Burn
A199
East Linton
A1
Dunbar 1650
East Barns
Pinkerton
Skateraw
Power Station
Thorntonloch
Church
Hopetoun Monument
Huntington
Elvingston
Haddington
Hailes
R. Tyne
St Martin's Kirk
E A S T
Pitcox
Spott
Doonhill Homestead
Brunt Hill 737
Dry Burn
Meadowmill
B6363
Luggate Burn
Stenton
Innerwick
Tranent
Macmerry
Penston
Gladsmuir
A199
B6471
St Mary's Pleasance
Reed Point
Cove
Siccar
Dunglass Collegiate Church
Cocklaw Hill 1046
Cockburnspath
Oldhamstocks
B6355
New Winton
New Town
Samuelston
Lennoxlove House
B6369
Morham
Papple
Whitelaw Hill
B6370
Garvald
L O T H I A N
B6371
A6093
Bolton
B6368
Colstoun House
Bransly Hill 1301
Cross
Pencaitland
Nunraw Abbey
White Castle Hillfort
Dunbar Common
Clints Dod 1307
Monynut Edge
803 Meikle Black Law
Glenkinchie Distillery
B6355
East Saltoun
West Saltoun
Gifford
Yester Castle
Spartleton Edge
Bothwell
Monynut
1283 Heart Law
Peastonbank
Peaston
Gilchriston
Longyester
Hopes Water
B6355
Water
Blackburn Rig
A1
Grantshouse
Humbie
B6368
Birns Water
H I L L S
Whiteadder Resr.
Cranshaws Hill 1245
Cranshaws
Abbey St Bathans
A6112
Fala Dam
B6457
B6458
Fala
Stobshiel Resr.
Lammer Law 1734
Hopes Resr.
Meikle Says Law 1755
Crib Law 1670
L A M M E R M U I R
Ellemford
Whiteadder
Whitchester
Edin's Hall Broch
Soutra Aisle
A68
Fala Moor
Dere Street Roman Road
Hunt Law 1625
Mutiny Stones
1593
Blythe Edge
Dye Water
Longformacus
Millburn Bridge
B6355
Preston
Cumledge Mill
B6365
Gilston
Carfrae
Hogs Law 1470
Soonhope Burn
UPLANDS
Watch Water Resr.
Dirrington Great Law 1307
Manderston
B6368
Jim Clark Room
Duns
Oxton
Addinston
Cleekhimin Bridge
S C O T T I S H
Dirrington Little Law
Gala Water
Edgarhope Wood
Scoured Rig
B6456
Gavinton
Nisbet Hill
Collie Law 1254
A697
SOUTHERN
Westruther
Polwarth
A6112
B O R D E R S
Fountainhall
Thirlestane
Halliburton
A6105
Fogo
Fogorig
B6460
A7
Lauder
B6362
Houndslow
Eden
Blackadder Water
Greenlaw
Leet Water
Lugate Water
Killochyett
A6089
Bassendean
Charterhall
M E R S
Stow
Pack Bridge
Old Kirk & Bishop's House
Leader Water
Nether Blainslie
Legerwood
Greenknowe Tower
Huntlywood
Gordon
A697
Leitholm
B6461
B6364
Lambden
A68
A6105
Great Law 1666
Hume
Hume Castle
Fans
Eccles
Sweethope Hill 730
Knowes Hill 1222
William Law 614
B710
Langshaw
B6397
Buckholm
A6089
Birgham
Wark Castle
Earlston
Mellerstain House
A698
Carham
B6461
A7
A72
Nenthorn
Stichill
Clovenfords
GALASHIELS
B6356
Smailholm
Ednam
R. Tweed
B6350
Kelso
James Thomson Obelisk
Hadden
Meigle Hill 1389
B6374
Lowood
Gattonside
Redpath
Col
L A U D E R D A L E

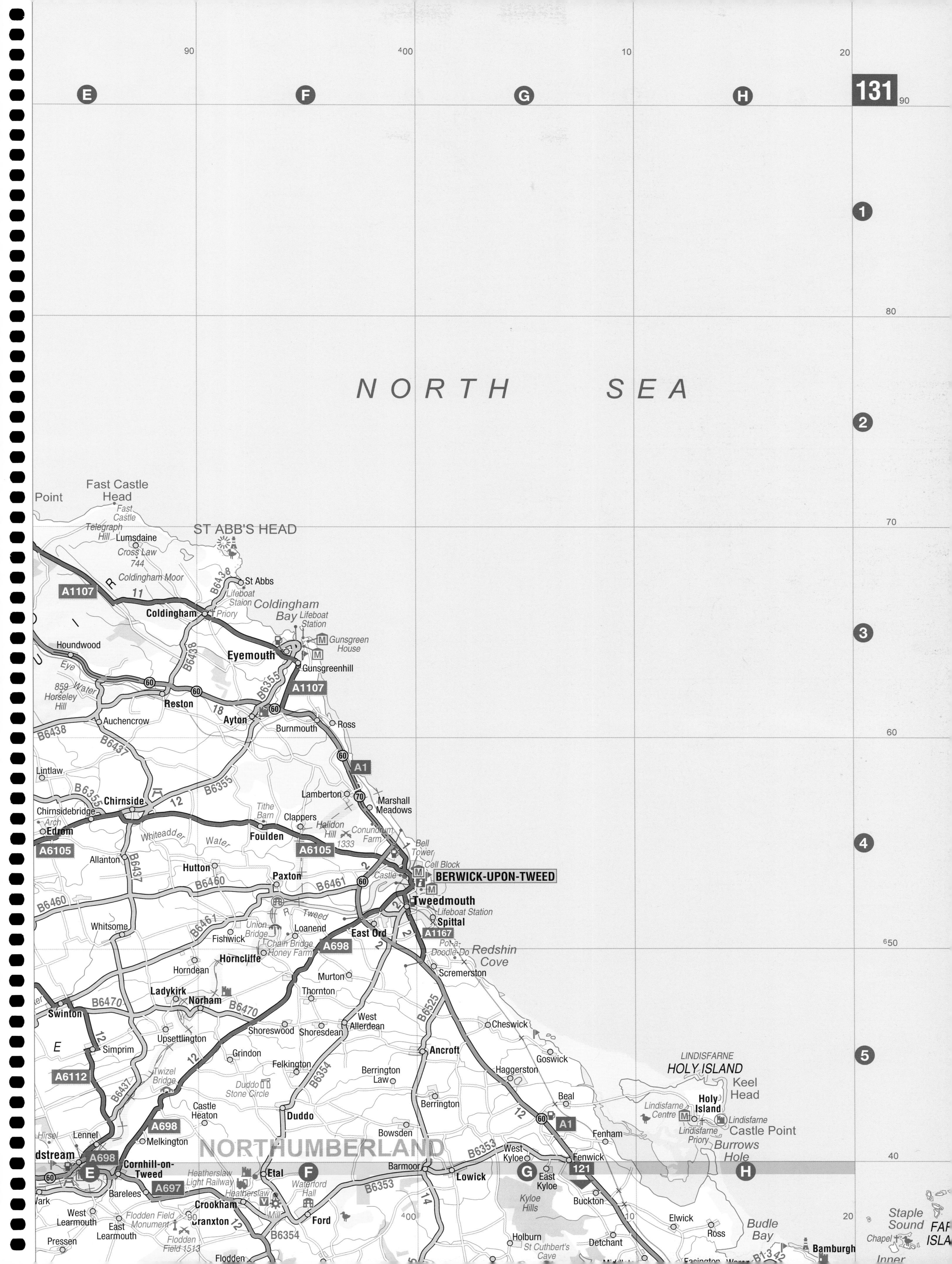
NORTH SEA
Fast Castle Head
ST ABB'S HEAD
St Abbs
Coldingham Bay
Coldingham
Eyemouth
Gunsgreenhill
Houndwood
Reston
Ayton
Burnmouth
Ross
Auchencrow
Lintlaw
Chirnside
Chirnsidebridge
Edrom
Allanton
Foulden
Lamberton
Marshall Meadows
Clappers
Halidon Hill
Hutton
Paxton
BERWICK-UPON-TWEED
Tweedmouth
Spittal
East Ord
Whitsome
Fishwick
Loanend
Horncliffe
Horndean
Redshin Cove
Scremerston
Murton
Ladykirk
Norham
Thornton
Swinton
West Allerdean
Shoreswood
Shoresdean
Cheswick
Simprim
Upsettlington
Grindon
Ancroft
Goswick
Felkington
Berrington Law
Haggerston
LINDISFARNE
HOLY ISLAND
Keel Head
Holy Island
Beal
Castle Heaton
Duddo
Berrington
Lindisfarne Castle Point
Fenham
Bowsden
Lennel
Melkington
NORTHUMBERLAND
Burrows Hole
Coldstream
Cornhill-on-Tweed
Etal
Barmoor
Lowick
West Kyloe
East Kyloe
Fenwick
Buckton
Barelees
Crookham
Ford
Kyloe Hills
Elwick
Ross
Budle Bay
Staple Sound
West Learmouth
East Learmouth
Branxton
Flodden Field 1513
Holburn
St Cuthbert's Cave
Detchant
Pressen
Flodden
Bamburgh
A1107
A6105
A6112
A698
A697
A1167
A1
B6438
B6437
B6355
B6460
B6461
B6470
B6354
B6353
B6525

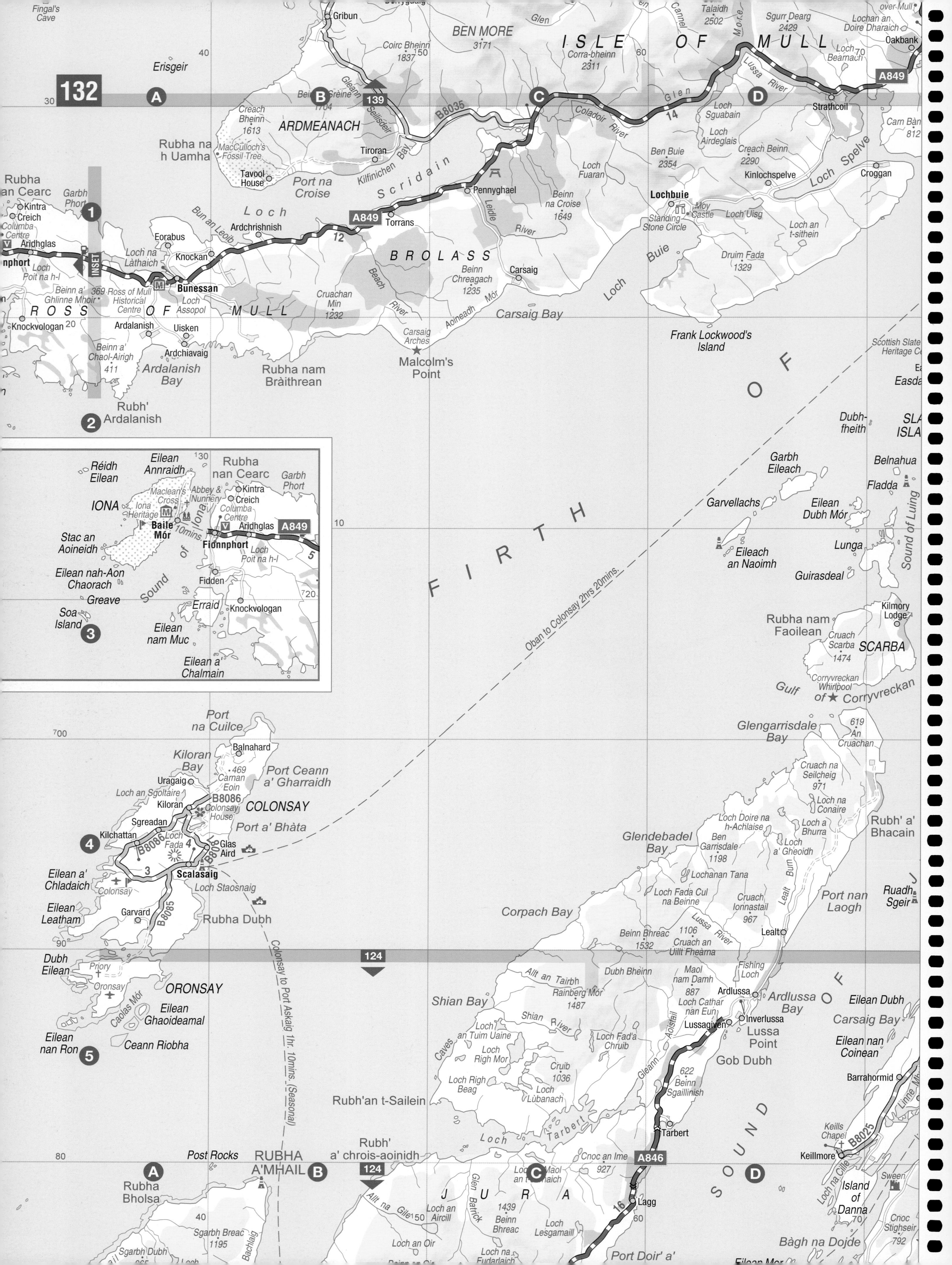

Fingal's Cave
Gribun
BEN MORE
3171
Glen
Cannel
Talaidh
2502
More
Sgurr Dearg
2429
Lochan an Doire Dharaich
Oakbank
ISLE OF MULL
Coirc Bheinn
1837
150
Corra-bheinn
2311
60
Loch Beamach
70
40
Erisgeir
132
A
B
C
D
Beinn Gréine
1704
139
Glen
Lussa River
A849
30
Creach Bheinn
1613
ARDMEANACH
Gleann Seilisdeir
B8035
Coladoir River
14
Loch Sguabain
Strathcoil
Carn Bàn
812
Rubha na h Uamha
MacCulloch's Fossil Tree
Tiroran
Kilfinichen Bay
Loch Airdeglais
Ben Buie
2354
Creach Beinn
2290
Tavool House
Port na Croise
Scridain
Loch Fuaran
Loch Spelve
Croggan
Kinlochspelve
Rubha an Cearc
Garbh Phort
1
Kintra
Creich
Columba Centre
Loch
Pennyghael
Beinn na Croise
1649
Lochbuie
Moy Castle
Loch Uisg
Standing Stone Circle
A849
Torrans
Bun an Leoib
Ardchrishnish
12
Leidle
River
Loch an t-sithein
Eorabus
Aridhglas
Loch na Làthaich
Knockan
BROLASS
Buie
Druim Fada
1329
INSET
Loch Poit na h-I
Beinn a' Ghlinne Mhóir
369
Ross of Mull Historical Centre
Bunessan
Loch Assopol
Beach River
Beinn Chreagach
1235
Carsaig
Loch
Cruachan Min
1232
ROSS OF MULL
Aoineadh Mór
Carsaig Bay
Knockvologan
20
Ardalanish
Uisken
River
Beinn a' Chaol-Airigh
411
Ardchiavaig
Carsaig Arches
Frank Lockwood's Island
Ardalanish Bay
Rubha nam Bràithrean
Malcolm's Point
Scottish Slate Heritage Centre
Easdale
2
Rubh' Ardalanish
OF
Réidh Eilean
Eilean Annraidh
130
Rubha nan Cearc
Garbh Phort
Kintra
Creich
Maclean's Cross
Abbey & Nunnery
IONA
Iona Heritage
Columba Centre
Baile Mór
Aridhglas
A849
10mins
Sound of Iona
Fionnphort
5
10
Stac an Aoineidh
Loch Poit na h-I
Eilean nah-Aon Chaoraich
Fidden
Greave
Sound
720
Erraid
Knockvologan
Soa Island
3
Eilean nam Muc
Eilean a' Chalmain
Dubh-fheith
Belnahua
Garbh Eileach
Fladda
Garvellachs
Eilean Dubh Mór
FIRTH
Sound of Luing
Lunga
Eileach an Naoimh
Guirasdeal
Kilmory Lodge
Rubha nam Faoilean
Cruach Scarba
1474
SCARBA
Oban to Colonsay 2hrs 20mins.
Corryvreckan Whirlpool
Gulf of Corryvreckan
Port na Cuilce
Glengarrisdale Bay
619
An Cruachan
700
Balnahard
Kiloran Bay
469
Carnan Eoin
Port Ceann a' Gharraidh
Uragaig
Cruach na Seilcheig
971
Loch an Sgoltaire
B8086
Loch na Conaire
Kiloran
Colonsay House
COLONSAY
Loch Doire na h-Achlaise
Loch a Bhurra
Sgreadan
Port a' Bhàta
Ben Garrisdale
1198
Rubh' a' Bhacain
4
Kilchattan
B8086
Loch Fada
4
Glas Aird
Glendebadel Bay
Loch a' Gheoidh
3
Scalasaig
Lochanan Tana
Eilean a' Chladaich
Colonsay
Loch Staosnaig
Loch Fada Cul na Beinne
Burn
Ruadh Sgeir
Port nan Laogh
Eilean Leatham
Garvard
B8085
Rubha Dubh
Corpach Bay
Cruach Ionnastail
967
Lealt
Beinn Bhreac
1106
Lussa River
Lealt
90
Cruach an Uillt Fheàrna
1532
124
Dubh Eilean
Priory
Fishing Loch
Allt an Tairbh
Dubh Bheinn
Maol nam Damh
887
Oronsay
ORONSAY
Rainberg Mór
1487
Ardlussa
Ardlussa Bay
OF
Eilean Dubh
Shian Bay
Caolas Mór
Eilean Ghaoideamal
Shian River
Loch Cathar nan Eun
Aoistail
Lussagiven
Inverlussa
Carsaig Bay
Eilean nan Ron
5
Ceann Riobha
Loch an Tuim Uaine
Loch Fad'a Chruib
Lussa Point
Eilean nan Coinean
Caves
Loch Righ Mor
Gob Dubh
Colonsay to Port Askaig 1hr. 10mins. (Seasonal)
Cruib
1036
Gleann
622
Beinn Sgaillinish
Barrahormid
Loch Righ Beag
Loch Lùbanach
Rubh'an t-Sailein
SOUND
Tarbert
Tarbert
Keills Chapel
B8025
Loch
Rubh' a' chrois-aoinidh
Cnoc an Ime
927
A846
Keillmore
80
Post Rocks
RUBHA A'MHAIL
Loch Maol an Fhaich
Loch na Cille
124
D
Sween
Rubha Bholsa
Glen Batrick
JURA
Lagg
Island of Danna
Allt na Gile
150
Loch an Aircill
1439
Beinn Bhreac
16
40
Loch Lesgamaill
60
70
Cnoc Stighseir
792
Sgarbh Breac
1195
Bachlaig
Loch an Oir
Sgarbh Dubh
Loch na Fudaraich
Port Doir' a'
Bàgh na Dojde

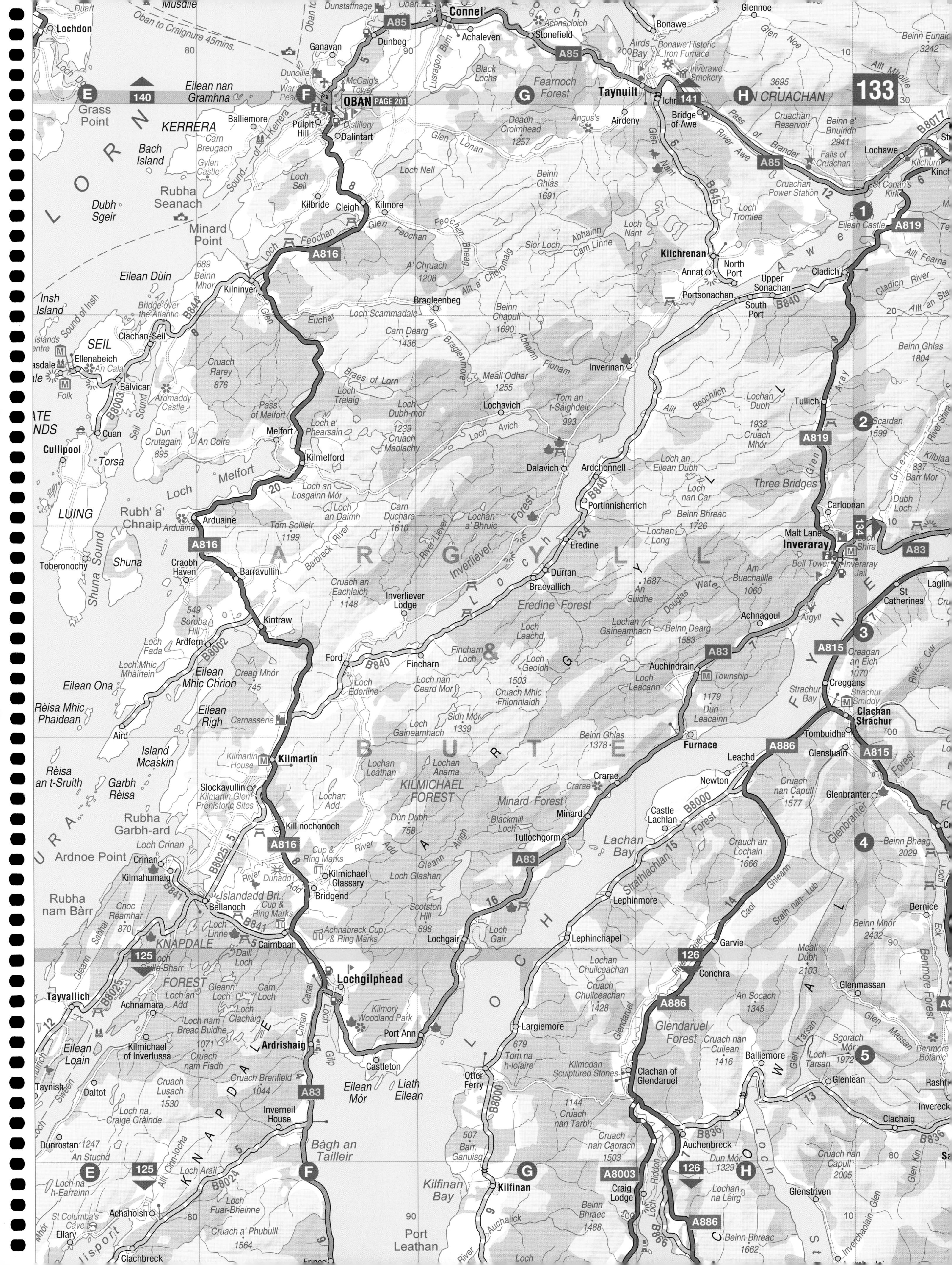

133
Lochdon
Oban to Craignure 45mins.
Dunstaffnage
Connel
A85
Dunbeg
Achaleven
Stonefield
Achnacloich
Glennoe
Bonawe
Glen Noe
Ganavan
Lusragon Burn
Black Lochs
Airds Bay
Bonawe Historic Iron Furnace
Inverawe Smokery
Beinn Eunaich 3242
Dunollie
McCaig's Tower
Fearnoch Forest
Taynuilt
3695
Allt Mhoille
140
Eilean nan Gramhna
OBAN PAGE 201
141
CRUACHAN
Grass Point
KERRERA
Balliemore
Pulpit Hill
Distillery
Dalintart
Deadh Croimhead 1257
Angus's
Airdeny
Ichrachan
Bridge of Awe
Pass of Brander
Cruachan Reservoir
Beinn a' Bhuiridh 2941
Falls of Cruachan
Lochawe
Kilchurn
Kinchrakine
B8077
Bach Island
Carn Breugach
Gylen Castle
Glen Lonan
River Awe
Loch Nell
Beinn Ghlas 1691
Glen Nant
B845
Cruachan Power Station
St Conan's Kirk
Rubha Seanach
Sound of Kerrera
Loch Seil
Kilbride
Cleigh
Kilmore
Glen Feochan
Feochan Bheag
Loch Tromlee
Loch Nant
Eilean Castle
A819
Dubh Sgeir
LORN
Minard Point
Loch Feochan
A816
Sior Loch
Abhainn Cam Linne
Kilchrenan
Annat
North Port
Cladich
Allt Fearna
Eilean Dùin
689 Beinn Mhor
Kilninver
A' Chruach 1208
Allt a' Chromaig
Upper Sonachan
Portsonachan
South Port
B840
Cladich River
Insh Island
Sound of Insh
Bridge over the Atlantic
B844
Bragleenbeg
Euchar
Loch Scammadale
Beinn Chapull 1690
Clachan-Seil
SEIL
Ellenabeich
An Cala
Balvicar
Folk
Carn Dearg 1436
Allt Braglenmore
Abhainn Fionain
Inverinan
Beinn Ghlas 1804
Cruach Rarey 876
Ardmaddy Castle
B8003
Braes of Lorn
Loch Tralaig
Meall Odhar 1255
Allt Beochlich
Lochan Dubh
Tullich
Pass of Melfort
Loch Dubh-mor
Lochavich
Tom an t-Saighdeir 993
Scardan 1599
Cuan
Seil Sound
Dun Crutagain 895
An Coire
Melfort
Loch a' Phearsain
1239 Cruach Maolachy
Loch Avich
1932 Cruach Mhór
A819
Cullipool
Torsa
Kilmelford
Dalavich
Ardchonnell
Loch an Eilean Dubh
Glen Aray
Kilblaa
837 Barr Mor
Loch Melfort
Loch an Losgainn Mór
Loch an Daimh
Carn Duchara 1610
Lochan a' Bhruic
Forest
Portinnisherrich
Loch nan Car
Three Bridges
Carloonan
Dubh Loch
LUING
Rubh' a' Chnaip
Arduaine
Tom Soillier 1199
Barbreck River
River Liever
B840
Beinn Bhreac 1726
Lochan Long
Malt Land
134
Inveraray
Loch Shira
A83
Shuna
Shuna Sound
Toberonochy
Craobh Haven
Barravullin
Cruach an Eachlaich 1148
Inverliever Forest
Eredine
Durran
Braevallich
1687 An Suidhe
Douglas Water
Am Buachaille 1060
Bell Tower
Inveraray Jail
St Catherines
ARGYLL
Inverliever Lodge
Eredine Forest
Loch Awe
549 Soroba Hill
Kintraw
Lochan Gaineamhach
Beinn Dearg 1583
Achnagoul
Argyll
Loch Fada
Ardfern
B8002
Loch Leachd
A83
A815
Creagan an Eich 1070
Loch Mhic Mhàirtein
Eilean Mhic Chrion
Creag Mhór 745
Ford
Fincham Loch
Fincharn
Loch Geoidh
Auchindrain
Township
River Cur
Eilean Ona
Loch Ederline
Loch nan Ceard Mor
1503 Cruach Mhic Fhionnlaidh
Loch Leacann
Creggans
Strachur Bay
Strachur Smiddy
Rèisa Mhic Phaidean
Eilean Righ
Carnasserie
Sidh Mór 1339
1179 Dun Leacainn
Clachan Strachur
Aird
Loch Gaineamhach
Beinn Ghlas 1378
Furnace
Tombuidhe
700
Island Mcaskin
Kilmartin House
Kilmartin
BUTE
Lochan Leathan
Lochan Anama
Leachd
A886
Glensluain
A815
Rèisa an t-Sruith
Garbh Rèisa
Slockavullin
Kilmartin Glen Prehistoric Sites
KILMICHAEL FOREST
Crarae
Newton
Cruach nan Capull 1577
Glenbranter
Rubha Garbh-ard
Lochan Add
Minard Forest
Castle Lachlan
B8000
Killinochonoch
Dùn Dubh 758
Blackmill Loch
Minard
Forest
Crauch an Lochain 1666
Loch Crinan
Tullochgorm
Lachan Bay
Beinn Bheag 2029
Ardnoe Point
Crinan
A816
A83
Strathlachlan
Kilmahumaig
B8025
River Add
Dunadd
Cup & Ring Marks
Kilmichael Glassary
Gleann Airigh
Loch Glashan
Ghleann
Rubha nam Bàrr
Bellanoch
Islandadd Bri.
Bridgend
Lephinmore
Strath nan-Lub
Caol
Bernice
Cnoc Reamhar 870
B841
Loch Linne
Scotston Hill 698
Lochgair
Loch Gair
Beinn Mhór 2432
Achnabreck Cup & Ring Marks
Cairnbaan
Lephinchapel
Garvie
KNAPDALE
125
Daill Loch
LOCH FYNE
Meall Dubh 2103
Gleann Sabhal
Lochgilphead
126
Conchra
Lochan Chuilceachan
FOREST
Gleann Loch
Carn Loch
Cruach Chuilceachan 1428
Glenmassan
Tayvallich
B8025
Achnamara
Loch an Add
Crinan Canal
A886
An Socach 1345
Loch Clachaig
Kilmory Woodland Park
Glendaruel
Benmore Forest
Loch nam Breac Buidhe
Port Ann
Largiemore
Glendaruel Forest
Glen Massan
Eilean Loain
Kilmichael of Inverlussa
1071 Cruach nam Fiadh
Ardrishaig
Loch Gilp
Castleton
679 Tom na h-Iolaire
Kilmodan Sculptured Stones
Cruach nan Cuilean 1416
Glen Tarsan
Loch Tarsan
Sgorach Mór 1972
Benmore Botanic
Taynish
Daltot
Cruach Lusach 1530
Cruach Brenfield 1044
Eilean Mór
Liath Eilean
Otter Ferry
Clachan of Glendaruel
Balliemore
Glenlean
Rashfield
A83
1144 Cruach nan Tarbh
Invereck
Loch na Craige Grainde
Inverneil House
B8000
Clachaig
507 Barr Ganuisg
Cruach nan Caorach 1503
B836
Auchenbreck
Dunrostan
1247 An Stuchd
Bàgh an Tailleir
Dun Mór 1329
Cruach nan Capull 2005
Loch na h-Earrainn
Allt Cinn-locha
B8024
Loch Arail
Kilfinan Bay
A8003
Craig Lodge
Kilfinan
Lochan na Leirg
Glenstriven
Achahoish
Loch Fuar-Bheinne
St Columba's Cave
Cruach a' Phubuill 1564
Port Leathan
Auchalick
Beinn Bhraec 1488
Loch Riddon
A886
B866
Beinn Bhreac 1662
Ellary
Clachbreck
Loch Striven

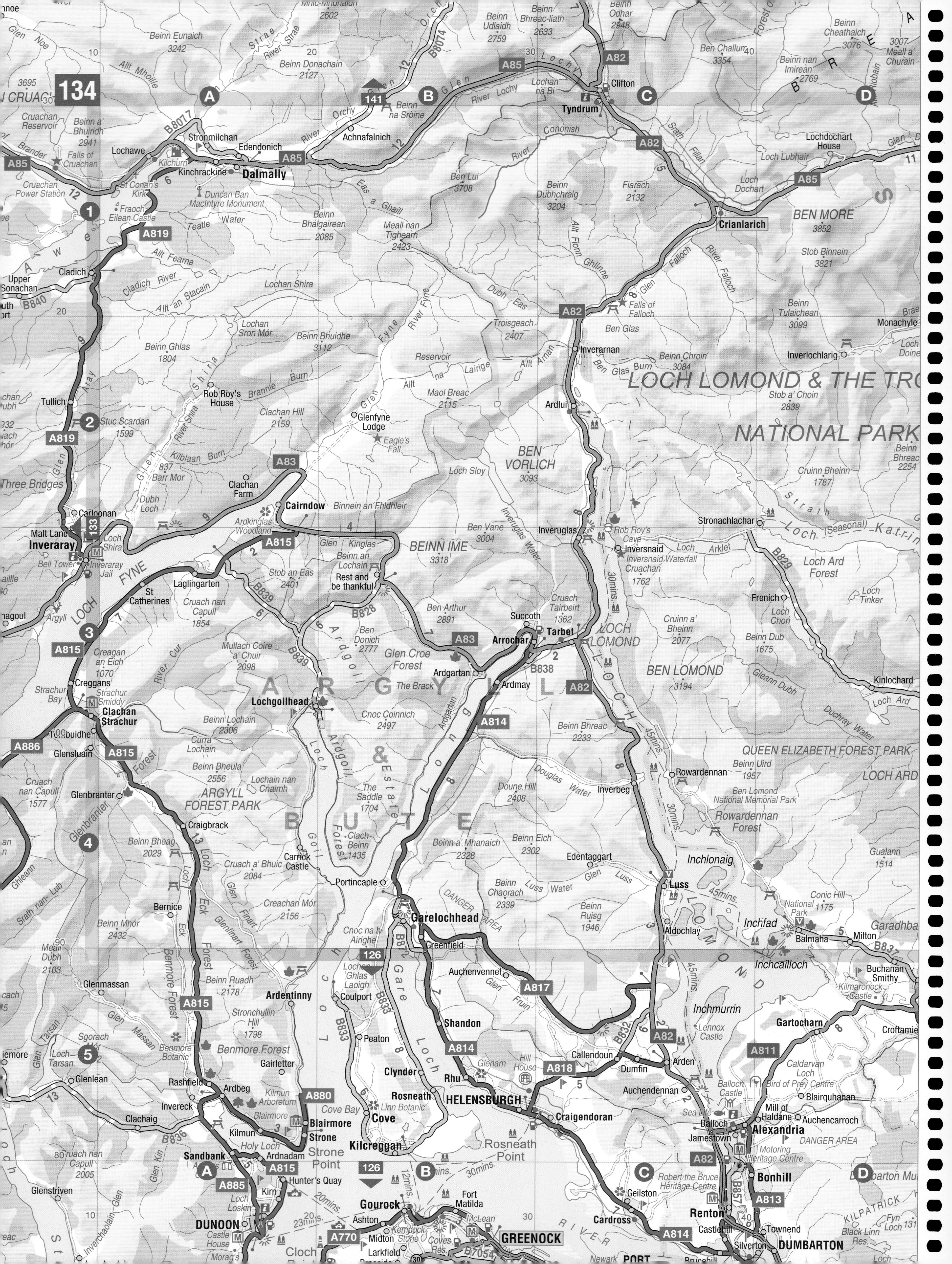
134
141
133
126
A
B
C
D
1
2
3
4
5
Beinn Eunaich
3242
Beinn Donachain
2127
Beinn Udlaidh
2759
Beinn Bhreac-liath
2633
Beinn Odhar
2948
Beinn Cheathaich
3076
Ben Challum
3354
Beinn nan Imirean
2769
BREADALBANE
Glen Noe
Allt Mhoille
River Strae
Glen Orchy
B8074
A85
A82
A819
A815
A83
A814
A886
A817
A818
A811
A813
A880
A885
A770
B8077
B840
B839
B828
B838
B833
B872
B832
B836
B829
B857
B7054
Cruachan Reservoir
Beinn a' Bhuiridh
2941
Falls of Cruachan
Lochawe
Stronmilchan
Edendonich
Kilchurn
Kinchrackine
Dalmally
Cruachan Power Station
St Conan's Kirk
Duncan Ban MacIntyre Monument
Fraoch Eilean Castle
Teatle Water
Achnafalnich
Beinn na Sròine
River Orchy
River Lochy
Lochan na Bi
Clifton
Tyndrum
Cononish
River Cononish
Strath Fillan
Lochdochart House
Loch Lubhair
Loch Dochart
Crianlarich
BEN MORE
3852
Stob Binnein
3821
Ben Lui
3708
Beinn Dubhchraig
3204
Fiarach
2132
Eas a Ghaill
Meall nan Tighearn
2423
Beinn Bhalgairean
2085
Allt Fionn Ghlinne
River Falloch
Glen Falloch
Falls of Falloch
Dubh Eas
Allt Fearna
Cladich
Cladich River
Upper Sonachan
Allt an Stacain
Lochan Shira
Lochan Sron Mór
Beinn Bhuidhe
3112
Beinn Ghlas
1804
Glen Fyne
River Fyne
Troisgeach
2407
Reservoir
Allt na Lairige
Allt Arnan
Inverarnan
Ben Glas
Ben Glas Burn
Beinn Chroin
3084
Beinn Tulaichean
3099
Monachyle
Inverlochlarig
Loch Doine
LOCH LOMOND & THE TROSSACHS NATIONAL PARK
Stob a' Choin
2839
Beinn Bhreac
2254
Cruinn Bheinn
1787
Glen Aray
Tullich
Stuc Scardan
1599
Glen Shira
River Shira
Rob Roy's House
Brannie Burn
Clachan Hill
2159
Glenfyne Lodge
Eagle's Fall
Maol Breac
2115
Ardlui
BEN VORLICH
3093
Loch Sloy
Kilblaan Burn
Barr Mor
837
Three Bridges
Dubh Loch
Clachan Farm
Cairndow
Binnein an Fhidhleir
Carloonan
Malt Lane
Inveraray
Loch Shira
Bell Tower
Inveraray Jail
Ardkinglas Woodland
Glen Kinglas
Beinn an Lochain
Rest and be thankful
Ben Vane
3004
BEINN IME
3318
Inveruglas Water
Inveruglas
Rob Roy's Cave
Inversnaid
Inversnaid Waterfall
Loch Arklet
Cruachan
1762
Stronachlachar
Loch Katrine (Seasonal)
Strath
Loch Ard Forest
Loch Tinker
Frenich
Loch Chon
LOCH FYNE
St Catherines
Laglingarten
Argyll
Cruach nan Capull
1854
Stob an Eas
2401
Ben Arthur
2891
Succoth
Cruach Tairbeirt
1362
Arrochar
Tarbet
LOCH LOMOND
30mins.
Cruinn a' Bheinn
2077
Beinn Dub
1675
BEN LOMOND
3194
Gleann Dubh
Kinlochard
Loch Ard
Duchray Water
Creagan an Eich
1070
Mullach Coire a' Chuir
2098
River Cur
Ben Donich
2777
Glen Croe Forest
Ardgartan
The Brack
Ardmay
Creggans
Strachur Bay
Strachur Smiddy
Clachan Strachur
Lochgoilhead
ARGYLL & BUTE
Cnoc Coinnich
2497
Beinn Lochain
2306
Beinn Bhreac
2233
Tornbuidhe
Glensluain
Curra Lochain
Beinn Bheula
2556
Lochain nan Cnaimh
Loch Goil
Ardgoil Estate
Loch Long
Douglas Water
Rowardennan
Beinn Uird
1957
QUEEN ELIZABETH FOREST PARK
LOCH ARD
Ben Lomond National Memorial Park
Rowardennan Forest
Cruach nan Capull
1577
Glenbranter
ARGYLL FOREST PARK
The Saddle
1704
Doune Hill
2408
Inverbeg
Craigbrack
Beinn Bheag
2029
Clach Beinn
1435
Beinn a' Mhanaich
2328
Beinn Eich
2302
Edentaggart
Inchlonaig
Gualann
1514
Cruach a' Bhuic
2084
Carrick Castle
Loch Eck
Portincaple
Beinn Chaorach
2339
Luss Water
Glen Luss
Luss
Conic Hill
1175
National Park
Creachan Mór
2156
Glen Finart
Garelochhead
DANGER AREA
Beinn Ruisg
1946
Aldochlay
Inchfad
Balmaha
Milton
Garadhban
Bernice
Beinn Mhór
2432
Cnoc na h-Airighe
Greenfield
Inchcailloch
Buchanan Smithy
Kilmaronock Castle
Meall Dubh
2103
Benmore Forest
Beinn Ruadh
2178
Ardentinny
Lochan Ghlas Laoigh
Coulport
Gare Loch
Auchenvennel
Glen Fruin
Inchmurrin
Glenmassan
Stronchullin Hill
1798
Shandon
Lennox Castle
Gartocharn
Croftamie
Sgorach Mór
Benmore Botanic
Glen Massan
Peaton
Callendoun
Dumfin
Arden
Loch Tarsan
Gairletter
Clynder
Glenarn
Hill House
Caldarvan Loch
Glenlean
Rashfield
Ardbeg
Kilmun Arboretum
Rosneath
HELENSBURGH
Auchendennan
Balloch Castle
Bird of Prey Centre
Blairquhanan
Invereck
Cove Bay
Linn Botanic
Cove
Craigendoran
Sea Life
Balloch
Mill of Haldane
Auchencarroch
Alexandria
Clachaig
Blairmore
Strone
Kilmun
Holy Loch
Kilcreggan
Rosneath Point
Jamestown
Motoring Heritage Centre
Sandbank
Ardnadam
Strone Point
Robert the Bruce Heritage Centre
Geilston
Bonhill
Hunter's Quay
Glenstriven
Kirn
Loch Loskin
Gourock
Fort Matilda
Renton
Castlehill
KILPATRICK
Fyn Loch
Black Linn Res.
Townend
DUNOON
Castle House
Ashton
Kempock Stone
McLean
GREENOCK
RIVER
Cardross
Silverton
DUMBARTON
Cloch
Midton
Larkfield
Coves Res.
PORT
12mins.
20mins.
23mins.
30mins.
45mins.

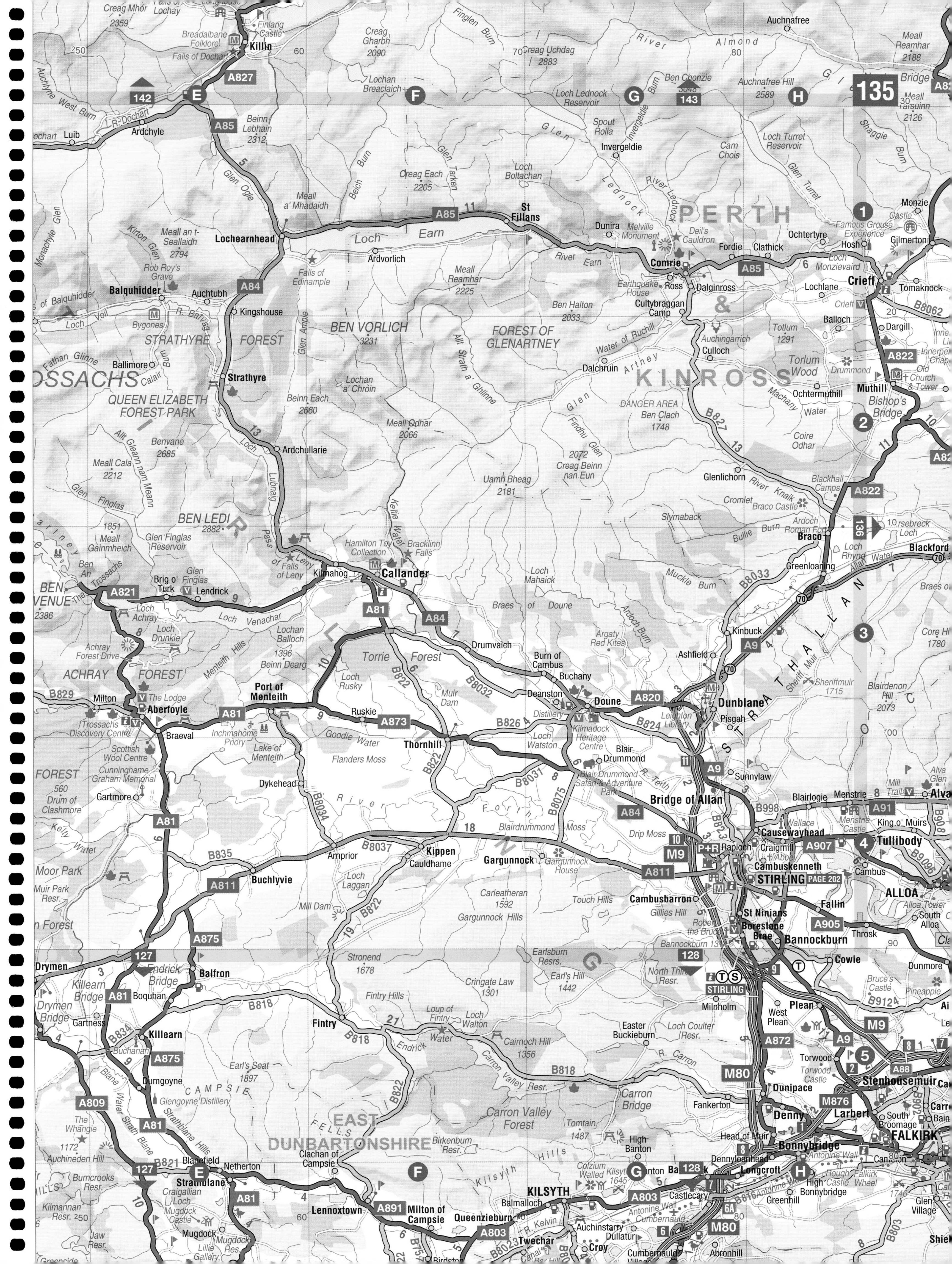

135
Creag Mhor 2359
Killin
Finlarig Castle
Breadalbane Folklore
Falls of Dochart
A827
142
143
E
F
G
H
Auchlyne West Burn
R. Dochart
Luib
Ardchyle
A85
Beinn Lebhain 2312
Glen Ogle
Creag Gharbh 2090
Lochan Breaclaich
Creag Uchdag 2883
Fingen Burn
River Almond
Auchnafree
Meall Reamhar 2188
Ben Chonzie 3048
Auchnafree Hill 2589
Loch Lednock Reservoir
Spout Rolla
Invergeldie
Glen Lednock
Loch Boltachan
Carn Chois
Loch Turret Reservoir
Glen Turret
Shaggie Burn
Meall Tarsuinn 2126
Creag Each 2205
Glen Tarken
Beich Burn
Meall a' Mhadaidh
St Fillans
Loch Earn
Lochearnhead
Ardvorlich
Falls of Edinample
Meall an t-Seallaidh 2794
Kirkton Glen
Monachyle Glen
Rob Roy's Grave
Balquhidder
Auchtubh
Kingshouse
A84
Loch Voil
Bygones
R. Balvag
STRATHYRE
FOREST
Ballimore
Strathyre
TROSSACHS
QUEEN ELIZABETH FOREST PARK
Glen Ample
BEN VORLICH 3231
Lochan a' Chròin
Beinn Each 2660
Meall Odhar 2066
Allt Strath a' Ghlinne
FOREST OF GLENARTNEY
Water of Ruchill
Dalchruin
Glen Artney
Dunira
Melville Monument
Deil's Cauldron
Comrie
Ross
Dalginross
Earthquake House
Cultybraggan Camp
Ben Halton 2033
River Earn
PERTH
&
KINROSS
Fordie
Clathick
Ochtertyre
Famous Grouse Experience
Monzie Castle
Monzie
Hosh
Gilmerton
Loch Monzievaird
Crieff
Tomaknock
Lochlane
B8062
Balloch
Dargill
Auchingarrich
Culloch
Totlum 1291
Torlum Wood
Drummond
A822
Muthill
Bishop's Bridge
Ochtermuthill
Machany Water
DANGER AREA
Ben Clach 1748
Glen Findhu
B827
Coire Odhar
Benvane 2685
Meall Cala 2212
Allt Gleann nam Meann
Ardchullarie
Loch Lubnaig
Glen Finglas
Uamh Bheag 2181
2072 Creag Beinn nan Eun
Glenlichorn
River Knaik
Blackhall Camps
Cromlet
Braco Castle
Slymaback
BEN LEDI 2882
Meall Gainmheich 1851
Glen Finglas Reservoir
Pass of Leny
Falls of Leny
Keltie Water
Hamilton Toy Collection
Bracklinn Falls
Callander
Kilmahog
Ardoch Roman Fort
Braco
Bullie Burn
Loch Rhynd
Allan Water
Blackford
Greenloaning
Muckle Burn
B8033
Loch Mahaick
Ben An
BEN VENUE 2386
The Trossachs
Brig o' Turk
Glen Finglas
Lendrick
A821
Loch Achray
Loch Venachar
Loch Drunkie
Achray Forest Drive
ACHRAY FOREST
Menteith Hills
Lochan Balloch 1396
Beinn Dearg
A81
A84
Braes of Doune
Drumvaich
Argaty Red Kites
Ardoch Burn
Kinbuck
Ashfield
A9
STRATHALLAN
Core Hill 1780
Torrie Forest
Loch Rusky
B822
B8032
Muir Dam
Burn of Cambus
Buchany
Deanston
Doune
A820
Dunblane
Leighton Library
Pisgah
Sheriffmuir 1715
Blairdenon Hill 2073
B829
Milton
The Lodge
Aberfoyle
Trossachs Discovery Centre
Braeval
Port of Menteith
Inchmahome Priory
Lake of Menteith
A873
Ruskie
Goodie Water
Flanders Moss
Thornhill
B826
Loch Watston
Kilmadock Heritage Centre
Blair Drummond
Blair Drummond Safari & Adventure Park
B8031
B8075
Sunnylaw
Scottish Wool Centre
Cunninghame Graham Memorial
Gartmore
Drum of Clashmore 560
Dykehead
B8034
River Forth
Blairdrummond Moss
Bridge of Allan
Drip Moss
Blairlogie
Menstrie
Alva
Mill Trail
A91
Menstrie Castle
King o' Muirs
Wallace
Causewayhead
Tullibody
B998
B823
Craigmill
Abbey
Cambuskenneth
A907
Kelty Water
Moor Park
B835
Arnprior
B8037
Kippen
Cauldhame
Gargunnock
Gargunnock House
M9
P+R
Raploch
STIRLING PAGE 202
A811
Buchlyvie
Muir Park Resr.
Loch Laggan
Mill Dam
Carleatheran 1592
Gargunnock Hills
Touch Hills
Cambusbarron
Gillies Hill
St Ninians
Robert the Bruce
Borestone
Brae
Bannockburn
Fallin
A905
Throsk
ALLOA
Alloa Tower
South Alloa
Cambus
A875
127
128
Drymen
Endrick Bridge
Balfron
Stronend 1678
Earlsburn Resrs.
North Third Resr.
Bannockburn 1314
STIRLING
Cowie
Dunmore
Killearn Bridge
Drymen Bridge
Boquhan
Gartness
B818
Fintry Hills
Cringate Law 1301
Earl's Hill 1442
Milnholm
Loup of Fintry
Loch Walton
Fintry
Endrick Water
Carron Valley Resr.
Cairnoch Hill 1356
Easter Buckieburn
Loch Coulter Resr.
R. Carron
West Plean
Plean
Bruce's Castle
Pineapple
B9124
A872
A9
M9
Torwood
Torwood Castle
Killearn
Buchanan
Earl's Seat 1897
CAMPSIE FELLS
Dumgoyne
Glengoyne Distillery
Strathblane Hills
Blane Water
A809
The Whangie
Auchineden Hill 1172
EAST DUNBARTONSHIRE
Birkenburn Resr.
Carron Valley Forest
Carron Bridge
Tomtain 1487
High Banton
Kilsyth Hills
Fankerton
M80
Dunipace
Denny
Head of Muir
M876
Larbert
Stenhousemuir
South Broomage
FALKIRK
Bonnybridge
Dennyloanhead
Longcroft
Antonine Wall
High Bonnybridge
Rough Castle
Falkirk Wheel
Camelon
Glen Village
Blanefield
Netherton
Strathblane
B821
Burncrooks Resr.
Craigallian Loch
Kilmannan Resr.
Mugdock Castle
Mugdock
Mugdock Res.
Lillie Gallery
Jaw Resr.
Clachan of Campsie
Lennoxtown
A891
Milton of Campsie
Queenzieburn
A803
KILSYTH
Balmalloch
Colzium Walled
Kilsyth 1645
Castlecary
Antonine Wall
Cumbernauld
Auchinstarry
Dullatur
Twechar
Croy
Abronhill
Greenhill
R. Kelvin
B803

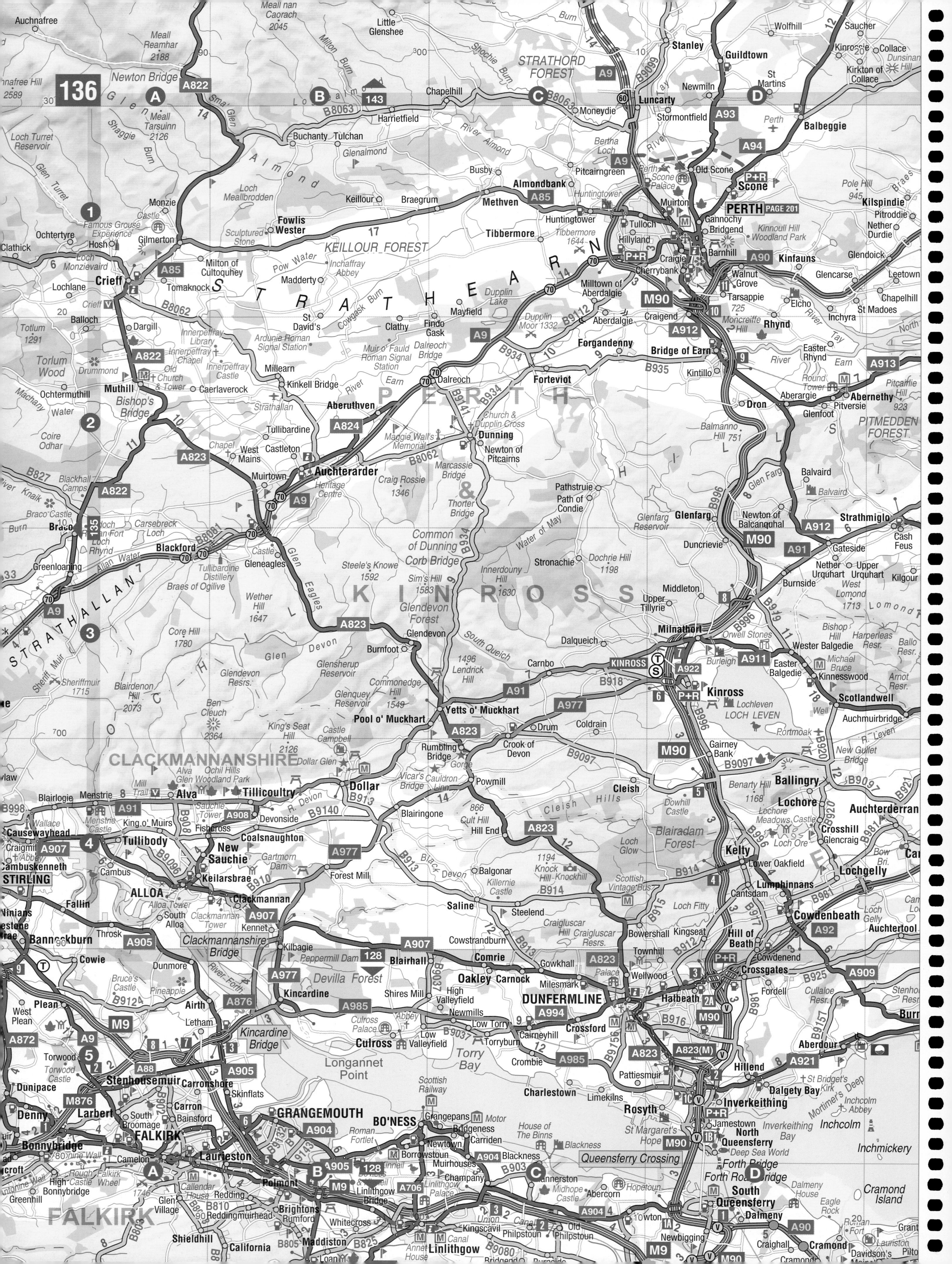

136
A
B
C
D
143
128
135
PERTH PAGE 201
Auchnafree
Meall nan Caorach 2045
Little Glenshee
Meall Reamhar 2188
Newton Bridge
Glen Shaggie
Meall Tarsuinn 2126
Loch Turret Reservoir
Glen Turret
Chapelhill
Harrietfield
Buchanty
Tulchan
Glenalmond
Moneydie
STRATHORD FOREST
Stanley
Luncarty
Stormontfield
Guildtown
Newmiln
St Martins
Wolfhill
Saucher
Kinrossie
Collace
Dunsinan Hill
Kirkton of Collace
Balbeggie
Perth
Old Scone
Scone
Pole Hill 945
Kilspindie
Pitroddie
Nether Durdie
Glendoick
Kinfauns
Glencarse
Leetown
Chapelhill
Inchyra
St Madoes
Elcho
Walnut Grove
Tarsappie
Moncreiffe Hill
Rhynd
Kinnoull Hill Woodland Park
Gannochy
Bridgend
Barnhill
Muirton
Scone Palace
Huntingtower
Tulloch
Hillyland
Craigie
Cherrybank
Craigend
Pitcairngreen
Almondbank
Busby
Bertha Loch
Methven
Braegrum
Keillour
Loch Meallbrodden
Monzie
Monzie Castle
Famous Grouse Experience
Gilmerton
Fowlis Wester
Sculptured Stone
KEILLOUR FOREST
Tibbermore
Tibbermore 1644
Ochtertyre
Hosh
Clathick
Loch Monzievaird
Lochlane
Crieff
Milton of Cultoquhey
Tomaknock
Pow Water
Inchaffray Abbey
Madderty
STRATHEARN
Dupplin Lake
Milltown of Aberdalgie
Aberdalgie
Dupplin Moor 1332
Mayfield
Clathy
Findo Gask
St David's
Cowgask Burn
Balloch
Dargill
Totlum 1291
Torlum Wood
Drummond
Innerpeffray Library
Ardunie Roman Signal Station
Innerpeffray Chapel
Innerpeffray Castle
Muir o' Fauld Roman Signal Station
Dalreoch Bridge
Forgandenny
Bridge of Earn
Kintillo
Forteviot
Millearn
Kinkell Bridge
Dalreoch
Old Church & Tower
Caerlaverock
Muthill
Bishop's Bridge
Ochtermuthill
Machany Water
Coire Odhar
Strathallan
Aberuthven
Tullibardine
PERTH
Church & Dupplin Cross
Dunning
Newton of Pitcairns
Maggie Wall's Memorial
Castleton
West Mains
Chapel
Muirtown
Auchterarder
Heritage Centre
Craig Rossie 1346
Marcassie Bridge
Thorter Bridge
Blackhall Camps
Braco Castle
Braco
Ardoch Roman Fort
Loch Rhynd
Carsebreck Loch
Blackford
Tullibardine Distillery
Braes of Ogilive
Castle
Gleneagles
Glen Eagles
Greenloaning
Allan Water
STRATHALLAN
Dron
Aberargie
Abernethy
Pitversie
Glenfoot
Pitcairlie Hill 923
PITMEDDEN FOREST
Balmanno Hill 751
Round Tower
Easter Rhynd
Earn
Balvaird
Pathstruie
Path of Condie
Glenfarg
Glen Farg
Glenfarg Reservoir
Newton of Balcanquhal
Duncrievie
Strathmiglo
Gateside
Cash Feus
Nether Urquhart
Upper Urquhart
Kilgour
Burnside
West Lomond 1713
Common of Dunning
Corb Bridge
Steele's Knowe 1592
Sim's Hill 1583
Innerdouny Hill 1630
Water of May
Stronachie
Dochrie Hill 1198
KINROSS
Glendevon Forest
Middleton
Upper Tillyrie
Milnathort
Orwell Stones
Bishop Hill
Harperleas Resr.
Ballo Resr.
Wester Balgedie
Easter Balgedie
Michael Bruce
Kinnesswood
Arnot Resr.
Scotlandwell
Auchmuirbridge
Wether Hill 1647
Core Hill 1780
Glendevon
Burnfoot
Glen Devon
Glensherup Reservoir
South Queich
1496 Lendrick Hill
Dalqueich
Carnbo
KINROSS
Burleigh
Kinross
Lochleven
LOCH LEVEN
Glendevon Resrs.
Sheriffmuir 1715
Blairdenon Hill 2073
Glenquey Reservoir
Commonedge Hill 1549
Yetts o' Muckhart
Pool o' Muckhart
Drum
Coldrain
Crook of Devon
Ben Cleuch 2364
King's Seat Hill 2126
Castle Campbell
Dollar Glen
Rumbling Bridge
Gorge
Portmoak
New Gullet Bridge
Gairney Bank
CLACKMANNANSHIRE
Alva Glen Woodland Park
Ochil Hills
Mill Trail
Alva
Tillicoultry
Dollar
Vicar's Bridge
Cauldron Linn
Powmill
Cleish Hills
Cleish
Benarty Hill 1168
Ballingry
Blairlogie
Menstrie
Menstrie Castle
Sauchie Tower
R. Devon
Blairingone
Dowhill Castle
Lochore
Lochore Meadows
Auchterderran
Crosshill
Glencraig
Causewayhead
Wallace
Craigmill
Abbey
Cambuskenneth
STIRLING
Tullibody
King o' Muirs
Fishcross
Devonside
Coalsnaughton
New Sauchie
Gartmorn Dam
866 Cult Hill
Hill End
Blairadam Forest
Loch Glow
Kelty
Loch Ore
Lower Oakfield
Lochgelly
Cambus
Keilarsbrae
ALLOA
Forest Mill
Black Devon
Balgonar
1194 Knock Hill
Knockhill
Killernie Castle
Scottish Vintage Bus
Lumphinnans
Cantsdam
Fallin
Alloa Tower
Clackmannan
Clackmannan Tower
South Alloa
Kennet
Saline
Steelend
Loch Fitty
Cowdenbeath
Loch Gelly
Auchtertool
Throsk
Bannockburn
Clackmannanshire Bridge
Kilbagie
Cowstrandburn
Craigluscar Hill
Craigluscar Resrs.
Bowershall
Kingseat
Hill of Beath
Cowie
Dunmore
Bruce's Castle
Pineapple
River Forth
Peppermill Dam
Blairhall
Comrie
Gowkhall
Townhill
Cowdenend
Crossgates
Fordell
Cullaloe Resr.
Stenhouse Resr.
Plean
West Plean
Airth
Letham
Devilla Forest
Kincardine
Shires Mill
High Valleyfield
Oakley
Carnock
Milesmark
Palace
Wellwood
DUNFERMLINE
Halbeath
Culross Palace
Abbey
Newmills
Low Torry
Low Valleyfield
Culross
Cairneyhill
Crossford
Torryburn
Torry Bay
Crombie
Aberdour
Kincardine Bridge
Torwood
Torwood Castle
Longannet Point
Hillend
Pattiesmuir
Dalgety Bay
St Bridget's Kirk
Mortimer's Deep
Inchcolm Abbey
Inchcolm
Inchmickery
Stenhousemuir
Carronshore
Skinflats
Scottish Railway
Charlestown
Limekilns
Rosyth
Inverkeithing
Dunipace
Larbert
Carron
Bainsford
South Broomage
GRANGEMOUTH
Grangepans
Motor
BO'NESS
Bridgeness
Carriden
Roman Fortlet
House of The Binns
Blackness
St Margaret's Hope
Jamestown
North Queensferry
Deep Sea World
Inverkeithing Bay
Denny
Bonnybridge
FALKIRK
Camelon
Laurieston
Newtown
Borrowstoun
Muirhouses
Queensferry Crossing
Forth Bridge
Forth Road Bridge
Dalmeny House
Eagle Rock
Cramond Island
Rough Castle
Falkirk Wheel
High Bonnybridge
Greenhill
Callendar House
Redding
Polmont
Champany
Linlithgow Bridge
Linlithgow Palace
Mannerston
Midhope Castle
Abercorn
Hopetoun
South Queensferry
Dalmeny
FALKIRK
Glen Village
Reddingmuirhead
Brightons
Rumford
Whitecross
Kingscavil
Philpstoun
Old Philpstoun
Union Canal
Newbigging
Craighall
Cramond
Lauriston
Davidson's
Shieldhill
California
Maddiston
Linlithgow
Annet House
Canal
Bridgend
Roman Fort
Grant
Pilto
Loan
M9
M90
M876
A9
A822
A85
A824
A823
A93
A94
A90
A912
A913
A91
A911
A922
A977
A91
A908
A907
A905
A876
A985
A88
A872
A904
A706
A994
A823(M)
A921
A909
A92
A803
A8
B8063
B8062
B934
B935
B9141
B8081
B9112
B9099
B8062
B996
B918
B919
B920
B9097
B9140
B913
B910
B9096
B908
B914
B915
B912
B917
B981
B925
B9037
B916
B9156
B9157
B903
B9124
B902
B9132
B9143
B805
B825
B8028
B9080
B810
B800

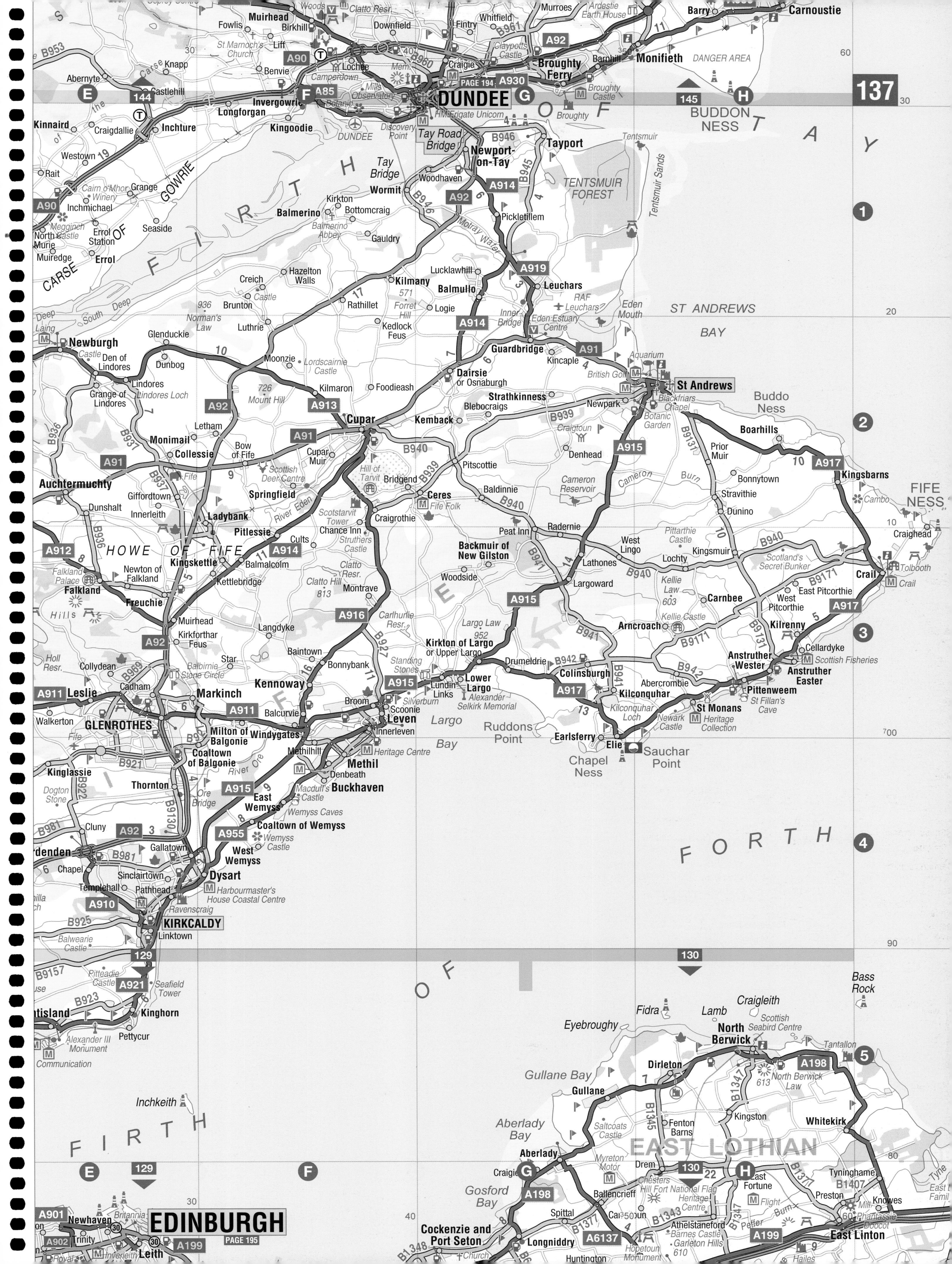
DUNDEE
PAGE 194
Muirhead
Birkhill
Fowlis
Liff
St Marnoch's Church
Downfield
Fintry
Whitfield
Murroes
Ardestie Earth House
Barry
Carnoustie
Claypotts Castle
Broughty Ferry
Barnhill
Monifieth
DANGER AREA
Broughty Castle
Broughty
BUDDON NESS
Craigie
Lochee
Benvie
Knapp
Abernyte
Castlehill
Camperdown
Mills Observatory
Invergowrie
Longforgan
Kingoodie
HMS Frigate Unicorn
Discovery Point
Tay Road Bridge
Kinnaird
Craigdallie
Inchture
Westown
Rait
Cairn o'Mhor Winery
Grange
Inchmichael
Megginch Castle
North Muirie
Errol Station
Muiredge
Errol
Seaside
CARSE OF GOWRIE
FIRTH OF TAY
Tay Bridge
Wormit
Woodhaven
Newport-on-Tay
Tayport
Tentsmuir
TENTSMUIR FOREST
Tentsmuir Sands
Kirkton
Bottomcraig
Balmerino
Balmerino Abbey
Gauldry
Pickletillem
Motray Water
Creich
Castle
Hazelton Walls
Kilmany
Lucklawhill
Balmullo
Leuchars
RAF Leuchars
Eden Mouth
ST ANDREWS BAY
Rathillet
Forret Hill
Logie
Inner Bridge
Eden Estuary Centre
Brunton
Norman's Law
Luthrie
Kedlock Feus
Deep Laing
Newburgh
Castle
Den of Lindores
Glenduckie
Dunbog
Moonzie
Lordscairnie Castle
Guardbridge
Kincaple
British Golf
Aquarium
St Andrews
Blackfriars Chapel
Botanic Garden
Buddo Ness
Lindores
Grange of Lindores
Lindores Loch
Mount Hill
Kilmaron
Foodieash
Dairsie or Osnaburgh
Strathkinness
Blebocraigs
Newpark
Craigtoun
Letham
Monimail
Collessie
Bow of Fife
Cupar
Cupar Muir
Kemback
Denhead
Prior Muir
Boarhills
Bonnytown
Kingsbarns
FIFE NESS
Cambo
Auchtermuchty
Fife
Scottish Deer Centre
Hill of Tarvit
Bridgend
Pitscottie
Cameron Reservoir
Cameron Burn
Stravithie
Dunino
Springfield
Ceres
Fife Folk
Baldinnie
Giffordtown
Dunshalt
Innerleith
Ladybank
River Eden
Scotstarvit Tower
Craigrothie
Peat Inn
Radernie
Pittarthie Castle
Craighead
HOWE OF FIFE
Pitlessie
Cults
Chance Inn
Struthers Castle
Backmuir of New Gilston
West Lingo
Kingsmuir
Scotland's Secret Bunker
Kingskettle
Balmalcolm
Clatto Resr.
Lathones
Lochty
Tolbooth
Falkland Palace
Newton of Falkland
Falkland
Kettlebridge
Clatto Hill
Montrave
Woodside
Largoward
Kellie Law
Crail
East Pitcorthie
West Pitcorthie
Freuchie
Carnbee
Hills
Muirhead
Langdyke
Carthurlie Resr.
Largo Law
Arncroach
Kellie Castle
Kilrenny
Kirkforthar Feus
Holl Resr.
Collydean
Baintown
Kirkton of Largo or Upper Largo
Drumeldrie
Cellardyke
Scottish Fisheries
Star
Balbirnie Stone Circle
Bonnybank
Standing Stones
Colinsburgh
Anstruther Wester
Anstruther Easter
Cadham
Kennoway
Lower Largo
Abercrombie
Pittenweem
Leslie
Markinch
Lundin Links
Alexander Selkirk Memorial
Kilconquhar
St Fillan's Cave
Walkerton
GLENROTHES
Balcurvie
Silverburn
Broom
Scoonie
Leven
Kilconquhar Loch
Newark Castle
St Monans
Heritage Collection
Milton of Balgonie
Windygates
Innerleven
Largo Bay
Ruddons Point
Earlsferry
Elie
Sauchar Point
Chapel Ness
Coaltown of Balgonie
Methilhill
Heritage Centre
Kinglassie
Thornton
Methil
Denbeath
River Ore
Dogton Stone
Ore Bridge
Macduff's Castle
Buckhaven
East Wemyss
Wemyss Caves
Cluny
Coaltown of Wemyss
Wemyss Castle
West Wemyss
Gallatown
Chapel
Sinclairtown
Dysart
Templehall
Pathhead
Harbourmaster's House Coastal Centre
Ravenscraig
KIRKCALDY
Linktown
Balwearie Castle
FIRTH OF FORTH
Pitteadie Castle
Seafield Tower
Kinghorn
Pettycur
Alexander III Monument
Communication
Bass Rock
Fidra
Lamb
Craigleith
Eyebroughy
Scottish Seabird Centre
North Berwick
Tantallon
Dirleton
North Berwick Law
Gullane Bay
Gullane
Fenton Barns
Kingston
Whitekirk
Inchkeith
Aberlady Bay
Saltcoats Castle
EAST LOTHIAN
Aberlady
Myreton Motor
Drem
Craigie
Chesters Hill Fort
National Flag Heritage Centre
East Fortune
Flight
Tyninghame
Gosford Bay
Ballencrieff
Preston
Knowes
Phantassie Doocot
Spittal
Athelstaneford
Barnes Castle
Garleton Hills
Peffer Burn
East Linton
Cockenzie and Port Seton
Longniddry
Hopetoun Monument
Huntington
Church
Hailes
EDINBURGH
PAGE 195
Newhaven
Britannia
Trinity
Leith
Royal
Inverleith
A90
A85
A92
A930
A914
A919
A91
A913
A915
A917
A912
A914
A916
A911
A955
A910
A921
A198
A6137
A199
A901
A902
A1
B953
B961
B960
B946
B945
B936
B937
B931
B939
B940
B941
B942
B9131
B9171
B969
B921
B922
B9130
B981
B925
B9157
B923
B1345
B1347
B1377
B1343
B1407
B1348
144
145
129
130

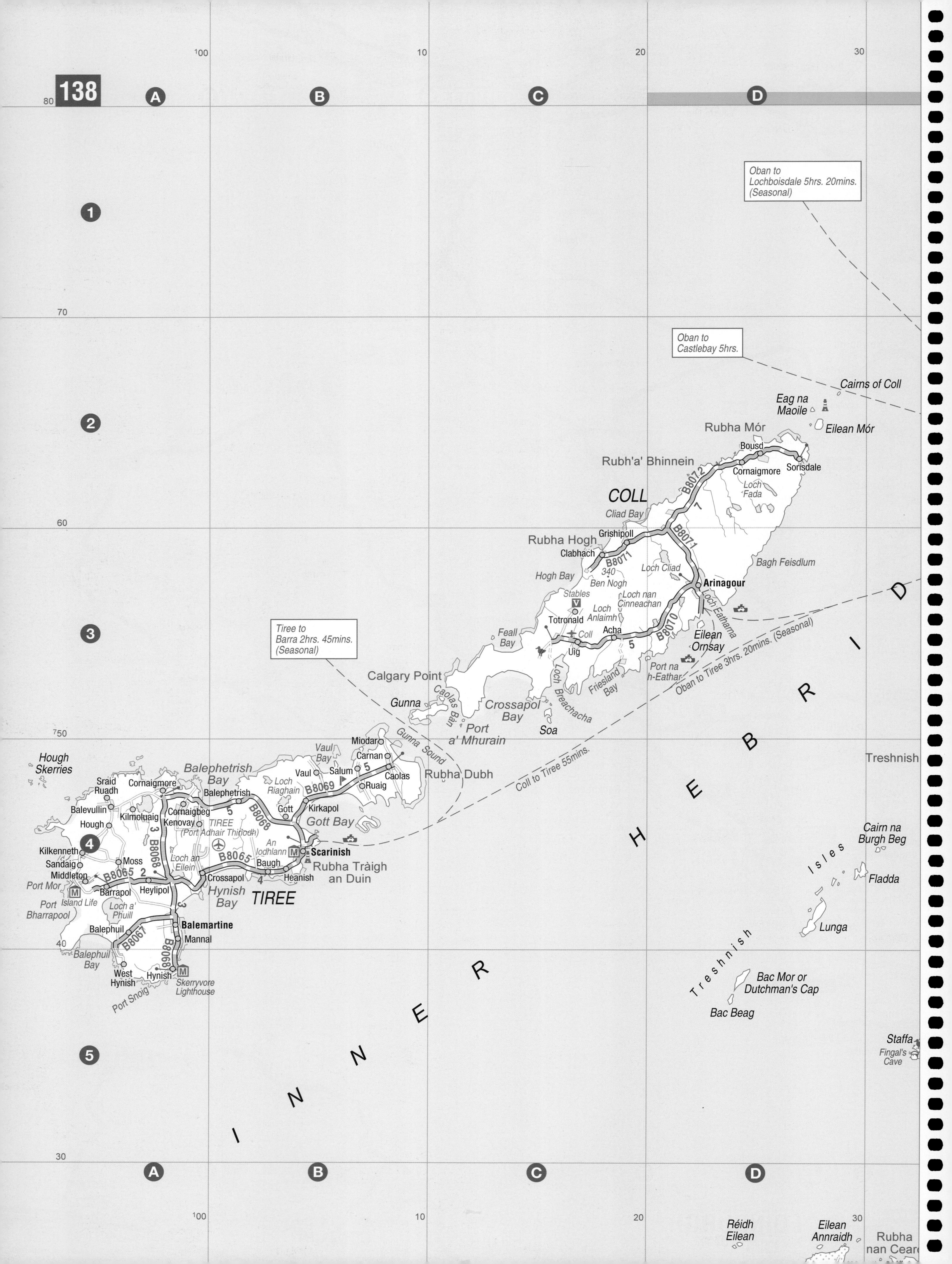

100   10   20   30

A   B   C   D

1

Oban to
Lochboisdale 5hrs. 20mins.
(Seasonal)

70

Oban to
Castlebay 5hrs.

Cairns of Coll

*Eag na
Maoile*

2   Rubha Mór   *Eilean Mór*

Bousd

Rubh'a' Bhinnein   Cornaigmore   Sorisdale

COLL   *Loch
Fada*

Cliad Bay   B8072   7

60   Grishipoll   B8071   *Bagh Feisdlum*

Rubha Hogh   Clabhach   B8071

Hogh Bay   340   *Loch Cliad*
Ben Nogh   **Arinagour**

3   Stables   *Loch nan
Cinneachan*

Tiree to   V   *Loch
Barra 2hrs. 45mins.   Totronald   Anlaimh*   B8070   *Eilean
(Seasonal)   Coll Acha   Ornsay*

*Feall   Uig 5
Bay*   *Port na
h-Eathar*

Calgary Point   *Oban to Tiree 3hrs. 20mins. (Seasonal)*

Gunna   *Caolas Bar*   *Crossapol
Bay*   *Friesland
Bay*

750   *Port
a' Mhurain*   *Soa*   **H**

Gunna Sound   Rubha Dubh   *Coll to Tiree 55mins.*   **E**   Treshnish

*Vaul
Bay*   Miodar   **B**

*Hough   *Balephetrish   Carnan 5
Skerries*   Bay*   Salum Caolas   **R**   *Cairn na
Sraid   Vaul   **I**   Burgh Beg*
Ruadh   Cornaigmore   *Loch   Ruaig   **D**
Balephetrish   Riaghain*   *Isles*
Balevullin   Cornaigbeg B8069 Gott   **E**   *Fladda*
Kilmoluaig Kenovay Gott Kirkapol
4   Hough   TIREE   *Gott Bay*   *Cairn na*
(Port Adhair Thiriodh)   **S**

An
Kilkenneth   Iodhlann B8065 M **Scarinish**   **H**   *Lunga*
Sandaig   Moss   Baugh
Middleton   B8065 2 *Loch an   Heanish   *Rubha Tràigh
Port Mor   Eilein*   Crossapol an Duin*
M   Island Life   4
Port   Barrapol Heylipol *Hynish   **Bac Mor or
Bharrapool* *Loch a'   Bay*   **TIREE**   Dutchman's Cap*
Phuill*
Balephuil   *Bac Beag*
40   Balephuil   B8067 **Balemartine**
Bay   B8068   Mannal
West   *Staffa*
Hynish   Hynish   M   *Fingal's
Cave*
Port Snoig   *Skerryvore
Lighthouse*

5

I N N E R

30

A   B   C   D

100   10   20   30

*Réidh
Eilean*   *Eilean
Annraidh*   *Rubha
nan Cearo*

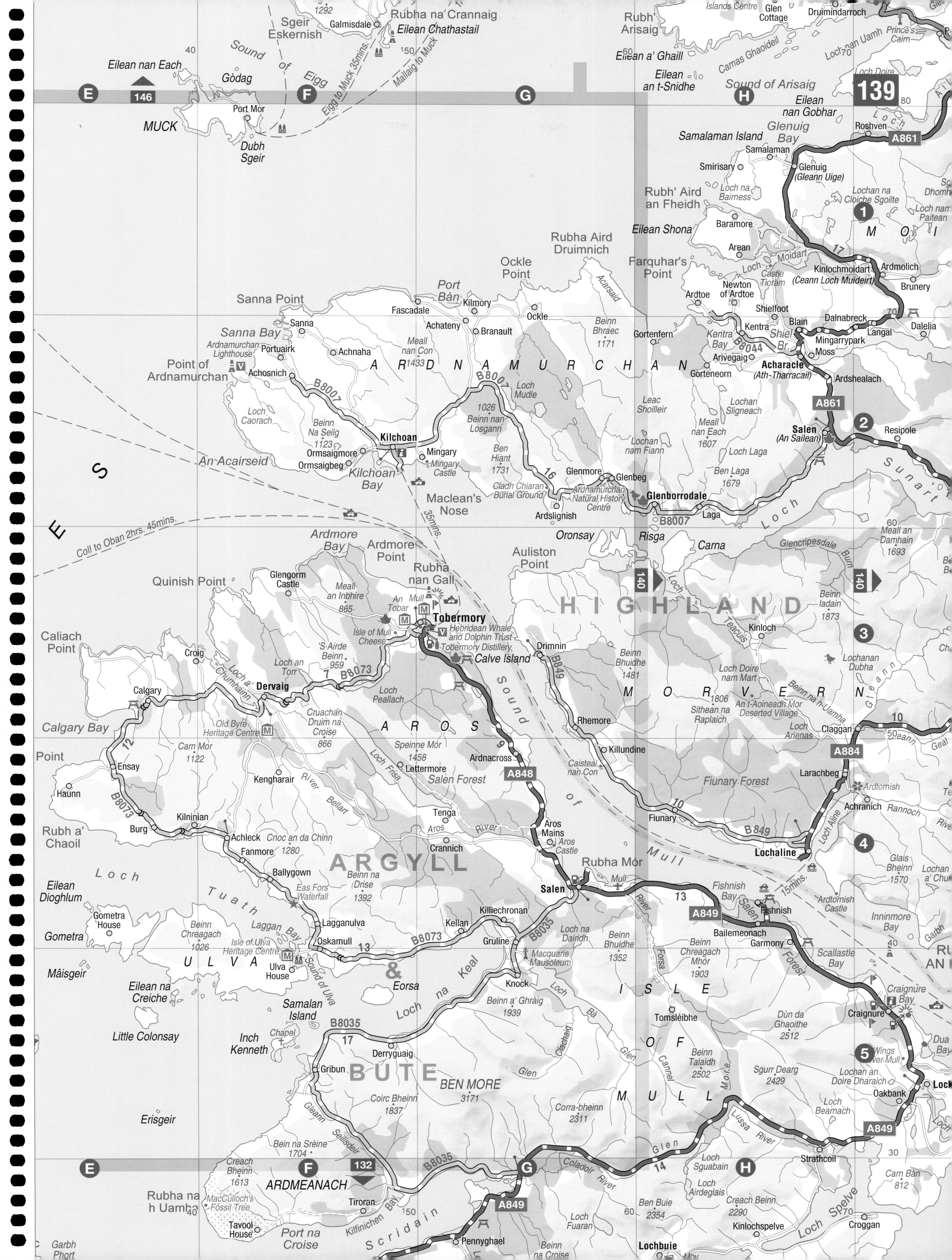

139
146
132
140
E
F
G
H
Rubha na Crannaig
Galmisdale
Eilean Chathastail
Sgeir Eskernish
Sound of Eigg
Eigg to Muck 35mins.
Mallaig to Muck
Eilean nan Each
Gòdag
Port Mor
MUCK
Dubh Sgeir
Rubh' Arisaig
Eilean a' Ghaill
Eilean an t-Snidhe
Sound of Arisaig
Camas Ghaoideil
Glen Cottage
Druimindarroch
Prince's Cairn
Loch nan Uamh
Loch Doire
Eilean nan Gobhar
Roshven
A861
Samalaman Island
Glenuig Bay
Samalaman
Smirisary
Glenuig (Gleann Uige)
Loch na Bairness
Lochan na Cloiche Sgoilte
Lochan nam Paitean
Rubh' Aird an Fheidh
Eilean Shona
Baramore
Arean
Loch Moidart
Castle Tioram
Kinlochmoidart (Ceann Loch Muideirt)
Ardmolich
Brunery
M O I
Rubha Aird Druimnich
Ockle Point
Farquhar's Point
Acarsaid
Newton of Ardtoe
Ardtoe
Shielfoot
Blain
Dalnabreck
Langal
Dalelia
Sanna Point
Port Bàn
Fascadale
Kilmory
Ockle
Achateny
Branault
Beinn Bhraec 1171
Gortenfern
Kentra
Kentra Bay
B8044
Shiel Br.
Mingarrypark
Moss
Arivegaig
Acharacle (Ath-Tharracail)
Gorteneorn
Ardshealach
Sanna Bay
Sanna
Ardnamurchan Lighthouse
Portuairk
Achnaha
Meall nan Con 1433
Point of Ardnamurchan
Achosnich
A R D N A M U R C H A N
B8007
Loch Mudle
Leac Shoilleir
Lochan Sligneach
Meall nan Each 1607
Loch Caorach
Beinn Na Seilg 1123
1026 Beinn nan Losgann
Kilchoan
Ben Hiant 1731
Lochan nam Fiann
Loch Laga
Salen (An Sailean)
Resipole
Ormsaigmore
Ormsaigbeg
Mingary
Mingary Castle
An Acairseid
Kilchoan Bay
Glenmore
Glenbeg
Ardnamurchan Natural History Centre
Glenborrodale
Cladh Chiaran Burial Ground
Ben Laga 1679
Maclean's Nose
Ardslignish
Laga
Loch Sunart
Coll to Oban 2hrs. 45mins.
35mins.
Ardmore Bay
Ardmore Point
Oronsay
Risga
Carna
Meall an Damhain 1693
Glencripesdale Burn
Auliston Point
Rubha nan Gall
Quinish Point
Glengorm Castle
Meall an Inbhire 865
H I G H L A N D
Loch Teacuis
Beinn Iadain 1873
An Tobar
Mull
Tobermory
Hebridean Whale and Dolphin Trust
Tobermory Distillery
Isle of Mull Cheese
Kinloch
Caliach Point
Croig
'S Airde Beinn 959
Calve Island
Drimnin
Beinn Bhuidhe 1481
Lochanan Dubha
Loch a' Chumhainn
Dervaig
Loch an Torr
B8073
Loch Doire nam Mart
Calgary
Loch Peallach
Sound of Mull
B849
M O R V E R N
Beinn na h-Uamha
Gleann
Cruachan Druim na Croise 866
1806 Sithean na Raplaich
An t-Aoineadh Mor Deserted Village
Old Byre Heritage Centre
A R O S
Rhemore
Loch Arienas
Claggan
Calgary Bay
Carn Mor 1122
Speinne Mòr 1458
Killundine
A884
Point
Ensay
Loch Frisa
Lettermore
Ardnacross
Caisteal nan Con
Kengharair
Salen Forest
A848
Fiunary Forest
Larachbeg
Ardtornish
Haunn
River Bellart
Tenga
Achranich
Rannoch
Kilninian
Aros River
Aros Mains
Aros Castle
Fiunary
Rubh a' Chaoil
Burg
Achleck
Cnoc an da Chinn 1280
Crannich
Loch Aline
Fanmore
ARGYLL
Rubha Mòr
Lochaline
Glais Bheinn 1570
Loch Tuath
Ballygowan
Beinn na Drise 1392
Mull
Salen
Fishnish Bay
Fishnish
15mins.
Lochan a' Chum
Eilean Dioghlum
Eas Fors Waterfall
Killiechronan
A849
Ardtornish Castle
Gometra House
Lagganulva
Kellan
Loch na Dairidh
Beinn Bhuidhe 1352
Bailemeonach
Garmony
Inninmore Bay
Gometra
Beinn Chreagach 1026
Laggan Bay
Oskamull
B8073
Gruline
B8035
Beinn Chreagach Mhòr 1903
Salen Forest
Scallastle Bay
Isle of Ulva Heritage Centre
U L V A
Ulva House
Sound of Ulva
Macquarie Mausoleum
Forsa River
Mâisgeir
&
Eorsa
Knock
Loch na Keal
I S L E
Craignure Bay
Eilean na Creiche
Samalan Island
Beinn a' Ghràig 1939
Tomsléibhe
Dùn da Ghaoithe 2512
Craignure
Little Colonsay
Inch Kenneth
Chapel
B8035
Derryguaig
O F
Beinn Talaidh 2502
Wings Over Mull
Gribun
BUTE
BEN MORE 3171
Glen Cannel
Sgurr Dearg 2429
Lochan an Doire Dharaich
Coirc Bheinn 1837
Corra-bheinn 2311
M U L L
Loch Beamach
Oakbank
Erisgeir
Gleann Seilisdeir
Glen More
Lussa River
A849
Bein na Srèine 1704
Strathcoil
Creach Bheinn 1613
ARDMEANACH
B8035
Coladoir River
Loch Sguabain
Carn Bàn 812
Rubha na h Uamha
MacCulloch's Fossil Tree
Tiroran
A849
Loch Airdeglais
Creach Beinn 2290
Ben Buie 2354
Loch Fuaran
Kilfinichen Bay
Loch Scridain
Kinlochspelve
Loch Spelve
Croggan
Tavool House
Port na Croise
Pennyghael
Beinn na Croise
Lochbuie
Garbh Phort

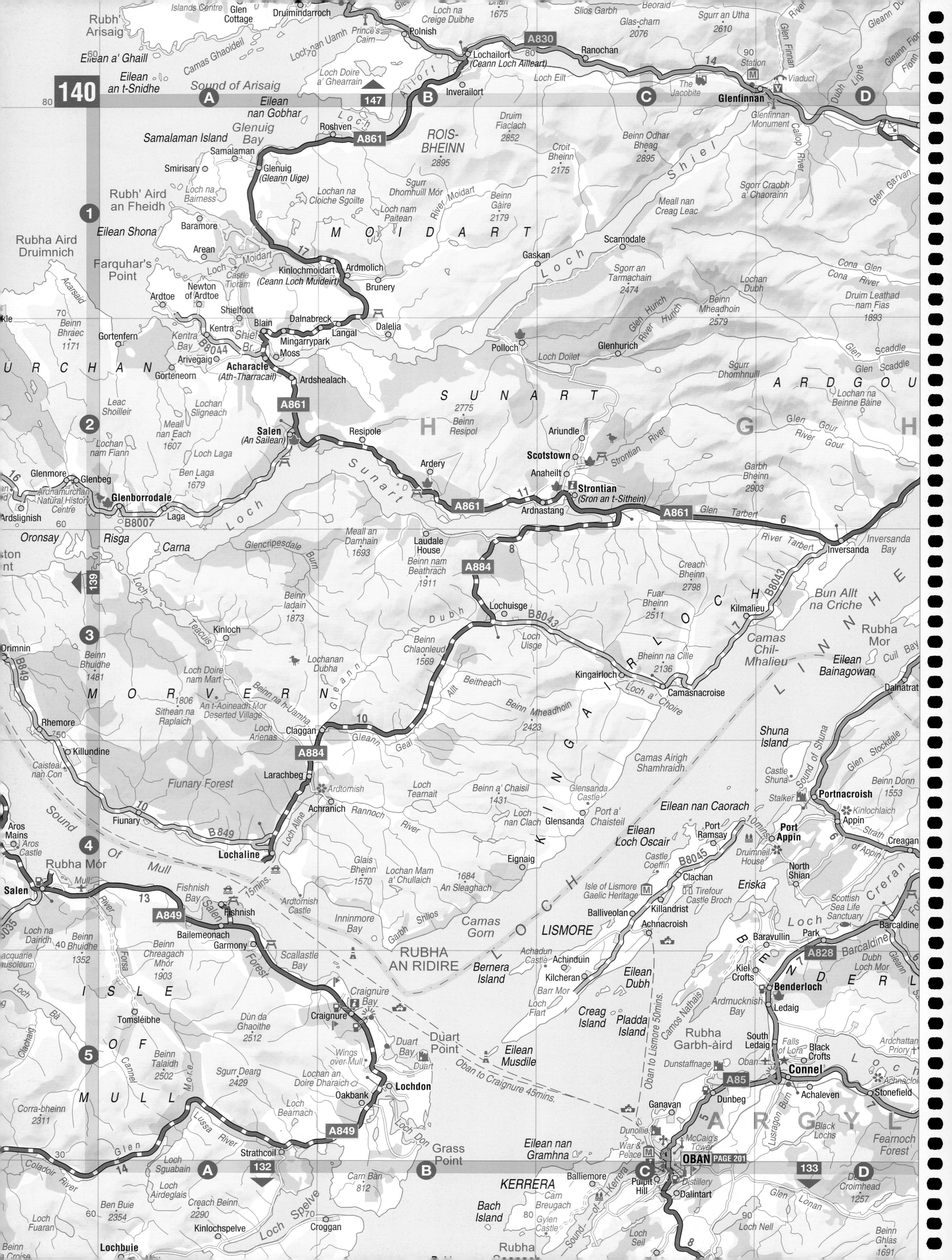
Rubh' Arisaig
Glen Cottage
Drumindarroch
Loch na Creige Duibhe
Polnish
Eilean a' Ghaill
Camas Ghaoideil
Loch nan Uamh
Prince's Cairn
Lochailort (Ceann Loch Ailleart)
A830
Ranochan
Glas-charn 2076
Sgurr an Utha 2610
Eilean an t-Snidhe
Sound of Arisaig
Loch Doire a' Ghearrain
147
Inverailort
Loch Eilt
The Jacobite
Station
Viaduct
Glenfinnan
Glenfinnan Monument
Eilean nan Gobhar
Glenuig Bay
Roshven
A861
ROIS-BHEINN 2895
Druim Fiaclach 2852
Croit Bheinn 2175
Beinn Odhar Bheag 2895
Samalaman Island
Samalaman
Smirisary
Glenuig (Gleann Uige)
Callop River
Rubh' Aird an Fheidh
Loch na Bairness
Lochan na Cloiche Sgoilte
Sgurr Dhomhnuill Mór
Loch nam Paitean
River Moidart
Beinn Gàire 2179
Meall nan Creag Leac
Sgorr Craobh a' Chaorainn
Glen Garvan
Rubha Aird Druimnich
Eilean Shona
Baramore
MOIDART
Arean
Farquhar's Point
Loch Moidart
Castle Tioram
Kinlochmoidart (Ceann Loch Muideirt)
Ardmolich
Brunery
Gaskan
Scamodale
Loch Shiel
Sgorr an Tarmachain 2474
Lochan Dubh
Cona Glen
Cona River
Druim Leathad nam Fias 1893
Newton of Ardtoe
Ardtoe
Shielfoot
Acarsaid
Beinn Bhraec 1171
Gortenfern
Kentra Bay
Kentra
Shiel Br.
Blain
Dalnabreck
Langal
Dalelia
Mingarrypark
Moss
Glen Hurich
River Hurich
Beinn Mheadhoin 2579
Polloch
Loch Doilet
Glenhurich
Glen Scaddle
B8044
Arivegaig
Acharacle (Ath-Tharracail)
Gorteneorn
Ardshealach
Sgurr Dhomhnuill
ARDGOUR
Lochan na Beinne Bàine
SUNART
Leac Shoilleir
Lochan Sligneach
A861
2775 Beinn Resipol
Meall nan Each 1607
Salen (An Sailean)
Resipole
Ariundle
Strontian River
Glen Gour
River Gour
Lochan nam Fiann
Loch Laga
Ben Laga 1679
Ardery
Scotstown
Anaheilt
Strontian (Sron an t-Sithein)
Garbh Bheinn 2903
Glenmore
Glenbeg
Ardnamurchan Natural History Centre
Glenborrodale
Ardslignish
Laga
B8007
Loch Sunart
Ardnastang
Glen Tarbert
Oronsay
Risga
Carna
Glencripesdale Burn
Meall an Damhain 1693
Laudale House
Beinn nam Beathrach 1911
A884
River Tarbert
Inversanda
Inversanda Bay
139
Creach Bheinn 2798
Bun Allt na Criche
Loch Teacuis
Beinn Iadain 1873
Fuar Bheinn 2511
Lochuisge
B8043
Kilmalieu
Loch Uisge
Dubh
Rubha Mor
Camas Chil-Mhalieu
Cuil Bay
Drimnin
Kinloch
Beinn Bhuidhe 1481
Loch Doire nam Mart
Lochanan Dubha
Beinn Chlaonleud 1569
Beitheach
Bheinn na Cille 2136
Kingairloch
Camasnacroise
Loch a' Choire
Eilean Bainagowan
Dalnatrat
B849
MORVERN
1806 Sithean na Raplaich
An t-Aoineadh Mor Deserted Village
Beinn na h-Uamha
Gleann Dubh
Beinn Mheadhoin 2423
KINGAIRLOCH
LOCH LINNHE
Rhemore
Killundine
Caisteal nan Con
Loch Arienas
Claggan
Gleann Geal
Shuna Island
Glen Stockdale
Fiunary Forest
Larachbeg
Ardtornish
Loch Teamait
Camas Airigh Shamhraidh
Castle Shuna
Sound of Shuna
Beinn Donn 1553
Achranich
Rannoch River
Beinn a' Chaisil 1431
Glensanda Castle
Port a' Chaisteil
Stalker
Portnacroish
Kinlochlaich
Appin
Fiunary
Loch Aline
Loch nan Clach
Glensanda
Eilean nan Caorach
Aros Mains
Aros Castle
B849
Lochaline
Eilean Loch Oscair
Port Ramsay
Port Appin
Strath of Appin
Creagan
Sound of Mull
Rubha Mór
Glais Bheinn 1570
Lochan Mam a' Chullaich
1684 An Sleaghach
Eignaig
Castle Coeffin
Drumneil House
North Shian
Salen
Mull
Fishnish Bay
15mins.
Fishnish
13
A849
Ardtornish Castle
Isle of Lismore Gaelic Heritage
Clachan
Tirefour Castle Broch
Eriska
Scottish Sea Life Sanctuary
Loch Creran
Barcaldine
Loch na Dairidh
Beinn Bhuidhe 1352
Bailemeonach
Garmony
Inninmore Bay
Garbh Shlios
Camas Gorn
LISMORE
Balliveolan
Killandrist
Achnacroish
Baravullin
Park
A828
Beinn Chreagach Mhór 1903
Scallastle Bay
Forest
RUBHA AN RIDIRE
Bernera Island
Achadun Castle
Achinduin
Kilcheran
Eilean Dubh
Kiel Crofts
Benderloch
Dubh Loch Mor
BENDERLOCH
ISLE OF MULL
Craignure Bay
Craignure
Tomsléibhe
Dùn da Ghaoithe 2512
Duart Point
Duart Bay
Duart
Barr Mor
Loch Fiart
Creag Island
Pladda Island
Oban to Lismore 50mins.
Camas Nathais
Ardmucknish Bay
Ledaig
Wings over Mull
Eilean Musdile
Rubha Garbh-àird
South Ledaig
Falls of Lora
Black Crofts
Ardchattan Priory
Beinn Talaidh 2502
Sgurr Dearg 2429
Lochan an Doire Dharaich
Oban to Craignure 45mins.
Dunstaffnage
Oban
Connel
A85
Achnacloich
Achaleven
Stonefield
Lochdon
Oakbank
Dunbeg
Corra-bheinn 2311
Loch Beamach
Ganavan
Lusragan Burn
ARGYLL
Black Lochs
A849
Lussa River
Loch Don
Grass Point
Dunollie
McCaig's Tower
War & Peace
Fearnoch Forest
Glen Forsa
Cannel
Strathcoil
Eilean nan Gramhna
OBAN PAGE 201
Glen Coladoir River
14
Loch Sguabain
132
Carn Ban 812
KERRERA
Balliemore
Pulpit Hill
Distillery
Dalintart
133
Croimhead 1257
Glen Lonan
Loch Airdeglais
Creach Beinn 2290
Bach Island
Carn Breugach
Sound of Kerrera
Gylen Castle
Loch Nell
Beinn Ghlas 1691
Ben Buie 2354
Loch Fuaran
Kinlochspelve
Loch Spelve
Croggan
Loch Seil
Rubha
Lochbuie
Beinn Croise

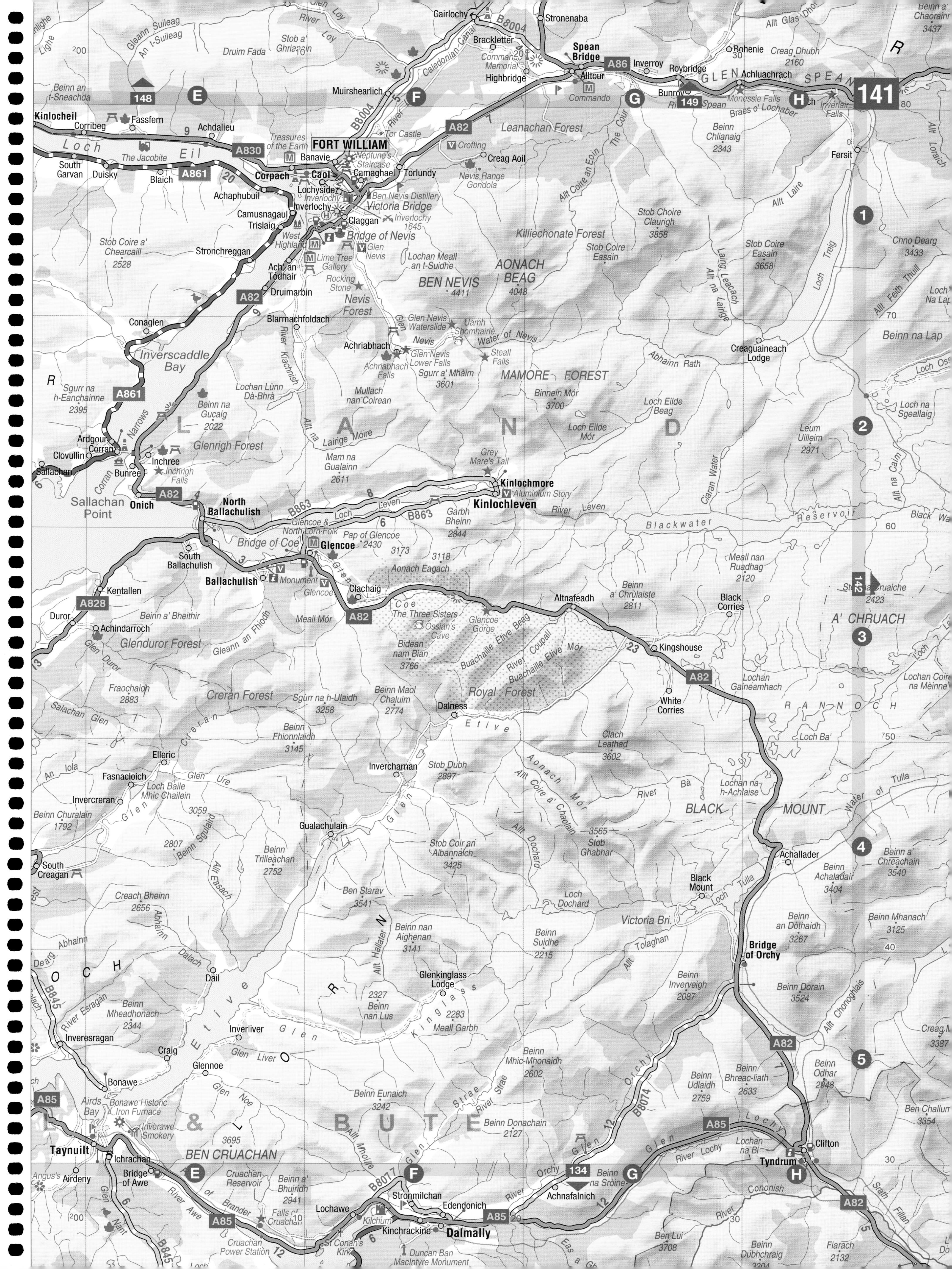

141
FORT WILLIAM
Gairlochy
Stronenaba
Spean Bridge
Brackletter
Commando Memorial
Highbridge
Alltour
Commando
A86
Inverroy
Roybridge
Bohenie
Creag Dhubh 2160
GLEN SPEAN
Achluachrach
Bunroy
Monessie Falls
Braes o' Lochaber
Inverlair Falls
Beinn a' Chaorainn 3437
Allt Glas Dhoire
B8004
Muirshearlich
Caledonian Canal
River Loy
Glen Loy
Stob a' Ghrianain
Druim Fada
Gleann Suileag
An t-Suileag
Beinn an t-Sneachda
Kinlocheil
Corribeg
Fassfern
Achdalieu
Loch Eil
The Jacobite
A830
A861
South Garvan
Duisky
Blaich
Corpach
Caol
Banavie
Treasures of the Earth
Neptune's Staircase
Camaghael
Torlundy
Tor Castle
A82
Leanachan Forest
Crofting
Creag Aoil
Nevis Range Gondola
Beinn Chlianaig 2343
Fersit
Allt Loraich
Achaphubuil
Lochyside
Inverlochy
Ben Nevis Distillery
Victoria Bridge
Camusnagaul
Trislaig
Claggan
Inverlochy 1645
West Highland
Bridge of Nevis
Glen Nevis
Lime Tree Gallery
Stob Coire a' Chearcaill 2528
Stronchreggan
Ach' an Todhair
Rocking Stone
Nevis Forest
Lochan Meall an t-Suidhe
BEN NEVIS 4411
AONACH BEAG 4048
Killiechonate Forest
Stob Coire Easain
Stob Choire Claurigh 3858
Stob Coire Easain 3658
Allt Coire an Eoin
The Cour
Allt Laire
Lairig Leacach
Allt na Lairige
Loch Treig
Chno Dearg 3433
Allt Feith Thuill
Loch Na Lap
Beinn na Lap
Druimarbin
Blarmachfoldach
Conaglen
Inverscaddle Bay
River Kiachnish
Glen Nevis Waterslide
Uamh Shomhairle
Water of Nevis
Achriabhach
Glen Nevis Lower Falls
Achriabhach Falls
Steall Falls
Sgurr a' Mhàim 3601
Abhainn Rath
Creaguaineach Lodge
Loch Ossian
Sgurr na h-Eanchainne 2395
A861
Lochan Lùnn Dà-Bhrà
Mullach nan Coirean
MAMORE FOREST
Binnein Mór 3700
Loch Eilde Beag
Loch na Sgeallaig
Beinn na Gucaig 2022
L A N D
Lairige Móire
Loch Eilde Mór
Leum Uilleim 2971
Narrows
Ardgour
Corran
Clovullin
Sallachan
Inchree
Inchree Falls
Bunree
Glenrigh Forest
Mam na Gualainn 2611
Grey Mare's Tail
Kinlochmore
Aluminium Story
Kinlochleven
Allt na Caim
Ciaran Water
Sallachan Point
Onich
North Ballachulish
B863
Loch Leven
River Leven
Garbh Bheinn 2844
Blackwater Reservoir
Black Water
Glencoe & North Lorn Folk
Pap of Glencoe 2430
Bridge of Coe
Glencoe
South Ballachulish
Ballachulish
Monument
Aonach Eagach
Glen Coe
Clachaig
Meall nan Ruadhag 2120
Stob a' Cruiche 2423
142
A' CHRUACH
Kentallen
A828
Duror
Beinn a' Bheithir
Achindarroch
Glenduror Forest
Glen Duror
Gleann an Fhiodh
Meall Mór
The Three Sisters
Ossian's Cave
Glencoe Gorge
Altnafeadh
Beinn a' Chrùlaiste 2811
Black Corries
Bidean nam Bian 3766
Buachaille Etive Beag
River Coupall
Buachaille Etive Mór
Royal Forest
Kingshouse
Lochan Gaineamhach
Lochan Coire na Mèinne
Fraochaidh 2883
Creran Forest
Sgùrr na h-Ulaidh 3258
Beinn Maol Chaluim 2774
Dalness
White Corries
R A N N O C H
Salachan Glen
Glen Etive
Beinn Fhionnlaidh 3145
Clach Leathad 3602
Loch Ba'
Elleric
River Creran
An Iola
Fasnacloich
Loch Baile Mhic Chailein
Glen Ure
Inverchamnan
Stob Dubh 2897
Aonach Mór
Allt Coire a' Chaorain
River Bà
Lochan na h-Achlaise
BLACK MOUNT
Water of Tulla
Invercreran
Beinn Churalain 1792
Glen Creran
3059
Gualachulain
Allt Dochard
3565
Stob Ghabhar
Achallader
South Creagan
2807
Beinn Sguliaird
Allt Easach
Beinn Trilleachan 2752
Stob Coir an Albannaich 3425
Black Mount
Loch Tulla
Beinn Achaladair 3404
Beinn a' Chreachain 3540
Creach Bheinn 2656
Abhainn
Ben Starav 3541
Loch Dochard
Victoria Bri.
Beinn an Dòthaidh 3267
Beinn Mhanach 3125
Beinn nan Aighenan 3141
Allt Hallater
Beinn Suidhe 2215
Allt Tolaghan
Bridge of Orchy
Dail
Glenkinglass Lodge
Beinn Inverveigh 2087
Beinn Dorain 3524
Allt Chonoghlais
B845
River Esragan
Beinn Mheadhonach 2344
2327 Beinn nan Lus
Kinglass
2283 Meall Garbh
Inveresragan
Inverliver
Glen Liver
Craig
Glennoe
Glen Noe
Beinn Mhic-Mhonaidh 2602
Beinn Udlaidh 2759
Beinn Bhreac-liath 2633
Beinn Odhar 2948
Creag Mhòr 3387
Bonawe
A85
Airds Bay
Bonawe Historic Iron Furnace
Inverawe Smokery
Beinn Eunaich 3242
River Strae
Glen Strae
Beinn Donachain 2127
B8074
River Orchy
Glen Orchy
Ben Challum 3354
ARGYLL & BUTE
Taynuilt
Ichrachan
3695
BEN CRUACHAN
Cruachan Reservoir
Allt Mhoille
Beinn na Sròine
A85
Glen Lochy
River Lochy
Lochan na Bi
Clifton
Tyndrum
Angus's
Airdeny
Bridge of Awe
River Awe
Pass of Brander
Beinn a' Bhuiridh 2941
Falls of Cruachan
B8077
Stronmilchan
Edendonich
134
Achnafalnich
Cononish
Strath Fillan
Glen Nant
Lochawe
Kilchurn
Kinchrackine
Dalmally
Cruachan Power Station
St Conan's Kirk
Duncan Ban MacIntyre Monument
Ben Lui 3708
Beinn Dubhchraig 3204
Fiarach 2132
Eas a' Ghaill

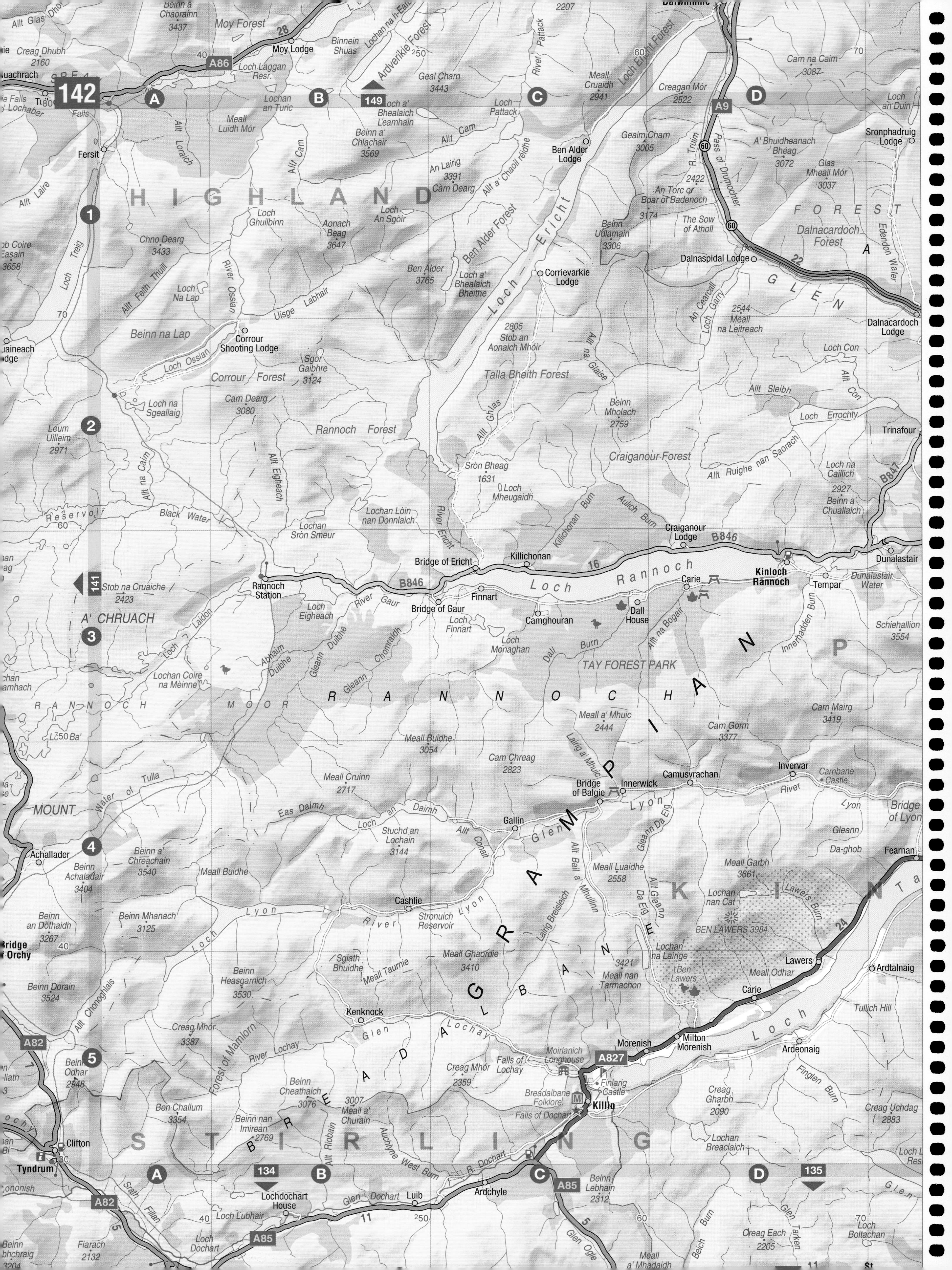

142
149
141
134
135
A
B
C
D
1
2
3
4
5
HIGHLAND
STIRLING
GRAMPIAN
BREADALBANE
RANNOCH MOOR
FOREST
GLEN
MOUNT
A' CHRUACH
Moy Forest
Moy Lodge
Loch Laggan Resr.
Ardverikie Forest
Geal Charn 3443
Lochan an Turic
Meall Luidh Mòr
Fersit
Loch Treig
Chno Dearg 3433
Loch Ghuilbinn
Aonach Beag 3647
Loch An Sgòir
Ben Alder Forest
Ben Alder 3765
Ben Alder Lodge
Loch Ericht
Corrievarkie Lodge
Beinn na Lap
Corrour Shooting Lodge
Loch Ossian
Corrour Forest
Sgor Gaibhre 3124
Carn Dearg 3080
Rannoch Forest
Talla Bheith Forest
Craiganour Forest
Rannoch Station
Bridge of Ericht
Bridge of Gaur
Killichonan
Finnart
Loch Rannoch
Carie
Kinloch Rannoch
Tempar
Dunalastair
Camghouran
Dall House
TAY FOREST PARK
Schiehallion 3554
Pass of Drumochter
Dalnaspidal Lodge
Dalnacardoch Lodge
Dalnacardoch Forest
Trinafour
Loch Errochty
Meall Buidhe 3054
Carn Gorm 3377
Carn Mairg 3419
Bridge of Balgie
Innerwick
Camusvrachan
Invervar
Bridge of Lyon
Gallin
Glen Lyon
Cashlie
Stronuich Reservoir
Loch Lyon
Meall Ghaordie 3410
Kenknock
Glen Lochay
Ben Lawers 3984
Lawers
Fearnan
Carie
Ardtalnaig
Morenish
Milton Morenish
Ardeonaig
Loch Tay
Killin
Finlarig Castle
Breadalbane Folklore
Falls of Dochart
Moirlanich Longhouse
Falls of Lochay
Tyndrum
Clifton
Bridge of Orchy
Achallader
Luib
Ardchyle
Lochdochart House
Glen Dochart
Loch Lubhair
A82
A827
A85
A86
A9
B846
B847

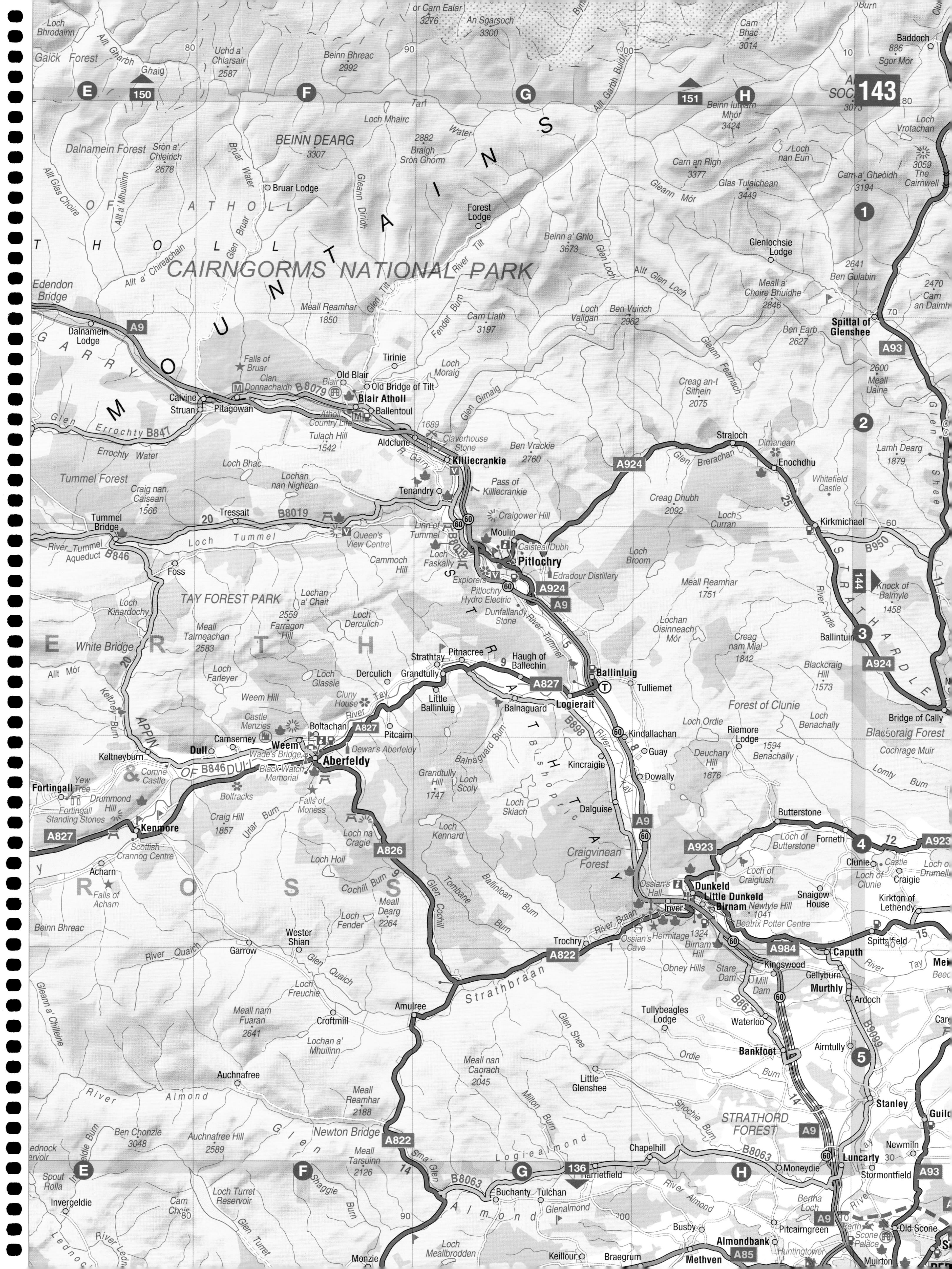
CAIRNGORMS NATIONAL PARK
MOUNTAINS
FOREST OF ATHOLL
GARRY
PERTH
STRATHARDLE
STRATHTAY
TAY FOREST PARK
Dalnamein Forest
Gaick Forest
Tummel Forest
Forest of Clunie
Craigvinean Forest
STRATHORD FOREST
BEINN DEARG 3307
Beinn Bhreac 2992
An Sgarsoch 3300
Carn Bhac 3014
Beinn Iutharn Mhòr 3424
Carn an Righ 3377
Glas Tulaichean 3449
Beinn a' Ghlo 3673
Carn a' Gheòidh 3194
The Cairnwell 3059
Ben Gulabin 2641
Ben Vuirich 2962
Ben Vrackie 2760
Carn Liath 3197
Meall Reamhar 1850
Farragon Hill 2559
Meall Tairneachan 2583
Craig nan Caisean 1566
Meall Dearg 2264
Meall nam Fuaran 2641
Ben Chonzie 3048
Meall nan Caorach 2045
Meall Reamhar 2188
Meall Tarsuinn 2126
Auchnafree Hill 2589
Birnam Hill 1324
Newtyle Hill 1041
Deuchary Hill 1676
Blackcraig Hill 1573
Knock of Balmyle 1458
Lamh Dearg 1879
Meall Uaine 2600
Ben Earb 2627
Creag Dhubh 2092
Creag nam Mial 1842
Grandtully Hill 1747
Craig Hill 1857
Tulach Hill 1542
Blair Atholl
Old Blair
Old Bridge of Tilt
Ballentoul
Calvine
Struan
Pitagowan
Killiecrankie
Pass of Killiecrankie
Tenandry
Aldclune
Pitlochry
Moulin
Edradour Distillery
Pitlochry Hydro Electric
Tummel Bridge
Tressait
Queen's View Centre
Foss
Ballinluig
Logierait
Tulliemet
Kindallachan
Guay
Dowally
Kincraigie
Dalguise
Dunkeld
Little Dunkeld
Birnam
Inver
Ossian's Hall
Ossian's Cave
Hermitage
Beatrix Potter Centre
Caputh
Spittalfield
Murthly
Kingswood
Gellyburn
Ardoch
Waterloo
Bankfoot
Airntully
Stanley
Luncarty
Moneydie
Stormontfield
Newmiln
Old Scone
Scone Palace
Almondbank
Methven
Pitcairngreen
Huntingtower
Busby
Braegrum
Keillour
Glenalmond
Buchanty
Tulchan
Harrietfield
Chapelhill
Aberfeldy
Weem
Dull
Camserney
Boltachan
Castle Menzies
Dewar's Aberfeldy
Black Watch Memorial
Falls of Moness
Wade's Bridge
Grandtully
Strathtay
Pitnacree
Derculich
Little Ballinluig
Balnaguard
Haugh of Ballechin
Pitcairn
Kenmore
Fortingall
Fortingall Standing Stones
Keltneyburn
Comrie Castle
Bolfracks
Drummond Hill
Scottish Crannog Centre
Acharn
Falls of Acharn
Garrow
Wester Shian
Amulree
Croftmill
Trochry
Auchnafree
Newton Bridge
Invergeldie
Monzie
Spittal of Glenshee
Kirkmichael
Enochdhu
Straloch
Dirnanean
Whitefield Castle
Ballintuim
Bridge of Cally
Butterstone
Forneth
Clunie
Craigie
Kirkton of Lethendy
Snaigow House
Riemore Lodge
Glenlochsie Lodge
Forest Lodge
Bruar Lodge
Dalnamein Lodge
Edendon Bridge
Tirinie
Clan Donnachaidh
Falls of Bruar
Atholl Country Life
Claverhouse Stone
Craigower Hill
Linn of Tummel
Explorers
Dunfallandy Stone
White Bridge
Tullybeagles Lodge
Little Glenshee
Loch Tummel
Loch Faskally
Loch Kinardochy
Loch Derculich
Loch Farleyer
Loch Glassie
Lochan a' Chait
Loch Bhac
Lochan nan Nighean
Loch Broom
Loch Curran
Loch Vallgan
Loch Moraig
Loch Ordie
Loch Benachally
Loch Kennard
Loch Skiach
Loch Scoly
Loch Hoil
Loch na Craigie
Loch Fender
Loch Freuchie
Lochan a' Mhuilinn
Loch of Butterstone
Loch of Craiglush
Loch of Clunie
Loch Turret Reservoir
Loch Meallbrodden
Loch Mhairc
Loch Vrotachan
Loch nan Eun
Loch Bhrodainn
Stare Dam
Mill Dam
Obney Hills
Strathbraan
River Tummel
River Tay
River Braan
River Almond
River Quaich
River Garry
River Tilt
River Ardle
Errochty Water
Glen Errochty
Glen Quaich
Glen Shee
Glen Tilt
Glen Cochill
Sma' Glen
Logiealmond
A9
A93
A822
A826
A827
A923
A924
A984
A85
B846
B847
B8019
B8079
B898
B950
B867
B8063
B9099
150
151
136
144
E
F
G
H
1
2
3
4
5

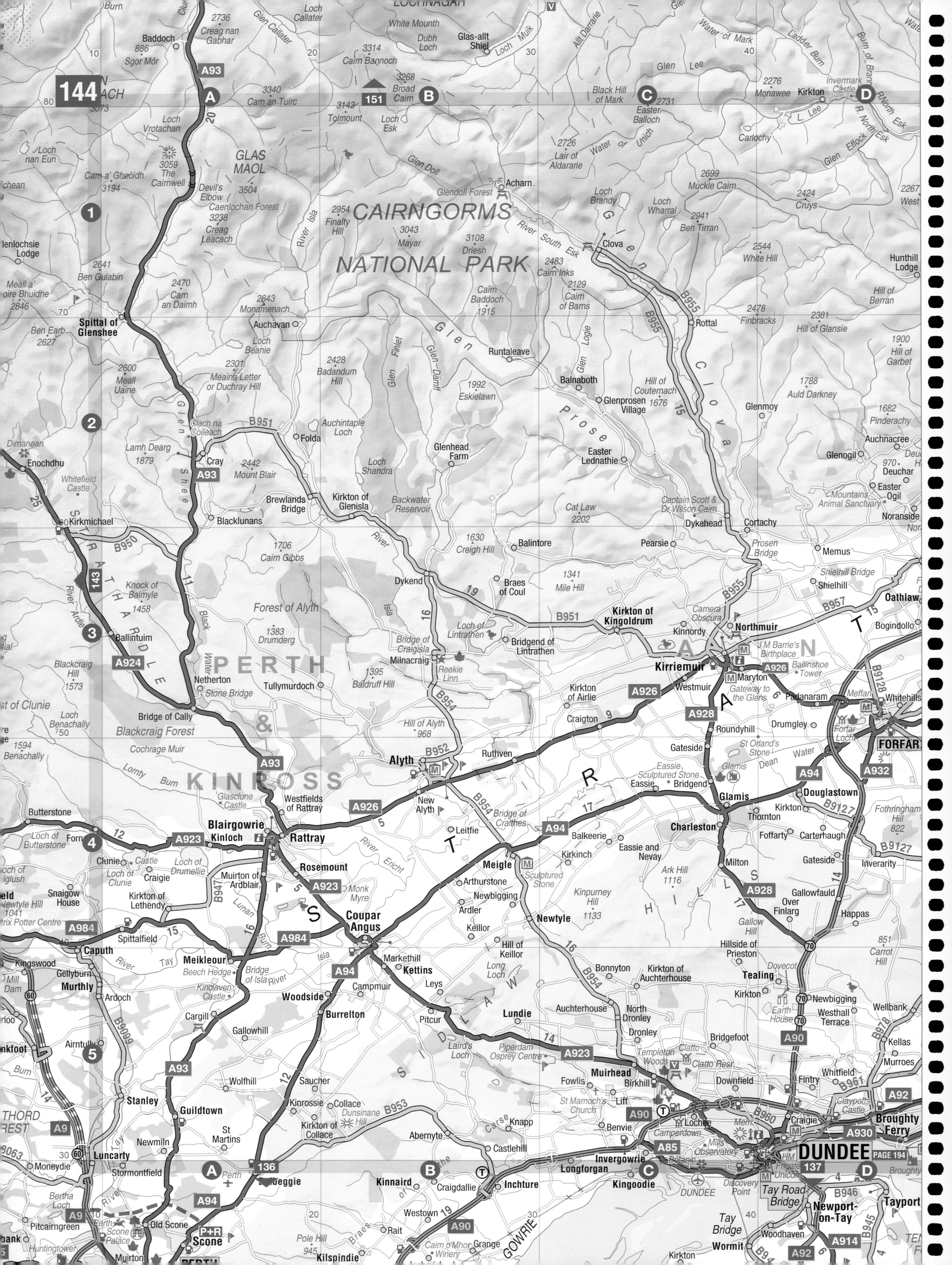
144
151
CAIRNGORMS
NATIONAL PARK
GLAS MAOL
Spittal of Glenshee
Kirkmichael
Blairgowrie
Rattray
Alyth
Coupar Angus
Kirriemuir
Glamis
Meigle
Newtyle
Dundee
FORFAR
Clova
Rottal
Cortachy
Northmuir
Kirkton of Kingoldrum
Bridge of Cally
Meikleour
Caputh
Murthly
Stanley
Guildtown
Scone
Luncarty
Burrelton
Woodside
Kettins
Lundie
Muirhead
Invergowrie
Kingoodie
Longforgan
Inchture
Kinnaird
Broughty Ferry
Newport-on-Tay
Tayport
Wormit
Tay Road Bridge
Tay Bridge
Tealing
Douglastown
Charleston
Padanaram
Oathlaw
PERTH
&
KINROSS
ANGUS
SIDLAW HILLS
STRATHARDLE
Glen Shee
Glen Clova
Glen Prosen
Glen Isla
Forest of Alyth
Blackcraig Forest
A93
A923
A926
A94
A984
A924
A928
A90
A85
A92
A932
A914
A9
B951
B955
B954
B952
B950
B947
B953
B9099
B957
B9127
B9128
B961
B960
B946
B945
B978
137
PAGE 194
136

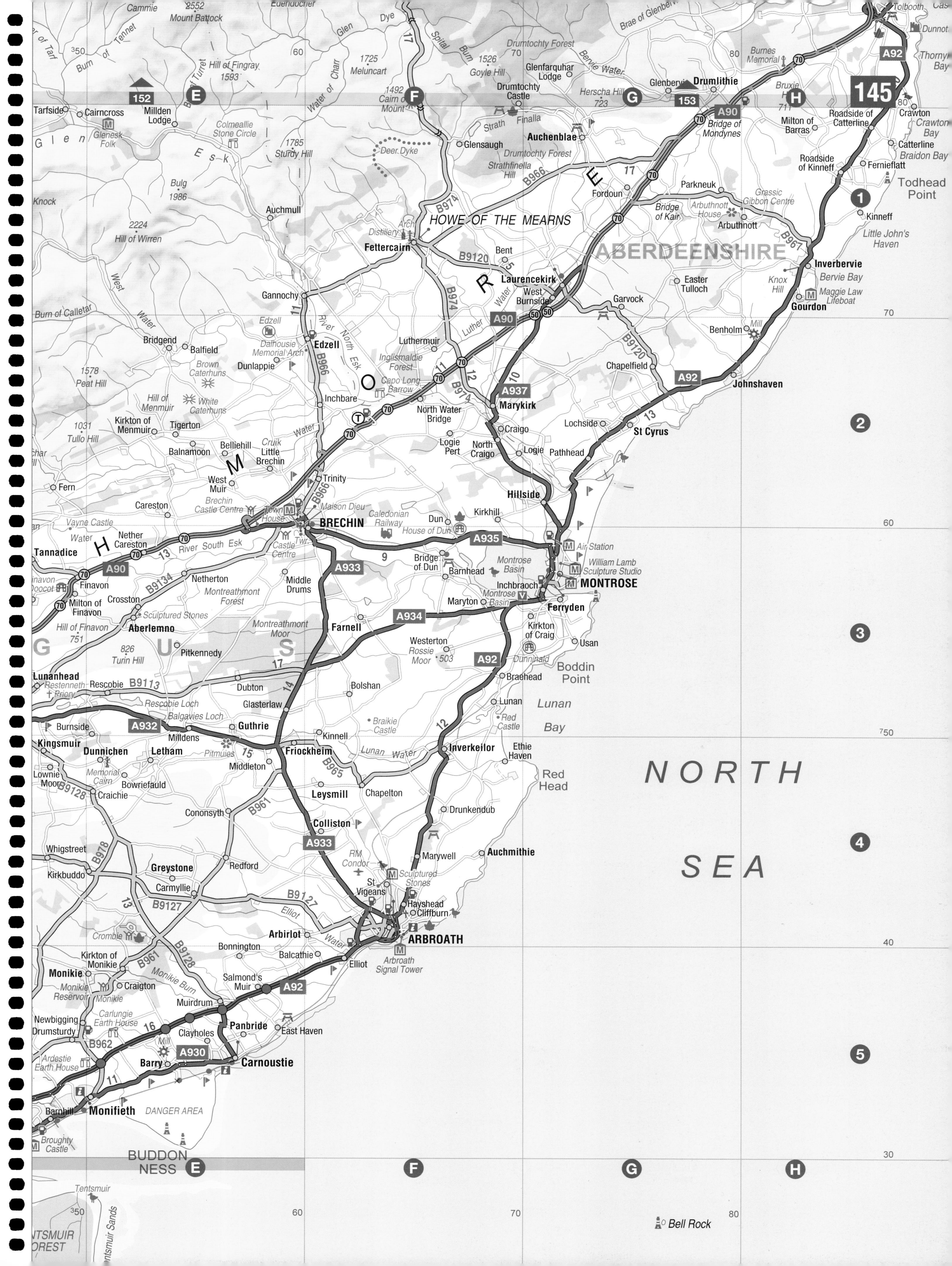

Cammie
2552
Mount Battock
Euendocher
Dye
Glen
Brae of Glenbervie
Tolbooth
Dunnot
Burn of Tennet
Burn
Hill of Fingray
1593
60
1725
Meluncart
Water of Charr
17
Spital Burn
1526
Goyle Hill
Drumtochty Forest
70
Bervie Water
Glenfarquhar Lodge
80
Burnes Memorial
70
A92
Thornyhive Bay
145
152
E
Millden Lodge
Burn of Turret
1492
Cairn o' Mount
F
Drumtochty Castle
Herscha Hill
723
G
Glenbervie
Drumlithie
153
A90
Bruxie Hill
711
H
Tarfside
Cairncross
Glenesk Folk
Colmeallie Stone Circle
Strath Finalla
Auchenblae
Bridge of Mondynes
Milton of Barras
Roadside of Catterline
Crawton
Crawton Bay
Catterline
Braidon Bay
Glen Esk
1785
Sturdy Hill
Deer Dyke
Glensaugh
Drumtochty Forest
Strathfinella Hill
B966
17
Fordoun
Roadside of Kinneff
Fernieflatt
Todhead Point
1
Bulg
1986
Knock
Auchmull
B974
HOWE OF THE MEARNS
Parkneuk
Bridge of Kair
Arbuthnott House
Grassic Gibbon Centre
Arbuthnott
Kinneff
Little John's Haven
2224
Hill of Wirren
Distillery
Arch
Fettercairn
B9120
Bent
ABERDEENSHIRE
B967
Inverbervie
Bervie Bay
West Water
Gannochy
Laurencekirk
West Burnside
Easter Tulloch
Knox Hill
Maggie Law Lifeboat
Gourdon
Garvock
70
Burn of Calletar
Edzell
A90
Luther Water
Bridgend
Balfield
Dalhousie Memorial Arch
Edzell
River North Esk
Luthermuir
Benholm
Mill
B9120
1578
Peat Hill
Brown Caterthuns
Dunlappie
B966
Inglismaldie Forest
Chapelfield
Capo Long Barrow
B974
A937
A92
Johnshaven
Hill of Menmuir
White Caterthuns
Inchbare
Marykirk
Kirkton of Menmuir
Tigerton
North Water Bridge
Craigo
Lochside
St Cyrus
2
1031
Tullo Hill
Balnamoon
Belliehill
Cruik Water
Little Brechin
Logie Pert
North Craigo
Logie
Pathhead
West Muir
Trinity
Fern
Hillside
Careston
Brechin Castle Centre
Town House
Maison Dieu
B966
Caledonian Railway
Dun
House of Dun
Kirkhill
Vayne Castle
BRECHIN
60
Nether Careston
Castle Centre
A935
Air Station
William Lamb Sculpture Studio
Tannadice
River South Esk
Twr
Bridge of Dun
Montrose Basin
A90
A933
Barnhead
MONTROSE
Finavon Doocot
Finavon
B9134
Netherton
Middle Drums
Inchbraach
Milton of Finavon
Crosston
Montreathmont Forest
Maryton
Montrose Basin
Ferryden
Sculptured Stones
A934
Hill of Finavon
751
Aberlemno
Montreathmont Moor
Farnell
Kirkton of Craig
Westerton
Usan
3
826
Turin Hill
Pitkennedy
Rossie Moor
503
A92
Dunninald
Boddin Point
Lunanhead
Restenneth Priory
Rescobie
B9113
Dubton
Bolshan
Braehead
Rescobie Loch
Glasterlaw
Lunan
Lunan Bay
Balgavies Loch
Red Castle
Burnside
A932
Guthrie
Kinnell
Braikie Castle
750
Kingsmuir
Milldens
Dunnichen
Letham
Pitmuies
Friockheim
Lunan Water
Inverkeilor
Ethie Haven
NORTH SEA
Lownie Moor
Memorial Cairn
Middleton
B965
Red Head
Bowriefauld
B9128
Craichie
Leysmill
Chapelton
Cononsyth
B961
Drunkendub
Colliston
Whigstreet
A933
Marywell
Auchmithie
4
B978
Kirkbuddo
Greystone
Redford
RM Condor
Sculptured Stones
Carmyllie
St Vigeans
B9127
Elliot Water
Hayshead
Cliffburn
Crombie
Arbirlot
ARBROATH
40
Bonnington
Kirkton of Monikie
Balcathie
Elliot
Arbroath Signal Tower
Monikie
B961
Monikie Burn
Salmond's Muir
A92
Monikie Reservoir
Craigton
Muirdrum
Newbigging
Carlungie Earth House
Drumsturdy
Panbride
East Haven
Clayholes
Mill
B962
A930
5
Ardestie Earth House
Barry
Carnoustie
Barnhill
Monifieth
DANGER AREA
Broughty Castle
BUDDON NESS
E
F
G
H
30
Tentsmuir
350
60
70
80
Tentsmuir Sands
TENTSMUIR FOREST
Bell Rock

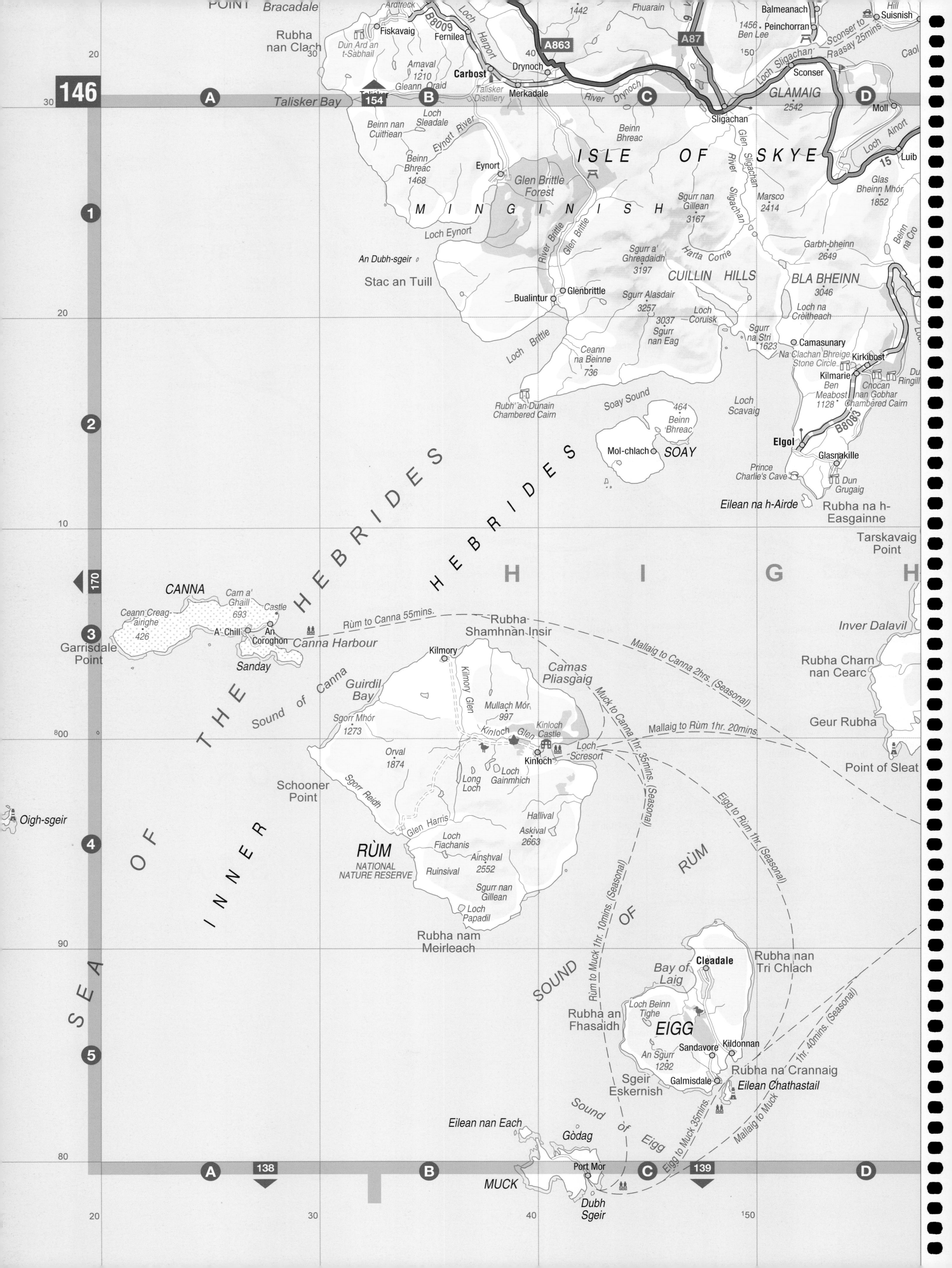

POINT *Bracadale*

Ardtreck

B8009

Loch Harport

1442

Fhuarain

Balmeanach

1456 Peinchorran

Sconser to Raasay 25mins

Hill • Suisnish

Fiskavaig

Fernilea

Rubha nan Clach 30

Dun Ard an t-Sabhail

Drynoch

A863

Carbost

A87

1456 Ben Lee

150

Sconser

Caol

Arnaval 1210

Gleann Oraid

Talisker Distillery

Merkadale

GLAMAIG 2542

Talisker

Talisker Bay

154

Drynoch

River

Loch Ainort

A

B

Sligachan

Loch Sligachan

C

Moll

D

Beinn nan Cuithean

Loch Sleadale

River Eynort

Beinn Bhreac

Glen Sligachan

Marsco 2414

15 • Luib

Glas Bheinn Mhór 1852

Eynort

Beinn Bhreac 1468

ISLE OF SKYE

Sgurr nan Gillean 3167

M I N G I N I S H

Beinn na Cro

1

20

Glen Brittle Forest

River Brittle

Glen Brittle

Sgurr a' Ghreadaidh 3197

Harta Corrie

Garbh-bheinn 2649

An Dubh-sgeir

Loch Eynort

CUILLIN HILLS

BLA BHEINN 3046

Stac an Tuill

Bualintur • Glenbrittle

Sgurr Alasdair 3257

Loch Coruisk

Loch na Crèitheach

Loch Brittle

3037 Sgurr nan Eag

Sgurr na Stri 1623

Camasunary

Na Clachan Bhreige Stone Circle

Kirkibost

2

Ceann na Beinne 736

Kilmarie

Ben Meabost 1128

Cnocan nan Gobhar

Chambered Cairn

Du Ringill

Rubh' an Dunain Chambered Cairn

Soay Sound

464 Beinn Bhreac

Loch Scavaig

Elgol

B8083

10

Mol-chlach

SOAY

Prince Charlie's Cave

Glasnakille

Dun Grugaig

Eilean na h-Airde

Rubha na h-Easgainne

Tarskavaig Point

170

T H E   H E B R I D E S

H E B R I D E S

H I G H

G

H

CANNA

Càrn a' Ghaill 693

Castle

Rubha Shamhnàn Insir

Mallaig to Canna 2hrs. (Seasonal)

Inver Dalavil

Ceann Creag-airighe 426

A' Chill

An Coroghon

Camas Pliasgaig

Rubha Charn nan Cearc

3

Garrisdale Point

Sanday

Canna Harbour

Rùm to Canna 55mins.

Kilmory

Muck to Canna 1hr. 35mins. (Seasonal)

Mallaig to Rùm 1hr. 20mins.

Geur Rubha

Sound of Canna

Guirdil Bay

Kilmory Glen

Mullach Mór 997

Kinloch Castle

800

Sgorr Mhór 1273

Kinloch Glen

Kinloch

Loch Scresort

Point of Sleat

T H E   I N N E R

Orval 1874

Long Loch

Loch Gainmhich

Eigg to Rùm 1hr. (Seasonal)

Oigh-sgeir

Sgorr Reidh

4

S E A   O F

Glen Harris

Loch Fiachanis

Hallival

Askival 2663

Schooner Point

RÙM

NATIONAL NATURE RESERVE

Ruinsival

Ainshval 2552

Sgurr nan Gillean

S O U N D   O F   R Ù M

90

Loch Papadil

Rubha nam Meirleach

Rùm to Muck 1hr. 10mins. (Seasonal)

Cleadale

Rubha nan Tri Chlach

Bay of Laig

Rubha an Fhasaidh

Loch Beinn Tighe

EIGG

5

An Sgurr 1292

Sandavore

Kildonnan

Eigg to Muck 35mins. (Seasonal)

Mallaig to Muck 1hr. 40mins. (Seasonal)

80

Galmisdale

Rubha na Crannaig

Eilean Chathastail

Sgeir Eskernish

Eilean nan Each

Sound of Eigg

A

138

B

Port Mor

C

139

D

Gòdag

MUCK

Dubh Sgeir

20

30

40

150

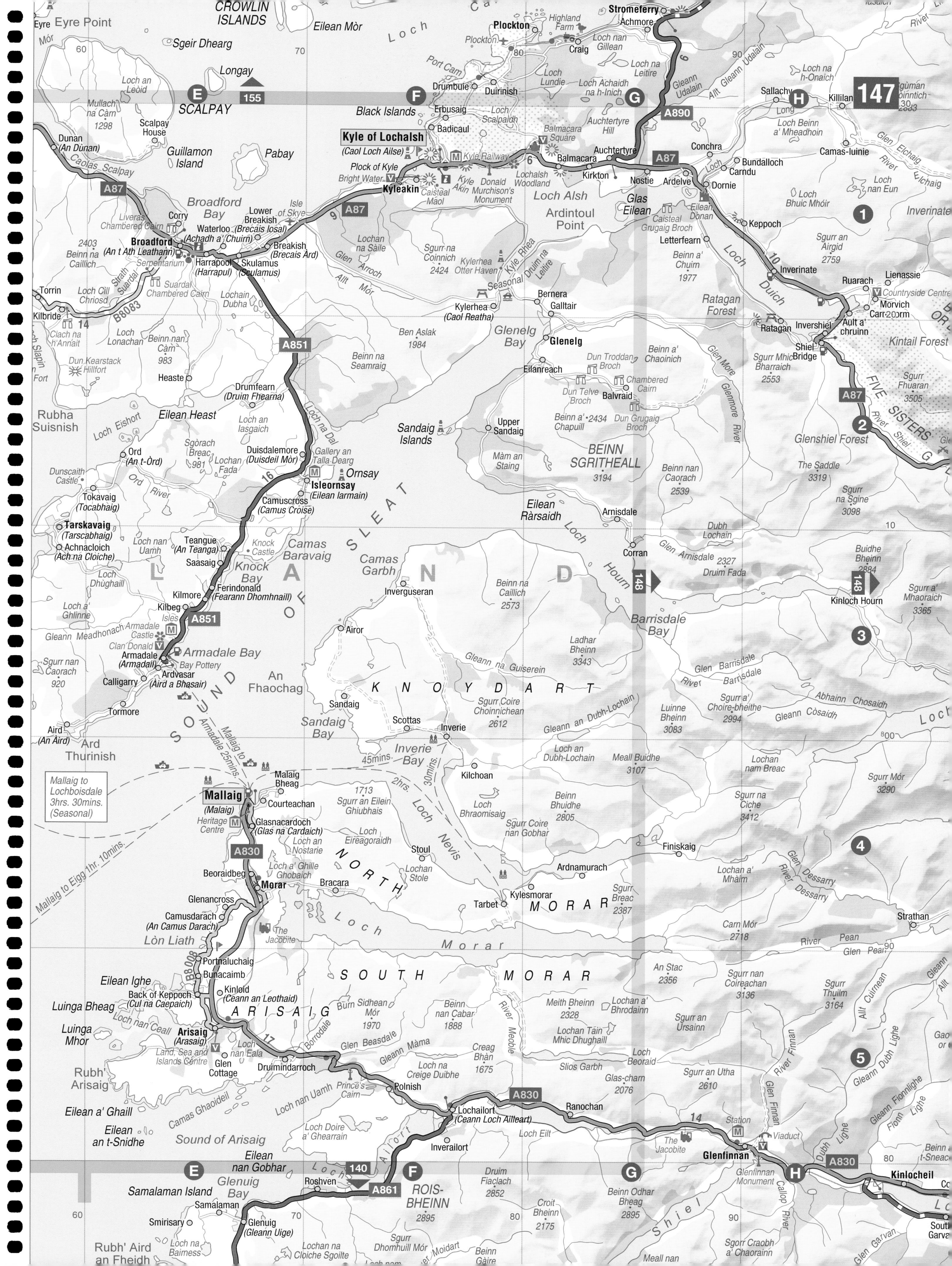

147
148
155
140
Kyle of Lochalsh
Mallaig
Mallaig to Lochboisdale 3hrs. 30mins. (Seasonal)
Plockton
Stromeferry
Broadford
Kyleakin
Isleornsay
Armadale
Glenelg
Arisaig
Morar
Glenfinnan
Lochailort
Kinlocheil
Inverie
Dornie
SCALPAY
CROWLIN ISLANDS
KNOYDART
NORTH MORAR
SOUTH MORAR
SOUND OF SLEAT
Loch Alsh
Loch Duich
Loch Hourn
Loch Nevis
Loch Morar
Sound of Arisaig
FIVE SISTERS
Kintail Forest
Glenshiel Forest
BEINN SGRITHEALL
Kinloch Hourn
A87
A851
A830
A890
A861
B8083
B8008

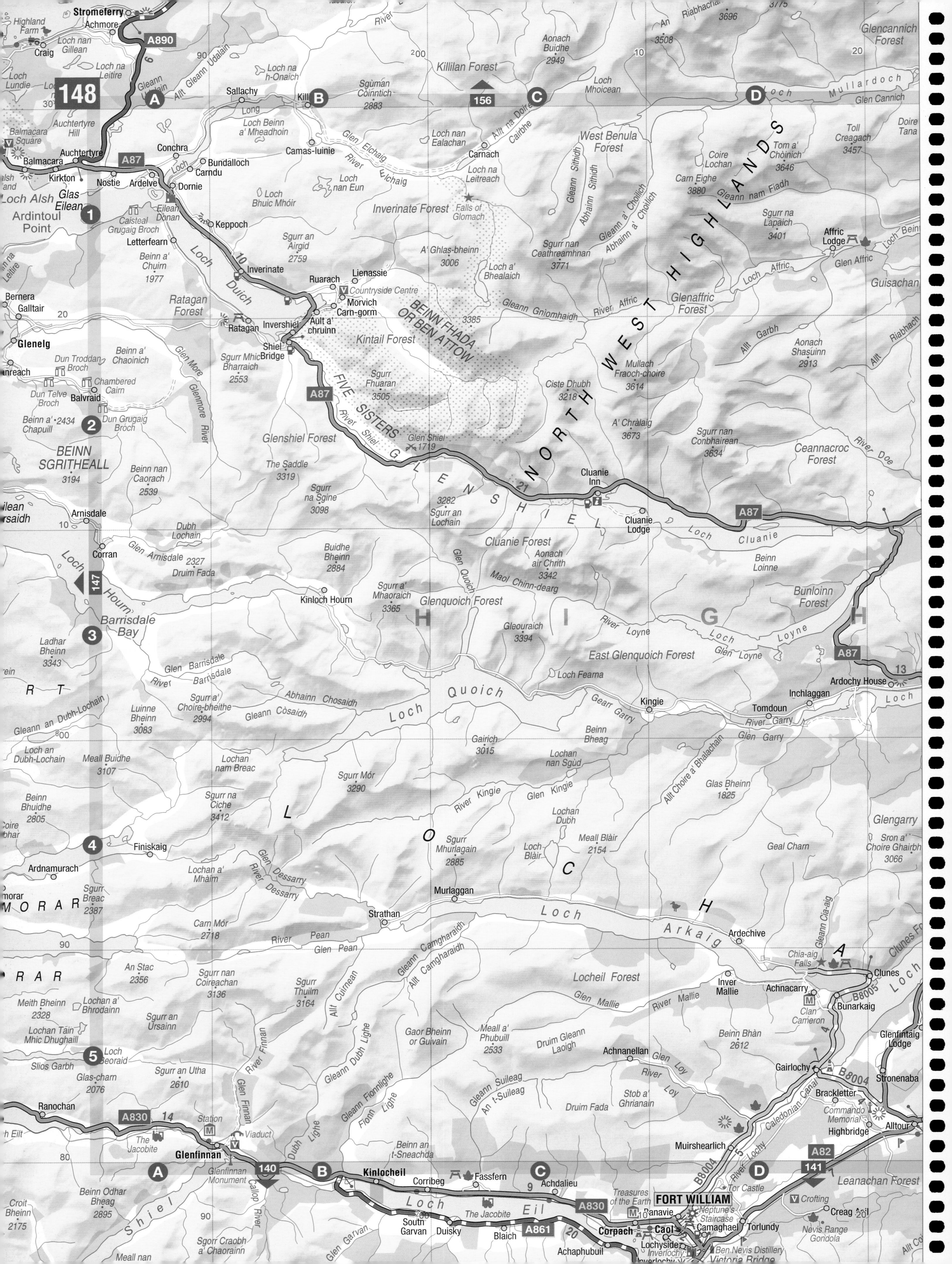

Stromeferry
Achmore
A890
Highland Farm
Craig
Loch nan Gillean
Loch na Leitire
Loch Lundie
148
Gleann Udalain
Allt Gleann Udalain
90
Loch na h-Onaich
Sallachy
Long
Killilan
Killilan Forest
Sgùman Còinntich
2883
156
Aonach Buidhe
2949
Loch Mhoicean
An Riabhachan
3508
3696
3775
Glencannich Forest
Loch Mullardoch
Glen Cannich
Auchtertyre Hill
Balmacara Square
Balmacara
Auchtertyre
A87
Conchra
Bundalloch
Carndu
Loch Beinn a' Mheadhoin
Camas-luinie
Glen Elchaig
River Elchaig
Loch nan Ealachan
Carnach
Allt na Doire Cairbhe
Loch na Leitreach
West Benula Forest
Gleann Sithidh
Abhainn Sithidh
Coire Lochan
Carn Eighe
3880
Tom a' Chòinich
3646
Toll Creagach
3457
Doire Tana
Kirkton
Nostie
Ardelve
Dornie
Loch Alsh
Glas Eilean
Eilean Donan
Ardintoul Point
Loch Long
Loch Bhuic Mhóir
Loch nan Eun
Inverinate Forest
Falls of Glomach
Gleann nam Fiadh
Sgurr na Lapaich
3401
Affric Lodge
Loch Beinn
Caisteal Grugaig Broch
Keppoch
Letterfearn
Beinn a' Chuirn
1977
Loch Duich
Inverinate
Sgurr an Airgid
2759
A' Ghlas-bheinn
3006
Loch a' Bhealaich
Sgurr nan Ceathreamhnan
3771
Gleann a' Choilich
Abhainn a' Choilich
NORTH WEST HIGHLANDS
Loch Affric
Glen Affric
Guisachan
Bernera
Galltair
Glenelg
Ratagan Forest
Ratagan
Ruarach
Lienassie
Countryside Centre
Morvich
Carn-gorm
Invershiel
Ault a' chruinn
Shiel Bridge
BEINN FHADA OR BEN ATTOW
3385
Gleann Gniomhaidh
River Affric
Glenaffric Forest
Kintail Forest
Dun Troddan Broch
Chambered Cairn
Beinn a' Chaoinich
Glen More
Glenmore River
Sgurr Mhic Bharraich
2553
Dun Telve Broch
Balvraid
Dun Grugaig Broch
Beinn a' Chapuill
2434
FIVE SISTERS
Sgurr Fhuaran
3505
Mullach Fraoch-choire
3614
Ciste Dhubh
3218
Allt Garbh
Aonach Shasuinn
2913
River Shiel
Glen Shiel
1719
Glenshiel Forest
A' Chràlaig
3673
Sgurr nan Conbhairean
3634
Ceannacroc Forest
River Doe
BEINN SGRITHEALL
3194
Beinn nan Caorach
2539
The Saddle
3319
Sgurr na Sgine
3098
3282
Sgurr an Lochain
GLEN SHIEL
Cluanie Inn
Cluanie Lodge
Loch Cluanie
Arnisdale
Dubh Lochain
Corran
Glen Arnisdale
2327
Druim Fada
Buidhe Bheinn
2884
Cluanie Forest
Aonach air Chrith
3342
Glen Quoich
Maol Chinn-dearg
Beinn Loinne
Bunloinn Forest
Loch Hourn
147
Kinloch Hourn
Sgurr a' Mhaoraich
3365
Glenquoich Forest
HIGH
Barrisdale Bay
Ladhar Bheinn
3343
Gleouraich
3394
River Loyne
Loch Loyne
Glen Loyne
East Glenquoich Forest
A87
Loch Fearna
Ardochy House
13
Inchlaggan
Glen Barrisdale
River Barrisdale
Sgurr a' Choire-bheithe
2994
Abhainn Chosaidh
Gleann Còsaidh
Loch Quoich
Gearr Garry
Kingie
Tomdoun
River Garry
Glen Garry
Beinn Bheag
Gleann an Dubh-Lochain
Luinne Bheinn
3083
Loch an Dubh-Lochain
Meall Buidhe
3107
Lochan nam Breac
Gairich
3015
Lochan nan Sgùd
Allt Choire a' Bhalachain
Glas Bheinn
1825
Sgurr Mór
3290
Beinn Bhuidhe
2805
Sgurr na Ciche
3412
River Kingie
Glen Kingie
Lochan Dubh
Glengarry
LOCH
Finiskaig
Sgurr Mhurlagain
2885
Loch Blàir
Meall Blàir
2154
Geal Charn
Sron a' Choire Ghairbh
3066
Ardnamurach
Lochan a' Mhàim
Glen Dessarry
River Dessarry
Sgurr Breac
2387
MORAR
Murlaggan
Strathan
Loch Arkaig
Carn Mór
2718
River Pean
Glen Pean
Gleann Camgharaidh
Allt Camgharaidh
Ardechive
Gleann Cia-aig
Chia-aig Falls
Clunes
Clunes Forest
An Stac
2356
Sgurr nan Coireachan
3136
Sgurr Thuilm
3164
Allt Cuirnean
Locheil Forest
Inver Mallie
Achnacarry
Clan Cameron
Bunarkaig
B8005
Meith Bheinn
2328
Lochan a' Bhrodainn
Sgurr an Ursainn
Glen Mallie
River Mallie
Lochan Tàin Mhic Dhughaill
River Finnan
Gleann Dubh Lighe
Gaor Bheinn or Gulvain
Meall a' Phubuill
2533
Druim Gleann Laoigh
Achnanellan
Beinn Bhàn
2612
Glenfintaig Lodge
Loch Beoraid
Slios Garbh
Glas-charn
2076
Sgurr an Utha
2610
Glen Finnan
Gleann Fionnlighe
Fionn Lighe
Gleann Suileag
An t-Suileag
Glen Loy
River Loy
Stob a' Ghrianain
Druim Fada
Gairlochy
B8004
Stronenaba
Caledonian Canal
Brackletter
Commando Memorial
Highbridge
Alltour
Ranochan
A830
14
Station
Viaduct
The Jacobite
Glenfinnan
Dubh Lighe
Beinn an t-Sneachda
Muirshearlich
A82
141
80
Glenfinnan Monument
140
Kinlocheil
Corribeg
Fassfern
Achdalieu
Tor Castle
Leanachan Forest
Crofting
Croit Bheinn
2175
Beinn Odhar Bheag
2895
Loch Shiel
Callop River
Loch Eil
The Jacobite
A830
Treasures of the Earth
FORT WILLIAM
Banavie
Neptune's Staircase
Creag Aoil
South Garvan
Duisky
Blaich
A861
Corpach
Caol
Camaghael
Torlundy
Nevis Range Gondola
Glen Garvan
Sgorr Craobh a' Chaorainn
Achaphubuil
Lochyside
Inverlochy
Ben Nevis Distillery
Victoria Bridge
Meall nan

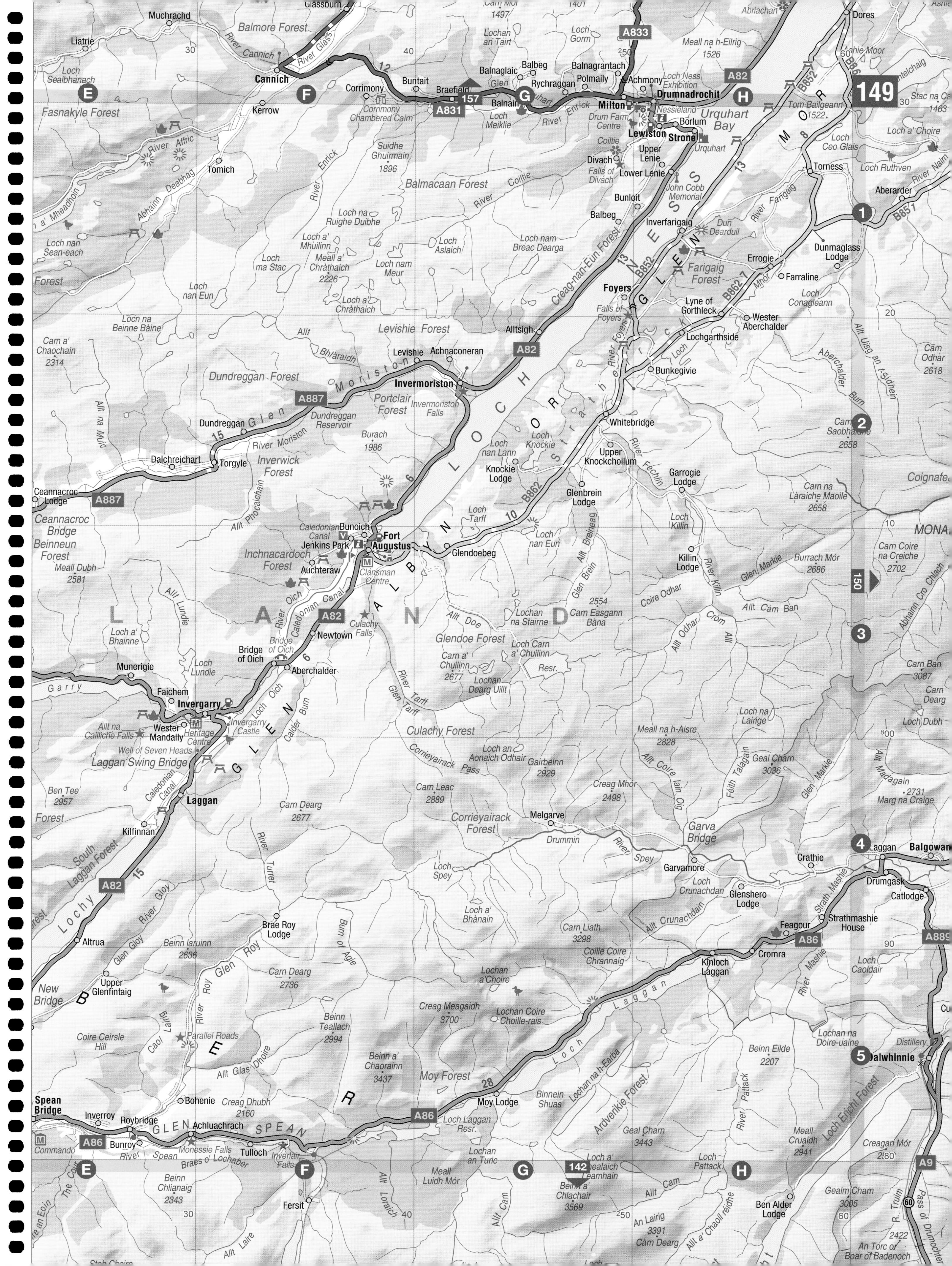
Glassburn
Muchrachd
Balmore Forest
Liatrie
River Cannich
River Glass
Loch Sealbhanach
Cannich
Fasnakyle Forest
Kerrow
Corrimony
Corrimony Chambered Cairn
Buntait
Braefield
157
A831
Balnaglaic
Balbeg
Glen
Balnain
Loch Meiklie
Balnagrantach
Polmaily
Rychraggan
River Enrick
Achmony
Drumnadrochit
Milton
Loch Ness Exhibition
Nessieland
Drum Farm Centre
Lewiston
Strone
Borlum
Urquhart Bay
Urquhart
Loch an Tairt
Lochan
1497
Loch Gorm
A833
Meall na h-Eilrig
1526
A82
Abriachan
Dores
Ashie Moor
B852
B862
Tom Balgeann
1522
Loch Ceo Glais
Loch a' Choire
Torness
Loch Ruthven
River Nairn
Aberarder
B851
Stac na Cailleach
1463
River Affric
Tomich
Abhainn Deabhag
Loch nan Sean-each
Forest
Suidhe Ghuirmain
1896
Balmacaan Forest
River Enrick
River Coiltie
Coiltie
Divach
Falls of Divach
Upper Lenie
Lower Lenie
John Cobb Memorial
Bunloit
Balbeg
Loch na Ruighe Duibhe
Loch a' Mhuilinn
Loch Aslaich
Loch nam Breac Dearga
Loch ma Stac
Meall a' Chràthaich
2226
Loch nam Meur
Loch nan Eun
Loch a' Chràthaich
Inverfarigaig
Dun Deardail
River Farigaig
Farigaig Forest
Errogie
Dunmaglass Lodge
Farraline
Loch Conagleann
Foyers
Falls of Foyers
Lyne of Gorthleck
Wester Aberchalder
Lochgarthside
Creag-nan-Eun Forest
Alltsigh
Locn na Beinne Bàine
Carn a' Chaochain
2314
Allt Bh'araidh
Levishie Forest
Levishie
Achnaconeran
Dundreggan Forest
Glen Moriston
A887
Invermoriston
Portclair Forest
Invermoriston Falls
Dundreggan Reservoir
Dundreggan
Allt na Muic
Burach
1986
River Moriston
Dalchreichart
Torgyle
Inverwick Forest
Ceannacroc Lodge
Ceannacroc Bridge
Beinneun Forest
Meall Dubh
2581
Allt Phocaichain
Inchnacardoch Forest
Caledonian Canal
Bunoich
Jenkins Park
Fort Augustus
Auchteraw
Clansman Centre
Glendoebeg
LOCH NESS
River Foyers
Stratherrick
Loch Mhòr
Bunkegivie
Aberchalder Burn
Allt Uisg an t-Sidhein
Carn Odhar
2618
Whitebridge
Upper Knockchoilum
Loch nan Lann
Loch Knockie
Knockie Lodge
River Fechlin
Garrogie Lodge
Glenbrein Lodge
Loch Tarff
B862
Loch nan Eun
Allt Breineag
Loch Killin
Killin Lodge
Carn Saobhaidhe
2658
Carn na Làraiche Maoile
2658
Coignafearn
MONADHLIATH
Carn Coire na Creiche
2702
Burrach Mór
2686
Glen Markie
150
River Killin
Glen Brein
Coire Odhar
2554
Carn Easgann Bàna
Lochan na Stairne
Allt Doe
Glendoe Forest
Loch Carn a' Chuilinn
Carn a' Chuilinn
2677
Resr.
Lochan Dearg Uillt
Allt Odhar
Allt Crom
Allt Càm Ban
Abhainn Cro Chlach
Carn Ban
3087
Carn Dearg
Loch Dubh
GREAT GLEN
LAND
River Oich
Caledonian Canal
A82
Newtown
Culachy Falls
Bridge of Oich
Loch a' Bhainne
Allt Lundie
Loch Lundie
Munerigie
Aberchalder
Garry
Faichem
Invergarry
Invergarry Castle
Loch Oich
Calder Burn
Wester Mandally
Heritage Centre
Allt na Cailliche Falls
Well of Seven Heads
Laggan Swing Bridge
River Tarff
Glen Tarff
Culachy Forest
Corrieyairack Pass
Loch an Aonaich Odhair
Gairbeinn
2929
Meall na h-Aisre
2828
Allt Coire Iain Oig
Lochan na Lairige
Féith Talagain
Geal Charn
3036
Glen Markie
Allt Madagain
2731
Marg na Craige
Ben Tee
2957
Laggan
Carn Leac
2889
Creag Mhòr
2498
Carn Dearg
2677
Corrieyairack Forest
Melgarve
Drummin
Garva Bridge
River Turret
Loch Spey
River Spey
Garvamore
Laggan
Balgowan
Crathie
Drumgask
Catlodge
Kilfinnan
South Laggan Forest
Loch Lochy
A82
River Gloy
Loch Crunachdan
Glenshero Lodge
Strath Mashie
Strathmashie House
Loch a' Bhànain
Brae Roy Lodge
Burn of Agie
Carn Liath
3298
Allt Crunachdain
Feagour
A86
A889
Altrua
Beinn Iaruinn
2636
Glen Gloy
Coille Coire Chrannaig
Cromra
Kinloch Laggan
Loch Caoldair
Upper Glenfintaig
New Bridge
Glen Roy
River Roy
Carn Dearg
2736
Lochan a' Choire
River Mashie
Loch Laggan
Creag Meagaidh
3700
Lochan Coire Choille-rais
Coire Ceirsle Hill
Caol Lairig
Parallel Roads
Beinn Teallach
2994
Lochan na Doire-uaine
Distillery
Dalwhinnie
Allt Glas Dhoire
Beinn a' Chaorainn
3437
Moy Forest
Beinn Eilde
2207
Loch Ericht Forest
River Pattack
Lochan na h-Earba
Ardverikie Forest
Spean Bridge
Bohenie
Creag Dhubh
2160
Moy Lodge
Binnein Shuas
Inverroy
Roybridge
Achluachrach
GLEN SPEAN
A86
Loch Laggan Resr.
Geal Charn
3443
Meall Cruaidh
2941
Creagan Mòr
2180
Commando
A86
Bunroy
Monessie Falls
Tulloch
Inverlair Falls
River Spean
Braes o' Lochaber
Lochan an Turic
Loch a' Bhealaich Leamhain
142
Loch Pattack
A9
Beinn Chlianaig
2343
Meall Luidh Mór
Beinn a' Chlachair
3569
Allt Cam
Fersit
Allt Loraich
Allt Cam
An Lairig
3391
Càrn Dearg
Allt a' Chaoil-réidhe
Ben Alder Lodge
Gealm Charn
3005
R. Truim
Pass of Drumochter
2422
An Torc or Boar of Badenoch
Allt Laire
The Cour
Stob Choire
E
F
G
H
1
2
3
4
5

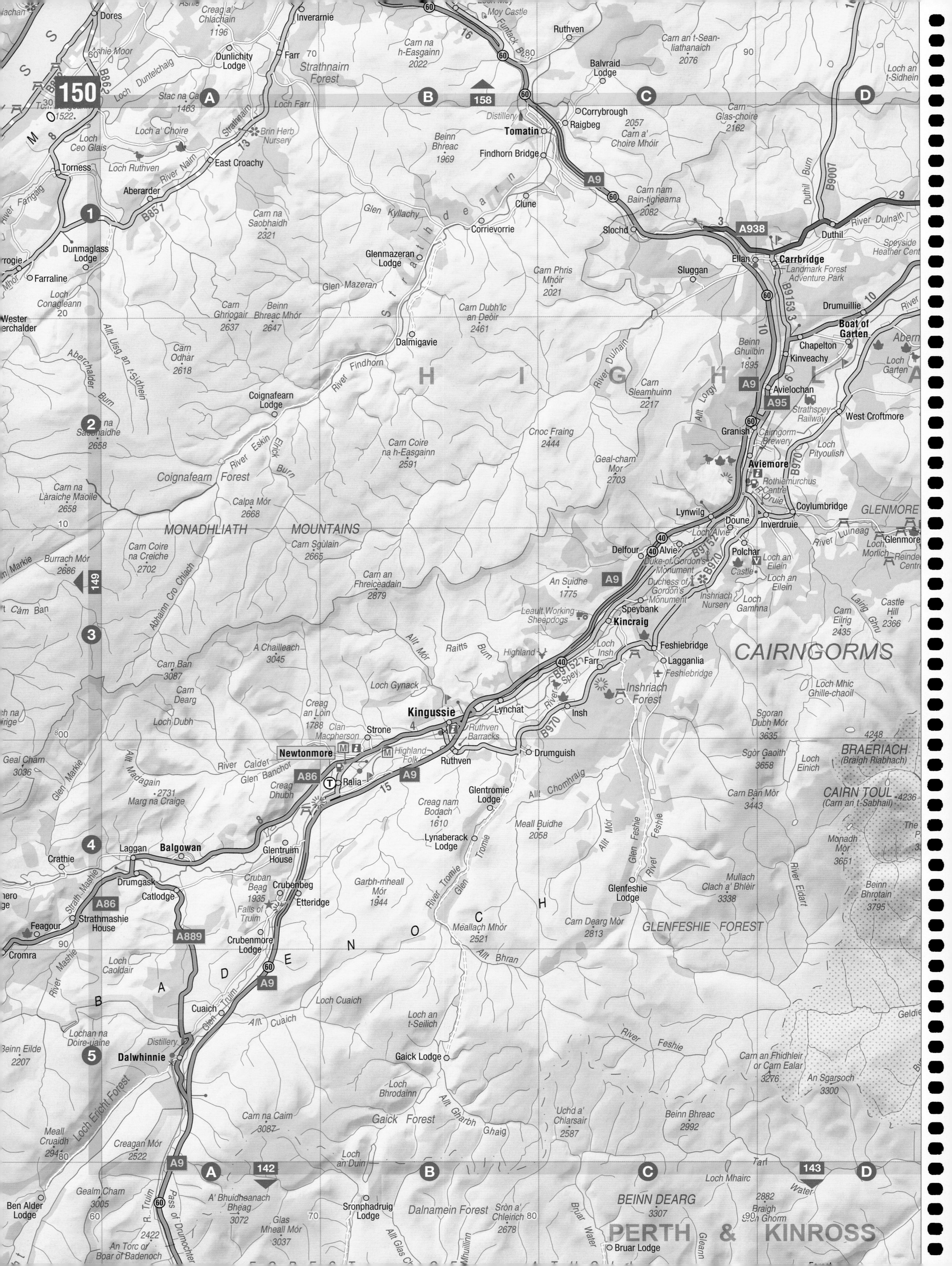
Dores
Creag a' Chlachain 1196
Inverarnie
Moy Castle
Funtack Burn
Ruthven
Carn an t-Sean-liathanaich 2076
Loch an t-Sidhein
Ashie Moor
Dunlichity Lodge
Farr
Strathnairn Forest
Carn na h-Easgainn 2022
Balvraid Lodge
Loch Duntelchaig
Stac na Cailleach 1463
Loch Farr
A
B
158
C
D
Carn Glas-choire 2162
Corrybrough
Raigbeg
Distillery
Tomatin
2057 Carn a' Choire Mhóir
Loch a' Choire
Brin Herb Nursery
Strathnairn
Beinn Bhreac 1969
Findhorn Bridge
Loch Ceo Glais
Torness
Loch Ruthven
East Croachy
River Nairn
A9
Carn nam Bain-tighearna 2082
Dulnain Burn
B9007
Aberarder
B851
River Fangaig
Clune
Carn na Saobhaidh 2321
Glen Kyllachy
Corrievorrie
Slochd
A938
Duthil
River Dulnain
Speyside Heather Centre
Dunmaglass Lodge
Glenmazeran Lodge
Ellan
Carrbridge
Landmark Forest Adventure Park
Farraline
Carn Phris Mhóir 2021
Sluggan
Loch Conagleann
Glen Mazeran
B9153
Western Aberchalder
Carn Ghriogair 2637
Beinn Bhreac Mhór 2647
Carn Dubh'Ic an Deòir 2461
Drumuillie
Boat of Garten
Allt Uisg an t-Sidhein
Strathdearn
Dalmigavie
Chapelton
Kinveachy
Beinn Ghuilbin 1895
Carn Odhar 2618
Aberchalder Burn
River Findhorn
River Dulnain
Loch Garten
H I G H L A
Carn Sleamhuinn 2217
Avielochan
A95
Coignafearn Lodge
Allt Lorgy
Strathspey Railway
West Croftmore
Carn na Saobhaidhe 2658
Carn Coire na h-Easgainn 2591
Cnoc Fraing 2444
Granish
Cairngorm Brewery
Loch Pityoulish
River Eskin
Elrick Burn
Geal-charn Mor 2703
Aviemore
Rothiemurchus Centre
B970
Coignafearn Forest
Carn na Làraiche Maoile 2658
Calpa Mór 2668
Lynwilg
Coylumbridge
Glenmore
Doune
Inverdruie
MONADHLIATH MOUNTAINS
Carn Coire na Creiche 2702
Carn Sgùlain 2665
Loch Alvie
Delfour
Alvie
Polchar
Loch an Eilein
River Luineag
Loch Morlich
Reindeer Centre
Burrach Mór 2686
Duke of Gordon's Monument
Castle
Carn an Fhreiceadain 2879
An Suidhe 1775
Duchess of Gordon's Monument
Loch an Eilein
149
Abhainn Cro Chlach
Inshriach Nursery
Loch Gamhna
Lairig Ghru
Castle Hill 2366
Carn Eilrig 2435
Leault Working Sheepdogs
Speybank
Kincraig
Càm Ban
Allt Mór
Raitts Burn
A Chailleach 3045
Highland Wildlife Park
Loch Insh
Feshiebridge
Lagganlia
Farr
CAIRNGORMS
Carn Ban 3087
Feshiebridge
B9152
River Spey
Loch Gynack
Carn Dearg
Loch Mhic Ghille-chaoil
Inshriach Forest
Creag an Loin 1788
Clan Macpherson
Kingussie
Lynchat
Insh
Sgoran Dubh Mór 3635
Loch Dubh
Strone
Ruthven Barracks
Newtonmore
Highland Folk
Drumguish
Sgòr Gaoith 3658
Loch Einich
BRAERIACH (Braigh Riabhach) 4248
Geal Charn 3036
River Calder
Ruthven
Glen Banchor
A86
Ralia
Allt Chomhraig
Carn Bàn Mòr 3443
CAIRN TOUL (Carn an t-Sabhail) 4236
Allt Madagain
Marg na Craige 2731
Creag Dhubh
Glentromie Lodge
Creag nam Bodach 1610
Meall Buidhe 2058
Glen Markie
Lynaberack Lodge
Allt Mór
Glen Feshie
River Feshie
Monadh Mór 3651
Crathie
Laggan
Balgowan
Glentruim House
Glen Tromie
Mullach Clach a' Bhlèir 3338
River Eidart
Beinn Bhrotain 3795
Drumgask
Strath Mashie
Cruban Beag 1935
Crubenbeg
Garbh-mheall Mór 1944
River Tromie
Glenfeshie Lodge
Catlodge
Etteridge
Falls of Truim
Carn Dearg Mòr 2813
GLENFESHIE FOREST
Feagour
Strathmashie House
A86
Meallach Mhór 2521
A889
Crubenmore Lodge
B A D E N O C H
Cromra
Allt Bhran
Loch Caoldair
River Mashie
A9
Cuaich
Loch Cuaich
Loch an t-Seilich
Allt Cuaich
River Feshie
Glen Truim
Distillery
Lochan na Doire-uaine
Dalwhinnie
Gaick Lodge
Carn an Fhidhleir or Carn Ealar 3276
Beinn Eilde 2207
An Sgarsoch 3300
Loch Ericht Forest
Loch Bhrodainn
Allt Gharbh Ghaig
Uchd a' Chlarsair 2587
Carn na Caim 3087
Gaick Forest
Beinn Bhreac 2992
Meall Cruaidh 2941
Creagan Mór 2522
Loch an Duin
Tarf Water
A9
A
142
B
C
143
D
Loch Mhairc
Gealm Charn 3005
A' Bhuidheanach Bheag 3072
BEINN DEARG 3307
Braigh Sròn Ghorm 2882
Ben Alder Lodge
Sronphadruig Lodge
Dalnamein Forest
Sròn a' Chleirich 2678
R. Truim
Pass of Drumochter
Glas Mheall Mór 3037
Bruar Water
PERTH & KINROSS
2422 An Torc or Boar of Badenoch
Allt Glas Choire
Bruar Lodge
Glen Banvie
1
2
3
4
5

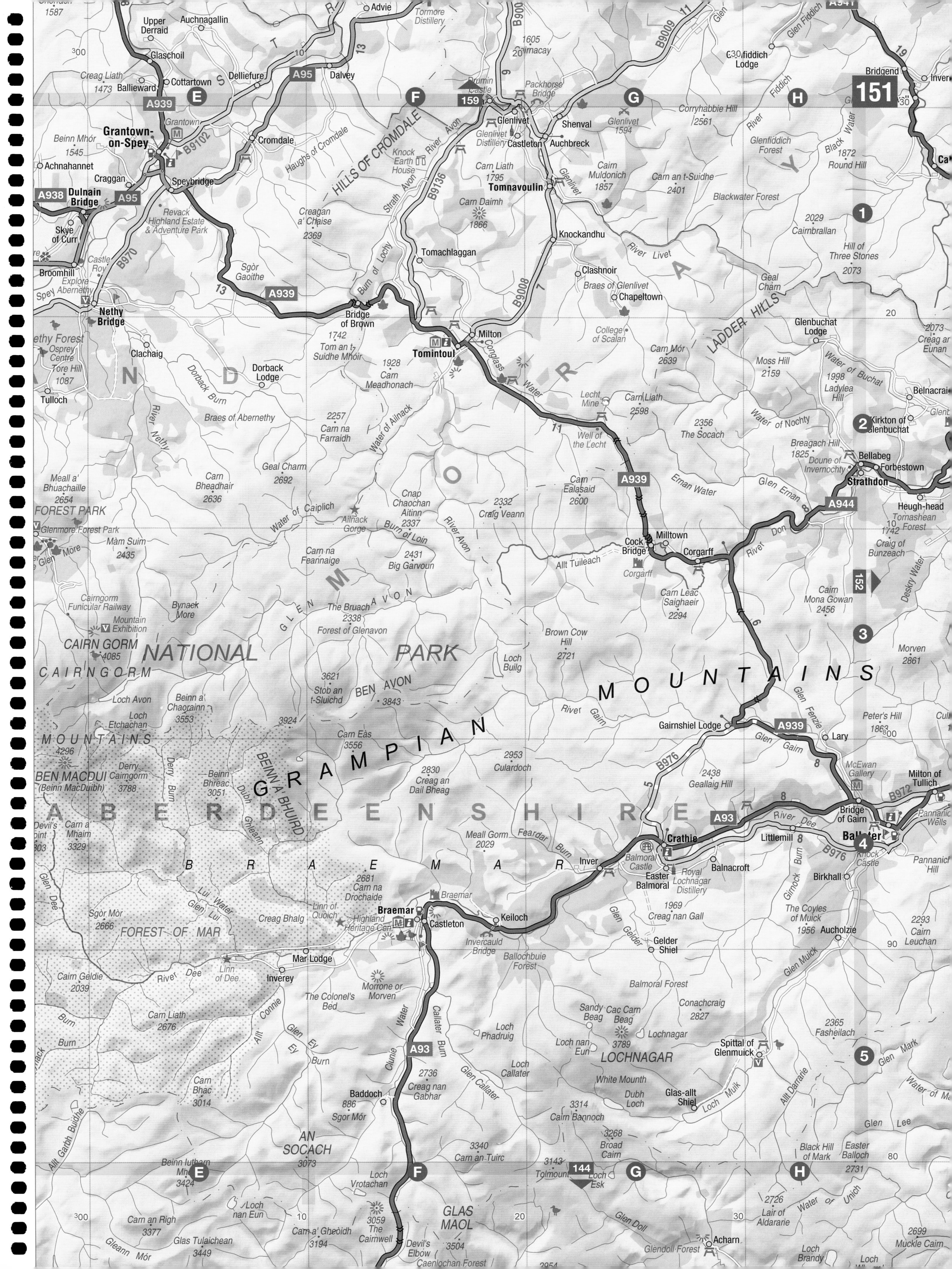
151
159
152
144
E
F
G
H
1
2
3
4
5
Advie
Tormore Distillery
Upper Derraid
Auchnagallin
Glaschoil
Creag Liath 1473
Ballieward
Cottartown
Delliefure
A95
Dalvey
A939
Grantown-on-Spey
Grantown
B9102
Cromdale
Haughs of Cromdale
HILLS OF CROMDALE
Beinn Mhòr 1545
Achnahannet
Craggan
Speybridge
A938
Dulnain Bridge
Skye of Curr
Revack Highland Estate & Adventure Park
Castle Roy
B970
Broomhill
Explore Abernethy
Spey
Nethy Bridge
Creagan a' Chaise 2369
Sgòr Gaoithe
Bridge of Brown
Burn of Lochy
Strath Avon
River Avon
Knock Earth House
B9136
Drumin Castle
Packhorse Bridge
1605 Cairnacay
B9009
Glenlivet
Glenlivet Distillery
Castleton
Auchbreck
Shenval
Glenlivet 1594
Carn Liath 1795
Carn Daimh 1866
Tomnavoulin
Cairn Muldonich 1857
Tomachlaggan
Knockandhu
Clashnoir
Braes of Glenlivet
Chapeltown
River Livet
B9008
Milton
Tomintoul
Conglass Water
College of Scalan
Corryhabbie Hill 2561
Glenfiddich Lodge
Glen Fiddich
Glenfiddich Forest
River Fiddich
Carn an t-Suidhe 2401
Blackwater Forest
Black Water
1872 Round Hill
Bridgend
2029 Cairnbrallan
Hill of Three Stones 2073
Geal Charn
LADDER HILLS
Glenbuchat Lodge
2073 Creag an Eunan
Water of Buchat
Moss Hill 2159
1998 Ladylea Hill
Belnacraig
Kirkton of Glenbuchat
Water of Nochty
Carn Mór 2639
Lecht Mine
Carn Liath 2598
Well of the Lecht
2356 The Socach
Breagach Hill 1825
Doune of Invernochty
Bellabeg
Forbestown
Strathdon
Heugh-head
Tornashean Forest
1742 Craig of Bunzeach
Glen Ernan
Ernan Water
A944
Deskry Water
Cairn Mona Gowan 2456
Morven 2861
Peter's Hill 1863
Lary
Glen Fenzie
Glenmore Forest Park
Abernethy Forest
Osprey Centre
Tore Hill 1087
Tulloch
Clachaig
Dorback Burn
Dorback Lodge
Braes of Abernethy
River Nethy
1742 Tom an t-Suidhe Mhóir
1928 Carn Meadhonach
2257 Carn na Farraidh
Water of Ailnack
Meall a' Bhuachaille 2654
Carn Bheadhair 2636
Geal Charn 2692
Cnap Chaochan Aitinn 2337
2332 Craig Veann
Carn Ealasaid 2600
A939
Water of Caiplich
Ailnack Gorge
Burn of Loin
River Avon
Màm Suim 2435
Carn na Feannaige
2431 Big Garvoun
Milltown
Cock Bridge
Corgarff
Allt Tuileach
River Don
Carn Leac Saighaeir 2294
Cairngorm Funicular Railway
Mountain Exhibition
Bynack More
GLEN AVON
The Brauch 2338
Forest of Glenavon
CAIRN GORM 4085
NATIONAL PARK
CAIRNGORM MOUNTAINS
Brown Cow Hill 2721
Loch Builg
Loch Avon
Loch Etchachan
Beinn a' Chaorainn 3553
3621 Stob an t-Sluichd
BEN AVON 3843
3924
River Gairn
Gairnshiel Lodge
Glen Gairn
B976
MOUNTAINS
GRAMPIAN
4296
BEN MACDUI (Beinn MacDuibh)
Derry Cairngorm 3788
Derry Burn
Beinn Bhreac 3051
BEINN A' BHUIRD
Carn Eàs 3556
2953 Culardoch
2830 Creag an Dail Bheag
2438 Geallaig Hill
McEwan Gallery
Milton of Tullich
B972
A93
River Dee
Bridge of Gairn
Ballater
Pannanich Wells
ABERDEENSHIRE
Devil's Point 3303
Carn a' Mhaim 3329
Glen Dee
BRAEMAR
Meall Gorm 2029
Feardar Burn
Crathie
Balmoral Castle
Inver
Easter Balmoral
Royal Lochnagar Distillery
Balnacroft
Littlemill
Knock Castle
Pannanich Hill
Birkhall
Girnock Burn
The Coyles of Muick 1956
Aucholzie
2293 Cairn Leuchan
2681 Carn na Drochaide
Braemar
Linn of Quoich
Highland Heritage Cen
Castleton
Keiloch
Invercauld Bridge
Ballochbuie Forest
1969 Creag nan Gall
Glen Gelder
Gelder Shiel
Glen Muick
Sgòr Mòr 2666
FOREST OF MAR
Glen Lui
Lui Water
Creag Bhalg
Mar Lodge
Linn of Dee
Inverey
Cairn Geldie 2039
River Dee
Morrone or Morven
The Colonel's Bed
Balmoral Forest
Sandy Beag
Cac Carn Beag 3789
Conachcraig 2827
2365 Fasheilach
Carn Liath 2676
Allt Connie
Glen Ey
Ey Burn
Clunie Water
Callater Burn
Loch Phadruig
Loch nan Eun
Lochnagar
LOCHNAGAR
Spittal of Glenmuick
Glen Mark
Water of Mark
Carn Bhac 3014
A93
2736 Creag nan Gabhar
Glen Callater
Loch Callater
White Mounth
Dubh Loch
Glas-allt Shiel
Loch Muick
Allt Darrarie
Baddoch 886
Sgor Mór
3314 Cairn Bannoch
3268 Broad Cairn
Glen Lee
Black Hill of Mark
Easter Balloch 2731
Allt Garbh Buidhe
AN SOCACH 3073
3340 Carn an Tuirc
3143 Tolmount
Loch Esk
Beinn Iutharn Mhòr 3424
Loch Vrotachan
2726 Lair of Aldararie
Water of Unich
Loch nan Eun
Carn an Righ 3377
3059 The Cairnwell
Carn a' Gheòidh 3194
GLAS MAOL 3504
Glen Doll
Acharn
Glendoll Forest
2699 Muckle Cairn
Loch Brandy
Glas Tulaichean 3449
Gleann Mór
Devil's Elbow
Caenlochan Forest

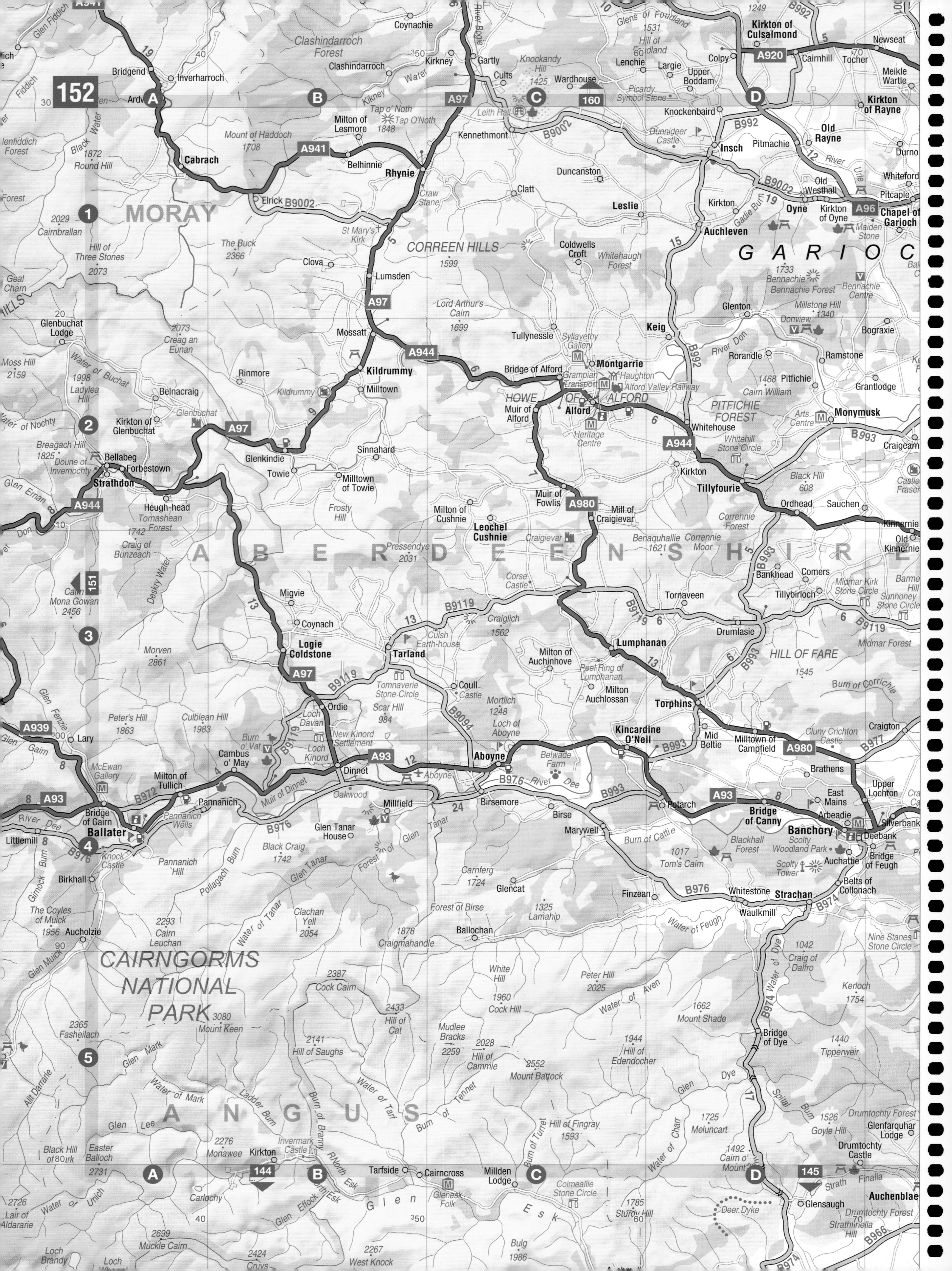

152
151
160
144
145
A
B
C
D
1
2
3
4
5
MORAY
GARIOCH
ABERDEENSHIRE
ANGUS
CAIRNGORMS NATIONAL PARK
Glen Fiddich
Bridgend
Inverharroch
Coynachie
Clashindarroch Forest
Clashindarroch
Kirkney
Gartly
Knockandy Hill 1425
Wardhouse
Cults
River Bogie
Glens of Foudland
1531 Hill of Foudland
Lenchie
Largie
Upper Boddam
Colpy
Kirkton of Culsalmond
1249
B992
A920
Cairnhill
Tocher
Newseat
Meikle Wartle
Kirkton of Rayne
Picardy Symbol Stone
Knockenbaird
Tap o' Noth
Tap O'Noth 1848
Milton of Lesmore
Leith Hall
Kennethmont
B9002
Dunnideer Castle
Insch
Pitmachie
Old Rayne
Durno
Black Water
Lienfiddich Forest
1872 Round Hill
Mount of Haddoch 1708
A941
Cabrach
Belhinnie
Rhynie
Duncanston
Clatt
Craw Stane
Elrick
B9002
Leslie
Kirkton
Gadie Burn
Oyne
Kirkton of Oyne
Old Westhall
Whiteford
Pitcaple
A96
Chapel of Garioch
Maiden Stone
Auchleven
2029 Cairnbrallan
Hill of Three Stones 2073
The Buck 2366
St Mary's Kirk
CORREEN HILLS
1599
Coldwells Croft
Whitehaugh Forest
Clova
Lumsden
1733 Bennachie
Bennachie Forest
Bennachie Centre
Geal Charn
A97
Lord Arthur's Cairn 1699
Glenton
Millstone Hill 1340
Donview
Glenbuchat Lodge
2073 Creag an Eunan
Mossatt
Tullynessle
Syllavethy Gallery
Keig
B992
River Don
Bograxie
Moss Hill 2159
Water of Buchat
1998 Ladylea Hill
Rinmore
Kildrummy
A944
Bridge of Alford
Montgarrie
Grampian Transport
Haughton
Alford Valley Railway
Rorandle
Ramstone
1468 Pitfichie
Cairn William
Grantlodge
Belnacraig
Kildrummy
Milltown
HOWE OF ALFORD
Muir of Alford
Alford
Heritage Centre
PITFICHIE FOREST
Arts Centre
Monymusk
Water of Nochty
Kirkton of Glenbuchat
Glenbuchat
Whitehouse
Whitehill Stone Circle
B993
Craigearn
Breagach Hill 1825
Doune of Invernochty
Bellabeg
Forbestown
Strathdon
Glenkindie
Towie
Sinnahard
Milltown of Towie
Kirkton
Tillyfourie
Black Hill 608
Castle Fraser
Glen Ernan
A944
Heugh-head
Tornashean Forest
1742 Craig of Bunzeach
Frosty Hill
Milton of Cushnie
Leochel Cushnie
Muir of Fowlis
A980
Mill of Craigievar
Craigievar
Corrennie Forest
Ordhead
Sauchen
Kinnernie
Old Kinnernie
Don
Pressendye 2031
Benaquhallie 1621
Corrennie Moor
Deskry Water
Cairn Mona Gowan 2456
Corse Castle
B993
Bankhead
Comers
Midmar Kirk Stone Circle
Barmekin Hill
Sunhoney Stone Circle
Tillybirloch
Tornaveen
Migvie
B9119
Craiglich 1562
Coynach
Culsh Earth-house
Tarland
Logie Coldstone
Milton of Auchinhove
Lumphanan
Peel Ring of Lumphanan
Drumlasie
HILL OF FARE
Midmar Forest
Morven 2861
Tomnaverie Stone Circle
Scar Hill 984
Coull Castle
Mortlich 1248
Milton Auchlossan
Burn of Corrichie
1545
Torphins
Glen Fenzie
Peter's Hill 1863
Culblean Hill 1983
Ordie
Loch Davan
New Kinord Settlement
Loch Kinord
B9094
Loch of Aboyne
Kincardine O'Neil
Mid Beltie
Milltown of Campfield
Cluny Crichton Castle
Craigton
B977
A939
Lary
Glen Gairn
Burn o' Vat
Cambus o' May
A93
Dinnet
Aboyne
Belwade Farm
River Dee
B993
A980
Brathens
Upper Lochton
McEwan Gallery
Milton of Tullich
B972
Pannanich
Pannanich Wells
Muir of Dinnet
Oakwood
Millfield
B976
Birsemore
Birse
Potarch
Bridge of Canny
East Mains
Arbeadie
Banchory
Silverbank
Deebank
Bridge of Gairn
Ballater
Littlemill
River Dee
Knock Castle
Glen Tanar House
Black Craig 1742
Glen Tanar
Forest of Glen Tanar
Marywell
Burn of Cattie
1017 Tom's Cairn
Blackhall Forest
Scolty Woodland Park
Scolty Tower
Auchattie
Bridge of Feugh
Birkhall
Pannanich Hill
Pollagach Burn
Carnferg 1724
Glencat
Finzean
B976
Whitestone
Strachan
Belts of Collonach
Girnock Burn
The Coyles of Muick 1956
Aucholzie
2293 Cairn Leuchan
Water of Tanar
Clachan Yell 2054
Forest of Birse
1325 Lamahip
Waulkmill
B974
Water of Feugh
1878 Craigmahandle
Ballochan
Nine Stanes Stone Circle
Glen Muick
2387 Cock Cairn
White Hill
Peter Hill 2025
1042 Craig of Dalfro
Kerloch 1754
2433 Hill of Cat
1960 Cock Hill
Water of Aven
1662 Mount Shade
Water of Dye
2365 Fasheilach
3080 Mount Keen
Mudlee Bracks 2259
2141 Hill of Saughs
2028 Hill of Cammie
1944 Hill of Edendocher
Bridge of Dye
1440 Tipperweir
Glen Mark
Water of Mark
2552 Mount Battock
Glen Dye
Spital Burn
Alt Darrarie
Ladder Burn
Burn of Branny
Water of Tarf
Burn of Tennet
Burn of Turret
Drumtochty Forest
1526 Goyle Hill
Glenfarquhar Lodge
Glen Lee
Hill of Fingray 1593
Water of Charr
1725 Meluncart
Drumtochty Castle
Black Hill of Mark
Easter Balloch
2276 Monawee
Kirkton
Invermark Castle
1492 Cairn o' Mount
2731
Tarfside
Cairncross
Millden Lodge
Strath Finella
Auchenblae
2726 Lair of Aldararie
Water of Unich
Carlochy
North Esk
Glen Effock
Glenesk Folk
Glen Esk
Colmeallie Stone Circle
1785 Sturdy Hill
Deer Dyke
Glensaugh
Drumtochty Forest
Strathfinella Hill
B966
2699 Muckle Cairn
Loch Brandy
2424 Cruys
2267 West Knock
Bulg 1986

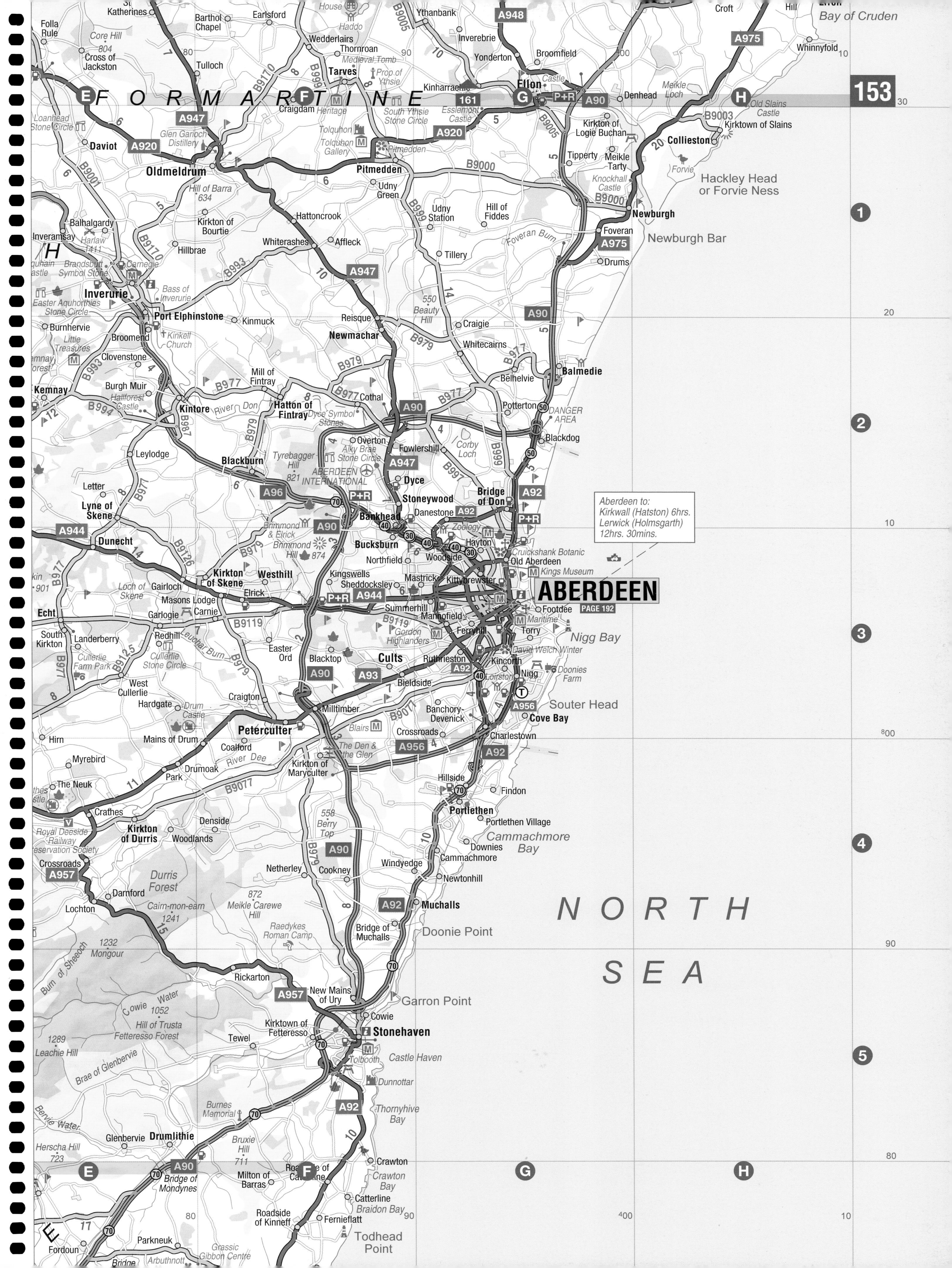
153
FORMARTINE
Bay of Cruden
Whinnyfold
Croft
Ythanbank
Inverebrie
Yonderton
Broomfield
Earlsford
Barthol Chapel
Katherines
Folla Rule
Core Hill
804
Cross of Jackson
Tulloch
Wedderlairs
Thornroan
Medieval Tomb
Haddo
Tarves
Prop of Ythsie
Kinharrachie
Ellon
Castle
Denhead
Meikle Loch
Old Slains Castle
Kirktown of Slains
Collieston
Forvie
Hackley Head or Forvie Ness
Kirkton of Logie Buchan
Tipperty
Meikle Tarty
Knockhall Castle
Newburgh
Foveran
Newburgh Bar
Drums
Craigdam
Heritage
South Ythsie Stone Circle
Esslemont Castle
Loanhead Stone Circle
Glen Garioch Distillery
Tolquhon
Tolquhon Gallery
Pitmedden
Daviot
Oldmeldrum
Hill of Barra
634
Udny Green
Udny Station
Hill of Fiddes
Tillery
Foveran Burn
Hattoncrook
Kirkton of Bourtie
Balhalgardy
Inveramsay
Harlaw 1411
Hillbrae
Whiterashes
Affleck
Brandsbutt Symbol Stone
Carnegie
Bass of Inverurie
Inverurie
Easter Aquhorthies Stone Circle
Port Elphinstone
Kinmuck
Reisque
Newmachar
550 Beauty Hill
Craigie
Whitecairns
Burnhervie
Broomend
Kinkell Church
Little Treasures
Clovenstone
Kemnay
Burgh Muir
Hallforest Castle
Kintore
River Don
Mill of Fintray
Hatton of Fintray
Cothal
Dyce Symbol Stones
Belhelvie
Balmedie
Potterton
DANGER AREA
Blackdog
Leylodge
Blackburn
Tyrebagger Hill 821
Overton
Aiky Brae Stone Circle
ABERDEEN INTERNATIONAL
Fowlershill
Corby Loch
Dyce
Stoneywood
Bridge of Don
Letter
Lyne of Skene
Danestone
Bankhead
Zoology
Dunecht
Brimmond & Elrick
Brimmond Hill 874
Bucksburn
Hayton
Northfield
Woodside
Cruickshank Botanic
Old Aberdeen
Kings Museum
Aberdeen to:
Kirkwall (Hatston) 6hrs.
Lerwick (Holmsgarth) 12hrs. 30mins.
Loch of Skene
Gairloch
Kirkton of Skene
Westhill
Kingswells
Sheddocksley
Mastrick
Kittybrewster
ABERDEEN
PAGE 192
Footdee
Echt
Masons Lodge
Elrick
Garlogie
Carnie
Summerhill
Mannofield
Maritime
Torry
Nigg Bay
South Kirkton
Landerberry
Redhill
Cullerlie Farm Park
Cullerlie Stone Circle
Leuchar Burn
Easter Ord
Gordon Highlanders
Ferryhill
David Welch Winter
Blacktop
Cults
Ruthrieston
Kincorth
Loirston
Nigg
Doonies Farm
West Cullerlie
Hardgate
Drum Castle
Craigton
Bieldside
Milltimber
Banchory-Devenick
Souter Head
Cove Bay
Hirn
Mains of Drum
Peterculter
Blairs
Crossroads
Charlestown
Myrebird
Coalford
River Dee
The Den & the Glen
Kirkton of Maryculter
Park
Drumoak
The Neuk
Hillside
Findon
Crathes
Portlethen
Portlethen Village
Royal Deeside Railway Preservation Society
Kirkton of Durris
Denside
Woodlands
558 Berry Top
Cammachmore Bay
Downies
Cammachmore
Crossroads
Durris Forest
Netherley
Cookney
Windyedge
Newtonhill
Darnford
872 Meikle Carewe Hill
Lochton
Cairn-mon-earn 1241
Muchalls
NORTH SEA
Raedykes Roman Camp
Bridge of Muchalls
Doonie Point
1232 Mongour
Burn of Sheeoch
Rickarton
New Mains of Ury
Garron Point
Cowie Water
1052
Hill of Trusta
Fetteresso Forest
Kirktown of Fetteresso
Cowie
Stonehaven
1289 Leachie Hill
Tewel
Tolbooth
Castle Haven
Brae of Glenbervie
Dunnottar
Thornyhive Bay
Burnes Memorial
Bervie Water
Glenbervie
Drumlithie
Bruxie Hill 711
Herscha Hill 723
Crawton
Bridge of Mondynes
Milton of Barras
Crawton Bay
Catterline
Braidon Bay
Roadside of Kinneff
Fernieflatt
Todhead Point
Parkneuk
Fordoun
Grassic Gibbon Centre
Arbuthnott
A90
A92
A93
A96
A944
A947
A948
A920
A956
A957
A975
B9000
B9001
B9003
B9005
B9077
B9119
B9125
B9126
B9170
B977
B979
B987
B993
B994
B997
B999
P+R
161
E
F
G
H
1
2
3
4
5

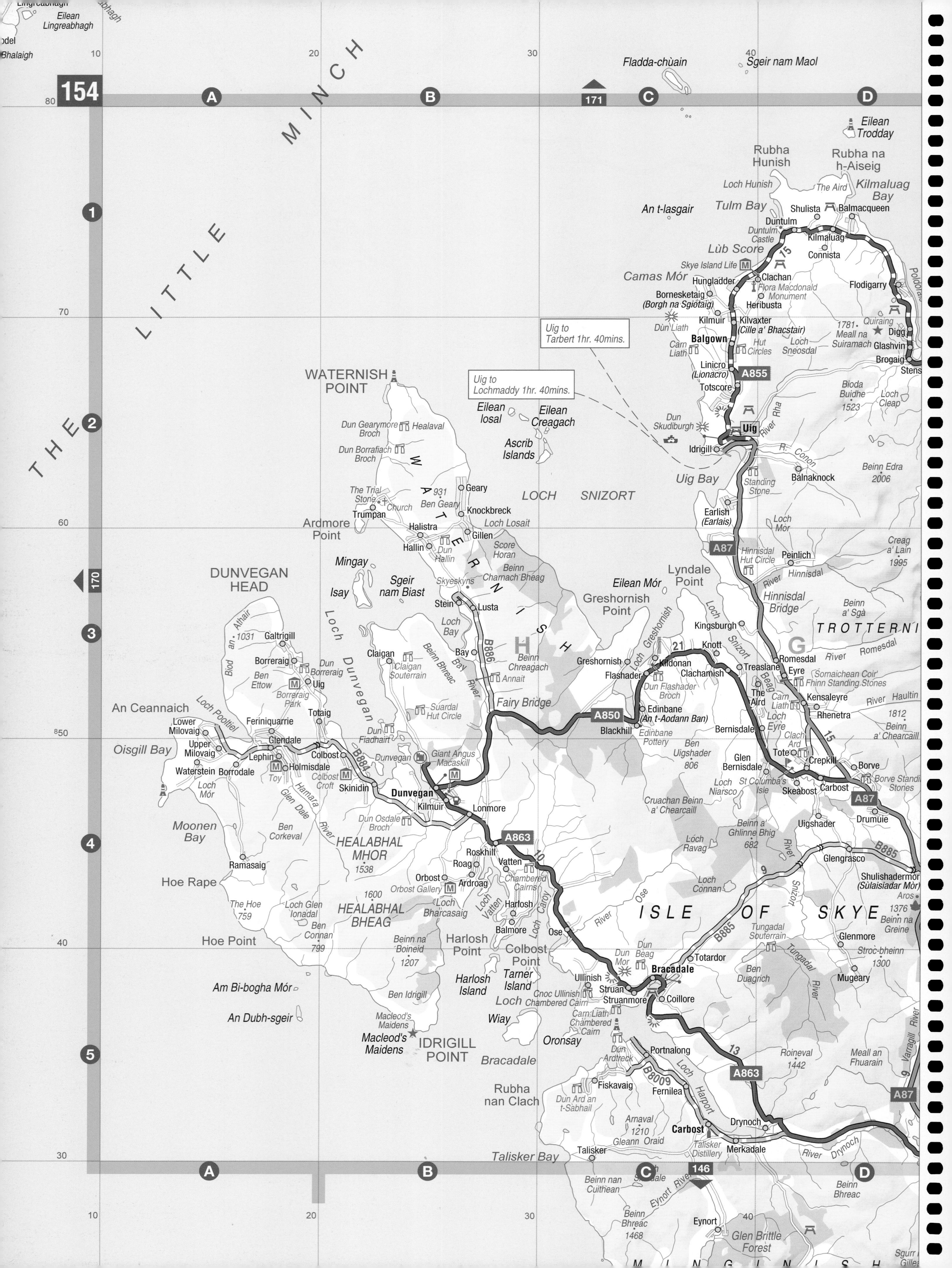

154
THE LITTLE MINCH
171
170
146
A
B
C
D
1
2
3
4
5
Eilean Lingreabhagh
Fladda-chùain
Sgeir nam Maol
Eilean Trodday
Rubha Hunish
Rubha na h-Aiseig
Loch Hunish
The Aird
Kilmaluag Bay
An t-Iasgair
Tulm Bay
Shulista
Balmacqueen
Duntulm
Duntulm Castle
Kilmaluag
Connista
Lùb Score
Skye Island Life
Camas Mór
Hungladder
Clachan
Flora Macdonald Monument
Borneskitaig (Borgh na Sgiotaig)
Heribusta
Flodigarry
Kilmuir
Kilvaxter (Cille a' Bhacstair)
Dùn Liath
Càrn Liath
Balgown
Hut Circles
Loch Sneosdal
1781 Meall na Suiramach
Quiraing
Digg
Glashvin
Brogaig
Stenscholl
Uig to Tarbert 1hr. 40mins.
Uig to Lochmaddy 1hr. 40mins.
Linicro (Lionacro)
A855
Totscore
Bioda Buidhe 1523
Loch Cleap
WATERNISH POINT
Eilean Iosal
Eilean Creagach
Ascrib Islands
Dun Skudiburgh
Uig
River Rha
Idrigill
R. Conon
Balnaknock
Beinn Edra 2006
Uig Bay
Standing Stone
Dun Gearymore Broch
Healaval
Dun Borrafiach Broch
WATERNISH
Geary
931 Ben Geary
Knockbreck
The Trial Stone
Church
Trumpan
LOCH SNIZORT
Earlish (Earlais)
Loch Mor
Ardmore Point
Halistra
Loch Losait
Gillen
Hallin
Dun Hallin
Score Horan
A87
Hinnisdal Hut Circle
Peinlich
Creag a' Lain 1995
Mingay
Isay
Sgeir nam Biast
Skyeskyns
Beinn Charnach Bheag
Eilean Mór
Lyndale Point
River Hinnisdal
Hinnisdal Bridge
Beinn a' Sgà
DUNVEGAN HEAD
Stein
Lusta
Greshornish Point
Loch Bay
Loch Dunvegan
Kingsburgh
TROTTERNISH
1031
Galtrigill
Biod an Athair
Claigan
Claigan Souterrain
Beinn Bhreac
Bay
Bay River
B886
Beinn Chreagach
Annait
Greshornish
Loch Greshornish
21
Knott
Kildonan
Flashader
Clachamish
Loch Snizort Beag
Treaslane
Romesdal
Eyre
River Romesdal
Somaichean Coir' Fhinn Standing Stones
Borreraig
Dun Borreraig
Ben Ettow
Borreraig Park
Uig
Dun Flashader Broch
The Aird
Carn Liath
Kensaleyre
River Haultin
An Ceannaich
Loch Pooltiel
Totaig
Suardal Hut Circle
Fairy Bridge
A850
Edinbane (An t-Aodann Ban)
Loch Eyre
Rhenetra
1812 Beinn a' Chearcaill
Lower Milovaig
Feriniquarrie
Glendale
Dun Fiadhairt
Blackhill
Edinbane Pottery
Bernisdale
Clach Ard
Upper Milovaig
Oisgill Bay
Lephin
Colbost
B884
Giant Angus Macaskill
Dunvegan
Ben Uigshader 806
Tote
Crepkill
Borve
Waterstein
Borrodale
Holmisdale
Toy
Colbost Croft
Glen Bernisdale
St Columba's Isle
Borve Standing Stones
Loch Mór
Skinidin
Dunvegan
Kilmuir
Lonmore
Loch Niarsco
Skeabost
Carbost
Glen Dale
Hamara River
Dun Osdale Broch
Cruachan Beinn a' Chearcaill
Uigshader
Drumuie
Moonen Bay
Ben Corkeval
HEALABHAL MHOR 1538
A863
Beinn a' Ghlinne Bhig 682
Loch Ravag
Glengrasco
B885
Ramasaig
Roskhill
Roag
Vatten
Snizort River
Shulishadermor (Sùlaisiadar Mòr)
Hoe Rape
Orbost
Orbost Gallery
Ardroag
Chambered Cairns
Loch Connan
Aros
1600
Loch Bharcasaig
Loch Vatten
Harlosh
Loch Caroy
1376 Beinn na Greine
The Hoe 759
Loch Glen Iondal
HEALABHAL BHEAG
River Ose
ISLE OF SKYE
Ben Connan 799
Balmore
Ose
Tungadal Souterrain
Glenmore
Hoe Point
Beinn na Boineid 1207
Harlosh Point
Colbost Point
Dun Mor
Dun Beag
Totardor
Stroc-bheinn 1300
Tarner Island
Harlosh Island
Ullinish
Bracadale
Ben Duagrich
Tungadal River
Mugeary
Am Bi-bogha Mór
Ben Idrigill
Cnoc Ullinish Chambered Cairn
Struan
Struanmore
Coillore
Loch Bracadale
Wiay
Càrn Liath Chambered Cairn
An Dubh-sgeir
Macleod's Maidens
IDRIGILL POINT
Oronsay
Dun Ardtreck
Portnalong
Roineval 1442
Meall an Fhuarain
Varragill River
A863
Rubha nan Clach
Fiskavaig
B8009
Fernilea
Loch Harport
A87
Dun Ard an t-Sabhail
Arnaval 1210
Carbost
Drynoch
Gleann Oraid
Talisker Distillery
Merkadale
River Drynoch
Talisker
Talisker Bay
Beinn nan Cuithean
Glen Eynort
Eynort River
Beinn Bhreac
Beinn Bhreac 1468
Eynort
Glen Brittle Forest
Sgurr Gillean

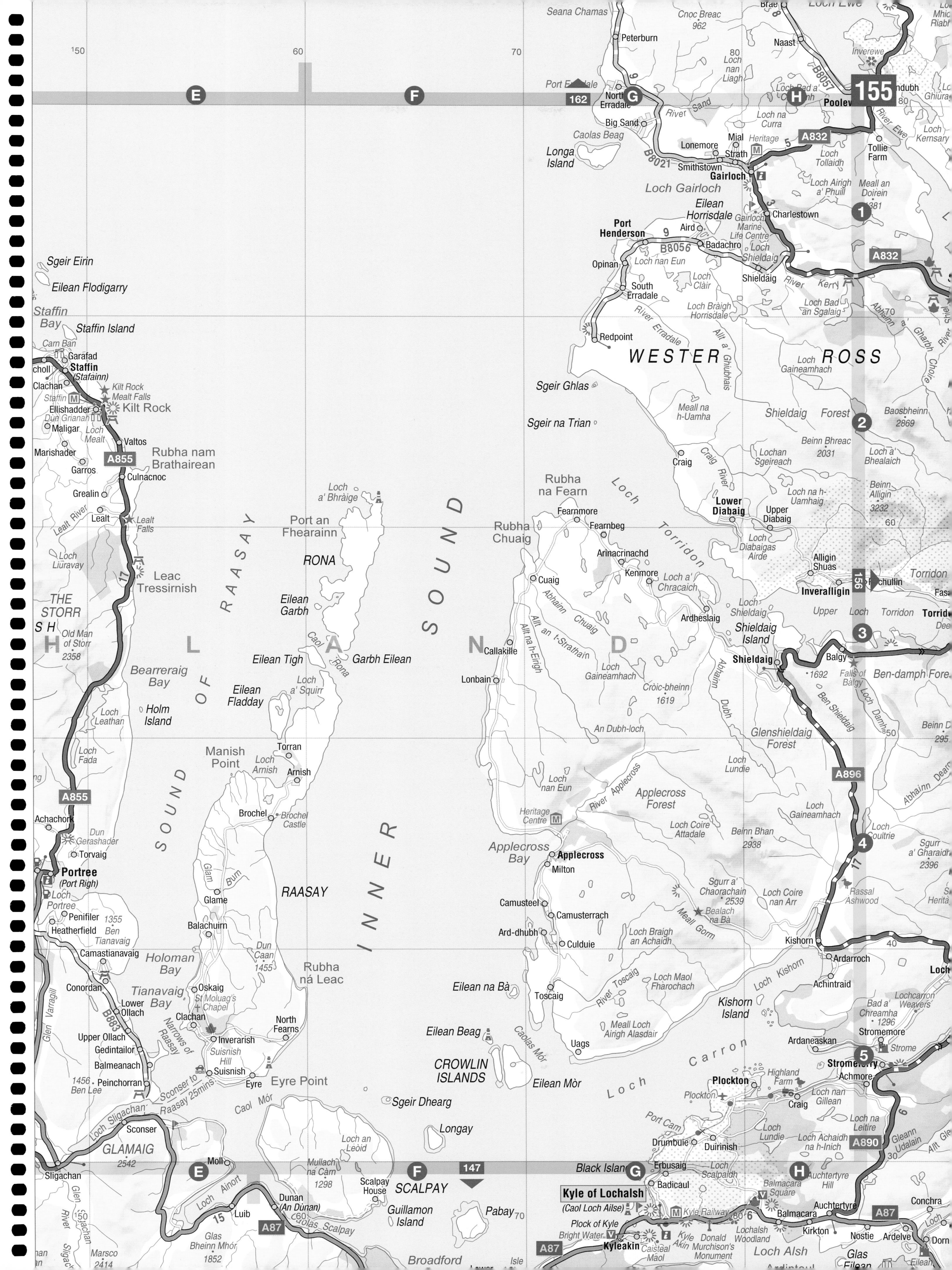

Seana Chamas · Cnoc Breac 962 · Brae · Loch Ewe

Peterburn · Naast · Inverewe · Loch Mhic Riabl

Port E..dale · 162 · North Erradale · G · River Sand · 80 Loch nan Liagh · A832 · B8057 · H · Poolev · 155

Big Sand · Mial · Heritage · Loch na Curra · A832 · Tollie Farm · River Ewe · Loch Kernsary

Caolas Beag · Lonemore · M · Loch Tollaidh

Longa Island · B8021 · Smithstown · Strath · Gairloch · i · Loch Airigh a' Phuill · Meall an Doirein 381 · 1

Loch Gairloch · Eilean Horrisdale · Gairloch Marine Life Centre · Charlestown

Port Henderson · 9 · Aird · Loch Shieldaig · A832

Opinan · B8056 · Badachro · Loch nan Eun · Shieldaig · River · Kerry

South Erradale · Loch Clàir

Loch Bràigh Horrisdale · Loch Bad an Sgalaig · 70

Redpoint · River Erradale · WESTER · ROSS · Loch Gaineamhach

Sgeir Eirin · Alt a' Ghiubhais · Baosbheinn 2869 · 2

Eilean Flodigarry · Sgeir Ghlas · Shieldaig Forest

Staffin Bay · Meall na h-Uamha · Beinn Bhreac 2031 · Lochan Sgeireach · Loch a' Bhealaich

Staffin Island · Sgeir na Trian · Beinn Alligin 3232 · 60

Carn Ban · Garafad · Staffin (Stafainn) · Craig · Craig River · Lochan Sgeireach

choll · Clachan · Kilt Rock Mealt Falls · Rubha na Fearn · Fearnmore · Loch Torridon · Lower Diabaig · Upper Diabaig · Loch na h-Uamhaig · Alligin Shuas · 156 · Torridon

Staffin M · Ellishadder · Dun Grianan · Fearnbeg · Loch Diabaigas Airde

Maligar · Loch Mealt · Valtos · Rubha Chuaig · Arinacrinachd · Kenmore · Loch a' Chracaich · Inveralligin · Upper Loch Torridon · Torrid

Marishader · Garros · A855 · Cuaig · Abhainn Chuaig · Loch Shieldaig · Shieldaig Island · 3

Grealin · Lealt · Callakille · Alt na h-Eirigh · Ardheslaig · Shieldaig · Balgy · Falls of Bàlgy · Ben-damph Fore..

Loch Liuravay · Port an Fhearainn · RONA · Lonbain · Loch Gaineamhach · 1692

THE STORR · Leac Tressirnish · Eilean Garbh · Cròic-bheinn 1619 · An Dubh-loch · Glenshieldaig Forest · Beinn.. 295.

Old Man of Storr 2358 · H · Eilean Tigh · Garbh Eilean · Loch Lundie · A896

Bearreraig Bay · Eilean Fladday · Loch a' Squirr · Loch nan Eun · Applecross Forest

Holm Island · Applecross Forest · Loch Gaineamhach · Loch Coultrie

Loch Leathan · Loch Fada · Torran · Manish Point · Loch Arnish · Arnish · River Applecross · Beinn Bhan 2938 · Loch Coire Attadale · 4

Achachork · Dun Gerashader · Brochel · Brochel Castle · Heritage Centre M · Applecross Bay · Applecross · Milton · Sgurr a' Chaorachain 2539 · Bealach na Bà · Rassal Ashwood · 17 · Sgurr a' Gharaidh 2396

Torvaig · Portree (Port Righ) · i · Glam Burn · Camusteel · Camusterrach · Loch Kishorn

Loch Portree · Glame · RAASAY · Ard-dhubh · Culduie · Kishorn · Ardarroch · Loch..

Penifiler 1355 · Heatherfield · Ben Tianavaig · Balachuirn · River Toscaig · Loch Braig an Achaidh · Loch Maol Fharochach · Achintraid · Lochcarron Weavers · Bad a' Chreamha 1296

Camastianavaig · Dun Caan 1455 · Rubha ná Leac · Eilean na Bà · Toscaig · Kishorn Island · Stromemore

Conordan · Holoman Bay · Oskaig · St Moluag's Chapel · Meall Loch Airigh Alasdair · Uags · Ardaneaskan · Strome

Lower Ollach · Tianavaig Bay · Clachan · North Fearns · Eilean Beag · Stromeferry · 5 · Achmore

Upper Ollach · B883 · Inverarish · Suisnish Hill · Eilean Mòr · Caolas Mòr · Plockton · Highland Farm

Gedintailor · Narrows of Raasay · Suisnish · CROWLIN ISLANDS · Plockton · Craig · Loch na Leitire

Balmeanach · Glen Varragill · Peinchorran · Eyre · Eyre Point · Sgeir Dhearg · A890 · 30

1456 Ben Lee · Sconser to Raasay 25mins · SOUND OF RAASAY · INNER SOUND · Longay · Black Island · G · Erbusaig · Loch Lundie · Loch Achaidh na h-Inich · Gleann ...dalain

Sligachan · Loch Sligachan · Sconser · Moll · Loch an Lèoid · E · 147 · F · SCALPAY · Drumbuie · Duirinish · H

GLAMAIG 2542 · Glen Sligachan · Loch Ainort · Mullach na' Càirn 1298 · Scalpay House · Kyle of Lochalsh (Caol Loch Ailse) · Badicaul · Balmacara Square · Auchtertyre Hill · Auchtertyre · A87

Marsco 2414 · Luib · Dunan (An Dùnan) · Guillamon Island · Pabay 70 · Plock of Kyle · Kyle Railway M · i · Balmacara · Kirkton · Conchra

A87 · 15 · A87 · Broadford · Bright Water V · Kyle Donald Murchison's Monument · Lochalsh Woodland V · Nostie · Ardelve

Glas Bheinn Mhór 1852 · Glas Scalpay · Kyleakin · Caisteal Màol · Loch Alsh · Glas Eilean · Ardintoul

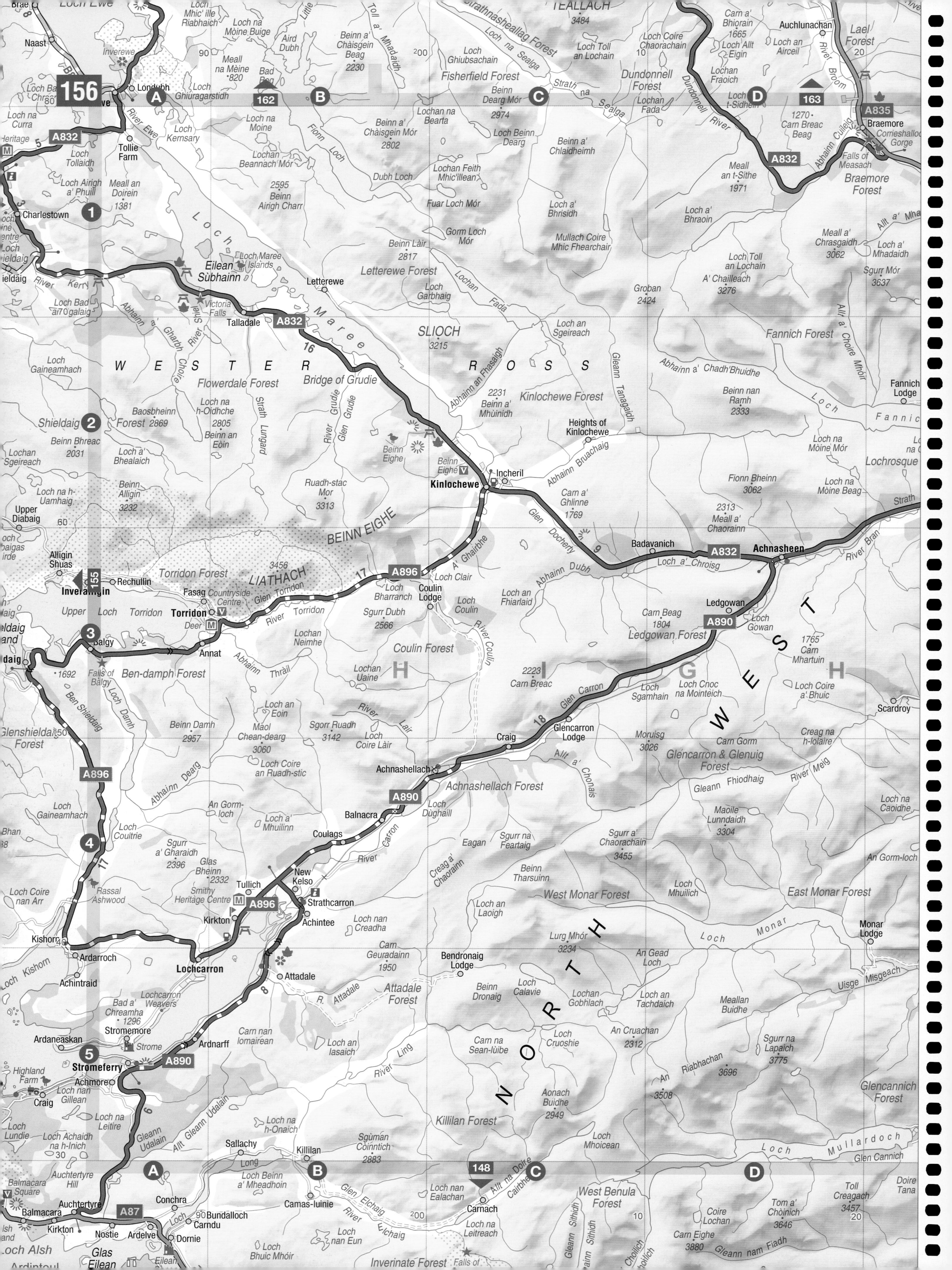

156
162
163
148
155
WESTER ROSS
HIGHLAND
NORTH WEST
Loch Ewe
Naast
Inverewe
Londubh
Poolewe
Tollie Farm
Charlestown
Loch Maree
Eilean Sùbhainn
Loch Maree Islands
Letterewe
Victoria Falls
Talladale
A832
A835
A896
A890
A87
Slioch 3215
Letterewe Forest
Fisherfield Forest
Strathnasheallag Forest
Dundonnell Forest
Braemore
Corrieshalloch Gorge
Falls of Measach
Braemore Forest
Auchlunachan
Lael Forest
Fannich Forest
Fannich Lodge
Loch Fannich
Lochrosque Forest
Kinlochewe Forest
Heights of Kinlochewe
Incheril
Kinlochewe
Beinn Eighe
Bridge of Grudie
Flowerdale Forest
Shieldaig
Upper Diabaig
Alligin Shuas
Inveralligin
Rechullin
Torridon Forest
Liathach
Fasag
Torridon
Upper Loch Torridon
Annat
Balgy
Falls of Balgy
Ben-damph Forest
Coulin Forest
Coulin Lodge
Loch Clair
Loch Coulin
Badavanich
Loch a' Chroisg
Achnasheen
Ledgowan
Ledgowan Forest
Loch Gowan
Scardroy
Glen Carron
Glencarron Lodge
Craig
Glencarron & Glenuig Forest
Achnashellach
Achnashellach Forest
Balnacra
Coulags
New Kelso
Strathcarron
Tullich
Kirkton
Achintee
Lochcarron
Kishorn
Ardarroch
Achintraid
Loch Kishorn
Attadale
Attadale Forest
Bendronaig Lodge
West Monar Forest
East Monar Forest
Loch Monar
Monar Lodge
Strome
Stromemore
Ardaneaskan
Stromeferry
Ardnarff
Achmore
Loch Carron
Killilan Forest
Killilan
Sallachy
Loch Long
Camas-luinie
Glen Elchaig
Carnach
West Benula Forest
Loch Mullardoch
Glen Cannich
Glencannich Forest
Auchtertyre
Balmacara
Balmacara Square
Kirkton
Nostie
Ardelve
Dornie
Conchra
Bundalloch
Carndu
Loch Alsh
Eilean Donan
Inverinate Forest

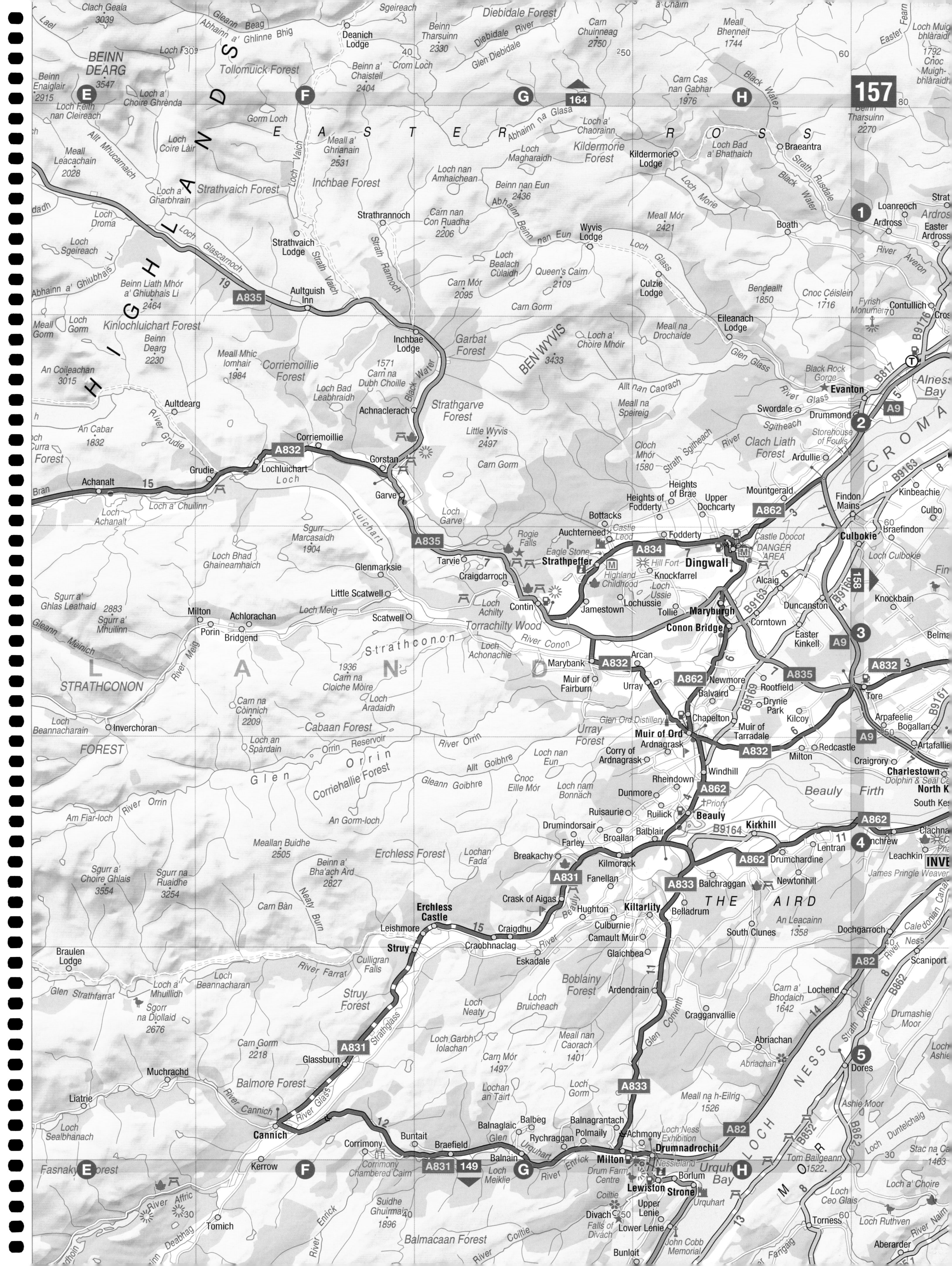

157
164
158
149
E
F
G
H
1
2
3
4
5
EASTER ROSS
HIGHLANDS
LAND
STRATHCONON
FOREST
THE AIRD
CROMA
Clach Geala 3039
Gleann Beag
Abhainn a' Ghlinne Bhig
Sgeireach
Deanich Lodge
Diebidale Forest
Diebidale River
Glen Diebidale
Beinn Tharsuinn 2330
Carn Chuinneag 2750
Meall Bhenneit 1744
Loch Muigh-bhlàraidh
1792 Cnoc Muigh-bhlàraidh
Easter Fearn
Beinn Tharsuinn 2270
BEINN DEARG 3547
Beinn Enaiglair 2915
Loch a' Choire Ghrènda
Loch Feith nan Cleireach
Tollomuick Forest
Beinn a' Chaisteil 2404
Crom Loch
Carn Cas nan Gabhar 1976
Black Water
Gorm Loch
Abhainn na Glasa
Loch a' Chaorainn
Kildermorie Forest
Kildermorie Lodge
Loch Bad a' Bhathaich
Braeantra
Strath Rusdale
Black Water
Loch Morie
Allt Mhucarnaich
Meall Leacachain 2028
Loch Coire Làir
Loch Vaich
Meall a' Ghrianain 2531
Loch Magharaidh
Inchbae Forest
Loch nan Amhaichean
Beinn nan Eun 2436
Strathvaich Forest
Loch a' Gharbhrain
Loch Droma
Carn nan Con Ruadha 2206
Abhainn Beinn nan Eun
Strathrannoch
Meall Mór 2421
Wyvis Lodge
Loch Glass
Boath
Loanreoch
Ardross
Easter Ardross
River Averon
Loch Sgeireach
Strathvaich Lodge
Strath Vaich
Strath Rannoch
Loch Bealach Cùlaidh
Queen's Cairn 2109
Culzie Lodge
Bendeallt 1850
Cnoc Céislein 1716
Fyrish Monument
Contullich
Loch Glascarnoch
Abhainn a' Ghiubhais Li
Beinn Liath Mhór a' Ghiubhais Li 2464
A835
Aultguish Inn
Carn Mór 2095
Carn Gorm
Eileanach Lodge
Meall Gorm
Loch Gorm
Kinlochluichart Forest
Inchbae Lodge
Garbat Forest
BEN WYVIS 3433
Loch a' Choire Mhóir
Meall na Drochaide
Glen Glass
B9176
Beinn Dearg 2230
Meall Mhic Iomhair 1984
Corriemoillie Forest
1571 Carn na Dubh Choille
Black Water
An Coileachan 3015
Loch Bad Leabhraidh
Allt nan Caorach
Black Rock Gorge
River Glass
B817
Evanton
Alness Bay
Aultdearg
Achnaclerach
Strathgarve Forest
Meall na Speireig
Swordale
Drummond
A9
River Grudie
An Cabar 1832
Little Wyvis 2497
Cloch Mhór 1580
Strath Sgitheach
Sgitheach River
Clach Liath Forest
Storehouse of Foulis
Ardullie
Corriemoillie
A832
Gorstan
Carn Gorm
B9163
Kinbeachie
Grudie
Lochluichart
Loch Luichart
Heights of Brae
Upper Dochcarty
Mountgerald
Findon Mains
Culbo
Achanalt
Loch a' Chuilinn
Garve
Heights of Fodderty
A862
Braefindon
Loch Achanalt
Loch Garve
Bottacks
Culbokie
Sgurr Marcasaidh 1904
A835
Rogie Falls
Auchterneed
Castle Leod
Fodderty
Castle Doocot
DANGER AREA
Loch Culbokie
Loch Bhad Ghaineamhaich
Tarvie
Eagle Stone
Strathpeffer
A834
Dingwall
Hill Fort
Knockfarrel
Highland Childhood
Loch Ussie
Glenmarksie
Craigdarroch
Alcaig
Knockbain
Sgurr a' Ghlas Leathaid 2883
Sgurr a' Mhuilinn
Little Scatwell
Loch Achilty
Contin
Jamestown
Lochussie
Tollie
Maryburgh
B9163
B9169
Duncanston
Milton
Porin
Achlorachan
Bridgend
Loch Meig
Scatwell
Torrachilty Wood
Conon Bridge
Corntown
Easter Kinkell
Gleann Meinich
River Meig
Strathconon
River Conon
Loch Achonachie
Marybank
A832
Arcan
Muir of Fairburn
Urray
A862
Newmore
Rootfield
A835
Tore
A832
B9161
1936 Carn na Cloiche Móire
Loch Aradaidh
Balvaird
Drynie Park
Carn na Còinnich 2209
Glen Ord Distillery
Chapelton
Kilcoy
Arpafeelie
Bogallan
Loch Beannacharain
Inverchoran
Cabaan Forest
Urray Forest
Muir of Ord
Muir of Tarradale
Loch an Spàrdain
Orrin Reservoir
River Orrin
Ardnagrask
A832
Redcastle
Artafallie
Glen Orrin
Corriehallie Forest
Allt Goibhre
Loch nan Eun
Corry of Ardnagrask
Windhill
Milton
Craigrory
Charlestown
Dolphin & Seal Ce
North K
Gleann Goibhre
Cnoc Eille Mór
Loch nam Bonnàch
Rheindown
Dunmore
A862
Priory
Beauly Firth
South Kes
River Orrin
Am Fiar-loch
An Gorm-loch
Ruisaurie
Ruilick
Beauly
Drumindorsair
Balblair
B9164
Kirkhill
A862
Clachna
Farley
Broallan
Lentran
Inchrew
Leachkin
INVE
Meallan Buidhe 2505
Beinn a' Bha'ach Ard 2827
Erchless Forest
Lochan Fada
Breakachy
Kilmorack
A862
Drumchardine
James Pringle Weaver
Sgurr a' Choire Ghlais 3554
Sgurr na Ruaidhe 3254
A831
Fanellan
A833
Balchraggan
Newtonhill
Crask of Aigas
Carn Bàn
Neaty Burn
Erchless Castle
River Beauly
Hughton
Kiltarlity
Belladrum
An Leacainn 1358
Leishmore
Craigdhu
Culburnie
South Clunes
Dochgarroch
Caledonian Canal
Struy
Craobhnaclag
River Beauly
Camault Muir
River Ness
Scaniport
Braulen Lodge
Culligran Falls
Eskadale
Glaichbea
A82
River Farrar
Loch Beannacharan
Boblainy Forest
Carn a' Bhodaich 1642
Lochend
B862
Glen Strathfarrar
Loch a' Mhuillidh
Sgorr na Diollaid 2676
Stuy Forest
Loch Bruicheach
Loch Neaty
Ardendrain
Glen Convinth
Cragganvallie
Drumashie Moor
Strath Dores
Carn Gorm 2218
Strathglass
A831
Loch Garbh Iolachan
Meall nan Caorach 1401
Abriachan
Abriachan
Glassburn
Carn Mór 1497
Dores
Loch Ness
Loch Ashie
Muchrachd
Balmore Forest
Lochan an Tairt
Loch Gorm
A833
Meall na h-Eilrig 1526
Ashie Moor
Liatrie
River Cannich
River Glass
Loch Duntelchaig
Loch Sealbhanach
Cannich
Buntait
Balnaglaic
Balbeg
Balnagrantach
Achmony
Loch Ness Exhibition
A82
B852
B862
Stac na Ca 1463
Corrimony
Braefield
Glen Urquhart
Rychraggan
Polmaily
Drumnadrochit
Tom Bailgeann 1522
Fasnakyle Forest
Kerrow
Corrimony Chambered Cairn
A831
Balnain
Loch Meiklie
River Enrick
Milton
Nessieland
Urquhart Bay
Drum Farm Centre
Borlum
Loch a' Choire
River Affric
Coiltie
Lewiston
Strone
Urquhart
Loch Ceo Glais
Tomich
Suidhe Ghuirmain 1896
Divach
Upper Lenie
Falls of Divach
Lower Lenie
Torness
Loch Ruthven
River Nairn
River Deabhag
River Enrick
Balmacaan Forest
Bunloit
John Cobb Memorial
Farigaig
Aberarder

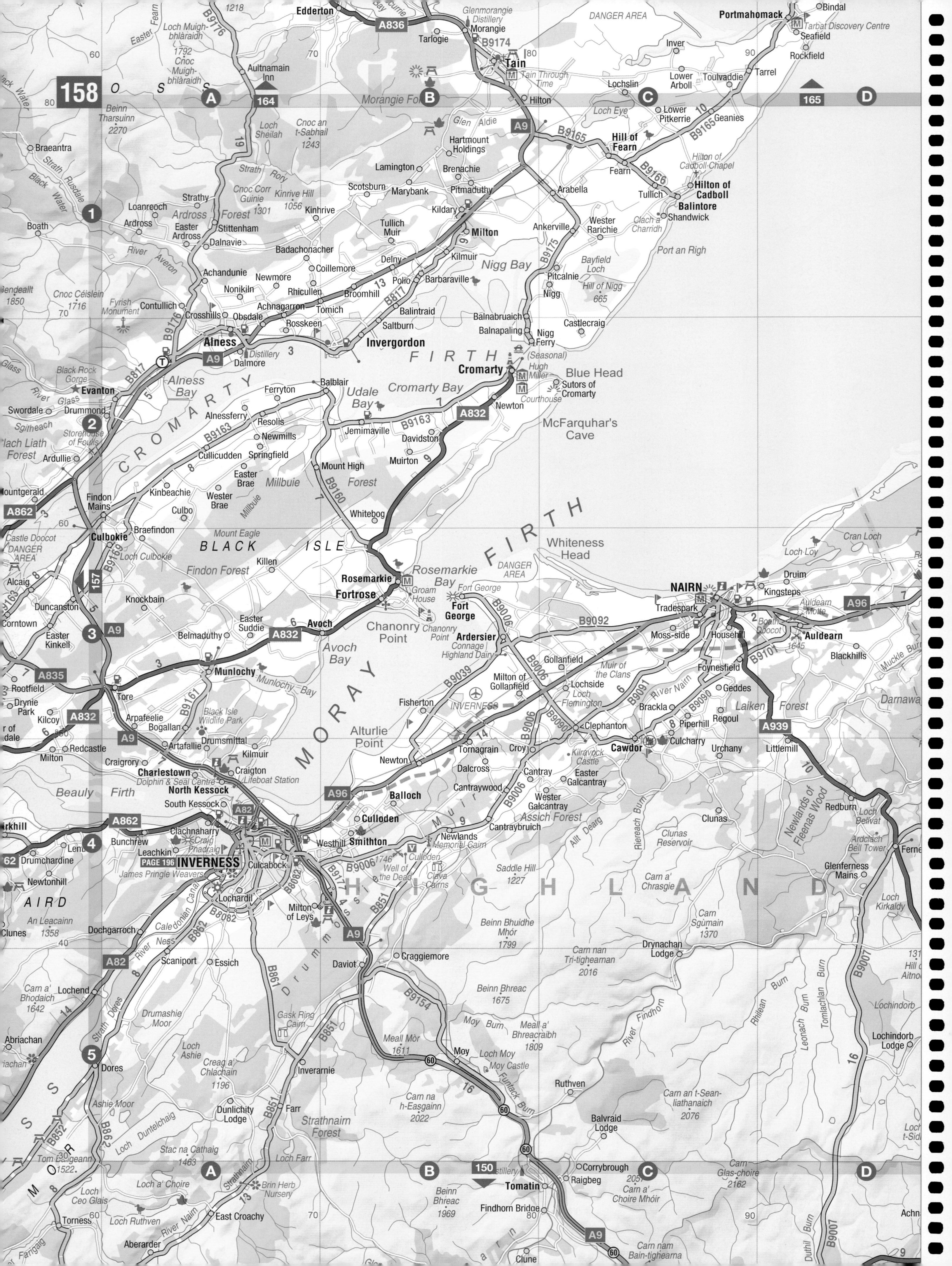
158
O S S
A
B
C
D
164
165
150
PAGE 196
Edderton
A836
Glenmorangie Distillery
Morangie
Tarlogie
B9174
Tain
Tain Through Time
DANGER AREA
Portmahomack
Bindal
Tarbat Discovery Centre
Seafield
Rockfield
Inver
Lower Arboll
Toulvaddie
Tarrel
Lochslin
Hilton
Loch Eye
Lower Pitkerrie
Geanies
B9165
Hill of Fearn
Fearn
B9166
Hilton of Cadboll Chapel
Hilton of Cadboll
Tullich
Balintore
Shandwick
Clach a' Charridh
Port an Righ
Easter Fearn
Loch Muigh-bhlàraidh
1792
Cnoc Muigh-bhlàraidh
B9176
Aultnamain Inn
Morangie Forest
Beinn Tharsuinn
2270
Loch Sheilah
Cnoc an t-Sabhail
1243
Glen Aldie
A9
Hartmount Holdings
Braeantra
Strath Rusdale
Black Water
Strath Rory
Cnoc Corr Guinie
1301
Kinrive Hill
1056
Lamington
Brenachie
Scotsburn
Marybank
Pitmaduthy
Arabella
Strathy
Loanreoch
Ardross Forest
Ardross
Easter Ardross
Stittenham
Kinrive
Kildary
Tullich Muir
Milton
Ankerville
Wester Rarichie
Boath
Dalnavie
River Averon
Badachonacher
Kilmuir
Delny
Nigg Bay
B9175
Bayfield Loch
Achandunie
Coillemore
Newmore
Barbaraville
Pitcalnie
Hill of Nigg
665
Bengeallt
1850
Cnoc Céislein
1716
Nonikiln
Rhicullen
Broomhill
Polio
B817
Nigg
Fyrish Monument
Contullich
Achnagarron
Tomich
Balintraid
Crosshills
Obsdale
Rosskeen
Saltburn
Balnabruaich
Balnapaling
Castlecraig
Nigg Ferry
Alness
Invergordon
Distillery
Dalmore
(Seasonal)
Black Rock Gorge
Alness Bay
CROMARTY FIRTH
Cromarty
Hugh Miller
Blue Head
Sutors of Cromarty
Courthouse
Evanton
River Glass
Swordale
Drummond
Ferryton
Balblair
Udale Bay
Cromarty Bay
Newton
A832
Alnessferry
Resolis
Jemimaville
B9163
Davidston
McFarquhar's Cave
Storehouse of Foulis
Newmills
Sgitheach
Clach Liath Forest
Cullicudden
Springfield
Muirton
Ardullie
Mount High
Easter Brae
Millbuie Forest
B9160
Kinbeachie
Findon Mains
Wester Brae
Culbo
Whitebog
Mountgerald
A862
Braefindon
Culbokie
Mount Eagle
Castle Doocot
DANGER AREA
BLACK ISLE
Loch Culbokie
Whiteness Head
Cran Loch
Loch Loy
B9169
Killen
Findon Forest
Rosemarkie
Rosemarkie Bay
DANGER AREA
MORAY FIRTH
Druim
Alcaig
Fortrose
Groam House
Fort George
NAIRN
Kingsteps
Duncanston
Knockbain
Tradespark
Auldearn Motte
A96
Corntown
Easter Suddie
Avoch
Chanonry Point
B9006
B9092
Boath Doocot
Easter Kinkell
Belmaduthy
A832
Ardersier
Moss-side
Househill
Auldearn
Blackhills
A9
Connage Highland Dairy
Avoch Bay
Gollanfield
Muir of the Clans
A835
B9101
Muckle Burn
Rootfield
Munlochy
Munlochy Bay
B9039
Milton of Gollanfield
Lochside
Loch Flemington
B9091
River Nairn
Foynesfield
Geddes
Drynie Park
Tore
Fisherton
INVERNESS
Brackla
B9090
Laiken Forest
Darnaway
Kilcoy
Arpafeelie
B9161
Black Isle Wildlife Park
Alturlie Point
Piperhill
Regoul
Bogallan
Clephanton
A939
Drumsmittal
Tornagrain
Croy
Cawdor
Culcharry
Urchany
Littlemill
Redcastle
Artafallie
Kilravock Castle
Milton
Kilmuir
Dalcross
Easter Galcantray
Craigrory
Charlestown
Craigton
Newton
Cantray
Dolphin & Seal Centre
Lifeboat Station
Cantraywood
Beauly Firth
North Kessock
Balloch
Wester Galcantray
Clunas
Redburn
Loch Belivat
South Kessock
A82
Assich Forest
Newlands of Fleenas Wood
Culloden
Cantraybruich
Rereach Burn
Kirkhill
A862
Clachnaharry
Craig Phadraig
Newlands
Memorial Cairn
Allt Dearg
Clunas Reservoir
Ardclach Bell Tower
Bunchrew
Westhill
Smithton
Lentran
Leachkin
INVERNESS
Culcaboch
B9006
1746
Culloden
Well of the Dead
Clava Cairns
Glenferness Mains
Ferness
Drumchardine
Newtonhill
James Pringle Weavers
B8082
B9177
B851
Saddle Hill
1227
Carn a' Chrasgie
HIGHLAND
AIRD
Lochardil
Milton of Leys
Loch Kirkaldy
An Leacainn
1358
Caledonian Canal
B8082
A9
Carn Sgùmain
1370
Clunes
Dochgarroch
River Ness
B862
Beinn Bhuidhe Mhòr
1799
Scaniport
Essich
Daviot
Craggiemore
Drynachan Lodge
Carn nan Tri-tighearnan
2016
B9007
A82
B861
Drummossie
Carn a' Bhodaich
1642
Lochend
B9154
Beinn Bhreac
1675
Lochindorb
Drumashie Moor
Moy Burn
Meall a' Bhreacraibh
1809
River Findhorn
Leonach Burn
Tomlachan Burn
Rhilean Burn
Abriachan
Strath Dores
Gask Ring Cairn
B851
Meall Mòr
1611
Moy
Loch Moy
Moy Castle
Lochindorb Lodge
Loch Ashie
Creag a' Chlachain
1196
Dores
Inverarnie
Funtack Burn
Ruthven
Ashie Moor
Dunlichity Lodge
B851
Farr
Carn na h-Easgainn
2022
Carn an t-Sean-liathanaich
2076
Strathnairn Forest
Balvraid Lodge
B852
B862
Loch Duntelchaig
Stac na Cathaig
1463
Tom Bailgeann
1522
Loch Farr
Corrybrough
Raigbeg
Carn Glas-choire
2162
Carn a' Choire Mhòir
2057
Loch a' Choire
Brin Herb Nursery
Strathnairn
Tomatin
Loch Ceo Glais
Beinn Bhreac
1969
Findhorn Bridge
Torness
Loch Ruthven
River Nairn
East Croachy
A9
Aberarder
Farigaig
Carn nam Bain-tighearna
Dulnain Burn
Clune
Achnahannet
B9007

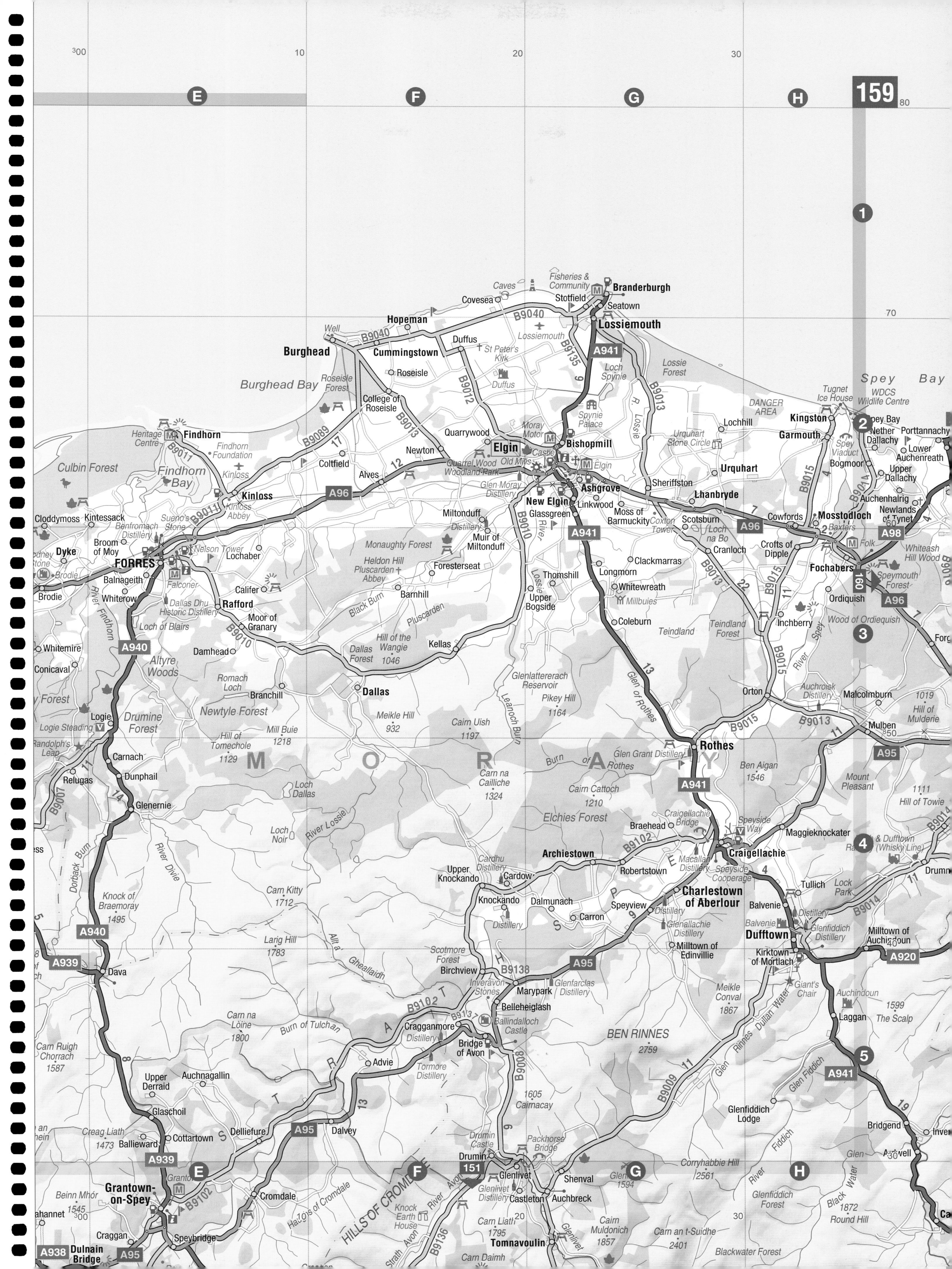

Lossiemouth
Elgin
Burghead
Hopeman
Burghead Bay
Findhorn
Kinloss
FORRES
Spey Bay
Fochabers
Mosstodloch
Lhanbryde
Rothes
Craigellachie
Charlestown of Aberlour
Dufftown
Archiestown
Dallas
M O R A Y
Grantown-on-Spey
Tomnavoulin
Glenlivet
BEN RINNES
Culbin Forest
Findhorn Bay

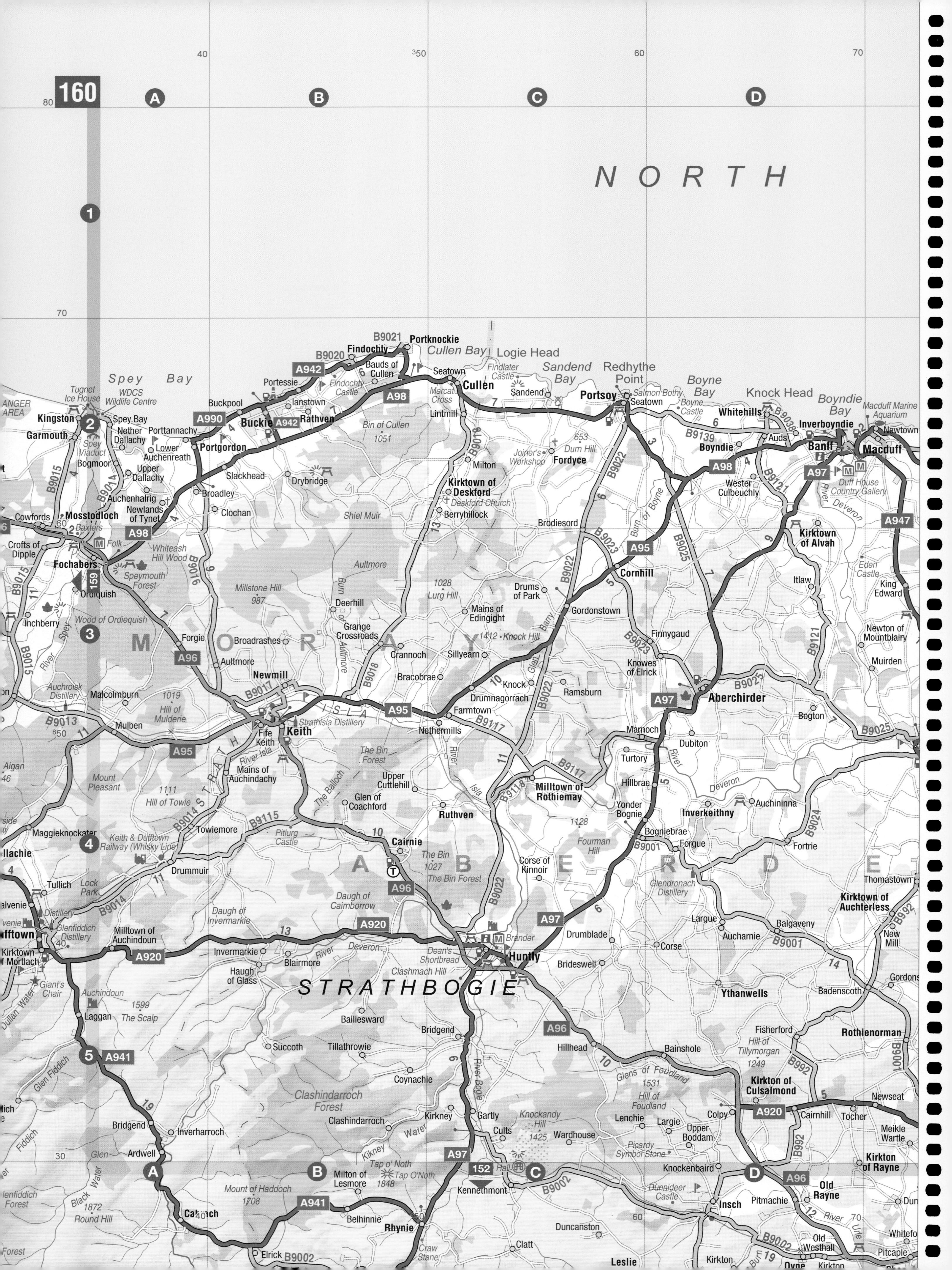

160
A
B
C
D
1
2
3
4
5
NORTH
Spey Bay
Tugnet Ice House
WDCS Wildlife Centre
Kingston
Garmouth
Spey Viaduct
Nether Dallachy
Upper Dallachy
Porttannachy
Lower Auchenreath
Portgordon
Bogmoor
Auchenhalrig
Newlands of Tynet
Mosstodloch
Baxters
Cowfords
Crofts of Dipple
Fochabers
Folk
Ordiquish
Speymouth Forest
Whiteash Hill Wood
Inchberry
Wood of Ordiequish
River Spey
MORAY
Auchroisk Distillery
Malcolmburn
Mulben
Aigan
Mount Pleasant
Maggieknockater
Keith & Dufftown Railway (Whisky Line)
Tullich
Lock Park
Dufftown
Distillery
Glenfiddich Distillery
Kirktown of Mortlach
Giant's Chair
Dullan Water
Auchindoun
Laggan
1599 The Scalp
Glen Fiddich
Bridgend
Ardwell
Inverharroch
Cabrach
Black Water
1872 Round Hill
Elrick
Forest
Buckpool
Buckie
Portessie
Ianstown
Rathven
Findochty
Findochty Castle
Bauds of Cullen
Portknockie
Cullen Bay
Logie Head
Findlater Castle
Sandend
Sandend Bay
Seatown
Cullen
Mercat Cross
Lintmill
Bin of Cullen 1051
Slackhead
Drybridge
Broadley
Clochan
Shiel Muir
Aultmore
Millstone Hill 987
Deerhill
Grange Crossroads
Broadrashes
Forgie
Aultmore
Newmill
Crannoch
Bracobrae
Keith
Fife Keith
Strathisla Distillery
ISLA
River Isla
Mains of Auchindachy
1019 Hill of Mulderie
1111 Hill of Towie
STRATH ISLA
Towiemore
Pitlurg Castle
Drummuir
Daugh of Invermarkie
Milltown of Auchindoun
Invermarkie
Haugh of Glass
Blairmore
River Deveron
Dean's Shortbread
Clashmach Hill
STRATHBOGIE
Bailiesward
Succoth
Tillathrowie
Bridgend
Coynachie
Clashindarroch Forest
Clashindarroch
Kirkney
Kirkney Water
Milton of Lesmore
Tap o' Noth
Tap O'Noth 1848
Mount of Haddoch 1708
Belhinnie
Rhynie
Craw Stane
The Bin Forest
The Balloch
Upper Cuttlehill
Glen of Coachford
Cairnie
The Bin 1027
The Bin Forest
Daugh of Cairnborrow
Ruthven
Nethermills
Farmtown
Drumnagorrach
Sillyearn
Knock
1412 Knock Hill
Mains of Edingight
1028 Lurg Hill
Berryhillock
Deskford Church
Kirktown of Deskford
Milton
Joiner's Workshop
Fordyce
653 Durn Hill
Portsoy
Redhythe Point
Salmon Bothy
Seatown
Boyne Castle
Boyne Bay
Knock Head
Whitehills
Boyndie Bay
Boyndie
Inverboyndie
Auds
Macduff Marine Aquarium
Newtown
Banff
Macduff
Wester Culbeuchly
Duff House Country Gallery
River Deveron
Burn of Boyne
Brodiesord
Drums of Park
Gordonstown
Cornhill
Burn of Barry
Glen
Ramsburn
Finnygaud
Knowes of Elrick
Aberchirder
Kirktown of Alvah
Itlaw
Eden Castle
King Edward
Newton of Mountblairy
Muirden
Bogton
Marnoch
Dubiton
Turtory
Hillbrae
River Deveron
Milltown of Rothiemay
Yonder Bognie
Bogniebrae
Forgue
Inverkeithny
Auchininna
1128 Fourman Hill
Corse of Kinnoir
Glendronach Distillery
Fortrie
Thomastown
Kirktown of Auchterless
ABERDEEN
Largue
Aucharnie
Balgaveny
New Mill
Drumblade
Corse
Brideswell
Brander
Huntly
Ythanwells
Badenscoth
Gordonstown
Hillhead
Bainshole
Glens of Foudland
1531 Hill of Foudland
Fisherford
Hill of Tillymorgan 1249
Rothienorman
Kirkton of Culsalmond
Newseat
Cairnhill
Tocher
Meikle Wartle
Colpy
Lenchie
Largie
Upper Boddam
Knockandy Hill 1425
Wardhouse
Gartly
Cults
Picardy Symbol Stone
Knockenbaird
Kirkton of Rayne
Old Rayne
Kennethmont
Dunnideer Castle
Insch
Pitmachie
River Urie
Duncanston
Clatt
Leslie
Kirkton
Old Westhall
Oyne
Pitcaple
Whitefo
River Bogie
B9021
B9020
A942
A98
A990
B9015
B9104
B9016
A96
B9017
B9013
A95
B9014
B9115
A920
A941
B9002
B9018
B9117
B9118
B9022
B9023
B9025
B9139
B9038
B9121
A97
A947
B9024
B9001
B992
152
159

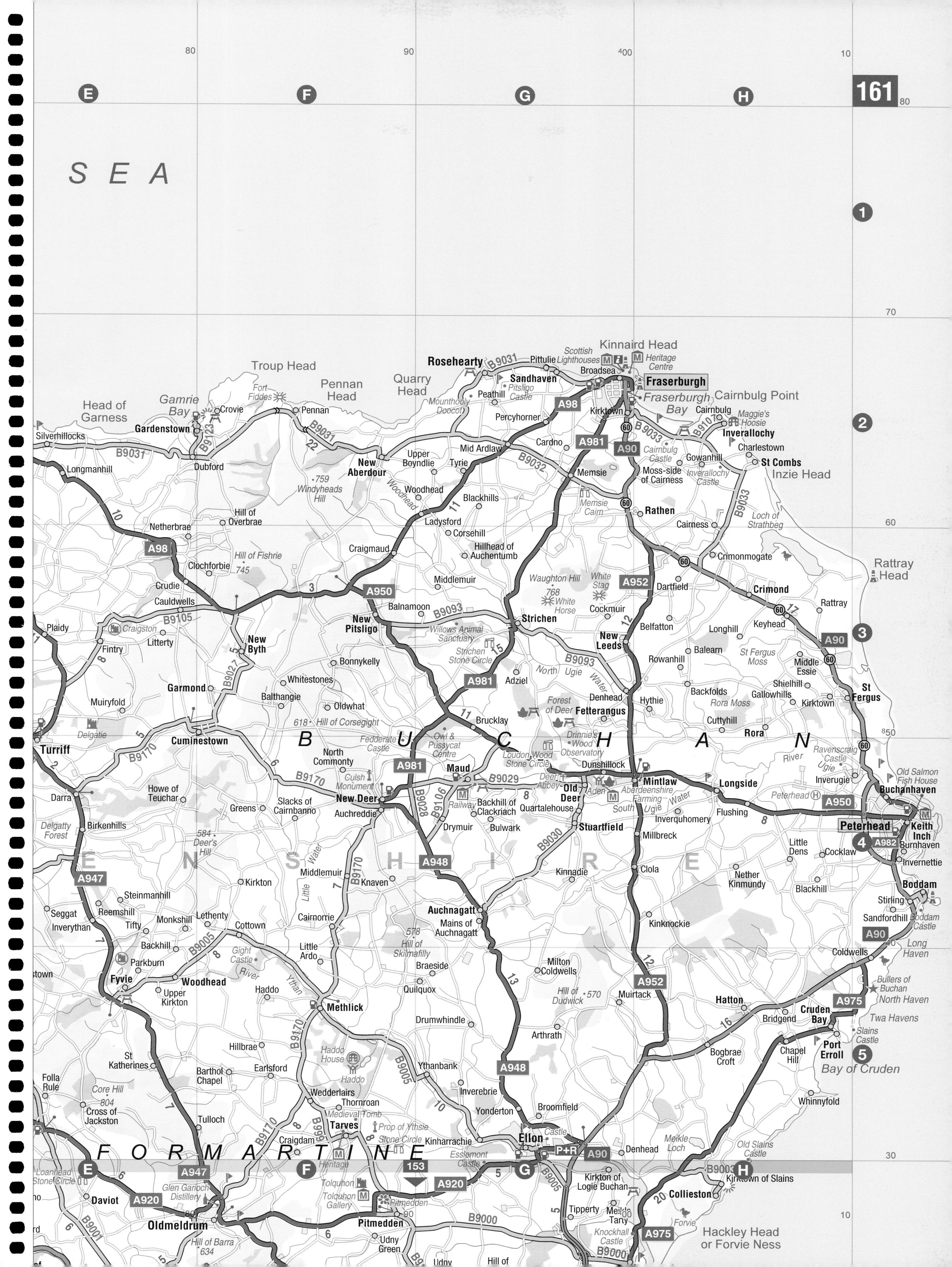
SEA
Troup Head
Pennan Head
Quarry Head
Head of Garness
Gamrie Bay
Gardenstown
Crovie
Pennan
Rosehearty
Sandhaven
Pittulie
Kinnaird Head
Scottish Lighthouses
Heritage Centre
Broadsea
Fraserburgh
Fraserburgh Bay
Cairnbulg Point
Cairnbulg
Inverallochy
Charlestown
St Combs
Inzie Head
Kirktown
Memsie
Rathen
Cairness
Loch of Strathbeg
Crimonmogate
Rattray Head
Crimond
Rattray
Strichen
New Leeds
Longside
Mintlaw
Peterhead
Buchanhaven
Boddam
Cruden Bay
Port Erroll
Bay of Cruden
Hatton
Ellon
Tarves
Methlick
Fyvie
Turriff
Cuminestown
New Deer
Maud
New Pitsligo
New Byth
New Aberdour
Oldmeldrum
Pitmedden
Collieston
Hackley Head or Forvie Ness
BUCHAN
FORMARTINE
ABERDEENSHIRE
A98
A981
A90
A950
A952
A948
A947
A920
A975
A982
B9031
B9032
B9033
B9093
B9029
B9170
B9005
B9000
153

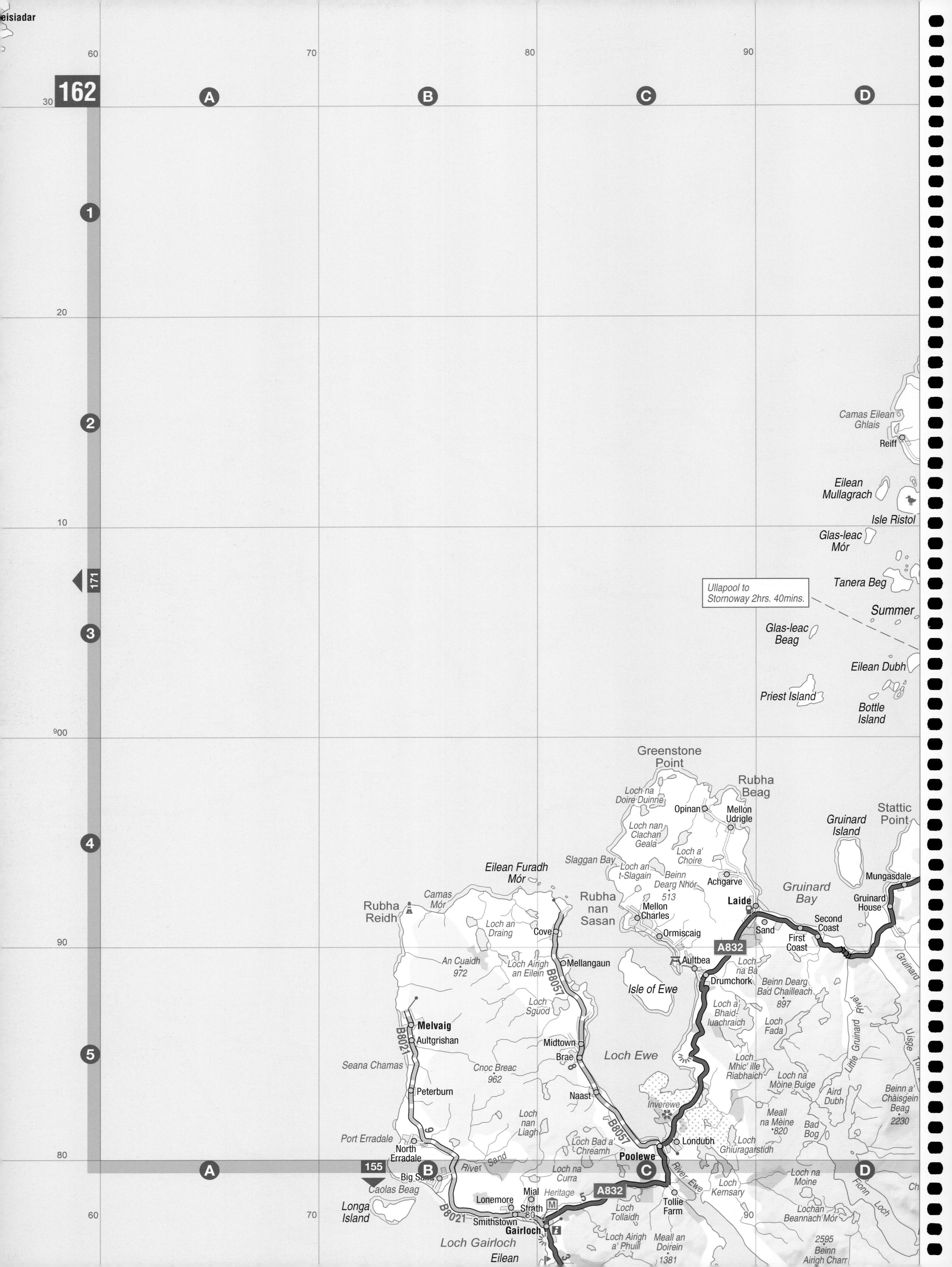

60
70
80
90

30

1

20

10

171

3

⁹00

Ullapool to
Stornoway 2hrs. 40mins.

*Camas Eilean
Ghlais*

Reiff

*Eilean
Mullagrach*

Isle Ristol

*Glas-leac
Mór*

Tanera Beg

Summer

*Glas-leac
Beag*

Eilean Dubh

Priest Island

*Bottle
Island*

4

*Greenstone
Point*

*Rubha
Beag*

*Loch na
Doire Duinne*

*Stattic
Point*

Opinan

Mellon
Udrigle

*Loch nan
Clachan Geala*

*Gruinard
Island*

*Loch a'
Choire*

Slaggan Bay

*Loch an
t-Slagain*

*Beinn
Dearg Nhór*
513

Achgarve

Mungasdale

*Eilean Furadh
Mór*

*Camas
Mór*

Rubha
Reidh

*Rubha nan
Sasan*

Mellon
Charles

Laide

*Gruinard
Bay*

Gruinard
House

Cove

Ormiscaig

Sand

Second
Coast

*Loch an
Draing*

90

An Cuaidh
972

*Loch Airigh
an Eilein*

Mellangaun

Aultbea

A832

First
Coast

*Loch
na Bà*

Drumchork

Isle of Ewe

*Beinn Dearg
Bad Chailleach*
897

*Loch
Sguod*

*Loch a'
Bhaid-
luachraich*

Melvaig

Aultgrishan

Midtown

Loch Ewe

*Loch
Fada*

5

Seana Chamas

Brae

Cnoc Breac
962

*Loch
Mhic'ille
Riabhaich*

*Loch na
Mòine Buige*

*Meall
na Mèine*
·820

*Beinn a'
Chàisgein
Beag*
2230

Peterburn

Naast

Inverewe

*Aird
Dubh*

*Bad
Bog*

*Loch
nan
Liagh*

*Meall
na Mèine*
·820

Port Erradale

North
Erradale

*Loch Bad a'
Chreamh*

Londubh

*Loch
Ghiuragarstidh*

*Bad
Bog*

Poolewe

80

155

Big Sand

River Sand

*Loch na
Curra*

A832

*Loch na
Moine*

*Longa
Island*

Caolas Beag

Lonemore

Mial

Strath

Heritage
M

5

Tollie
Farm

*Loch
Kernsary*

*Lochan
Beannach Mòr*

Smithstown

*Loch
Tollaidh*

*Meall an
Doirein*
1381

60

70

80

90

2595
*Beinn
Airigh Charr*

Gairloch

Loch Gairloch

Eilean

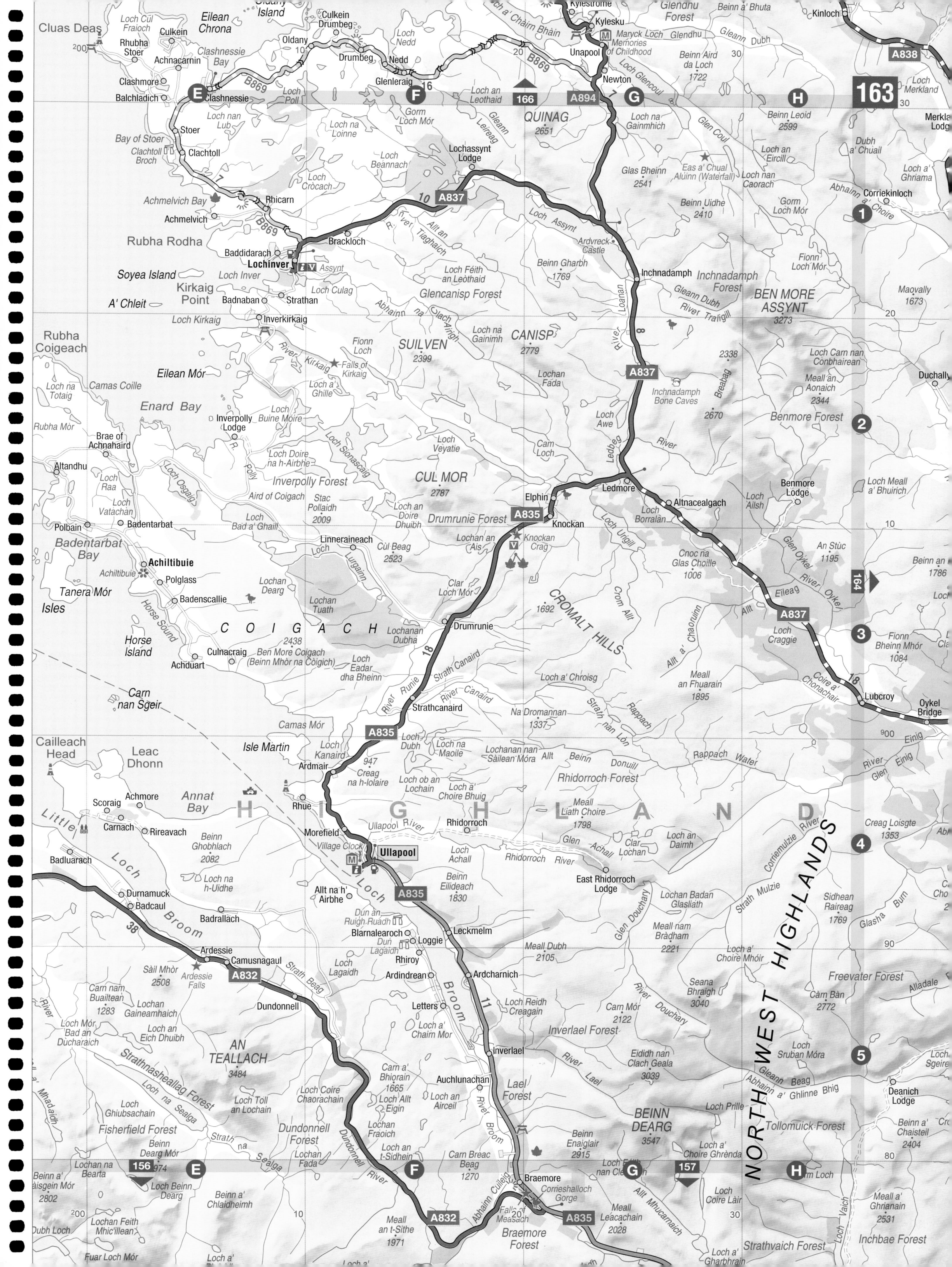
163
166
164
156
157
E
F
G
H
1
2
3
4
5
Kylestrome
Kylesku
Glendhu Forest
Beinn a' Bhuta
Kinloch
A838
Loch Merkland
Merkland Lodge
Oldany Island
Culkein Drumbeg
Cluas Deas
Loch Cùl Fraioch
Culkein
Eilean Chrona
Rhubha Stoer
Clashnessie Bay
Achnacarnin
Oldany
Drumbeg
Loch Nedd
Nedd
Glenleraig
Unapool
Maryck Loch
Memories of Childhood
Glendhu
Gleann Dubh
Beinn Aird da Loch 1722
Newton
Loch Glencoul
Clashmore
Balchladich
Clashnessie
B869
Loch Poll
Loch an Leothaid
A894
Loch na Gainmhich
Glen Coul
Beinn Leoid 2599
Gorm Loch Mór
QUINAG 2651
Loch nan Lub
Stoer
Bay of Stoer
Clachtoll
Clachtoll Broch
Loch na Loinne
Gleann Leireag
Lochassynt Lodge
Loch Beannach
Loch Crócach
Eas a' Chual Aluinn (Waterfall)
Glas Bheinn 2541
Loch an Eircill
Loch nan Caorach
Dubh a' Chuail
Loch a' Ghriama
Corriekinloch
Abhainn a' Choire
Gorm Loch Mór
Achmelvich Bay
Rhicarn
A837
Achmelvich
Rubha Rodha
Brackloch
River Tiaghaich
Allt an Tiaghaich
Loch Assynt
Beinn Uidhe 2410
Ardvreck Castle
Baddidarach
Lochinver
Assynt
Soyea Island
Loch Inver
Kirkaig Point
Badnaban
Strathan
Loch Culag
A' Chleit
Loch Féith an Leòthaid
Beinn Gharbh 1769
Inchnadamph
Inchnadamph Forest
Fionn Loch Mór
Glencanisp Forest
Gleann Dubh
River Traligill
BEN MORE ASSYNT 3273
Maovally 1673
Loch Kirkaig
Inverkirkaig
Abhainn na Clach Airigh
Loch na Gainimh
CANISP 2779
River Loanan
Rubha Coigeach
Fionn Loch
SUILVEN 2399
River Kirkaig
Falls of Kirkaig
2338
Loch Carn nan Conbhairean
Eilean Mór
Loch a' Ghille
Lochan Fada
Meall an Aonaich 2344
Duchally
Loch na Totaig
Camas Coille
Inchnadamph Bone Caves
Breabag
Enard Bay
Inverpolly Lodge
Loch Buine Moire
2670
Benmore Forest
Loch Awe
Rubha Mòr
Brae of Achnahaird
Loch Sionascaig
Loch Veyatie
Cam Loch
River
Ledbeg
Altandhu
Loch Doire na h-Airbhe
Loch Raa
Loch Osgaig
Inverpolly Forest
CUL MOR 2787
Ledmore
Loch Meall a' Bhuirich
Benmore Lodge
Elphin
Altnacealgach
Loch Ailsh
Loch Vatachan
Aird of Coigach
Stac Pollaidh 2009
Loch an Doire Dhuibh
Loch Borralan
Polbain
Badentarbat
Loch Bad a' Ghaill
Drumrunie Forest
A835
Knockan
Loch Urigill
10
Badentarbat Bay
Linneraineach
Loch Lurgainn
Cùl Beag 2523
Lochan an Ais
Knockan Crag
Cnoc na Glas Choille 1006
Glen Oykel
An Stùc 1195
Beinn an 1786
Achiltibuie
Polglass
Tanera Mór
Isles
Lochan Dearg
Clar Loch Mór
Crom Allt
River Oykel
Eileag
Badenscallie
Lochan Tuath
1692
Allt a' Chaoruinn
Drumrunie
Horse Sound
COIGACH
Lochanan Dubha
2438
CROMALT HILLS
Loch Craggie
Fionn Bheinn Mhór 1084
Horse Island
Achduart
Culnacraig
Ben More Coigach (Beinn Mhòr na Còigich)
Loch Eadar dha Bheinn
Strath Canaird
Loch a' Chroisg
Meall an Fhuarain 1895
Coire a' Chonachair
18
Lubcroy
Oykel Bridge
Carn nan Sgeir
River Runie
Strathcanaird
River Canaird
Na Dromannan 1337
Strath nan Lon
Rappach
Camas Mór
Loch Kanaird
Loch Dubh
Loch na Maoile
Lochanan nan Sàilean Mòra
Allt Beinn Donuill
Rappach Water
Einig
River Einig
Glen Einig
Cailleach Head
Leac Dhonn
Isle Martin
Ardmair
947 Creag na h-Iolaire
Loch ob an Lochain
Loch a' Choire Bhuig
Rhidorroch Forest
Annat Bay
Achmore
Scoraig
Rhue
HIGHLAND
Meall Liath Choire 1798
Creag Loisgte 1353
Little Loch Broom
Carnach
Rireavach
Ullapool River
Rhidorroch
Corriemulzie River
Morefield
Village Clock
Ullapool
Loch Achall
Glen Achall
Clar Lochan
Loch an Daimh
Beinn Ghobhlach 2082
Badluarach
Rhidorroch River
East Rhidorroch Lodge
Loch na h-Uidhe
Loch Broom
A835
Beinn Eilideach 1830
Glen Douchary
Lochan Badan Glasliath
Strath Mulzie
Sidhean Raireag 1769
Glasha Burn
Durnamuck
Allt na h' Airbhe
Badcaul
Dun an Ruigh Ruadh
Meall nam Bradham 2221
Badrallach
Blarnalearoch
Leckmelm
Loggie
Dun Lagaidh
NORTHWEST HIGHLANDS
Ardessie
Camusnagaul
Rhiroy
Meall Dubh 2105
Loch a' Choire Mhóir
Loch Lagaidh
Ardindrean
Ardcharnich
Sàil Mhòr 2508
Ardessie Falls
A832
Strath Beag
Seana Bhraigh 3040
Freevater Forest
Alladale
Càrn Bàn 2772
Carn nam Buailtean 1283
Lochan Gaineamhaich
Dundonnell
Letters
Broom
11
Loch Reidh Creagain
Carn Mór 2122
River Douchary
Loch an Eich Dhuibh
Loch a' Chairn Mor
Inverlael Forest
Loch Mór Bad an Dùcharaich
AN TEALLACH 3484
Inverlael
Eididh nan Clach Geala 3039
Loch Sruban Mòra
Strathnasheallag Forest
Loch Coire Chaorachain
Carn a' Bhiorain 1665
Auchlunachan
River Lael
Gleann Beag
Deanich Lodge
Loch na Sealga
Loch Toll an Lochain
Loch Allt Eigin
Loch an Airceil
Lael Forest
Abhainn a' Ghlinne Bhig
Loch Ghiubsachain
Lochan Fraoich
River Broom
BEINN DEARG 3547
Loch Prille
Tollomuick Forest
Fisherfield Forest
Dundonnell Forest
Loch an t-Sidhein
Beinn Enaiglair 2915
Loch a' Choire Ghrènda
Beinn a' Chaisteil 2404
Beinn Dearg Mór 2974
Strath na Sealga
Lochan Fada
Carn Breac Beag 1270
Loch nan Cleith
Lochan na Bearta
Dundonnell River
Braemore
Corrieshalloch Gorge
Allt Mhucarnaich
Loch Beinn Dearg
Beinn a' Chlaidheimh
Abhainn Cuileig
Falls of Measach
Meall Leacachain 2028
Loch Coire Làir
Meall a' Ghrianain 2531
Lochan Feith Mhic'illean
Meall an t-Sithe 1971
Braemore Forest
Strathvaich Forest
Inchbae Forest
Loch Vaich
Loch a' Gharbhrain
Fuar Loch Mór

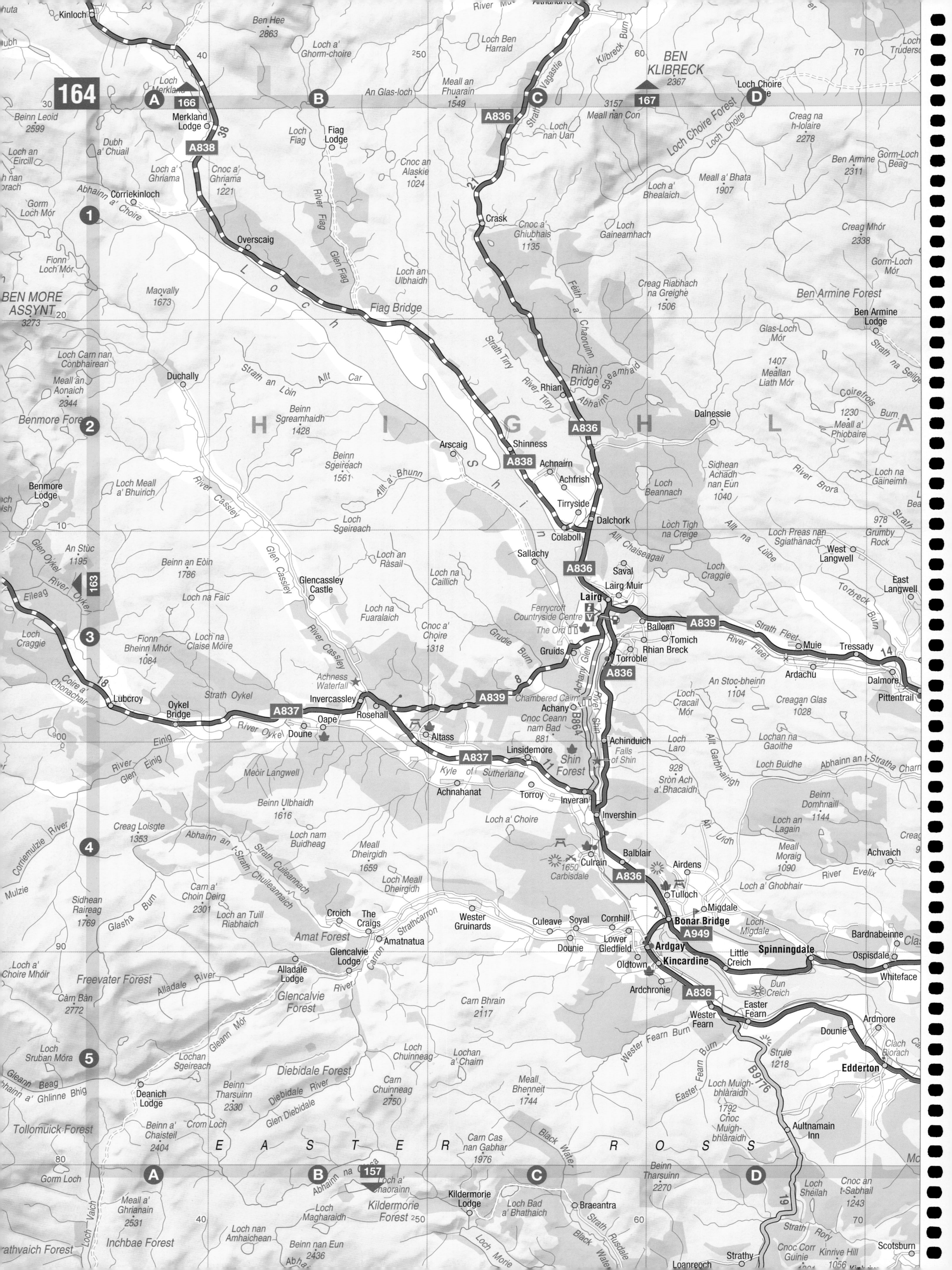
164
Kinloch
Ben Hee
2863
Loch a' Ghorm-choire
Loch Ben Harrald
BEN KLIBRECK
2367
Loch Merkland
166
Merkland Lodge
A838
An Glas-loch
Meall an Fhuarain
1549
A836
Strath Vagastie
3157
Meall nan Con
167
Loch Choire Lodge
Loch Choire Forest
Loch Choire
Creag na h-Iolaire
2278
Beinn Leoid
2599
Dubh a' Chuail
Loch Fiag
Fiag Lodge
Loch nan Uan
Loch an Eircill
Loch a' Ghriama
Cnoc a' Ghriama
1221
Cnoc an Alaskie
1024
Ben Armine
2311
Gorm-Loch Beag
Meall a' Bhata
1907
Corriekinloch
Abhainn a' Choire
Gorm Loch Mór
River Fiag
Loch a' Bhealaich
Crask
Cnoc a' Ghiubhais
1135
Loch Gaineamhach
Creag Mhór
2338
Overscaig
Glen Fiag
Fionn Loch Mór
Loch an Ulbhaidh
Gorm-Loch Mór
Maovally
1673
BEN MORE ASSYNT
3273
Loch Shin
Fiag Bridge
Creag Riabhach na Greighe
1506
Féith a' Chaoruinn
Ben Armine Forest
Ben Armine Lodge
Glas-Loch Mór
Strath na Seilge
Loch Carn nan Conbhairean
Meall an Aonaich
2344
Duchally
Strath an Lòin
Allt Car
Strath Tirry
River Tirry
Rhian
Rhian Bridge
Abhainn Sgeamhaidh
1407
Meallan Liath Mór
Coirefrois
Benmore Forest
HIGHLAND
Beinn Sgreamhaidh
1428
Shinness
Dalnessie
1230
Meall a' Phiobaire
Burn
Arscaig
Achnairn
Achfrish
Beinn Sgeireach
1561
Allt a' Bhunn
Loch Beannach
Sidhean Achadh nan Eun
1040
River Brora
Loch na Gaineimh
Benmore Lodge
Loch Meall a' Bhuirich
River Cassley
Tirryside
Dalchork
Colaboll
Loch Sgeireach
Loch Tigh na Creige
Allt na Lùibe
978
Grumby Rock
Strath
Loch Preas nan Sgiathanach
West Langwell
Glen Oykel
An Stùc
1195
Beinn an Eòin
1786
Glen Cassley
Loch an Ràsail
Loch na Caillich
Sallachy
Allt Chaiseagail
Saval
Loch Craggie
East Langwell
163
River Oykel
Eileag
Loch na Faic
Glencassley Castle
Lairg
Lairg Muir
Torbreck Burn
Loch na Fuaralaich
Ferrycroft Countryside Centre
The Ord
Balloan
A839
Tomich
Rhian Breck
Strath Fleet
River Fleet
Muie
Tressady
Loch Craggie
Fionn Bheinn Mhór
1084
Loch na Claise Móire
Cnoc a' Choire
1318
Grudie Burn
Gruids
Torroble
Ardachu
Dalmore
Pittentrail
Coire a' Chonachair
Lubcroy
Oykel Bridge
Strath Oykel
Achness Waterfall
Invercassley
Rosehall
Chambered Cairn
Achany
Achany Glen
River Shin
An Stoc-bheinn
1104
Loch Cracail Mór
Creagan Glas
1028
A837
Oape
Doune
Altass
Cnoc Ceann nam Bad
881
B864
Achinduich
Loch Laro
Lochan na Gaoithe
River Einig
Glen Einig
Meòir Langwell
Linsidemore
Kyle of Sutherland
Shin Forest
Falls of Shin
928
Sròn Ach a' Bhacaidh
Allt Garbh-airigh
Loch Buidhe
Abhainn an t-Stratha Charnaig
Beinn Ulbhaidh
1616
Achnahanat
Torroy
Invershin
Inveran
Beinn Domhnaill
1144
Corriemulzie River
Creag Loisgte
1353
Abhainn an t-Strath Chuileannaich
Loch nam Buidheag
Meall Dheirgidh
1659
Loch a' Choire
Loch an Lagain
Allt an Ulidh
Meall Moraig
1090
Achvaich
Strath Cuileannach
Loch Meall Dheirgidh
1650
Carbisdale
Culrain
Balblair
Airdens
River Evelix
Mulzie
Sidhean Raireag
1769
Glasha Burn
Carn a' Choin Deirg
2301
Loch an Tuill Riabhaich
Croich
The Craigs
Strathcarron
Wester Gruinards
Tulloch
Loch a' Ghobhair
Migdale
Bonar Bridge
Amat Forest
Amatnatua
Culeave
Soyal
Cornhill
Lower Gledfield
Ardgay
A949
Loch Migdale
Little Creich
Spinningdale
Bardnabeinne
Ospisdale
Dounie
Glencalvie Lodge
Oldtown
Kincardine
Whiteface
Loch a' Choire Mhóir
Freevater Forest
Alladale River
Alladale Lodge
River Carron
Glencalvie Forest
Ardchronie
Dun Creich
Càrn Bàn
2772
Gleann Mór
Carn Bhrain
2117
Wester Fearn
Easter Fearn
Ardmore
Dounie
Clach Biorach
Wester Fearn Burn
Loch Sruban Móra
Lochan Sgeireach
Loch Chuinneag
Lochan a' Chairn
Struie
1218
Edderton
Gleann Beag
Abhainn a' Ghlinne Bhig
Diebidale Forest
Diebidale River
Deanich Lodge
Beinn Tharsuinn
2330
Carn Chuinneag
2750
Glen Diebidale
Meall Bhenneit
1744
Easter Fearn Burn
Loch Mugh-bhlàraidh
1792
Cnoc Mugh-bhlàraidh
B9176
Aultnamain Inn
Tollomuick Forest
Beinn a' Chaisteil
2404
Crom Loch
Carn Cas nan Gabhar
1976
Black Water
EASTER ROSS
157
Beinn Tharsuinn
2270
Gorm Loch
Meall a' Ghrianain
2531
Abhainn na Glasa
Loch a' Chaorainn
Kildermorie Lodge
Loch Bad a' Bhathaich
Braeantra
Loch Sheilah
Cnoc an t-Sabhail
1243
Loch Magharaidh
Kildermorie Forest
Strath Rusdale
Loch Vaich
Loch nan Amhaichean
Beinn nan Eun
2436
Loch Morie
Strath Rory
Inchbae Forest
Strathvaich Forest
Loanreoch
Strathy
Cnoc Corr Guinie
Kinrive Hill
1056
Scotsburn

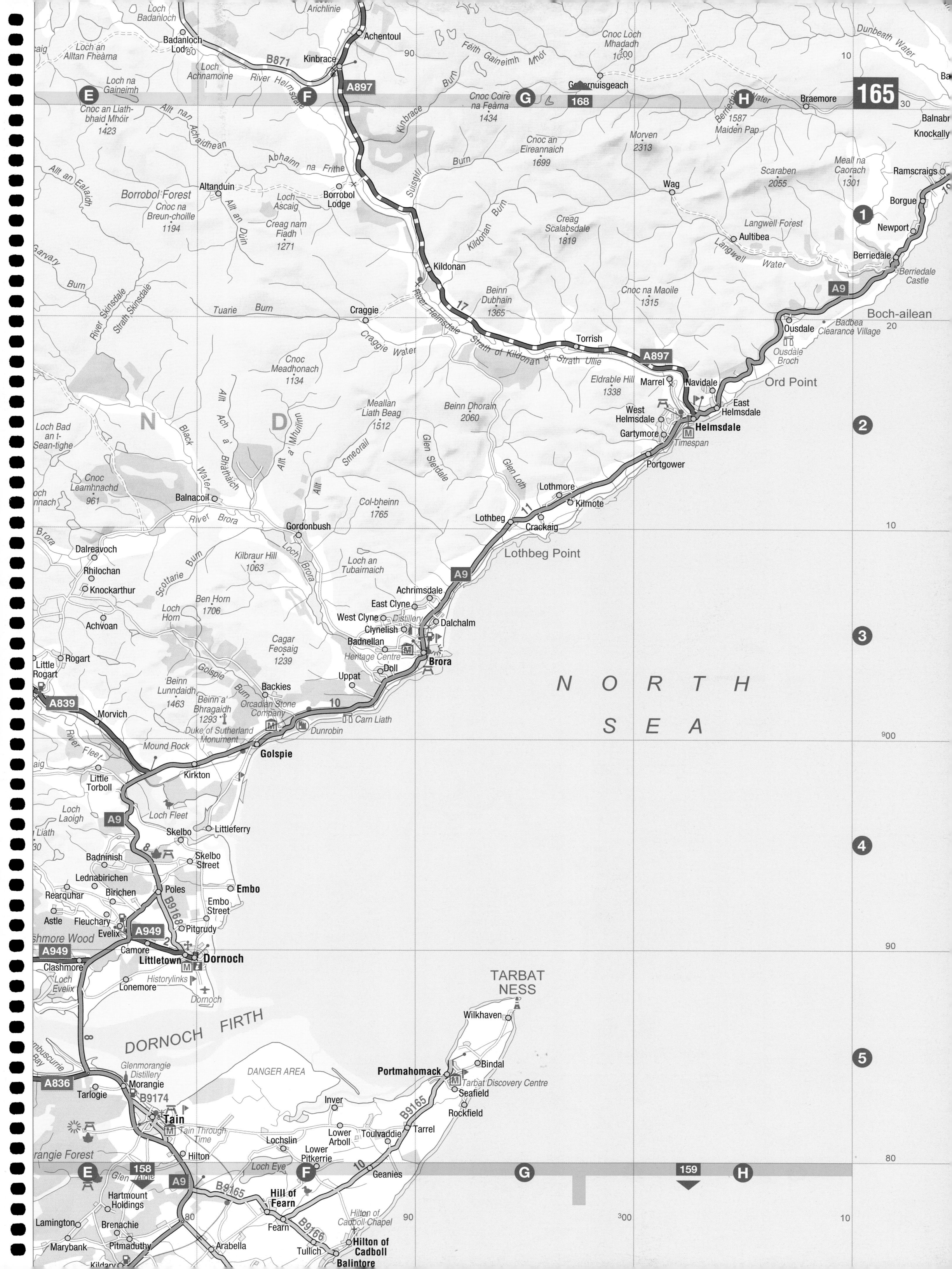
165
168
159
158
NORTH SEA
DORNOCH FIRTH
TARBAT NESS
Helmsdale
Brora
Golspie
Dornoch
Tain
Portmahomack
Embo
Kinbrace
Achentoul
Kildonan
Borrobol Lodge
Altanduin
Borrobol Forest
Craggie
Torrish
Marrel
Navidale
East Helmsdale
West Helmsdale
Gartymore
Timespan
Portgower
Lothmore
Kilmote
Lothbeg
Crackaig
Lothbeg Point
Ord Point
Ousdale
Badbea Clearance Village
Boch-ailean
Berriedale
Berriedale Castle
Newport
Borgue
Ramscraigs
Knockally
Braemore
Wag
Aultibea
Langwell Forest
Morven 2313
Scaraben 2055
Maiden Pap 1587
Achrimsdale
East Clyne
West Clyne
Clynelish
Dalchalm
Badnellan
Heritage Centre
Doll
Uppat
Backies
Carn Liath
Dunrobin
Duke of Sutherland Monument
Mound Rock
Kirkton
Little Torboll
Loch Fleet
Skelbo
Littleferry
Skelbo Street
Badninish
Lednabirichen
Birichen
Poles
Rearquhar
Astle
Fleuchary
Evelix
Embo Street
Pitgrudy
Camore
Littletown
Clashmore
Lonemore
Historylinks
Morvich
Rogart
Little Rogart
Achvoan
Knockarthur
Rhilochan
Dalreavoch
Balnacoil
Gordonbush
Wilkhaven
Bindal
Seafield
Rockfield
Tarbat Discovery Centre
Tarrel
Toulvaddie
Inver
Lower Arboll
Lochslin
Lower Pitkerrie
Geanies
Hilton
Glenmorangie Distillery
Morangie
Tarlogie
Tain Through Time
Hill of Fearn
Fearn
Tullich
Hilton of Cadboll
Balintore
Hartmount Holdings
Brenachie
Lamington
Marybank
Pitmaduthy
Arabella
DANGER AREA
A9
A897
A839
A949
A836
B871
B9168
B9174
B9165
B9166

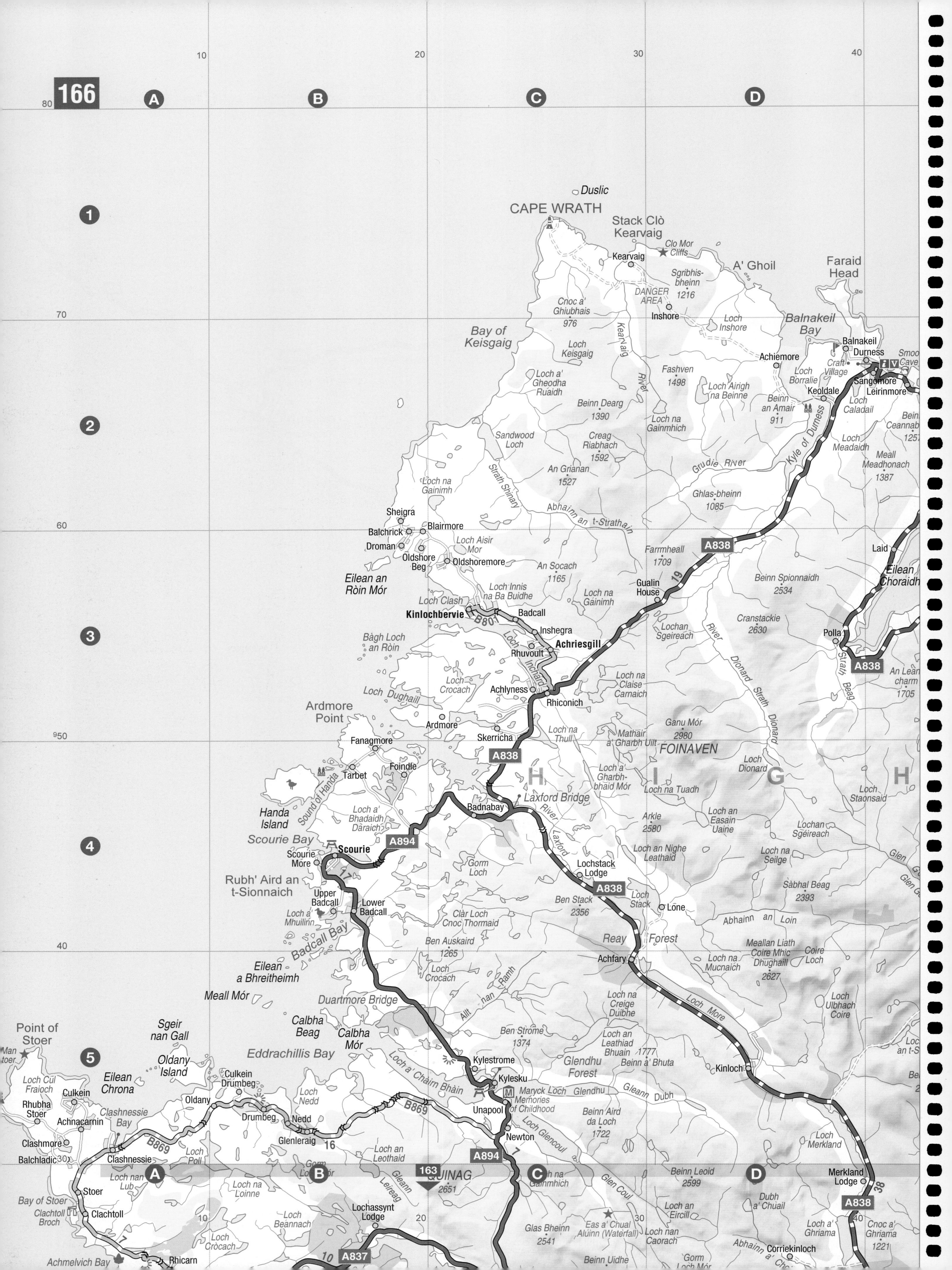

A
B
C
D
1
2
3
4
5
10
20
30
40
80
70
60
50
Duslic
CAPE WRATH
Stack Clò Kearvaig
Clo Mor Cliffs
Kearvaig
A' Ghoil
Faraid Head
Sgribhis-bheinn 1216
DANGER AREA
Inshore
Cnoc a' Ghiubhais 976
Bay of Keisgaig
Loch Keisgaig
Kearvaig River
Loch Inshore
Balnakeil Bay
Balnakeil
Durness
Achiemore
Craft Village
Fashven 1498
Loch Borralie
Sangomore
Leirinmore
Loch a' Gheodha Ruaidh
Loch Airigh na Beinne
Keoldale
Loch Caladail
Beinn Dearg 1390
Beinn an Amair 911
Loch na Gainmhich
Kyle of Durness
Sandwood Loch
Creag Riabhach 1592
Loch Meadaidh
Meall Meadhonach 1387
Strath Shinary
An Grianan 1527
Grudie River
Loch na Gainimh
Ghlas-bheinn 1085
Abhainn an t-Strathain
Sheigra
Balchrick
Blairmore
Droman
Loch Aisir Mor
Oldshore Beg
Oldshoremore
An Socach 1165
Farrmheall 1709
A838
Laid
Eilean an Ròin Mór
Gualin House
Beinn Spionnaidh 2534
Eilean Choraidh
Loch Innis na Ba Buidhe
Loch na Gainimh
Loch Clash
Kinlochbervie
B801
Badcall
Lochan Sgeireach
Cranstackie 2630
Inshegra
Polla
Bàgh Loch an Ròin
Achriesgill
Rhuvoult
River Dionard
Strath Beag
Loch Inchard
Loch Crocach
Loch na Claise Carnaich
An Lean charm 1705
Loch Dughaill
Achlyness
Rhiconich
Ardmore Point
Ardmore
Ganu Mór 2980
Strath Dionard
Skerricha
Loch na Thull
Mathair a' Gharbh Uilt
FOINAVEN
Fanagmore
Loch Dionard
Foindle
Tarbet
H
I
G
H
Loch a' Gharbh-bhaid Mór
Loch na Tuadh
Loch Staonsaid
Sound of Handa
Laxford Bridge
Badnabay
Handa Island
Loch a' Bhadaidh Daraich
River Laxford
Arkle 2580
Loch an Easain Uaine
Lochan Sgéireach
Scourie Bay
Scourie
A894
Scourie More
Loch an Nighe Leathaid
Loch na Seilge
Gorm Loch
Lochstack Lodge
Rubh' Aird an t-Sionnaich
Sàbhal Beag 2393
Upper Badcall
Lower Badcall
Loch Stack
Ben Stack 2356
Lone
Loch a' Mhuilinn
Clàr Loch
Cnoc Thormaid
Abhainn an Loin
Badcall Bay
Ben Auskaird 1265
Reay Forest
Meallan Liath Coire Mhic Dhughaill 2627
Coire Loch
Eilean a Bhreitheimh
Loch Crocach
Achfary
Loch na Mucnaich
Meall Mór
Allt nan Ramh
Loch Ulbhach Coire
Duartmore Bridge
Loch na Creige Duibhe
Loch More
Point of Stoer
Sgeir nan Gall
Calbha Beag
Calbha Mór
Ben Strome 1374
Loch an Leathiad Bhuain
Eddrachillis Bay
Kylestrome
Glendhu Forest
1777 Beinn a' Bhuta
Kinloch
Oldany Island
Eilean Chrona
Loch Cùl Fraioch
Culkein Drumbeg
Loch a' Chàirn Bhàin
Kylesku
Maryck Loch
Glendhu
Culkein
Memories of Childhood
Gleann Dubh
Rhubha Stoer
Clashnessie Bay
Oldany
Loch Nedd
Drumbeg
Nedd
B869
Unapool
Beinn Aird da Loch 1722
Achnacarnin
Loch Glencoul
Clashmore
B869
Glenleraig
16
Newton
Loch Merkland
Balchladich
Clashnessie
Loch Poll
Loch an Leothaid
A894
7
163
QUINAG 2651
Glen Coul
Beinn Leoid 2599
Merkland Lodge
Loch nan Lub
Loch na Loinne
Gleann Leireag
38
Stoer
Bay of Stoer
Clachtoll Broch
Clachtoll
Loch Beannach
Lochassynt Lodge
Dubh a' Chuail
A838
Loch an Eircill
Eas a' Chual Aluinn (Waterfall)
Loch a' Ghriama
Cnoc a' Ghriama 1221
Loch Cròcach
Glas Bheinn 2541
Loch nan Caorach
Corriekinloch
Achmelvich Bay
Rhicarn
A837
10
Beinn Uidhe

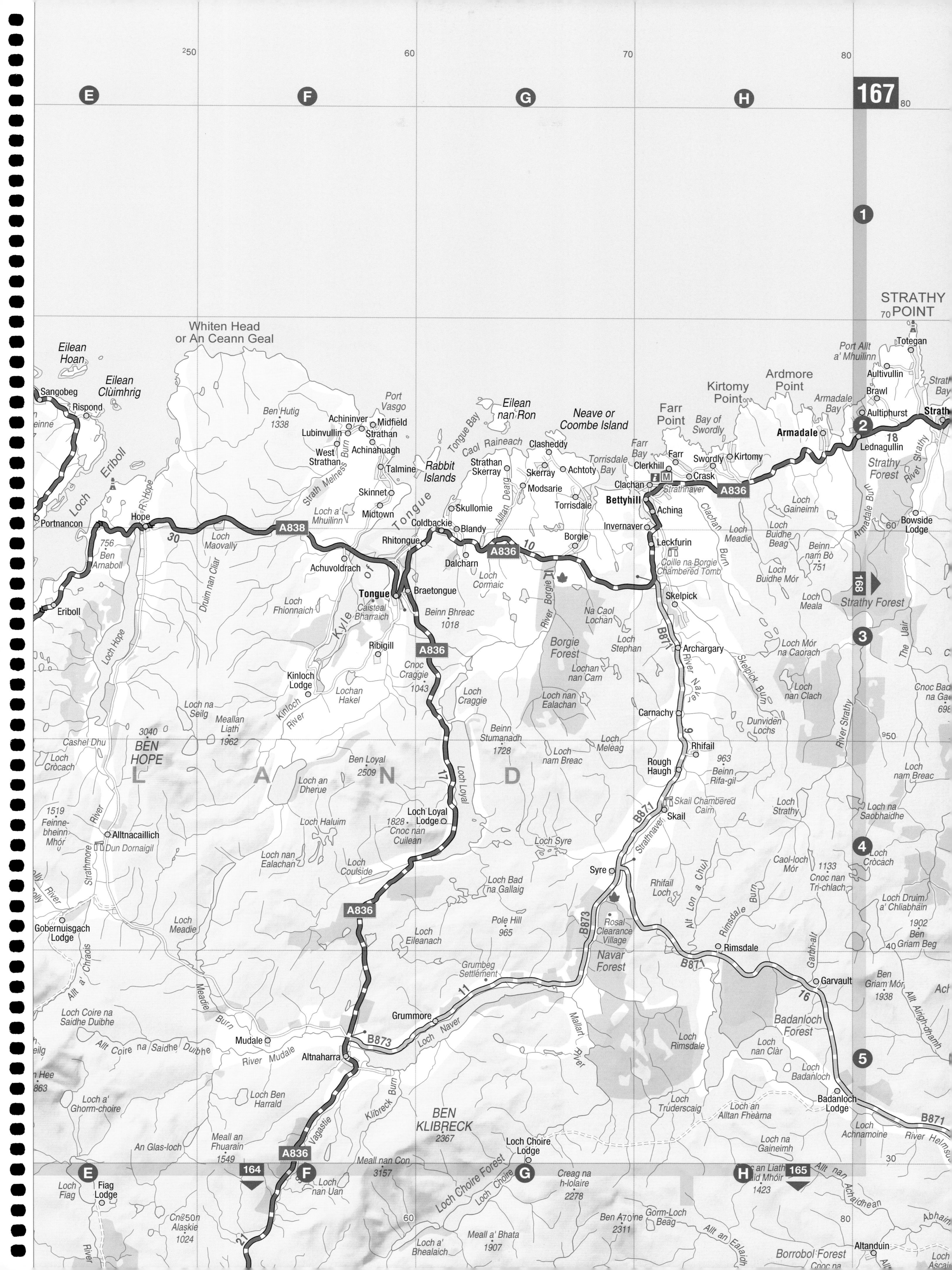

STRATHY POINT
Whiten Head or An Ceann Geal
Eilean Hoan
Eilean Clùimhrig
Sangobeg
Rispond
Loch Eriboll
Portnancon
Hope
Eriboll
Ben Hutig 1338
Achininver
Midfield
Lubinvullin
Strathan
West Strathan
Achinahuagh
Talmine
Port Vasgo
Rabbit Islands
Skinnet
Midtown
Kyle of Tongue
Tongue Bay
Eilean nan Ron
Neave or Coombe Island
Farr Point
Kirtomy Point
Ardmore Point
Armadale Bay
Armadale
Totegan
Port Allt a' Mhuilinn
Aultivullin
Brawl
Aultiphurst
Lednagullin
Strathy Forest
Clasheddy
Skerray
Achtoty
Modsarie
Torrisdale
Torrisdale Bay
Farr Bay
Farr
Clerkhill
Swordly
Bay of Swordly
Kirtomy
Crask
Clachan
Bettyhill
Achina
Invernaver
Leckfurin
Coille na Borgie Chambered Tomb
Skelpick
Strathan Skerray
Caol Raineach
Skullomie
Coldbackie
Blandy
Rhitongue
Dalcharn
Borgie
A838
A836
B871
B873
Loch Maovally
Achuvoldrach
Tongue
Braetongue
Caisteal Bharraich
Beinn Bhreac 1018
Ribigill
Cnoc Craggie 1043
Kinloch Lodge
Lochan Hakel
Loch Craggie
Borgie Forest
Na Caol Lochan
Loch Stephan
Archargary
River Naver
Loch Fhionnaich
Loch na Seilg
Meallan Liath 1962
BEN HOPE 3040
Cashel Dhu
Loch Crocach
L A N D
Ben Loyal 2509
Loch an Dherue
Loch Loyal
Loch Loyal Lodge
Cnoc nan Cuilean 1828
Loch Haluim
Beinn Stumanadh 1728
Loch nam Breac
Loch Meleag
Carnachy
Rhifail
Rough Haugh
Beinn Rifa-gil 963
Skail Chambered Cairn
Skail
Loch Syre
Syre
Rosal Clearance Village
Navar Forest
Rimsdale
Garvault
Badanloch Forest
Loch Badanloch
Badanloch Lodge
Alltnacaillich
Dun Dornaigil
Strathmore River
Feinne-bheinn Mhór 1519
Loch nan Ealachan
Loch Coulside
Loch Bad na Gallaig
Pole Hill 965
Loch Eileanach
Grumbeg Settlement
Gobernuisgach Lodge
Loch Meadie
Grummore
Loch Naver
Mudale
River Mudale
Altnaharra
Loch Ben Harrald
BEN KLIBRECK 2367
Loch Coire na Saidhe Duibhe
Loch a' Ghorm-choire
Meall an Fhuarain 1549
An Glas-loch
Loch Choire Lodge
Loch Choire Forest
Meall nan Con 3157
Loch Rimsdale
Loch Truderscaig
Loch an Alltan Fhearna
Loch nan Clàr
Loch Achnamoine
Loch na Gaineimh
River Helmsdale
Loch Fiag
Fiag Lodge
Loch nan Uan
Creag na h-Ioiaire 2278
Ben Armine 2311
Gorm-Loch Beag
Meall a' Bhata 1907
Loch a' Bhealaich
Cnoc Alaskie 1024
Borrobol Forest
Altanduin
Loch Mór na Caorach
Loch nan Clach
Dunviden Lochs
Loch Strathy
Loch na Saobhaidhe
Loch Crocach
Caol-loch Mór
Cnoc nan Tri-chlach 1133
Loch Druim a' Chliabhain
Ben Griam Beg 1902
Ben Griam Mór 1938
Beinn nam Bò 751
Loch Meala
Loch Buidhe Mór
Loch Buidhe Beag
Loch Gaineimh
Loch Meadie
Bowside Lodge
Strathy Forest
168
164
165

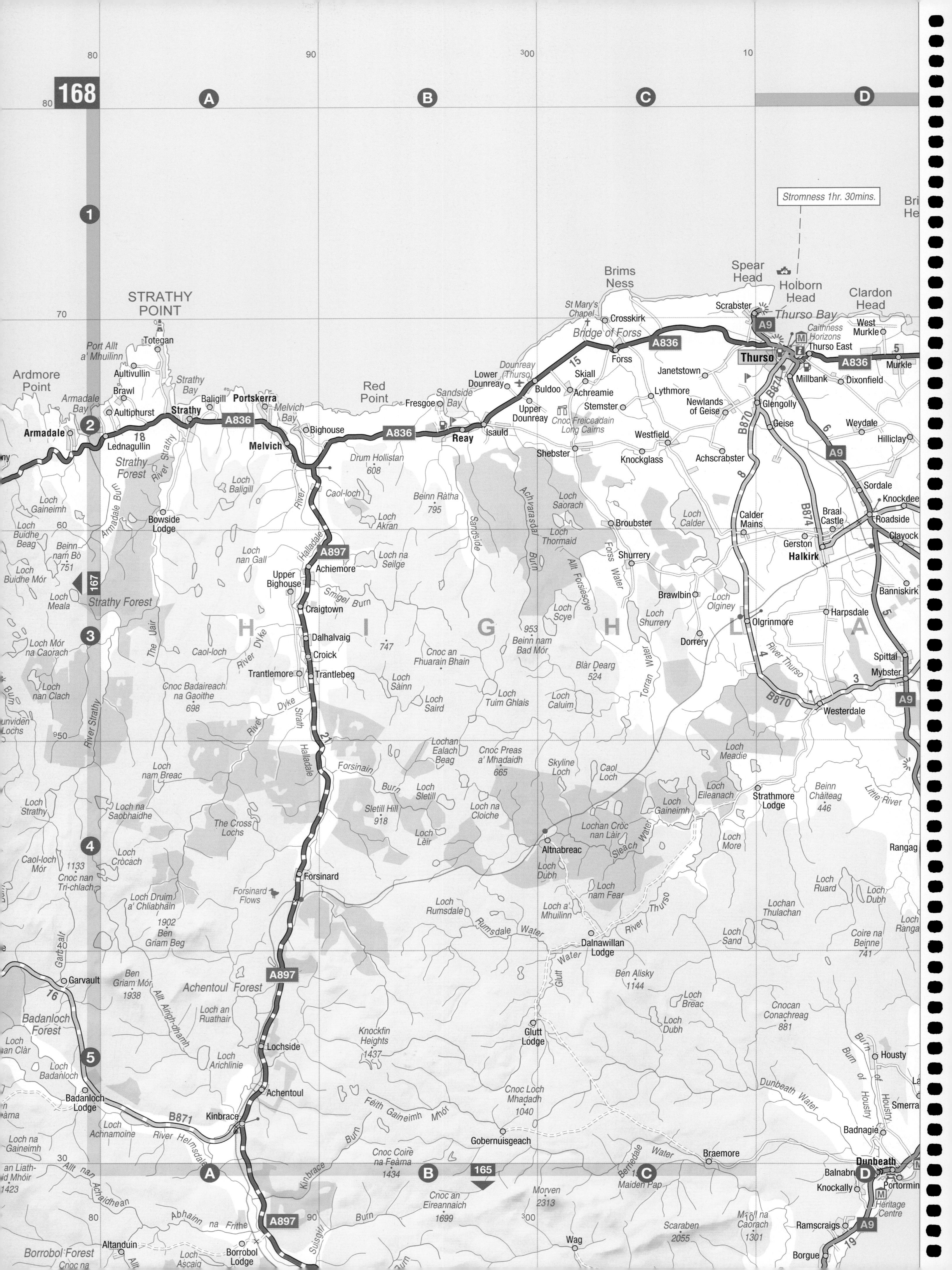

STRATHY POINT
Ardmore Point
Armadale
Strathy
Portskerra
Melvich
Bighouse
Red Point
Fresgoe
Reay
Isauld
Lower Dounreay
Dounreay (Thurso)
Upper Dounreay
Buldoo
Brims Ness
Crosskirk
Bridge of Forss
Forss
A836
Spear Head
Holborn Head
Clardon Head
Scrabster
Thurso Bay
Thurso
Thurso East
Caithness Horizons
West Murkle
Murkle
Stromness 1hr. 30mins.
Millbank
Dixonfield
Janetstown
Lythmore
Skiall
Achreamie
Stemster
Newlands of Geise
Glengolly
Geise
Weydale
Hilliclay
Cnoc Freiceadain Long Cairns
Shebster
Westfield
Knockglass
Achscrabster
Drum Hollistan 608
Beinn Ràtha 795
Loch Saorach
Broubster
Loch Calder
Calder Mains
Braal Castle
Sordale
Knockdee
Roadside
Clayock
Gerston
Halkirk
Shurrery
Brawlbin
Loch Olginey
Olgrinmore
Harpsdale
Banniskirk
Dorrery
Spittal
Mybster
Westerdale
A9
B874
B870
HIGHLAND
Lednagullin
Strathy Forest
Totegan
Port Allt a' Mhuilinn
Aultivullin
Strathy Bay
Brawl
Baligill
Aultiphurst
Armadale Bay
Loch Baligill
Bowside Lodge
Loch Gaineimh
Loch Buidhe Beag
Beinn nam Bò 751
Loch Buidhe Mór
Loch Meala
Strathy Forest
Caol-loch
Loch Akran
A897
Achiemore
Upper Bighouse
Loch nan Gall
Loch na Seilge
Craigtown
Dalhalvaig
Croick
Trantlemore
Trantlebeg
747
Cnoc an Fhuarain Bhain
953 Beinn nam Bad Mór
Blàr Dearg 524
Loch Mór na Caorach
Loch nan Clach
Cnoc Badaireach na Gaoithe 698
Loch Sàinn
Loch Saird
Loch Tuim Ghlais
Loch Caluim
Loch Meadie
Lochan Ealach Beag
Cnoc Preas a' Mhadaidh 665
Skyline Loch
Caol Loch
Loch nam Breac
Loch Sletill
Sletill Hill 918
Loch na Cloiche
Loch Eileanach
Strathmore Lodge
Beinn Châiteag 446
Loch Strathy
Loch na Saobhaidhe
The Cross Lochs
Loch Lèir
Lochan Cròc nan Làir
Loch Gaineimh
Altnabreac
Loch More
Rangag
Loch Cròcach
Caol-loch Mór
1133 Cnoc nan Tri-chlach
Forsinard
Forsinard Flows
Loch Dubh
Loch nam Fear
Loch Ruard
Loch Dubh
Loch Druim a' Chliabhain
1902 Ben Griam Beg
Loch Rumsdale
Loch a' Mhuilinn
Lochan Thulachan
Loch Sand
Coire na Beinne 741
Dalnawillan Lodge
Garvault
Ben Griam Mór 1938
Achentoul Forest
Ben Alisky 1144
Badanloch Forest
Loch an Ruathair
Knockfin Heights 1437
Glutt Lodge
Loch Breac
Loch Dubh
Cnocan Conachreag 881
Lochside
Loch Arichlinie
Loch Badanloch
Badanloch Lodge
Achentoul
Kinbrace
B871
Cnoc Loch Mhadadh 1040
Houstry
Dunbeath Water
Badnagie
Loch Achnamoine
Gobernuisgeach
Braemore
Dunbeath
Balnabruich
Knockally
Portormin
Heritage Centre
Cnoc Coire na Feàrna 1434
Maiden Pap
Cnoc an Eireannaich 1699
Morven 2313
Scaraben 2055
Meall na Caorach 1301
Ramscraigs
Altanduin
Borrobol Forest
Borrobol Lodge
Wag
Borgue
165
167

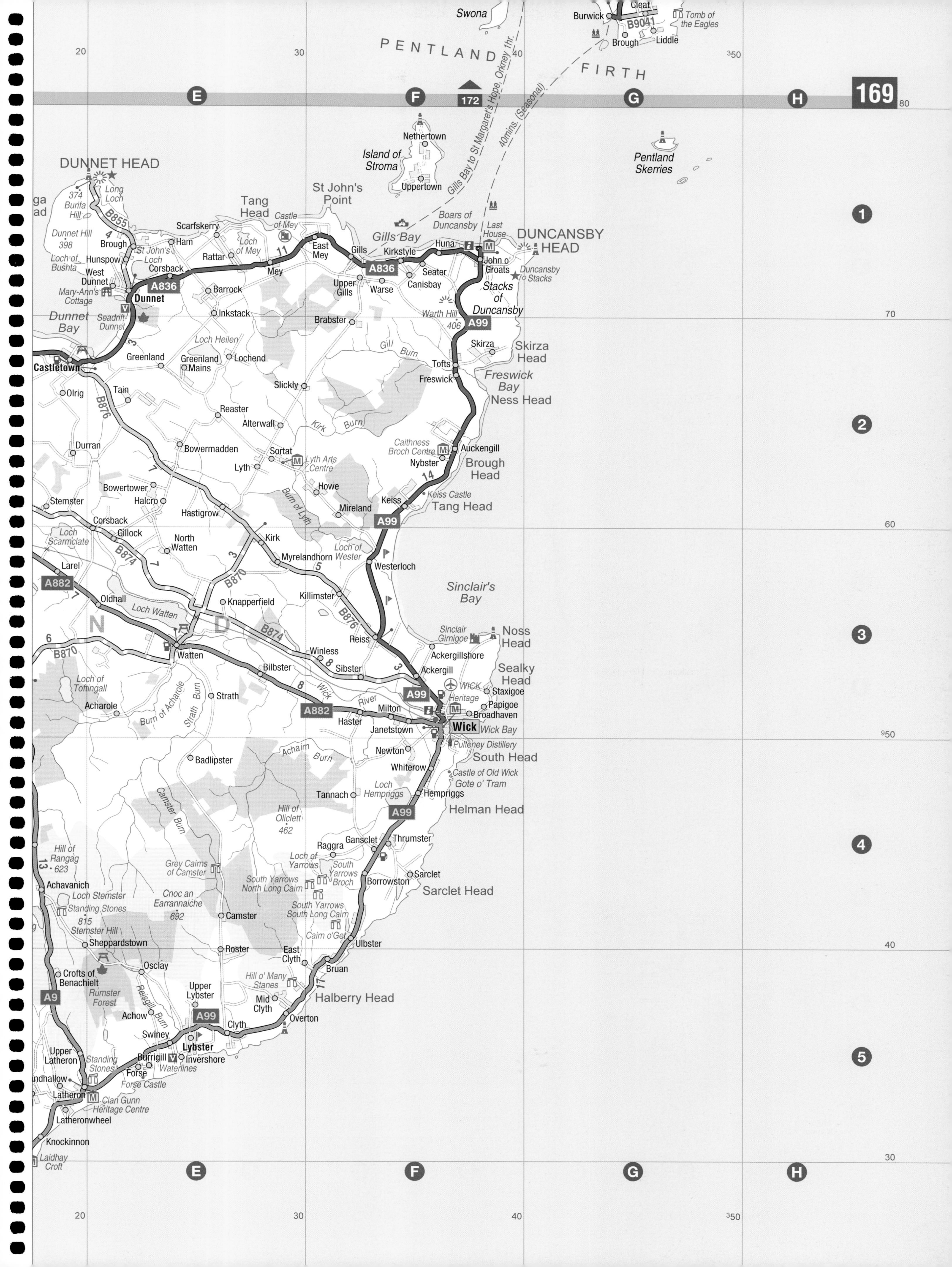
PENTLAND FIRTH
Swona
Burwick
Cleat
B9041
Tomb of the Eagles
Brough
Liddle
172
Gills Bay to St Margaret's Hope, Orkney 1hr.
40mins. (Seasonal)
Nethertown
Island of Stroma
Uppertown
Pentland Skerries
DUNNET HEAD
Long Loch
374 Burifa Hill
Dunnet Hill 398
Brough
B855
Loch of Bushta
Hunspow
West Dunnet
Mary-Ann's Cottage
Dunnet
St John's Loch
Corsback
Ham
Scarfskerry
Tang Head
Castle of Mey
Loch of Mey
Rattar
Mey
A836
Barrock
Inkstack
St John's Point
East Mey
Gills
Gills Bay
Kirkstyle
Huna
Boars of Duncansby
Last House
DUNCANSBY HEAD
John o' Groats
Duncansby Stacks
Stacks of Duncansby
Seater
Canisbay
Upper Gills
Warse
Brabster
Warth Hill 406
A99
Dunnet Bay
Seadrift Dunnet
Castletown
Greenland
Greenland Mains
Loch Heilen
Lochend
Slickly
Gil Burn
Skirza
Skirza Head
Tofts
Freswick
Freswick Bay
Ness Head
Olrig
Tain
B876
Reaster
Alterwall
Kirk Burn
Durran
Bowermadden
Sortat
Lyth Arts Centre
Lyth
Caithness Broch Centre
Auckengill
Nybster
Brough Head
Bowertower
Halcro
Stemster
Hastigrow
Howe
Burn of Lyth
Mireland
Keiss
Keiss Castle
Tang Head
Corsback
Gillock
Loch Scarmclate
North Watten
Kirk
B874
Larel
A882
Myrelandhorn
Loch of Wester
Westerloch
B870
Knapperfield
Killimster
Sinclair's Bay
Oldhall
Loch Watten
Reiss
Sinclair Girnigoe
Noss Head
Ackergillshore
Watten
Winless
Sibster
Bilbster
Ackergill
Sealky Head
WICK
Heritage
Staxigoe
Papigoe
Broadhaven
Loch of Toftingall
Acharole
Burn of Acharole
Strath Burn
Strath
Wick River
Milton
Haster
Janetstown
Wick
Wick Bay
Pulteney Distillery
South Head
Badlipster
Achairn Burn
Newton
Whiterow
Castle of Old Wick
Gote o' Tram
Camster Burn
Hill of Oliclett 462
Loch Hempriggs
Tannach
Hempriggs
Helman Head
Hill of Rangag 623
Raggra
Ganselet
Thrumster
Grey Cairns of Camster
Loch of Yarrows
South Yarrows Broch
South Yarrows North Long Cairn
Sarclet
Sarclet Head
Borrowston
Achavanich
Loch Stemster
Standing Stones
Cnoc an Earrannaiche 692
815 Stemster Hill
Camster
South Yarrows South Long Cairn
Cairn o'Get
Ulbster
Sheppardstown
Roster
East Clyth
Oscley
Bruan
Crofts of Benachielt
Rumster Forest
Hill o' Many Stanes
Halberry Head
A9
Achow
Reisgill Burn
Upper Lybster
Mid Clyth
Overton
Swiney
Clyth
Upper Latheron
Standing Stones
Burrigill
Lybster
Invershore
Forse
Waterlines
Forse Castle
Latheron
Clan Gunn Heritage Centre
Latheronwheel
Knockinnon
Laidhay Croft
E
F
G
H
1
2
3
4
5
20
30
40
350
80
70
60
950
40
30

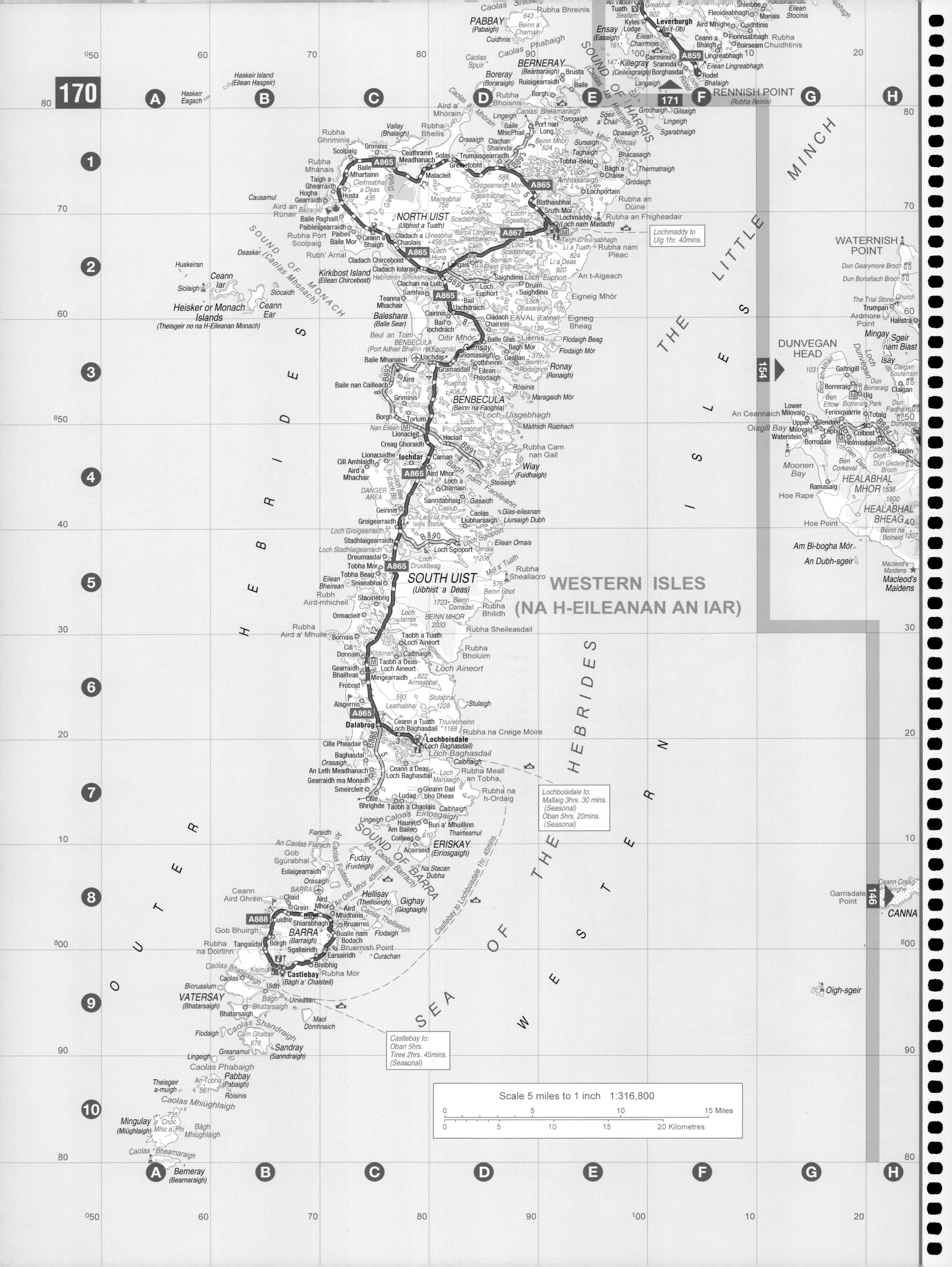

170
PABBAY
(Pabaigh)
BERNERAY
(Bearnaraigh)
SOUND OF HARRIS
Leverburgh
(An t-Ob)
Ensay
(Easaigh)
Killegray
(Ceileagraigh)
A859
RENNISH POINT
(Rubha Reinis)
171
Haskeir Island
(Eilean Hasgeir)
Haskeir Eagach
Boreray
(Boraraigh)
Vallay
(Bhalaigh)
Griminis
Scolpaig
A865
Solas
Malacleit
Ceathramh Meadhanach
Greinetobht
Trumaisgearraidh
B893
Lochportain
Blathaisbhal
Lochmaddy
(Loch nam Madadh)
NORTH UIST
(Uibhist a Tuath)
A867
Lochmaddy to Uig 1hr. 40mins.
Causamul
Huskeiran
Siolaigh
Ceann Iar
Heisker or Monach Islands
(Theisgeir no na H-Eileanan Monach)
Ceann Ear
SOUND OF MONACH
(Caolas Mhonach)
Kirkibost Island
(Eilean Chircebost)
Cladach Chirceboist
Cladach Iolaraigh
Clachan na Luib
B894
Langais
Saighdinis
Loch Euphort
Eigneig Mhòr
Eigneig Bheag
Baleshare
(Baile Sear)
Cairinis
EAVAL
(Eabhal)
Grimsay
(Griomasaigh)
Flodaigh Beag
Flodaigh Mòr
Ronay
(Ronaigh)
Baile Mhanaich
Uachdar
BENBECULA
(Port Adhair Bheinn na Faoghla)
Baile nan Cailleach
B892
Griminis
BENBECULA
(Beinn na Faoghla)
Loch Uisgebhagh
Borgh
Torlum
Nan Eilean
Lionacleit
Creag Ghoraidh
B891
Rubha Cam nan Gall
Lionacuidhe
Iochdar
Carnan
Cill Amhlaidh
Aird a' Mhachair
A865
Aird Mhor
Loch a Charnain
Wiay
(Fuidhaigh)
DANGER AREA
Sanndabhaig
Geirinis
Groigearraidh
Caolas Liubharsaigh
Loch Groigearraidh
Stadhlaigearraidh
B890
Loch Sgioport
Eilean Ornais
Dreumasdal
Tobha Mòr
Tobha Beag
Sniseabhal
Eilean Bheirean
Staoinebrig
SOUTH UIST
(Uibhist a Deas)
Rubha Sheallacro
BEINN MHOR
2033
Ormacleit
Rubha Bhilidh
Rubha Aird a' Mhuile
Bornais
Rubha Sheileasdail
Cill Donnain
Taobh a Tuath Loch Aineort
Taobh a Deas Loch Aineort
Loch Aineort
Gearraidh Bhailteas
Frobost
Mingearraidh
Stulaigh
Aisgernis
Dalabrog
Ceann a Tuath Loch Baghasdail
Rubha na Creige Mòire
Lochboisdale
(Loch Baghasdail)
Cille Pheadair
B888
Baghasdal
Orasaigh
An Leth Meadhanach
Gearraidh ma Monadh
Smeircleit
Ceann a Deas Loch Baghasdail
Rubha Meall an Tobha
Rubha na h-Ordaig
Cille Bhrighde
Ludag
Taobh a Chaolais
Lochboisdale to: Mallaig 3hrs. 30 mins. (Seasonal) Oban 5hrs. 20mins. (Seasonal)
Eriosgaigh
ERISKAY
(Eiriosgaigh)
Am Baile
Coilleag
Acairseid
Fiaraidh
Gob Sgùrabhal
Eolaigearraidh
Fuday
(Fuideigh)
SOUND OF BARRA
(An Caolas Barrach)
Na Stacan Dubha
BARRA
Hellisay
(Theilisaigh)
Gighay
(Gioghaigh)
Ceann Aird Ghrèin
Cliaid
Grein
A888
Cuidhir
Bagh Shiarabhagh
Bruairnis
Gob Bhuirgh
Rubha na Doirlinn
Tangasdal
Borgh
BARRA
(Barraigh)
Buaile nam Bodach
Bruernish Point
Flodaigh
Curachan
Sgallairidh
Earsairidh
Breibhig
Castlebay
(Bàgh a' Chaisteil)
Rubha Mòr
Castlebay to Lochboisdale 1hr. 45mins.
Bioruaslum
VATERSAY
(Bhatarsaigh)
Uidh
Uineasan
Maol Dòmhnaich
Castlebay to: Oban 5hrs. Tiree 2hrs. 45mins. (Seasonal)
Caolas Shandraigh
Flodaigh
Greanamul
Sandray
(Sanndraigh)
Lingeigh
Caolas Phabaigh
Pabbay
(Pabaigh)
Theisgeir a-muigh
Roisinis
Caolas Mhiùghlaigh
Mingulay
(Miùghlaigh)
Bàgh Mhiùghlaigh
Caolas Bhearnaraigh
Berneray
(Bearnaraigh)
OUTER HEBRIDES
SEA OF THE HEBRIDES
THE LITTLE MINCH
WESTERN ISLES
(NA H-EILEANAN AN IAR)
THE WESTERN ISLES
WATERNISH POINT
DUNVEGAN HEAD
154
Galtrigill
Borreraig
Claigan
Lower Milovaig
Upper Milovaig
Glendale
Waterstein
Colbost
Skinidin
Totaig
Dunvegan
Moonen Bay
Ramasaig
HEALABHAL MHOR
HEALABHAL BHEAG
Hoe Rape
Hoe Point
Am Bi-bogha Mór
An Dubh-sgeir
Macleod's Maidens
Mingay
Isay
Trumpan
Halistra
Oisgill Bay
An Ceannaich
146
Garrisdale Point
CANNA
Oigh-sgeir
Scale 5 miles to 1 inch 1:316,800
0 5 10 15 Miles
0 5 10 15 20 Kilometres

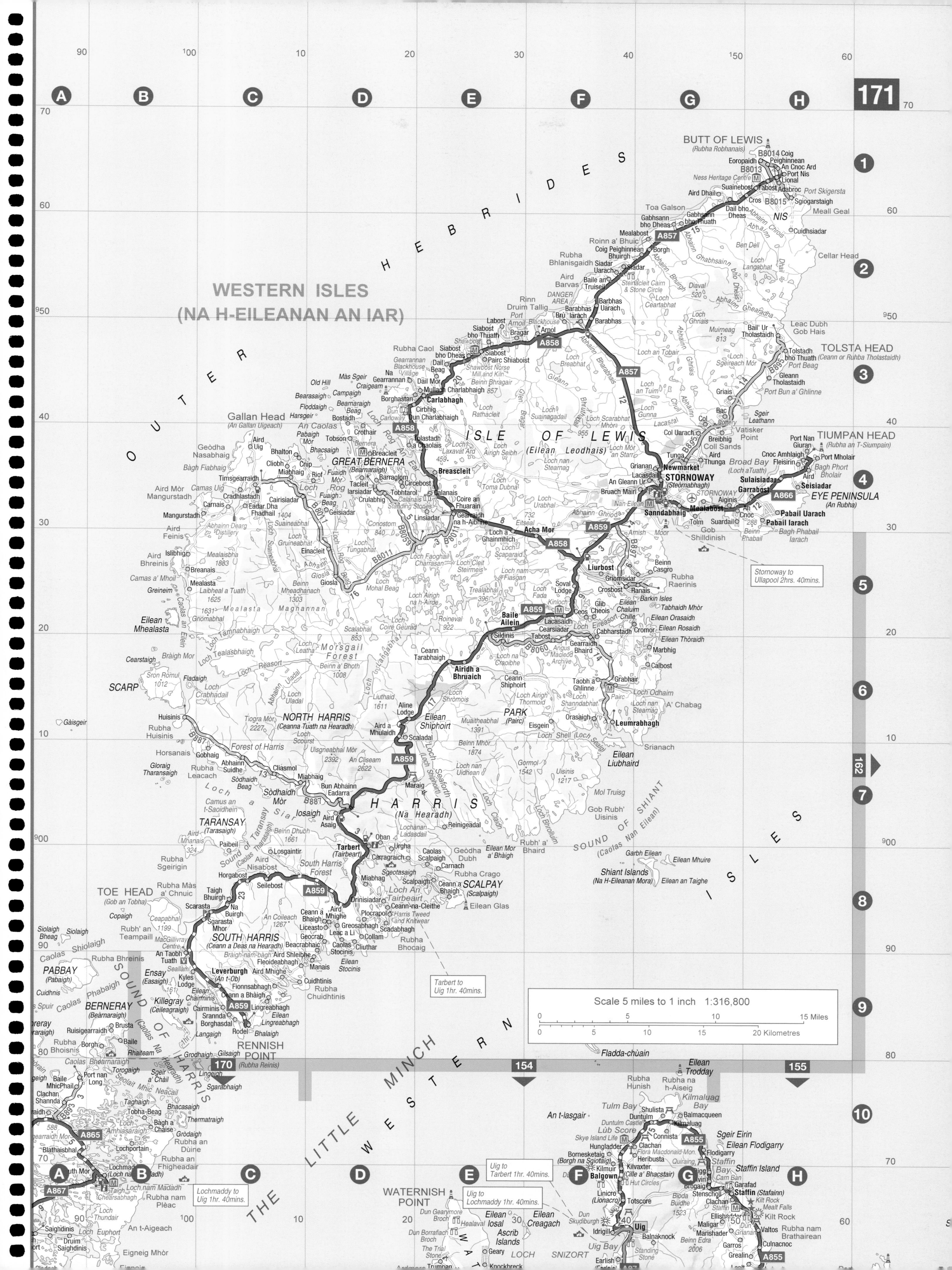
171
WESTERN ISLES
(NA H-EILEANAN AN IAR)
OUTER HEBRIDES
BUTT OF LEWIS
(Rubha Robhanais)
Port Skigersta
NIS
Cellar Head
Toa Galson
TOLSTA HEAD
(Ceann or Rubha Tholastaidh)
Gallan Head
(An Gallan Uigeach)
ISLE OF LEWIS
(Eilean Leodhais)
GREAT BERNERA
(Bearnaraigh)
TIUMPAN HEAD
(Rubha an T-Siumpain)
Broad Bay
(Loch aTuath)
STORNOWAY
(Steòrnabhagh)
EYE PENINSULA
(An Rubha)
Stornoway to
Ullapool 2hrs. 40mins.
Eilean Mhealasta
SCARP
NORTH HARRIS
(Ceanna Tuath na Hearadh)
Forest of Harris
PARK
(Pairc)
Eilean Liubhaird
HARRIS
(Nà Hearadh)
TARANSAY
(Tarasaigh)
Tarbert
(Tairbeart)
SOUND OF SHIANT
(Caolas Nan Eilean)
Shiant Islands
(Na H-Eileanan Mora)
SCALPAY
(Scalpaigh)
Eilean Glas
TOE HEAD
(Gob an Tobha)
SOUTH HARRIS
(Ceann a Deas na Hearadh)
PABBAY
(Pabaigh)
BERNERAY
(Beàrnaraigh)
SOUND OF HARRIS
Leverburgh
(An t-Ob)
RENNISH POINT
(Rubha Reinis)
Tarbert to
Uig 1hr. 40mins.
Scale 5 miles to 1 inch 1:316,800
15 Miles
20 Kilometres
THE LITTLE MINCH
WESTERN ISLES
Lochmaddy to
Uig 1hr. 40mins.
Uig to
Tarbert 1hr. 40mins.
Uig to
Lochmaddy 1hr. 40mins.
WATERNISH POINT
Ascrib Islands
Staffin Island
Eilean Flodigarry
Uig
A857
A858
A859
A866
A865
A867
A855
B8011
B8060
170
154
155
162

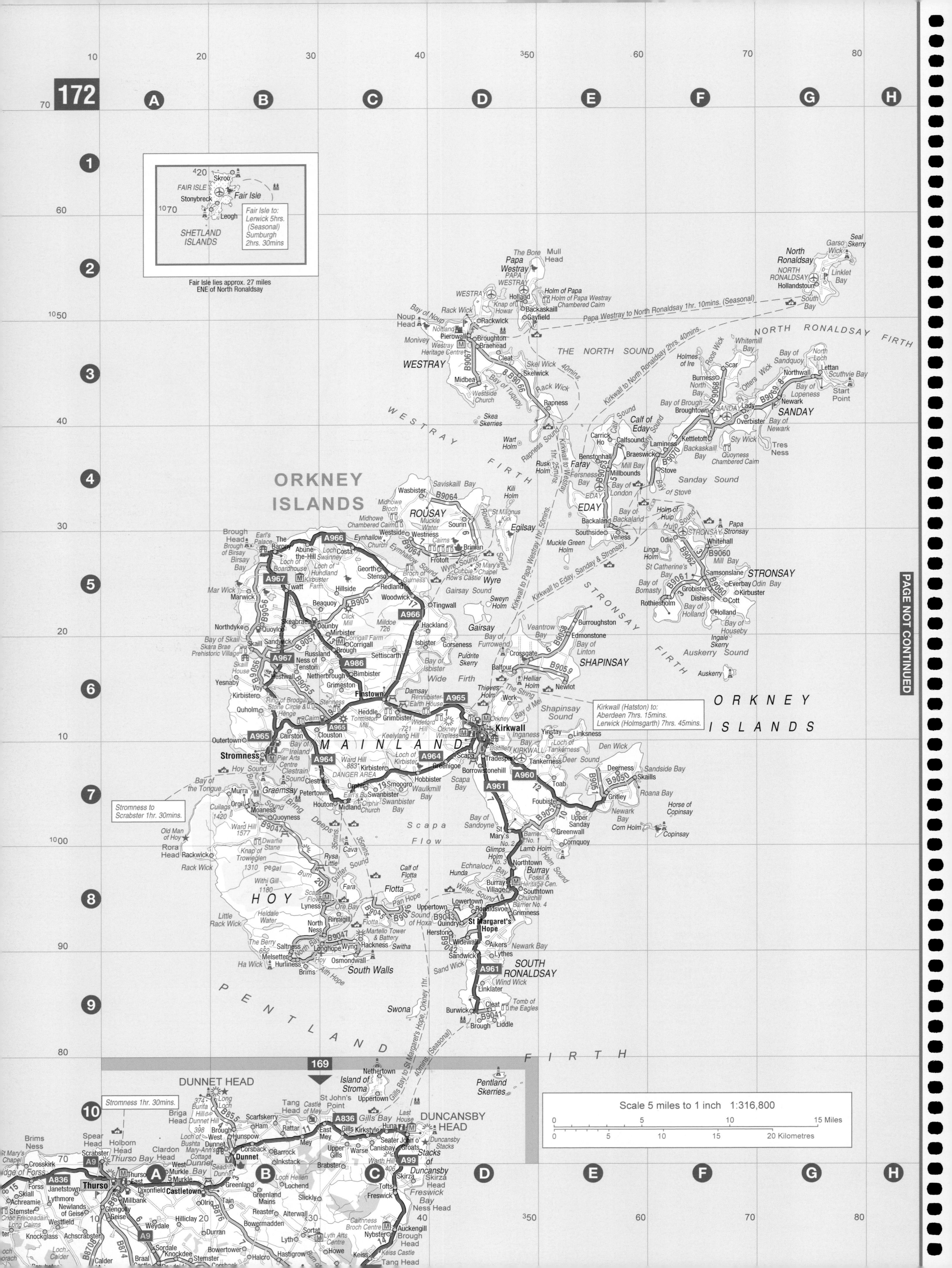

ORKNEY ISLANDS

PAGE NOT CONTINUED

Fair Isle to:
Lerwick 5hrs. (Seasonal)
Sumburgh 2hrs. 30mins.

Fair Isle lies approx. 27 miles
ENE of North Ronaldsay

FAIR ISLE
Skroo
Stonybreck
Fair Isle
Leogh
SHETLAND ISLANDS

WESTRAY
PAPA WESTRAY
North Ronaldsay
NORTH RONALDSAY
Linklet Bay
Hollandstoun
Seal Skerry
Garso Wick

The Bore   Mull Head
Papa Westray
Holm of Papa
Holm of Papa Westray Chambered Cairn
Holland
Backaskaill
Gayfield
Rack Wick
South Bay

Papa Westray to North Ronaldsay 1hr. 10mins. (Seasonal)

NORTH RONALDSAY FIRTH
Whitemill Bay
Bay of Sandquoy
North Loch
Lettan
Scuthvie Bay
Start Point
Northwall
Bay of Lopeness

Noup Head
Bay of Noup
Monivey
Pierowall
Broughton
Braehead
Cleat
Skel Wick
Skelwick
Midbea
Westside Church
Bay of Tuquoy
Rack Wick
Rapness
Skea Skerries
Wart Holm

Westray Heritage Centre

THE NORTH SOUND

Kirkwall to North Ronaldsay 2hrs. 40mins.

Roos Wick
Scar
Holmes of Ire
Burness
North Bay
SANDAY
Lady
Newark
Bay of Brough
Broughtown
Kettletoft
Overbister
Sty Wick
Quoyness Chambered Cairn
Bay of Newark
Tres Ness

WESTRAY FIRTH
Rapness Sound
Kirkwall to Westray 1hr. 25mins.
Calf Sound
Calf of Eday
Carrick Ho
Calfsound
Laminess
Backaskaill Bay
Sanday Sound

ORKNEY ISLANDS

Saviskaill Bay
B906A
Wasbister
Kili Holm
Rusk Holm
Faray
Fersness Bay
EDAY
Bay of London
Bay of Stove
Stove
Millbounds
Mill Bay
Benstonhall
Southside
Veness
Backaland
Bay of Backaland
Holm of Huip
Huip Sound

ROUSAY
Midhowe Broch
Midhowe Chambered Cairn
Muckle Water
St Magnus Kirk
Sourin
Cairns
Westside
Westness
Frotoft
Brinian
Egilsay
Muckle Green Holm

STRONSAY
Papa Stronsay
Whitehall
B9060
Mill Bay
Linga Holm
St Catherine's Bay
Samsonslane
Everbay
Odin Bay
Kirbuster
Grobister
Dishes
Cott
Bay of Holland
Rothiesholm
Holland
Bay of Houseby
Ingale Skerry
Auskerry Sound
Auskerry

Odie
STRONSAY FIRTH

Kirkwall to Eday, Sanday & Stronsay

Eynhallow
Eynhallow Sound
Wyre
Cubbie Row's Castle
Chapel
Wyre Sound
Gairsay
Gairsay Sound
Swein Holm
Rendall
Sweyn Holm
Veantrow Bay
Edmonstone
Burroughston
Bay of Furrowend
Crossgate
Bay of Linton
Balfour
SHAPINSAY
Helliar Holm
Newlot
Work
The String
Thieves Holm
Shapinsay Sound

Bay of Mel

ORKNEY ISLANDS

Kirkwall (Hatston) to:
Aberdeen 7hrs. 15mins.
Lerwick (Holmsgarth) 7hrs. 45mins.

Brough Head
Earl's Palace
The Barony
Brough of Birsay
A966
Abune-the-Hill
Loch of Swannay
Loch Costa
Birsay Bay
A967
Loch of Boardhouse
Loch of Hundland
Kirbuster
Twatt
Marwick
Mar Wick
B9056
Beaquoy
Skeabrae
Dounby
Click Mill
Milldoe 726
Hillside
Woodwick
Tingwall
Redland
Geortth
Stenso
Broch of Gurness
A966
Hackland
Northdyke
Quoyloo
Skaill
Sandwick
Corrigall Farm
Mirbister
Corrigall
Brough
Settiscarth
Isbister
Gorseness
Bay of Isbister
Puldrite Skerry
Balfour
Crossgate

Bay of Skaill
Skara Brae Prehistoric Village
Skaill House
A967
Russland
Ness of Tenston
Netherbrough
A986
Bimbister
Grimeston
Damsay
Rennibister
Earth House
Wide Firth

Yesnaby
Westveil
B9055
Voy
Kirbister
Finstown
Stenness
Ring of Brodgar Stone Circle & Henge
Heddle
Tormiston Mill
Grimbister
Orkney
Wireless Mus
A965

Outertown
A965
Cairston
Clouston
Tongataston
721 Hill
Keelylang Hill
Orkney

Stromness
MAINLAND
Loch of Kirbister
Grimbister
KIRKWALL
Inganess
Distillery
Yinstay
Linksness

Pier Arts Centre
Clestrain
Bay of Ireland
Ward Hill 883
Kirbister
A964
Breenoge
Borrowstonehill
Scapa
Tradespark
Tankerness
Deer Sound
Den Wick

Hoy Sound
Sound
Orphir
Bu
Swanbister
Smoogro
Hobbister
Scapa Bay
A961
A960
Deerness
Sandside Bay
Skaills

Murra
Graemsay
Petertown
Houton
Midland
Orphir Church
Swanbister Bay
Waulkmill Bay
Foubister
Toab
Gritley
B9050
Roana Bay

Bay of the Tongue
Orgil
Moaness
Quoyness
Cuilags 1420
Brinkie's
Ward Hill 1577
Deepdale
Cava
Scapa Flow
Bay of Sandoyne
St Mary's
Upper Sanday
Greenwall
Cornquoy
Newark Bay
Horse of Copinsay

Old Man of Hoy
Dwarfie Stane
Rora Head
Rackwick
Knap of Trowieglen 1310
Pegal
Rysa Little
Gutter Sound
Fara
Flotta
Calf of Flotta
Glimps Holm
Lamb Holm
Northtown
Barrier No. 1
Barrier No. 2
Barrier No. 3
Corn Holm
Copinsay

HOY
Little Rack Wick
Heldale Water
Withi Gill 1180
Burn
Scad Head
North Ness
Lyness
Rinnigill
Ore Bay
Pan Hope
Sound of Hoxa
Uppertown
Lowertown
Ronaldsvoe
BURRAY
Burray Village
Fossil & Heritage Cen.
Southtown
Churchill Barrier No. 4
Grimness
Water Sound
Echnaloch Bay
Hunda
Quindry

The Berry 652
Saltness
Melsetter
Hurliness
Longhope
B9047
Wyng
Hackness
Martello Tower & Battery
Osmondwall
Hoy
Brims
Ha Wick
South Walls
Swona
Switem
Herston
St Margaret's Hope
A961
Widewall
Sandwick
Lythes
SOUTH RONALDSAY
Sand Wick
Wind Wick
Burwick
Cleat
Tomb of the Eagles
Brough
Liddle
Linklater
B9041

Stromness to Scrabster 1hr. 30mins.

Stromness to St Margaret's Hope, Orkney 1hr.
Gills Bay to St Margaret's Hope (Seasonal) 40mins.

PENTLAND FIRTH

Stromness 1hr. 30mins.

169

DUNNET HEAD
Long Loch
Burifa Hill 374
Briga Head
Dunnet Hill 398
Castle of Mey
Tang Head
St John's Point
Uppertown
Netherton
Island of Stroma
Pentland Skerries
DUNCANSBY HEAD

Scale 5 miles to 1 inch   1:316,800
0   5   10   15 Miles
0   5   10   15   20 Kilometres

Scarfskerry
West Dunnet
Hunspow
Scaup
Brough
Ham
Rattar
East Mey
Gills Bay
Kirkstyle
Huna
Canisbay
Seater
John o'Groats
Duncansby Head
Stacks of Duncansby
Skirza Head

A836
Dunnet
Loch of Bushta
Mary-Ann's Cottage
Barrock
Upper Gills
Warse
Corsback
A99
Last House

Spear Head
Holborn Head
Clardon
Thurso Bay
Murkle
Castlehill
Dunnet
Seadrift
Brims Ness
St Mary's Chapel
Crosskirk
Bridge of Forss
A836
Thurso
Dixonfield
Castletown
Olrig
Tain
Greenland
Lochend
Slickly
Freswick
Tofts
Keiss
Auckengill
Nybster
Keiss Castle
Tang Head

Skaill
Millbank
Janetstown
A9
Scrabster
Achreamie
Forss
Lythmore
Newlands of Geise
Geise
Westfield
Braal
Knockglass
Long Cairns
Glengolly
Hilliclay
Durran
Bowermadden
Greenland Mains
Reaster
Alterwall
Warth Hill
Skirza
Ness Head
Freswick Bay
Caithness Broch Centre
Lyth Arts Centre
Lyth
Howe

Brims Ness
West Murkle
Weydale
A9
Sordale
Halcro
Bowertower
Stemster
Corsback
Lyth
Hastigrow
Kirk
Achscrabster
B7043
B876
Sortat
B874

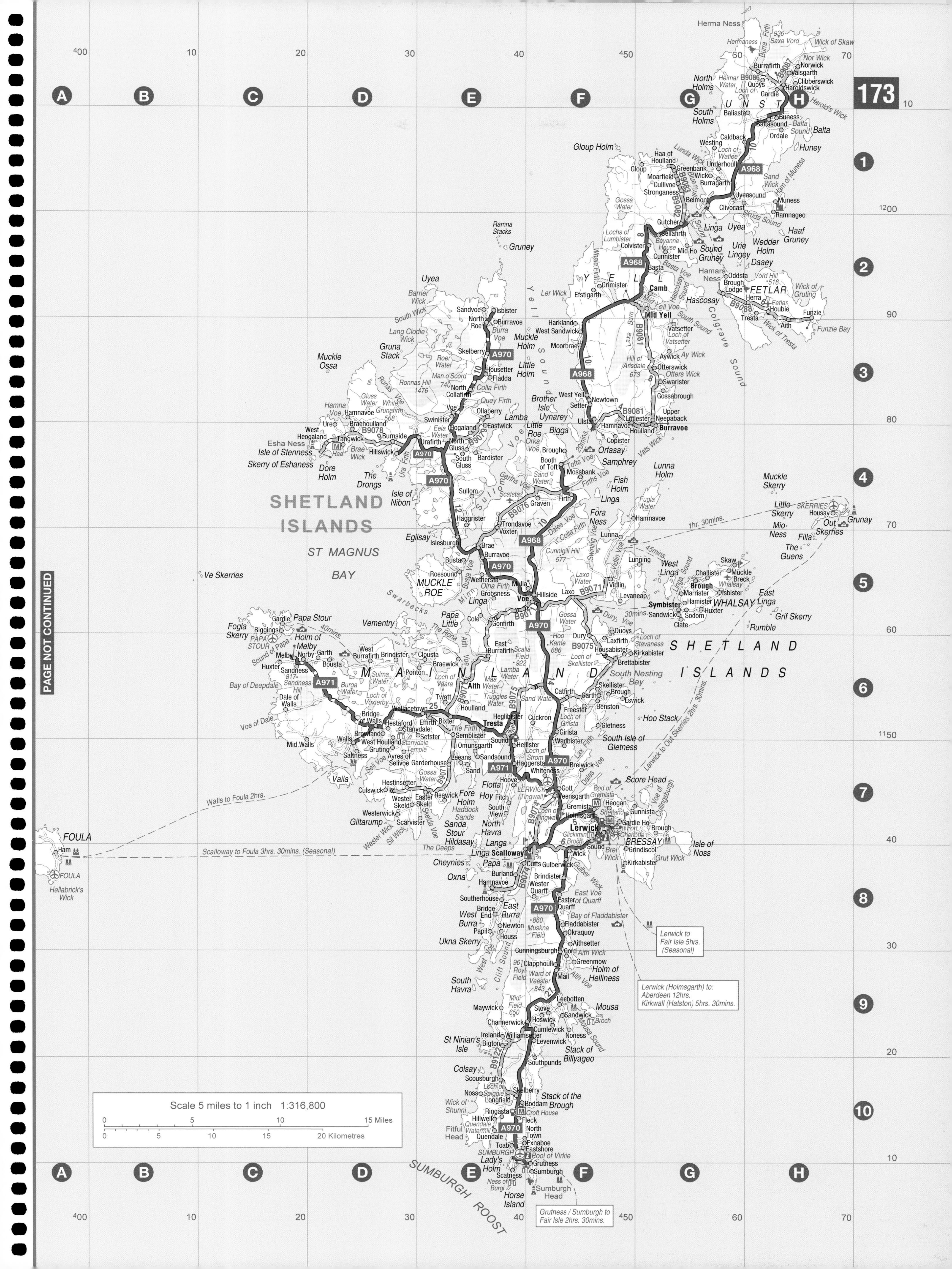

173
PAGE NOT CONTINUED
SHETLAND ISLANDS
ST MAGNUS BAY
MAINLAND
SHETLAND ISLANDS
UNST
YELL
FETLAR
WHALSAY
BRESSAY
MUCKLE ROE
Papa Stour
FOULA
Herma Ness
Saxa Vord
Wick of Skaw
Haroldswick
Norwick
Baltasound
Balta
Huney
Uyeasound
Muness
Haaf Gruney
Gloup Holm
Gutcher
Cullivoe
Linga
Uyea
Mid Yell
Hascosay
Colgrave Sound
Burravoe
Lunna Holm
Muckle Skerry
Out Skerries
Grunay
Housay
Ramna Stacks
Gruney
Uyea
North Roe
Muckle Ossa
Gruna Stack
Ronas Hill 1476
Hillswick
Esha Ness
Isle of Stenness
Skerry of Eshaness
Dore Holm
The Drongs
Isle of Nibon
Sullom
Brae
Voe
Ve Skerries
Vementry
Papa Little
Aith
Walls
Vaila
Tresta
Symbister
Grif Skerry
Rumble
Score Head
Lerwick
Isle of Noss
Scalloway
Cheynies
Oxna
West Burra
East Burra
Ukna Skerry
South Havra
Mousa
Holm of Helliness
St Ninian's Isle
Colsay
Stack of Billyageo
Stack of the Brough
Fitful Head
Lady's Holm
Horse Island
Sumburgh Head
SUMBURGH ROOST
A968
A970
A971
B9081
B9075
B9071
B9074
Walls to Foula 2hrs.
Scalloway to Foula 3hrs. 30mins. (Seasonal)
Lerwick to Fair Isle 5hrs. (Seasonal)
Lerwick (Holmsgarth) to: Aberdeen 12hrs. Kirkwall (Hatston) 5hrs. 30mins.
Grutness / Sumburgh to Fair Isle 2hrs. 30mins.
Lerwick to Out Skerries 2hrs. 30mins.
1hr. 30mins.
Scale 5 miles to 1 inch 1:316,800
0 5 10 15 Miles
0 5 10 15 20 Kilometres
A B C D E F G H
1 2 3 4 5 6 7 8 9 10
400 10 20 30 40 450 60 70
1200 90 80 70 60 1150 40 30 20 10

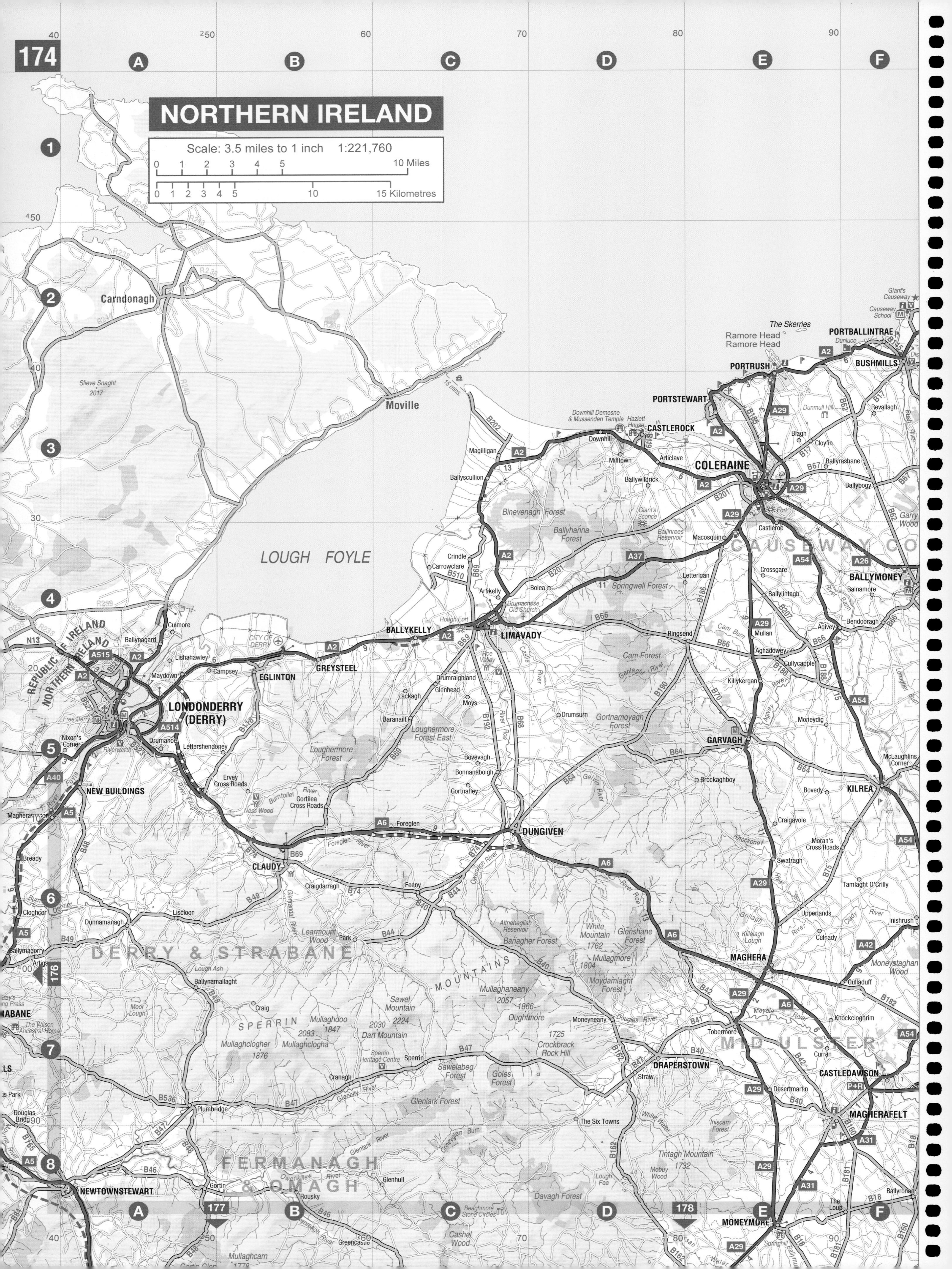
NORTHERN IRELAND
Scale: 3.5 miles to 1 inch 1:221,760
10 Miles
15 Kilometres
LOUGH FOYLE
Carndonagh
Moville
Slieve Snaght 2017
The Skerries
Ramore Head
PORTBALLINTRAE
PORTRUSH
BUSHMILLS
PORTSTEWART
Giant's Causeway
Causeway School
Downhill Demesne & Mussenden Temple
Hazlett House
CASTLEROCK
COLERAINE
Downhill
Magilligan
Ballyscullion
Binevenagh Forest
Ballyhanna Forest
Macosquin
Castleroe
CAUSEWAY CO
BALLYMONEY
Crindle
Carrowclare
Artikelly
Bolea
Springwell Forest
Letterloan
Crossgare
Ballylintagh
Drumachose Old Church
BALLYKELLY
LIMAVADY
Ringsend
Mullan
Aghadowey
Agivey
Bendooragh
Cam Forest
Cullycapple
Killykergan
Culmore
Ballynagard
Lishahawley
Campsey
Maydown
EGLINTON
GREYSTEEL
REPUBLIC OF IRELAND
NORTHERN IRELAND
LONDONDERRY (DERRY)
Drumraighland
Glenhead
Lackagh
Moys
Baranailt
Loughermore Forest East
Loughermore Forest
Drumsurn
Gortnamoyagh Forest
Moneydig
GARVAGH
Nixon's Corner
Drumahoe
Lettershendoney
Ervey Cross Roads
Gortilea Cross Roads
Ness Wood
Bovevagh
Bonnanaboigh
Gortnahey
Brockaghboy
McLaughlins Corner
KILREA
Bovedy
NEW BUILDINGS
Foreglen
DUNGIVEN
Craigavole
Moran's Cross Roads
CLAUDY
Swatragh
Craigdarragh
Feeny
Tamlaght O'Crilly
Bready
Cloghcor
Liscloon
Dunnamanagh
Learmount Wood
Park
Altnaheglish Reservoir
Banagher Forest
White Mountain 1762
Glenshane Forest
Mullagmore 1804
Moydamlaght Forest
Upperlands
Inishrush
Culnady
MAGHERA
Moneystaghan Wood
Gulladuff
DERRY & STRABANE
Ballymagorry
Lough Ash
Ballynamallaght
Craig
MOUNTAINS
Mullaghaneany 2057
Sawel Mountain 2224
1866 Oughtmore
SPERRIN
Mullaghdoo 1847
2083
2030 Dart Mountain
Mullaghclogher 1876
Mullaghclogha
Moneyneany
Tobermore
MID ULSTER
Knockcloghrim
1725 Crockbrack Rock Hill
Sperrin Heritage Centre
Sperrin
Sawelabeg Forest
Goles Forest
Cranagh
DRAPERSTOWN
Straw
Curran
CASTLEDAWSON
Desertmartin
Glenlark Forest
Plumbridge
The Six Towns
Inniscarn Forest
MAGHERAFELT
Tintagh Mountain 1732
Mobuy Wood
Lough Fea
FERMANAGH & OMAGH
Gortin
Glenhull
Rousky
NEWTOWNSTEWART
Davagh Forest
Beaghmore Stone Circles
The Loup
Ballyronan
MONEYMORE
Springhill
Cashel Wood
Greencastle
Mullaghcarn
176
177
178

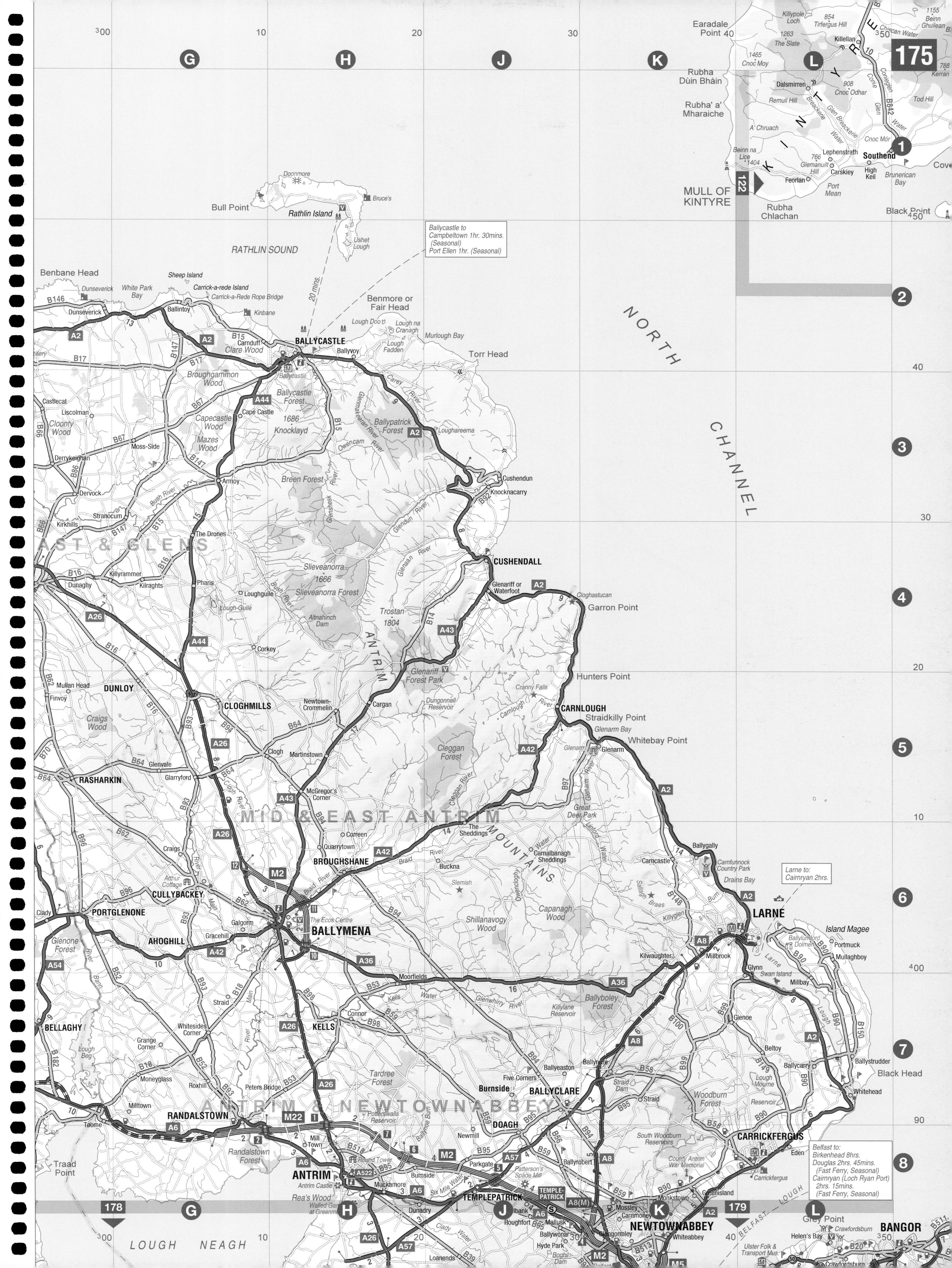
G
H
J
K
L
NORTH CHANNEL
RATHLIN SOUND
Rathlin Island
Bull Point
Doonmore
Bruce's
Ushet Lough
Ballycastle to Campbeltown 1hr. 30mins. (Seasonal)
Port Ellen 1hr. (Seasonal)
20 mins.
Benbane Head
Sheep Island
Carrick-a-rede Island
Carrick-a-Rede Rope Bridge
White Park Bay
Dunseverick
Ballintoy
Kinbane
Benmore or Fair Head
Lough Doo
Lough na Cranagh
Lough Fadden
Murlough Bay
Torr Head
BALLYCASTLE
Ballyvoy
Carnduff
Clare Wood
Broughgammon Wood
Ballycastle Forest
1686 Knocklayd
Cape Castle
Castlecat
Liscolman
Cloonty Wood
Capecastle Wood
Mazes Wood
Moss-Side
Derrykeighan
Ballypatrick Forest
Loughareema
Carey River
Glenmakeeran River
Owencam River
Breen Forest
Armoy
Dervock
Stranocum
Kirkhills
Bush River
The Drones
CAUSEWAY COAST & GLENS
Cushendun
Knocknacarry
Glendun River
Glenaan River
CUSHENDALL
Slieveanorra
1666
Slieveanorra Forest
Trostan 1804
Altnahinch Dam
Glenariff or Waterfoot
Cloghastucan
Garron Point
Killyrammer
Dunaghy
Kilraghts
Pharis
Loughguile
Lough-Guile
Corkey
ANTRIM
Glenariff Forest Park
Hunters Point
Cranny Falls
Dungonnell Reservoir
CARNLOUGH
Straidkilly Point
Glenarm Bay
Whitebay Point
Glenarm
Mullan Head
Finvoy
DUNLOY
CLOGHMILLS
Newtown-Crommelin
Cargan
Craigs Wood
Clogh
Martinstown
Cleggan Forest
Glenvale
Glarryford
RASHARKIN
McGregor's Corner
MID & EAST ANTRIM
Correen
Quarrytown
The Sheddings
Great Deer Park
MOUNTAINS
Carnalbanagh Sheddings
Ballygally
Carnfunnock Country Park
Drains Bay
Carncastle
Craigs
Arthur Cottage
CULLYBACKEY
BROUGHSHANE
Buckna
Slemish
Shillanavogy Wood
Capanagh Wood
Larne to: Cairnryan 2hrs.
LARNE
Island Magee
Ballylumford Dolmen
Portmuck
Mullaghboy
Clady
PORTGLENONE
Glenone Forest
AHOGHILL
Galgorm
Gracehill
The Ecos Centre
BALLYMENA
Moorfields
Kilwaughter
Millbrook
Glynn
Swan Island
Millbay
Ballyboley Forest
Killylane Reservoir
Glenwhirry River
Kells Water
Straid
BELLAGHY
Whitesides Corner
Grange Corner
Lough Beg
Connor
KELLS
Glenoe
Beltoy
Ballystrudder
Ballycarry
Black Head
Whitehead
Moneyglass
Roxhill
Peters Bridge
Tardree Forest
Five Corners
Burnside
BALLYCLARE
Ballyeaston
Ballynure
Straid Dam
Lough Mourne
Woodburn Forest
Reservoir
ANTRIM & NEWTOWNABBEY
Milltown
Toome
RANDALSTOWN
Potterswalls Reservoir
Mill Town
Randalstown Forest
Traad Point
DOAGH
Newmill
South Woodburn Reservoirs
CARRICKFERGUS
Eden
County Antrim War Memorial
Carrickfergus
Belfast to: Birkenhead 8hrs. Douglas 2hrs. 45mins. (Fast Ferry, Seasonal) Cairnryan (Loch Ryan Port) 2hrs. 15mins. (Fast Ferry, Seasonal)
ANTRIM
Antrim Castle
Round Tower
Muckamore
Rea's Wood
Walled Garden at Greenmount
Parkgate
Patterson's Spade Mill
TEMPLEPATRICK
Ballyrobert
Monkstown
Greenisland
Mossley
Carnmoney
NEWTOWNABBEY
Whiteabbey
Glengormley
Ballywonard
Hyde Park
Mallusk
Roughfort
Dunadry
Clady Water
Six Mile Water
Loanends
LOUGH NEAGH
BELFAST LOUGH
Grey Point
Crawfordsburn
Helen's Bay
BANGOR
Ulster Folk & Transport Mus.
Earadale Point
Killypole Loch
854 Tirfergus Hill
1263 The Slate
Killellan
1465 Cnoc Moy
Dalsmirren
908 Cnoc Odhar
Remuil Hill
A' Chruach
Conieglen Water
Tod Hill
Cnoc Mòr
Lephenstrath
Southend
Beinn na Lice
1404
766 Glemanuilt Hill
Carskiey
High Keil
Brunerican Bay
Feorlan
Port Mean
Rubha Dùin Bhàin
Rubha' a' Mharaiche
MULL OF KINTYRE
Rubha Chlachan
Black Point
KINTYRE
1155 Beinn Ghuilean
788 Kerran
Chiscan Water
122
178
179
A2
A26
A36
A42
A43
A44
A6
A8
M2
M22
B15
B16
B17
B94
B95

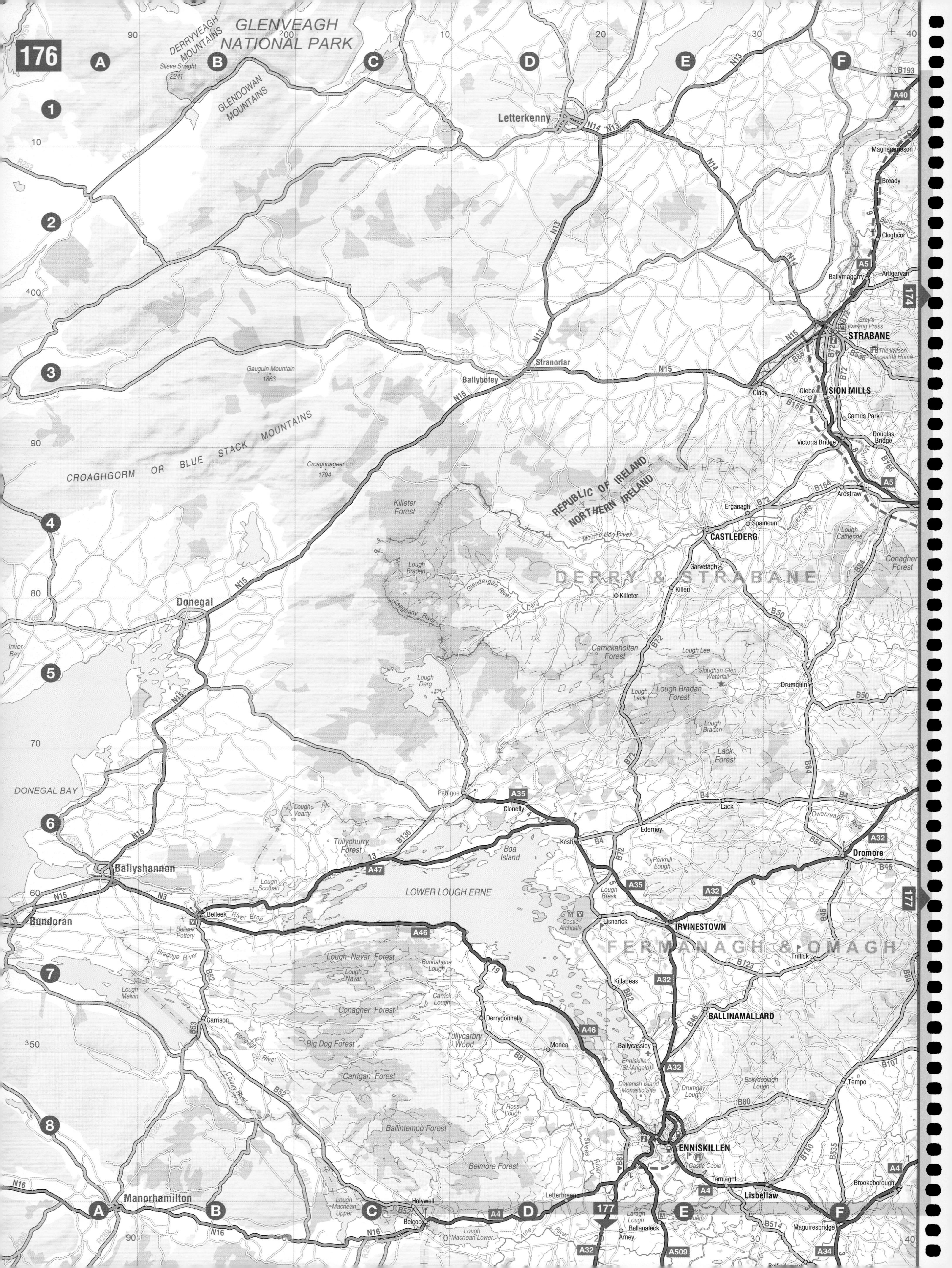
GLENVEAGH
NATIONAL PARK
DERRYVEAGH
MOUNTAINS
Slieve Snaght
2241
GLENDOWAN
MOUNTAINS
Letterkenny
Magheramason
Bready
Cloghcor
Artigarvan
Ballymagorry
Gray's
Printing Press
STRABANE
The Wilson
Ancestral Home
Stranorlar
Ballybofey
Gauguin Mountain
1863
Clady
Glebe
SION MILLS
Camus Park
Victoria Bridge
Douglas
Bridge
CROAGHGORM OR BLUE STACK MOUNTAINS
Croaghnageer
1794
REPUBLIC OF IRELAND
NORTHERN IRELAND
Killeter
Forest
Ardstraw
Erganagh
Spamount
CASTLEDERG
Lough
Catherine
Mourne Beg River
Lough
Bradan
Garvetagh
Conagher
Forest
DERRY & STRABANE
Killen
Killeter
Glendergan River
Leaghany River
River Derg
Donegal
Inver
Bay
Carrickaholten
Forest
Lough Lee
Sloughan Glen
Waterfall
Lough
Derg
Lough
Lack
Lough Bradan
Forest
Drumquin
Lough
Bradan
Lack
Forest
DONEGAL BAY
Pettigoe
Clonelly
Lack
Lough
Vearty
Tullychurry
Forest
Owenreagh
River
Boa
Island
Kesh
Ederney
Dromore
Ballyshannon
Parkhill
Lough
Lough
Scolban
LOWER LOUGH ERNE
Lough
Bresk
Bundoran
Belleek
River Erne
Belleek
Pottery
Castle
Archdale
Lisnarick
IRVINESTOWN
Bradoge River
Lough Navar Forest
Lough
Navar
Bunnahone
Lough
FERMANAGH & OMAGH
Trillick
Lough
Melvin
Carrick
Lough
Killadeas
Conagher Forest
Garrison
Derrygonnelly
BALLINAMALLARD
Roogagh
River
Big Dog Forest
Tullycarbry
Wood
Monea
Ballycassidy
Enniskillen
(St. Angelo)
Carrigan Forest
Devenish Island
Monastic Site
Ballydoolagh
Lough
Tempo
Drumgay
Lough
Ross
Lough
Ballintempo Forest
ENNISKILLEN
Belmore Forest
Castle Coole
Tamlaght
Brookeborough
Manorhamilton
Lough
Macnean
Upper
Holywell
Letterbreen
Lisbellaw
Belcoo
Lough
Macnean Lower
Laragh
Lough
Bellanaleck
Arney
Maguiresbridge
174
177

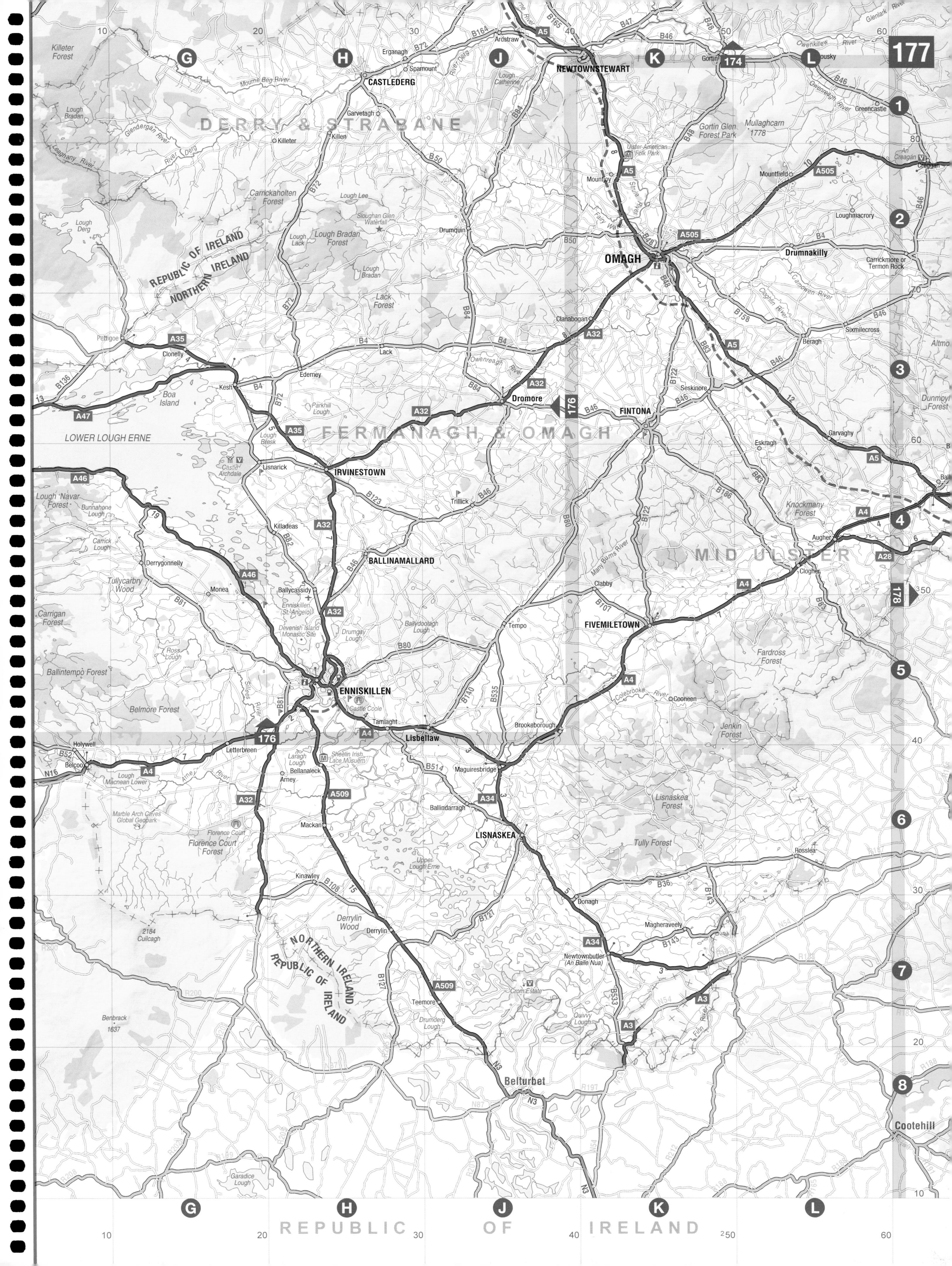
DERRY & STRABANE
FERMANAGH & OMAGH
MID ULSTER
REPUBLIC OF IRELAND
NORTHERN IRELAND
NEWTOWNSTEWART
CASTLEDERG
OMAGH
Drumnakilly
Dromore
FINTONA
IRVINESTOWN
BALLINAMALLARD
FIVEMILETOWN
ENNISKILLEN
Lisbellaw
LISNASKEA
Newtownbutler (An Baile Nua)
Belturbet
Cootehill
LOWER LOUGH ERNE
Boa Island
Upper Lough Erne
Lough Derg
Kesh
Pettigoe
Ederney
Lack
Tempo
Brookeborough
Maguiresbridge
Belcoo
Letterbreen
Derrygonnelly
Monea
Derrylin
Teemore
Kinawley
Donagh
Clogher
Augher
Seskinore
Beragh
Sixmilecross
Mountfield
Gortin
Ardstraw
Erganagh
Spamount
Killen
Killeter
Castle Coole
Florence Court Forest
Tully Forest
Lisnaskea Forest
Jenkin Forest
Fardross Forest
Knockmany Forest
Gortin Glen Forest Park
Mullaghcarn 1778
Cuilcagh 2184
Benbrack 1637
Marble Arch Caves Global Geopark
Ulster American Folk Park
Crom Estate
Sheelin Irish Lace Museum
Devenish Island Monastic Site
Sloughan Glen Waterfall
Belmore Forest
Ballintempo Forest
Lough Navar Forest
Carrigan Forest
Lough Bradan Forest
Lack Forest
Carrickaholten Forest
Killeter Forest
Tullycarbry Wood
Derrylin Wood
Mourne Beg River
Camowen River
Owenreagh River
Colebrooke River
Finn River

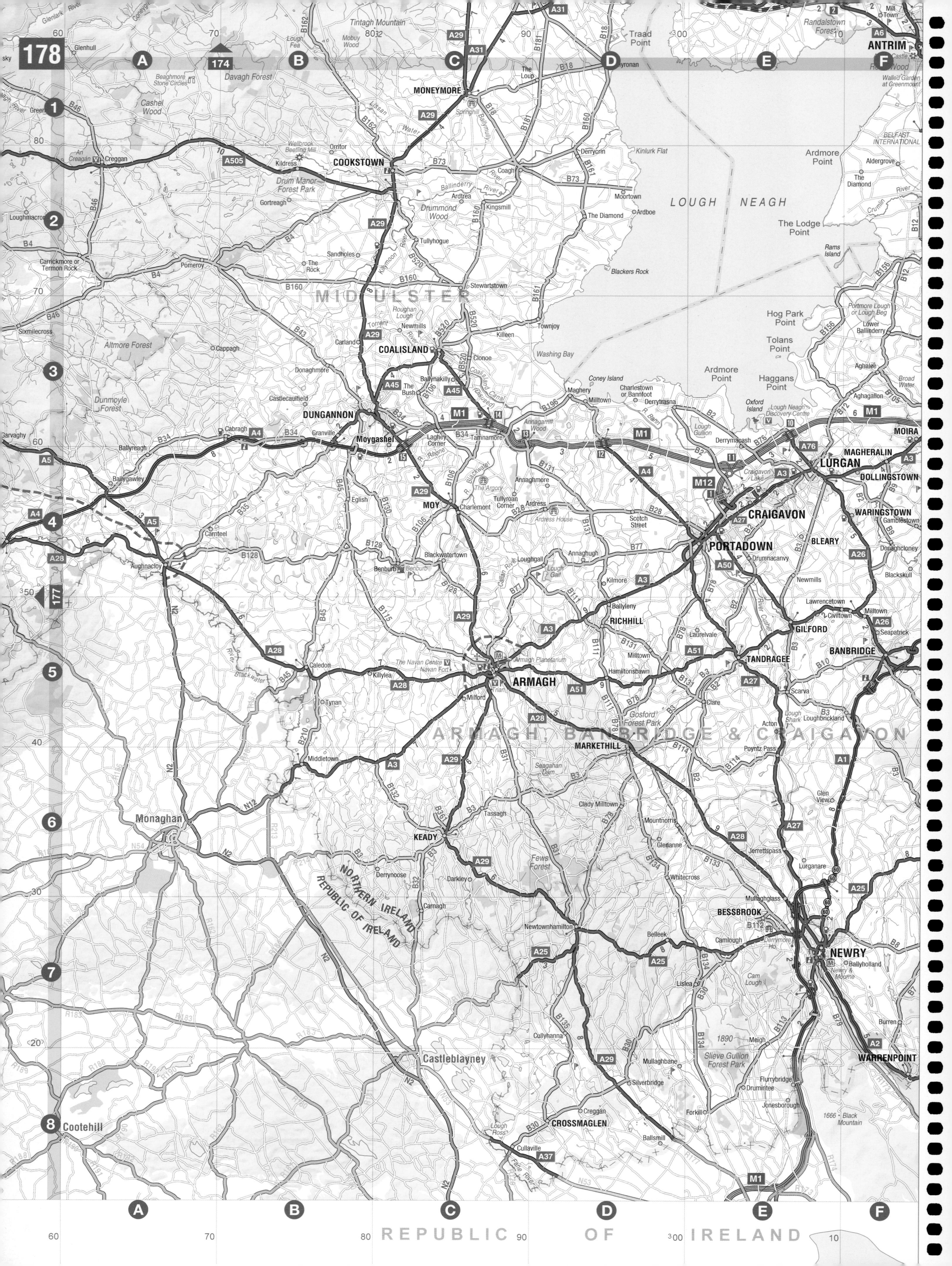
178
174
177
A
B
C
D
E
F
1
2
3
4
5
6
7
8
MONEYMORE
COOKSTOWN
Drum Manor Forest Park
Kildress
Orritor
Creggan
Cashel Wood
Davagh Forest
Tintagh Mountain
Traad Point
ANTRIM
Randalstown Forest
BELFAST INTERNATIONAL
Ardmore Point
Aldergrove
The Diamond
LOUGH NEAGH
The Lodge Point
Rams Island
Coagh
Ardtrea
Kingsmill
Drummond Wood
Moortown
Ardboe
The Diamond
Kinlurk Flat
Derrycrin
Blackers Rock
Tullyhogue
Sandholes
The Rock
Pomeroy
Carrickmore or Termon Rock
Loughmacrory
Gortreagh
Stewartstown
MID ULSTER
Roughan Lough
Newmills
Carland
COALISLAND
Clonoe
Killeen
Townjoy
Washing Bay
Hog Park Point
Tolans Point
Ardmore Point
Haggans Point
Portmore Lough or Lough Beg
Lower Ballinderry
Aghalee
Aghagallon
Broad Water
Sixmilecross
Altmore Forest
Cappagh
Donaghmore
Castlecaulfield
Dunmoyle Forest
DUNGANNON
Ballynakilly
The Bush
Coalisland Canal
Annagarriff Wood
Maghery
Milltown
Coney Island
Charlestown or Bannfoot
Derrytrasna
Lough Gullion
Oxford Island
Lough Neagh Discovery Centre
MOIRA
MAGHERALIN
LURGAN
DOLLINGSTOWN
Cabragh
Granville
Moygashel
Laghey Corner
Tamnamore
Derrymacash
Craigavon Lake
CRAIGAVON
WARINGSTOWN
Gamblestown
Ballyreagh
Ballygawley
The Argory
Annaghmore
Tullyroan Corner
Ardress
Ardress House
Charlemont
MOY
Eglish
Scotch Street
PORTADOWN
BLEARY
Drumnacanvy
Donaghcloney
Carnteel
Aughnacloy
Blackwatertown
Benburb
Loughgall
Lough Gall
Annaghugh
Kilmore
Blackskull
Newmills
Ballyleny
RICHHILL
Laurelvale
Lawrencetown
Milltown
Civiltown
GILFORD
Seapatrick
BANBRIDGE
TANDRAGEE
Milltown
Hamiltonsbawn
Caledon
Killylea
The Navan Centre
Navan Fort
Armagh Planetarium
ARMAGH
Milford
Tynan
Blackwater
Clare
Scarva
Lough Shark
Loughbrickland
Acton
Gosford Forest Park
MARKETHILL
ARMAGH, BANBRIDGE & CRAIGAVON
Poyntz Pass
Middletown
Seaghan Dam
Clady Milltown
Glen View
Monaghan
Tassagh
KEADY
Mountnorris
Glenanne
Jerrettspass
Derrynoose
Darkley
Fews Forest
Whitecross
Lurganare
NORTHERN IRELAND
REPUBLIC OF IRELAND
Carnagh
Mullaghglass
BESSBROOK
Newtownhamilton
Belleek
Camlough
Derrymore Ho.
NEWRY
Ballyholland
Newry & Mourne
Lislea
Cam Lough
Cullyhanna
Meigh
Slieve Gullion Forest Park
Burren
WARRENPOINT
Castleblayney
Mullaghbane
Silverbridge
Flurrybridge
Drumintee
Jonesborough
Black Mountain
Forkill
Creggan
CROSSMAGLEN
Lough Ross
Cullaville
Ballsmill
Cootehill
REPUBLIC OF IRELAND

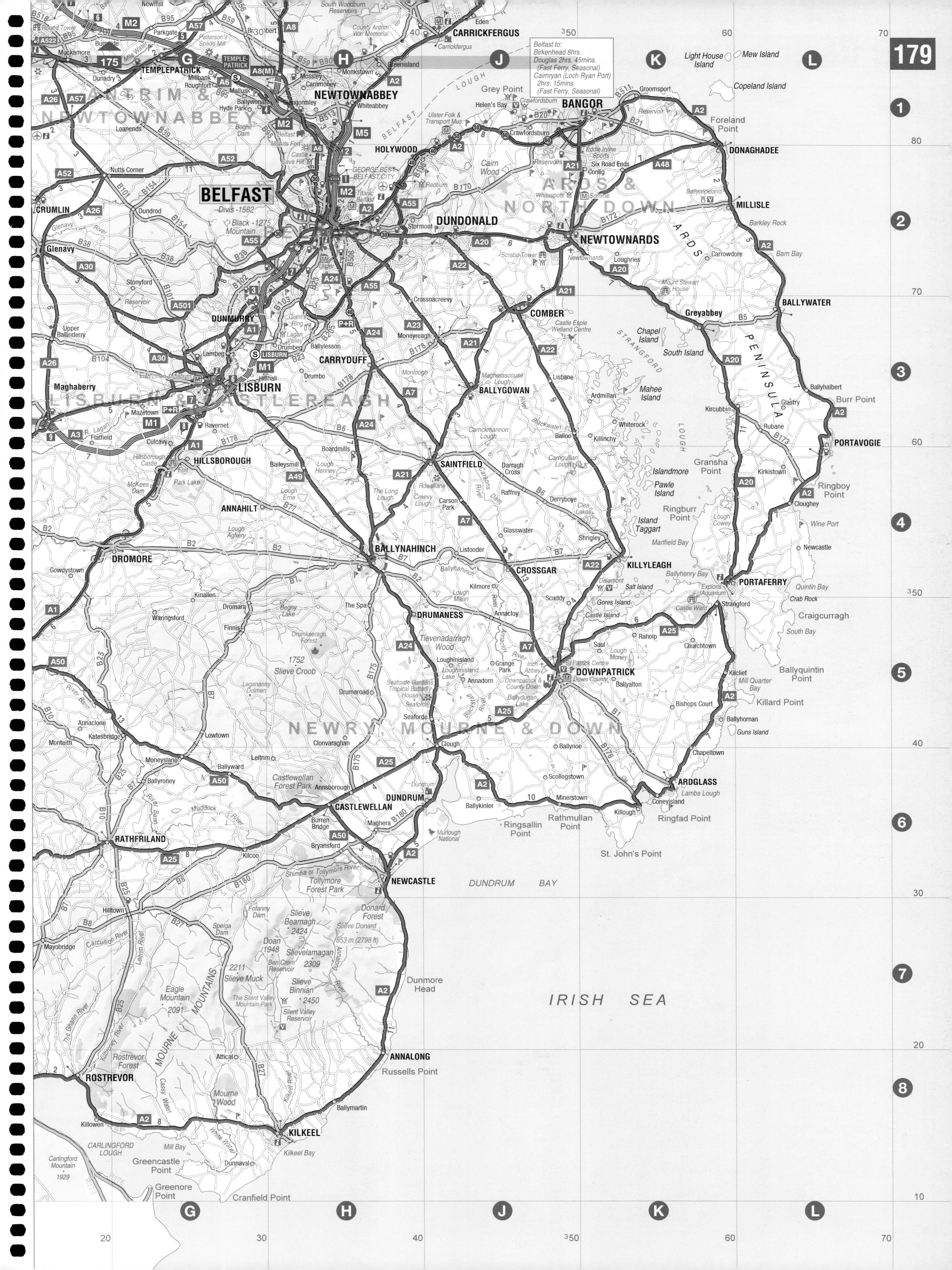
Belfast to:
Birkenhead 8hrs.
Douglas 2hrs. 45mins.
(Fast Ferry, Seasonal)
Cairnryan (Loch Ryan Port)
2hrs. 15mins.
(Fast Ferry, Seasonal)
CARRICKFERGUS
Light House Island
Mew Island
Copeland Island
Grey Point
BANGOR
Groomsport
Foreland Point
DONAGHADEE
TEMPLEPATRICK
NEWTOWNABBEY
ANTRIM & NEWTOWNABBEY
BELFAST LOUGH
HOLYWOOD
BELFAST
Divis 1562
Black Mountain 1275
CRUMLIN
Glenavy
Nutts Corner
Dundrod
Stonyford
ARDS & NORTH DOWN
MILLISLE
Barkley Rock
DUNDONALD
NEWTOWNARDS
Carrowdore
Barn Bay
Mount Stewart House
BALLYWATER
COMBER
Greyabbey
Chapel Island
South Island
STRANGFORD
ARDS PENINSULA
DUNMURRY
CARRYDUFF
Maghaberry
LISBURN
LISBURN & CASTLEREAGH
BALLYGOWAN
Mahee Island
Ballyhalbert
Burr Point
Kircubbin
PORTAVOGIE
HILLSBOROUGH
SAINTFIELD
Islandmore
Pawle Island
Gransha Point
Ringboy Point
Cloughey
ANNAHILT
Ringburr Point
Island Taggart
Kirkistown
Wine Port
DROMORE
BALLYNAHINCH
CROSSGAR
KILLYLEAGH
Newcastle
PORTAFERRY
Quintin Bay
Crab Rock
Craigcurragh
South Bay
Strangford
DRUMANESS
Tievenadarragh Wood
Slieve Croob 1752
DOWNPATRICK
Ballyquintin Point
Killard Point
Ballyhornan
Guns Island
Chapeltown
NEWRY, MOURNE & DOWN
Clough
Katesbridge
Rathfriland
Castlewellan Forest Park
DUNDRUM
CASTLEWELLAN
ARDGLASS
Killough
Coneyisland
Ringfad Point
Ringsallin Point
Rathmullan Point
St. John's Point
RATHFRILAND
NEWCASTLE
DUNDRUM BAY
Tollymore Forest Park
Donard Forest
Slieve Bearnagh 2424
Slieve Donard 853 m (2798 ft)
Doan 1948
Slievelamagan 2309
Slieve Muck 2211
Slieve Binnian 2450
Eagle Mountain 2091
MOURNE MOUNTAINS
Dunmore Head
IRISH SEA
ANNALONG
Russells Point
ROSTREVOR
Rostrevor Forest
Mourne Wood
KILKEEL
Kilkeel Bay
Ballymartin
CARLINGFORD LOUGH
Carlingford Mountain 1929
Greencastle Point
Greenore Point
Cranfield Point
G
H
J
K
L
1
2
3
4
5
6
7
8
20
30
40
350
60
70

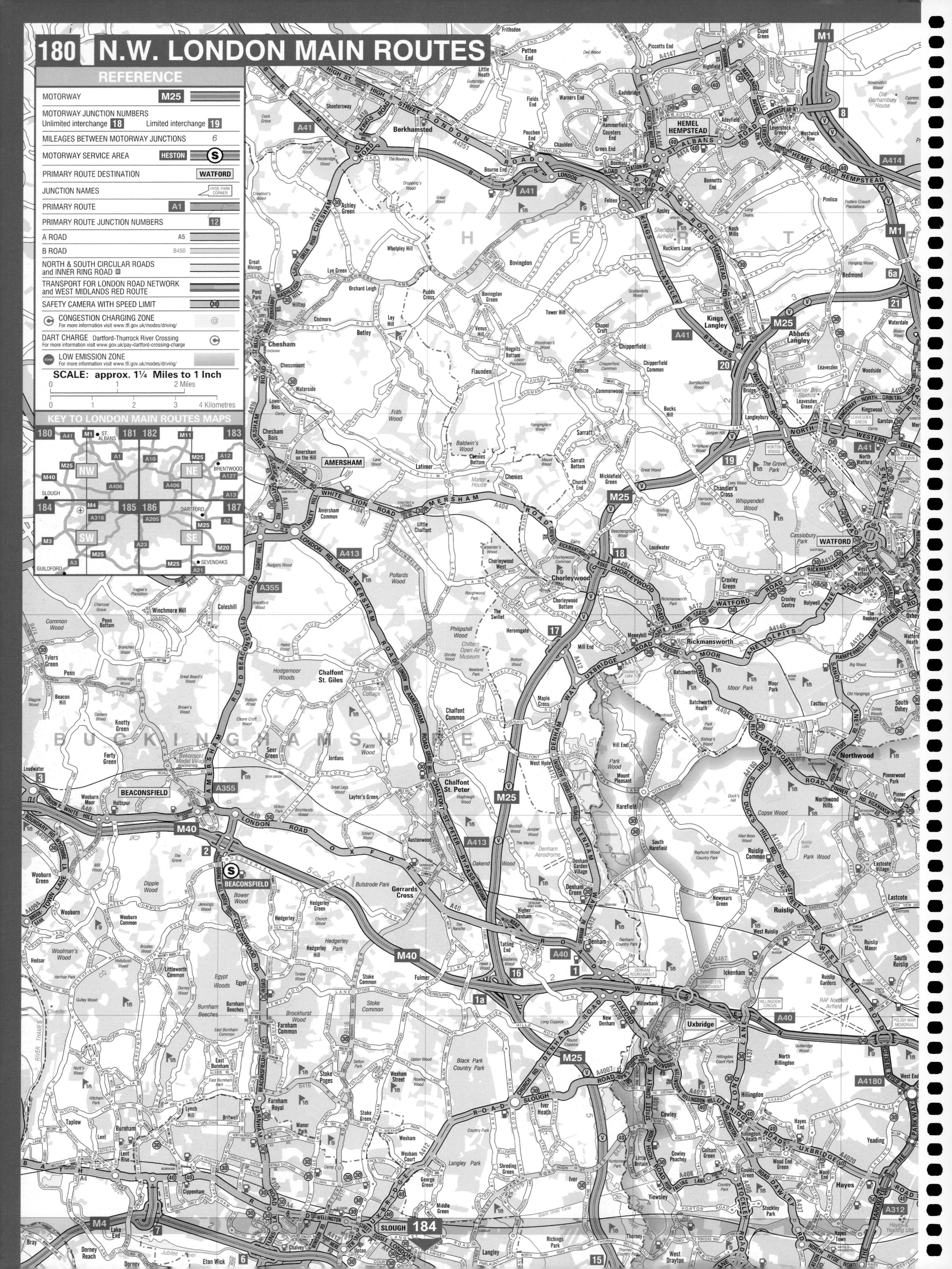

REFERENCE

MOTORWAY	M25
MOTORWAY JUNCTION NUMBERS	
Unlimited interchange 18 Limited interchange 19	
MILEAGES BETWEEN MOTORWAY JUNCTIONS	6
MOTORWAY SERVICE AREA	HESTON Ⓢ
PRIMARY ROUTE DESTINATION	WATFORD
JUNCTION NAMES	HYDE PARK CORNER
PRIMARY ROUTE	A1
PRIMARY ROUTE JUNCTION NUMBERS	12
A ROAD	A5
B ROAD	B450
NORTH & SOUTH CIRCULAR ROADS and INNER RING ROAD	Ⓡ
TRANSPORT FOR LONDON ROAD NETWORK and WEST MIDLANDS RED ROUTE	
SAFETY CAMERA WITH SPEED LIMIT	30
© CONGESTION CHARGING ZONE For more information visit www.tfl.gov.uk/modes/driving/	
© DART CHARGE Dartford-Thurrock River Crossing For more information visit www.gov.uk/pay-dartford-crossing-charge	
LEZ LOW EMISSION ZONE For more information visit www.tfl.gov.uk/modes/driving/	

SCALE: approx. 1¼ Miles to 1 Inch

0 — 1 — 2 Miles

0 — 1 — 2 — 3 — 4 Kilometres

KEY TO LONDON MAIN ROUTES MAPS

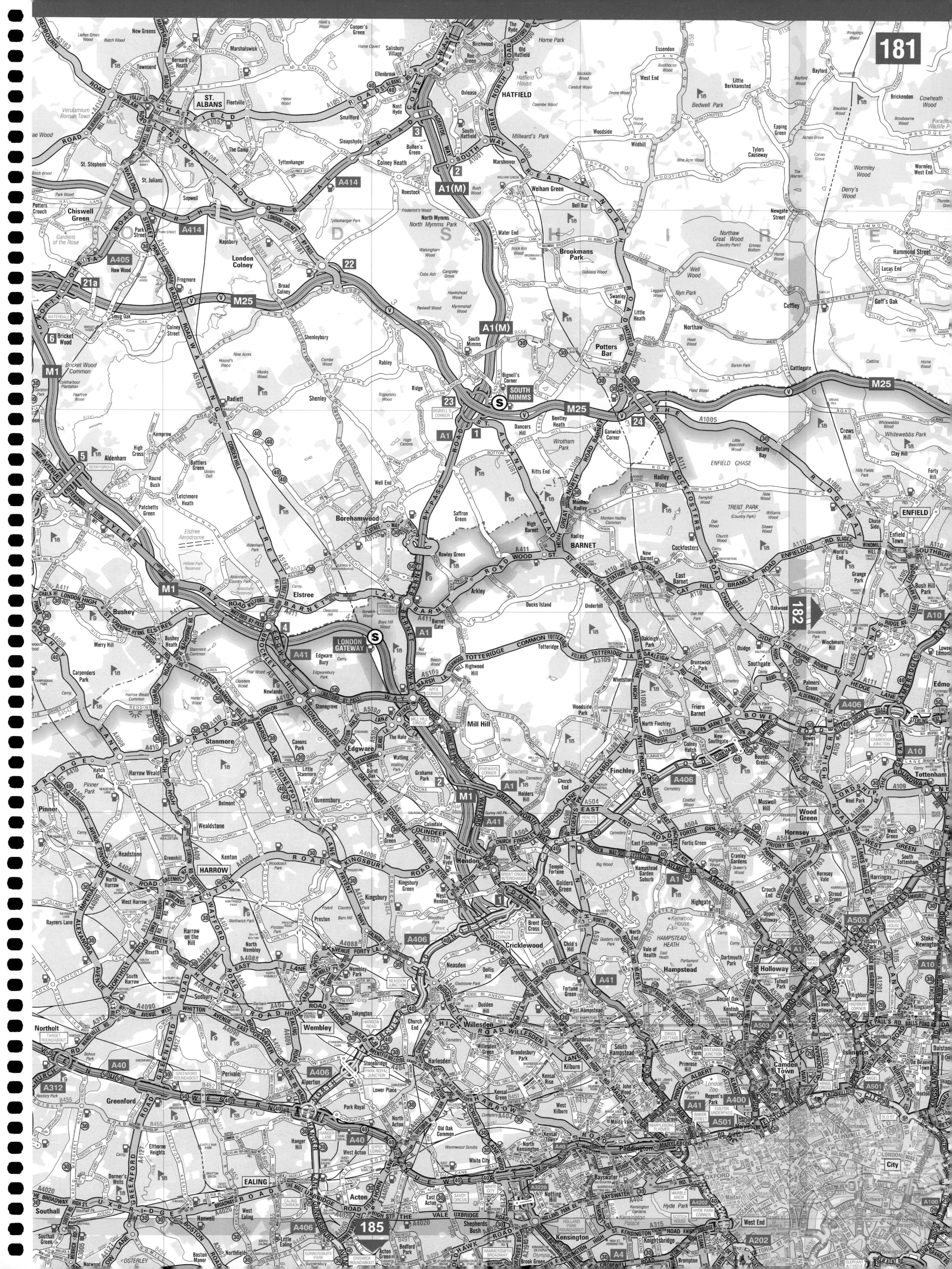
181
182
185
St. Albans
Hatfield
Hatfield House
Welham Green
Brookmans Park
London Colney
Colney Heath
Potters Bar
South Mimms
Cuffley
Goff's Oak
Enfield
Southbury
Borehamwood
Elstree
Radlett
Shenley
Aldenham
Bushey
Bushey Heath
Stanmore
Edgware
Mill Hill
Barnet
High Barnet
Hadley Wood
Cockfosters
East Barnet
New Barnet
Oakwood
Southgate
Palmers Green
Winchmore Hill
Whetstone
Totteridge
Finchley
Friern Barnet
New Southgate
Muswell Hill
Wood Green
Hornsey
Tottenham
Highgate
Hampstead
Holloway
Islington
Camden Town
Kilburn
Willesden
Cricklewood
Hendon
Colindale
Kingsbury
Kenton
Harrow
Pinner
Wealdstone
Harrow Weald
Wembley
Sudbury
Alperton
Northolt
Greenford
Perivale
Ealing
Acton
Southall
Hanwell
Paddington
Marylebone
Bayswater
Notting Hill
Kensington
Knightsbridge
Shepherds Bush
White City
Harlesden
Neasden
Chiswell Green
Park Street
Bricket Wood
Enfield Chase
Trent Park
Whitewebbs Park
Northaw
Cattlegate
Crews Hill
Bayford
Brickendon
Essendon
Little Berkhamsted
M25
M1
A1(M)
A1
A41
A406
A40
A414
A405
A411
A10
A503
A5109
A4020
A202
A4
HERTFORDSHIRE
LONDON GATEWAY
SOUTH MIMMS

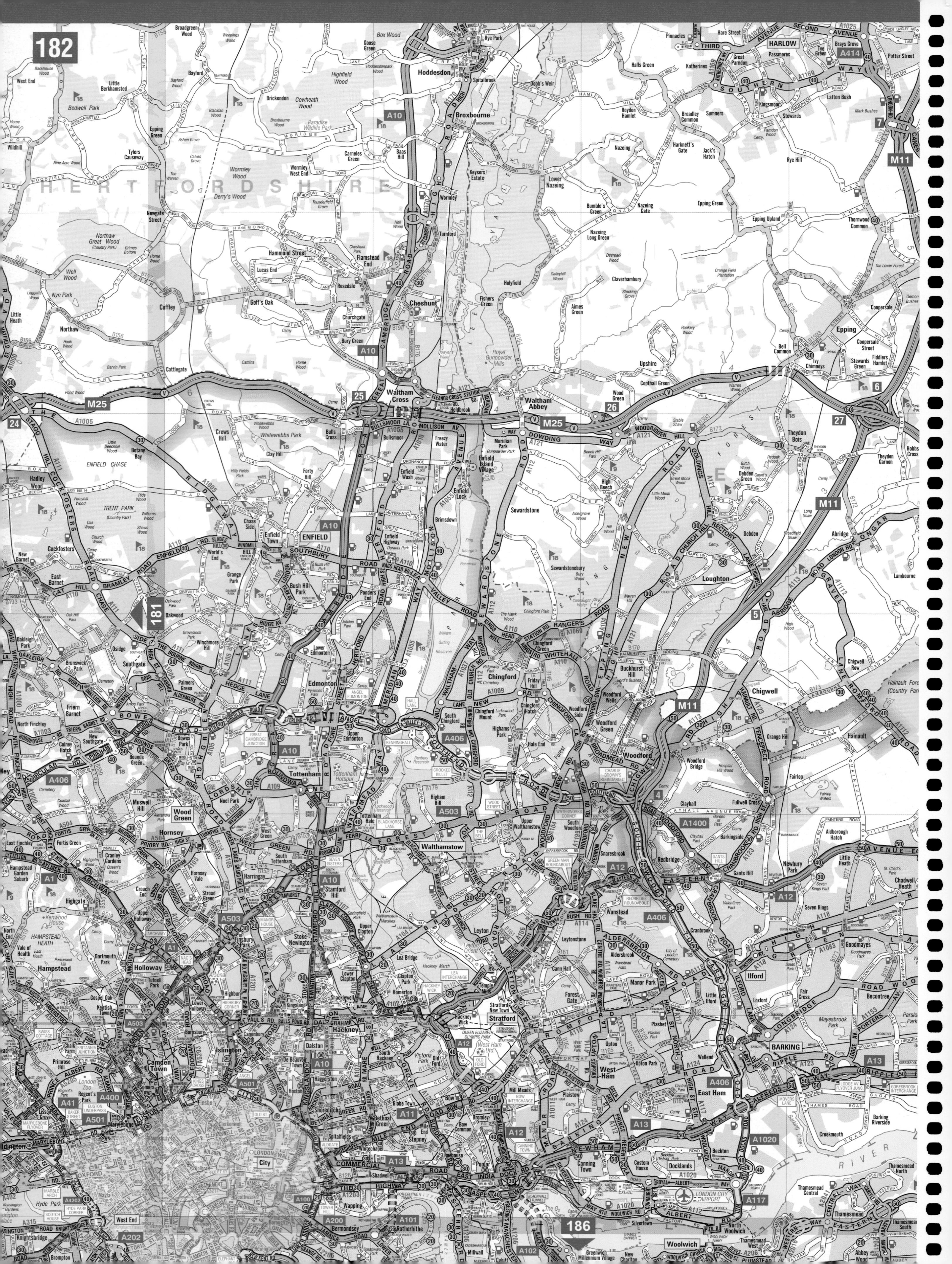
HERTFORDSHIRE
Hoddesdon
Broxbourne
Rye Park
Spitalbrook
Wormley
Turnford
Cheshunt
Flamstead End
Goff's Oak
Cuffley
Rosedale
Hammond Street
Churchgate
Bury Green
Waltham Cross
Waltham Abbey
Holdbrook
Crews Hill
Bulls Cross
Botany Bay
ENFIELD CHASE
Hadley Wood
Cockfosters
New Barnet
East Barnet
Enfield Town
ENFIELD
Southbury
Enfield Wash
Enfield Lock
Enfield Highway
Brimsdown
Ponders End
Bush Hill Park
Winchmore Hill
Southgate
Oakwood
Osidge
Palmers Green
Friern Barnet
Edmonton
Lower Edmonton
Upper Edmonton
Chingford
Sewardstone
Loughton
Buckhurst Hill
Chigwell
Woodford
Woodford Green
Woodford Bridge
Highams Park
Walthamstow
Tottenham
Tottenham Hale
Wood Green
Muswell Hill
Hornsey
Harringay
Stoke Newington
Stamford Hill
Upper Clapton
Lower Clapton
Leyton
Leytonstone
Wanstead
Snaresbrook
Redbridge
Gants Hill
Ilford
Barkingside
Seven Kings
Goodmayes
Chadwell Heath
Hainault
Chigwell Row
Abridge
Theydon Bois
Epping
Coopersale
Harlow
Nazeing
Lower Nazeing
Roydon Hamlet
Broadley Common
Epping Green
Hampstead
Highgate
Holloway
Islington
Camden Town
Kentish Town
Finsbury Park
Highbury
Dalston
Hackney
Homerton
Stratford
West Ham
Upton Park
East Ham
Barking
Plaistow
Canning Town
Poplar
Bow
Stepney
Bethnal Green
Shoreditch
Whitechapel
City
Marylebone
Regent's Park
Hyde Park
Knightsbridge
Bermondsey
Rotherhithe
Wapping
Millwall
Docklands
Beckton
Silvertown
North Woolwich
Woolwich
Thamesmead
Creekmouth
LONDON CITY AIRPORT
RIVER THAMES
M25
M11
A10
A406
A12
A13
EPPING FOREST

181
186

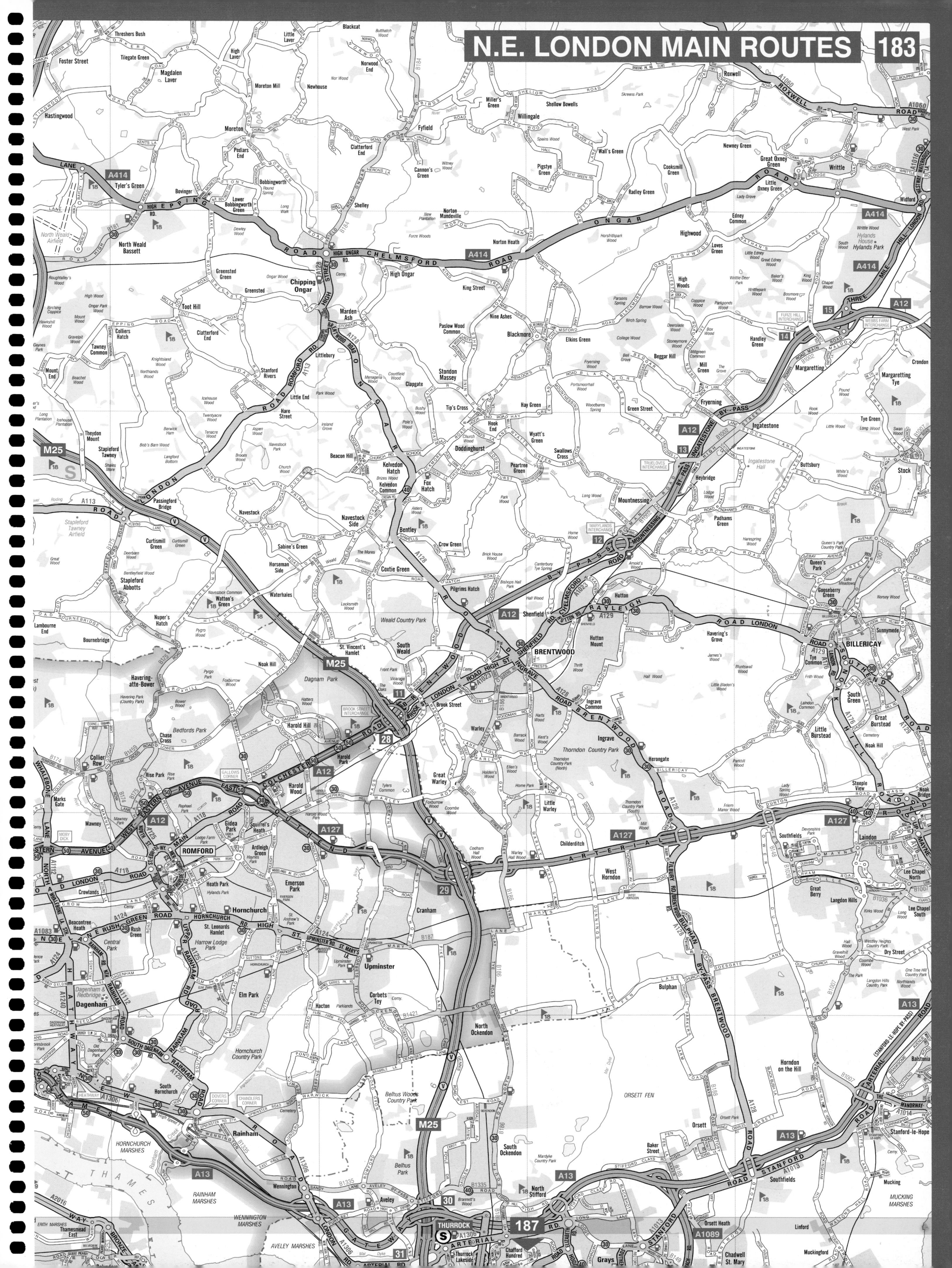

Threshers Bush
Blackcat
Little Laver
Foster Street
Tilegate Green
High Laver
Magdalen Laver
Moreton Mill
Norwood End
Newhouse
Roxwell
Miller's Green
Shellow Bowells
Hastingwood
Moreton
Fyfield
Willingale
Wall's Green
Newney Green
Clatterford End
Cannon's Green
Pigstye Green
Cooksmill Green
Great Oxney Green
Writtle
Tyler's Green
Bovinger
Pedlars End
Bobbingworth
Lower Bobbingworth Green
Shelley
Radley Green
Little Oxney Green
Widford
Norton Mandeville
Edney Common
North Weald Bassett
North Weald Airfield
Norton Heath
Highwood
Loves Green
Hylands Park
Greensted Green
High Ongar
Chipping Ongar
King Street
High Woods
Greensted
Toot Hill
Marden Ash
Nine Ashes
Colliers Hatch
Clatterford End
Paslow Wood Common
Blackmore
Elkins Green
Handley Green
Tawney Common
Littlebury
Beggar Hill
Margaretting
Crondon
Mount End
Stanford Rivers
Clapgate
Stondon Massey
Mill Green
Margaretting Tye
Little End
Fryerning
Hare Street
Tip's Cross
Hay Green
Green Street
Ingatestone
Tye Green
Theydon Mount
Hook End
Wyatt's Green
Stapleford Tawney
Beacon Hill
Kelvedon Hatch
Doddinghurst
Swallows Cross
Buttsbury
Peartree Green
Heybridge
Stock
Kelvedon Common
Fox Hatch
Passingford Bridge
Navestock
Mountnessing
Navestock Side
Bentley
Padhams Green
Stapleford Tawney Airfield
Curtismill Green
Sabine's Green
Crow Green
Horseman Side
Coxtie Green
Queen's Park
Stapleford Abbotts
Pilgrims Hatch
Gooseberry Green
Waterhales
Watton's Green
Shenfield
Hutton
Lambourne End
Nuper's Hatch
Weald Country Park
Sunnymede
Bournebridge
Hutton Mount
Havering's Grove
BILLERICAY
St. Vincent's Hamlet
South Weald
BRENTWOOD
Tye Common
Noak Hill
Havering-atte-Bower
Dagnam Park
Brook Street
Ingrave Common
South Green
Harold Hill
Great Burstead
Bedfords Park
Chase Cross
Warley
Ingrave
Thorndon Country Park
Herongate
Little Burstead
Collier Row
Harold Park
Noak Hill
Rise Park
Great Warley
Harold Wood
Marks Gate
Gidea Park
Squirrel's Heath
Little Warley
Steeple View
Noak Bridge
Mawney
Childerditch
Southfields
Laindon
ROMFORD
Ardleigh Green
West Horndon
Lee Chapel North
Heath Park
Emerson Park
Crowlands
Hornchurch
Cranham
Great Berry
Langdon Hills
Lee Chapel South
Beacontree Heath
Rush Green
St. Leonards Hamlet
Central Park
Harrow Lodge Park
Upminster
Dry Street
Dagenham
Elm Park
Corbets Tey
Bulphan
Hacton
North Ockendon
Hornchurch Country Park
Horndon on the Hill
South Hornchurch
Belhus Woods Country Park
ORSETT FEN
Rainham
Orsett
Stanford-le-Hope
HORNCHURCH MARSHES
South Ockendon
Baker Street
Belhus Park
Southfields
Mucking
RAINHAM MARSHES
Wennington
North Stifford
Aveley
MUCKING MARSHES
WENNINGTON MARSHES
Thamesmead East
THURROCK
Orsett Heath
Linford
AVELEY MARSHES
Chafford Hundred
Grays
Muckingford
Chadwell St. Mary
Thurrock Lakeside
M25
A414
A12
A127
A13
A128
A1089
187

180

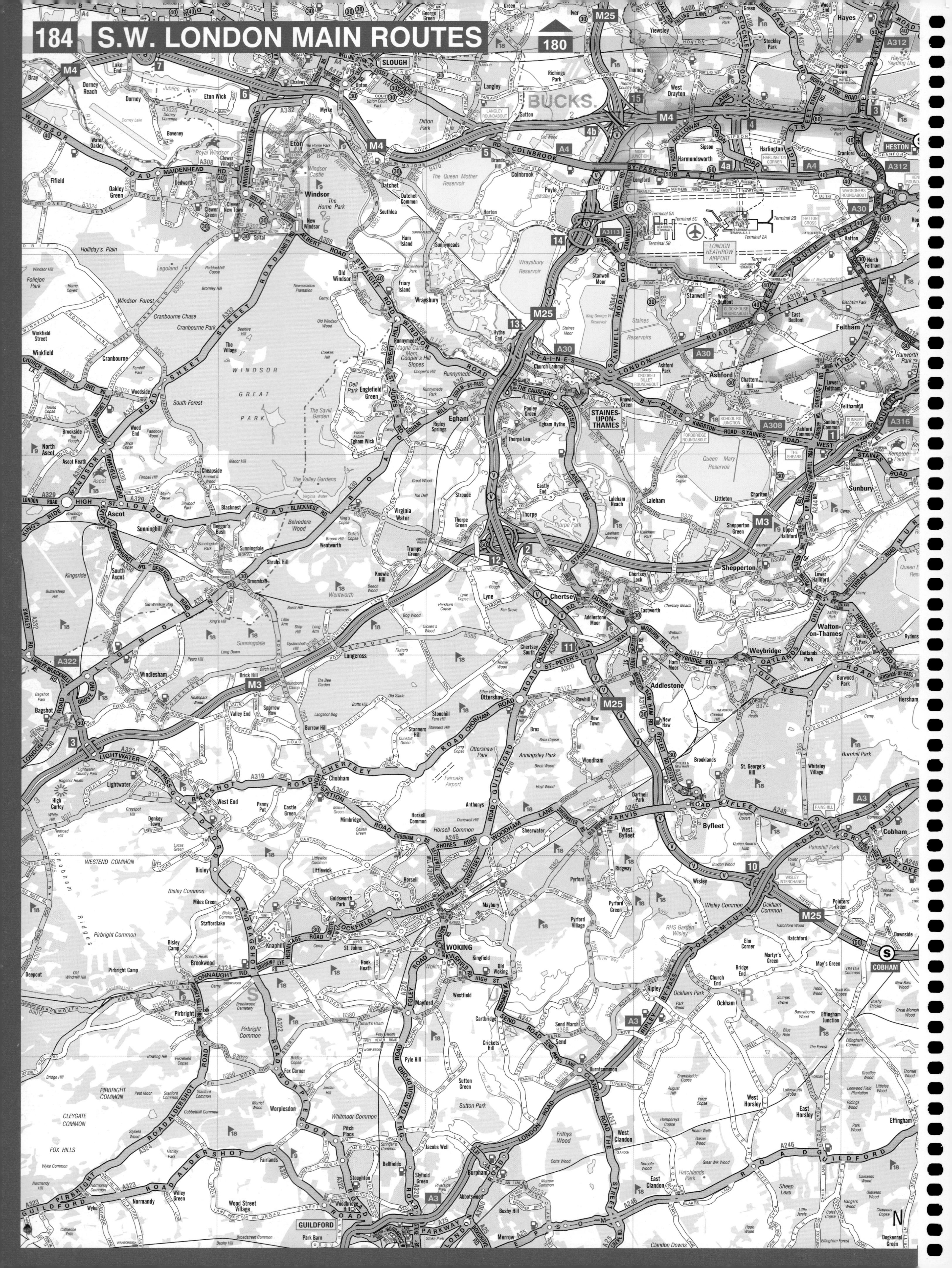
SLOUGH
BUCKS
M4
M25
M3
A4
A30
A308
A312
A316
A3
A322
A320
A245
A246
A329
A332
HESTON
Hayes
Yiewsley
West Drayton
Harmondsworth
Harlington
Cranford
Langley
Colnbrook
Datchet
Eton
Windsor
Dorney
Bray
Fifield
Oakley Green
Old Windsor
Wraysbury
Egham
Englefield Green
Virginia Water
Staines
STAINES-UPON-THAMES
Ashford
Stanwell
Feltham
Sunbury
Shepperton
Laleham
Thorpe
Chertsey
Addlestone
Weybridge
Walton-on-Thames
Hersham
Byfleet
West Byfleet
Woking
Cobham
Ripley
Ockham
Send
Burpham
GUILDFORD
COBHAM
Ascot
Sunninghill
Sunningdale
South Ascot
Windlesham
Bagshot
Lightwater
Chobham
Bisley
Knaphill
Brookwood
Pirbright
Worplesdon
Normandy
Wood Street Village
Fairlands
Longcross
Lyne
Ottershaw
Woodham
Pyrford
Mayford
West Horsley
East Horsley
Effingham
West Clandon
East Clandon
Merrow
WINDSOR GREAT PARK
LONDON HEATHROW AIRPORT
Queen Mother Reservoir
Wraysbury Reservoir
Queen Mary Reservoir
Legoland
Wentworth
Fairoaks Airport
RHS Garden Wisley
Wisley Common
Ockham Common
Bisley Common
Pirbright Common
Chobham Ridges
WESTEND COMMON
PIRBRIGHT COMMON
CLEYGATE COMMON
FOX HILLS
Whitmoor Common
Sutton Park

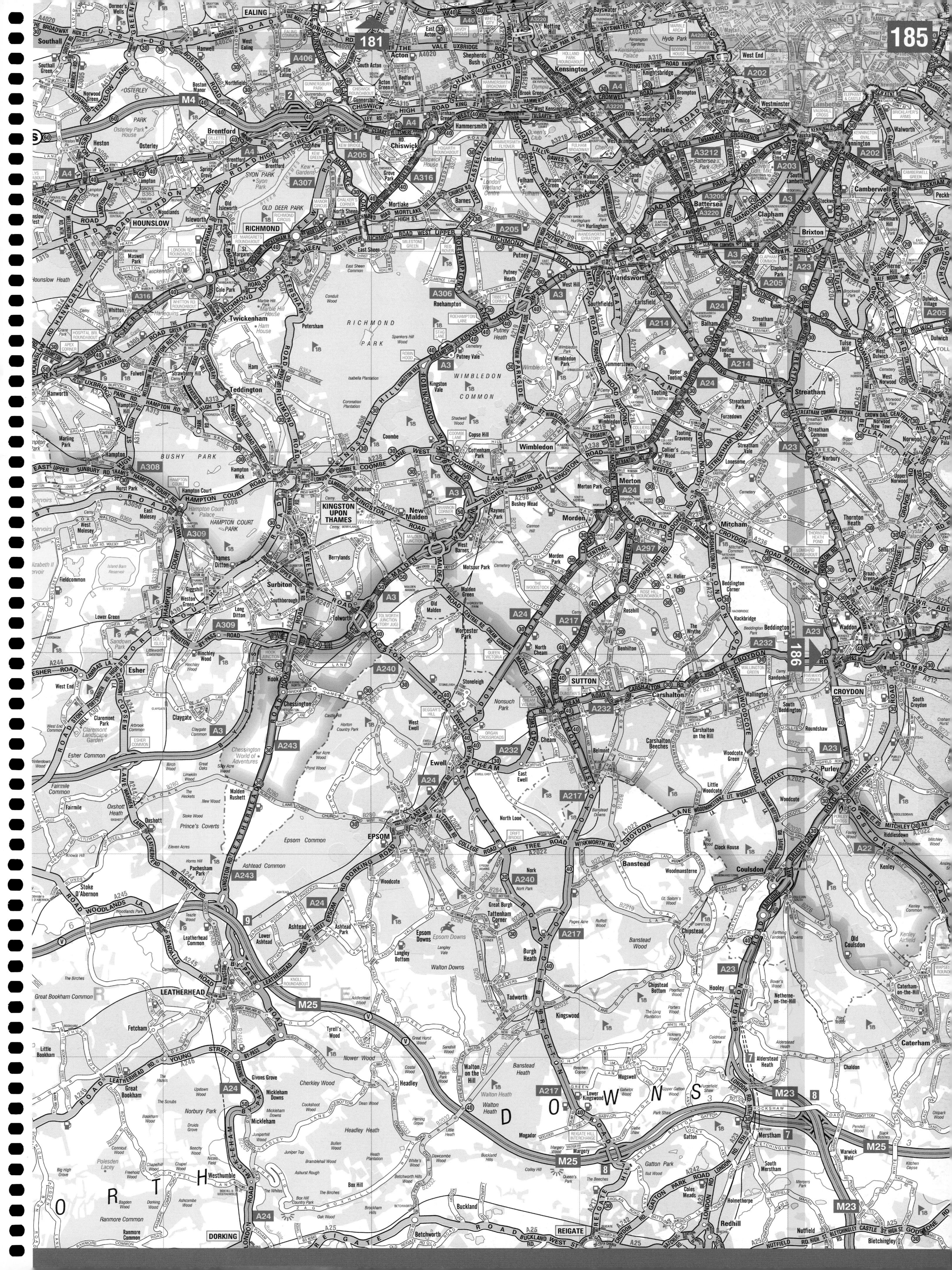
181
186
Ealing
Southall
Hanwell
West Ealing
Acton
Shepherds Bush
Notting Hill
Bayswater
Hyde Park
West End
Kensington
Knightsbridge
Westminster
Brompton
Chelsea
Pimlico
Vauxhall
Lambeth
Walworth
Kennington
Camberwell
Hammersmith
Chiswick
Brentford
Heston
Osterley
Hounslow
Isleworth
Richmond
Mortlake
Barnes
Fulham
Putney
Battersea
Clapham
Brixton
Wandsworth
Roehampton
Sheen
East Sheen
Twickenham
Petersham
Richmond Park
Wimbledon Common
Wimbledon
Teddington
Hampton
Bushy Park
Hampton Wick
Kingston upon Thames
Norbiton
New Malden
Coombe
Merton
Morden
Tooting
Balham
Streatham
Norwood
Mitcham
Thornton Heath
Croydon
Surbiton
Tolworth
Thames Ditton
East Molesey
West Molesey
Esher
Claygate
Chessington
Worcester Park
Cheam
Sutton
Carshalton
Wallington
Beddington
Purley
Coulsdon
Ewell
Epsom
Epsom Downs
Banstead
Ashtead
Leatherhead
Oxshott
Fetcham
Great Bookham
Mickleham
Dorking
Headley
Walton on the Hill
Tadworth
Kingswood
Chipstead
Reigate
Redhill
Merstham
Caterham
Kenley
Old Coulsdon
Bletchingley
Nutfield
Buckland
Betchworth
Westhumble
NORTH DOWNS
M4
M25
M23
A3
A24
A23
A217
A240
A243
A232

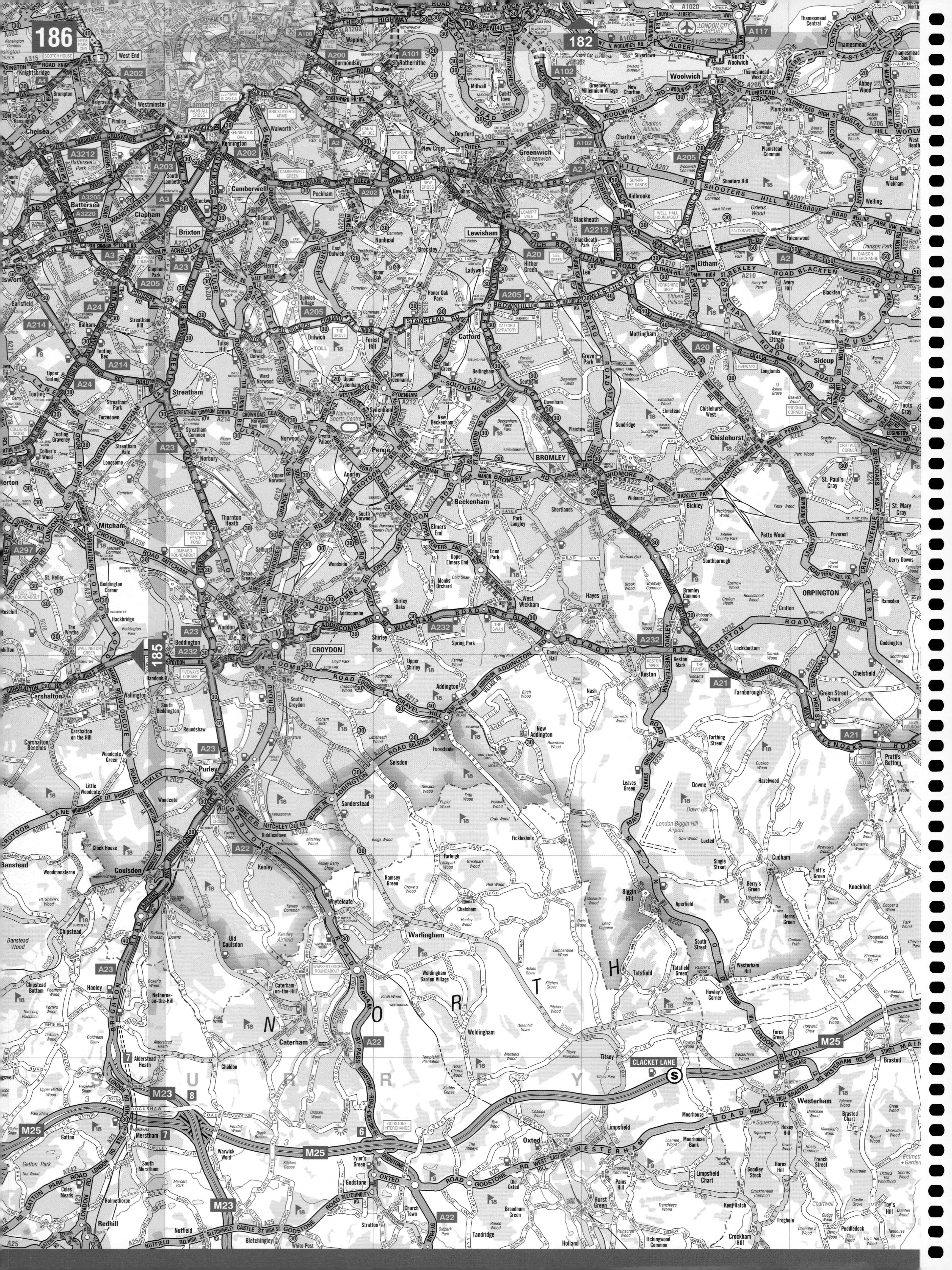
186
182
185
West End
Knightsbridge
Chelsea
Westminster
Lambeth
Pimlico
Brompton
Belgravia
Vauxhall
Kennington
Walworth
Bermondsey
Rotherhithe
Wapping
Shadwell
Millwall
Cubitt Town
Deptford
New Cross
Greenwich
Silvertown
North Woolwich
Woolwich
Charlton
Plumstead
Thamesmead
Abbey Wood
Battersea
Clapham
Stockwell
Camberwell
Peckham
Brixton
Nunhead
Brockley
Lewisham
Lee
Blackheath
Kidbrooke
Eltham
Shooters Hill
Welling
Falconwood
Sidcup
Balham
Tooting
Streatham
Dulwich
Forest Hill
Catford
Sydenham
Penge
Anerley
Norwood
Beckenham
Bromley
Chislehurst
Mottingham
Grove Park
Plaistow
Sundridge
Shortlands
Mitcham
Thornton Heath
Selhurst
Woodside
Croydon
Addiscombe
Shirley
West Wickham
Hayes
Keston
Bickley
Petts Wood
Orpington
St. Paul's Cray
St. Mary Cray
Locksbottom
Farnborough
Chelsfield
Green Street Green
Pratt's Bottom
Waddon
Beddington
Wallington
Carshalton
Hackbridge
South Croydon
Purley
Sanderstead
Selsdon
Addington
New Addington
Coulsdon
Kenley
Whyteleafe
Warlingham
Chelsham
Biggin Hill
Tatsfield
Westerham
Brasted
Oxted
Limpsfield
Godstone
Caterham
Chaldon
Merstham
Redhill
Nutfield
Bletchingley
Chipstead
Banstead
Woodmansterne
Hooley
London Biggin Hill Airport
London City Airport
Clacket Lane
NORTH
SURREY
M25
M23
A23
A21
A20
A2
A22
A232
A205

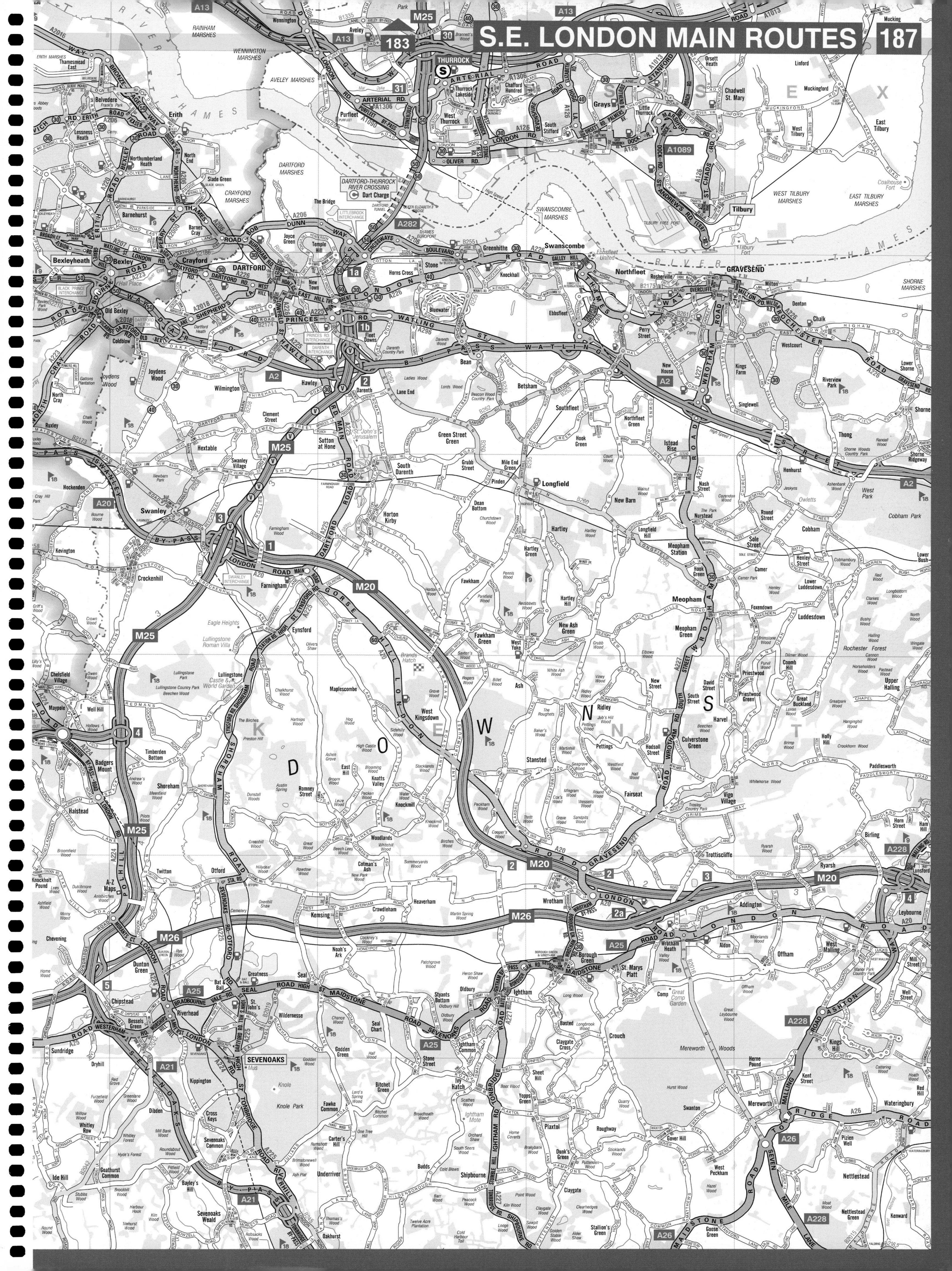

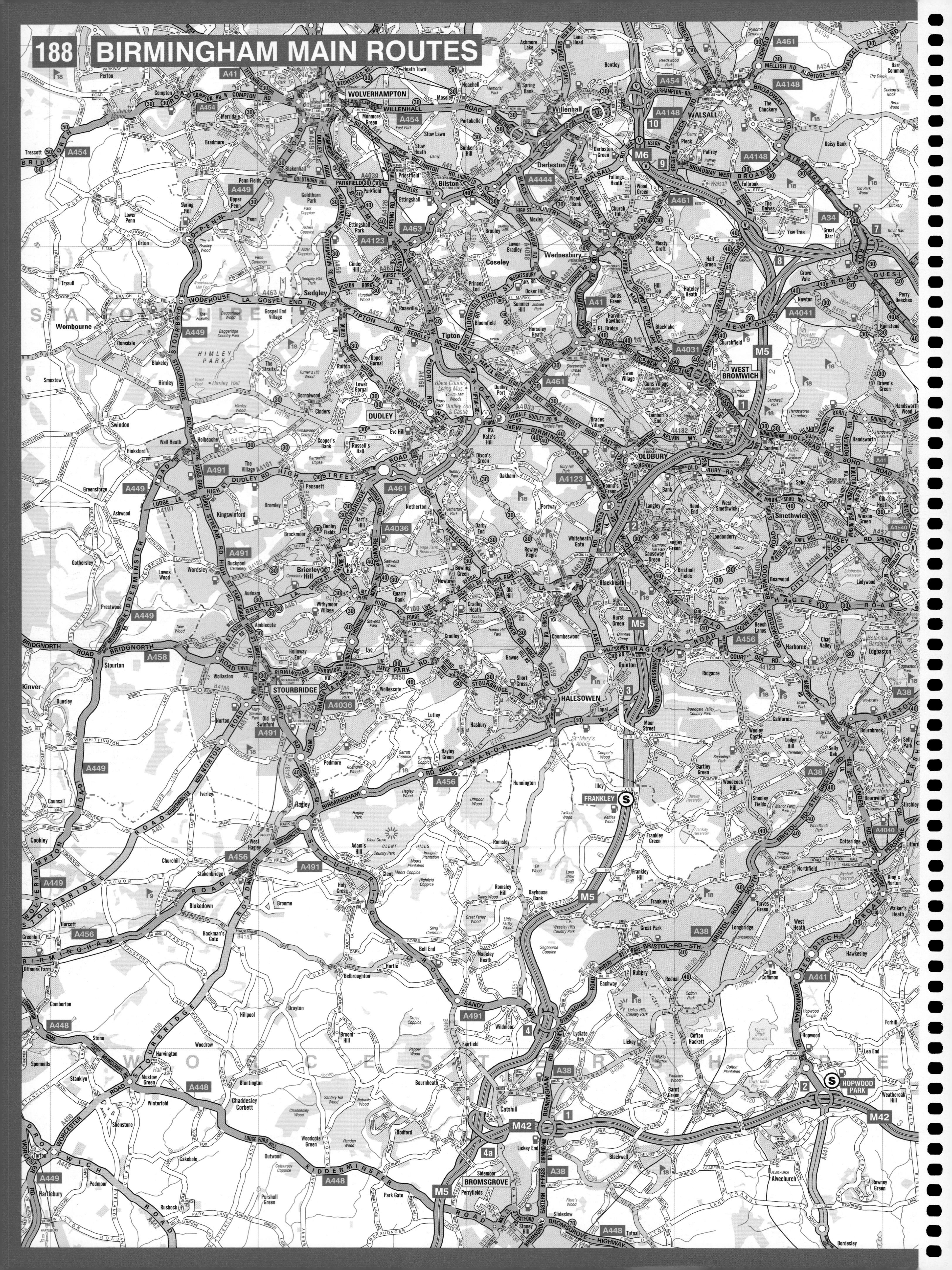
WOLVERHAMPTON
WALSALL
Willenhall
Darlaston
Bilston
Wednesbury
Coseley
Sedgley
Tipton
DUDLEY
WEST BROMWICH
OLDBURY
Smethwick
STAFFORDSHIRE
Wombourne
HIMLEY PARK
Kingswinford
Brierley Hill
Netherton
Rowley Regis
Blackheath
Halesowen
HALESOWEN
STOURBRIDGE
Lye
Cradley
Quinton
Harborne
Edgbaston
Bearwood
Northfield
Longbridge
Rubery
Hagley
Kinver
Stourton
Belbroughton
Catshill
BROMSGROVE
Alvechurch
Bordesley
WORCESTERSHIRE
FRANKLEY
HOPWOOD PARK
M5
M6
M42
A449
A491
A456
A458
A38
A41
A454
A461
A4123
A448
A441

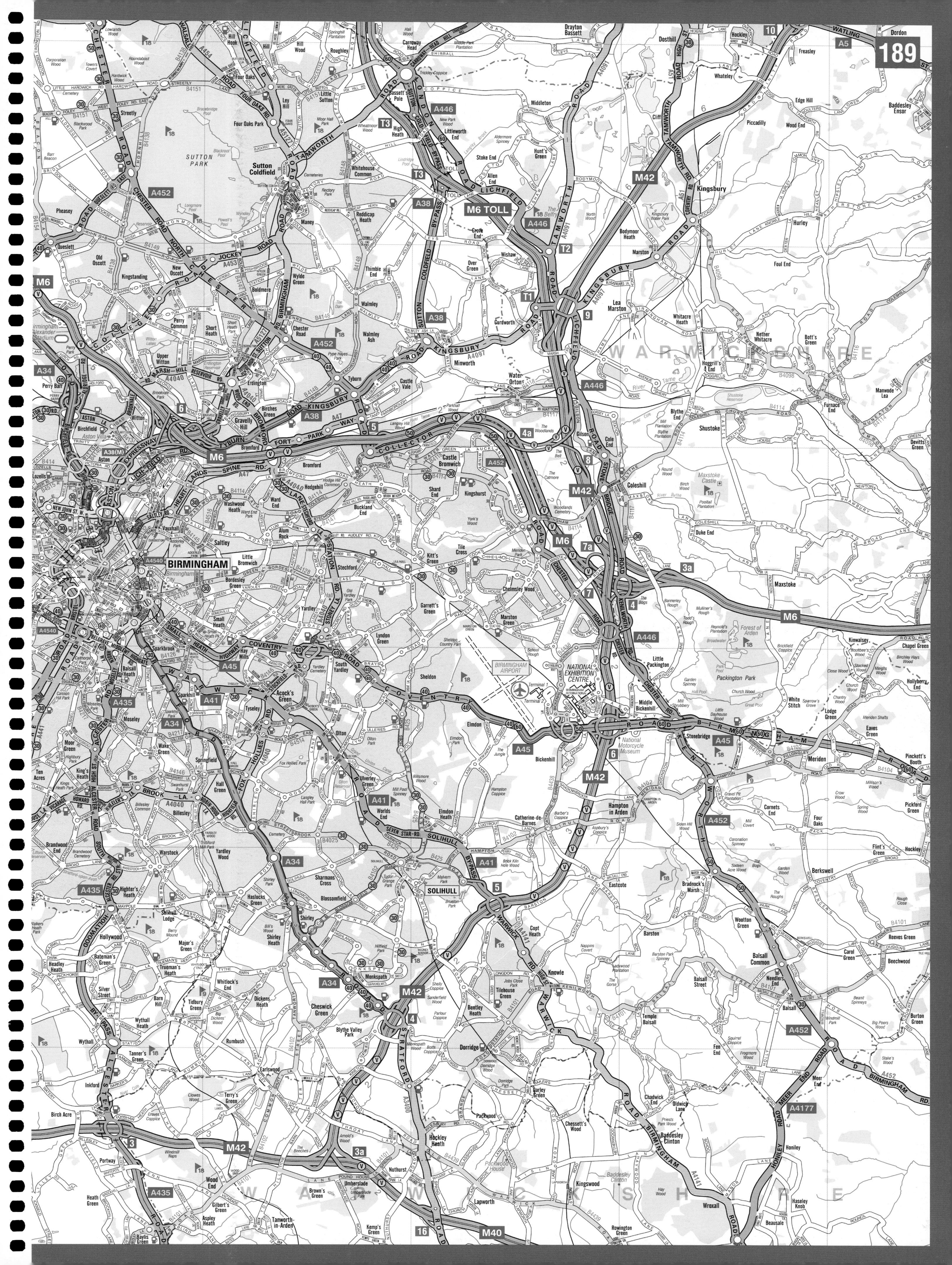

BIRMINGHAM
WARWICKSHIRE
Sutton Coldfield
SUTTON PARK
Four Oaks
Four Oaks Park
Streetly
Little Sutton
Ley Hill
Hill Hook
Hill Wood
Roughley
Carroway Head
Bassett's Pole
Drayton Bassett
Dosthill
Hockley
Dordon
Freasley
Whateley
Edge Hill
Baddesley Ensor
Piccadilly
Wood End
Middleton
Hunt's Green
Stoke End
Allen End
Littleworth End
High Heath
Whitehouse Common
Kingsbury
Hurley
Foul End
Bodymoor Heath
Marston
Lea Marston
Whitacre Heath
Nether Whitacre
Bott's Green
Hoggrill's End
Manwode Lea
Furnace End
Devitts Green
Shustoke
Blythe End
Maxstoke Castle
Coleshill
Cole End
Duke End
Maxstoke
Pheasey
Queslett
Old Oscott
Kingstanding
New Oscott
Boldmere
Wylde Green
Maney
Reddicap Heath
Thimble End
Walmley
Walmley Ash
Minworth
Water Orton
Curdworth
Wishaw
Over Green
Grove End
Perry Common
Short Heath
Upper Witton
Erdington
Tyburn
Castle Vale
Chester Road
Pype Hayes
Perry Barr
Witton
Birchfield
Aston
Lozells
Gravelly Hill
Birches Green
Bromford
Castle Bromwich
Hodgehill
Shard End
Kingshurst
Ward End
Washwood Heath
Buckland End
Alum Rock
Saltley
Vauxhall
Little Bromwich
Stechford
Kitt's Green
Tile Cross
Chelmsley Wood
Marston Green
Bordesley Green
Small Heath
Sparkbrook
Balsall Heath
Yardley
Garrett's Green
Lyndon Green
Hay Mills
South Yardley
Sheldon
Sparkhill
Tyseley
Acock's Green
Moseley
Olton
Elmdon
Bickenhill
Little Packington
Packington Park
Middle Bickenhill
Kinwalsey
Chapel Green
Hollyberry End
Eaves Green
Meriden
Pinckett's Booth
Millison's Wood
Pickford Green
Four Oaks
Cornets End
Hampton in Arden
Catherine-de-Barnes
Elmdon Heath
Ulverley Green
Worlds End
Hall Green
Springfield
Wake Green
Moor Green
Billesley
Yardley Wood
Warstock
Highter's Heath
Brandwood End
King's Heath
Ten Acres
Stirchley
Shirley
Shirley Heath
Sharmans Cross
Blossomfield
Haslucks Green
Major's Green
Solihull
SOLIHULL
Solihull Lodge
Hollywood
Bateman's Green
Headley Heath
Silver Street
Barn Hill
Trueman's Heath
Whitlock's End
Dickens Heath
Tidbury Green
Wythall
Wythall Heath
Cheswick Green
Monkspath
Blythe Valley Park
Dorridge
Bentley Heath
Copt Heath
Knowle
Eastcote
Barston
Bradnock's Marsh
Berkswell
Wootton Green
Balsall Common
Reeves Green
Carol Green
Beechwood
Needlers End
Balsall
Burton Green
Temple Balsall
Balsall Street
Fen End
Meer End
Chadwick End
Oldwich Lane
Baddesley Clinton
Honiley
Haseley Knob
Beausale
Wroxall
Kingswood
Lapworth
Rowington Green
Hockley Heath
Darley Green
Chessett's Wood
Packwood
Nuthurst
Umberslade
Brown's Green
Earlswood
Terry's Green
Tanworth-in-Arden
Kemp's Green
Aspley Heath
Gilbert's Green
Wood End
Inkford
Tanner's Green
Rumbush
Birch Acre
Portway
Heath Green
Baylis Green
Hockley
Flint's Green
BIRMINGHAM AIRPORT
NATIONAL EXHIBITION CENTRE
National Motorcycle Museum
M6
M6 TOLL
M42
M40
A38(M)
A38
A446
A452
A453
A34
A41
A45
A47
A435
A4540
A4177
A5
T1
T2
T3

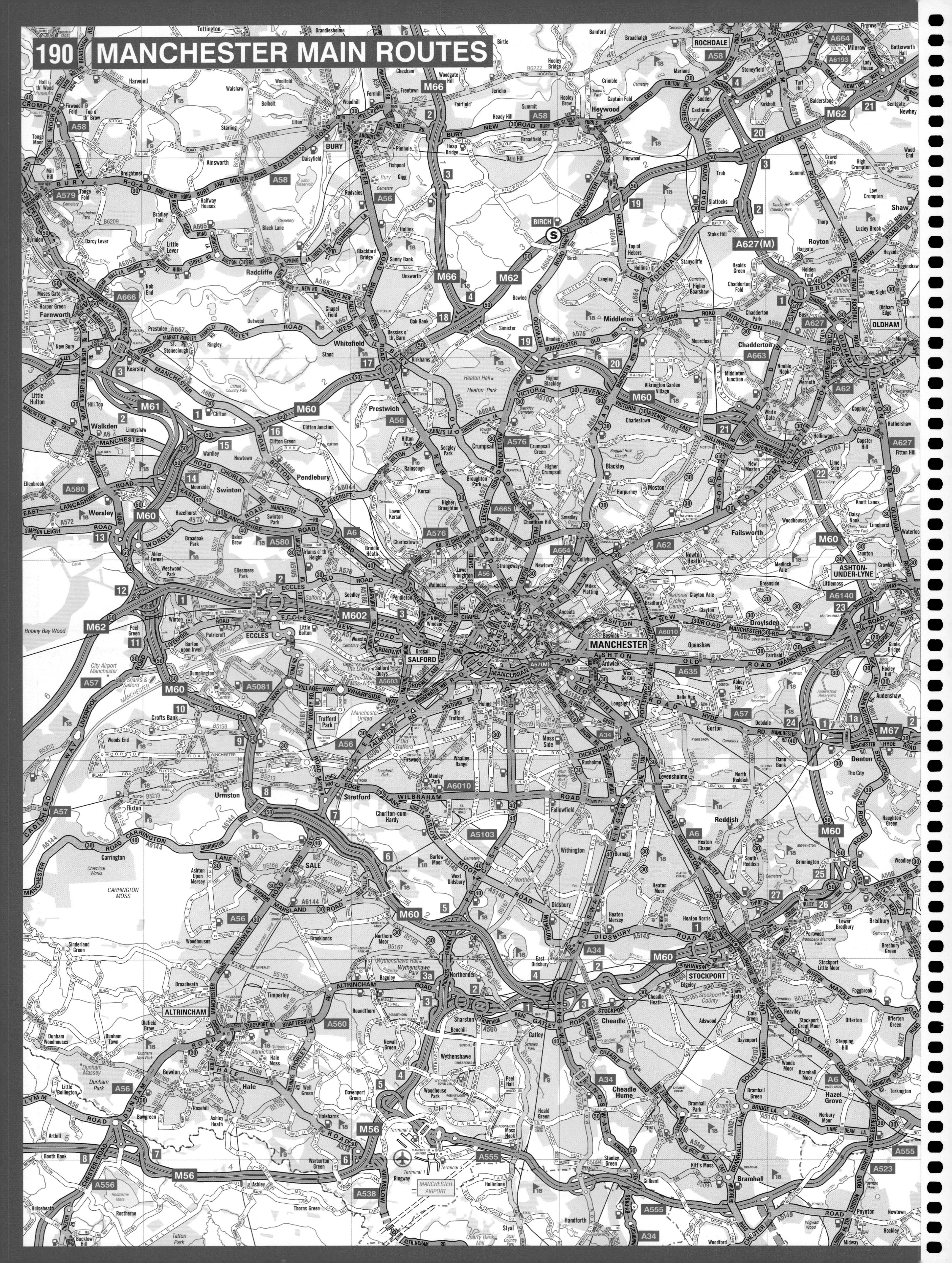
190
MANCHESTER MAIN ROUTES
MANCHESTER
SALFORD
BURY
ROCHDALE
OLDHAM
STOCKPORT
ALTRINCHAM
ASHTON-UNDER-LYNE
ECCLES
SALE
Middleton
Heywood
Radcliffe
Whitefield
Prestwich
Swinton
Worsley
Walkden
Farnworth
Urmston
Stretford
Denton
Cheadle
Wythenshawe
MANCHESTER AIRPORT
M60
M62
M66
M61
M602
M67
M56
A627(M)
A57(M)
Trafford Park
Chorlton-cum-Hardy
Didsbury
Levenshulme
Gorton
Droylsden
Failsworth
Chadderton
Royton
Shaw
Hazel Grove
Bramhall
Cheadle Hulme
Gatley
Hale
Timperley
Carrington
Flixton
Manchester United

City & Town Centre Plans

Aberdeen....192
Bath....192
Birmingham....192
Blackpool....192
Bournemouth....192
Bradford....192
Brighton & Hove....192
Bristol....193
Cambridge....193
Canterbury....193
Cardiff (Caerdydd)....193
Carlisle....193
Cheltenham....193
Chester....194
Coventry....194
Derby....194
Dover....194
Dumfries....194
Dundee....194
Durham....194
Eastbourne....194
Edinburgh....195
Exeter....195
Folkestone....195
Glasgow....195
Gloucester....195
Guildford....195
Harrogate....196
Inverness....196
Ipswich....196
Kilmarnock....196
Kingston upon Hull....196
Leeds....196
Leicester....196
Lincoln....197
Liverpool....197
London....198-199
Manchester....197
Medway Towns....197
Middlesbrough....197
Milton Keynes....200
Newcastle Upon Tyne....197
Newport (Casnewydd)....200
Northampton....200
Norwich....200
Nottingham....200
Oban....201
Oxford....200
Perth....201
Peterborough....201
Plymouth....201
Portsmouth....201
Preston....201
Reading....201
Salisbury....201
Sheffield....202
Shrewsbury....202
Southampton....202
Stirling....202
Stoke-on-Trent....202
Stratford-upon-Avon....202
Sunderland....202
Swansea (Abertawe)....203
Swindon....203
Taunton....203
Winchester....203
Windsor....203
Wolverhampton....203
Worcester....203
York....203

Port Plans

Harwich....204
Kingston upon Hull....204
Newcastle upon Tyne....204
Newhaven....204
Pembroke Dock (Doc Penfro)....204
Poole....204
Portsmouth....204
Weymouth....204

Additional port plans included with city and town plans:

Aberdeen....192
Dover....194
Liverpool....197
Oban....201
Plymouth....201
Southampton....202

Airport Plans

Birmingham....205
East Midlands....205
Glasgow....205
London Gatwick....205
London Heathrow....205
London Luton....205
London Stansted....205
Manchester....205

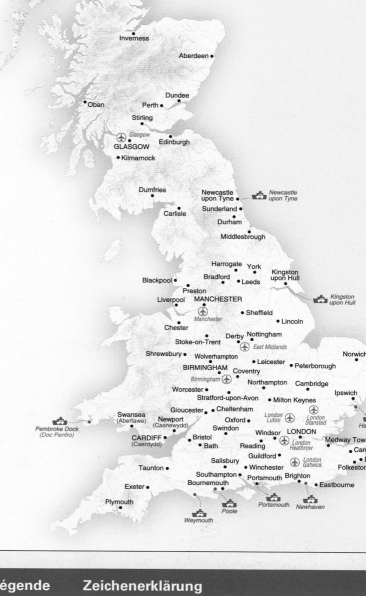

Reference to City & Town Plans   Légende   Zeichenerklärung

Motorway — Autoroute — Autobahn (M1)

Motorway Under Construction — Autoroute en construction — Autobahn im Bau

Motorway Proposed — Autoroute prévue — Geplante Autobahn

Motorway Junctions with Numbers — Unlimited Interchange 4 — Limited Interchange 5
Autoroute échangeur numéroté — Echangeur complet — Echangeur partiel
Autobahnanschlußstelle mit Nummer — Unbeschränkter Fahrtrichtungswechsel — Beschränkter Fahrtrichtungswechsel

Primary Route — Route à grande circulation — Hauptverkehrsstraße (A41)

Dual Carriageways (A & B roads) — Route à double chaussées séparées (route A & B) — Zweispurige Schnellstraße (A- und B- Straßen)

Class A Road — Route de type A — A-Straße (A129)

Class B Road — Route de type B — B-Straße (B177)

Major Roads Under Construction — Route prioritaire en construction — Hauptverkehrsstraße im Bau

Major Roads Proposed — Route prioritaire prévue — Geplante Hauptverkehrsstraße

Minor Roads — Route secondaire — Nebenstraße

Safety Camera — Radars de contrôle de vitesse — Sicherheitskamera (30)

Restricted Access — Accès réglementé — Beschränkte Zufahrt

Pedestrianized Road & Main Footway — Rue piétonne et chemin réservé aux piétons — Fußgängerstraße und Fußweg

One Way Streets — Sens unique — Einbahnstraße

Fuel Station — Station service — Tankstelle

Toll — Barrière de péage — Gebührenpflichtig (TOLL)

Railway & Station — Voie ferrée et gare — Eisenbahnlinie und Bahnhof

Underground / Metro & DLR Station — Station de métro et DLR — U-Bahnstation und DLR-Station (DLR)

Level Crossing & Tunnel — Passage à niveau et tunnel — Bahnübergang und Tunnel

Tram Stop & One Way Tram Stop — Arrêt de tramway — Straßenbahnhaltestelle

Built-up Area — Agglomération — Geschloßene Ortschaft

Abbey, Cathedral, Priory etc — Abbaye, cathédrale, prieuré etc — Abtei, Kathedrale, Kloster usw

Airport — Aéroport — Flughafen

Bus Station — Gare routière — Bushaltestelle

Car Park (selection of) — Sélection de parkings — Auswahl von Parkplatz (P)

Church — Eglise — Kirche

City Wall — Murs d'enceinte — Stadtmauer

Congestion Charging Zone — Zone de péage urbain — City-Maut Zone

Ferry (vehicular) (foot only)
Bac (véhicules) (piétons)
Fähre (autos) (nur für Personen)

Golf Course — Terrain de golf — Golfplatz (9, 18)

Heliport — Héliport — Hubschrauberlandeplatz

Hospital — Hôpital — Krankenhaus (H)

Lighthouse — Phare — Leuchtturm

Market — Marché — Markt

National Trust Property (open) NT — (restricted opening) NT — (National Trust for Scotland) NTS NTS
National Trust Property (ouvert) (heures d'ouverture) (National Trust for Scotland)
National Trust- Eigentum (geöffnet) (beschränkte Öffnungszeit) (National Trust for Scotland)

Park & Ride — Parking relais — Auswahl von Parkplatz (P+R)

Place of Interest — Curiosité — Sehenswürdigkeit

Police Station — Commissariat de police — Polizeirevier

Post Office — Bureau de poste — Postamt

Shopping Area (main street & precinct) — Quartier commerçant (rue et zone principales) — Einkaufsviertel (hauptgeschäftsstraße, fußgängerzone)

Shopmobility — Shopmobility — Shopmobility

Toilet — Toilettes — Toilette

Tourist Information Centre — Syndicat d'initiative — Information (i)

Viewpoint — Vue panoramique — Aussichtspunkt

Visitor Information Centre — Centre d'information touristique — Besucherzentrum (V)

ABERDEEN

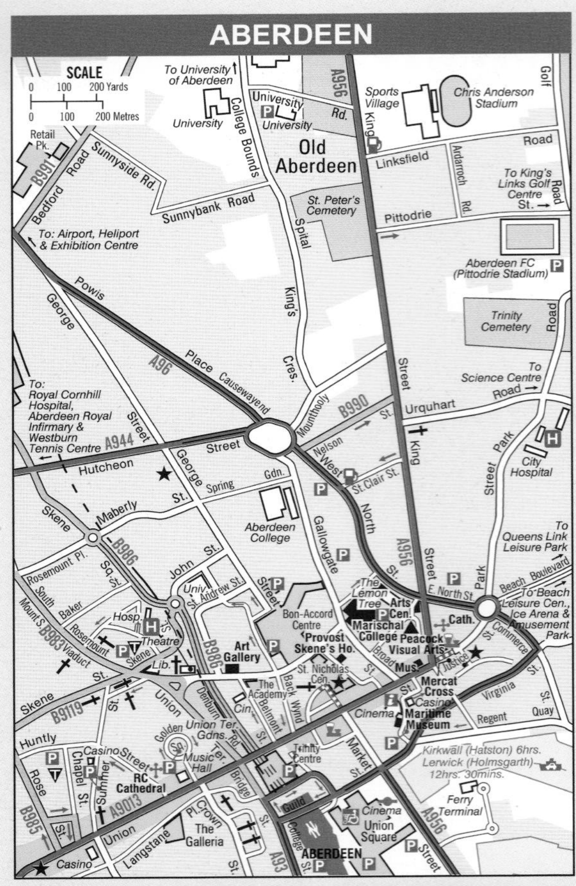

BATH

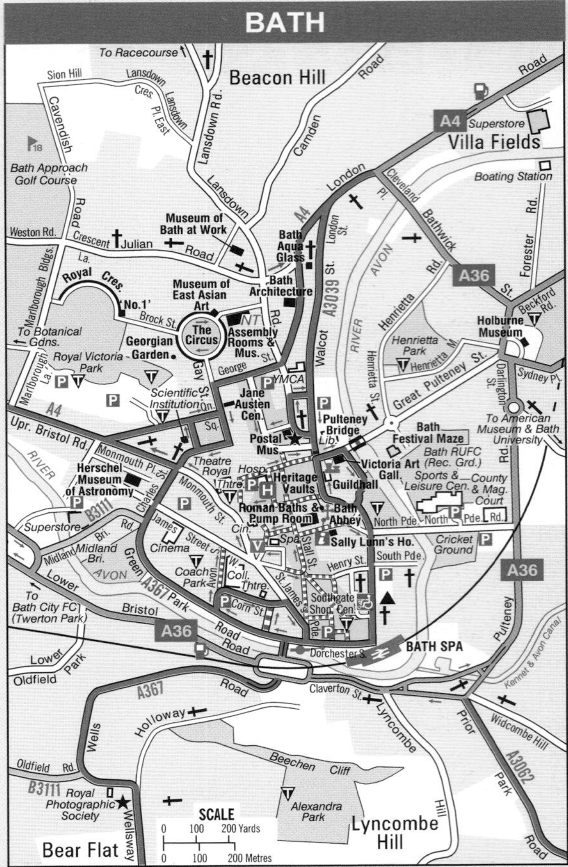

BLACKPOOL

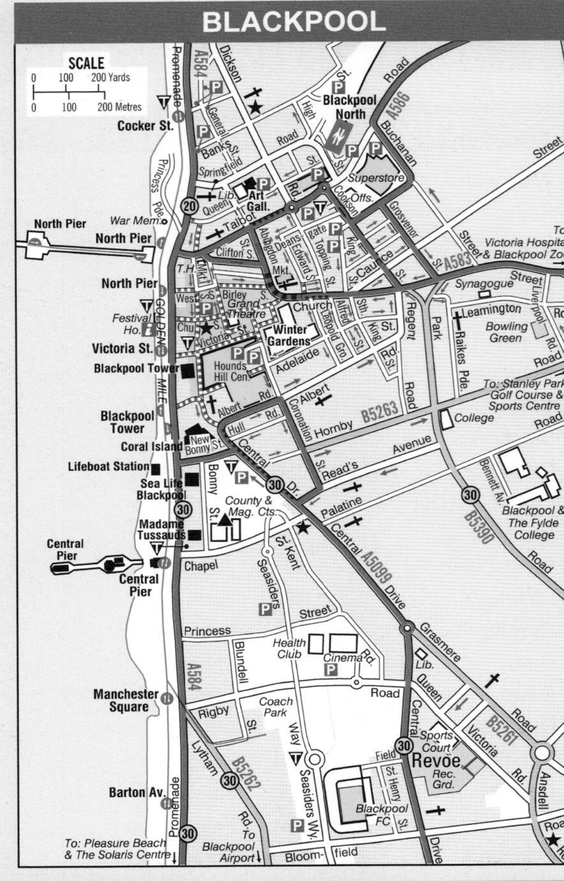

BIRMINGHAM (CITY CENTRE)

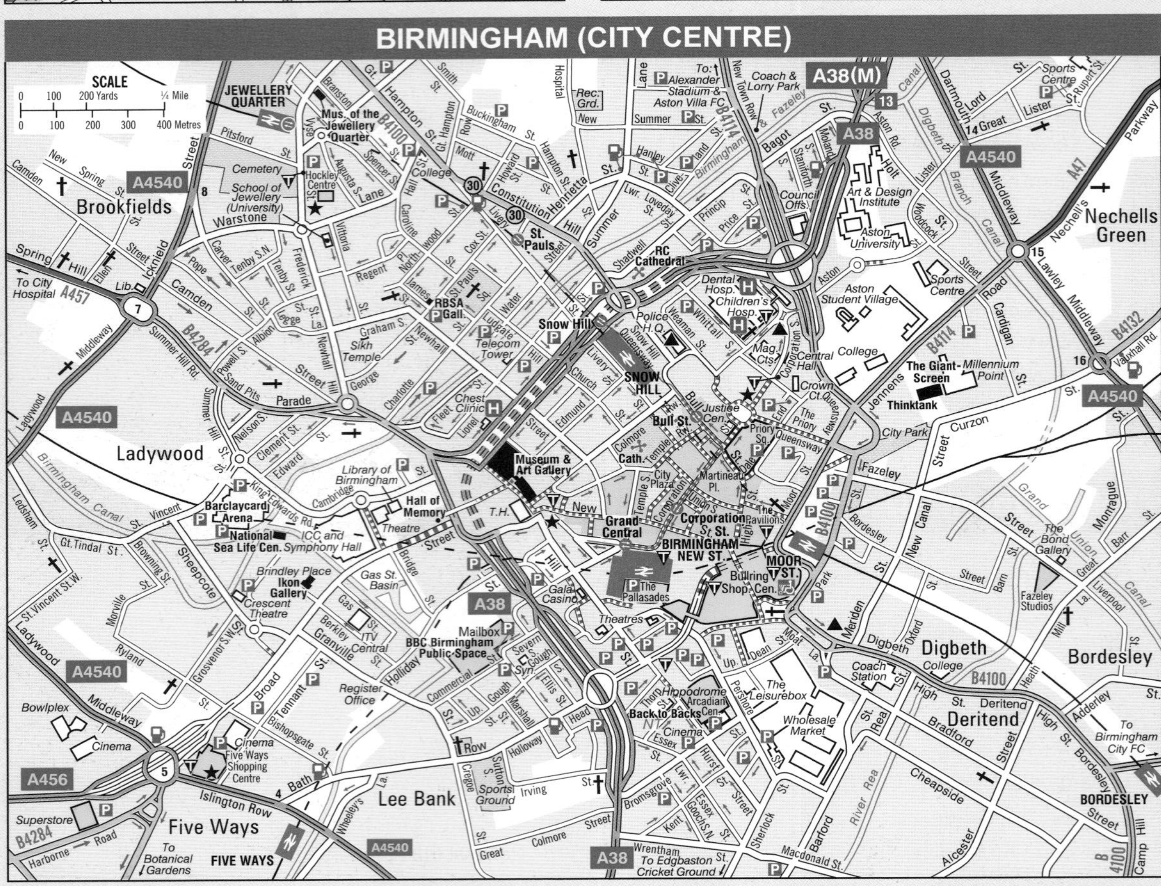

BOURNEMOUTH

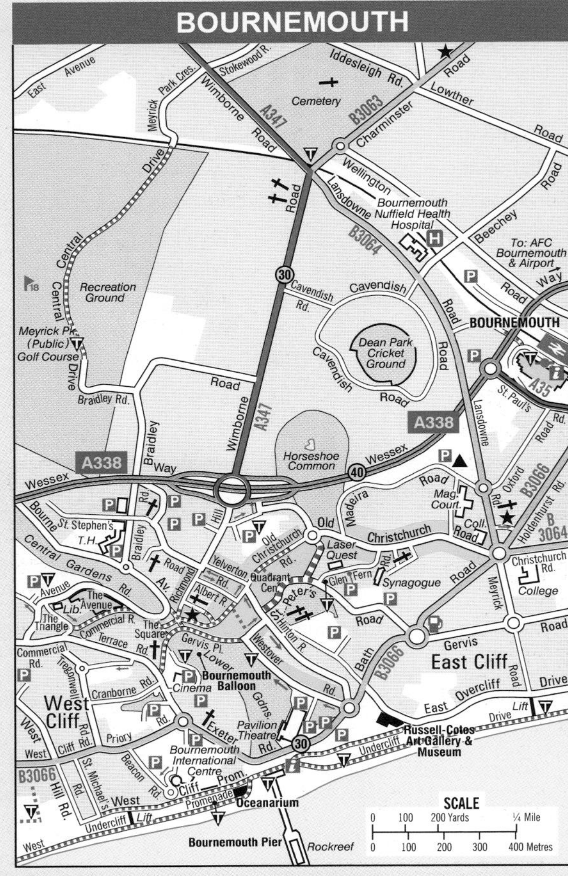

BRADFORD

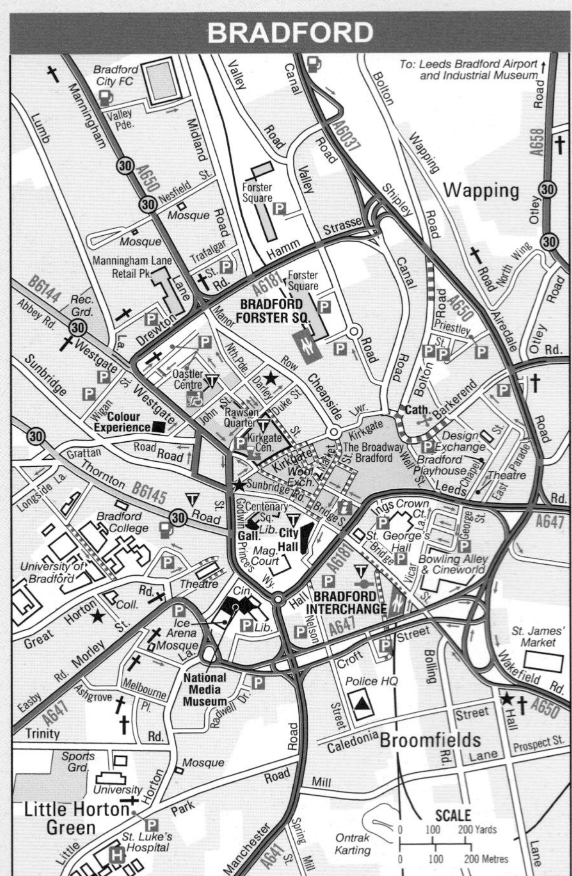

BRIGHTON and HOVE

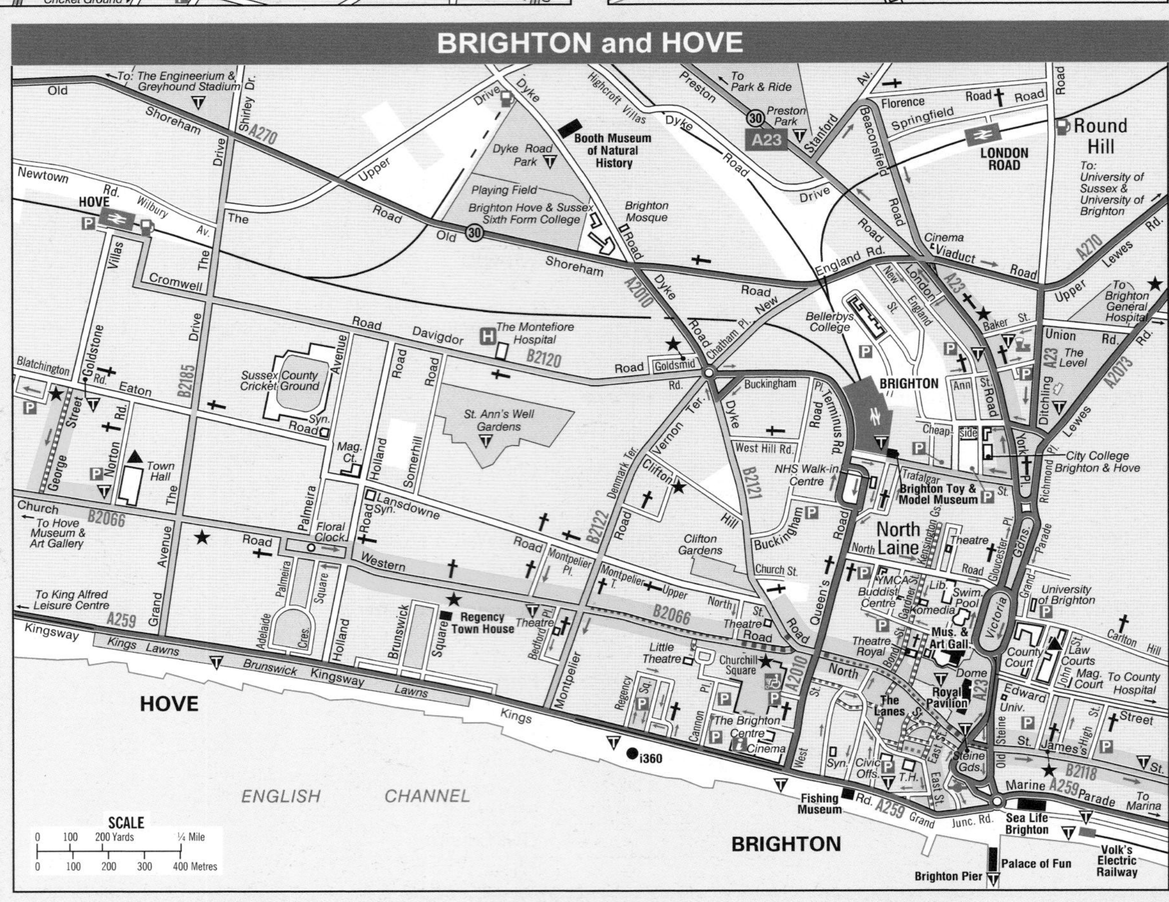

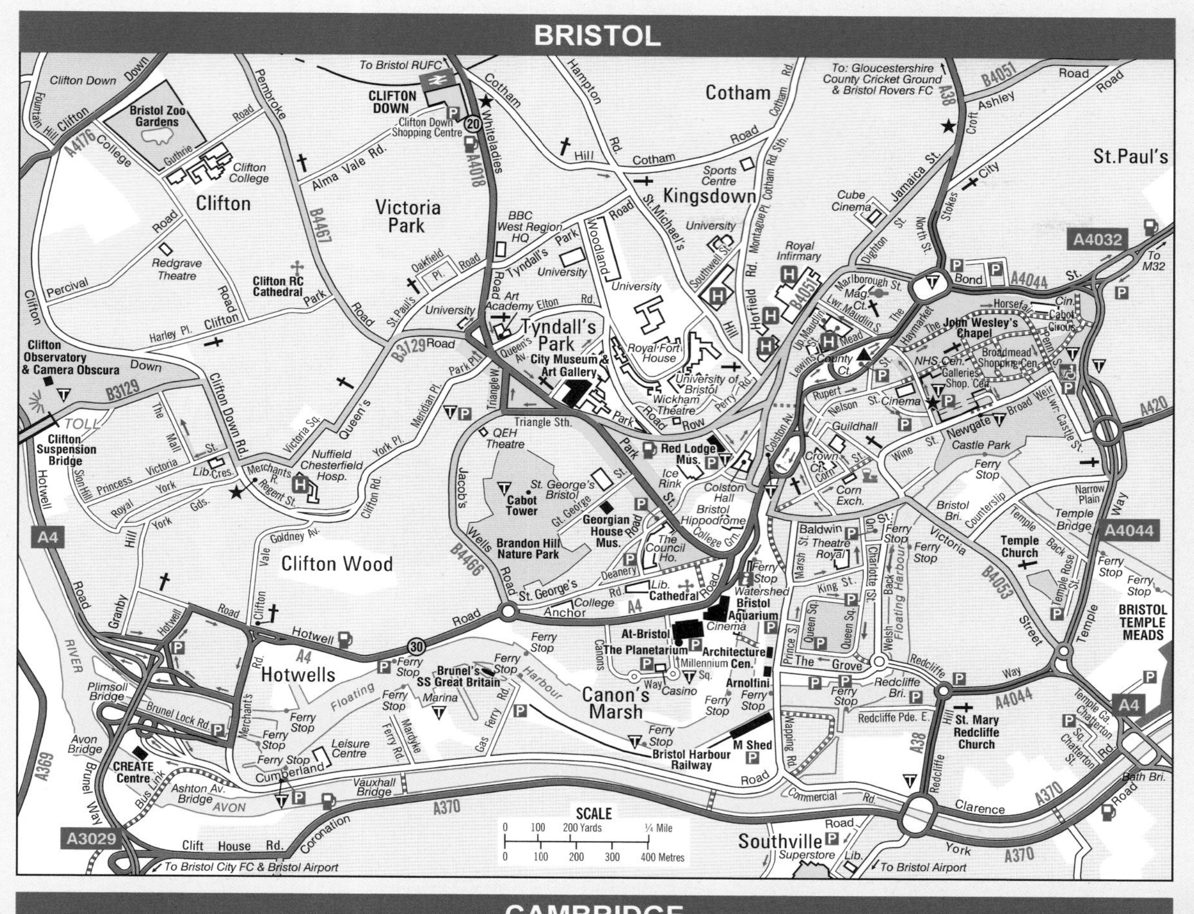
BRISTOL
Clifton Down
Bristol Zoo Gardens
Clifton College
Clifton
Cotham
Kingsdown
Victoria Park
St.Paul's
Redgrave Theatre
Clifton RC Cathedral
Clifton Observatory & Camera Obscura
Clifton Suspension Bridge
Tyndall's Park
City Museum & Art Gallery
Royal Infirmary
John Wesley's Chapel
Broadmead Shopping Cen.
Cabot Tower
Brandon Hill Nature Park
Georgian House Mus.
Red Lodge Mus.
Clifton Wood
Colston Hall
Bristol Hippodrome
Council Ho.
Cathedral
Bristol Aquarium
At-Bristol
The Planetarium
Millennium Sq.
Architecture Cen.
Arnolfini
Hotwells
Brunel's SS Great Britain
Canon's Marsh
Temple Church
Bristol Temple Meads
St. Mary Redcliffe Church
Bristol Harbour Railway
M Shed
CREATE Centre
Southville
Clarence
A4
A4032
A4044
A3029
A370
To Bristol City FC & Bristol Airport
To Bristol Airport
SCALE
200 Yards
¼ Mile
400 Metres

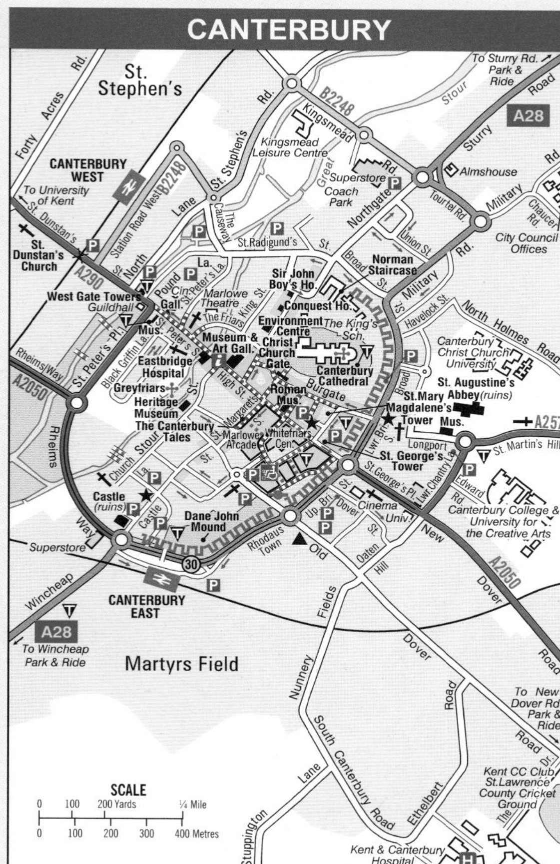
CANTERBURY
St. Stephen's
Kingsmead Leisure Centre
Almshouse
A28
Canterbury West
To University of Kent
City Council Offices
St. Dunstan's Church
West Gate Towers
Norman Staircase
Sir John Boys Ho.
Conquest Ho.
Marlowe Theatre
Museum & Art Gall.
Christ Church Gate
Eastbridge Hospital
Canterbury Cathedral
Canterbury Christ Church University
Greyfriars
Heritage Museum
The Canterbury Tales
Roman Mus.
St. Augustine's Abbey (ruins)
St.Mary Magdalene's Tower
St. George's Tower
Castle (ruins)
Dane John Mound
Canterbury College & University for the Creative Arts
Canterbury East
A28
To Wincheap Park & Ride
Martyrs Field
A257
A2050
To New Dover Rd. Park & Ride
Kent CC Club St.Lawrence County Cricket Ground
Kent & Canterbury Hospital
SCALE
200 Yards
¼ Mile
400 Metres

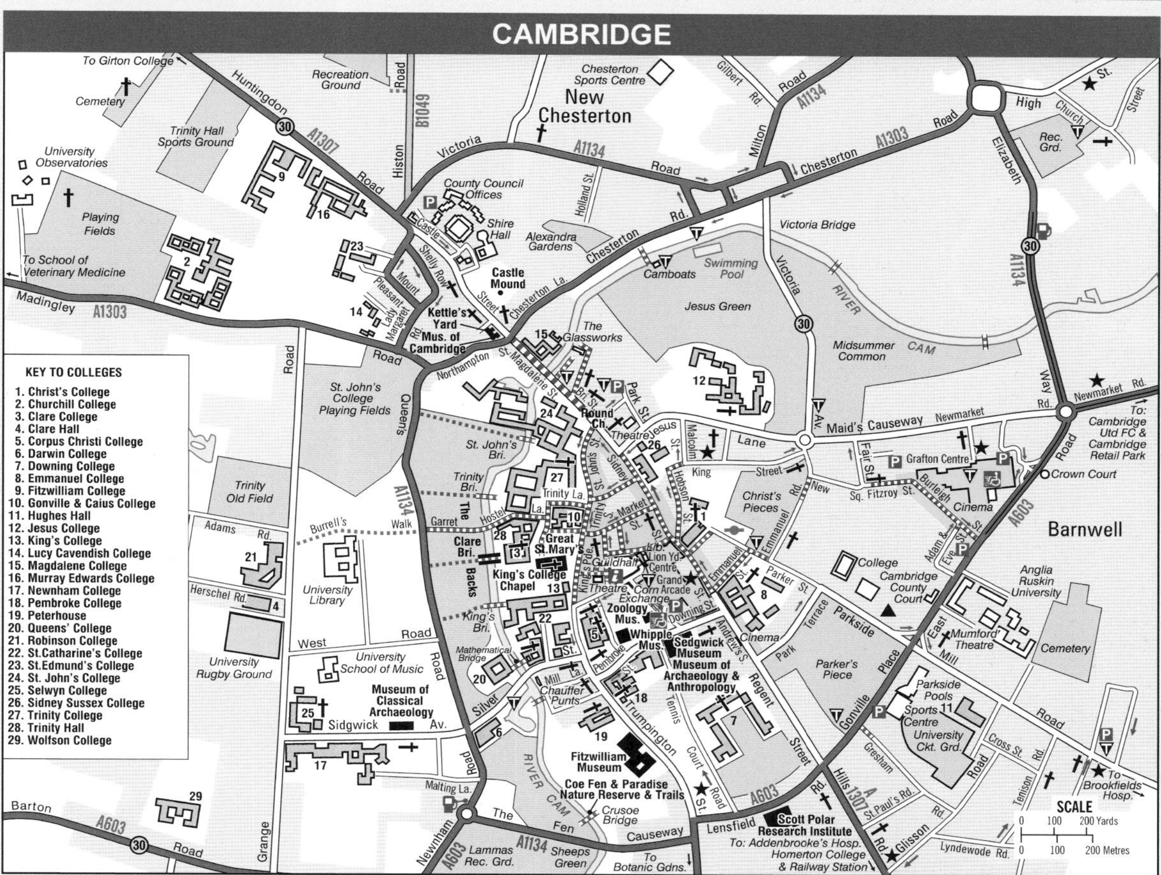
CAMBRIDGE
To Girton College
Recreation Ground
Chesterton Sports Centre
New Chesterton
Trinity Hall Sports Ground
University Observatories
Playing Fields
To School of Veterinary Medicine
County Council Offices
Shire Hall
Alexandra Gardens
Castle Mound
Kettle's Yard
Mus. of Cambridge
Victoria Bridge
Jesus Green
Midsummer Common
The Glassworks
St. John's College Playing Fields
Maid's Causeway
Grafton Centre
Christ's Pieces
Trinity Old Field
Round Ch.
Great St.Mary's
King's College Chapel
Zoology Mus.
Whipple Mus.
Sedgwick Museum
Museum of Archaeology & Anthropology
University Library
University Rugby Ground
University School of Music
Museum of Classical Archaeology
Fitzwilliam Museum
Coe Fen & Paradise Nature Reserve & Trails
Parker's Piece
Mumford Theatre
Anglia Ruskin University
Barnwell
Parkside Pools
University Ckt. Grd.
Scott Polar Research Institute
To: Addenbrooke's Hosp. Homerton College & Railway Station
To Botanic Gdns.
Lammas Rec. Grd.
Sheeps Green
Cemetery
To: Cambridge Utd FC & Cambridge Retail Park
KEY TO COLLEGES
1. Christ's College
2. Churchill College
3. Clare College
4. Clare Hall
5. Corpus Christi College
6. Darwin College
7. Downing College
8. Emmanuel College
9. Fitzwilliam College
10. Gonville & Caius College
11. Hughes Hall
12. Jesus College
13. King's College
14. Lucy Cavendish College
15. Magdalene College
16. Murray Edwards College
17. Newnham College
18. Pembroke College
19. Peterhouse
20. Queens' College
21. Robinson College
22. St.Catharine's College
23. St.Edmund's College
24. St. John's College
25. Selwyn College
26. Sidney Sussex College
27. Trinity College
28. Trinity Hall
29. Wolfson College
SCALE
200 Yards
200 Metres

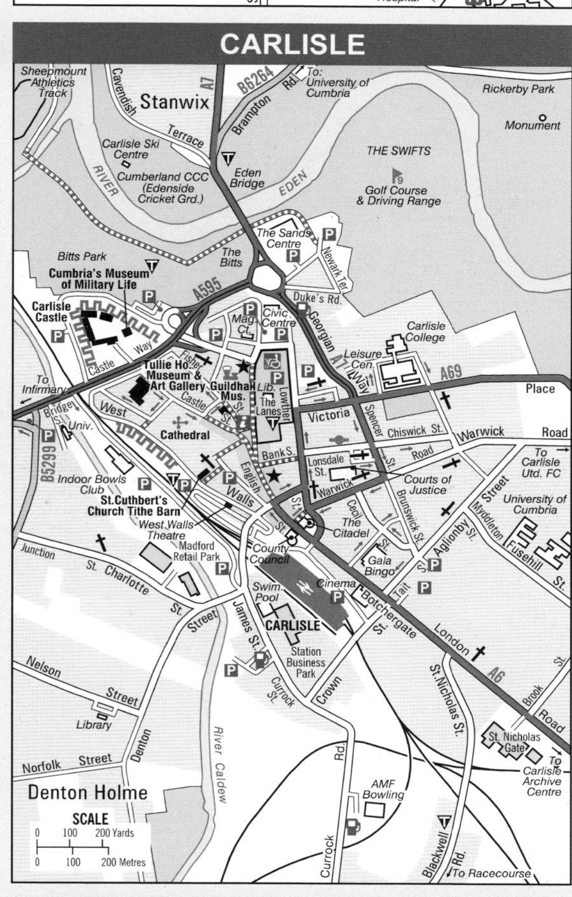
CARLISLE
Sheepmount Athletics Track
Stanwix
To: University of Cumbria
Rickerby Park
Monument
Carlisle Ski Centre
Cumberland CCC (Edenside Cricket Grd.)
THE SWIFTS
Golf Course & Driving Range
Eden Bridge
The Sands Centre
Bitts Park
Cumbria's Museum of Military Life
The Bitts
Carlisle Castle
Civic Centre
Carlisle College
Tullie Ho. Museum & Art Gallery
Guildhall Mus.
Cathedral
Leisure Cen.
Carlisle Utd. FC
University of Cumbria
Courts of Justice
St.Cuthbert's Church
Tithe Barn
West Walls Theatre
Madford Retail Park
The Citadel
Gala Bingo
Carlisle
Station Business Park
Denton Holme
Library
AMF Bowling
St. Nicholas Gate
Carlisle Archive Centre
To Racecourse
SCALE
200 Yards
200 Metres

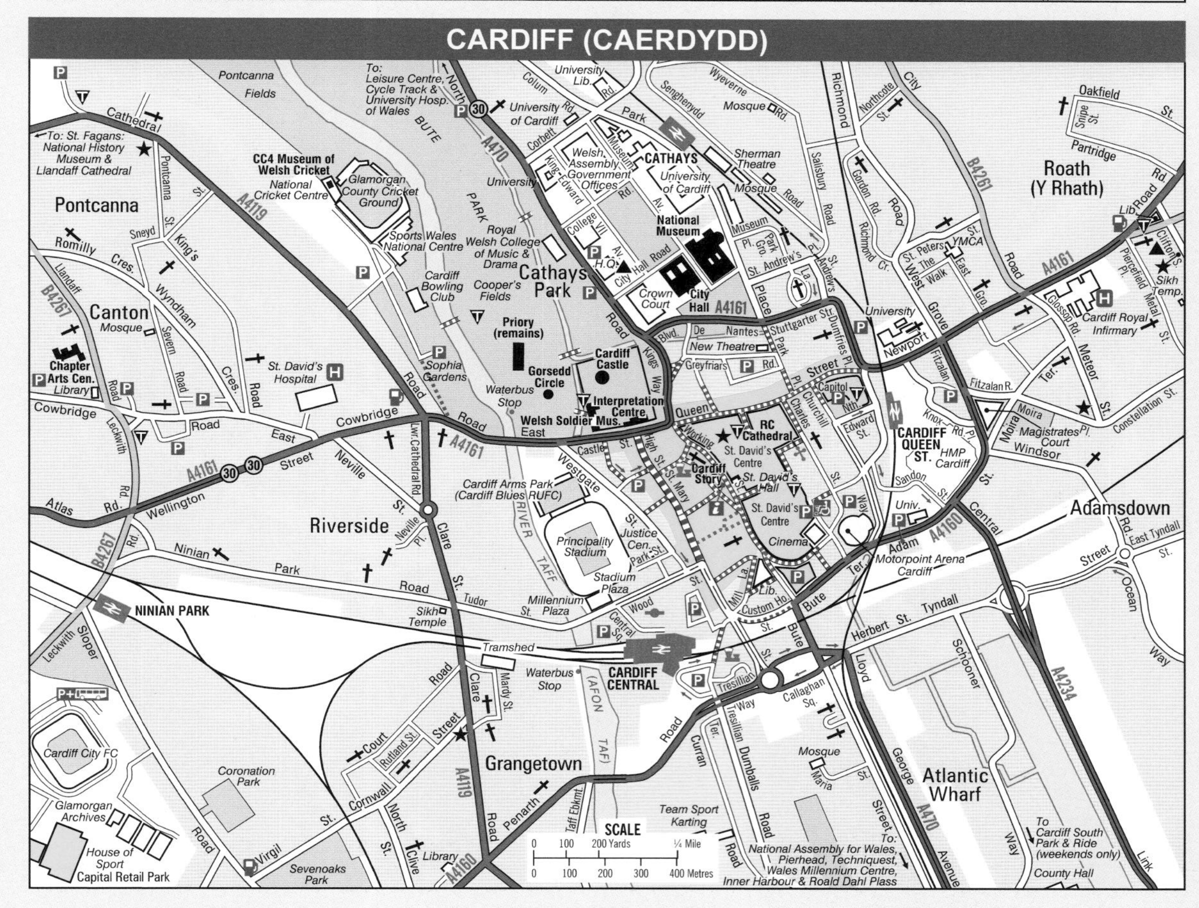
CARDIFF (CAERDYDD)
Pontcanna Fields
To: Leisure Centre, Cycle Track & University Hosp. of Wales
To: St. Fagans: National History Museum & Llandaff Cathedral
CC4 Museum of Welsh Cricket
Glamorgan County Cricket Ground
National Cricket Centre
Sports Wales National Centre
Pontcanna
Canton
Mosque
Chapter Arts Cen.
Cathays
University of Cardiff
Welsh Assembly Government Offices
Sherman Theatre
National Museum
Royal Welsh College of Music & Drama
Cathays Park
City Hall
Crown Court
Roath (Y Rhath)
Cardiff Royal Infirmary
Cardiff Bowling Club
Cooper's Fields
Priory (remains)
Gorsedd Circle
Cardiff Castle
Interpretation Centre
Welsh Soldier Mus.
RC Cathedral
New Theatre
Cardiff Queen St.
HMP Cardiff
Magistrates' Court
St. David's Hospital
Sophia Gardens
Riverside
Cardiff Arms Park (Cardiff Blues RUFC)
Principality Stadium
St. David's Centre
Justice Cen.
Cardiff Story
Motorpoint Arena Cardiff
Adamsdown
Ninian Park
Tramshed
Millennium Plaza
Cardiff Central
Cardiff City FC
Coronation Park
Grangetown
Atlantic Wharf
Glamorgan Archives
House of Sport
Sevenoaks Park
Capital Retail Park
Team Sport Karting
National Assembly for Wales, Pierhead, Techniquest, Wales Millennium Centre, Inner Harbour & Roald Dahl Plass
To Cardiff South Park & Ride (weekends only)
County Hall
SCALE
200 Yards
¼ Mile
400 Metres

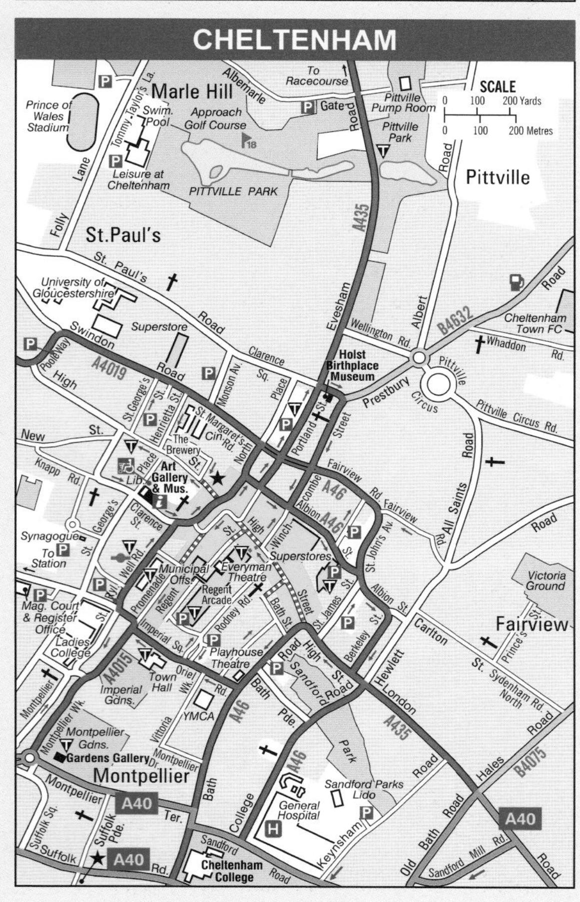
CHELTENHAM
To Racecourse
Marle Hill
Prince of Wales Stadium
Pittville Pump Room
Pittville Park
Approach Golf Course
Leisure at Cheltenham
PITTVILLE PARK
Pittville
St.Paul's
University of Gloucestershire
Superstore
Cheltenham Town FC
Holst Birthplace Museum
Art Gallery & Mus.
Municipal Offs.
Everyman Theatre
Regent Arcade
Playhouse Theatre
To Station
Victoria Ground
Fairview
Town Hall
Imperial Gdns.
Montpellier Gdns.
Gardens Gallery
Montpellier
General Hospital
Sandford Parks Lido
Cheltenham College
A40
A46
A435
A4019
SCALE
200 Yards
200 Metres

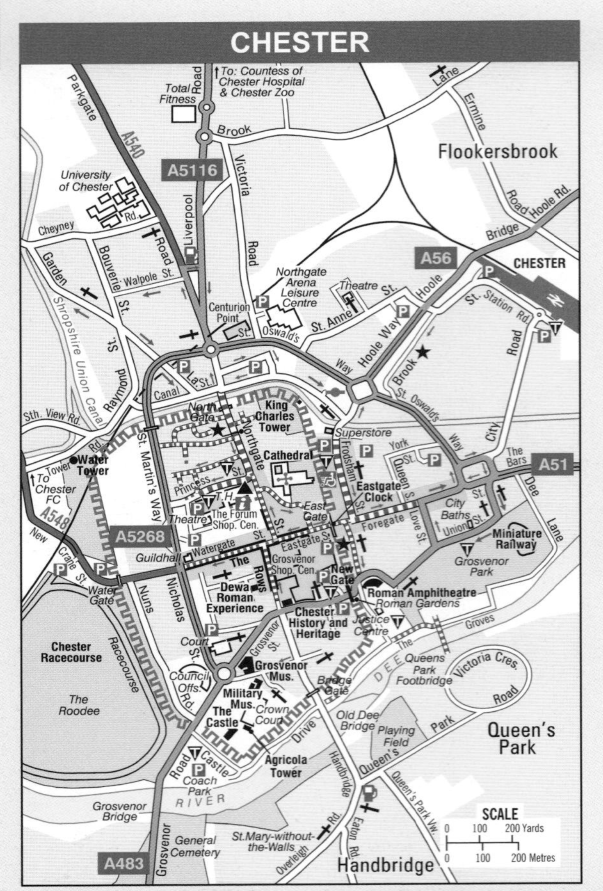
CHESTER
To: Countess of Chester Hospital & Chester Zoo
Flookersbrook
University of Chester
A5116
A56
CHESTER
Northgate Arena Leisure Centre
King Charles Tower
Cathedral
Eastgate Clock
A51
Water Tower
A5268
Miniature Railway
Grosvenor Park
Dewa Roman Experience
Roman Amphitheatre
Roman Gardens
Chester History and Heritage
Chester Racecourse
The Roodee
Grosvenor Mus.
Military Mus.
The Castle
Agricola Tower
Queen's Park
Grosvenor Bridge
General Cemetery
St.Mary-without-the-Walls
Handbridge
A483
SCALE
0 100 200 Yards
0 100 200 Metres

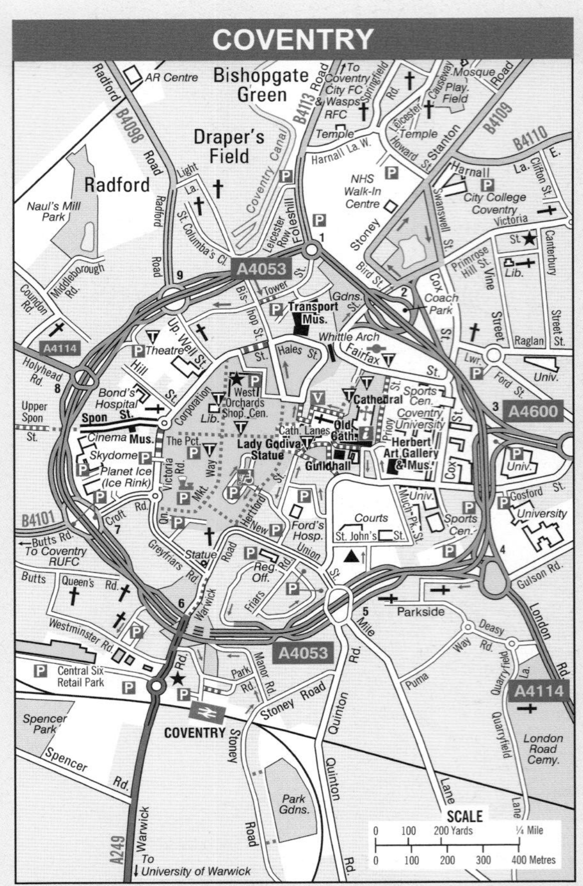
COVENTRY
Bishopgate Green
Draper's Field
Radford
Naul's Mill Park
A4053
Transport Mus.
Whittle Arch
Cathedral
Lady Godiva Statue
Guildhall
Herbert Art Gallery & Mus.
Spon St.
Skydome
Planet Ice (Ice Rink)
A4600
Courts
Parkside
A4114
COVENTRY
Central Six Retail Park
Spencer Park
Park Gdns.
London Road Cemy.
To University of Warwick
SCALE
0 100 200 Yards ¼ Mile
0 100 200 300 400 Metres

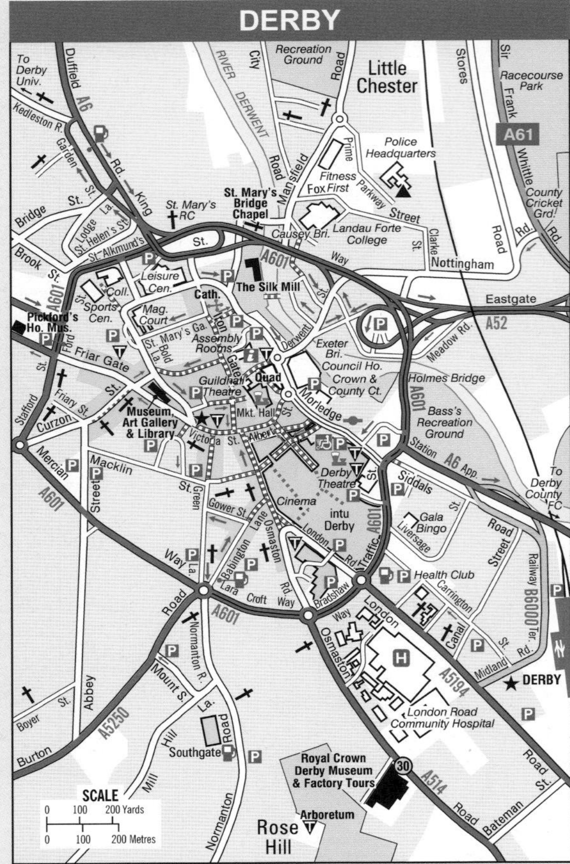
DERBY
To Derby Univ.
Recreation Ground
Little Chester
Racecourse Park
A61
Police Headquarters
St. Mary's Bridge Chapel
The Silk Mill
Cath.
Eastgate
Pickford's Ho. Mus.
Museum Art Gallery & Library
Derby Theatre
intu Derby
Bass's Recreation Ground
A52
A601
A6
DERBY
London Road Community Hospital
Royal Crown Derby Museum & Factory Tours
Arboretum
Rose Hill
SCALE
0 100 200 Yards
0 100 200 Metres

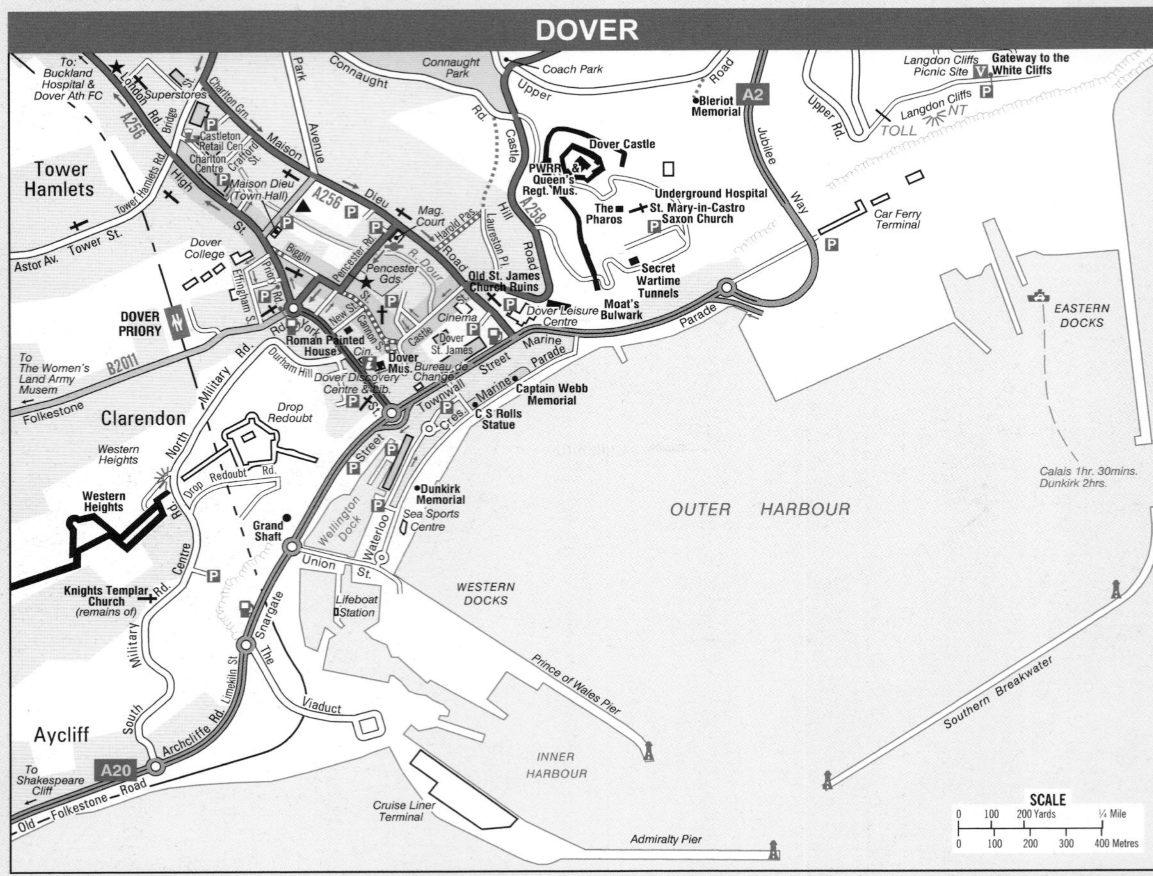
DOVER
To: Buckland Hospital & Dover Ath FC
Tower Hamlets
Connaught Park
Coach Park
Bleriot Memorial
A2
Langdon Cliffs Picnic Site
Gateway to the White Cliffs
Dover Castle
PWRR & Queen's Regt. Mus.
The Pharos
Underground Hospital
St. Mary-in-Castro Saxon Church
Secret Wartime Tunnels
Car Ferry Terminal
EASTERN DOCKS
DOVER PRIORY
Old St. James Church Ruins
Moat's Bulwark
Roman Painted House
Dover Mus.
Captain Webb Memorial
C S Rolls Statue
Clarendon
Drop Redoubt
Western Heights
Grand Shaft
Dunkirk Memorial
Sea Sports Centre
OUTER HARBOUR
Calais 1hr. 30mins. Dunkirk 2hrs.
Knights Templar Church (remains of)
WESTERN DOCKS
Lifeboat Station
Prince of Wales Pier
Southern Breakwater
INNER HARBOUR
Aycliff
A20
To Shakespeare Cliff
Cruise Liner Terminal
Admiralty Pier
SCALE
0 100 200 Yards ¼ Mile
0 100 200 300 400 Metres

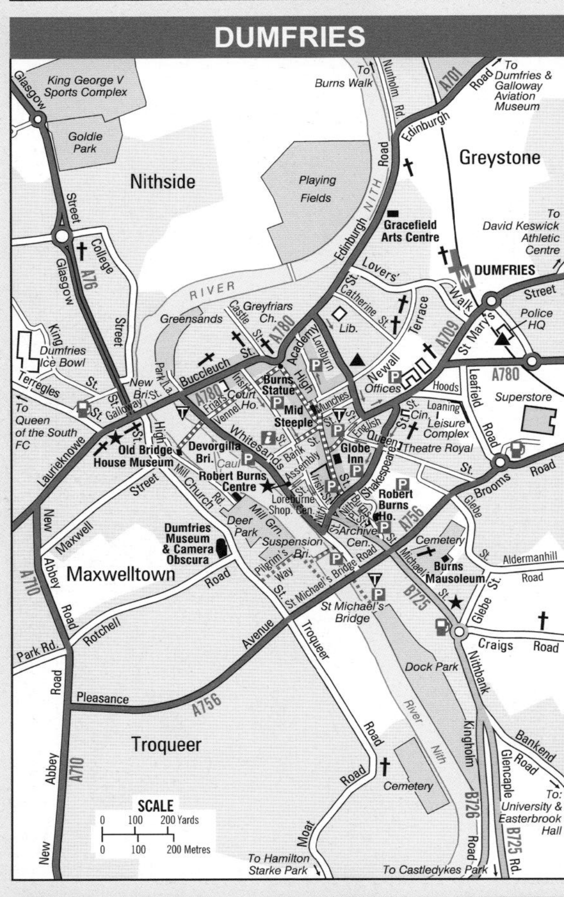
DUMFRIES
King George V Sports Complex
To: Dumfries & Galloway Aviation Museum
Burns Walk
Goldie Park
Nithside
Greystone
Playing Fields
Gracefield Arts Centre
To David Keswick Athletic Centre
DUMFRIES
Police HQ
Dumfries Ice Bowl
Burns Statue
Mid Steeple
Superstore
To Queen of the South FC
Old Bridge House Museum
Devorgilla Bri.
Globe Inn
Theatre Royal
Robert Burns Centre
Robert Burns Ho.
Dumfries Museum & Camera Obscura
Maxwelltown
Burns Mausoleum
St Michael's Bridge
Dock Park
Troqueer
A756
A710
To: University & Easterbrook Hall
To Hamilton Starke Park
To Castledykes Park
SCALE
0 100 200 Yards
0 100 200 Metres

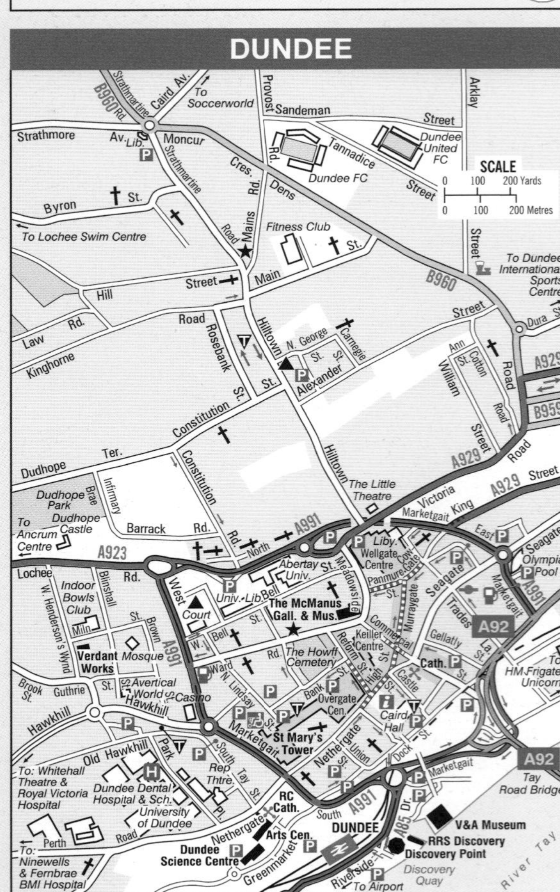
DUNDEE
To: Soccerworld
Dundee United FC
Dundee FC
To Lochee Swim Centre
To Dundee International Sports Centre
A929
B959
The Little Theatre
To Ancrum Centre
Indoor Bowls Club
Verdant Works
The McManus Gall. & Mus.
A92
HM Frigate Unicorn
Olympia Pool
To: Whitehall Theatre & Royal Victoria Hospital
Dundee Dental Hospital & Sch.
University of Dundee
To: Ninewells & Fernbrae BMI Hospital
Dundee Science Centre
V&A Museum
RRS Discovery
Discovery Point
DUNDEE
Tay Road Bridge
River Tay
SCALE
0 100 200 Yards
0 100 200 Metres

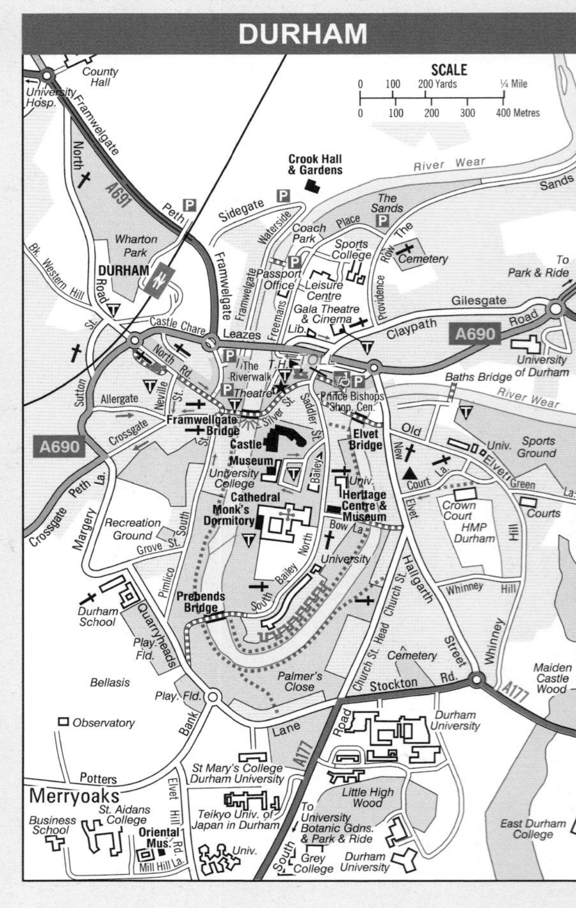
DURHAM
County Hall
Crook Hall & Gardens
River Wear
The Sands
Wharton Park
DURHAM
Gala Theatre & Cinema
A690
Gilesgate
To Park & Ride
University of Durham
Baths Bridge
Framwellgate Bridge
Castle
Cathedral
Elvet Bridge
Heritage Centre & Museum
Crown Court
HMP Durham
Prebends Bridge
Durham School
Observatory
Maiden Castle Wood
A177
Merryoaks
Oriental Mus.
Durham University
East Durham College
SCALE
0 100 200 Yards ¼ Mile
0 100 200 300 400 Metres

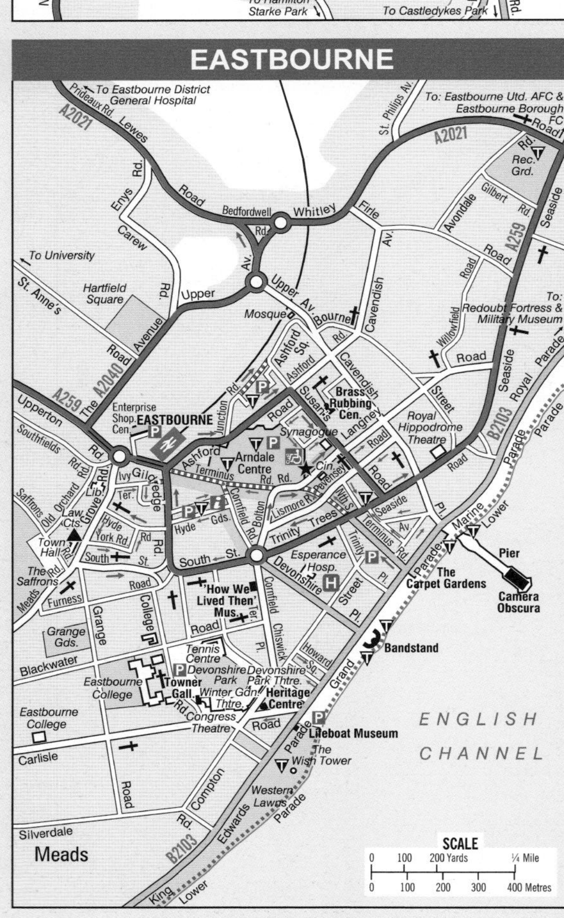
EASTBOURNE
To Eastbourne District General Hospital
To: Eastbourne Utd. AFC & Eastbourne Borough F.C.
A2021
To University
Hartfield Square
Redoubt Fortress & Military Museum
EASTBOURNE
Enterprise Shop. Cen.
Arndale Centre
Brass Rubbing Cen.
Royal Hippodrome Theatre
How We Lived Then Mus.
Esperance Hosp.
Pier
The Carpet Gardens
Camera Obscura
Bandstand
Towner Gall.
Devonshire Park
Congress Theatre
Eastbourne College
Lifeboat Museum
The Wish Tower
Western Lawns
ENGLISH CHANNEL
Meads
SCALE
0 100 200 Yards ¼ Mile
0 100 200 300 400 Metres

EDINBURGH

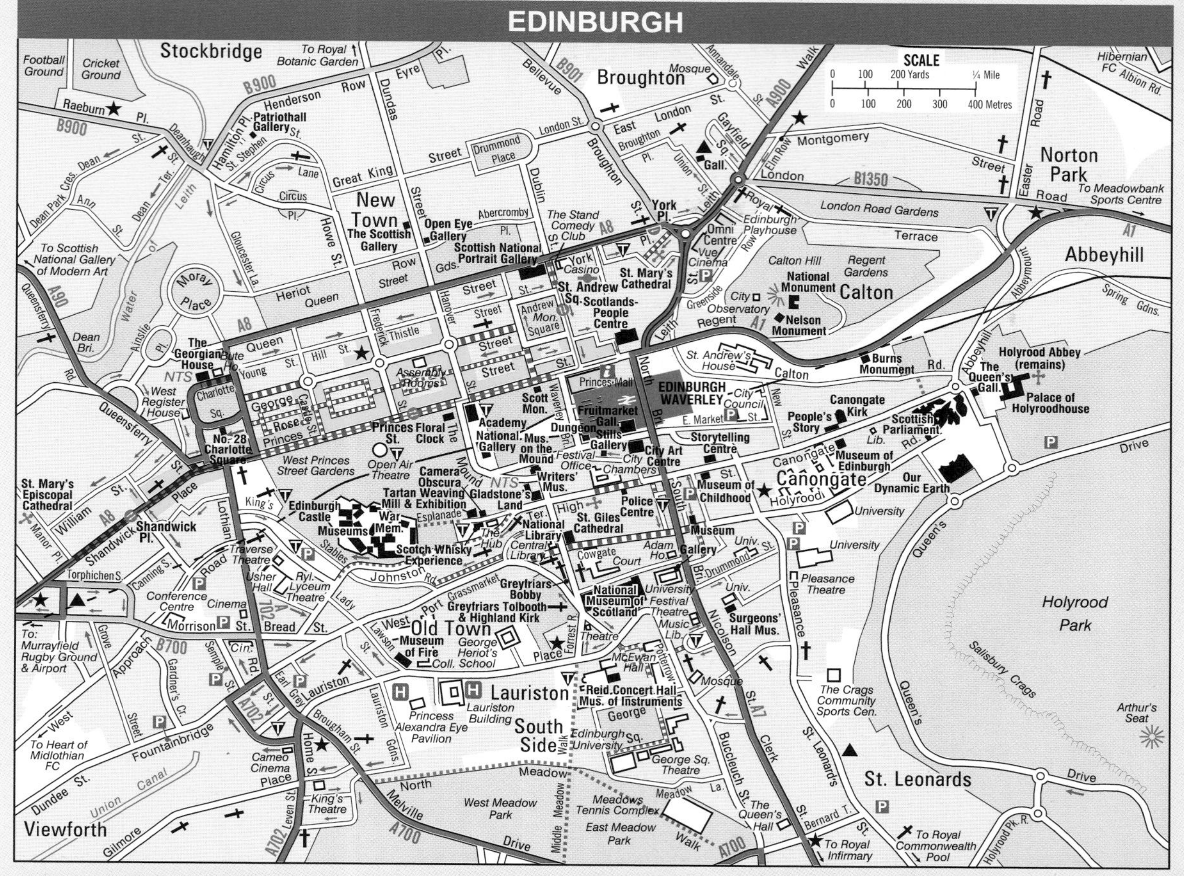

FOLKESTONE

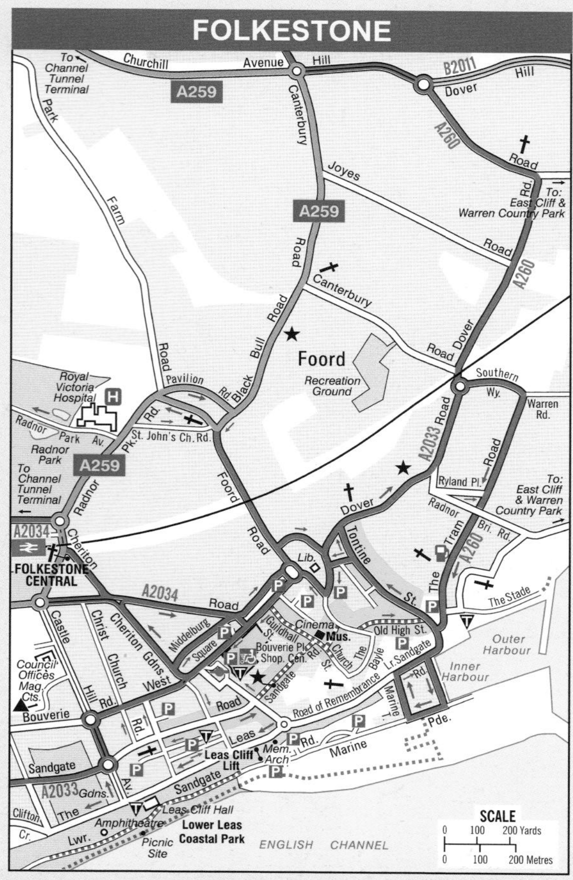

EXETER

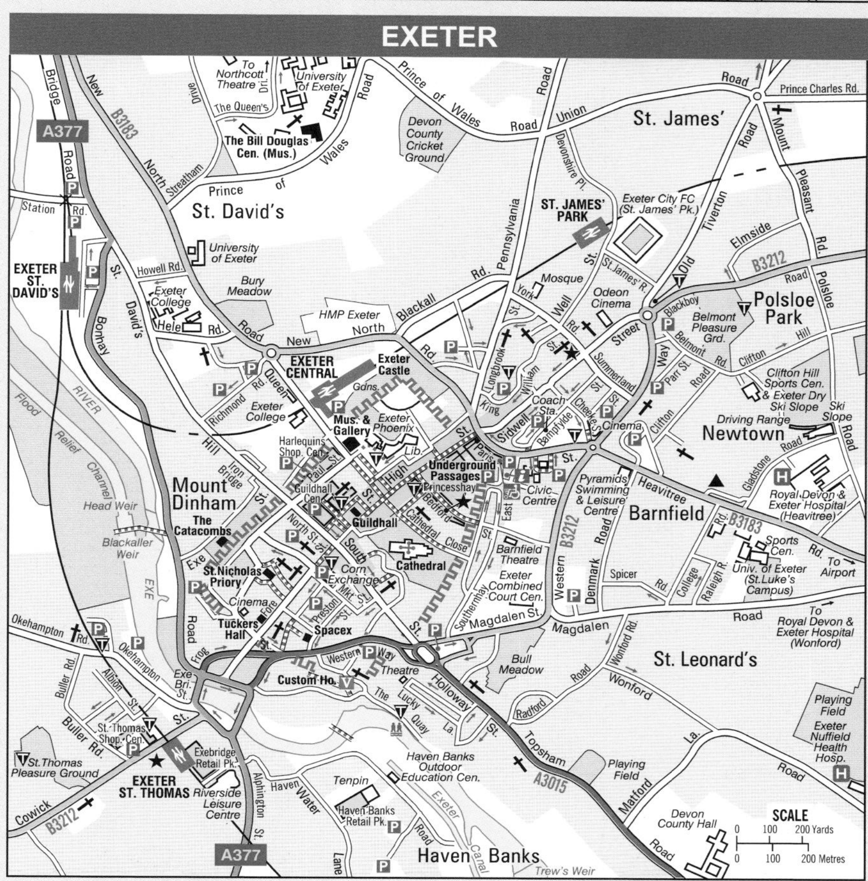

GUILDFORD

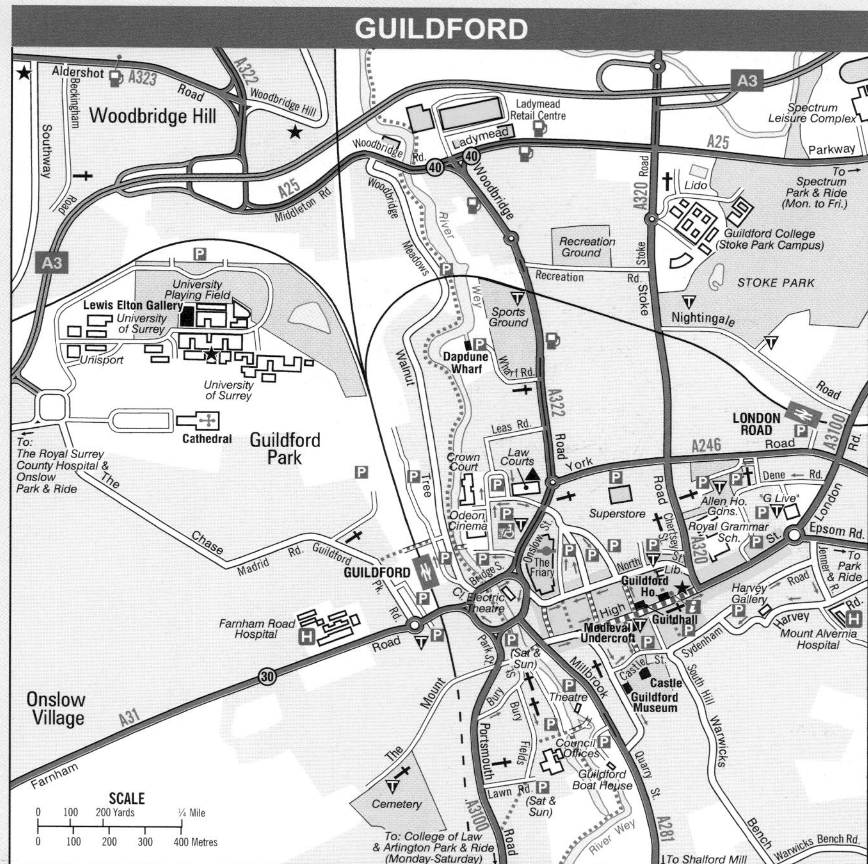

GLASGOW

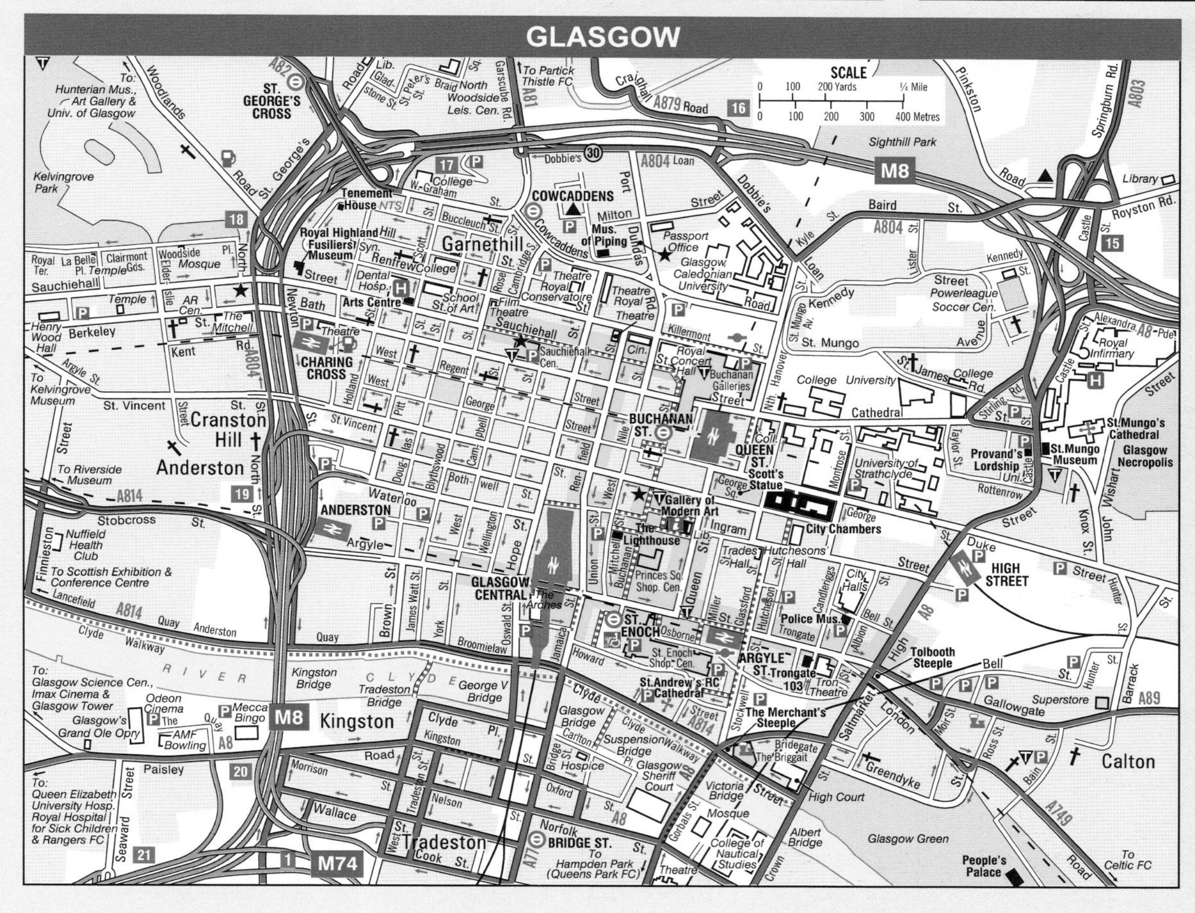

GLOUCESTER

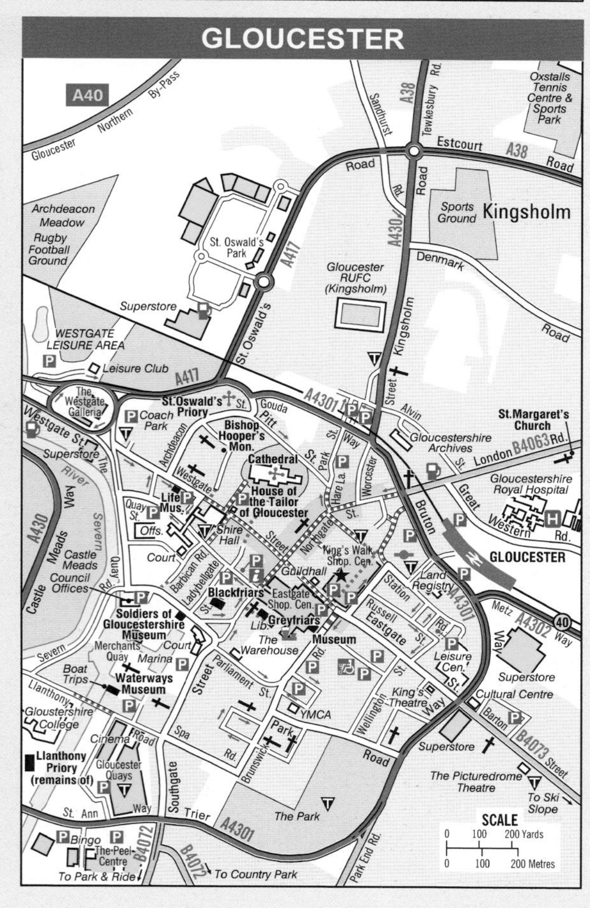

HARROGATE
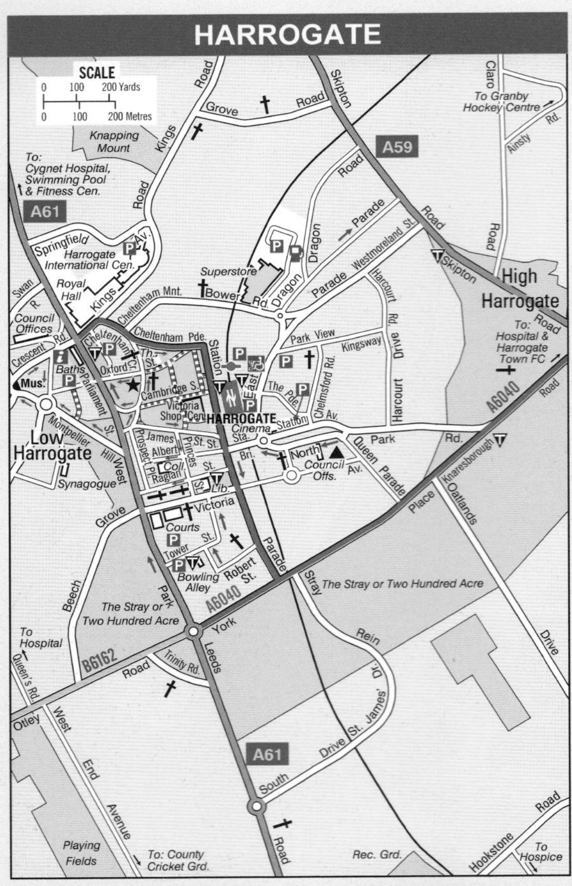

INVERNESS
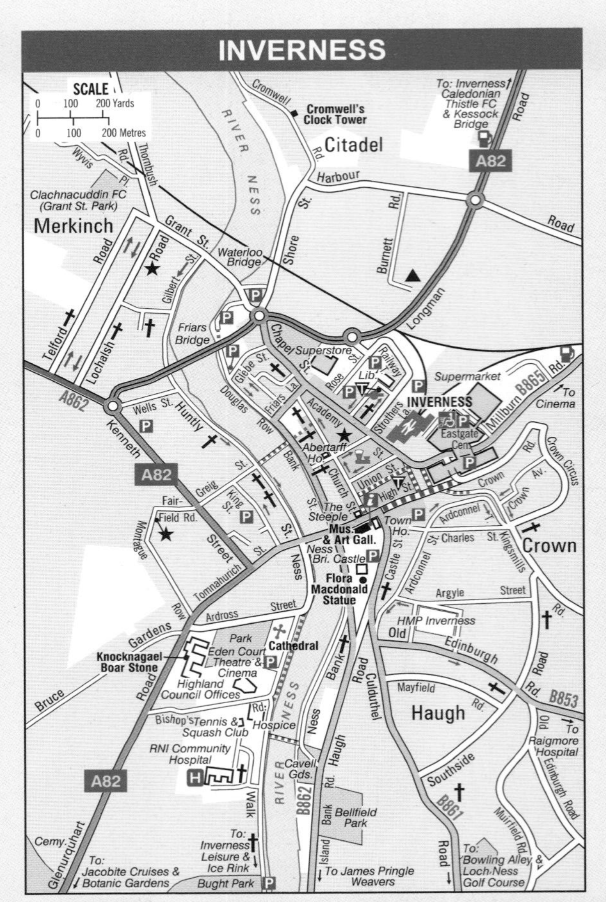

IPSWICH
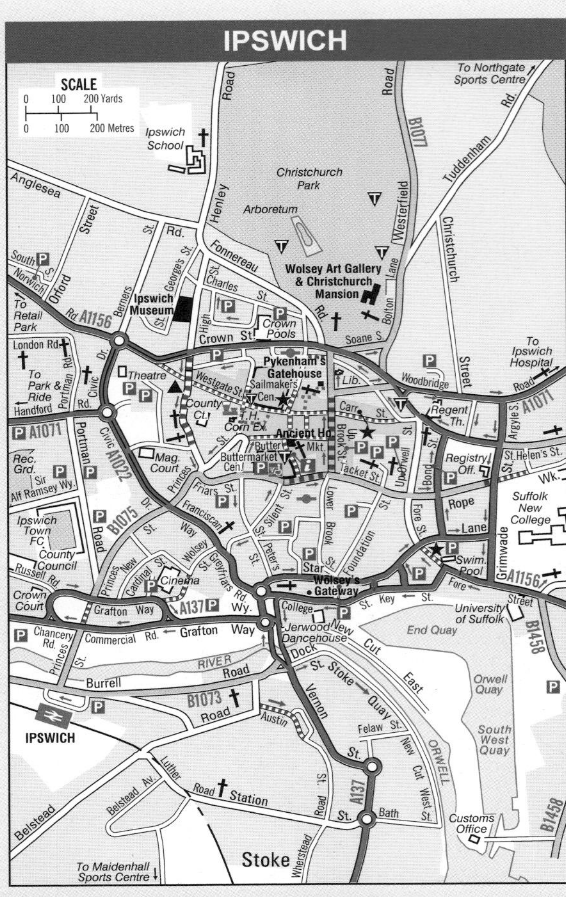

KILMARNOCK
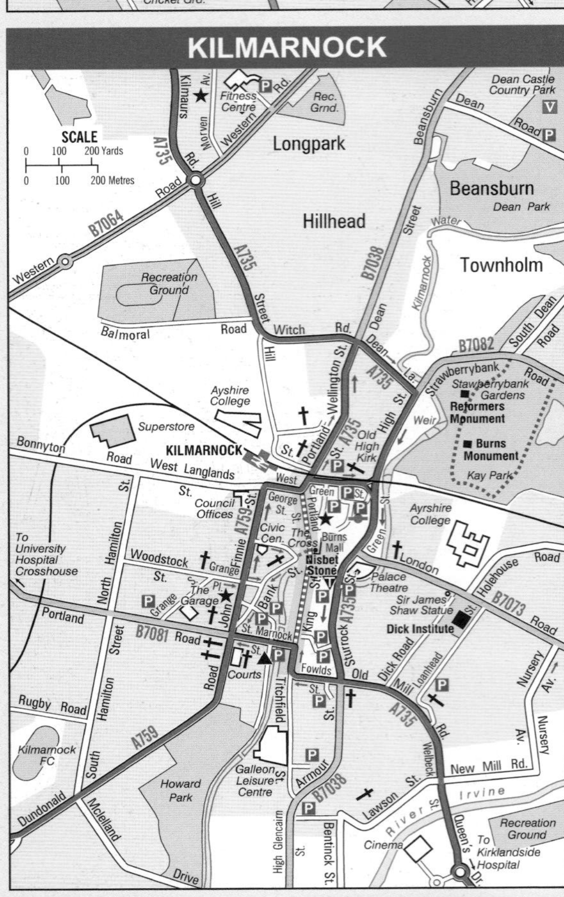

LEEDS
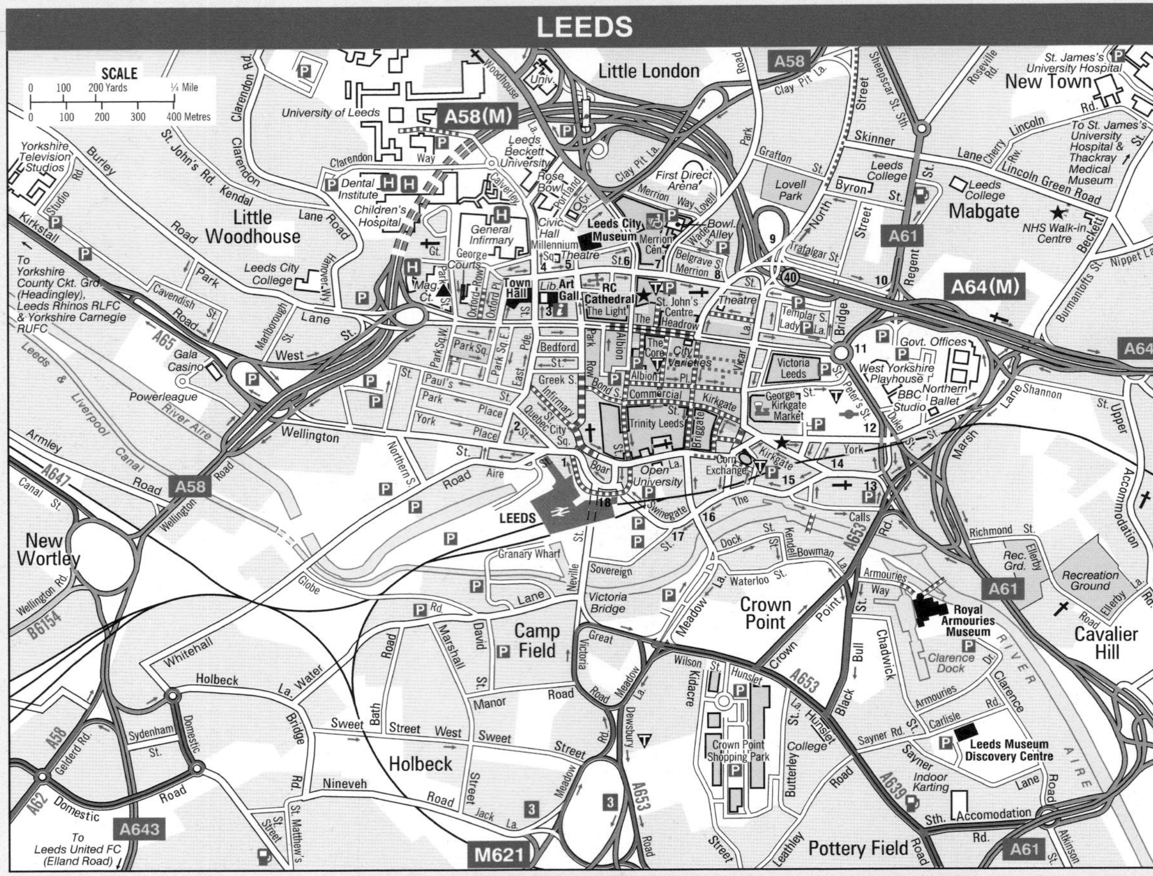

KINGSTON UPON HULL
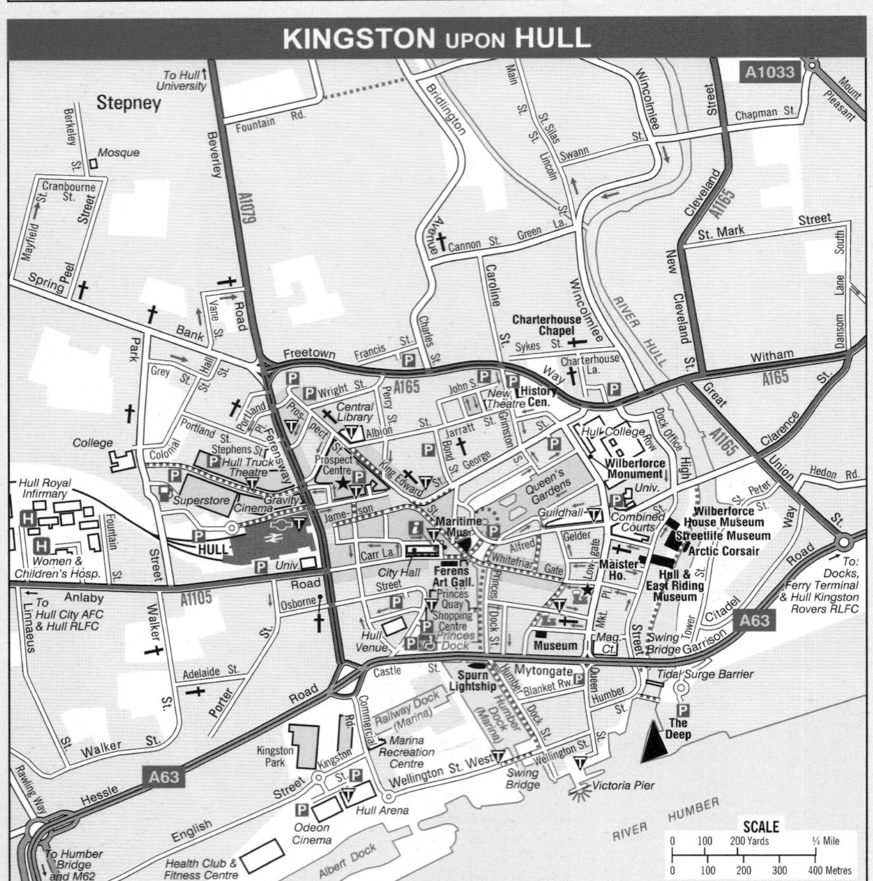

LEICESTER
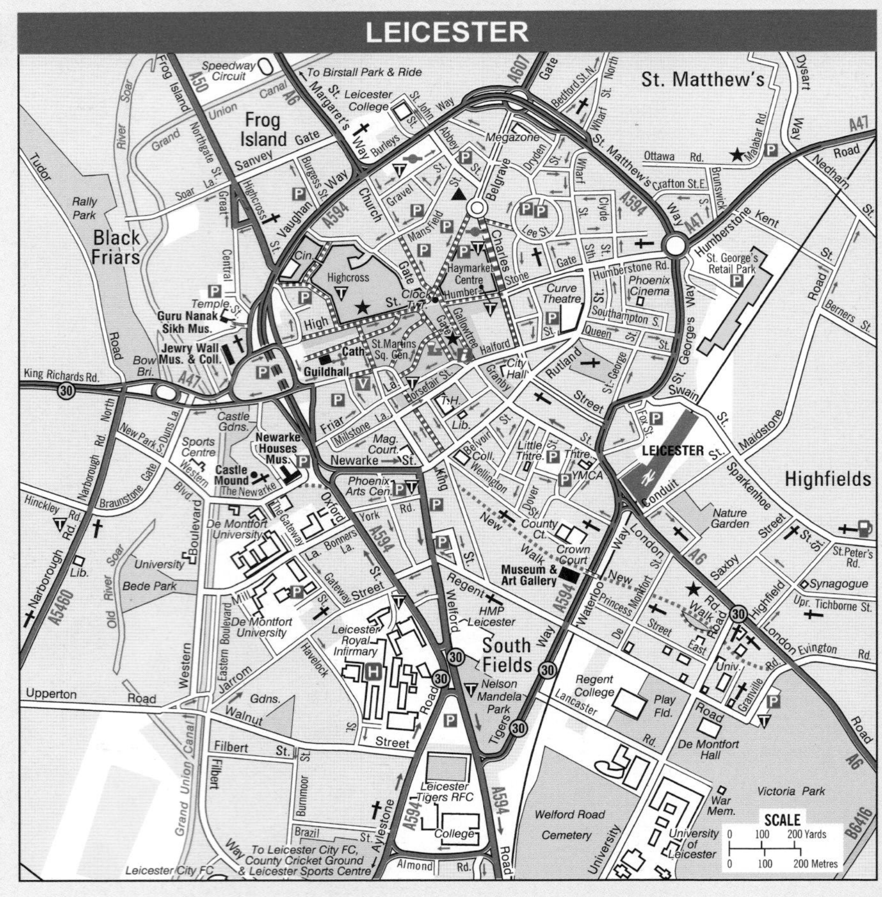

LINCOLN

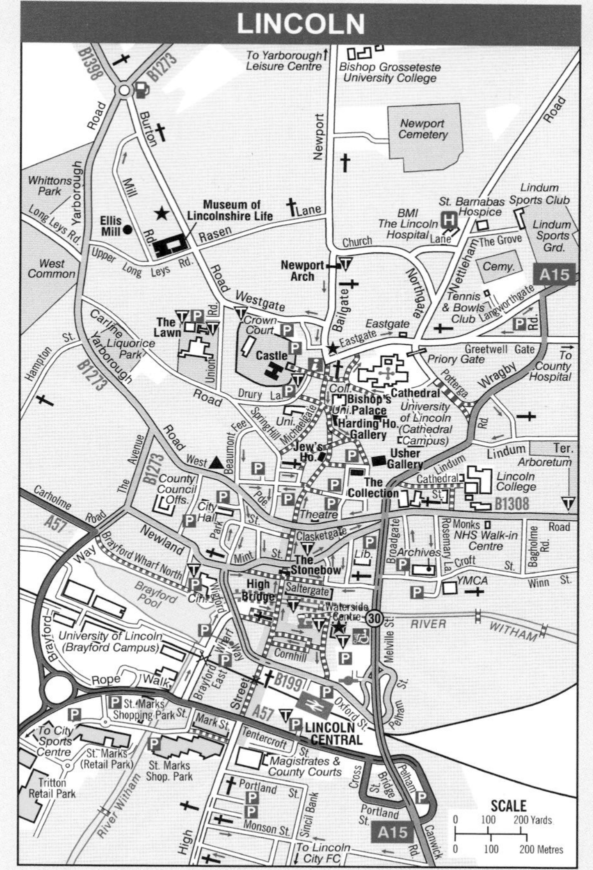

LIVERPOOL

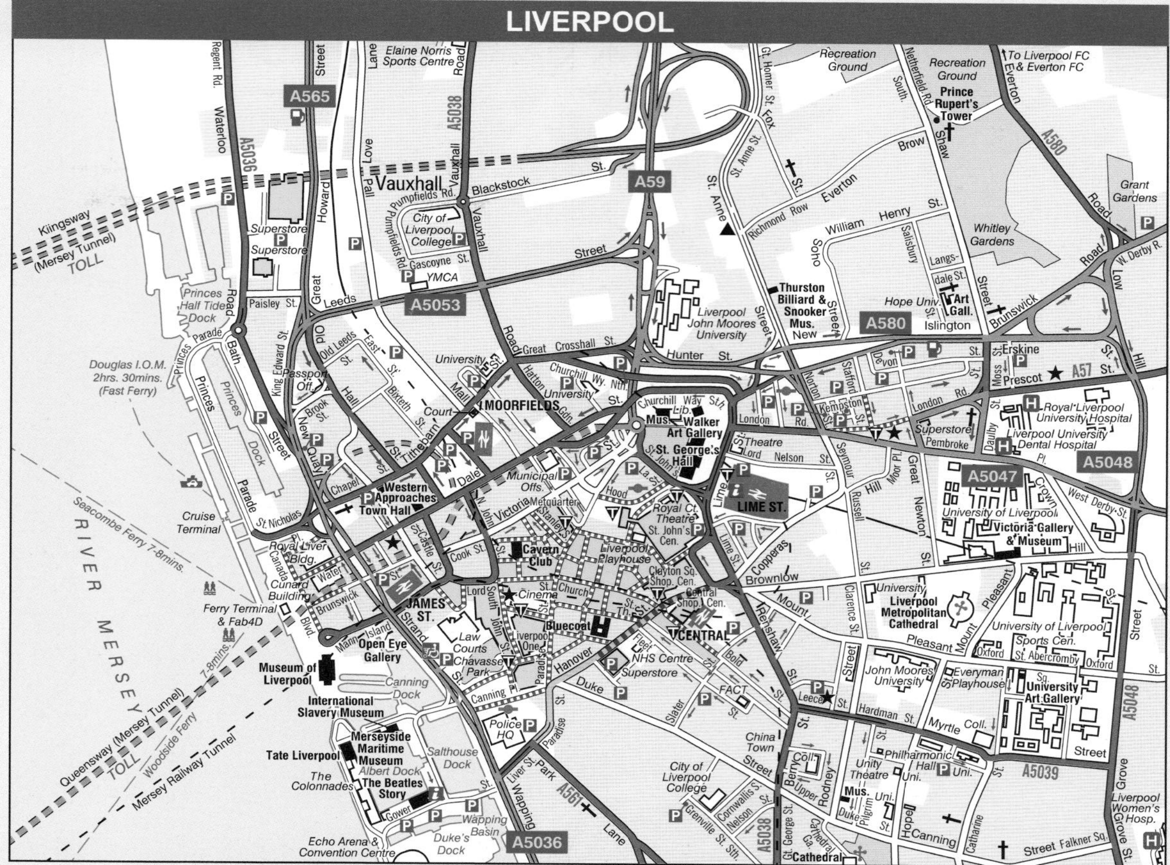

MANCHESTER (CITY CENTRE)

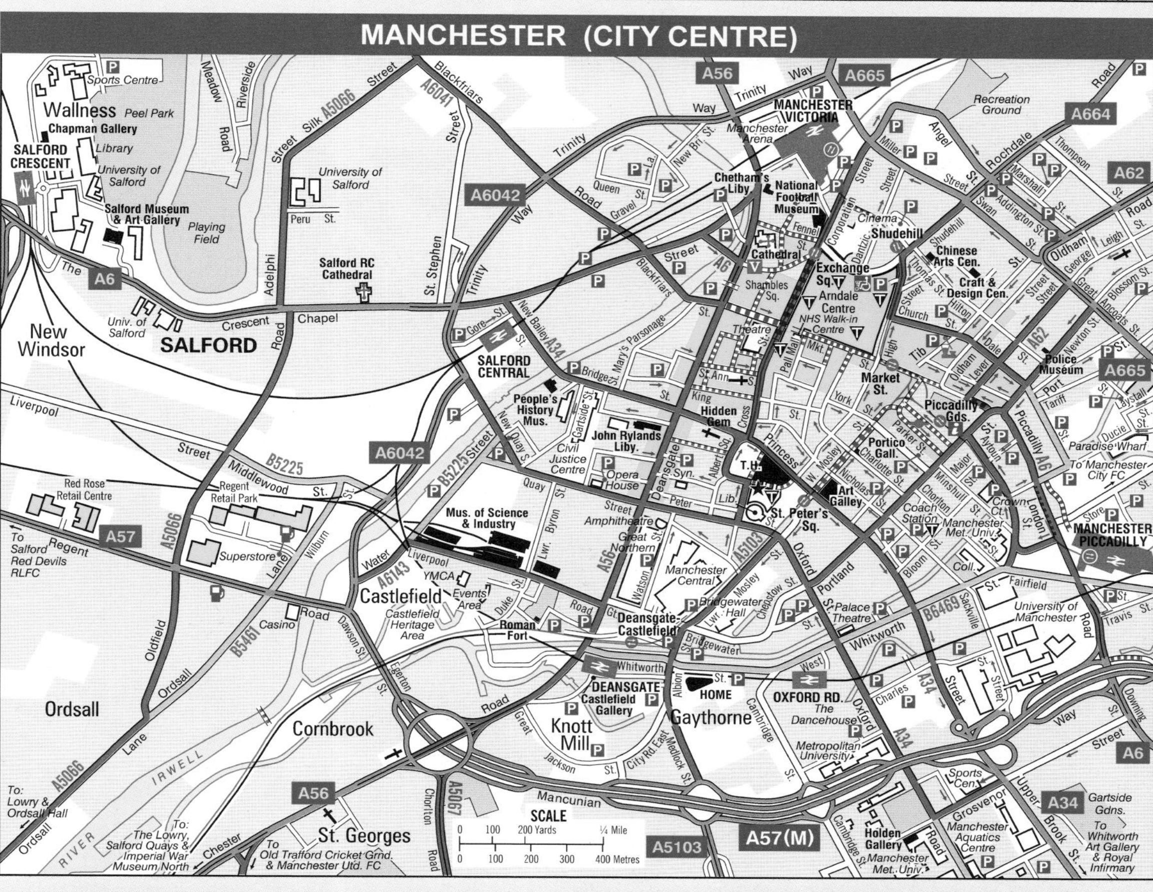

MIDDLESBROUGH

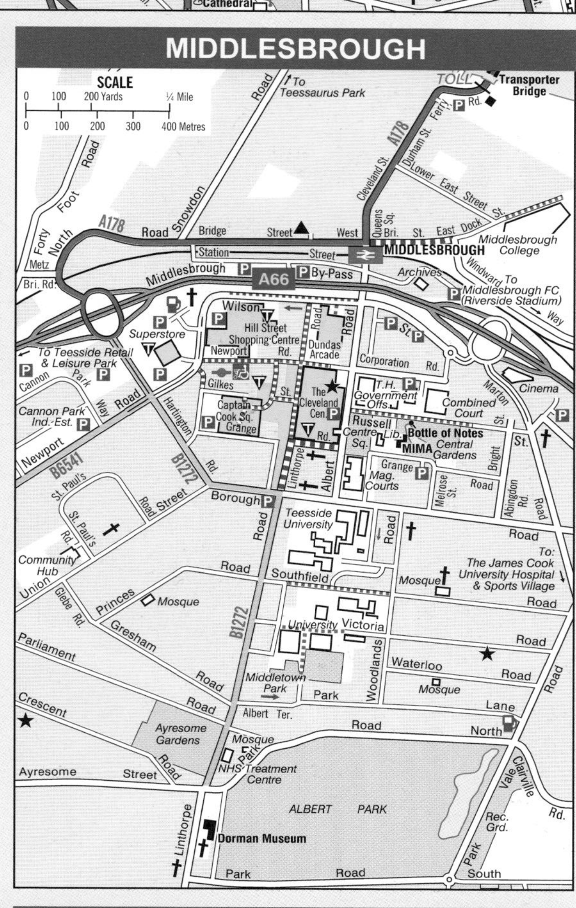

MEDWAY TOWNS

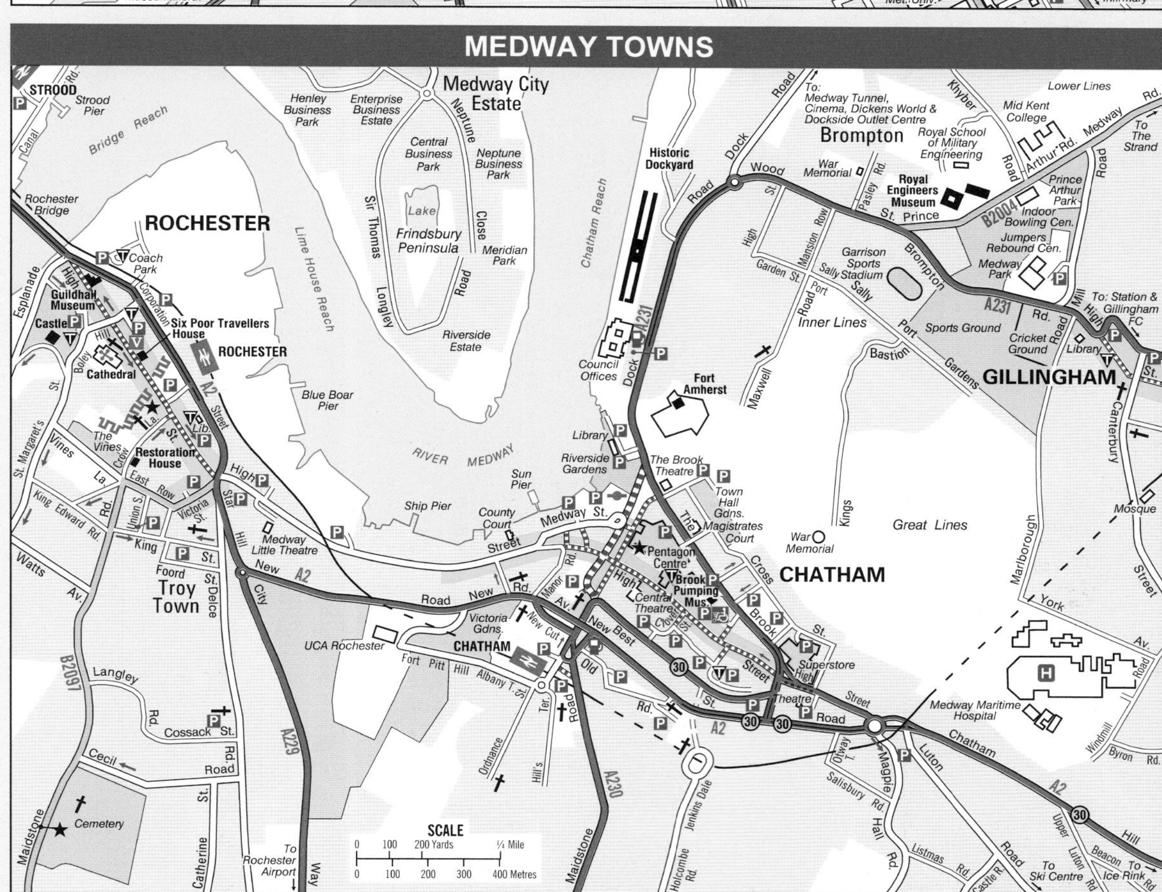

NEWCASTLE UPON TYNE

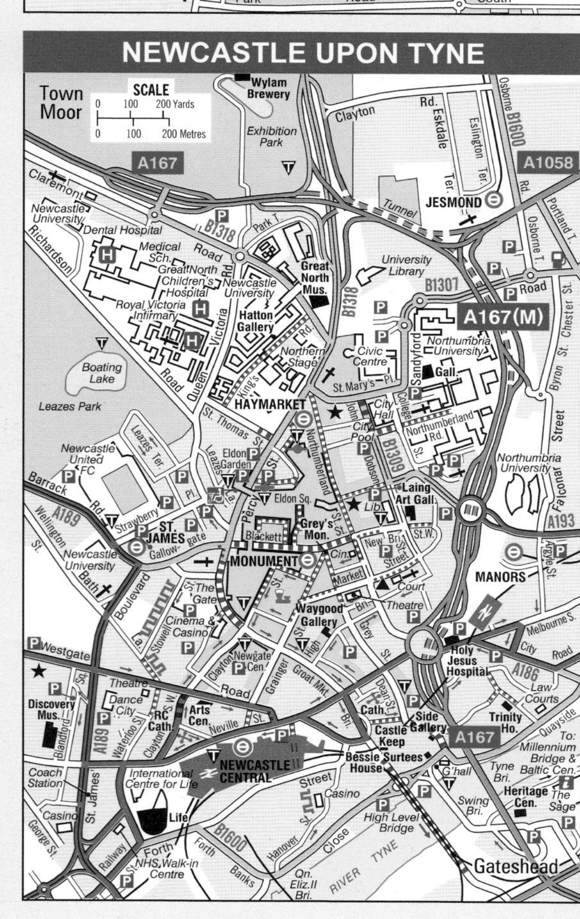

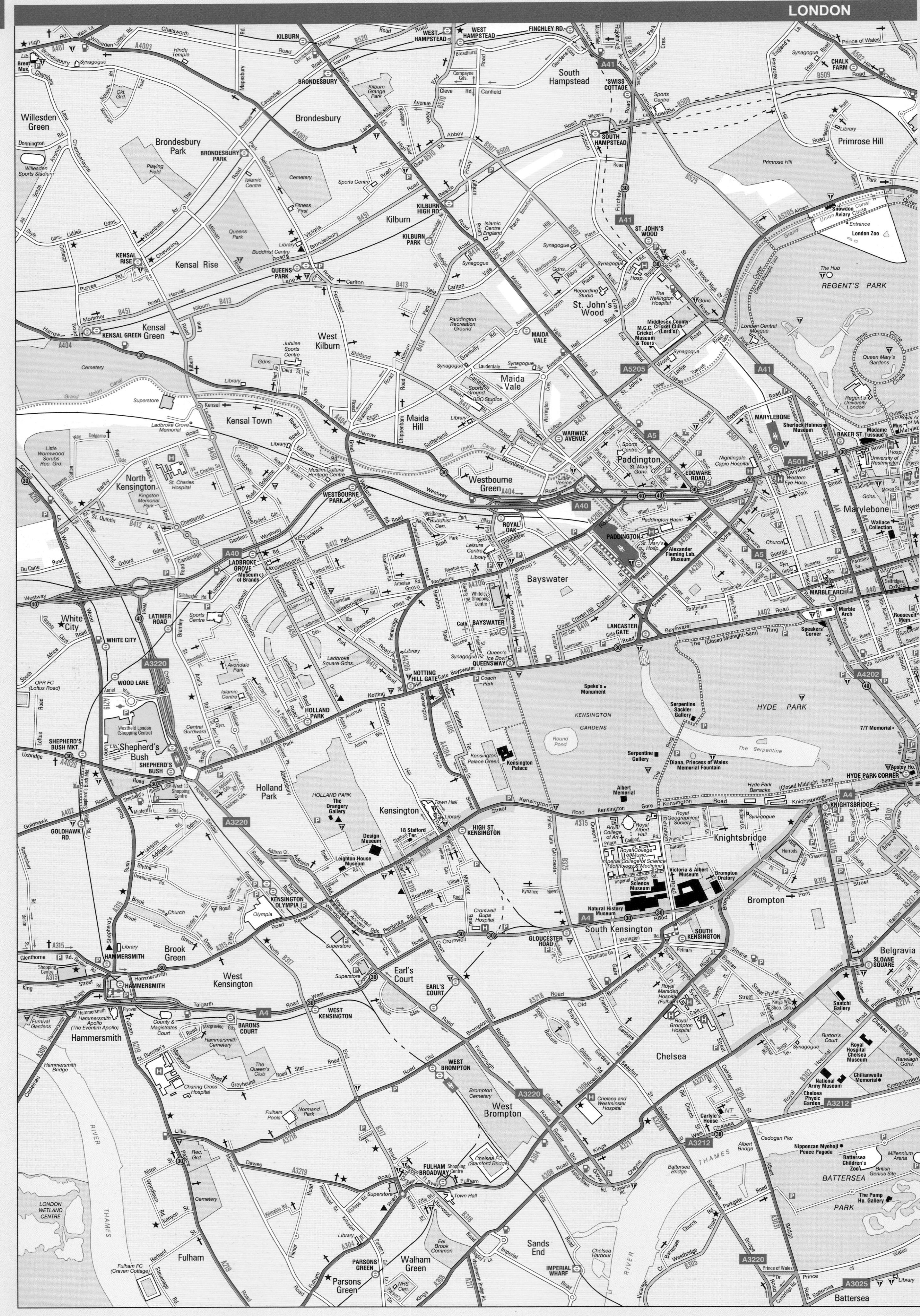
Willesden Green
Brondesbury Park
Brondesbury
Kilburn
South Hampstead
Primrose Hill
Kensal Rise
Kensal Green
West Kilburn
St. John's Wood
Maida Vale
REGENT'S PARK
London Zoo
Kensal Town
Maida Hill
North Kensington
Westbourne Green
Paddington
Marylebone
Bayswater
White City
HYDE PARK
KENSINGTON GARDENS
The Serpentine
Shepherd's Bush
Holland Park
Kensington
Knightsbridge
Brompton
South Kensington
Belgravia
Brook Green
West Kensington
Earl's Court
Hammersmith
Chelsea
West Brompton
BATTERSEA PARK
Fulham
Sands End
Walham Green
Parsons Green
Battersea
THAMES

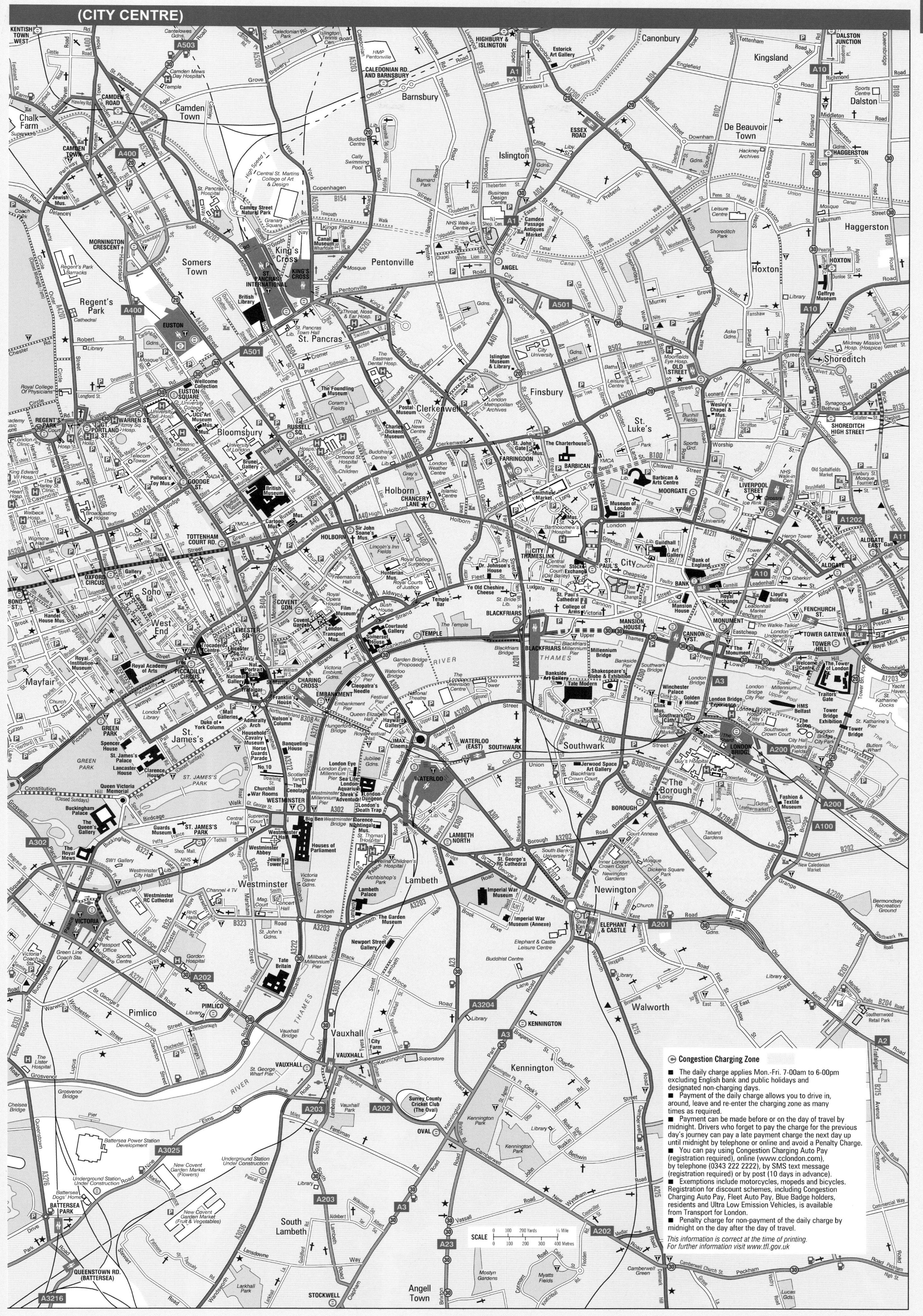
Congestion Charging Zone
■ The daily charge applies Mon.-Fri. 7-00am to 6-00pm excluding English bank and public holidays and designated non-charging days.
■ Payment of the daily charge allows you to drive in, around, leave and re-enter the charging zone as many times as required.
■ Payment can be made before or on the day of travel by midnight. Drivers who forget to pay the charge for the previous day's journey can pay a late payment charge the next day up until midnight by telephone or online and avoid a Penalty Charge.
■ You can pay using Congestion Charging Auto Pay (registration required), online (www.cclondon.com), by telephone (0343 222 2222), by SMS text message (registration required) or by post (10 days in advance).
■ Exemptions include motorcycles, mopeds and bicycles. Registration for discount schemes, including Congestion Charging Auto Pay, Fleet Auto Pay, Blue Badge holders, residents and Ultra Low Emission Vehicles, is available from Transport for London.
■ Penalty charge for non-payment of the daily charge by midnight on the day after the day of travel.
This information is correct at the time of printing.
For further information visit www.tfl.gov.uk
SCALE
0 100 200 Yards ½ Mile
0 100 200 300 400 Metres
Canonbury
Kingsland
Dalston
Camden Town
Barnsbury
Islington
De Beauvoir Town
Haggerston
Somers Town
King's Cross
Pentonville
Hoxton
Regent's Park
St. Pancras
Shoreditch
Finsbury
Clerkenwell
St. Luke's
Bloomsbury
Holborn
City
Soho
West End
Mayfair
St. James's
Southwark
The Borough
Westminster
Lambeth
Newington
Pimlico
Walworth
Vauxhall
Kennington
South Lambeth
Angell Town

MILTON KEYNES
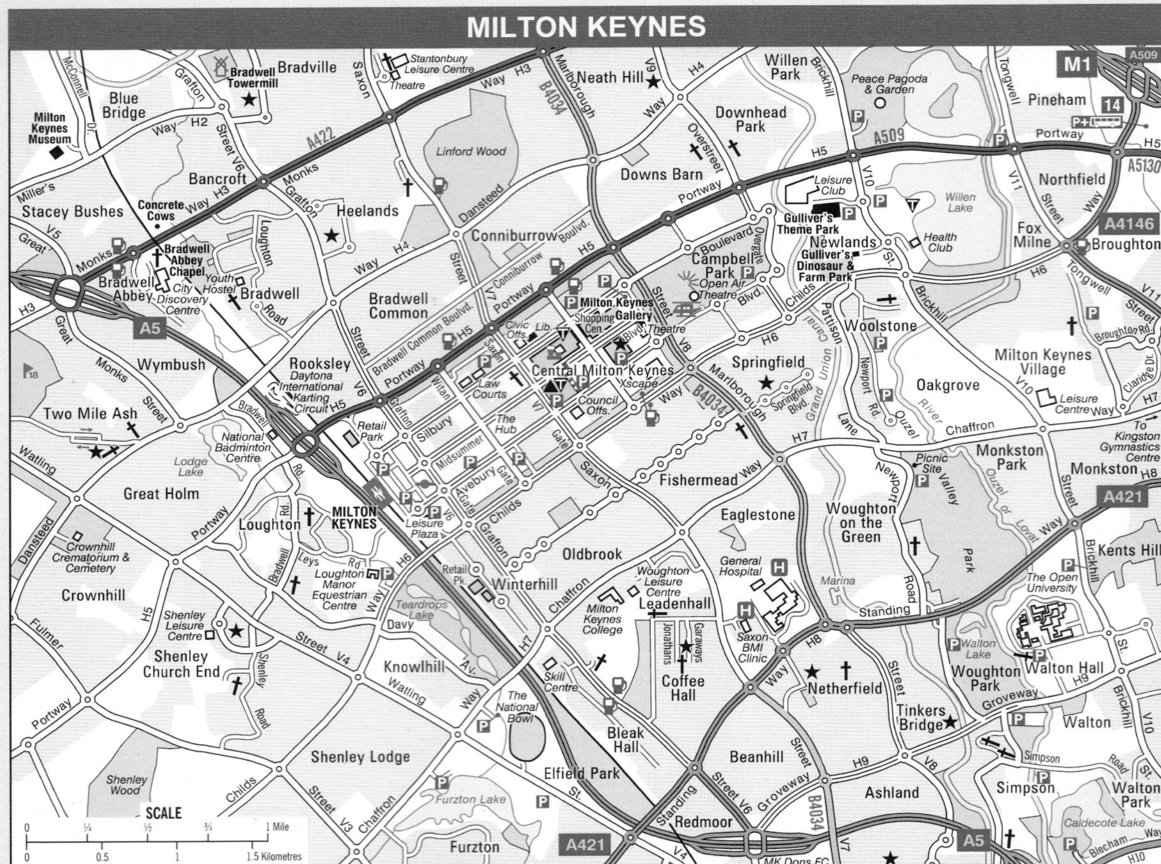

NEWPORT (CASNEWYDD)
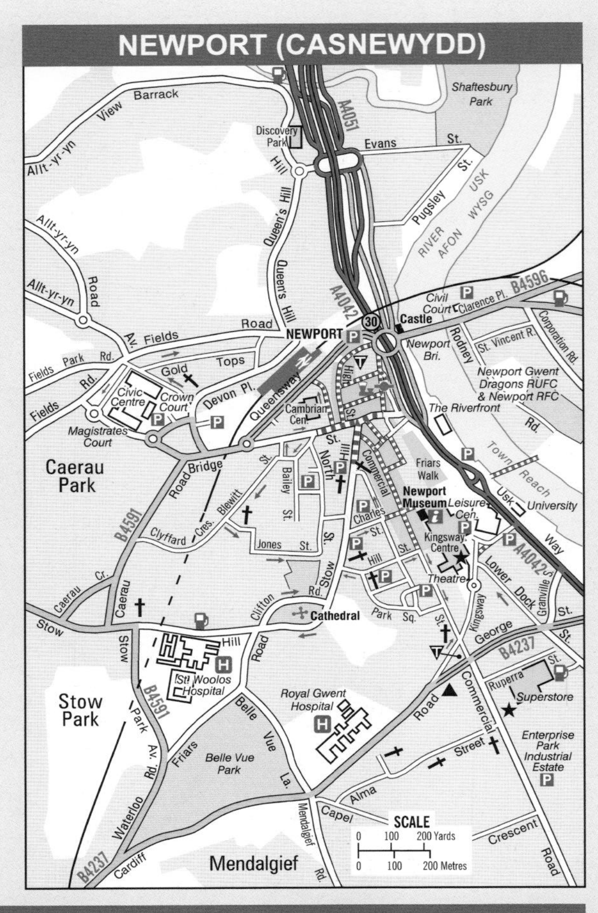

NORWICH
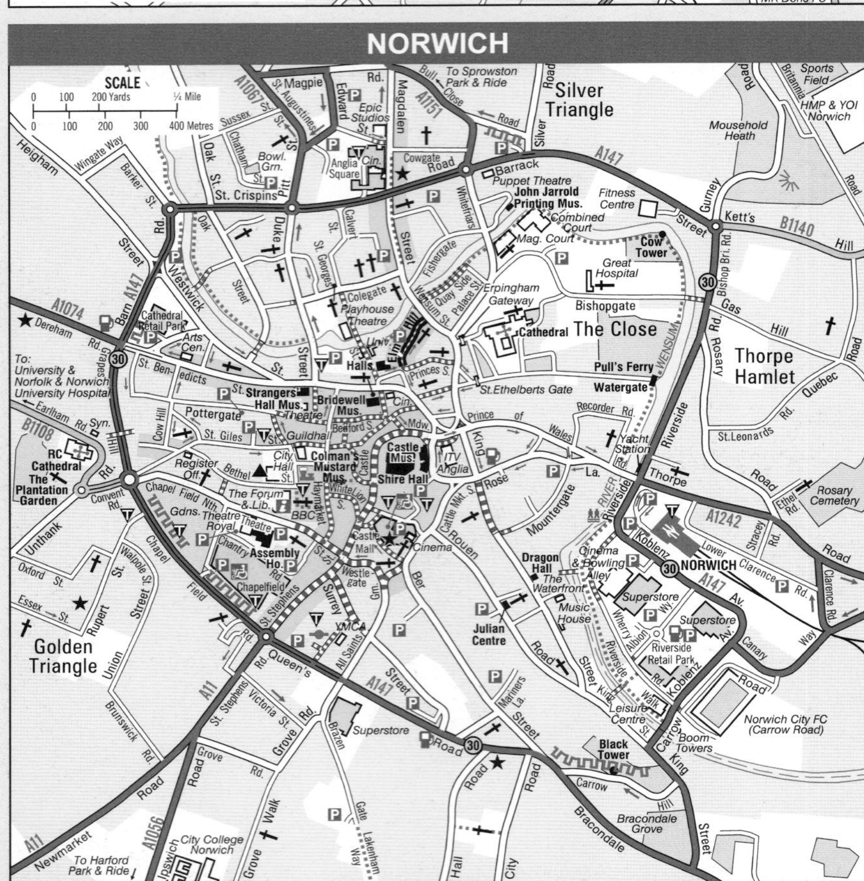

NOTTINGHAM
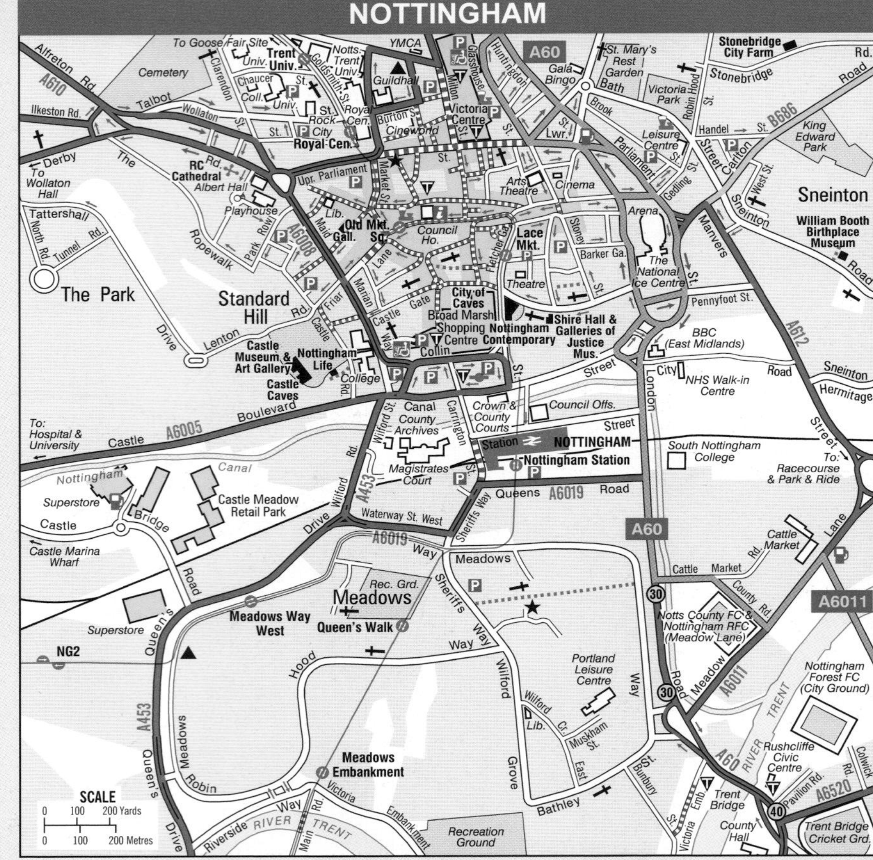

NORTHAMPTON
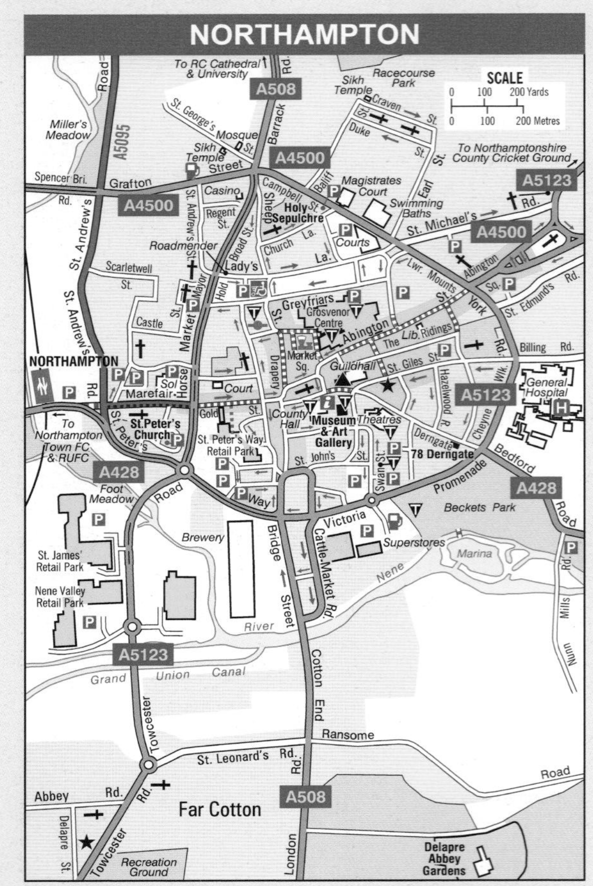

OXFORD
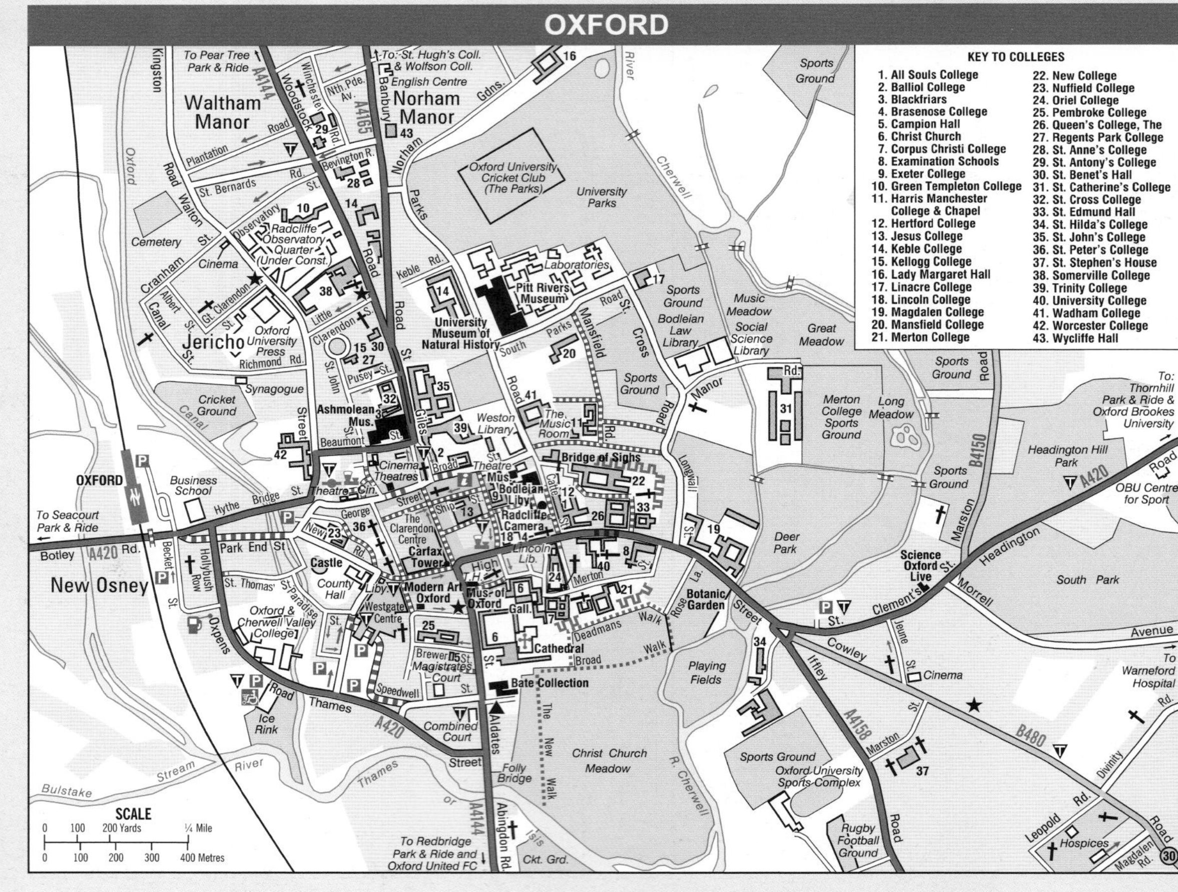

OBAN
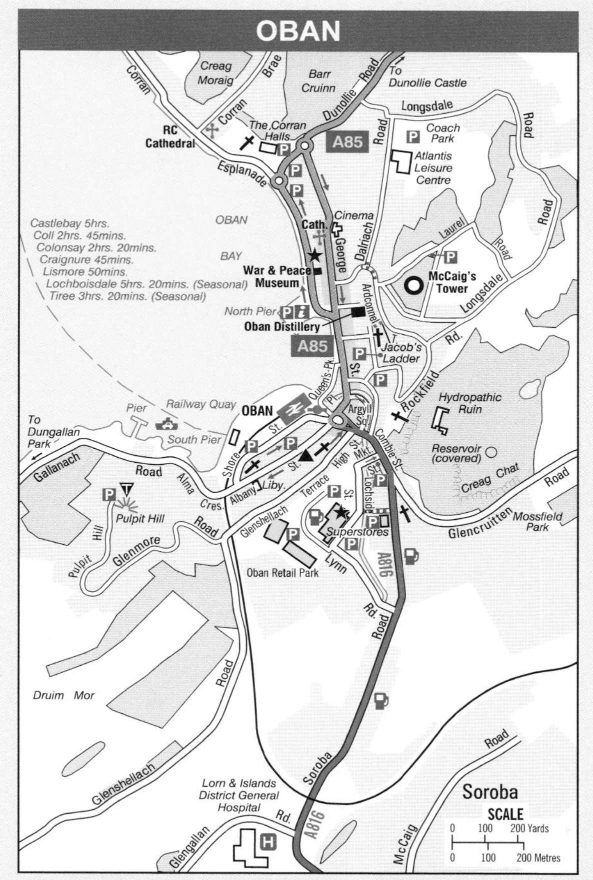

PERTH
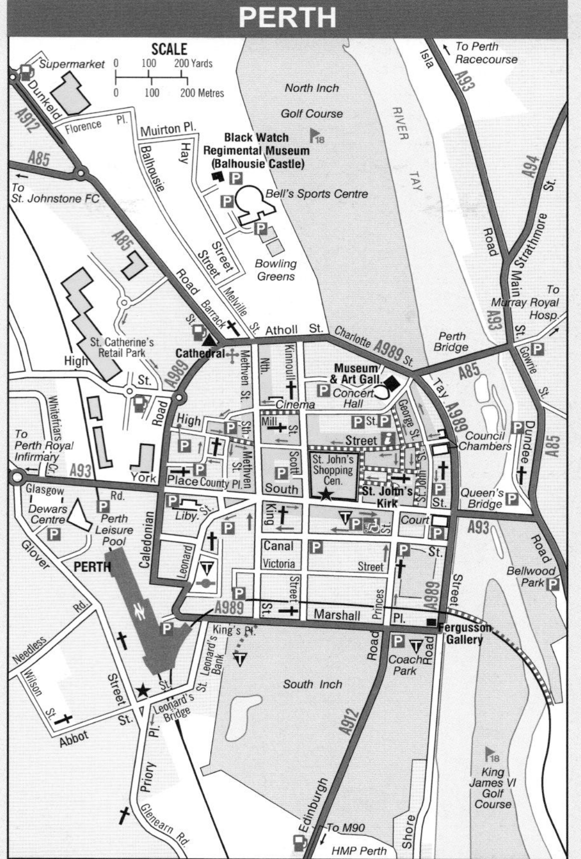

PETERBOROUGH
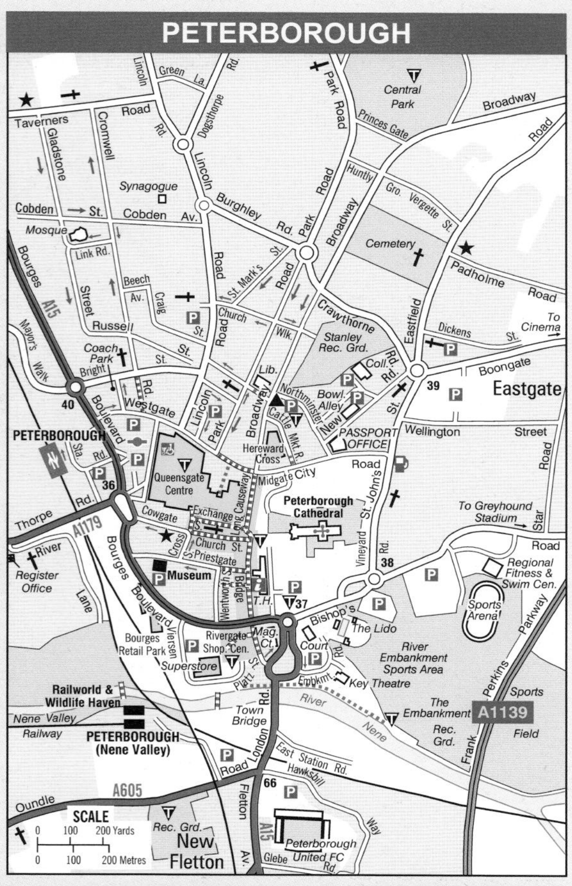

PLYMOUTH
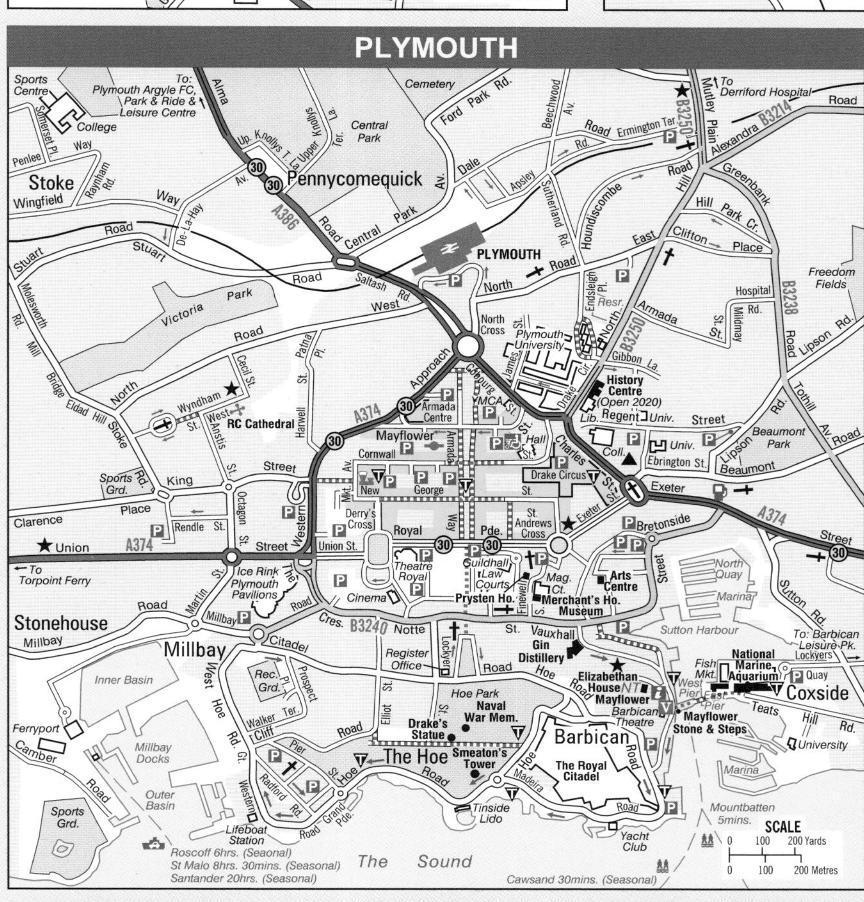

PORTSMOUTH
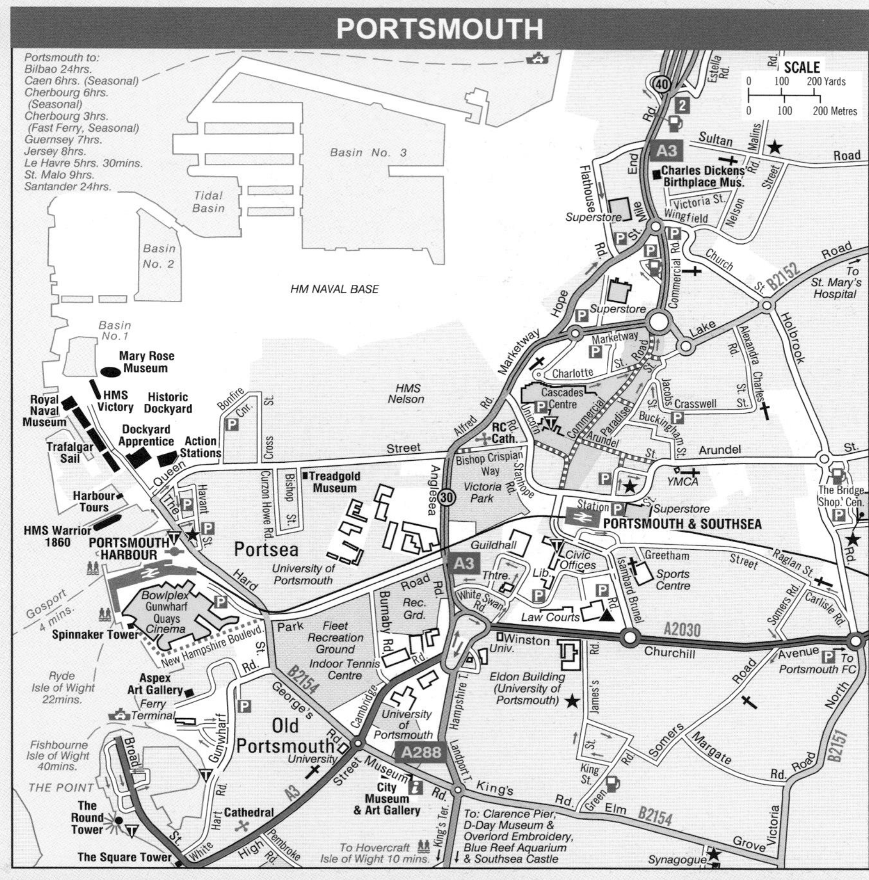

PRESTON
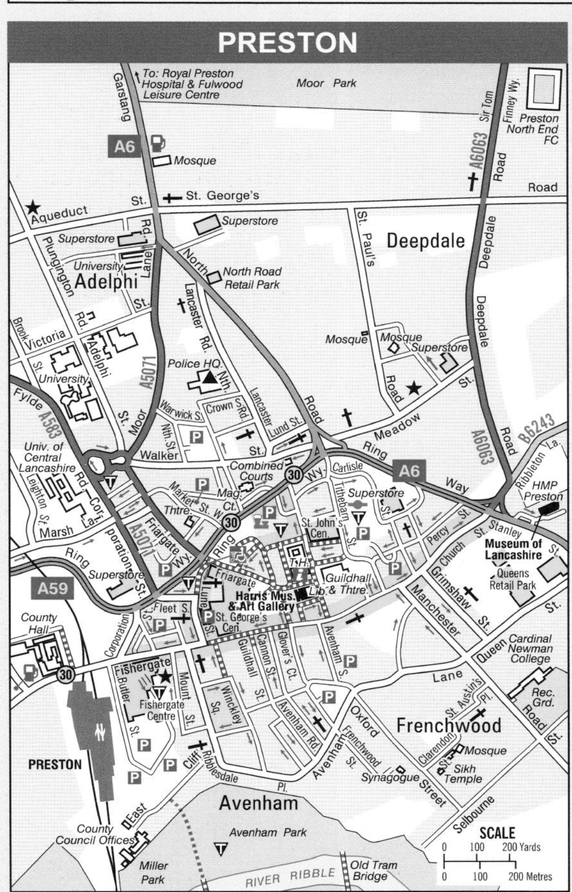

READING
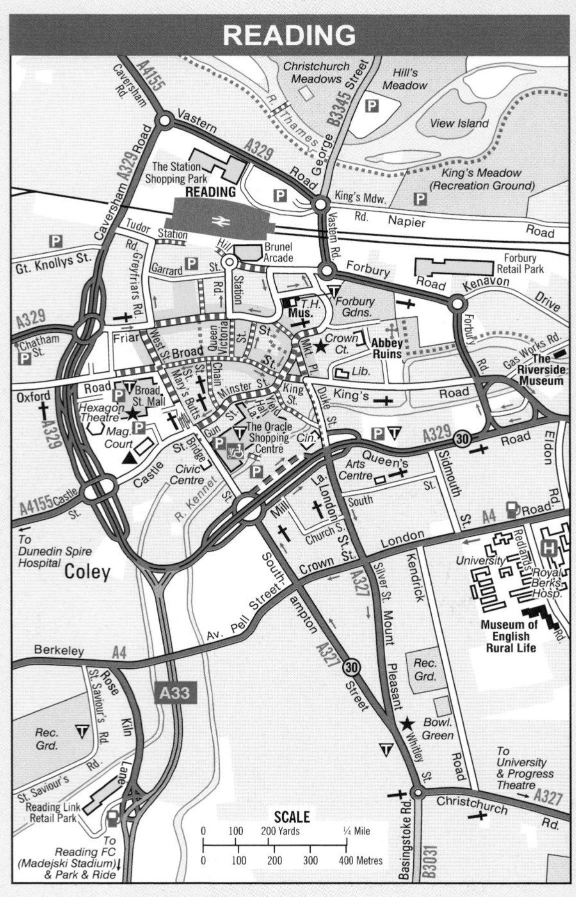

SALISBURY
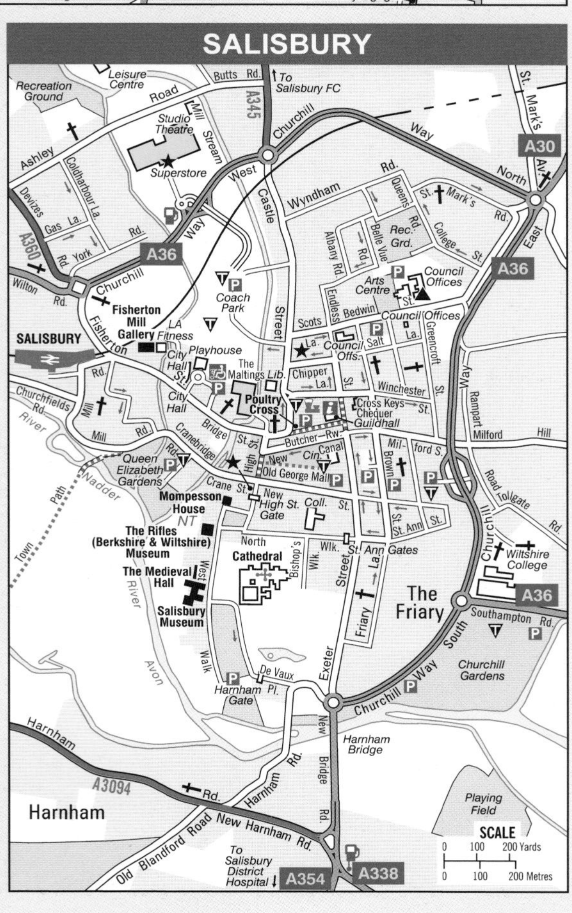

SHEFFIELD

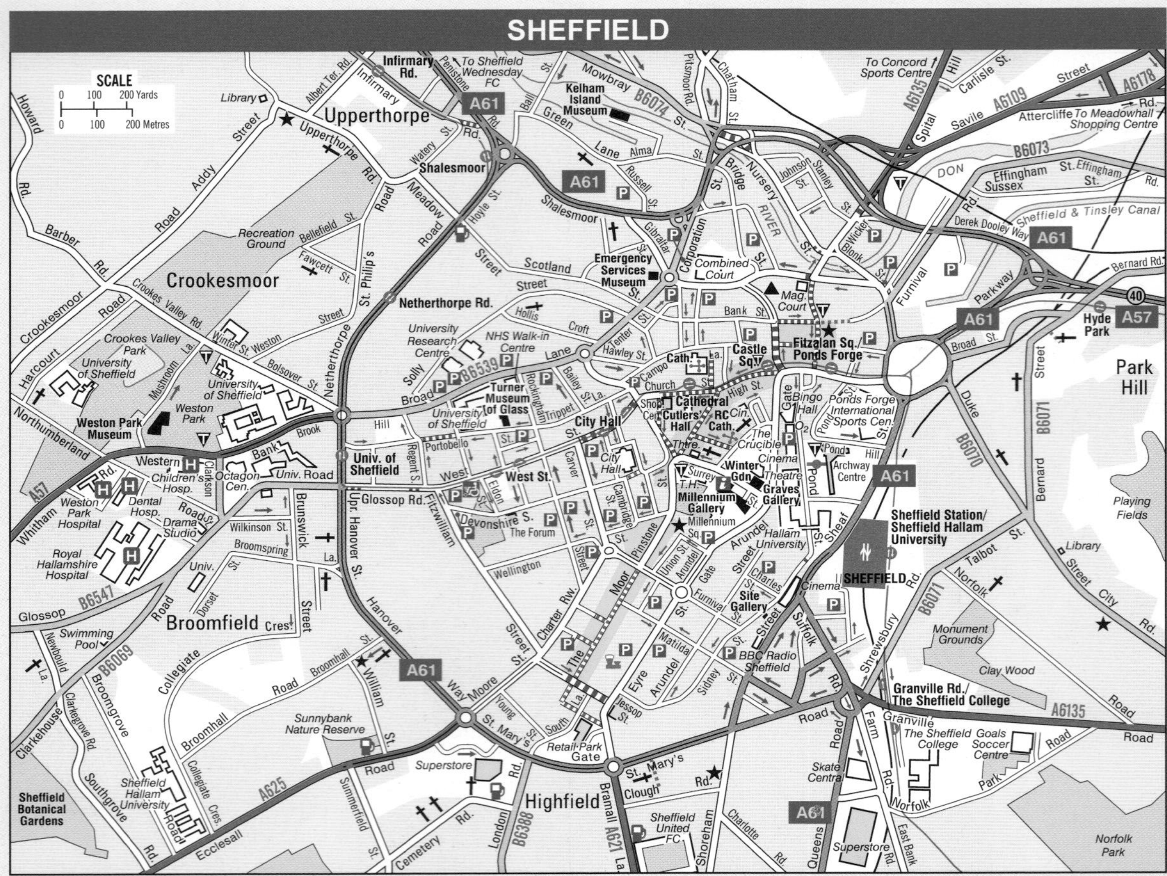

SHREWSBURY

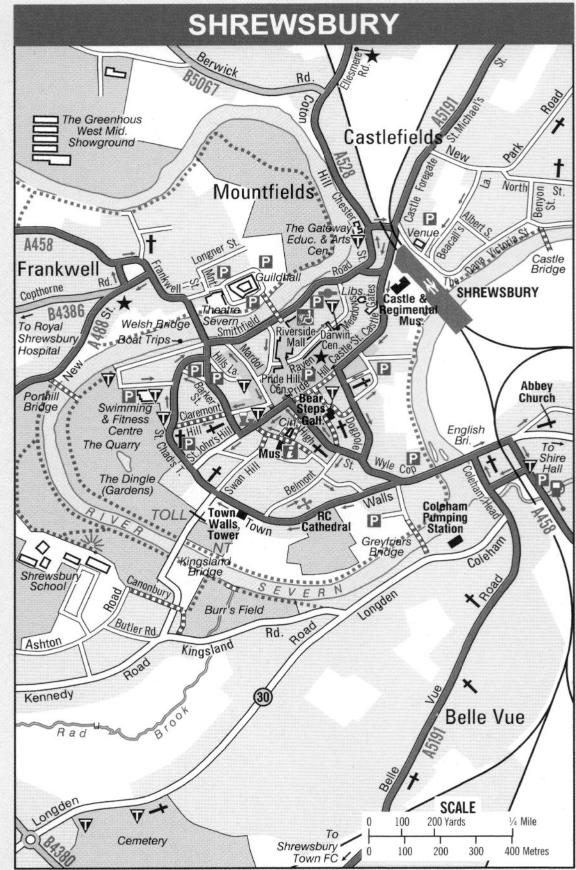

SOUTHAMPTON

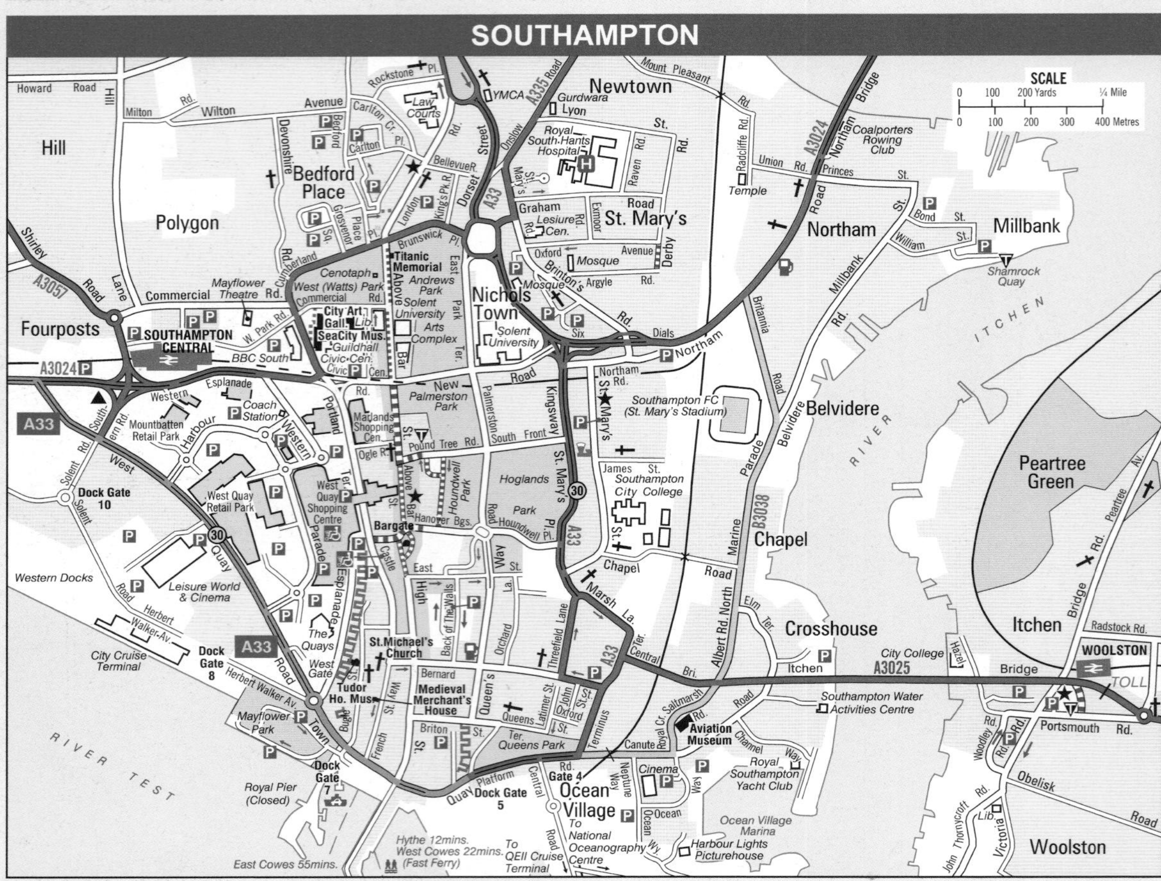

STIRLING

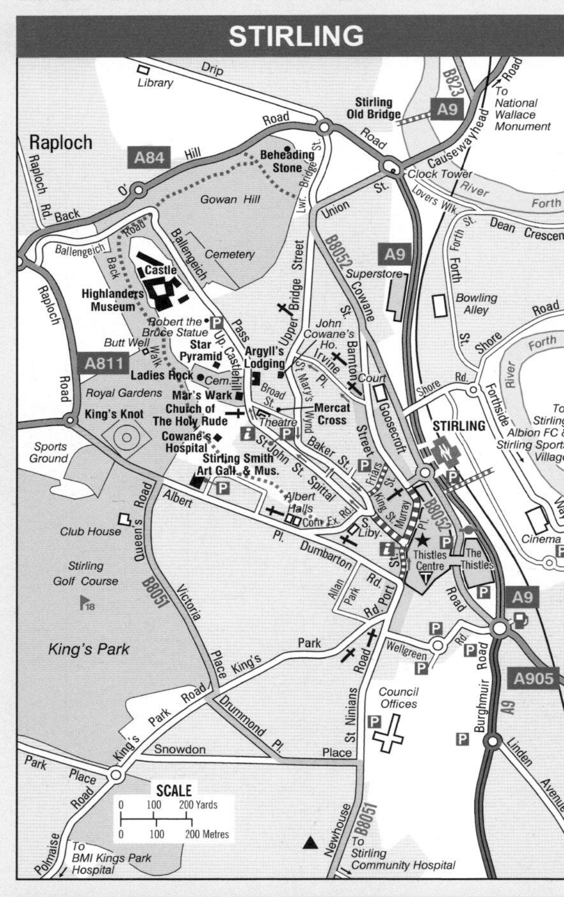

STOKE-ON-TRENT

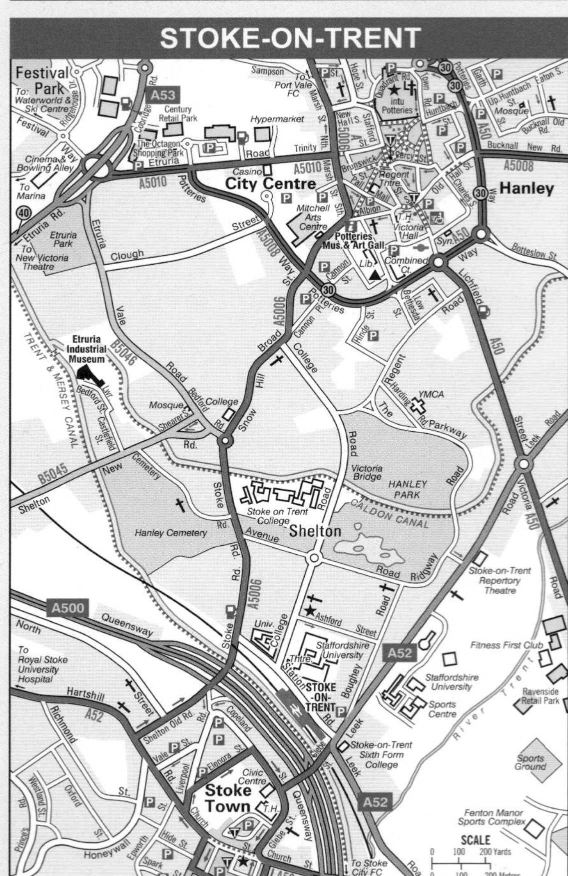

STRATFORD UPON AVON

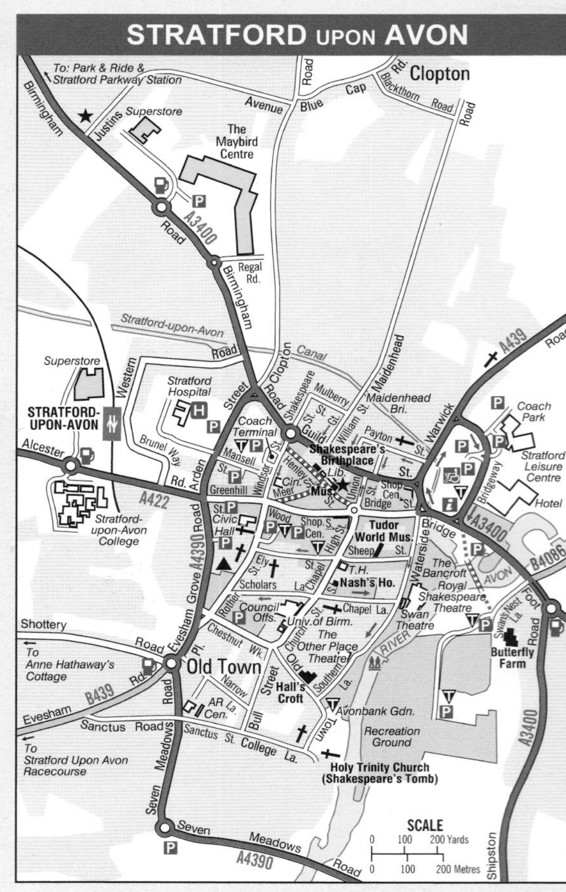

SUNDERLAND

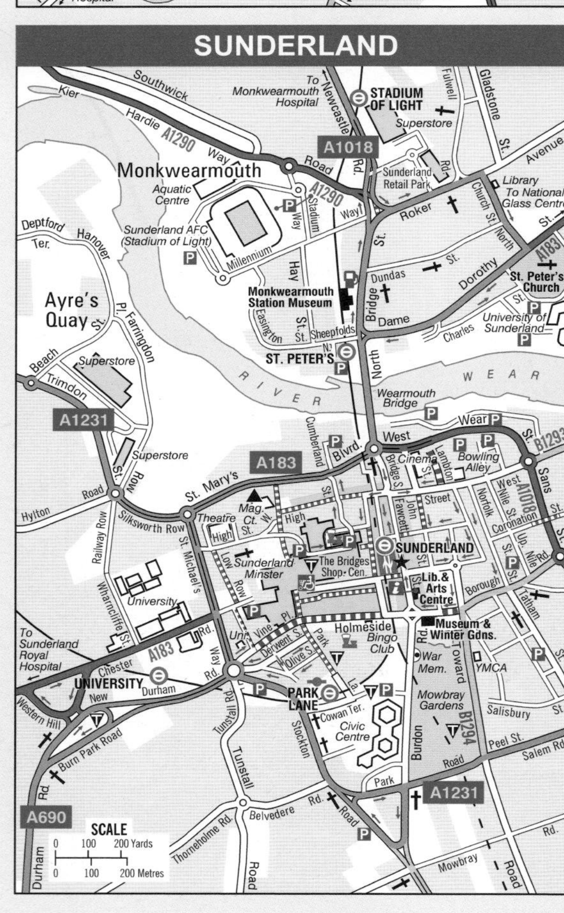

SWANSEA (ABERTAWE)
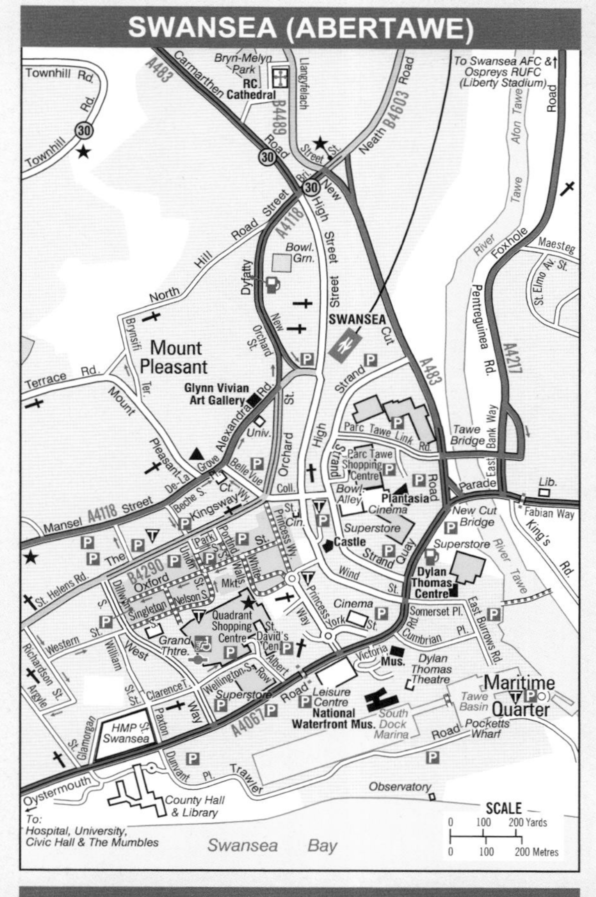

SWINDON
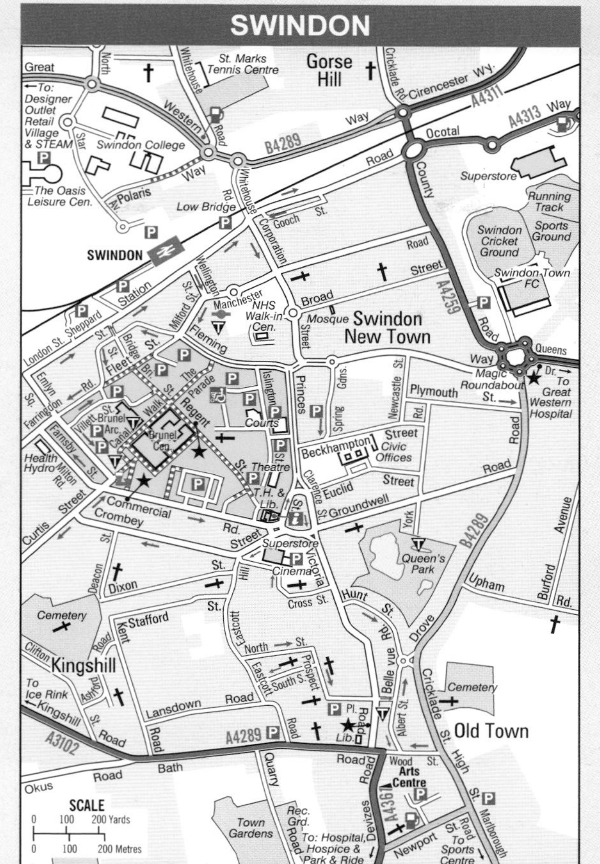

TAUNTON
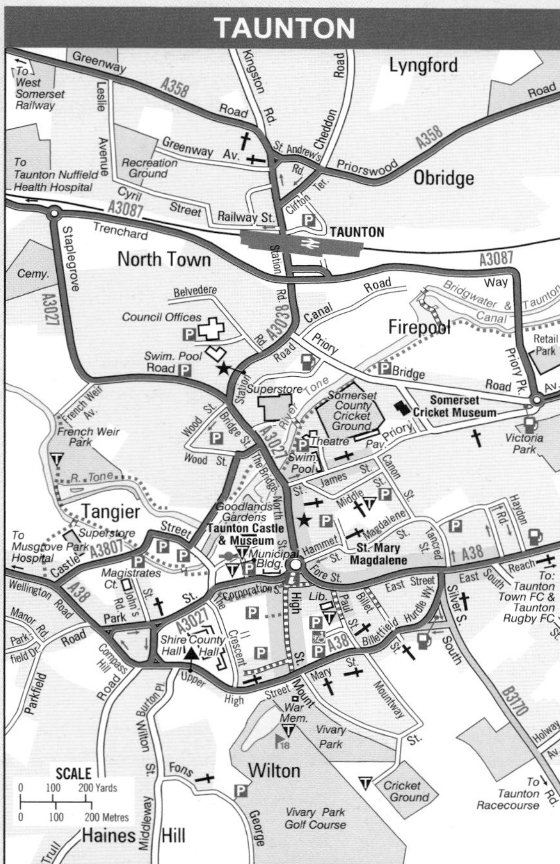

WINCHESTER
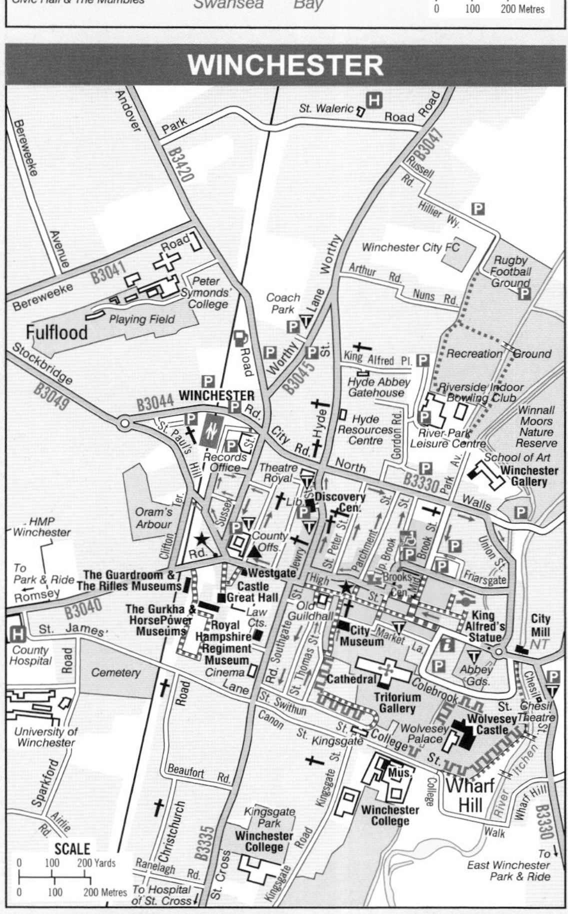

WINDSOR
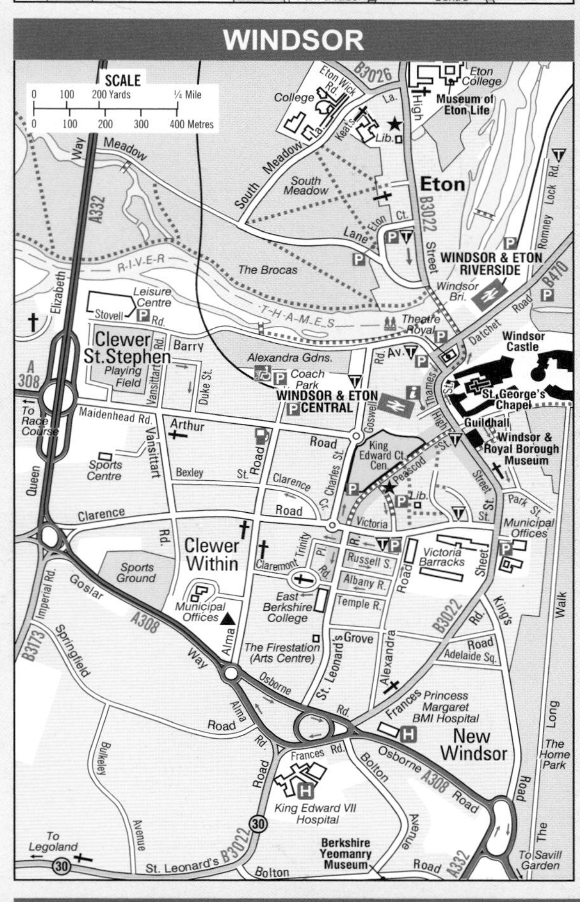

WOLVERHAMPTON
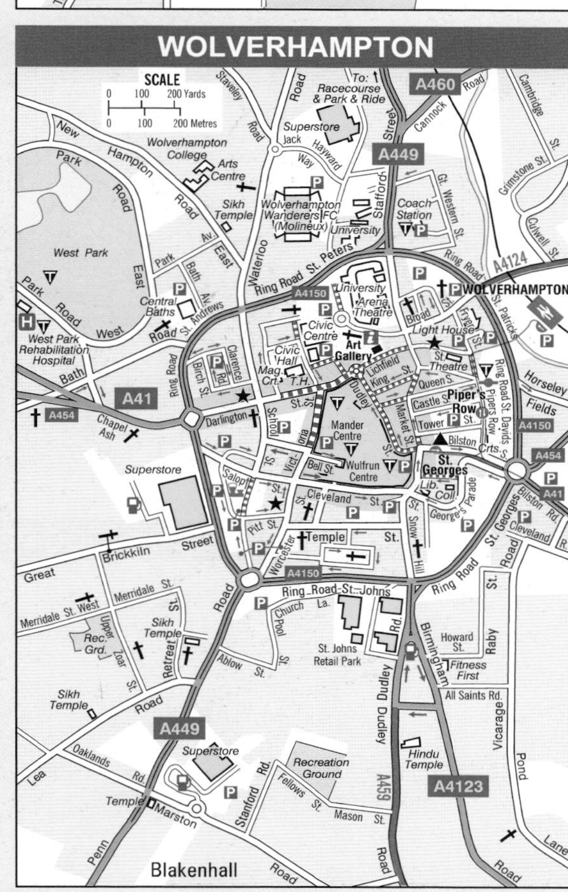

WORCESTER
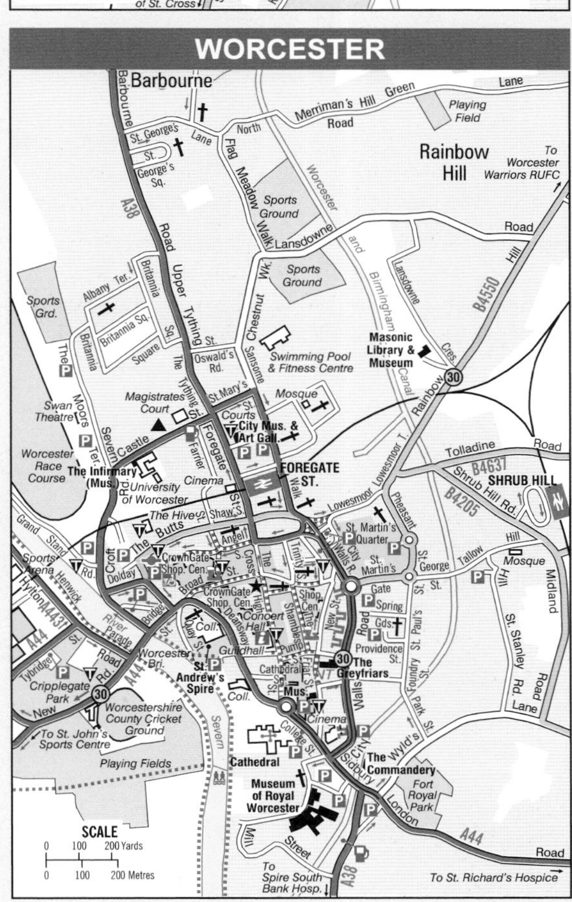

YORK
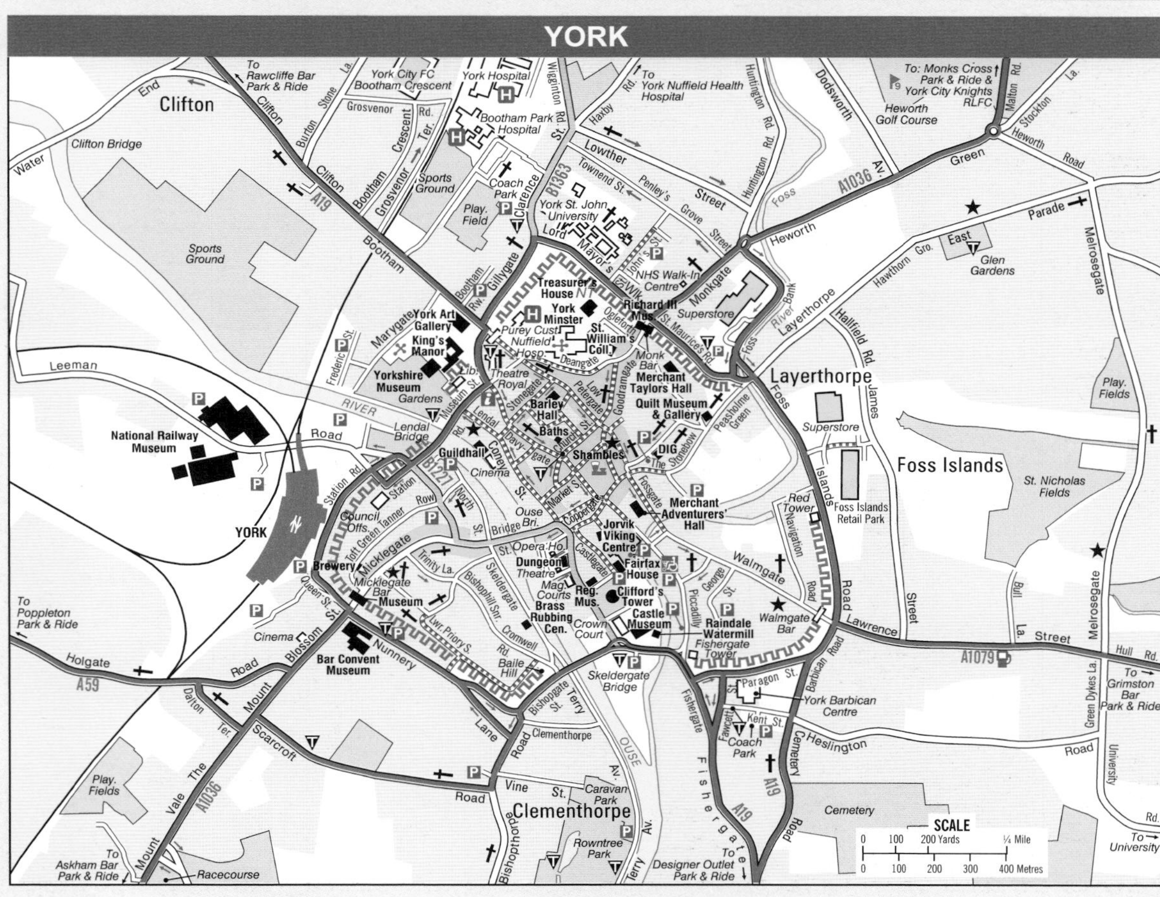

HARWICH

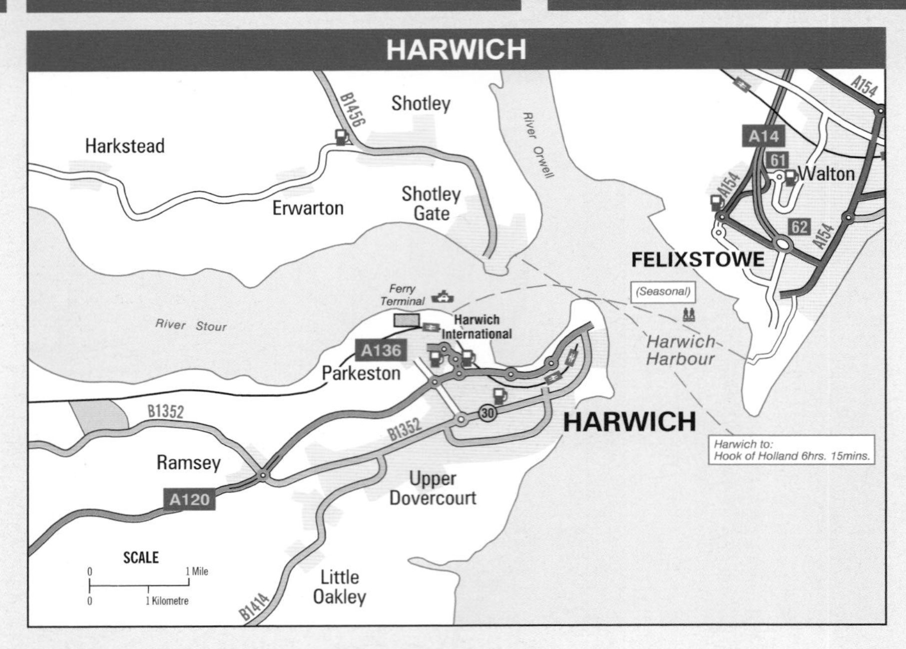

KINGSTON UPON HULL

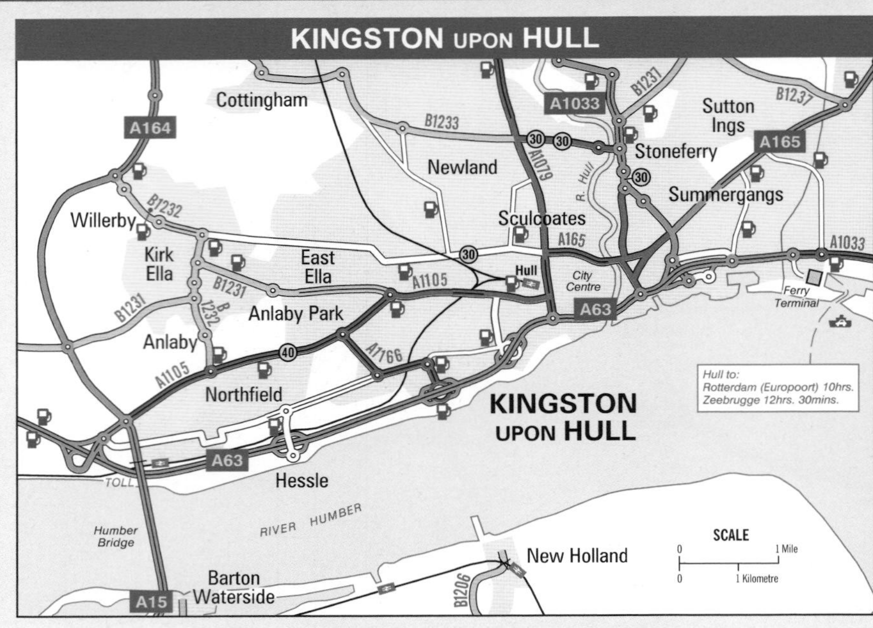

NEWCASTLE UPON TYNE

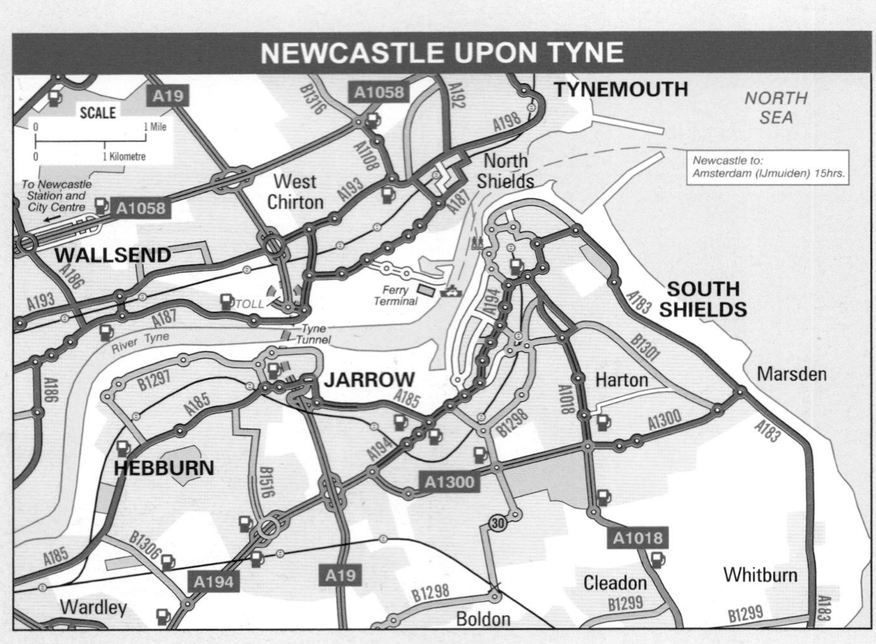

NEWHAVEN

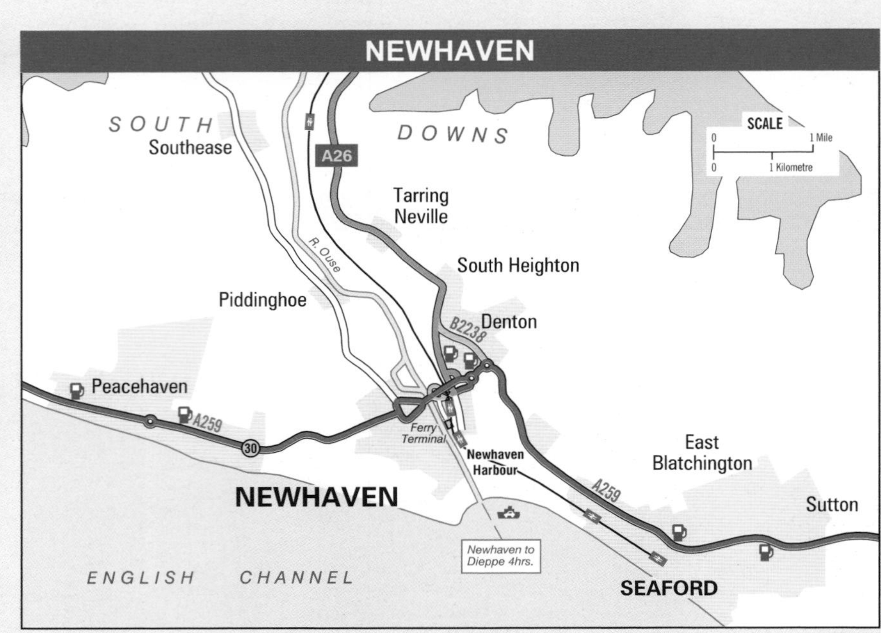

PEMBROKE DOCK (DOC PENFRO)

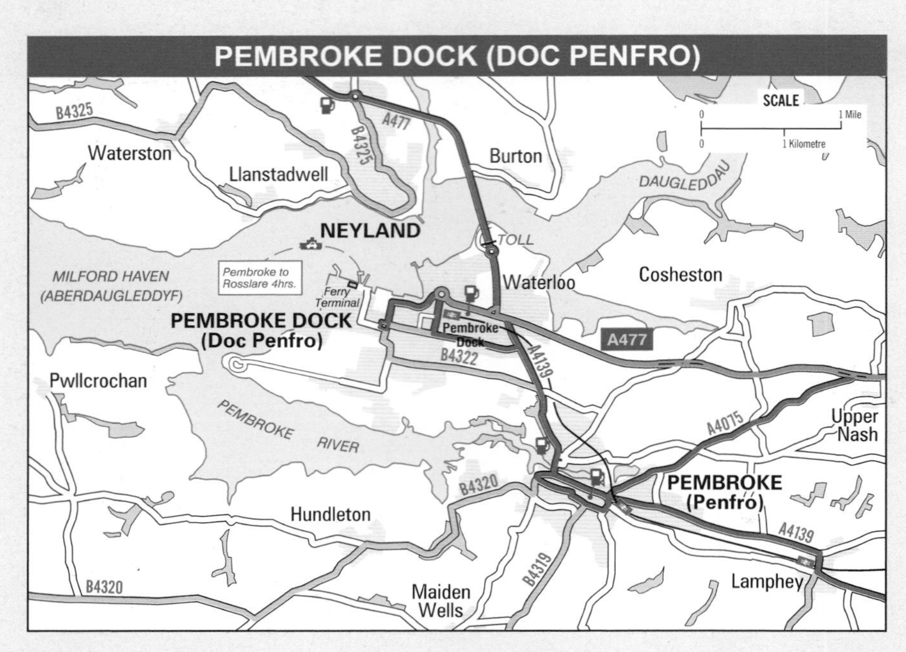

POOLE

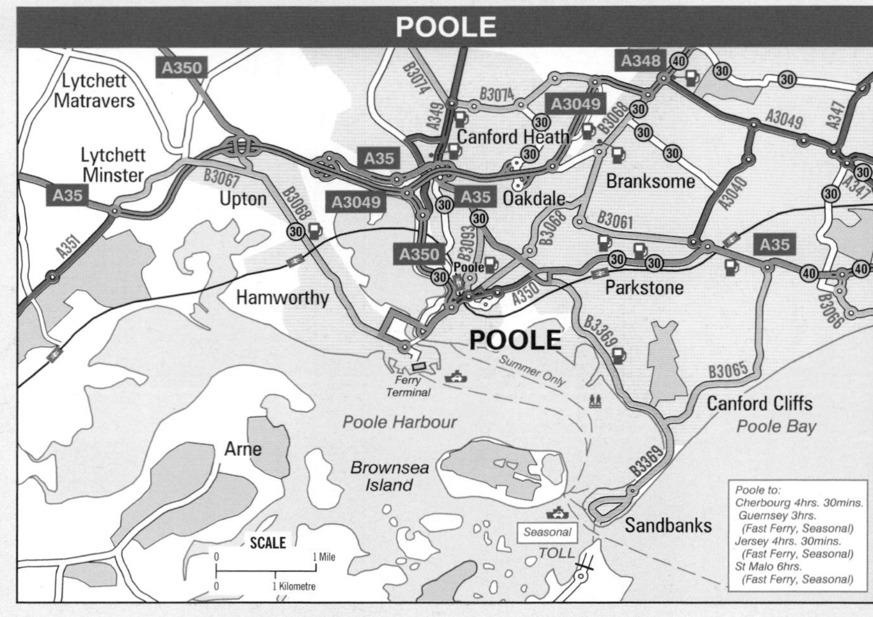

PORTSMOUTH

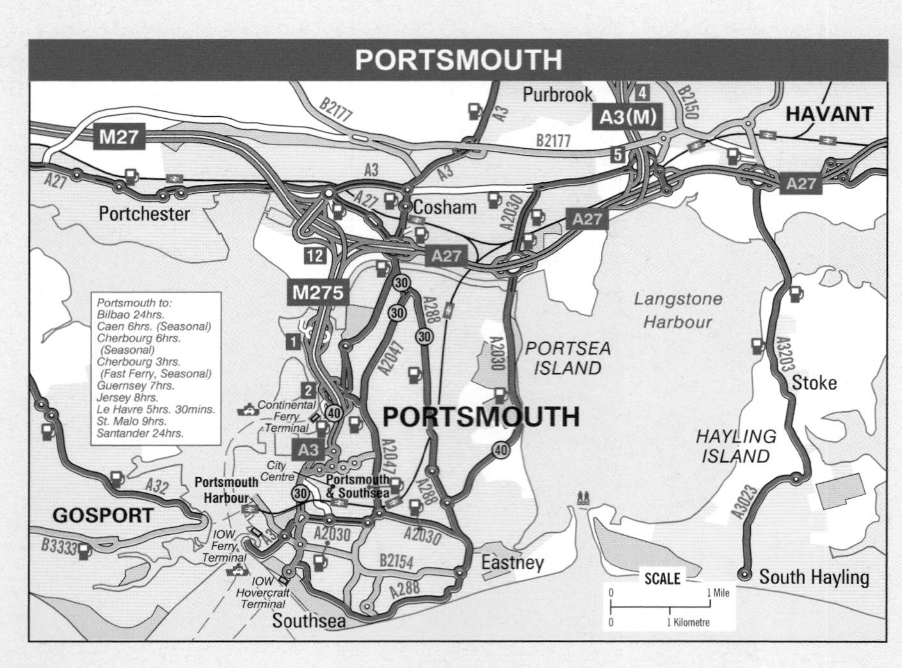

WEYMOUTH

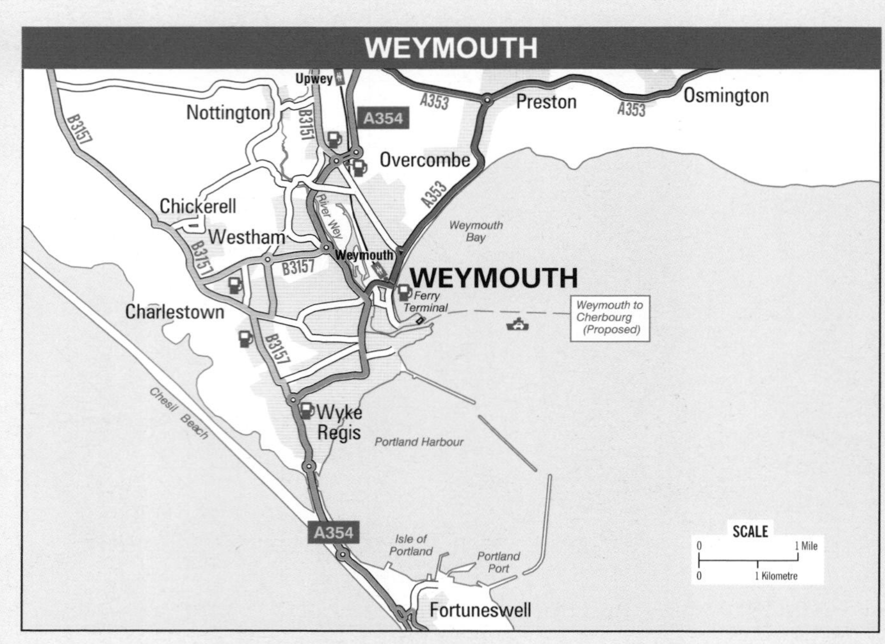

BIRMINGHAM

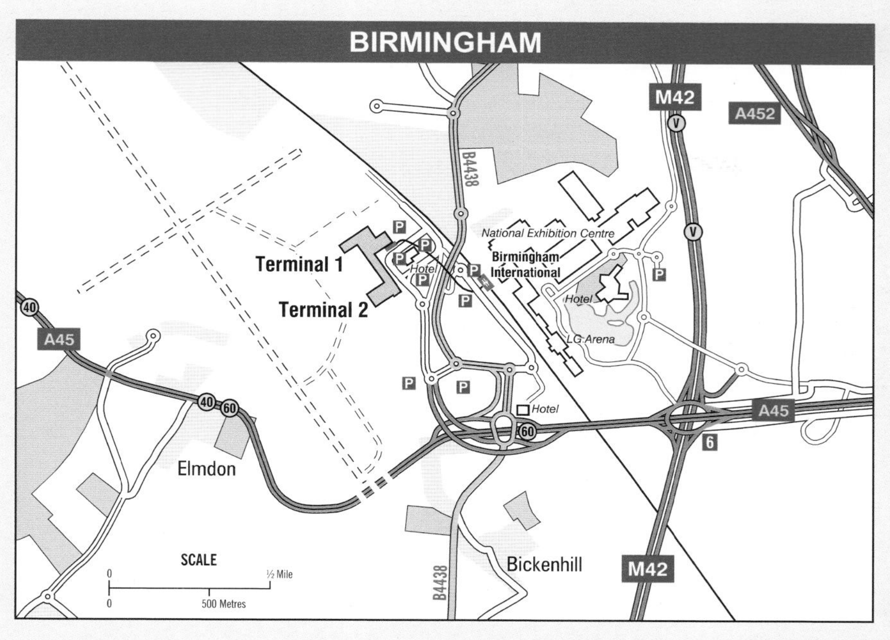

EAST MIDLANDS

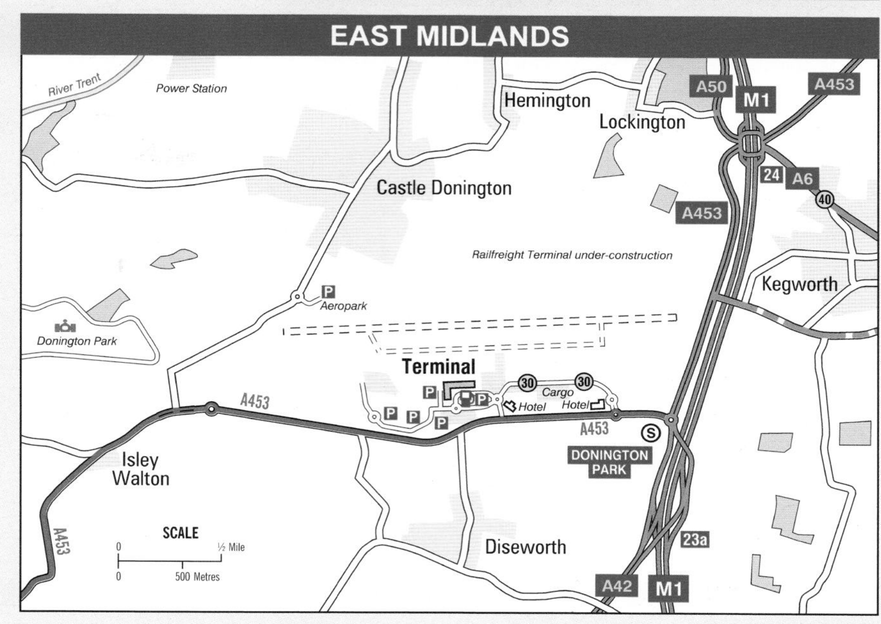

GLASGOW

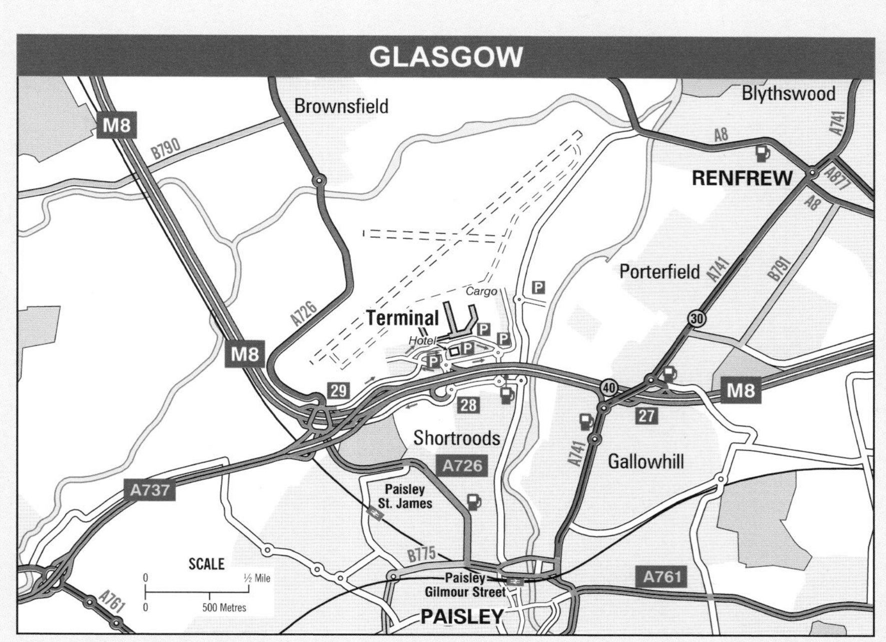

LONDON GATWICK

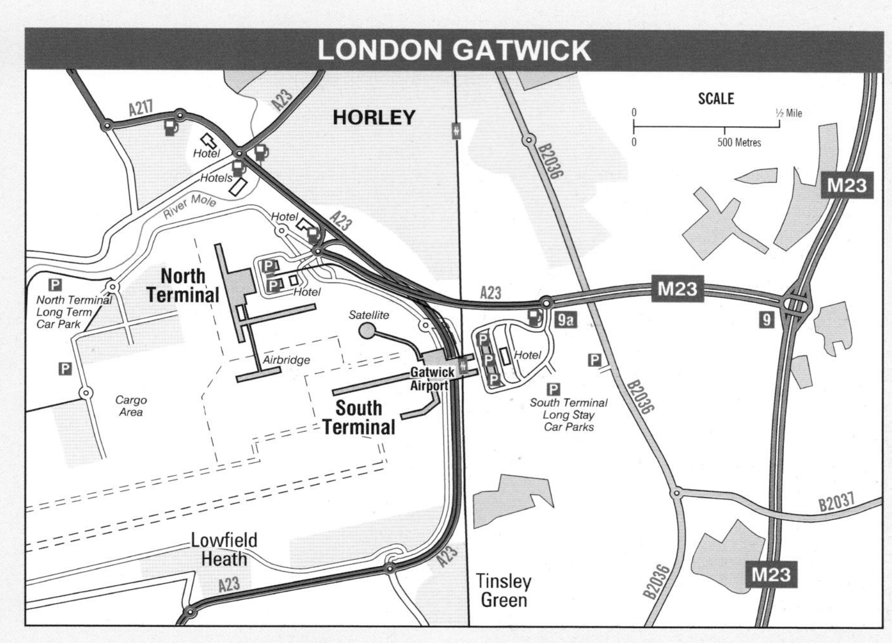

LONDON HEATHROW

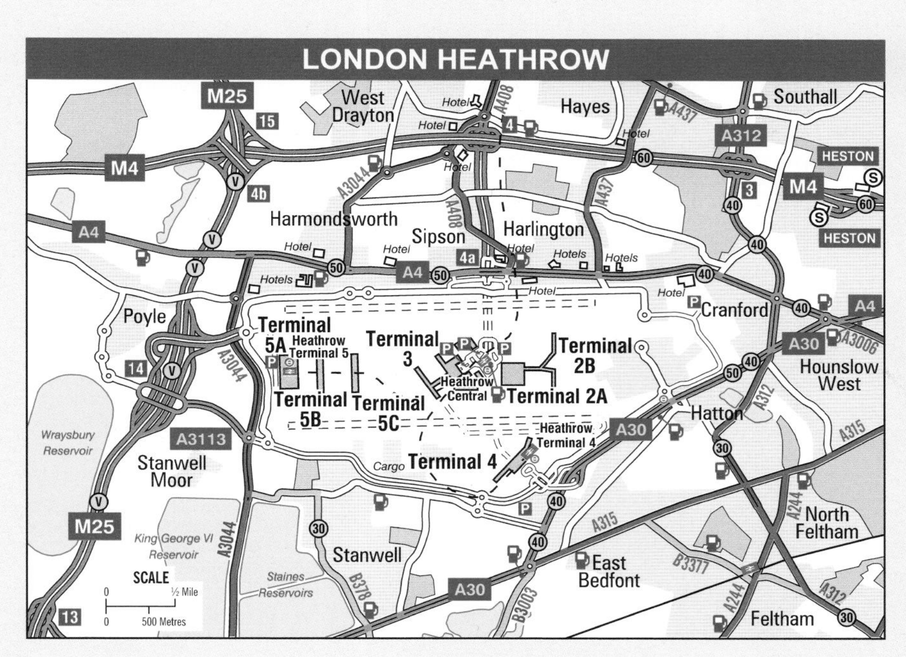

LONDON LUTON

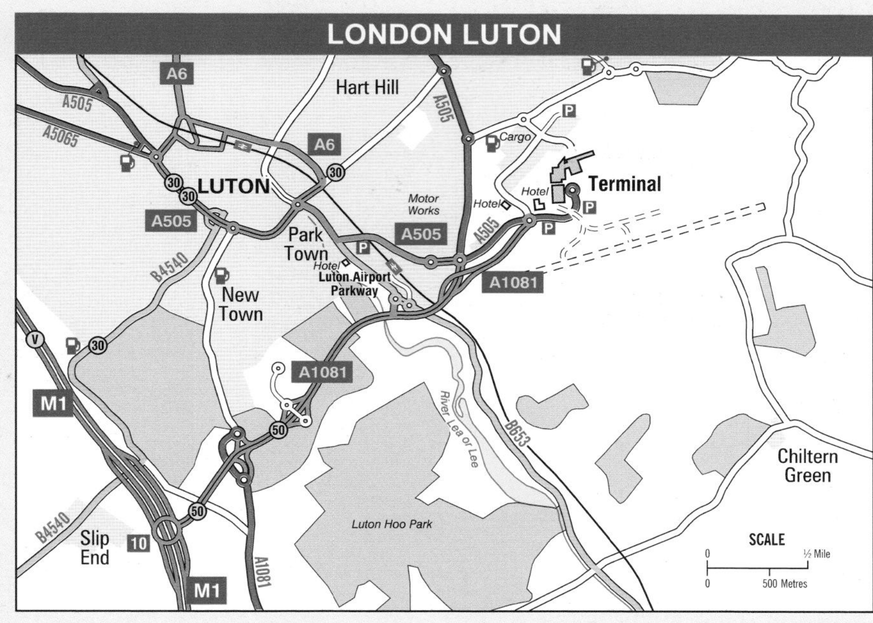

LONDON STANSTED

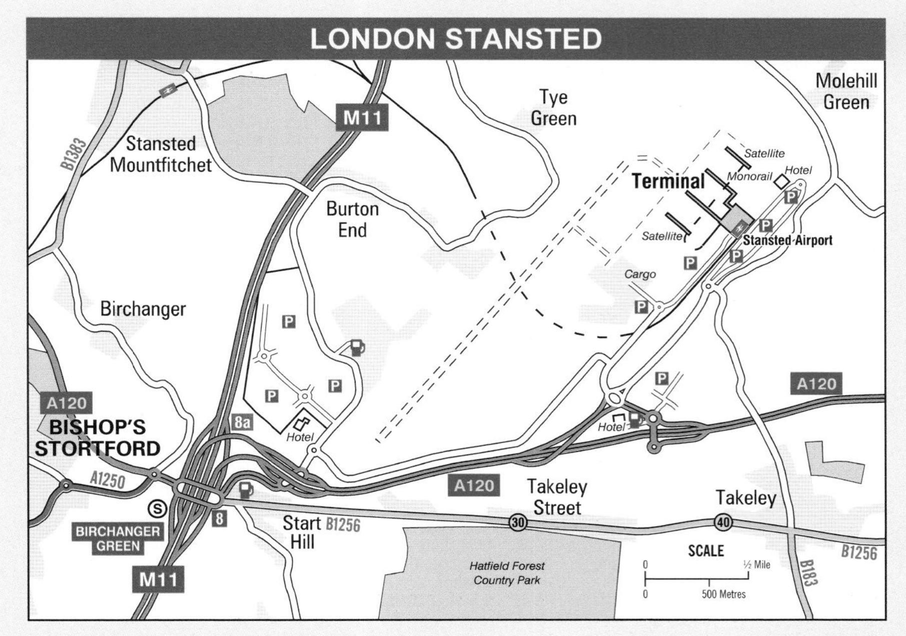

MANCHESTER

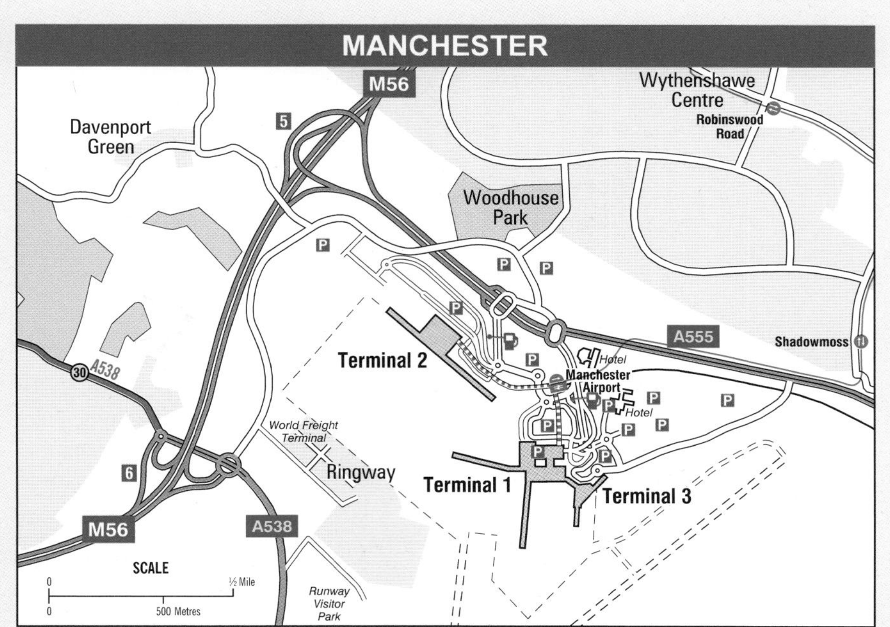

INDEX TO CITIES, TOWNS, VILLAGES, HAMLETS, LOCATIONS, AIRPORTS & PORTS

(1) A strict alphabetical order is used e.g. An Dùnan follows Andreas but precedes Andwell.

(2) The map reference given refers to the actual map square in which the town spot or built-up area is located and not to the place name.

(3) Major towns and destinations are shown in bold, i.e. **Aberdeen.** *Aber* **192** (3G **153**)
Page references for Town Plan entries are shown first.

(4) Where two or more places of the same name occur in the same County or Unitary Authority, the nearest large town is also given; e.g. Achiemore. *High* nr. Durness . . . .2D **166** indicates that Achiemore is located in square 2D on page **166** and is situated near Durness in the Unitary Authority of Highland.

(5) Only one reference is given although due to page overlaps the place may appear on more than one page.

COUNTIES and UNITARY AUTHORITIES with the abbreviations used in this index

Aberdeen : *Aber*
Aberdeenshire : *Abers*
Angus : *Ang*
Antrim & Newtownabbey : *Ant*
Ards & North Down : *Ards*
Argyll & Bute : *Arg*
Armagh, Banbridge & Craigavon : *Arm*
Bath & N E Somerset : *Bath*
Bedford : *Bed*
Belfast : *Bel*
Blackburn with Darwen : *Bkbn*
Blackpool : *Bkpl*
Blaenau Gwent : *Blae*
Bournemouth : *Bour*
Bracknell Forest : *Brac*
Bridgend : *B'end*
Brighton & Hove : *Brig*
Bristol : *Bris*
Buckinghamshire : *Buck*
Caerphilly : *Cphy*
Cambridgeshire : *Cambs*
Cardiff : *Card*
Carmarthenshire : *Carm*
Causeway Coast & Glens : *Caus*
Central Bedfordshire : *C Beds*
Ceredigion : *Cdgn*
Cheshire East : *Ches E*
Cheshire West & Chester : *Ches W*
Clackmannanshire : *Clac*
Conwy : *Cnwy*
Cornwall : *Corn*
Cumbria : *Cumb*
Darlington : *Darl*
Denbighshire : *Den*
Derby : *Derb*
Derbyshire : *Derbs*
Derry & Strabane : *Derr*
Devon : *Devn*
Dorset : *Dors*
Dumfries & Galloway : *Dum*
Dundee : *D'dee*
Durham : *Dur*
East Ayrshire : *E Ayr*
East Dunbartonshire : *E Dun*
East Lothian : *E Lot*
East Renfrewshire : *E Ren*
East Riding of Yorkshire : *E Yor*
East Sussex : *E Sus*
Edinburgh : *Edin*
Essex : *Essx*
Falkirk : *Falk*
Fermanagh & Omagh : *Ferm*
Fife : *Fife*
Flintshire : *Flin*
Glasgow : *Glas*
Gloucestershire : *Glos*
Greater London : *G Lon*
Greater Manchester : *G Man*
Gwynedd : *Gwyn*
Halton : *Hal*
Hampshire : *Hants*
Hartlepool : *Hart*
Herefordshire : *Here*
Hertfordshire : *Herts*
Highland : *High*
Inverclyde : *Inv*
Isle of Anglesey : *IOA*
Isle of Man : *IOM*
Isle of Wight : *IOW*
Isles of Scilly : *IOS*
Kent : *Kent*
Kingston upon Hull : *Hull*
Lancashire : *Lanc*
Leicester : *Leic*
Leicestershire : *Leics*
Lincolnshire : *Linc*
Lisburn & Castlereagh : *Lis*
Luton : *Lutn*
Medway : *Medw*
Merseyside : *Mers*
Merthyr Tydfil : *Mer T*
Mid & East Antrim : *ME Ant*
Middlesbrough : *Midd*
Midlothian : *Midl*
Mid Ulster : *M Ulst*
Milton Keynes : *Mil*
Monmouthshire : *Mon*
Moray : *Mor*
Neath Port Talbot : *Neat*
Newport : *Newp*
Newry, Mourne & Down : *New M*
Norfolk : *Norf*
Northamptonshire : *Nptn*
North Ayrshire : *N Ayr*
North East Lincolnshire : *NE Lin*
North Lanarkshire : *N Lan*
North Lincolnshire : *N Lin*
North Somerset : *N Som*
Northumberland : *Nmbd*
North Yorkshire : *N Yor*
Nottingham : *Nott*
Nottinghamshire : *Notts*
Orkney : *Orkn*
Oxfordshire : *Oxon*
Pembrokeshire : *Pemb*
Perth & Kinross : *Per*
Peterborough : *Pet*
Plymouth : *Plym*
Poole : *Pool*
Portsmouth : *Port*
Powys : *Powy*
Reading : *Read*
Redcar & Cleveland : *Red C*
Renfrewshire : *Ren*
Rhondda Cynon Taff : *Rhon*
Rutland : *Rut*
Scottish Borders : *Bord*
Shetland : *Shet*
Shropshire : *Shrp*
Slough : *Slo*
Somerset : *Som*
Southampton : *Sotn*
South Ayrshire : *S Ayr*
Southend-on-Sea : *S'end*
South Gloucestershire : *S Glo*
South Lanarkshire : *S Lan*
South Yorkshire : *S Yor*
Staffordshire : *Staf*
Stirling : *Stir*
Stockton-on-Tees : *Stoc T*
Stoke-on-Trent : *Stoke*
Suffolk : *Suff*
Surrey : *Surr*
Swansea : *Swan*
Swindon : *Swin*
Telford & Wrekin : *Telf*
Thurrock : *Thur*
Torbay : *Torb*
Torfaen : *Torf*
Tyne & Wear : *Tyne*
Vale of Glamorgan, The : *V Glam*
Warrington : *Warr*
Warwickshire : *Warw*
West Berkshire : *W Ber*
West Dunbartonshire : *W Dun*
Western Isles : *W Isl*
West Lothian : *W Lot*
West Midlands : *W Mid*
West Sussex : *W Sus*
West Yorkshire : *W Yor*
Wiltshire : *Wilts*
Windsor & Maidenhead : *Wind*
Wokingham : *Wok*
Worcestershire : *Worc*
Wrexham : *Wrex*
York : *York*

INDEX

A

Abbas Combe. Som 4C 22
Abberley. Worc 4B 60
Abberley Common. Worc 4B 60
Abberton. Essx 4D 54
Abberton. Worc 5D 61
Abberwick. Nmbd 3F 121
Abbess Roding. Essx 4F 53
Abbey. Devn 1E 13
Abbey-cwm-hir. Powy 3C 58
Abbeydale. S Yor 2H 85
Abbeydale Park. S Yor 2H 85
Abbey Dore. Here 2G 47
Abbey Gate. Devn 3F 13
Abbey Hulton. Stoke 1D 72
Abbey St Bathans. Bord 3D 130
Abbeystead. Lanc 4E 97
Abbeytown. Cumb 4C 112
Abbey Village. Lanc 2E 91
Abbey Wood. G Lon 3F 39
Abbots Bickington. Devn 1D 11
Abbots Bromley. Staf 3E 73
Abbotsbury. Dors 4A 14
Abbotsham. Devn 4E 19
Abbotskerswell. Devn 2E 9
Abbots Langley. Herts 5A 52
Abbots Leigh. N Som 4A 34
Abbotsley. Cambs 5B 64
Abbots Morton. Worc 5E 61
Abbots Ripton. Cambs 3B 64
Abbot's Salford. Warw 5E 61
Abbotstone. Hants 3D 24
Abbots Worthy. Hants 3C 24
Abbotts Ann. Hants 2B 24
Abcott. Shrp 3F 59
Abdon. Shrp 2H 59
Abenhall. Glos 4B 48
Aber. Cdgn 1E 45
Aberaeron. Cdgn 4D 56
Aberafan. Neat 3G 31
Aberaman. Rhon 5D 46
Aberangell. Gwyn 4H 69
Aberarad. Carm 1H 43
Aberarder. High 1A 150
Aberargie. Per 2D 136
Aberarth. Cdgn 4D 57
Aberavon. Neat 3G 31
Aber-banc. Cdgn 1D 44
Aberbargoed. Cphy 2E 33
Aberbechan. Powy 1D 58
Aberbeeg. Blae 5F 47
Aberbowlan. Carm 2G 45
Aberbran. Powy 3C 46
Abercanaid. Mer T 5D 46
Abercarn. Cphy 2F 33
Abercastle. Pemb 1C 42
Abercegir. Powy 5H 69
Aberchalder. High 3F 149
Aberchirder. Abers 3D 160
Aberchwiler. Den 4C 82
Abercorn. W Lot 2D 129
Abercraf. Powy 4B 46
Abercregan. Neat 2B 32
Abercrombie. Fife 3H 137
Abercwmboi. Rhon 2D 32
Abercych. Pemb 1C 44
Abercynon. Rhon 2D 32
Aber-Cywarch. Gwyn 4A 70
Aberdalgie. Per 1C 136
Aberdar. Rhon 5C 46
Aberdare. Rhon 5C 46
Aberdaron. Gwyn 3A 68
Aberdaugleddau. Pemb 4D 42
Aberdeen. Aber 192 (3G 153)
Aberdeen International Airport.
  Aber 2F 153
Aberdesach. Gwyn 5D 80
Aberdour. Fife 1E 129
Aberdovey. Gwyn 1F 57
Aberdulais. Neat 5A 46
Aberdyfi. Gwyn 1F 57
Aberedw. Powy 1D 46
Abereiddy. Pemb 1B 42
Abererch. Gwyn 2C 68
Aberfan. Mer T 5D 46
Aberfeldy. Per 4F 143
Aberffraw. IOA 4C 80
Aberffrwd. Cdgn 3F 57
Aberford. W Yor 1E 93
Aberfoyle. Stir 3E 135
Abergarw. B'end 3C 32
Abergarwed. Neat 5B 46
Abergavenny. Mon 4G 47
Abergele. Cnwy 3B 82
Aber-Giâr. Carm 1F 45
Abergorlech. Carm 2F 45
Abergwaun. Pemb 1D 42
Abergwesyn. Powy 5A 58
Abergwili. Carm 3E 45
Abergwynfi. Neat 2B 32
Abergwyngregyn. Gwyn 3F 81
Abergynolwyn. Gwyn 5F 69
Aberhafesp. Powy 1C 58
Aberhonddu. Powy 3D 46
Aberhosan. Powy 1H 57
Aberkenfig. B'end 3B 32
Aberlady. E Lot 1A 130
Aberlemno. Ang 3E 145
Aberllefenni. Gwyn 5G 69
Abermaw. Gwyn 4F 69
Abermeurig. Cdgn 5E 57
Aber-miwl. Powy 1D 58
Abermule. Powy 1D 58
Abernant. Carm 2H 43
Abernant. Rhon 5D 46
Abernethy. Per 2D 136
Abernyte. Per 5B 144
Aber-oer. Wrex 1E 71
Aberpennar. Rhon 2D 32
Aberporth. Cdgn 5B 56
Aberriw. Powy 5D 70
Abersoch. Gwyn 3C 68
Abersychan. Torf 5F 47
Abertawe. Swan 203 (3F 31)
Aberteifi. Cdgn 1B 44
Aberthin. V Glam 4D 32
Abertillery. Blae 5F 47
Abertridwr. Cphy 3E 32
Abertridwr. Powy 4C 70
Abertyleri. Blae 5F 47
Abertysswg. Cphy 5E 47
Aberuthven. Per 2B 136
Aber Village. Powy 3E 46
Aberwheeler. Den 4C 82
Aberyscir. Powy 3C 46
Aberystwyth. Cdgn 2E 57
Abhainn Suidhe. W Isl 7C 171
Abingdon-on-Thames.
  Oxon 2C 36
Abinger Common. Surr 1C 26
Abinger Hammer. Surr 1B 26
Abington. S Lan 2B 118
Abington Pigotts. Cambs 1D 52
Ab Kettleby. Leics 3E 74
Ab Lench. Worc 5E 61
Ablington. Glos 5G 49
Ablington. Wilts 2G 23
Abney. Derbs 3F 85
Aboyne. Abers 4C 152
Abram. G Man 4E 90
Abriachan. High 5H 157
Abridge. Essx 1F 39
Abronhill. N Lan 2A 128
Abson. S Glo 4C 34
Abthorpe. Nptn 1E 51
Abune-the-Hill. Orkn 5B 172
Aby. Linc 3D 88
Acairseid. W Isl 8C 170
Acaster Malbis. York 5H 99
Acaster Selby. N Yor 5H 99
Accott. Devn 3G 19
Accrington. Lanc 2F 91
Acha. Arg 3C 138
Achachork. High 4D 155
Achadh a' Chuirn. High 1E 147
Achahoish. Arg 2F 125
Achaleven. Arg 5D 140
Achallader. Arg 4H 141
Acha Mor. W Isl 5F 171
Achanalt. High 2E 157
Achandunie. High 1A 158
Ach' an Todhair. High 1E 141
Achany. High 3C 164
Achaphubuil. High 1E 141
Acharacle. High 2A 140
Acharn. Ang 1B 144
Acharn. Per 4E 143
Acharole. High 3E 169
Achateny. High 2G 139
Achavanich. High 4D 169
Achdalieu. High 1E 141
Achduart. High 3E 163
Achentoul. High 5A 168
Achfary. High 5C 166
Achfrish. High 2C 164
Achgarve. High 4C 162
Achiemore. High
  nr. Durness 2D 166
  nr. Thurso 3A 168
A' Chill. High 3A 146
Achiltibuie. High 3E 163
Achina. High 2H 167
Achinahuagh. High 2F 167
Achindarroch. High 3E 141
Achinduich. High 3C 164
Achinduin. Arg 5C 140
Achininver. High 2F 167
Achintee. High 4B 156
Achintraid. High 5H 155
Achleck. Arg 4F 139
Achlorachan. High 3F 157
Achluachrach. High 5E 149
Achlyness. High 3C 166
Achmelvich. High 1E 163
Achmony. High 5H 157
Achmore. High
  nr. Stromeferry 5A 156
  nr. Ullapool 4E 163
Achnacarnin. High 1E 163
Achnacarry. High 5D 148
Achnaclerach. High 2G 157
Achnacloich. High 3D 147
Ach na Cloiche. High 3D 147
Achnaconeran. High 2G 149
Achnacroish. Arg 4C 140
Achnafalnich. Arg 1B 134
Achnagarron. High 1A 158
Achnagoul. Arg 3H 133
Achnaha. High 2F 139
Achnahanat. High 4C 164
Achnahannet. High 1D 151
Achnairn. High 2C 164
Achnamara. Arg 1F 125
Achnanellan. High 5C 148
Achnasheen. High 3D 156
Achnashellach. High 4C 156
Achosnich. High 2F 139
Achow. High 5E 169
Achranich. High 4B 140
Achreamie. High 2C 168
Achriabhach. High 2F 141
Achriesgill. High 3C 166
Achrimsdale. High 3G 165
Achscrabster. High 2C 168
Achtoty. High 2G 167
Achurch. Nptn 2H 63
Achuvoldrach. High 3F 167
Achvaich. High 4E 164
Achvoan. High 3E 165
Ackenthwaite. Cumb 1E 97
Ackergill. High 3F 169
Ackergillshore. High 3F 169
Acklam. Midd 3B 106
Acklam. N Yor 3B 100
Ackleton. Shrp 1B 60
Acklington. Nmbd 4G 121
Ackton. W Yor 2E 93
Ackworth Moor Top.
  W Yor 3E 93
Acle. Norf 4G 79
Acocks Green. W Mid 2F 61
Acol. Kent 4H 41
Acomb. Nmbd 3C 114
Acomb. York 4H 99
Aconbury. Here 2A 48
Acre. G Man 4H 91
Acre. Lanc 2F 91
Acrefair. Wrex 1E 71
Acrise. Kent 1F 29
Acton. Arm 5E 178
Acton. Ches E 5A 84
Acton. Dors 5E 15
Acton. G Lon 2C 38
Acton. Shrp 2F 59
Acton. Staf 1C 72
Acton. Suff 1B 54
Acton. Worc 4C 60
Acton. Wrex 5F 83
Acton Beauchamp. Here 5A 60
Acton Bridge. Ches W 3H 83
Acton Burnell. Shrp 5H 71
Acton Green. Here 5A 60
Acton Pigott. Shrp 5H 71
Acton Round. Shrp 1A 60
Acton Scott. Shrp 2G 59
Acton Trussell. Staf 4D 72
Acton Turville. S Glo 3D 34
Adabroc. W Isl 1H 171
Adam's Hill. Worc 3D 60
Adbaston. Staf 3B 72
Adber. Dors 4B 22
Adderbury. Oxon 2C 50
Adderley. Shrp 2A 72
Adderstone. Nmbd 1F 121
Addiewell. W Lot 3C 128
Addingham. W Yor 5C 98
Addington. Buck 3F 51
Addington. G Lon 4E 39
Addington. Kent 5A 40
Addinston. Bord 4B 130
Addiscombe. G Lon 4E 39
Addlestone. Surr 4B 38
Addlethorpe. Linc 4E 89
Adeney. Telf 4B 72
Adfa. Powy 5C 70
Adforton. Here 3G 59
Adgestone. IOW 4D 16
Adisham. Kent 5G 41
Adlestrop. Glos 3H 49
Adlingfleet. E Yor 2B 94
Adlington. Ches E 2D 84
Adlington. Lanc 3E 90
Admaston. Staf 3E 73
Admaston. Telf 4A 72
Admington. Warw 1H 49
Adpar. Cdgn 1D 44
Adsborough. Som 4F 21
Adstock. Buck 2F 51
Adstone. Nptn 5C 62
Adversane. W Sus 3B 26
Advie. High 5F 159
Adwalton. W Yor 2C 92
Adwell. Oxon 2E 37
Adwick le Street. S Yor 4F 93
Adwick upon Dearne.
  S Yor 4E 93
Adziel. Abers 3G 161
Ae. Dum 1A 112
Affleck. Abers 1F 153
Affpuddle. Dors 3D 14
Affric Lodge. High 1D 148
Afon-wen. Flin 3D 82
Agglethorpe. N Yor 1C 98
Aghagallon. Arm 3F 178
Aghalee. Lis 3F 178
Aglionby. Cumb 4F 113
Ahoghill. ME Ant 6G 175
Aigburth. Mers 2F 83
Aiginis. W Isl 4G 171
Aike. E Yor 5E 101
Aikers. Orkn 8D 172
Aiketgate. Cumb 5F 113
Aikhead. Cumb 5D 112
Aikton. Cumb 4D 112
Ailey. Here 1G 47
Ailsworth. Pet 1A 64
Ainderby Quernhow.
  N Yor 1F 99
Ainderby Steeple. N Yor 5A 106
Aingers Green. Essx 3E 54
Ainsdale. Mers 3B 90
Ainsdale-on-Sea. Mers 3B 90
Ainstable. Cumb 5G 113
Ainsworth. G Man 3F 91
Ainthorpe. N Yor 4E 107
Aintree. Mers 1F 83
Aird. Arg 3E 133
Aird. Dum 3F 109
Aird. High
  nr. Port Henderson 1G 155
  nr. Tarskavaig 3D 147
Aird, The. High 3D 154
Aird. W Isl
  on Benbecula 3C 170
  on Isle of Lewis 4H 171
Àird a Bhasair. High 3E 147
Aird a Mhachair. W Isl 4C 170
Aird a Mhulaidh. W Isl 6D 171
Aird Asaig. W Isl 7D 171
Aird Dhail. W Isl 1G 171
Airdens. High 4D 164
Airdeny. Arg 1G 133
Aird Mhidhinis. W Isl 8C 170
Aird Mhighe. W Isl
  nr. Ceann a Bhaigh 8D 171
  nr. Fionnsabhagh 9C 171
Aird Mhor. W Isl
  on Barra 8C 170
  on South Uist 4D 170
Airdrie. N Lan 3A 128
Aird Shleibhe. W Isl 9D 171
Aird Thunga. W Isl 4G 171
Aird Uig. W Isl 4C 171
Airedale. W Yor 2E 93
Airidh a Bhruaich. W Isl 6E 171
Airies. Dum 3E 109
Airmyn. E Yor 2H 93
Airntully. Per 5H 143
Airor. High 3F 147
Airth. Falk 1C 128
Airton. N Yor 4B 98
Aisby. Linc
  nr. Gainsborough 1F 87
  nr. Grantham 2H 75
Aisgernis. W Isl 6C 170
Aish. Devn
  nr. Buckfastleigh 2C 8
  nr. Totnes 3E 9
Aisholt. Som 3E 21
Aiskew. N Yor 1E 99
Aislaby. N Yor
  nr. Pickering 1B 100
  nr. Whitby 4F 107
Aislaby. Stoc T 3B 106
Aisthorpe. Linc 2G 87
Aith. Shet
  on Fetlar 3H 173
  on Mainland 6E 173
Aithsetter. Shet 8F 173
Akeld. Nmbd 2D 120
Akeley. Buck 2F 51
Akenham. Suff 1E 55
Albaston. Corn 5E 11
Alberbury. Shrp 4F 71
Albert Town. Pemb 3D 42
Albert Village. Leics 4H 73
Albourne. W Sus 4D 26
Albrighton. Shrp
  nr. Shrewsbury 4G 71
  nr. Telford 5C 72
Alburgh. Norf 2E 67
Albury. Herts 3E 53
Albury. Surr 1B 26
Albyfield. Cumb 4G 113
Alby Hill. Norf 2D 78
Alcaig. High 3H 157
Alcaston. Shrp 2G 59
Alcester. Warw 5E 61
Alciston. E Sus 5G 27
Alcombe. Som 2C 20
Alconbury. Cambs 3A 64
Alconbury Weston. Cambs 3A 64
Aldborough. Norf 2D 78
Aldborough. N Yor 3G 99
Aldbourne. Wilts 4A 36
Aldbrough. E Yor 1F 95
Aldbrough St John. N Yor 3F 105
Aldbury. Herts 4H 51
Aldcliffe. Lanc 3D 96
Aldclune. Per 2G 143
Aldeburgh. Suff 5G 67
Aldeby. Norf 1G 67
Aldenham. Herts 1C 38
Alderbury. Wilts 4G 23
Aldercar. Derbs 1B 74
Alderford. Norf 4D 78
Alderholt. Dors 1G 15
Alderley. Glos 2C 34
Alderley Edge. Ches E 3C 84
Aldermaston. W Ber 5D 36
Aldermaston Soke. Hants 5E 36
Aldermaston Wharf. W Ber 5E 36
Alderminster. Warw 1H 49
Alder Moor. Staf 3G 73
Aldersey Green. Ches W 5G 83
Aldershot. Hants 1G 25
Alderton. Glos 2F 49
Alderton. Nptn 1F 51
Alderton. Shrp 3G 71
Alderton. Suff 1G 55
Alderton. Wilts 3D 34
Alderton Fields. Glos 2F 49
Alderwasley. Derbs 5H 85
Aldfield. N Yor 3E 99
Aldford. Ches W 5G 83
Aldgate. Rut 5G 75
Aldham. Essx 3C 54
Aldham. Suff 1D 54
Aldingbourne. W Sus 5A 26
Aldingham. Cumb 2B 96
Aldington. Kent 2E 29
Aldington. Worc 1F 49
Aldington Frith. Kent 2E 29
Aldochlay. Arg 4C 134
Aldon. Shrp 3G 59
Aldoth. Cumb 5C 112
Aldreth. Cambs 3D 64
Aldridge. W Mid 5E 73
Aldringham. Suff 4G 67
Aldsworth. Glos 4G 49
Aldsworth. W Sus 2F 17
Aldwark. Derbs 5G 85
Aldwark. N Yor 3G 99
Aldwick. W Sus 3H 17
Aldwincle. Nptn 2H 63
Aldworth. W Ber 4D 36
Alexandria. W Dun 1E 127
Aley. Som 3E 21
Aley Green. C Beds 4A 52
Alfardisworthy. Devn 1C 10
Alfington. Devn 3E 12
Alfold. Surr 2B 26
Alfold Bars. W Sus 2B 26
Alfold Crossways. Surr 2B 26
Alford. Abers 2C 152
Alford. Linc 3D 88
Alford. Som 3B 22
Alfreton. Derbs 5B 86
Alfrick. Worc 5B 60
Alfrick Pound. Worc 5B 60
Alfriston. E Sus 5G 27
Algarkirk. Linc 2B 76
Alhampton. Som 3B 22
Aline Lodge. W Isl 6D 171
Alkborough. N Lin 2B 94
Alkerton. Oxon 1B 50
Alkham. Kent 1G 29
Alkington. Shrp 2H 71
Alkmonton. Derbs 2F 73
Alladale Lodge. High 5B 164
Allaleigh. Devn 3E 9
Allanbank. N Lan 4B 128
Allanton. N Lan 4B 128
Allanton. Bord 4E 131
Allaston. Glos 5B 48
Allbrook. Hants 4C 24
All Cannings. Wilts 5F 35
Allendale Town. Nmbd 4B 114
Allen End. Warw 1F 61
Allenheads. Nmbd 5B 114
Allensford. Dur 5D 115
Allen's Green. Herts 4E 53
Allensmore. Here 2H 47
Allenton. Derb 2A 74
Aller. Som 4H 21
Allerby. Cumb 1B 102
Allercombe. Devn 3D 12
Allerford. Som 2C 20
Allerston. N Yor 1C 100
Allerthorpe. E Yor 5B 100
Allerton. Mers 2G 83
Allerton. W Yor 1B 92
Allerton Bywater. W Yor 2E 93
Allerton Mauleverer. N Yor 4G 99
Allesley. W Mid 2G 61
Allestree. Derb 2H 73
Allet. Corn 4B 6
Allexton. Leics 5F 75
Allgreave. Ches E 4D 84
Allhallows. Medw 3C 40
Allhallows-on-Sea. Medw 3C 40
Alligin Shuas. High 3H 155
Allimore Green. Staf 4C 72
Allington. Kent 5B 40
Allington. Linc 1F 75
Allington. Wilts
  nr. Amesbury 3H 23
  nr. Devizes 5F 35
Allithwaite. Cumb 2C 96
Alloa. Clac 4A 136
Allonby. Cumb 5B 112
Allostock. Ches W 3B 84
Alloway. S Ayr 3C 116
Allowenshay. Som 1G 13
All Saints South Elmham.
  Suff 2F 67
Allscott. Shrp 1B 60
Allscott. Telf 4A 72
All Stretton. Shrp 1G 59
Allt. Carm 5F 45
Alltami. Flin 4E 83
Alltgobhlach. N Ayr 5G 125
Alltmawr. Powy 1D 46
Alltnacaillich. High 4E 167
Allt na h' Airbhe. High 4F 163
Alltour. High 5E 148
Alltsigh. High 2G 149
Alltwalis. Carm 2E 45
Alltwen. Neat 5H 45
Alltyblacca. Cdgn 1F 45
Allt-y-goed. Pemb 1B 44
Almeley. Here 5F 59
Almeley Wooton. Here 5F 59
Almer. Dors 3E 15
Almholme. S Yor 4F 93
Almington. Staf 2B 72
Alminstone Cross. Devn 4D 18
Almodington. W Sus 3G 17
Almondbank. Per 1C 136
Almondbury. W Yor 3B 92
Almondsbury. S Glo 3B 34
Alne. N Yor 3G 99
Alness. High 2A 158
Alnessferry. High 2A 158
Alnham. Nmbd 3D 121
Alnmouth. Nmbd 3G 121
Alnwick. Nmbd 3F 121
Alphamstone. Essx 2B 54
Alpheton. Suff 5A 66
Alphington. Devn 3C 12
Alpington. Norf 5E 79
Alport. Derbs 4G 85
Alport. Powy 1E 59
Alpraham. Ches E 5H 83
Alresford. Essx 3D 54
Alrewas. Staf 4F 73
Alsager. Ches E 5B 84
Alsagers Bank. Staf 1C 72
Alsop en le Dale. Derbs 5F 85
Alston. Cumb 5A 114
Alston. Devn 2G 13
Alstone. Glos 2E 49
Alstone. Som 2G 21
Alstonefield. Staf 5F 85
Alston Sutton. Som 1H 21
Alswear. Devn 4H 19
Altandhu. High 2D 163
Altanduin. High 1F 165
Altarnun. Corn 4C 10
Altass. High 3B 164
Alterwall. High 2E 169
Altgaltraig. Arg 2B 126
Altham. Lanc 1F 91
Althorne. Essx 1D 40
Althorpe. N Lin 4B 94
Altnabreac. High 4C 168
Altnacealgach. High 2G 163
Altnafeadh. High 3G 141
Altnaharra. High 5F 167
Altofts. W Yor 2D 93
Alton. Derbs 4A 86
Alton. Hants 3F 25
Alton. Staf 1E 73
Alton Barnes. Wilts 5G 35
Altonhill. E Ayr 1D 116
Alton Pancras. Dors 2C 14
Alton Priors. Wilts 5G 35
Altrincham. G Man 2B 84
Altrua. High 4E 149
Alva. Clac 4A 136
Alvanley. Ches W 3G 83
Alvaston. Derb 2A 74
Alvechurch. Worc 3E 61
Alvecote. Warw 5G 73
Alvediston. Wilts 4E 23
Alveley. Shrp 2B 60
Alverdiscott. Devn 4F 19
Alverstoke. Hants 3D 16
Alverstone. IOW 4D 16
Alverthorpe. W Yor 2D 92
Alverton. Notts 1E 75
Alves. Mor 2F 159
Alvescot. Oxon 5A 50
Alveston. S Glo 3B 34
Alveston. Warw 5G 61
Alvie. High 3C 150
Alvingham. Linc 1C 88
Alvington. Glos 5B 48
Alwalton. Cambs 1A 64
Alweston. Dors 1B 14
Alwington. Devn 4E 19
Alwinton. Nmbd 4D 120
Alwoodley. W Yor 5E 99
Alyth. Per 4B 144
Amatnatua. High 4B 164
Am Baile. W Isl 7C 170
Ambaston. Derbs 2B 74
Ambergate. Derbs 5H 85
Amber Hill. Linc 1B 76
Amberley. Glos 5D 48
Amberley. W Sus 4B 26
Amble. Nmbd 4G 121
Amblecote. W Mid 2C 60
Ambler Thorn. W Yor 2A 92
Ambleside. Cumb 4E 103
Ambleston. Pemb 2E 43
Ambrosden. Oxon 4E 50
Amcotts. N Lin 3B 94
Amersham. Buck 1A 38
Amerton. Staf 3D 73
Amesbury. Wilts 2G 23
Amisfield. Dum 1B 112
Amlwch. IOA 1D 80
Amlwch Port. IOA 1D 80
Ammanford. Carm 4G 45
Amotherby. N Yor 2B 100
Ampfield. Hants 4B 24
Ampleforth. N Yor 2H 99
Ampleforth College. N Yor 2H 99
Ampney Crucis. Glos 5F 49
Ampney St Mary. Glos 5F 49
Ampney St Peter. Glos 5F 49
Amport. Hants 2A 24
Ampthill. C Beds 2A 52
Ampton. Suff 3A 66
Amroth. Pemb 4F 43
Amulree. Per 5G 143
Amwell. Herts 4B 52
Anaheilt. High 2C 140
An Aird. High 3D 147
An Baile Nua. Ferm 7K 177
An Camus Darach. High 4E 147
Ancaster. Linc 1G 75
Anchor. Shrp 2D 58
Anchorsholme. Lanc 5C 96
Anchor Street. Norf 3F 79
An Cnoc. W Isl 4G 171
An Cnoc Ard. W Isl 1H 171
An Coroghon. High 3A 146
Ancroft. Nmbd 5G 131
Ancrum. Bord 2A 120
Ancton. W Sus 5A 26
Anderby. Linc 3E 89
Anderby Creek. Linc 3E 89
Anderson. Dors 3D 15
Anderton. Ches W 3A 84
Andertons Mill. Lanc 3D 90
Andover. Hants 2B 24
Andover Down. Hants 2B 24
Andoversford. Glos 4F 49
Andreas. IOM 2D 108
An Dùnan. High 1D 147
Andwell. Hants 1E 25
Anelog. Gwyn 3A 68
Anfield. Mers 1F 83
Angarrack. Corn 3C 4
Angelbank. Shrp 3H 59
Angersleigh. Som 1E 13
Angerton. Cumb 4D 112
Angle. Pemb 4C 42
An Gleann Ur. W Isl 4G 171
Angmering. W Sus 5B 26
Angmering-on-Sea. W Sus 5B 26
Angram. N Yor
  nr. Keld 5B 104
  nr. York 5H 99
Anick. Nmbd 3C 114
Ankerbold. Derbs 4A 86
Ankerville. High 1C 158
Anlaby. E Yor 2D 94
Anlaby Park. Hull 2D 94
An Leth Meadhanach.
  W Isl 7C 170
Anmer. Norf 3G 77
Anmore. Hants 1E 17
Annacloy. New M 5J 179
Annadorn. New M 5J 179
Annaghmore. Arm 4D 178
Annaghugh. Arm 4D 178
Annahilt. Lis 4G 179
Annalong. New M 8H 179
Annan. Dum 3D 112
Annaside. Cumb 1A 96
Annat. Arg 1H 133
Annat. High 3A 156
Annathill. N Lan 2A 128
Anna Valley. Hants 2B 24
Annbank. S Ayr 2D 116
Annesley. Notts 5C 86
Annesley Woodhouse.
  Notts 5C 86
Annfield Plain. Dur 4E 115
Annsborough. New M 6H 179
Annscroft. Shrp 5G 71
An Sailean. High 2A 140
Ansdell. Lanc 2B 90
Ansford. Som 3B 22

Bishop Middleham. Dur 1A 106
Bishopmill. Mor 2G 159
Bishop Monkton. N Yor 3F 99
Bishop Norton. Linc 1G 87
Bishopsbourne. Kent 5F 41
Bishops Cannings. Wilts 5F 35
Bishop's Castle. Shrp 2F 59
Bishop's Caundle. Dors 1B 14
Bishop's Cleeve. Glos 3E 49
Bishops Court. New M 5K 179
Bishop's Down. Dors 1B 14
Bishop's Frome. Here 1B 48
Bishop's Green. Essx 4G 53
Bishop's Green. Hants 5D 36
Bishop's Hull. Som 4F 21
Bishop's Itchington. Warw 5A 62
Bishops Lydeard. Som 4E 21
Bishop's Norton. Glos 3D 48
Bishop's Nympton. Devn 4A 20
Bishop's Offley. Staf 3B 72
Bishop's Stortford. Herts 3E 53
Bishop's Sutton. Hants 3E 24
Bishop's Tachbrook. Warw 4H 61
Bishop's Tawton. Devn 3F 19
Bishopsteignton. Devn 5C 12
Bishopstoke. Hants 1C 16
Bishopston. Swan 4E 31
Bishopstone. Buck 4G 51
Bishopstone. E Sus 5F 27
Bishopstone. Here 1H 47
Bishopstone. Swin 3H 35
Bishopstone. Wilts 4F 23
Bishopstrow. Wilts 2D 23
Bishop Sutton. Bath 1A 22
Bishop's Waltham. Hants 1D 16
Bishopswood. Som 1F 13
Bishops Wood. Staf 5C 72
Bishopsworth. Bris 5A 34
Bishop Thornton. N Yor 3E 99
Bishopthorpe. York 5H 99
Bishopton. Darl 2A 106
Bishopton. Dum 5B 110
Bishopton. N Yor 2E 99
Bishopton. Ren 2F 127
Bishopton. Warw 5F 61
Bishop Wilton. E Yor 4B 100
Bishton. Newp 3G 33
Bishton. Staf 3E 73
Bisley. Glos 5E 49
Bisley. Surr 5A 38
Bispham. Bkpl 5C 96
Bispham Green. Lanc 3C 90
Bissoe. Corn 4B 6
Bisterne. Hants 2G 15
Bisterne Close. Hants 2H 15
Bitchfield. Linc 3G 75
Bittadon. Devn 2F 19
Bittaford. Devn 3C 8
Bittering. Norf 4B 78
Bitterley. Shrp 3H 59
Bitterne. Sotn 1C 16
Bitteswell. Leics 2C 62
Bitton. S Glo 5B 34
Bix. Oxon 3F 37
Bixter. Shet 6E 173
Blaby. Leics 1C 62
Blackawton. Devn 3E 9
Black Bank. Cambs 2E 65
Black Barn. Linc 3D 76
Blackborough. Devn 2D 12
Blackborough. Norf 4F 77
Blackborough End. Norf 4F 77
Black Bourton. Oxon 5A 50
Blackboys. E Sus 3G 27
Blackbrook. Derbs 1H 73
Blackbrook. Mers 1H 83
Blackbrook. Staf 2B 72
Blackbrook. Surr 1C 26
Blackburn. Abers 2F 153
Blackburn. Bkbn 2E 91
Blackburn. W Lot 3C 128
Black Callerton. Tyne 3E 115
Black Carr. Norf 1C 66
Black Clauchrie. S Ayr 1H 109
Black Corries. High 3G 141
Black Crofts. Arg 5D 140
Black Cross. Corn 2D 6
Blackden Heath. Ches E 3B 84
Blackditch. Oxon 5C 50
Blackdog. Abers 2G 153
Black Dog. Devn 2B 12
Blackdown. Dors 2G 13
Blackdyke. Cumb 4C 112
Blacker Hill. S Yor 4D 92
Blackfen. G Lon 3F 39
Blackfield. Hants 2C 16
Blackford. Cumb 3E 113
Blackford. Per 3A 136
Blackford. Shrp 2H 59
Blackford. Som
  nr. Burnham-on-Sea 2H 21
  nr. Wincanton 4B 22
Blackfordby. Leics 4H 73
Blackgang. IOW 5C 16
Blackhall. Edin 2F 129
Blackhall. Ren 3F 127
Blackhall Colliery. Dur 1B 106
Blackhall Mill. Tyne 4E 115
Blackhall Rocks. Dur 1B 106
Blackham. E Sus 2F 27
Blackheath. Essx 3D 54
Blackheath. G Lon 3E 39
Blackheath. Suff 3G 67
Blackheath. Surr 1B 26
Blackheath. W Mid 2D 61
Black Heddon. Nmbd 2D 115
Blackhill. Abers 4H 161
Blackhill. High 3C 154
Black Hill. Warw 5G 61
Blackhills. Abers 2G 161
Blackhills. High 3D 158
Blackjack. Linc 2B 76
Blackland. Wilts 5F 35
Black Lane. G Man 4F 91
Blackleach. Lanc 1C 90
Blackley. G Man 4G 91
Blackley. W Yor 3B 92
Blacklunans. Per 2A 144
Blackmill. B'end 3C 32
Blackmoor. G Man 4E 91
Blackmoor. Hants 3F 25
Blackmoor Gate. Devn 2G 19
Blackmore. Essx 5G 53
Blackmore End. Essx 2H 53
Blackmore End. Herts 4B 52
Black Mount. Arg 4G 141
Blackness. Falk 2D 128
Blacknest. Hants 2F 25
Blackney. Dors 3H 13
Blacknoll. Dors 4D 14
Black Notley. Essx 3A 54
Blacko. Lanc 5A 98
Black Pill. Swan 3F 31
Blackpool. Bkpl 192 (1B 90)
Blackpool. Devn 4E 9
Blackpool Airport. Lanc 1B 90
Blackpool Corner. Dors 3G 13
Blackpool Gate. Cumb 2G 113
Blackridge. W Lot 3B 128
Blackrock. Arg 3B 124
Blackrock. Mon 4F 47
Blackrod. G Man 3E 90
Blackshaw. Dum 3B 112
Blackshaw Head. W Yor 2H 91
Blackshaw Moor. Staf 5E 85
Blackskull. Arm 4F 178
Blacksmith's Green. Suff 4D 66
Blacksnape. Bkbn 2F 91
Blackstone. W Sus 4D 26
Black Street. Suff 2H 67
Black Tar. Pemb 4D 43
Blackthorn. Oxon 4E 50
Blackthorpe. Suff 4B 66
Blacktoft. E Yor 2B 94
Blacktop. Aber 3F 153
Black Torrington. Devn 2E 11
Blacktown. Newp 3F 33
Blackwall Tunnel. G Lon 2E 39
Blackwater. Corn 4B 6
Blackwater. Hants 1G 25
Blackwater. IOW 4D 16
Blackwater. Som 1F 13
Blackwaterfoot. N Ayr 3C 122
Blackwatertown. Arm 4C 178
Blackwell. Darl 3F 105
Blackwell. Derbs
  nr. Alfreton 5B 86
  nr. Buxton 3F 85
Blackwell. Som 4D 20
Blackwell. Warw 1H 49
Blackwell. Worc 3D 61
Blackwood. Cphy 2E 33
Blackwood. Dum 1G 111
Blackwood. S Lan 5A 128
Blackwood Hill. Staf 5D 84
Blacon. Ches W 4F 83
Bladnoch. Dum 4B 110
Bladon. Oxon 4C 50
Blaenannerch. Cdgn 1C 44
Blaenau Dolwyddelan. Cnwy 5F 81
Blaenau Ffestiniog. Gwyn 1G 69
Blaenavon. Torf 5F 47
Blaenawey. Mon 4F 47
Blaen Celyn. Cdgn 5C 56
Blaen Clydach. Rhon 2C 32
Blaencwm. Rhon 2C 32
Blaendulais. Neat 5B 46
Blaenffos. Pemb 1F 43
Blaengarw. B'end 2C 32
Blaen-geuffordd. Cdgn 2F 57
Blaengwrach. Neat 5B 46
Blaengwynfi. Neat 2B 32
Blaenllechau. Rhon 2C 32
Blaenpennal. Cdgn 4F 57
Blaenplwyf. Cdgn 3E 57
Blaenporth. Cdgn 1C 44
Blaenrhondda. Rhon 5C 46
Blaenwaun. Carm 2G 43
Blaen-y-coed. Carm 2H 43
Blagdon. N Som 1A 22
Blagdon. Torb 2E 9
Blagdon Hill. Som 1F 13
Blagill. Cumb 5A 114
Blaguegate. Lanc 4C 90
Blaich. High 1E 141
Blain. High 2A 140
Blaina. Blae 5F 47
Blair Atholl. Per 2F 143
Blair Drummond. Stir 4G 135
Blairgowrie. Per 4A 144
Blairhall. Fife 1D 128
Blairingone. Per 4B 136
Blairlogie. Stir 4H 135
Blairmore. Abers 5B 160
Blairmore. Arg 1C 126
Blairmore. High 3B 166
Blairquhanan. W Dun 1F 127
Blaisdon. Glos 4C 48
Blakebrook. Worc 3C 60
Blakedown. Worc 3C 60
Blake End. Essx 3H 53
Blakemere. Here 1G 47
Blakeney. Glos 5B 48
Blakeney. Norf 1C 78
Blakenhall. Ches E 1B 72
Blakeshall. Worc 2C 60
Blakesley. Nptn 5D 62
Blanchland. Nmbd 4C 114
Blandford Camp. Dors 2E 15
Blandford Forum. Dors 2D 15
Blandford St Mary. Dors 2D 15
Bland Hill. N Yor 4E 98
Blandy. High 2G 167
Blanefield. Stir 2G 127
Blankney. Linc 4H 87
Blantyre. S Lan 4H 127
Blarmachfoldach. High 2E 141
Blarnalearoch. High 4F 163
Blashford. Hants 2G 15
Blaston. Leics 1F 63
Blatchbridge. Som 2C 22
Blathaisbhal. W Isl 1D 170
Blatherwycke. Nptn 1G 63
Blawith. Cumb 1B 96
Blaxhall. Suff 5F 67
Blaxton. S Yor 4G 93
Blaydon. Tyne 3E 115
Bleadney. Som 2H 21
Bleadon. N Som 1G 21
Blean. Kent 4F 41
Bleary. Arm 4E 178
Bleasby. Linc 2A 88
Bleasby. Notts 1E 74
Bleasby Moor. Linc 2A 88
Blebocraigs. Fife 2G 137
Bleddfa. Powy 4E 58
Bledington. Glos 3H 49
Bledlow. Buck 5F 51
Bledlow Ridge. Buck 2F 37
Blencarn. Cumb 1H 103
Blencogo. Cumb 5C 112
Blendworth. Hants 1F 17
Blennerhasset. Cumb 5C 112
Bletchingdon. Oxon 4D 50
Bletchingley. Surr 5E 39
Bletchley. Mil 2G 51
Bletchley. Shrp 2A 72
Bletherston. Pemb 2E 43
Bletsoe. Bed 5H 63
Blewbury. Oxon 3D 36
Blickling. Norf 3D 78
Blidworth. Notts 5C 86
Blindburn. Nmbd 3C 120
Blindcrake. Cumb 1C 102
Blindley Heath. Surr 1E 27
Blindmoor. Som 1F 13
Blisland. Corn 5B 10
Blissford. Hants 1G 15
Bliss Gate. Worc 3B 60
Blists Hill. Telf 5A 72
Blisworth. Nptn 5E 63
Blithbury. Staf 3E 73
Blitterlees. Cumb 4C 112
Blockley. Glos 2G 49
Blofield. Norf 5F 79
Blofield Heath. Norf 4F 79
Blo' Norton. Norf 3C 66
Bloomfield. Bord 2H 119
Blore. Staf 1F 73
Blount's Green. Staf 2E 73
Bloxham. Oxon 2C 50
Bloxholm. Linc 5H 87
Bloxwich. W Mid 5D 73
Bloxworth. Dors 3D 15
Blubberhouses. N Yor 4D 98
Blue Anchor. Som 2D 20
Blue Anchor. Swan 3E 31
Blue Bell Hill. Kent 4B 40
Blue Row. Essx 4D 54
Bluetown. Kent 5D 40
Blundeston. Suff 1H 67
Blunham. C Beds 5A 64
Blunsdon St Andrew. Swin 3G 35
Bluntington. Worc 3C 60
Bluntisham. Cambs 3C 64
Blunts. Corn 2H 7
Blurton. Stoke 1C 72
Blyborough. Linc 1G 87
Blyford. Suff 3G 67
Blymhill. Staf 4C 72
Blymhill Lawns. Staf 4C 72
Blyth. Nmbd 1G 115
Blyth. Notts 2D 86
Blyth. Bord 5E 129
Blyth Bank. Bord 5E 129
Blyth Bridge. Bord 5E 129
Blythburgh. Suff 3G 67
Blythe Bridge. Staf 1D 72
Blythe, The. Staf 3E 73
Blythe Marsh. Staf 1D 72
Blyton. Linc 1F 87
Boardmills. Lis 4H 179
Boarhills. Fife 2H 137
Boarhunt. Hants 2E 16
Boarshead. E Sus 2G 27
Boar's Head. G Man 4D 90
Boars Hill. Oxon 5C 50
Boarstall. Buck 4E 51
Boasley Cross. Devn 3E 11
Boath. High 1H 157
Boat of Garten. High 2D 150
Bobbing. Kent 4C 40
Bobbington. Staf 1C 60
Bobbingworth. Essx 5F 53
Bocaddon. Corn 3F 7
Bocking. Essx 3A 54
Bocking Churchstreet. Essx 3A 54
Boddam. Abers 4H 161
Boddam. Shet 10E 173
Boddington. Glos 3D 49
Bodedern. IOA 2C 80
Bodelwyddan. Den 3C 82
Bodenham. Here 5H 59
Bodenham. Wilts 4G 23
Bodewryd. IOA 1C 80
Bodfari. Den 3C 82
Bodffordd. IOA 3D 80
Bodham. Norf 1D 78
Bodiam. E Sus 3B 28
Bodicote. Oxon 2C 50
Bodieve. Corn 1D 6
Bodinnick. Corn 3F 7
Bodle Street Green. E Sus 4A 28
Bodmin. Corn 2E 7
Bodnant. Cnwy 3H 81
Bodney. Norf 1H 65
Bodorgan. IOA 4C 80
Bodrane. Corn 2G 7
Bodsham. Kent 1F 29
Boduan. Gwyn 2C 68
Bodymoor Heath. Warw 1F 61
Bog, The. Shrp 1F 59
Bogallan. High 3A 158
Bogbrae Croft. Abers 5H 161
Bogend. S Ayr 1C 116
Boghall. Midl 3F 129
Boghall. W Lot 3C 128
Boghead. S Lan 5A 128
Bogindollo. Ang 3D 144
Bogmoor. Mor 2A 160
Bogniebrae. Abers 4C 160
Bognor Regis. W Sus 3H 17
Bograxie. Abers 2E 152
Bogside. N Lan 4B 128
Bogton. Abers 3D 160
Bogue. Dum 1D 110
Bohenie. High 5E 149
Bohortha. Corn 5C 6
Boirseam. W Isl 9C 171
Bokiddick. Corn 2E 7
Bolam. Dur 2E 105
Bolam. Nmbd 1D 115
Bolberry. Devn 5C 8
Bold Heath. Mers 2H 83
Boldon. Tyne 3G 115
Boldon Colliery. Tyne 3G 115
Boldre. Hants 3B 16
Boldron. Dur 3D 104
Bole. Notts 2E 87
Bolehall. Staf 5G 73
Bolehill. Derbs 5G 85
Bolenowe. Corn 5A 6
Boleside. Bord 1G 119
Bolham. Devn 1C 12
Bolham Water. Devn 1E 13
Bolingey. Corn 3B 6
Bollington. Ches E 3D 84
Bolney. W Sus 3D 26
Bolnhurst. Bed 5H 63
Bolshan. Ang 3F 145
Bolsover. Derbs 3B 86
Bolsterstone. S Yor 1G 85
Bolstone. Here 2A 48
Boltachan. Per 3F 143
Boltby. N Yor 1G 99
Bolton. Cumb 2H 103
Bolton. E Lot 2B 130
Bolton. E Yor 4B 100
Bolton. G Man 4F 91
Bolton. Nmbd 3F 121
Bolton Abbey. N Yor 4C 98
Bolton-by-Bowland. Lanc 5G 97
Boltonfellend. Cumb 3F 113
Boltongate. Cumb 5D 112
Bolton Green. Lanc 3D 90
Bolton-le-Sands. Lanc 3D 97
Bolton Low Houses. Cumb 5D 112
Bolton New Houses. Cumb 5D 112
Bolton-on-Swale. N Yor 5F 105
Bolton Percy. N Yor 5H 99
Bolton Town End. Lanc 3D 97
Bolton upon Dearne. S Yor 4E 93
Bolton Wood Lane. Cumb 5D 112
Bolventor. Corn 5B 10
Bomarsund. Nmbd 1F 115
Bomere Heath. Shrp 4G 71
Bonar Bridge. High 4D 164
Bonawe. Arg 5E 141
Bonby. N Lin 3D 94
Boncath. Pemb 1G 43
Bonchester Bridge. Bord 3H 119
Bonchurch. IOW 5D 16
Bond End. Staf 4F 73
Bondleigh. Devn 2G 11
Bonds. Lanc 5D 97
Bonehill. Devn 5H 11
Bonehill. Staf 5F 73
Bo'ness. Falk 1C 128
Boney Hay. Staf 4E 73
Bonham. Wilts 3C 22
Bonhill. W Dun 2E 127
Boningale. Shrp 5C 72
Bonjedward. Bord 2A 120
Bonkle. N Lan 4B 128
Bonnanaboigh. Caus 5C 174
Bonnington. Ang 5E 145
Bonnington. Edin 3E 129
Bonnington. Kent 2E 29
Bonnybank. Fife 3F 137
Bonnybridge. Falk 1B 128
Bonnykelly. Abers 3F 161
Bonnyrigg. Midl 3G 129
Bonnyton. Ang 5C 144
Bonnytown. Fife 2H 137
Bonsall. Derbs 5G 85
Bont. Mon 4G 47
Bontddu. Gwyn 4F 69
Bont Dolgadfan. Powy 5A 70
Y Bont-Faen. V Glam 4C 32
Bontgoch. Cdgn 2F 57
Bonthorpe. Linc 3D 89
Bontnewydd. Cdgn 4F 57
Bont-newydd. Cnwy 3C 82
Bont Newydd. Gwyn 1G 69
Bontnewydd. Gwyn 4D 81
Bontuchel. Den 5C 82
Bonvilston. V Glam 4D 32
Bon-y-maen. Swan 3F 31
Booker. Buck 2G 37
Booley. Shrp 3H 71
Boorley Green. Hants 1D 16
Boosbeck. Red C 3D 106
Boot. Cumb 4C 102
Booth. W Yor 2A 92
Boothby Graffoe. Linc 5G 87
Boothby Pagnell. Linc 2G 75
Booth Green. Ches E 2D 84
Booth of Toft. Shet 4F 173
Boothstown. G Man 4F 91
Boothville. Nptn 4E 63
Bootle. Cumb 1A 96
Bootle. Mers 1F 83
Booton. Norf 3D 78
Booze. N Yor 4D 104
Boquhan. Stir 1G 127
Boraston. Shrp 3A 60
Borden. Kent 4C 40
Borden. W Sus 4G 25
Bordlands. Bord 5E 129
Bordley. N Yor 3B 98
Bordon. Hants 3F 25
Boreham. Essx 5A 54
Boreham. Wilts 2D 23
Boreham Street. E Sus 4A 28
Borehamwood. Herts 1C 38
Boreland. Dum 5D 118
Boreston. Devn 3D 8
Borestone Brae. Stir 4G 135
Boreton. Shrp 5H 71
Borgh. W Isl
  on Barra 8B 170
  on Benbecula 3C 170
  on Berneray 1E 170
  on Isle of Lewis 2G 171
Borghasdal. W Isl 9C 171
Borghastan. W Isl 3D 171
Borgh na Sgiotaig. High 1C 154
Borgie. High 3G 167
Borgue. Dum 5D 110
Borgue. High 1H 165
Borley. Essx 1B 54
Borley Green. Essx 1B 54
Borley Green. Suff 4B 66
Borlum. High 1H 149
Bornais. W Isl 6C 170
Bornesketaig. High 1C 154
Boroughbridge. N Yor 3F 99
Borough Green. Kent 5H 39
Borreraig. High 3A 154
Borrobol Lodge. High 1F 165
Borrodale. High 4A 154
Borrowash. Derbs 2B 74
Borrowby. N Yor
  nr. Northallerton 1G 99
  nr. Whitby 3E 107
Borrowston. High 4F 169
Borrowstonehill. Orkn 7D 172
Borrowstoun. Falk 1C 128
Borstal. Medw 4B 40
Borth. Cdgn 2F 57
Borthwick. Midl 4G 129
Borth-y-Gest. Gwyn 2E 69
Borve. High 4D 154
Borwick. Lanc 2E 97
Bosbury. Here 1B 48
Boscastle. Corn 3A 10
Boscombe. Bour 3G 15
Boscombe. Wilts 3H 23
Boscoppa. Corn 3E 7
Bosham. W Sus 2G 17
Bosherston. Pemb 5D 42
Bosley. Ches E 4D 84
Bossall. N Yor 3B 100
Bossiney. Corn 4A 10
Bossingham. Kent 1F 29
Bossington. Som 2B 20
Bostadh. W Isl 3D 171
Bostock Green. Ches W 4A 84
Boston. Linc 1C 76
Boston Spa. W Yor 5G 99
Boswarthen. Corn 3B 4
Boswinger. Corn 4D 6
Botallack. Corn 3A 4
Botany Bay. G Lon 1D 39
Botcheston. Leics 5B 74
Botesdale. Suff 3C 66
Bothal. Nmbd 1F 115
Bothampstead. W Ber 4D 36
Bothamsall. Notts 3D 86
Bothel. Cumb 1C 102
Bothenhampton. Dors 3H 13
Bothwell. S Lan 4A 128
Botley. Buck 5H 51
Botley. Hants 1D 16
Botley. Oxon 5C 50
Botloe's Green. Glos 3C 48
Botolph Claydon. Buck 3F 51
Botolphs. W Sus 5C 26
Bottacks. High 2G 157
Bottesford. Leics 2F 75
Bottesford. N Lin 4B 94
Bottisham. Cambs 4E 65
Bottlesford. Wilts 1G 23
Bottomcraig. Fife 1F 137
Bottom o' th' Moor. G Man 3E 91
Botton. N Yor 4D 107
Botton Head. Lanc 3F 97
Bottreaux Mill. Devn 4B 20
Botus Fleming. Corn 2A 8
Botwnnog. Gwyn 2B 68
Bough Beech. Kent 1F 27
Boughrood. Powy 2E 47
Boughspring. Glos 2A 34
Boughton. Norf 5F 77
Boughton. Nptn 4E 63
Boughton. Notts 4D 86
Boughton Aluph. Kent 1E 29
Boughton Green. Kent 5B 40
Boughton Lees. Kent 1E 28
Boughton Malherbe. Kent 1C 28
Boughton Monchelsea. Kent 5B 40
Boughton under Blean. Kent 5E 41
Boulby. Red C 3E 107
Bouldnor. IOW 4B 16
Bouldon. Shrp 2H 59
Boulmer. Nmbd 3G 121
Boulston. Pemb 3D 42
Boultham. Linc 4G 87
Boulton. Derb 2A 74
Boundary. Staf 1D 73
Bounds. Here 2B 48
Bourn. Cambs 5C 64
Bournbrook. W Mid 2E 61
Bourne. Linc 3H 75
Bourne, The. Surr 2G 25
Bourne End. Bed 4H 63
Bourne End. Buck 3G 37
Bourne End. C Beds 1H 51
Bourne End. Herts 5A 52
Bournemouth. Bour 192 (3F 15)
Bournemouth Airport. Dors 3G 15
Bournes Green. Glos 5E 49
Bournes Green. S'end 2D 40
Bournheath. Worc 3D 60
Bournmoor. Dur 4G 115
Bournville. W Mid 2E 61
Bourton. Dors 3C 22
Bourton. N Som 5G 33
Bourton. Oxon 3H 35
Bourton. Shrp 1H 59
Bourton. Wilts 5F 35
Bourton on Dunsmore. Warw 3B 62
Bourton-on-the-Hill. Glos 2G 49
Bourton-on-the-Water. Glos 3G 49
Bousd. Arg 2D 138
Bousta. Shet 6D 173
Boustead Hill. Cumb 4D 112
Bouth. Cumb 1C 96
Bouthwaite. N Yor 2D 98
Boveney. Buck 3A 38
Boveridge. Dors 1F 15
Boverton. V Glam 5C 32
Bovey Tracey. Devn 5B 12
Bovingdon. Herts 5A 52
Bovingdon Green. Buck 3G 37
Bovinger. Essx 5F 53
Bovington Camp. Dors 4D 14
Bow. Devn 2H 11
Bowbank. Dur 2C 104
Bow Brickhill. Mil 2H 51
Bowbridge. Glos 5D 48
Bowburn. Dur 1A 106
Bowcombe. IOW 4C 16
Bowd. Devn 4E 12
Bowden. Devn 4E 9
Bowden. Bord 1H 119
Bowden Hill. Wilts 5E 35
Bowdens. Som 4H 21
Bowderdale. Cumb 4H 103
Bowdon. G Man 2B 84
Bower. Nmbd 1A 114
Bowerchalke. Wilts 4F 23
Bowerhill. Wilts 5E 35
Bower Hinton. Som 1H 13
Bowermadden. High 2E 169
Bowers. Staf 2C 72
Bowers Gifford. Essx 2B 40
Bowershall. Fife 4C 136
Bowertower. High 2E 169
Bowes. Dur 3C 104
Bowgreave. Lanc 5D 97
Bowhousebog. N Lan 4B 128
Bowithick. Corn 4B 10
Bowland Bridge. Cumb 1D 96
Bowlees. Dur 2C 104
Bowley. Here 5H 59
Bowlhead Green. Surr 2A 26
Bowling. W Dun 2F 127
Bowling. W Yor 1B 92
Bowling Bank. Wrex 1F 71
Bowling Green. Worc 5C 60
Bowlish. Som 2B 22
Bowmanstead. Cumb 5E 102
Bowmore. Arg 4B 124
Bowness-on-Solway. Cumb 3D 112
Bowness-on-Windermere. Cumb 5F 103
Bow of Fife. Fife 2F 137
Bowriefauld. Ang 4E 145
Bowscale. Cumb 1E 103
Bowsden. Nmbd 5F 131
Bowside Lodge. High 2A 168
Bowston. Cumb 5F 103
Bow Street. Cdgn 2F 57
Bowthorpe. Norf 5D 78
Box. Glos 5D 48
Box. Wilts 5D 34
Boxbush. Glos 3B 48
Box End. Bed 1A 52
Boxford. Suff 1C 54
Boxford. W Ber 4C 36
Boxgrove. W Sus 5A 26
Box Hill. Wilts 5D 34
Boxley. Kent 5B 40
Boxmoor. Herts 5A 52
Box's Shop. Corn 2C 10
Boxted. Essx 2C 54
Boxted. Suff 5H 65
Boxted Cross. Essx 2D 54
Boxworth. Cambs 4C 64
Boxworth End. Cambs 4C 64
Boyden End. Suff 5G 65
Boyden Gate. Kent 4G 41
Boylestone. Derbs 2F 73
Boylestonfield. Derbs 2F 73
Boyndie. Abers 2D 160
Boynton. E Yor 3F 101
Boys Hill. Dors 1B 14
Boythorpe. Derbs 4A 86
Boyton. Corn 3D 10
Boyton. Suff 1G 55
Boyton. Wilts 3E 23
Boyton Cross. Essx 5G 53
Boyton End. Essx 2G 53
Boyton End. Suff 1H 53
Bozeat. Nptn 5G 63
Braaid. IOM 4C 108
Braal Castle. High 3D 168
Brabling Green. Suff 4E 67
Brabourne. Kent 1F 29
Brabourne Lees. Kent 1E 29
Brabster. High 2F 169
Bracadale. High 5C 154
Bracara. High 4F 147
Braceborough. Linc 4H 75
Bracebridge. Linc 4G 87
Bracebridge Heath. Linc 4G 87
Braceby. Linc 2H 75
Bracewell. Lanc 5A 98
Brackenber. Cumb 3A 104
Brackenfield. Derbs 5A 86
Brackenlands. Cumb 5D 112
Brackenthwaite. Cumb 5D 112
Brackenthwaite. N Yor 4E 99
Brackla. B'end 4C 32
Brackla. High 3C 158
Bracklesham. W Sus 3G 17
Brackletter. High 5D 148
Brackley. Nptn 2D 50
Brackley Hatch. Nptn 1E 51
Brackloch. High 1F 163
Bracknell. Brac 5G 37
Braco. Per 3H 135
Bracobrae. Mor 3C 160
Bracon. N Lin 4A 94
Bracon Ash. Norf 1D 66
Bradbourne. Derbs 5G 85
Bradbury. Dur 2A 106
Bradda. IOM 4A 108
Bradden. Nptn 1E 51
Bradenham. Buck 2G 37
Bradenham. Norf 5B 78
Bradenstoke. Wilts 4F 35
Bradfield. Essx 2E 55
Bradfield. Norf 2E 79
Bradfield. W Ber 4E 36
Bradfield Combust. Suff 5A 66
Bradfield Green. Ches E 5A 84
Bradfield Heath. Essx 3E 55
Bradfield St Clare. Suff 5B 66
Bradfield St George. Suff 4B 66
Bradford. Derbs 4G 85
Bradford. Devn 2E 11
Bradford. Nmbd 1F 121
Bradford. W Yor 192 (1B 92)
Bradford Abbas. Dors 1A 14
Bradford Barton. Devn 1B 12
Bradford Leigh. Wilts 5D 34
Bradford-on-Avon. Wilts 5D 34
Bradford-on-Tone. Som 4E 21
Bradford Peverell. Dors 3B 14
Bradiford. Devn 3F 19
Brading. IOW 4E 16
Bradley. Ches W 3H 83
Bradley. Derbs 1G 73
Bradley. Glos 2C 34
Bradley. Hants 2E 25
Bradley. NE Lin 4F 95
Bradley. N Yor 1C 98
Bradley. Staf 4C 72
Bradley. W Mid 1D 60
Bradley. W Yor 2B 92
Bradley. Wrex 5F 83
Bradley Cross. Som 1H 21
Bradley Green. Ches W 1H 71
Bradley Green. Som 3F 21
Bradley Green. Warw 5G 73
Bradley Green. Worc 4D 61
Bradley in the Moors. Staf 1E 73
Bradley Mount. Ches E 3D 84
Bradley Stoke. S Glo 3B 34
Bradlow. Here 2C 48
Bradmore. Notts 2C 74
Bradmore. W Mid 1C 60
Bradninch. Devn 2D 12
Bradnop. Staf 5E 85
Bradpole. Dors 3H 13
Bradshaw. G Man 3F 91
Bradstone. Devn 4D 11
Bradwall Green. Ches E 4B 84
Bradway. S Yor 2H 85
Bradwell. Derbs 2F 85
Bradwell. Essx 3B 54
Bradwell. Mil 2G 51
Bradwell. Norf 5H 79
Bradwell-on-Sea. Essx 5D 54
Bradwell Waterside. Essx 5C 54
Bradworthy. Devn 1D 10
Brae. High 5C 162
Brae. Shet 5E 173
Braeantra. High 1H 157
Braefield. High 5G 157
Braefindon. High 3A 158
Braegrum. Per 1C 136
Braehead. Ang 3F 145
Braehead. Dum 4B 110
Braehead. Mor 4G 159
Braehead. Orkn 3D 172
Braehead. S Lan
  nr. Coalburn 1H 117
  nr. Forth 4C 128
Braehoulland. Shet 4D 173
Braemar. Abers 4F 151
Braemore. High
  nr. Dunbeath 5C 168
  nr. Ullapool 1D 156
Brae of Achnahaird. High 2E 163
Brae Roy Lodge. High 4F 149
Braeside. Abers 5G 161
Braeside. Inv 2D 126
Braes of Coul. Ang 3B 144
Braeswick. Orkn 4F 172
Braetongue. High 3F 167
Braeval. Stir 3E 135
Braevallich. Arg 3G 133
Braewick. Shet 6E 173
Brafferton. Darl 2F 105
Brafferton. N Yor 2G 99
Brafield-on-the-Green. Nptn 5F 63
Bragar. W Isl 3E 171
Bragbury End. Herts 3C 52
Bragleenbeg. Arg 1G 133
Braichmelyn. Gwyn 4F 81
Braides. Lanc 4D 96
Braidwood. S Lan 5B 128
Braigo. Arg 3A 124
Brailsford. Derbs 1G 73
Braintree. Essx 3A 54
Braiseworth. Suff 3D 66
Braishfield. Hants 4B 24
Braithwaite. Cumb 2D 102
Braithwaite. S Yor 3G 93
Braithwaite. W Yor 5C 98
Braithwell. S Yor 1C 86
Brakefield Green. Norf 5C 78
Bramber. W Sus 4C 26
Brambridge. Hants 4C 24
Bramcote. Notts 2C 74
Bramcote. Warw 2B 62
Bramdean. Hants 4E 24
Bramerton. Norf 5E 79
Bramfield. Herts 4C 52
Bramfield. Suff 3F 67
Bramford. Suff 1E 54
Bramhall. G Man 2C 84
Bramham. W Yor 5G 99
Bramhope. W Yor 5E 99
Bramley. Hants 1E 25
Bramley. S Yor 1B 86
Bramley. Surr 1B 26
Bramley. W Yor 1C 92
Bramley Green. Hants 1E 25
Bramley Head. N Yor 4D 98
Bramley Vale. Derbs 4B 86
Bramling. Kent 5G 41
Brampford Speke. Devn 3C 12
Brampton. Cambs 3B 64
Brampton. Cumb
  nr. Appleby-in-Westmorland 2H 103
  nr. Carlisle 3G 113
Brampton. Linc 3F 87
Brampton. Norf 3E 78
Brampton. S Yor 4E 93
Brampton. Suff 2G 67
Brampton Abbotts. Here 3B 48
Brampton Ash. Nptn 2E 63
Brampton Bryan. Here 3F 59
Brampton en le Morthen. S Yor 2B 86
Bramshall. Staf 2E 73
Bramshaw. Hants 1A 16
Bramshill. Hants 5F 37
Bramshott. Hants 3G 25
Branault. High 2G 139
Brancaster. Norf 1G 77
Brancaster Staithe. Norf 1G 77
Brancepeth. Dur 1F 105
Branch End. Nmbd 3D 114
Branchill. Mor 3E 159
Brand End. Linc 1C 76
Branderburgh. Mor 1G 159
Brandesburton. E Yor 5F 101
Brandeston. Suff 4E 67
Brand Green. Glos 3C 48
Brandhill. Shrp 3G 59
Brandis Corner. Devn 2E 11
Brandish Street. Som 2C 20
Brandiston. Norf 3D 78
Brandon. Dur 1F 105
Brandon. Linc 1G 75
Brandon. Nmbd 3E 121
Brandon. Suff 2G 65
Brandon. Warw 3B 62
Brandon Bank. Cambs 2F 65
Brandon Creek. Norf 1F 65
Brandon Parva. Norf 5C 78
Brandsby. N Yor 2H 99
Brandy Wharf. Linc 1H 87
Brane. Corn 4B 4
Bran End. Essx 3G 53
Branksome. Pool 3F 15
Bransbury. Hants 2C 24
Bransby. Linc 3F 87
Branscombe. Devn 4E 13
Bransford. Worc 5B 60
Bransgore. Hants 3G 15
Bransholme. Hull 1E 94
Bransley. Shrp 3A 60
Branston. Leics 3F 75
Branston. Linc 4H 87
Branston. Staf 3G 73
Branston Booths. Linc 4H 87
Branstone. IOW 4D 16
Bransty. Cumb 3A 102
Brant Broughton. Linc 5G 87
Brantham. Suff 2E 54
Branthwaite. Cumb
  nr. Caldbeck 1D 102
  nr. Workington 2B 102
Brantingham. E Yor 2C 94
Branton. Nmbd 3E 121
Branton. S Yor 4G 93
Branton Green. N Yor 3G 99
Branxholme. Bord 3G 119
Branxton. Nmbd 1C 120
Brassington. Derbs 5G 85
Brasted. Kent 5F 39
Brasted Chart. Kent 5F 39
Bratch, The. Staf 1C 60
Brathens. Abers 4D 152
Bratoft. Linc 4D 88
Brattleby. Linc 2G 87
Bratton. Som 2C 20
Bratton. Telf 4A 72
Bratton. Wilts 1E 23
Bratton Clovelly. Devn 3E 11
Bratton Fleming. Devn 3G 19
Bratton Seymour. Som 4B 22
Braughing. Herts 3D 53
Braulen Lodge. High 5E 157
Braunston. Nptn 4C 62
Braunstone Town. Leics 5C 74
Braunston-in-Rutland. Rut 5F 75
Braunton. Devn 3E 19
Brawby. N Yor 2B 100
Brawl. High 2A 168
Brawlbin. High 3C 168
Bray. Wind 3A 38
Braybrooke. Nptn 2E 63
Brayford. Devn 3G 19
Bray Shop. Corn 5D 10
Braystones. Cumb 4B 102
Brayton. N Yor 1G 93
Bray Wick. Wind 4G 37
Brazacott. Corn 3C 10
Brea. Corn 4A 6
Breach. W Sus 2F 17

Breachwood Green—Burton End

Breachwood Green. Herts 3B 52
Breacleit. W Isl 4D 171
Breaden Heath. Shrp 2G 71
Breadsall. Derbs 1A 74
Breadstone. Glos 5C 48
Breage. Corn 4D 4
Breakachy. High 4G 157
Breakish. High 1E 147
Bream. Glos 5B 48
Breamore. Hants 1G 15
Bream's Meend. Glos 5B 48
Brean. Som 1F 21
Breanais. W Isl 5B 171
Brearton. N Yor 3F 99
Breascleit. W Isl 4E 171
Breaston. Derbs 2B 74
Brecais Àrd. High 1E 147
Brecais Iosal. High 1E 147
Brechfa. Carm 2F 45
Brechin. Ang 3F 145
Breckles. Norf 1B 66
Brecon. Powy 3D 46
Bredbury. G Man 1D 84
Brede. E Sus 4C 28
Bredenbury. Here 5A 60
Bredfield. Suff 5E 67
Bredgar. Kent 4C 40
Bredhurst. Kent 4B 40
Bredicot. Worc 5D 60
Bredon. Worc 2E 49
Bredon's Norton. Worc 2E 49
Bredwardine. Here 1G 47
Breedon on the Hill. Leics 3B 74
Breibhig. W Isl
on Barra 9B 170
on Isle of Lewis 4G 171
Breich. W Lot 3C 128
Breightmet. G Man 4F 91
Breighton. E Yor 1H 93
Breinton. Here 2H 47
Breinton Common. Here 2H 47
Breiwick. Shet 7F 173
Brelston Green. Here 3A 48
Bremhill. Wilts 4E 35
Brenachie. High 1B 158
Brenchley. Kent 1A 28
Brendon. Devn 2A 20
Brent Cross. G Lon 2D 38
Brent Eleigh. Suff 1C 54
Brentford. G Lon 3C 38
Brentingby. Leics 4E 75
Brent Knoll. Som 1G 21
Brent Pelham. Herts 2E 53
Brentwood. Essx 1G 39
Brenzett. Kent 3E 28
Brereton. Staf 4E 73
Brereton Cross. Staf 4E 73
Brereton Green. Ches E 4B 84
Brereton Heath. Ches E 4C 84
Bressingham. Norf 2C 66
Bretby. Derbs 3G 73
Bretford. Warw 3B 62
Bretforton. Worc 1F 49
Bretherdale Head. Cumb 4G 103
Bretherton. Lanc 2C 90
Brettabister. Shet 6F 173
Brettenham. Norf 2B 66
Brettenham. Suff 5B 66
Bretton. Flin 4F 83
Bretton. Pet 5A 76
Brewlands Bridge. Ang 2A 144
Brewood. Staf 5C 72
Briantspuddle. Dors 3D 14
Bricket Wood. Herts 5B 52
Bricklehampton. Worc 1E 49
Bride. IOM 1D 108
Bridekirk. Cumb 1C 102
Bridell. Pemb 1B 44
Bridestowe. Devn 4F 11
Brideswell. Abers 5C 160
Bridford. Devn 4B 12
Bridge. Corn 4A 6
Bridge. Kent 5F 41
Bridge. Som 2G 13
Bridge End. Bed 5H 63
Bridge End. Cumb
nr. Broughton in Furness 5D 102
nr. Dalston 5E 113
Bridge End. Linc 2A 76
Bridge End. Shet 8E 173
Bridgefoot. Ang 5C 144
Bridgefoot. Cumb 2B 102
Bridge Green. Essx 2E 53
Bridgehampton. Som 4A 22
Bridge Hewick. N Yor 2F 99
Bridgehill. Dur 4D 115
Bridgemary. Hants 2D 16
Bridgemere. Ches E 1B 72
Bridgemont. Derbs 2E 85
Bridgend. Abers
nr. Huntly 5C 160
nr. Peterhead 5H 161
Bridgend. Ang
nr. Brechin 2E 145
nr. Kirriemuir 4C 144
Bridgend. Arg
nr. Lochgilphead 4F 133
on Islay 3B 124
Bridgend. B'end 3C 32
Bridgend. Cumb 3E 103
Bridgend. Devn 4B 8
Bridgend. Fife 2F 137
Bridgend. High 3F 157
Bridgend. Mor 5A 160
Bridgend. Per 1D 136
Bridgend. W Lot 2D 128
Bridgend of Lintrathen.
Ang 3B 144
Bridgeness. Falk 1D 128
Bridge of Alford. Abers 2C 152
Bridge of Allan. Stir 4G 135
Bridge of Avon. Mor 5F 159
Bridge of Awe. Arg 1H 133
Bridge of Balgie. Per 4C 142
Bridge of Brown. High 1F 151
Bridge of Cally. Per 3A 144
Bridge of Canny. Abers 4D 152
Bridge of Dee. Dum 3E 111
Bridge of Don. Aber 2G 153
Bridge of Dun. Ang 3F 145
Bridge of Dye. Abers 5D 152
Bridge of Earn. Per 2D 136
Bridge of Ericht. Per 3C 142
Bridge of Feugh. Abers 4E 152
Bridge of Gairn. Abers 4A 152
Bridge of Gaur. Per 3C 142
Bridge of Muchalls. Abers 4F 153
Bridge of Oich. High 3F 149
Bridge of Orchy. Arg 5H 141
Bridge of Walls. Shet 6D 173
Bridge of Weir. Ren 3E 127
Bridge Reeve. Devn 1G 11
Bridgerule. Devn 2C 10
Bridge Sollers. Here 1H 47
Bridge Street. Suff 1B 54
Bridgetown. Devn 2E 9
Bridgetown. Som 3C 20
Bridge Town. Warw 5G 61
Bridge Trafford. Ches W 3G 83
Bridgeyate. S Glo 4B 34
Bridgham. Norf 2B 66
Bridgnorth. Shrp 1B 60
Bridgtown. Staf 5D 73
Bridgwater. Som 3G 21
Bridlington. E Yor 3F 101
Bridport. Dors 3H 13
Bridstow. Here 3A 48
Brierfield. Lanc 1G 91
Brierley. Glos 4B 48
Brierley. Here 5G 59
Brierley. S Yor 3E 93
Brierley Hill. W Mid 2D 60
Brierton. Hart 1B 106
Briestfield. W Yor 3C 92
Brigg. N Lin 4D 94
Briggate. Norf 3F 79
Briggswath. N Yor 4F 107
Brigham. Cumb 1B 102
Brigham. E Yor 4E 101
Brighouse. W Yor 2B 92
Brighstone. IOW 4C 16
Brightgate. Derbs 5G 85
Brighthampton. Oxon 5B 50
Brightholmlee. S Yor 1G 85
Brightley. Devn 3G 11
Brightling. E Sus 3A 28
Brightlingsea. Essx 4D 54
Brighton. Brig 192 (5E 27)
Brighton. Corn 3D 6
Brighton Hill. Hants 2E 24
Brightons. Falk 2C 128
Brightwalton. W Ber 4C 36
Brightwalton Green. W Ber 4C 36
Brightwell. Suff 1F 55
Brightwell Baldwin. Oxon 2E 37
Brightwell-cum-Sotwell.
Oxon 2D 36
Brigmerston. Wilts 2G 23
Brignall. Dur 3D 104
Brig o' Turk. Stir 3E 135
Brigsley. NE Lin 4F 95
Brigsteer. Cumb 1D 97
Brigstock. Nptn 2G 63
Brill. Buck 4E 51
Brill. Corn 4E 5
Brilley. Here 1F 47
Brimaston. Pemb 2D 42
Brimfield. Here 4H 59
Brimington. Derbs 3B 86
Brimley. Devn 5A 12
Brimpsfield. Glos 4E 49
Brimpton. W Ber 5D 36
Brims. Orkn 9B 172
Brimscombe. Glos 5D 48
Brimstage. Mers 2F 83
Brincliffe. S Yor 2H 85
Brind. E Yor 1H 93
Brindister. Shet
nr. West Burrafirth 6D 173
nr. West Lerwick 8F 173
Brindle. Lanc 2D 90
Brindley. Ches E 5H 83
Brindley Ford. Stoke 5C 84
Brineton. Staf 4C 72
Bringhurst. Leics 1F 63
Bringsty Common. Here 5A 60
Brington. Cambs 3H 63
Brinian. Orkn 5D 172
Brinningham. Norf 2C 78
Brinkhill. Linc 3C 88
Brinkley. Cambs 5F 65
Brinklow. Warw 3B 62
Brinkworth. Wilts 3F 35
Brinscall. Lanc 2E 91
Brinscombe. Som 1H 21
Brinsley. Notts 1B 74
Brinsworth. S Yor 2B 86
Brinton. Norf 2C 78
Brisco. Cumb 4F 113
Brisley. Norf 3B 78
Brislington. Bris 4B 34
Brissenden Green. Kent 2D 28
Bristol. Bris 193 (4A 34)
Bristol Airport. N Som 5A 34
Briston. Norf 2C 78
Britannia. Lanc 2G 91
Britford. Wilts 4G 23
Brithdir. Cphy 5E 47
Brithdir. Cdgn 1D 44
Brithdir. Gwyn 4G 69
Briton Ferry. Neat 3G 31
Britwell Salome. Oxon 2E 37
Brixham. Torb 3F 9
Brixton. Devn 3B 8
Brixton. G Lon 3E 39
Brixton Deverill. Wilts 3D 22
Brixworth. Nptn 3E 63
Brize Norton. Oxon 5B 50
Broad Alley. Worc 4C 60
Broad Blunsdon. Swin 2G 35
Broadbottom. G Man 1D 85
Broadbridge. W Sus 2G 17
Broadbridge Heath. W Sus 2C 26
Broad Campden. Glos 2G 49
Broad Chalke. Wilts 4F 23
Broadclyst. Devn 3C 12
Broadfield. Inv 2E 127
Broadfield. Pemb 4F 43
Broadfield. W Sus 2D 26
Broadford. High 1E 147
Broadford Bridge. W Sus 3B 26
Broadgate. Cumb 1A 96
Broad Green. Cambs 5F 65
Broad Green. C Beds 1H 51
Broad Green. Worc
nr. Bromsgrove 3D 61
nr. Worcester 5B 60
Broadhaven. High 3F 169
Broad Haven. Pemb 3C 42
Broadheath. G Man 2B 84
Broad Heath. Staf 3C 72
Broadheath. Worc 4A 60
Broadheath Common.
Worc 5C 60
Broadhembury. Devn 2E 12
Broadhempston. Devn 2E 9
Broad Hill. Cambs 3E 65
Broad Hinton. Wilts 4G 35
Broadholme. Derbs 1A 74
Broadholme. Linc 3F 87
Broadlay. Carm 5D 44
Broad Laying. Hants 5C 36
Broadley. Lanc 3G 91
Broadley. Mor 2A 160
Broadley Common. Essx 5E 53
Broad Marston. Worc 1G 49
Broadmayne. Dors 4C 14
Broadmere. Hants 2E 24
Broadmoor. Pemb 4E 43
Broad Oak. Carm 3F 45
Broad Oak. Cumb 5C 102
Broad Oak. Devn 3D 12
Broad Oak. Dors 1C 14
Broadoak. Dors 3H 13
Broad Oak. E Sus
nr. Hastings 4C 28
nr. Heathfield 3H 27
Broadoak. Glos 4B 48
Broadoak. Hants 1D 16
Broad Oak. Here 3H 47
Broad Oak. Kent 4F 41
Broadrashes. Mor 3B 160
Broadsea. Abers 2G 161
Broad's Green. Essx 4G 53
Broadshard. Som 1H 13
Broadstairs. Kent 4H 41
Broadstone. Pool 3F 15
Broadstone. Shrp 2H 59
Broad Street. E Sus 4C 28
Broad Street. Kent
nr. Ashford 1F 29
nr. Maidstone 5C 40
Broad Street Green. Essx 5B 54
Broad Town. Wilts 4F 35
Broadwas. Worc 5B 60
Broadwath. Cumb 4F 113
Broadway. Carm
nr. Kidwelly 5D 45
nr. Laugharne 4G 43
Broadway. Pemb 3C 42
Broadway. Som 1G 13
Broadway. Suff 3F 67
Broadway. Worc 2F 49
Broadwell. Glos
nr. Cinderford 4A 48
nr. Stow-on-the-Wold 3H 49
Broadwell. Oxon 5A 50
Broadwell. Warw 4B 62
Broadwell House. Nmbd 4C 114
Broadwey. Dors 4B 14
Broadwindsor. Dors 2H 13
Broadwoodkelly. Devn 2G 11
Broadwoodwidger. Devn 4E 11
Broallan. High 4G 157
Brobury. Here 1G 47
Brochel. High 4E 155
Brockaghboy. Caus 5E 174
Brockamin. Worc 5B 60
Brockbridge. Hants 1E 16
Brockdish. Norf 3E 66
Brockencote. Worc 3C 60
Brockenhurst. Hants 2A 16
Brocketsbrae. S Lan 1H 117
Brockford Street. Suff 4D 66
Brockhall. Nptn 4D 62
Brockham. Surr 1C 26
Brockhampton. Glos
nr. Bishop's Cleeve 3E 49
nr. Sevenhampton 3F 49
Brockhampton. Here 2A 48
Brockhill. Bord 2F 119
Brockholes. W Yor 3B 92
Brockhurst. Hants 2D 16
Brocklesby. Linc 3E 95
Brockley. N Som 5H 33
Brockley Corner. Suff 3H 65
Brockley Green. Suff
nr. Bury St Edmunds 1H 53
nr. Haverhill 5H 65
Brockleymoor. Cumb 1F 103
Brockmoor. W Mid 2D 60
Brockton. Shrp
nr. Bishop's Castle 2F 59
nr. Madeley 5B 72
nr. Much Wenlock 1H 59
nr. Pontesbury 5F 71
Brockton. Staf 2C 72
Brockton. Telf 4B 72
Brockweir. Glos 5A 48
Brockworth. Glos 4D 49
Brocton. Staf 4D 72
Brodick. N Ayr 2E 123
Brodie. Mor 3D 159
Brodiesord. Abers 3C 160
Brodsworth. S Yor 4F 93
Brogaig. High 2D 154
Brogborough. C Beds 2H 51
Brokenborough. Wilts 3E 35
Broken Cross. Ches E 3C 84
Bromborough. Mers 2F 83
Bromdon. Shrp 2A 60
Brome. Suff 3D 66
Brome Street. Suff 3D 66
Bromeswell. Suff 5F 67
Bromfield. Cumb 5C 112
Bromfield. Shrp 3G 59
Bromford. W Mid 1F 61
Bromham. Bed 5H 63
Bromham. Wilts 5E 35
Bromley. G Lon 4F 39
Bromley. Herts 3E 53
Bromley. Shrp 1B 60
Bromley Cross. G Man 3F 91
Bromley Green. Kent 2D 28
Bromley Wood. Staf 3F 73
Brompton. Medw 4B 40
Brompton. N Yor
nr. Northallerton 5A 106
nr. Scarborough 1D 100
Brompton. Shrp 5H 71
Brompton-on-Swale.
N Yor 5F 105
Brompton Ralph. Som 3D 20
Brompton Regis. Som 3C 20
Bromsash. Here 3B 48
Bromsberrow. Glos 2C 48
Bromsberrow Heath. Glos 2C 48
Bromsgrove. Worc 3D 60
Bromstead Heath. Staf 4B 72
Bromyard. Here 5A 60
Bromyard Downs. Here 5A 60
Bronaber. Gwyn 2G 69
Broncroft. Shrp 2H 59
Brongest. Cdgn 1D 44
Brongwyn. Cdgn 1C 44
Bronington. Wrex 2G 71
Bronllys. Powy 2E 47
Bronnant. Cdgn 4F 57
Bronwydd Arms. Carm 3E 45
Bronydd. Powy 1F 47
Bronygarth. Shrp 2E 71
Brook. Carm 4G 43
Brook. Hants
nr. Cadnam 1A 16
nr. Romsey 4B 24
Brook. IOW 4B 16
Brook. Kent 1E 29
Brook. Surr
nr. Guildford 1B 26
nr. Haslemere 2A 26
Brooke. Norf 1E 67
Brooke. Rut 5F 75
Brookeborough. Ferm 8F 176
Brookenby. Linc 1B 88
Brookend. Glos 5B 48
Brook End. Worc 1D 48
Brookfield. Lanc 1D 90
Brookfield. Ren 3F 127
Brookhouse. Lanc 3E 97
Brookhouse. S Yor 2C 86
Brookhouse Green. Ches E 4C 84
Brookhouses. Staf 1D 73
Brookhurst. Mers 2F 83
Brookland. Kent 3D 28
Brooklands. G Man 1B 84
Brooklands. Shrp 1H 71
Brookmans Park. Herts 5C 52
Brooks. Powy 1D 58
Brooksby. Leics 4D 74
Brooks Green. W Sus 3C 26
Brook Street. Essx 1G 39
Brook Street. Kent 2D 28
Brook Street. W Sus 3E 27
Brookthorpe. Glos 4D 48
Brookville. Norf 1G 65
Brookwood. Surr 5A 38
Broom. C Beds 1B 52
Broom. Fife 3F 137
Broom. Warw 5E 61
Broome. Norf 1F 67
Broome. Shrp
nr. Cardington 1H 59
nr. Craven Arms 2G 59
Broome. Worc 3D 60
Broomedge. Warr 2B 84
Broomend. Abers 2E 153
Broomer's Corner. W Sus 3C 26
Broomfield. Abers 5G 161
Broomfield. Essx 4H 53
Broomfield. Kent
nr. Herne Bay 4F 41
nr. Maidstone 5C 40
Broomfield. Som 3F 21
Broomfleet. E Yor 2B 94
Broom Green. Norf 3B 78
Broomhall. Ches E 1A 72
Broomhall. Wind 4A 38
Broomhaugh. Nmbd 3D 114
Broom Hill. Dors 2F 15
Broomhill. High
nr. Grantown-on-Spey 1D 151
nr. Invergordon 1B 158
Broomhill. Norf 5F 77
Broomhill. S Yor 4E 93
Broom Hill. Worc 3D 60
Broomhillbank. Dum 5D 118
Broomholm. Norf 2F 79
Broomlands. Dum 4C 118
Broomley. Nmbd 3D 114
Broom of Moy. Mor 3E 159
Broompark. Dur 5F 115
Broom's Green. Glos 2C 48
Brora. High 3G 165
Broseley. Shrp 5A 72
Brotherhouse Bar. Linc 4B 76
Brotheridge Green. Worc 1D 48
Brotherlee. Dur 1C 104
Brothertoft. Linc 1B 76
Brotherton. N Yor 2E 93
Brotton. Red C 3D 107
Broubster. High 2C 168
Brough. Cumb 3A 104
Brough. Derbs 2F 85
Brough. E Yor 2C 94
Brough. High 1E 169
Brough. Notts 5F 87
Brough. Orkn
nr. Finstown 6C 172
nr. St Margaret's Hope 9D 172
Brough. Shet
nr. Benston 6F 173
nr. Booth of Toft 4F 173
on Bressay 7G 173
on Whalsay 5G 173
Broughall. Shrp 1H 71
Brougham. Cumb 2G 103
Brough Lodge. Shet 2G 173
Broughshane. ME Ant 6H 175
Brough Sowerby. Cumb 3A 104
Broughton. Cambs 3B 64
Broughton. Flin 4F 83
Broughton. Hants 3B 24
Broughton. Lanc 1D 90
Broughton. Mil 2G 51
Broughton. Nptn 3F 63
Broughton. N Lin 4C 94
Broughton. N Yor
nr. Malton 2B 100
nr. Skipton 4B 98
Broughton. Orkn 3D 172
Broughton. Oxon 2C 50
Broughton. Bord 1D 118
Broughton. Staf 2B 72
Broughton. V Glam 4C 32
Broughton Astley. Leics 1C 62
Broughton Beck. Cumb 1B 96
Broughton Cross. Cumb 1B 102
Broughton Gifford. Wilts 5D 35
Broughton Green. Worc 4D 60
Broughton Hackett. Worc 5D 60
Broughton in Furness.
Cumb 1B 96
Broughton Mills. Cumb 5D 102
Broughton Moor. Cumb 1B 102
Broughton Park. G Man 4G 91
Broughton Poggs. Oxon 5H 49
Broughtown. Orkn 3F 172
Broughty Ferry. D'dee 5D 144
Browland. Shet 6D 173
Brownbread Street. E Sus 4A 28
Brown Candover. Hants 3D 24
Brown Edge. Lanc 3B 90
Brown Edge. Staf 5D 84
Brownhill. Bkbn 1E 91
Brownhill. Shrp 3G 71
Brownhills. Shrp 2A 72
Brownhills. W Mid 5E 73
Brown Knowl. Ches W 5G 83
Brownlow. Ches E 4C 84
Brownlow Heath. Ches E 4C 84
Brown's Green. W Mid 1E 61
Brownshill. Glos 5D 49
Brownston. Devn 3C 8
Brownstone. Devn 2A 12
Browston Green. Norf 5G 79
Broxa. N Yor 5G 107
Broxbourne. Herts 5D 52
Broxburn. E Lot 2C 130
Broxburn. W Lot 2D 128
Broxholme. Linc 3G 87
Broxted. Essx 3F 53
Broxton. Ches W 5G 83
Broxwood. Here 5F 59
Broyle Side. E Sus 4F 27
Brù. W Isl 3F 171
Bruach Mairi. W Isl 4G 171
Bruairnis. W Isl 8C 170
Bruan. High 5F 169
Bruar Lodge. Per 1F 143
Brucehill. W Dun 2E 127
Brucklay. Abers 3G 161
Bruera. Ches W 4G 83
Bruern Abbey. Oxon 3A 50
Bruichladdich. Arg 3A 124
Bruisyard. Suff 4F 67
Bruisyard Street. Suff 4F 67
Brund. Staf 4F 85
Brundall. Norf 5F 79
Brundish. Norf 1F 67
Brundish. Suff 4E 67
Brundish Street. Suff 3E 67
Brunery. High 1B 140
Brunswick Village. Tyne 2F 115
Brunthwaite. W Yor 5C 98
Bruntingthorpe. Leics 1D 62
Brunton. Fife 1F 137
Brunton. Nmbd 2G 121
Brunton. Wilts 1H 23
Brushford. Devn 2G 11
Brushford. Som 4C 20
Brusta. W Isl 1E 170
Bruton. Som 3B 22
Bryansford. New M 6H 179
Bryanston. Dors 2D 14
Bryant's Bottom. Buck 2G 37
Brydekirk. Dum 2C 112
Brymbo. Cnwy 3H 81
Brymbo. Wrex 5E 83
Brympton D'Evercy. Som 1A 14
Bryn. Carm 5F 45
Bryn. G Man 4D 90
Bryn. Neat 2B 32
Bryn. Shrp 2E 59
Brynamman. Carm 4H 45
Brynberian. Pemb 1F 43
Brynbryddan. Neat 2A 32
Bryncae. Rhon 3C 32
Bryncethin. B'end 3C 32
Bryncir. Gwyn 1D 69
Bryncoch. Neat 3G 31
Bryncroes. Gwyn 2B 68
Bryncrug. Gwyn 5F 69
Bryn Du. IOA 3C 80
Bryn Eden. Gwyn 3G 69
Bryneglwys. Den 1D 70
Bryn Eglwys. Gwyn 4F 81
Brynford. Flin 3D 82
Bryn Gates. G Man 4D 90
Bryn Golau. Rhon 3D 32
Bryngwran. IOA 3C 80
Bryngwyn. Mon 5G 47
Bryngwyn. Powy 1E 47
Bryn-henllan. Pemb 1E 43
Brynhoffnant. Cdgn 5C 56
Bryn-llwyn. Den 2C 82
Brynllywarch. Powy 2D 58
Brynmawr. Blae 4E 47
Bryn-mawr. Gwyn 2B 68
Brynmenyn. B'end 3C 32
Brynmill. Swan 3F 31
Brynna. Rhon 3C 32
Brynrefail. Gwyn 4E 81
Brynrefail. IOA 2D 81
Brynsadler. Rhon 3D 32
Bryn-Saith Marchog. Den 5C 82
Brynsiencyn. IOA 4D 81
Brynteg. IOA 2D 81
Brynteg. Wrex 5F 83
Brynygwenyn. Mon 4G 47
Bryn-y-maen. Cnwy 3H 81
Buaile nam Bodach. W Isl 8C 170
Bualintur. High 1C 146
Bubbenhall. Warw 3A 62
Bubwith. E Yor 1H 93
Buccleuch. Bord 3F 119
Buchanan Smithy. Stir 1F 127
Buchanhaven. Abers 4H 161
Buchanty. Per 1B 136
Buchany. Stir 3G 135
Buchley. E Dun 2G 127
Buchlyvie. Stir 4E 135
Buckabank. Cumb 5E 113
Buckden. Cambs 4A 64
Buckden. N Yor 2B 98
Buckenham. Norf 5F 79
Buckerell. Devn 2E 12
Buckfast. Devn 2D 8
Buckfastleigh. Devn 2D 8
Buckhaven. Fife 4F 137
Buckholm. Bord 1G 119
Buckholt. Here 4A 48
Buckhorn Weston. Dors 4C 22
Buckhurst Hill. Essx 1F 39
Buckie. Mor 2B 160
Buckingham. Buck 2E 51
Buckland. Buck 4G 51
Buckland. Glos 2F 49
Buckland. Here 5H 59
Buckland. Herts 2D 52
Buckland. Kent 1H 29
Buckland. Oxon 2B 36
Buckland. Surr 5D 38
Buckland Brewer. Devn 4E 19
Buckland Common. Buck 5H 51
Buckland Dinham. Som 1C 22
Buckland Filleigh. Devn 2E 11
Buckland in the Moor.
Devn 5H 11
Buckland Monachorum.
Devn 2A 8
Buckland Newton. Dors 2B 14
Buckland Ripers. Dors 4B 14
Buckland St Mary. Som 1F 13
Buckland-tout-Saints. Devn 4D 8
Bucklebury. W Ber 4D 36
Bucklegate. Linc 2C 76
Buckleigh. Devn 4E 19
Buckler's Hard. Hants 3C 16
Bucklesham. Suff 1F 55
Buckley. Flin 4E 83
Buckley Green. Warw 4F 61
Buckley Hill. Mers 1F 83
Bucklow Hill. Ches E 2B 84
Buckminster. Leics 3F 75
Bucknall. Linc 4A 88
Bucknall. Stoke 1D 72
Bucknell. Oxon 3D 50
Bucknell. Shrp 3F 59
Buckpool. Mor 2B 160
Bucksburn. Aber 3F 153
Buck's Cross. Devn 4D 18
Bucks Green. W Sus 2B 26
Buckshaw Village. Lanc 2D 90
Bucks Hill. Herts 5A 52
Bucks Horn Oak. Hants 2G 25
Buck's Mills. Devn 4D 19
Buckton. E Yor 2F 101
Buckton. Here 3F 59
Buckton. Nmbd 1E 121
Buckton Vale. G Man 4H 91
Buckworth. Cambs 3A 64
Budby. Notts 4D 86
Bude. Corn 2C 10
Budge's Shop. Corn 3H 7
Budlake. Devn 2C 12
Budle. Nmbd 1F 121
Budleigh Salterton. Devn 4D 12
Budock Water. Corn 5B 6
Buerton. Ches E 1A 72
Buffler's Holt. Buck 2E 51
Bugbrooke. Nptn 5D 62
Buglawton. Ches E 4C 84
Bugle. Corn 3E 6
Bugthorpe. E Yor 4B 100
Buildwas. Shrp 5A 72
Builth Road. Powy 5C 58
Builth Wells. Powy 5C 58
Bulbourne. Herts 4H 51
Bulby. Linc 3H 75
Bulcote. Notts 1D 74
Buldoo. High 2B 168
Bulford. Wilts 2G 23
Bulford Camp. Wilts 2G 23
Bulkeley. Ches E 5H 83
Bulkington. Warw 2A 62
Bulkington. Wilts 1E 23
Bulkworthy. Devn 1D 11
Bullamoor. N Yor 5A 106
Bull Bay. IOA 1D 80
Bullbridge. Derbs 5A 86
Bullgill. Cumb 1B 102
Bull Hill. Hants 3B 16
Bullinghope. Here 2A 48
Bull's Green. Herts 4C 52
Bullwood. Arg 2C 126
Bulmer. Essx 1B 54
Bulmer. N Yor 3A 100
Bulmer Tye. Essx 2B 54
Bulphan. Thur 2H 39
Bulverhythe. E Sus 5B 28
Bulwark. Abers 4G 161
Bulwell. Nott 1C 74
Bulwick. Nptn 1G 63
Bumble's Green. Essx 5E 53
Bun Abhainn Eadarra.
W Isl 7D 171
Bunacaimb. High 5E 147
Bun a' Mhuillinn. W Isl 7C 170
Bunarkaig. High 5D 148
Bunbury. Ches E 5H 83
Bunchrew. High 4A 158
Bundalloch. High 1A 148
Buness. Shet 1H 173
Bunessan. Arg 1A 132
Bungay. Suff 2F 67
Bunkegivie. High 2H 149
Bunker's Hill. Cambs 5D 76
Bunkers Hill. Linc 5B 88
Bunker's Hill. Suff 5H 79
Bunloit. High 1H 149
Bunnahabhain. Arg 2C 124
Bunny. Notts 3C 74
Bunoich. High 3F 149
Bunree. High 2E 141
Bunroy. High 5E 149
Buntait. High 5G 157
Buntingford. Herts 3D 52
Bunting's Green. Essx 2B 54
Bunwell. Norf 1D 66
Burbage. Derbs 3E 85
Burbage. Leics 1B 62
Burbage. Wilts 5H 35
Burcher. Here 4F 59
Burchett's Green. Wind 3G 37
Burcombe. Wilts 3F 23
Burcot. Oxon 2D 36
Burcot. Worc 3D 61
Burcote. Shrp 1B 60
Burcott. Buck 3G 51
Burcott. Som 2A 22
Burdale. N Yor 3C 100
Burdrop. Oxon 2B 50
Bures. Suff 2C 54
Burf, The. Worc 4C 60
Burford. Oxon 4A 50
Burford. Shrp 4H 59
Burg. Arg 4E 139
Burgate Great Green. Suff 3C 66
Burgate Little Green. Suff 3C 66
Burgess Hill. W Sus 4E 27
Burgh. Suff 5E 67
Burgh by Sands. Cumb 4E 113
Burgh Castle. Norf 5G 79
Burghclere. Hants 5C 36
Burghead. Mor 2F 159
Burghfield. W Ber 5E 37
Burghfield Common.
W Ber 5E 37
Burghfield Hill. W Ber 5E 37
Burgh Heath. Surr 5D 38
Burghill. Here 1H 47
Burgh le Marsh. Linc 4E 89
Burgh Muir. Abers 2E 153
Burgh next Aylsham. Norf 3E 78
Burgh on Bain. Linc 2B 88
Burgh St Margaret. Norf 4G 79
Burgh St Peter. Norf 1G 67
Burghwallis. S Yor 3F 93
Burham. Kent 4B 40
Buriton. Hants 4F 25
Burland. Ches E 5A 84
Burland. Shet 8E 173
Burlawn. Corn 2D 6
Burleigh. Glos 5D 48
Burleigh. Wind 4G 37
Burlescombe. Devn 1D 12
Burleston. Dors 3C 14
Burlestone. Devn 4E 9
Burley. Hants 2H 15
Burley. Rut 4F 75
Burley. W Yor 1C 92
Burleydam. Ches E 1A 72
Burley Gate. Here 1A 48
Burley in Wharfedale.
W Yor 5D 98
Burley Street. Hants 2H 15
Burley Woodhead. W Yor 5D 98
Burlingjobb. Powy 5E 59
Burlington. Shrp 4B 72
Burlton. Shrp 3G 71
Burmantofts. W Yor 1D 92
Burmarsh. Kent 2F 29
Burmington. Warw 2A 50
Burn. N Yor 2F 93
Burnage. G Man 1C 84
Burnaston. Derbs 2G 73
Burnbanks. Cumb 3G 103
Burnby. E Yor 5C 100
Burncross. S Yor 1H 85
Burneside. Cumb 5G 103
Burness. Orkn 3F 172
Burneston. N Yor 1F 99
Burnett. Bath 5B 34
Burnfoot. E Ayr 4D 116
Burnfoot. Per 3B 136
Burnfoot. Bord
nr. Hawick 3H 119
nr. Roberton 3G 119
Burngreave. S Yor 2A 86
Burnham. Buck 2A 38
Burnham. N Lin 3D 94
Burnham Deepdale. Norf 1H 77
Burnham Green. Herts 4C 52
Burnham Market. Norf 1H 77
Burnham Norton. Norf 1H 77
Burnham-on-Crouch.
Essx 1D 40
Burnham-on-Sea. Som 2G 21
Burnham Overy Staithe.
Norf 1H 77
Burnham Overy Town.
Norf 1H 77
Burnham Thorpe. Norf 1A 78
Burnhaven. Abers 4H 161
Burnhead. Dum 5A 118
Burnhervie. Abers 2E 153
Burnhill Green. Staf 5B 72
Burnhope. Dur 5E 115
Burnhouse. N Ayr 4E 127
Burniston. N Yor 5H 107
Burnley. Lanc 1G 91
Burnmouth. Bord 3F 131
Burn Naze. Lanc 5C 96
Burn of Cambus. Stir 3G 135
Burnopfield. Dur 4E 115
Burnsall. N Yor 3C 98
Burnside. Ang 3E 145
Burnside. Ant
nr. Antrim 8H 175
nr. Ballyclare 7J 175
Burnside. E Ayr 3E 117
Burnside. Per 3D 136
Burnside. Shet 4D 173
Burnside. S Lan 4H 127
Burnside. W Lot
nr. Broxburn 2D 129
nr. Winchburgh 2D 128
Burntcommon. Surr 5B 38
Burntheath. Derbs 2G 73
Burnt Heath. Essx 3D 54
Burnt Hill. W Ber 4D 36
Burnt Houses. Dur 2E 105
Burntisland. Fife 1F 129
Burnt Oak. G Lon 1D 38
Burnton. E Ayr 4D 117
Burntstalk. Norf 2G 77
Burntwood. Staf 5E 73
Burntwood Green. Staf 5E 73
Burnt Yates. N Yor 3E 99
Burnwynd. Edin 3E 129
Burpham. Surr 5B 38
Burpham. W Sus 5B 26
Burradon. Nmbd 4D 121
Burradon. Tyne 2F 115
Burrafirth. Shet 1H 173
Burragarth. Shet 1G 173
Burras. Corn 5A 6
Burraton. Corn 3A 8
Burravoe. Shet
nr. North Roe 3E 173
on Mainland 5E 173
on Yell 4G 173
Burray Village. Orkn 8D 172
Burrells. Cumb 3H 103
Burrelton. Per 5A 144
Burren. New M 7F 178
Burren Bridge. New M 6H 179
Burridge. Hants 1D 16
Burridge. Som 2G 13
Burrigill. High 5E 169
Burrill. N Yor 1E 99
Burringham. N Lin 4B 94
Burrington. Devn 1G 11
Burrington. Here 3G 59
Burrington. N Som 1H 21
Burrough End. Cambs 5F 65
Burrough Green. Cambs 5F 65
Burrough on the Hill. Leics 4E 75
Burroughston. Orkn 5E 172
Burrow. Devn 4D 12
Burrow. Som 2C 20
Burrowbridge. Som 4G 21
Burrowhill. Surr 4A 38
Burry. Swan 3D 30
Burry Green. Swan 3D 30
Burry Port. Carm 5E 45
Burscough. Lanc 3C 90
Burscough Bridge. Lanc 3C 90
Bursea. E Yor 1B 94
Burshill. E Yor 5E 101
Bursledon. Hants 2C 16
Burslem. Stoke 1C 72
Burstall. Suff 1D 54
Burstock. Dors 2H 13
Burston. Devn 2H 11
Burston. Norf 2D 66
Burston. Staf 2D 72
Burstow. Surr 1E 27
Burstwick. E Yor 2F 95
Burtersett. N Yor 1A 98
Burtholme. Cumb 3G 113
Burthorpe. Suff 4G 65
Burthwaite. Cumb 5F 113
Burtle. Som 2H 21
Burtoft. Linc 2B 76
Burton. Ches W
nr. Kelsall 4H 83
nr. Neston 3F 83
Burton. Dors
nr. Christchurch 3G 15
nr. Dorchester 3B 14
Burton. Nmbd 1F 121
Burton. Pemb 4D 43
Burton. Som 2E 21
Burton. Wilts
nr. Chippenham 4D 34
nr. Warminster 3D 22
Burton. Wrex 5F 83
Burton Agnes. E Yor 3F 101
Burton Bradstock. Dors 4H 13
Burton-by-Lincoln. Linc 3G 87
Burton Coggles. Linc 3G 75
Burton Constable. E Yor 1E 95
Burton Corner. Linc 1C 76
Burton End. Cambs 1G 53
Burton End. Essx 3F 53

210 A-Z Great Britain Road Atlas

Burton Fleming—Chapelton

Burton Fleming. E Yor 2E 101
Burton Green. Warw 3G 61
Burton Green. Wrex 5F 83
Burton Hastings. Warw 2B 62
Burton-in-Kendal. Cumb 2E 97
Burton in Lonsdale. N Yor 2F 97
Burton Joyce. Notts 1D 74
Burton Latimer. Nptn 3G 63
Burton Lazars. Leics 4E 75
Burton Leonard. N Yor 3F 99
Burton on the Wolds. Leics 3C 74
Burton Overy. Leics 1D 62
Burton Pedwardine. Linc 1A 76
Burton Pidsea. E Yor 1F 95
Burton Salmon. N Yor 2E 93
Burton's Green. Essx 3B 54
Burton Stather. N Lin 3B 94
Burton upon Stather. N Lin 3B 94
Burton upon Trent. Staf 3G 73
Burton Wolds. Leics 3D 74
Burtonwood. Warr 1H 83
Burwardsley. Ches W 5H 83
Burwarton. Shrp 2A 60
Burwash. E Sus 3A 28
Burwash Common. E Sus 3H 27
Burwash Weald. E Sus 3A 28
Burwell. Cambs 4E 65
Burwell. Linc 3C 88
Burwen. IOA 1D 80
Burwick. Orkn 9D 172
Bury. Cambs 2B 64
Bury. G Man 3G 91
Bury. Som 4C 20
Bury. W Sus 4B 26
Burybank. Staf 2C 72
Bury End. Worc 2F 49
Bury Green. Herts 3E 53
Bury St Edmunds. Suff 4H 65
Burythorpe. N Yor 3B 100
Busbridge. Surr 1A 26
Busby. E Ren 4G 127
Busby. Per 1C 136
Buscot. Oxon 2H 35
Bush. Corn 2C 10
Bush, The. M Ulst 3C 178
Bush Bank. Here 5G 59
Bushbury. W Mid 5D 72
Bushby. Leics 5D 74
Bushey. Dors 4E 15
Bushey. Herts 1C 38
Bushey Heath. Herts 1C 38
Bush Green. Norf
 nr. Attleborough 1C 66
 nr. Harleston 2E 66
Bush Green. Suff 5B 66
Bushley. Worc 2D 49
Bushley Green. Worc 2D 48
Bushmead. Bed 4A 64
Bushmills. Caus 2F 174
Bushmoor. Shrp 2G 59
Bushton. Wilts 4F 35
Bushy Common. Norf 4B 78
Busk. Cumb 5H 113
Buslingthorpe. Linc 2H 87
Bussage. Glos 5D 49
Bussex. Som 3G 21
Busta. Shet 5E 173
Butcher's Cross. E Sus 3G 27
Butcombe. N Som 5A 34
Bute Town. Cphy 5E 46
Butleigh. Som 3A 22
Butleigh Wootton. Som 3A 22
Butlers Marston. Warw 1B 50
Butley. Suff 5F 67
Butley High Corner. Suff 1G 55
Butlocks Heath. Hants 2C 16
Butterburn. Cumb 2H 113
Buttercrambe. N Yor 4B 100
Butterknowle. Dur 2E 105
Butterleigh. Devn 2C 12
Buttermere. Cumb 3C 102
Buttermere. Wilts 5B 36
Buttershaw. W Yor 2B 92
Butterstone. Per 4H 143
Butterton. Staf
 nr. Leek 5E 85
 nr. Stoke-on-Trent 1C 72
Butterwick. Dur 2A 106
Butterwick. Linc 1C 76
Butterwick. N Yor
 nr. Malton 2B 100
 nr. Weaverthorpe 2D 101
Butteryhaugh. Nmbd 5A 120
Butt Green. Ches E 5A 84
Buttington. Powy 5E 71
Buttonbridge. Shrp 3B 60
Buttonoak. Shrp 3B 60
Buttsash. Hants 2C 16
Butt's Green. Essx 5A 54
Butt Yeats. Lanc 3E 97
Buxhall. Suff 5C 66
Buxted. E Sus 3F 27
Buxton. Derbs 3E 85
Buxton. Norf 3E 79
Buxworth. Derbs 2E 85
Bwcle. Flin 4E 83
Bwlch. Powy 3E 47
Bwlchderwin. Gwyn 1D 68
Bwlchgwyn. Wrex 5E 83
Bwlch-Llan. Cdgn 5E 57
Bwlchnewydd. Carm 3D 44
Bwlchtocyn. Gwyn 3C 68
Bwlch-y-cibau. Powy 4D 70
Bwlchyddar. Powy 3D 70
Bwlch-y-fadfa. Cdgn 1E 45
Bwlch-y-ffridd. Powy 1C 58
Bwlch y Garreg. Powy 1C 58
Bwlch-y-groes. Pemb 1G 43
Bwlch-y-sarnau. Powy 3C 58
Bybrook. Kent 1E 28
Byermoor. Tyne 4E 115
Byers Garth. Dur 5G 115
Byers Green. Dur 1F 105
Byfield. Nptn 5C 62
Byfleet. Surr 4B 38
Byford. Here 1G 47
Bygrave. Herts 2C 52
Byker. Tyne 3F 115
Byland Abbey. N Yor 2H 99
Bylchau. Cnwy 4B 82
Byley. Ches W 4B 84
Bynea. Carm 3E 31
Byram. N Yor 2E 93
Byrness. Nmbd 4B 120
Bystock. Devn 4D 12
Bythorn. Cambs 3H 63
Byton. Here 4F 59
Bywell. Nmbd 3D 114
Byworth. W Sus 3A 26

C

Cabharstadh. W Isl 6F 171
Cabourne. Linc 4E 95
Cabrach. Arg 3C 124
Cabrach. Mor 1A 152
Cabragh. M Ulst 3B 178
Cabus. Lanc 5D 97
Cadbury. Devn 2C 12
Cadder. E Dun 2H 127
Caddington. C Beds 4A 52
Caddonfoot. Bord 1G 119
Cadeby. Leics 5B 74
Cadeby. S Yor 4F 93
Cadeleigh. Devn 2C 12
Cade Street. E Sus 3H 27
Cadgwith. Corn 5E 5
Cadham. Fife 3E 137
Cadishead. G Man 1B 84
Cadle. Swan 3F 31
Cadley. Lanc 1D 90
Cadley. Wilts
 nr. Ludgershall 1H 23
 nr. Marlborough 5H 35
Cadmore End. Buck 2F 37
Cadnam. Hants 1A 16
Cadney. N Lin 4D 94
Cadole. Flin 4E 82
Cadoxton-juxta-Neath. Neat 2A 32
Cadwell. Herts 2B 52
Cadwst. Den 2C 70
Caeathro. Gwyn 4E 81
Caehopkin. Powy 4B 46
Caenby. Linc 2H 87
Caerau. B'end 2B 32
Caerau. Card 4E 33
Cae'r-bont. Powy 4B 46
Cae'r-bryn. Carm 4F 45
Caerdeon. Gwyn 4F 69
Caerdydd. Card 193 (4E 33)
Caerfarchell. Pemb 2B 42
Caerffili. Cphy 3E 33
Caerfyrddin. Carm 4E 45
Caergeiliog. IOA 3C 80
Caergwrle. Flin 5F 83
Caergybi. IOA 2B 80
Caerlaverock. Per 2A 136
Caerleon. Newp 2G 33
Caerlleon. Carm 2G 43
Caerllion. Newp 2G 33
Caernarfon. Gwyn 4D 81
Caerphilly. Cphy 3E 33
Caersws. Powy 1C 58
Caerwedros. Cdgn 5C 56
Caerwent. Mon 2H 33
Caerwys. Flin 3D 82
Caim. IOA 2F 81
Caio. Carm 2G 45
Cairinis. W Isl 2D 170
Cairisiadar. W Isl 4C 171
Cairminis. W Isl 9C 171
Cairnbaan. Arg 4F 133
Cairnbulg. Abers 2H 161
Cairncross. Ang 1D 145
Cairndow. Arg 2A 134
Cairness. Abers 2H 161
Cairneyhill. Fife 1D 128
Cairngarroch. Dum 5F 109
Cairnhill. Abers 5D 160
Cairnie. Abers 4B 160
Cairnorrie. Abers 4F 161
Cairnryan. Dum 3F 109
Cairston. Orkn 6B 172
Caister-on-Sea. Norf 4H 79
Caistor. Linc 4E 94
Caistor St Edmund. Norf 5E 79
Caistron. Nmbd 4D 121
Cakebole. Worc 3C 60
Calais Street. Suff 1C 54
Calanais. W Isl 4E 171
Calbost. W Isl 6G 171
Calbourne. IOW 4C 16
Calceby. Linc 3C 88
Calcot. Glos 4F 49
Calcot Row. W Ber 4E 37
Calcott. Kent 4F 41
Calcott. Shrp 4G 71
Caldback. Shet 1H 173
Caldbeck. Cumb 1E 102
Caldbergh. N Yor 1C 98
Caldecote. Cambs
 nr. Cambridge 5C 64
 nr. Peterborough 2A 64
Caldecote. Herts 2C 52
Caldecote. Nptn 5D 62
Caldecote. Warw 1A 62
Caldecott. Nptn 4G 63
Caldecott. Oxon 2C 36
Caldecott. Rut 1F 63
Calderbank. N Lan 3A 128
Calder Bridge. Cumb 4B 102
Calderbrook. G Man 3H 91
Caldercruix. N Lan 3B 128
Calder Grove. W Yor 3D 92
Calder Mains. High 3C 168
Caldermill. S Lan 5H 127
Calder Vale. Lanc 5E 97
Calderwood. S Lan 4H 127
Caldicot. Mon 3H 33
Caldwell. Derbs 4G 73
Caldwell. N Yor 3E 105
Caldy. Mers 2E 83
Calebrack. Cumb 1E 103
Caledon. M Ulst 5B 178
Calf Heath. Staf 5D 72
Calford Green. Suff 1G 53
Calfsound. Orkn 4E 172
Calgary. Arg 3E 139
Califer. Mor 3E 159
California. Cambs 2E 65
California. Falk 2C 128
California. Norf 4H 79
California. Suff 1E 55
Calke. Derbs 3A 74
Callakille. High 3F 155
Callaly. Nmbd 4E 121
Callander. Stir 3F 135
Callaughton. Shrp 1A 60
Callendoun. Arg 1E 127
Callestick. Corn 3B 6
Calligarry. High 3E 147
Callington. Corn 2H 7
Callingwood. Staf 3F 73
Callow. Here 2H 47
Callowell. Glos 5D 48
Callow End. Worc 1D 48
Callow Hill. Wilts 3F 35
Callow Hill. Worc
 nr. Bewdley 3B 60
 nr. Redditch 4E 61
Calmore. Hants 1B 16
Calmsden. Glos 5F 49
Calne. Wilts 4E 35
Calow. Derbs 3B 86
Calshot. Hants 2C 16
Calstock. Corn 2A 8
Calstone Wellington. Wilts 5F 35
Calthorpe. Norf 2D 78
Calthorpe Street. Norf 3G 79
Calthwaite. Cumb 5F 113
Calton. N Yor 4B 98
Calton. Staf 5F 85
Calveley. Ches E 5H 83
Calver. Derbs 3G 85
Calverhall. Shrp 2A 72
Calverleigh. Devn 1C 12
Calverley. W Yor 1C 92
Calvert. Buck 3E 51
Calverton. Mil 2F 51
Calverton. Notts 1D 74
Calvine. Per 2F 143
Calvo. Cumb 4C 112
Cam. Glos 2C 34
Camaghael. High 1F 141
Camas-luinie. High 1B 148
Camasnacroise. High 3C 140
Camastianavaig. High 5E 155
Camasunary. High 2D 146
Camault Muir. High 4H 157
Camb. Shet 2G 173
Camber. E Sus 4D 28
Camberley. Surr 5G 37
Camberwell. G Lon 3E 39
Camblesforth. N Yor 2G 93
Cambo. Nmbd 1D 114
Cambois. Nmbd 1G 115
Camborne. Corn 5A 6
Cambourne. Cambs 5C 64
Cambridge. Cambs 193 (5D 64)
Cambridge. Glos 5C 48
Cambrose. Corn 4A 6
Cambus. Clac 4A 136
Cambusbarron. Stir 4G 135
Cambuskenneth. Stir 4H 135
Cambuslang. S Lan 3H 127
Cambusnethan. N Lan 4B 128
Cambus o' May. Abers 4B 152
Camden Town. G Lon 2D 39
Cameley. Bath 1B 22
Camelford. Corn 4B 10
Camelon. Falk 1B 128
Camelsdale. W Sus 3G 25
Camer's Green. Worc 2C 48
Camerton. Bath 1B 22
Camerton. Cumb 1B 102
Camerton. E Yor 2F 95
Camghouran. Per 3C 142
Camlough. New M 7E 178
Cammachmore. Abers 4G 153
Cammeringham. Linc 2G 87
Camore. High 4E 165
Camp, The. Glos 5E 49
Campbelton. N Ayr 4C 126
Campbeltown. Arg 3B 122
Campbeltown Airport. Arg 3A 122
Cample. Dum 5A 118
Campmuir. Per 5B 144
Campsall. S Yor 3F 93
Campsea Ashe. Suff 5F 67
Camps End. Cambs 1G 53
Campsey. Derr 4A 174
Campton. C Beds 2B 52
Camptoun. E Lot 2B 130
Camptown. Bord 3A 120
Camrose. Pemb 2D 42
Camserney. Per 4F 143
Camster. High 4E 169
Camus Croise. High 2E 147
Camuscross. High 2E 147
Camusdarach. High 4E 147
Camusnagaul. High
 nr. Fort William 1E 141
 nr. Little Loch Broom 5E 163
Camus Park. Derr 3F 176
Camusteel. High 4G 155
Camusterrach. High 4G 155
Camusvrachan. Per 4D 142
Canada. Hants 1A 16
Canadia. E Sus 4B 28
Canaston Bridge. Pemb 3E 43
Candlesby. Linc 4D 88
Candle Street. Suff 3C 66
Candy Mill. S Lan 5D 128
Cane End. Oxon 4E 37
Canewdon. Essx 1D 40
Canford Cliffs. Pool 4F 15
Canford Heath. Pool 3F 15
Canford Magna. Pool 3F 15
Cangate. Norf 4F 79
Canham's Green. Suff 4C 66
Canholes. Derbs 3E 85
Canisbay. High 1F 169
Canley. W Mid 3H 61
Cann. Dors 4D 22
Cann Common. Dors 4D 23
Cannich. High 5F 157
Cannington. Som 3F 21
Cannock. Staf 4D 73
Cannock Wood. Staf 4E 73
Canonbie. Dum 2E 113
Canon Bridge. Here 1H 47
Canon Frome. Here 1B 48
Canon Pyon. Here 1H 47
Canons Ashby. Nptn 5C 62
Canonstown. Corn 3C 4
Canterbury. Kent 193 (5F 41)
Cantley. Norf 5F 79
Cantley. S Yor 4G 93
Cantlop. Shrp 5H 71
Canton. Card 4E 33
Cantray. High 4B 158
Cantraybruich. High 4B 158
Cantraywood. High 4B 158
Cantsdam. Fife 4D 136
Cantsfield. Lanc 2F 97
Canvey Island. Essx 2B 40
Canwick. Linc 4G 87
Canworthy Water. Corn 3C 10
Caol. High 1F 141
Caolas. Arg 4B 138
Caolas. W Isl 9B 170
Caolas Liubharsaigh. W Isl 4D 170
Caolas Scalpaigh. W Isl 8E 171
Caolas Stocinis. W Isl 8D 171
Caol Ila. Arg 2C 124
Caol Loch Ailse. High 1F 147
Caol Reatha. High 1F 147
Capel. Kent 1H 27
Capel. Surr 1C 26
Capel Bangor. Cdgn 2F 57
Capel Betws Lleucu. Cdgn 5F 57
Capel Coch. IOA 2D 80
Capel Curig. Cnwy 5G 81
Capel Cynon. Cdgn 1D 45
Capel Dewi. Carm 3E 45
Capel Dewi. Cdgn
 nr. Aberystwyth 2F 57
 nr. Llandysul 1E 45
Capel Garmon. Cnwy 5H 81
Capel Green. Suff 1G 55
Capel Gwyn. IOA 3C 80
Capel Gwynfe. Carm 3H 45
Capel Hendre. Carm 4F 45
Capel Isaac. Carm 3F 45
Capel Iwan. Carm 1G 43
Capel-le-Ferne. Kent 2G 29
Capel Llanilltern. Card 4D 32
Capel Mawr. IOA 3D 80
Capel Newydd. Pemb 1G 43
Capel St Andrew. Suff 1G 55
Capel St Mary. Suff 2D 54
Capel Seion. Carm 4F 45
Capel Seion. Cdgn 3F 57
Capel Uchaf. Gwyn 1D 68
Capel-y-ffin. Powy 2F 47
Capenhurst. Ches W 3F 83
Capernwray. Lanc 2E 97
Capheaton. Nmbd 1D 114
Cappagh. M Ulst 3A 178
Cappercleuch. Bord 2E 119
Capplegill. Dum 4D 118
Capton. Devn 3E 9
Capton. Som 3D 20
Caputh. Per 5H 143
Caradon Town. Corn 5C 10
Carbis Bay. Corn 3C 4
Carbost. High
 nr. Loch Harport 5C 154
 nr. Portree 4D 154
Carbrook. S Yor 2A 86
Carbrooke. Norf 5B 78
Carburton. Notts 3D 86
Carcluie. S Ayr 3C 116
Car Colston. Notts 1E 74
Carcroft. S Yor 4F 93
Cardenden. Fife 4E 136
Cardeston. Shrp 4F 71
Cardewlees. Cumb 4E 113
Cardiff. Card 193 (4E 33)
Cardiff Airport. V Glam 5D 32
Cardigan. Cdgn 1B 44
Cardinal's Green. Cambs 1G 53
Cardington. Bed 1A 52
Cardington. Shrp 1H 59
Cardinham. Corn 2F 7
Cardno. Abers 2G 161
Cardow. Mor 4F 159
Cardross. Arg 2E 127
Cardurnock. Cumb 4C 112
Careby. Linc 4H 75
Careston. Ang 2E 145
Carew. Pemb 4E 43
Carew Cheriton. Pemb 4E 43
Carew Newton. Pemb 4E 43
Carey. Here 2A 48
Carfin. N Lan 4A 128
Carfrae. Bord 4B 130
Cargan. ME Ant 5H 175
Cargate Green. Norf 4F 79
Cargenbridge. Dum 2G 111
Cargill. Per 5A 144
Cargo. Cumb 4E 113
Cargreen. Corn 2A 8
Carham. Nmbd 1C 120
Carhampton. Som 2D 20
Carharrack. Corn 4B 6
Carie. Per
 nr. Loch Rannah 3D 142
 nr. Loch Tay 5D 142
Carisbrooke. IOW 4C 16
Cark. Cumb 2C 96
Carkeel. Corn 2A 8
Carlabhagh. W Isl 3E 171
Carland Cross. Corn 3C 6
Carlbury. Darl 3F 105
Carlby. Linc 4H 75
Carlecotes. S Yor 4B 92
Carleen. Corn 4D 4
Carlesmoor. N Yor 2D 98
Carleton. Cumb
 nr. Carlisle 4F 113
 nr. Egremont 4B 102
 nr. Penrith 2G 103
Carleton. Lanc 5C 96
Carleton. N Yor 5B 98
Carleton. W Yor 2E 93
Carleton Forehoe. Norf 5C 78
Carleton Rode. Norf 1D 66
Carleton St Peter. Norf 5F 79
Carlidnack. Corn 4E 5
Carlingcott. Bath 1B 22
Carlin How. Red C 3E 107
Carlisle. Cumb 193 (4F 113)
Carloonan. Arg 2H 133
Carlops. Bord 4E 129
Carlton. Bed 5G 63
Carlton. Cambs 5F 65
Carlton. Leics 5A 74
Carlton. N Yor
 nr. Helmsley 1A 100
 nr. Middleham 1C 98
 nr. Selby 2G 93
Carlton. Notts 1D 74
Carlton. S Yor 3D 92
Carlton. Stoc T 2A 106
Carlton. Suff 4F 67
Carlton. W Yor 2D 92
Carlton Colville. Suff 1H 67
Carlton Curlieu. Leics 1D 62
Carlton Husthwaite. N Yor 2G 99
Carlton in Cleveland. N Yor 4C 106
Carlton in Lindrick. Notts 2C 86
Carlton-le-Moorland. Linc 5G 87
Carlton Miniott. N Yor 1F 99
Carlton-on-Trent. Notts 4F 87
Carlton Scroop. Linc 1G 75
Carluke. S Lan 4B 128
Carlyon Bay. Corn 3E 7
Carmarthen. Carm 4E 45
Carmel. Carm 4F 45
Carmel. Flin 3D 82
Carmel. Gwyn 5D 81
Carmel. IOA 2C 80
Carmichael. S Lan 1B 118
Carmunnock. Glas 4H 127
Carmyle. Glas 3H 127
Carmyllie. Ang 4E 145
Carnaby. E Yor 3F 101
Carnach. High
 nr. Lochcarron 1C 148
 nr. Ullapool 4E 163
Carnach. Mor 4E 159
Carnach. W Isl 8E 171
Carnachy. High 3H 167
Carnain. Arg 3B 124
Carnais. W Isl 4C 171
Carnan. Arg 4B 138
Carnan. W Isl 4C 170
Carnbee. Fife 3H 137
Carnbo. Per 3C 136
Carn Brea Village. Corn 4A 6
Carndu. High 1A 148
Carnduff. Caus 2G 175
Carne. Corn 5D 6
Carnell. S Ayr 1D 116
Carnforth. Lanc 2E 97
Carn-gorm. High 1B 148
Carnhedryn. Pemb 2C 42
Carnhell Green. Corn 3D 4
Carnie. Abers 3F 153
Carnkie. Corn
 nr. Falmouth 5B 6
 nr. Redruth 5A 6
Carnkief. Corn 3B 6
Carnlough. ME Ant 5J 175
Carnmoney. Ant 1H 179
Carno. Powy 1B 58
Carnock. Fife 1D 128
Carnon Downs. Corn 4B 6
Carnoustie. Ang 5E 145
Carnteel. M Ulst 4A 178
Carntyne. Glas 3H 127
Carnwath. S Lan 5C 128
Carnyorth. Corn 3A 4
Carol Green. W Mid 3G 61
Carpalla. Corn 3D 6
Carperby. N Yor 1C 98
Carradale. Arg 2C 122
Carragraich. W Isl 8D 171
Carrbridge. High 1D 150
Carr Cross. Lanc 3B 90
Carreglefn. IOA 2C 80
Carrhouse. N Lin 4A 94
Carrick Castle. Arg 4A 134
Carrickfergus. ME Ant 8L 175
Carrick Ho. Orkn 4E 172
Carrickmore. Ferm 2A 178
Carriden. Falk 1D 128
Carrington. G Man 1B 84
Carrington. Linc 5C 88
Carrington. Midl 3G 129
Carrog. Cnwy 1G 69
Carrog. Den 1D 70
Carron. Falk 1B 128
Carron. Mor 4G 159
Carronbridge. Dum 5A 118
Carronshore. Falk 1B 128
Carrowclare. Caus 4C 174
Carrowdore. Ards 2K 179
Carrow Hill. Mon 2H 33
Carr Shield. Nmbd 5B 114
Carrutherstown. Dum 2C 112
Carr Vale. Derbs 4B 86
Carrville. Dur 5G 115
Carryduff. Lis 3H 179
Carsaig. Arg 1C 132
Carscreugh. Dum 3H 109
Carsegowan. Dum 4B 110
Carse House. Arg 3F 125
Carseriggan. Dum 3A 110
Carsethorn. Dum 4A 112
Carshalton. G Lon 4D 39
Carsington. Derbs 5G 85
Carskiey. Arg 5A 122
Carsluith. Dum 4B 110
Carson Park. New M 4J 179
Carsphairn. Dum 5E 117
Carstairs. S Lan 5C 128
Carstairs Junction. S Lan 5C 128
Cartbridge. Surr 5B 38
Carterhaugh. Ang 4D 144
Carter's Clay. Hants 4B 24
Carterton. Oxon 5A 50
Carterway Heads. Nmbd 4D 114
Carthew. Corn 3E 6
Carthorpe. N Yor 1F 99
Cartington. Nmbd 4E 121
Cartland. S Lan 5B 128
Cartmel. Cumb 2C 96
Cartmel Fell. Cumb 1D 96
Cartworth. W Yor 4B 92
Carwath. Cumb 5E 112
Carway. Carm 5E 45
Carwinley. Cumb 2F 113
Cascob. Powy 4E 59
Cas-gwent. Mon 2A 34
Cash Feus. Fife 3E 136
Cashlie. Per 4B 142
Cashmoor. Dors 1E 15
Cas-Mael. Pemb 2E 43
Casnewydd. Newp 200 (3G 33)
Cassington. Oxon 4C 50
Cassop. Dur 1A 106
Castell. Cnwy 4G 81
Castell. Den 4D 82
Castell Hendre. Pemb 2E 43
Castell-Nedd. Neat 2A 32
Castell Newydd Emlyn. Carm 1D 44
Castell-y-bwch. Torf 2F 33
Casterton. Cumb 2F 97
Castle. Som 2A 22
Castle Acre. Norf 4H 77
Castle Ashby. Nptn 5F 63
Castlebay. W Isl 9B 170
Castle Bolton. N Yor 5D 104
Castle Bromwich. W Mid 2F 61
Castle Bytham. Linc 4G 75
Castlebythe. Pemb 2E 43
Castle Caereinion. Powy 5D 70
Castle Camps. Cambs 1G 53
Castle Carrock. Cumb 4G 113
Castlecary. N Lan 2A 128
Castle Cary. Som 3B 22
Castlecaulfield. M Ulst 3B 178
Castle Combe. Wilts 4D 34
Castlecraig. High 2C 158
Castledawson. M Ulst 7F 174
Castlederg. Derr 4E 176
Castle Donington. Leics 3B 74
Castle Douglas. Dum 3E 111
Castle Eaton. Swin 2G 35
Castle Eden. Dur 1B 106
Castleford. W Yor 2E 93
Castle Frome. Here 1B 48
Castle Green. Surr 4A 38
Castle Green. Warw 3G 61
Castle Gresley. Derbs 4G 73
Castle Heaton. Nmbd 5F 131
Castle Hedingham. Essx 2A 54
Castle Hill. Kent 1A 28
Castlehill. Per 5B 144
Castlehill. S Lan 4B 128
Castle Hill. Suff 1E 55
Castlehill. W Dun 2E 127
Castle Kennedy. Dum 4G 109
Castle Lachlan. Arg 4H 133
Castlemartin. Pemb 5D 42
Castlemilk. Glas 4H 127
Castlemorris. Pemb 1D 42
Castlemorton. Worc 2C 48
Castle O'er. Dum 5E 119
Castle Park. N Yor 3F 107
Castlerigg. Cumb 2D 102
Castle Rising. Norf 3F 77
Castlerock. Caus 3D 174
Castleroe. Caus 4E 174
Castleside. Dur 5D 115
Castlethorpe. Mil 1F 51
Castleton. Abers 4F 151
Castleton. Arg 1G 125
Castleton. Derbs 2F 85
Castleton. G Man 3G 91
Castleton. Mor 1F 151
Castleton. Newp 3F 33
Castleton. N Yor 4D 107
Castleton. Per 2B 136
Castletown. Cumb 1G 103
Castletown. Dors 5B 14
Castletown. High 2D 169
Castletown. IOM 5B 108
Castletown. Tyne 4G 115
Castlewellan. New M 6H 179
Castley. N Yor 5E 99
Caston. Norf 1B 66
Castor. Pet 1A 64
Catacol. N Ayr 5H 125
Catbrook. Mon 5A 48
Catchems End. Worc 3B 60
Catchgate. Dur 4E 115
Catcleugh. Nmbd 4B 120
Catcliffe. S Yor 2B 86
Catcott. Som 3G 21
Caterham. Surr 5E 39
Catfield. Norf 3F 79
Catfield Common. Norf 3F 79
Catfirth. Shet 6F 173
Catford. G Lon 3E 39
Catforth. Lanc 1C 90
Cathcart. Glas 3G 127
Cathedine. Powy 3E 47
Catherine-de-Barnes. W Mid 2F 61
Catherington. Hants 1E 17
Catherston Leweston. Dors 3G 13
Catherton. Shrp 3A 60
Catisfield. Hants 2D 16
Catlodge. High 4A 150
Catlowdy. Cumb 2F 113
Catmore. W Ber 3C 36
Caton. Devn 5A 12
Caton. Lanc 3E 97
Catrine. E Ayr 2E 117
Cat's Ash. Newp 2G 33
Catsfield. E Sus 4B 28
Catsgore. Som 4A 22
Catshill. Worc 3D 60
Cattal. N Yor 4G 99
Cattawade. Suff 2E 54
Catterall. Lanc 5E 97
Catterick. N Yor 5F 105
Catterick Bridge. N Yor 5F 105
Catterick Garrison. N Yor 5E 105
Catterlen. Cumb 1F 103
Catterline. Abers 1H 145
Catterton. N Yor 5H 99
Catteshall. Surr 1A 26
Catthorpe. Leics 3C 62
Cattistock. Dors 3A 14
Catton. Nmbd 4B 114
Catton. N Yor 2F 99
Catwick. E Yor 5F 101
Catworth. Cambs 3H 63
Caudle Green. Glos 4E 49
Caulcott. Oxon 3D 50
Cauldhame. Stir 4F 135
Cauldmill. Bord 3H 119
Cauldon. Staf 1E 73
Cauldon Lowe. Staf 1E 73
Cauldwells. Abers 3E 161
Caulkerbush. Dum 4G 111
Caulside. Dum 1F 113
Caunsall. Worc 2C 60
Caunton. Notts 4E 87
Causewayend. S Lan 1C 118
Causewayhead. Stir 4H 135
Causey Park. Nmbd 5F 121
Caute. Devn 1E 11
Cautley. Cumb 5H 103
Cavendish. Suff 1B 54
Cavendish Bridge. Leics 3B 74
Cavenham. Suff 3G 65
Caversfield. Oxon 3D 50
Caversham. Read 4F 37
Caversham Heights. Read 4F 37
Caverswall. Staf 1D 72
Cawdor. High 3C 158
Cawkwell. Linc 2B 88
Cawood. N Yor 1F 93
Cawsand. Corn 3A 8
Cawston. Norf 3D 78
Cawston. Warw 3B 62
Cawthorne. N Yor 1B 100
Cawthorne. S Yor 4C 92
Cawthorpe. Linc 3H 75
Cawton. N Yor 2A 100
Caxton. Cambs 5C 64
Caynham. Shrp 3H 59
Caythorpe. Linc 1G 75
Caythorpe. Notts 1D 74
Cayton. N Yor 1E 101
Ceallan. W Isl 3D 170
Ceann a Bhaigh. W Isl
 on North Uist 2C 170
 on Scalpay 8E 171
 on South Harris 8D 171
Ceann a Bhàigh. W Isl 9C 171
Ceannacroc Lodge. High 2E 149
Ceann a Deas Loch Baghasdail. W Isl 7C 170
Ceann an Leothaid. High 5E 147
Ceann a Tuath Loch Baghasdail. W Isl 6C 170
Ceann Loch Ailleart. High 5F 147
Ceann Loch Muideirt. High 1B 140
Ceann-na-Cleithe. W Isl 8D 171
Ceann Shiphoirt. W Isl 6E 171
Ceann Tarabhaigh. W Isl 6E 171
Cearsiadar. W Isl 5F 171
Ceathramh Meadhanach. W Isl 1D 170
Cefn Berain. Cnwy 4B 82
Cefn-brith. Cnwy 5B 82
Cefn-bryn-brain. Carm 4H 45
Cefn Bychan. Cphy 2F 33
Cefn-bychan. Flin 4D 82
Cefncaeau. Carm 3E 31
Cefn Canol. Powy 2E 71
Cefn Coch. Powy 5C 70
Cefn-coch. Powy 3D 70
Cefn-coed-y-cymmer. Mer T 5D 46
Cefn Cribwr. B'end 3B 32
Cefn-ddwysarn. Gwyn 2B 70
Cefn Einion. Shrp 2E 59
Cefneithin. Carm 4F 45
Cefngorwydd. Powy 1C 46
Cefn Llwyd. Cdgn 2F 57
Cefn-mawr. Wrex 1E 71
Cefn-y-bedd. Flin 5F 83
Cefn-y-coed. Powy 1D 58
Cefn-y-pant. Carm 2F 43
Cegidfa. Powy 4E 70
Ceinewydd. Cdgn 5C 56
Cellan. Cdgn 1G 45
Cellardyke. Fife 3H 137
Cellarhead. Staf 1D 72
Cemaes. IOA 1C 80
Cemmaes. Powy 5H 69
Cemmaes Road. Powy 5H 69
Cenarth. Cdgn 1C 44
Cenin. Gwyn 1D 68
Ceos. W Isl 5F 171
Ceres. Fife 2G 137
Ceri. Powy 2D 58
Cerist. Powy 2B 58
Cerne Abbas. Dors 2B 14
Cerney Wick. Glos 2F 35
Cerrigceinwen. IOA 3D 80
Cerrigydrudion. Cnwy 1B 70
Cess. Norf 4G 79
Cessford. Bord 2B 120
Ceunant. Gwyn 4E 81
Chaceley. Glos 2D 48
Chacewater. Corn 4B 6
Chackmore. Buck 2E 51
Chacombe. Nptn 1C 50
Chadderton. G Man 4H 91
Chaddesden. Derb 2A 74
Chaddesden Common. Derb 2A 74
Chaddesley Corbett. Worc 3C 60
Chaddlehanger. Devn 5E 11
Chaddleworth. W Ber 4C 36
Chadlington. Oxon 3B 50
Chadshunt. Warw 5H 61
Chadstone. Nptn 5F 63
Chad Valley. W Mid 2E 61
Chadwell. Leics 3E 75
Chadwell. Shrp 4B 72
Chadwell Heath. G Lon 2F 39
Chadwell St Mary. Thur 3H 39
Chadwick End. W Mid 3G 61
Chadwick Green. Mers 1H 83
Chaffcombe. Som 1G 13
Chafford Hundred. Thur 3H 39
Chagford. Devn 4H 11
Chailey. E Sus 4E 27
Chainbridge. Cambs 5D 76
Chain Bridge. Linc 1C 76
Chainhurst. Kent 1B 28
Chalbury. Dors 2F 15
Chalbury Common. Dors 2F 15
Chaldon. Surr 5E 39
Chaldon Herring. Dors 4C 14
Chale. IOW 5C 16
Chale Green. IOW 5C 16
Chalfont Common. Buck 1B 38
Chalfont St Giles. Buck 1A 38
Chalfont St Peter. Buck 2B 38
Chalford. Glos 5D 49
Chalgrove. Oxon 2E 37
Chalk. Kent 3A 40
Chalk End. Essx 4G 53
Chalk Hill. Glos 3G 49
Challaborough. Devn 4C 8
Challacombe. Devn 2G 19
Challister. Shet 5G 173
Challoch. Dum 3A 110
Challock. Kent 5E 40
Chalton. C Beds
 nr. Bedford 5A 64
 nr. Luton 3A 52
Chalton. Hants 1F 17
Chalvington. E Sus 5G 27
Champany. Falk 2D 128
Chance Inn. Fife 2F 137
Chancery. Cdgn 3E 57
Chandler's Cross. Herts 1B 38
Chandler's Cross. Worc 2C 48
Chandler's Ford. Hants 4C 24
Chanlockfoot. Dum 4G 117
Channel's End. Bed 5A 64
Channel Tunnel. Kent 2F 29
Channerwick. Shet 9F 173
Chantry. Som 2C 22
Chantry. Suff 1E 55
Chapel. Cumb 1D 102
Chapel. Fife 4E 137
Chapel Allerton. Som 1H 21
Chapel Allerton. W Yor 1C 92
Chapel Amble. Corn 1D 6
Chapel Brampton. Nptn 4E 63
Chapelbridge. Cambs 1B 64
Chapel Chorlton. Staf 2C 72
Chapel Cleeve. Som 2D 20
Chapel End. C Beds 1A 52
Chapel-en-le-Frith. Derbs 2E 85
Chapelfield. Abers 2G 145
Chapelgate. Linc 3D 76
Chapel Green. Warw
 nr. Coventry 2G 61
 nr. Southam 4B 62
Chapel Haddlesey. N Yor 2F 93
Chapelhall. N Lan 3A 128
Chapel Hill. Abers 5H 161
Chapel Hill. Linc 5B 88
Chapel Hill. Mon 5A 48
Chapelhill. Per
 nr. Glencarse 1E 136
 nr. Harrietfield 5H 143
Chapelknowe. Dum 2E 112
Chapel Lawn. Shrp 3F 59
Chapel le Dale. N Yor 2G 97
Chapel Milton. Derbs 2E 85
Chapel of Garioch. Abers 1E 152
Chapel Row. W Ber 5D 36
Chapels. Cumb 1B 96
Chapel St Leonards. Linc 3E 89
Chapel Stile. Cumb 4E 102
Chapelthorpe. W Yor 3D 92
Chapelton. Ang 4F 145
Chapelton. Devn 4F 19

Chapelton—Colby

Chapelton. High
nr. Grantown-on-Spey 2D 150
nr. Inverness 3H 157
Chapelton. S Lan 5H 127
Chapeltown. Bkbn 3F 91
Chapel Town. Corn 3C 6
Chapeltown. Mor 1G 151
Chapeltown. New M 6K 179
Chapeltown. S Yor 1A 86
Chapmanslade. Wilts 2D 22
Chapmans Well. Devn 3D 10
Chapmore End. Herts 4D 52
Chappel. Essx 3B 54
Chard. Som 2G 13
Chard Junction. Dors 2G 13
Chardstock. Devn 2G 13
Charfield. S Glo 2C 34
Charing. Kent 1D 28
Charing Heath. Kent 1D 28
Charing Hill. Kent 5D 40
Charingworth. Glos 2H 49
Charlbury. Oxon 4B 50
Charlcombe. Bath 5C 34
Charlcutt. Wilts 4E 35
Charlecote. Warw 5G 61
Charlemont. Arm 4C 178
Charles. Devn 3G 19
Charlesfield. Dum 3C 112
Charleshill. Surr 2G 25
Charleston. Ang 4C 144
Charleston. Ren 3F 127
Charlestown. Aber 3G 153
Charlestown. Abers 2H 161
Charlestown. Corn 3E 7
Charlestown. Dors 5B 14
Charlestown. Fife 1D 128
Charlestown. G Man 4G 91
Charlestown. High
nr. Gairloch 1H 155
nr. Inverness 4A 158
Charlestown. W Yor 2H 91
Charlestown of Aberlour. Mor 4G 159
Charles Tye. Suff 5C 66
Charlesworth. Derbs 1E 85
Charlton. G Lon 3F 39
Charlton. Hants 2B 24
Charlton. Herts 3B 52
Charlton. Nptn 2D 50
Charlton. Nmbd 1B 114
Charlton. Oxon 3C 36
Charlton. Som
nr. Radstock 1B 22
nr. Shepton Mallet 2B 22
nr. Taunton 4F 21
Charlton. Telf 4H 71
Charlton. W Sus 1G 17
Charlton. Wilts
nr. Malmesbury 3E 35
nr. Pewsey 1G 23
nr. Shaftesbury 4E 23
Charlton. Worc
nr. Evesham 1F 49
nr. Stourport-on-Severn 3C 60
Charlton Abbots. Glos 3F 49
Charlton Adam. Som 4A 22
Charlton All Saints. Wilts 4G 23
Charlton Down. Dors 3B 14
Charlton Horethorne. Som 4B 22
Charlton Kings. Glos 3E 49
Charlton Mackrell. Som 4A 22
Charlton Marshall. Dors 2E 15
Charlton Musgrove. Som 4C 22
Charlton-on-Otmoor. Oxon 4D 50
Charlton on the Hill. Dors 2D 15
Charlwood. Hants 3E 25
Charlwood. Surr 1D 26
Charlynch. Som 3F 21
Charminster. Dors 3B 14
Charmouth. Dors 3G 13
Charndon. Buck 3E 51
Charney Bassett. Oxon 2B 36
Charnock Green. Lanc 3D 90
Charnock Richard. Lanc 3D 90
Charsfield. Suff 5E 67
Chart, The. Kent 5F 39
Chart Corner. Kent 5B 40
Charter Alley. Hants 1D 24
Charterhouse. Som 1H 21
Charterville Allotments. Oxon 4B 50
Chartham. Kent 5F 41
Chartham Hatch. Kent 5F 41
Chartridge. Buck 5H 51
Chart Sutton. Kent 5B 40
Charvil. Wok 4F 37
Charwelton. Nptn 5C 62
Chase Terrace. Staf 5E 73
Chasetown. Staf 5E 73
Chastleton. Oxon 3H 49
Chasty. Devn 2D 10
Chatburn. Lanc 5G 97
Chatcull. Staf 2B 72
Chatham. Medw ... **Medway Towns 197** (4B 40)
Chatham Green. Essx 4H 53
Chathill. Nmbd 2F 121
Chatley. Worc 4C 60
Chattenden. Medw 3B 40
Chatteris. Cambs 2C 64
Chattisham. Suff 1D 54
Chatton. Nmbd 2E 121
Chatwall. Shrp 1H 59
Chaulden. Herts 5A 52
Chaul End. C Beds 3A 52
Chawleigh. Devn 1H 11
Chawley. Oxon 5C 50
Chawston. Bed 5A 64
Chawton. Hants 3F 25
Chaxhill. Glos 4C 48
Cheadle. G Man 2C 84
Cheadle. Staf 1E 73
Cheadle Hulme. G Man 2C 84
Cheam. G Lon 4D 38
Cheapside. Wind 4A 38
Chearsley. Buck 4F 51
Chebsey. Staf 3C 72
Checkendon. Oxon 3E 37
Checkley. Ches E 1B 72
Checkley. Here 2A 48
Checkley. Staf 2E 73
Chedburgh. Suff 5G 65
Cheddar. Som 1H 21
Cheddington. Buck 4H 51
Cheddleton. Staf 5D 84
Cheddon Fitzpaine. Som 4F 21
Chedglow. Wilts 2E 35
Chedgrave. Norf 1F 67
Chedington. Dors 2H 13
Chediston. Suff 3F 67
Chediston Green. Suff 3F 67
Chedworth. Glos 4F 49
Chedzoy. Som 3G 21
Cheeseman's Green. Kent 2E 29
Cheetham Hill. G Man 4G 91
Cheglinch. Devn 2F 19
Cheldon. Devn 1H 11
Chelford. Ches E 3C 84
Chellaston. Derb 2A 74
Chellington. Bed 5G 63
Chelmarsh. Shrp 2B 60
Chelmick. Shrp 1G 59
Chelmondiston. Suff 2F 55
Chelmorton. Derbs 4F 85
Chelmsford. Essx 5H 53
Chelsea. G Lon 3D 38
Chelsfield. G Lon 4F 39
Chelsham. Surr 5E 39
Chelston. Som 4E 21
Chelsworth. Suff 1C 54
Cheltenham. Glos **193** (3E 49)
Chelveston. Nptn 4G 63
Chelvey. N Som 5H 33
Chelwood. Bath 5B 34
Chelwood Common. E Sus 3F 27
Chelwood Gate. E Sus 3F 27
Chelworth. Wilts 2E 35
Chelworth Lower Green. Wilts 2F 35
Chelworth Upper Green. Wilts 2F 35
Chelynch. Som 2B 22
Cheney Longville. Shrp 2G 59
Chenies. Buck 1B 38
Chepstow. Mon 2A 34
Chequerfield. W Yor 2E 93
Chequers Corner. Norf 5D 77
Cherhill. Wilts 4F 35
Cherington. Glos 2E 35
Cherington. Warw 2A 50
Cheriton. Devn 2H 19
Cheriton. Hants 4D 24
Cheriton. Kent 2G 29
Cheriton. Pemb 5D 43
Cheriton. Swan 3D 30
Cheriton Bishop. Devn 3A 12
Cheriton Cross. Devn 3A 12
Cheriton Fitzpaine. Devn 2B 12
Cherrington. Telf 3A 72
Cherrybank. Per 1D 136
Cherry Burton. E Yor 5D 101
Cherry Green. Herts 3D 52
Cherry Hinton. Cambs 5D 65
Cherry Willingham. Linc 3H 87
Chertsey. Surr 4B 38
Cheselbourne. Dors 3C 14
Chesham. Buck 5H 51
Chesham. G Man 3G 91
Chesham Bois. Buck 1A 38
Cheshunt. Herts 5D 52
Cheslyn Hay. Staf 5D 73
Chessetts Wood. Warw 3F 61
Chessington. G Lon 4C 38
Chester. Ches W **194** (4G 83)
Chesterblade. Som 2B 22
Chesterfield. Derbs 3A 86
Chesterfield. Staf 5F 73
Chesterhope. Nmbd 1B 114
Chester-le-Street. Dur 4F 115
Chester Moor. Dur 5F 115
Chesters. Bord 3A 120
Chesterton. Cambs
nr. Cambridge 4D 64
nr. Peterborough 1A 64
Chesterton. Glos 5F 49
Chesterton. Oxon 3D 50
Chesterton. Shrp 1B 60
Chesterton. Staf 1C 72
Chesterton Green. Warw 5H 61
Chesterwood. Nmbd 3B 114
Chestfield. Kent 4F 41
Cheston. Devn 3C 8
Cheswardine. Shrp 2B 72
Cheswell. Telf 4B 72
Cheswick. Nmbd 5G 131
Cheswick Green. W Mid 3F 61
Chetnole. Dors 2B 14
Chettiscombe. Devn 1C 12
Chettisham. Cambs 2E 65
Chettle. Dors 1E 15
Chetton. Shrp 1A 60
Chetwode. Buck 3E 51
Chetwynd Aston. Telf 4B 72
Cheveley. Cambs 4F 65
Chevening. Kent 5F 39
Chevington. Suff 5G 65
Chevithorne. Devn 1C 12
Chew Magna. Bath 5A 34
Chew Moor. G Man 4E 91
Chew Stoke. Bath 5A 34
Chewton Keynsham. Bath 5B 34
Chewton Mendip. Som 1A 22
Chichacott. Devn 3G 11
Chicheley. Mil 1H 51
Chichester. W Sus 2G 17
Chickerell. Dors 4B 14
Chickering. Suff 3E 66
Chicklade. Wilts 3E 23
Chicksands. C Beds 2B 52
Chickward. Here 5E 59
Chidden. Hants 1E 17
Chiddingfold. Surr 2A 26
Chiddingly. E Sus 4G 27
Chiddingstone. Kent 1G 27
Chiddingstone Causeway. Kent 1G 27
Chiddingstone Hoath. Kent 1F 27
Chideock. Dors 3H 13
Chidgley. Som 3D 20
Chidham. W Sus 2F 17
Chieveley. W Ber 4C 36
Chignal St James. Essx 5G 53
Chignal Smealy. Essx 4G 53
Chigwell. Essx 1F 39
Chigwell Row. Essx 1F 39
Chilbolton. Hants 3B 24
Chilcomb. Hants 4D 24
Chilcombe. Dors 3A 14
Chilcompton. Som 1B 22
Chilcote. Leics 4G 73
Childer Thornton. Ches W 3F 83
Child Okeford. Dors 1D 14
Childrey. Oxon 3B 36
Child's Ercall. Shrp 3A 72
Childswickham. Worc 2F 49
Childwall. Mers 2G 83
Childwick Green. Herts 4B 52
Chilfrome. Dors 3A 14
Chilgrove. W Sus 1G 17
Chilham. Kent 5E 41
Chilhampton. Wilts 3F 23
Chilla. Devn 2E 11
Chilland. Hants 3D 24
Chillaton. Devn 4E 11
Chillenden. Kent 5G 41
Chillerton. IOW 4C 16
Chillesford. Suff 5F 67
Chillingham. Nmbd 2E 121
Chillington. Devn 4D 9
Chillington. Som 1G 13
Chilmark. Wilts 3E 23
Chilmington Green. Kent 1D 28
Chilson. Oxon 4B 50
Chilsworthy. Corn 5E 11
Chilsworthy. Devn 2D 10
Chiltern Green. C Beds 4B 52
Chilthorne Domer. Som 1A 14
Chilton. Buck 4E 51
Chilton. Devn 2B 12
Chilton. Dur 2F 105
Chilton. Oxon 3C 36
Chilton Candover. Hants 2D 24
Chilton Cantelo. Som 4A 22
Chilton Foliat. Wilts 4B 36
Chilton Lane. Dur 1A 106
Chilton Polden. Som 3G 21
Chilton Street. Suff 1A 54
Chilton Trinity. Som 3F 21
Chilwell. Notts 2C 74
Chilworth. Hants 1C 16
Chilworth. Surr 1B 26
Chimney. Oxon 5B 50
Chimney Street. Suff 1H 53
Chineham. Hants 1E 25
Chingford. G Lon 1E 39
Chinley. Derbs 2E 85
Chinnor. Oxon 5F 51
Chipley. Som 4E 20
Chipnall. Shrp 2B 72
Chippenham. Cambs 4F 65
Chippenham. Wilts 4E 35
Chipperfield. Herts 5A 52
Chipping. Herts 2D 52
Chipping. Lanc 5F 97
Chipping Campden. Glos 2G 49
Chipping Hill. Essx 4B 54
Chipping Norton. Oxon 3B 50
Chipping Ongar. Essx 5F 53
Chipping Sodbury. S Glo 3C 34
Chipping Warden. Nptn 1C 50
Chipstable. Som 4D 20
Chipstead. Kent 5G 39
Chipstead. Surr 5D 38
Chirbury. Shrp 1E 59
Chirk. Wrex 2E 71
Chirmorie. S Ayr 2H 109
Chirnside. Bord 4E 131
Chirnsidebridge. Bord 4E 131
Chirton. Wilts 1F 23
Chisbridge Cross. Buck 3G 37
Chisbury. Wilts 5A 36
Chiselborough. Som 1H 13
Chiseldon. Swin 4G 35
Chiselhampton. Oxon 2D 36
Chiserley. W Yor 2A 92
Chislehurst. G Lon 3F 39
Chislet. Kent 4G 41
Chiswell. Dors 5B 14
Chiswell Green. Herts 5B 52
Chiswick. G Lon 3D 38
Chisworth. Derbs 1D 85
Chitcombe. E Sus 3C 28
Chithurst. W Sus 4G 25
Chittering. Cambs 4D 65
Chitterley. Devn 2C 12
Chitterne. Wilts 2E 23
Chittlehamholt. Devn 4G 19
Chittlehampton. Devn 4G 19
Chittoe. Wilts 5E 35
Chivelstone. Devn 5D 9
Chivenor. Devn 3F 19
Chobham. Surr 4A 38
Cholderton. Wilts 2H 23
Cholesbury. Buck 5H 51
Chollerford. Nmbd 2C 114
Chollerton. Nmbd 2C 114
Cholsey. Oxon 3D 36
Cholstrey. Here 5G 59
Chop Gate. N Yor 5C 106
Choppington. Nmbd 1F 115
Chopwell. Tyne 4E 115
Chorley. Ches E 5H 83
Chorley. Lanc 3D 90
Chorley. Shrp 2A 60
Chorley. Staf 4E 73
Chorleywood. Herts 1B 38
Chorlton. Ches E 5B 84
Chorlton-cum-Hardy. G Man 1C 84
Chorlton Lane. Ches W 1G 71
Choulton. Shrp 2F 59
Chrishall. Essx 2E 53
Christchurch. Cambs 1D 65
Christchurch. Dors 3G 15
Christchurch. Glos 4A 48
Christian Malford. Wilts 4E 35
Christleton. Ches W 4G 83
Christmas Common. Oxon 2F 37
Christon. N Som 1G 21
Christon Bank. Nmbd 2G 121
Christow. Devn 4B 12
Chryston. N Lan 2H 127
Chuck Hatch. E Sus 2F 27
Chudleigh. Devn 5B 12
Chudleigh Knighton. Devn 5B 12
Chulmleigh. Devn 1G 11
Chunal. Derbs 1E 85
Church. Lanc 2F 91
Churcham. Glos 4C 48
Church Aston. Telf 4B 72
Church Brampton. Nptn 4E 62
Church Brough. Cumb 3A 104
Church Broughton. Derbs 2G 73
Church Corner. Suff 2G 67
Church Crookham. Hants 1G 25
Churchdown. Glos 3D 49
Church Eaton. Staf 4C 72
Church End. Cambs
nr. Cambridge 5D 65
nr. Over 3C 64
nr. Sawtry 2B 64
nr. Wisbech 5C 76
Church End. C Beds
nr. Stotfold 2B 52
nr. Totternhoe 3H 51
Church End. E Yor 4E 101
Church End. Essx
nr. Braintree 3H 53
nr. Great Dunmow 3G 53
nr. Saffron Walden 1F 53
Churchend. Essx 1E 40
Church End. Glos 5C 48
Church End. Hants 1E 25
Church End. Linc
nr. Donington 2B 76
nr. North Somercotes 1D 88
Church End. Norf 4E 77
Church End. Warw
nr. Coleshill 1G 61
nr. Nuneaton 1G 61
Church End. Wilts 4F 35
Church Enstone. Oxon 3B 50
Church Fenton. N Yor 1F 93
Church Green. Devn 3E 13
Church Gresley. Derbs 4G 73
Church Hanborough. Oxon 4C 50
Church Hill. Ches W 4A 84
Church Hill. Worc 4E 61
Church Hougham. Kent 1G 29
Church Houses. N Yor 5D 106
Churchill. Devn
nr. Axminster 2G 13
nr. Barnstaple 2F 19
Churchill. N Som 1H 21
Churchill. Oxon 3A 50
Churchill. Worc
nr. Kidderminster 3C 60
nr. Worcester 5D 60
Churchinford. Som 1F 13
Church Knowle. Dors 4E 15
Church Laneham. Notts 3F 87
Church Langley. Essx 5E 53
Church Langton. Leics 1E 62
Church Lawford. Warw 3B 62
Church Lawton. Ches E 5C 84
Church Leigh. Staf 2E 73
Church Lench. Worc 5E 61
Church Mayfield. Staf 1F 73
Church Minshull. Ches E 4A 84
Church Norton. W Sus 3G 17
Churchover. Warw 2C 62
Church Preen. Shrp 1H 59
Church Pulverbatch. Shrp 5G 71
Churchstanton. Som 1E 13
Church Stoke. Powy 1E 59
Churchstow. Devn 4D 8
Church Stowe. Nptn 5D 62
Church Street. Kent 3B 40
Church Stretton. Shrp 1G 59
Churchtown. Cumb 5E 113
Churchtown. Derbs 4G 85
Churchtown. Devn 2G 19
Churchtown. IOM 2D 108
Churchtown. Lanc 5D 97
Church Town. Leics 4A 74
Churchtown. Mers 3B 90
Churchtown. New M 5K 179
Church Town. N Lin 4A 94
Churchtown. Shrp 2E 59
Church Village. Rhon 3D 32
Church Warsop. Notts 4C 86
Church Westcote. Glos 3H 49
Church Wilne. Derbs 2B 74
Churnsike Lodge. Nmbd 2H 113
Churston Ferrers. Torb 3F 9
Churt. Surr 3G 25
Churton. Ches W 5G 83
Churwell. W Yor 2C 92
Chute Standen. Wilts 1B 24
Chwilog. Gwyn 2D 68
Chwitffordd. Flin 3D 82
Chyandour. Corn 3B 4
Cilan Uchaf. Gwyn 3B 68
Cilcain. Flin 4D 82
Cilcennin. Cdgn 4E 57
Cilfrew. Neat 5A 46
Cilfynydd. Rhon 2D 32
Cilgerran. Pemb 1B 44
Cilgeti. Pemb 4F 43
Cilgwyn. Carm 3H 45
Cilgwyn. Pemb 1E 43
Ciliau Aeron. Cdgn 5D 57
Cill Amhlaidh. W Isl 4C 170
Cill Donnain. W Isl 6C 170
Cille a' Bhacstair. High 2C 154
Cille Bhrighde. W Isl 7C 170
Cille Pheadair. W Isl 7C 170
Cilmaengwyn. Neat 5H 45
Cilmeri. Powy 5C 58
Cilmery. Powy 5C 58
Cilrhedyn. Pemb 1G 43
Cilsan. Carm 3F 45
Ciltalgarth. Gwyn 1A 70
Ciltwrch. Powy 1E 47
Cilybebyll. Neat 5H 45
Cilycwm. Carm 1A 46
Cimla. Neat 2A 32
Cinderford. Glos 4B 48
Cinderhill. Derbs 1A 74
Cippenham. Slo 2A 38
Cippyn. Pemb 1B 44
Cirbhig. W Isl 3D 171
Circebost. W Isl 4D 171
Cirencester. Glos 5F 49
City, The. Buck 2F 37
City. Powy 1E 58
City. V Glam 4C 32
City Airport. G Lon 2F 39
City Centre. Stoke ... **Stoke 202** (1C 72)
City Dulas. IOA 2D 80
City of Derry Airport. Derr 4B 174
City of London. G Lon ... **London 199** (2E 39)
Civiltown. Arm 5F 178
Clabby. Ferm 4K 177
Clabhach. Arg 3C 138
Clachaig. Arg 1C 126
Clachaig. High
nr. Kinlochleven 3F 141
nr. Nethy Bridge 2E 151
Clachamish. High 3C 154
Clachan. Arg
on Kintyre 4F 125
on Lismore 4C 140
Clachan. High
nr. Bettyhill 2H 167
nr. Staffin 2D 155
nr. Uig 1D 154
on Raasay 5E 155
Clachan Farm. Arg 2A 134
Clachan na Luib. W Isl 2D 170
Clachan of Campsie. E Dun 2H 127
Clachan of Glendaruel. Arg 1A 126
Clachan-Seil. Arg 2E 133
Clachan Shannda. W Isl 1D 170
Clachan Strachur. Arg 3H 133
Clachbreck. Arg 2F 125
Clachnaharry. High 4A 158
Clachtoll. High 1E 163
Clackmannan. Clac 4B 136
Clackmannanshire Bridge. Clac 1C 128
Clackmarras. Mor 3G 159
Clacton-on-Sea. Essx 4E 55
Cladach a Chaolais. W Isl 2C 170
Cladach Chairinis. W Isl 3D 170
Cladach Chirceboist. W Isl 2C 170
Cladach Iolaraigh. W Isl 2C 170
Cladich. Arg 1H 133
Cladswell. Worc 5E 61
Clady. Derr 5E 176
Clady. M Ulst 6F 175
Claggan. High
nr. Fort William 1F 141
nr. Lochaline 3B 140
Claigan. High 3B 154
Clandown. Bath 1B 22
Clanfield. Hants 1E 17
Clanfield. Oxon 5A 50
Clanville. Hants 2B 24
Clanville. Som 3B 22
Claonaig. Arg 4G 125
Clapgate. Dors 2F 15
Clapgate. Herts 3E 53
Clapham. Bed 5H 63
Clapham. Devn 4B 12
Clapham. G Lon 3D 39
Clapham. N Yor 3G 97
Clapham. W Sus 5B 26
Clap Hill. Kent 2E 29
Clappers. Bord 4F 131
Clappersgate. Cumb 4E 103
Clapphoull. Shet 9F 173
Clapton. Som
nr. Crewkerne 2H 13
nr. Radstock 1B 22
Clapton in Gordano. N Som 4H 33
Clapton-on-the-Hill. Glos 4G 49
Clapworthy. Devn 4G 19
Clara Vale. Tyne 3E 115
Clarbeston. Pemb 2E 43
Clarbeston Road. Pemb 2E 43
Clarborough. Notts 2E 87
Clare. Arm 5E 178
Clare. Suff 1A 54
Clarebrand. Dum 3E 111
Clarencefield. Dum 3B 112
Clarilaw. Bord 3H 119
Clark's Green. Surr 2C 26
Clark's Hill. Linc 3C 76
Clarkston. E Ren 4G 127
Clasheddy. High 2G 167
Clashindarroch. Abers 5B 160
Clashmore. High
nr. Dornoch 5E 165
nr. Stoer 1E 163
Clashnessie. High 5A 166
Clashnoir. Mor 1G 151
Clate. Shet 5G 173
Clathick. Per 1H 135
Clathy. Per 2B 136
Clatt. Abers 1C 152
Clatter. Powy 1B 58
Clatterford. IOW 4C 16
Clatworthy. Som 3D 20
Claudy. Derr 6B 174
Claughton. Lanc
nr. Caton 3E 97
nr. Garstang 5E 97
Claughton. Mers 2E 83
Claverdon. Warw 4F 61
Claverham. N Som 5H 33
Clavering. Essx 2E 53
Claverley. Shrp 1B 60
Claverton. Bath 5C 34
Clawdd-coch. V Glam 4D 32
Clawdd-newydd. Den 5C 82
Clawson Hill. Leics 3E 75
Clawton. Devn 3D 10
Claxby. Linc
nr. Alford 3D 88
nr. Market Rasen 1A 88
Claxton. Norf 5F 79
Claxton. N Yor 3A 100
Claybrooke Magna. Leics 2B 62
Claybrooke Parva. Leics 2B 62
Clay Common. Suff 2G 67
Clay Coton. Nptn 3C 62
Clay Cross. Derbs 4A 86
Claydon. Oxon 5B 62
Claydon. Suff 5D 66
Clay End. Herts 3D 52
Claygate. Dum 2E 113
Claygate. Kent 1B 28
Claygate. Surr 4C 38
Claygate Cross. Kent 5H 39
Clayhall. Hants 3E 16
Clayhanger. Devn 4D 20
Clayhanger. W Mid 5E 73
Clayhidon. Devn 1E 13
Clay Hill. Bris 4B 34
Clayhill. E Sus 3C 28
Clayhill. Hants 2B 16
Clayhithe. Cambs 4E 65
Clayholes. Ang 5E 145
Clay Lake. Linc 3B 76
Clayock. High 3D 168
Claypits. Glos 5C 48
Claypole. Linc 1F 75
Claythorpe. Linc 3D 88
Clayton. G Man 1C 84
Clayton. S Yor 4E 93
Clayton. Staf 1C 72
Clayton. W Sus 4E 27
Clayton. W Yor 1B 92
Clayton Green. Lanc 2D 90
Clayton-le-Moors. Lanc 1F 91
Clayton-le-Woods. Lanc 2D 90
Clayton West. W Yor 3C 92
Clayworth. Notts 2E 87
Cleadale. High 5C 146
Cleadon. Tyne 3G 115
Clearbrook. Devn 2B 8
Clearwell. Glos 5A 48
Cleasby. N Yor 3F 105
Cleat. Orkn
nr. Braehead 3D 172
nr. St Margaret's Hope 9D 172
Cleatlam. Dur 3E 105
Cleator. Cumb 3B 102
Cleator Moor. Cumb 3B 102
Cleckheaton. W Yor 2B 92
Cleedownton. Shrp 2H 59
Cleehill. Shrp 3H 59
Cleekhimin. N Lan 4A 128
Clee St Margaret. Shrp 2H 59
Cleestanton. Shrp 3H 59
Cleethorpes. NE Lin 4G 95
Cleeton St Mary. Shrp 3A 60
Cleeve. N Som 5H 33
Cleeve. Oxon 3E 36
Cleeve Hill. Glos 3E 49
Cleeve Prior. Worc 1F 49
Clehonger. Here 2H 47
Cleigh. Arg 1F 133
Cleish. Per 4C 136
Cleland. N Lan 4B 128
Clench Common. Wilts 5G 35
Clenchwarton. Norf 3E 77
Clennell. Nmbd 4D 120
Clent. Worc 3D 60
Cleobury Mortimer. Shrp 3A 60
Cleobury North. Shrp 2A 60
Clephanton. High 3C 158
Clerkhill. High 2H 167
Clestrain. Orkn 7C 172
Clevancy. Wilts 4F 35
Clevedon. N Som 4H 33
Cleveley. Oxon 3B 50
Cleveleys. Lanc 5C 96
Clevelode. Worc 1D 48
Cleverton. Wilts 3E 35
Clewer. Som 1H 21
Cley next the Sea. Norf 1C 78
Cliaid. W Isl 8B 170
Cliasmol. W Isl 7C 171
Clibberswick. Shet 1H 173
Cliburn. Cumb 2G 103
Cliddesden. Hants 2E 25
Clieves Hills. Lanc 4B 90
Cliff. Warw 1G 61
Cliffburn. Ang 4F 145
Cliffe. Medw 3B 40
Cliffe. N Yor
nr. Darlington 3F 105
nr. Selby 1G 93
Cliff End. E Sus 4C 28
Cliffe Woods. Medw 3B 40
Clifford. Here 1F 47
Clifford. W Yor 5G 99
Clifford Chambers. Warw 5F 61
Clifford's Mesne. Glos 3C 48
Cliffsend. Kent 4H 41
Clifton. Bris 4A 34
Clifton. C Beds 2B 52
Clifton. Cumb 2G 103
Clifton. Derbs 1F 73
Clifton. Devn 2G 19
Clifton. G Man 4F 91
Clifton. Lanc 1C 90
Clifton. Nmbd 1F 115
Clifton. N Yor 5D 98
Clifton. Nott 2C 74
Clifton. Oxon 2C 50
Clifton. S Yor 1C 86
Clifton. Stir 5H 141
Clifton. W Yor 2B 92
Clifton. Worc 1D 48
Clifton. York 4H 99
Clifton Campville. Staf 4G 73
Clifton Hampden. Oxon 2D 36
Clifton Hill. Worc 4B 60
Clifton Reynes. Mil 5G 63
Clifton upon Dunsmore. Warw 3C 62
Clifton upon Teme. Worc 4B 60
Cliftonville. Kent 3H 41
Cliftonville. Norf 2F 79
Climping. W Sus 5A 26
Climpy. S Lan 4C 128
Clink. Som 2C 22
Clint. N Yor 4E 99
Clint Green. Norf 4C 78
Clintmains. Bord 1A 120
Cliobh. W Isl 4C 171
Clipiau. Gwyn 4H 69
Clippesby. Norf 4G 79
Clippings Green. Norf 4C 78
Clipsham. Rut 4G 75
Clipston. Nptn 2E 62
Clipston. Notts 2D 74
Clipstone. Notts 4C 86
Clitheroe. Lanc 5G 97
Cliuthar. W Isl 8D 171
Clive. Shrp 3H 71
Clivocast. Shet 1G 173
Clixby. Linc 4D 94
Clocaenog. Den 5C 82
Clochan. Mor 2B 160
Clochforbie. Abers 3F 161
Clock Face. Mers 1H 83
Cloddiau. Powy 5E 70
Cloddymoss. Mor 2D 159
Clodock. Here 3G 47
Cloford. Som 2C 22
Clogh. ME Ant 5G 175
Clogher. M Ulst 4L 177
Cloghmills. Caus 5G 175
Clola. Abers 4H 161
Clonoe. M Ulst 3C 178
Clonvaraghan. New M 5H 179
Clophill. C Beds 2A 52
Clopton. Nptn 2H 63
Clopton Corner. Suff 5E 66
Clopton Green. Suff 5G 65
Closeburn. Dum 5A 118
Close Clark. IOM 4B 108
Closworth. Som 1A 14
Clothall. Herts 2C 52
Clotton. Ches W 4H 83
Clough. G Man 3H 91
Clough. New M 5J 179
Clough. W Yor 3A 92
Cloughey. Ards 4L 179
Clough Foot. W Yor 2H 91
Cloughton. N Yor 5H 107
Cloughton Newlands. N Yor 5H 107
Clousta. Shet 6E 173
Clouston. Orkn 6B 172
Clova. Abers 1B 152
Clova. Ang 1C 144
Clovelly. Devn 4D 18
Clovenfords. Bord 1G 119
Clovenstone. Abers 2E 153
Clovullin. High 2E 141
Clowne. Derbs 3B 86
Clows Top. Worc 3B 60
Cloy. Wrex 1F 71
Cloyfin. Caus 3E 174
Cluanie Inn. High 2A 150
Cluanie Lodge. High 2C 148
Cluddley. Telf 4A 72
Y Clun. Neat 5B 46
Clun. Shrp 2F 59
Clunas. High 4C 158
Clunbury. Shrp 2F 59
Clunderwen. Pemb 3F 43
Clune. High 1B 150
Clunes. High 5E 148
Clungunford. Shrp 3F 59
Clunie. Per 4A 144
Clunton. Shrp 2F 59
Cluny. Fife 4E 137
Clutton. Bath 1B 22
Clutton. Ches W 5G 83
Clwt-y-bont. Gwyn 4E 81
Clwydfagwyr. Mer T 5D 46
Clydach. Mon 4F 47
Clydach. Swan 5G 45
Clydach Vale. Rhon 2C 32
Clydebank. W Dun 3G 127
Clydey. Pemb 1G 43
Clyffe Pypard. Wilts 4F 35
Clynder. Arg 1D 126
Clyne. Neat 5B 46
Clynelish. High 3F 165
Clynnog-fawr. Gwyn 1D 68
Clyro. Powy 1F 47
Clyst Honiton. Devn 3C 12
Clyst Hydon. Devn 2D 12
Clyst St George. Devn 4C 12
Clyst St Lawrence. Devn 2D 12
Clyst St Mary. Devn 3C 12
Clyth. High 5E 169
Cnip. W Isl 4C 171
Cnoc Amhlaigh. W Isl 4H 171
Cnwcau. Pemb 1C 44
Cnwch Coch. Cdgn 3F 57
Coad's Green. Corn 5C 10
Coagh. M Ulst 2C 178
Coal Aston. Derbs 3A 86
Coalbrookdale. Telf 5A 72
Coalbrookvale. Blae 5E 47
Coalburn. S Lan 1H 117
Coalburns. Tyne 3E 115
Coalcleugh. Nmbd 5B 114
Coaley. Glos 5C 48
Coalford. Abers 4F 153
Coalhall. E Ayr 3D 116
Coalhill. Essx 1B 40
Coalisland. M Ulst 3C 178
Coalpit Heath. S Glo 3B 34
Coal Pool. W Mid 5E 73
Coalport. Telf 5B 72
Coalsnaughton. Clac 4B 136
Coaltown of Balgonie. Fife 4F 137
Coaltown of Wemyss. Fife 4F 137
Coalville. Leics 4B 74
Coalway. Glos 4A 48
Coanwood. Nmbd 4H 113
Coat. Som 4H 21
Coatbridge. N Lan 3A 128
Coatdyke. N Lan 3A 128
Coate. Swin 3G 35
Coate. Wilts 5F 35
Coates. Cambs 1C 64
Coates. Glos 5E 49
Coates. Linc 2G 87
Coates. W Sus 4A 26
Coatham. Red C 2C 106
Coatham Mundeville. Darl 2F 105
Cobbaton. Devn 4G 19
Coberley. Glos 4E 49
Cobhall Common. Here 2H 47
Cobham. Kent 4A 40
Cobham. Surr 5C 38
Cobnash. Here 4G 59
Coburg. Devn 5B 12
Cockayne. N Yor 5D 106
Cockayne Hatley. C Beds 1C 52
Cock Bank. Wrex 1F 71
Cock Bridge. Abers 3G 151
Cockburnspath. Bord 2D 130
Cock Clarks. Essx 5B 54
Cockenzie and Port Seton. E Lot 2H 129
Cockerham. Lanc 4D 96
Cockermouth. Cumb 1C 102
Cockernhoe. Herts 3B 52
Cockfield. Dur 2E 105
Cockfield. Suff 5B 66
Cockfosters. G Lon 1D 39
Cock Gate. Here 4G 59
Cock Green. Essx 4G 53
Cocking. W Sus 1G 17
Cocking Causeway. W Sus 1G 17
Cockington. Torb 2E 9
Cocklake. Som 2H 21
Cocklaw. Abers 4H 161
Cocklaw. Nmbd 2C 114
Cockley Beck. Cumb 4D 102
Cockley Cley. Norf 5G 77
Cockmuir. Abers 3G 161
Cockpole Green. Wok 3F 37
Cockshutford. Shrp 2H 59
Cockshutt. Shrp 3G 71
Cockthorpe. Norf 1B 78
Cockwood. Devn 4C 12
Cockyard. Derbs 3E 85
Cockyard. Here 2H 47
Codda. Corn 5B 10
Coddenham. Suff 5D 66
Coddenham Green. Suff 5D 66
Coddington. Ches W 5G 83
Coddington. Here 1C 48
Coddington. Notts 5F 87
Codford. Wilts 3E 23
Codicote. Herts 4C 52
Codmore Hill. W Sus 3B 26
Codnor. Derbs 1B 74
Codrington. S Glo 4C 34
Codsall. Staf 5C 72
Codsall Wood. Staf 5C 72
Coed Duon. Cphy 2E 33
Coedely. Rhon 3D 32
Coedglasson. Powy 4C 58
Coedkernew. Newp 3F 33
Coed Morgan. Mon 4G 47
Coedpoeth. Wrex 5E 83
Coedway. Powy 4F 71
Coed-y-bryn. Cdgn 1D 44
Coed-y-paen. Mon 2G 33
Coed Ystumgwern. Gwyn 3E 69
Coelbren. Powy 4B 46
Coffinswell. Devn 2E 9
Cofton Hackett. Worc 3E 61
Cogan. V Glam 4E 33
Cogenhoe. Nptn 4F 63
Cogges. Oxon 5B 50
Coggeshall. Essx 3B 54
Coggeshall Hamlet. Essx 3B 54
Coggins Mill. E Sus 3G 27
Coignafearn Lodge. High 2A 150
Coig Peighinnean. W Isl 1H 171
Coig Peighinnean Bhuirgh. W Isl 2G 171
Coilleag. W Isl 7C 170
Coillemore. High 1A 158
Coillore. High 5C 154
Coire an Fhuarain. W Isl 4E 171
Coity. B'end 3C 32
Cokhay Green. Derbs 3G 73
Col. W Isl 3G 171
Colaboll. High 2C 164
Colan. Corn 2C 6
Colaton Raleigh. Devn 4D 12
Colbost. High 4B 154
Colburn. N Yor 5E 105
Colby. Cumb 2H 103
Colby. IOM 4B 108
Colby. Norf 2E 78

212 A-Z Great Britain Road Atlas

Colchester—Cross Green

Colchester. Essx 3D 54
Cold Ash. W Ber 5D 36
Cold Ashby. Nptn 3D 62
Cold Ashton. S Glo 4C 34
Cold Aston. Glos 4G 49
Coldbackie. High 3G 167
Cold Blow. Pemb 3F 43
Cold Brayfield. Mil 5G 63
Cold Cotes. N Yor 2G 97
Coldean. Brig 5E 27
Coldeast. Devn 5B 12
Colden. W Yor 2H 91
Colden Common. Hants 4C 24
Coldfair Green. Suff 4G 67
Coldham. Cambs 5D 76
Coldham. Staf 5C 72
Cold Hanworth. Linc 2H 87
Coldharbour. Corn 4B 6
Cold Harbour. Dors 3E 15
Coldharbour. Glos 5A 48
Coldharbour. Kent 5G 39
Coldharbour. Surr 1C 26
Cold Hatton. Telf 3A 72
Cold Hatton Heath. Telf 3A 72
Cold Hesledon. Dur 5H 115
Cold Hiendley. W Yor 3D 92
Cold Higham. Nptn 5D 62
Coldingham. Bord 3F 131
Cold Kirby. N Yor 1H 99
Coldmeece. Staf 2C 72
Cold Northcott. Corn 4C 10
Cold Norton. Essx 5B 54
Cold Overton. Leics 4F 75
Coldrain. Per 3C 136
Coldred. Kent 1G 29
Coldridge. Devn 2G 11
Cold Row. Lanc 5C 96
Coldstream. Bord 5E 131
Coldwaltham. W Sus 4B 26
Coldwell. Here 2H 47
Coldwells. Abers 5H 161
Coldwells Croft. Abers 1C 152
Cole. Shet 5E 173
Cole. Som 3B 22
Colebatch. Shrp 2F 59
Colebrook. Devn 2D 12
Colebrooke. Devn 3A 12
Coleburn. Mor 3G 159
Coleby. Linc 4G 87
Coleby. N Lin 3B 94
Cole End. Warw 2G 61
Coleford. Devn 2A 12
Coleford. Glos 4A 48
Coleford. Som 2B 22
Colegate End. Norf 2D 66
Cole Green. Herts 4C 52
Cole Henley. Hants 1C 24
Colehill. Dors 2F 15
Coleman Green. Herts 4B 52
Coleman's Hatch. E Sus 2F 27
Colemere. Shrp 2G 71
Colemore. Hants 3F 25
Colemore Green. Shrp 1B 60
Coleorton. Leics 4B 74
Coleraine. Caus 3E 174
Colerne. Wilts 4D 34
Colesbourne. Glos 4F 49
Colesden. Bed 5A 64
Coles Green. Worc 5B 60
Coleshill. Buck 1A 38
Coleshill. Oxon 2H 35
Coleshill. Warw 2G 61
Colestocks. Devn 2D 12
Colethrop. Glos 4D 48
Coley. Bath 1A 22
Colgate. W Sus 2D 26
Colinsburgh. Fife 3G 137
Colinton. Edin 3F 129
Colintraive. Arg 2B 126
Colkirk. Norf 3B 78
Collace. Per 5B 144
Collam. W Isl 8D 171
Collaton. Devn 5D 8
Collaton St Mary. Torb 2E 9
College of Roseisle. Mor 2F 159
Collessie. Fife 2E 137
Collier Row. G Lon 1F 39
Colliers End. Herts 3D 52
Collier Street. Kent 1B 28
Colliery Row. Tyne 5G 115
Collieston. Abers 1H 153
Collin. Dum 2B 112
Collingbourne Ducis. Wilts 1H 23
Collingbourne Kingston. Wilts 1H 23
Collingham. Notts 4F 87
Collingham. W Yor 5F 99
Collingtree. Nptn 5E 63
Collins Green. Warr 1H 83
Collins Green. Worc 5B 60
Colliston. Ang 4F 145
Colliton. Devn 2D 12
Collydean. Fife 3E 137
Collyweston. Nptn 5G 75
Colmonell. S Ayr 1G 109
Colmworth. Bed 5A 64
Colnbrook. Slo 3B 38
Colne. Cambs 3C 64
Colne. Lanc 5A 98
Colne Engaine. Essx 2B 54
Colney. Norf 5D 78
Colney Heath. Herts 5C 52
Colney Street. Herts 5B 52
Coln Rogers. Glos 5F 49
Coln St Aldwyns. Glos 5G 49
Coln St Dennis. Glos 4F 49
Colpitts Grange. Nmbd 4C 114
Colpy. Abers 5D 160
Colscott. Devn 1D 10
Colsterdale. N Yor 1D 98
Colsterworth. Linc 3G 75
Colston Bassett. Notts 2E 74
Colstoun House. E Lot 2B 130
Coltfield. Mor 2F 159
Colthouse. Cumb 5E 103
Coltishall. Norf 4E 79
Coltness. N Lan 4B 128
Colton. Cumb 1C 96
Colton. Norf 5D 78
Colton. N Yor 5H 99
Colton. Staf 3E 73
Colton. W Yor 1D 92
Colt's Hill. Kent 1H 27
Col Uarach. W Isl 4G 171
Colvend. Dum 4F 111
Colvister. Shet 2G 173
Colwall. Here 1C 48
Colwall Green. Here 1C 48
Colwell. Nmbd 2C 114
Colwich. Staf 3E 73
Colwick. Notts 1D 74
Colwinston. V Glam 4C 32
Colworth. W Sus 5A 26
Colwyn Bay. Cnwy 3A 82
Colyford. Devn 3F 13
Colyton. Devn 3F 13
Combe. Devn 2D 8
Combe. Here 4F 59
Combe. Oxon 4C 50
Combe. W Ber 5B 36
Combe Almer. Dors 3E 15
Combebow. Devn 4E 11
Combe Down. Bath 5C 34
Combe Fishacre. Devn 2E 9
Combe Florey. Som 3E 21
Combe Hay. Bath 5C 34
Combeinteignhead. Devn 5C 12
Combe Martin. Devn 2F 19
Combe Moor. Here 4F 59
Comber. Ards 3J 179
Combe Raleigh. Devn 2E 13
Comberbach. Ches W 3A 84
Comberford. Staf 5F 73
Comberton. Cambs 5C 64
Comberton. Here 4G 59
Combe St Nicholas. Som 1G 13
Combpyne. Devn 3F 13
Combridge. Staf 2E 73
Combrook. Warw 5H 61
Combs. Derbs 3E 85
Combs. Suff 5C 66
Combs Ford. Suff 5C 66
Combwich. Som 2F 21
Comers. Abers 3D 152
Comhampton. Worc 4C 60
Comins Coch. Cdgn 2F 57
Comley. Shrp 1G 59
Commercial End. Cambs 4E 65
Commins. Powy 3D 70
Commins Coch. Powy 5H 69
Common, The. Wilts
nr. Salisbury 3H 23
nr. Swindon 3F 35
Commondale. N Yor 3D 106
Common End. Cumb 2B 102
Common Hill. Here 2A 48
Common Moor. Corn 2G 7
Commonside. Ches W 3H 83
Common Side. Derbs 3H 85
Commonside. Derbs 1G 73
Compstall. G Man 1D 84
Compton. Devn 2E 9
Compton. Hants 4C 24
Compton. Staf 2C 60
Compton. Surr 1A 26
Compton. W Ber 4D 36
Compton. W Sus 1F 17
Compton. Wilts 1G 23
Compton Abbas. Dors 1D 15
Compton Abdale. Glos 4F 49
Compton Bassett. Wilts 4F 35
Compton Beauchamp. Oxon 3A 36
Compton Bishop. Som 1G 21
Compton Chamberlayne. Wilts 4F 23
Compton Dando. Bath 5B 34
Compton Dundon. Som 3H 21
Compton Greenfield. S Glo 3A 34
Compton Martin. Bath 1A 22
Compton Pauncefoot. Som 4B 22
Compton Valence. Dors 3A 14
Comrie. Fife 1D 128
Comrie. Per 1G 135
Conaglen. High 2E 141
Conchra. Arg 1B 126
Conchra. High 1A 148
Conder Green. Lanc 4D 96
Conderton. Worc 2E 49
Condicote. Glos 3G 49
Condorrat. N Lan 2A 128
Condover. Shrp 5G 71
Coneyhurst. W Sus 3C 26
Coneyisland. New M 6K 179
Coneysthorpe. N Yor 2B 100
Coneythorpe. N Yor 4F 99
Coney Weston. Suff 3B 66
Conford. Hants 3G 25
Congdon's Shop. Corn 5C 10
Congerstone. Leics 5A 74
Congham. Norf 3G 77
Congleton. Ches E 4C 84
Congl-y-wal. Gwyn 1G 69
Congresbury. N Som 5H 33
Congreve. Staf 4D 72
Conham. S Glo 4B 34
Conicaval. Mor 3D 159
Coningsby. Linc 5B 88
Conington. Cambs
nr. Fenstanton 4C 64
nr. Sawtry 2A 64
Conisbrough. S Yor 1C 86
Conisby. Arg 3A 124
Conisholme. Linc 1D 88
Coniston. Cumb 5E 102
Coniston. E Yor 1E 95
Coniston Cold. N Yor 4B 98
Conistone. N Yor 3B 98
Conlig. Ards 2K 179
Connah's Quay. Flin 3E 83
Connel. Arg 5D 140
Connel Park. E Ayr 3F 117
Connista. High 1D 154
Connor. ME Ant 7H 175
Connor Downs. Corn 3C 4
Conock. Wilts 1F 23
Conon Bridge. High 3H 157
Cononley. N Yor 5B 98
Cononsyth. Ang 4E 145
Conordan. High 5E 155
Consall. Staf 1D 73
Consett. Dur 4E 115
Constable Burton. N Yor 5E 105
Constantine. Corn 4E 5
Constantine Bay. Corn 1C 6
Contin. High 3G 157
Contullich. High 1A 158
Conwy. Cnwy 3G 81
Conyer. Kent 4D 40
Conyer's Green. Suff 4A 66
Cooden. E Sus 5B 28
Cooil. IOM 4C 108
Cookbury. Devn 2E 11
Cookbury Wick. Devn 2D 11
Cookham. Wind 3G 37
Cookham Dean. Wind 3G 37
Cookham Rise. Wind 3G 37
Cookhill. Worc 5E 61
Cookley. Suff 3F 67
Cookley. Worc 2C 60
Cookley Green. Oxon 2E 37
Cookney. Abers 4F 153
Cooksbridge. E Sus 4F 27
Cooksey Green. Worc 4D 60
Cookshill. Staf 1D 72
Cooksmill Green. Essx 5G 53
Cookstown. M Ulst 2C 178
Coolham. W Sus 3C 26
Cooling. Medw 3B 40
Cooling Street. Medw 3B 40
Coombe. Corn
nr. Bude 1C 10
nr. St Austell 3D 6
nr. Truro 4C 6
Coombe. Devn
nr. Sidmouth 3E 12
nr. Teignmouth 5C 12
Coombe. Glos 2C 34
Coombe. Hants 4E 25
Coombe. Wilts 1G 23
Coombe Bissett. Wilts 4G 23
Coombe Hill. Glos 3D 49
Coombe Keynes. Dors 4D 14
Coombes. W Sus 5C 26
Coopersale. Essx 5E 53
Coopersale Street. Essx 5E 53
Cooper's Corner. Kent 1F 27
Cooper Street. Kent 5H 41
Cootham. W Sus 4B 26
Copalder Corner. Cambs 1C 64
Copdock. Suff 1E 54
Copford. Essx 3C 54
Copford Green. Essx 3C 54
Copgrove. N Yor 3F 99
Copister. Shet 4F 173
Cople. Bed 1B 52
Copley. Dur 2D 105
Coplow Dale. Derbs 3F 85
Copmanthorpe. York 5H 99
Copp. Lanc 1C 90
Coppathorne. Corn 2C 10
Coppenhall. Ches E 5B 84
Coppenhall. Staf 4D 72
Coppenhall Moss. Ches E 5B 84
Copperhouse. Corn 3C 4
Coppicegate. Shrp 2B 60
Coppingford. Cambs 2A 64
Copplestone. Devn 2A 12
Coppull. Lanc 3D 90
Coppull Moor. Lanc 3D 90
Copsale. W Sus 3C 26
Copshaw Holm. Bord 1F 113
Copster Green. Lanc 1E 91
Copston Magna. Warw 2B 62
Copt Green. Warw 4F 61
Copthall Green. Essx 5E 53
Copt Heath. W Mid 3F 61
Copt Hewick. N Yor 2F 99
Copthill. Dur 5B 114
Copthorne. W Sus 2E 27
Coptiviney. Shrp 2G 71
Copy's Green. Norf 2B 78
Copythorne. Hants 1B 16
Corbridge. Nmbd 3C 114
Corby. Nptn 2F 63
Corby Glen. Linc 3G 75
Cordon. N Ayr 2E 123
Coreley. Shrp 3A 60
Corfe. Som 1F 13
Corfe Castle. Dors 4E 15
Corfe Mullen. Dors 3E 15
Corfton. Shrp 2G 59
Corgarff. Abers 3G 151
Corhampton. Hants 4E 24
Corkey. Caus 4G 175
Corlae. Dum 5F 117
Corlannau. Neat 2A 32
Corley. Warw 2H 61
Corley Ash. Warw 2G 61
Corley Moor. Warw 2G 61
Cormiston. S Lan 1C 118
Cornaa. IOM 3D 108
Cornaigbeg. Arg 4A 138
Cornaigmore. Arg
on Coll 2D 138
on Tiree 4A 138
Corner Row. Lanc 1C 90
Corney. Cumb 5C 102
Cornforth. Dur 1A 106
Cornhill. Abers 3C 160
Cornhill. High 4C 164
Cornhill-on-Tweed. Nmbd 1C 120
Cornholme. W Yor 2H 91
Cornish Hall End. Essx 2G 53
Cornquoy. Orkn 7E 172
Cornriggs. Dur 5B 114
Cornsay. Dur 5E 115
Cornsay Colliery. Dur 5E 115
Corntown. High 3H 157
Corntown. V Glam 4C 32
Cornwell. Oxon 3A 50
Cornwood. Devn 3C 8
Cornworthy. Devn 3E 9
Corpach. High 1E 141
Corpusty. Norf 3D 78
Corra. Dum 3F 111
Corran. High
nr. Arnisdale 2E 141
nr. Fort William 3A 148
Corrany. IOM 3D 108
Corribeg. High 1D 141
Corrie. N Ayr 5B 126
Corrie Common. Dum 1D 112
Corriecravie. N Ayr 3D 122
Corriekinloch. High 1A 164
Corriemoillie. High 2F 157
Corrievarkie Lodge. Per 1C 142
Corrievorrie. High 1B 150
Corrigall. Orkn 6C 172
Corrimony. High 5F 157
Corringham. Linc 1F 87
Corringham. Thur 2B 40
Corris. Gwyn 5G 69
Corris Uchaf. Gwyn 5G 69
Corrour Shooting Lodge. High 2B 142
Corry. High 1E 147
Corrybrough. High 1C 150
Corrygills. N Ayr 2E 123
Corry of Ardnagrask. High 4H 157
Corsback. High
nr. Dunnet 1E 169
nr. Halkirk 3E 169
Corscombe. Dors 2A 14
Corse. Abers 4D 160
Corse. Glos 3C 48
Corsehill. Abers 3G 161
Corse Lawn. Worc 2D 48
Corse of Kinnoir. Abers 4C 160
Corsham. Wilts 4D 34
Corsley. Wilts 2D 22
Corsley Heath. Wilts 2D 22
Corsock. Dum 2E 111
Corston. Bath 5B 34
Corston. Wilts 3E 35
Corstorphine. Edin 2F 129
Cortachy. Ang 3C 144
Corton. Suff 1H 67
Corton. Wilts 2E 23
Corton Denham. Som 4B 22
Corwar House. S Ayr 1H 109
Corwen. Den 1C 70
Coryates. Dors 4B 14
Coryton. Devn 4E 11
Coryton. Thur 2B 40
Cosby. Leics 1C 62
Coscote. Oxon 3D 36
Coseley. W Mid 1D 60
Cosgrove. Nptn 1F 51
Cosham. Port 2E 17
Cosheston. Pemb 4E 43
Coskills. N Lin 3D 94
Cosmeston. V Glam 5E 33
Cossall. Notts 1B 74
Cossington. Leics 4D 74
Cossington. Som 2G 21
Costa. Orkn 5C 172
Costessey. Norf 4D 78
Costock. Notts 3C 74
Coston. Leics 3F 75
Coston. Norf 5C 78
Cote. Oxon 5B 50
Cotebrook. Ches W 4H 83
Cotehill. Cumb 4F 113
Cotes. Cumb 1D 97
Cotes. Leics 3C 74
Cotes. Staf 2C 72
Cotesbach. Leics 2C 62
Cotes Heath. Staf 2C 72
Cotford St Luke. Som 4E 21
Cotgrave. Notts 2D 74
Cothal. Abers 2F 153
Cotham. Notts 1E 75
Cothelstone. Som 3E 21
Cotheridge. Worc 5B 60
Cotherstone. Dur 3D 104
Cothill. Oxon 2C 36
Cotland. Mon 5A 48
Cotleigh. Devn 2F 13
Cotmanhay. Derbs 1B 74
Coton. Cambs 5D 64
Coton. Nptn 3D 62
Coton. Staf
nr. Gnosall 3C 72
nr. Stone 2D 73
nr. Tamworth 5F 73
Coton Clanford. Staf 3C 72
Coton Hayes. Staf 2D 73
Coton Hill. Shrp 4G 71
Coton in the Clay. Staf 3F 73
Coton in the Elms. Derbs 4G 73
Cotonwood. Shrp 2H 71
Cotonwood. Staf 3C 72
Cott. Devn 2D 9
Cott. Orkn 5F 172
Cottam. E Yor 3D 101
Cottam. Lanc 1D 90
Cottam. Notts 3F 87
Cottartown. High 5E 159
Cottarville. Nptn 4E 63
Cottenham. Cambs 4D 64
Cotterdale. N Yor 5B 104
Cottered. Herts 3D 52
Cotterstock. Nptn 1H 63
Cottesbrooke. Nptn 3E 62
Cottesmore. Rut 4G 75
Cotteylands. Devn 1C 12
Cottingham. E Yor 1D 94
Cottingham. Nptn 1F 63
Cottingley. W Yor 1B 92
Cottisford. Oxon 2D 50
Cotton. Staf 1E 73
Cotton. Suff 4C 66
Cotton End. Bed 1A 52
Cottown. Abers 4F 161
Cotts. Devn 2A 8
Cotwalton. Staf 2D 72
Couch's Mill. Corn 3F 7
Coughton. Here 3A 48
Coughton. Warw 4E 61
Coulags. High 4B 156
Coulby Newham. Midd 3C 106
Coulderton. Cumb 4A 102
Coulin Lodge. High 3C 156
Coull. Abers 3C 152
Coulport. Arg 1D 126
Coulsdon. G Lon 5D 39
Coulston. Wilts 1E 23
Coulter. S Lan 1C 118
Coultings. Som 2F 21
Coulton. N Yor 2A 100
Cound. Shrp 5H 71
Coundon. Dur 2F 105
Coundon Grange. Dur 2F 105
Countersett. N Yor 1B 98
Countess. Wilts 2G 23
Countess Cross. Essx 2B 54
Countesthorpe. Leics 1C 62
Countisbury. Devn 2H 19
Coupar Angus. Per 4B 144
Coupe Green. Lanc 2D 90
Coupland. Cumb 3A 104
Coupland. Nmbd 1D 120
Cour. Arg 5G 125
Courance. Dum 5C 118
Court-at-Street. Kent 2E 29
Courteachan. High 4E 147
Courteenhall. Nptn 5E 63
Court Henry. Carm 3F 45
Courtsend. Essx 1E 41
Courtway. Som 3F 21
Cousland. Midl 3G 129
Cousley Wood. E Sus 2A 28
Coustonn. Arg 2B 126
Cove. Arg 1D 126
Cove. Devn 1C 12
Cove. Hants 1G 25
Cove. High 4C 162
Cove. Bord 2D 130
Cove Bay. Aber 3G 153
Covehithe. Suff 2H 67
Coven. Staf 5D 72
Coveney. Cambs 2D 65
Covenham St Bartholomew. Linc 1C 88
Covenham St Mary. Linc 1C 88
Coven Heath. Staf 5D 72
Coventry. W Mid 194 (3H 61)
Coverack. Corn 5E 5
Coverham. N Yor 1D 98
Covesea. Mor 1F 159
Covingham. Swin 3G 35
Covington. Cambs 3H 63
Covington. S Lan 1B 118
Cowan Bridge. Lanc 2F 97
Cowan Head. Cumb 5F 103
Cowbar. Red C 3E 107
Cowbeech. E Sus 4H 27
Cowbit. Linc 4B 76
Cowbridge. V Glam 4C 32
Cowden. Kent 1F 27
Cowdenbeath. Fife 4D 136
Cowdenburn. Bord 4F 129
Cowdenend. Fife 4D 136
Cowers Lane. Derbs 1H 73
Cowes. IOW 3C 16
Cowesby. N Yor 1G 99
Cowfold. W Sus 3D 26
Cowfords. Mor 2H 159
Cowgill. Cumb 1G 97
Cowie. Abers 5F 153
Cowie. Stir 1B 128
Cowlam. E Yor 3D 100
Cowley. Devn 3C 12
Cowley. Glos 4E 49
Cowley. G Lon 2B 38
Cowley. Oxon 5D 50
Cowley. Staf 4C 72
Cowleymoor. Devn 1C 12
Cowling. Lanc 3D 90
Cowling. N Yor
nr. Bedale 1E 99
nr. Glusburn 5B 98
Cowlinge. Suff 5G 65
Cowmes. W Yor 3B 92
Cowpe. Lanc 2G 91
Cowpen. Nmbd 1F 115
Cowpen Bewley. Stoc T 2B 106
Cowplain. Hants 1E 17
Cowshill. Dur 5B 114
Cowslip Green. N Som 5H 33
Cowstrandburn. Fife 4C 136
Cowthorpe. N Yor 4G 99
Coxall. Here 3F 59
Coxbank. Ches E 1A 72
Coxbench. Derbs 1A 74
Cox Common. Suff 2G 67
Coxford. Norf 3H 77
Coxgreen. Staf 2C 60
Cox Green. Surr 2B 26
Cox Green. Tyne 4G 115
Coxheath. Kent 5B 40
Coxhoe. Dur 1A 106
Coxley. Som 2A 22
Coxwold. N Yor 2H 99
Coychurch. B'end 3C 32
Coylton. S Ayr 3D 116
Coylumbridge. High 2D 150
Coynach. Abers 3B 152
Coynachie. Abers 5B 160
Coytrahen. B'end 3B 32
Crabbs Cross. Worc 4E 61
Crabgate. Norf 3C 78
Crab Orchard. Dors 2F 15
Crabtree. W Sus 3D 26
Crabtree Green. Wrex 1F 71
Crackaig. High 2G 165
Crackenthorpe. Cumb 2H 103
Crackington Haven. Corn 3B 10
Crackley. Staf 5C 84
Crackley. Warw 3G 61
Crackleybank. Shrp 4B 72
Crackpot. N Yor 5C 104
Cracoe. N Yor 3B 98
Craddock. Devn 1D 12
Cradhlastadh. W Isl 4C 171
Cradley. Here 1C 48
Cradley. W Mid 2D 60
Cradoc. Powy 2D 46
Crafthole. Corn 3H 7
Crafton. Buck 4G 51
Cragabus. Arg 5B 124
Crag Foot. Lanc 2D 97
Craggan. High 1E 151
Cragganmore. Mor 5F 159
Cragganvallie. High 5H 157
Craggie. High 2F 165
Craggiemore. High 5B 158
Cragg Vale. W Yor 2A 92
Craghead. Dur 4F 115
Crai. Powy 3B 46
Craichie. Ang 4E 145
Craig. Arg 5E 141
Craig. Dum 2D 111
Craig. High
nr. Achnashellach 4C 156
nr. Lower Diabaig 2G 155
nr. Stromeferry 5H 155
Craiganour Lodge. Per 3D 142
Craigavon. Arm 4E 178
Craigbrack. Arg 4A 134
Craig-Cefn-Parc. Swan 5G 45
Craigdallie. Per 1E 137
Craigdam. Abers 5F 161
Craigdarragh. Derr 6B 174
Craigdarroch. E Ayr 4F 117
Craigdarroch. High 3G 157
Craigdhu. High 4G 157
Craigearn. Abers 2E 152
Craigellachie. Mor 4G 159
Craigend. Per 1D 136
Craigendoran. Arg 1E 126
Craigends. Ren 3F 127
Craigenputtock. Dum 1E 111
Craigens. E Ayr 3E 117
Craighall. Edin 2E 129
Craighead. Fife 2H 137
Craighouse. Arg 3D 124
Craigie. Abers 2G 153
Craigie. D'dee 5D 144
Craigie. Per
nr. Blairgowrie 4A 144
nr. Perth 1D 136
Craigie. S Ayr 1D 116
Craigielaw. E Lot 2A 130
Craiglemine. Dum 5B 110
Craig-llwyn. Shrp 3E 71
Craiglockhart. Edin 2F 129
Craig Lodge. Arg 2B 126
Craigmalloch. E Ayr 5D 117
Craigmaud. Abers 3F 161
Craigmill. Stir 4H 135
Craigmillar. Edin 2F 129
Craigmore. Arg 3C 126
Craigmuie. Dum 1E 111
Craignair. Dum 3F 111
Craignant. Shrp 2E 71
Craigneuk. N Lan
nr. Airdrie 3A 128
nr. Motherwell 4A 128
Craignure. Arg 5B 140
Craigo. Ang 2F 145
Craigrory. High 4A 158
Craigrothie. Fife 2F 137
Craigs. Dum 2D 112
Craigs, The. High 4B 164
Craigshill. W Lot 3D 128
Craigton. Aber 3F 153
Craigton. Abers 3E 152
Craigton. Ang
nr. Carnoustie 5E 145
nr. Kirriemuir 3C 144
Craigton. High 4A 158
Craigtown. High 3A 168
Craig-y-Duke. Neat 5H 45
Craig-y-nos. Powy 4B 46
Craik. Bord 4F 119
Crail. Fife 3H 137
Crailing. Bord 2A 120
Crailinghall. Bord 2A 120
Crakehill. N Yor 2G 99
Crakemarsh. Staf 2E 73
Crambe. N Yor 3B 100
Crambeck. N Yor 3B 100
Cramlington. Nmbd 2F 115
Cramond. Edin 2E 129
Cramond Bridge. Edin 2E 129
Cranage. Ches E 4B 84
Cranagh. Derr 7B 174
Cranberry. Staf 2C 72
Cranborne. Dors 1F 15
Cranbourne. Brac 3A 38
Cranbrook. Devn 3D 12
Cranbrook. Kent 2B 28
Cranbrook Common. Kent 2B 28
Crane Moor. S Yor 4D 92
Crane's Corner. Norf 4B 78
Cranfield. C Beds 1H 51
Cranford. G Lon 3C 38
Cranford St Andrew. Nptn 3G 63
Cranford St John. Nptn 3G 63
Cranham. Glos 4D 49
Cranham. G Lon 2G 39
Crank. Mers 1H 83
Cranleigh. Surr 2B 26
Cranley. Suff 3D 66
Cranloch. Mor 3G 159
Cranmer Green. Suff 3C 66
Cranmore. IOW 3C 16
Cranmore. Linc 5A 76
Crannich. Arg 4G 139
Crannoch. Mor 3B 160
Cranoe. Leics 1E 63
Cransford. Suff 4F 67
Cranshaws. Bord 3C 130
Cranstal. IOM 1D 108
Crantock. Corn 2B 6
Cranwell. Linc 1H 75
Cranwich. Norf 1G 65
Cranworth. Norf 5B 78
Craobh Haven. Arg 3E 133
Craobhnaclag. High 4G 157
Crapstone. Devn 2B 8
Crarae. Arg 4G 133
Crask. High
nr. Bettyhill 2H 167
nr. Lairg 1C 164
Crask of Aigas. High 4G 157
Craster. Nmbd 2G 121
Craswall. Here 2F 47
Cratfield. Suff 3F 67
Crathes. Abers 4E 153
Crathie. Abers 4G 151
Crathie. High 4H 149
Crathorne. N Yor 4B 106
Craven Arms. Shrp 2G 59
Crawcrook. Tyne 3E 115
Crawford. Lanc 4C 90
Crawford. S Lan 2B 118
Crawforddyke. S Lan 4B 128
Crawfordjohn. S Lan 2A 118
Crawfordsburn. Ards 1J 179
Crawick. Dum 3G 117
Crawley. Devn 2F 13
Crawley. Hants 3C 24
Crawley. Oxon 4B 50
Crawley. W Sus 2D 26
Crawley Down. W Sus 2E 27
Crawley End. Essx 1E 53
Crawley Side. Dur 5C 114
Crawshawbooth. Lanc 2G 91
Crawton. Abers 5F 153
Cray. N Yor 2B 98
Cray. Per 2A 144
Crayford. G Lon 3G 39
Crayke. N Yor 2H 99
Craymere Beck. Norf 2C 78
Crays Hill. Essx 1B 40
Cray's Pond. Oxon 3E 37
Crazies Hill. Wok 3F 37
Creacombe. Devn 1B 12
Creagan. Arg 4D 140
Creag Aoil. High 1F 141
Creag Ghoraidh. W Isl 4C 170
Creaguaineach Lodge. High 2H 141
Creamore Bank. Shrp 2H 71
Creaton. Nptn 3E 62
Creca. Dum 2D 112
Credenhill. Here 1H 47
Crediton. Devn 2B 12
Creebridge. Dum 3B 110
Creech. Dors 4E 15
Creech Heathfield. Som 4F 21
Creech St Michael. Som 4F 21
Creed. Corn 4D 6
Creekmoor. Pool 3E 15
Creekmouth. G Lon 2F 39
Creeting St Mary. Suff 5C 66
Creeting St Peter. Suff 5C 66
Creeton. Linc 3H 75
Creetown. Dum 4B 110
Creggan. Ferm 2A 178
Creggan. New M 8D 178
Creggans. Arg 3H 133
Cregneash. IOM 5A 108
Cregrina. Powy 5D 58
Creich. Arg 2B 132
Creich. Fife 1F 137
Creighton. Staf 2E 73
Creigiau. Card 3D 32
Cremyll. Corn 3A 8
Crendell. Dors 1F 15
Crepkill. High 4D 154
Cressage. Shrp 5H 71
Cressbrook. Derbs 3F 85
Cresselly. Pemb 4E 43
Cressing. Essx 3A 54
Cresswell. Nmbd 5G 121
Cresswell. Staf 2D 73
Cresswell Quay. Pemb 4E 43
Creswell. Derbs 3C 86
Creswell Green. Staf 4E 73
Cretingham. Suff 4E 67
Crewe. Ches E 5B 84
Crewe-by-Farndon. Ches W 5G 83
Crewgreen. Powy 4F 71
Crewkerne. Som 2H 13
Crews Hill. G Lon 5D 52
Crewton. Derb 2A 74
Crianlarich. Stir 1C 134
Cribbs Causeway. S Glo 3A 34
Cribyn. Cdgn 5E 57
Criccieth. Gwyn 2D 69
Crich. Derbs 5A 86
Crichton. Midl 3G 129
Crick. Mon 2H 33
Crick. Nptn 3C 62
Crickadarn. Powy 1D 46
Cricket Hill. Hants 5G 37
Cricket Malherbie. Som 1G 13
Cricket St Thomas. Som 2G 13
Crickham. Som 2H 21
Crickheath. Shrp 3E 71
Crickhowell. Powy 4F 47
Cricklade. Wilts 2G 35
Cricklewood. G Lon 2D 38
Cridling Stubbs. N Yor 2F 93
Crieff. Per 1A 136
Criftins. Shrp 2F 71
Criggion. Powy 4E 71
Crigglestone. W Yor 3D 92
Crimchard. Som 2G 13
Crimdon Park. Dur 1B 106
Crimond. Abers 3H 161
Crimonmogate. Abers 3H 161
Crimplesham. Norf 5F 77
Crimscote. Warw 1H 49
Crinan. Arg 4E 133
Cringleford. Norf 5D 78
Crinow. Pemb 3F 43
Cripplesease. Corn 3C 4
Cripplestyle. Dors 1F 15
Cripp's Corner. E Sus 3B 28
Croanford. Corn 5A 10
Crockenhill. Kent 4G 39
Crocker End. Oxon 3F 37
Crockerhill. Hants 2D 16
Crockernwell. Devn 3A 12
Crocker's Ash. Here 4A 48
Crockerton. Wilts 2D 22
Crocketford. Dum 2F 111
Crockey Hill. York 5A 100
Crockham Hill. Kent 5F 39
Crockhurst Street. Kent 1H 27
Crockleford Heath. Essx 3D 54
Croeserw. Neat 2B 32
Croes-Goch. Pemb 1C 42
Croes Hywel. Mon 4G 47
Croes-lan. Cdgn 1D 45
Croesor. Gwyn 1F 69
Croesoswallt. Shrp 3E 71
Croesyceiliog. Carm 4E 45
Croesyceiliog. Torf 2G 33
Croes-y-mwyalch. Torf 2G 33
Croesywaun. Gwyn 5E 81
Croford. Som 4E 20
Croft. Leics 1C 62
Croft. Linc 4E 89
Croft. Warr 1A 84
Croftamie. Stir 1F 127
Croftfoot. Glas 3G 127
Croftmill. Per 5F 143
Crofton. Cumb 4E 112
Crofton. W Yor 3D 93
Crofton. Wilts 5A 36
Croft-on-Tees. N Yor 4F 105
Crofts. Dum 2E 111
Crofts of Benachielt. High 5D 169
Crofts of Dipple. Mor 3H 159
Crofty. Swan 3E 31
Croggan. Arg 1E 132
Croglin. Cumb 5G 113
Croich. High 4B 164
Croick. High 3A 168
Croig. Arg 3E 139
Cromarty. High 2B 158
Crombie. Fife 1D 128
Cromdale. High 1E 151
Cromer. Herts 3C 52
Cromer. Norf 1E 78
Cromford. Derbs 5G 85
Cromhall. S Glo 2B 34
Cromor. W Isl 5G 171
Cromra. High 5H 149
Cromwell. Notts 4E 87
Cronberry. E Ayr 2F 117
Crondall. Hants 2F 25
Cronk, The. IOM 2C 108
Cronk-y-Voddy. IOM 3C 108
Cronton. Mers 2G 83
Crook. Cumb 5F 103
Crook. Dur 1E 105
Crookdake. Cumb 5C 112
Crooke. G Man 4D 90
Crookedholm. E Ayr 1D 116
Crooked Soley. Wilts 4B 36
Crookes. S Yor 2H 85
Crookgate Bank. Dur 4E 115
Crookhall. Dur 4E 115
Crookham. Nmbd 1D 120
Crookham. W Ber 5D 36
Crookham Village. Hants 1F 25
Crooklands. Cumb 1E 97
Crook of Devon. Per 3C 136
Crookston. Glas 3G 127
Cropredy. Oxon 1C 50
Cropston. Leics 4C 74
Cropthorne. Worc 1E 49
Cropton. N Yor 1B 100
Cropwell Bishop. Notts 2D 74
Cropwell Butler. Notts 2D 74
Cros. W Isl 1H 171
Crosbie. N Ayr 4D 126
Crosbost. W Isl 5F 171
Crosby. Cumb 1B 102
Crosby. IOM 4C 108
Crosby. Mers 1F 83
Crosby. N Lin 3B 94
Crosby Court. N Yor 5A 106
Crosby Garrett. Cumb 4A 104
Crosby Ravensworth. Cumb 3H 103
Crosby Villa. Cumb 1B 102
Croscombe. Som 2A 22
Crosland Moor. W Yor 3B 92
Cross. Som 1H 21
Crossaig. Arg 4G 125
Crossapol. Arg 4A 138
Cross Ash. Mon 4H 47
Cross-at-Hand. Kent 1B 28
Crossbush. W Sus 5B 26
Crosscanonby. Cumb 1B 102
Crossdale Street. Norf 2E 79
Cross End. Essx 2B 54
Crossens. Mers 2B 90
Crossford. Fife 1D 128
Crossford. S Lan 5B 128
Cross Foxes. Gwyn 4G 69
Crossgar. New M 4J 179
Crossgate. Orkn 6D 172
Crossgate. Staf 2D 72
Crossgatehall. E Lot 3G 129
Crossgates. Fife 1E 129
Crossgates. N Yor 1E 101
Crossgates. Powy 4C 58
Cross Gates. W Yor 1D 92
Crossgill. Lanc 3E 97
Cross Green. Devn 4D 11
Cross Green. Staf 5D 72

Cross Green—Dovercourt

Cross Green. Suff
nr. Cockfield 5A 66
nr. Hitcham 5B 66
Cross Hands. Carm 4F 45
Crosshands. Carm 2F 43
Crosshands. E Ayr 1D 117
Cross Hill. Derbs 1B 74
Crosshill. E Ayr 2D 117
Crosshill. Fife 4D 136
Cross Hill. Glos 2A 34
Crosshill. S Ayr 4C 116
Crosshills. High 1A 158
Cross Hills. N Yor 5C 98
Cross Holme. N Yor 5C 106
Crosshouse. E Ayr 1C 116
Cross Houses. Shrp 5H 71
Crossings. Cumb 2G 113
Cross in Hand. E Sus 3G 27
Cross Inn. Cdgn
nr. Aberaeron 4E 57
nr. New Quay 5C 56
Cross Inn. Rhon 3D 32
Crosskeys. Cphy 2F 33
Crosskirk. High 2C 168
Crosslands. Cumb 1C 96
Cross Lane Head. Shrp 1B 60
Cross Lanes. Corn 4D 5
Cross Lanes. Dur 3D 104
Cross Lanes. N Yor 3H 99
Crosslanes. Shrp 4F 71
Cross Lanes. Wrex 1F 71
Crosslee. Ren 3F 127
Crossmaglen. New M 8D 178
Crossmichael. Dum 3E 111
Crossmoor. Lanc 1C 90
Crossnacreevy. Lis 3H 179
Cross Oak. Powy 3E 46
Cross of Jackston. Abers 5E 161
Cross o' th' Hands. Derbs 1G 73
Crossroads. Abers
nr. Aberdeen 3G 153
nr. Banchory 4E 153
Crossroads. E Ayr 1D 116
Cross Side. Devn 4B 20
Cross Street. Suff 3D 66
Crosston. Ang 3E 145
Cross Town. Ches E 3B 84
Crossway. Mon 4H 47
Crossway. Powy 5C 58
Crossway Green. Mon 2A 34
Crossway Green. Worc 4C 60
Crossways. Dors 4C 14
Crosswell. Pemb 1F 43
Crosswood. Cdgn 3F 57
Crosthwaite. Cumb 5F 103
Croston. Lanc 3C 90
Crostwick. Norf 4E 79
Crostwight. Norf 3F 79
Crothair. W Isl 4D 171
Crouch. Kent 5H 39
Croucheston. Wilts 4F 23
Crouch Hill. Dors 1C 14
Croughton. Nptn 2D 50
Crovie. Abers 2F 161
Crow. Hants 2G 15
Crowan. Corn 3D 4
Crowborough. E Sus 2G 27
Crowcombe. Som 3E 21
Crowcroft. Worc 5B 60
Crowdecote. Derbs 4F 85
Crowden. Derbs 1E 85
Crowden. Devn 3E 11
Crowdhill. Hants 1C 16
Crowdon. N Yor 5G 107
Crow Edge. S Yor 4B 92
Crow End. Cambs 5C 64
Crowfield. Nptn 1E 50
Crowfield. Suff 5D 66
Crow Green. Essx 1G 39
Crow Hill. Here 3B 48
Crowhurst. E Sus 4B 28
Crowhurst. Surr 1E 27
Crowhurst Lane End. Surr 1E 27
Crowland. Linc 4B 76
Crowland. Suff 3C 66
Crowlas. Corn 3C 4
Crowle. N Lin 3A 94
Crowle. Worc 5D 60
Crowle Green. Worc 5D 60
Crowmarsh Gifford. Oxon 3E 36
Crown Corner. Suff 3E 67
Crownthorpe. Norf 5C 78
Crowntown. Corn 3D 4
Crows-an-wra. Corn 4A 4
Crowshill. Norf 5B 78
Crowthorne. Brac 5G 37
Crowton. Ches W 3H 83
Croxall. Staf 4F 73
Croxby. Linc 1A 88
Croxdale. Dur 1F 105
Croxden. Staf 2E 73
Croxley Green. Herts 1B 38
Croxton. Cambs 4B 64
Croxton. Norf
nr. Fakenham 2B 78
nr. Thetford 2A 66
Croxton. N Lin 3D 94
Croxton. Staf 2B 72
Croxtonbank. Staf 2B 72
Croxton Green. Ches E 5H 83
Croxton Kerrial. Leics 3F 75
Croy. High 4B 158
Croy. N Lan 2A 128
Croyde. Devn 3E 19
Croydon. Cambs 1D 52
Croydon. G Lon 4E 39
Crubenbeg. High 4A 150
Crubenmore Lodge. High 4A 150
Cruckmeole. Shrp 5G 71
Cruckton. Shrp 4G 71
Cruden Bay. Abers 5H 161
Crudgington. Telf 4A 72
Crudie. Abers 3E 161
Crudwell. Wilts 2E 35
Cruft. Devn 3E 11
Crug. Powy 3D 58
Crughywel. Powy 4F 47
Crugmeer. Corn 1D 6
Crugybar. Carm 2G 45
Crug-y-byddar. Powy 2D 58
Crulabhig. W Isl 4D 171
Crumlin. Ant 2F 179
Crumlin. Cphy 2F 33
Crumpsall. G Man 4G 91
Crumpsbrook. Shrp 3A 60
Crundale. Kent 1E 29
Crundale. Pemb 3D 42
Cruwys Morchard. Devn 1B 12
Crux Easton. Hants 1C 24
Cruxton. Dors 3B 14
Crwbin. Carm 4E 45
Cryers Hill. Buck 2G 37
Crymych. Pemb 1F 43
Crynant. Neat 5A 46
Crystal Palace. G Lon 3E 39
Cuaich. High 5A 150
Cuaig. High 3G 155
Cuan. Arg 2E 133
Cubbington. Warw 4H 61
Cubert. Corn 3B 6
Cubley. S Yor 4C 92
Cubley Common. Derbs 2F 73
Cublington. Buck 3G 51
Cublington. Here 2G 47
Cuckfield. W Sus 3E 27
Cucklington. Som 4C 22
Cuckney. Notts 3C 86
Cuckron. Shet 6F 173
Cuddesdon. Oxon 5E 50
Cuddington. Buck 4F 51
Cuddington. Ches W 3A 84
Cuddington Heath. Ches W 1G 71
Cuddy Hill. Lanc 1C 90
Cudham. G Lon 5F 39
Cudlipptown. Devn 5F 11
Cudworth. Som 1G 13
Cudworth. S Yor 4D 93
Cudworth. Surr 1D 26
Cuerdley Cross. Warr 2H 83
Cuffley. Herts 5D 52
Cuidhir. W Isl 8B 170
Cuidhsiadar. W Isl 2H 171
Cuidhtinis. W Isl 9C 171
Culbo. High 2A 158
Culbokie. High 3A 158
Culburnie. High 4G 157
Culcabock. High 4A 158
Culcavy. Lis 3G 179
Culcharry. High 3C 158
Culcheth. Warr 1A 84
Culduie. High 4G 155
Culeave. High 4C 164
Culford. Suff 3H 65
Culgaith. Cumb 2H 103
Culham. Oxon 2D 36
Culkein. High 1E 163
Culkein Drumbeg. High 5B 166
Culkerton. Glos 2E 35
Cullaville. New M 8C 178
Cullen. Mor 2C 160
Cullercoats. Tyne 2G 115
Cullicudden. High 2A 158
Cullingworth. W Yor 1A 92
Cullipool. Arg 2E 133
Cullivoe. Shet 1G 173
Culloch. Per 2G 135
Culloden. High 4B 158
Cullompton. Devn 2D 12
Cullybackey. ME Ant 6G 175
Cullycapple. Caus 4E 174
Cullyhanna. New M 7D 178
Culm Davy. Devn 1E 13
Culmington. Shrp 2G 59
Culmore. Derr 4A 174
Culmstock. Devn 1E 12
Cul na Caepaich. High 5E 147
Culnacnoc. High 2E 155
Culnacraig. High 3E 163
Culnady. M Ulst 6E 174
Culrain. High 4C 164
Culross. Fife 1C 128
Culroy. S Ayr 3C 116
Culswick. Shet 7D 173
Cults. Aber 3F 153
Cults. Abers 5C 160
Cults. Fife 3F 137
Cultybraggan Camp. Per 1G 135
Culver. Devn 3B 12
Culverlane. Devn 2D 8
Culverstone Green. Kent 4H 39
Culverthorpe. Linc 1H 75
Culworth. Nptn 1D 50
Culzie Lodge. High 1H 157
Cumberlow Green. Herts 2D 52
Cumbernauld. N Lan 2A 128
Cumbernauld Village. N Lan 2A 128
Cumberworth. Linc 3E 89
Cumdivock. Cumb 5E 113
Cuminestown. Abers 3F 161
Cumledge Mill. Bord 4D 130
Cumlewick. Shet 9F 173
Cummersdale. Cumb 4E 113
Cummertrees. Dum 3C 112
Cummingstown. Mor 2F 159
Cumnock. E Ayr 2E 117
Cumnor. Oxon 5C 50
Cumrew. Cumb 4G 113
Cumwhinton. Cumb 4F 113
Cumwhitton. Cumb 4G 113
Cundall. N Yor 2G 99
Cunninghamhead. N Ayr 5E 127
Cunning Park. S Ayr 3C 116
Cunningsburgh. Shet 9F 173
Cunnister. Shet 2G 173
Cupar. Fife 2F 137
Cupar Muir. Fife 2F 137
Cupernham. Hants 4B 24
Curbar. Derbs 3G 85
Curborough. Staf 4F 73
Curbridge. Hants 1D 16
Curbridge. Oxon 5B 50
Curdridge. Hants 1D 16
Curdworth. Warw 1F 61
Curland. Som 1F 13
Curland Common. Som 1F 13
Curran. M Ulst 7E 174
Curridge. W Ber 4C 36
Currie. Edin 3E 129
Curry Mallet. Som 4G 21
Curry Rivel. Som 4G 21
Curtisden Green. Kent 1B 28
Curtisknowle. Devn 3D 8
Cury. Corn 4D 5
Cusgarne. Corn 4B 6
Cushendall. Caus 4J 175
Cushendun. Caus 3J 175
Cusop. Here 1F 47
Cusworth. S Yor 4F 93
Cutcombe. Som 3C 20
Cuthill. E Lot 2G 129
Cutiau. Gwyn 4F 69
Cutlers Green. Essx 2F 53
Cutmadoc. Corn 2E 7
Cutnall Green. Worc 4C 60
Cutsdean. Glos 2F 49
Cutthorpe. Derbs 3H 85
Cuttiford's Door. Som 1G 13
Cuttivett. Corn 2H 7
Cutts. Shet 8E 173
Cuttybridge. Pemb 3D 42
Cuttyhill. Abers 3H 161
Cuxham. Oxon 2E 37
Cuxton. Medw 4B 40
Cuxwold. Linc 4E 95
Cwm. Blae 5E 47
Cwm. Den 3C 82
Cwm. Powy 1E 59
Cwmafan. Neat 2A 32
Cwmaman. Rhon 2C 32
Cwmann. Carm 1F 45
Cwmbach. Carm 2G 43
Cwmbach. Powy 2E 47
Cwmbach. Rhon 5D 46
Cwmbach Llechrhyd. Powy 5C 58
Cwmbelan. Powy 2B 58
Cwmbran. Torf 2F 33
Cwmbrwyno. Cdgn 2G 57
Cwm Capel. Carm 5E 45
Cwmcarn. Cphy 2F 33
Cwmcarvan. Mon 5H 47
Cwm-celyn. Blae 5F 47
Cwmcerdinen. Swan 5G 45
Cwm-Cewydd. Gwyn 4A 70
Cwm-cou. Cdgn 1C 44
Cwmcych. Pemb 1G 43
Cwmdare. Rhon 5C 46
Cwmdu. Carm 2G 45
Cwmdu. Powy 3E 47
Cwmduad. Carm 2D 45
Cwm Dulais. Swan 5G 45
Cwmerfyn. Cdgn 2F 57
Cwmfelin. B'end 3B 32
Cwmfelin Boeth. Carm 3F 43
Cwmfelinfach. Cphy 2E 33
Cwmfelin Mynach. Carm 2G 43
Cwmffrwd. Carm 4E 45
Cwmgiedd. Powy 4A 46
Cwmgors. Neat 4H 45
Cwmgwili. Carm 4F 45
Cwmgwrach. Neat 5B 46
Cwmhiraeth. Carm 1H 43
Cwmifor. Carm 3G 45
Cwmisfael. Carm 4E 45
Cwm-Llinau. Powy 5H 69
Cwmllynfell. Neat 4H 45
Cwm-mawr. Carm 4F 45
Cwm-miles. Carm 2F 43
Cwmorgan. Carm 1G 43
Cwmparc. Rhon 2C 32
Cwm Penmachno. Cnwy 1G 69
Cwmpennar. Rhon 5D 46
Cwm Plysgog. Pemb 1B 44
Cwmrhos. Powy 3E 47
Cwmsychpant. Cdgn 1E 45
Cwmsyfiog. Cphy 5E 47
Cwmsymlog. Cdgn 2F 57
Cwmtillery. Blae 5F 47
Cwm-twrch Isaf. Powy 5A 46
Cwm-twrch Uchaf. Powy 4A 46
Cwmwysg. Powy 3B 46
Cwm-y-glo. Gwyn 4E 81
Cwmyoy. Mon 3G 47
Cwmystwyth. Cdgn 3G 57
Cwrt. Gwyn 5F 69
Cwrtnewydd. Cdgn 1E 45
Cwrt-y-Cadno. Carm 1G 45
Cydweli. Carm 5E 45
Cyffylliog. Den 5C 82
Cymau. Flin 5E 83
Cymer. Neat 2B 32
Cymmer. Neat 2B 32
Cymmer. Rhon 2D 32
Cyncoed. Card 3E 33
Cynghordy. Carm 2B 46
Cynheidre. Carm 5E 45
Cynonville. Neat 2B 32
Cynwyd. Den 1C 70
Cynwyl Elfed. Carm 3D 44
Cywarch. Gwyn 4A 70

D

Dacre. Cumb 2F 103
Dacre. N Yor 3D 98
Dacre Banks. N Yor 3D 98
Daddry Shield. Dur 1B 104
Dadford. Buck 2E 51
Dadlington. Leics 1B 62
Dafen. Carm 5F 45
Daffy Green. Norf 5B 78
Dagdale. Staf 2E 73
Dagenham. G Lon 2F 39
Daggons. Dors 1G 15
Daglingworth. Glos 5E 49
Dagnall. Buck 4H 51
Dagtail End. Worc 4E 61
Dail. Arg 5E 141
Dail Beag. W Isl 3E 171
Dail bho Dheas. W Isl 1G 171
Dailly. S Ayr 4B 116
Dail Mor. W Isl 3E 171
Dairsie. Fife 2G 137
Daisy Bank. W Mid 1E 61
Daisy Hill. G Man 4E 91
Daisy Hill. W Yor 1B 92
Dalabrog. W Isl 6C 170
Dalavich. Arg 2G 133
Dalbeattie. Dum 3F 111
Dalblair. E Ayr 3F 117
Dalbury. Derbs 2G 73
Dalby. IOM 4B 108
Dalby Wolds. Leics 3D 74
Dalchalm. High 3G 165
Dalcharn. High 3G 167
Dalchork. High 2C 164
Dalchreichart. High 2E 149
Dalchruin. Per 2G 135
Dalcross. High 4B 158
Dalderby. Linc 4B 88
Dale. Cumb 5G 113
Dale. Pemb 4C 42
Dale Abbey. Derbs 2B 74
Dalebank. Derbs 4A 86
Dale Bottom. Cumb 2D 102
Dale Head. Cumb 3F 103
Dalehouse. N Yor 3E 107
Dalelia. High 2B 140
Dale of Walls. Shet 6C 173
Dalgarven. N Ayr 5D 126
Dalgety Bay. Fife 1E 129
Dalginross. Per 1G 135
Dalguise. Per 4G 143
Dalhalvaig. High 3A 168
Dalham. Suff 4G 65
Dalintart. Arg 1F 133
Dalkeith. Midl 3G 129
Dallas. Mor 3F 159
Dalleagles. E Ayr 3E 117
Dall House. Per 3C 142
Dallinghoo. Suff 5E 67
Dallington. E Sus 4A 28
Dallow. N Yor 2D 98
Dalmally. Arg 1A 134
Dalmarnock. Glas 3H 127
Dalmellington. E Ayr 4D 117
Dalmeny. Edin 2E 129
Dalmigavie. High 2B 150
Dalmilling. S Ayr 2C 116
Dalmore. High
nr. Alness 2A 158
nr. Rogart 3E 164
Dalmuir. W Dun 2F 127
Dalmunach. Mor 4G 159
Dalnabreck. High 2B 140
Dalnacardoch Lodge. Per 1E 142
Dalnamein Lodge. Per 2E 143
Dalnaspidal Lodge. Per 1D 142
Dalnatrat. High 3D 140
Dalnavie. High 1A 158
Dalnawillan Lodge. High 4C 168
Dalness. High 3F 141
Dalnessie. High 2D 164
Dalqueich. Per 3C 136
Dalquhairn. S Ayr 5C 116
Dalreavoch. High 3E 165
Dalreoch. Per 2C 136
Dalry. Edin 2F 129
Dalry. N Ayr 5D 126
Dalrymple. E Ayr 3C 116
Dalscote. Nptn 5D 62
Dalserf. S Lan 4B 128
Dalsmirren. Arg 4A 122
Dalston. Cumb 4E 113
Dalswinton. Dum 1G 111
Dalton. Dum 2C 112
Dalton. Lanc 4C 90
Dalton. Nmbd
nr. Hexham 4C 114
nr. Ponteland 2E 115
Dalton. N Yor
nr. Richmond 4E 105
nr. Thirsk 2G 99
Dalton. S Lan 4H 127
Dalton. S Yor 1B 86
Dalton-in-Furness. Cumb 2B 96
Dalton-le-Dale. Dur 5H 115
Dalton Magna. S Yor 1B 86
Dalton-on-Tees. N Yor 4F 105
Dalton Piercy. Hart 1B 106
Daltot. Arg 1F 125
Dalvey. High 5F 159
Dalwhinnie. High 5A 150
Dalwood. Devn 2F 13
Damerham. Hants 1G 15
Damgate. Norf
nr. Acle 5G 79
nr. Martham 4G 79
Dam Green. Norf 2C 66
Damhead. Mor 3E 159
Danaway. Kent 4C 40
Danbury. Essx 5A 54
Danby. N Yor 4E 107
Danby Botton. N Yor 4D 107
Danby Wiske. N Yor 5A 106
Danderhall. Midl 3G 129
Danebank. Ches E 2D 85
Danebridge. Ches E 4D 84
Dane End. Herts 3D 52
Danehill. E Sus 3F 27
Danesford. Shrp 1B 60
Daneshill. Hants 1E 25
Danesmoor. Derbs 4B 86
Danestone. Aber 2G 153
Dangerous Corner. Lanc 3D 90
Daniel's Water. Kent 1D 28
Dan's Castle. Dur 1E 105
Danzey Green. Warw 4F 61
Dapple Heath. Staf 3E 73
Daren. Powy 4F 47
Darenth. Kent 3G 39
Daresbury. Hal 2H 83
Darfield. S Yor 4E 93
Dargate. Kent 4E 41
Dargill. Per 2A 136
Darite. Corn 2G 7
Darkley. Arm 6C 178
Darlaston. W Mid 1D 61
Darley. N Yor 4E 98
Darley Abbey. Derb 2H 73
Darley Bridge. Derbs 4G 85
Darley Dale. Derbs 4G 85
Darley Head. N Yor 4D 98
Darlingscott. Warw 1H 49
Darlington. Darl 3F 105
Darliston. Shrp 2H 71
Darlton. Notts 3E 87
Darmsden. Suff 5C 66
Darnall. S Yor 2A 86
Darnford. Abers 4E 153
Darnford. Staf 5F 73
Darnhall. Ches W 4A 84
Darnick. Bord 1H 119
Darowen. Powy 5H 69
Darra. Abers 4E 161
Darracott. Devn 3E 19
Darragh Cross. New M 4J 179
Darras Hall. Nmbd 2E 115
Darrington. W Yor 2E 93
Darrow Green. Norf 2E 67
Darsham. Suff 4G 67
Dartfield. Abers 3H 161
Dartford. Kent 3G 39
Dartford-Thurrock River Crossing. Kent 3G 39
Dartington. Devn 2D 9
Dartmeet. Devn 5G 11
Dartmouth. Devn 3E 9
Darton. S Yor 3D 92
Darvel. E Ayr 1E 117
Darwen. Bkbn 2E 91
Dassels. Herts 3D 53
Datchet. Wind 3A 38
Datchworth. Herts 4C 52
Datchworth Green. Herts 4C 52
Daubhill. G Man 4F 91
Dauntsey. Wilts 3E 35
Dauntsey Green. Wilts 3E 35
Dauntsey Lock. Wilts 3E 35
Dava. Mor 5E 159
Davenham. Ches W 3A 84
Daventry. Nptn 4C 62
Davidson's Mains. Edin 2F 129
Davidston. High 2B 158
Davidstow. Corn 4B 10
David's Well. Powy 3C 58
Davington. Dum 4E 119
Daviot. Abers 1E 153
Daviot. High 5B 158
Davyhulme. G Man 1B 84
Daw Cross. N Yor 4E 99
Dawdon. Dur 5H 115
Dawesgreen. Surr 1D 26
Dawley. Telf 5A 72
Dawlish. Devn 5C 12
Dawlish Warren. Devn 5C 12
Dawn. Cnwy 3A 82
Daws Heath. Essx 2C 40
Dawshill. Worc 5C 60
Daw's House. Corn 4D 10
Dawsmere. Linc 2D 76
Dayhills. Staf 2D 72
Dayhouse Bank. Worc 3D 60
Daylesford. Glos 3H 49
Daywall. Shrp 2E 71
Ddol. Flin 3D 82
Ddol Cownwy. Powy 4C 70
Deadman's Cross. C Beds 1B 52
Deadwater. Nmbd 5A 120
Deaf Hill. Dur 1A 106
Deal. Kent 5H 41
Dean. Cumb 2B 102
Dean. Devn
nr. Combe Martin 2G 19
nr. Lynton 2H 19
Dean. Dors 1E 15
Dean. Hants
nr. Bishop's Waltham 1D 16
nr. Winchester 3C 24
Dean. Oxon 3B 50
Dean. Som 2B 22
Dean Bank. Dur 1F 105
Deanburnhaugh. Bord 3F 119
Dean Cross. Devn 2F 19
Deane. Hants 1D 24
Deanich Lodge. High 5A 164
Deanland. Dors 1E 15
Deanlane End. W Sus 1F 17
Dean Park. Shrp 4A 60
Dean Prior. Devn 2D 8
Dean Row. Ches E 2C 84
Deans. W Lot 3D 128
Deanscales. Cumb 2B 102
Deanshanger. Nptn 1F 51
Deanston. Stir 3G 135
Dearham. Cumb 1B 102
Dearne Valley. S Yor 4D 93
Debach. Suff 5E 67
Debden. Essx 2F 53
Debden Green. Essx
nr. Loughton 1F 39
nr. Saffron Walden 2F 53
Debenham. Suff 4D 66
Dechmont. W Lot 2D 128
Deddington. Oxon 2C 50
Dedham. Essx 2D 54
Dedham Heath. Essx 2D 54
Deebank. Abers 4D 152
Deene. Nptn 1G 63
Deenethorpe. Nptn 1G 63
Deepcar. S Yor 1G 85
Deepcut. Surr 5A 38
Deepdale. Cumb 1G 97
Deepdale. N Lin 3D 94
Deepdale. N Yor 2A 98
Deeping Gate. Pet 5A 76
Deeping St James. Linc 4A 76
Deeping St Nicholas. Linc 4B 76
Deerhill. Mor 3B 160
Deerhurst. Glos 3D 48
Deerhurst Walton. Glos 3D 49
Deerness. Orkn 7E 172
Defford. Worc 1E 49
Defynnog. Powy 3C 46
Deganwy. Cnwy 3G 81
Deighton. N Yor 4A 106
Deighton. W Yor 3B 92
Deighton. York 5A 100
Deiniolen. Gwyn 4E 81
Delabole. Corn 4A 10
Delamere. Ches W 4H 83
Delfour. High 3C 150
Dell, The. Suff 1G 67
Delliefure. High 5E 159
Delly End. Oxon 4B 50
Delny. High 1B 158
Delph. G Man 4H 91
Delves. Dur 5E 115
Delves, The. W Mid 1E 61
Delvin End. Essx 2A 54
Dembleby. Linc 2H 75
Demelza. Corn 2D 6
Den, The. N Ayr 4E 127
Denaby Main. S Yor 1B 86
Denbeath. Fife 4F 137
Denbigh. Den 4C 82
Denbury. Devn 2E 9
Denby. Derbs 1A 74
Denby Common. Derbs 1B 74
Denby Dale. W Yor 4C 92
Denchworth. Oxon 2B 36
Dendron. Cumb 2B 96
Deneside. Dur 5H 115
Denford. Nptn 3G 63
Dengie. Essx 5C 54
Denham. Buck 2B 38
Denham. Suff
nr. Bury St Edmunds 4G 65
nr. Eye 3D 66
Denham Green. Buck 2B 38
Denham Street. Suff 3D 66
Denhead. Abers
nr. Ellon 5G 161
nr. Strichen 3G 161
Denhead. Fife 2G 137
Denholm. Bord 3H 119
Denholme. W Yor 1A 92
Denholme Clough. W Yor 1A 92
Denholme Gate. W Yor 1A 92
Denio. Gwyn 2C 68
Denmead. Hants 1E 17
Dennington. Suff 4E 67
Denny. Falk 1B 128
Denny End. Cambs 4D 65
Dennyloanhead. Falk 1B 128
Den of Lindores. Fife 2E 137
Denshaw. G Man 3H 91
Denside. Abers 4F 153
Densole. Kent 1G 29
Denston. Suff 5G 65
Denstone. Staf 1F 73
Denstroude. Kent 4F 41
Dent. Cumb 1G 97
Denton. Cambs 2A 64
Denton. Darl 3F 105
Denton. E Sus 5F 27
Denton. G Man 1D 84
Denton. Kent 1G 29
Denton. Linc 2F 75
Denton. Norf 2E 67
Denton. Nptn 5F 63
Denton. N Yor 5D 98
Denton. Oxon 5D 50
Denver. Norf 5F 77
Denwick. Nmbd 3G 121
Deopham. Norf 5C 78
Deopham Green. Norf 1C 66
Depden. Suff 5G 65
Depden Green. Suff 5G 65
Deptford. G Lon 3E 39
Deptford. Wilts 3F 23
Derby. Derb 194 (2A 74)
Derbyhaven. IOM 5B 108
Derculich. Per 3F 143
Dereham. Norf 4B 78
Deri. Cphy 5E 47
Derril. Devn 2D 10
Derringstone. Kent 1G 29
Derrington. Shrp 1A 60
Derrington. Staf 3C 72
Derriton. Devn 2D 10
Derry. Derr 5A 174
Derryboye. New M 4J 179
Derrycrin. M Ulst 2D 178
Derrygonnelly. Ferm 7D 176
Derryguaig. Arg 5F 139
Derry Hill. Wilts 4E 35
Derrykeighan. Caus 3F 175
Derrylin. Ferm 7H 177
Derrymacash. Arm 4E 178
Derrythorpe. N Lin 4B 94
Derrytrasna. Arm 3D 178
Dersingham. Norf 2F 77
Dervaig. Arg 3F 139
Dervock. Caus 3F 175
Derwen. Den 5C 82
Derwen Gam. Cdgn 5D 56
Derwenlas. Powy 1G 57
Desborough. Nptn 2F 63
Desertmartin. M Ulst 7E 174
Desford. Leics 5B 74
Detchant. Nmbd 1E 121
Dethick. Derbs 5H 85
Detling. Kent 5B 40
Deuchar. Ang 2D 144
Deuddwr. Powy 4E 71
Devauden. Mon 2H 33
Devil's Bridge. Cdgn 3G 57
Devitts Green. Warw 1G 61
Devizes. Wilts 5F 35
Devonport. Plym 3A 8
Devonside. Clac 4B 136
Devoran. Corn 5B 6
Dewartown. Midl 3G 129
Dewlish. Dors 3C 14
Dewsall Court. Here 2H 47
Dewsbury. W Yor 2C 92
Dexbeer. Devn 2C 10
Dhoon. IOM 3D 108
Dhoor. IOM 2D 108
Dhowin. IOM 1D 108
Dial Green. W Sus 3A 26
Dial Post. W Sus 4C 26
Diamond, The. M Ulst 2D 178
Dibberford. Dors 2H 13
Dibden. Hants 2C 16
Dibden Purlieu. Hants 2C 16
Dickleburgh. Norf 2D 66
Didbrook. Glos 2F 49
Didcot. Oxon 2D 36
Diddington. Cambs 4A 64
Diddlebury. Shrp 2H 59
Didley. Here 2H 47
Didling. W Sus 1G 17
Didmarton. Glos 3D 34
Didsbury. G Man 1C 84
Didworthy. Devn 2C 8
Digby. Linc 5H 87
Digg. High 2D 154
Diggle. G Man 4A 92
Digmoor. Lanc 4C 90
Digswell. Herts 4C 52
Dihewyd. Cdgn 5D 57
Dilham. Norf 3F 79
Dilhorne. Staf 1D 72
Dillarburn. S Lan 5B 128
Dillington. Cambs 4A 64
Dilston. Nmbd 3C 114
Dilton Marsh. Wilts 2D 22
Dilwyn. Here 5G 59
Dimmer. Som 3B 22
Dimple. G Man 3F 91
Dinas. Carm 1G 43
Dinas. Gwyn
nr. Caernarfon 5D 81
nr. Tudweiliog 2B 68
Dinas Cross. Pemb 1E 43
Dinas Dinlle. Gwyn 5D 80
Dinas Mawddwy. Gwyn 4A 70
Dinas Powys. V Glam 4E 33
Dinbych. Den 4C 82
Dinbych-y-Pysgod. Pemb 4F 43
Dinckley. Lanc 1E 91
Dinder. Som 2A 22
Dinedor. Here 2A 48
Dinedor Cross. Here 2A 48
Dingestow. Mon 4H 47
Dingle. Mers 2F 83
Dingleden. Kent 2C 28
Dingleton. Bord 1H 119
Dingley. Nptn 2E 63
Dingwall. High 3H 157
Dinmael. Cnwy 1C 70
Dinnet. Abers 4B 152
Dinnington. Som 1H 13
Dinnington. S Yor 2C 86
Dinnington. Tyne 2F 115
Dinorwig. Gwyn 4E 81
Dinton. Buck 4F 51
Dinton. Wilts 3F 23
Dinworthy. Devn 1D 10
Dipley. Hants 1F 25
Dippen. Arg 2B 122
Dippenhall. Surr 2G 25
Dippertown. Devn 4E 11
Dippin. N Ayr 3E 123
Dipple. S Ayr 4B 116
Diptford. Devn 3D 8
Dipton. Dur 4E 115
Dirleton. E Lot 1B 130
Dirt Pot. Nmbd 5B 114
Discoed. Powy 4E 59
Diseworth. Leics 3B 74
Dishes. Orkn 5F 172
Dishforth. N Yor 2F 99
Disley. Ches E 2D 85
Diss. Norf 3D 66
Disserth. Powy 5C 58
Distington. Cumb 2B 102
Ditchampton. Wilts 3F 23
Ditcheat. Som 3B 22
Ditchingham. Norf 1F 67
Ditchling. E Sus 4E 27
Ditteridge. Wilts 5D 34
Dittisham. Devn 3E 9
Ditton. Hal 2G 83
Ditton. Kent 5B 40
Ditton Green. Cambs 5F 65
Ditton Priors. Shrp 2A 60
Divach. High 1G 149
Dixonfield. High 2D 168
Dixton. Glos 2E 49
Dixton. Mon 4A 48
Dizzard. Corn 3B 10
Doagh. Ant 8J 175
Dobcross. G Man 4H 91
Dobs Hill. Flin 4F 83
Dobson's Bridge. Shrp 2G 71
Dobwalls. Corn 2G 7
Doccombe. Devn 4A 12
Dochgarroch. High 4A 158
Docking. Norf 2G 77
Docklow. Here 5H 59
Dockray. Cumb 2E 103
Doc Penfro. Pemb 204 (4D 42)
Dodbrooke. Devn 4D 8
Doddenham. Worc 5B 60
Doddinghurst. Essx 1G 39
Doddington. Cambs 1C 64
Doddington. Kent 5D 40
Doddington. Linc 3G 87
Doddington. Nmbd 1D 121
Doddington. Shrp 3A 60
Doddiscombsleigh. Devn 4B 12
Doddshill. Norf 2G 77
Dodford. Nptn 4D 62
Dodford. Worc 3D 60
Dodington. Som 2E 21
Dodington. S Glo 3C 34
Dodleston. Ches W 4F 83
Dods Leigh. Staf 2E 73
Dodworth. S Yor 4D 92
Doe Lea. Derbs 4B 86
Dogdyke. Linc 5B 88
Dogmersfield. Hants 1F 25
Dogsthorpe. Pet 5B 76
Dog Village. Devn 3C 12
Dolanog. Powy 4C 70
Dolau. Powy 4D 58
Dolau. Rhon 3D 32
Dolbenmaen. Gwyn 1E 69
Doley. Staf 3B 72
Dol-fâch. Powy 5B 70
Dolfach. Powy 3B 58
Dolfor. Powy 2D 58
Dolgarrog. Cnwy 4G 81
Dolgellau. Gwyn 4G 69
Dolgoch. Gwyn 5F 69
Dol-gran. Carm 2E 45
Dolhelfa. Powy 3B 58
Doll. High 3F 165
Dollar. Clac 4B 136
Dolley Green. Powy 4E 59
Dollingstown. Arm 4F 178
Dollwen. Cdgn 2F 57
Dolphin. Flin 3D 82
Dolphinholme. Lanc 4E 97
Dolphinton. S Lan 5E 129
Dolton. Devn 1F 11
Dolwen. Cnwy 3A 82
Dolwyddelan. Cnwy 5G 81
Dol-y-Bont. Cdgn 2F 57
Dolyhir. Powy 5E 59
Domgay. Powy 4E 71
Donagh. Ferm 7J 177
Donaghadee. Ards 2K 179
Donaghcloney. Arm 4F 178
Donaghmore. M Ulst 3B 178
Doncaster. S Yor 4F 93
Doncaster Sheffield Airport. S Yor 1D 86
Donhead St Andrew. Wilts 4E 23
Donhead St Mary. Wilts 4E 23
Doniford. Som 2D 20
Donington. Linc 2B 76
Donington. Shrp 5C 72
Donington Eaudike. Linc 2B 76
Donington le Heath. Leics 4B 74
Donington on Bain. Linc 2B 88
Donington South Ing. Linc 2B 76
Donisthorpe. Leics 4H 73
Donkey Street. Kent 2F 29
Donkey Town. Surr 4A 38
Donna Nook. Linc 1D 88
Donnington. Glos 3G 49
Donnington. Here 2C 48
Donnington. Shrp 5H 71
Donnington. Telf 4B 72
Donnington. W Ber 5C 36
Donnington. W Sus 2G 17
Donyatt. Som 1G 13
Doomsday Green. W Sus 2C 26
Doonfoot. S Ayr 3C 116
Doonholm. S Ayr 3C 116
Dorback Lodge. High 2E 151
Dorchester. Dors 3B 14
Dorchester on Thames. Oxon 2D 36
Dordon. Warw 5G 73
Dore. S Yor 2H 85
Dores. High 5H 157
Dorking. Surr 1C 26
Dorking Tye. Suff 2C 54
Dormansland. Surr 1F 27
Dormans Park. Surr 1E 27
Dormanstown. Red C 2C 106
Dormington. Here 1A 48
Dormston. Worc 5D 61
Dorn. Glos 2H 49
Dorney. Buck 3A 38
Dornie. High 1A 148
Dornoch. High 5E 165
Dornock. Dum 3D 112
Dorrery. High 3C 168
Dorridge. W Mid 3F 61
Dorrington. Linc 5H 87
Dorrington. Shrp 5G 71
Dorsington. Warw 1G 49
Dorstone. Here 1G 47
Dorton. Buck 4E 51
Dosthill. Staf 5G 73
Dotham. IOA 3C 80
Dottery. Dors 3H 13
Doublebois. Corn 2F 7
Dougarie. N Ayr 2C 122
Doughton. Glos 2D 35
Douglas. IOM 4C 108
Douglas. S Lan 1H 117
Douglas Bridge. Derr 3F 176
Douglastown. Ang 4D 144
Douglas Water. S Lan 1A 118
Doulting. Som 2B 22
Dounby. Orkn 5B 172
Doune. High
nr. Kingussie 2C 150
nr. Lairg 3B 164
Doune. Stir 3G 135
Dounie. High
nr. Bonar Bridge 4C 164
nr. Tain 5D 164
Dounreay. High 2B 168
Doura. N Ayr 5E 127
Dousland. Devn 2B 8
Dovaston. Shrp 3F 71
Dove Holes. Derbs 3E 85
Dovenby. Cumb 1B 102
Dover. Kent 194 (1H 29)
Dovercourt. Essx 2F 55

Doverdale—Edgcott

Doverdale. Worc 4C 60
Doveridge. Derbs 2F 73
Doversgreen. Surr 1D 26
Dowally. Per 4H 143
Dowbridge. Lanc 1C 90
Dowdeswell. Glos 4F 49
Dowlais. Mer T 5D 46
Dowland. Devn 1F 11
Dowlands. Devn 3F 13
Dowles. Worc 3B 60
Dowlesgreen. Wok 5G 37
Dowlish Wake. Som 1G 13
Down, The. Shrp 1A 60
Downall Green. Mers 4D 90
Down Ampney. Glos 2G 35
Downderry. Corn
nr. Looe 3H 7
nr. St Austell 3D 6
Downe. G Lon 4F 39
Downend. IOW 4D 16
Downend. S Glo 4B 34
Downend. W Ber 4C 36
Down Field. Cambs 3F 65
Downfield. D'dee 5C 144
Downgate. Corn
nr. Kelly Bray 5D 10
nr. Upton Cross 5C 10
Downham. Essx 1B 40
Downham. Lanc 5G 97
Downham. Nmbd 1C 120
Downham Market. Norf 5F 77
Down Hatherley. Glos 3D 48
Downhead. Som
nr. Frome 2B 22
nr. Yeovil 4A 22
Downhill. Caus 3D 174
Downholland Cross. Lanc 4B 90
Downholme. N Yor 5E 105
Downies. Abers 4G 153
Downley. Buck 2G 37
Downpatrick. New M 5J 179
Down St Mary. Devn 2H 11
Downside. Som
nr. Chilcompton 1B 22
nr. Shepton Mallet 2B 22
Downside. Surr 5C 38
Down Thomas. Devn 3B 8
Downton. Hants 3A 16
Downton. Wilts 4G 23
Downton on the Rock. Here 3G 59
Dowsby. Linc 3A 76
Dowsdale. Linc 4B 76
Dowthwaitehead. Cumb 2E 103
Doxey. Staf 3D 72
Doxford. Nmbd 2F 121
Doynton. S Glo 4C 34
Drabblegate. Norf 3E 78
Draethen. Cphy 3F 33
Draffan. S Lan 5A 128
Dragonby. N Lin 3C 94
Dragon's Green. W Sus 3C 26
Drakelow. Worc 2C 60
Drakemyre. N Ayr 4D 126
Drakes Broughton. Worc 1E 49
Drakes Cross. Worc 3E 61
Drakewalls. Corn 5E 11
Draperstown. M Ulst 7D 174
Draughton. Nptn 3E 63
Draughton. N Yor 4C 98
Drax. N Yor 2G 93
Draycot. Oxon 5E 51
Draycote. Warw 3B 62
Draycot Foliat. Swin 4G 35
Draycott. Derbs 2B 74
Draycott. Glos 2G 49
Draycott. Shrp 1C 60
Draycott. Som
nr. Cheddar 1H 21
nr. Yeovil 4A 22
Draycott. Worc 1D 48
Draycott in the Clay. Staf 3F 73
Draycott in the Moors. Staf 1D 73
Drayford. Devn 1A 12
Drayton. Leics 1F 63
Drayton. Linc 2B 76
Drayton. Norf 4D 78
Drayton. Nptn 4C 62
Drayton. Oxon
nr. Abingdon 2C 36
nr. Banbury 1C 50
Drayton. Port 2E 17
Drayton. Som 4H 21
Drayton. Warw 5F 61
Drayton. Worc 3D 60
Drayton Bassett. Staf 5F 73
Drayton Beauchamp. Buck 4H 51
Drayton Parslow. Buck 3G 51
Drayton St Leonard. Oxon 2D 36
Drebley. N Yor 4C 98
Dreenhill. Pemb 3D 42
Y Dref. Gwyn 2D 69
Drefach. Carm
nr. Meidrim 4F 45
nr. Newcastle Emlyn 2D 44
nr. Tumble 2G 43
Drefach. Cdgn 1E 45
Dreghorn. N Ayr 1C 116
Drellingore. Kent 1G 29
Drem. E Lot 2B 130
Y Drenewydd. Powy 1D 58
Dreumasdal. W Isl 5C 170
Drewsteignton. Devn 3H 11
Driby. Linc 3C 88
Driffield. E Yor 4E 101
Driffield. Glos 2F 35
Drift. Corn 4B 4
Drigg. Cumb 5B 102
Drighlington. W Yor 2C 92
Drimnin. High 3G 139
Drimpton. Dors 2H 13
Dringhoe. E Yor 4F 101
Drinisiadar. W Isl 8D 171
Drinkstone. Suff 4B 66
Drinkstone Green. Suff 4B 66
Drointon. Staf 3E 73
Droitwich Spa. Worc 4C 60
Droman. High 3B 166
Dromara. Lis 5G 179
Dromore. Arm 4G 179
Dromore. Ferm 6F 176
Dron. Per 2D 136
Dronfield. Derbs 3A 86
Dronfield Woodhouse. Derbs 3H 85
Drongan. E Ayr 3D 116
Dronley. Ang 5C 144
Droop. Dors 2C 14
Drope. V Glam 4E 32
Droxford. Hants 1E 16
Droylsden. G Man 1C 84
Druggers End. Worc 2C 48
Druid. Den 1C 70
Druid's Heath. W Mid 5E 73
Druidston. Pemb 3C 42
Druim. High 3D 158
Druimarbin. High 1E 141
Druim Fhearna. High 2E 147
Druimindarroch. High 5E 147
Druim Saighdinis. W Isl 2D 170
Drum. Per 3C 136
Drumaness. New M 5H 179
Drumaroad. New M 5H 179
Drumbeg. High 5B 166
Drumblade. Abers 4C 160
Drumbo. Lis 3H 179
Drumbuie. Dum 1C 110
Drumbuie. High 5G 155
Drumburgh. Cumb 4D 112
Drumburn. Dum 3A 112
Drumchapel. Glas 2G 127
Drumchardine. High 4H 157
Drumchork. High 5C 162
Drumclog. S Lan 1F 117
Drumeldrie. Fife 3G 137
Drumelzier. Bord 1D 118
Drumfearn. High 2E 147
Drumgask. High 4A 150
Drumgelloch. N Lan 3A 128
Drumgley. Ang 3D 144
Drumguish. High 4B 150
Drumin. Mor 5F 159
Drumindorsair. High 4G 157
Drumintee. New M 8E 178
Drumlamford House. S Ayr 2H 109
Drumlasie. Abers 3D 152
Drumlemble. Arg 4A 122
Drumlithie. Abers 5E 153
Drummoddie. Dum 5A 110
Drummond. High 2A 158
Drummore. Dum 5E 109
Drummuir. Mor 4A 160
Drumnacanvy. Arm 4E 178
Drumnadrochit. High 5H 157
Drumnagorrach. Mor 3C 160
Drumnakilly. Ferm 2L 177
Drumoak. Abers 4E 153
Drumquin. Ferm 5E 176
Drumraighland. Caus 4C 174
Drumrunie. High 3F 163
Drumry. W Dun 2G 127
Drums. Abers 1G 153
Drumsleet. Dum 2G 111
Drumsmittal. High 4A 158
Drums of Park. Abers 3C 160
Drumsturdy. Ang 5D 145
Drumsurn. Caus 5D 174
Drumtochty Castle. Abers 5D 152
Drumuie. High 4D 154
Drumuillie. High 1D 150
Drumvaich. Stir 3F 135
Drumwhindle. Abers 5G 161
Drunkendub. Ang 4F 145
Drury. Flin 4E 83
Drury Square. Norf 4B 78
Drybeck. Cumb 3H 103
Drybridge. Mor 2B 160
Drybridge. N Ayr 1C 116
Drybrook. Glos 4B 48
Drybrook. Here 4A 48
Dryburgh. Bord 1H 119
Dry Doddington. Linc 1F 75
Dry Drayton. Cambs 4C 64
Drym. Corn 3D 4
Drymen. Stir 1F 127
Drymuir. Abers 4G 161
Drynachan Lodge. High 5C 158
Drynie Park. High 3H 157
Drynoch. High 5D 154
Dry Sandford. Oxon 5C 50
Dryslwyn. Carm 3F 45
Dry Street. Essx 2A 40
Dryton. Shrp 5H 71
Dubford. Abers 2E 161
Dubiton. Abers 3D 160
Dubton. Ang 3E 145
Duchally. High 2A 164
Duck End. Essx 3G 53
Duckington. Ches W 5G 83
Ducklington. Oxon 5B 50
Duckmanton. Derbs 3B 86
Duck Street. Hants 2B 24
Dudbridge. Glos 5D 48
Duddenhoe End. Essx 2E 53
Duddingston. Edin 2F 129
Duddington. Nptn 5G 75
Duddleswell. E Sus 3F 27
Duddo. Nmbd 5F 131
Duddon. Ches W 4H 83
Duddon Bridge. Cumb 1A 96
Dudleston. Shrp 2F 71
Dudleston Heath. Shrp 2F 71
Dudley. Tyne 2F 115
Dudley. W Mid 2D 60
Dudston. Shrp 1E 59
Dudwells. Pemb 2D 42
Duffield. Derbs 1H 73
Duffryn. Neat 2B 32
Dufftown. Mor 4H 159
Duffus. Mor 2F 159
Dufton. Cumb 2H 103
Duggleby. N Yor 3C 100
Duirinish. High 5G 155
Duisdalemore. High 2E 147
Duisdeil Mòr. High 2E 147
Duisky. High 1E 141
Dukesfield. Nmbd 4C 114
Dukestown. Blae 5E 47
Dukinfield. G Man 1D 84
Dulas. IOA 2D 81
Dulcote. Som 2A 22
Dulford. Devn 2D 12
Dull. Per 4F 143
Dullatur. N Lan 2A 128
Dullingham. Cambs 5F 65
Dullingham Ley. Cambs 5F 65
Dulnain Bridge. High 1D 151
Duloe. Bed 4A 64
Duloe. Corn 3G 7
Dulverton. Som 4C 20
Dulwich. G Lon 3E 39
Dumbarton. W Dun 2F 127
Dumbleton. Glos 2F 49
Dumfin. Arg 1E 127
Dumfries. Dum 194 (2A 112)
Dumgoyne. Stir 1G 127
Dummer. Hants 2D 24
Dumpford. W Sus 4G 25
Dun. Ang 2F 145
Dunadry. Ant 1F 179
Dunaghy. Caus 4F 175
Dunagoil. Arg 4B 126
Dunalastair. Per 3E 142
Dunan. High 1D 147
Dunball. Som 2G 21
Dunbar. E Lot 2C 130
Dunbeath. High 5D 168
Dunbeg. Arg 5C 140
Dunblane. Stir 3G 135
Dunbog. Fife 2E 137
Dunbridge. Hants 4B 24
Duncanston. Abers 1C 152
Duncanston. High 3H 157
Dun Charlabhaigh. W Isl 3D 171
Dunchideock. Devn 4B 12
Dunchurch. Warw 3B 62
Duncote. Nptn 5D 62
Duncow. Dum 1A 112
Duncrievie. Per 3D 136
Duncton. W Sus 4A 26
Dundee. D'dee 194 (5D 144)
Dundee Airport. D'dee 1F 137
Dundon. Som 3H 21
Dundonald. Lis 2J 179
Dundonald. S Ayr 1C 116
Dundonnell. High 5E 163
Dundraw. Cumb 5D 112
Dundreggan. High 2F 149
Dundrennan. Dum 5E 111
Dundridge. Hants 1D 16
Dundrod. Lis 2G 179
Dundrum. New M 6J 179
Dundry. N Som 5A 34
Dunecht. Abers 3E 153
Dunfermline. Fife 1D 129
Dunford Bridge. S Yor 4B 92
Dungannon. M Ulst 3B 178
Dungate. Kent 5D 40
Dunge. Wilts 1D 23
Dungeness. Kent 4E 29
Dungiven. Caus 6C 174
Dungworth. S Yor 2G 85
Dunham-on-the-Hill. Ches W 3G 83
Dunham-on-Trent. Notts 3F 87
Dunhampton. Worc 4C 60
Dunham Town. G Man 2B 84
Dunham Woodhouses. G Man 2B 84
Dunholme. Linc 3H 87
Dunino. Fife 2H 137
Dunipace. Falk 1B 128
Dunira. Per 1G 135
Dunkeld. Per 4H 143
Dunkerton. Bath 1C 22
Dunkeswell. Devn 2E 13
Dunkeswick. N Yor 5F 99
Dunkirk. Kent 5E 41
Dunkirk. S Glo 3C 34
Dunkirk. Staf 5C 84
Dunkirk. Wilts 5E 35
Dunk's Green. Kent 5H 39
Dunlappie. Ang 2E 145
Dunley. Hants 1C 24
Dunley. Worc 4B 60
Dunlichity Lodge. High 5A 158
Dunlop. E Ayr 5F 127
Dunloy. Caus 5G 175
Dunmaglass Lodge. High 1H 149
Dunmore. Arg 3F 125
Dunmore. Falk 1B 128
Dunmore. High 4H 157
Dunmurry. Bel 3G 179
Dunnamanagh. Derr 6A 174
Dunnaval. New M 8G 179
Dunnet. High 1E 169
Dunnichen. Ang 4E 145
Dunning. Per 2C 136
Dunnington. E Yor 4F 101
Dunnington. Warw 5E 61
Dunnington. York 4A 100
Dunningwell. Cumb 1A 96
Dunnockshaw. Lanc 2G 91
Dunoon. Arg 2C 126
Dunphail. Mor 4E 159
Dunragit. Dum 4G 109
Dunrostan. Arg 1F 125
Duns. Bord 4D 130
Dunsby. Linc 3A 76
Dunscar. G Man 3F 91
Dunscore. Dum 1F 111
Dunscroft. S Yor 4G 93
Dunsdale. Red C 3D 106
Dunsden Green. Oxon 4F 37
Dunsfold. Surr 2B 26
Dunsford. Devn 4B 12
Dunshalt. Fife 2E 137
Dunshillock. Abers 4G 161
Dunsley. N Yor 3F 107
Dunsley. Staf 2C 60
Dunsmore. Buck 5G 51
Dunsop Bridge. Lanc 4F 97
Dunstable. C Beds 3A 52
Dunstal. Staf 3E 73
Dunstall. Staf 3F 73
Dunstall Green. Suff 4G 65
Dunstall Hill. W Mid 5D 72
Dunstan. Nmbd 3G 121
Dunster. Som 2C 20
Duns Tew. Oxon 3C 50
Dunston. Linc 4H 87
Dunston. Norf 5E 79
Dunston. Staf 4D 72
Dunston. Tyne 3F 115
Dunstone. Devn 3B 8
Dunston Heath. Staf 4D 72
Dunsville. S Yor 4G 93
Dunswell. E Yor 1D 94
Dunsyre. S Lan 5D 128
Dunterton. Devn 5D 11
Duntisbourne Abbots. Glos 5E 49
Duntisbourne Leer. Glos 5E 49
Duntisbourne Rouse. Glos 5E 49
Duntish. Dors 2B 14
Duntocher. W Dun 2F 127
Dunton. Buck 3G 51
Dunton. C Beds 1C 52
Dunton. Norf 2A 78
Dunton Bassett. Leics 1C 62
Dunton Green. Kent 5G 39
Dunton Patch. Norf 2A 78
Duntulm. High 1D 154
Dunure. S Ayr 3B 116
Dunvant. Swan 3E 31
Dunvegan. High 4B 154
Dunwich. Suff 3G 67
Dunwood. Staf 5D 84
Durdar. Cumb 4F 113
Durgates. E Sus 2H 27
Durham. Dur 194 (5F 115)
Durham Tees Valley Airport. Darl 3A 106
Durisdeer. Dum 4A 118
Durisdeermill. Dum 4A 118
Durkar. W Yor 3D 92
Durleigh. Som 3F 21
Durley. Hants 1D 16
Durley. Wilts 5H 35
Durley Street. Hants 1D 16
Durlow Common. Here 2B 48
Durnamuck. High 4E 163
Durness. High 2E 166
Durno. Abers 1E 152
Durns Town. Hants 3A 16
Duror. High 3D 141
Durran. Arg 3G 133
Durran. High 2D 169
Durrant Green. Kent 2C 28
Durrants. Hants 1F 17
Durrington. W Sus 5C 26
Durrington. Wilts 2G 23
Dursley. Glos 2C 34
Dursley Cross. Glos 4B 48
Durston. Som 4F 21
Durweston. Dors 2D 14
Dury. Shet 6F 173
Duston. Nptn 4E 63
Duthil. High 1D 150
Dutlas. Powy 3E 58
Duton Hill. Essx 3G 53
Dutson. Corn 4D 10
Dutton. Ches W 3H 83
Duxford. Cambs 1E 53
Duxford. Oxon 2B 36
Dwygyfylchi. Cnwy 3G 81
Dwyran. IOA 4D 80
Dyce. Aber 2F 153
Dyffryn. B'end 2B 32
Dyffryn. Carm 2H 43
Dyffryn. Pemb 1D 42
Dyffryn. V Glam 4D 32
Dyffryn Ardudwy. Gwyn 3E 69
Dyffryn Castell. Cdgn 2G 57
Dyffryn Ceidrych. Carm 3H 45
Dyffryn Cellwen. Neat 5B 46
Dyke. Linc 3A 76
Dyke. Mor 3D 159
Dykehead. Ang 2C 144
Dykehead. N Lan 3B 128
Dykehead. Stir 4E 135
Dykend. Ang 3B 144
Dykesfield. Cumb 4E 112
Dylife. Powy 1A 58
Dymchurch. Kent 3F 29
Dymock. Glos 2C 48
Dyrham. S Glo 4C 34
Dysart. Fife 4F 137
Dyserth. Den 3C 82

E

Eachwick. Nmbd 2E 115
Eadar Dha Fhadhail. W Isl 4C 171
Eagland Hill. Lanc 5D 96
Eagle. Linc 4F 87
Eagle Barnsdale. Linc 4F 87
Eagle Moor. Linc 4F 87
Eaglescliffe. Stoc T 3B 106
Eaglesfield. Cumb 2B 102
Eaglesfield. Dum 2D 112
Eaglesham. E Ren 4G 127
Eaglethorpe. Nptn 1H 63
Eagley. G Man 3F 91
Eairy. IOM 4B 108
Eakley Lanes. Mil 5F 63
Eakring. Notts 4D 86
Ealand. N Lin 3A 94
Ealing. G Lon 2C 38
Eallabus. Arg 3B 124
Eals. Nmbd 4H 113
Eamont Bridge. Cumb 2G 103
Earby. Lanc 5B 98
Earcroft. Bkbn 2E 91
Eardington. Shrp 1B 60
Eardisland. Here 5G 59
Eardisley. Here 1G 47
Eardiston. Shrp 3F 71
Eardiston. Worc 4A 60
Earith. Cambs 3C 64
Earlais. High 2C 154
Earle. Nmbd 2D 121
Earlesfield. Linc 2G 75
Earlestown. Mers 1H 83
Earley. Wok 4F 37
Earlham. Norf 5D 78
Earlish. High 2C 154
Earls Barton. Nptn 4F 63
Earls Colne. Essx 3B 54
Earls Common. Worc 5D 60
Earl's Croome. Worc 1D 48
Earlsdon. W Mid 3H 61
Earlsferry. Fife 3G 137
Earlsford. Abers 5F 161
Earl's Green. Suff 4C 66
Earlsheaton. W Yor 2C 92
Earl Shilton. Leics 1B 62
Earl Soham. Suff 4E 67
Earl Sterndale. Derbs 4E 85
Earlston. E Ayr 1D 116
Earlston. Bord 1H 119
Earl Stonham. Suff 5D 66
Earlstoun. Dum 1D 110
Earlswood. Mon 2H 33
Earlswood. Warw 3F 61
Earlyvale. Bord 4F 129
Earnley. W Sus 3G 17
Earsairidh. W Isl 9C 170
Earsdon. Tyne 2G 115
Earsham. Norf 2F 67
Earsham Street. Suff 3E 67
Earswick. York 4A 100
Eartham. W Sus 5A 26
Earthcott Green. S Glo 3B 34
Easby. N Yor
nr. Great Ayton 4C 106
nr. Richmond 4E 105
Easdale. Arg 2E 133
Easebourne. W Sus 4G 25
Easenhall. Warw 3B 62
Eashing. Surr 1A 26
Easington. Buck 4E 51
Easington. Dur 5H 115
Easington. E Yor 3G 95
Easington. Nmbd 1F 121
Easington. Oxon
nr. Banbury 2C 50
nr. Watlington 2E 37
Easington. Red C 3E 107
Easington Colliery. Dur 5H 115
Easington Lane. Tyne 5G 115
Easingwold. N Yor 2H 99
Eassie. Ang 4C 144
Eassie and Nevay. Ang 4C 144
East Aberthaw. V Glam 5D 32
Eastacombe. Devn 4F 19
Eastacott. Devn 4G 19
East Allington. Devn 4D 8
East Anstey. Devn 4B 20
East Anton. Hants 2B 24
East Appleton. N Yor 5F 105
East Ardsley. W Yor 2D 92
East Ashley. Devn 1G 11
East Ashling. W Sus 2G 17
East Aston. Hants 2C 24
East Ayton. N Yor 1D 101
East Barkwith. Linc 2A 88
East Barnby. N Yor 3F 107
East Barnet. G Lon 1D 39
East Barns. E Lot 2D 130
East Barsham. Norf 2B 78
East Beach. W Sus 3G 17
East Beckham. Norf 2D 78
East Bedfont. G Lon 3B 38
East Bennan. N Ayr 3D 123
East Bergholt. Suff 2D 54
East Bierley. W Yor 2C 92
East Bilney. Norf 4B 78
East Blatchington. E Sus 5F 27
East Bloxworth. Dors 3D 15
East Boldre. Hants 2B 16
East Bolton. Nmbd 3F 121
Eastbourne. Darl 3F 105
Eastbourne. E Sus 194 (5H 27)
East Brent. Som 1G 21
East Bridge. Suff 4G 67
East Bridgford. Notts 1D 74
East Briscoe. Dur 3C 104
East Buckland. Devn
nr. Barnstaple 3G 19
nr. Thurlestone 4C 8
East Budleigh. Devn 4D 12
Eastburn. W Yor 5C 98
East Burnham. Buck 2A 38
East Burrafirth. Shet 6E 173
East Burton. Dors 4D 14
Eastbury. Herts 1B 38
Eastbury. W Ber 4B 36
East Butsfield. Dur 5E 115
East Butterleigh. Devn 2C 12
East Butterwick. N Lin 4B 94
Eastby. N Yor 4C 98
East Calder. W Lot 3D 129
East Carleton. Norf 5D 78
East Carlton. Nptn 2F 63
East Carlton. W Yor 5E 98
East Chaldon. Dors 4C 14
East Challow. Oxon 3B 36
East Charleton. Devn 4D 8
East Chelborough. Dors 2A 14
East Chiltington. E Sus 4E 27
East Chinnock. Som 1H 13
East Chisenbury. Wilts 1G 23
Eastchurch. Kent 3D 40
East Clandon. Surr 5B 38
East Claydon. Buck 3F 51
East Clevedon. N Som 4H 33
East Clyne. High 3F 165
East Clyth. High 5E 169
East Coker. Som 1A 14
Eastcombe. Glos 5D 49
East Combe. Som 3E 21
East Common. N Yor 1G 93
East Compton. Som 2B 22
East Cornworthy. Devn 3E 9
Eastcote. G Lon 2C 38
Eastcote. Nptn 5D 62
Eastcote. W Mid 3F 61
Eastcott. Corn 1C 10
Eastcott. Wilts 1F 23
East Cottingwith. E Yor 5B 100
Eastcourt. Wilts
nr. Pewsey 5H 35
nr. Tetbury 2E 35
East Cowes. IOW 3D 16
East Cowick. E Yor 2G 93
East Cowton. N Yor 4A 106
East Cramlington. Nmbd 2F 115
East Cranmore. Som 2B 22
East Creech. Dors 4E 15
East Croachy. High 1A 150
East Dean. E Sus 5G 27
East Dean. Glos 3B 48
East Dean. Hants 4A 24
East Dean. W Sus 4A 26
East Down. Devn 2G 19
East Drayton. Notts 3E 87
East Dundry. N Som 5A 34
East Ella. Hull 2D 94
East End. Cambs 3C 64
East End. Dors 3E 15
East End. E Yor
nr. Ulrome 4F 101
nr. Withernsea 2F 95
East End. Hants
nr. Lymington 3B 16
nr. Newbury 5C 36
East End. Herts 3E 53
East End. Kent
nr. Minster 3D 40
nr. Tenterden 2C 28
East End. N Som 4H 33
East End. Oxon 4B 50
East End. Som 1A 22
East End. Suff 2E 54
Easter Ardross. High 1A 158
Easter Balgedie. Per 3D 136
Easter Balmoral. Abers 4G 151
Easter Brae. High 2A 158
Easter Buckieburn. Stir 1A 128
Easter Compton. S Glo 3A 34
Easter Fearn. High 5D 164
Easter Galcantray. High 4C 158
Eastergate. W Sus 5A 26
Easterhouse. Glas 3H 127
Easter Howgate. Midl 3F 129
Easter Kinkell. High 3H 157
Easter Lednathie. Ang 2C 144
Easter Ogil. Ang 2D 144
Easter Ord. Abers 3F 153
Easter Quarff. Shet 8F 173
Easter Rhynd. Per 2D 136
Easter Skeld. Shet 7E 173
Easter Suddie. High 3A 158
Easterton. Wilts 1F 23
Eastertown. Som 1G 21
Easter Tulloch. Abers 1G 145
Easter Everleigh. Wilts 1H 23
East Farleigh. Kent 5B 40
East Farndon. Nptn 2E 62
East Ferry. Linc 1F 87
Eastfield. N Lan
nr. Caldercruix 3B 128
nr. Harthill 3B 128
Eastfield. N Yor 1E 101
Eastfield. S Lan 3H 127
Eastfield Hall. Nmbd 4G 121
East Fortune. E Lot 2B 130
East Garforth. W Yor 1E 93
East Garston. W Ber 4B 36
Eastgate. Dur 1C 104
Eastgate. Norf 3D 78
East Ginge. Oxon 3C 36
East Gores. Essx 3B 54
East Goscote. Leics 4D 74
East Grafton. Wilts 5A 36
East Green. Suff 5F 65
East Grimstead. Wilts 4H 23
East Grinstead. W Sus 2E 27
East Guldeford. E Sus 3D 28
East Haddon. Nptn 4D 62
East Hagbourne. Oxon 3D 36
East Halton. N Lin 2E 95
East Ham. G Lon 2F 39
Eastham. Mers 2F 83
Eastham. Worc 4A 60
Eastham Ferry. Mers 2F 83
Easthampstead. Brac 5G 37
Easthampton. Here 4G 59
East Hanney. Oxon 2C 36
East Hanningfield. Essx 5A 54
East Hardwick. W Yor 3E 93
East Harling. Norf 2B 66
East Harlsey. N Yor 5B 106
East Harptree. Bath 1A 22
East Hartford. Nmbd 2F 115
East Harting. W Sus 1G 17
East Hatch. Wilts 4E 23
East Hatley. Cambs 5B 64
Easthaugh. Norf 4C 78
East Hauxwell. N Yor 5E 105
East Haven. Ang 5E 145
Eastheath. Wok 5G 37
East Heckington. Linc 1A 76
East Hedleyhope. Dur 5E 115
East Helmsdale. High 2H 165
East Hendred. Oxon 3C 36
East Heslerton. N Yor 2D 100
East Hoathly. E Sus 4G 27
East Holme. Dors 4D 15
Easthope. Shrp 1H 59
Easthorpe. Essx 3C 54
Easthorpe. Leics 2F 75
East Horrington. Som 2A 22
East Horsley. Surr 5B 38
East Horton. Nmbd 1E 121
Easthouses. Midl 3G 129
East Howe. Bour 3F 15
East Huntspill. Som 2G 21
East Hyde. C Beds 4B 52
East Ilsley. W Ber 3C 36
Eastington. Devn 2H 11
Eastington. Glos
nr. Northleach 4G 49
nr. Stonehouse 5C 48
East Keal. Linc 4C 88
East Kennett. Wilts 5G 35
East Keswick. W Yor 5F 99
East Kilbride. S Lan 4H 127
East Kirkby. Linc 4C 88
East Knapton. N Yor 2C 100
East Knighton. Dors 4D 14
East Knowstone. Devn 4B 20
East Knoyle. Wilts 3D 23
East Kyloe. Nmbd 1E 121
East Lambrook. Som 1H 13
East Langdon. Kent 1H 29
East Langton. Leics 1E 63
East Langwell. High 3E 164
East Lavant. W Sus 2G 17
East Lavington. W Sus 4A 26
East Layton. N Yor 4E 105
Eastleach Martin. Glos 5H 49
Eastleach Turville. Glos 5G 49
East Leake. Notts 3C 74
East Learmouth. Nmbd 1C 120
East Leigh. Devn
nr. Crediton 2G 11
nr. Modbury 3C 8
Eastleigh. Devn 4E 19
Eastleigh. Hants 1C 16
East Lexham. Norf 4A 78
East Lilburn. Nmbd 2E 121
Eastling. Kent 5D 40
East Linton. E Lot 2B 130
East Liss. Hants 4F 25
East Lockinge. Oxon 3C 36
East Looe. Corn 3G 7
East Lound. N Lin 1E 87
East Lulworth. Dors 4D 14
East Lutton. N Yor 3D 100
East Lydford. Som 3A 22
East Lyng. Som 4G 21
East Mains. Abers 4D 152
East Malling. Kent 5B 40
East Marden. W Sus 1G 17
East Markham. Notts 3E 87
East Marton. N Yor 4B 98
East Meon. Hants 4E 25
East Mersea. Essx 4D 54
East Mey. High 1F 169
East Midlands Airport. Leics 205 (3B 74)
East Molesey. Surr 4C 38
Eastmoor. Norf 5G 77
East Morden. Dors 3E 15
East Morton. W Yor 5D 98
East Ness. N Yor 2A 100
East Newton. E Yor 1F 95
East Newton. N Yor 2A 100
Eastney. Port 3E 17
Eastnor. Here 2C 48
East Norton. Leics 5E 75
East Nynehead. Som 4E 21
East Oakley. Hants 1D 24
Eastoft. N Lin 3B 94
East Ogwell. Devn 5B 12
Easton. Cambs 3A 64
Easton. Cumb
nr. Burgh by Sands 4D 112
nr. Longtown 2F 113
Easton. Devn 4H 11
Easton. Dors 5B 14
Easton. Hants 3D 24
Easton. Linc 3G 75
Easton. Norf 4D 78
Easton. Som 2A 22
Easton. Suff 5E 67
Easton. Wilts 4D 35
Easton Grey. Wilts 3D 35
Easton-in-Gordano. N Som 4A 34
Easton Maudit. Nptn 5F 63
Easton on the Hill. Nptn 5H 75
Easton Royal. Wilts 5H 35
East Orchard. Dors 1D 14
East Ord. Nmbd 4F 131
East Panson. Devn 3D 10
East Peckham. Kent 1A 28
East Pennard. Som 3A 22
East Perry. Cambs 4A 64
East Pitcorthie. Fife 3H 137
East Portlemouth. Devn 5D 8
East Prawle. Devn 5D 9
East Preston. W Sus 5B 26
East Putford. Devn 1D 10
East Quantoxhead. Som 2E 21
East Rainton. Tyne 5G 115
East Ravendale. NE Lin 1B 88
East Raynham. Norf 3A 78
Eastrea. Cambs 1B 64
East Rhidorroch Lodge. High 4G 163
Eastriggs. Dum 3D 112
East Rigton. W Yor 5F 99
Eastrington. E Yor 2A 94
East Rounton. N Yor 4B 106
East Row. N Yor 3F 107
East Rudham. Norf 3H 77
East Runton. Norf 1D 78
East Ruston. Norf 3F 79
Eastry. Kent 5H 41
East Saltoun. E Lot 3A 130
East Shaws. Dur 3D 105
East Shefford. W Ber 4B 36
Eastshore. Shet 10E 173
East Sleekburn. Nmbd 1F 115
East Somerton. Norf 4G 79
East Stockwith. Linc 1E 87
East Stoke. Dors 4D 14
East Stoke. Notts 1E 75
East Stoke. Som 1H 13
East Stour. Dors 4D 22
East Stourmouth. Kent 4G 41
East Stowford. Devn 4G 19
East Stratton. Hants 2D 24
East Studdal. Kent 1H 29
East Taphouse. Corn 2F 7
East-the-Water. Devn 4E 19
East Thirston. Nmbd 5F 121
East Tilbury. Thur 3A 40
East Tisted. Hants 3F 25
East Torrington. Linc 2A 88
East Tuddenham. Norf 4C 78
East Tytherley. Hants 4A 24
East Tytherton. Wilts 4E 35
East Village. Devn 2B 12
Eastville. Linc 5D 88
East Wall. Shrp 1H 59
East Walton. Norf 4G 77
East Week. Devn 3G 11
Eastwell. Leics 3E 75
East Wellow. Hants 4B 24
East Wemyss. Fife 4F 137
East Whitburn. W Lot 3C 128
Eastwick. Herts 4E 53
Eastwick. Shet 4E 173
East Williamston. Pemb 4E 43
East Winch. Norf 4F 77
East Winterslow. Wilts 3H 23
East Wittering. W Sus 3F 17
East Witton. N Yor 1D 98
Eastwood. Notts 1B 74
Eastwood. S'end 2C 40
East Woodburn. Nmbd 1C 114
Eastwood End. Cambs 1D 64
East Woodhay. Hants 5C 36
East Woodlands. Som 2C 22
East Worldham. Hants 3F 25
East Worlington. Devn 1A 12
East Wretham. Norf 1B 66
East Youlstone. Devn 1C 10
Eathorpe. Warw 4A 62
Eaton. Ches E 4C 84
Eaton. Ches W 4H 83
Eaton. Leics 3E 75
Eaton. Norf
nr. Heacham 2F 77
nr. Norwich 5E 78
Eaton. Notts 3E 86
Eaton. Oxon 5C 50
Eaton. Shrp
nr. Bishop's Castle 2F 59
nr. Church Stretton 2H 59
Eaton Bishop. Here 2H 47
Eaton Bray. C Beds 3H 51
Eaton Constantine. Shrp 5H 71
Eaton Hastings. Oxon 2A 36
Eaton Socon. Cambs 5A 64
Eaton upon Tern. Shrp 3A 72
Eau Brink. Norf 4E 77
Eaves Green. W Mid 2G 61
Ebberley Hill. Devn 1F 11
Ebberston. N Yor 1C 100
Ebbesbourne Wake. Wilts 4E 23
Ebblake. Dors 2G 15
Ebbsfleet. Kent 3H 39
Ebbw Vale. Blae 5E 47
Ebchester. Dur 4E 115
Ebernoe. W Sus 3A 26
Ebford. Devn 4C 12
Ebley. Glos 5D 48
Ebnal. Ches W 1G 71
Ebrington. Glos 1G 49
Ecchinswell. Hants 1D 24
Ecclefechan. Dum 2C 112
Eccles. G Man 1B 84
Eccles. Kent 4B 40
Eccles. Bord 5D 130
Ecclesall. S Yor 2H 85
Ecclesfield. S Yor 1A 86
Eccles Green. Here 1G 47
Eccleshall. Staf 3C 72
Eccleshill. W Yor 1B 92
Ecclesmachan. W Lot 2D 128
Eccles on Sea. Norf 3G 79
Eccles Road. Norf 1C 66
Eccleston. Ches W 4G 83
Eccleston. Lanc 3D 90
Eccleston. Mers 1G 83
Eccup. W Yor 5E 99
Echt. Abers 3E 153
Eckford. Bord 2B 120
Eckington. Derbs 3B 86
Eckington. Worc 1E 49
Ecton. Nptn 4F 63
Edale. Derbs 2F 85
Eday Airport. Orkn 4E 172
Edburton. W Sus 4D 26
Edderside. Cumb 5C 112
Edderton. High 5E 164
Eddington. Kent 4F 41
Eddington. W Ber 5B 36
Eddleston. Bord 5F 129
Eddlewood. S Lan 4A 128
Edenbridge. Kent 1F 27
Edendonich. Arg 1A 134
Edenfield. Lanc 3F 91
Edenhall. Cumb 1G 103
Edenham. Linc 3H 75
Edensor. Derbs 3G 85
Edentaggart. Arg 4C 134
Edenthorpe. S Yor 4G 93
Eden Vale. Dur 1B 106
Edern. Gwyn 2B 68
Ederney. Ferm 6E 176
Edgarley. Som 3A 22
Edgbaston. W Mid 2E 61
Edgcott. Buck 3E 51

Edgcott—Flaxley Green

Edgcott. *Som* 3B **20**
Edge. *Glos* 5D **48**
Edge. *Shrp* 5F **71**
Edgebolton. *Shrp* 3H **71**
Edge End. *Glos* 4A **48**
Edgefield. *Norf* 2C **78**
Edgefield Street. *Norf* 2C **78**
Edge Green. *Ches W* 5G **83**
Edgehead. *Midl* 3G **129**
Edgeley. *Shrp* 1H **71**
Edgeside. *Lanc* 2G **91**
Edgeworth. *Glos* 5E **49**
Edgiock. *Worc* 4E **61**
Edgmond. *Telf* 4B **72**
Edgmond Marsh. *Telf* 3B **72**
Edgton. *Shrp* 2F **59**
Edgware. *G Lon* 1C **38**
Edgworth. *Bkbn* 3F **91**
Edinbane. *High* 3C **154**
Edinburgh. *Edin* **195** (2F **129**)
Edinburgh Airport. *Edin* 2E **129**
Edingale. *Staf* 4G **73**
Edingley. *Notts* 5D **86**
Edingthorpe. *Norf* 2F **79**
Edington. *Som* 3G **21**
Edington. *Wilts* 1E **23**
Edingworth. *Som* 1G **21**
Edistone. *Devn* 4C **18**
Edithmead. *Som* 2G **21**
Edith Weston. *Rut* 5G **75**
Edlaston. *Derbs* 1F **73**
Edlesborough. *Buck* 4H **51**
Edlingham. *Nmbd* 4F **121**
Edlington. *Linc* 3B **88**
Edmondsham. *Dors* 1F **15**
Edmondsley. *Dur* 5F **115**
Edmondthorpe. *Leics* 4F **75**
Edmonstone. *Orkn* 5E **172**
Edmonton. *Corn* 1D **6**
Edmonton. *G Lon* 1E **39**
Edmundbyers. *Dur* 4D **114**
Ednam. *Bord* 1B **120**
Ednaston. *Derbs* 1G **73**
Edney Common. *Essx* 5G **53**
Edrom. *Bord* 4E **131**
Edstaston. *Shrp* 2H **71**
Edstone. *Warw* 4F **61**
Edwalton. *Notts* 2C **74**
Edwardstone. *Suff* 1C **54**
Edwardsville. *Mer T* 2D **32**
Edwinsford. *Carm* 2G **45**
Edwinstowe. *Notts* 4D **86**
Edworth. *C Beds* 1C **52**
Edwyn Ralph. *Here* 5A **60**
Edzell. *Ang* 2F **145**
Efail-fach. *Neat* 2A **32**
Efail Isaf. *Rhon* 3D **32**
Efailnewydd. *Gwyn* 2C **68**
Efail-rhyd. *Powy* 3D **70**
Efailwen. *Carm* 2F **43**
Efenechtyd. *Den* 5D **82**
Effingham. *Surr* 5C **38**
Effingham Common. *Surr* 5C **38**
Effirth. *Shet* 6E **173**
Efflinch. *Staf* 4F **73**
Efford. *Devn* 2B **12**
Efstigarth. *Shet* 2F **173**
Egbury. *Hants* 1C **24**
Egdon. *Worc* 5D **60**
Egerton. *G Man* 3F **91**
Egerton. *Kent* 1D **28**
Egerton Forstal. *Kent* 1C **28**
Eggborough. *N Yor* 2F **93**
Eggbuckland. *Plym* 3A **8**
Eggesford. *Devn* 1G **11**
Eggington. *C Beds* 3H **51**
Egginton. *Derbs* 3G **73**
Egglescliffe. *Stoc T* 3B **106**
Eggleston. *Dur* 2C **104**
Egham. *Surr* 3B **38**
Egham Hythe. *Surr* 3B **38**
Egleton. *Rut* 5F **75**
Eglingham. *Nmbd* 3F **121**
Eglinton. *Derr* 4B **174**
Eglish. *M Ulst* 4B **178**
Egloshayle. *Corn* 5A **10**
Egloskerry. *Corn* 4C **10**
Eglwysbach. *Cnwy* 3H **81**
Eglwys-Brewis. *V Glam* 5D **32**
Eglwys Fach. *Cdgn* 1F **57**
Eglwyswrw. *Pemb* 1F **43**
Egmanton. *Notts* 4E **87**
Egmere. *Norf* 2B **78**
Egremont. *Cumb* 3B **102**
Egremont. *Mers* 1F **83**
Egton. *N Yor* 4F **107**
Egton Bridge. *N Yor* 4F **107**
Egypt. *Buck* 2A **38**
Egypt. *Hants* 2C **24**
Eight Ash Green. *Essx* 3C **54**
Eight Mile Burn. *Midl* 4E **129**
Eignaig. *High* 4B **140**
Eilanreach. *High* 2G **147**
Eildon. *Bord* 1H **119**
Eileanach Lodge. *High* 2H **157**
Eilean Fhlodaigh. *W Isl* 3D **170**
Eilean Iarmain. *High* 2F **147**
Einacleit. *W Isl* 5D **171**
Eisgein. *W Isl* 6F **171**
Eisingrug. *Gwyn* 2F **69**
Elan Village. *Powy* 4B **58**
Elberton. *S Glo* 3B **34**
Elbridge. *W Sus* 5A **26**
Elburton. *Plym* 3B **8**
Elcho. *Per* 1D **136**
Elcombe. *Swin* 3G **35**
Elcot. *W Ber* 5B **36**
Eldernell. *Cambs* 1C **64**
Eldersfield. *Worc* 2D **48**
Elderslie. *Ren* 3F **127**
Elder Street. *Essx* 2F **53**
Eldon. *Dur* 2F **105**
Eldroth. *N Yor* 3G **97**
Eldwick. *W Yor* 5D **98**
Elfhowe. *Cumb* 5F **103**
Elford. *Nmbd* 1F **121**
Elford. *Staf* 4F **73**
Elford Closes. *Cambs* 3D **65**
Elgin. *Mor* 2G **159**
Elgol. *High* 2D **146**
Elham. *Kent* 1F **29**
Elie. *Fife* 3G **137**
Eling. *Hants* 1B **16**
Eling. *W Ber* 4D **36**
Elishaw. *Nmbd* 5C **120**
Elizafield. *Dum* 2B **112**
Elkesley. *Notts* 3D **86**
Elkington. *Nptn* 3D **62**
Elkins Green. *Essx* 5G **53**
Elkstone. *Glos* 4E **49**
Ellan. *High* 1C **150**
Elland. *W Yor* 2B **92**
Ellary. *Arg* 2F **125**
Ellastone. *Staf* 1F **73**
Ellbridge. *Corn* 2A **8**
Ellel. *Lanc* 4D **97**
Ellemford. *Bord* 3D **130**
Ellenabeich. *Arg* 2E **133**
Ellenborough. *Cumb* 1B **102**
Ellenbrook. *Herts* 5C **52**
Ellenhall. *Staf* 3C **72**
Ellen's Green. *Surr* 2B **26**
Ellerbeck. *N Yor* 5B **106**
Ellerburn. *N Yor* 1C **100**
Ellerby. *N Yor* 3E **107**
Ellerdine. *Telf* 3A **72**
Ellerdine Heath. *Telf* 3A **72**
Ellerhayes. *Devn* 2C **12**
Elleric. *Arg* 4E **141**
Ellerker. *E Yor* 2C **94**
Ellerton. *E Yor* 1H **93**
Ellerton. *Shrp* 3B **72**
Ellerton-on-Swale. *N Yor* 5F **105**
Ellesborough. *Buck* 5G **51**
Ellesmere. *Shrp* 2G **71**
Ellesmere Port. *Ches W* 3G **83**
Ellingham. *Hants* 2G **15**
Ellingham. *Norf* 1F **67**
Ellingham. *Nmbd* 2F **121**
Ellingstring. *N Yor* 1D **98**
Ellington. *Cambs* 3A **64**
Ellington. *Nmbd* 5G **121**
Ellington Thorpe. *Cambs* 3A **64**
Elliot. *Ang* 5F **145**
Ellisfield. *Hants* 2E **25**
Ellishadder. *High* 2E **155**
Ellistown. *Leics* 4B **74**
Ellon. *Abers* 5G **161**
Ellonby. *Cumb* 1F **103**
Ellough. *Suff* 2G **67**
Elloughton. *E Yor* 2C **94**
Ellwood. *Glos* 5A **48**
Elm. *Cambs* 5D **76**
Elmbridge. *Glos* 4D **48**
Elmbridge. *Worc* 4D **60**
Elmdon. *Essx* 2E **53**
Elmdon. *W Mid* 2F **61**
Elmdon Heath. *W Mid* 2F **61**
Elmesthorpe. *Leics* 1B **62**
Elmfield. *IOW* 3E **16**
Elm Hill. *Dors* 4D **22**
Elmhurst. *Staf* 4F **73**
Elmley Castle. *Worc* 1E **49**
Elmley Lovett. *Worc* 4C **60**
Elmore. *Glos* 4C **48**
Elmore Back. *Glos* 4C **48**
Elm Park. *G Lon* 2G **39**
Elmscott. *Devn* 4C **18**
Elmsett. *Suff* 1D **54**
Elmstead. *Essx* 3D **54**
Elmstead Heath. *Essx* 3D **54**
Elmstead Market. *Essx* 3D **54**
Elmsted. *Kent* 1F **29**
Elmstone. *Kent* 4G **41**
Elmstone Hardwicke. *Glos* 3E **49**
Elmswell. *E Yor* 4D **101**
Elmswell. *Suff* 4B **66**
Elmton. *Derbs* 3C **86**
Elphin. *High* 2G **163**
Elphinstone. *E Lot* 2G **129**
Elrick. *Abers* 3F **153**
Elrick. *Mor* 1B **152**
Elrig. *Dum* 5A **110**
Elsdon. *Nmbd* 5D **120**
Elsecar. *S Yor* 1A **86**
Elsenham. *Essx* 3F **53**
Elsfield. *Oxon* 4D **50**
Elsham. *N Lin* 3D **94**
Elsing. *Norf* 4C **78**
Elslack. *N Yor* 5B **98**
Elsrickle. *S Lan* 5D **128**
Elstead. *Surr* 1A **26**
Elsted. *W Sus* 1G **17**
Elsted Marsh. *W Sus* 4G **25**
Elsthorpe. *Linc* 3H **75**
Elstob. *Dur* 2A **106**
Elston. *Devn* 2A **12**
Elston. *Lanc* 1E **90**
Elston. *Notts* 1E **75**
Elston. *Wilts* 2F **23**
Elstone. *Devn* 1G **11**
Elstow. *Bed* 1A **52**
Elstree. *Herts* 1C **38**
Elstronwick. *E Yor* 1F **95**
Elswick. *Lanc* 1C **90**
Elswick. *Tyne* 3F **115**
Elsworth. *Cambs* 4C **64**
Elterwater. *Cumb* 4E **103**
Eltham. *G Lon* 3F **39**
Eltisley. *Cambs* 5B **64**
Elton. *Cambs* 1H **63**
Elton. *Ches W* 3G **83**
Elton. *Derbs* 4G **85**
Elton. *Glos* 4C **48**
Elton. *G Man* 3F **91**
Elton. *Here* 3G **59**
Elton. *Notts* 2E **75**
Elton. *Stoc T* 3B **106**
Elton Green. *Ches W* 3G **83**
Eltringham. *Nmbd* 3D **115**
Elvanfoot. *S Lan* 3B **118**
Elvaston. *Derbs* 2B **74**
Elveden. *Suff* 3H **65**
Elvetham Heath. *Hants* 1F **25**
Elvingston. *E Lot* 2A **130**
Elvington. *Kent* 5G **41**
Elvington. *York* 5B **100**
Elwick. *Hart* 1B **106**
Elwick. *Nmbd* 1F **121**
Elworth. *Ches E* 4B **84**
Elworth. *Dors* 4A **14**
Elworthy. *Som* 3D **20**
Ely. *Cambs* 2E **65**
Ely. *Card* 4E **33**
Emberton. *Mil* 1G **51**
Embleton. *Cumb* 1C **102**
Embleton. *Hart* 2B **106**
Embleton. *Nmbd* 2G **121**
Embo. *High* 4F **165**
Emborough. *Som* 1B **22**
Embo Street. *High* 4F **165**
Embsay. *N Yor* 4C **98**
Emery Down. *Hants* 2A **16**
Emley. *W Yor* 3C **92**
Emmbrook. *Wok* 5F **37**
Emmer Green. *Read* 4F **37**
Emmington. *Oxon* 5F **51**
Emneth. *Norf* 5D **77**
Emneth Hungate. *Norf* 5E **77**
Empingham. *Rut* 5G **75**
Empshott. *Hants* 3F **25**
Emsworth. *Hants* 2F **17**
Enborne. *W Ber* 5C **36**
Enborne Row. *W Ber* 5C **36**
Enchmarsh. *Shrp* 1H **59**
Enderby. *Leics* 1C **62**
Endmoor. *Cumb* 1E **97**
Endon. *Staf* 5D **84**
Endon Bank. *Staf* 5D **84**
Enfield. *G Lon* 1E **39**
Enfield Wash. *G Lon* 1E **39**
Enford. *Wilts* 1G **23**
Engine Common. *S Glo* 3B **34**
Englefield. *W Ber* 4E **37**
Englefield Green. *Surr* 3A **38**
Englesea-brook. *Ches E* 5B **84**
English Bicknor. *Glos* 4A **48**
Englishcombe. *Bath* 5C **34**
English Frankton. *Shrp* 3G **71**
Enham Alamein. *Hants* 2B **24**
Enmore. *Som* 3F **21**
Ennerdale Bridge. *Cumb* 3B **102**
Enniscaven. *Corn* 3D **6**
Enniskillen. *Ferm* 8E **176**
Enoch. *Dum* 4A **118**
Enochdhu. *Per* 2H **143**
Ensay. *Arg* 4E **139**
Ensbury. *Bour* 3F **15**
Ensdon. *Shrp* 4G **71**
Ensis. *Devn* 4F **19**
Enson. *Staf* 3D **72**
Enstone. *Oxon* 3B **50**
Enterkinfoot. *Dum* 4A **118**
Enville. *Staf* 2C **60**
Eolaigearraidh. *W Isl* 8C **170**
Eorabus. *Arg* 1A **132**
Eoropaidh. *W Isl* 1H **171**
Epney. *Glos* 4C **48**
Epperstone. *Notts* 1D **74**
Epping. *Essx* 5E **53**
Epping Green. *Essx* 5E **53**
Epping Green. *Herts* 5C **52**
Epping Upland. *Essx* 5E **53**
Eppleby. *N Yor* 3E **105**
Eppleworth. *E Yor* 1D **94**
Epsom. *Surr* 4D **38**
Epwell. *Oxon* 1B **50**
Epworth. *N Lin* 4A **94**
Epworth Turbary. *N Lin* 4A **94**
Erbistock. *Wrex* 1F **71**
Erbusaig. *High* 1F **147**
Erchless Castle. *High* 4G **157**
Erdington. *W Mid* 1F **61**
Eredine. *Arg* 3G **133**
Eriboll. *High* 3E **167**
Ericstane. *Dum* 3C **118**
Eridge Green. *E Sus* 2G **27**
Erines. *Arg* 2G **125**
Eriswell. *Suff* 3G **65**
Erith. *G Lon* 3G **39**
Erlestoke. *Wilts* 1E **23**
Ermine. *Linc* 3G **87**
Ermington. *Devn* 3C **8**
Ernesettle. *Plym* 3A **8**
Erpingham. *Norf* 2D **78**
Erriott Wood. *Kent* 5D **40**
Errogie. *High* 1H **149**
Errol. *Per* 1E **137**
Errol Station. *Per* 1E **137**
Erskine. *Ren* 2F **127**
Erskine Bridge. *Ren* 2F **127**
Ervie. *Dum* 3F **109**
Erwarton. *Suff* 2F **55**
Erwood. *Powy* 1D **46**
Eryholme. *N Yor* 4A **106**
Eryrys. *Den* 5E **82**
Escalls. *Corn* 4A **4**
Escomb. *Dur* 1E **105**
Escrick. *N Yor* 5A **100**
Esgair. *Carm*
nr. Carmarthen 3D **45**
nr. St Clears 3G **43**
Esgairgeiliog. *Powy* 5G **69**
Esh. *Dur* 5E **115**
Esher. *Surr* 4C **38**
Esholt. *W Yor* 5D **98**
Eshott. *Nmbd* 5G **121**
Eshton. *N Yor* 4B **98**
Esh Winning. *Dur* 5E **115**
Eskadale. *High* 5G **157**
Eskbank. *Midl* 3G **129**
Eskdale Green. *Cumb* 4C **102**
Eskdalemuir. *Dum* 5E **119**
Eskham. *Linc* 1C **88**
Esknish. *Arg* 3B **124**
Esk Valley. *N Yor* 4F **107**
Eslington Hall. *Nmbd* 3E **121**
Esprick. *Lanc* 1C **90**
Essendine. *Rut* 4H **75**
Essendon. *Herts* 5C **52**
Essich. *High* 5A **158**
Essington. *Staf* 5D **72**
Eston. *Red C* 3C **106**
Estover. *Plym* 3B **8**
Eswick. *Shet* 6F **173**
Etal. *Nmbd* 1D **120**
Etchilhampton. *Wilts* 5F **35**
Etchingham. *E Sus* 3B **28**
Etchinghill. *Kent* 2F **29**
Etchinghill. *Staf* 4E **73**
Etherley Dene. *Dur* 2E **105**
Ethie Haven. *Ang* 4F **145**
Etling Green. *Norf* 4C **78**
Etloe. *Glos* 5B **48**
Eton. *Wind* 3A **38**
Eton Wick. *Wind* 3A **38**
Etteridge. *High* 4A **150**
Ettersgill. *Dur* 2B **104**
Ettiley Heath. *Ches E* 4B **84**
Ettington. *Warw* 1A **50**
Etton. *E Yor* 5D **101**
Etton. *Pet* 5A **76**
Ettrick. *Bord* 3E **119**
Ettrickbridge. *Bord* 2F **119**
Etwall. *Derbs* 2G **73**
Eudon Burnell. *Shrp* 2B **60**
Eudon George. *Shrp* 2A **60**
Euston. *Suff* 3A **66**
Euxton. *Lanc* 3D **90**
Evanstown. *B'end* 3C **32**
Evanton. *High* 2A **158**
Evedon. *Linc* 1H **75**
Evelix. *High* 4E **165**
Evendine. *Here* 1C **48**
Evenjobb. *Powy* 4E **59**
Evenley. *Nptn* 2D **50**
Evenlode. *Glos* 3H **49**
Even Swindon. *Swin* 3G **35**
Evenwood. *Dur* 2E **105**
Evenwood Gate. *Dur* 2E **105**
Everbay. *Orkn* 5F **172**
Evercreech. *Som* 3B **22**
Everdon. *Nptn* 5C **62**
Everingham. *E Yor* 5C **100**
Everleigh. *Wilts* 1H **23**
Everley. *N Yor* 1D **100**
Eversholt. *C Beds* 2H **51**
Evershot. *Dors* 2A **14**
Eversley. *Hants* 5F **37**
Eversley Centre. *Hants* 5F **37**
Eversley Cross. *Hants* 5F **37**
Everthorpe. *E Yor* 1C **94**
Everton. *C Beds* 5B **64**
Everton. *Hants* 3A **16**
Everton. *Mers* 1F **83**
Everton. *Notts* 1D **86**
Evertown. *Dum* 2E **113**
Evesbatch. *Here* 1B **48**
Evesham. *Worc* 1F **49**
Evington. *Leic* 5D **74**
Ewden Village. *S Yor* 1G **85**
Ewdness. *Shrp* 1B **60**
Ewell. *Surr* 4D **38**
Ewell Minnis. *Kent* 1G **29**
Ewelme. *Oxon* 2E **37**
Ewen. *Glos* 2F **35**
Ewenny. *V Glam* 4C **32**
Ewerby. *Linc* 1A **76**
Ewes. *Dum* 5F **119**
Ewesley. *Nmbd* 5E **121**
Ewhurst. *Surr* 1B **26**
Ewhurst Green. *E Sus* 3B **28**
Ewhurst Green. *Surr* 2B **26**
Ewlo. *Flin* 4E **83**
Ewloe. *Flin* 4E **83**
Ewood Bridge. *Lanc* 2F **91**
Eworthy. *Devn* 3E **11**
Ewshot. *Hants* 1G **25**
Ewyas Harold. *Here* 3G **47**
Exbourne. *Devn* 2G **11**
Exbury. *Hants* 2C **16**
Exceat. *E Sus* 5G **27**
Exebridge. *Som* 4C **20**
Exelby. *N Yor* 1E **99**
Exeter. *Devn* **195** (3C **12**)
Exeter Airport. *Devn* 3D **12**
Exford. *Som* 3B **20**
Exfords Green. *Shrp* 5G **71**
Exhall. *Warw* 5F **61**
Exlade Street. *Oxon* 3E **37**
Exminster. *Devn* 4C **12**
Exmouth. *Devn* 4D **12**
Exnaboe. *Shet* 10E **173**
Exning. *Suff* 4F **65**
Exton. *Devn* 4C **12**
Exton. *Hants* 4E **24**
Exton. *Rut* 4G **75**
Exton. *Som* 3C **20**
Exwick. *Devn* 3C **12**
Eyam. *Derbs* 3G **85**
Eydon. *Nptn* 5C **62**
Eye. *Here* 4G **59**
Eye. *Pet* 5B **76**
Eye. *Suff* 3D **66**
Eye Green. *Pet* 5B **76**
Eyemouth. *Bord* 3F **131**
Eyeworth. *C Beds* 1C **52**
Eyhorne Street. *Kent* 5C **40**
Eyke. *Suff* 5F **67**
Eynesbury. *Cambs* 5A **64**
Eynort. *High* 1B **146**
Eynsford. *Kent* 4G **39**
Eynsham. *Oxon* 5C **50**
Eyre. *High*
on Isle of Skye 3D **154**
on Raasay 5E **155**
Eythorne. *Kent* 1G **29**
Eyton. *Here* 4G **59**
Eyton. *Shrp*
nr. Bishop's Castle 2F **59**
nr. Shrewsbury 4F **71**
Eyton. *Wrex* 1F **71**
Eyton on Severn. *Shrp* 5H **71**
Eyton upon the Weald Moors. *Telf* 4A **72**

F

Faccombe. *Hants* 1B **24**
Faceby. *N Yor* 4B **106**
Faddiley. *Ches E* 5H **83**
Fadmoor. *N Yor* 1A **100**
Fagwyr. *Swan* 5G **45**
Faichem. *High* 3E **149**
Faifley. *W Dun* 2G **127**
Fail. *S Ayr* 2D **116**
Failand. *N Som* 4A **34**
Failford. *S Ayr* 2D **116**
Failsworth. *G Man* 4H **91**
Fairbourne. *Gwyn* 4F **69**
Fairbourne Heath. *Kent* 5C **40**
Fairburn. *N Yor* 2E **93**
Fairfield. *Derbs* 3E **85**
Fairfield. *Kent* 3D **28**
Fairfield. *Worc*
nr. Bromsgrove 3D **60**
nr. Evesham 1F **49**
Fairford. *Glos* 5G **49**
Fair Green. *Norf* 4F **77**
Fair Hill. *Cumb* 1G **103**
Fairhill. *S Lan* 4A **128**
Fair Isle Airport. *Shet* 1B **172**
Fairlands. *Surr* 5A **38**
Fairlie. *N Ayr* 4D **126**
Fairlight. *E Sus* 4C **28**
Fairlight Cove. *E Sus* 4C **28**
Fairmile. *Devn* 3D **12**
Fairmile. *Surr* 4C **38**
Fairmilehead. *Edin* 3F **129**
Fair Oak. *Devn* 1D **12**
Fair Oak. *Hants*
nr. Eastleigh 1C **16**
nr. Kingsclere 5D **36**
Fairoak. *Staf* 2B **72**
Fair Oak Green. *Hants* 5E **37**
Fairseat. *Kent* 4H **39**
Fairstead. *Essx* 4A **54**
Fairstead. *Norf* 4F **77**
Fairwarp. *E Sus* 3F **27**
Fairwater. *Card* 4E **33**
Fairy Cross. *Devn* 4E **19**
Fakenham. *Norf* 3B **78**
Fakenham Magna. *Suff* 3B **66**
Fala. *Midl* 3H **129**
Fala Dam. *Midl* 3H **129**
Falcon. *Here* 2B **48**
Faldingworth. *Linc* 2H **87**
Falfield. *S Glo* 2B **34**
Y Fali. *IOA* 3B **80**
Falkenham. *Suff* 2F **55**
Falkirk. *Falk* 1B **128**
Falkland. *Fife* 3E **137**
Fallin. *Stir* 4H **135**
Fallowfield. *G Man* 1C **84**
Falmer. *E Sus* 5E **27**
Falmouth. *Corn* 5C **6**
Falsgrave. *N Yor* 1E **101**
Falstone. *Nmbd* 1A **114**
Fanagmore. *High* 4B **166**
Fancott. *C Beds* 3A **52**
Fanellan. *High* 4G **157**
Fangdale Beck. *N Yor* 5C **106**
Fangfoss. *E Yor* 4B **100**
Fankerton. *Falk* 1A **128**
Fanmore. *Arg* 4F **139**
Fanner's Green. *Essx* 4G **53**
Fannich Lodge. *High* 2E **156**
Fans. *Bord* 5C **130**
Farcet. *Cambs* 1B **64**
Far Cotton. *Nptn* 5E **63**
Fareham. *Hants* 2D **16**
Farewell. *Staf* 4E **73**
Far Forest. *Worc* 3B **60**
Farforth. *Linc* 3C **88**
Far Green. *Glos* 5C **48**
Far Hoarcross. *Staf* 3F **73**
Faringdon. *Oxon* 2A **36**
Farington. *Lanc* 2D **90**
Farlam. *Cumb* 4G **113**
Farleigh. *N Som* 5H **33**
Farleigh. *Surr* 4E **39**
Farleigh Hungerford. *Som* 1D **22**
Farleigh Wallop. *Hants* 2E **24**
Farleigh Wick. *Wilts* 5D **34**
Farlesthorpe. *Linc* 3D **88**
Farleton. *Cumb* 1E **97**
Farleton. *Lanc* 3E **97**
Farley. *High* 4G **157**
Farley. *Shrp*
nr. Shrewsbury 5F **71**
nr. Telford 5A **72**
Farley. *Staf* 1E **73**
Farley. *Wilts* 4H **23**
Farley Green. *Suff* 5G **65**
Farley Green. *Surr* 1B **26**
Farley Hill. *Wok* 5F **37**
Farley's End. *Glos* 4C **48**
Farlington. *N Yor* 3A **100**
Farlington. *Port* 2E **17**
Farlow. *Shrp* 2A **60**
Farmborough. *Bath* 5B **34**
Farmcote. *Glos* 3F **49**
Farmcote. *Shrp* 1B **60**
Farmington. *Glos* 4G **49**
Far Moor. *G Man* 4D **90**
Farmoor. *Oxon* 5C **50**
Farmtown. *Mor* 3C **160**
Farnah Green. *Derbs* 1H **73**
Farnborough. *G Lon* 4F **39**
Farnborough. *Hants* 1G **25**
Farnborough. *Warw* 1C **50**
Farnborough. *W Ber* 3C **36**
Farncombe. *Surr* 1A **26**
Farndish. *Bed* 4G **63**
Farndon. *Ches W* 5G **83**
Farndon. *Notts* 5E **87**
Farnell. *Ang* 3F **145**
Farnham. *Dors* 1E **15**
Farnham. *Essx* 3E **53**
Farnham. *N Yor* 3F **99**
Farnham. *Suff* 4F **67**
Farnham. *Surr* 2G **25**
Farnham Common. *Buck* 2A **38**
Farnham Green. *Essx* 3E **53**
Farnham Royal. *Buck* 2A **38**
Farnhill. *N Yor* 5C **98**
Farningham. *Kent* 4G **39**
Farnley. *N Yor* 5E **98**
Farnley Tyas. *W Yor* 3B **92**
Farnsfield. *Notts* 5D **86**
Farnworth. *G Man* 4F **91**
Farnworth. *Hal* 2H **83**
Far Oakridge. *Glos* 5E **49**
Farr. *High*
nr. Bettyhill 2H **167**
nr. Inverness 5A **158**
nr. Kingussie 3C **150**
Farraline. *High* 1H **149**
Farringdon. *Devn* 3D **12**
Farrington. *Dors* 1D **14**
Farrington Gurney. *Bath* 1B **22**
Far Sawrey. *Cumb* 5E **103**
Farsley. *W Yor* 1C **92**
Farthinghoe. *Nptn* 2D **50**
Farthingstone. *Nptn* 5D **62**
Farthorpe. *Linc* 3B **88**
Fartown. *W Yor* 3B **92**
Farway. *Devn* 3E **13**
Fasag. *High* 3A **156**
Fascadale. *High* 1G **139**
Fasnacloich. *Arg* 4E **141**
Fassfern. *High* 1E **141**
Fatfield. *Tyne* 4G **115**
Faugh. *Cumb* 4G **113**
Fauld. *Staf* 3F **73**
Fauldhouse. *W Lot* 3C **128**
Faulkbourne. *Essx* 4A **54**
Faulkland. *Som* 1C **22**
Fauls. *Shrp* 2H **71**
Faverdale. *Darl* 3F **105**
Faversham. *Kent* 4E **40**
Fawdington. *N Yor* 2G **99**
Fawfieldhead. *Staf* 4E **85**
Fawkham Green. *Kent* 4G **39**
Fawler. *Oxon* 4B **50**
Fawley. *Buck* 3F **37**
Fawley. *Hants* 2C **16**
Fawley. *W Ber* 3B **36**
Fawley Chapel. *Here* 3A **48**
Fawton. *Corn* 2F **7**
Faxfleet. *E Yor* 2B **94**
Faygate. *W Sus* 2D **26**
Fazakerley. *Mers* 1F **83**
Fazeley. *Staf* 5F **73**
Feagour. *High* 4H **149**
Fearann Dhomhnaill. *High* 3E **147**
Fearby. *N Yor* 1D **98**
Fearn. *High* 1C **158**
Fearnan. *Per* 4E **142**
Fearnbeg. *High* 3G **155**
Fearnhead. *Warr* 1A **84**
Fearnmore. *High* 2G **155**
Featherstone. *Staf* 5D **72**
Featherstone. *W Yor* 2E **93**
Featherstone Castle. *Nmbd* 3H **113**
Feckenham. *Worc* 4E **61**
Feeny. *Caus* 6C **174**
Feering. *Essx* 3B **54**
Feetham. *N Yor* 5C **104**
Feizor. *N Yor* 3G **97**
Felbridge. *Surr* 2E **27**
Felbrigg. *Norf* 2E **78**
Felcourt. *Surr* 1E **27**
Felden. *Herts* 5A **52**
Felhampton. *Shrp* 2G **59**
Felindre. *Carm*
nr. Llandeilo 3F **45**
nr. Llandovery 2G **45**
nr. Newcastle Emlyn 2D **44**
Felindre. *Powy* 2D **58**
Felindre. *Swan* 5G **45**
Felindre Farchog. *Pemb* 1F **43**
Felinfach. *Cdgn* 5E **57**
Felinfach. *Powy* 2D **46**
Felinfoel. *Carm* 5F **45**
Felingwmisaf. *Carm* 3F **45**
Felingwmuchaf. *Carm* 3F **45**
Y Felinheli. *Gwyn* 4E **81**
Felin Newydd. *Powy*
nr. Newtown 5C **70**
nr. Oswestry 3E **70**
Felin Wnda. *Cdgn* 1D **44**
Felinwynt. *Cdgn* 5B **56**
Felixkirk. *N Yor* 1G **99**
Felixstowe. *Suff* 2F **55**
Felixstowe Ferry. *Suff* 2G **55**
Felkington. *Nmbd* 5F **131**
Fell End. *Cumb* 5A **104**
Felling. *Tyne* 3F **115**
Fell Side. *Cumb* 1E **102**
Felmersham. *Bed* 5G **63**
Felmingham. *Norf* 3E **79**
Felpham. *W Sus* 3H **17**
Felsham. *Suff* 5B **66**
Felsted. *Essx* 3G **53**
Feltham. *G Lon* 3C **38**
Felthamhill. *Surr* 3B **38**
Felthorpe. *Norf* 4D **78**
Felton. *Here* 1A **48**
Felton. *N Som* 5A **34**
Felton. *Nmbd* 4F **121**
Felton Butler. *Shrp* 4F **71**
Feltwell. *Norf* 1G **65**
Fenay Bridge. *W Yor* 3B **92**
Fence. *Lanc* 1G **91**
Fence Houses. *Tyne* 4G **115**
Fencott. *Oxon* 4D **50**
Fen Ditton. *Cambs* 4D **65**
Fen Drayton. *Cambs* 4C **64**
Fen End. *Linc* 3B **76**
Fen End. *W Mid* 3G **61**
Fenham. *Nmbd* 5G **131**
Fenham. *Tyne* 3F **115**
Fenhouses. *Linc* 1B **76**
Feniscowles. *Bkbn* 2E **91**
Feniton. *Devn* 3D **12**
Fenn Green. *Shrp* 2B **60**
Y Fenni. *Mon* 4G **47**
Fenn's Bank. *Wrex* 2H **71**
Fenn Street. *Medw* 3B **40**
Fenny Bentley. *Derbs* 5F **85**
Fenny Bridges. *Devn* 3E **12**
Fenny Compton. *Warw* 5B **62**
Fenny Drayton. *Leics* 1H **61**
Fenny Stratford. *Mil* 2G **51**
Fenrother. *Nmbd* 5F **121**
Fenstanton. *Cambs* 4C **64**
Fen Street. *Norf* 1C **66**
Fenton. *Cambs* 3C **64**
Fenton. *Cumb* 4G **113**
Fenton. *Linc*
nr. Caythorpe 5F **87**
nr. Saxilby 3F **87**
Fenton. *Nmbd* 1D **120**
Fenton. *Notts* 2E **87**
Fenton. *Stoke* 1C **72**
Fentonadle. *Corn* 5A **10**
Fenton Barns. *E Lot* 1B **130**
Fenwick. *E Ayr* 5F **127**
Fenwick. *Nmbd*
nr. Berwick-upon-Tweed 5G **131**
nr. Hexham 2D **114**
Fenwick. *S Yor* 3F **93**
Feochaig. *Arg* 4B **122**
Feock. *Corn* 5C **6**
Feolin Ferry. *Arg* 3C **124**
Feorlan. *Arg* 5A **122**
Ferindonald. *High* 3E **147**
Feriniquarrie. *High* 3A **154**
Fern. *Ang* 2D **145**
Ferndale. *Rhon* 2C **32**
Ferndown. *Dors* 2F **15**
Ferness. *High* 4D **158**
Fernham. *Oxon* 2A **36**
Fernhill. *W Sus* 1E **27**
Fernhill Heath. *Worc* 5C **60**
Fernhurst. *W Sus* 4G **25**
Fernieflatt. *Abers* 1H **145**
Ferniegair. *S Lan* 4A **128**
Fernilea. *High* 5C **154**
Fernilee. *Derbs* 3E **85**
Ferrensby. *N Yor* 3F **99**
Ferriby Sluice. *N Lin* 2C **94**
Ferring. *W Sus* 5B **26**
Ferrybridge. *W Yor* 2E **93**
Ferryden. *Ang* 3G **145**
Ferryhill. *Aber* 3G **153**
Ferry Hill. *Cambs* 2C **64**
Ferryhill. *Dur* 1F **105**
Ferryhill Station. *Dur* 1A **106**
Ferryside. *Carm* 4D **44**
Ferryton. *High* 2A **158**
Fersfield. *Norf* 2C **66**
Fersit. *High* 1A **142**
Y Ferwig. *Cdgn* 1B **44**
Feshiebridge. *High* 3C **150**
Fetcham. *Surr* 5C **38**
Fetterangus. *Abers* 3G **161**
Fettercairn. *Abers* 1F **145**
Fewcott. *Oxon* 3D **50**
Fewston. *N Yor* 4D **98**
Ffairfach. *Carm* 3G **45**
Ffair Rhos. *Cdgn* 4G **57**
Ffaldybrenin. *Carm* 1G **45**
Ffarmers. *Carm* 1G **45**
Ffawyddog. *Powy* 4F **47**
Y Fflint. *Flin* 3E **83**
Ffodun. *Powy* 5E **71**
Ffont-y-gari. *V Glam* 5D **32**
Y Ffor. *Gwyn* 2C **68**
Fforest. *Carm* 5F **45**
Fforest-fach. *Swan* 3F **31**
Fforest Goch. *Neat* 5H **45**
Ffostrasol. *Cdgn* 1D **44**
Ffos-y-ffin. *Cdgn* 4D **56**
Ffrith. *Flin* 5E **83**
Ffwl-y-mwn. *V Glam* 5D **32**
Ffynnongroyw. *Flin* 2D **82**
Ffynnon Gynydd. *Powy* 1E **47**
Ffynnon-oer. *Cdgn* 5E **57**
Fiag Lodge. *High* 1B **164**
Fidden. *Arg* 2B **132**
Fiddington. *Glos* 2E **49**
Fiddington. *Som* 2F **21**
Fiddleford. *Dors* 1D **14**
Fiddlers Hamlet. *Essx* 5E **53**
Field. *Staf* 2E **73**
Field Assarts. *Oxon* 4B **50**
Field Broughton. *Cumb* 1C **96**
Field Dalling. *Norf* 2C **78**
Fieldhead. *Cumb* 1F **103**
Field Head. *Leics* 5B **74**
Fifehead Magdalen. *Dors* 4C **22**
Fifehead Neville. *Dors* 1C **14**
Fifehead St Quintin. *Dors* 1C **14**
Fife Keith. *Mor* 3B **160**
Fifield. *Oxon* 4H **49**
Fifield. *Wilts* 1G **23**
Fifield. *Wind* 3A **38**
Fifield Bavant. *Wilts* 4F **23**
Figheldean. *Wilts* 2G **23**
Filby. *Norf* 4G **79**
Filey. *N Yor* 1F **101**
Filford. *Dors* 3H **13**
Filgrave. *Mil* 1G **51**
Filkins. *Oxon* 5H **49**
Filleigh. *Devn*
nr. Crediton 1H **11**
nr. South Molton 4G **19**
Fillingham. *Linc* 2G **87**
Fillongley. *Warw* 2G **61**
Filton. *S Glo* 4B **34**
Fimber. *E Yor* 3C **100**
Finavon. *Ang* 3D **145**
Fincham. *Norf* 5F **77**
Finchampstead. *Wok* 5F **37**
Fincharn. *Arg* 3G **133**
Finchdean. *Hants* 1F **17**
Finchingfield. *Essx* 2G **53**
Finchley. *G Lon* 1D **38**
Findern. *Derbs* 2H **73**
Findhorn. *Mor* 2E **159**
Findhorn Bridge. *High* 1C **150**
Findochty. *Mor* 2B **160**
Findo Gask. *Per* 1C **136**
Findon. *Abers* 4G **153**
Findon. *W Sus* 5C **26**
Findon Mains. *High* 2A **158**
Findon Valley. *W Sus* 5C **26**
Finedon. *Nptn* 3G **63**
Fingal Street. *Suff* 3E **66**
Fingest. *Buck* 2F **37**
Finghall. *N Yor* 1D **98**
Fingland. *Cumb* 4D **112**
Fingland. *Dum* 3G **117**
Finglesham. *Kent* 5H **41**
Fingringhoe. *Essx* 3D **54**
Finiskaig. *High* 4A **148**
Finmere. *Oxon* 2E **51**
Finnart. *Per* 3C **142**
Finningham. *Suff* 4C **66**
Finningley. *S Yor* 1D **86**
Finnygaud. *Abers* 3D **160**
Finsbury. *G Lon* 2E **39**
Finstall. *Worc* 4D **61**
Finsthwaite. *Cumb* 1C **96**
Finstock. *Oxon* 4B **50**
Finstown. *Orkn* 6C **172**
Fintona. *Ferm* 3K **177**
Fintry. *Abers* 3E **161**
Fintry. *D'dee* 5D **144**
Fintry. *Stir* 1H **127**
Finvoy. *Caus* 5F **175**
Finwood. *Warw* 4F **61**
Finzean. *Abers* 4D **152**
Fionnphort. *Arg* 2B **132**
Fionnsabhagh. *W Isl* 9C **171**
Firbeck. *S Yor* 2C **86**
Firby. *N Yor*
nr. Bedale 1E **99**
nr. Malton 3B **100**
Firgrove. *G Man* 3H **91**
Firle. *E Sus* 5F **27**
Firsby. *Linc* 4D **88**
Firsdown. *Wilts* 3H **23**
First Coast. *High* 4D **162**
Firth. *Shet* 4F **173**
Fir Tree. *Dur* 1E **105**
Fishbourne. *IOW* 3D **16**
Fishbourne. *W Sus* 2G **17**
Fishburn. *Dur* 1A **106**
Fishcross. *Clac* 4A **136**
Fisherford. *Abers* 5D **160**
Fisherrow. *E Lot* 2G **129**
Fisher's Pond. *Hants* 4C **24**
Fisher's Row. *Lanc* 5D **96**
Fisherstreet. *W Sus* 2A **26**
Fisherton. *High* 3B **158**
Fisherton. *S Ayr* 3B **116**
Fisherton de la Mere. *Wilts* 3E **23**
Fishguard. *Pemb* 1D **42**
Fishlake. *S Yor* 3G **93**
Fishley. *Norf* 4G **79**
Fishnish. *Arg* 4A **140**
Fishpond Bottom. *Dors* 3G **13**
Fishponds. *Bris* 4B **34**
Fishpool. *Glos* 3B **48**
Fishpool. *G Man* 3G **91**
Fishpools. *Powy* 4D **58**
Fishtoft. *Linc* 1C **76**
Fishtoft Drove. *Linc* 1C **76**
Fishwick. *Bord* 4F **131**
Fiskavaig. *High* 5C **154**
Fiskerton. *Linc* 3H **87**
Fiskerton. *Notts* 5E **87**
Fitch. *Shet* 7E **173**
Fitling. *E Yor* 1F **95**
Fittleton. *Wilts* 2G **23**
Fittleworth. *W Sus* 4B **26**
Fitton End. *Cambs* 4D **76**
Fitz. *Shrp* 4G **71**
Fitzhead. *Som* 4E **20**
Fitzwilliam. *W Yor* 3E **93**
Fiunary. *High* 4A **140**
Five Ash Down. *E Sus* 3F **27**
Five Ashes. *E Sus* 3G **27**
Five Bells. *Som* 2D **20**
Five Bridges. *Here* 1B **48**
Fivehead. *Som* 4G **21**
Fivelanes. *Corn* 4C **10**
Fivemiletown. *M Ulst* 5K **177**
Five Oak Green. *Kent* 1H **27**
Five Oaks. *W Sus* 3B **26**
Five Roads. *Carm* 5E **45**
Five Ways. *Warw* 3G **61**
Flack's Green. *Essx* 4A **54**
Flackwell Heath. *Buck* 3G **37**
Fladbury. *Worc* 1E **49**
Fladda. *Shet* 3E **173**
Fladdabister. *Shet* 8F **173**
Flagg. *Derbs* 4F **85**
Flamborough. *E Yor* 2G **101**
Flamstead. *Herts* 4A **52**
Flansham. *W Sus* 5A **26**
Flasby. *N Yor* 4B **98**
Flash. *Staf* 4E **85**
Flashader. *High* 3C **154**
Flatt, The. *Cumb* 2G **113**
Flaunden. *Herts* 5A **52**
Flawborough. *Notts* 1E **75**
Flawith. *N Yor* 3G **99**
Flax Bourton. *N Som* 5A **34**
Flaxby. *N Yor* 4F **99**
Flaxholme. *Derbs* 1H **73**
Flaxley. *Glos* 4B **48**
Flaxley Green. *Staf* 4E **73**

Hailey—Hessett

Hailey. Herts 4D 52
Hailey. Oxon 4B 50
Hailsham. E Sus 5G 27
Hail Weston. Cambs 4A 64
Hainault. G Lon 1F 39
Hainford. Norf 4E 78
Hainton. Linc 2A 88
Hainworth. W Yor 1A 92
Haisthorpe. E Yor 3F 101
Hakin. Pemb 4C 42
Halam. Notts 5D 86
Halbeath. Fife 1E 129
Halberton. Devn 1D 12
Halcro. High 2E 169
Hale. Cumb 2E 97
Hale. G Man 2B 84
Hale. Hal 2G 83
Hale. Hants 1G 15
Hale. Surr 2G 25
Hale Bank. Hal 2G 83
Halebarns. G Man 2B 84
Hales. Norf 1F 67
Hales. Staf 2B 72
Halesgate. Linc 3C 76
Hales Green. Derbs 1F 73
Halesowen. W Mid 2D 60
Hale Street. Kent 1A 28
Halesworth. Suff 3F 67
Halewood. Mers 2G 83
Halford. Shrp 2G 59
Halford. Warw 1A 50
Halfpenny. Cumb 1E 97
Halfpenny Furze. Carm 3G 43
Halfpenny Green. Staf 1C 60
Halfway. Carm
nr. Llandeilo 2G 45
nr. Llandovery 2B 46
Halfway. S Yor 2B 86
Halfway. W Ber 5C 36
Halfway House. Shrp 4F 71
Halfway Houses. Kent 3D 40
Halgabron. Corn 4A 10
Halifax. W Yor 2A 92
Halistra. High 3B 154
Halket. E Ayr 4F 127
Halkirk. High 3D 168
Halkyn. Flin 3E 82
Hall. E Ren 4F 127
Hallam Fields. Derbs 1B 74
Halland. E Sus 4G 27
Hallands, The. N Lin 2D 94
Hallaton. Leics 1E 63
Hallatrow. Bath 1B 22
Hallbank. Cumb 5H 103
Hallbankgate. Cumb 4G 113
Hall Dunnerdale. Cumb 5D 102
Hallen. S Glo 3A 34
Hall End. Bed 1A 52
Hallgarth. Dur 5G 115
Hall Green. Ches E 5C 84
Hall Green. Norf 2D 66
Hall Green. W Mid 2F 61
Hall Green. W Yor 3D 92
Hall Green. Wrex 1G 71
Halliburton. Bord 5C 130
Hallin. High 3B 154
Halling. Medw 4B 40
Hallington. Linc 2C 88
Hallington. Nmbd 2C 114
Halloughton. Notts 5D 86
Hallow. Worc 5C 60
Hallow Heath. Worc 5C 60
Hallowsgate. Ches W 4H 83
Hallsands. Devn 5E 9
Hall's Green. Herts 3C 52
Hallspill. Devn 4E 19
Hallthwaites. Cumb 1A 96
Hall Waberthwaite. Cumb 5C 102
Hallwood Green. Glos 2B 48
Hallworthy. Corn 4B 10
Hallyne. Bord 5E 129
Halmer End. Staf 1C 72
Halmond's Frome. Here 1B 48
Halmore. Glos 5B 48
Halnaker. W Sus 5A 26
Halsall. Lanc 3B 90
Halse. Nptn 1D 50
Halse. Som 4E 21
Halsetown. Corn 3C 4
Halsham. E Yor 2F 95
Halsinger. Devn 3F 19
Halstead. Essx 2B 54
Halstead. Kent 4F 39
Halstead. Leics 5E 75
Halstock. Dors 2A 14
Halsway. Som 3E 21
Haltcliff Bridge. Cumb 1E 103
Haltham. Linc 4B 88
Haltoft End. Linc 1C 76
Halton. Buck 5G 51
Halton. Hal 2H 83
Halton. Lanc 3E 97
Halton. Nmbd 3C 114
Halton. W Yor 1D 92
Halton. Wrex 2F 71
Halton East. N Yor 4C 98
Halton Fenside. Linc 4D 88
Halton Gill. N Yor 2A 98
Halton Holegate. Linc 4D 88
Halton Lea Gate. Nmbd 4H 113
Halton Moor. W Yor 1D 92
Halton Shields. Nmbd 3D 114
Halton West. N Yor 4H 97
Haltwhistle. Nmbd 3A 114
Halvergate. Norf 5G 79
Halwell. Devn 3D 9
Halwill. Devn 3E 11
Halwill Junction. Devn 3E 11
Ham. Devn 2F 13
Ham. Glos 2B 34
Ham. G Lon 3C 38
Ham. High 1E 169
Ham. Kent 5H 41
Ham. Plym 3A 8
Ham. Shet 8A 173
Ham. Som
nr. Ilminster 1F 13
nr. Taunton 4F 21
nr. Wellington 4E 21
Ham. Wilts 5B 36
Hambleden. Buck 3F 37
Hambledon. Hants 1E 17
Hambledon. Surr 2A 26
Hamble-le-Rice. Hants 2C 16
Hambleton. Lanc 5C 96
Hambleton. N Yor 1F 93
Hambridge. Som 4G 21
Hambrook. S Glo 4B 34
Hambrook. W Sus 2F 17
Ham Common. Dors 4D 22
Hameringham. Linc 4C 88
Hamerton. Cambs 3A 64
Ham Green. Here 1C 48
Ham Green. Kent 4C 40
Ham Green. N Som 4A 34
Ham Green. Worc 4E 61
Ham Hill. Kent 4A 40
Hamilton. Leic 5D 74
Hamilton. S Lan 4A 128
Hamiltonsbawn. Arm 5D 178
Hamister. Shet 5G 173
Hammer. W Sus 3G 25
Hammersmith. G Lon 3D 38
Hammerwich. Staf 5E 73
Hammerwood. E Sus 2F 27
Hammill. Kent 5G 41
Hammond Street. Herts 5D 52
Hammoon. Dors 1D 14
Hamnavoe. Shet
nr. Braehoulland 3D 173
nr. Burland 8E 173
nr. Lunna 4F 173
on Yell 3F 173
Hamp. Som 3G 21
Hampden Park. E Sus 5G 27
Hampen. Glos 4F 49
Hamperden End. Essx 2F 53
Hamperley. Shrp 2G 59
Hampnett. Glos 4F 49
Hampole. S Yor 3F 93
Hampreston. Dors 3F 15
Hampstead. G Lon 2D 38
Hampstead Norreys.
W Ber 4D 36
Hampsthwaite. N Yor 4E 99
Hampton. Devn 3F 13
Hampton. G Lon 3C 38
Hampton. Kent 4F 41
Hampton. Shrp 2B 60
Hampton. Swin 2G 35
Hampton. Worc 1F 49
Hampton Bishop. Here 2A 48
Hampton Fields. Glos 2D 35
Hampton Hargate. Pet 1A 64
Hampton Heath. Ches W 1H 71
Hampton in Arden. W Mid 2G 61
Hampton Loade. Shrp 2B 60
Hampton Lovett. Worc 4C 60
Hampton Lucy. Warw 5G 61
Hampton Magna. Warw 4G 61
Hampton on the Hill.
Warw 4G 61
Hampton Poyle. Oxon 4D 50
Hampton Wick. G Lon 4C 38
Hamptworth. Wilts 1H 15
Hamrow. Norf 3B 78
Hamsey. E Sus 4F 27
Hamsey Green. Surr 5E 39
Hamstall Ridware. Staf 4F 73
Hamstead. IOW 3C 16
Hamstead. W Mid 1E 61
Hamstead Marshall. W Ber 5C 36
Hamsterley. Dur
nr. Consett 4E 115
nr. Wolsingham 1E 105
Hamsterley Mill. Dur 4E 115
Hamstreet. Kent 2E 28
Ham Street. Som 3A 22
Hamworthy. Pool 3E 15
Hanbury. Staf 3F 73
Hanbury. Worc 4D 60
Hanbury Woodend. Staf 3F 73
Hanby. Linc 2H 75
Hanchurch. Staf 1C 72
Hand and Pen. Devn 3D 12
Handbridge. Ches W 4G 83
Handcross. W Sus 2D 26
Handforth. Ches E 2C 84
Handley. Ches W 5G 83
Handley. Derbs 4A 86
Handsacre. Staf 4E 73
Handsworth. S Yor 2B 86
Handsworth. W Mid 1E 61
Handy Cross. Buck 2G 37
Hanford. Dors 1D 14
Hanford. Stoke 1C 72
Hangersley. Hants 2G 15
Hanging Houghton. Nptn 3E 63
Hanging Langford. Wilts 3F 23
Hangleton. Brig 5D 26
Hangleton. W Sus 5B 26
Hanham. S Glo 4B 34
Hanham Green. S Glo 4B 34
Hankelow. Ches E 1A 72
Hankerton. Wilts 2E 35
Hankham. E Sus 5H 27
Hanley. Stoke . . . **Stoke 202** (1C 72)
Hanley Castle. Worc 1D 48
Hanley Childe. Worc 4A 60
Hanley Swan. Worc 1D 48
Hanley William. Worc 4A 60
Hanlith. N Yor 3B 98
Hanmer. Wrex 2G 71
Hannaborough. Devn 2F 11
Hannaford. Devn 4G 19
Hannah. Linc 3E 89
Hannington. Hants 1D 24
Hannington. Nptn 3F 63
Hannington. Swin 2G 35
Hannington Wick. Swin 2G 35
Hanscombe End. C Beds 2B 52
Hanslope. Mil 1G 51
Hanthorpe. Linc 3H 75
Hanwell. G Lon 2C 38
Hanwell. Oxon 1C 50
Hanwood. Shrp 5G 71
Hanworth. G Lon 3C 38
Hanworth. Norf 2D 78
Happas. Ang 4D 144
Happendon. S Lan 1A 118
Happisburgh. Norf 2F 79
Happisburgh Common.
Norf 3F 79
Hapsford. Ches W 3G 83
Hapton. Lanc 1F 91
Hapton. Norf 1D 66
Harberton. Devn 3D 9
Harbertonford. Devn 3D 9
Harbledown. Kent 5F 41
Harborne. W Mid 2E 61
Harborough Magna. Warw 3B 62
Harbottle. Nmbd 4D 120
Harbourneford. Devn 2D 8
Harbours Hill. Worc 4D 60
Harbridge. Hants 1G 15
Harbury. Warw 4A 62
Harby. Leics 2E 75
Harby. Notts 3F 87
Harcombe. Devn 3E 13
Harcombe Bottom. Devn 3G 13
Harcourt. Corn 5C 6
Harden. W Yor 1A 92
Hardenhuish. Wilts 4E 35
Hardgate. Abers 3E 153
Hardgate. Dum 3F 111
Hardham. W Sus 4B 26
Hardingham. Norf 5C 78
Hardingstone. Nptn 5E 63
Hardings Wood. Staf 5C 84
Hardington. Som 1C 22
Hardington Mandeville.
Som 1A 14
Hardington Marsh. Som 2A 14
Hardington Moor. Som 1A 14
Hardley. Hants 2C 16
Hardley Street. Norf 5F 79
Hardmead. Mil 1H 51
Hardraw. N Yor 5B 104
Hardstoft. Derbs 4B 86
Hardway. Hants 2E 16
Hardway. Som 3C 22
Hardwick. Buck 4G 51
Hardwick. Cambs 5C 64
Hardwick. Norf 2E 66
Hardwick. Nptn 4F 63
Hardwick. Oxon
nr. Bicester 3D 50
nr. Witney 5B 50
Hardwick. Shrp 1F 59
Hardwick. S Yor 2B 86
Hardwick. Stoc T 2B 106
Hardwick. W Mid 1E 61
Hardwicke. Glos
nr. Cheltenham 3E 49
nr. Gloucester 4C 48
Hardwicke. Here 1F 47
Hardwick Village. Notts 3D 86
Hardy's Green. Essx 3C 54
Hare. Som 1F 13
Hareby. Linc 4C 88
Hareden. Lanc 4F 97
Harefield. G Lon 1B 38
Hare Green. Essx 3D 54
Hare Hatch. Wok 4G 37
Harehill. Derbs 2F 73
Harehills. W Yor 1D 92
Harehope. Nmbd 2E 121
Harelaw. Dum 2F 113
Harelaw. Dur 4E 115
Hareplain. Kent 2C 28
Haresceugh. Cumb 5H 113
Harescombe. Glos 4D 48
Haresfield. Glos 4D 48
Haresfinch. Mers 1H 83
Hareshaw. N Lan 3B 128
Hare Street. Essx 5E 53
Hare Street. Herts 3D 53
Harewood. W Yor 5F 99
Harewood End. Here 3A 48
Harford. Devn 3C 8
Hargate. Norf 1D 66
Hargatewall. Derbs 3F 85
Hargrave. Ches W 4G 83
Hargrave. Nptn 3H 63
Hargrave. Suff 5G 65
Harker. Cumb 3E 113
Harkland. Shet 3F 173
Harkstead. Suff 2E 55
Harlaston. Staf 4G 73
Harlaxton. Linc 2F 75
Harlech. Gwyn 2E 69
Harlequin. Notts 2D 74
Harlescott. Shrp 4H 71
Harleston. Devn 4D 9
Harleston. Norf 2E 67
Harleston. Suff 4C 66
Harlestone. Nptn 4E 62
Harley. Shrp 5H 71
Harley. S Yor 1A 86
Harling Road. Norf 2B 66
Harlington. C Beds 2A 52
Harlington. G Lon 3B 38
Harlington. S Yor 4E 93
Harlosh. High 4B 154
Harlow. Essx 4E 53
Harlow Hill. Nmbd 3D 115
Harlsey Castle. N Yor 5B 106
Harlthorpe. E Yor 1H 93
Harlton. Cambs 5C 64
Harlyn Bay. Corn 1C 6
Harman's Cross. Dors 4E 15
Harmby. N Yor 1D 98
Harmer Green. Herts 4C 52
Harmer Hill. Shrp 3G 71
Harmondsworth. G Lon 3B 38
Harmston. Linc 4G 87
Harnage. Shrp 5H 71
Harnham. Nmbd 1D 115
Harnham. Wilts 4G 23
Harnhill. Glos 5F 49
Harold Hill. G Lon 1G 39
Haroldston West. Pemb 3C 42
Haroldswick. Shet 1H 173
Harold Wood. G Lon 1G 39
Harome. N Yor 1A 100
Harpenden. Herts 4B 52
Harpford. Devn 3D 12
Harpham. E Yor 3E 101
Harpley. Norf 3G 77
Harpley. Worc 4A 60
Harpole. Nptn 4D 62
Harpsdale. High 3D 168
Harpsden. Oxon 3F 37
Harpswell. Linc 2G 87
Harpurhey. G Man 4G 91
Harpur Hill. Derbs 3E 85
Harraby. Cumb 4F 113
Harracott. Devn 4F 19
Harrapool. High 1E 147
Harrapul. High 1E 147
Harrietfield. Per 1B 136
Harrietsham. Kent 5C 40
Harrington. Cumb 2A 102
Harrington. Linc 3C 88
Harrington. Nptn 2E 63
Harringworth. Nptn 1G 63
Harriseahead. Staf 5C 84
Harriston. Cumb 5C 112
Harrogate. N Yor **196** (4F 99)
Harrold. Bed 5G 63
Harrop Dale. G Man 4A 92
Harrow. G Lon 2C 38
Harrowbarrow. Corn 2H 7
Harrowden. Bed 1A 52
Harrowgate Hill. Darl 3F 105
Harrow on the Hill. G Lon 2C 38
Harrow Weald. G Lon 1C 38
Harry Stoke. S Glo 4B 34
Harston. Cambs 5D 64
Harston. Leics 2F 75
Harswell. E Yor 5C 100
Hart. Hart 1B 106
Hartburn. Nmbd 1D 115
Hartburn. Stoc T 3B 106
Hartest. Suff 5H 65
Hartfield. E Sus 2F 27
Hartford. Cambs 3B 64
Hartford. Ches W 3A 84
Hartford. Som 4C 20
Hartford Bridge. Hants 1F 25
Hartford End. Essx 4G 53
Harthill. Ches W 5H 83
Harthill. N Lan 3C 128
Harthill. S Yor 2B 86
Hartington. Derbs 4F 85
Hartland. Devn 4C 18
Hartland Quay. Devn 4C 18
Hartle. Worc 3D 60
Hartlebury. Worc 3C 60
Hartlepool. Hart 1C 106
Hartley. Cumb 4A 104
Hartley. Kent
nr. Cranbrook 2B 28
nr. Dartford 4H 39
Hartley. Nmbd 2G 115
Hartley Green. Staf 3D 73
Hartley Mauditt. Hants 3F 25
Hartley Wespall. Hants 1E 25
Hartley Wintney. Hants 1F 25
Hartlip. Kent 4C 40
Hartmount Holdings.
High 1B 158
Hartoft End. N Yor 5E 107
Harton. N Yor 3B 100
Harton. Shrp 2G 59
Harton. Tyne 3G 115
Hartpury. Glos 3D 48
Hartshead. W Yor 2B 92
Hartshill. Warw 1H 61
Hartshorne. Derbs 3H 73
Hartsop. Cumb 3F 103
Hart Station. Hart 1B 106
Hartswell. Som 4D 20
Hartwell. Nptn 5E 63
Hartwood. Lanc 3D 90
Hartwood. N Lan 4B 128
Harvel. Kent 4A 40
Harvington. Worc
nr. Evesham 1F 49
nr. Kidderminster 3C 60
Harwell. Oxon 3C 36
Harwich. Essx **204** (2F 55)
Harwood. Dur 1B 104
Harwood. G Man 3F 91
Harwood Dale. N Yor 5G 107
Harworth. Notts 1D 86
Hascombe. Surr 2A 26
Haselbech. Nptn 3E 62
Haselbury Plucknett. Som 1H 13
Haseley. Warw 4G 61
Hasfield. Glos 3D 48
Hasguard. Pemb 4C 42
Haskayne. Lanc 4B 90
Hasketon. Suff 5E 67
Hasland. Derbs 4A 86
Haslemere. Surr 2A 26
Haslingden. Lanc 2F 91
Haslingfield. Cambs 5D 64
Haslington. Ches E 5B 84
Hassall. Ches E 5B 84
Hassall Green. Ches E 5B 84
Hassell Street. Kent 1E 29
Hassendean. Bord 2H 119
Hassingham. Norf 5F 79
Hassness. Cumb 3C 102
Hassocks. W Sus 4E 27
Hassop. Derbs 3G 85
Haster. High 3F 169
Hasthorpe. Linc 4D 89
Hastigrow. High 2E 169
Hastingleigh. Kent 1E 29
Hastings. E Sus 5C 28
Hastingwood. Essx 5E 53
Hastoe. Herts 5H 51
Haston. Shrp 3H 71
Haswell. Dur 5G 115
Haswell Plough. Dur 5G 115
Hatch. C Beds 1B 52
Hatch Beauchamp. Som 4G 21
Hatch End. G Lon 1C 38
Hatch Green. Som 1G 13
Hatching Green. Herts 4B 52
Hatchmere. Ches W 3H 83
Hatch Warren. Hants 2E 24
Hatcliffe. NE Lin 4F 95
Hatfield. Here 5H 59
Hatfield. Herts 5C 52
Hatfield. S Yor 4G 93
Hatfield. Worc 5C 60
Hatfield Broad Oak. Essx 4F 53
Hatfield Garden Village.
Herts 5C 52
Hatfield Heath. Essx 4F 53
Hatfield Hyde. Herts 4C 52
Hatfield Peverel. Essx 4A 54
Hatfield Woodhouse.
S Yor 4G 93
Hatford. Oxon 2B 36
Hatherden. Hants 1B 24
Hatherleigh. Devn 2F 11
Hathern. Leics 3B 74
Hatherop. Glos 5G 49
Hathersage. Derbs 2G 85
Hathersage Booths. Derbs 2G 85
Hatherton. Ches E 1A 72
Hatherton. Staf 4D 72
Hatley St George. Cambs 5B 64
Hatt. Corn 2H 7
Hattersley. G Man 1D 85
Hattingley. Hants 3E 25
Hatton. Abers 5H 161
Hatton. Derbs 2G 73
Hatton. G Lon 3B 38
Hatton. Linc 3A 88
Hatton. Shrp 1G 59
Hatton. Warr 2A 84
Hatton. Warw 4G 61
Hattoncrook. Abers 1F 153
Hatton Heath. Ches W 4G 83
Hatton of Fintray. Abers 2F 153
Haugh. E Ayr 2D 117
Haugh. Linc 3D 88
Haugham. Linc 2C 88
Haugh Head. Nmbd 2E 121
Haughley. Suff 4C 66
Haughley Green. Suff 4C 66
Haugh of Ballechin. Per 3G 143
Haugh of Glass. Mor 5B 160
Haugh of Urr. Dum 3F 111
Haughton. Ches E 5H 83
Haughton. Notts 3D 86
Haughton. Shrp
nr. Bridgnorth 1A 60
nr. Oswestry 3F 71
nr. Shifnal 5B 72
nr. Shrewsbury 4H 71
Haughton. Staf 3C 72
Haughton Green. G Man 1D 84
Haughton le Skerne. Darl 3A 106
Haultwick. Herts 3D 52
Haunn. Arg 4E 139
Haunn. W Isl 7C 170
Haunton. Staf 4G 73
Hauxton. Cambs 5D 64
Havannah. Ches E 4C 84
Havant. Hants 2F 17
Haven. Here 5G 59
Haven, The. W Sus 2B 26
Haven Bank. Linc 5B 88
Havenstreet. IOW 3D 16
Havercroft. W Yor 3D 93
Haverfordwest. Pemb 3D 42
Haverhill. Suff 1G 53
Haverigg. Cumb 2A 96
Havering-Atte-Bower.
G Lon 1G 39
Havering's Grove. Essx 1A 40
Haversham. Mil 1G 51
Haverthwaite. Cumb 1C 96
Haverton Hill. Stoc T 2B 106
Havyatt. Som 3A 22
Hawarden. Flin 4F 83
Hawbridge. Worc 1E 49
Hawcoat. Cumb 2B 96
Hawcross. Glos 2C 48
Hawen. Cdgn 1D 44
Hawes. N Yor 1A 98
Hawes Green. Norf 1E 67
Hawick. Bord 3H 119
Hawkchurch. Devn 2G 13
Hawkedon. Suff 5G 65
Hawkenbury. Kent 1C 28
Hawkeridge. Wilts 1D 22
Hawkerland. Devn 4D 12
Hawkesbury. S Glo 3C 34
Hawkesbury. Warw 2A 62
Hawkesbury Upton. S Glo 3C 34
Hawkes End. W Mid 2G 61
Hawk Green. G Man 2D 84
Hawkhurst. Kent 2B 28
Hawkhurst Common.
E Sus 4G 27
Hawkinge. Kent 1G 29
Hawkley. Hants 4F 25
Hawkridge. Som 3B 20
Hawksdale. Cumb 5E 113
Hawkshaw. G Man 3F 91
Hawkshead. Cumb 5E 103
Hawkshead Hill. Cumb 5E 103
Hawkswick. N Yor 2B 98
Hawksworth. Notts 1E 75
Hawksworth. W Yor 5D 98
Hawkwell. Essx 1C 40
Hawley. Hants 1G 25
Hawley. Kent 3G 39
Hawling. Glos 3F 49
Hawnby. N Yor 1H 99
Haworth. W Yor 1A 92
Hawstead. Suff 5A 66
Hawthorn. Dur 5H 115
Hawthorn Hill. Brac 4G 37
Hawthorn Hill. Linc 5B 88
Hawthorpe. Linc 3H 75
Hawton. Notts 5E 87
Haxby. York 4A 100
Haxey. N Lin 1E 87
Haybridge. Shrp 3A 60
Haybridge. Som 2A 22
Haydock. Mers 1H 83
Haydon. Bath 1B 22
Haydon. Dors 1B 14
Haydon. Som 4F 21
Haydon Bridge. Nmbd 3B 114
Haydon Wick. Swin 3G 35
Haye. Corn 2H 7
Hayes. G Lon
nr. Bromley 4F 39
Hayes. G Lon
nr. Uxbridge 2B 38
Hayfield. Derbs 2E 85
Hay Green. Norf 4E 77
Hayhill. E Ayr 3D 116
Haylands. IOW 3D 16
Hayle. Corn 3C 4
Hayley Green. W Mid 2D 60
Hayling Island. Hants 3F 17
Hayne. Devn 2B 12
Haynes. C Beds 1A 52
Haynes West End. C Beds 1A 52
Hay-on-Wye. Powy 1F 47
Hayscastle. Pemb 2C 42
Hayscastle Cross. Pemb 2D 42
Hayshead. Ang 4F 145
Hay Street. Herts 3D 53
Hayton. Aber 3G 153
Hayton. Cumb
nr. Aspatria 5C 112
nr. Brampton 4G 113
Hayton. E Yor 5C 100
Hayton. Notts 2E 87
Hayton's Bent. Shrp 2H 59
Haytor Vale. Devn 5A 12
Haytown. Devn 1D 11
Haywards Heath. W Sus 3E 27
Haywood. S Lan 4C 128
Hazelbank. S Lan 5B 128
Hazelbury Bryan. Dors 2C 14
Hazeleigh. Essx 5B 54
Hazeley. Hants 1F 25
Hazel Grove. G Man 2D 84
Hazelhead. S Yor 4B 92
Hazelslade. Staf 4E 73
Hazel Street. Kent 2A 28
Hazelton Walls. Fife 1F 137
Hazelwood. Derbs 1H 73
Hazlemere. Buck 2G 37
Hazler. Shrp 1G 59
Hazlerigg. Tyne 2F 115
Hazles. Staf 1E 73
Hazleton. Glos 4F 49
Hazon. Nmbd 4F 121
Heacham. Norf 2F 77
Headbourne Worthy. Hants 3C 24
Headcorn. Kent 1C 28
Headingley. W Yor 1C 92
Headington. Oxon 5D 50
Headlam. Dur 3E 105
Headless Cross. Worc 4E 61
Headley. Hants
nr. Haslemere 3G 25
nr. Kingsclere 5D 36
Headley. Surr 5D 38
Headley Down. Hants 3G 25
Headley Heath. Worc 3E 61
Headley Park. Bris 5A 34
Head of Muir. Falk 1B 128
Headon. Notts 3E 87
Heads Nook. Cumb 4F 113
Heage. Derbs 5A 86
Healaugh. N Yor
nr. Grinton 5D 104
nr. York 5H 99
Heald Green. G Man 2C 84
Heale. Devn 2G 19
Healey. G Man 3G 91
Healey. Nmbd 4D 114
Healey. N Yor 1D 98
Healeyfield. Dur 5D 114
Healing. NE Lin 3F 95
Heamoor. Corn 3B 4
Heanish. Arg 4B 138
Heanor. Derbs 1B 74
Heanton Punchardon.
Devn 3F 19
Heapham. Linc 2F 87
Heartsease. Powy 4D 58
Heasley Mill. Devn 3H 19
Heaste. High 2E 147
Heath. Derbs 4B 86
Heath, The. Norf
nr. Buxton 3E 79
nr. Fakenham 3B 78
nr. Hevingham 3D 78
Heath, The. Staf 2E 73
Heath, The. Suff 2E 55
Heath and Reach. C Beds 3H 51
Heath Common. W Sus 4C 26
Heathcote. Derbs 4F 85
Heath Cross. Devn 3H 11
Heathencote. Nptn 1F 51
Heath End. Hants 5D 36
Heath End. Leics 3A 74
Heath End. W Mid 5E 73
Heather. Leics 4A 74
Heatherfield. High 4D 155
Heatherton. Derb 2H 73
Heathfield. Cambs 1E 53
Heathfield. Cumb 5C 112
Heathfield. Devn 5B 12
Heathfield. E Sus 3G 27
Heathfield. Ren 3E 126
Heathfield. Som
nr. Lydeard St Lawrence
3E 21
nr. Norton Fitzwarren 4E 21
Heath Green. Worc 3E 61
Heathhall. Dum 2A 112
Heath Hayes. Staf 4E 73
Heath Hill. Shrp 4B 72
Heath House. Som 2H 21
Heathrow Airport.
G Lon **205** (3B 38)
Heathstock. Devn 2F 13
Heathton. Shrp 1C 60
Heathtop. Derbs 2G 73
Heath Town. W Mid 1D 60
Heatley. Staf 3E 73
Heatley. Warr 2B 84
Heaton. Lanc 3D 96
Heaton. Staf 4D 84
Heaton. Tyne 3F 115
Heaton. W Yor 1B 92
Heaton Moor. G Man 1C 84
Heaton's Bridge. Lanc 3C 90
Heaverham. Kent 5G 39
Heavitree. Devn 3C 12
Hebburn. Tyne 3G 115
Hebden. N Yor 3C 98
Hebden Bridge. W Yor 2H 91
Hebden Green. Ches W 4A 84
Hebing End. Herts 3D 52
Hebron. Carm 2F 43
Hebron. Nmbd 1E 115
Heck. Dum 1B 112
Heckdyke. Notts 1E 87
Heckfield. Hants 5F 37
Heckfield Green. Suff 3D 66
Heckfordbridge. Essx 3C 54
Heckington. Linc 1A 76
Heckmondwike. W Yor 2C 92
Heddington. Wilts 5E 35
Heddle. Orkn 6C 172
Heddon. Devn 4G 19
Heddon-on-the-Wall.
Nmbd 3E 115
Hedenham. Norf 1F 67
Hedge End. Hants 1C 16
Hedgerley. Buck 2A 38
Hedging. Som 4G 21
Hedley on the Hill. Nmbd 4D 115
Hednesford. Staf 4E 73
Hedon. E Yor 2E 95
Hegdon Hill. Here 5H 59
Heglibister. Shet 6E 173
Heighington. Darl 2F 105
Heighington. Linc 4H 87
Heightington. Worc 3B 60
Heights of Brae. High 2H 157
Heights of Fodderty.
High 2H 157
Heights of Kinlochewe.
High 2C 156
Heiton. Bord 1B 120
Hele. Devn
nr. Exeter 2C 12
nr. Holsworthy 3D 10
nr. Ilfracombe 2F 19
Hele. Torb 2F 9
Helen's Bay. Ards 1J 179
Helensburgh. Arg 1D 126
Helford. Corn 4E 5
Helhoughton. Norf 3A 78
Helions Bumpstead. Essx 1G 53
Helland. Corn 5A 10
Helland. Som 4G 21
Hellandbridge. Corn 5A 10
Hellesdon. Norf 4E 78
Hellesveor. Corn 2C 4
Hellidon. Nptn 5C 62
Hellifield. N Yor 4A 98
Hellingly. E Sus 4G 27
Hellington. Norf 5F 79
Hellister. Shet 7E 173
Helmdon. Nptn 1D 50
Helmingham. Suff 5D 66
Helmington Row. Dur 1E 105
Helmsdale. High 2H 165
Helmshore. Lanc 2F 91
Helmsley. N Yor 1A 100
Helperby. N Yor 3G 99
Helperthorpe. N Yor 2D 100
Helpringham. Linc 1A 76
Helpston. Pet 5A 76
Helsby. Ches W 3G 83
Helsey. Linc 3E 89
Helston. Corn 4D 4
Helstone. Corn 4A 10
Helton. Cumb 2G 103
Helwith. N Yor 4D 105
Helwith Bridge. N Yor 3H 97
Helygain. Flin 3E 82
Hem, The. Shrp 5B 72
Hemblington. Norf 4F 79
Hemel Hempstead. Herts 5A 52
Hemerdon. Devn 3B 8
Hemingbrough. N Yor 1G 93
Hemingby. Linc 3B 88
Hemingfield. S Yor 4D 93
Hemingford Abbots.
Cambs 3B 64
Hemingford Grey. Cambs 3B 64
Hemingstone. Suff 5D 66
Hemington. Leics 3B 74
Hemington. Nptn 2H 63
Hemington. Som 1C 22
Hemley. Suff 1F 55
Hemlington. Midd 3B 106
Hempholme. E Yor 4E 101
Hempnall. Norf 1E 67
Hempnall Green. Norf 1E 67
Hempriggs. High 4F 169
Hemp's Green. Essx 3C 54
Hempstead. Essx 2G 53
Hempstead. Medw 4B 40
Hempstead. Norf
nr. Holt 2D 78
nr. Stalham 3G 79
Hempsted. Glos 4D 48
Hempton. Norf 3B 78
Hempton. Oxon 2C 50
Hemsby. Norf 4G 79
Hemswell. Linc 1G 87
Hemswell Cliff. Linc 2G 87
Hemsworth. Dors 2E 15
Hemsworth. W Yor 3E 93
Hemyock. Devn 1E 13
Henallt. Carm 3E 45
Henbury. Bris 4A 34
Henbury. Ches E 3C 84
Hendomen. Powy 1E 58
Hendon. G Lon 2D 38
Hendon. Tyne 4H 115
Hendra. Corn 3D 6
Hendre. B'end 3C 32
Hendreforgan. Rhon 3C 32
Hendy. Carm 5F 45
Heneglwys. IOA 3D 80
Henfeddau Fawr. Pemb 1G 43
Henfield. S Glo 4B 34
Henfield. W Sus 4D 26
Henford. Devn 3D 10
Hengoed. Cphy 2E 33
Hengoed. Shrp 2E 71
Hengrave. Suff 4H 65
Henham. Essx 3F 53
Heniarth. Powy 5D 70
Henlade. Som 4F 21
Henley. Dors 2B 14
Henley. Shrp
nr. Church Stretton 2G 59
nr. Ludlow 3H 59
Henley. Som 3H 21
Henley. Suff 5D 66
Henley. W Sus 4G 25
Henley Down. E Sus 4B 28
Henley-in-Arden. Warw 4F 61
Henley-on-Thames. Oxon 3F 37
Henley Street. Kent 4A 40
Henllan. Cdgn 1D 44
Henllan. Den 4C 82
Henllan. Mon 3F 47
Henllan Amgoed. Carm 3F 43
Henllys. Torf 2F 33
Henlow. C Beds 2B 52
Hennock. Devn 4B 12
Henny Street. Essx 2B 54
Henryd. Cnwy 3G 81
Henry's Moat. Pemb 2E 43
Hensall. N Yor 2F 93
Henshaw. Nmbd 3A 114
Hensingham. Cumb 3A 102
Henstead. Suff 2G 67
Hensting. Hants 4C 24
Henstridge. Som 1C 14
Henstridge Ash. Som 4C 22
Henstridge Bowden. Som 4B 22
Henstridge Marsh. Som 4C 22
Henton. Oxon 5F 51
Henton. Som 2H 21
Henwood. Corn 5C 10
Heogan. Shet 7F 173
Heolgerrig. Mer T 5D 46
Heol Senni. Powy 3C 46
Heol-y-Cyw. B'end 3C 32
Hepburn. Nmbd 2E 121
Hepple. Nmbd 4D 121
Hepscott. Nmbd 1F 115
Heptonstall. W Yor 2H 91
Hepworth. Suff 3B 66
Hepworth. W Yor 4B 92
Herbrandston. Pemb 4C 42
Hereford. Here 2A 48
Heribusta. High 1D 154
Heriot. Bord 4H 129
Hermiston. Edin 2E 129
Hermitage. Dors 2B 14
Hermitage. Bord 5H 119
Hermitage. W Ber 4D 36
Hermitage. W Sus 2F 17
Hermon. Carm
nr. Llandeilo 3G 45
nr. Newcastle Emlyn 2D 44
Hermon. IOA 4C 80
Hermon. Pemb 1G 43
Herne. Kent 4F 41
Herne Bay. Kent 4F 41
Herne Common. Kent 4F 41
Herne Pound. Kent 5A 40
Herner. Devn 4F 19
Hernhill. Kent 4E 41
Herodsfoot. Corn 2G 7
Heronden. Kent 5G 41
Herongate. Essx 1H 39
Heronsford. S Ayr 1G 109
Heronsgate. Herts 1B 38
Heron's Ghyll. E Sus 3F 27
Herra. Shet 2H 173
Herriard. Hants 2E 25
Herringfleet. Suff 1G 67
Herringswell. Suff 4G 65
Herrington. Tyne 4G 115
Hersden. Kent 4G 41
Hersham. Corn 2C 10
Hersham. Surr 4C 38
Herstmonceux. E Sus 4H 27
Herston. Dors 5F 15
Herston. Orkn 8D 172
Hertford. Herts 4D 52
Hertford Heath. Herts 4D 52
Hertingfordbury. Herts 4D 52
Hesketh. Lanc 2C 90
Hesketh Bank. Lanc 2C 90
Hesketh Lane. Lanc 5F 97
Hesket Newmarket. Cumb 1E 103
Heskin Green. Lanc 3D 90
Hesleden. Dur 1B 106
Hesleyside. Nmbd 1B 114
Heslington. York 4A 100
Hessay. York 4H 99
Hessenford. Corn 3H 7
Hessett. Suff 4B 66

Hessilhead—Hulland Ward

Hessilhead. N Ayr 4E 127
Hessle. E Yor 2D 94
Hestaford. Shet 6D 173
Hest Bank. Lanc 3D 96
Hester's Way. Glos 3E 49
Hestinsetter. Shet 7D 173
Heston. G Lon 3C 38
Hestwall. Orkn 6B 172
Heswall. Mers 2E 83
Hethe. Oxon 3D 50
Hethelpit Cross. Glos 3C 48
Hethersett. Norf 5D 78
Hethersgill. Cumb 3F 113
Hetherside. Cumb 3F 113
Hethpool. Nmbd 2C 120
Hett. Dur 1F 105
Hetton. N Yor 4B 98
Hetton-le-Hole. Tyne 5G 115
Hetton Steads. Nmbd 1E 121
Heugh. Nmbd 2D 115
Heugh-head. Abers 2A 152
Heveningham. Suff 3F 67
Hever. Kent 1F 27
Heversham. Cumb 1D 97
Hevingham. Norf 3D 78
Hewas Water. Corn 4D 6
Hewelsfield. Glos 5A 48
Hewish. N Som 5H 33
Hewish. Som 2H 13
Hewood. Dors 2G 13
Heworth. York 4A 100
Hexham. Nmbd 3C 114
Hextable. Kent 3G 39
Hexton. Herts 2B 52
Hexworthy. Devn 5G 11
Heybridge. Essx
  nr. Brentwood 1H 39
  nr. Maldon 5B 54
Heybridge Basin. Essx 5B 54
Heybrook Bay. Devn 4A 8
Heydon. Cambs 1E 53
Heydon. Norf 3D 78
Heydour. Linc 2H 75
Heylipol. Arg 4A 138
Heyop. Powy 3E 59
Heysham. Lanc 3D 96
Heyshott. W Sus 1G 17
Heytesbury. Wilts 2E 23
Heythrop. Oxon 3B 50
Heywood. G Man 3G 91
Heywood. Wilts 1D 22
Hibaldstow. N Lin 4C 94
Hickleton. S Yor 4E 93
Hickling. Norf 3G 79
Hickling. Notts 3D 74
Hickling Green. Norf 3G 79
Hickling Heath. Norf 3G 79
Hickstead. W Sus 3D 26
Hidcote Bartrim. Glos 1G 49
Hidcote Boyce. Glos 1G 49
Higford. Shrp 5B 72
High Ackworth. W Yor 3E 93
Higham. Derbs 5A 86
Higham. Kent 3B 40
Higham. Lanc 1G 91
Higham. S Yor 4D 92
Higham. Suff
  nr. Ipswich 2D 54
  nr. Newmarket 4G 65
Higham Dykes. Nmbd 2E 115
Higham Ferrers. Nptn 4G 63
Higham Gobion. C Beds 2B 52
Higham on the Hill. Leics 1A 62
Highampton. Devn 2E 11
Higham Wood. Kent 1H 27
High Angerton. Nmbd 1D 115
High Auldgirth. Dum 1G 111
High Bankhill. Cumb 5G 113
High Banton. N Lan 1A 128
High Barnet. G Lon 1D 38
High Beech. Essx 1F 39
High Bentham. N Yor 3F 97
High Bickington. Devn 4G 19
High Biggins. Cumb 2E 97
High Birkwith. N Yor 2G 97
High Blantyre. S Lan 4H 127
High Bonnybridge. Falk 2B 128
High Borrans. Cumb 4F 103
High Bradfield. S Yor 1G 85
High Bray. Devn 3G 19
Highbridge. Cumb 5E 113
Highbridge. High 5E 148
Highbridge. Som 2G 21
Highbrook. W Sus 2E 27
High Brooms. Kent 1G 27
High Bullen. Devn 4F 19
Highburton. W Yor 3B 92
Highbury. Som 2B 22
High Buston. Nmbd 4G 121
High Callerton. Nmbd 2E 115
High Carlingill. Cumb 4H 103
High Catton. E Yor 4B 100
High Church. Nmbd 1E 115
Highclere. Hants 5C 36
Highcliffe. Dors 3H 15
High Cogges. Oxon 5B 50
High Common. Norf 5B 78
High Coniscliffe. Darl 3F 105
High Crosby. Cumb 4F 113
High Cross. Hants 4F 25
High Cross. Herts 4D 52
High Easter. Essx 4G 53
High Eggborough. N Yor 2F 93
High Ellington. N Yor 1D 98
Higher Alham. Som 2B 22
Higher Ansty. Dors 2C 14
Higher Ashton. Devn 4B 12
Higher Ballam. Lanc 1B 90
Higher Bartle. Lanc 1D 90
Higher Bockhampton.
  Dors 3C 14
Higher Bojewyan. Corn 3A 4
High Ercall. Telf 4H 71
Higher Cheriton. Devn 2E 12
Higher Clovelly. Devn 4D 18
Higher Compton. Plym 3A 8
Higher Dean. Devn 2D 8
Higher Dinting. Derbs 1E 85
Higher Dunstone. Devn 5H 11
Higher End. G Man 4D 90
Higherford. Lanc 5A 98
Higher Gabwell. Devn 2F 9
Higher Halstock Leigh.
  Dors 2A 14
Higher Heysham. Lanc 3D 96
Higher Hurdsfield. Ches E 3D 84
Higher Kingcombe. Dors 3A 14
Higher Kinnerton. Flin 4F 83
Higher Melcombe. Dors 2C 14
Higher Penwortham. Lanc 2D 90
Higher Porthpean. Corn 3E 7
Higher Poynton. Ches E 2D 84
Higher Shotton. Flin 4F 83
Higher Shurlach. Ches W 3A 84
Higher Slade. Devn 2F 19
Higher Tale. Devn 2D 12
Highertown. Corn 4C 6
Higher Town. IOS 1B 4
Higher Town. Som 2C 20
Higher Vexford. Som 3E 20
Higher Walton. Lanc 2D 90
Higher Walton. Warr 2H 83
Higher Whatcombe. Dors 2D 14
Higher Wheelton. Lanc 2E 90
Higher Whiteleigh. Corn 3C 10
Higher Whitley. Ches W 2A 84
Higher Wincham. Ches W 3A 84
Higher Wraxall. Dors 2A 14
Higher Wych. Ches W 1G 71
Higher Yalberton. Torb 3E 9
High Etherley. Dur 2E 105
High Ferry. Linc 1C 76
Highfield. E Yor 1H 93
Highfield. N Ayr 4E 126
Highfield. Tyne 4E 115
Highfields Caldecote.
  Cambs 5C 64
High Gallowhill. E Dun 2H 127
High Garrett. Essx 3A 54
Highgate. G Lon 2D 39
Highgate. N Ayr 4E 127
Highgate. Powy 1D 58
High Grange. Dur 1E 105
High Green. Cumb 4F 103
High Green. Norf 5D 78
High Green. Shrp 2B 60
High Green. S Yor 1H 85
High Green. W Yor 3B 92
High Green. Worc 1D 49
Highgreen Manor. Nmbd 5C 120
High Halden. Kent 2C 28
High Halstow. Medw 3B 40
High Ham. Som 3H 21
High Harrington. Cumb 2B 102
High Haswell. Dur 5G 115
High Hatton. Shrp 3A 72
High Hawsker. N Yor 4G 107
High Hesket. Cumb 5F 113
High Hesleden. Dur 1B 106
High Hoyland. S Yor 3C 92
High Hunsley. E Yor 1C 94
High Hurstwood. E Sus 3F 27
High Hutton. N Yor 3B 100
High Ireby. Cumb 1D 102
High Keil. Arg 5A 122
High Kelling. Norf 2D 78
High Kilburn. N Yor 2H 99
High Knipe. Cumb 3G 103
High Lands. Dur 2E 105
Highlands, The. Shrp 2A 60
Highlane. Ches E 4C 84
Highlane. Derbs 2B 86
High Lane. G Man 2D 84
High Lane. Worc 4A 60
High Laver. Essx 5F 53
Highlaws. Cumb 5C 112
Highleadon. Glos 3C 48
High Legh. Ches E 2B 84
Highleigh. W Sus 3G 17
High Leven. Stoc T 3B 106
Highley. Shrp 2B 60
High Littleton. Bath 1B 22
High Longthwaite. Cumb 5D 112
High Lorton. Cumb 2C 102
High Marishes. N Yor 2C 100
High Marnham. Notts 3F 87
High Melton. S Yor 4F 93
High Mickley. Nmbd 3D 115
Highmoor. Cumb 5D 112
Highmoor. Oxon 3F 37
Highmoor Cross. Oxon 3F 37
Highmoor Hill. Mon 3H 33
Highnam. Glos 4C 48
High Newport. Tyne 4G 115
High Newton. Cumb 1D 96
High Newton-by-the-Sea.
  Nmbd 2G 121
High Nibthwaite. Cumb 1B 96
High Offley. Staf 3B 72
High Ongar. Essx 5F 53
High Onn. Staf 4C 72
High Orchard. Glos 4D 48
High Park. Mers 3B 90
High Roding. Essx 4G 53
High Row. Cumb 1E 103
High Salvington. W Sus 5C 26
High Scales. Cumb 5C 112
High Shaw. N Yor 5B 104
High Shincliffe. Dur 5F 115
High Side. Cumb 1D 102
High Spen. Tyne 3E 115
Highsted. Kent 4D 40
High Stoop. Dur 5E 115
High Street. Corn 3D 6
High Street. Suff
  nr. Aldeburgh 5G 67
  nr. Bungay 2F 67
  nr. Yoxford 3G 67
Highstreet Green. Essx 2A 54
High Street Green. Suff 5C 66
Highstreet Green. Surr 2A 26
Hightae. Dum 2B 112
High Throston. Hart 1B 106
Hightown. Ches E 4C 84
Hightown. Mers 4A 90
High Town. Staf 4D 73
Hightown Green. Suff 5B 66
High Toynton. Linc 4B 88
High Trewhitt. Nmbd 4E 121
High Valleyfield. Fife 1D 128
Highway. Here 1H 47
Highweek. Devn 5B 12
High Westwood. Dur 4E 115
Highwood. Staf 2E 73
Highwood. Worc 4A 60
High Worsall. N Yor 4A 106
Highworth. Swin 2H 35
High Wray. Cumb 5E 103
High Wych. Herts 4E 53
High Wycombe. Buck 2G 37
Hilborough. Norf 5H 77
Hilcott. Wilts 1G 23
Hildenborough. Kent 1G 27
Hildersham. Cambs 1F 53
Hilderstone. Staf 2D 72
Hilderthorpe. E Yor 3F 101
Hilfield. Dors 2B 14
Hilgay. Norf 1F 65
Hill, The. Cumb 1A 96
Hill. S Glo 2B 34
Hill. Warw 4B 62
Hill. Worc 1E 49
Hillam. N Yor 2F 93
Hillbeck. Cumb 3A 104
Hillberry. IOM 4C 108
Hillborough. Kent 4G 41
Hillbourne. Pool 3F 15
Hillbrae. Abers
  nr. Aberchirder 4D 160
  nr. Inverurie 1E 153
  nr. Methlick 5F 161
Hill Brow. Hants 4F 25
Hillbutts. Dors 2E 15
Hillclifflane. Derbs 1G 73
Hillcommon. Som 4E 21
Hill Deverill. Wilts 2D 22
Hilldyke. Linc 1C 76
Hill End. Dur 1D 104
Hill End. Fife 4C 136
Hillend. Fife 1E 129
Hill End. N Lan 3B 128
Hill End. N Yor 4C 98
Hillend. Shrp 1C 60
Hillend. Swan 3D 30
Hillersland. Glos 4A 48
Hillerton. Devn 3H 11
Hillesden. Buck 3E 51
Hillesley. Glos 3C 34
Hillfarrance. Som 4E 21
Hill Gate. Here 3H 47
Hill Green. Essx 2E 53
Hill Green. W Ber 4C 36
Hillhall. Lis 3G 179
Hillhead. Abers 5C 160
Hillhead. Devn 3F 9
Hill Head. Hants 2D 16
Hillhead. S Ayr 3D 116
Hillhead of Auchentumb.
  Abers 3G 161
Hilliard's Cross. Staf 4F 73
Hilliclay. High 2D 168
Hillingdon. G Lon 2B 38
Hillington. Glas 3G 127
Hillington. Norf 3G 77
Hillmorton. Warw 3C 62
Hill of Beath. Fife 4D 136
Hill of Fearn. High 1C 158
Hill of Fiddes. Abers 1G 153
Hill of Keillor. Ang 4B 144
Hill of Overbrae. Abers 2F 161
Hill Ridware. Staf 4E 73
Hillsborough. Lis 4G 179
Hillsborough. S Yor 1H 85
Hillside. Abers 4G 153
Hillside. Ang 2G 145
Hillside. Devn 2D 8
Hillside. Mers 3B 90
Hillside. Orkn 5C 172
Hillside. Shet 5F 173
Hillside. Shrp 2A 60
Hill Side. W Yor 3B 92
Hillside. Worc 4B 60
Hillside of Prieston. Ang 5C 144
Hill Somersal. Derbs 2F 73
Hillstown. Derbs 4B 86
Hillstreet. Hants 1B 16
Hillswick. Shet 4D 173
Hill Top. Dur
  nr. Barnard Castle 2C 104
  nr. Durham 5F 115
  nr. Stanley 4E 115
Hilltown. New M 7G 179
Hill View. Dors 3E 15
Hillwell. Shet 10E 173
Hill Wootton. Warw 4H 61
Hillyland. Per 1C 136
Hilmarton. Wilts 4F 35
Hilperton. Wilts 1D 22
Hilperton Marsh. Wilts 1D 22
Hilsea. Port 2E 17
Hilston. E Yor 1F 95
Hiltingbury. Hants 4C 24
Hilton. Cambs 4B 64
Hilton. Cumb 2A 104
Hilton. Derbs 2G 73
Hilton. Dors 2C 14
Hilton. Dur 2E 105
Hilton. High 5E 165
Hilton. Shrp 1B 60
Hilton. Staf 5E 73
Hilton. Stoc T 3B 106
Hilton of Cadboll. High 1C 158
Himbleton. Worc 5D 60
Himley. Staf 1C 60
Hincaster. Cumb 1E 97
Hinchwick. Glos 2G 49
Hinckley. Leics 1B 62
Hinderclay. Suff 3C 66
Hinderwell. N Yor 3E 107
Hindford. Shrp 2F 71
Hindhead. Surr 3G 25
Hindley. G Man 4E 90
Hindley. Nmbd 4D 114
Hindley Green. G Man 4E 91
Hindlip. Worc 5C 60
Hindolveston. Norf 3C 78
Hindon. Wilts 3E 23
Hindringham. Norf 2B 78
Hingham. Norf 5C 78
Hinksford. Staf 2C 60
Hinstock. Shrp 3A 72
Hintlesham. Suff 1D 54
Hinton. Hants 3H 15
Hinton. Here 2G 47
Hinton. Nptn 5C 62
Hinton. Shrp 5G 71
Hinton. S Glo 4C 34
Hinton Ampner. Hants 4D 24
Hinton Blewett. Bath 1A 22
Hinton Charterhouse. Bath 1C 22
Hinton-in-the-Hedges.
  Nptn 2D 50
Hinton Martell. Dors 2F 15
Hinton on the Green. Worc 1F 49
Hinton Parva. Swin 3H 35
Hinton St George. Som 1H 13
Hinton St Mary. Dors 1C 14
Hinton Waldrist. Oxon 2B 36
Hints. Shrp 3A 60
Hints. Staf 5F 73
Hinwick. Bed 4G 63
Hinxhill. Kent 1E 29
Hinxton. Cambs 1E 53
Hinxworth. Herts 1C 52
Hipley. Hants 1E 16
Hipperholme. W Yor 2B 92
Hipsburn. Nmbd 3G 121
Hipswell. N Yor 5E 105
Hiraeth. Carm 2F 43
Hirn. Abers 3E 153
Hirnant. Powy 3C 70
Hirst. N Lan 3B 128
Hirst. Nmbd 1F 115
Hirst Courtney. N Yor 2G 93
Hirwaen. Den 4D 82
Hirwaun. Rhon 5C 46
Hiscott. Devn 4F 19
Histon. Cambs 4D 64
Hitcham. Suff 5B 66
Hitchin. Herts 3B 52
Hittisleigh. Devn 3H 11
Hittisleigh Barton. Devn 3H 11
Hive. E Yor 1B 94
Hixon. Staf 3E 73
Hoaden. Kent 5G 41
Hoar Cross. Staf 3F 73
Hoarwithy. Here 3A 48
Hoath. Kent 4G 41
Yr Hôb. Flin 5F 83
Hobarris. Shrp 3F 59
Hobbister. Orkn 7C 172
Hobbles Green. Suff 5G 65
Hobbs Cross. Essx 1F 39
Hobkirk. Bord 3H 119
Hobson. Dur 4E 115
Hoby. Leics 4D 74
Hockering. Norf 4C 78
Hockering Heath. Norf 4C 78
Hockerton. Notts 5E 86
Hockley. Essx 1C 40
Hockley. Staf 5G 73
Hockley. W Mid 3G 61
Hockley Heath. W Mid 3F 61
Hockliffe. C Beds 3H 51
Hockwold cum Wilton.
  Norf 2G 65
Hockworthy. Devn 1D 12
Hoddesdon. Herts 5D 52
Hoddlesden. Bkbn 2F 91
Hoddomcross. Dum 2C 112
Hodgeston. Pemb 5E 43
Hodley. Powy 1D 58
Hodnet. Shrp 3A 72
Hodsoll Street. Kent 4H 39
Hodson. Swin 3G 35
Hodthorpe. Derbs 3C 86
Hoe. Norf 4B 78
Hoe, The. Plym 3A 8
Hoe Gate. Hants 1E 17
Hoff. Cumb 3H 103
Hoffleet Stow. Linc 2B 76
Hogaland. Shet 4E 173
Hogben's Hill. Kent 5E 41
Hoggard's Green. Suff 5A 66
Hoggeston. Buck 3G 51
Hoggrill's End. Warw 1G 61
Hogha Gearraidh. W Isl 1C 170
Hoghton. Lanc 2E 90
Hoghton Bottoms. Lanc 2E 91
Hognaston. Derbs 5G 85
Hogsthorpe. Linc 3E 89
Hogstock. Dors 2E 15
Holbeach. Linc 3C 76
Holbeach Bank. Linc 3C 76
Holbeach Clough. Linc 3C 76
Holbeach Drove. Linc 4C 76
Holbeach Hurn. Linc 3C 76
Holbeach St Johns. Linc 4C 76
Holbeach St Marks. Linc 2C 76
Holbeach St Matthew. Linc 2D 76
Holbeck. Notts 3C 86
Holbeck. W Yor 1C 92
Holbeck Woodhouse.
  Notts 3C 86
Holberrow Green. Worc 5E 61
Holbeton. Devn 3C 8
Holborn. G Lon 2E 39
Holbrook. Derbs 1A 74
Holbrook. S Yor 2B 86
Holbrook. Suff 2E 55
Holburn. Nmbd 1E 121
Holbury. Hants 2C 16
Holcombe. Devn 5C 12
Holcombe. G Man 3F 91
Holcombe. Som 2B 22
Holcombe Brook. G Man 3F 91
Holcombe Rogus. Devn 1D 12
Holcot. Nptn 4E 63
Holden. Lanc 5G 97
Holdenby. Nptn 4D 62
Holder's Green. Essx 3G 53
Holdgate. Shrp 2H 59
Holdingham. Linc 1H 75
Holditch. Dors 2G 13
Holemoor. Devn 2E 11
Hole Street. W Sus 4C 26
Holford. Som 2E 21
Holker. Cumb 2C 96
Holkham. Norf 1A 78
Hollacombe. Devn 2D 11
Holland. Orkn
  on Papa Westray 2D 172
  on Stronsay 5F 172
Holland Fen. Linc 1B 76
Holland Lees. Lanc 4D 90
Holland-on-Sea. Essx 4F 55
Holland Park. W Mid 5E 73
Hollandstoun. Orkn 2G 172
Hollesley. Suff 1G 55
Hollinfare. Warr 1A 84
Hollingbourne. Kent 5C 40
Hollingbury. Brig 5E 27
Hollingdon. Buck 3G 51
Hollingrove. E Sus 3A 28
Hollington. Derbs 2G 73
Hollington. E Sus 4B 28
Hollington. Staf 2E 73
Hollington Grove. Derbs 2G 73
Hollingworth. G Man 1E 85
Hollins. Derbs 3H 85
Hollins. G Man
  nr. Bury 4G 91
  nr. Middleton 4G 91
Hollinsclough. Staf 4E 85
Hollinswood. Telf 5B 72
Hollinthorpe. W Yor 1D 93
Hollinwood. G Man 4H 91
Hollinwood. Shrp 2H 71
Hollocombe. Devn 1G 11
Holloway. Derbs 5H 85
Hollowell. Nptn 3D 62
Hollow Meadows. S Yor 2G 85
Hollows. Dum 2E 113
Hollybush. Cphy 5E 47
Hollybush. E Ayr 3C 116
Hollybush. Worc 2C 48
Holly End. Norf 5D 77
Holly Hill. N Yor 4E 105
Hollyhurst. Shrp 1H 71
Hollym. E Yor 2G 95
Hollywood. Worc 3E 61
Holmacott. Devn 4F 19
Holmbridge. W Yor 4B 92
Holmbury St Mary. Surr 1C 26
Holmbush. Corn 3E 7
Holmcroft. Staf 3D 72
Holme. Cambs 2A 64
Holme. Cumb 2E 97
Holme. N Lin 4C 94
Holme. N Yor 1F 99
Holme. Notts 5F 87
Holme. W Yor 4B 92
Holmebridge. Dors 4D 15
Holme Chapel. Lanc 2G 91
Holme Hale. Norf 5A 78
Holme Lacy. Here 2A 48
Holme Marsh. Here 5F 59
Holmend. Dum 4C 118
Holme next the Sea. Norf 1G 77
Holme-on-Spalding-Moor.
  E Yor 1B 94
Holme on the Wolds.
  E Yor 5D 100
Holme Pierrepont. Notts 2D 74
Holmer. Here 1A 48
Holmer Green. Buck 1A 38
Holmes. Lanc 3C 90
Holme St Cuthbert. Cumb 5C 112
Holmes Chapel. Ches E 4B 84
Holmesfield. Derbs 3H 85
Holmeswood. Lanc 3C 90
Holmewood. Derbs 4B 86
Holmfirth. W Yor 4B 92
Holmhead. E Ayr 2E 117
Holmisdale. High 4A 154
Holm of Drumlanrig.
  Dum 5H 117
Holmpton. E Yor 2G 95
Holmrook. Cumb 5B 102
Holmsgarth. Shet 7F 173
Holmside. Dur 5F 115
Holmwrangle. Cumb 5G 113
Holne. Devn 2D 8
Holsworthy. Devn 2D 10
Holsworthy Beacon. Devn 2D 10
Holt. Dors 2F 15
Holt. Norf 2C 78
Holt. Wilts 5D 34
Holt. Worc 4C 60
Holt. Wrex 5G 83
Holtby. York 4A 100
Holt End. Hants 3E 25
Holt End. Worc 4E 61
Holt Fleet. Worc 4C 60
Holt Green. Lanc 4B 90
Holt Heath. Dors 2F 15
Holt Heath. Worc 4C 60
Holton. Oxon 5D 50
Holton. Som 4B 22
Holton. Suff 3F 67
Holton cum Beckering.
  Linc 2A 88
Holton Heath. Dors 3E 15
Holton le Clay. Linc 4F 95
Holton le Moor. Linc 1H 87
Holton St Mary. Suff 2D 54
Holt Pound. Hants 2G 25
Holtsmere End. Herts 4A 52
Holtye. E Sus 2F 27
Holwell. Dors 1C 14
Holwell. Herts 2B 52
Holwell. Leics 3E 75
Holwell. Oxon 5H 49
Holwell. Som 2C 22
Holwick. Dur 2C 104
Holworth. Dors 4C 14
Holybourne. Hants 2F 25
Holy City. Devn 2G 13
Holy Cross. Worc 3D 60
Holyfield. Essx 5D 53
Holyhead. IOA 2B 80
Holy Island. Nmbd 5H 131
Holymoorside. Derbs 4H 85
Holyport. Wind 4G 37
Holystone. Nmbd 4D 120
Holytown. N Lan 3A 128
Holywell. Cambs 3C 64
Holywell. Corn 3B 6
Holywell. Dors 2A 14
Holywell. Flin 3D 82
Holywell. Glos 2C 34
Holywell. Nmbd 2G 115
Holywell. Warw 4F 61
Holywell Green. W Yor 3A 92
Holywell Lake. Som 4E 20
Holywell Row. Suff 3G 65
Holywood. Ards 2J 179
Holywood. Dum 1G 111
Homer. Shrp 5A 72
Homer Green. Mers 4B 90
Homersfield. Suff 2E 67
Hom Green. Here 3A 48
Homington. Wilts 4G 23
Honeyborough. Pemb 4D 42
Honeybourne. Worc 1G 49
Honeychurch. Devn 2G 11
Honeydon. Bed 5A 64
Honey Hill. Kent 4F 41
Honey Street. Wilts 5G 35
Honey Tye. Suff 2C 54
Honeywick. C Beds 3H 51
Honiley. Warw 3G 61
Honing. Norf 3F 79
Honingham. Norf 4D 78
Honington. Linc 1G 75
Honington. Suff 3B 66
Honington. Warw 1A 50
Honiton. Devn 2E 13
Honley. W Yor 3B 92
Honnington. Telf 4B 72
Hoo. Suff 5E 67
Hoobrook. Worc 3C 60
Hood Green. S Yor 4D 92
Hooe. E Sus 5A 28
Hooe. Plym 3B 8
Hooe Common. E Sus 4A 28
Hoo Green. Ches E 2B 84
Hoohill. Bkpl 1B 90
Hook. Cambs 1D 64
Hook. E Yor 2A 94
Hook. G Lon 4C 38
Hook. Hants
  nr. Basingstoke 1F 25
  nr. Fareham 2D 16
Hook. Pemb 3D 43
Hook. Wilts 3F 35
Hook-a-Gate. Shrp 5G 71
Hook Bank. Worc 1D 48
Hooke. Dors 2A 14
Hooker Gate. Tyne 4E 115
Hookgate. Staf 2B 72
Hook Green. Kent
  nr. Lamberhurst 2A 28
  nr. Meopham 4H 39
  nr. Southfleet 3H 39
Hook Norton. Oxon 2B 50
Hook's Cross. Herts 3C 52
Hook Street. Glos 2B 34
Hookway. Devn 3B 12
Hookwood. Surr 1D 26
Hoole. Ches W 4G 83
Hooley. Surr 5D 39
Hooley Bridge. G Man 3G 91
Hooley Brow. G Man 3G 91
Hoo St Werburgh. Medw 3B 40
Hooton. Ches W 3F 83
Hooton Levitt. S Yor 1C 86
Hooton Pagnell. S Yor 4E 93
Hooton Roberts. S Yor 1B 86
Hoove. Shet 7E 173
Hope. Derbs 2F 85
Hope. Flin 5F 83
Hope. High 2E 167
Hope. Powy 5E 71
Hope. Shrp 5F 71
Hope. Staf 5F 85
Hope Bagot. Shrp 3H 59
Hope Bowdler. Shrp 1G 59
Hopedale. Staf 5F 85
Hope Green. Ches E 2D 84
Hopeman. Mor 2F 159
Hope Mansell. Here 4B 48
Hopesay. Shrp 2F 59
Hope's Green. Essx 2B 40
Hopetown. W Yor 2D 93
Hope under Dinmore. Here 5H 59
Hopley's Green. Here 5F 59
Hopperton. N Yor 4G 99
Hop Pole. Linc 4A 76
Hopstone. Shrp 1B 60
Hopton. Derbs 5G 85
Hopton. Powy 1E 59
Hopton. Shrp
  nr. Oswestry 3F 71
  nr. Wem 3H 71
Hopton. Staf 3D 72
Hopton. Suff 3B 66
Hopton Cangeford. Shrp 2H 59
Hopton Castle. Shrp 3F 59
Hoptonheath. Shrp 3F 59
Hopton Heath. Staf 3D 72
Hopton on Sea. Norf 5H 79
Hopton Wafers. Shrp 3A 60
Hopwas. Staf 5F 73
Hopwood. Worc 3E 61
Horam. E Sus 4G 27
Horbling. Linc 2A 76
Horbury. W Yor 3C 92
Horcott. Glos 5G 49
Horden. Dur 5H 115
Horderley. Shrp 2G 59
Hordle. Hants 3A 16
Hordley. Shrp 2F 71
Horeb. Carm
  nr. Brechfa 3F 45
  nr. Llanelli 5E 45
Horeb. Cdgn 1D 45
Horfield. Bris 4A 34
Horgabost. W Isl 8C 171
Horham. Suff 3E 66
Horkstow. N Lin 3C 94
Horley. Oxon 1C 50
Horley. Surr 1D 27
Horn Ash. Dors 2G 13
Hornblotton Green. Som 3A 22
Hornby. Lanc 3E 97
Hornby. N Yor
  nr. Appleton Wiske 4A 106
  nr. Catterick Garrison 5F 105
Horncastle. Linc 4B 88
Hornchurch. G Lon 2G 39
Horncliffe. Nmbd 5F 131
Horndean. Hants 1F 17
Horndean. Bord 5E 131
Horndon. Devn 4F 11
Horndon on the Hill. Thur 2A 40
Horne. Surr 1E 27
Horner. Som 2C 20
Horning. Norf 4F 79
Horninghold. Leics 1F 63
Horninglow. Staf 3G 73
Horningsea. Cambs 4D 65
Horningsham. Wilts 2D 22
Horningtoft. Norf 3B 78
Hornsbury. Som 1G 13
Hornsby. Cumb 4G 113
Hornsbygate. Cumb 4G 113
Horns Corner. Kent 3B 28
Horns Cross. Devn 4D 19
Hornsea. E Yor 5G 101
Hornsea Burton. E Yor 5G 101
Hornsey. G Lon 2E 39
Hornton. Oxon 1B 50
Horpit. Swin 3H 35
Horrabridge. Devn 2B 8
Horringer. Suff 4H 65
Horringford. IOW 4D 16
Horrocks Fold. G Man 3F 91
Horrocksford. Lanc 5G 97
Horsbrugh Ford. Bord 1E 119
Horsebridge. Devn 5E 11
Horsebridge. Hants 3B 24
Horsebrook. Staf 4C 72
Horsecastle. N Som 5H 33
Horsehay. Telf 5A 72
Horseheath. Cambs 1G 53
Horsehouse. N Yor 1C 98
Horsell. Surr 5A 38
Horseman's Green. Wrex 1G 71
Horsenden. Buck 5F 51
Horseway. Cambs 2D 64
Horsey. Norf 3G 79
Horsey. Som 3G 21
Horsford. Norf 4D 78
Horsforth. W Yor 1C 92
Horsham. W Sus 2C 26
Horsham. Worc 5B 60
Horsham St Faith. Norf 4E 78
Horsington. Linc 4A 88
Horsington. Som 4C 22
Horsley. Derbs 1A 74
Horsley. Glos 2D 34
Horsley. Nmbd
  nr. Prudhoe 3D 115
  nr. Rochester 5C 120
Horsley Cross. Essx 3E 54
Horsleycross Street. Essx 3E 54
Horsleyhill. Bord 3H 119
Horsleyhope. Dur 5D 114
Horsley Woodhouse.
  Derbs 1A 74
Horsmonden. Kent 1A 28
Horspath. Oxon 5D 50
Horstead. Norf 4E 79
Horsted Keynes. W Sus 3E 27
Horton. Buck 4H 51
Horton. Dors 2F 15
Horton. Lanc 4A 98
Horton. Nptn 5F 63
Horton. Shrp 2G 71
Horton. Som 1G 13
Horton. S Glo 3C 34
Horton. Staf 5D 84
Horton. Swan 4D 30
Horton. Wilts 5F 35
Horton. Wind 3B 38
Horton Cross. Som 1G 13
Horton-cum-Studley. Oxon 4D 50
Horton Grange. Nmbd 2F 115
Horton Green. Ches W 1G 71
Horton Heath. Hants 1C 16
Horton in Ribblesdale.
  N Yor 2H 97
Horton Kirby. Kent 4G 39
Hortonwood. Telf 4A 72
Horwich. G Man 3E 91
Horwich End. Derbs 2E 85
Horwood. Devn 4F 19
Hoscar. Lanc 3C 90
Hose. Leics 3E 75
Hosh. Per 1A 136
Hosta. W Isl 1C 170
Hoswick. Shet 9F 173
Hotham. E Yor 1B 94
Hothfield. Kent 1D 28
Hoton. Leics 3C 74
Houbie. Shet 2H 173
Hough. Arg 4A 138
Hough. Ches E
  nr. Crewe 5B 84
  nr. Wilmslow 3C 84
Hougham. Linc 1F 75
Hough Green. Hal 2G 83
Hough-on-the-Hill. Linc 1G 75
Houghton. Cambs 3B 64
Houghton. Cumb 4F 113
Houghton. Hants 3B 24
Houghton. Nmbd 3E 115
Houghton. Pemb 4D 43
Houghton. W Sus 4B 26
Houghton Bank. Darl 2F 105
Houghton Conquest.
  C Beds 1A 52
Houghton Green. E Sus 3D 28
Houghton-le-Side. Darl 2F 105
Houghton-le-Spring.
  Tyne 4G 115
Houghton on the Hill.
  Leics 5D 74
Houghton Regis. C Beds 3A 52
Houghton St Giles. Norf 2B 78
Houlland. Shet
  on Mainland 6E 173
  on Yell 4G 173
Houlsyke. N Yor 4E 107
Hound. Hants 2C 16
Hound Green. Hants 1F 25
Houndslow. Bord 5C 130
Houndsmoor. Som 4E 21
Houndwood. Bord 3E 131
Hounsdown. Hants 1B 16
Hounslow. G Lon 3C 38
Housabister. Shet 6F 173
Housay. Shet 4H 173
Househill. High 3C 158
Housetter. Shet 3E 173
Houss. Shet 8E 173
Houston. Ren 3F 127
Housty. High 5D 168
Houton. Orkn 7C 172
Hove. Brig 192 (5D 27)
Hoveringham. Notts 1D 74
Hoveton. Norf 4F 79
Hovingham. N Yor 2A 100
How. Cumb 4G 113
How Caple. Here 2B 48
Howden. E Yor 2H 93
Howden-le-Wear. Dur 1E 105
Howe, The. Cumb 1D 96
Howe. High 2F 169
Howe, The. IOM 5A 108
Howe. Norf 5E 79
Howe. N Yor 1F 99
Howe Green. Essx 5H 53
Howegreen. Essx 5B 54
Howe Green. Warw 2H 61
Howell. Linc 1A 76
How End. C Beds 1A 52
Howe of Teuchar. Abers 4E 161
Howes. Dum 3C 112
Howe Street. Essx
  nr. Chelmsford 4G 53
  nr. Finchingfield 2G 53
Howey. Powy 5C 58
Howgate. Midl 4F 129
Howgill. Lanc 5H 97
Howgill. N Yor 4C 98
How Green. Kent 1F 27
How Hill. Norf 4F 79
Howick. Nmbd 3G 121
Howle. Telf 3A 72
Howle Hill. Here 3B 48
Howleigh. Som 1F 13
Howlett End. Essx 2F 53
Howley. Som 2F 13
Howley. Warr 2A 84
Hownam. Bord 3B 120
Howsham. N Lin 4D 94
Howsham. N Yor 3B 100
Howtel. Nmbd 1C 120
Howt Green. Kent 4C 40
Howton. Here 3H 47
Howwood. Ren 3E 127
Hoxne. Suff 3D 66
Hoylake. Mers 2E 82
Hoyland. S Yor 4D 92
Hoylandswaine. S Yor 4C 92
Hoyle. W Sus 4A 26
Hubberholme. N Yor 2B 98
Hubberston. Pemb 4C 42
Hubbert's Bridge. Linc 1B 76
Huby. N Yor
  nr. Harrogate 5E 99
  nr. York 3H 99
Hucclecote. Glos 4D 48
Hucking. Kent 5C 40
Hucknall. Notts 1C 74
Huddersfield. W Yor 3B 92
Huddington. Worc 5D 60
Huddlesford. Staf 5F 73
Hudswell. N Yor 4E 105
Huggate. E Yor 4C 100
Hugglescote. Leics 4B 74
Hughenden Valley. Buck 2G 37
Hughley. Shrp 1H 59
Hughton. High 4G 157
Hugh Town. IOS 1B 4
Hugus. Corn 4B 6
Huish. Devn 1F 11
Huish. Wilts 5G 35
Huish Champflower. Som 4D 20
Huish Episcopi. Som 4H 21
Huisinis. W Isl 6B 171
Hulcote. Nptn 1F 51
Hulcott. Buck 4G 51
Hulham. Devn 4D 12
Hull. Hull 196 (2E 94)
Hulland. Derbs 1G 73
Hulland Moss. Derbs 1G 73
Hulland Ward. Derbs 1G 73

Hullavington—Kincraigie

Hullavington. Wilts 3D 35
Hullbridge. Essx 1C 40
Hulme. G Man 1C 84
Hulme. Staf 1D 72
Hulme End. Staf 5F 85
Hulme Walfield. Ches E 4C 84
Hulverstone. IOW 4B 16
Hulver Street. Suff 2G 67
Humber. Devn 5C 12
Humber. Here 5H 59
Humber Bridge. N Lin 2D 94
Humberside Airport. N Lin 3D 94
Humberston. NE Lin 4G 95
Humberstone. Leic 5D 74
Humbie. E Lot 3A 130
Humbleton. E Yor 1F 95
Humbleton. Nmbd 2D 121
Humby. Linc 2H 75
Hume. Bord 5D 130
Humshaugh. Nmbd 2C 114
Huna. High 1F 169
Huncoat. Lanc 1F 91
Huncote. Leics 1C 62
Hundall. Derbs 3A 86
Hunderthwaite. Dur 2C 104
Hundleby. Linc 4C 88
Hundle Houses. Linc 5B 88
Hundleton. Pemb 4D 42
Hundon. Suff 1H 53
Hundred, The. Here 4H 59
Hundred Acres. Hants 1D 16
Hundred House. Powy 5D 58
Hungarton. Leics 5D 74
Hungerford. Hants 1G 15
Hungerford. Shrp 2H 59
Hungerford. Som 2D 20
Hungerford. W Ber 5B 36
Hungerford Newtown.
W Ber 4B 36
Hunger Hill. G Man 4E 91
Hungerton. Linc 2F 75
Hungladder. High 1C 154
Hungryhatton. Shrp 3A 72
Hunmanby. N Yor 2E 101
Hunmanby Sands. N Yor 2F 101
Hunningham. Warw 4A 62
Hunnington. Worc 2D 60
Hunny Hill. IOW 4C 16
Hunsdon. Herts 4E 53
Hunsdonbury. Herts 4E 53
Hunsingore. N Yor 4G 99
Hunslet. W Yor 1D 92
Hunslet Carr. W Yor 1D 92
Hunsonby. Cumb 1G 103
Hunspow. High 1E 169
Hunstanton. Norf 1F 77
Hunstanworth. Dur 5C 114
Hunston. Suff 4B 66
Hunston. W Sus 2G 17
Hunstrete. Bath 5B 34
Hunt End. Worc 4E 61
Hunterfield. Midl 3G 129
Hunters Forstal. Kent 4F 41
Hunter's Quay. Arg 2C 126
Huntham. Som 4G 21
Hunthill Lodge. Ang 1D 144
Huntingdon. Cambs 3B 64
Huntingfield. Suff 3F 67
Huntingford. Wilts 4D 22
Huntington. Ches W 4G 83
Huntington. E Lot 2A 130
Huntington. Here 5E 59
Huntington. Staf 4D 72
Huntington. Telf 5A 72
Huntington. York 4A 100
Huntingtower. Per 1C 136
Huntley. Glos 4C 48
Huntley. Staf 1E 73
Huntly. Abers 5C 160
Huntlywood. Bord 5C 130
Hunton. Hants 3C 24
Hunton. Kent 1B 28
Hunton. N Yor 5E 105
Hunton Bridge. Herts 1B 38
Hunt's Corner. Norf 2C 66
Huntscott. Som 2C 20
Hunt's Cross. Mers 2G 83
Hunts Green. Warw 1F 61
Huntsham. Devn 4D 20
Huntshaw. Devn 4F 19
Huntspill. Som 2G 21
Huntstile. Som 3F 21
Huntworth. Som 3G 21
Hunwick. Dur 1E 105
Hunworth. Norf 2C 78
Hurcott. Som
nr. Ilminster 1G 13
nr. Somerton 4A 22
Hurdcott. Wilts 3G 23
Hurdley. Powy 1E 59
Hurdsfield. Ches E 3D 84
Hurlet. Glas 3G 127
Hurley. Warw 1G 61
Hurley. Wind 3G 37
Hurlford. E Ayr 1D 116
Hurliness. Orkn 9B 172
Hurlston Green. Lanc 3C 90
Hurn. Dors 3G 15
Hursey. Dors 2H 13
Hursley. Hants 4C 24
Hurst. G Man 4H 91
Hurst. N Yor 4D 104
Hurst. Som 1H 13
Hurst. Wok 4F 37
Hurstbourne Priors. Hants 2C 24
Hurstbourne Tarrant.
Hants 1B 24
Hurst Green. Ches E 1H 71
Hurst Green. E Sus 3B 28
Hurst Green. Essx 4D 54
Hurst Green. Lanc 1E 91
Hurst Green. Surr 5E 39
Hurstley. Here 1G 47
Hurstpierpoint. W Sus 4D 27
Hurstway Common. Here 1G 47
Hurst Wickham. W Sus 4D 27
Hurstwood. Lanc 1G 91
Hurtmore. Surr 1A 26
Hurworth-on-Tees. Darl 3A 106
Hurworth Place. Darl 4F 105
Hury. Dur 3C 104
Husbands Bosworth. Leics 2D 62
Husborne Crawley. C Beds 2H 51
Husthwaite. N Yor 2H 99
Hutcherleigh. Devn 3D 9
Hut Green. N Yor 2F 93
Huthwaite. Notts 5B 86
Huttoft. Linc 3E 89
Hutton. Cumb 2F 103
Hutton. E Yor 4E 101
Hutton. Essx 1H 39
Hutton. Lanc 2C 90
Hutton. N Som 1G 21
Hutton. Bord 4F 131
Hutton Bonville. N Yor 4A 106
Hutton Buscel. N Yor 1D 100
Hutton Conyers. N Yor 2F 99
Hutton Cranswick. E Yor 4E 101
Hutton End. Cumb 1F 103
Hutton Gate. Red C 3C 106
Hutton Henry. Dur 1B 106
Hutton-le-Hole. N Yor 1B 100
Hutton Magna. Dur 3E 105
Hutton Mulgrave. N Yor 4F 107
Hutton Roof. Cumb
nr. Kirkby Lonsdale 2E 97
nr. Penrith 1E 103
Hutton Rudby. N Yor 4B 106
Huttons Ambo. N Yor 3B 100
Hutton Sessay. N Yor 2G 99
Hutton Village. Red C 3D 106
Hutton Wandesley. N Yor 4H 99
Huxham. Devn 3C 12
Huxham Green. Som 3A 22
Huxley. Ches W 4H 83
Huxter. Shet
on Mainland 6C 173
on Whalsay 5G 173
Huyton. Mers 1G 83
Hwlffordd. Pemb 3D 42
Hycemoor. Cumb 1A 96
Hyde. Glos
nr. Stroud 5D 49
nr. Winchcombe 3F 49
Hyde. G Man 1D 84
Hyde Heath. Buck 5H 51
Hyde Lea. Staf 4D 72
Hyde Park. S Yor 4F 93
Hydestile. Surr 1A 26
Hyndford Bridge. S Lan 5C 128
Hynish. Arg 5A 138
Hyssington. Powy 1F 59
Hythe. Hants 2C 16
Hythe. Kent 2F 29
Hythe End. Wind 3B 38
Hythie. Abers 3H 161
Hyton. Cumb 1A 96

I

Ianstown. Mor 2B 160
Iarsiadar. W Isl 4D 171
Ibberton. Dors 2C 14
Ible. Derbs 5G 85
Ibrox. Glas 3G 127
Ibsley. Hants 2G 15
Ibstock. Leics 4B 74
Ibstone. Buck 2F 37
Ibthorpe. Hants 1B 24
Iburndale. N Yor 4F 107
Ibworth. Hants 1D 24
Icelton. N Som 5G 33
Ichrachan. Arg 5E 141
Ickburgh. Norf 1H 65
Ickenham. G Lon 2B 38
Ickenthwaite. Cumb 1C 96
Ickford. Buck 5E 51
Ickham. Kent 5G 41
Ickleford. Herts 2B 52
Icklesham. E Sus 4C 28
Ickleton. Cambs 1E 53
Icklingham. Suff 3G 65
Ickwell. C Beds 1B 52
Icomb. Glos 3H 49
Idbury. Oxon 4H 49
Iddesleigh. Devn 2F 11
Ide. Devn 3B 12
Ideford. Devn 5B 12
Ide Hill. Kent 5F 39
Iden. E Sus 3D 28
Iden Green. Kent
nr. Benenden 2C 28
nr. Goudhurst 2B 28
Idle. W Yor 1B 92
Idless. Corn 4C 6
Idlicote. Warw 1A 50
Idmiston. Wilts 3G 23
Idole. Carm 4E 45
Idridgehay. Derbs 1G 73
Idrigill. High 2C 154
Idstone. Oxon 3A 36
Iffley. Oxon 5D 50
Ifield. W Sus 2D 26
Ifieldwood. W Sus 2D 26
Ifold. W Sus 2B 26
Iford. E Sus 5F 27
Ifton Heath. Shrp 2F 71
Ightfield. Shrp 2H 71
Ightham. Kent 5G 39
Iken. Suff 5G 67
Ilam. Staf 5F 85
Ilchester. Som 4A 22
Ilderton. Nmbd 2E 121
Ilford. G Lon 2F 39
Ilford. Som 1G 13
Ilfracombe. Devn 2F 19
Ilkeston. Derbs 1B 74
Ilketshall St Andrew. Suff 2F 67
Ilketshall St Lawrence. Suff 2F 67
Ilketshall St Margaret. Suff 2F 67
Ilkley. W Yor 5D 98
Illand. Corn 5C 10
Illey. W Mid 2D 61
Illidge Green. Ches E 4B 84
Illington. Norf 2B 66
Illingworth. W Yor 2A 92
Illogan. Corn 4A 6
Illogan Highway. Corn 4A 6
Illston on the Hill. Leics 1E 62
Ilmer. Buck 5F 51
Ilmington. Warw 1H 49
Ilminster. Som 1G 13
Ilsington. Devn 5A 12
Ilsington. Dors 3C 14
Ilston. Swan 3E 31
Ilton. N Yor 2D 98
Ilton. Som 1G 13
Imachar. N Ayr 5G 125
Imber. Wilts 2E 23
Immingham. NE Lin 3E 95
Immingham Dock. NE Lin 3F 95
Impington. Cambs 4D 64
Ince. Ches W 3G 83
Ince Blundell. Mers 4B 90
Ince-in-Makerfield.
G Man 4D 90
Inchbae Lodge. High 2G 157
Inchbare. Ang 2F 145
Inchberry. Mor 3H 159
Inchbraoch. Ang 3G 145
Inchbrook. Glos 5D 48
Incheril. High 2C 156
Inchinnan. Ren 3F 127
Inchlaggan. High 3D 148
Inchmichael. Per 1E 137
Inchnadamph. High 1G 163
Inchree. High 2E 141
Inchture. Per 1E 137
Inchyra. Per 1D 136
Indian Queens. Corn 3D 6
Ingatestone. Essx 1H 39
Ingbirchworth. S Yor 4C 92
Ingestre. Staf 3D 73
Ingham. Linc 2G 87
Ingham. Norf 3F 79
Ingham. Suff 3A 66
Ingham Corner. Norf 3F 79
Ingleborough. Norf 4D 76
Ingleby. Derbs 3H 73
Ingleby Arncliffe. N Yor 4B 106
Ingleby Barwick. Stoc T 3B 106
Ingleby Greenhow. N Yor 4C 106
Ingleigh Green. Devn 2G 11
Inglemire. Hull 1D 94
Inglesbatch. Bath 5C 34
Ingleton. Dur 2E 105
Ingleton. N Yor 2F 97
Inglewhite. Lanc 5E 97
Ingoe. Nmbd 2D 114
Ingol. Lanc 1D 90
Ingoldisthorpe. Norf 2F 77
Ingoldmells. Linc 4E 89
Ingoldsby. Linc 2H 75
Ingon. Warw 5G 61
Ingram. Nmbd 3E 121
Ingrave. Essx 1H 39
Ingrow. W Yor 1A 92
Ings. Cumb 5F 103
Ingst. S Glo 3A 34
Ingthorpe. Rut 5G 75
Ingworth. Norf 3D 78
Inishrush. M Ulst 6F 174
Inkberrow. Worc 5E 61
Inkford. Worc 3E 61
Inkpen. W Ber 5B 36
Inkstack. High 1E 169
Innellan. Arg 3C 126
Inner Hope. Devn 5C 8
Innerleith. Fife 2E 137
Innerleithen. Bord 1F 119
Innerleven. Fife 3F 137
Innermessan. Dum 3F 109
Innerwick. E Lot 2D 130
Innerwick. Per 4C 142
Innsworth. Glos 3D 48
Insch. Abers 1D 152
Insh. High 3C 150
Inshegra. High 3C 166
Inshore. High 1D 166
Inskip. Lanc 1C 90
Instow. Devn 3E 19
Intwood. Norf 5D 78
Inver. Abers 4G 151
Inver. High 5F 165
Inver. Per 4H 143
Inverailort. High 5F 147
Inveralligin. High 3H 155
Inverallochy. Abers 2H 161
Inveramsay. Abers 1E 153
Inveran. High 4C 164
Inveraray. Arg 3H 133
Inverarish. High 5E 155
Inverarity. Ang 4D 144
Inverarnan. Stir 2C 134
Inverarnie. High 5A 158
Inverbeg. Arg 4C 134
Inverbervie. Abers 1H 145
Inverboyndie. Abers 2D 160
Invercassley. High 3B 164
Invercharnan. High 4F 141
Inverchoran. High 3E 157
Invercreran. Arg 4E 141
Inverdruie. High 2D 150
Inverebrie. Abers 5G 161
Invereck. Arg 1C 126
Inveresk. E Lot 2G 129
Inveresragan. Arg 5D 141
Inverey. Abers 5E 151
Inverfarigaig. High 1H 149
Invergarry. High 3F 149
Invergeldie. Per 1G 135
Invergordon. High 2B 158
Invergowrie. Per 5C 144
Inverguseran. High 3F 147
Inverharroch. Mor 5A 160
Inverie. High 3F 147
Inverinan. Arg 2G 133
Inverinate. High 1B 148
Inverkeilor. Ang 4F 145
Inverkeithing. Fife 1E 129
Inverkeithny. Abers 4D 160
Inverkip. Inv 2D 126
Inverkirkaig. High 2E 163
Inverlael. High 5F 163
Inverliever Lodge. Arg 3F 133
Inverliver. Arg 5E 141
Inverlochlarig. Stir 2D 134
Inverlochy. High 1F 141
Inverlussa. Arg 1E 125
Inver Mallie. High 5D 148
Invermarkie. Abers 5B 160
Invermoriston. High 2G 149
Invernaver. High 2H 167
Inverneil House. Arg 1G 125
Inverness. High 196 (4A 158)
Inverness Airport. High 3B 158
Invernettie. Abers 4H 161
Inverpolly Lodge. High 2E 163
Inverquhomery. Abers 4H 161
Inverroy. High 5E 149
Inversanda. High 3D 140
Invershiel. High 2B 148
Invershore. High 5E 169
Inversnaid. Stir 3C 134
Inverugie. Abers 4H 161
Inveruglas. Arg 3C 134
Inverurie. Abers 1E 153
Invervar. Per 4D 142
Inverythan. Abers 4E 161
Inwardleigh. Devn 3F 11
Inworth. Essx 4B 54
Iochdar. W Isl 4C 170
Iping. W Sus 4G 25
Ipplepen. Devn 2E 9
Ipsden. Oxon 3E 37
Ipstones. Staf 1E 73
Ipswich. Suff 196 (1E 55)
Irby. Mers 2E 83
Irby in the Marsh. Linc 4D 88
Irby upon Humber.
NE Lin 4E 95
Irchester. Nptn 4G 63
Ireby. Cumb 1D 102
Ireby. Lanc 2F 97
Ireland. Shet 9E 173
Ireleth. Cumb 2B 96
Ireshopeburn. Dur 1B 104
Ireton Wood. Derbs 1G 73
Irlam. G Man 1B 84
Irnham. Linc 3H 75
Iron Acton. S Glo 3B 34
Iron Bridge. Cambs 1D 65
Ironbridge. Telf 5A 72
Iron Cross. Warw 5E 61
Ironville. Derbs 5B 86
Irstead. Norf 3F 79
Irthington. Cumb 3F 113
Irthlingborough. Nptn 3G 63
Irton. N Yor 1E 101
Irvine. N Ayr 1C 116
Irvine Mains. N Ayr 1C 116
Irvinestown. Ferm 7E 176
Isabella Pit. Nmbd 1G 115
Isauld. High 2B 168
Isbister. Orkn 6C 172
Isbister. Shet
on Mainland 2E 173
on Whalsay 5G 173
Isfield. E Sus 4F 27
Isham. Nptn 3F 63
Island Carr. N Lin 4C 94
Islay Airport. Arg 4B 124
Isle Abbotts. Som 4G 21
Isle Brewers. Som 4G 21
Isleham. Cambs 3F 65
Isle of Man Airport. IOM 5B 108
Isle of Thanet. Kent 4H 41
Isle of Whithorn. Dum 5B 110
Isle of Wight. IOW 4C 16
Isleornsay. High 2F 147
Islesburgh. Shet 5E 173
Isles of Scilly (St Mary's) Airport.
IOS 1B 4
Islesteps. Dum 2A 112
Isleworth. G Lon 3C 38
Isley Walton. Leics 3B 74
Islibhig. W Isl 5B 171
Islington. G Lon 2E 39
Islington. Telf 3B 72
Islip. Nptn 3G 63
Islip. Oxon 4D 50
Isombridge. Telf 4A 72
Istead Rise. Kent 4H 39
Itchen. Sotn 1C 16
Itchen Abbas. Hants 3D 24
Itchenor. W Sus 2F 17
Itchen Stoke. Hants 3D 24
Itchingfield. W Sus 3C 26
Itchington. S Glo 3B 34
Itlaw. Abers 3D 160
Itteringham. Norf 2D 78
Itteringham Common.
Norf 3D 78
Itton. Devn 3G 11
Itton Common. Mon 2H 33
Ivegill. Cumb 5F 113
Ivelet. N Yor 5C 104
Iverchaolain. Arg 2B 126
Iver Heath. Buck 2B 38
Iveston. Dur 4E 115
Ivetsey Bank. Staf 4C 72
Ivinghoe. Buck 4H 51
Ivinghoe Aston. Buck 4H 51
Ivington. Here 5G 59
Ivington Green. Here 5G 59
Ivybridge. Devn 3C 8
Ivychurch. Kent 3E 29
Ivy Hatch. Kent 5G 39
Ivy Todd. Norf 5A 78
Iwade. Kent 4D 40
Iwerne Courtney. Dors 1D 14
Iwerne Minster. Dors 1D 14
Ixworth. Suff 3B 66
Ixworth Thorpe. Suff 3B 66

J

Jackfield. Shrp 5A 72
Jack Hill. N Yor 4D 98
Jacksdale. Notts 5B 86
Jackton. S Lan 4G 127
Jacobstow. Corn 3B 10
Jacobstowe. Devn 2F 11
Jacobs Well. Surr 5A 38
Jameston. Pemb 5E 43
Jamestown. Dum 5F 119
Jamestown. Fife 1E 129
Jamestown. High 3G 157
Jamestown. W Dun 1E 127
Janetstown. High
nr. Thurso 2C 168
nr. Wick 3F 169
Jarrow. Tyne 3G 115
Jarvis Brook. E Sus 3G 27
Jasper's Green. Essx 3H 53
Jaywick. Essx 4E 55
Jedburgh. Bord 2A 120
Jeffreyston. Pemb 4E 43
Jemimaville. High 2B 158
Jenkins Park. High 3F 149
Jersey Marine. Neat 3G 31
Jesmond. Tyne 3F 115
Jevington. E Sus 5G 27
Jingle Street. Mon 4H 47
Jockey End. Herts 4A 52
Jodrell Bank. Ches E 3B 84
Johnby. Cumb 1F 103
John O'Gaunts. W Yor 2D 92
John o' Groats. High 1F 169
John's Cross. E Sus 3B 28
Johnshaven. Abers 2G 145
Johnson Street. Norf 4F 79
Johnston. Pemb 3D 42
Johnstone. Ren 3F 127
Johnstonebridge. Dum 5C 118
Johnstown. Carm 4E 45
Johnstown. Wrex 1F 71
Jonesborough. New M 8E 178
Joppa. Edin 2G 129
Joppa. S Ayr 3D 116
Jordan Green. Norf 3C 78
Jordans. Buck 1A 38
Jordanston. Pemb 1D 42
Jump. S Yor 4D 93
Jumpers Common. Dors 3G 15
Juniper. Nmbd 4C 114
Juniper Green. Edin 3E 129
Jurby East. IOM 2C 108
Jurby West. IOM 2C 108
Jury's Gap. E Sus 4D 28

K

Kaber. Cumb 3A 104
Kaimend. S Lan 5C 128
Kaimes. Edin 3F 129
Kaimrig End. Bord 5D 129
Kames. Arg 2A 126
Kames. E Ayr 2F 117
Katesbridge. Arm 5G 179
Kea. Corn 4C 6
Keadby. N Lin 3B 94
Keady. Arm 6C 178
Keal Cotes. Linc 4C 88
Kearsley. G Man 4F 91
Kearsney. Kent 1G 29
Kearstwick. Cumb 1F 97
Kearton. N Yor 5C 104
Kearvaig. High 1C 166
Keasden. N Yor 3G 97
Keason. Corn 2H 7
Keckwick. Hal 2H 83
Keddington. Linc 2C 88
Keddington Corner. Linc 2C 88
Kedington. Suff 1H 53
Kedleston. Derbs 1H 73
Kedlock Feus. Fife 2F 137
Keekle. Cumb 3B 102
Keelby. Linc 3E 95
Keele. Staf 1C 72
Keeley Green. Bed 1A 52
Keeston. Pemb 3D 42
Keevil. Wilts 1E 23
Kegworth. Leics 3B 74
Kehelland. Corn 2D 4
Keig. Abers 2D 152
Keighley. W Yor 5C 98
Keilarsbrae. Clac 4A 136
Keillmore. Arg 1E 125
Keillor. Per 4B 144
Keillour. Per 1B 136
Keills. Arg 3C 124
Keiloch. Abers 4F 151
Keils. Arg 3D 124
Keinton Mandeville. Som 3A 22
Keir Mill. Dum 5A 118
Keirsleywell Row. Nmbd 4A 114
Keisby. Linc 3H 75
Keisley. Cumb 2A 104
Keiss. High 2F 169
Keith. Mor 3B 160
Keith Inch. Abers 4H 161
Kelbrook. Lanc 5B 98
Kelby. Linc 1H 75
Keld. Cumb 3G 103
Keld. N Yor 4B 104
Keldholme. N Yor 1B 100
Kelfield. N Lin 4B 94
Kelfield. N Yor 1F 93
Kelham. Notts 5E 87
Kellacott. Devn 4E 11
Kellan. Arg 4G 139
Kellas. Ang 5D 144
Kellas. Mor 3F 159
Kellaton. Devn 5E 9
Kelleth. Cumb 4H 103
Kelling. Norf 1C 78
Kellingley. N Yor 2F 93
Kellington. N Yor 2F 93
Kelloe. Dur 1A 106
Kelloholm. Dum 3G 117
Kells. Cumb 3A 102
Kells. ME Ant 7H 175
Kelly. Devn 4D 11
Kelly Bray. Corn 5D 10
Kelmarsh. Nptn 3E 63
Kelmscott. Oxon 2H 35
Kelsale. Suff 4F 67
Kelsall. Ches W 4H 83
Kelshall. Herts 2D 52
Kelsick. Cumb 4C 112
Kelso. Bord 1B 120
Kelstedge. Derbs 4H 85
Kelstern. Linc 1B 88
Kelsterton. Flin 3E 83
Kelston. Bath 5C 34
Keltneyburn. Per 4E 143
Kelton. Dum 2A 112
Kelton Hill. Dum 4E 111
Kelty. Fife 4D 136
Kelvedon. Essx 4B 54
Kelvedon Hatch. Essx 1G 39
Kelvinside. Glas 3G 127
Kelynack. Corn 3A 4
Kemback. Fife 2G 137
Kemberton. Shrp 5B 72
Kemble. Glos 2E 35
Kemerton. Worc 2E 49
Kemeys Commander.
Mon 5G 47
Kemnay. Abers 2E 153
Kempe's Corner. Kent 1E 29
Kempley. Glos 3B 48
Kempley Green. Glos 3B 48
Kempsey. Worc 1D 48
Kempsford. Glos 2G 35
Kemps Green. Warw 3F 61
Kempshott. Hants 2E 24
Kempston. Bed 1A 52
Kempston Hardwick. Bed 1A 52
Kempton. Shrp 2F 59
Kemp Town. Brig 5E 27
Kemsing. Kent 5G 39
Kemsley. Kent 4D 40
Kenardington. Kent 2D 28
Kenchester. Here 1H 47
Kencot. Oxon 5A 50
Kendal. Cumb 5G 103
Kendleshire. S Glo 4B 34
Kendray. S Yor 4D 92
Kenfig. B'end 3B 32
Kenfig Hill. B'end 3B 32
Kengharair. Arg 4F 139
Kenilworth. Warw 3G 61
Kenknock. Stir 5B 142
Kenley. G Lon 5E 39
Kenley. Shrp 5H 71
Kenmore. High 3G 155
Kenmore. Per 4E 143
Kenn. Devn 4C 12
Kenn. N Som 5H 33
Kennacraig. Arg 3G 125
Kenneggy Downs. Corn 4C 4
Kennerleigh. Devn 2B 12
Kennet. Clac 4B 136
Kennethmont. Abers 1C 152
Kennett. Cambs 4G 65
Kennford. Devn 4C 12
Kenninghall. Norf 2C 66
Kennington. Kent 1E 28
Kennington. Oxon 5D 50
Kennoway. Fife 3F 137
Kennyhill. Suff 3F 65
Kennythorpe. N Yor 3B 100
Kenovay. Arg 4A 138
Kensaleyre. High 3D 154
Kensington. G Lon 3D 38
Kenstone. Shrp 3H 71
Kensworth. C Beds 4A 52
Kensworth Common.
C Beds 4A 52
Kentallen. High 3E 141
Kentchurch. Here 3H 47
Kentford. Suff 4G 65
Kentisbeare. Devn 2D 12
Kentisbury. Devn 2G 19
Kentisbury Ford. Devn 2G 19
Kentmere. Cumb 4F 103
Kenton. Devn 4C 12
Kenton. G Lon 2C 38
Kenton. Suff 4D 66
Kenton Bankfoot. Tyne 3F 115
Kentra. High 2A 140
Kentrigg. Cumb 5G 103
Kents Bank. Cumb 2C 96
Kent's Green. Glos 3C 48
Kent's Oak. Hants 4B 24
Kent Street. E Sus 4B 28
Kent Street. Kent 5A 40
Kent Street. W Sus 3D 26
Kenwick. Shrp 2G 71
Kenwyn. Corn 4C 6
Kenyon. Warr 1A 84
Keoldale. High 2D 166
Keppoch. High 1B 148
Kepwick. N Yor 5B 106
Keresley. W Mid 2H 61
Keresley Newland. Warw 2H 61
Keristal. IOM 4C 108
Kerne Bridge. Here 4A 48
Kerridge. Ches E 3D 84
Kerris. Corn 4B 4
Kerrow. High 5F 157
Kerry. Powy 2D 58
Kerrycroy. Arg 3C 126
Kerry's Gate. Here 2G 47
Kersall. Notts 4E 86
Kersbrook. Devn 4D 12
Kerse. Ren 4E 127
Kersey. Suff 1D 54
Kershopefoot. Cumb 1F 113
Kersoe. Worc 1E 49
Kerswell. Devn 2D 12
Kerswell Green. Worc 1D 48
Kesgrave. Suff 1F 55
Kesh. Ferm 6D 176
Kessingland. Suff 2H 67
Kessingland Beach. Suff 2H 67
Kestle. Corn 4D 6
Kestle Mill. Corn 3C 6
Keston. G Lon 4F 39
Keswick. Cumb 2D 102
Keswick. Norf
nr. North Walsham 2F 79
nr. Norwich 5E 78
Ketsby. Linc 3C 88
Kettering. Nptn 3F 63
Ketteringham. Norf 5D 78
Kettins. Per 5B 144
Kettlebaston. Suff 5B 66
Kettlebridge. Fife 3F 137
Kettlebrook. Staf 5G 73
Kettleburgh. Suff 4E 67
Kettleholm. Dum 2C 112
Kettleness. N Yor 3F 107
Kettleshulme. Ches E 3D 85
Kettlesing. N Yor 4E 98
Kettlesing Bottom. N Yor 4E 99
Kettlestone. Norf 2B 78
Kettlethorpe. Linc 3F 87
Kettletoft. Orkn 4F 172
Kettlewell. N Yor 2B 98
Ketton. Rut 5G 75
Kew. G Lon 3C 38
Kewaigue. IOM 4C 108
Kewstoke. N Som 5G 33
Kexbrough. S Yor 4C 92
Kexby. Linc 2F 87
Kexby. York 4B 100
Keyford. Som 2C 22
Key Green. Ches E 4C 84
Key Green. N Yor 4F 107
Keyham. Leics 5D 74
Keyhaven. Hants 3B 16
Keyhead. Abers 3H 161
Keyingham. E Yor 2F 95
Keymer. W Sus 4E 27
Keynsham. Bath 5B 34
Keysoe. Bed 4H 63
Keysoe Row. Bed 4H 63
Key's Toft. Linc 5D 89
Keyston. Cambs 3H 63
Key Street. Kent 4C 40
Keyworth. Notts 2D 74
Kibblesworth. Tyne 4F 115
Kibworth Beauchamp.
Leics 1D 62
Kibworth Harcourt. Leics 1D 62
Kidbrooke. G Lon 3F 39
Kidburngill. Cumb 2B 102
Kiddemore Green. Staf 5C 72
Kidderminster. Worc 3C 60
Kiddington. Oxon 3C 50
Kidd's Moor. Norf 5D 78
Kidlington. Oxon 4C 50
Kidmore End. Oxon 4E 37
Kidnal. Ches W 1G 71
Kidsgrove. Staf 5C 84
Kidstones. N Yor 1B 98
Kidwelly. Carm 5E 45
Kiel Crofts. Arg 5D 140
Kielder. Nmbd 5A 120
Kilbagie. Fife 4B 136
Kilbarchan. Ren 3F 127
Kilbeg. High 3E 147
Kilberry. Arg 3F 125
Kilbirnie. N Ayr 4E 126
Kilbride. Arg 1F 133
Kilbride. High 1D 147
Kilbucho Place. Bord 1C 118
Kilburn. Derbs 1A 74
Kilburn. G Lon 2D 38
Kilburn. N Yor 2H 99
Kilby. Leics 1D 62
Kilchattan. Arg 4A 132
Kilchattan Bay. Arg 4C 126
Kilchenzie. Arg 3A 122
Kilcheran. Arg 5C 140
Kilchiaran. Arg 3A 124
Kilchoan. High
nr. Inverie 4F 147
nr. Tobermory 2F 139
Kilchoman. Arg 3A 124
Kilchrenan. Arg 1H 133
Kilclief. New M 5K 179
Kilconquhar. Fife 3G 137
Kilcoo. New M 6G 179
Kilcot. Glos 3B 48
Kilcoy. High 3H 157
Kilcreggan. Arg 1D 126
Kildale. N Yor 4D 106
Kildary. High 1B 158
Kildermorie Lodge. High 1H 157
Kildonan. Dum 4F 109
Kildonan. High
nr. Helmsdale 1G 165
on Isle of Skye 3C 154
Kildonan. N Ayr 3E 123
Kildonnan. High 5C 146
Kildrummy. Abers 2B 152
Kildwick. N Yor 5C 98
Kilfillan. Dum 4H 109
Kilfinan. Arg 2H 125
Kilfinnan. High 4E 149
Kilgetty. Pemb 4F 43
Kilgour. Fife 3E 136
Kilgrammie. S Ayr 4B 116
Kilham. E Yor 3E 101
Kilham. Nmbd 1C 120
Kilkeel. New M 8H 179
Kilkenneth. Arg 4A 138
Kilkhampton. Corn 1C 10
Killadeas. Ferm 7E 176
Killamarsh. Derbs 2B 86
Killandrist. Arg 4C 140
Killay. Swan 3F 31
Killean. Arg 5E 125
Killearn. Stir 1G 127
Killeen. M Ulst 3C 178
Killellan. Arg 4A 122
Killen. Derr 4E 176
Killen. High 3A 158
Killerby. Darl 3E 105
Killeter. Derr 4E 176
Killichonan. Per 3C 142
Killiechronan. Arg 4G 139
Killiecrankie. Per 2G 143
Killilan. High 5B 156
Killimster. High 3F 169
Killin. Stir 5C 142
Killinchy. Ards 3K 179
Killinghall. N Yor 4E 99
Killington. Cumb 1F 97
Killingworth. Tyne 2F 115
Killin Lodge. High 3H 149
Killinochonoch. Arg 4F 133
Killochyett. Bord 5A 130
Killough. New M 6K 179
Killowen. New M 8F 179
Killundine. High 4G 139
Killyleagh. Arm 5B 178
Killyleagh. New M 4K 179
Killyrammer. Caus 4F 175
Kilmacolm. Inv 3E 127
Kilmahog. Stir 3F 135
Kilmahumaig. Arg 4E 133
Kilmalieu. High 3C 140
Kilmaluag. High 1D 154
Kilmany. Fife 1F 137
Kilmarie. High 2D 146
Kilmarnock. E Ayr 196 (1D 116)
Kilmaron. Fife 2F 137
Kilmartin. Arg 4F 133
Kilmaurs. E Ayr 5F 127
Kilmelford. Arg 2F 133
Kilmeny. Arg 3B 124
Kilmersdon. Som 1B 22
Kilmeston. Hants 4D 24
Kilmichael Glassary. Arg 4F 133
Kilmichael of Inverlussa.
Arg 1F 125
Kilmington. Devn 3F 13
Kilmington. Wilts 3C 22
Kilmoluaig. Arg 4A 138
Kilmorack. High 4G 157
Kilmore. Arg 1F 133
Kilmore. Arm 4D 178
Kilmore. High 3E 147
Kilmore. New M 4J 179
Kilmory. Arg 2F 125
Kilmory. High
nr. Kilchoan 1G 139
on Rùm 3B 146
Kilmory. N Ayr 3D 122
Kilmory Lodge. Arg 3E 132
Kilmote. High 2G 165
Kilmuir. High
nr. Dunvegan 4B 154
nr. Invergordon 1B 158
nr. Inverness 4A 158
nr. Uig 1C 154
Kilmun. Arg 1C 126
Kilnave. Arg 2A 124
Kilncadzow. S Lan 5B 128
Kilndown. Kent 2B 28
Kiln Green. Here 4B 48
Kiln Green. Wok 4G 37
Kilnhill. Cumb 1D 102
Kilnhurst. S Yor 1B 86
Kilninian. Arg 4E 139
Kilninver. Arg 1F 133
Kiln Pit Hill. Nmbd 4D 114
Kilnsea. E Yor 3H 95
Kilnsey. N Yor 3B 98
Kilnwick. E Yor 5D 101
Kiloran. Arg 4A 132
Kilpatrick. N Ayr 3D 122
Kilpeck. Here 2H 47
Kilpin. E Yor 2A 94
Kilpin Pike. E Yor 2A 94
Kilrea. Caus 5F 174
Kilrenny. Fife 3H 137
Kilsby. Nptn 3C 62
Kilspindie. Per 1E 136
Kilstay. Dum 5G 109
Kilsyth. N Lan 2A 128
Kiltarlity. High 4H 157
Kilton. Som 2E 21
Kilton Thorpe. Red C 3D 107
Kilvaxter. High 2C 154
Kilve. Som 2E 21
Kilvington. Notts 1F 75
Kilwinning. N Ayr 5D 126
Kimberley. Norf 5C 78
Kimberley. Notts 1B 74
Kimblesworth. Dur 5F 115
Kimble Wick. Buck 5G 51
Kimbolton. Cambs 4H 63
Kimbolton. Here 4H 59
Kimcote. Leics 2C 62
Kimmeridge. Dors 5E 15
Kimmerston. Nmbd 1D 120
Kimpton. Hants 2A 24
Kimpton. Herts 4B 52
Kinallen. Arm 5G 179
Kinawley. Ferm 6H 177
Kinbeachie. High 2A 158
Kinbrace. High 5A 168
Kinbuck. Stir 3G 135
Kincaple. Fife 2G 137
Kincardine. Fife 1C 128
Kincardine. High 5D 164
Kincardine Bridge. Falk 1C 128
Kincardine O'Neil. Abers 4C 152
Kinchrackine. Arg 1A 134
Kincorth. Aber 3G 153
Kincraig. High 3C 150
Kincraigie. Per 4G 143

Ledsham—Llangybi

Ledsham. *Ches W* 3F **83**
Ledsham. *W Yor* 2E **93**
Ledston. *W Yor* 2E **93**
Ledstone. *Devn* 4D **8**
Ledwell. *Oxon* 3C **50**
Lee, The. *Buck* 5H **51**
Lee. *Devn*
nr. Ilfracombe 2E **19**
nr. South Molton 4B **20**
Lee. *G Lon* 3E **39**
Lee. *Hants* 1B **16**
Lee. *Lanc* 4E **97**
Lee. *Shrp* 2G **71**
Leeans. *Shet* 7E **173**
Leebotten. *Shet* 9F **173**
Leebotwood. *Shrp* 1G **59**
Lee Brockhurst. *Shrp* 3H **71**
Leece. *Cumb* 3B **96**
Leechpool. *Mon* 3A **34**
Lee Clump. *Buck* 5H **51**
Leeds. *Kent* 5C **40**
Leeds. *W Yor* **196** (1C **92**)
Leeds Bradford Airport.
W Yor 5E **99**
Leedstown. *Corn* 3D **4**
Leegomery. *Telf* 4A **72**
Lee Head. *Derbs* 1E **85**
Leek. *Staf* 5D **85**
Leekbrook. *Staf* 5D **85**
Leek Wootton. *Warw* 4G **61**
Lee Mill. *Devn* 3B **8**
Leeming. *N Yor* 1E **99**
Leeming Bar. *N Yor* 5F **105**
Lee Moor. *Devn* 2B **8**
Lee Moor. *W Yor* 2D **92**
Lee-on-the-Solent. *Hants* 2D **16**
Lees. *Derbs* 2G **73**
Lees. *G Man* 4H **91**
Lees, The. *Kent* 5E **40**
Lees. *W Yor* 1A **92**
Leeswood. *Flin* 4E **83**
Leetown. *Per* 1E **136**
Leftwich. *Ches W* 3A **84**
Legbourne. *Linc* 2C **88**
Legburthwaite. *Cumb* 3E **102**
Legerwood. *Bord* 5B **130**
Legsby. *Linc* 2A **88**
Leicester. *Leic* **196** (5C **74**)
Leicester Forest East.
Leics 5C **74**
Leigh. *Dors* 2B **14**
Leigh, The. *Glos* 3D **48**
Leigh. *G Man* 4E **91**
Leigh. *Kent* 1G **27**
Leigh. *Shrp* 5F **71**
Leigh. *Surr* 1D **26**
Leigh. *Wilts* 2F **35**
Leigh. *Worc* 5B **60**
Leigham. *Plym* 3B **8**
Leigh Beck. *Essx* 2C **40**
Leigh Common. *Som* 4C **22**
Leigh Delamere. *Wilts* 4D **35**
Leigh Green. *Kent* 2D **28**
Leighland Chapel. *Som* 3D **20**
Leigh-on-Sea. *S'end* 2C **40**
Leigh Park. *Hants* 2F **17**
Leigh Sinton. *Worc* 5B **60**
Leighterton. *Glos* 2D **34**
Leighton. *N Yor* 2D **98**
Leighton. *Powy* 5E **71**
Leighton. *Shrp* 5A **72**
Leighton. *Som* 2C **22**
Leighton Bromswold.
Cambs 3A **64**
Leighton Buzzard. *C Beds* 3H **51**
Leigh-upon-Mendip. *Som* 2B **22**
Leinthall Earls. *Here* 4G **59**
Leinthall Starkes. *Here* 4G **59**
Leintwardine. *Here* 3G **59**
Leire. *Leics* 1C **62**
Leirinmore. *High* 2E **166**
Leishmore. *High* 4G **157**
Leiston. *Suff* 4G **67**
Leitfie. *Per* 4B **144**
Leith. *Edin* 2F **129**
Leitholm. *Bord* 5D **130**
Leitrim. *New M* 6H **179**
Lelant. *Corn* 3C **4**
Lelant Downs. *Corn* 3C **4**
Lelley. *E Yor* 1F **95**
Lem Hill. *Shrp* 3B **60**
Lemington. *Tyne* 3E **115**
Lempitlaw. *Bord* 1B **120**
Lemsford. *Herts* 4C **52**
Lenacre. *Cumb* 1F **97**
Lenchie. *Abers* 5C **160**
Lenchwick. *Worc* 1F **49**
Lendalfoot. *S Ayr* 1G **109**
Lendrick. *Stir* 3E **135**
Lenham. *Kent* 5C **40**
Lenham Heath. *Kent* 1D **28**
Lenimore. *N Ayr* 5G **125**
Lennel. *Bord* 5E **131**
Lennoxtown. *E Dun* 2H **127**
Lenton. *Linc* 2H **75**
Lentran. *High* 4H **157**
Lenwade. *Norf* 4C **78**
Lenzie. *E Dun* 2H **127**
Leochel Cushnie. *Abers* 2C **152**
Leogh. *Shet* 1B **172**
Leominster. *Here* 5G **59**
Leonard Stanley. *Glos* 5D **48**
Lepe. *Hants* 3C **16**
Lephenstrath. *Arg* 5A **122**
Lephin. *High* 4A **154**
Lephinchapel. *Arg* 4G **133**
Lephinmore. *Arg* 4G **133**
Leppington. *N Yor* 3B **100**
Lepton. *W Yor* 3C **92**
Lerryn. *Corn* 3F **7**
Lerwick. *Shet* 7F **173**
Lerwick (Tingwall) Airport.
Shet 7F **173**
Lesbury. *Nmbd* 3G **121**
Leslie. *Abers* 1C **152**
Leslie. *Fife* 3E **137**
Lesmahagow. *S Lan* 1H **117**
Lesnewth. *Corn* 3B **10**
Lessingham. *Norf* 3F **79**
Lessonhall. *Cumb* 4D **112**
Leswalt. *Dum* 3F **109**
Letchmore Heath. *Herts* 1C **38**
Letchworth Garden City.
Herts 2C **52**
Letcombe Bassett. *Oxon* 3B **36**
Letcombe Regis. *Oxon* 3B **36**
Letham. *Ang* 4E **145**
Letham. *Falk* 1B **128**
Letham. *Fife* 2F **137**
Lethanhill. *E Ayr* 3D **116**
Lethenty. *Abers* 4F **161**
Letheringham. *Suff* 5E **67**
Letheringsett. *Norf* 2C **78**
Lettaford. *Devn* 4H **11**
Lettan. *Orkn* 3G **172**
Letter. *Abers* 2E **153**
Letterewe. *High* 1B **156**
Letterfearn. *High* 1A **148**
Lettermore. *Arg* 4F **139**
Letters. *High* 5F **163**
Lettershendoney. *Derr* 5B **174**
Letterston. *Pemb* 2D **42**
Letton. *Here*
nr. Kington 1G **47**
nr. Leintwardine 3F **59**
Letty Green. *Herts* 4C **52**
Letwell. *S Yor* 2C **86**
Leuchars. *Fife* 1G **137**
Leumrabhagh. *W Isl* 6F **171**
Leusdon. *Devn* 5H **11**
Levaneap. *Shet* 5F **173**
Levedale. *Staf* 4C **72**
Leven. *E Yor* 5F **101**
Leven. *Fife* 3F **137**
Levencorroch. *N Ayr* 3E **123**
Levenhall. *E Lot* 2G **129**
Levens. *Cumb* 1D **97**
Levens Green. *Herts* 3D **52**
Levenshulme. *G Man* 1C **84**
Levenwick. *Shet* 9F **173**
Leverburgh. *W Isl* 9C **171**
Leverington. *Cambs* 4D **76**
Leverton. *Linc* 1C **76**
Leverton. *W Ber* 4B **36**
Leverton Lucasgate. *Linc* 1D **76**
Leverton Outgate. *Linc* 1D **76**
Levington. *Suff* 2F **55**
Levisham. *N Yor* 5F **107**
Levishie. *High* 2G **149**
Lew. *Oxon* 5B **50**
Lewaigue. *IOM* 2D **108**
Lewannick. *Corn* 4C **10**
Lewdown. *Devn* 4E **11**
Lewes. *E Sus* 4F **27**
Leweston. *Pemb* 2D **42**
Lewisham. *G Lon* 3E **39**
Lewiston. *High* 1H **149**
Lewistown. *B'end* 3C **32**
Lewknor. *Oxon* 2F **37**
Leworthy. *Devn*
nr. Barnstaple 3G **19**
nr. Holsworthy 2D **10**
Lewson Street. *Kent* 4D **40**
Lewthorn Cross. *Devn* 5A **12**
Lewtrenchard. *Devn* 4E **11**
Ley. *Corn* 2F **7**
Leybourne. *Kent* 5A **40**
Leyburn. *N Yor* 5E **105**
Leycett. *Staf* 1B **72**
Leyfields. *Staf* 5G **73**
Ley Green. *Herts* 3B **52**
Ley Hill. *Buck* 5H **51**
Leyland. *Lanc* 2D **90**
Leylodge. *Abers* 2E **153**
Leymoor. *W Yor* 3B **92**
Leys. *Per* 5B **144**
Leysdown-on-Sea. *Kent* 3E **41**
Leysmill. *Ang* 4F **145**
Leyton. *G Lon* 2E **39**
Leytonstone. *G Lon* 2F **39**
Lezant. *Corn* 5D **10**
Leziate. *Norf* 4F **77**
Lhanbryde. *Mor* 2G **159**
Lhen, The. *IOM* 1C **108**
Liatrie. *High* 5E **157**
Libanus. *Powy* 3C **46**
Libberton. *S Lan* 5C **128**
Libbery. *Worc* 5D **60**
Liberton. *Edin* 3F **129**
Liceasto. *W Isl* 8D **171**
Lichfield. *Staf* 5F **73**
Lickey. *Worc* 3D **61**
Lickey End. *Worc* 3D **60**
Lickfold. *W Sus* 3A **26**
Liddaton. *Devn* 4E **11**
Liddington. *Swin* 3H **35**
Liddle. *Orkn* 9D **172**
Lidgate. *Suff* 5G **65**
Lidgett. *Notts* 4D **86**
Lidham Hill. *E Sus* 4C **28**
Lidlington. *C Beds* 2H **51**
Lidsey. *W Sus* 5A **26**
Lidstone. *Oxon* 3B **50**
Lienassie. *High* 1B **148**
Liff. *Ang* 5C **144**
Lifford. *W Mid* 2E **61**
Lifton. *Devn* 4D **11**
Liftondown. *Devn* 4D **10**
Lighthorne. *Warw* 5H **61**
Light Oaks. *Stoke* 5D **84**
Lightwater. *Surr* 4A **38**
Lightwood. *Staf* 1E **73**
Lightwood. *Stoke* 1D **72**
Lightwood Green. *Ches E* 1A **72**
Lightwood Green. *Wrex* 1F **71**
Lilbourne. *Nptn* 3C **62**
Lilburn Tower. *Nmbd* 2E **121**
Lillesdon. *Som* 4G **21**
Lilleshall. *Telf* 4B **72**
Lilley. *Herts* 3B **52**
Lilliesleaf. *Bord* 2H **119**
Lillingstone Dayrell. *Buck* 2F **51**
Lillingstone Lovell. *Buck* 1F **51**
Lillington. *Dors* 1B **14**
Lilstock. *Som* 2E **21**
Lilybank. *Inv* 2E **126**
Lilyhurst. *Shrp* 4B **72**
Limavady. *Caus* 4C **174**
Limbrick. *Lanc* 3E **90**
Limbury. *Lutn* 3A **52**
Limekilnburn. *S Lan* 4A **128**
Limekilns. *Fife* 1D **129**
Limerigg. *Falk* 2B **128**
Limestone Brae. *Nmbd* 5A **114**
Lime Street. *Worc* 2D **48**
Limington. *Som* 4A **22**
Limpenhoe. *Norf* 5F **79**
Limpley Stoke. *Wilts* 5C **34**
Limpsfield. *Surr* 5F **39**
Limpsfield Chart. *Surr* 5F **39**
Linburn. *W Lot* 3E **129**
Linby. *Notts* 5C **86**
Linchmere. *W Sus* 3G **25**
Lincluden. *Dum* 2A **112**
Lincoln. *Linc* **197** (3G **87**)
Lincomb. *Worc* 4C **60**
Lindale. *Cumb* 1D **96**
Lindal in Furness. *Cumb* 2B **96**
Lindean. *Bord* 1G **119**
Linden. *Glos* 4D **48**
Lindfield. *W Sus* 3E **27**
Lindford. *Hants* 3G **25**
Lindores. *Fife* 2E **137**
Lindridge. *Worc* 4A **60**
Lindsell. *Essx* 3G **53**
Lindsey. *Suff* 1C **54**
Lindsey Tye. *Suff* 1C **54**
Linford. *Hants* 2G **15**
Linford. *Thur* 3A **40**
Lingague. *IOM* 4B **108**
Lingdale. *Red C* 3D **106**
Lingen. *Here* 4F **59**
Lingfield. *Surr* 1E **27**
Lingreabhagh. *W Isl* 9C **171**
Lingwood. *Norf* 5F **79**
Lingy Close. *Cumb* 4E **113**
Linicro. *High* 2C **154**
Linkend. *Worc* 2D **48**
Linkenholt. *Hants* 1B **24**
Linkinhorne. *Corn* 5D **10**
Linklater. *Orkn* 9D **172**
Linksness. *Orkn* 6E **172**
Linktown. *Fife* 4E **137**
Linkwood. *Mor* 2G **159**
Linley. *Shrp*
nr. Bishop's Castle 1F **59**
nr. Bridgnorth 1A **60**
Linley Green. *Here* 5A **60**
Linlithgow. *W Lot* 2C **128**
Linlithgow Bridge. *Falk* 2C **128**
Linneraineach. *High* 3F **163**
Linshiels. *Nmbd* 4C **120**
Linsiadar. *W Isl* 4E **171**
Linsidemore. *High* 4C **164**
Linslade. *C Beds* 3H **51**
Linstead Parva. *Suff* 3F **67**
Linstock. *Cumb* 4F **113**
Linthwaite. *W Yor* 3B **92**
Lintlaw. *Bord* 4E **131**
Lintmill. *Mor* 2C **160**
Linton. *Cambs* 1F **53**
Linton. *Derbs* 4G **73**
Linton. *Here* 3B **48**
Linton. *Kent* 1B **28**
Linton. *N Yor* 3B **98**
Linton. *Bord* 2B **120**
Linton. *W Yor* 5F **99**
Linton Colliery. *Nmbd* 5G **121**
Linton Hill. *Here* 3B **48**
Linton-on-Ouse. *N Yor* 3G **99**
Lintzford. *Dur* 4E **115**
Lintzgarth. *Dur* 5C **114**
Linwood. *Hants* 2G **15**
Linwood. *Linc* 2A **88**
Linwood. *Ren* 3F **127**
Lionacleit. *W Isl* 4C **170**
Lionacro. *High* 2C **154**
Lionacuidhe. *W Isl* 4C **170**
Lional. *W Isl* 1H **171**
Liphook. *Hants* 3G **25**
Lipley. *Shrp* 2B **72**
Lipyeate. *Som* 1B **22**
Liquo. *N Lan* 4B **128**
Lisbane. *Ards* 3J **179**
Lisbellaw. *Ferm* 8F **176**
Lisburn. *Lis* 3G **179**
Liscard. *Mers* 1F **83**
Liscolman. *Caus* 3F **175**
Liscombe. *Som* 3B **20**
Lishahawley. *Derr* 4A **174**
Liskeard. *Corn* 2G **7**
Lislea. *New M* 7E **178**
Lisle Court. *Hants* 3B **16**
Lisnarick. *Ferm* 7D **176**
Lisnaskea. *Ferm* 6J **177**
Liss. *Hants* 4F **25**
Lissett. *E Yor* 4F **101**
Liss Forest. *Hants* 4F **25**
Lissington. *Linc* 2A **88**
Liston. *Essx* 1B **54**
Listooder. *New M* 4J **179**
Lisvane. *Card* 3E **33**
Liswerry. *Newp* 3G **33**
Litcham. *Norf* 4A **78**
Litchard. *B'end* 3C **32**
Litchborough. *Nptn* 5D **62**
Litchfield. *Hants* 1C **24**
Litherland. *Mers* 1F **83**
Litlington. *Cambs* 1D **52**
Litlington. *E Sus* 5G **27**
Littemill. *Nmbd* 3G **121**
Litterty. *Abers* 3E **161**
Little Abington. *Cambs* 1F **53**
Little Addington. *Nptn* 3G **63**
Little Airmyn. *N Yor* 2H **93**
Little Alne. *Warw* 4F **61**
Little Ardo. *Abers* 5F **161**
Little Asby. *Cumb* 4H **103**
Little Aston. *Staf* 5E **73**
Little Atherfield. *IOW* 4C **16**
Little Ayton. *N Yor* 3C **106**
Little Baddow. *Essx* 5A **54**
Little Badminton. *S Glo* 3D **34**
Little Ballinluig. *Per* 3G **143**
Little Bampton. *Cumb* 4D **112**
Little Bardfield. *Essx* 2G **53**
Little Barford. *Bed* 5A **64**
Little Barningham. *Norf* 2D **78**
Little Barrington. *Glos* 4H **49**
Little Barrow. *Ches W* 4G **83**
Little Barugh. *N Yor* 2B **100**
Little Bavington. *Nmbd* 2C **114**
Little Bealings. *Suff* 1F **55**
Littlebeck. *Cumb* 3H **103**
Little Bedwyn. *Wilts* 5A **36**
Little Bentley. *Essx* 3E **54**
Little Berkhamsted. *Herts* 5C **52**
Little Billing. *Nptn* 4F **63**
Little Billington. *C Beds* 3H **51**
Little Birch. *Here* 2A **48**
Little Bispham. *Bkpl* 5C **96**
Little Blakenham. *Suff* 1E **54**
Little Blencow. *Cumb* 1F **103**
Little Bognor. *W Sus* 3B **26**
Little Bolas. *Shrp* 3A **72**
Little Bollington. *Ches E* 2B **84**
Little Bookham. *Surr* 5C **38**
Littleborough. *Devn* 1B **12**
Littleborough. *G Man* 3H **91**
Littleborough. *Notts* 2F **87**
Littlebourne. *Kent* 5G **41**
Little Bourton. *Oxon* 1C **50**
Little Bowden. *Leics* 2E **63**
Little Bradley. *Suff* 5F **65**
Little Brampton. *Shrp* 2F **59**
Little Brechin. *Ang* 2E **145**
Littlebredy. *Dors* 4A **14**
Little Brickhill. *Mil* 2H **51**
Little Bridgeford. *Staf* 3C **72**
Little Brington. *Nptn* 4D **62**
Little Bromley. *Essx* 3D **54**
Little Broughton. *Cumb* 1B **102**
Little Budworth. *Ches W* 4H **83**
Little Burstead. *Essx* 1A **40**
Little Burton. *E Yor* 5F **101**
Littlebury. *Essx* 2F **53**
Littlebury Green. *Essx* 2E **53**
Little Bytham. *Linc* 4H **75**
Little Canfield. *Essx* 3F **53**
Little Canford. *Dors* 3F **15**
Little Carlton. *Linc* 2C **88**
Little Carlton. *Notts* 5E **87**
Little Casterton. *Rut* 5H **75**
Little Catwick. *E Yor* 5F **101**
Little Catworth. *Cambs* 3A **64**
Little Cawthorpe. *Linc* 2C **88**
Little Chalfont. *Buck* 1A **38**
Little Chart. *Kent* 1D **28**
Little Chesterford. *Essx* 1F **53**
Little Cheverell. *Wilts* 1E **23**
Little Chishill. *Cambs* 2E **53**
Little Clacton. *Essx* 4E **55**
Little Clanfield. *Oxon* 5A **50**
Little Clifton. *Cumb* 2B **102**
Little Coates. *NE Lin* 4F **95**
Little Comberton. *Worc* 1E **49**
Little Common. *E Sus* 5B **28**
Little Compton. *Warw* 2A **50**
Little Cornard. *Suff* 2B **54**
Littlecote. *Buck* 3G **51**
Littlecott. *Wilts* 1G **23**
Little Cowarne. *Here* 5A **60**
Little Coxwell. *Oxon* 2A **36**
Little Crakehall. *N Yor* 5F **105**
Little Crawley. *Mil* 1H **51**
Little Creich. *High* 5D **164**
Little Cressingham. *Norf* 5A **78**
Little Crosby. *Mers* 4B **90**
Little Crosthwaite. *Cumb* 2D **102**
Little Cubley. *Derbs* 2F **73**
Little Dalby. *Leics* 4E **75**
Little Dawley. *Telf* 5A **72**
Littledean. *Glos* 4B **48**
Little Dens. *Abers* 4H **161**
Little Dewchurch. *Here* 2A **48**
Little Ditton. *Cambs* 5F **65**
Little Down. *Hants* 1B **24**
Little Downham. *Cambs* 2E **65**
Little Drayton. *Shrp* 2A **72**
Little Driffield. *E Yor* 4E **101**
Little Dunham. *Norf* 4A **78**
Little Dunkeld. *Per* 4H **143**
Little Dunmow. *Essx* 3G **53**
Little Easton. *Essx* 3G **53**
Little Eaton. *Derbs* 1A **74**
Little Eccleston. *Lanc* 5D **96**
Little Ellingham. *Norf* 1C **66**
Little Elm. *Som* 2C **22**
Little End. *Essx* 5F **53**
Little Everdon. *Nptn* 5C **62**
Little Eversden. *Cambs* 5C **64**
Little Faringdon. *Oxon* 5H **49**
Little Fencote. *N Yor* 5F **105**
Little Fenton. *N Yor* 1F **93**
Littleferry. *High* 4F **165**
Little Fransham. *Norf* 4B **78**
Little Gaddesden. *Herts* 4H **51**
Little Garway. *Here* 3H **47**
Little Gidding. *Cambs* 2A **64**
Little Glemham. *Suff* 5F **67**
Little Glenshee. *Per* 5G **143**
Little Gransden. *Cambs* 5B **64**
Little Green. *Suff* 3C **66**
Little Green. *Wrex* 1G **71**
Little Grimsby. *Linc* 1C **88**
Little Habton. *N Yor* 2B **100**
Little Hadham. *Herts* 3E **53**
Little Hale. *Linc* 1A **76**
Little Hallingbury. *Essx* 4E **53**
Littleham. *Devn*
nr. Bideford 4E **19**
nr. Exmouth 4D **12**
Little Hampden. *Buck* 5G **51**
Littlehampton. *W Sus* 5B **26**
Little Haresfield. *Glos* 5D **48**
Little Harrowden. *Nptn* 3F **63**
Little Haseley. *Oxon* 5E **51**
Little Hatfield. *E Yor* 5F **101**
Little Hautbois. *Norf* 3E **79**
Little Haven. *Pemb* 3C **42**
Little Hay. *Staf* 5F **73**
Little Hayfield. *Derbs* 2E **85**
Little Haywood. *Staf* 3E **73**
Little Heath. *W Mid* 2H **61**
Little Heck. *N Yor* 2F **93**
Littlehempston. *Devn* 2E **9**
Little Herbert's. *Glos* 4E **49**
Little Hereford. *Here* 4H **59**
Little Horkesley. *Essx* 2C **54**
Little Hormead. *Herts* 3D **53**
Little Horsted. *E Sus* 4F **27**
Little Horton. *W Yor* 1B **92**
Little Horwood. *Buck* 2F **51**
Little Houghton. *Nptn* 5F **63**
Littlehoughton. *Nmbd* 3G **121**
Little Houghton. *S Yor* 4E **93**
Little Hucklow. *Derbs* 3F **85**
Little Hulton. *G Man* 4F **91**
Little Irchester. *Nptn* 4G **63**
Little Kelk. *E Yor* 3E **101**
Little Kimble. *Buck* 5G **51**
Little Kineton. *Warw* 5H **61**
Little Kingshill. *Buck* 2G **37**
Little Langdale. *Cumb* 4E **102**
Little Langford. *Wilts* 3F **23**
Little Laver. *Essx* 5F **53**
Little Lawford. *Warw* 3B **62**
Little Leigh. *Ches W* 3A **84**
Little Leighs. *Essx* 4H **53**
Little Leven. *E Yor* 5E **101**
Little Lever. *G Man* 4F **91**
Little Linford. *Mil* 1G **51**
Little London. *Buck* 4E **51**
Little London. *E Sus* 4G **27**
Little London. *Hants*
nr. Andover 2B **24**
nr. Basingstoke 1E **24**
Little London. *Linc*
nr. Long Sutton 3D **76**
nr. Spalding 3B **76**
Little London. *Norf*
nr. North Walsham 2E **79**
nr. Northwold 1G **65**
nr. Saxthorpe 2D **78**
nr. Southery 1F **65**
Little London. *Powy* 2C **58**
Little Longstone. *Derbs* 3F **85**
Little Malvern. *Worc* 1C **48**
Little Maplestead. *Essx* 2B **54**
Little Marcle. *Here* 2B **48**
Little Marlow. *Buck* 3G **37**
Little Massingham. *Norf* 3G **77**
Little Melton. *Norf* 5D **78**
Littlemill. *Abers* 4H **151**
Littlemill. *E Ayr* 3D **116**
Littlemill. *High* 4D **158**
Little Mill. *Mon* 5G **47**
Little Milton. *Oxon* 5E **50**
Little Missenden. *Buck* 1A **38**
Littlemoor. *Derbs* 4A **86**
Littlemoor. *Dors* 4B **14**
Littlemore. *Oxon* 5D **50**
Little Mountain. *Flin* 4E **83**
Little Musgrave. *Cumb* 3A **104**
Little Ness. *Shrp* 4G **71**
Little Neston. *Ches W* 3E **83**
Little Newcastle. *Pemb* 2D **43**
Little Newsham. *Dur* 3E **105**
Little Oakley. *Essx* 3F **55**
Little Oakley. *Nptn* 2F **63**
Little Onn. *Staf* 4C **72**
Little Ormside. *Cumb* 3A **104**
Little Orton. *Cumb* 4E **113**
Little Orton. *Leics* 5H **73**
Little Ouse. *Cambs* 2F **65**
Little Ouseburn. *N Yor* 3G **99**
Littleover. *Derb* 2H **73**
Little Packington. *Warw* 2G **61**
Little Paxton. *Cambs* 4A **64**
Little Petherick. *Corn* 1D **6**
Little Plumpton. *Lanc* 1B **90**
Little Plumstead. *Norf* 4F **79**
Little Ponton. *Linc* 2G **75**
Littleport. *Cambs* 2E **65**
Little Posbrook. *Hants* 2D **16**
Little Potheridge. *Devn* 1F **11**
Little Preston. *Nptn* 5C **62**
Little Raveley. *Cambs* 3B **64**
Little Reynoldston. *Swan* 4D **31**
Little Ribston. *N Yor* 4F **99**
Little Rissington. *Glos* 4G **49**
Little Rogart. *High* 3E **165**
Little Rollright. *Oxon* 2A **50**
Little Ryburgh. *Norf* 3B **78**
Little Ryle. *Nmbd* 3E **121**
Little Ryton. *Shrp* 5G **71**
Little Salkeld. *Cumb* 1G **103**
Little Sampford. *Essx* 2G **53**
Little Sandhurst. *Brac* 5G **37**
Little Saredon. *Staf* 5D **72**
Little Saxham. *Suff* 4G **65**
Little Scatwell. *High* 3F **157**
Little Shelford. *Cambs* 5D **64**
Little Shoddesden. *Hants* 2A **24**
Little Singleton. *Lanc* 1B **90**
Little Smeaton. *N Yor* 3F **93**
Little Snoring. *Norf* 2B **78**
Little Sodbury. *S Glo* 3C **34**
Little Somborne. *Hants* 3B **24**
Little Somerford. *Wilts* 3E **35**
Little Soudley. *Shrp* 3B **72**
Little Stainforth. *N Yor* 3H **97**
Little Stainton. *Darl* 3A **106**
Little Stanney. *Ches W* 3G **83**
Little Staughton. *Bed* 4A **64**
Little Steeping. *Linc* 4D **88**
Littlester. *Shet* 3G **173**
Little Stoke. *Staf* 2D **72**
Littlestone-on-Sea. *Kent* 3E **29**
Little Stonham. *Suff* 4D **66**
Little Stretton. *Leics* 5D **74**
Little Stretton. *Shrp* 1G **59**
Little Strickland. *Cumb* 3G **103**
Little Stukeley. *Cambs* 3B **64**
Little Sugnall. *Staf* 2C **72**
Little Sutton. *Ches W* 3F **83**
Little Sutton. *Linc* 3D **76**
Little Swinburne. *Nmbd* 2C **114**
Little Tew. *Oxon* 3B **50**
Little Tey. *Essx* 3B **54**
Little Thetford. *Cambs* 3E **65**
Little Thirkleby. *N Yor* 2G **99**
Little Thornage. *Norf* 2C **78**
Little Thornton. *Lanc* 5C **96**
Littlethorpe. *Leics* 1C **62**
Littlethorpe. *N Yor* 3F **99**
Little Thorpe. *W Yor* 2B **92**
Little Thurlow. *Suff* 5F **65**
Little Thurrock. *Thur* 3H **39**
Littleton. *Ches W* 4G **83**
Littleton. *Hants* 3C **24**
Littleton. *Som* 3H **21**
Littleton. *Surr*
nr. Guildford 1A **26**
nr. Staines 4B **38**
Littleton Drew. *Wilts* 3D **34**
Littleton Pannell. *Wilts* 1F **23**
Littleton-upon-Severn.
S Glo 3A **34**
Little Torboll. *High* 4E **165**
Little Torrington. *Devn* 1E **11**
Little Totham. *Essx* 4B **54**
Little Town. *Cumb* 3D **102**
Littletown. *Dur* 5G **115**
Littletown. *High* 5E **165**
Little Town. *Lanc* 1E **91**
Little Twycross. *Leics* 5H **73**
Little Urswick. *Cumb* 2B **96**
Little Wakering. *Essx* 2D **40**
Little Walden. *Essx* 1F **53**
Little Waldingfield. *Suff* 1C **54**
Little Walsingham. *Norf* 2B **78**
Little Waltham. *Essx* 4H **53**
Little Warley. *Essx* 1H **39**
Little Weighton. *E Yor* 1C **94**
Little Wenham. *Suff* 2D **54**
Little Wenlock. *Telf* 5A **72**
Little Whelnetham. *Suff* 4A **66**
Little Whittingham Green.
Suff 3E **67**
Littlewick Green. *Wind* 4G **37**
Little Wilbraham. *Cambs* 5E **65**
Littlewindsor. *Dors* 2H **13**
Little Wisbeach. *Linc* 2A **76**
Little Witcombe. *Glos* 4E **49**
Little Witley. *Worc* 4B **60**
Little Wittenham. *Oxon* 2D **36**
Little Wolford. *Warw* 2A **50**
Littleworth. *Bed* 1A **52**
Littleworth. *Glos* 2G **49**
Littleworth. *Oxon* 2B **36**
Littleworth. *Staf*
nr. Cannock 4E **73**
nr. Eccleshall 3B **72**
nr. Stafford 3D **72**
Littleworth. *W Sus* 3C **26**
Littleworth. *Worc*
nr. Redditch 4D **61**
nr. Worcester 5C **60**
Little Wratting. *Suff* 1G **53**
Little Wymondley. *Herts* 3C **52**
Little Wyrley. *Staf* 5E **73**
Little Yeldham. *Essx* 2A **54**
Littley Green. *Essx* 4G **53**
Litton. *Derbs* 3F **85**
Litton. *N Yor* 2B **98**
Litton. *Som* 1A **22**
Litton Cheney. *Dors* 3A **14**
Liurbost. *W Isl* 5F **171**
Liverpool. *Mers* **197** (1F **83**)
Liverpool John Lennon Airport.
Mers 2G **83**
Liversedge. *W Yor* 2B **92**
Liverton. *Devn* 5B **12**
Liverton. *Red C* 3E **107**
Liverton Mines. *Red C* 3E **107**
Livingston. *W Lot* 3D **128**
Livingston Village. *W Lot* 3D **128**
Lixwm. *Flin* 3D **82**
Lizard. *Corn* 5E **5**
Llaingoch. *IOA* 2B **80**
Llaithddu. *Powy* 2C **58**
Llampha. *V Glam* 4C **32**
Llan. *Powy* 5A **70**
Llanaber. *Gwyn* 4F **69**
Llanaelhaearn. *Gwyn* 1C **68**
Llanaeron. *Cdgn* 4D **57**
Llanafan. *Cdgn* 3F **57**
Llanafan-fawr. *Powy* 5B **58**
Llanafan-fechan. *Powy* 5B **58**
Llanallgo. *IOA* 2D **81**
Llanandras. *Powy* 4F **59**
Llananno. *Powy* 3C **58**
Llanarmon. *Gwyn* 2D **68**
Llanarmon Dyffryn Ceiriog.
Wrex 2D **70**
Llanarmon-yn-Ial. *Den* 5D **82**
Llanarth. *Cdgn* 5D **56**
Llanarth. *Mon* 4G **47**
Llanarthne. *Carm* 3F **45**
Llanasa. *Flin* 2D **82**
Llanbabo. *IOA* 2C **80**
Llanbadarn Fawr. *Cdgn* 2F **57**
Llanbadarn Fynydd. *Powy* 3D **58**
Llanbadarn-y-garreg. *Powy* 1E **46**
Llanbadoc. *Mon* 5G **47**
Llanbadrig. *IOA* 1C **80**
Llanbeder. *Newp* 2G **33**
Llanbedr. *Gwyn* 3E **69**
Llanbedr. *Powy*
nr. Crickhowell 3F **47**
nr. Hay-on-Wye 1E **47**
Llanbedr-Dyffryn-Clwyd.
Den 5D **82**
Llanbedrgoch. *IOA* 2E **81**
Llanbedrog. *Gwyn* 2C **68**
Llanbedr Pont Steffan.
Cdgn 1F **45**
Llanbedr-y-cennin. *Cnwy* 4G **81**
Llanberis. *Gwyn* 4E **81**
Llanbethery. *V Glam* 5D **32**
Llanbister. *Powy* 3D **58**
Llanblethian. *V Glam* 4C **32**
Llanboidy. *Carm* 2G **43**
Llanbradach. *Cphy* 2E **33**
Llanbrynmair. *Powy* 5A **70**
Llanbydderi. *V Glam* 5D **32**
Llancadle. *V Glam* 5D **32**
Llancarfan. *V Glam* 4D **32**
Llancatal. *V Glam* 5D **32**
Llancayo. *Mon* 5G **47**
Llancloudy. *Here* 3H **47**
Llancoch. *Powy* 3E **58**
Llancynfelyn. *Cdgn* 1F **57**
Llandaff. *Card* 4E **33**
Llandanwg. *Gwyn* 3E **69**
Llandarcy. *Neat* 3G **31**
Llandawke. *Carm* 3G **43**
Llanddaniel Fab. *IOA* 3D **81**
Llanddarog. *Carm* 4F **45**
Llanddeiniol. *Cdgn* 3E **57**
Llanddeiniolen. *Gwyn* 4E **81**
Llandderfel. *Gwyn* 2B **70**
Llanddeusant. *Carm* 3A **46**
Llanddeusant. *IOA* 2C **80**
Llanddew. *Powy* 2D **46**
Llanddewi. *Swan* 4D **30**
Llanddewi Brefi. *Cdgn* 5F **57**
Llanddewi'r Cwm. *Powy* 1D **46**
Llanddewi Rhydderch.
Mon 4G **47**
Llanddewi Velfrey. *Pemb* 3F **43**
Llanddewi Ystradenni.
Powy 4D **58**
Llanddoged. *Cnwy* 4H **81**
Llanddona. *IOA* 3E **81**
Llanddowror. *Carm* 3G **43**
Llanddulas. *Cnwy* 3B **82**
Llanddwywe. *Gwyn* 3E **69**
Llanddyfnan. *IOA* 3E **81**
Llandecwyn. *Gwyn* 2F **69**
Llandefaelog Fach. *Powy* 2D **46**
Llandefaelog-tre'r-graig.
Powy 2E **47**
Llandefalle. *Powy* 2E **46**
Llandegfan. *IOA* 3E **81**
Llandegla. *Den* 5D **82**
Llandegley. *Powy* 4D **58**
Llandegveth. *Mon* 2G **33**
Llandeilo. *Carm* 3G **45**
Llandeilo Graban. *Powy* 1D **46**
Llandeilo'r Fan. *Powy* 2B **46**
Llandeloy. *Pemb* 2C **42**
Llandenny. *Mon* 5H **47**
Llandevaud. *Newp* 2H **33**
Llandevenny. *Mon* 3H **33**
Llandilo. *Pemb* 2F **43**
Llandinabo. *Here* 3A **48**
Llandinam. *Powy* 2C **58**
Llandissilio. *Pemb* 2F **43**
Llandogo. *Mon* 5A **48**
Llandough. *V Glam*
nr. Cowbridge 4C **32**
nr. Penarth 4E **33**
Llandovery. *Carm* 2A **46**
Llandow. *V Glam* 4C **32**
Llandre. *Cdgn* 2F **57**
Llandrillo. *Den* 2C **70**
Llandrillo-yn-Rhos. *Cnwy* 2H **81**
Llandrindod. *Powy* 4C **58**
Llandrindod Wells. *Powy* 4C **58**
Llandrinio. *Powy* 4E **71**
Llandudno. *Cnwy* 2G **81**
Llandudno Junction. *Cnwy* 3G **81**
Llandudoch. *Pemb* 1B **44**
Llandw. *V Glam* 4C **32**
Llandwrog. *Gwyn* 5D **80**
Llandybie. *Carm* 4G **45**
Llandyfaelog. *Carm* 4E **45**
Llandyfan. *Carm* 4G **45**
Llandyfriog. *Cdgn* 1D **44**
Llandyfrydog. *IOA* 2D **80**
Llandygai. *Gwyn* 3F **81**
Llandygwydd. *Cdgn* 1C **44**
Llandynan. *Den* 1D **70**
Llandyrnog. *Den* 4D **82**
Llandysilio. *Powy* 4E **71**
Llandyssil. *Powy* 1D **58**
Llandysul. *Cdgn* 1E **45**
Llanedeyrn. *Card* 3F **33**
Llaneglwys. *Powy* 2D **46**
Llanegryn. *Gwyn* 5F **69**
Llanegwad. *Carm* 3F **45**
Llaneilian. *IOA* 1D **80**
Llanelian-yn-Rhos. *Cnwy* 3A **82**
Llanelidan. *Den* 5D **82**
Llanelieu. *Powy* 2E **47**
Llanellen. *Mon* 4G **47**
Llanelli. *Carm* 3E **31**
Llanelltyd. *Gwyn* 4G **69**
Llanelly. *Mon* 4F **47**
Llanelly Hill. *Mon* 4F **47**
Llanelwedd. *Powy* 5C **58**
Llan-Elwy. *Den* 3C **82**
Llanenddwyn. *Gwyn* 3E **69**
Llanengan. *Gwyn* 3B **68**
Llanerch. *Powy* 1F **59**
Llanerchymedd. *IOA* 2D **80**
Llanerfyl. *Powy* 5C **70**
Llaneuddog. *IOA* 2D **80**
Llanfachraeth. *IOA* 2C **80**
Llanfachreth. *Gwyn* 3G **69**
Llanfaelog. *IOA* 3C **80**
Llanfaelrhys. *Gwyn* 3B **68**
Llanfaenor. *Mon* 4H **47**
Llanfaes. *IOA* 3F **81**
Llanfaes. *Powy* 3D **46**
Llanfaethlu. *IOA* 2C **80**
Llanfaglan. *Gwyn* 4D **80**
Llanfair. *Gwyn* 3E **69**
Llanfair. *Here* 1F **47**
Llanfair Caereinion. *Powy* 5D **70**
Llanfair Clydogau. *Cdgn* 5F **57**
Llanfair Dyffryn Clwyd.
Den 5D **82**
Llanfairfechan. *Cnwy* 3F **81**
Llanfair-Nant-Gwyn. *Pemb* 1F **43**
Llanfair Pwllgwyngyll. *IOA* 3E **81**
Llanfair Talhaiarn. *Cnwy* 3B **82**
Llanfair Waterdine. *Shrp* 3E **59**
Llanfair-ym-Muallt. *Powy* 5C **58**
Llanfairyneubwll. *IOA* 3C **80**
Llanfairynghornwy. *IOA* 1C **80**
Llanfallteg. *Carm* 3F **43**
Llanfallteg West. *Carm* 3F **43**
Llanfaredd. *Powy* 5C **58**
Llanfarian. *Cdgn* 3E **57**
Llanfechain. *Powy* 3D **70**
Llanfechell. *IOA* 1C **80**
Llanfendigaid. *Gwyn* 5E **69**
Llanferres. *Den* 4D **82**
Llan Ffestiniog. *Gwyn* 1G **69**
Llanfflewyn. *IOA* 2C **80**
Llanfihangel-ar-Arth. *Carm* 2E **45**
Llanfihangel Glyn Myfyr.
Cnwy 1B **70**
Llanfihangel Nant Bran.
Powy 2C **46**
Llanfihangel-Nant-Melan.
Powy 5D **58**
Llanfihangel near Rogiet.
Mon 3H **33**
Llanfihangel Rhydithon.
Powy 4D **58**
Llanfihangel Tal-y-llyn.
Powy 3E **46**
Llanfihangel-uwch-Gwili.
Carm 3E **45**
Llanfihangel-y-Creuddyn.
Cdgn 3F **57**
Llanfihangel-yng-Ngwynfa.
Powy 4C **70**
Llanfihangel yn Nhowyn.
IOA 3C **80**
Llanfihangel-y-pennant. *Gwyn*
nr. Golan 1E **69**
nr. Tywyn 5F **69**
Llanfihangel-y-traethau.
Gwyn 2E **69**
Llanfilo. *Powy* 2E **46**
Llanfleiddan. *V Glam* 4C **32**
Llanfoist. *Mon* 4F **47**
Llanfor. *Gwyn* 2B **70**
Llanfrechfa. *Torf* 2G **33**
Llanfrothen. *Gwyn* 1F **69**
Llanfrynach. *Powy* 3D **46**
Llanfwrog. *Den* 5D **82**
Llanfwrog. *IOA* 2C **80**
Llanfyllin. *Powy* 4D **70**
Llanfynydd. *Carm* 3F **45**
Llanfynydd. *Flin* 5E **83**
Llanfyrnach. *Pemb* 1G **43**
Llangadfan. *Powy* 4C **70**
Llangadog. *Carm*
nr. Llandovery 3H **45**
nr. Llanelli 5E **45**
Llangadwaladr. *IOA* 4C **80**
Llangadwaladr. *Powy* 2D **70**
Llangaffo. *IOA* 4D **80**
Llangain. *Carm* 4D **45**
Llangammarch Wells.
Powy 1C **46**
Llangan. *V Glam* 4C **32**
Llangarron. *Here* 3A **48**
Llangasty-Talyllyn. *Powy* 3E **47**
Llangathen. *Carm* 3F **45**
Llangattock. *Powy* 4F **47**
Llangattock Lingoed. *Mon* 3G **47**
Llangattock-Vibon-Avel.
Mon 4H **47**
Llangedwyn. *Powy* 3D **70**
Llangefni. *IOA* 3D **80**
Llangeinor. *B'end* 3C **32**
Llangeitho. *Cdgn* 5F **57**
Llangeler. *Carm* 2D **44**
Llangelynin. *Gwyn* 5E **69**
Llangendeirne. *Carm* 4E **45**
Llangennech. *Carm* 5F **45**
Llangennith. *Swan* 3D **30**
Llangenny. *Powy* 4F **47**
Llangernyw. *Cnwy* 4A **82**
Llangian. *Gwyn* 3B **68**
Llangiwg. *Neat* 5H **45**
Llangloffan. *Pemb* 1D **42**
Llanglydwen. *Carm* 2F **43**
Llangoed. *IOA* 3F **81**
Llangoedmor. *Cdgn* 1B **44**
Llangollen. *Den* 1E **70**
Llangolman. *Pemb* 2F **43**
Llangorse. *Powy* 3E **47**
Llangorwen. *Cdgn* 2F **57**
Llangovan. *Mon* 5H **47**
Llangower. *Gwyn* 2B **70**
Llangranog. *Cdgn* 5C **56**
Llangristiolus. *IOA* 3D **80**
Llangrove. *Here* 4A **48**
Llangua. *Mon* 3G **47**
Llangunllo. *Powy* 3E **58**
Llangunnor. *Carm* 3E **45**
Llangurig. *Powy* 3B **58**
Llangwm. *Cnwy* 1B **70**
Llangwm. *Mon* 5H **47**
Llangwm. *Pemb* 4D **43**
Llangwm-isaf. *Mon* 5H **47**
Llangwnnadl. *Gwyn* 2B **68**
Llangwyfan. *Den* 4D **82**
Llangwyfan-isaf. *IOA* 4C **80**
Llangwyllog. *IOA* 3D **80**
Llangwyryfon. *Cdgn* 3F **57**
Llangybi. *Cdgn* 5F **57**
Llangybi. *Gwyn* 1D **68**

Llangybi—Maghera

Llangybi. Mon 2G 33
Llangyfelach. Swan 3F 31
Llangynhafal. Den 4D 82
Llangynidr. Powy 4E 47
Llangynin. Carm 3G 43
Llangynog. Carm 3H 43
Llangynog. Powy 3C 70
Llangynwyd. B'end 3B 32
Llanhamlach. Powy 3D 46
Llanharan. Rhon 3D 32
Llanharry. Rhon 3D 32
Llanhennock. Mon 2G 33
Llanhilleth. Blae 5F 47
Llanidloes. Powy 2B 58
Llaniestyn. Gwyn 2B 68
Llanigon. Powy 1F 47
Llanilar. Cdgn 3F 57
Llanilid. Rhon 3C 32
Llanilltud Fawr. V Glam 5C 32
Llanishen. Card 3E 33
Llanishen. Mon 5H 47
Llanllawddog. Carm 3E 45
Llanllechid. Gwyn 4F 81
Llanllowell. Mon 2G 33
Llanllugan. Powy 5C 70
Llanllwch. Carm 4D 45
Llanllwchaiarn. Powy 1D 58
Llanllwni. Carm 2E 45
Llanllyfni. Gwyn 5D 80
Llanmadoc. Swan 3D 30
Llanmaes. V Glam 5C 32
Llanmartin. Newp 3G 33
Llanmerwig. Powy 1D 58
Llanmihangel. V Glam 4C 32
Llan-mill. Pemb 3F 43
Llanmiloe. Carm 4G 43
Llanmorlais. Swan 3E 31
Llannefydd. Cnwy 3B 82
Llannon. Carm 5F 45
Llan-non. Cdgn 4E 57
Llannor. Gwyn 2C 68
Llanover. Mon 5G 47
Llanpumsaint. Carm 3E 45
Llanrhaeadr. Den 4C 82
Llanrhaeadr-ym-Mochnant. Powy 3D 70
Llanrhian. Pemb 1C 42
Llanrhidian. Swan 3D 31
Llanrhos. Cnwy 2G 81
Llanrhyddlad. IOA 2C 80
Llanrhystud. Cdgn 4E 57
Llanrothal. Here 4H 47
Llanrug. Gwyn 4E 81
Llanrumney. Card 3F 33
Llanrwst. Cnwy 4G 81
Llansadurnen. Carm 3G 43
Llansadwrn. Carm 2G 45
Llansadwrn. IOA 3E 81
Llansaint. Carm 5D 45
Llansamlet. Swan 3F 31
Llansanffraid Glan Conwy. Cnwy 3H 81
Llansannan. Cnwy 4B 82
Llansannor. V Glam 4C 32
Llansantffraed. Cdgn 4E 57
Llansantffraed. Powy 3E 46
Llansantffraed Cwmdeuddwr. Powy 4B 58
Llansantffraed-in-Elwel. Powy 5C 58
Llansantffraid-ym-Mechain. Powy 3E 70
Llansawel. Carm 2G 45
Llansawel. Neat 3G 31
Llansilin. Powy 3E 70
Llansoy. Mon 5H 47
Llanspyddid. Powy 3D 46
Llanstadwell. Pemb 4D 42
Llansteffan. Carm 4D 44
Llanstephan. Powy 1E 46
Llantarnam. Torf 2G 33
Llanteg. Pemb 3F 43
Llanthony. Mon 3F 47
Llantilio Crossenny. Mon 4G 47
Llantilio Pertholey. Mon 4G 47
Llantood. Pemb 1B 44
Llantrisant. Mon 2G 33
Llantrisant. Rhon 3D 32
Llantrithyd. V Glam 4D 32
Llantwit Fardre. Rhon 3D 32
Llantwit Major. V Glam 5C 32
Llanuwchllyn. Gwyn 2A 70
Llanvaches. Newp 2H 33
Llanvair Discoed. Mon 2H 33
Llanvapley. Mon 4G 47
Llanvetherine. Mon 4G 47
Llanveynoe. Here 2G 47
Llanvihangel Crucorney. Mon 3G 47
Llanvihangel Gobion. Mon 5G 47
Llanvihangel Ystern-Llewern. Mon 4H 47
Llanwarne. Here 3A 48
Llanwddyn. Powy 4C 70
Llanwenarth. Mon 4F 47
Llanwenog. Cdgn 1E 45
Llanwern. Newp 3G 33
Llanwinio. Carm 2G 43
Llanwnda. Gwyn 5D 80
Llanwnda. Pemb 1D 42
Llanwnnen. Cdgn 1F 45
Llanwnog. Powy 1C 58
Llanwrda. Carm 2H 45
Llanwrin. Powy 5G 69
Llanwrthwl. Powy 4B 58
Llanwrtud. Powy 1B 46
Llanwrtyd. Powy 1B 46
Llanwrtyd Wells. Powy 1B 46
Llanwyddelan. Powy 5C 70
Llanyblodwel. Shrp 3E 71
Llanybri. Carm 3H 43
Llanybydder. Carm 1F 45
Llanycefn. Pemb 2E 43
Llanychaer. Pemb 1D 43
Llanycil. Gwyn 2B 70
Llanymawddwy. Gwyn 4B 70
Llanymddyfri. Carm 2A 46
Llanymynech. Powy 3E 71
Llanynghenedl. IOA 2C 80
Llanynys. Den 4D 82
Llan-y-pwll. Wrex 5F 83
Llanyrafon. Torf 2G 33
Llanyre. Powy 4C 58
Llanystumdwy. Gwyn 2D 68
Llanywern. Powy 3E 46
Llawhaden. Pemb 3E 43
Llawndy. Flin 2D 82
Llawnt. Shrp 2E 71
Llawr Dref. Gwyn 3B 68
Llawryglyn. Powy 1B 58
Llay. Wrex 5F 83
Llechfaen. Powy 3D 46
Llechryd. Cphy 5E 46
Llechryd. Cdgn 1C 44
Llechrydau. Wrex 2E 71
Lledrod. Cdgn 3F 57
Llethrid. Swan 3E 31
Llidiad-Nenog. Carm 2F 45
Llidiardau. Gwyn 2A 70
Llidiart y Parc. Den 1D 70
Llithfaen. Gwyn 1C 68
Lloc. Flin 3D 82
Llong. Flin 4E 83
Llowes. Powy 1E 47
Lloyney. Powy 3E 59
Llundain-fach. Cdgn 5E 57
Llwydcoed. Rhon 5C 46
Llwyncelyn. Cdgn 5D 56
Llwyncelyn. Swan 5G 45
Llwyndafydd. Cdgn 5C 56
Llwynderw. Powy 5E 70
Llwyn-du. Mon 4F 47
Llwyngwril. Gwyn 5E 69
Llwynhendy. Carm 3E 31
Llwynmawr. Wrex 2E 71
Llwyn-on Village. Mer T 4D 46
Llwyn-têg. Carm 5F 45
Llwyn-y-brain. Carm 3F 43
Llwynygog. Powy 1A 58
Llwyn-y-groes. Cdgn 5E 57
Llwynypia. Rhon 2C 32
Llynclys. Shrp 3E 71
Llynfaes. IOA 3D 80
Llysfaen. Cnwy 3A 82
Llyswen. Powy 2E 47
Llysworney. V Glam 4C 32
Llys-y-fran. Pemb 2E 43
Llywel. Powy 2B 46
Llywernog. Cdgn 2G 57
Loan. Falk 2C 128
Loanend. Nmbd 4F 131
Loanhead. Midl 3F 129
Loaningfoot. Dum 4A 112
Loanreoch. High 1A 158
Loans. S Ayr 1C 116
Loansdean. Nmbd 1E 115
Lobb. Devn 3E 19
Lobhillcross. Devn 4E 11
Lochaber. Mor 3E 159
Loch a Charnain. W Isl 4D 170
Loch a Ghainmhich. W Isl 5E 171
Lochailort. High 5F 147
Lochaline. High 4A 140
Lochans. Dum 4F 109
Locharbriggs. Dum 1A 112
Lochardil. High 4A 158
Lochassynt Lodge. High 1F 163
Lochavich. Arg 2G 133
Lochawe. Arg 1A 134
Loch Baghasdail. W Isl 7C 170
Lochboisdale. W Isl 7C 170
Lochbuie. Arg 1D 132
Lochcarron. High 5A 156
Loch Choire Lodge. High 5G 167
Lochdochart House. Stir 1D 134
Lochdon. Arg 5B 140
Lochearnhead. Stir 1E 135
Lochee. D'dee 5C 144
Lochend. High
nr. Inverness 5H 157
nr. Thurso 2E 169
Locherben. Dum 5B 118
Loch Euphort. W Isl 2D 170
Lochfoot. Dum 2F 111
Lochgair. Arg 4G 133
Lochgarthside. High 2H 149
Lochgelly. Fife 4D 136
Lochgilphead. Arg 1G 125
Lochgoilhead. Arg 3A 134
Loch Head. Dum 5A 110
Lochhill. Mor 2G 159
Lochindorb Lodge. High 5D 158
Lochinver. High 1E 163
Lochlane. Per 1H 135
Loch Lomond. Arg 3C 134
Loch Loyal Lodge. High 4G 167
Lochluichart. High 2F 157
Lochmaben. Dum 1B 112
Lochmaddy. W Isl 2E 170
Loch nam Madadh. W Isl 2E 170
Lochore. Fife 4D 136
Lochportain. W Isl 1E 170
Lochranza. N Ayr 4H 125
Loch Sgioport. W Isl 5D 170
Lochside. Abers 2G 145
Lochside. High
nr. Achentoul 5A 168
nr. Nairn 3C 158
Lochslin. High 5F 165
Lochstack Lodge. High 4C 166
Lochton. Abers 4E 153
Lochty. Fife 3H 137
Lochuisge. High 3B 140
Lochussie. High 3G 157
Lochwinnoch. Ren 4E 127
Lochyside. High 1F 141
Lockengate. Corn 2E 7
Lockerbie. Dum 1C 112
Lockeridge. Wilts 5G 35
Lockerley. Hants 4A 24
Lockhills. Cumb 5G 113
Locking. N Som 1G 21
Lockington. E Yor 5D 101
Lockington. Leics 3B 74
Lockleywood. Shrp 3A 72
Locksgreen. IOW 3C 16
Locks Heath. Hants 2D 16
Lockton. N Yor 5F 107
Loddington. Leics 5E 75
Loddington. Nptn 3F 63
Loddiswell. Devn 4D 8
Loddon. Norf 1F 67
Lode. Cambs 4E 65
Loders. Dors 3H 13
Lodsworth. W Sus 3A 26
Lofthouse. N Yor 2D 98
Lofthouse. W Yor 2D 92
Lofthouse Gate. W Yor 2D 92
Loftus. Red C 3E 107
Logan. E Ayr 2E 117
Loganlea. W Lot 3C 128
Logaston. Here 5F 59
Loggerheads. Staf 2B 72
Loggie. High 4F 163
Logie. Ang 2F 145
Logie. Fife 1G 137
Logie. Mor 3E 159
Logie Coldstone. Abers 3B 152
Logie Pert. Ang 2F 145
Logierait. Per 3G 143
Login. Carm 2F 43
Lolworth. Cambs 4C 64
Lonbain. High 3F 155
Londesborough. E Yor 5C 100
London. G Lon 198-199 (2E 39)
London Apprentice. Corn 3E 6
London Ashford Airport. Kent 3E 29
London City Airport. G Lon 2F 39
London Colney. Herts 5B 52
Londonderry. Derr 5A 174
Londonderry. N Yor 1F 99
London Gatwick Airport. W Sus 205 (1D 26)
London Heathrow Airport. G Lon 205 (3B 38)
London Luton Airport. Lutn 205 (3B 52)
London Southend Airport. Essx 2C 40
London Stansted Airport. Essx 205 (3F 53)
Londonthorpe. Linc 2G 75
Londubh. High 5C 162
Lone. High 4D 166
Lonemore. High
nr. Dornoch 5E 165
nr. Gairloch 1G 155
Long Ashton. N Som 4A 34
Long Bank. Worc 3B 60
Longbar. N Ayr 4E 127
Long Bennington. Linc 1F 75
Longbenton. Tyne 3F 115
Longborough. Glos 3G 49
Long Bredy. Dors 3A 14
Longbridge. Warw 4G 61
Longbridge. W Mid 3E 61
Longbridge Deverill. Wilts 2D 22
Long Buckby. Nptn 4D 62
Long Buckby Wharf. Nptn 4D 62
Longburgh. Cumb 4E 112
Longburton. Dors 1B 14
Long Clawson. Leics 3E 74
Longcliffe. Derbs 5G 85
Long Common. Hants 1D 16
Long Compton. Staf 3C 72
Long Compton. Warw 2A 50
Longcot. Oxon 2A 36
Long Crendon. Buck 5E 51
Long Crichel. Dors 1E 15
Longcroft. Cumb 4D 112
Longcroft. Falk 2A 128
Longcross. Surr 4A 38
Longdale. Cumb 4H 103
Longdales. Cumb 5G 113
Longden. Shrp 5G 71
Longden Common. Shrp 5G 71
Long Ditton. Surr 4C 38
Longdon. Staf 4E 73
Longdon. Worc 2D 48
Longdon Green. Staf 4E 73
Longdon on Tern. Telf 4A 72
Longdown. Devn 3B 12
Longdowns. Corn 5B 6
Long Drax. N Yor 2G 93
Long Duckmanton. Derbs 3B 86
Long Eaton. Derbs 2B 74
Longfield. Kent 4H 39
Longfield. Shet 10E 173
Longfield Hill. Kent 4H 39
Longford. Derbs 2G 73
Longford. Glos 3D 48
Longford. G Lon 3B 38
Longford. Shrp 2A 72
Longford. Telf 4B 72
Longford. W Mid 2A 62
Longforgan. Per 5C 144
Longformacus. Bord 4C 130
Longframlington. Nmbd 4F 121
Long Gardens. Essx 2B 54
Long Green. Ches W 3G 83
Long Green. Worc 2D 48
Longham. Dors 3F 15
Longham. Norf 4B 78
Long Hanborough. Oxon 4C 50
Longhedge. Wilts 2D 22
Longhill. Abers 3H 161
Longhirst. Nmbd 1F 115
Longhope. Glos 4B 48
Longhope. Orkn 8C 172
Longhorsley. Nmbd 5F 121
Longhoughton. Nmbd 3G 121
Long Itchington. Warw 4B 62
Longlands. Cumb 1D 102
Longlane. Derbs 2G 73
Long Lane. Telf 4A 72
Longlane. W Ber 4C 36
Long Lawford. Warw 3B 62
Long Lease. N Yor 4G 107
Longley Green. Worc 5B 60
Long Load. Som 4H 21
Longmanhill. Abers 2E 161
Long Marston. Herts 4G 51
Long Marston. N Yor 4H 99
Long Marston. Warw 1G 49
Long Marton. Cumb 2H 103
Long Meadow. Cambs 4E 65
Long Meadowend. Shrp 2G 59
Long Melford. Suff 1B 54
Longmoor Camp. Hants 3F 25
Longmorn. Mor 3G 159
Longmoss. Ches E 3C 84
Long Newnton. Glos 2E 35
Longnewton. Bord 2H 119
Long Newton. Stoc T 3A 106
Longney. Glos 4C 48
Longniddry. E Lot 2H 129
Longnor. Shrp 5G 71
Longnor. Staf
nr. Leek 4E 85
nr. Stafford 4C 72
Longparish. Hants 2C 24
Longpark. Cumb 3F 113
Long Preston. N Yor 4H 97
Longridge. Lanc 1E 90
Longridge. Staf 4D 72
Longridge. W Lot 3C 128
Longriggend. N Lan 2B 128
Long Riston. E Yor 5F 101
Longrock. Corn 3C 4
Longsdon. Staf 5D 84
Longshaw. G Man 4D 90
Longshaw. Staf 1E 73
Longside. Abers 4H 161
Longslow. Shrp 2A 72
Longstanton. Cambs 4C 64
Longstock. Hants 3B 24
Longstowe. Cambs 5C 64
Long Stratton. Norf 1D 66
Long Street. Mil 1F 51
Longstreet. Wilts 1G 23
Long Sutton. Hants 2F 25
Long Sutton. Linc 3D 76
Long Sutton. Som 4H 21
Longthorpe. Pet 1A 64
Long Thurlow. Suff 4C 66
Longthwaite. Cumb 2F 103
Longton. Lanc 2C 90
Longton. Stoke 1D 72
Longtown. Cumb 3E 113
Longtown. Here 3G 47
Longville in the Dale. Shrp 1H 59
Long Whatton. Leics 3B 74
Longwick. Buck 5F 51
Long Wittenham. Oxon 2D 36
Longwitton. Nmbd 1D 115
Longworth. Oxon 2B 36
Longyester. E Lot 3B 130
Lonmore. High 4B 154
Looe. Corn 3G 7
Loose. Kent 5B 40
Loosegate. Linc 3C 76
Loosley Row. Buck 5G 51
Lopcombe Corner. Wilts 3A 24
Lopen. Som 1H 13
Loppington. Shrp 3G 71
Lorbottle. Nmbd 4E 121
Lordington. W Sus 2F 17
Loscoe. Derbs 1B 74
Loscombe. Dors 3A 14
Losgaintir. W Isl 8C 171
Lossiemouth. Mor 2G 159
Lossit. Arg 4A 124
Lostock Gralam. Ches W 3A 84
Lostock Green. Ches W 3A 84
Lostock Hall. Lanc 2D 90
Lostock Junction. G Man 4E 91
Lostwithiel. Corn 3F 7
Lothbeg. High 2G 165
Lothersdale. N Yor 5B 98
Lothianbridge. Midl 3G 129
Lothianburn. Midl 3F 129
Lothmore. High 2G 165
Lottisham. Som 3A 22
Loudwater. Buck 1A 38
Loughborough. Leics 4C 74
Loughbrickland. Arm 5F 178
Loughgall. Arm 4D 178
Loughguile. Caus 4G 175
Loughinisland. New M 5J 179
Loughmacrory. Ferm 2L 177
Loughor. Swan 3E 31
Loughries. Ards 2K 179
Loughton. Essx 1F 39
Loughton. Mil 2G 51
Loughton. Shrp 2A 60
Lound. Linc 4H 75
Lound. Notts 2D 86
Lound. Suff 1H 67
Lount. Leics 4A 74
Loup, The. M Ulst 1D 178
Louth. Linc 2C 88
Love Clough. Lanc 2G 91
Lovedean. Hants 1E 17
Lover. Wilts 4H 23
Loversall. S Yor 1C 86
Loves Green. Essx 5G 53
Loveston. Pemb 4E 43
Lovington. Som 3A 22
Low Ackworth. W Yor 3E 93
Low Angerton. Nmbd 1D 115
Low Ardwell. Dum 5F 109
Low Ballochdowan. S Ayr 2F 109
Lowbands. Glos 2C 48
Low Barlings. Linc 3H 87
Low Bell End. N Yor 5E 107
Low Bentham. N Yor 3F 97
Low Borrowbridge. Cumb 4H 103
Low Bradfield. S Yor 1G 85
Low Bradley. N Yor 5C 98
Low Braithwaite. Cumb 5F 113
Low Brunton. Nmbd 2C 114
Low Burnham. N Lin 4A 94
Lowca. Cumb 2A 102
Low Catton. E Yor 4B 100
Low Coniscliffe. Darl 3F 105
Low Coylton. S Ayr 3D 116
Low Crosby. Cumb 4F 113
Low Dalby. N Yor 1C 100
Lowdham. Notts 1D 74
Low Dinsdale. Darl 3A 106
Lowe. Shrp 2H 71
Low Ellington. N Yor 1E 98
Lower Amble. Corn 1D 6
Lower Ansty. Dors 2C 14
Lower Arboll. High 5F 165
Lower Arncott. Oxon 4E 50
Lower Ashton. Devn 4B 12
Lower Assendon. Oxon 3F 37
Lower Auchenreath. Mor 2A 160
Lower Badcall. High 4B 166
Lower Ballam. Lanc 1B 90
Lower Ballinderry. Lis 3F 178
Lower Basildon. W Ber 4E 36
Lower Beeding. W Sus 3D 26
Lower Benefield. Nptn 2G 63
Lower Bentley. Worc 4D 61
Lower Beobridge. Shrp 1B 60
Lower Bockhampton. Dors 3C 14
Lower Boddington. Nptn 5B 62
Lower Bordean. Hants 4E 25
Lower Brailes. Warw 2B 50
Lower Breakish. High 1E 147
Lower Broadheath. Worc 5C 60
Lower Brynamman. Neat 4H 45
Lower Bullingham. Here 2A 48
Lower Bullington. Hants 2C 24
Lower Burgate. Hants 1G 15
Lower Cam. Glos 5C 48
Lower Catesby. Nptn 5C 62
Lower Chapel. Powy 2D 46
Lower Cheriton. Devn 2E 12
Lower Chicksgrove. Wilts 3E 23
Lower Chute. Wilts 1B 24
Lower Clopton. Warw 5F 61
Lower Common. Hants 2E 25
Lower Crossings. Derbs 2E 85
Lower Cumberworth. W Yor 4C 92
Lower Darwen. Bkbn 2E 91
Lower Dean. Bed 4H 63
Lower Dean. Devn 2D 8
Lower Diabaig. High 2G 155
Lower Dicker. E Sus 4G 27
Lower Dounreay. High 2B 168
Lower Down. Shrp 2F 59
Lower Dunsforth. N Yor 3G 99
Lower East Carleton. Norf 5D 78
Lower Egleton. Here 1B 48
Lower Ellastone. Staf 1F 73
Lower End. Nptn 4F 63
Lower Everleigh. Wilts 1G 23
Lower Eype. Dors 3H 13
Lower Failand. N Som 4A 34
Lower Faintree. Shrp 2A 60
Lower Farringdon. Hants 3F 25
Lower Foxdale. IOM 4B 108
Lower Frankton. Shrp 2F 71
Lower Froyle. Hants 2F 25
Lower Gabwell. Devn 2F 9
Lower Gledfield. High 4C 164
Lower Godney. Som 2H 21
Lower Gravenhurst. C Beds 2B 52
Lower Green. Essx 2E 53
Lower Green. Norf 2B 78
Lower Green. W Ber 5B 36
Lower Halstow. Kent 4C 40
Lower Hardres. Kent 5F 41
Lower Hardwick. Here 5G 59
Lower Hartshay. Derbs 5A 86
Lower Hawthwaite. Cumb 1B 96
Lower Haysden. Kent 1G 27
Lower Hayton. Shrp 2H 59
Lower Hergest. Here 5E 59
Lower Heyford. Oxon 3C 50
Lower Heysham. Lanc 3D 96
Lower Higham. Kent 3B 40
Lower Holbrook. Suff 2E 55
Lower Holditch. Dors 2G 13
Lower Hordley. Shrp 3F 71
Lower Horncroft. W Sus 4B 26
Lower Horsebridge. E Sus 4G 27
Lower Kilcott. Glos 3C 34
Lower Killeyan. Arg 5A 124
Lower Kingcombe. Dors 3A 14
Lower Kingswood. Surr 5D 38
Lower Kinnerton. Ches W 4F 83
Lower Langford. N Som 5H 33
Lower Largo. Fife 3G 137
Lower Layham. Suff 1D 54
Lower Ledwyche. Shrp 3H 59
Lower Leigh. Staf 2E 73
Lower Lemington. Glos 2H 49
Lower Lenie. High 1H 149
Lower Ley. Glos 4C 48
Lower Llanfadog. Powy 4B 58
Lower Lode. Glos 2D 49
Lower Lovacott. Devn 4F 19
Lower Loxhore. Devn 3G 19
Lower Loxley. Staf 2E 73
Lower Lydbrook. Glos 4A 48
Lower Lye. Here 4G 59
Lower Machen. Newp 3F 33
Lower Maes-coed. Here 2G 47
Lower Meend. Glos 5A 48
Lower Midway. Derbs 3H 73
Lower Milovaig. High 3A 154
Lower Moor. Worc 1E 49
Lower Morton. S Glo 2B 34
Lower Mountain. Flin 5F 83
Lower Nazeing. Essx 5D 53
Lower Netchwood. Shrp 1A 60
Lower Nyland. Dors 4C 22
Lower Oakfield. Fife 4D 136
Lower Oddington. Glos 3H 49
Lower Ollach. High 5E 155
Lower Penarth. V Glam 5E 33
Lower Penn. Staf 1C 60
Lower Pennington. Hants 3B 16
Lower Peover. Ches W 3B 84
Lower Pilsley. Derbs 4B 86
Lower Pitkerrie. High 1C 158
Lower Place. G Man 3H 91
Lower Quinton. Warw 1G 49
Lower Rainham. Medw 4C 40
Lower Raydon. Suff 2D 54
Lower Seagry. Wilts 3E 35
Lower Shelton. C Beds 1H 51
Lower Shiplake. Oxon 4F 37
Lower Shuckburgh. Warw 4B 62
Lower Sketty. Swan 3F 31
Lower Slade. Devn 2F 19
Lower Slaughter. Glos 3G 49
Lower Soudley. Glos 4B 48
Lower Stanton St Quintin. Wilts 3E 35
Lower Stoke. Medw 3C 40
Lower Stondon. C Beds 2B 52
Lower Stonnall. Staf 5E 73
Lower Stow Bedon. Norf 1B 66
Lower Street. Norf 2E 79
Lower Strensham. Worc 1E 49
Lower Sundon. C Beds 3A 52
Lower Swanwick. Hants 2C 16
Lower Swell. Glos 3G 49
Lower Tale. Devn 2D 12
Lower Tean. Staf 2E 73
Lower Thurlton. Norf 1G 67
Lower Thurnham. Lanc 4D 96
Lower Thurvaston. Derbs 2G 73
Lowertown. Corn 4D 4
Lower Town. Here 1B 48
Lower Town. IOS 1B 4
Lowertown. Orkn 8D 172
Lower Town. Pemb 1D 42
Lower Tysoe. Warw 1B 50
Lower Upham. Hants 1D 16
Lower Upnor. Medw 3B 40
Lower Vexford. Som 3E 20
Lower Walton. Warr 2A 84
Lower Wear. Devn 4C 12
Lower Weare. Som 1H 21
Lower Welson. Here 5E 59
Lower Whatcombe. Dors 2D 14
Lower Whitley. Ches W 3A 84
Lower Wield. Hants 2E 25
Lower Withington. Ches E 4C 84
Lower Woodend. Buck 3G 37
Lower Woodford. Wilts 3G 23
Lower Wraxall. Dors 2A 14
Lower Wych. Ches W 1G 71
Lower Wyche. Worc 1C 48
Lowesby. Leics 5E 74
Lowestoft. Suff 1H 67
Loweswater. Cumb 2C 102
Low Etherley. Dur 2E 105
Lowfield Heath. W Sus 1D 26
Lowford. Hants 1C 16
Low Fulney. Linc 3B 76
Low Gate. Nmbd 3C 114
Lowgill. Cumb 5H 103
Lowgill. Lanc 3F 97
Low Grantley. N Yor 2E 99
Low Green. N Yor 4E 98
Low Habberley. Worc 3C 60
Low Ham. Som 4H 21
Low Hameringham. Linc 4C 88
Low Hawsker. N Yor 4G 107
Low Hesket. Cumb 5F 113
Low Hesleyhurst. Nmbd 5E 121
Lowick. Cumb 1B 96
Lowick. Nptn 2G 63
Lowick. Nmbd 1E 121
Lowick Bridge. Cumb 1B 96
Lowick Green. Cumb 1B 96
Low Knipe. Cumb 2G 103
Low Leighton. Derbs 2E 85
Low Lorton. Cumb 2C 102
Low Marishes. N Yor 2C 100
Low Marnham. Notts 4F 87
Low Mill. N Yor 5D 106
Low Moor. Lanc 5G 97
Low Moor. W Yor 2B 92
Low Moorsley. Tyne 5G 115
Low Newton-by-the-Sea. Nmbd 2G 121
Lownie Moor. Ang 4D 145
Lowood. Bord 1H 119
Low Row. Cumb
nr. Brampton 3G 113
nr. Wigton 5C 112
Low Row. N Yor 5C 104
Lowsonford. Warw 4F 61
Low Street. Norf 5C 78
Lowther. Cumb 2G 103
Lowthorpe. E Yor 3E 101
Lowton. Devn 2G 11
Lowton. G Man 1A 84
Lowton. Som 1E 13
Lowton Common. G Man 1A 84
Low Torry. Fife 1D 128
Low Toynton. Linc 3B 88
Low Valleyfield. Fife 1C 128
Low Westwood. Dur 4E 115
Low Whinnow. Cumb 4E 112
Low Wood. Cumb 1C 96
Low Worsall. N Yor 4A 106
Low Wray. Cumb 4E 103
Loxbeare. Devn 1C 12
Loxhill. Surr 2B 26
Loxhore. Devn 3G 19
Loxley. S Yor 2H 85
Loxley. Warw 5G 61
Loxley Green. Staf 2E 73
Loxton. N Som 1G 21
Loxwood. W Sus 2B 26
Lubcroy. High 3A 164
Lubenham. Leics 2E 62
Lubinvullin. High 2F 167
Luccombe. Som 2C 20
Luccombe Village. IOW 4D 16
Lucker. Nmbd 1F 121
Luckett. Corn 5D 11
Luckington. Wilts 3D 34
Lucklawhill. Fife 1G 137
Luckwell Bridge. Som 3C 20
Lucton. Here 4G 59
Ludag. W Isl 7C 170
Ludborough. Linc 1B 88
Ludchurch. Pemb 3F 43
Luddenden. W Yor 2A 92
Luddenden Foot. W Yor 2A 92
Luddenham. Kent 4D 40
Ludderburn. Cumb 5F 103
Luddesdown. Kent 4A 40
Luddington. N Lin 3B 94
Luddington. Warw 5F 61
Luddington in the Brook. Nptn 2A 64
Ludford. Linc 2A 88
Ludford. Shrp 3H 59
Ludgershall. Buck 4E 51
Ludgershall. Wilts 1A 24
Ludgvan. Corn 3C 4
Ludham. Norf 4F 79
Ludlow. Shrp 3H 59
Ludstone. Shrp 1C 60
Ludwell. Wilts 4E 23
Ludworth. Dur 5G 115
Luffenhall. Herts 3C 52
Luffincott. Devn 3D 10
Lugar. E Ayr 2E 117
Luggate Burn. E Lot 2C 130
Lugg Green. Here 4G 59
Luggiebank. N Lan 2A 128
Lugton. E Ayr 4F 127
Lugwardine. Here 1A 48
Luib. High 1D 146
Luib. Stir 1D 135
Lulham. Here 1H 47
Lullington. Derbs 4G 73
Lullington. E Sus 5G 27
Lullington. Som 1C 22
Lulsgate Bottom. N Som 5A 34
Lulsley. Worc 5B 60
Lulworth Camp. Dors 4D 14
Lumb. Lanc 2G 91
Lumby. N Yor 1E 93
Lumphanan. Abers 3C 152
Lumphinnans. Fife 4D 136
Lumsdaine. Bord 3E 131
Lumsden. Abers 1B 152
Lunan. Ang 3F 145
Lunanhead. Ang 3D 145
Luncarty. Per 1C 136
Lund. E Yor 5D 100
Lund. N Yor 1G 93
Lundie. Ang 5B 144
Lundin Links. Fife 3G 137
Lundy Green. Norf 1E 67
Lunna. Shet 5F 173
Lunning. Shet 5G 173
Lunnon. Swan 4E 31
Lunsford. Kent 5A 40
Lunsford's Cross. E Sus 4B 28
Lunt. Mers 4B 90
Luppitt. Devn 2E 13
Lupridge. Devn 3D 8
Lupset. W Yor 3D 92
Lupton. Cumb 1E 97
Lurgan. Arm 4E 178
Lurganare. New M 6E 178
Lurgashall. W Sus 3A 26
Lurley. Devn 1C 12
Lusby. Linc 4C 88
Luscombe. Devn 3D 9
Luson. Devn 4C 8
Luss. Arg 4C 134
Lussagiven. Arg 1E 125
Lusta. High 3B 154
Lustleigh. Devn 4A 12
Luston. Here 4G 59
Luthermuir. Abers 2F 145
Luthrie. Fife 2F 137
Lutley. Staf 2C 60
Luton. Devn
nr. Honiton 2D 12
nr. Teignmouth 5C 12
Luton. Lutn 3A 52
Luton Airport. Lutn 205 (3B 52)
Lutterworth. Leics 2C 62
Lutton. Devn
nr. Ivybridge 3B 8
nr. South Brent 2C 8
Lutton. Linc 3D 76
Lutton. Nptn 2A 64
Lutton Gowts. Linc 3D 76
Lutworthy. Devn 1A 12
Luxborough. Som 3C 20
Luxley. Glos 3B 48
Luxulyan. Corn 3E 7
Lybster. High 5E 169
Lydbury North. Shrp 2F 59
Lydcott. Devn 3G 19
Lydd. Kent 3E 29
Lydd Airport. Kent 3E 29
Lydden. Kent
nr. Dover 1G 29
nr. Margate 4H 41
Lyddington. Rut 1F 63
Lydd-on-Sea. Kent 3E 29
Lydeard St Lawrence. Som 3E 21
Lyde Green. Hants 1F 25
Lydford. Devn 4F 11
Lydford Fair Place. Som 3A 22
Lydgate. G Man 4H 91
Lydgate. W Yor 2H 91
Lydham. Shrp 1F 59
Lydiard Millicent. Wilts 3F 35
Lydiate. Mers 4B 90
Lydiate Ash. Worc 3D 61
Lydlinch. Dors 1C 14
Lydmarsh. Som 2G 13
Lydney. Glos 5B 48
Lydstep. Pemb 5E 43
Lye, The. Shrp 1A 60
Lye. W Mid 2D 60
Lye Green. Buck 5H 51
Lye Green. E Sus 2G 27
Lye Head. Worc 3B 60
Lyford. Oxon 2B 36
Lyham. Nmbd 1E 121
Lylestone. N Ayr 5E 127
Lymbridge Green. Kent 1F 29
Lyme Regis. Dors 3G 13
Lyminge. Kent 1F 29
Lymington. Hants 3B 16
Lyminster. W Sus 5B 26
Lymm. Warr 2A 84
Lymore. Hants 3A 16
Lympne. Kent 2F 29
Lympsham. Som 1G 21
Lympstone. Devn 4C 12
Lynaberack Lodge. High 4B 150
Lynbridge. Devn 2H 19
Lynch. Som 2C 20
Lynchat. High 3B 150
Lynch Green. Norf 5D 78
Lyndhurst. Hants 2B 16
Lyndon. Rut 5G 75
Lyne. Bord 5F 129
Lyne. Surr 4B 38
Lyneal. Shrp 2G 71
Lyne Down. Here 2B 48
Lyneham. Oxon 3A 50
Lyneham. Wilts 4F 35
Lyneholmeford. Cumb 2G 113
Lynemouth. Nmbd 5G 121
Lyne of Gorthleck. High 1H 149
Lyne of Skene. Abers 2E 153
Lynesack. Dur 2D 105
Lyness. Orkn 8C 172
Lyng. Norf 4C 78
Lyngate. Norf
nr. North Walsham 2E 79
nr. Worstead 3F 79
Lynmouth. Devn 2H 19
Lynn. Staf 5E 73
Lynn. Telf 4B 72
Lynsted. Kent 4D 40
Lynstone. Corn 2C 10
Lynton. Devn 2H 19
Lynwilg. High 2C 150
Lyon's Gate. Dors 2B 14
Lyonshall. Here 5F 59
Lytchett Matravers. Dors 3E 15
Lytchett Minster. Dors 3E 15
Lyth. High 2E 169
Lytham. Lanc 2B 90
Lytham St Anne's. Lanc 2B 90
Lythe. N Yor 3F 107
Lythes. Orkn 9D 172
Lythmore. High 2C 168

M

Mabe Burnthouse. Corn 5B 6
Mabie. Dum 2A 112
Mablethorpe. Linc 2E 89
Macbiehill. Bord 4E 129
Macclesfield. Ches E 3D 84
Macclesfield Forest. Ches E 3D 84
Macduff. Abers 2E 160
Machan. S Lan 4A 128
Macharioch. Arg 5B 122
Machen. Cphy 3F 33
Machrie. N Ayr 2C 122
Machrihanish. Arg 3A 122
Machroes. Gwyn 3C 68
Machynlleth. Powy 5G 69
Mackerye End. Herts 4B 52
Mackworth. Derb 2H 73
Macmerry. E Lot 2H 129
Macosquin. Caus 4E 174
Madderty. Per 1B 136
Maddington. Wilts 2F 23
Maddiston. Falk 2C 128
Madehurst. W Sus 4A 26
Madeley. Staf 1B 72
Madeley. Telf 5A 72
Madeley Heath. Staf 1B 72
Madeley Heath. Worc 3D 60
Madford. Devn 1E 13
Madingley. Cambs 4C 64
Madley. Here 2H 47
Madresfield. Worc 1D 48
Madron. Corn 3B 4
Maenaddwyn. IOA 2D 80
Maenclochog. Pemb 2E 43
Maendy. V Glam 4D 32
Maenporth. Corn 4E 5
Maentwrog. Gwyn 1F 69
Maen-y-groes. Cdgn 5C 56
Maer. Staf 2B 72
Maerdy. Carm 3G 45
Maerdy. Cnwy 1C 70
Maerdy. Rhon 2C 32
Maesbrook. Shrp 3F 71
Maesbury. Shrp 3F 71
Maesbury Marsh. Shrp 3F 71
Maes-glas. Flin 3D 82
Maesgwyn-Isaf. Powy 4D 70
Maeshafn. Den 4E 82
Maes Llyn. Cdgn 1D 44
Maesmynis. Powy 1D 46
Maesteg. B'end 2B 32
Maestir. Cdgn 1F 45
Maesybont. Carm 4F 45
Maesycrugiau. Carm 1E 45
Maesycwmmer. Cphy 2E 33
Maesyrhandir. Powy 1C 58
Magdalen Laver. Essx 5F 53
Maggieknockater. Mor 4H 159
Maghaberry. Lis 3F 179
Magham Down. E Sus 4H 27
Maghera. M Ulst 6E 174
Maghera. New M 6H 179

Magherafelt—Milton

Magherafelt. M Ulst 7E 174
Magheralin. Arm 4F 178
Magheramason. Derr 1F 176
Magheraveely. Ferm 7K 177
Maghery. Arm 3D 178
Maghull. Mers 4B 90
Magna Park. Leics 2C 62
Magor. Mon 3H 33
Magpie Green. Suff 3C 66
Maguiresbridge. Ferm 6J 177
Magwyr. Mon 3H 33
Maidenbower. W Sus 2D 27
Maiden Bradley. Wilts 3D 22
Maidencombe. Torb 2F 9
Maidenhayne. Devn 3F 13
Maidenhead. Wind 3G 37
Maiden Law. Dur 5E 115
Maiden Newton. Dors 3A 14
Maidens. S Ayr 4B 116
Maiden's Green. Brac 4G 37
Maidensgrove. Oxon 3F 37
Maidenwell. Corn 5B 10
Maidenwell. Linc 3C 88
Maiden Wells. Pemb 5D 42
Maidford. Nptn 5D 62
Maids Moreton. Buck 2F 51
Maidstone. Kent 5B 40
Maidwell. Nptn 3E 63
Mail. Shet 9F 173
Maindee. Newp 3G 33
Mainsforth. Dur 1A 106
Mains of Auchindachy. Mor 4B 160
Mains of Auchnagatt. Abers 4G 161
Mains of Drum. Abers 4F 153
Mains of Edingight. Mor 3C 160
Mainsriddle. Dum 4G 111
Mainstone. Shrp 2E 59
Maisemore. Glos 3D 48
Major's Green. Worc 3F 61
Makeney. Derbs 1A 74
Makerstoun. Bord 1A 120
Malacleit. W Isl 1C 170
Malaig. High 4E 147
Malaig Bheag. High 4E 147
Malborough. Devn 5D 8
Malcoff. Derbs 2E 85
Malcolmburn. Mor 3A 160
Malden Rushett. G Lon 4C 38
Maldon. Essx 5B 54
Malham. N Yor 3B 98
Maligar. High 2D 155
Malinslee. Telf 5A 72
Mallaig. High 4E 147
Malleny Mills. Edin 3E 129
Mallows Green. Essx 3E 53
Malltraeth. IOA 4D 80
Mallusk. Ant 1G 179
Mallwyd. Gwyn 4A 70
Malmesbury. Wilts 3E 35
Malmsmead. Devn 2A 20
Malpas. Ches W 1G 71
Malpas. Corn 4C 6
Malpas. Newp 2G 33
Malswick. Glos 3C 48
Maltby. S Yor 1C 86
Maltby. Stoc T 3B 106
Maltby le Marsh. Linc 2D 88
Malt Lane. Arg 3H 133
Maltman's Hill. Kent 1D 28
Malton. N Yor 2B 100
Malvern Link. Worc 1C 48
Malvern Wells. Worc 1C 48
Mamble. Worc 3A 60
Mamhilad. Mon 5G 47
Manaccan. Corn 4E 5
Manafon. Powy 5D 70
Manais. W Isl 9D 171
Manaton. Devn 4A 12
Manby. Linc 2C 88
Mancetter. Warw 1H 61
Manchester. G Man 197 (1C 84)
Manchester Airport. G Man 205 (2C 84)
Mancot. Flin 4F 83
Manea. Cambs 2D 65
Maney. W Mid 1F 61
Manfield. N Yor 3F 105
Mangotsfield. S Glo 4B 34
Mangurstadh. W Isl 4C 171
Mankinholes. W Yor 2H 91
Manley. Ches W 3H 83
Manmoel. Cphy 5E 47
Mannal. Arg 4A 138
Mannerston. Falk 2D 128
Manningford Bohune. Wilts 1G 23
Manningford Bruce. Wilts 1G 23
Manningham. W Yor 1B 92
Mannings Heath. W Sus 3D 26
Mannington. Dors 2F 15
Manningtree. Essx 2E 54
Mannofield. Aber 3G 153
Manorbier. Pemb 5E 43
Manorbier Newton. Pemb 5E 43
Manordeilo. Carm 3G 45
Manorowen. Pemb 1D 42
Manor Park. G Lon 2F 39
Mansell Gamage. Here 1G 47
Mansell Lacy. Here 1H 47
Mansergh. Cumb 1F 97
Mansewood. Glas 3G 127
Mansfield. E Ayr 3F 117
Mansfield. Notts 4C 86
Mansfield Woodhouse. Notts 4C 86
Mansriggs. Cumb 1B 96
Manston. Dors 1D 14
Manston. Kent 4H 41
Manston. W Yor 1D 92
Manswood. Dors 2E 15
Manthorpe. Linc
nr. Bourne 4H 75
nr. Grantham 2G 75
Manton. N Lin 4C 94
Manton. Notts 3C 86
Manton. Rut 5F 75
Manton. Wilts 5G 35
Manuden. Essx 3E 53
Maperton. Som 4B 22
Maplebeck. Notts 4E 86
Maple Cross. Herts 1B 38
Mapledurham. Oxon 4E 37
Mapledurwell. Hants 1E 25
Maplehurst. W Sus 3C 26
Maplescombe. Kent 4G 39
Mapleton. Derbs 1F 73
Mapperley. Derbs 1B 74
Mapperley. Nott 1C 74
Mapperley Park. Nott 1C 74
Mapperton. Dors
nr. Beaminster 3A 14
nr. Poole 3E 15
Mappleborough Green. Warw 4E 61
Mappleton. E Yor 5G 101
Mapplewell. S Yor 4D 92
Mappowder. Dors 2C 14
Maraig. W Isl 7E 171
Marazion. Corn 3C 4
Marbhig. W Isl 6G 171
Marbury. Ches E 1H 71
March. Cambs 1D 64
Marcham. Oxon 2C 36
Marchamley. Shrp 3H 71
Marchington. Staf 2F 73
Marchington Woodlands. Staf 3F 73
Marchwiel. Wrex 1F 71
Marchwood. Hants 1B 16
Marcross. V Glam 5C 32
Marden. Here 1A 48
Marden. Kent 1B 28
Marden. Wilts 1F 23
Marden Beech. Kent 1B 28
Marden Thorn. Kent 1B 28
Mardu. Shrp 2E 59
Mardy. Mon 4G 47
Marefield. Leics 5E 75
Mareham le Fen. Linc 4B 88
Mareham on the Hill. Linc 4B 88
Marehay. Derbs 1B 74
Marehill. W Sus 4B 26
Maresfield. E Sus 3F 27
Marfleet. Hull 2E 95
Marford. Wrex 5F 83
Margam. Neat 3A 32
Margaret Marsh. Dors 1D 14
Margaret Roding. Essx 4F 53
Margaretting. Essx 5G 53
Margaretting Tye. Essx 5G 53
Margate. Kent 3H 41
Margery. Surr 5D 38
Margnaheglish. N Ayr 2E 123
Marham. Norf 5G 77
Marhamchurch. Corn 2C 10
Marholm. Pet 5A 76
Marian Cwm. Den 3C 82
Mariandyrys. IOA 2F 81
Marian-glas. IOA 2E 81
Mariansleigh. Devn 4H 19
Marian-y-de. Gwyn 2C 68
Marian-y-mor. Gwyn 2C 68
Marine Town. Kent 3D 40
Marishader. High 2D 155
Marjoriebanks. Dum 1B 112
Mark. Dum 4G 109
Mark. Som 2G 21
Markbeech. Kent 1F 27
Markby. Linc 3D 89
Mark Causeway. Som 2G 21
Mark Cross. E Sus 2G 27
Markeaton. Derb 2H 73
Market Bosworth. Leics 5B 74
Market Deeping. Linc 4A 76
Market Drayton. Shrp 2A 72
Market End. Warw 2H 61
Market Harborough. Leics 2E 63
Markethill. Arm 6D 178
Markethill. Per 5B 144
Market Lavington. Wilts 1F 23
Market Overton. Rut 4F 75
Market Rasen. Linc 2A 88
Market Stainton. Linc 2B 88
Market Weighton. E Yor 5C 100
Market Weston. Suff 3B 66
Markfield. Leics 4B 74
Markham. Cphy 5E 47
Markinch. Fife 3E 137
Markington. N Yor 3E 99
Marksbury. Bath 5B 34
Mark's Corner. IOW 3C 16
Marks Tey. Essx 3C 54
Markwell. Corn 3H 7
Markyate. Herts 4A 52
Marlborough. Wilts 5G 35
Marlcliff. Warw 5E 61
Marldon. Devn 2E 9
Marle Green. E Sus 4G 27
Marlesford. Suff 5F 67
Marley Green. Ches E 1H 71
Marley Hill. Tyne 4F 115
Marlingford. Norf 5D 78
Mar Lodge. Abers 5E 151
Marloes. Pemb 4B 42
Marlow. Buck 3G 37
Marlow. Here 3F 59
Marlow Bottom. Buck 3G 37
Marlow Common. Buck 3G 37
Marlpit Hill. Kent 1F 27
Marlpits. E Sus 3F 27
Marlpool. Derbs 1B 74
Marnhull. Dors 1C 14
Marnoch. Abers 3C 160
Marnock. N Lan 3A 128
Marple. G Man 2D 84
Marr. S Yor 4F 93
Marrel. High 2H 165
Marrick. N Yor 5D 105
Marrister. Shet 5G 173
Marros. Carm 4G 43
Marsden. Tyne 3G 115
Marsden. W Yor 3A 92
Marsett. N Yor 1B 98
Marsh. Buck 5G 51
Marsh. Devn 1F 13
Marsh, The. Powy 1F 59
Marsh, The. Shrp 3A 72
Marshall Meadows. Nmbd 4F 131
Marshalsea. Dors 2G 13
Marshalswick. Herts 5B 52
Marsham. Norf 3D 78
Marshaw. Lanc 4E 97
Marsh Baldon. Oxon 2D 36
Marsh Benham. W Ber 5C 36
Marshborough. Kent 5H 41
Marshbrook. Shrp 2G 59
Marshchapel. Linc 1C 88
Marshfield. Newp 3F 33
Marshfield. S Glo 4C 34
Marshgate. Corn 3B 10
Marsh Gibbon. Buck 3E 51
Marsh Green. Devn 3D 12
Marsh Green. Kent 1F 27
Marsh Green. Staf 5C 84
Marsh Green. Telf 4A 72
Marsh Lane. Derbs 3B 86
Marshside. Kent 4G 41
Marshside. Mers 3B 90
Marsh Side. Norf 1G 77
Marsh Street. Som 2C 20
Marshwood. Dors 3G 13
Marske. N Yor 4E 105
Marske-by-the-Sea. Red C 2D 106
Marston. Ches W 3A 84
Marston. Here 5F 59
Marston. Linc 1F 75
Marston. Oxon 5D 50
Marston. Staf
nr. Stafford 3D 72
nr. Wheaton Aston 4C 72
Marston. Warw 1G 61
Marston. Wilts 1E 23
Marston Doles. Warw 5B 62
Marston Green. W Mid 2F 61
Marston Hill. Glos 2G 35
Marston Jabbett. Warw 2A 62
Marston Magna. Som 4A 22
Marston Meysey. Wilts 2G 35
Marston Montgomery. Derbs 2F 73
Marston Moretaine. C Beds 1H 51
Marston on Dove. Derbs 3G 73
Marston St Lawrence. Nptn 1D 50
Marston Stannett. Here 5H 59
Marston Trussell. Nptn 2D 62
Marstow. Here 4A 48
Marsworth. Buck 4H 51
Marten. Wilts 1A 24
Marthall. Ches E 3C 84
Martham. Norf 4G 79
Marthwaite. Cumb 5H 103
Martin. Hants 1F 15
Martin. Kent 1H 29
Martin. Linc
nr. Horncastle 4B 88
nr. Metheringham 5A 88
Martindale. Cumb 3F 103
Martin Dales. Linc 4A 88
Martin Drove End. Hants 4F 23
Martinhoe. Devn 2G 19
Martinhoe Cross. Devn 2G 19
Martin Hussingtree. Worc 4C 60
Martin Mill. Kent 1H 29
Martinscroft. Warr 2A 84
Martin's Moss. Ches E 4C 84
Martinstown. Dors 4B 14
Martinstown. ME Ant 5H 175
Martlesham. Suff 1F 55
Martlesham Heath. Suff 1F 55
Martletwy. Pemb 3E 43
Martley. Worc 4B 60
Martock. Som 1H 13
Marton. Ches E 4C 84
Marton. Cumb 2B 96
Marton. E Yor
nr. Bridlington 3G 101
nr. Hull 1E 95
Marton. Linc 2F 87
Marton. Midd 3C 106
Marton. N Yor
nr. Boroughbridge 3G 99
nr. Pickering 1B 100
Marton. Shrp
nr. Myddle 3G 71
nr. Worthen 5E 71
Marton. Warw 4B 62
Marton Abbey. N Yor 3H 99
Marton-le-Moor. N Yor 2F 99
Martyr's Green. Surr 5B 38
Martyr Worthy. Hants 3D 24
Marwick. Orkn 5B 172
Marwood. Devn 3F 19
Marybank. High
nr. Dingwall 3G 157
nr. Invergordon 1B 158
Maryburgh. High 3H 157
Maryfield. Corn 3A 8
Maryhill. Glas 3G 127
Marykirk. Abers 2F 145
Marylebone. G Lon 2D 39
Marylebone. G Man 4D 90
Marypark. Mor 5F 159
Maryport. Cumb 1B 102
Maryport. Dum 5E 109
Marystow. Devn 4E 11
Mary Tavy. Devn 5F 11
Maryton. Ang
nr. Kirriemuir 3C 144
nr. Montrose 3F 145
Marywell. Abers 4C 152
Marywell. Ang 4F 145
Masham. N Yor 1E 98
Mashbury. Essx 4G 53
Masongill. N Yor 2F 97
Masons Lodge. Abers 3F 153
Mastin Moor. Derbs 3B 86
Mastrick. Aber 3G 153
Matching. Essx 4F 53
Matching Green. Essx 4F 53
Matching Tye. Essx 4F 53
Matfen. Nmbd 2D 114
Matfield. Kent 1A 28
Mathern. Mon 2A 34
Mathon. Here 1C 48
Mathry. Pemb 1C 42
Matlaske. Norf 2D 78
Matlock. Derbs 5G 85
Matlock Bath. Derbs 5G 85
Matterdale End. Cumb 2E 103
Mattersey. Notts 2D 86
Mattersey Thorpe. Notts 2D 86
Mattingley. Hants 1F 25
Mattishall. Norf 4C 78
Mattishall Burgh. Norf 4C 78
Mauchline. E Ayr 2D 117
Maud. Abers 4G 161
Maudlin. Corn 2E 7
Maugersbury. Glos 3G 49
Maughold. IOM 2D 108
Maulden. C Beds 2A 52
Maulds Meaburn. Cumb 3H 103
Maunby. N Yor 1F 99
Maund Bryan. Here 5H 59
Mautby. Norf 4G 79
Mavesyn Ridware. Staf 4E 73
Mavis Enderby. Linc 4C 88
Mawbray. Cumb 5B 112
Mawdesley. Lanc 3C 90
Mawdlam. B'end 3B 32
Mawgan. Corn 4E 5
Mawgan Porth. Corn 2C 6
Maw Green. Ches E 5B 84
Mawla. Corn 4B 6
Mawnan. Corn 4E 5
Mawnan Smith. Corn 4E 5
Mawsley Village. Nptn 3E 63
Mawthorpe. Linc 3D 88
Maxey. Pet 5A 76
Maxstoke. Warw 2G 61
Maxted Street. Kent 1F 29
Maxton. Kent 1G 29
Maxton. Bord 1A 120
Maxwellheugh. Bord 1B 120
Maxwelltown. Dum 2A 112
Maxworthy. Corn 3C 10
Mayals. Swan 4F 31
Maybole. S Ayr 4C 116
Maybush. Sotn 1B 16
Maydown. Derr 5A 174
Mayes Green. Surr 2C 26
Mayfield. E Sus 3G 27
Mayfield. Midl 3G 129
Mayfield. Per 1C 136
Mayfield. Staf 1F 73
Mayford. Surr 5A 38
Mayhill. Swan 3F 31
Mayland. Essx 5C 54
Maylandsea. Essx 5C 54
Maynard's Green. E Sus 4G 27
Mayobridge. New M 7F 179
Maypole. IOS 1B 4
Maypole. Kent 4G 41
Maypole. Mon 4H 47
Maypole Green. Norf 1G 67
Maypole Green. Suff 5B 66
Maywick. Shet 9E 173
Mazetown. Lis 3G 179
Mead. Devn 1C 10
Meadgate. Bath 1B 22
Meadle. Buck 5G 51
Meadowbank. Ches W 4A 84
Meadowfield. Dur 1F 105
Meadow Green. Here 5B 60
Meadowmill. E Lot 2H 129
Meadows. Nott 2C 74
Meadowtown. Shrp 5F 71
Meadwell. Devn 4E 11
Meaford. Staf 2C 72
Mealabost. W Isl
nr. Borgh 2G 171
nr. Stornoway 4G 171
Mealasta. W Isl 5B 171
Meal Bank. Cumb 5G 103
Mealrigg. Cumb 5C 112
Mealsgate. Cumb 5D 112
Meanwood. W Yor 1C 92
Mearbeck. N Yor 3H 97
Meare. Som 2H 21
Meare Green. Som
nr. Curry Mallet 4F 21
nr. Stoke St Gregory 4G 21
Mears Ashby. Nptn 4F 63
Measham. Leics 4H 73
Meath Green. Surr 1D 27
Meathop. Cumb 1D 96
Meaux. E Yor 1D 94
Meavy. Devn 2B 8
Medbourne. Leics 1E 63
Medburn. Nmbd 2E 115
Meddon. Devn 1C 10
Meden Vale. Notts 4C 86
Medlam. Linc 5C 88
Medlicott. Shrp 1G 59
Medmenham. Buck 3G 37
Medomsley. Dur 4E 115
Medstead. Hants 3E 25
Medway Towns. Medw 197 (4B 40)
Meerbrook. Staf 4D 85
Meer End. W Mid 3G 61
Meers Bridge. Linc 2D 89
Meesden. Herts 2E 53
Meeson. Telf 3A 72
Meeth. Devn 2F 11
Meeting Green. Suff 5G 65
Meeting House Hill. Norf 3F 79
Meidrim. Carm 2G 43
Meifod. Powy 4D 70
Meigh. New M 7E 178
Meigle. Per 4B 144
Meikle Earnock. S Lan 4A 128
Meikle Kilchattan Butts. Arg 4B 126
Meikleour. Per 5A 144
Meikle Tarty. Abers 1G 153
Meikle Wartle. Abers 5E 160
Meinciau. Carm 4E 45
Meir. Stoke 1D 72
Meir Heath. Staf 1D 72
Melbourn. Cambs 1D 53
Melbourne. Derbs 3A 74
Melbourne. E Yor 5B 100
Melbury Abbas. Dors 4D 23
Melbury Bubb. Dors 2A 14
Melbury Osmond. Dors 2A 14
Melbury Sampford. Dors 2A 14
Melby. Shet 6C 173
Melchbourne. Bed 4H 63
Melcombe Bingham. Dors 2C 14
Melcombe Regis. Dors 4B 14
Meldon. Devn 3F 11
Meldon. Nmbd 1E 115
Meldreth. Cambs 1D 53
Melfort. Arg 2F 133
Melgarve. High 4G 149
Meliden. Den 2C 82
Melinbyrhedyn. Powy 1H 57
Melincourt. Neat 5B 46
Melin-y-coed. Cnwy 4H 81
Melin-y-ddol. Powy 5C 70
Melin-y-wig. Den 1C 70
Melkington. Nmbd 5E 131
Melkinthorpe. Cumb 2G 103
Melkridge. Nmbd 3A 114
Melksham. Wilts 5E 35
Mellangaun. High 5C 162
Melldalloch. Arg 2H 125
Mellguards. Cumb 5F 113
Melling. Lanc 2E 97
Melling. Mers 4B 90
Melling Mount. Mers 4C 90
Mellis. Suff 3C 66
Mellon Charles. High 4C 162
Mellon Udrigle. High 4C 162
Mellor. G Man 2D 85
Mellor. Lanc 1E 91
Mellor Brook. Lanc 1E 91
Mells. Som 2C 22
Melmerby. Cumb 1H 103
Melmerby. N Yor
nr. Middleham 1C 98
nr. Ripon 2F 99
Melplash. Dors 3H 13
Melrose. Bord 1H 119
Melsetter. Orkn 9B 172
Melsonby. N Yor 4E 105
Meltham. W Yor 3B 92
Meltham Mills. W Yor 3B 92
Melton. E Yor 2C 94
Melton. Suff 5E 67
Meltonby. E Yor 4B 100
Melton Constable. Norf 2C 78
Melton Mowbray. Leics 4E 75
Melton Ross. N Lin 3D 94
Melvaig. High 5B 162
Melverley. Shrp 4F 71
Melverley Green. Shrp 4F 71
Melvich. High 2A 168
Membury. Devn 2F 13
Memsie. Abers 2G 161
Memus. Ang 3D 144
Menabilly. Corn 3E 7
Menai Bridge. IOA 3E 81
Mendham. Suff 2E 67
Mendlesham. Suff 4D 66
Mendlesham Green. Suff 4C 66
Menethorpe. N Yor 3B 100
Menheniot. Corn 2G 7
Menithwood. Worc 4B 60
Menna. Corn 3D 6
Mennock. Dum 4H 117
Menston. W Yor 5D 98
Menstrie. Clac 4H 135
Menthorpe. N Yor 1H 93
Mentmore. Buck 4H 51
Meole Brace. Shrp 4G 71
Meols. Mers 1E 83
Meon. Hants 2D 16
Meonstoke. Hants 1E 16
Meopham. Kent 4H 39
Meopham Green. Kent 4H 39
Meopham Station. Kent 4H 39
Mepal. Cambs 2D 64
Meppershall. C Beds 2B 52
Merbach. Here 1G 47
Mercaston. Derbs 1G 73
Merchiston. Edin 2F 129
Mere. Ches E 2B 84
Mere. Wilts 3D 22
Mere Brow. Lanc 3C 90
Mereclough. Lanc 1G 91
Mere Green. W Mid 1F 61
Mere Green. Worc 4D 60
Mere Heath. Ches W 3A 84
Mereside. Bkpl 1B 90
Meretown. Staf 3B 72
Mereworth. Kent 5A 40
Meriden. W Mid 2G 61
Merkadale. High 5C 154
Merkland. S Ayr 5B 116
Merkland Lodge. High 1A 164
Merley. Pool 3F 15
Merlin's Bridge. Pemb 3D 42
Merridge. Som 3F 21
Merrington. Shrp 3G 71
Merrion. Pemb 5D 42
Merriott. Som 1H 13
Merrivale. Devn 5F 11
Merrow. Surr 5B 38
Merrybent. Darl 3F 105
Merry Lees. Leics 5B 74
Merrymeet. Corn 2G 7
Mersham. Kent 2E 29
Merstham. Surr 5D 39
Merston. W Sus 2G 17
Merstone. IOW 4D 16
Merther. Corn 4C 6
Merthyr. Carm 3D 44
Merthyr Cynog. Powy 2C 46
Merthyr Dyfan. V Glam 4E 32
Merthyr Mawr. B'end 4B 32
Merthyr Tudful. Mer T 5D 46
Merthyr Tydfil. Mer T 5D 46
Merthyr Vale. Mer T 5D 46
Merton. Devn 1F 11
Merton. G Lon 4D 38
Merton. Norf 1B 66
Merton. Oxon 4D 50
Meshaw. Devn 1A 12
Messing. Essx 4B 54
Messingham. N Lin 4B 94
Metcombe. Devn 3D 12
Metfield. Suff 2E 67
Metherell. Corn 2A 8
Metheringham. Linc 4H 87
Methil. Fife 4F 137
Methilhill. Fife 4F 137
Methley. W Yor 2D 93
Methley Junction. W Yor 2D 93
Methlick. Abers 5F 161
Methven. Per 1C 136
Methwold. Norf 1G 65
Methwold Hythe. Norf 1G 65
Mettingham. Suff 2F 67
Metton. Norf 2D 78
Mevagissey. Corn 4E 6
Mexborough. S Yor 4E 93
Mey. High 1E 169
Meysey Hampton. Glos 2G 35
Miabhag. W Isl 8D 171
Miabhaig. W Isl
nr. Cliasmol 7C 171
nr. Timsgearraidh 4C 171
Mial. High 1G 155
Michaelchurch. Here 3A 48
Michaelchurch Escley. Here 2G 47
Michaelchurch-on-Arrow. Powy 5E 59
Michaelston-le-Pit. V Glam 4E 33
Michaelston-y-Fedw. Newp 3F 33
Michaelstow. Corn 5A 10
Michelcombe. Devn 2C 8
Micheldever. Hants 3D 24
Micheldever Station. Hants 2D 24
Michelmersh. Hants 4B 24
Mickfield. Suff 4D 66
Micklebring. S Yor 1C 86
Mickleby. N Yor 3F 107
Micklefield. W Yor 1E 93
Micklefield Green. Herts 1B 38
Mickleham. Surr 5C 38
Mickleover. Derb 2H 73
Micklethwaite. Cumb 4D 112
Micklethwaite. W Yor 5D 98
Mickleton. Dur 2C 104
Mickleton. Glos 1G 49
Mickletown. W Yor 2D 93
Mickle Trafford. Ches W 4G 83
Mickley. N Yor 2E 99
Mickley Green. Suff 5H 65
Mickley Square. Nmbd 3D 115
Mid Ardlaw. Abers 2G 161
Midbea. Orkn 3D 172
Mid Beltie. Abers 3D 152
Mid Calder. W Lot 3D 129
Mid Clyth. High 5E 169
Middle Assendon. Oxon 3F 37
Middle Aston. Oxon 3C 50
Middle Barton. Oxon 3C 50
Middlebie. Dum 2D 112
Middle Chinnock. Som 1H 13
Middle Claydon. Buck 3F 51
Middlecliffe. S Yor 4E 93
Middlecott. Devn 4H 11
Middle Drums. Ang 3E 145
Middle Duntisbourne. Glos 5E 49
Middle Essie. Abers 3H 161
Middleforth Green. Lanc 2D 90
Middleham. N Yor 1D 98
Middle Handley. Derbs 3B 86
Middle Harling. Norf 2B 66
Middlehope. Shrp 2G 59
Middle Littleton. Worc 1F 49
Middle Maes-coed. Here 2G 47
Middlemarsh. Dors 2B 14
Middle Marwood. Devn 3F 19
Middle Mayfield. Staf 1F 73
Middlemoor. Devn 5E 11
Middlemuir. Abers
nr. New Deer 4F 161
nr. Strichen 3G 161
Middle Rainton. Tyne 5G 115
Middle Rasen. Linc 2H 87
Middles, The. Dur 4F 115
Middlesbrough. Midd 197 (3B 106)
Middlesceugh. Cumb 5E 113
Middleshaw. Cumb 1E 97
Middlesmoor. N Yor 2C 98
Middlestone. Dur 1F 105
Middlestone Moor. Dur 1F 105
Middle Stoughton. Som 2H 21
Middlestown. W Yor 3C 92
Middle Street. Glos 5C 48
Middle Taphouse. Corn 2F 7
Middleton. Ang 4E 145
Middleton. Arg 4A 138
Middleton. Cumb 1F 97
Middleton. Derbs
nr. Bakewell 4F 85
nr. Wirksworth 5G 85
Middleton. Essx 2B 54
Middleton. G Man 4G 91
Middleton. Hants 2C 24
Middleton. Hart 1C 106
Middleton. Here 4H 59
Middleton. IOW 4B 16
Middleton. Lanc 4D 96
Middleton. Midl 4G 129
Middleton. Norf 4F 77
Middleton. Nptn 2F 63
Middleton. Nmbd
nr. Belford 1F 121
nr. Morpeth 1D 114
Middleton. N Yor
nr. Ilkley 5D 98
nr. Pickering 1B 100
Middleton. Per 3D 136
Middleton. Shrp
nr. Ludlow 3H 59
nr. Oswestry 3F 71
Middleton. Suff 4G 67
Middleton. Swan 4D 30
Middleton. Warw 1F 61
Middleton. W Yor 2C 92
Middleton Cheney. Nptn 1D 50
Middleton Green. Staf 2D 73
Middleton-in-Teesdale. Dur 2C 104
Middleton One Row. Darl 3A 106
Middleton-on-Leven. N Yor 4B 106
Middleton-on-Sea. W Sus 5A 26
Middleton on the Hill. Here 4H 59
Middleton-on-the-Wolds. E Yor 5D 100
Middleton Priors. Shrp 1A 60
Middleton Quernhow. N Yor 2F 99
Middleton St George. Darl 3A 106
Middleton Scriven. Shrp 2A 60
Middleton Stoney. Oxon 3D 50
Middleton Tyas. N Yor 4F 105
Middletown. Arm 6B 178
Middletown. Cumb 4A 102
Middle Town. IOS 1B 4
Middletown. Powy 4F 71
Middle Tysoe. Warw 1B 50
Middle Wallop. Hants 3A 24
Middlewich. Ches E 4B 84
Middle Winterslow. Wilts 3H 23
Middlewood. Corn 5C 10
Middlewood. S Yor 1H 85
Middle Woodford. Wilts 3G 23
Middlewood Green. Suff 4C 66
Middleyard. Glos 5D 48
Middlezoy. Som 3G 21
Middridge. Dur 2F 105
Midelney. Som 4H 21
Midfield. High 2F 167
Midford. Bath 5C 34
Mid Garrary. Dum 2C 110
Midge Hall. Lanc 2D 90
Midgeholme. Cumb 4H 113
Midgham. W Ber 5D 36
Midgley. W Yor
nr. Halifax 2A 92
nr. Horbury 3C 92
Mid Ho. Shet 2G 173
Midhopestones. S Yor 1G 85
Midhurst. W Sus 4G 25
Mid Kirkton. N Ayr 4C 126
Mid Lambrook. Som 1H 13
Midland. Orkn 7C 172
Mid Lavant. W Sus 2G 17
Midlem. Bord 2H 119
Midney. Som 4A 22
Midsomer Norton. Bath 1B 22
Midton. Inv 2D 126
Midtown. High
nr. Poolewe 5C 162
nr. Tongue 2F 167
Midville. Linc 5C 88
Mid Walls. Shet 7C 173
Mid Yell. Shet 2G 173
Migdale. High 4D 164
Migvie. Abers 3B 152
Milborne Port. Som 1B 14
Milborne St Andrew. Dors 3D 14
Milborne Wick. Som 4B 22
Milbourne. Nmbd 2E 115
Milbourne. Wilts 3E 35
Milburn. Cumb 2H 103
Milbury Heath. S Glo 2B 34
Milby. N Yor 3G 99
Milcombe. Oxon 2C 50
Milden. Suff 1C 54
Mildenhall. Suff 3G 65
Mildenhall. Wilts 5H 35
Milebrook. Powy 3F 59
Milebush. Kent 1B 28
Mile End. Cambs 2F 65
Mile End. Essx 3C 54
Mileham. Norf 4B 78
Mile Oak. Brig 5D 26
Miles Green. Staf 5C 84
Miles Hope. Here 4H 59
Milesmark. Fife 1D 128
Mile Town. Kent 3D 40
Milfield. Nmbd 1D 120
Milford. Arm 5C 178
Milford. Derbs 1A 74
Milford. Devn 4C 18
Milford. Powy 1C 58
Milford. Staf 3D 72
Milford. Surr 1A 26
Milford Haven. Pemb 4D 42
Milford on Sea. Hants 3A 16
Milkwall. Glos 5A 48
Milkwell. Wilts 4E 23
Milland. W Sus 4G 25
Millbank. Ant 1G 179
Millbank. High 2D 168
Mill Bank. W Yor 2A 92
Millbay. ME Ant 7L 175
Millbeck. Cumb 2D 102
Millbounds. Orkn 4E 172
Millbreck. Abers 4H 161
Millbridge. Surr 2G 25
Millbrook. C Beds 2A 52
Millbrook. Corn 3A 8
Millbrook. G Man 1D 85
Millbrook. ME Ant 6K 175
Millbrook. Sotn 1B 16
Mill Common. Suff 2G 67
Mill Corner. E Sus 3C 28
Milldale. Staf 5F 85
Millden Lodge. Ang 1E 145
Milldens. Ang 3E 145
Millearn. Per 2B 136
Mill End. Buck 3F 37
Mill End. Cambs 5F 65
Mill End. Glos 4G 49
Mill End. Herts 2D 52
Millerhill. Midl 3G 129
Miller's Dale. Derbs 3F 85
Millers Green. Derbs 5G 85
Millerston. Glas 3H 127
Millfield. Abers 4B 152
Millfield. Pet 5A 76
Millgate. Lanc 3G 91
Mill Green. Essx 5G 53
Mill Green. Norf 2D 66
Mill Green. Shrp 3A 72
Mill Green. Staf 3E 73
Mill Green. Suff 1C 54
Millhall. Here 1F 47
Millhall. E Ren 4G 127
Millhayes. Devn
nr. Honiton 2F 13
nr. Wellington 1E 13
Millhead. Lanc 2D 97
Millheugh. S Lan 4A 128
Mill Hill. Bkbn 2E 91
Mill Hill. G Lon 1D 38
Millholme. Cumb 5G 103
Millhouse. Arg 2A 126
Millhouse. Cumb 1E 103
Millhousebridge. Dum 1C 112
Millhouses. S Yor 2H 85
Millikenpark. Ren 3F 127
Millington. E Yor 4C 100
Millington Green. Derbs 1G 73
Millisle. Ards 2K 179
Mill Knowe. Arg 3B 122
Mill Lane. Hants 1F 25
Millmeece. Staf 2C 72
Mill of Craigievar. Abers 2C 152
Mill of Fintray. Abers 2F 153
Mill of Haldane. W Dun 1F 127
Millom. Cumb 1A 96
Millow. C Beds 1C 52
Millpool. Corn 5B 10
Millport. N Ayr 4C 126
Mill Side. Cumb 1D 96
Mill Street. Norf
nr. Lyng 4C 78
nr. Swanton Morley 4C 78
Millthorpe. Derbs 3H 85
Millthorpe. Linc 2A 76
Millthrop. Cumb 5H 103
Milltimber. Aber 3F 153
Milltown. Abers
nr. Corgarff 3G 151
nr. Lumsden 2B 152
Mill Town. Ant 8H 175
Milltown. Ant 7G 175
Milltown. Arm
nr. Banbridge 5F 178
nr. Coalisland 3D 178
nr. Richhill 5D 178
Milltown. Corn 3F 7
Milltown. Derbs 4A 86
Milltown. Devn 3F 19
Milltown. Dum 2E 113
Milltown of Aberdalgie. Per 1C 136
Milltown of Auchindoun. Mor 4A 160
Milltown of Campfield. Abers 3D 152
Milltown of Edinvillie. Mor 4G 159
Milltown of Rothiemay. Mor 4C 160
Milltown of Towie. Abers 2B 152
Milnacraig. Ang 3B 144
Milnathort. Per 3D 136
Milngavie. E Dun 2G 127
Milnholm. Stir 1A 128
Milnrow. G Man 3H 91
Milnthorpe. Cumb 1D 97
Milnthorpe. W Yor 3D 92
Milson. Shrp 3A 60
Milstead. Kent 5D 40
Milston. Wilts 2G 23
Milthorpe. Nptn 1D 50
Milton. Ang 4C 144
Milton. Cambs 4D 65
Milton. Cumb
nr. Brampton 3G 113
nr. Crooklands 1E 97
Milton. Derbs 3H 73
Milton. Dum
nr. Crocketford 2F 111
nr. Glenluce 4H 109
Milton. Glas 3G 127
Milton. High
nr. Achnasheen 3F 157
nr. Applecross 4G 155
nr. Drumnadrochit 5G 157
nr. Invergordon 1B 158
nr. Inverness 4H 157
nr. Wick 3F 169
Milton. Mor
nr. Cullen 2C 160
nr. Tomintoul 2F 151
Milton. N Som 5G 33
Milton. Notts 3E 86

Milton—New Cowper

Milton. Oxon
nr. Bloxham 2C 50
nr. Didcot 2C 36
Milton. Pemb 4E 43
Milton. Port 3E 17
Milton. Som 4H 21
Milton. S Ayr 2D 116
Milton. Stir
nr. Aberfoyle 3E 135
nr. Drymen 4D 134
Milton. Stoke 5D 84
Milton. W Dun 2F 127
Milton Abbas. Dors 2D 14
Milton Abbot. Devn 5E 11
Milton Auchlossan. Abers 3C 152
Milton Bridge. Midl 3F 129
Milton Bryan. C Beds 2H 51
Milton Clevedon. Som 3B 22
Milton Coldwells. Abers 5G 161
Milton Combe. Devn 2A 8
Milton Common. Oxon 5E 51
Milton Damerel. Devn 1D 11
Miltonduff. Mor 2F 159
Milton End. Glos 5G 49
Milton Ernest. Bed 5H 63
Milton Green. Ches W 5G 83
Milton Hill. Devn 5C 12
Milton Hill. Oxon 2C 36
Milton Keynes. Mil 200 (2G 51)
Milton Keynes Village. Mil 2G 51
Milton Lilbourne. Wilts 5G 35
Milton Malsor. Nptn 5E 63
Milton Morenish. Per 5D 142
Milton of Auchinhove.
Abers 3C 152
Milton of Balgonie. Fife 3F 137
Milton of Barras. Abers 1H 145
Milton of Campsie. E Dun 2H 127
Milton of Cultoquhey. Per 1A 136
Milton of Cushnie. Abers 2C 152
Milton of Finavon. Ang 3D 145
Milton of Gollanfield.
High 3B 158
Milton of Lesmore. Abers 1B 152
Milton of Leys. High 4A 158
Milton of Tullich. Abers 4A 152
Milton on Stour. Dors 4C 22
Milton Regis. Kent 4C 40
Milton Street. E Sus 5G 27
Milton-under-Wychwood.
Oxon 4A 50
Milverton. Som 4E 20
Milverton. Warw 4H 61
Milwich. Staf 2D 72
Mimbridge. Surr 4A 38
Minard. Arg 4G 133
Minchington. Dors 1E 15
Minchinhampton. Glos 5D 48
Mindrum. Nmbd 1C 120
Minehead. Som 2C 20
Minera. Wrex 5E 83
Minerstown. New M 6J 179
Minety. Wilts 2F 35
Minffordd. Gwyn 2E 69
Mingarrypark. High 2A 140
Mingary. High 2G 139
Mingearraidh. W Isl 6C 170
Miningsby. Linc 4C 88
Minions. Corn 5C 10
Minishant. S Ayr 3C 116
Minllyn. Gwyn 4A 70
Minnigaff. Dum 3B 110
Minorca. IOM 3D 108
Minskip. N Yor 3F 99
Minstead. Hants 1A 16
Minsted. W Sus 4G 25
Minster. Kent
nr. Ramsgate 4H 41
Minster. Kent
nr. Sheerness 3D 40
Minsteracres. Nmbd 4D 114
Minsterley. Shrp 5F 71
Minster Lovell. Oxon 4B 50
Minsterworth. Glos 4C 48
Minterne Magna. Dors 2B 14
Minterne Parva. Dors 2B 14
Minting. Linc 3A 88
Mintlaw. Abers 4H 161
Minto. Bord 2H 119
Minton. Shrp 1G 59
Minwear. Pemb 3E 43
Minworth. W Mid 1F 61
Miodar. Arg 4B 138
Mirbister. Orkn 5C 172
Mirehouse. Cumb 3A 102
Mireland. High 2F 169
Mirfield. W Yor 3C 92
Miserden. Glos 5E 49
Miskin. Rhon 3D 32
Misson. Notts 1D 86
Misterton. Leics 2C 62
Misterton. Notts 1E 87
Misterton. Som 2H 13
Mistley. Essx 2E 54
Mistley Heath. Essx 2E 55
Mitcham. G Lon 4D 39
Mitcheldean. Glos 4B 48
Mitchell. Corn 3C 6
Mitchel Troy. Mon 4H 47
Mitcheltroy Common. Mon 5H 47
Mitford. Nmbd 1E 115
Mithian. Corn 3B 6
Mitton. Staf 4C 72
Mixbury. Oxon 2E 50
Mixenden. W Yor 2A 92
Mixon. Staf 5E 85
Moaness. Orkn 7B 172
Moarfield. Shet 1G 173
Moat. Cumb 2F 113
Moats Tye. Suff 5C 66
Mobberley. Ches E 3B 84
Mobberley. Staf 1E 73
Moccas. Here 1G 47
Mochdre. Cnwy 3H 81
Mochdre. Powy 2C 58
Mochrum. Dum 5A 110
Mockbeggar. Hants 2G 15
Mockerkin. Cumb 2B 102
Modbury. Devn 3C 8
Moddershall. Staf 2D 72
Modsarie. High 2G 167
Moelfre. Cnwy 3B 82
Moelfre. IOA 2E 81
Moelfre. Powy 3D 70
Moffat. Dum 4C 118
Moggerhanger. C Beds 1B 52
Mogworthy. Devn 1B 12
Moira. Leics 4H 73
Moira. Lis 3F 178
Molash. Kent 5E 41
Mol-chlach. High 2C 146
Mold. Flin 4E 83
Molehill Green. Essx 3F 53
Molescroft. E Yor 5E 101
Molesden. Nmbd 1E 115
Molesworth. Cambs 3H 63
Moll. High 1D 146
Molland. Devn 4B 20
Mollington. Ches W 3F 83
Mollington. Oxon 1C 50
Mollinsburn. N Lan 2A 128
Monachty. Cdgn 4E 57
Monachyle. Stir 2D 135
Monar Lodge. High 4E 156
Monaughty. Powy 4E 59
Monea. Ferm 7D 176
Monewden. Suff 5E 67
Moneydie. Per 1C 136
Moneyglass. Ant 7G 175
Moneymore. M Ulst 1C 178
Moneyneany. M Ulst 7D 174
Moneyreagh. Lis 3J 179
Moneyrow Green. Wind 4G 37
Moneyslane. Arm 6G 179
Moniaive. Dum 5G 117
Monifieth. Ang 5E 145
Monikie. Ang 5E 145
Monimail. Fife 2E 137
Monington. Pemb 1B 44
Monk Bretton. S Yor 4D 92
Monken Hadley. G Lon 1D 38
Monk Fryston. N Yor 2F 93
Monk Hesleden. Dur 1B 106
Monkhide. Here 1B 48
Monkhill. Cumb 4E 113
Monkhopton. Shrp 1A 60
Monkland. Here 5G 59
Monkleigh. Devn 4E 19
Monknash. V Glam 4C 32
Monkokehampton. Devn 2F 11
Monkseaton. Tyne 2G 115
Monks Eleigh. Suff 1C 54
Monk's Gate. W Sus 3D 26
Monk's Heath. Ches E 3C 84
Monk Sherborne. Hants 1E 24
Monkshill. Abers 4E 161
Monksilver. Som 3D 20
Monks Kirby. Warw 2B 62
Monk Soham. Suff 4E 66
Monk Soham Green. Suff 4E 66
Monkspath. W Mid 3F 61
Monks Risborough. Buck 5G 51
Monksthorpe. Linc 4D 88
Monkstown. Ant 1H 179
Monk Street. Essx 3G 53
Monkswood. Mon 5G 47
Monkton. Devn 2E 13
Monkton. Kent 4G 41
Monkton. Pemb 4D 42
Monkton. S Ayr 2C 116
Monkton Combe. Bath 5C 34
Monkton Deverill. Wilts 3D 22
Monkton Farleigh. Wilts 5D 34
Monkton Heathfield. Som 4F 21
Monktonhill. S Ayr 2C 116
Monkton Up Wimborne.
Dors 1F 15
Monkton Wyld. Dors 3G 13
Monkwearmouth. Tyne 4G 115
Monkwood. Dors 3H 13
Monkwood. Hants 3E 25
Monmarsh. Here 1A 48
Monmouth. Mon 4A 48
Monnington on Wye. Here 1G 47
Monreith. Dum 5A 110
Montacute. Som 1H 13
Monteith. Arm 5F 179
Montford. Arg 3C 126
Montford. Shrp 4G 71
Montford Bridge. Shrp 4G 71
Montgarrie. Abers 2C 152
Montgarswood. E Ayr 2E 117
Montgomery. Powy 1E 58
Montgreenan. N Ayr 5E 127
Montrave. Fife 3F 137
Montrose. Ang 3G 145
Monxton. Hants 2B 24
Monyash. Derbs 4F 85
Monymusk. Abers 2D 152
Monzie. Per 1A 136
Moodiesburn. N Lan 2H 127
Moon's Green. Kent 3C 28
Moonzie. Fife 2F 137
Moor, The. Kent 3B 28
Moor. Som 1H 13
Moor Allerton. W Yor 1C 92
Moorbath. Dors 3H 13
Moorbrae. Shet 3F 173
Moorby. Linc 4B 88
Moorcot. Here 5F 59
Moor Crichel. Dors 2E 15
Moor Cross. Devn 3C 8
Moordown. Bour 3F 15
Moore. Hal 2H 83
Moorend. Dum 2D 112
Moor End. E Yor 1B 94
Moorend. Glos
nr. Dursley 5C 48
nr. Gloucester 4D 48
Moorends. S Yor 3G 93
Moorfields. ME Ant 7H 175
Moorgate. S Yor 1B 86
Moorgreen. Hants 1C 16
Moorgreen. Notts 1B 74
Moor Green. Wilts 5D 34
Moorhaigh. Notts 4C 86
Moorhall. Derbs 3H 85
Moorhampton. Here 1G 47
Moorhouse. Cumb
nr. Carlisle 4E 113
nr. Wigton 4D 112
Moorhouse. Notts 4E 87
Moorhouse. Surr 5F 39
Moorhouses. Linc 5B 88
Moorland. Som 3G 21
Moorlinch. Som 3H 21
Moor Monkton. N Yor 4H 99
Moor of Granary. Mor 3E 159
Moor Row. Cumb
nr. Whitehaven 3B 102
nr. Wigton 5D 112
Moorsholm. Red C 3D 107
Moorside. Dors 1C 14
Moorside. G Man 4H 91
Moortown. Devn 3D 10
Moortown. Hants 2G 15
Moortown. IOW 4C 16
Moortown. Linc 1H 87
Moortown. M Ulst 2D 178
Moortown. Telf 4A 72
Moortown. W Yor 1D 92
Morangie. High 5E 165
Morar. High 4E 147
Morborne. Cambs 1A 64
Morchard Bishop. Devn 2A 12
Morcombelake. Dors 3H 13
Morcott. Rut 5G 75
Morda. Shrp 3E 71
Morden. G Lon 4D 38
Mordiford. Here 2A 48
Mordon. Dur 2A 106
More. Shrp 1F 59
Morebath. Devn 4C 20
Morebattle. Bord 2B 120
Morecambe. Lanc 3D 96
Morefield. High 4F 163
Moreleigh. Devn 3D 8
Morenish. Per 5C 142
Moresby Parks. Cumb 3A 102
Morestead. Hants 4D 24
Moreton. Dors 4D 14
Moreton. Essx 5F 53
Moreton. Here 4H 59
Moreton. Mers 1E 83
Moreton. Oxon 5E 51
Moreton. Staf 4B 72
Moreton Corbet. Shrp 3H 71
Moretonhampstead. Devn 4A 12
Moreton-in-Marsh. Glos 2H 49
Moreton Jeffries. Here 1B 48
Moreton Morrell. Warw 5H 61
Moreton on Lugg. Here 1A 48
Moreton Pinkney. Nptn 1D 50
Moreton Say. Shrp 2A 72
Moreton Valence. Glos 5C 48
Morfa. Cdgn 5C 56
Morfa Bach. Carm 4D 44
Morfa Bychan. Gwyn 2E 69
Morfa Glas. Neat 5B 46
Morfa Nefyn. Gwyn 1B 68
Morganstown. Card 3E 33
Morgan's Vale. Wilts 4G 23
Morham. E Lot 2B 130
Moriah. Cdgn 3F 57
Morland. Cumb 2G 103
Morley. Ches E 2C 84
Morley. Derbs 1A 74
Morley. Dur 2E 105
Morley. W Yor 2C 92
Morley St Botolph. Norf 1C 66
Morningside. Edin 2F 129
Morningside. N Lan 4B 128
Morningthorpe. Norf 1E 66
Morpeth. Nmbd 1F 115
Morrey. Staf 4F 73
Morridge Side. Staf 5E 85
Morridge Top. Staf 4E 85
Morrington. Dum 1F 111
Morris Green. Essx 2H 53
Morriston. Swan 3F 31
Morston. Norf 1C 78
Mortehoe. Devn 2E 19
Morthen. S Yor 2B 86
Mortimer. W Ber 5E 37
Mortimer's Cross. Here 4G 59
Mortimer West End. Hants 5E 37
Mortomley. S Yor 1H 85
Morton. Cumb
nr. Calthwaite 1F 103
nr. Carlisle 4E 113
Morton. Derbs 4B 86
Morton. Linc
nr. Bourne 3H 75
nr. Gainsborough 1F 87
nr. Lincoln 4F 87
Morton. Norf 4D 78
Morton. Notts 5E 87
Morton. Shrp 3E 71
Morton. S Glo 2B 34
Morton Bagot. Warw 4F 61
Morton Mill. Shrp 3H 71
Morton-on-Swale. N Yor 5A 106
Morton Tinmouth. Dur 2E 105
Morvah. Corn 3B 4
Morval. Corn 3G 7
Morvich. High
nr. Golspie 3E 165
nr. Shiel Bridge 1B 148
Morvil. Pemb 1E 43
Morville. Shrp 1A 60
Morwenstow. Corn 1C 10
Morwick. Nmbd 4G 121
Mosborough. S Yor 2B 86
Moscow. E Ayr 5F 127
Mose. Shrp 1B 60
Mosedale. Cumb 1E 103
Moseley. W Mid
nr. Birmingham 2E 61
nr. Wolverhampton 5D 72
Moseley. Worc 5C 60
Moss. Arg 4A 138
Moss. High 2A 140
Moss. S Yor 3F 93
Moss. Wrex 5F 83
Mossatt. Abers 2B 152
Moss Bank. Mers 1H 83
Mossbank. Shet 4F 173
Mossblown. S Ayr 2D 116
Mossbrow. G Man 2B 84
Mossburnford. Bord 3A 120
Mossdale. Dum 2D 110
Mossedge. Cumb 3F 113
Mossend. N Lan 3A 128
Mossgate. Staf 2D 72
Moss Lane. Ches E 3D 84
Mossley. Ant 1H 179
Mossley. Ches E 4C 84
Mossley. G Man 4H 91
Mossley Hill. Mers 2F 83
Moss of Barmuckity. Mor 2G 159
Mosspark. Glas 3G 127
Mosspaul. Bord 5G 119
Moss-Side. Caus 3G 175
Moss Side. Cumb 4C 112
Moss Side. G Man 1C 84
Moss-side. High 3C 158
Moss Side. Lanc
nr. Blackpool 1B 90
nr. Preston 2D 90
Moss Side. Mers 4B 90
Moss-side of Cairness.
Abers 2H 161
Mosstodloch. Mor 2H 159
Mosswood. Nmbd 4D 114
Mossy Lea. Lanc 3D 90
Mosterton. Dors 2H 13
Moston. Shrp 3H 71
Moston Green. Ches E 4B 84
Mostyn. Flin 2D 82
Mostyn Quay. Flin 2D 82
Motcombe. Dors 4D 22
Mothecombe. Devn 4C 8
Motherby. Cumb 2F 103
Motherwell. N Lan 4A 128
Mottingham. G Lon 3F 39
Mottisfont. Hants 4B 24
Mottistone. IOW 4C 16
Mottram in Longdendale.
G Man 1D 85
Mottram St Andrew.
Ches E 3C 84
Mott's Mill. E Sus 2G 27
Mouldsworth. Ches W 3H 83
Moulin. Per 3G 143
Moulsecoomb. Brig 5E 27
Moulsford. Oxon 3D 36
Moulsoe. Mil 1H 51
Moulton. Ches W 4A 84
Moulton. Linc 3C 76
Moulton. Nptn 4E 63
Moulton. N Yor 4F 105
Moulton. Suff 4F 65
Moulton. V Glam 4D 32
Moulton Chapel. Linc 4B 76
Moulton Eaugate. Linc 4C 76
Moulton St Mary. Norf 5F 79
Moulton Seas End. Linc 3C 76
Mount. Corn
nr. Bodmin 2F 7
nr. Newquay 3B 6
Mountain Ash. Rhon 2D 32
Mountain Cross. Bord 5E 129
Mountain Street. Kent 5E 41
Mountain Water. Pemb 2D 42
Mount Ambrose. Corn 4B 6
Mountbenger. Bord 2F 119
Mountblow. W Dun 2F 127
Mount Bures. Essx 2C 54
Mountfield. E Sus 3B 28
Mountfield. Ferm 2L 177
Mountgerald. High 2H 157
Mount Hawke. Corn 4B 6
Mount High. High 2A 158
Mountjoy. Corn 2C 6
Mountjoy. Ferm 2K 177
Mount Lothian. Midl 4F 129
Mountnessing. Essx 1H 39
Mountnorris. Arm 6D 178
Mounton. Mon 2A 34
Mount Pleasant. Buck 2E 51
Mount Pleasant. Ches E 5C 84
Mount Pleasant. Derbs
nr. Derby 1H 73
nr. Swadlincote 4G 73
Mount Pleasant. E Sus 4F 27
Mount Pleasant. Hants 3A 16
Mount Pleasant. Norf 1B 66
Mount Skippett. Oxon 4B 50
Mountsorrel. Leics 4C 74
Mount Stuart. Arg 4C 126
Mousehole. Corn 4B 4
Mouswald. Dum 2B 112
Mow Cop. Ches E 5C 84
Mowden. Darl 3F 105
Mowhaugh. Bord 2C 120
Mowmacre Hill. Leic 5C 74
Mowsley. Leics 2D 62
Moy. High 5B 158
Moy. M Ulst 4C 178
Moygashel. M Ulst 3C 178
Moylgrove. Pemb 1B 44
Moy Lodge. High 5G 149
Muasdale. Arg 5E 125
Muchalls. Abers 4G 153
Much Birch. Here 2A 48
Much Cowarne. Here 1B 48
Much Dewchurch. Here 2H 47
Muchelney. Som 4H 21
Muchelney Ham. Som 4H 21
Much Hadham. Herts 4E 53
Much Hoole. Lanc 2C 90
Muchlarnick. Corn 3G 7
Much Marcle. Here 2B 48
Muchrachd. High 5E 157
Much Wenlock. Shrp 5A 72
Mucking. Thur 2A 40
Muckle Breck. Shet 5G 173
Muckleford. Dors 3B 14
Mucklestone. Staf 2B 72
Muckleton. Norf 2H 77
Muckleton. Shrp 3H 71
Muckley. Shrp 1A 60
Muckley Corner. Staf 5E 73
Muckton. Linc 2C 88
Mudale. High 5F 167
Muddiford. Devn 3F 19
Mudeford. Dors 3G 15
Mudford. Som 1A 14
Mudgley. Som 2H 21
Mugdock. Stir 2G 127
Mugeary. High 5D 154
Mugginton. Derbs 1G 73
Muggintonlane End. Derbs 1G 73
Muggleswick. Dur 4D 114
Mugswell. Surr 5D 38
Muie. High 3D 164
Muirden. Abers 3E 160
Muirdrum. Ang 5E 145
Muiredge. Per 1E 137
Muirend. Glas 3G 127
Muirhead. Ang 5C 144
Muirhead. Fife 3E 137
Muirhead. N Lan 3H 127
Muirhouses. Falk 1D 128
Muirkirk. E Ayr 2F 117
Muir of Alford. Abers 2C 152
Muir of Fairburn. High 3G 157
Muir of Fowlis. Abers 2C 152
Muir of Miltonduff. Mor 3F 159
Muir of Ord. High 3H 157
Muir of Tarradale. High 3H 157
Muirshearlich. High 5D 148
Muirtack. Abers 5G 161
Muirton. High 2B 158
Muirton. Per 1D 136
Muirton of Ardblair. Per 4A 144
Muirtown. Per 2B 136
Muiryfold. Abers 3E 161
Muker. N Yor 5C 104
Mulbarton. Norf 5D 78
Mulben. Mor 3A 160
Mulindry. Arg 4B 124
Mulla. Shet 5F 173
Mullach Charlabhaigh.
W Isl 3E 171
Mullacott. Devn 2F 19
Mullaghbane. New M 8D 178
Mullaghboy. ME Ant 6L 175
Mullaghglass. New M 7E 178
Mullion. Corn 5D 5
Mullion Cove. Corn 5D 4
Mumbles. Swan 4F 31
Mumby. Linc 3E 89
Munderfield Row. Here 5A 60
Munderfield Stocks. Here 5A 60
Mundesley. Norf 2F 79
Mundford. Norf 1H 65
Mundham. Norf 1F 67
Mundon. Essx 5B 54
Munerigie. High 3E 149
Muness. Shet 1H 173
Mungasdale. High 4D 162
Mungrisdale. Cumb 1E 103
Munlochy. High 3A 158
Munsley. Here 1B 48
Munslow. Shrp 2H 59
Murchington. Devn 4G 11
Murcot. Worc 1F 49
Murcott. Oxon 4D 50
Murdishaw. Hal 2H 83
Murieston. W Lot 3D 128
Murkle. High 2D 168
Murlaggan. High 4C 148
Murra. Orkn 7B 172
Murray, The. S Lan 4H 127
Murrayfield. Edin 2F 129
Murrell Green. Hants 1F 25
Murroes. Ang 5D 144
Murrow. Cambs 5C 76
Mursley. Buck 3G 51
Murthly. Per 5H 143
Murton. Cumb 2A 104
Murton. Dur 5G 115
Murton. Nmbd 5F 131
Murton. Swan 4E 31
Murton. York 4A 100
Musbury. Devn 3F 13
Muscoates. N Yor 1A 100
Muscott. Nptn 4D 62
Musselburgh. E Lot 2G 129
Muston. Leics 2F 75
Muston. N Yor 2E 101
Mustow Green. Worc 3C 60
Muswell Hill. G Lon 2D 39
Mutehill. Dum 5D 111
Mutford. Suff 2G 67
Muthill. Per 2A 136
Mutterton. Devn 2D 12
Muxton. Telf 4B 72
Mwmbwls. Swan 4F 31
Mybster. High 3D 168
Myddfai. Carm 2A 46
Myddle. Shrp 3G 71
Mydroilyn. Cdgn 5D 56
Myerscough. Lanc 1C 90
Mylor Bridge. Corn 5C 6
Mylor Churchtown. Corn 5C 6
Mynachlog-ddu. Pemb 1F 43
Mynydd-bach. Mon 2H 33
Mynydd Isa. Flin 4E 83
Mynyddislwyn. Cphy 2E 33
Mynydd Llandegai. Gwyn 4F 81
Mynydd Mechell. IOA 1C 80
Mynydd-y-briw. Powy 3D 70
Mynyddygarreg. Carm 5E 45
Mynytho. Gwyn 2C 68
Myrebird. Abers 4E 153
Myrelandhorn. High 3E 169
Mytchett. Surr 1G 25
Mythe, The. Glos 2D 49
Mytholmroyd. W Yor 2A 92
Myton-on-Swale. N Yor 3G 99
Mytton. Shrp 4G 71

N

Naast. High 5C 162
Na Buirgh. W Isl 8C 171
Naburn. York 5H 99
Nab Wood. W Yor 1B 92
Nackington. Kent 5F 41
Nacton. Suff 1F 55
Nafferton. E Yor 4E 101
Na Gearrannan. W Isl 3D 171
Nailbridge. Glos 4B 48
Nailsbourne. Som 4F 21
Nailsea. N Som 4H 33
Nailstone. Leics 5B 74
Nailsworth. Glos 2D 34
Nairn. High 3C 158
Nalderswood. Surr 1D 26
Nancegollan. Corn 3D 4
Nancledra. Corn 3B 4
Nangreaves. G Man 3G 91
Nanhyfer. Pemb 1E 43
Nannerch. Flin 4D 82
Nanpantan. Leics 4C 74
Nanpean. Corn 3D 6
Nanstallon. Corn 2E 7
Nant-ddu. Powy 4D 46
Nanternis. Cdgn 5C 56
Nantgaredig. Carm 3E 45
Nantgarw. Rhon 3E 33
Nant Glas. Powy 4B 58
Nantglyn. Den 4C 82
Nantgwyn. Powy 3B 58
Nantlle. Gwyn 5E 81
Nantmawr. Shrp 3E 71
Nantmel. Powy 4C 58
Nantmor. Gwyn 1F 69
Nant Peris. Gwyn 5F 81
Nantwich. Ches E 5A 84
Nant-y-bai. Carm 1A 46
Nant-y-bwch. Blae 4E 47
Nant-y-Derry. Mon 5G 47
Nant-y-dugoed. Powy 4B 70
Nant-y-felin. Cnwy 3F 81
Nantyffyllon. B'end 2B 32
Nantyglo. Blae 4E 47
Nant-y-meichiaid. Powy 4D 70
Nant-y-moel. B'end 2C 32
Nant-y-pandy. Cnwy 3F 81
Naphill. Buck 2G 37
Nappa. N Yor 4A 98
Napton on the Hill. Warw 4B 62
Narberth. Pemb 3F 43
Narberth Bridge. Pemb 3F 43
Narborough. Leics 1C 62
Narborough. Norf 4G 77
Narkurs. Corn 3H 7
Narth, The. Mon 5A 48
Narthwaite. Cumb 5A 104
Nasareth. Gwyn 5D 80
Naseby. Nptn 3D 62
Nash. Buck 2F 51
Nash. Here 4F 59
Nash. Kent 5G 41
Nash. Newp 3G 33
Nash. Shrp 3A 60
Nash Lee. Buck 5G 51
Nassington. Nptn 1H 63
Nasty. Herts 3D 52
Natcott. Devn 4C 18
Nateby. Cumb 4A 104
Nateby. Lanc 5D 96
Nately Scures. Hants 1F 25
Natland. Cumb 1E 97
Naughton. Suff 1D 54
Naunton. Glos 3G 49
Naunton. Worc 2D 49
Naunton Beauchamp.
Worc 5D 60
Navenby. Linc 5G 87
Navestock. Essx 1G 39
Navestock Side. Essx 1G 39
Navidale. High 2H 165
Nawton. N Yor 1A 100
Nayland. Suff 2C 54
Nazeing. Essx 5E 53
Neacroft. Hants 3G 15
Nealhouse. Cumb 4E 113
Neal's Green. Warw 2H 61
Near Sawrey. Cumb 5E 103
Neasden. G Lon 2D 38
Neasham. Darl 3A 106
Neath. Neat 2A 32
Neath Abbey. Neat 3G 31
Neatishead. Norf 3F 79
Neaton. Norf 5B 78
Nebo. Cdgn 4E 57
Nebo. Cnwy 5H 81
Nebo. Gwyn 5D 81
Nebo. IOA 1D 80
Necton. Norf 5A 78
Nedd. High 5B 166
Nedderton. Nmbd 1F 115
Nedging. Suff 1D 54
Nedging Tye. Suff 1D 54
Needham. Norf 2E 67
Needham Market. Suff 5C 66
Needham Street. Suff 4G 65
Needingworth. Cambs 3C 64
Needwood. Staf 3F 73
Neen Savage. Shrp 3A 60
Neen Sollars. Shrp 3A 60
Neenton. Shrp 2A 60
Nefyn. Gwyn 1C 68
Neilston. E Ren 4F 127
Neithrop. Oxon 1C 50
Nelly Andrews Green.
Powy 5E 71
Nelson. Cphy 2E 32
Nelson. Lanc 1G 91
Nelson Village. Nmbd 2F 115
Nemphlar. S Lan 5B 128
Nempnett Thrubwell. Bath 5A 34
Nene Terrace. Linc 5B 76
Nenthall. Cumb 5A 114
Nenthead. Cumb 5A 114
Nenthorn. Bord 1A 120
Nercwys. Flin 4E 83
Neribus. Arg 4A 124
Nerston. S Lan 4H 127
Nesbit. Nmbd 1D 121
Nesfield. N Yor 5C 98
Ness. Ches W 3F 83
Nesscliffe. Shrp 4F 71
Ness of Tenston. Orkn 6B 172
Neston. Ches W 3E 83
Neston. Wilts 5D 34
Nethanfoot. S Lan 5B 128
Nether Alderley. Ches E 3C 84
Netheravon. Wilts 2G 23
Nether Blainslie. Bord 5B 130
Netherbrae. Abers 3E 161
Netherbrough. Orkn 6C 172
Nether Broughton. Leics 3D 74
Netherburn. S Lan 5B 128
Nether Burrow. Lanc 2F 97
Netherbury. Dors 3H 13
Netherby. Cumb 2E 113
Nether Careston. Ang 3E 145
Nether Cerne. Dors 3B 14
Nether Compton. Dors 1A 14
Nethercote. Glos 3G 49
Nethercote. Warw 4C 62
Nethercott. Devn 3E 19
Nethercott. Oxon 3C 50
Nether Dallachy. Mor 2A 160
Nether Durdie. Per 1E 136
Nether End. Derbs 3G 85
Netherend. Glos 5A 48
Nether Exe. Devn 2C 12
Netherfield. E Sus 4B 28
Netherfield. Notts 1D 74
Nethergate. Norf 3C 78
Netherhampton. Wilts 4G 23
Nether Handley. Derbs 3B 86
Nether Haugh. S Yor 1B 86
Nether Heage. Derbs 5A 86
Nether Heyford. Nptn 5D 62
Netherhouses. Cumb 1B 96
Nether Howcleugh. S Lan 3C 118
Nether Kellet. Lanc 3E 97
Nether Kinmundy. Abers 4H 161
Netherland Green. Staf 2F 73
Nether Langwith. Notts 3C 86
Netherlaw. Dum 5E 111
Netherley. Abers 4F 153
Nethermill. Dum 1B 112
Nethermills. Mor 3C 160
Nether Moor. Derbs 4A 86
Nether Padley. Derbs 3G 85
Netherplace. E Ren 4G 127
Nether Poppleton. York 4H 99
Netherseal. Derbs 4G 73
Nether Silton. N Yor 5B 106
Nether Stowey. Som 3E 21
Nether Street. Essx 4F 53
Netherstreet. Wilts 5E 35
Netherthird. E Ayr 3E 117
Netherthong. W Yor 4B 92
Netherton. Ang 3E 145
Netherton. Cumb 1B 102
Netherton. Devn 5B 12
Netherton. Hants 1B 24
Netherton. Here 3A 48
Netherton. Mers 1F 83
Netherton. N Lan 4A 128
Netherton. Nmbd 4D 121
Netherton. Per 3A 144
Netherton. Shrp 2B 60
Netherton. Stir 2G 127
Netherton. W Mid 2D 60
Netherton. W Yor
nr. Armitage Bridge 3B 92
nr. Horbury 3C 92
Netherton. Worc 1E 49
Nethertown. Cumb 4A 102
Nethertown. High 1F 169
Nethertown. Staf 4F 73
Nether Urquhart. Fife 3D 136
Nether Wallop. Hants 3B 24
Nether Wasdale. Cumb 4C 102
Nether Welton. Cumb 5E 113
Nether Westcote. Glos 3H 49
Nether Whitacre. Warw 1G 61
Nether Winchendon. Buck 4F 51
Netherwitton. Nmbd 5F 121
Nether Worton. Oxon 2C 50
Nethy Bridge. High 1E 151
Netley. Shrp 5G 71
Netley Abbey. Hants 2C 16
Netley Marsh. Hants 1B 16
Nettlebed. Oxon 3F 37
Nettlebridge. Som 2B 22
Nettlecombe. Dors 3A 14
Nettlecombe. IOW 5D 16
Nettleden. Herts 4A 52
Nettleham. Linc 3H 87
Nettlestead. Kent 5A 40
Nettlestead Green. Kent 5A 40
Nettlestone. IOW 3E 16
Nettlesworth. Dur 5F 115
Nettleton. Linc 4E 94
Nettleton. Wilts 4D 34
Netton. Devn 4B 8
Netton. Wilts 3G 23
Neuadd. Powy 5C 70
Neuk, The. Abers 4E 153
Nevendon. Essx 1B 40
Nevern. Pemb 1E 43
New Abbey. Dum 3A 112
New Aberdour. Abers 2F 161
New Addington. G Lon 4E 39
Newall. W Yor 5E 98
New Alresford. Hants 3D 24
New Alyth. Per 4B 144
Newark. Orkn 3G 172
Newark. Pet 5B 76
Newark-on-Trent. Notts 5E 87
New Arley. Warw 2G 61
Newarthill. N Lan 4A 128
New Ash Green. Kent 4H 39
New Balderton. Notts 5F 87
New Barn. Kent 4H 39
New Barnetby. N Lin 3D 94
Newbattle. Midl 3G 129
New Bewick. Nmbd 2E 121
Newbie. Dum 3C 112
Newbiggin. Cumb
nr. Appleby 2H 103
nr. Barrow-in-Furness 3B 96
nr. Cumrew 5G 113
nr. Penrith 2F 103
nr. Seascale 5B 102
Newbiggin. Dur
nr. Consett 5E 115
nr. Holwick 2C 104
Newbiggin. Nmbd 5C 114
Newbiggin. N Yor
nr. Askrigg 5C 104
nr. Filey 1F 101
nr. Thoralby 1B 98
Newbiggin-by-the-Sea.
Nmbd 1G 115
Newbigging. Ang
nr. Monikie 5D 145
nr. Newtyle 4B 144
nr. Tealing 5D 144
Newbigging. Edin 2E 129
Newbigging. S Lan 5D 128
Newbiggin-on-Lune.
Cumb 4A 104
Newbold. Derbs 3A 86
Newbold. Leics 4B 74
Newbold on Avon. Warw 3B 62
Newbold on Stour. Warw 1H 49
Newbold Pacey. Warw 5G 61
Newbold Verdon. Leics 5B 74
New Bolingbroke. Linc 5C 88
Newborough. IOA 4D 80
Newborough. Pet 5B 76
Newborough. Staf 3F 73
Newbottle. Nptn 2D 50
Newbottle. Tyne 4G 115
New Boultham. Linc 3G 87
Newbourne. Suff 1F 55
New Brancepeth. Dur 5F 115
Newbridge. Cphy 2F 33
Newbridge. Cdgn 5E 57
Newbridge. Corn 3B 4
New Bridge. Dum 2G 111
Newbridge. Edin 2E 129
Newbridge. Hants 1A 16
Newbridge. IOW 4C 16
Newbridge. N Yor 1C 100
Newbridge. Pemb 1D 42
Newbridge. Wrex 1E 71
Newbridge Green. Worc 2D 48
Newbridge-on-Usk. Mon 2G 33
Newbridge on Wye. Powy 5C 58
New Brighton. Flin 4E 83
New Brighton. Hants 2F 17
New Brighton. Mers 1F 83
New Brinsley. Notts 5B 86
Newbrough. Nmbd 3B 114
New Broughton. Wrex 5F 83
New Buckenham. Norf 1C 66
New Buildings. Derr 5A 174
Newbuildings. Devn 2A 12
Newburgh. Abers 1G 153
Newburgh. Fife 2E 137
Newburgh. Lanc 3C 90
Newburn. Tyne 3E 115
Newbury. W Ber 5C 36
Newbury. Wilts 2D 22
Newby. Cumb 2G 103
Newby. N Yor
nr. Ingleton 2G 97
nr. Scarborough 1E 101
nr. Stokesley 3C 106
Newby Bridge. Cumb 1C 96
Newby Cote. N Yor 2G 97
Newby East. Cumb 4F 113
Newby Head. Cumb 2G 103
New Byth. Abers 3F 161
Newby West. Cumb 4E 113
Newby Wiske. N Yor 1F 99
Newcastle. Ards 4L 179
Newcastle. B'end 3B 32
Newcastle. Mon 4H 47
Newcastle. New M 6H 179
Newcastle. Shrp 2E 59
Newcastle Emlyn. Carm 1D 44
Newcastle International Airport.
Tyne 2E 115
Newcastleton. Bord 1F 113
Newcastle-under-Lyme.
Staf 1C 72
Newcastle upon Tyne.
Tyne 197 (3F 115)
Newchapel. Pemb 1G 43
Newchapel. Powy 2B 58
Newchapel. Staf 5C 84
Newchapel. Surr 1E 27
New Cheriton. Hants 4D 24
Newchurch. Carm 3D 45
Newchurch. Here 5F 59
Newchurch. IOW 4D 16
Newchurch. Kent 2E 29
Newchurch. Lanc 2G 91
Newchurch. Mon 2H 33
Newchurch. Powy 5E 58
Newchurch. Staf 3F 73
Newchurch in Pendle.
Lanc 1G 91
New Costessey. Norf 4D 78
Newcott. Devn 2F 13
New Cowper. Cumb 5C 112

Newcraighall—Old Bridge of Tilt

Newcraighall. *Edin* 2G 129
New Crofton. *W Yor* 3D 93
New Cross. *Cdgn* 3F 57
New Cross. *Som* 1H 13
New Cumnock. *E Ayr* 3F 117
New Deer. *Abers* 4F 161
New Denham. *Buck* 2B 38
Newdigate. *Surr* 1C 26
New Duston. *Nptn* 4E 62
New Earswick. *York* 4A 100
New Edlington. *S Yor* 1C 86
New Elgin. *Mor* 2G 159
New Ellerby. *E Yor* 1E 95
Newell Green. *Brac* 4G 37
New Eltham. *G Lon* 3F 39
New End. *Warw* 4F 61
New End. *Worc* 5E 61
Newenden. *Kent* 3C 28
New England. *Essx* 1H 53
New England. *Pet* 5A 76
Newent. *Glos* 3C 48
New Ferry. *Mers* 2F 83
Newfield. *Dur*
nr. Chester-le-Street 4F 115
nr. Willington 1F 105
Newfound. *Hants* 1D 24
New Fryston. *W Yor* 2E 93
Newgale. *Pemb* 2C 42
New Galloway. *Dum* 2D 110
Newgate. *Norf* 1C 78
Newgate Street. *Herts* 5D 52
New Greens. *Herts* 5B 52
New Grimsby. *IOS* 1A 4
New Hainford. *Norf* 4E 78
Newhall. *Ches E* 1A 72
Newhall. *Derbs* 3G 73
Newham. *Nmbd* 2F 121
New Hartley. *Nmbd* 2G 115
Newhaven. *Derbs* 4F 85
Newhaven. *E Sus* 204 (5F 27)
Newhaven. *Edin* 2F 129
New Haw. *Surr* 4B 38
New Hedges. *Pemb* 4F 43
New Herrington. *Tyne* 4G 115
Newhey. *G Man* 3H 91
New Holkham. *Norf* 2A 78
New Holland. *N Lin* 2D 94
Newholm. *N Yor* 3F 107
New Houghton. *Derbs* 4C 86
New Houghton. *Norf* 3G 77
Newhouse. *N Lan* 3A 128
New Houses. *N Yor* 2H 97
New Hutton. *Cumb* 5G 103
New Hythe. *Kent* 5B 40
Newick. *E Sus* 3F 27
Newingreen. *Kent* 2F 29
Newington. *Edin* 2F 129
Newington. *Kent*
nr. Folkestone 2F 29
nr. Sittingbourne 4C 40
Newington. *Notts* 1D 86
Newington. *Oxon* 2E 36
Newington Bagpath. *Glos* 2D 34
New Inn. *Carm* 2E 45
New Inn. *Mon* 5H 47
New Inn. *N Yor* 2H 97
New Inn. *Torf* 2G 33
New Invention. *Shrp* 3E 59
New Kelso. *High* 4B 156
New Lanark. *S Lan* 5B 128
Newland. *Glos* 5A 48
Newland. *Hull* 1D 94
Newland. *N Yor* 2G 93
Newland. *Som* 3B 20
Newland. *Worc* 1C 48
Newlandrig. *Midl* 3G 129
Newlands. *Cumb* 1E 103
Newlands. *High* 4B 158
Newlands. *Nmbd* 4D 115
Newlands. *Staf* 3E 73
Newlands of Geise. *High* 2C 168
Newlands of Tynet. *Mor* 2A 160
Newlands Park. *IOA* 2B 80
New Lane. *Lanc* 3C 90
New Lane End. *Warr* 1A 84
New Langholm. *Dum* 1E 113
New Leake. *Linc* 5D 88
New Leeds. *Abers* 3G 161
New Lenton. *Nott* 2C 74
New Longton. *Lanc* 2D 90
Newlot. *Orkn* 6E 172
New Luce. *Dum* 3G 109
Newlyn. *Corn* 4B 4
Newmachar. *Abers* 2F 153
Newmains. *N Lan* 4B 128
New Mains of Ury. *Abers* 5F 153
New Malden. *G Lon* 4D 38
Newman's Green. *Suff* 1B 54
Newmarket. *Suff* 4F 65
Newmarket. *W Isl* 4G 171
New Marske. *Red C* 2D 106
New Marton. *Shrp* 2F 71
New Micklefield. *W Yor* 1E 93
New Mill. *Abers* 4E 160
Newmill. *Ant* 8J 175
New Mill. *Corn* 3B 4
New Mill. *Herts* 4H 51
Newmill. *Mor* 3B 160
Newmill. *Bord* 3G 119
New Mill. *W Yor* 4B 92
New Mill. *Wilts* 5G 35
Newmillerdam. *W Yor* 3D 92
Newmills. *Arm* 4E 178
New Mills. *Corn* 3C 6
New Mills. *Derbs* 2E 85
Newmills. *Fife* 1D 128
Newmills. *High* 2A 158
Newmills. *M Ulst* 3C 178
New Mills. *Mon* 5A 48
New Mills. *Powy* 5C 70
Newmiln. *Per* 5A 144
Newmilns. *E Ayr* 1E 117
New Milton. *Hants* 3H 15
New Mistley. *Essx* 2E 54
New Moat. *Pemb* 2E 43
Newmore. *High*
nr. Dingwall 3H 157
nr. Invergordon 1A 158
Newnham. *Cambs* 5D 64
Newnham. *Glos* 4B 48
Newnham. *Hants* 1F 25
Newnham. *Herts* 2C 52
Newnham. *Kent* 5D 40
Newnham. *Nptn* 5C 62
Newnham. *Warw* 4F 61
Newnham Bridge. *Worc* 4A 60
New Ollerton. *Notts* 4D 86
New Oscott. *W Mid* 1E 61
Newpark. *Fife* 2G 137
New Park. *N Yor* 4E 99
New Pitsligo. *Abers* 3F 161
New Polzeath. *Corn* 1D 6
Newport. *Corn* 4D 10
Newport. *Devn* 3F 19
Newport. *E Yor* 1B 94
Newport. *Essx* 2F 53
Newport. *Glos* 2B 34
Newport. *High* 1H 165
Newport. *IOW* 4D 16
Newport. *Newp* 200 (3G 33)
Newport. *Norf* 4H 79
Newport. *Pemb* 1E 43
Newport. *Som* 4G 21
Newport. *Telf* 4B 72
Newport-on-Tay. *Fife* 1G 137
Newport Pagnell. *Mil* 1G 51
Newpound Common. *W Sus* 3B 26
New Prestwick. *S Ayr* 2C 116
New Quay. *Cdgn* 5C 56
Newquay. *Corn* 2C 6
Newquay Cornwall Airport. *Corn* 2C 6
New Rackheath. *Norf* 4E 79
New Radnor. *Powy* 4E 58
New Rent. *Cumb* 1F 103
New Ridley. *Nmbd* 4D 114
New Romney. *Kent* 3E 29
New Rossington. *S Yor* 1D 86
New Row. *Cdgn* 3G 57
Newry. *New M* 7E 178
New Sauchie. *Clac* 4A 136
Newsbank. *Ches E* 4C 84
Newseat. *Abers* 5E 160
Newsham. *Lanc* 1D 90
Newsham. *Nmbd* 2G 115
Newsham. *N Yor*
nr. Richmond 3E 105
nr. Thirsk 1F 99
New Sharlston. *W Yor* 2D 93
Newsholme. *E Yor* 2H 93
Newsholme. *Lanc* 4H 97
New Shoreston. *Nmbd* 1F 121
New Springs. *G Man* 4D 90
Newstead. *Notts* 5C 86
Newstead. *Bord* 1H 119
New Stevenston. *N Lan* 4A 128
New Street. *Here* 5F 59
Newstreet Lane. *Shrp* 2A 72
New Swanage. *Dors* 4F 15
New Swannington. *Leics* 4B 74
Newthorpe. *N Yor* 1E 93
Newthorpe. *Notts* 1B 74
Newton. *Arg* 4H 133
Newton. *B'end* 4B 32
Newton. *Cambs*
nr. Cambridge 1E 53
nr. Wisbech 4D 76
Newton. *Ches W*
nr. Chester 4G 83
nr. Tattenhall 5H 83
Newton. *Cumb* 2B 96
Newton. *Derbs* 5B 86
Newton. *Dors* 1C 14
Newton. *Dum*
nr. Annan 2D 112
nr. Moffat 5D 118
Newton. *G Man* 1D 84
Newton. *Here*
nr. Ewyas Harold 2G 47
nr. Leominster 5H 59
Newton. *High*
nr. Cromarty 2B 158
nr. Inverness 4B 158
nr. Kylestrome 5C 166
nr. Wick 4F 169
Newton. *Lanc*
nr. Blackpool 1B 90
nr. Carnforth 2E 97
nr. Clitheroe 4F 97
Newton. *Linc* 2H 75
Newton. *Mers* 2E 83
Newton. *Mor* 2F 159
Newton. *Norf* 4H 77
Newton. *Nptn* 2F 63
Newton. *Nmbd* 3D 114
Newton. *Notts* 1D 74
Newton. *Bord* 2A 120
Newton. *Shet* 8E 173
Newton. *Shrp*
nr. Bridgnorth 1B 60
nr. Wem 2G 71
Newton. *Som* 3E 20
Newton. *S Lan*
nr. Glasgow 3H 127
nr. Lanark 1B 118
Newton. *Staf* 3E 73
Newton. *Suff* 1C 54
Newton. *Swan* 4F 31
Newton. *Warw* 3C 62
Newton. *W Lot* 2D 129
Newton. *Wilts* 4H 23
Newton Abbot. *Devn* 5B 12
Newtonairds. *Dum* 1F 111
Newton Arlosh. *Cumb* 4D 112
Newton Aycliffe. *Dur* 2F 105
Newton Bewley. *Hart* 2B 106
Newton Blossomville. *Mil* 5G 63
Newton Bromswold. *Nptn* 4G 63
Newton Burgoland. *Leics* 5A 74
Newton by Toft. *Linc* 2H 87
Newton Ferrers. *Devn* 4B 8
Newton Flotman. *Norf* 1E 66
Newtongrange. *Midl* 3G 129
Newton Green. *Mon* 2A 34
Newton Hall. *Dur* 5F 115
Newton Hall. *Nmbd* 3D 114
Newton Harcourt. *Leics* 1D 62
Newton Heath. *G Man* 4G 91
Newtonhill. *Abers* 4G 153
Newtonhill. *High* 4H 157
Newton Hill. *W Yor* 2D 92
Newton Ketton. *Darl* 2A 106
Newton Kyme. *N Yor* 5G 99
Newton-le-Willows. *Mers* 1H 83
Newton-le-Willows. *N Yor* 1E 98
Newton Longville. *Buck* 2G 51
Newton Mearns. *E Ren* 4G 127
Newtonmore. *High* 4B 150
Newton Morrell. *N Yor* 4F 105
Newton Mulgrave. *N Yor* 3E 107
Newton of Ardtoe. *High* 1A 140
Newton of Balcanquhal. *Per* 2D 136
Newton of Beltrees. *Ren* 4E 127
Newton of Falkland. *Fife* 3E 137
Newton of Mountblairy. *Abers* 3D 160
Newton of Pitcairns. *Per* 2C 136
Newton-on-Ouse. *N Yor* 4H 99
Newton-on-Rawcliffe. *N Yor* 5F 107
Newton on the Hill. *Shrp* 3G 71
Newton-on-the-Moor. *Nmbd* 4F 121
Newton on Trent. *Linc* 3F 87
Newton Poppleford. *Devn* 4D 12
Newton Purcell. *Oxon* 2E 51
Newton Regis. *Warw* 5G 73
Newton Reigny. *Cumb* 1F 103
Newton Rigg. *Cumb* 1F 103
Newton St Cyres. *Devn* 3B 12
Newton St Faith. *Norf* 4E 78
Newton St Loe. *Bath* 5C 34
Newton St Petrock. *Devn* 1E 11
Newton Solney. *Derbs* 3G 73
Newton Stacey. *Hants* 2C 24
Newton Stewart. *Dum* 3B 110
Newton Toney. *Wilts* 2H 23
Newton Tony. *Wilts* 2H 23
Newton Tracey. *Devn* 4F 19
Newton under Roseberry. *Red C* 3C 106
Newton upon Ayr. *S Ayr* 2C 116
Newton upon Derwent. *E Yor* 5B 100
Newton Valence. *Hants* 3F 25
Newton-with-Scales. *Lanc* 1C 90
Newtown. *Abers* 2E 160
Newtown. *Cambs* 4H 63
Newtown. *Corn* 5C 10
Newtown. *Cumb*
nr. Aspatria 5B 112
nr. Brampton 3G 113
nr. Penrith 2G 103
Newtown. *Derbs* 2D 85
Newtown. *Devn* 4A 20
New Town. *Dors* 1E 15
Newtown. *Dors* 2H 13
New Town. *E Lot* 2H 129
Newtown. *Falk* 1C 128
Newtown. *Glos*
nr. Lydney 5B 48
nr. Tewkesbury 2E 49
Newtown. *Hants*
nr. Bishop's Waltham 1D 16
nr. Liphook 3G 25
nr. Lyndhurst 1A 16
nr. Newbury 5C 36
nr. Romsey 4B 24
nr. Warsash 2C 16
nr. Wickham 1E 16
Newtown. *Here*
nr. Little Dewchurch 2A 48
nr. Stretton Grandison 1B 48
Newtown. *High* 3F 149
Newtown. *IOM* 4C 108
Newtown. *IOW* 3C 16
Newtown. *Lanc* 3D 90
New Town. *Lutn* 3A 52
Newtown. *Nmbd*
nr. Rothbury 4E 121
nr. Wooler 2E 121
Newtown. *Pool* 3F 15
Newtown. *Powy* 1D 58
Newtown. *Rhon* 2D 32
Newtown. *Shet* 3F 173
Newtown. *Shrp* 2G 71
Newtown. *Som* 1F 13
Newtown. *Staf*
nr. Biddulph 4D 84
nr. Cannock 5D 73
nr. Longnor 4E 85
New Town. *W Yor* 2E 93
Newtown. *Wilts* 4E 23
Newtownabbey. *Ant* 1H 179
Newtownards. *Ards* 2J 179
Newtownbutler. *Ferm* 7K 177
Newtown-Crommelin. *ME Ant* 5H 175
Newtownhamilton. *New M* 7D 178
Newtown-in-St Martin. *Corn* 4E 5
Newtown Linford. *Leics* 5C 74
Newtown St Boswells. *Bord* 1H 119
Newtownstewart. *Derr* 8A 174
Newtown Unthank. *Leics* 5B 74
New Tredegar. *Cphy* 5E 47
Newtyle. *Ang* 4B 144
New Village. *E Yor* 1D 94
New Village. *S Yor* 4F 93
New Walsoken. *Cambs* 5D 76
New Waltham. *NE Lin* 4F 95
New Winton. *E Lot* 2H 129
New World. *Cambs* 1C 64
New Yatt. *Oxon* 4B 50
Newyears Green. *G Lon* 2B 38
New York. *Linc* 5B 88
New York. *Tyne* 2G 115
Nextend. *Here* 5F 59
Neyland. *Pemb* 4D 42
Nib Heath. *Shrp* 4G 71
Nicholashayne. *Devn* 1E 12
Nicholaston. *Swan* 4E 31
Nidd. *N Yor* 3F 99
Niddrie. *Edin* 2G 129
Niddry. *W Lot* 2D 129
Nigg. *Aber* 3G 153
Nigg. *High* 1C 158
Nigg Ferry. *High* 2B 158
Nightcott. *Som* 4B 20
Nimmer. *Som* 1G 13
Nine Ashes. *Essx* 5F 53
Ninebanks. *Nmbd* 4A 114
Nine Elms. *Swin* 3G 35
Ninemile Bar. *Dum* 2F 111
Nine Mile Burn. *Midl* 4E 129
Ninfield. *E Sus* 4B 28
Ningwood. *IOW* 4C 16
Nisbet. *Bord* 2A 120
Nisbet Hill. *Bord* 4D 130
Niton. *IOW* 5D 16
Nitshill. *Glas* 3G 127
Niwbwrch. *IOA* 4D 80
Nixon's Corner. *Derr* 5A 174
Noak Hill. *G Lon* 1G 39
Nobold. *Shrp* 4G 71
Nobottle. *Nptn* 4D 62
Nocton. *Linc* 4H 87
Nogdam End. *Norf* 5F 79
Noke. *Oxon* 4D 50
Nolton. *Pemb* 3C 42
Nolton Haven. *Pemb* 3C 42
No Man's Heath. *Ches W* 1H 71
No Man's Heath. *Warw* 5G 73
Nomansland. *Devn* 1B 12
Nomansland. *Wilts* 1A 16
Noneley. *Shrp* 3G 71
Noness. *Shet* 9F 173
Nonikiln. *High* 1A 158
Nonington. *Kent* 5G 41
Nook. *Cumb*
nr. Longtown 2F 113
nr. Milnthorpe 1E 97
Noranside. *Ang* 2D 144
Norbreck. *Bkpl* 5C 96
Norbridge. *Here* 1C 48
Norbury. *Ches E* 1H 71
Norbury. *Derbs* 1F 73
Norbury. *Shrp* 1F 59
Norbury. *Staf* 3B 72
Norby. *N Yor* 1G 99
Norby. *Shet* 6C 173
Norcross. *Lanc* 5C 96
Nordelph. *Norf* 5E 77
Norden. *G Man* 3G 91
Nordley. *Shrp* 1A 60
Norham. *Nmbd* 5F 131
Norland Town. *W Yor* 2A 92
Norley. *Ches W* 3H 83
Norleywood. *Hants* 3B 16
Normanby. *N Lin* 3B 94
Normanby. *N Yor* 1B 100
Normanby. *Red C* 3C 106
Normanby-by-Spital. *Linc* 2H 87
Normanby le Wold. *Linc* 1A 88
Norman Cross. *Cambs* 1A 64
Normandy. *Surr* 5A 38
Norman's Bay. *E Sus* 5A 28
Norman's Green. *Devn* 2D 12
Normanton. *Derb* 2H 73
Normanton. *Leics* 1F 75
Normanton. *Notts* 5E 86
Normanton. *W Yor* 2D 93
Normanton le Heath. *Leics* 4A 74
Normanton-on-Cliffe. *Linc* 1G 75
Normanton on Soar. *Notts* 3C 74
Normanton-on-the-Wolds. *Notts* 2D 74
Normanton on Trent. *Notts* 4E 87
Normoss. *Lanc* 1B 90
Norrington Common. *Wilts* 5D 35
Norris Green. *Mers* 1F 83
Norris Hill. *Leics* 4H 73
Norristhorpe. *W Yor* 2C 92
Northacre. *Norf* 1B 66
Northall. *Buck* 3H 51
Northallerton. *N Yor* 5A 106
Northam. *Devn* 4E 19
Northam. *Sotn* 1C 16
Northampton. *Nptn* 200 (4E 63)
North Anston. *S Yor* 2C 86
North Ascot. *Brac* 4A 38
North Aston. *Oxon* 3C 50
Northaw. *Herts* 5C 52
Northay. *Som* 1F 13
North Baddesley. *Hants* 4B 24
North Balfern. *Dum* 4B 110
North Ballachulish. *High* 2E 141
North Barrow. *Som* 4B 22
North Barsham. *Norf* 2B 78
Northbeck. *Linc* 1H 75
North Benfleet. *Essx* 2B 40
North Bersted. *W Sus* 5A 26
North Berwick. *E Lot* 1B 130
North Bitchburn. *Dur* 1E 105
North Blyth. *Nmbd* 1G 115
North Boarhunt. *Hants* 1E 16
North Bockhampton. *Dors* 3G 15
Northborough. *Pet* 5A 76
Northbourne. *Kent* 5H 41
Northbourne. *Oxon* 3D 36
North Bovey. *Devn* 4H 11
North Bowood. *Dors* 3H 13
North Bradley. *Wilts* 1D 22
North Brentor. *Devn* 4E 11
North Brewham. *Som* 3C 22
Northbrook. *Oxon* 3C 50
North Brook End. *Cambs* 1C 52
North Broomhill. *Nmbd* 4G 121
North Buckland. *Devn* 2E 19
North Burlingham. *Norf* 4F 79
North Cadbury. *Som* 4B 22
North Carlton. *Linc* 3G 87
North Cave. *E Yor* 1B 94
North Cerney. *Glos* 5F 49
North Chailey. *E Sus* 3E 27
Northchapel. *W Sus* 3A 26
North Charford. *Hants* 1G 15
North Charlton. *Nmbd* 2F 121
North Cheriton. *Som* 4B 22
North Chideock. *Dors* 3H 13
Northchurch. *Herts* 5H 51
North Cliffe. *E Yor* 1B 94
North Clifton. *Notts* 3F 87
North Close. *Dur* 1F 105
North Cockerington. *Linc* 1C 88
North Coker. *Som* 1A 14
North Collafirth. *Shet* 3E 173
North Common. *E Sus* 3E 27
North Commonty. *Abers* 4F 161
North Coombe. *Devn* 1B 12
North Cornelly. *B'end* 3B 32
North Cotes. *Linc* 4G 95
Northcott. *Devn*
nr. Boyton 3D 10
nr. Culmstock 1D 12
Northcourt. *Oxon* 2D 36
North Cove. *Suff* 2G 67
North Cowton. *N Yor* 4F 105
North Craigo. *Ang* 2F 145
North Crawley. *Mil* 1H 51
North Cray. *G Lon* 3F 39
North Creake. *Norf* 2A 78
North Curry. *Som* 4G 21
North Dalton. *E Yor* 4D 100
North Deighton. *N Yor* 4F 99
North Dronley. *Ang* 5C 144
North Duffield. *N Yor* 1G 93
Northdyke. *Orkn* 5B 172
Northedge. *Derbs* 4A 86
North Elkington. *Linc* 1B 88
North Elmham. *Norf* 3B 78
North Elmsall. *W Yor* 3E 93
Northend. *Buck* 2F 37
North End. *E Yor* 1F 95
North End. *Essx*
nr. Great Dunmow 4G 53
nr. Great Yeldham 2A 54
North End. *Hants* 5C 36
North End. *Leics* 4C 74
North End. *Linc* 1B 76
North End. *Norf* 1B 66
North End. *N Som* 5H 33
North End. *Port* 2E 17
Northend. *Warw* 5A 62
North End. *W Sus* 5C 26
North End. *Wilts* 2F 35
North Erradale. *High* 5B 162
North Evington. *Leic* 5D 74
North Fambridge. *Essx* 1C 40
North Fearns. *High* 5E 155
North Featherstone. *W Yor* 2E 93
North Feorline. *N Ayr* 3D 122
North Ferriby. *E Yor* 2C 94
Northfield. *Aber* 3F 153
Northfield. *E Yor* 2D 94
Northfield. *Som* 3F 21
Northfield. *W Mid* 3E 61
Northfleet. *Kent* 3H 39
North Frodingham. *E Yor* 4F 101
Northgate. *Linc* 3A 76
North Gluss. *Shet* 4E 173
North Gorley. *Hants* 1G 15
North Green. *Norf* 2E 66
North Green. *Suff*
nr. Framlingham 4F 67
nr. Halesworth 3F 67
nr. Saxmundham 4F 67
North Greetwell. *Linc* 3H 87
North Grimston. *N Yor* 3C 100
North Halling. *Medw* 4B 40
North Hayling. *Hants* 2F 17
North Hazelrigg. *Nmbd* 1E 121
North Heasley. *Devn* 3H 19
North Heath. *W Sus* 3B 26
North Hill. *Corn* 5C 10
North Holmwood. *Surr* 1C 26
North Huish. *Devn* 3D 8
North Hykeham. *Linc* 4G 87
Northiam. *E Sus* 3C 28
Northill. *C Beds* 1B 52
Northington. *Hants* 3D 24
North Kelsey. *Linc* 4D 94
North Kelsey Moor. *Linc* 4D 94
North Kessock. *High* 4A 158
North Killingholme. *N Lin* 3E 95
North Kilvington. *N Yor* 1G 99
North Kilworth. *Leics* 2D 62
North Kyme. *Linc* 5A 88
North Lancing. *W Sus* 5C 26
Northlands. *Linc* 5C 88
Northleach. *Glos* 4G 49
North Lee. *Buck* 5G 51
North Lees. *N Yor* 2E 99
Northleigh. *Devn*
nr. Barnstaple 3G 19
nr. Honiton 3E 13
North Leigh. *Kent* 1F 29
North Leigh. *Oxon* 4B 50
North Leverton. *Notts* 2E 87
Northlew. *Devn* 3F 11
North Littleton. *Worc* 1F 49
North Lopham. *Norf* 2C 66
North Luffenham. *Rut* 5G 75
North Marden. *W Sus* 1G 17
North Marston. *Buck* 3F 51
North Middleton. *Midl* 4G 129
North Middleton. *Nmbd* 2E 121
North Molton. *Devn* 4H 19
North Moor. *N Yor* 1D 100
Northmoor. *Oxon* 5C 50
Northmoor Green. *Som* 3G 21
North Moreton. *Oxon* 3D 36
Northmuir. *Ang* 3C 144
North Mundham. *W Sus* 2G 17
North Murie. *Per* 1E 137
North Muskham. *Notts* 5E 87
North Ness. *Orkn* 8C 172
North Newbald. *E Yor* 1C 94
North Newington. *Oxon* 2C 50
North Newnton. *Wilts* 1G 23
North Newton. *Som* 3F 21
Northney. *Hants* 2F 17
North Nibley. *Glos* 2C 34
North Oakley. *Hants* 1D 24
North Ockendon. *G Lon* 2G 39
Northolt. *G Lon* 2C 38
Northop. *Flin* 4E 83
Northop Hall. *Flin* 4E 83
North Ormesby. *Midd* 3C 106
North Ormsby. *Linc* 1B 88
Northorpe. *Linc*
nr. Bourne 4H 75
nr. Donington 2B 76
nr. Gainsborough 1F 87
North Otterington. *N Yor* 1F 99
Northover. *Som*
nr. Glastonbury 3H 21
nr. Yeovil 4A 22
North Owersby. *Linc* 1H 87
Northowram. *W Yor* 2B 92
North Perrott. *Som* 2H 13
North Petherton. *Som* 3F 21
North Petherwin. *Corn* 4C 10
North Pickenham. *Norf* 5A 78
North Piddle. *Worc* 5D 60
North Poorton. *Dors* 3A 14
North Port. *Arg* 1H 133
Northport. *Dors* 4E 15
North Queensferry. *Fife* 1E 129
North Radworthy. *Devn* 3A 20
North Rauceby. *Linc* 1H 75
Northrepps. *Norf* 2E 79
North Rigton. *N Yor* 5E 99
North Rode. *Ches E* 4C 84
North Roe. *Shet* 3E 173
North Ronaldsay Airport. *Orkn* 2G 172
North Row. *Cumb* 1D 102
North Runcton. *Norf* 4F 77
North Sannox. *N Ayr* 5B 126
North Scale. *Cumb* 2A 96
North Scarle. *Linc* 4F 87
North Seaton. *Nmbd* 1F 115
North Seaton Colliery. *Nmbd* 1F 115
North Sheen. *G Lon* 3C 38
North Shian. *Arg* 4D 140
North Shields. *Tyne* 3G 115
North Shoebury. *S'end* 2D 40
North Shore. *Bkpl* 1B 90
North Side. *Cumb* 2B 102
North Skelton. *Red C* 3D 106
North Somercotes. *Linc* 1D 88
North Stainley. *N Yor* 2E 99
North Stainmore. *Cumb* 3B 104
North Stifford. *Thur* 2H 39
North Stoke. *Bath* 5C 34
North Stoke. *Oxon* 3E 36
North Stoke. *W Sus* 4B 26
Northstowe. *Cambs* 4D 64
North Street. *Hants* 3E 25
North Street. *Kent* 5E 40
North Street. *Medw* 3C 40
North Street. *W Ber* 4E 37
North Sunderland. *Nmbd* 1G 121
North Tamerton. *Corn* 3D 10
North Tawton. *Devn* 2G 11
North Thoresby. *Linc* 1B 88
North Tidworth. *Wilts* 2H 23
North Town. *Devn* 2F 11
Northtown. *Orkn* 8D 172
North Town. *Shet* 10E 173
North Tuddenham. *Norf* 4C 78
North Walbottle. *Tyne* 3E 115
Northwall. *Orkn* 3G 172
North Walney. *Cumb* 3A 96
North Walsham. *Norf* 2E 79
North Waltham. *Hants* 2D 24
North Warnborough. *Hants* 1F 25
North Water Bridge. *Ang* 2F 145
North Watten. *High* 3E 169
Northway. *Glos* 2E 49
Northway. *Swan* 4E 31
North Weald Bassett. *Essx* 5F 53
North Weston. *N Som* 4H 33
North Weston. *Oxon* 5E 51
North Wheatley. *Notts* 2E 87
North Whilborough. *Devn* 2E 9
Northwich. *Ches W* 3A 84
North Wick. *Bath* 5A 34
Northwick. *Som* 2G 21
Northwick. *S Glo* 3A 34
North Widcombe. *Bath* 1A 22
North Willingham. *Linc* 2A 88
North Wingfield. *Derbs* 4B 86
North Witham. *Linc* 3G 75
Northwold. *Norf* 1G 65
Northwood. *Derbs* 4G 85
Northwood. *G Lon* 1B 38
Northwood. *IOW* 3C 16
Northwood. *Kent* 4H 41
Northwood. *Shrp* 2G 71
Northwood. *Stoke* 1C 72
Northwood Green. *Glos* 4C 48
North Wootton. *Dors* 1B 14
North Wootton. *Norf* 3F 77
North Wootton. *Som* 2A 22
North Wraxall. *Wilts* 4D 34
North Wroughton. *Swin* 3G 35
North Yardhope. *Nmbd* 4D 120
Norton. *Devn* 3E 9
Norton. *Glos* 3D 48
Norton. *Hal* 2H 83
Norton. *Herts* 2C 52
Norton. *IOW* 4B 16
Norton. *Mon* 3H 47
Norton. *Nptn* 4D 62
Norton. *Notts* 3C 86
Norton. *Powy* 4F 59
Norton. *Shrp*
nr. Ludlow 2G 59
nr. Madeley 5B 72
nr. Shrewsbury 5H 71
Norton. *S Yor*
nr. Askern 3F 93
nr. Sheffield 2A 86
Norton. *Stoc T* 2B 106
Norton. *Suff* 4B 66
Norton. *Swan* 4F 31
Norton. *W Sus*
nr. Selsey 3G 17
nr. Westergate 5A 26
Norton. *Wilts* 3D 35
Norton. *Worc*
nr. Evesham 1F 49
nr. Worcester 5C 60
Norton Bavant. *Wilts* 2E 23
Norton Bridge. *Staf* 2C 72
Norton Canes. *Staf* 5E 73
Norton Canon. *Here* 1G 47
Norton Corner. *Norf* 3C 78
Norton Disney. *Linc* 5F 87
Norton East. *Staf* 5E 73
Norton Ferris. *Wilts* 3C 22
Norton Fitzwarren. *Som* 4E 21
Norton Green. *IOW* 4B 16
Norton Green. *Stoke* 5D 84
Norton Hawkfield. *Bath* 5A 34
Norton Heath. *Essx* 5F 53
Norton in Hales. *Shrp* 2B 72
Norton in the Moors. *Stoke* 5C 84
Norton-Juxta-Twycross. *Leics* 5H 73
Norton-le-Clay. *N Yor* 2G 99
Norton Lindsey. *Warw* 4G 61
Norton Little Green. *Suff* 4B 66
Norton Malreward. *Bath* 5B 34
Norton Mandeville. *Essx* 5F 53
Norton-on-Derwent. *N Yor* 2B 100
Norton St Philip. *Som* 1C 22
Norton Subcourse. *Norf* 1G 67
Norton sub Hamdon. *Som* 1H 13
Norton Woodseats. *S Yor* 2A 86
Norwell. *Notts* 4E 87
Norwell Woodhouse. *Notts* 4E 87
Norwich. *Norf* 200 (5E 79)
Norwich Airport. *Norf* 4E 79
Norwick. *Shet* 1H 173
Norwood. *Derbs* 2B 86
Norwood Green. *W Yor* 2B 92
Norwood Hill. *Surr* 1D 26
Norwood Park. *Som* 3A 22
Norwoodside. *Cambs* 1D 64
Noseley. *Leics* 1E 63
Noss. *Shet* 10E 173
Noss Mayo. *Devn* 4B 8
Nosterfield. *N Yor* 1E 99
Nostie. *High* 1A 148
Notgrove. *Glos* 3G 49
Nottage. *B'end* 4B 32
Nottingham. *Nott* 200 (1C 74)
Nottington. *Dors* 4B 14
Notton. *Dors* 3B 14
Notton. *W Yor* 3D 92
Notton. *Wilts* 5E 35
Nounsley. *Essx* 4A 54
Noutard's Green. *Worc* 4B 60
Nox. *Shrp* 4G 71
Noyadd Trefawr. *Cdgn* 1C 44
Nuffield. *Oxon* 3E 37
Nunburnholme. *E Yor* 5C 100
Nuncargate. *Notts* 5C 86
Nunclose. *Cumb* 5F 113
Nuneaton. *Warw* 1A 62
Nuneham Courtenay. *Oxon* 2D 36
Nun Monkton. *N Yor* 4H 99
Nunnerie. *S Lan* 3B 118
Nunney. *Som* 2C 22
Nunnington. *N Yor* 2A 100
Nunnykirk. *Nmbd* 5E 121
Nunsthorpe. *NE Lin* 4F 95
Nunthorpe. *Midd* 3C 106
Nunthorpe. *York* 4H 99
Nunton. *Wilts* 4G 23
Nunwick. *Nmbd* 2B 114
Nunwick. *N Yor* 2F 99
Nupend. *Glos* 5C 48
Nursling. *Hants* 1B 16
Nursted. *Hants* 4F 25
Nursteed. *Wilts* 5F 35
Nurston. *V Glam* 5D 32
Nutbourne. *W Sus*
nr. Chichester 2F 17
nr. Pulborough 4B 26
Nutfield. *Surr* 5E 39
Nuthall. *Notts* 1C 74
Nuthampstead. *Herts* 2E 53
Nuthurst. *Warw* 3F 61
Nuthurst. *W Sus* 3C 26
Nutley. *E Sus* 3F 27
Nuttall. *G Man* 3F 91
Nutwell. *S Yor* 4G 93
Nybster. *High* 2F 169
Nyetimber. *W Sus* 3G 17
Nyewood. *W Sus* 4G 25
Nymet Rowland. *Devn* 2H 11
Nymet Tracey. *Devn* 2H 11
Nympsfield. *Glos* 5D 48
Nynehead. *Som* 4E 21
Nyton. *W Sus* 5A 26

O

Oadby. *Leics* 5D 74
Oad Street. *Kent* 4C 40
Oakamoor. *Staf* 1E 73
Oakbank. *Arg* 5B 140
Oakbank. *W Lot* 3D 129
Oakdale. *Cphy* 2E 33
Oakdale. *Pool* 3F 15
Oake. *Som* 4E 21
Oaken. *Staf* 5C 72
Oakenclough. *Lanc* 5E 97
Oakengates. *Telf* 4A 72
Oakenholt. *Flin* 3E 83
Oakenshaw. *Dur* 1F 105
Oakenshaw. *W Yor* 2B 92
Oakerthorpe. *Derbs* 5A 86
Oakford. *Cdgn* 5D 56
Oakford. *Devn* 4C 20
Oakfordbridge. *Devn* 4C 20
Oakgrove. *Ches E* 4D 84
Oakham. *Rut* 5F 75
Oakhanger. *Ches E* 5B 84
Oakhanger. *Hants* 3F 25
Oakhill. *Som* 2B 22
Oakington. *Cambs* 4D 64
Oaklands. *Powy* 5C 58
Oakle Street. *Glos* 4C 48
Oakley. *Bed* 5H 63
Oakley. *Buck* 4E 51
Oakley. *Fife* 1D 128
Oakley. *Hants* 1D 24
Oakley. *Suff* 3D 66
Oakley Green. *Wind* 3A 38
Oakley Park. *Powy* 2B 58
Oakmere. *Ches W* 4H 83
Oakridge Lynch. *Glos* 5E 49
Oaks. *Shrp* 5G 71
Oaksey. *Wilts* 2E 35
Oaks Green. *Derbs* 2F 73
Oakshaw Ford. *Cumb* 2G 113
Oakshott. *Hants* 4F 25
Oakthorpe. *Leics* 4H 73
Oak Tree. *Darl* 3A 106
Oakwood. *Derb* 2A 74
Oakwood. *W Yor* 1D 92
Oakwoodhill. *Surr* 2C 26
Oakworth. *W Yor* 1A 92
Oape. *High* 3B 164
Oare. *Kent* 4E 40
Oare. *Som* 2B 20
Oare. *W Ber* 4D 36
Oare. *Wilts* 5G 35
Oareford. *Som* 2B 20
Oasby. *Linc* 2H 75
Oath. *Som* 4G 21
Oathlaw. *Ang* 3D 145
Oatlands. *N Yor* 4F 99
Oban. *Arg* 201 (1F 133)
Oban. *W Isl* 7D 171
Oborne. *Dors* 1B 14
Obsdale. *High* 2A 158
Obthorpe. *Linc* 4H 75
Occlestone Green. *Ches W* 4A 84
Occold. *Suff* 3D 66
Ochiltree. *E Ayr* 2E 117
Ochtermuthill. *Per* 2H 135
Ochtertyre. *Per* 1H 135
Ockbrook. *Derbs* 2B 74
Ockeridge. *Worc* 4B 60
Ockham. *Surr* 5B 38
Ockle. *High* 1G 139
Ockley. *Surr* 1C 26
Ocle Pychard. *Here* 1A 48
Octofad. *Arg* 4A 124
Octomore. *Arg* 4A 124
Octon. *E Yor* 3E 101
Odcombe. *Som* 1A 14
Odd Down. *Bath* 5C 34
Oddingley. *Worc* 5D 60
Oddington. *Oxon* 4D 50
Oddsta. *Shet* 2G 173
Odell. *Bed* 5G 63
Odie. *Orkn* 5F 172
Odiham. *Hants* 1F 25
Odsey. *Cambs* 2C 52
Odstock. *Wilts* 4G 23
Odstone. *Leics* 5A 74
Offchurch. *Warw* 4A 62
Offenham. *Worc* 1F 49
Offenham Cross. *Worc* 1F 49
Offerton. *G Man* 2D 84
Offerton. *Tyne* 4G 115
Offham. *E Sus* 4E 27
Offham. *Kent* 5A 40
Offham. *W Sus* 5B 26
Offleyhay. *Staf* 3C 72
Offley Hoo. *Herts* 3B 52
Offleymarsh. *Staf* 3B 72
Offord Cluny. *Cambs* 4B 64
Offord D'Arcy. *Cambs* 4B 64
Offton. *Suff* 1D 54
Offwell. *Devn* 3E 13
Ogbourne Maizey. *Wilts* 4G 35
Ogbourne St Andrew. *Wilts* 4G 35
Ogbourne St George. *Wilts* 4H 35
Ogden. *G Man* 3H 91
Ogle. *Nmbd* 2E 115
Ogmore. *V Glam* 4B 32
Ogmore-by-Sea. *V Glam* 4B 32
Ogmore Vale. *B'end* 2C 32
Okeford Fitzpaine. *Dors* 1D 14
Okehampton. *Devn* 3F 11
Okehampton Camp. *Devn* 3F 11
Okraquoy. *Shet* 8F 173
Okus. *Swin* 3G 35
Old. *Nptn* 3E 63
Old Aberdeen. *Aber* 3G 153
Old Alresford. *Hants* 3D 24
Oldany. *High* 5B 166
Old Arley. *Warw* 1G 61
Old Basford. *Nott* 1C 74
Old Basing. *Hants* 1E 25
Oldberrow. *Warw* 4F 61
Old Bewick. *Nmbd* 2E 121
Old Bexley. *G Lon* 3F 39
Old Blair. *Per* 2F 143
Old Bolingbroke. *Linc* 4C 88
Oldborough. *Devn* 2A 12
Old Brampton. *Derbs* 3H 85
Old Bridge of Tilt. *Per* 2F 143

Old Bridge of Urr—Perrott's Brook

Old Bridge of Urr. Dum 3E 111
Old Brumby. N Lin 4B 94
Old Buckenham. Norf 1C 66
Old Burghclere. Hants 1C 24
Oldbury. Shrp 1B 60
Oldbury. Warw 1H 61
Oldbury. W Mid 2D 61
Oldbury-on-Severn. S Glo 2B 34
Oldbury on the Hill. Glos 3D 34
Old Byland. N Yor 1H 99
Old Cassop. Dur 1A 106
Oldcastle. Mon 3G 47
Oldcastle Heath. Ches W 1G 71
Old Catton. Norf 4E 79
Old Clee. NE Lin 4F 95
Old Cleeve. Som 2D 20
Old Colwyn. Cnwy 3A 82
Oldcotes. Notts 2C 86
Old Coulsdon. G Lon 5E 39
Old Dailly. S Ayr 5B 116
Old Dalby. Leics 3D 74
Old Dam. Derbs 3F 85
Old Deer. Abers 4G 161
Old Dilton. Wilts 2D 22
Old Down. S Glo 3B 34
Oldeamere. Cambs 1C 64
Old Edlington. S Yor 1C 86
Old Eldon. Dur 2F 105
Old Ellerby. E Yor 1E 95
Old Fallings. W Mid 5D 72
Oldfallow. Staf 4D 73
Old Felixstowe. Suff 2G 55
Oldfield. Shrp 2A 60
Oldfield. Worc 4C 60
Old Fletton. Pet 1A 64
Oldford. Som 1C 22
Old Forge. Here 4A 48
Old Glossop. Derbs 1E 85
Old Goole. E Yor 2H 93
Old Gore. Here 3B 48
Old Graitney. Dum 3E 112
Old Grimsby. IOS 1A 4
Oldhall. High 3E 169
Old Hall Street. Norf 2F 79
Oldham. G Man 4H 91
Oldhamstocks. E Lot 2D 130
Old Heathfield. E Sus 3G 27
Old Hill. W Mid 2D 60
Old Hunstanton. Norf 1F 77
Oldhurst. Cambs 3B 64
Old Hutton. Cumb 1E 97
Old Kea. Corn 4C 6
Old Kilpatrick. W Dun 2F 127
Old Kinnernie. Abers 3E 152
Old Knebworth. Herts 3C 52
Oldland. S Glo 4B 34
Old Laxey. IOM 3D 108
Old Leake. Linc 5D 88
Old Lenton. Nott 2C 74
Old Llanberis. Gwyn 5F 81
Old Malton. N Yor 2B 100
Oldmeldrum. Abers 1F 153
Old Micklefield. W Yor 1E 93
Old Mill. Corn 5D 10
Oldmixon. N Som 1G 21
Old Monkland. N Lan 3A 128
Old Newton. Suff 4C 66
Old Park. Telf 5A 72
Old Pentland. Midl 3F 129
Old Philpstoun. W Lot 2D 128
Old Quarrington. Dur 1A 106
Old Radnor. Powy 5E 59
Old Rayne. Abers 1D 152
Oldridge. Devn 3B 12
Old Romney. Kent 3E 29
Old Scone. Per 1D 136
Oldshore Beg. High 3B 166
Oldshoremore. High 3C 166
Old Snydale. W Yor 2E 93
Old Sodbury. S Glo 3C 34
Old Somerby. Linc 2G 75
Old Spital. Dur 3C 104
Oldstead. N Yor 1H 99
Old Stratford. Nptn 1F 51
Old Swan. Mers 1F 83
Old Swarland. Nmbd 4F 121
Old Tebay. Cumb 4H 103
Old Town. Cumb 5F 113
Old Town. E Sus 5G 27
Oldtown. High 5C 164
Old Town. IOS 1B 4
Old Town. Nmbd 5C 120
Old Trafford. G Man 1C 84
Old Tupton. Derbs 4A 86
Oldwall. Cumb 3F 113
Oldwalls. Swan 3D 31
Old Warden. C Beds 1B 52
Oldways End. Som 4B 20
Old Westhall. Abers 1D 152
Old Weston. Cambs 3H 63
Oldwhat. Abers 3F 161
Old Windsor. Wind 3A 38
Old Wives Lees. Kent 5E 41
Old Woking. Surr 5B 38
Oldwood Common. Worc 4H 59
Old Woodstock. Oxon 4C 50
Olgrinmore. High 3C 168
Oliver's Battery. Hants 4C 24
Ollaberry. Shet 3E 173
Ollerton. Ches E 3B 84
Ollerton. Notts 4D 86
Ollerton. Shrp 3A 72
Olmarch. Cdgn 5F 57
Olmstead Green. Cambs 1G 53
Olney. Mil 5F 63
Olrig. High 2D 169
Olton. W Mid 2F 61
Olveston. S Glo 3B 34
Omagh. Ferm 2K 177
Ombersley. Worc 4C 60
Ompton. Notts 4D 86
Omunsgarth. Shet 7E 173
Onchan. IOM 4D 108
Onecote. Staf 5E 85
Onehouse. Suff 5C 66
Onen. Mon 4H 47
Ongar Hill. Norf 3E 77
Ongar Street. Here 4F 59
Onibury. Shrp 3G 59
Onich. High 2E 141
Onllwyn. Neat 4B 46
Onneley. Staf 1B 72
Onslow Green. Essx 4G 53
Onslow Village. Surr 1A 26
Onthank. E Ayr 1D 116
Openwoodgate. Derbs 1A 74
Opinan. High
nr. Gairloch 1G 155
nr. Laide 4C 162
Orasaigh. W Isl 6F 171
Orbost. High 4B 154
Orby. Linc 4D 89
Orchard Hill. Devn 4E 19
Orchard Portman. Som 4F 21
Orcheston. Wilts 2F 23
Orcop. Here 3H 47
Orcop Hill. Here 3H 47
Ord. High 2E 147
Ordale. Shet 1H 173
Ordhead. Abers 2D 152
Ordie. Abers 3B 152
Ordiquish. Mor 3H 159
Ordley. Nmbd 4C 114
Ordsall. Notts 3E 86
Ore. E Sus 4C 28
Oreton. Shrp 2A 60
Orford. Suff 1H 55
Orford. Warr 1A 84
Organford. Dors 3E 15
Orgil. Orkn 7B 172
Orgreave. Staf 4F 73
Oridge Street. Glos 3C 48
Orlestone. Kent 2D 28
Orleton. Here 4G 59
Orleton. Worc 4A 60
Orleton Common. Here 4G 59
Orlingbury. Nptn 3F 63
Ormacleit. W Isl 5C 170
Ormathwaite. Cumb 2D 102
Ormesby. Red C 3C 106
Ormesby St Margaret. Norf 4G 79
Ormesby St Michael. Norf 4G 79
Ormiscaig. High 4C 162
Ormiston. E Lot 3H 129
Ormsaigbeg. High 2F 139
Ormsaigmore. High 2F 139
Ormsary. Arg 2F 125
Ormsgill. Cumb 2A 96
Ormskirk. Lanc 4C 90
Orphir. Orkn 7C 172
Orpington. G Lon 4F 39
Orrell. G Man 4D 90
Orrell. Mers 1F 83
Orrisdale. IOM 2C 108
Orsett. Thur 2H 39
Orslow. Staf 4C 72
Orston. Notts 1E 75
Orthwaite. Cumb 1D 102
Orton. Cumb 4H 103
Orton. Mor 3H 159
Orton. Nptn 3F 63
Orton. Staf 1C 60
Orton Longueville. Pet 1A 64
Orton-on-the-Hill. Leics 5H 73
Orton Waterville. Pet 1A 64
Orton Wistow. Pet 1A 64
Orwell. Cambs 5C 64
Osbaldeston. Lanc 1E 91
Osbaldwick. York 4A 100
Osbaston. Leics 5B 74
Osbaston. Shrp 3F 71
Osbournby. Linc 2H 75
Osclay. High 5E 169
Oscroft. Ches W 4H 83
Ose. High 4C 154
Osgathorpe. Leics 4B 74
Osgodby. Linc 1H 87
Osgodby. N Yor
nr. Scarborough 1E 101
nr. Selby 1G 93
Oskaig. High 5E 155
Oskamull. Arg 5F 139
Osleston. Derbs 2G 73
Osmaston. Derb 2A 74
Osmaston. Derbs 1G 73
Osmington. Dors 4C 14
Osmington Mills. Dors 4C 14
Osmondthorpe. W Yor 1D 92
Osmondwall. Orkn 9C 172
Osmotherley. N Yor 5B 106
Osnaburgh. Fife 2G 137
Ospisdale. High 5E 164
Ospringe. Kent 4E 40
Ossett. W Yor 2C 92
Ossington. Notts 4E 87
Ostend. Essx 1D 40
Ostend. Norf 2F 79
Osterley. G Lon 3C 38
Oswaldkirk. N Yor 2A 100
Oswaldtwistle. Lanc 2F 91
Oswestry. Shrp 3E 71
Otby. Linc 1A 88
Otford. Kent 5G 39
Otham. Kent 5B 40
Otherton. Staf 4D 72
Othery. Som 3G 21
Otley. Suff 5E 66
Otley. W Yor 5E 98
Otterbourne. Hants 4C 24
Otterburn. Nmbd 5C 120
Otterburn. N Yor 4A 98
Otterburn Camp. Nmbd 5C 120
Otterburn Hall. Nmbd 5C 120
Otter Ferry. Arg 1H 125
Otterford. Som 1F 13
Otterham. Corn 3B 10
Otterhampton. Som 2F 21
Otterham Quay. Medw 4C 40
Ottershaw. Surr 4B 38
Otterspool. Mers 2F 83
Otterswick. Shet 3G 173
Otterton. Devn 4D 12
Otterwood. Hants 2C 16
Ottery St Mary. Devn 3E 12
Ottinge. Kent 1F 29
Ottringham. E Yor 2F 95
Oughterby. Cumb 4D 112
Oughtershaw. N Yor 1A 98
Oughterside. Cumb 5C 112
Oughtibridge. S Yor 1H 85
Oughtrington. Warr 2A 84
Oulston. N Yor 2H 99
Oulton. Cumb 4D 112
Oulton. Norf 3D 78
Oulton. Staf
nr. Gnosall Heath 3B 72
nr. Stone 2D 72
Oulton. Suff 1H 67
Oulton. W Yor 2D 92
Oulton Broad. Suff 1H 67
Oulton Street. Norf 3D 78
Oundle. Nptn 2H 63
Ousby. Cumb 1H 103
Ousdale. High 2H 165
Ousden. Suff 5G 65
Ousefleet. E Yor 2B 94
Ouston. Dur 4F 115
Ouston. Nmbd
nr. Bearsbridge 4A 114
nr. Stamfordham 2D 114
Outer Hope. Devn 4C 8
Outertown. Orkn 6B 172
Outgate. Cumb 5E 103
Outhgill. Cumb 4A 104
Outlands. Staf 2B 72
Outlane. W Yor 3A 92
Out Newton. E Yor 2G 95
Out Rawcliffe. Lanc 5D 96
Outwell. Norf 5E 77
Outwick. Hants 1G 15
Outwood. Surr 1E 27
Outwood. W Yor 2D 92
Outwood. Worc 3D 60
Outwoods. Leics 4B 74
Outwoods. Staf 4B 72
Ouzlewell Green. W Yor 2D 92
Ovenden. W Yor 2A 92
Over. Cambs 3C 64
Over. Ches W 4A 84
Over. Glos 4D 48
Over. S Glo 3A 34
Overbister. Orkn 3F 172
Over Burrows. Derbs 2G 73
Overbury. Worc 2E 49
Overcombe. Dors 4B 14
Over Compton. Dors 1A 14
Over End. Cambs 1H 63
Over Finlarg. Ang 4D 144
Overgreen. Derbs 3H 85
Over Green. Warw 1F 61
Over Haddon. Derbs 4G 85
Over Hulton. G Man 4E 91
Over Kellet. Lanc 2E 97
Over Kiddington. Oxon 3C 50
Overleigh. Som 3H 21
Overley. Staf 4F 73
Over Monnow. Mon 4A 48
Over Norton. Oxon 3B 50
Over Peover. Ches E 3B 84
Overpool. Ches W 3F 83
Overscaig. High 1B 164
Overseal. Derbs 4G 73
Over Silton. N Yor 5B 106
Oversland. Kent 5E 41
Overstone. Nptn 4F 63
Over Stowey. Som 3E 21
Overstrand. Norf 1E 79
Over Stratton. Som 1H 13
Over Street. Wilts 3F 23
Overthorpe. Nptn 1C 50
Overton. Aber 2F 153
Overton. Ches W 3H 83
Overton. Hants 2D 24
Overton. High 5E 169
Overton. Lanc 4D 96
Overton. N Yor 4H 99
Overton. Shrp
nr. Bridgnorth 2A 60
nr. Ludlow 3H 59
Overton. Swan 4D 30
Overton. W Yor 3C 92
Overton. Wrex 1F 71
Overtown. Lanc 2F 97
Overtown. N Lan 4B 128
Overtown. Swin 4G 35
Over Wallop. Hants 3A 24
Over Whitacre. Warw 1G 61
Over Worton. Oxon 3C 50
Oving. Buck 3F 51
Oving. W Sus 5A 26
Ovingdean. Brig 5E 27
Ovingham. Nmbd 3D 115
Ovington. Dur 3E 105
Ovington. Essx 1A 54
Ovington. Hants 3D 24
Ovington. Norf 5B 78
Ovington. Nmbd 3D 114
Owen's Bank. Staf 3G 73
Ower. Hants
nr. Holbury 2C 16
nr. Totton 1B 16
Owermoigne. Dors 4C 14
Owlbury. Shrp 1F 59
Owler Bar. Derbs 3G 85
Owlerton. S Yor 1H 85
Owlsmoor. Brac 5G 37
Owlswick. Buck 5F 51
Owmby. Linc 4D 94
Owmby-by-Spital. Linc 2H 87
Ownham. W Ber 4C 36
Owrytn. Wrex 1F 71
Owslebury. Hants 4D 24
Owston. Leics 5E 75
Owston. S Yor 3F 93
Owston Ferry. N Lin 4B 94
Owstwick. E Yor 1F 95
Owthorne. E Yor 2G 95
Owthorpe. Notts 2D 74
Owton Manor. Hart 2B 106
Oxborough. Norf 5G 77
Oxbridge. Dors 3H 13
Oxcombe. Linc 3C 88
Oxen End. Essx 3G 53
Oxenhall. Glos 3C 48
Oxenholme. Cumb 5G 103
Oxenhope. W Yor 1A 92
Oxen Park. Cumb 1C 96
Oxenpill. Som 2H 21
Oxenton. Glos 2E 49
Oxenwood. Wilts 1B 24
Oxford. Oxon **200** (5D 50)
Oxgangs. Edin 3F 129
Oxhey. Herts 1C 38
Oxhill. Warw 1B 50
Oxley. W Mid 5D 72
Oxley Green. Essx 4C 54
Oxley's Green. E Sus 3A 28
Oxlode. Cambs 2D 65
Oxnam. Bord 3B 120
Oxshott. Surr 4C 38
Oxspring. S Yor 4C 92
Oxted. Surr 5E 39
Oxton. Mers 2F 83
Oxton. N Yor 5H 99
Oxton. Notts 5D 86
Oxton. Bord 4A 130
Oxwich. Swan 4D 31
Oxwich Green. Swan 4D 31
Oxwick. Norf 3B 78
Oykel Bridge. High 3A 164
Oyne. Abers 1D 152
Oystermouth. Swan 4F 31
Ozleworth. Glos 2C 34

P

Pabail Iarach. W Isl 4H 171
Pabail Uarach. W Isl 4H 171
Pachesham Park. Surr 5C 38
Packers Hill. Dors 1C 14
Packington. Leics 4A 74
Packmoor. Stoke 5C 84
Packmores. Warw 4G 61
Packwood. W Mid 3F 61
Packwood Gullet. W Mid 3F 61
Padanaram. Ang 3D 144
Padbury. Buck 2F 51
Paddington. G Lon 2D 38
Paddington. Warr 2A 84
Paddlesworth. Kent 2F 29
Paddock. Kent 5D 40
Paddockhole. Dum 1D 112
Paddock Wood. Kent 1A 28
Paddolgreen. Shrp 2H 71
Padeswood. Flin 4E 83
Padiham. Lanc 1F 91
Padside. N Yor 4D 98
Padson. Devn 3F 11
Padstow. Corn 1D 6
Padworth. W Ber 5E 36
Page Bank. Dur 1F 105
Pagham. W Sus 3G 17
Paglesham Churchend. Essx 1D 40
Paglesham Eastend. Essx 1D 40
Paibeil. W Isl
on North Uist 2C 170
on Taransay 8C 171
Paiblesgearraidh. W Isl 2C 170
Paignton. Torb 2E 9
Pailton. Warw 2B 62
Paine's Corner. E Sus 3H 27
Painleyhill. Staf 2E 73
Painscastle. Powy 1E 47
Painshawfield. Nmbd 3D 114
Painsthorpe. E Yor 4C 100
Painswick. Glos 5D 48
Painter's Forstal. Kent 5D 40
Painthorpe. W Yor 3D 92
Pairc Shiaboist. W Isl 3E 171
Paisley. Ren 3F 127
Pakefield. Suff 1H 67
Pakenham. Suff 4B 66
Pale. Gwyn 2B 70
Palehouse Common. E Sus 4F 27
Palestine. Hants 2A 24
Paley Street. Wind 4G 37
Palgowan. Dum 1A 110
Palgrave. Suff 3D 66
Pallington. Dors 3C 14
Palmarsh. Kent 2F 29
Palmer Moor. Derbs 2F 73
Palmers Cross. W Mid 5C 72
Palmerstown. V Glam 5E 33
Palnackie. Dum 4F 111
Palnure. Dum 3B 110
Palterton. Derbs 4B 86
Pamber End. Hants 1E 24
Pamber Green. Hants 1E 24
Pamber Heath. Hants 5E 36
Pamington. Glos 2E 49
Pamphill. Dors 2E 15
Pampisford. Cambs 1E 53
Panborough. Som 2H 21
Panbride. Ang 5E 145
Pancrasweek. Devn 2C 10
Pandy. Gwyn
nr. Bala 2A 70
nr. Tywyn 5F 69
Pandy. Mon 3G 47
Pandy. Powy 5B 70
Pandy. Wrex 2D 70
Pandy Tudur. Cnwy 4A 82
Panfield. Essx 3H 53
Pangbourne. W Ber 4E 37
Pannal. N Yor 4F 99
Pannal Ash. N Yor 4E 99
Pannanich. Abers 4A 152
Pant. Shrp 3E 71
Pant. Wrex 1E 71
Pantasaph. Flin 3D 82
Pant Glas. Gwyn 1D 68
Pant-glas. Shrp 2E 71
Pantgwyn. Carm 3F 45
Pantgwyn. Cdgn 1C 44
Pant-lasau. Swan 5G 45
Panton. Linc 3A 88
Pant-pastynog. Den 4C 82
Pantperthog. Gwyn 5G 69
Pant-teg. Carm 3E 45
Pant-y-Caws. Carm 2F 43
Pant-y-dwr. Powy 3B 58
Pant-y-ffridd. Powy 5D 70
Pantyffynnon. Carm 4G 45
Pantygasseg. Torf 5F 47
Pant-y-llyn. Carm 4G 45
Pant-yr-awel. B'end 3C 32
Pant y Wacco. Flin 3D 82
Panxworth. Norf 4F 79
Papa Stour Airport. Shet 6C 173
Papa Westray Airport. Orkn 2D 172
Papcastle. Cumb 1C 102
Papigoe. High 3F 169
Papil. Shet 8E 173
Papple. E Lot 2B 130
Papplewick. Notts 5C 86
Papworth Everard. Cambs 4B 64
Papworth St Agnes. Cambs 4B 64
Par. Corn 3E 7
Paramour Street. Kent 4G 41
Parbold. Lanc 3C 90
Parbrook. Som 3A 22
Parbrook. W Sus 3B 26
Parc. Gwyn 2A 70
Parcllyn. Cdgn 5B 56
Parc-Seymour. Newp 2H 33
Pardown. Hants 2D 24
Pardshaw. Cumb 2B 102
Parham. Suff 4F 67
Park. Abers 4E 153
Park. Arg 4D 140
Park. Derr 6B 174
Park. Dum 5B 118
Park Bottom. Corn 4A 6
Parkburn. Abers 5E 161
Park Corner. E Sus 2G 27
Park Corner. Oxon 3E 37
Parkend. Glos 5B 48
Park End. Nmbd 2B 114
Parkeston. Essx 2F 55
Parkfield. Corn 2H 7
Parkgate. Ant 8J 175
Parkgate. Ches W 3E 83
Parkgate. Cumb 5D 112
Parkgate. Dum 1B 112
Park Gate. Hants 2D 16
Parkgate. Surr 1D 26
Park Gate. Worc 3D 60
Parkhall. W Dun 2F 127
Parkham. Devn 4D 19
Parkham Ash. Devn 4D 18
Parkhead. Cumb 5E 113
Parkhead. Glas 3H 127
Park Hill. Mers 4C 90
Parkhouse. Mon 5A 48
Parkhurst. IOW 3C 16
Park Lane. G Man 4F 91
Park Lane. Staf 5C 72
Parkmill. Swan 4E 31
Park Mill. W Yor 3C 92
Parkneuk. Abers 1G 145
Parkside. N Lan 4B 128
Parkstone. Pool 3F 15
Park Street. Herts 5B 52
Park Street. W Sus 2C 26
Park Town. Oxon 5D 50
Park Village. Nmbd 3H 113
Parkway. Here 2C 48
Parley Cross. Dors 3F 15
Parmoor. Buck 3F 37
Parr. Mers 1H 83
Parracombe. Devn 2G 19
Parrog. Pemb 1E 43
Parsonage Green. Essx 4H 53
Parsonby. Cumb 1C 102
Parson Cross. S Yor 1H 85
Parson Drove. Cambs 5C 76
Partick. Glas 3G 127
Partington. G Man 1B 84
Partney. Linc 4D 88
Parton. Cumb
nr. Whitehaven 2A 102
nr. Wigton 4D 112
Parton. Dum 2D 111
Partridge Green. W Sus 4C 26
Parwich. Derbs 5F 85
Passenham. Nptn 2F 51
Passfield. Hants 3G 25
Passingford Bridge. Essx 1G 39
Paston. Norf 2F 79
Pasturefields. Staf 3D 73
Patchacott. Devn 3E 11
Patcham. Brig 5E 27
Patchetts Green. Herts 1C 38
Patching. W Sus 5B 26
Patchole. Devn 2G 19
Patchway. S Glo 3B 34
Pateley Bridge. N Yor 3D 98
Pathe. Som 3G 21
Pathfinder Village. Devn 3B 12
Pathhead. Abers 2G 145
Pathhead. E Ayr 3F 117
Pathhead. Fife 4E 137
Pathhead. Midl 3G 129
Pathlow. Warw 5F 61
Path of Condie. Per 2C 136
Pathstruie. Per 2C 136
Patmore Heath. Herts 3E 53
Patna. E Ayr 3D 116
Patney. Wilts 1F 23
Patrick. IOM 3B 108
Patrick Brompton. N Yor 5F 105
Patrington. E Yor 2G 95
Patrington Haven. E Yor 2G 95
Patrixbourne. Kent 5F 41
Patterdale. Cumb 3E 103
Pattiesmuir. Fife 1D 129
Pattingham. Staf 1C 60
Pattishall. Nptn 5D 62
Pattiswick. Essx 3B 54
Patton Bridge. Cumb 5G 103
Paul. Corn 4B 4
Paulerspury. Nptn 1F 51
Paull. E Yor 2E 95
Paulton. Bath 1B 22
Pauperhaugh. Nmbd 5F 121
Pave Lane. Telf 4B 72
Pavenham. Bed 5G 63
Pawlett. Som 2G 21
Pawston. Nmbd 1C 120
Paxford. Glos 2G 49
Paxton. Bord 4F 131
Payhembury. Devn 2D 12
Paythorne. Lanc 4H 97
Payton. Som 4E 20
Peacehaven. E Sus 5F 27
Peak Dale. Derbs 3E 85
Peak Forest. Derbs 3F 85
Peak Hill. Linc 4B 76
Peakirk. Pet 5A 76
Pearsie. Ang 3C 144
Peasedown St John. Bath 1C 22
Peaseland Green. Norf 4C 78
Peasemore. W Ber 4C 36
Peasenhall. Suff 4F 67
Pease Pottage. W Sus 2D 26
Peaslake. Surr 1B 26
Peasley Cross. Mers 1H 83
Peasmarsh. E Sus 3C 28
Peasmarsh. Som 1G 13
Peasmarsh. Surr 1A 26
Peaston. E Lot 3H 129
Peastonbank. E Lot 3H 129
Peathill. Abers 2G 161
Peat Inn. Fife 3G 137
Peatling Magna. Leics 1C 62
Peatling Parva. Leics 2C 62
Peaton. Arg 1D 126
Peaton. Shrp 2H 59
Peats Corner. Suff 4D 66
Pebmarsh. Essx 2B 54
Pebworth. Worc 1G 49
Pecket Well. W Yor 2H 91
Peckforton. Ches E 5H 83
Peckham Bush. Kent 5A 40
Peckleton. Leics 5B 74
Pedair-ffordd. Powy 3D 70
Pedham. Norf 4F 79
Pedlinge. Kent 2F 29
Pedmore. W Mid 2D 60
Pedwell. Som 3H 21
Peebles. Bord 5F 129
Peel. IOM 3B 108
Peel. Bord 1G 119
Peel Common. Hants 2D 16
Peening Quarter. Kent 3C 28
Peggs Green. Leics 4B 74
Pegsdon. C Beds 2B 52
Pegswood. Nmbd 1F 115
Peinchorran. High 5E 155
Peinlich. High 3D 154
Pelaw. Tyne 3F 115
Pelcomb Bridge. Pemb 3D 42
Pelcomb Cross. Pemb 3D 42
Peldon. Essx 4C 54
Pelsall. W Mid 5E 73
Pelton. Dur 4F 115
Pelutho. Cumb 5C 112
Pelynt. Corn 3G 7
Pemberton. Carm 5F 45
Pembrey. Carm 5E 45
Pembridge. Here 5F 59
Pembroke. Pemb 4D 43
Pembroke Dock. Pemb **204** (4D 42)
Pembroke Ferry. Pemb 4D 42
Pembury. Kent 1H 27
Penallt. Mon 4A 48
Penally. Pemb 5F 43
Penalt. Here 3A 48
Penalum. Pemb 5F 43
Penare. Corn 4D 6
Penarth. V Glam 4E 33
Penbeagle. Corn 3C 4
Penberth. Corn 4B 4
Pen-bont Rhydybeddau. Cdgn 2F 57
Penbryn. Cdgn 5B 56
Pencader. Carm 2E 45
Pen-cae. Cdgn 5D 56
Pencaenewydd. Gwyn 1D 68
Pencaerau. Neat 3G 31
Pencaitland. E Lot 3H 129
Pencarnisiog. IOA 3C 80
Pencarreg. Carm 1F 45
Pencarrow. Corn 4B 10
Pencelli. Powy 3D 46
Pen-clawdd. Swan 3E 31
Pencoed. B'end 3C 32
Pencombe. Here 5H 59
Pencraig. Here 3A 48
Pencraig. Powy 3C 70
Pendeen. Corn 3A 4
Pendeford. W Mid 5C 72
Penderyn. Rhon 5C 46
Pendine. Carm 4G 43
Pendlebury. G Man 4F 91
Pendleton. G Man 1C 84
Pendleton. Lanc 1F 91
Pendock. Worc 2C 48
Pendoggett. Corn 5A 10
Pendomer. Som 1A 14
Pendoylan. V Glam 4D 32
Pendre. B'end 3C 32
Penegoes. Powy 5G 69
Penelewey. Corn 4C 6
Penffordd. Pemb 2E 43
Penffordd-Lâs. Powy 1A 58
Penfro. Pemb 4D 43
Pengam. Cphy 2E 33
Pengam. Card 4F 33
Penge. G Lon 3E 39
Pengelly. Corn 4A 10
Pengenffordd. Powy 2E 47
Pengersick. Corn 4C 4
Pengorffwysfa. IOA 1D 80
Pengover Green. Corn 2G 7
Pengwern. Den 3C 82
Penhale. Corn
nr. Mullion 5D 5
nr. St Austell 3D 6
Penhale Camp. Corn 3B 6
Penhallow. Corn 3B 6
Penhalvean. Corn 5B 6
Penhelig. Gwyn 1F 57
Penhill. Swin 3G 35
Penhow. Newp 2H 33
Penhurst. E Sus 4A 28
Peniarth. Gwyn 5F 69
Penicuik. Midl 3F 129
Peniel. Carm 3E 45
Penifiler. High 4D 155
Peninver. Arg 3B 122
Penisa'r Waun. Gwyn 4E 81
Penistone. S Yor 4C 92
Penketh. Warr 2H 83
Penkill. S Ayr 5B 116
Penkridge. Staf 4D 72
Penley. Wrex 2G 71
Penllech. Gwyn 2B 68
Penllergaer. Swan 3F 31
Pen-llyn. IOA 2C 80
Penmachno. Cnwy 5G 81
Penmaen. Swan 4E 31
Penmaenmawr. Cnwy 3G 81
Penmaenpool. Gwyn 4F 69
Penmaen Rhos. Cnwy 3A 82
Pen-marc. V Glam 5D 32
Penmark. V Glam 5D 32
Penmarth. Corn 5B 6
Penmon. IOA 2F 81
Penmorfa. Gwyn 1E 69
Penmynydd. IOA 3E 81
Penn. Buck 1A 38
Penn. Dors 3G 13
Penn. W Mid 1C 60
Pennal. Gwyn 5G 69
Pennan. Abers 2F 161
Pennant. Cdgn 4E 57
Pennant. Den 2C 70
Pennant. Gwyn 3B 70
Pennant. Powy 1A 58
Pennant Melangell. Powy 3C 70
Pennar. Pemb 4D 42
Pennard. Swan 4E 31
Pennerley. Shrp 1F 59
Pennington. Cumb 2B 96
Pennington. G Man 1A 84
Pennington. Hants 3B 16
Pennorth. Powy 3E 46
Penn Street. Buck 1A 38
Pennsylvania. Devn 3C 12
Pennsylvania. S Glo 4C 34
Penny Bridge. Cumb 1C 96
Pennycross. Plym 3A 8
Pennygate. Norf 3F 79
Pennyghael. Arg 1C 132
Penny Hill. Linc 3C 76
Pennylands. Lanc 4C 90
Pennymoor. Devn 1B 12
Pennyvenie. E Ayr 4D 117
Pennywell. Tyne 4G 115
Penparc. Cdgn 1C 44
Penparcau. Cdgn 2E 57
Pen-pedair-heol. Cphy 2E 33
Penperlleni. Mon 5G 47
Penpillick. Corn 3E 7
Penpol. Corn 5C 6
Penpoll. Corn 3F 7
Penponds. Corn 3D 4
Penpont. Corn 5A 10
Penpont. Dum 5H 117
Penpont. Powy 3C 46
Penprysg. B'end 3C 32
Penquit. Devn 3C 8
Penrherber. Carm 1G 43
Penrhiw. Pemb 1C 44
Penrhiwceiber. Rhon 2D 32
Pen-Rhiw-fawr. Neat 4H 45
Penrhiw-llan. Cdgn 1D 44
Penrhiw-pal. Cdgn 1D 44
Penrhos. Gwyn 2C 68
Penrhos. Here 5F 59
Penrhos. IOA 2B 80
Penrhos. Mon 4H 47
Penrhos. Powy 4B 46
Penrhos Garnedd. Gwyn 3E 81
Penrhyn. IOA 1C 80
Penrhyn Bay. Cnwy 2H 81
Penrhyn-coch. Cdgn 2F 57
Penrhyndeudraeth. Gwyn 2F 69
Penrhyn-side. Cnwy 2H 81
Penrice. Swan 4D 31
Penrith. Cumb 2G 103
Penrose. Corn 1C 6
Penruddock. Cumb 2F 103
Penryn. Corn 5B 6
Pen-sarn. Carm 4E 45
Pen-sarn. Gwyn 3E 69
Pensax. Worc 4B 60
Pensby. Mers 2E 83
Penselwood. Som 3C 22
Pensford. Bath 5B 34
Pensham. Worc 1E 49
Penshaw. Tyne 4G 115
Penshurst. Kent 1G 27
Pensilva. Corn 2G 7
Pensnett. W Mid 2D 60
Penston. E Lot 2H 129
Penstone. Devn 2A 12
Pentewan. Corn 4E 6
Pentir. Gwyn 4E 81
Pentire. Corn 2B 6
Pentlepoir. Pemb 4F 43
Pentlow. Essx 1B 54
Pentney. Norf 4G 77
Penton Mewsey. Hants 2B 24
Pentraeth. IOA 3E 81
Pentre. Powy
nr. Church Stoke 1E 59
nr. Kerry 2D 58
nr. Mochdre 2C 58
Pentre. Rhon 2C 32
Pentre. Shrp 4F 71
Pentre. Wrex
nr. Chirk 1E 71
nr. Llanarmon Dyffryn Ceiriog 2D 70
Pentrebach. Carm 2B 46
Pentre-bach. Cdgn 1F 45
Pentrebach. Mer T 5D 46
Pentre-bach. Powy 2C 46
Pentrebach. Swan 5G 45
Pentre Berw. IOA 3D 80
Pentre-bont. Cnwy 5G 81
Pentrecagal. Carm 1D 44
Pentre-celyn. Den 5D 82
Pentre-clawdd. Shrp 2E 71
Pentreclwydau. Neat 5B 46
Pentre-cwrt. Carm 2D 45
Pentre Dolau Honddu. Powy 1C 46
Pentre-dwr. Swan 3F 31
Pentrefelin. Carm 3F 45
Pentrefelin. Cdgn 1G 45
Pentrefelin. Cnwy 3H 81
Pentrefelin. Gwyn 2E 69
Pentrefoelas. Cnwy 5A 82
Pentre Galar. Pemb 1F 43
Pentregat. Cdgn 5C 56
Pentre Gwenlais. Carm 4G 45
Pentre Gwynfryn. Gwyn 3E 69
Pentre Halkyn. Flin 3E 82
Pentre Hodre. Shrp 3F 59
Pentre-Llanrhaeadr. Den 4C 82
Pentre Llifior. Powy 1D 58
Pentrellwyn. IOA 2E 81
Pentre-llwyn-llwyd. Powy 5B 58
Pentre-llyn-cymmer. Cnwy 5B 82
Pentre Meyrick. V Glam 4C 32
Pentre-piod. Gwyn 2A 70
Pentre-poeth. Newp 3F 33
Pentre'r beirdd. Powy 4D 70
Pentre'r-felin. Powy 2C 46
Pentre-tafarn-y-fedw. Cnwy 4H 81
Pentre-ty-gwyn. Carm 2B 46
Pentre-uchaf. Gwyn 2C 68
Pentrich. Derbs 5A 86
Pentridge. Dors 1F 15
Pen-twyn. Cphy 5F 47
Pentwyn. Cphy 5E 46
Pentwyn. Card 3F 33
Pentyrch. Card 3E 32
Pentywyn. Carm 4G 43
Penuwch. Cdgn 4E 57
Penwithick. Corn 3E 7
Penwyllt. Powy 4B 46
Pen-y-banc. Carm 3G 45
Penybanc. Carm 4G 45
Pen-y-bont. Carm 2H 43
Pen-y-bont. Powy 3E 70
Penybont. Powy 4D 58
Pen-y-Bont Ar Ogwr. B'end 3C 32
Penybontfawr. Powy 3C 70
Penybryn. Cphy 2E 33
Pen-y-bryn. Pemb 1B 44
Pen-y-bryn. Wrex 1E 71
Pen-y-cae. Powy 4B 46
Penycae. Wrex 1E 71
Pen-y-cae mawr. Mon 2H 33
Penycaerau. Gwyn 3A 68
Pen-y-cefn. Flin 3D 82
Pen-y-clawdd. Mon 5H 47
Pen-y-coedcae. Rhon 3D 32
Penycwm. Pemb 2C 42
Pen-y-Darren. Mer T 5D 46
Pen-y-fai. B'end 3B 32
Pen-y-ffordd. Flin 2D 82
Penyffordd. Flin 4F 83
Penyffridd. Gwyn 5E 81
Pen-y-garn. Cdgn 2F 57
Pen-y-garnedd. IOA 3E 81
Penygarnedd. Powy 3D 70
Pen-y-graig. Gwyn 2B 68
Penygraig. Rhon 2C 32
Penygraigwen. IOA 2D 80
Pen-y-groes. Carm 4F 45
Penygroes. Gwyn 5D 80
Penygroes. Pemb 1F 43
Pen-y-Mynydd. Carm 5E 45
Penymynydd. Flin 4F 83
Penyrheol. Cphy 3E 33
Pen-yr-heol. Mon 4H 47
Penyrheol. Swan 3E 31
Penysarn. IOA 1D 80
Pen-y-stryt. Den 5D 82
Penywaun. Rhon 5C 46
Penzance. Corn 3B 4
Peopleton. Worc 5D 60
Peover Heath. Ches E 3B 84
Peper Harow. Surr 1A 26
Peplow. Shrp 3A 72
Pepper Arden. N Yor 4F 105
Perceton. N Ayr 5E 127
Percyhorner. Abers 2G 161
Perham Down. Wilts 2A 24
Periton. Som 2C 20
Perkinsville. Dur 4F 115
Perlethorpe. Notts 3D 86
Perranarworthal. Corn 5B 6
Perranporth. Corn 3B 6
Perranuthnoe. Corn 4C 4
Perranwell. Corn 5B 6
Perranzabuloe. Corn 3B 6
Perrott's Brook. Glos 5F 49

Perry—Ramsey

Perry. W Mid 1E 61
Perry Barr. W Mid 1E 61
Perry Crofts. Staf 5G 73
Perry Green. Essx 3B 54
Perry Green. Herts 4E 53
Perry Green. Wilts 3E 35
Perry Street. Kent 3H 39
Perry Street. Som 2G 13
Perrywood. Kent 5E 41
Pershall. Staf 3C 72
Pershore. Worc 1E 49
Pertenhall. Bed 4H 63
Perth. Per 201 (1D 136)
Perthy. Shrp 2F 71
Perton. Staf 1C 60
Pertwood. Wilts 3D 23
Peterborough. Pet 201 (1A 64)
Peterburn. High 5B 162
Peterchurch. Here 2G 47
Peterculter. Aber 3F 153
Peterhead. Abers 4H 161
Peterlee. Dur 5H 115
Petersfield. Hants 4F 25
Petersfinger. Wilts 4G 23
Peters Green. Herts 4B 52
Peters Marland. Devn 1E 11
Peterstone Wentlooge.
Newp 3F 33
Peterston-super-Ely.
V Glam 4D 32
Peterstow. Here 3A 48
Peters Village. Kent 4B 40
Peter Tavy. Devn 5F 11
Petertown. Orkn 7C 172
Petham. Kent 5F 41
Petherwin Gate. Corn 4C 10
Petrockstowe. Devn 2F 11
Petsoe End. Mil 1G 51
Pett. E Sus 4C 28
Pettaugh. Suff 5D 66
Pett Bottom. Kent 5F 41
Petteridge. Kent 1A 28
Pettinain. S Lan 5C 128
Pettistree. Suff 5E 67
Petton. Devn 4D 20
Petton. Shrp 3G 71
Petts Wood. G Lon 4F 39
Pettycur. Fife 1F 129
Pettywell. Norf 3C 78
Petworth. W Sus 3A 26
Pevensey. E Sus 5H 27
Pevensey Bay. E Sus 5A 28
Pewsey. Wilts 5G 35
Pheasants Hill. Buck 3F 37
Philadelphia. Tyne 4G 115
Philham. Devn 4C 18
Philiphaugh. Bord 2G 119
Phillack. Corn 3C 4
Philleigh. Corn 5C 6
Philpstoun. W Lot 2D 128
Phocle Green. Here 3B 48
Phoenix Green. Hants 1F 25
Pibsbury. Som 4H 21
Pibwrlwyd. Carm 4E 45
Pica. Cumb 2B 102
Piccadilly. Warw 1G 61
Piccadilly Corner. Norf 2E 67
Piccotts End. Herts 5A 52
Pickering. N Yor 1B 100
Picket Piece. Hants 2B 24
Picket Post. Hants 2G 15
Pickford. W Mid 2G 61
Pickhill. N Yor 1F 99
Picklenash. Glos 3C 48
Picklescott. Shrp 1G 59
Pickletillem. Fife 1G 137
Pickmere. Ches E 3A 84
Pickstock. Telf 3B 72
Pickwell. Devn 2E 19
Pickwell. Leics 4E 75
Pickworth. Linc 2H 75
Pickworth. Rut 4G 75
Picton. Ches W 3G 83
Picton. Flin 2D 82
Picton. N Yor 4B 106
Pict's Hill. Som 4H 21
Piddinghoe. E Sus 5F 27
Piddington. Buck 2G 37
Piddington. Nptn 5F 63
Piddington. Oxon 4E 51
Piddlehinton. Dors 3C 14
Piddletrenthide. Dors 2C 14
Pidley. Cambs 3C 64
Pidney. Dors 2C 14
Pie Corner. Here 4A 60
Piercebridge. Darl 3F 105
Pierowall. Orkn 3D 172
Pigdon. Nmbd 1E 115
Pightley. Som 3F 21
Pikehall. Derbs 5F 85
Pikeshill. Hants 2A 16
Pilford. Dors 2F 15
Pilgrims Hatch. Essx 1G 39
Pilham. Linc 1F 87
Pill, The. Mon 3H 33
Pill. N Som 4A 34
Pillaton. Corn 2H 7
Pillaton. Staf 4D 72
Pillerton Hersey. Warw 1B 50
Pillerton Priors. Warw 1A 50
Pilleth. Powy 4E 59
Pilley. Hants 3B 16
Pilley. S Yor 4D 92
Pillgwenlly. Newp 3G 33
Pilling. Lanc 5D 96
Pilling Lane. Lanc 5C 96
Pillowell. Glos 5B 48
Pillwell. Dors 1C 14
Pilning. S Glo 3A 34
Pilsbury. Derbs 4F 85
Pilsdon. Dors 3H 13
Pilsgate. Pet 5H 75
Pilsley. Derbs
nr. Bakewell 3G 85
nr. Clay Cross 4B 86
Pilson Green. Norf 4F 79
Piltdown. E Sus 3F 27
Pilton. Edin 2F 129
Pilton. Nptn 2H 63
Pilton. Rut 5G 75
Pilton. Som 2A 22
Pilton Green. Swan 4D 30
Pimperne. Dors 2E 15
Pinchbeck. Linc 3B 76
Pinchbeck Bars. Linc 3A 76
Pinchbeck West. Linc 3B 76
Pinfold. Lanc 3B 90
Pinford End. Suff 5H 65
Pinged. Carm 5E 45
Pinhoe. Devn 3C 12
Pinkerton. E Lot 2D 130
Pinkneys Green. Wind 3G 37
Pinley. W Mid 3A 62
Pinley Green. Warw 4G 61
Pinmill. Suff 2F 55
Pinmore. S Ayr 5B 116
Pinner. G Lon 2C 38
Pins Green. Worc 1C 48
Pinsley Green. Ches E 1H 71
Pinvin. Worc 1E 49
Pinwherry. S Ayr 1G 109
Pinxton. Derbs 5B 86
Pipe and Lyde. Here 1A 48
Pipe Aston. Here 3G 59
Pipe Gate. Shrp 1B 72
Pipehill. Staf 5E 73
Piperhill. High 3C 158
Pipe Ridware. Staf 4E 73
Pipers Pool. Corn 4C 10
Pipewell. Nptn 2F 63
Pippacott. Devn 3F 19
Pipton. Powy 2E 47
Pirbright. Surr 5A 38
Pirnmill. N Ayr 5G 125
Pirton. Herts 2B 52
Pirton. Worc 1D 49
Pisgah. Stir 3G 135
Pishill. Oxon 3F 37
Pistyll. Gwyn 1C 68
Pitagowan. Per 2F 143
Pitcairn. Per 3F 143
Pitcairngreen. Per 1C 136
Pitcalnie. High 1C 158
Pitcaple. Abers 1E 152
Pitchcombe. Glos 5D 48
Pitchcott. Buck 3F 51
Pitchford. Shrp 5H 71
Pitch Green. Buck 5F 51
Pitch Place. Surr 5A 38
Pitcombe. Som 3B 22
Pitcox. E Lot 2C 130
Pitcur. Per 5B 144
Pitfichie. Abers 2D 152
Pitgrudy. High 4E 165
Pitkennedy. Ang 3E 145
Pitlessie. Fife 3F 137
Pitlochry. Per 3G 143
Pitmachie. Abers 1D 152
Pitmaduthy. High 1B 158
Pitmedden. Abers 1F 153
Pitminster. Som 1F 13
Pitnacree. Per 3G 143
Pitney. Som 4H 21
Pitroddie. Per 1E 136
Pitscottie. Fife 2G 137
Pitsea. Essx 2B 40
Pitsford. Nptn 4E 63
Pitsford Hill. Som 3E 20
Pitsmoor. S Yor 2A 86
Pitstone. Buck 4H 51
Pitt. Hants 4C 24
Pitt Court. Glos 2C 34
Pittentrail. High 3E 164
Pittenweem. Fife 3H 137
Pittington. Dur 5G 115
Pitton. Swan 4D 30
Pitton. Wilts 3H 23
Pittswood. Kent 1H 27
Pittulie. Abers 2G 161
Pittville. Glos 3E 49
Pitversie. Per 2D 136
Pityme. Corn 1D 6
Pity Me. Dur 5F 115
Pixey Green. Suff 3E 67
Pixley. Here 2B 48
Place Newton. N Yor 2C 100
Plaidy. Abers 3E 161
Plaidy. Corn 3G 7
Plain Dealings. Pemb 3E 43
Plains. N Lan 3A 128
Plainsfield. Som 3E 21
Plaish. Shrp 1H 59
Plaistow. Here 2B 48
Plaistow. W Sus 2B 26
Plaitford. Wilts 1A 16
Plastow Green. Hants 5D 36
Plas yn Cefn. Den 3C 82
Platt, The. E Sus 2G 27
Platt Bridge. G Man 4E 90
Platt Lane. Shrp 2H 71
Platts Common. S Yor 4D 92
Platt's Heath. Kent 5C 40
Plawsworth. Dur 5F 115
Plaxtol. Kent 5H 39
Playden. E Sus 3D 28
Playford. Suff 1F 55
Play Hatch. Oxon 4F 37
Playing Place. Corn 4C 6
Playley Green. Glos 2C 48
Plealey. Shrp 5G 71
Plean. Stir 1B 128
Pleasington. Bkbn 2E 91
Pleasley. Derbs 4C 86
Pledgdon Green. Essx 3F 53
Plenmeller. Nmbd 3A 114
Pleshey. Essx 4G 53
Plockton. High 5H 155
Plocrapol. W Isl 8D 171
Ploughfield. Here 1G 47
Plowden. Shrp 2F 59
Ploxgreen. Shrp 5F 71
Pluckley. Kent 1D 28
Plucks Gutter. Kent 4G 41
Plumbland. Cumb 1C 102
Plumbridge. Derr 7A 174
Plumgarths. Cumb 5F 103
Plumley. Ches E 3B 84
Plummers Plain. W Sus 3D 26
Plumpton. Cumb 1F 103
Plumpton. E Sus 4E 27
Plumpton. Nptn 1D 50
Plumpton Foot. Cumb 1F 103
Plumpton Green. E Sus 4E 27
Plumpton Head. Cumb 1G 103
Plumstead. G Lon 3F 39
Plumstead. Norf 2D 78
Plumtree. Notts 2D 74
Plumtree Park. Notts 2D 74
Plungar. Leics 2E 75
Plush. Dors 2C 14
Plushabridge. Corn 5D 10
Plwmp. Cdgn 5C 56
Plymouth. Plym 201 (3A 8)
Plympton. Plym 3B 8
Plymstock. Plym 3B 8
Plymtree. Devn 2D 12
Pockley. N Yor 1A 100
Pocklington. E Yor 5C 100
Pode Hole. Linc 3B 76
Podimore. Som 4A 22
Podington. Bed 4G 63
Podmore. Staf 2B 72
Poffley End. Oxon 4B 50
Point Clear. Essx 4D 54
Pointon. Linc 2A 76
Pokesdown. Bour 3G 15
Polbae. Dum 2H 109
Polbain. High 3E 163
Polbathic. Corn 3H 7
Polbeth. W Lot 3D 128
Polbrock. Corn 2E 6
Polchar. High 3C 150
Polebrook. Nptn 2H 63
Pole Elm. Worc 1D 48
Polegate. E Sus 5G 27
Pole Moor. W Yor 3A 92
Poles. High 4E 165
Polesworth. Warw 5G 73
Polglass. High 3E 163
Polgooth. Corn 3D 6
Poling. W Sus 5B 26
Poling Corner. W Sus 5B 26
Polio. High 1B 158
Polkerris. Corn 3E 7
Polla. High 3D 166
Pollard Street. Norf 2F 79
Pollicott. Buck 4F 51
Pollington. E Yor 3G 93
Polloch. High 2B 140
Pollok. Glas 3G 127
Pollokshaws. Glas 3G 127
Pollokshields. Glas 3G 127
Polmaily. High 5G 157
Polmassick. Corn 4D 6
Polmont. Falk 2C 128
Polnessan. E Ayr 3D 116
Polnish. High 5F 147
Polperro. Corn 3G 7
Polruan. Corn 3F 7
Polscoe. Corn 2F 7
Polsham. Som 2A 22
Polskeoch. Dum 4F 117
Polstead. Suff 2C 54
Polstead Heath. Suff 1C 54
Poltesco. Corn 5E 5
Poltimore. Devn 3C 12
Polton. Midl 3F 129
Polwarth. Bord 4D 130
Polyphant. Corn 4C 10
Polzeath. Corn 1D 6
Pomeroy. M Ulst 2A 178
Ponde. Powy 2E 46
Pondersbridge. Cambs 1B 64
Ponders End. G Lon 1E 39
Pond Street. Essx 2E 53
Pondtail. Hants 1G 25
Ponsanooth. Corn 5B 6
Ponsongath. Corn 5E 5
Ponsworthy. Devn 5H 11
Pontamman. Carm 4G 45
Pontantwn. Carm 4E 45
Pontardawe. Neat 5H 45
Pontarddulais. Swan 5F 45
Pontarfynach. Cdgn 3G 57
Pont-ar-gothi. Carm 3F 45
Pont ar Hydfer. Powy 3B 46
Pontarllechau. Carm 3H 45
Pontarsais. Carm 3E 45
Pontblyddyn. Flin 4E 83
Pontbren Llwyd. Rhon 5C 46
Pont-Cyfyng. Cnwy 5G 81
Pontdolgoch. Powy 1C 58
Pontefract. W Yor 2E 93
Ponteland. Nmbd 2E 115
Ponterwyd. Cdgn 2G 57
Pontesbury. Shrp 5G 71
Pontesford. Shrp 5G 71
Pontfadog. Wrex 2E 71
Pontfaen. Pemb 1E 43
Pont-faen. Powy 2C 46
Pont-Faen. Shrp 2E 71
Pontgarreg. Cdgn 5C 56
Pont-Henri. Carm 5E 45
Ponthir. Torf 2G 33
Ponthirwaun. Cdgn 1C 44
Pont-iets. Carm 5E 45
Pontllanfraith. Cphy 2E 33
Pontlliw. Swan 5G 45
Pont Llogel. Powy 4C 70
Pontllyfni. Gwyn 5D 80
Pontlottyn. Cphy 5E 46
Pontneddfechan. Powy 5C 46
Pont-newydd. Carm 5E 45
Pont-newydd. Flin 4D 82
Pontnewydd. Torf 2F 33
Ponton. Shet 6E 173
Pont Pen-y-benglog. Gwyn 4F 81
Pontrhydfendigaid. Cdgn 4G 57
Pont Rhyd-y-cyff. B'end 3B 32
Pontrhydyfen. Neat 2A 32
Pont-rhyd-y-groes. Cdgn 3G 57
Pontrhydyrun. Torf 2F 33
Pont-Rhythallt. Gwyn 4E 81
Pontrilas. Here 3G 47
Pontrilas Road. Here 3G 47
Pontrobert. Powy 4D 70
Pont-rug. Gwyn 4E 81
Ponts Green. E Sus 4A 28
Pontshill. Here 3B 48
Pont-Sian. Cdgn 1E 45
Pontsticill. Mer T 4D 46
Pont-Walby. Neat 5B 46
Pontwelly. Carm 2E 45
Pontwgan. Cnwy 3G 81
Pontyates. Carm 5E 45
Pontyberem. Carm 4F 45
Pontybodkin. Flin 5E 83
Pontyclun. Rhon 3D 32
Pontycymer. B'end 2C 32
Pontyglazier. Pemb 1F 43
Pontygwaith. Rhon 2D 32
Pont-y-pant. Cnwy 5G 81
Pontypool. Torf 2F 33
Pontypridd. Rhon 3D 32
Pontypwl. Torf 2F 33
Pontywaun. Cphy 2F 33
Pooksgreen. Hants 1B 16
Pool. Corn 4A 6
Pool. W Yor 5E 99
Poole. N Yor 2E 93
Poole. Pool 204 (3F 15)
Poole. Som 4E 21
Poole Keynes. Glos 2E 35
Poolend. Staf 5D 84
Poolewe. High 5C 162
Pooley Bridge. Cumb 2F 103
Poolfold. Staf 5C 84
Pool Head. Here 5H 59
Pool Hey. Lanc 3B 90
Poolhill. Glos 3C 48
Poolmill. Here 3A 48
Pool o' Muckhart. Clac 3C 136
Pool Quay. Powy 4E 71
Poolsbrook. Derbs 3B 86
Pool Street. Essx 2A 54
Pootings. Kent 1F 27
Pope Hill. Pemb 3D 42
Pope's Hill. Glos 4B 48
Popeswood. Brac 5G 37
Popham. Hants 2D 24
Poplar. G Lon 2E 39
Popley. Hants 1E 25
Porchfield. IOW 3C 16
Porin. High 3F 157
Poringland. Norf 5E 79
Porkellis. Corn 5A 6
Porlock. Som 2B 20
Porlock Weir. Som 2B 20
Portachoillan. Arg 4F 125
Port Adhair Bheinn na Faoghla.
W Isl 3C 170
Port Adhair Thirlodh. Arg 4B 138
Portadown. Arm 4E 178
Portaferry. Ards 4K 179
Port Ann. Arg 1H 125
Port Appin. Arg 4D 140
Port Asgaig. Arg 3C 124
Port Askaig. Arg 3C 124
Portavadie. Arg 3H 125
Portavogie. Ards 3L 179
Portballintrae. Caus 2F 174
Port Bannatyne. Arg 3B 126
Portbury. N Som 4A 34
Port Carlisle. Cumb 3D 112
Port Charlotte. Arg 4A 124
Portchester. Hants 2E 16
Port Clarence. Stoc T 2B 106
Port Driseach. Arg 2A 126
Port Dundas. Glas 3G 127
Port Ellen. Arg 5B 124
Port Elphinstone. Abers 1E 153
Portencalzie. Dum 2F 109
Portencross. N Ayr 5C 126
Port Erin. IOM 5A 108
Port Erroll. Abers 5H 161
Porter's Fen Corner. Norf 5E 77
Portesham. Dors 4B 14
Portessie. Mor 2B 160
Port e Vullen. IOM 2D 108
Port-Eynon. Swan 4D 30
Portfield. Som 4H 21
Portfield Gate. Pemb 3D 42
Portgate. Devn 4E 11
Port Gaverne. Corn 4A 10
Port Glasgow. Inv 2E 127
Portglenone. ME Ant 6F 175
Portgordon. Mor 2A 160
Portgower. High 2H 165
Porth. Corn 2C 6
Porth. Rhon 2D 32
Porthaethwy. IOA 3E 81
Porthallow. Corn
nr. Looe 3G 7
nr. St Keverne 4E 5
Porthcawl. B'end 4B 32
Porthceri. V Glam 5D 32
Porthcothan. Corn 1C 6
Porthcurno. Corn 4A 4
Port Henderson. High 1G 155
Porthgain. Pemb 1C 42
Porthgwarra. Corn 4A 4
Porthill. Shrp 4G 71
Porthkerry. V Glam 5D 32
Porthleven. Corn 4D 4
Porthllechog. IOA 1D 80
Porthmadog. Gwyn 2E 69
Porthmeor. Corn 3B 4
Porth Navas. Corn 4E 5
Portholland. Corn 4D 6
Porthoustock. Corn 4F 5
Porthtowan. Corn 4A 6
Porth Tywyn. Carm 5E 45
Porth-y-felin. IOA 2B 80
Porthyrhyd. Carm
nr. Carmarthen 4F 45
nr. Llandovery 2H 45
Porth-y-waen. Shrp 3E 71
Portincaple. Arg 4B 134
Portington. E Yor 1A 94
Portinnisherrich. Arg 2G 133
Portinscale. Cumb 2D 102
Port Isaac. Corn 1D 6
Portishead. N Som 4H 33
Portknockie. Mor 2B 160
Port Lamont. Arg 2B 126
Portlethen. Abers 4G 153
Portlethen Village. Abers 4G 153
Portling. Dum 4F 111
Port Lion. Pemb 4D 43
Portloe. Corn 5D 6
Port Logan. Dum 5F 109
Portmahomack. High 5G 165
Portmead. Swan 3F 31
Portmeirion. Gwyn 2E 69
Portmellon. Corn 4E 6
Port Mholair. W Isl 4H 171
Port Mor. High 1F 139
Portmore. Hants 3B 16
Port Mulgrave. N Yor 3E 107
Portnacroish. Arg 4D 140
Portnahaven. Arg 4A 124
Portnalong. High 5C 154
Portnaluchaig. High 5E 147
Portnancon. High 2E 167
Port Nan Giuran. W Isl 4H 171
Port nan Long. W Isl 1D 170
Port Nis. W Isl 1H 171
Portobello. Edin 2G 129
Portobello. W Yor 3D 92
Port of Menteith. Stir 3E 135
Porton. Wilts 3G 23
Portormin. High 5D 168
Portpatrick. Dum 4F 109
Port Quin. Corn 1D 6
Port Ramsay. Arg 4C 140
Portreath. Corn 4A 6
Portree. High 4D 155
Port Righ. High 4D 155
Portrush. Caus 3E 174
Port St Mary. IOM 5B 108
Portscatho. Corn 5C 6
Portsea. Port 2E 17
Port Seton. E Lot 2H 129
Portskerra. High 2A 168
Portskewett. Mon 3A 34
Portslade-by-Sea. Brig 5D 26
Portsmouth. Port 201 (2E 17)
Portsmouth. W Yor 2H 91
Port Soderick. IOM 4C 108
Port Solent. Port 2E 17
Portsonachan. Arg 1H 133
Portsoy. Abers 2C 160
Portstewart. Caus 3E 174
Port Sunlight. Mers 2F 83
Portswood. Sotn 1C 16
Port Talbot. Neat 3A 32
Porttannachy. Mor 2A 160
Port Tennant. Swan 3F 31
Portuairk. High 2F 139
Portway. Here 1H 47
Portway. Worc 3E 61
Port Wemyss. Arg 4A 124
Port William. Dum 5A 110
Portwrinkle. Corn 3H 7
Poslingford. Suff 1A 54
Postbridge. Devn 5G 11
Postcombe. Oxon 2F 37
Post Green. Dors 3E 15
Postling. Kent 2F 29
Postlip. Glos 3F 49
Post-Mawr. Cdgn 5D 56
Postwick. Norf 5E 79
Potarch. Abers 4D 152
Potsgrove. C Beds 3H 51
Potten End. Herts 5A 52
Potter Brompton. N Yor 2D 101
Pottergate Street. Norf 1D 66
Potterhanworth. Linc 4H 87
Potterhanworth Booths.
Linc 4H 87
Potter Heigham. Norf 4G 79
Potter Hill. Leics 3E 75
Potteries, The. Stoke 1C 72
Potterne. Wilts 1E 23
Potterne Wick. Wilts 1F 23
Potternewton. W Yor 1D 92
Potters Bar. Herts 5C 52
Potters Brook. Lanc 4D 97
Potter's Cross. Staf 2C 60
Potters Crouch. Herts 5B 52
Potter Somersal. Derbs 2F 73
Potterspury. Nptn 1F 51
Potter Street. Essx 5E 53
Potterton. Abers 2G 153
Potthorpe. Norf 3B 78
Pottle Street. Wilts 2D 22
Potto. N Yor 4B 106
Potton. C Beds 1C 52
Pott Row. Norf 3G 77
Pott Shrigley. Ches E 3D 84
Poughill. Corn 2C 10
Poughill. Devn 2B 12
Poulner. Hants 2G 15
Poulshot. Wilts 1E 23
Poulton. Glos 5G 49
Poulton-le-Fylde. Lanc 1B 90
Pound Bank. Worc 3B 60
Poundbury. Dors 3B 14
Poundfield. E Sus 2G 27
Poundgate. E Sus 3F 27
Pound Green. E Sus 3G 27
Pound Green. Suff 5G 65
Pound Hill. W Sus 2D 27
Poundland. S Ayr 1G 109
Poundon. Buck 3E 51
Poundsgate. Devn 5H 11
Poundstock. Corn 3C 10
Pound Street. Hants 5C 36
Pounsley. E Sus 3G 27
Powburn. Nmbd 3E 121
Powderham. Devn 4C 12
Powerstock. Dors 3A 14
Powfoot. Dum 3C 112
Powick. Worc 5C 60
Powmill. Per 4C 136
Poxwell. Dors 4C 14
Poyle. Slo 3B 38
Poynings. W Sus 4D 26
Poyntington. Dors 4B 22
Poynton. Ches E 2D 84
Poynton. Telf 4H 71
Poynton Green. Telf 4H 71
Poyntz Pass. Arm 6E 178
Poystreet Green. Suff 5B 66
Praa Sands. Corn 4C 4
Pratt's Bottom. G Lon 4F 39
Praze-an-Beeble. Corn 3D 4
Prees. Shrp 2H 71
Preesall. Lanc 5C 96
Preesall Park. Lanc 5C 96
Prees Green. Shrp 2H 71
Prees Higher Heath. Shrp 2H 71
Prendergast. Pemb 3D 42
Prendwick. Nmbd 3E 121
Pren-gwyn. Cdgn 1E 45
Prenteg. Gwyn 1E 69
Prenton. Mers 2F 83
Prescot. Mers 1G 83
Prescott. Devn 1D 12
Prescott. Shrp 3G 71
Preshute. Wilts 5G 35
Pressen. Nmbd 1C 120
Prestatyn. Den 2C 82
Prestbury. Ches E 3D 84
Prestbury. Glos 3E 49
Presteigne. Powy 4F 59
Presthope. Shrp 1H 59
Prestleigh. Som 2B 22
Preston. Brig 5E 27
Preston. Devn 5B 12
Preston. Dors 4C 14
Preston. E Lot
nr. East Linton 2B 130
nr. Prestonpans 2G 129
Preston. E Yor 1E 95
Preston. Glos 5F 49
Preston. Herts 3B 52
Preston. Kent
nr. Canterbury 4G 41
nr. Faversham 4E 41
Preston. Lanc 201 (2D 90)
Preston. Nmbd 2F 121
Preston. Rut 5F 75
Preston. Bord 4D 130
Preston. Shrp 4H 71
Preston. Suff 5B 66
Preston. Wilts
nr. Aldbourne 4A 36
nr. Lyneham 4F 35
Preston Bagot. Warw 4F 61
Preston Bissett. Buck 3E 51
Preston Bowyer. Som 4E 21
Preston Brockhurst. Shrp 3H 71
Preston Brook. Hal 2H 83
Preston Candover. Hants 2E 24
Preston Capes. Nptn 5C 62
Preston Cross. Glos 2B 48
Preston Gubbals. Shrp 4G 71
Preston-le-Skerne. Dur 2A 106
Preston Marsh. Here 1A 48
Prestonmill. Dum 4A 112
Preston on Stour. Warw 1H 49
Preston on the Hill. Hal 2H 83
Preston on Wye. Here 1G 47
Prestonpans. E Lot 2G 129
Preston Plucknett. Som 1A 14
Preston-under-Scar.
N Yor 5D 104
Preston upon the Weald Moors.
Telf 4A 72
Preston Wynne. Here 1A 48
Prestwich. G Man 4G 91
Prestwick. Nmbd 2E 115
Prestwick. S Ayr 2C 116
Prestwold. Leics 3C 74
Prestwood. Buck 5G 51
Prestwood. Staf 1F 73
Price Town. B'end 2C 32
Prickwillow. Cambs 2E 65
Priddy. Som 1A 22
Priestcliffe. Derbs 3F 85
Priesthill. Glas 3G 127
Priest Hutton. Lanc 2E 97
Priestland. E Ayr 1E 117
Priest Weston. Shrp 1E 59
Priestwood. Brac 4G 37
Priestwood. Kent 4A 40
Primethorpe. Leics 1C 62
Primrose Green. Norf 4C 78
Primrose Hill. Glos 5B 48
Primrose Hill. Lanc 4B 90
Primrose Valley. N Yor 2F 101
Primsidemill. Bord 2C 120
Princes Gate. Pemb 3F 43
Princes Risborough. Buck 5G 51
Princethorpe. Warw 3B 62
Princetown. Devn 5F 11
Prinsted. W Sus 2F 17
Prion. Den 4C 82
Prior Muir. Fife 2H 137
Prior's Frome. Here 2A 48
Priors Halton. Shrp 3G 59
Priors Hardwick. Warw 5B 62
Priorslee. Telf 4B 72
Priors Marston. Warw 5B 62
Prior's Norton. Glos 3D 48
Priory, The. W Ber 5B 36
Priory Wood. Here 1F 47
Priston. Bath 5B 34
Pristow Green. Norf 2D 66
Prittlewell. S'end 2C 40
Privett. Hants 4E 25
Prixford. Devn 3F 19
Probus. Corn 4C 6
Prospect. Cumb 5C 112
Prospect Village. Staf 4E 73
Provanmill. Glas 3H 127
Prudhoe. Nmbd 3D 115
Publow. Bath 5B 34
Puckeridge. Herts 3D 53
Puckington. Som 1G 13
Pucklechurch. S Glo 4B 34
Puckrup. Glos 2D 49
Puddinglake. Ches W 4B 84
Puddington. Ches W 3F 83
Puddington. Devn 1B 12
Puddlebrook. Glos 4B 48
Puddledock. Norf 1C 66
Puddletown. Dors 3C 14
Pudleston. Here 5H 59
Pudsey. W Yor 1C 92
Pulborough. W Sus 4B 26
Puleston. Telf 3B 72
Pulford. Ches W 5F 83
Pulham. Dors 2C 14
Pulham Market. Norf 2D 66
Pulham St Mary. Norf 2E 66
Pulley. Shrp 5G 71
Pulloxhill. C Beds 2A 52
Pulpit Hill. Arg 1F 133
Pulverbatch. Shrp 5G 71
Pumpherston. W Lot 3D 128
Pumsaint. Carm 1G 45
Puncheston. Pemb 2E 43
Puncknowle. Dors 4A 14
Punnett's Town. E Sus 3H 27
Purbrook. Hants 2E 17
Purfleet. Thur 3G 39
Puriton. Som 2G 21
Purleigh. Essx 5B 54
Purley. G Lon 4E 39
Purley on Thames. W Ber 4E 37
Purlogue. Shrp 3E 59
Purl's Bridge. Cambs 2D 65
Purse Caundle. Dors 1B 14
Purslow. Shrp 2F 59
Purston Jaglin. W Yor 3E 93
Purtington. Som 2G 13
Purton. Glos
nr. Lydney 5B 48
nr. Sharpness 5B 48
Purton. Wilts 3F 35
Purton Stoke. Wilts 2F 35
Pury End. Nptn 1F 51
Pusey. Oxon 2B 36
Putley. Here 2B 48
Putney. G Lon 3D 38
Putsborough. Devn 2E 19
Puttenham. Herts 4G 51
Puttenham. Surr 1A 26
Puttock End. Essx 1B 54
Puttock's End. Essx 4F 53
Puxey. Dors 1C 14
Puxton. N Som 5H 33
Pwll. Carm 5E 45
Pwll. Powy 5D 70
Pwllcrochan. Pemb 4D 42
Pwll-glas. Den 5D 82
Pwllgloyw. Powy 2D 46
Pwllheli. Gwyn 2C 68
Pwllmeyric. Mon 2A 34
Pwlltrap. Carm 3G 43
Pwll-y-glaw. Neat 2A 32
Pyecombe. W Sus 4D 27
Pye Corner. Herts 4E 53
Pye Corner. Newp 3G 33
Pye Green. Staf 4D 73
Pyewipe. NE Lin 3F 95
Pyle. B'end 3B 32
Pyle. IOW 5C 16
Pyle Hill. Surr 5A 38
Pylle. Som 3B 22
Pymoor. Cambs 2D 65
Pymore. Dors 3H 13
Pyrford. Surr 5B 38
Pyrford Village. Surr 5B 38
Pyrton. Oxon 2E 37
Pytchley. Nptn 3F 63
Pyworthy. Devn 2D 10

Q

Quabbs. Shrp 2E 58
Quadring. Linc 2B 76
Quadring Eaudike. Linc 2B 76
Quainton. Buck 3F 51
Quaking Houses. Dur 4E 115
Quarley. Hants 2A 24
Quarndon. Derbs 1H 73
Quarrendon. Buck 4G 51
Quarrier's Village. Inv 3E 127
Quarrington. Linc 1H 75
Quarrington Hill. Dur 1A 106
Quarry, The. Glos 2C 34
Quarry Bank. W Mid 2D 60
Quarrywood. Mor 2F 159
Quartalehouse. Abers 4G 161
Quarter. N Ayr 3C 126
Quarter. S Lan 4A 128
Quatford. Shrp 1B 60
Quatt. Shrp 2B 60
Quebec. Dur 5E 115
Quedgeley. Glos 4D 48
Queen Adelaide. Cambs 2E 65
Queenborough. Kent 3D 40
Queen Camel. Som 4A 22
Queen Charlton. Bath 5B 34
Queen Dart. Devn 1B 12
Queenhill. Worc 2D 48
Queen Oak. Dors 3C 22
Queensbury. W Yor 1B 92
Queensferry Crossing.
Edin 2E 129
Queensferry. Flin 4F 83
Queenstown. Bkpl 1B 90
Queen Street. Kent 1A 28
Queenzieburn. N Lan 2H 127
Quemerford. Wilts 5F 35
Quendale. Shet 10E 173
Quendon. Essx 2F 53
Queniborough. Leics 4D 74
Quenington. Glos 5G 49
Quernmore. Lanc 3E 97
Quethiock. Corn 2H 7
Quholm. Orkn 6B 172
Quick's Green. W Ber 4D 36
Quidenham. Norf 2C 66
Quidhampton. Hants 1D 24
Quidhampton. Wilts 3G 23
Quilquox. Abers 5G 161
Quina Brook. Shrp 2H 71
Quindry. Orkn 8D 172
Quine's Hill. IOM 4C 108
Quinton. Nptn 5E 63
Quinton. W Mid 2D 61
Quintrell Downs. Corn 2C 6
Quixhill. Staf 1F 73
Quoditch. Devn 3E 11
Quorn. Leics 4C 74
Quorndon. Leics 4C 74
Quothquan. S Lan 1B 118
Quoyloo. Orkn 5B 172
Quoyness. Orkn 7B 172
Quoys. Shet
on Mainland 5F 173
on Unst 1H 173

R

Rableyheath. Herts 4C 52
Raby. Cumb 4C 112
Raby. Mers 3F 83
Rachan Mill. Bord 1D 118
Rachub. Gwyn 4F 81
Rack End. Oxon 5C 50
Rackenford. Devn 1B 12
Rackham. W Sus 4B 26
Rackheath. Norf 4E 79
Racks. Dum 2B 112
Rackwick. Orkn
on Hoy 8B 172
on Westray 3D 172
Radbourne. Derbs 2G 73
Radcliffe. G Man 4F 91
Radcliffe. Nmbd 4G 121
Radcliffe on Trent. Notts 2D 74
Radclive. Buck 2E 51
Radernie. Fife 3G 137
Radfall. Kent 4F 41
Radford. Bath 1B 22
Radford. Nott 1C 74
Radford. Oxon 3C 50
Radford. W Mid 2H 61
Radford. Worc 5E 61
Radford Semele. Warw 4H 61
Radipole. Dors 4B 14
Radlett. Herts 1C 38
Radley. Oxon 2D 36
Radnage. Buck 2F 37
Radstock. Bath 1B 22
Radstone. Nptn 1D 50
Radway. Warw 1B 50
Radway Green. Ches E 5B 84
Radwell. Bed 5H 63
Radwell. Herts 2C 52
Radwinter. Essx 2G 53
Radyr. Card 3E 33
RAF Coltishall. Norf 3E 79
Rafford. Mor 3E 159
Raffrey. New M 4J 179
Ragdale. Leics 4D 74
Ragdon. Shrp 1G 59
Ragged Appleshaw. Hants 2B 24
Raggra. High 4F 169
Raglan. Mon 5H 47
Ragnall. Notts 3F 87
Raholp. New M 5K 179
Raigbeg. High 1C 150
Rainford. Mers 4C 90
Rainford Junction. Mers 4C 90
Rainham. G Lon 2G 39
Rainham. Medw 4C 40
Rainhill. Mers 1G 83
Rainow. Ches E 3D 84
Rainton. N Yor 2F 99
Rainworth. Notts 5C 86
Raisbeck. Cumb 4H 103
Raise. Cumb 5A 114
Rait. Per 1E 137
Raithby. Linc 2C 88
Raithby by Spilsby. Linc 4C 88
Raithwaite. N Yor 3F 107
Rake. W Sus 4G 25
Rake End. Staf 4E 73
Rakeway. Staf 1E 73
Rakewood. G Man 3H 91
Ralia. High 4B 150
Ram Alley. Wilts 5H 35
Ramasaig. High 4A 154
Rame. Corn
nr. Millbrook 4A 8
nr. Penryn 5B 6
Ram Lane. Kent 1D 28
Ramnageo. Shet 1H 173
Rampisham. Dors 2A 14
Rampside. Cumb 3B 96
Rampton. Cambs 4D 64
Rampton. Notts 3E 87
Ramsbottom. G Man 3F 91
Ramsburn. Mor 3C 160
Ramsbury. Wilts 4A 36
Ramscraigs. High 1H 165
Ramsdean. Hants 4F 25
Ramsdell. Hants 1D 24
Ramsden. Oxon 4B 50
Ramsden. Worc 1E 49
Ramsden Bellhouse. Essx 1B 40
Ramsden Heath. Essx 1B 40
Ramsey. Cambs 2B 64

Saffron Walden—Shieldmuir

Saffron Walden. Essx 2F 53
Sageston. Pemb 4E 43
Saham Hills. Norf 5B 78
Saham Toney. Norf 5A 78
Saighdinis. W Isl 2D 170
Saighton. Ches W 4G 83
Sain Dunwyd. V Glam 5C 32
Sain Hilari. V Glam 4D 32
St Abbs. Bord 3F 131
St Agnes. Corn 3B 6
St Albans. Herts 5B 52
St Allen. Corn 3C 6
St Andrews. Fife 2H 137
St Andrews Major. V Glam 4E 33
St Anne's. Lanc 2B 90
St Ann's. Dum 5C 118
St Ann's Chapel. Corn 5E 11
St Ann's Chapel. Devn 4C 8
St Anthony. Corn 5C 6
St Anthony-in-Meneage.
Corn 4E 5
St Arvans. Mon 2A 34
St Asaph. Den 3C 82
Sain Tathan. V Glam 5D 32
St Athan. V Glam 5D 32
St Austell. Corn 3E 6
St Bartholomew's Hill.
Wilts 4E 23
St Bees. Cumb 3A 102
St Blazey. Corn 3E 7
St Blazey Gate. Corn 3E 7
St Boswells. Bord 1H 119
St Breock. Corn 1D 6
St Breward. Corn 5A 10
St Briavels. Glos 5A 48
St Brides. Pemb 3B 42
St Brides Major. V Glam 4B 32
St Bride's Netherwent.
Mon 3H 33
St Bride's-super-Ely.
V Glam 4D 32
St Brides Wentlooge.
Newp 3F 33
St Budeaux. Plym 3A 8
Saintbury. Glos 2G 49
St Buryan. Corn 4B 4
St Catherine. Bath 4C 34
St Catherines. Arg 3A 134
St Clears. Carm 3G 43
St Cleer. Corn 2G 7
St Clement. Corn 4C 6
St Clether. Corn 4C 10
St Colmac. Arg 3B 126
St Columb Major. Corn 2D 6
St Columb Minor. Corn 2C 6
St Columb Road. Corn 3D 6
St Combs. Abers 2H 161
St Cross. Hants 4C 24
St Cross South Elmham.
Suff 2E 67
St Cyrus. Abers 2G 145
St Davids. Pemb 2B 42
St David's. Per 1B 136
St Day. Corn 4B 6
St Dennis. Corn 3D 6
St Dogmaels. Pemb 1B 44
St Dominick. Corn 2H 7
St Donat's. V Glam 5C 32
St Edith's Marsh. Wilts 5E 35
St Endellion. Corn 1D 6
St Enoder. Corn 3C 6
St Erme. Corn 4C 6
St Erney. Corn 3H 7
St Erth. Corn 3C 4
St Erth Praze. Corn 3C 4
St Ervan. Corn 1C 6
St Eval. Corn 2C 6
St Ewe. Corn 4D 6
St Fagans. Card 4E 32
St Fergus. Abers 3H 161
Saintfield. New M 4J 179
St Fillans. Per 1F 135
St Florence. Pemb 4E 43
St Gennys. Corn 3B 10
St George. Cnwy 3B 82
St George's. N Som 5G 33
St Georges. V Glam 4D 32
St George's Hill. Surr 4B 38
St Germans. Corn 3H 7
St Giles in the Wood. Devn 1F 11
St Giles on the Heath.
Devn 3D 10
St Giles's Hill. Hants 4C 24
St Gluvias. Corn 5B 6
St Harmon. Powy 3B 58
St Helena. Warw 5G 73
St Helen Auckland. Dur 2E 105
St Helens. Cumb 1B 102
St Helen's. E Sus 4C 28
St Helens. IOW 4E 17
St Helens. Mers 1H 83
St Hilary. Corn 3C 4
St Hilary. V Glam 4D 32
Saint Hill. Devn 2D 12
Saint Hill. W Sus 2E 27
St Illtyd. Blae 5F 47
St Ippolyts. Herts 3B 52
St Ishmael. Carm 5D 44
St Ishmael's. Pemb 4C 42
St Issey. Corn 1D 6
St Ive. Corn 2H 7
St Ives. Cambs 3C 64
St Ives. Corn 2C 4
St Ives. Dors 2G 15
St James' End. Nptn 4E 63
St James South Elmham.
Suff 2F 67
St Jidgey. Corn 2D 6
St John. Corn 3A 8
St John's. IOM 3B 108
St John's. Worc 5C 60
St John's Chapel. Devn 4F 19
St John's Chapel. Dur 1B 104
St John's Fen End. Norf 4E 77
St John's Town of Dalry.
Dum 1D 110
St Judes. IOM 2C 108
St Just. Corn 3A 4
St Just in Roseland. Corn 5C 6
St Katherines. Abers 5E 161
St Keverne. Corn 4E 5
St Kew. Corn 5A 10
St Kew Highway. Corn 5A 10
St Keyne. Corn 2G 7
St Lawrence. Corn 2E 7
St Lawrence. Essx 5C 54
St Lawrence. IOW 5D 16
St Leonards. Buck 5H 51
St Leonards. Dors 2G 15
St Leonards. E Sus 5B 28
St Levan. Corn 4A 4
St Lythans. V Glam 4E 32
St Mabyn. Corn 5A 10
St Madoes. Per 1D 136
St Margarets. Here 2G 47
St Margaret's. Herts 4A 52
St Margarets. Herts 4D 53
St Margaret's. Wilts 5H 35
St Margaret's at Cliffe. Kent 1H 29
St Margaret's Hope. Orkn 8D 172
St Margaret South Elmham.
Suff 2F 67
St Mark's. IOM 4B 108
St Martin. Corn
nr. Helston 4E 5
nr. Looe 3G 7
St Martins. Per 5A 144
St Martin's. Shrp 2F 71
St Mary Bourne. Hants 1C 24
St Marychurch. Torb 2F 9
St Mary Church. V Glam 4D 32
St Mary Cray. G Lon 4F 39
St Mary Hill. V Glam 4C 32
St Mary Hoo. Medw 3C 40
St Mary in the Marsh. Kent 3E 29
St Mary's. Orkn 7D 172
St Mary's Bay. Kent 3E 29
St Marys Platt. Kent 5H 39
St Maughan's Green. Mon 4H 47
St Mawes. Corn 5C 6
St Mawgan. Corn 2C 6
St Mellion. Corn 2H 7
St Mellons. Card 3F 33
St Merryn. Corn 1C 6
St Mewan. Corn 3D 6
St Michael Caerhays. Corn 4D 6
St Michael Penkevil. Corn 4C 6
St Michaels. Kent 2C 28
St Michaels. Torb 3E 9
St Michaels. Worc 4H 59
St Michael's on Wyre. Lanc 5D 96
St Michael South Elmham.
Suff 2F 67
St Minver. Corn 1D 6
St Monans. Fife 3H 137
St Neot. Corn 2F 7
St Neots. Cambs 4A 64
St Newlyn East. Corn 3C 6
St Nicholas. Pemb 1C 42
St Nicholas. V Glam 4D 32
St Nicholas at Wade. Kent 4G 41
St Nicholas South Elmham.
Suff 2F 67
St Ninians. Stir 4G 135
St Olaves. Norf 1G 67
St Osyth. Essx 4E 54
St Osyth Heath. Essx 4E 55
St Owen's Cross. Here 3A 48
St Paul's Cray. G Lon 4F 39
St Paul's Walden. Herts 3B 52
St Peter's. Kent 4H 41
St Peter The Great. Worc 5C 60
St Petrox. Pemb 5D 42
St Pinnock. Corn 2G 7
St Quivox. S Ayr 2C 116
St Ruan. Corn 5E 5
St Stephen. Corn 3D 6
St Stephens. Corn
nr. Launceston 4D 10
nr. Saltash 3A 8
St Teath. Corn 4A 10
St Thomas. Devn 3C 12
St Thomas. Swan 3F 31
St Tudy. Corn 5A 10
St Twynnells. Pemb 5D 42
St Veep. Corn 3F 7
St Vigeans. Ang 4F 145
St Wenn. Corn 2D 6
St Weonards. Here 3H 47
St Winnolls. Corn 3H 7
St Winnow. Corn 3F 7
Salcombe. Devn 5D 8
Salcombe Regis. Devn 4E 13
Salcott. Essx 4C 54
Sale. G Man 1B 84
Saleby. Linc 3D 88
Sale Green. Worc 5D 60
Salehurst. E Sus 3B 28
Salem. Carm 3G 45
Salem. Cdgn 2F 57
Salen. Arg 4G 139
Salen. High 2A 140
Salesbury. Lanc 1E 91
Saleway. Worc 5D 60
Salford. C Beds 2H 51
Salford. G Man
Manchester 197 (1C 84)
Salford. Oxon 3A 50
Salford Priors. Warw 5E 61
Salfords. Surr 1D 27
Salhouse. Norf 4F 79
Saligo. Arg 3A 124
Saline. Fife 4C 136
Salisbury. Wilts 201 (3G 23)
Salkeld Dykes. Cumb 1G 103
Sallachan. High 2D 141
Sallachy. High
nr. Lairg 3C 164
nr. Stromeferry 5B 156
Salle. Norf 3D 78
Salmonby. Linc 3C 88
Salmond's Muir. Ang 5E 145
Salperton. Glos 3F 49
Salph End. Bed 5H 63
Salsburgh. N Lan 3B 128
Salt. Staf 3D 72
Salta. Cumb 5B 112
Saltaire. W Yor 1B 92
Saltash. Corn 3A 8
Saltburn. High 2B 158
Saltburn-by-the-Sea.
Red C 2D 106
Saltby. Leics 3F 75
Saltcoats. Cumb 5B 102
Saltcoats. N Ayr 5D 126
Saltdean. Brig 5E 27
Salt End. E Yor 2E 95
Salter. Lanc 3F 97
Salterforth. Lanc 5A 98
Salters Lode. Norf 5E 77
Salterswall. Ches W 4A 84
Salterton. Wilts 3G 23
Saltfleet. Linc 1D 88
Saltfleetby All Saints. Linc 1D 88
Saltfleetby St Clements.
Linc 1D 88
Saltfleetby St Peter. Linc 2D 88
Saltford. Bath 5B 34
Salthouse. Norf 1C 78
Saltmarshe. E Yor 2A 94
Saltness. Orkn 9B 172
Saltness. Shet 7D 173
Saltney. Flin 4F 83
Salton. N Yor 2B 100
Saltrens. Devn 4E 19
Saltwick. Nmbd 2E 115
Saltwood. Kent 2F 29
Salum. Arg 4B 138
Salwarpe. Worc 4C 60
Salwayash. Dors 3H 13
Samalaman. High 1A 140
Sambourne. Warw 4E 61
Sambourne. Wilts 2D 22
Sambrook. Telf 3B 72
Samhia. W Isl 2C 170
Samlesbury. Lanc 1D 90
Samlesbury Bottoms. Lanc 2E 90
Sampford Arundel. Som 1E 12
Sampford Brett. Som 2D 20
Sampford Courtenay. Devn 2G 11
Sampford Peverell. Devn 1D 12
Sampford Spiney. Devn 5F 11
Samsonslane. Orkn 5F 172
Samuelston. E Lot 2A 130
Sanaigmore. Arg 2A 124
Sancreed. Corn 4B 4
Sancton. E Yor 1C 94
Sand. High 4D 162
Sand. Shet 7E 173
Sand. Som 2H 21
Sandaig. Arg 4A 138
Sandaig. High 3F 147
Sandale. Cumb 5D 112
Sandal Magna. W Yor 3D 92
Sandavore. High 5C 146
Sanday Airport. Orkn 3F 172
Sandbach. Ches E 4B 84
Sandbank. Arg 1C 126
Sandbanks. Pool 4F 15
Sandend. Abers 2C 160
Sanderstead. G Lon 4E 39
Sandfields. Neat 3G 31
Sandford. Cumb 3A 104
Sandford. Devn 2B 12
Sandford. Dors 4E 15
Sandford. Hants 2G 15
Sandford. IOW 4D 16
Sandford. N Som 1H 21
Sandford. Shrp
nr. Oswestry 3F 71
nr. Whitchurch 2H 71
Sandford. S Lan 5A 128
Sandfordhill. Abers 4H 161
Sandford-on-Thames.
Oxon 5D 50
Sandford Orcas. Dors 4B 22
Sandford St Martin. Oxon 3C 50
Sandgate. Kent 2F 29
Sandgreen. Dum 4C 110
Sandhaven. Abers 2G 161
Sandhead. Dum 4F 109
Sandhill. Cambs 2E 65
Sandhills. Dors 1B 14
Sandhills. Oxon 5D 50
Sandhills. Surr 2A 26
Sandhoe. Nmbd 3C 114
Sand Hole. E Yor 1B 94
Sandholes. M Ulst 2B 178
Sandholme. E Yor 1B 94
Sandholme. Linc 2C 76
Sandhurst. Brac 5G 37
Sandhurst. Glos 3D 48
Sandhurst. Kent 3B 28
Sandhurst Cross. Kent 3B 28
Sand Hutton. N Yor 4A 100
Sandhutton. N Yor 1F 99
Sandiacre. Derbs 2B 74
Sandilands. Linc 2E 89
Sandiway. Ches W 3A 84
Sandleheath. Hants 1G 15
Sandling. Kent 5B 40
Sandlow Green. Ches E 4B 84
Sandness. Shet 6C 173
Sandon. Essx 5H 53
Sandon. Herts 2D 52
Sandon. Staf 3D 72
Sandonbank. Staf 3D 72
Sandown. IOW 4D 16
Sandplace. Corn 3G 7
Sandridge. Herts 4B 52
Sandringham. Norf 3F 77
Sands, The. Surr 2G 25
Sandsend. N Yor 3F 107
Sandside. Cumb 2C 96
Sandsound. Shet 7E 173
Sandtoft. N Lin 4H 93
Sandvoe. Shet 2E 173
Sandway. Kent 5C 40
Sandwich. Kent 5H 41
Sandwick. Cumb 3F 103
Sandwick. Orkn
on Mainland 6B 172
on South Ronaldsay 9D 172
Sandwick. Shet
on Mainland 9F 173
on Whalsay 5G 173
Sandwith. Cumb 3A 102
Sandy. Carm 5E 45
Sandy. C Beds 1B 52
Sandy Bank. Linc 5B 88
Sandycroft. Flin 4F 83
Sandy Cross. Here 5A 60
Sandygate. Devn 5B 12
Sandygate. IOM 2C 108
Sandy Haven. Pemb 4C 42
Sandyhills. Dum 4F 111
Sandylands. Lanc 3D 96
Sandylane. Swan 4E 31
Sandy Lane. Wilts 5E 35
Sandystones. Bord 2H 119
Sandyway. Here 3H 47
Sangobeg. High 2E 167
Sangomore. High 2E 167
Sankyn's Green. Worc 4B 60
Sanna. High 2F 139
Sanndabhaig. W Isl
on Isle of Lewis 4G 171
on South Uist 4D 170
Sannox. N Ayr 5B 126
Sanquhar. Dum 3G 117
Santon. Cumb 4B 102
Santon Bridge. Cumb 4C 102
Santon Downham. Suff 2H 65
Sapcote. Leics 1B 62
Sapey Common. Here 4B 60
Sapiston. Suff 3B 66
Sapley. Cambs 3B 64
Sapperton. Derbs 2F 73
Sapperton. Glos 5E 49
Sapperton. Linc 2H 75
Saracen's Head. Linc 3C 76
Sarclet. High 4F 169
Sardis. Carm 5F 45
Sardis. Pemb
nr. Milford Haven 4D 42
nr. Tenby 4F 43
Sarisbury Green. Hants 2D 16
Sarn. B'end 3C 32
Sarn. Powy 1E 58
Sarnau. Carm 3E 45
Sarnau. Cdgn 5C 56
Sarnau. Gwyn 2B 70
Sarnau. Powy
nr. Brecon 2D 46
nr. Welshpool 4E 71
Sarn Bach. Gwyn 3C 68
Sarnesfield. Here 5F 59
Sarn Meyllteyrn. Gwyn 2B 68
Saron. Carm
nr. Ammanford 4G 45
nr. Newcastle Emlyn 2D 45
Saron. Gwyn
nr. Bethel 4E 81
nr. Bontnewydd 5D 80
Sarratt. Herts 1B 38
Sarre. Kent 4G 41
Sarsden. Oxon 3A 50
Satley. Dur 5E 115
Satron. N Yor 5C 104
Satterleigh. Devn 4G 19
Satterthwaite. Cumb 5E 103
Satwell. Oxon 3F 37
Sauchen. Abers 2D 152
Saucher. Per 5A 144
Saughall. Ches W 3F 83
Saughtree. Bord 5H 119
Saul. Glos 5C 48
Saul. New M 5K 179
Saundby. Notts 2E 87
Saundersfoot. Pemb 4F 43
Saunderton. Buck 5F 51
Saunderton Lee. Buck 2G 37
Saunton. Devn 3E 19
Sausthorpe. Linc 4C 88
Saval. High 3C 164
Saverley Green. Staf 2D 72
Sawbridge. Warw 4C 62
Sawbridgeworth. Herts 4E 53
Sawdon. N Yor 1D 100
Sawley. Derbs 2B 74
Sawley. Lanc 5G 97
Sawley. N Yor 3E 99
Sawston. Cambs 1E 53
Sawtry. Cambs 2A 64
Saxby. Leics 3F 75
Saxby. Linc 2H 87
Saxby All Saints. N Lin 3C 94
Saxelby. Leics 3D 74
Saxelbye. Leics 3D 74
Saxham Street. Suff 4C 66
Saxilby. Linc 3F 87
Saxlingham. Norf 2C 78
Saxlingham Green. Norf 1E 67
Saxlingham Nethergate.
Norf 1E 67
Saxlingham Thorpe. Norf 1E 66
Saxmundham. Suff 4F 67
Saxondale. Notts 1D 74
Saxon Street. Cambs 5F 65
Saxtead. Suff 4E 67
Saxtead Green. Suff 4E 67
Saxthorpe. Norf 2D 78
Saxton. N Yor 1E 93
Sayers Common. W Sus 4D 26
Scackleton. N Yor 2A 100
Scadabhagh. W Isl 8D 171
Scaddy. New M 5J 179
Scaftworth. Notts 1D 86
Scagglethorpe. N Yor 2C 100
Scaitcliffe. Lanc 2F 91
Scaladal. W Isl 6D 171
Scalasaig. Arg 4A 132
Scalby. E Yor 2B 94
Scalby. N Yor 5H 107
Scalby Mills. N Yor 5H 107
Scaldwell. Nptn 3E 63
Scaleby. Cumb 3F 113
Scaleby Hill. Cumb 3F 113
Scale Houses. Cumb 5G 113
Scales. Cumb
nr. Barrow-in-Furness 2B 96
nr. Keswick 2E 103
Scalford. Leics 3E 75
Scaling. N Yor 3E 107
Scaling Dam. Red C 3E 107
Scalloway. Shet 8F 173
Scalpaigh. W Isl 8E 171
Scalpay House. High 1E 147
Scamblesby. Linc 3B 88
Scamodale. High 1C 140
Scampston. N Yor 2C 100
Scampton. Linc 3G 87
Scaniport. High 5A 158
Scapa. Orkn 7D 172
Scapegoat Hill. W Yor 3A 92
Scar. Orkn 3F 172
Scarasta. W Isl 8C 171
Scarborough. N Yor 1E 101
Scarcliffe. Derbs 4B 86
Scarcroft. W Yor 5F 99
Scardroy. High 3E 156
Scarfskerry. High 1E 169
Scargill. Dur 3D 104
Scarinish. Arg 4B 138
Scarisbrick. Lanc 3B 90
Scarning. Norf 4B 78
Scarrington. Notts 1E 75
Scarth Hill. Lanc 4C 90
Scartho. NE Lin 4F 95
Scarva. Arm 5E 178
Scarvister. Shet 7E 173
Scatness. Shet 10E 173
Scatwell. High 3F 157
Scaur. Dum 4F 111
Scawby. N Lin 4C 94
Scawby Brook. N Lin 4C 94
Scawsby. S Yor 4F 93
Scawton. N Yor 1H 99
Scaynes Hill. W Sus 3E 27
Scethrog. Powy 3E 46
Scholar Green. Ches E 5C 84
Scholes. G Man 4D 90
Scholes. W Yor
nr. Bradford 2B 92
nr. Holmfirth 4B 92
nr. Leeds 1D 93
Scholey Hill. W Yor 2D 93
School Aycliffe. Darl 2F 105
School Green. Ches W 4A 84
School Green. Essx 2H 53
Scissett. W Yor 3C 92
Scleddau. Pemb 1D 42
Scofton. Notts 2D 86
Scole. Norf 3D 66
Scollogstown. New M 6J 179
Scolpaig. W Isl 1C 170
Scolton. Pemb 2D 43
Scone. Per 1D 136
Sconser. High 5E 155
Scoonie. Fife 3F 137
Scopwick. Linc 5H 87
Scoraig. High 4E 163
Scorborough. E Yor 5E 101
Scorrier. Corn 4B 6
Scorriton. Devn 2D 8
Scorton. Lanc 5E 97
Scorton. N Yor 4F 105
Sco Ruston. Norf 3E 79
Scotbheinn. W Isl 3D 170
Scotby. Cumb 4F 113
Scotch Corner. N Yor 4F 105
Scotch Street. Arm 4D 178
Scotforth. Lanc 3D 97
Scot Hay. Staf 1C 72
Scothern. Linc 3H 87
Scotland End. Oxon 2B 50
Scotlandwell. Per 3D 136
Scot Lane End. G Man 4E 91
Scotsburn. High 1B 158
Scotsburn. Mor 2G 159
Scotsdike. Cumb 2E 113
Scot's Gap. Nmbd 1D 114
Scotstoun. Glas 3G 127
Scotstown. High 2C 140
Scotswood. Tyne 3F 115
Scottas. High 3F 147
Scotter. Linc 4B 94
Scotterthorpe. Linc 4B 94
Scottlethorpe. Linc 3H 75
Scotton. Linc 1F 87
Scotton. N Yor
nr. Catterick Garrison 5E 105
nr. Harrogate 4F 99
Scottow. Norf 3E 79
Scoulton. Norf 5B 78
Scounslow Green. Staf 3E 73
Scourie. High 4B 166
Scourie More. High 4B 166
Scousburgh. Shet 10E 173
Scout Green. Cumb 4G 103
Scouthead. G Man 4H 91
Scrabster. High 1C 168
Scrafield. Linc 4C 88
Scrainwood. Nmbd 4D 121
Scrane End. Linc 1C 76
Scraptoft. Leics 5D 74
Scratby. Norf 4H 79
Scrayingham. N Yor 3B 100
Scredington. Linc 1H 75
Scremby. Linc 4D 88
Scremerston. Nmbd 5G 131
Screveton. Notts 1E 75
Scrivelsby. Linc 4B 88
Scriven. N Yor 4F 99
Scronkey. Lanc 5D 96
Scrooby. Notts 1D 86
Scropton. Derbs 2F 73
Scrub Hill. Linc 5B 88
Scruton. N Yor 5F 105
Scuggate. Cumb 2F 113
Sculamus. High 1E 147
Sculcoates. Hull 1D 94
Sculthorpe. Norf 2B 78
Scunthorpe. N Lin 3B 94
Scurlage. Swan 4D 30
Sea. Som 1G 13
Seaborough. Dors 2H 13
Seabridge. Staf 1C 72
Seabrook. Kent 2F 29
Seaburn. Tyne 3H 115
Seacombe. Mers 1F 83
Seacroft. Linc 4E 89
Seacroft. W Yor 1D 92
Seadyke. Linc 2C 76
Seafield. High 5G 165
Seafield. Midl 3F 129
Seafield. S Ayr 2C 116
Seafield. W Lot 3D 128
Seaford. E Sus 5F 27
Seaforde. New M 5J 179
Seaforth. Mers 1F 83
Seagrave. Leics 4D 74
Seaham. Dur 5H 115
Seahouses. Nmbd 1G 121
Seal. Kent 5G 39
Sealand. Flin 4F 83
Seale. Surr 2G 25
Seamer. N Yor
nr. Scarborough 1E 101
nr. Stokesley 3B 106
Seamill. N Ayr 5D 126
Sea Mills. Bris 4A 34
Sea Palling. Norf 3G 79
Seapatrick. Arm 5F 178
Searby. Linc 4D 94
Seasalter. Kent 4E 41
Seascale. Cumb 4B 102
Seaside. Per 1E 137
Seater. High 1F 169
Seathorne. Linc 4E 89
Seathwaite. Cumb
nr. Buttermere 3D 102
nr. Ulpha 5D 102
Seatle. Cumb 1C 96
Seatoller. Cumb 3D 102
Seaton. Corn 3H 7
Seaton. Cumb 1B 102
Seaton. Devn 3F 13
Seaton. Dur 4G 115
Seaton. E Yor 5F 101
Seaton. Nmbd 2G 115
Seaton. Rut 1G 63
Seaton Burn. Tyne 2F 115
Seaton Carew. Hart 2C 106
Seaton Delaval. Nmbd 2G 115
Seaton Junction. Devn 3F 13
Seaton Ross. E Yor 5B 100
Seaton Sluice. Nmbd 2G 115
Seatown. Abers 2C 160
Seatown. Dors 3H 13
Seatown. Mor
nr. Cullen 2C 160
nr. Lossiemouth 1G 159
Seave Green. N Yor 4C 106
Seaview. IOW 3E 17
Seaville. Cumb 4C 112
Seavington St Mary. Som 1H 13
Seavington St Michael.
Som 1H 13
Seawick. Essx 4E 55
Sebastopol. Torf 2F 33
Sebergham. Cumb 5E 113
Seckington. Warw 5G 73
Second Coast. High 4D 162
Sedbergh. Cumb 5H 103
Sedbury. Glos 2A 34
Sedbusk. N Yor 5B 104
Sedgeberrow. Worc 2F 49
Sedgebrook. Linc 2F 75
Sedgefield. Dur 2A 106
Sedgeford. Norf 2G 77
Sedgehill. Wilts 4D 22
Sedgley. W Mid 1D 60
Sedgwick. Cumb 1E 97
Sedlescombe. E Sus 4B 28
Seend. Wilts 5E 35
Seend Cleeve. Wilts 5E 35
Seer Green. Buck 1A 38
Seething. Norf 1F 67
Sefster. Shet 6E 173
Sefton. Mers 4B 90
Sefton Park. Mers 2F 83
Segensworth. Hants 2D 16
Seggat. Abers 4E 161
Seghill. Nmbd 2F 115
Seifton. Shrp 2G 59
Seighford. Staf 3C 72
Seilebost. W Isl 8C 171
Seisdon. Staf 1C 60
Seisiadar. W Isl 4H 171
Selattyn. Shrp 2E 71
Selborne. Hants 3F 25
Selby. N Yor 1G 93
Selham. W Sus 3A 26
Selkirk. Bord 2G 119
Sellack. Here 3A 48
Sellafirth. Shet 2G 173
Sellick's Green. Som 1F 13
Sellindge. Kent 2F 29
Selling. Kent 5E 41
Sells Green. Wilts 5E 35
Selly Oak. W Mid 2E 61
Selmeston. E Sus 5G 27
Selsdon. G Lon 4E 39
Selsey. W Sus 3G 17
Selsfield Common. W Sus 2E 27
Selside. Cumb 5G 103
Selside. N Yor 2G 97
Selsley. Glos 5D 48
Selsted. Kent 1G 29
Selston. Notts 5B 86
Selworthy. Som 2C 20
Semblister. Shet 6E 173
Semer. Suff 1D 54
Semington. Wilts 5D 35
Semley. Wilts 4D 23
Sempringham. Linc 2A 76
Send. Surr 5B 38
Send Marsh. Surr 5B 38
Senghenydd. Cphy 2E 32
Sennen. Corn 4A 4
Sennen Cove. Corn 4A 4
Sennybridge. Powy 3C 46
Serlby. Notts 2D 86
Seskinore. Ferm 3K 177
Sessay. N Yor 2G 99
Setchey. Norf 4F 77
Setley. Hants 2B 16
Setter. Shet 3F 173
Settiscarth. Orkn 6C 172
Settle. N Yor 3H 97
Settrington. N Yor 2C 100
Seven Ash. Som 3E 21
Sevenhampton. Glos 3F 49
Sevenhampton. Swin 2H 35
Sevenoaks. Kent 5G 39
Sevenoaks Weald. Kent 5G 39
Seven Sisters. Neat 5B 46
Seven Springs. Glos 4E 49
Severn Beach. S Glo 3A 34
Severn Stoke. Worc 1D 48
Sevington. Kent 1E 29
Sewards End. Essx 2F 53
Sewardstone. Essx 1E 39
Sewell. C Beds 3H 51
Sewerby. E Yor 3G 101
Seworgan. Corn 5B 6
Sewstern. Leics 3F 75
Sgallairidh. W Isl 9B 170
Sgarasta Mhor. W Isl 8C 171
Sgiogarstaigh. W Isl 1H 171
Sgreadan. Arg 4A 132
Shabbington. Buck 5E 51
Shackerley. Shrp 5C 72
Shackerstone. Leics 5A 74
Shackleford. Surr 1A 26
Shadforth. Dur 5G 115
Shadingfield. Suff 2G 67
Shadoxhurst. Kent 2D 28
Shadsworth. Bkbn 2F 91
Shadwell. Norf 2B 66
Shadwell. W Yor 1D 92
Shaftesbury. Dors 4D 22
Shafton. S Yor 3D 93
Shafton Two Gates. S Yor 3D 93
Shaggs. Dors 4D 14
Shakesfield. Glos 2B 48
Shalbourne. Wilts 5B 36
Shalcombe. IOW 4B 16
Shalden. Hants 2E 25
Shaldon. Devn 5C 12
Shalfleet. IOW 4C 16
Shalford. Essx 3H 53
Shalford. Surr 1B 26
Shalford Green. Essx 3H 53
Shallowford. Devn 2H 19
Shallowford. Staf 3C 72
Shalmsford Street. Kent 5E 41
Shalstone. Buck 2E 51
Shamley Green. Surr 1B 26
Shandon. Arg 1D 126
Shandwick. High 1C 158
Shangton. Leics 1E 62
Shankhouse. Nmbd 2F 115
Shanklin. IOW 4D 16
Shannochie. N Ayr 3D 123
Shap. Cumb 3G 103
Shapwick. Dors 2E 15
Shapwick. Som 3H 21
Sharcott. Wilts 1G 23
Shardlow. Derbs 2B 74
Shareshill. Staf 5D 72
Sharlston. W Yor 3D 93
Sharlston Common. W Yor 3D 93
Sharnal Street. Medw 3B 40
Sharnbrook. Bed 5G 63
Sharneyford. Lanc 2G 91
Sharnford. Leics 1B 62
Sharnhill Green. Dors 2C 14
Sharoe Green. Lanc 1D 90
Sharow. N Yor 2F 99
Sharpenhoe. C Beds 2A 52
Sharperton. Nmbd 4D 120
Sharpness. Glos 5B 48
Sharp Street. Norf 3F 79
Sharpthorne. W Sus 2E 27
Sharrington. Norf 2C 78
Shatterford. Worc 2B 60
Shatton. Derbs 2F 85
Shaugh Prior. Devn 2B 8
Shavington. Ches E 5B 84
Shaw. G Man 4H 91
Shaw. W Ber 5C 36
Shaw. Wilts 5D 35
Shawbirch. Telf 4A 72
Shawbury. Shrp 3H 71
Shawell. Leics 2C 62
Shawford. Hants 4C 24
Shawforth. Lanc 2G 91
Shaw Green. Lanc 3D 90
Shawhead. Dum 2F 111
Shaw Mills. N Yor 3E 99
Shawwood. E Ayr 2E 117
Shearington. Dum 3B 112
Shearsby. Leics 1D 62
Shearston. Som 3F 21
Shebbear. Devn 2E 11
Shebdon. Staf 3B 72
Shebster. High 2C 168
Sheddocksley. Aber 3F 153
Shedfield. Hants 1D 16
Shedog. N Ayr 2D 122
Sheen. Staf 4F 85
Sheepbridge. Derbs 3A 86
Sheep Hill. Dur 4E 115
Sheepscar. W Yor 1D 92
Sheepscombe. Glos 4D 49
Sheepstor. Devn 2B 8
Sheepwash. Devn 2E 11
Sheepwash. Nmbd 1F 115
Sheepway. N Som 4H 33
Sheepy Magna. Leics 5H 73
Sheepy Parva. Leics 5H 73
Sheering. Essx 4F 53
Sheerness. Kent 3D 40
Sheerwater. Surr 4B 38
Sheet. Hants 4F 25
Sheffield. S Yor 202 (2A 86)
Sheffield Bottom. W Ber 5E 37
Sheffield Green. E Sus 3F 27
Shefford. C Beds 2B 52
Shefford Woodlands.
W Ber 4B 36
Sheigra. High 2B 166
Sheinton. Shrp 5A 72
Shelderton. Shrp 3G 59
Sheldon. Derbs 4F 85
Sheldon. Devn 2E 12
Sheldon. W Mid 2F 61
Sheldwich. Kent 5E 40
Sheldwich Lees. Kent 5E 40
Shelf. W Yor 2B 92
Shelfanger. Norf 2D 66
Shelfield. Warw 4F 61
Shelfield. W Mid 5E 73
Shelford. Notts 1D 74
Shelford. Warw 2B 62
Shell. Worc 5D 60
Shelley. Suff 2D 54
Shelley. W Yor 3C 92
Shell Green. Hal 2H 83
Shellingford. Oxon 2B 36
Shellow Bowells. Essx 5G 53
Shelsley Beauchamp.
Worc 4B 60
Shelsley Walsh. Worc 4B 60
Shelthorpe. Leics 4C 74
Shelton. Bed 4H 63
Shelton. Norf 1E 67
Shelton. Notts 1E 75
Shelton. Shrp 4G 71
Shelton Green. Norf 1E 67
Shelton Lock. Derb 2A 74
Shelve. Shrp 1F 59
Shelwick. Here 1A 48
Shelwick Green. Here 1A 48
Shenfield. Essx 1H 39
Shenington. Oxon 1B 50
Shenley. Herts 5B 52
Shenley Brook End. Mil 2G 51
Shenleybury. Herts 5B 52
Shenley Church End. Mil 2G 51
Shenmore. Here 2G 47
Shennanton. Dum 3A 110
Shenstone. Staf 5F 73
Shenstone. Worc 3C 60
Shenstone Woodend. Staf 5F 73
Shenton. Leics 5A 74
Shenval. Mor 1G 151
Shepeau Stow. Linc 4C 76
Shephall. Herts 3C 52
Shepherd's Bush. G Lon 2D 38
Shepherd's Gate. Norf 4E 77
Shepherd's Green. Oxon 3F 37
Shepherd's Port. Norf 2F 77
Shepherdswell. Kent 1G 29
Shepley. W Yor 4B 92
Sheppardstown. High 4D 169
Shepperdine. S Glo 2B 34
Shepperton. Surr 4B 38
Shepreth. Cambs 1D 53
Shepshed. Leics 4B 74
Shepton Beauchamp. Som 1H 13
Shepton Mallet. Som 2B 22
Shepton Montague. Som 3B 22
Shepway. Kent 5B 40
Sheraton. Dur 1B 106
Sherborne. Dors 1B 14
Sherborne. Glos 4G 49
Sherborne. Som 1A 22
Sherborne Causeway.
Dors 4D 22
Sherborne St John. Hants 1E 24
Sherbourne. Warw 4G 61
Sherburn. Dur 5G 115
Sherburn. N Yor 2D 100
Sherburn Hill. Dur 5G 115
Sherburn in Elmet. N Yor 1E 93
Shere. Surr 1B 26
Shereford. Norf 3A 78
Sherfield English. Hants 4A 24
Sherfield on Loddon.
Hants 1E 25
Sherford. Devn 4D 9
Sherford. Dors 3E 15
Sheriffhales. Shrp 4B 72
Sheriff Hutton. N Yor 3A 100
Sheriffston. Mor 2G 159
Sheringham. Norf 1D 78
Sherington. Mil 1G 51
Shermanbury. W Sus 4D 26
Shernal Green. Worc 4D 60
Shernborne. Norf 2G 77
Sherrington. Wilts 3E 23
Sherston. Wilts 3D 34
Sherwood. Nott 1C 74
Sherwood Green. Devn 4F 19
Shettleston. Glas 3H 127
Shevington. G Man 4D 90
Shevington Moor. G Man 3D 90
Shevington Vale. G Man 4D 90
Sheviock. Corn 3H 7
Shide. IOW 4C 16
Shiel Bridge. High 2B 148
Shieldaig. High
nr. Charlestown 1H 155
nr. Torridon 3H 155
Shieldhill. Dum 1B 112
Shieldhill. Falk 2B 128
Shieldhill. S Lan 5D 128
Shieldmuir. N Lan 4A 128

Shielfoot—Stainsacre

Shielfoot. High 1A 140
Shielhill. Abers 3H 161
Shielhill. Ang 3D 144
Shifnal. Shrp 5B 72
Shilbottle. Nmbd 4F 121
Shilbottle Grange. Nmbd 4G 121
Shildon. Dur 2F 105
Shillford. E Ren 4F 127
Shillingford. Devn 4C 20
Shillingford. Oxon 2D 36
Shillingford St George. Devn 4C 12
Shillingstone. Dors 1D 14
Shillington. C Beds 2B 52
Shillmoor. Nmbd 4C 120
Shilton. Oxon 5A 50
Shilton. Warw 2B 62
Shilvinghampton. Dors 4B 14
Shilvington. Nmbd 1E 115
Shimpling. Norf 2D 66
Shimpling. Suff 5A 66
Shimpling Street. Suff 5A 66
Shincliffe. Dur 5F 115
Shiney Row. Tyne 4G 115
Shinfield. Wok 5F 37
Shingay. Cambs 1D 52
Shingham. Norf 5G 77
Shingle Street. Suff 1G 55
Shinner's Bridge. Devn 2D 9
Shinness. High 2C 164
Shipbourne. Kent 5G 39
Shipdham. Norf 5B 78
Shipham. Som 1H 21
Shiphay. Torb 2E 9
Shiplake. Oxon 4F 37
Shipley. Derbs 1B 74
Shipley. Nmbd 3F 121
Shipley. Shrp 1C 60
Shipley. W Sus 3C 26
Shipley. W Yor 1B 92
Shipley Bridge. Surr 1E 27
Shipmeadow. Suff 2F 67
Shippon. Oxon 2C 36
Shipston-on-Stour. Warw 1A 50
Shipton. Buck 3F 51
Shipton. Glos 4F 49
Shipton. N Yor 4H 99
Shipton. Shrp 1H 59
Shipton Bellinger. Hants 2H 23
Shipton Gorge. Dors 3H 13
Shipton Green. W Sus 3G 17
Shipton Moyne. Glos 3D 35
Shipton-on-Cherwell. Oxon 4C 50
Shiptonthorpe. E Yor 5C 100
Shipton-under-Wychwood. Oxon 4A 50
Shirburn. Oxon 2E 37
Shirdley Hill. Lanc 3B 90
Shire. Cumb 1H 103
Shirebrook. Derbs 4C 86
Shiregreen. S Yor 1A 86
Shirehampton. Bris 4A 34
Shiremoor. Tyne 2G 115
Shirenewton. Mon 2H 33
Shireoaks. Notts 2C 86
Shires Mill. Fife 1D 128
Shirkoak. Kent 2D 28
Shirland. Derbs 5A 86
Shirley. Derbs 1G 73
Shirley. Sotn 1B 16
Shirley. W Mid 3F 61
Shirleywich. Staf 3D 73
Shirl Heath. Here 5G 59
Shirrell Heath. Hants 1D 16
Shirwell. Devn 3F 19
Shiskine. N Ayr 3D 122
Shobdon. Here 4F 59
Shobnall. Staf 3G 73
Shobrooke. Devn 2B 12
Shoby. Leics 3D 74
Shocklach. Ches W 1G 71
Shoeburyness. S'end 2D 40
Sholden. Kent 5H 41
Sholing. Sotn 1C 16
Sholver. G Man 4H 91
Shoot Hill. Shrp 4G 71
Shop. Corn
nr. Bude 1C 10
nr. Padstow 1C 6
Shop. Devn 1D 11
Shopford. Cumb 2G 113
Shoreditch. G Lon 2E 39
Shoreditch. Som 4F 21
Shoregill. Cumb 4A 104
Shoreham. Kent 4G 39
Shoreham-by-Sea. W Sus 5D 26
Shoresdean. Nmbd 5F 131
Shoreswood. Nmbd 5F 131
Shorncote. Glos 2F 35
Shorne. Kent 3A 40
Shorne Ridgeway. Kent 3A 40
Shortacombe. Devn 4F 11
Shortbridge. E Sus 3F 27
Shortgate. E Sus 4F 27
Short Green. Norf 2C 66
Shorthampton. Oxon 3B 50
Short Heath. Derbs 4H 73
Short Heath. W Mid
nr. Erdington 1E 61
nr. Wednesfield 5D 73
Shortlanesend. Corn 4C 6
Shorton. Torb 2E 9
Shortstown. Bed 1A 52
Shortwood. S Glo 4B 34
Shorwell. IOW 4C 16
Shoscombe. Bath 1C 22
Shotesham. Norf 1E 67
Shotgate. Essx 1B 40
Shotley. Suff 2F 55
Shotley Bridge. Dur 4D 115
Shotleyfield. Nmbd 4D 114
Shotley Gate. Suff 2F 55
Shottenden. Kent 5E 41
Shottermill. Surr 3G 25
Shottery. Warw 5F 61
Shotteswell. Warw 1C 50
Shottisham. Suff 1G 55
Shottle. Derbs 1H 73
Shotton. Dur
nr. Peterlee 1B 106
nr. Sedgefield 2A 106
Shotton. Flin 4F 83
Shotton. Nmbd
nr. Morpeth 2F 115
nr. Town Yetholm 1C 120
Shotton Colliery. Dur 5G 115
Shotts. N Lan 3B 128
Shotwick. Ches W 3F 83
Shouldham. Norf 5F 77
Shouldham Thorpe. Norf 5F 77
Shoulton. Worc 5C 60
Shrawardine. Shrp 4G 71
Shrawley. Worc 4C 60
Shreding Green. Buck 2B 38
Shrewley. Warw 4G 61
Shrewsbury. Shrp 202 (4G 71)
Shrewton. Wilts 2F 23
Shrigley. New M 4K 179
Shripney. W Sus 5A 26
Shrivenham. Oxon 3H 35
Shropham. Norf 1B 66
Shroton. Dors 1D 14
Shrub End. Essx 3C 54
Shucknall. Here 1A 48
Shudy Camps. Cambs 1G 53
Shulishadermor. High 4D 155
Shulista. High 1D 154
Shurdington. Glos 4E 49
Shurlock Row. Wind 4G 37
Shurrery. High 3C 168
Shurton. Som 2F 21
Shustoke. Warw 1G 61
Shute. Devn
nr. Axminster 3F 13
nr. Crediton 2B 12
Shutford. Oxon 1B 50
Shut Heath. Staf 3C 72
Shuthonger. Glos 2D 49
Shutlanehead. Staf 1C 72
Shutlanger. Nptn 1F 51
Shutt Green. Staf 5C 72
Shuttington. Warw 5G 73
Shuttlewood. Derbs 3B 86
Shuttleworth. G Man 3G 91
Siabost. W Isl 3E 171
Siabost bho Dheas. W Isl 3E 171
Siabost bho Thuath. W Isl 3E 171
Siadar. W Isl 2F 171
Siadar Uarach. W Isl 2F 171
Sibbaldbie. Dum 1C 112
Sibbertoft. Nptn 2D 62
Sibdon Carwood. Shrp 2G 59
Sibertswold. Kent 1G 29
Sibford Ferris. Oxon 2B 50
Sibford Gower. Oxon 2B 50
Sible Hedingham. Essx 2A 54
Sibsey. Linc 5C 88
Sibsey Fen Side. Linc 5C 88
Sibson. Cambs 1H 63
Sibson. Leics 5A 74
Sibster. High 3F 169
Sibthorpe. Notts 1E 75
Sibton. Suff 4F 67
Sicklesmere. Suff 4A 66
Sicklinghall. N Yor 5F 99
Sid. Devn 4E 13
Sidbury. Devn 3E 13
Sidbury. Shrp 2A 60
Sidcot. N Som 1H 21
Sidcup. G Lon 3F 39
Siddick. Cumb 1B 102
Siddington. Ches E 3C 84
Siddington. Glos 2F 35
Side of the Moor. G Man 3F 91
Sidestrand. Norf 2E 79
Sidford. Devn 3E 13
Sidlesham. W Sus 3G 17
Sidley. E Sus 5B 28
Sidlow. Surr 1D 26
Sidmouth. Devn 4E 13
Sigford. Devn 5A 12
Sigglesthorne. E Yor 5F 101
Sighthill. Edin 2E 129
Signingstone. V Glam 4C 32
Signet. Oxon 4H 49
Silchester. Hants 5E 37
Sildinis. W Isl 6E 171
Sileby. Leics 4D 74
Silecroft. Cumb 1A 96
Silfield. Norf 1D 66
Silian. Cdgn 5E 57
Silkstone. S Yor 4C 92
Silkstone Common. S Yor 4C 92
Silksworth. Tyne 4G 115
Silk Willoughby. Linc 1H 75
Silloth. Cumb 4C 112
Sills. Nmbd 4C 120
Sillyearn. Mor 3C 160
Silpho. N Yor 5G 107
Silsden. W Yor 5C 98
Silsoe. C Beds 2A 52
Silverbank. Abers 4E 152
Silverbridge. New M 8D 178
Silverburn. Midl 3F 129
Silverdale. Lanc 2D 96
Silverdale. Staf 1C 72
Silverdale Green. Lanc 2D 96
Silver End. Essx 4B 54
Silver End. W Mid 2D 60
Silvergate. Norf 3D 78
Silver Green. Norf 1E 67
Silverhillocks. Abers 2E 161
Silverley's Green. Suff 3E 67
Silverstone. Nptn 1E 51
Silverton. Devn 2C 12
Silverton. W Dun 2F 127
Silvington. Shrp 3A 60
Simm's Cross. Hal 2H 83
Simm's Lane End. Mers 4D 90
Simonburn. Nmbd 2B 114
Simonsbath. Som 3A 20
Simonstone. Lanc 1F 91
Simprim. Bord 5E 131
Simpson. Pemb 3C 42
Simpson Cross. Pemb 3C 42
Sinclairston. E Ayr 3D 116
Sinclairtown. Fife 4E 137
Sinderby. N Yor 1F 99
Sinderhope. Nmbd 4B 114
Sindlesham. Wok 5F 37
Sinfin. Derb 2H 73
Singleborough. Buck 2F 51
Singleton. Kent 1D 28
Singleton. Lanc 1B 90
Singleton. W Sus 1G 17
Singlewell. Kent 3A 40
Sinkhurst Green. Kent 1C 28
Sinnahard. Abers 2B 152
Sinnington. N Yor 1B 100
Sinton Green. Worc 4C 60
Sion Mills. Derr 3F 176
Sipson. G Lon 3B 38
Sirhowy. Blae 4E 47
Sisland. Norf 1F 67
Sissinghurst. Kent 2B 28
Siston. S Glo 4B 34
Sithney. Corn 4D 4
Sittingbourne. Kent 4D 40
Six Ashes. Staf 2B 60
Six Bells. Blae 5F 47
Six Hills. Leics 3D 74
Sixhills. Linc 2A 88
Six Mile Bottom. Cambs 5E 65
Sixmilecross. Ferm 3L 177
Sixpenny Handley. Dors 1E 15
Sizewell. Suff 4G 67
Skail. High 4H 167
Skaill. Orkn 6B 172
Skaills. Orkn 7E 172
Skares. E Ayr 3E 117
Skateraw. E Lot 2D 130
Skaw. Shet 5G 173
Skeabost. High 4D 154
Skeabrae. Orkn 5B 172
Skeeby. N Yor 4E 105
Skeffington. Leics 5E 75
Skeffling. E Yor 3G 95
Skegby. Notts
nr. Mansfield 4B 86
nr. Tuxford 3E 87
Skegness. Linc 4E 89
Skelberry. Shet
nr. Boddam 10E 173
nr. Housetter 3E 173
Skelbo. High 4E 165
Skelbo Street. High 4E 165
Skelbrooke. S Yor 3F 93
Skeldyke. Linc 2C 76
Skelfhill. Bord 4G 119
Skellingthorpe. Linc 3G 87
Skellister. Shet 6F 173
Skellorn Green. Ches E 2D 84
Skellow. S Yor 3F 93
Skelmanthorpe. W Yor 3C 92
Skelmersdale. Lanc 4C 90
Skelmorlie. N Ayr 3C 126
Skelpick. High 3H 167
Skelton. Cumb 1F 103
Skelton. E Yor 2A 94
Skelton. N Yor
nr. Richmond 4D 105
nr. Ripon 3F 99
Skelton. Red C 3D 106
Skelton. York 4H 99
Skelton Green. Red C 3D 106
Skelwick. Orkn 3D 172
Skelwith Bridge. Cumb 4E 103
Skendleby. Linc 4D 88
Skendleby Psalter. Linc 3D 88
Skenfrith. Mon 3H 47
Skerne. E Yor 4E 101
Skeroblingarry. Arg 3B 122
Skerray. High 2G 167
Skerricha. High 3C 166
Skerries Airport. Shet 4H 173
Skerton. Lanc 3D 97
Sketchley. Leics 1B 62
Sketty. Swan 3F 31
Skewen. Neat 3G 31
Skewsby. N Yor 2A 100
Skeyton. Norf 3E 79
Skeyton Corner. Norf 3E 79
Skiall. High 2C 168
Skidbrooke. Linc 1D 88
Skidbrooke North End. Linc 1D 88
Skidby. E Yor 1D 94
Skilgate. Som 4C 20
Skillington. Linc 3F 75
Skinburness. Cumb 4C 112
Skinflats. Falk 1C 128
Skinidin. High 4B 154
Skinnet. High 2F 167
Skinningrove. Red C 3E 107
Skipness. Arg 4G 125
Skippool. Lanc 5C 96
Skiprigg. Cumb 5E 113
Skipsea. E Yor 4F 101
Skipsea Brough. E Yor 4F 101
Skipton. N Yor 4B 98
Skipton-on-Swale. N Yor 2F 99
Skipwith. N Yor 1G 93
Skirbeck. Linc 1C 76
Skirbeck Quarter. Linc 1C 76
Skirlaugh. E Yor 1E 95
Skirling. Bord 1C 118
Skirmett. Buck 2F 37
Skirpenbeck. E Yor 4B 100
Skirwith. Cumb 1H 103
Skirwith. N Yor 2G 97
Skirza. High 2F 169
Skitby. Cumb 3F 113
Skitham. Lanc 5D 96
Skittle Green. Buck 5F 51
Skroo. Shet 1B 172
Skulamus. High 1E 147
Skullomie. High 2G 167
Skyborry Green. Shrp 3E 59
Skye Green. Essx 3B 54
Skye of Curr. High 1D 151
Slack, The. Dur 2E 105
Slack. W Yor 2H 91
Slackhall. Derbs 2E 85
Slack Head. Cumb 2D 97
Slackhead. Mor 2B 160
Slackholme End. Linc 3E 89
Slacks of Cairnbanno. Abers 4F 161
Slad. Glos 5D 48
Slade. Swan 4D 31
Slade, The. W Ber 5D 36
Slade End. Oxon 2D 36
Slade Field. Cambs 2C 64
Slade Green. G Lon 3G 39
Slade Heath. Staf 5D 72
Slade Hooton. S Yor 2C 86
Sladesbridge. Corn 5A 10
Slaggyford. Nmbd 4H 113
Slaidburn. Lanc 4G 97
Slaid Hill. W Yor 5F 99
Slaithwaite. W Yor 3A 92
Slaley. Derbs 5G 85
Slaley. Nmbd 4C 114
Slamannan. Falk 2B 128
Slapton. Buck 3H 51
Slapton. Devn 4E 9
Slapton. Nptn 1E 51
Slattocks. G Man 4G 91
Slaugham. W Sus 3D 26
Slaughterbridge. Corn 4B 10
Slaughterford. Wilts 4D 34
Slawston. Leics 1E 63
Sleaford. Hants 3G 25
Sleaford. Linc 1H 75
Sleagill. Cumb 3G 103
Sleap. Shrp 3G 71
Sledmere. E Yor 3D 100
Sleightholme. Dur 3C 104
Sleights. N Yor 4F 107
Slepe. Dors 3E 15
Slickly. High 2E 169
Sliddery. N Ayr 3D 122
Sligachan. High 1C 146
Slimbridge. Glos 5C 48
Slindon. Staf 2C 72
Slindon. W Sus 5A 26
Slinfold. W Sus 2C 26
Slingsby. N Yor 2A 100
Slip End. C Beds 4A 52
Slipton. Nptn 3G 63
Slitting Mill. Staf 4E 73
Slochd. High 1C 150
Slockavullin. Arg 4F 133
Sloley. Norf 3E 79
Sloncombe. Devn 4H 11
Sloothby. Linc 3D 89
Slough. Slo 3A 38
Slough Green. Som 4F 21
Slough Green. W Sus 3D 27
Sluggan. High 1C 150
Slyne. Lanc 3D 97
Smailholm. Bord 1A 120
Smallbridge. G Man 3H 91
Smallbrook. Devn 3B 12
Smallburgh. Norf 3F 79
Smallburn. E Ayr 2F 117
Smalldale. Derbs 3E 85
Small Dole. W Sus 4D 26
Smalley. Derbs 1B 74
Smallfield. Surr 1E 27
Small Heath. W Mid 2E 61
Smallholm. Dum 2C 112
Small Hythe. Kent 2C 28
Smallrice. Staf 2D 72
Smallridge. Devn 2G 13
Smallwood Hey. Lanc 5C 96
Smallworth. Norf 2C 66
Smannell. Hants 2B 24
Smardale. Cumb 4A 104
Smarden. Kent 1C 28
Smarden Bell. Kent 1C 28
Smart's Hill. Kent 1G 27
Smeatharpe. Devn 1F 13
Smeeth. Kent 2E 29
Smeeth, The. Norf 4E 77
Smeeton Westerby. Leics 1D 62
Smeircleit. W Isl 7C 170
Smerral. High 5D 168
Smestow. Staf 1C 60
Smethwick. W Mid 2E 61
Smirisary. High 1A 140
Smisby. Derbs 4H 73
Smitham Hill. Bath 1A 22
Smith End Green. Worc 5B 60
Smithfield. Cumb 3F 113
Smith Green. Lanc 4D 97
Smithies, The. Shrp 1A 60
Smithincott. Devn 1D 12
Smith's Green. Essx 3F 53
Smithstown. High 1G 155
Smithton. High 4B 158
Smithwood Green. Suff 5B 66
Smithy Bridge. G Man 3H 91
Smithy Green. Ches E 3B 84
Smithy Lane Ends. Lanc 3C 90
Smockington. Leics 2B 62
Smoogro. Orkn 7C 172
Smythe's Green. Essx 4C 54
Snaigow House. Per 4H 143
Snailbeach. Shrp 5F 71
Snailwell. Cambs 4F 65
Snainton. N Yor 1D 100
Snaith. E Yor 2G 93
Snape. N Yor 1E 99
Snape. Suff 5F 67
Snape Green. Lanc 3B 90
Snapper. Devn 3F 19
Snarestone. Leics 5H 73
Snarford. Linc 2H 87
Snargate. Kent 3D 28
Snave. Kent 3E 28
Sneachill. Worc 5D 60
Snead. Powy 1F 59
Snead Common. Worc 4B 60
Sneaton. N Yor 4F 107
Sneatonthorpe. N Yor 4G 107
Snelland. Linc 2H 87
Snelston. Derbs 1F 73
Snetterton. Norf 1B 66
Snettisham. Norf 2F 77
Snibston. Leics 4B 74
Sniseabhal. W Isl 5C 170
Snitter. Nmbd 4E 121
Snitterby. Linc 1G 87
Snitterfield. Warw 5G 61
Snitton. Shrp 3H 59
Snodhill. Here 1G 47
Snodland. Kent 4B 40
Snods Edge. Nmbd 4D 114
Snowshill. Glos 2F 49
Snow Street. Norf 2C 66
Snydale. W Yor 2E 93
Soake. Hants 1E 17
Soar. Carm 3G 45
Soar. Gwyn 2F 69
Soar. IOA 3C 80
Soar. Powy 2C 46
Soberton. Hants 1E 16
Soberton Heath. Hants 1E 16
Sockbridge. Cumb 2G 103
Sockburn. Darl 4A 106
Sodom. Den 3C 82
Sodom. Shet 5G 173
Soham. Cambs 3E 65
Soham Cotes. Cambs 3E 65
Solas. W Isl 1D 170
Soldon Cross. Devn 1D 10
Soldridge. Hants 3E 25
Solent Breezes. Hants 2D 16
Sole Street. Kent
nr. Meopham 4A 40
nr. Waltham 1E 29
Solihull. W Mid 2F 61
Sollers Dilwyn. Here 5G 59
Sollers Hope. Here 2B 48
Sollom. Lanc 3C 90
Solva. Pemb 2B 42
Somerby. Leics 4E 75
Somerby. Linc 4D 94
Somercotes. Derbs 5B 86
Somerford. Dors 3G 15
Somerford. Staf 5C 72
Somerford Keynes. Glos 2F 35
Somerley. W Sus 3G 17
Somerleyton. Suff 1G 67
Somersal Herbert. Derbs 2F 73
Somersby. Linc 3C 88
Somersham. Cambs 3C 64
Somersham. Suff 1D 54
Somerton. Oxon 3C 50
Somerton. Som 4H 21
Somerton. Suff 5H 65
Sompting. W Sus 5C 26
Sonning. Wok 4F 37
Sonning Common. Oxon 3F 37
Sonning Eye. Oxon 4F 37
Sookholme. Notts 4C 86
Sopley. Hants 3G 15
Sopworth. Wilts 3D 34
Sorbie. Dum 5B 110
Sordale. High 2D 168
Sorisdale. Arg 2D 138
Sorn. E Ayr 2E 117
Sornhill. E Ayr 1E 117
Sortat. High 2E 169
Sotby. Linc 3B 88
Sots Hole. Linc 4A 88
Sotterley. Suff 2G 67
Soudley. Shrp
nr. Church Stretton 1G 59
nr. Market Drayton 3B 72
Soughton. Flin 4E 83
Soulbury. Buck 3G 51
Soulby. Cumb
nr. Appleby 3A 104
nr. Penrith 2F 103
Souldern. Oxon 2D 50
Souldrop. Bed 4G 63
Sound. Ches E 1A 72
Sound. Shet
nr. Lerwick 7F 173
nr. Tresta 6E 173
Soundwell. S Glo 4B 34
Sourhope. Bord 2C 120
Sourin. Orkn 4D 172
Sour Nook. Cumb 5E 113
Sourton. Devn 3F 11
Soutergate. Cumb 1B 96
South Acre. Norf 4H 77
Southall. G Lon 3C 38
South Allington. Devn 5D 9
South Alloa. Falk 4A 136
Southam. Glos 3E 49
Southam. Warw 4B 62
South Ambersham. W Sus 3A 26
Southampton. Sotn 202 (1C 16)
Southampton Airport. Hants 1C 16
Southannan. N Ayr 4D 126
South Anston. S Yor 2C 86
South Ascot. Wind 4A 38
South Baddesley. Hants 3B 16
South Balfern. Dum 4B 110
South Ballachulish. High 3E 141
South Bank. Red C 2C 106
South Barrow. Som 4B 22
South Benfleet. Essx 2B 40
South Bents. Tyne 3H 115
South Bersted. W Sus 5A 26
Southborough. Kent 1G 27
Southbourne. Bour 3G 15
Southbourne. W Sus 2F 17
South Bowood. Dors 3H 13
South Brent. Devn 3C 8
South Brewham. Som 3C 22
South Broomage. Falk 1B 128
South Broomhill. Nmbd 5G 121
Southburgh. Norf 5B 78
South Burlingham. Norf 5F 79
Southburn. E Yor 4D 101
South Cadbury. Som 4B 22
South Carlton. Linc 3G 87
South Cave. E Yor 1C 94
South Cerney. Glos 2F 35
South Chailey. E Sus 4E 27
South Chard. Som 2G 13
South Charlton. Nmbd 2F 121
South Cheriton. Som 4B 22
South Church. Dur 2F 105
Southchurch. S'end 2D 40
South Cleatlam. Dur 3E 105
South Cliffe. E Yor 1B 94
South Clifton. Notts 3F 87
South Clunes. High 4H 157
South Cockerington. Linc 2C 88
South Common. Devn 2G 13
South Cornelly. B'end 3B 32
Southcott. Devn
nr. Great Torrington 1E 11
nr. Okehampton 3F 11
Southcott. Wilts 1G 23
Southcourt. Buck 4G 51
South Cove. Suff 2G 67
South Creagan. Arg 4D 141
South Creake. Norf 2A 78
South Crosland. W Yor 3B 92
South Croxton. Leics 4D 74
South Dalton. E Yor 5D 100
South Darenth. Kent 4G 39
Southdean. Bord 4A 120
Southdown. Bath 5C 34
South Duffield. N Yor 1G 93
Southease. E Sus 5F 27
South Elkington. Linc 2B 88
South Elmsall. W Yor 3E 93
Southend. Arg 5A 122
South End. Cumb 3B 96
Southend. Glos 2C 34
South End. N Lin 2E 94
Southend. W Ber 4D 36
Southend Airport. Essx 2C 40
Southend-on-Sea. S'end 2C 40
Southerfield. Cumb 5C 112
Southerhouse. Shet 8E 173
Southerly. Devn 4F 11
Southernden. Kent 1C 28
Southerndown. V Glam 4B 32
Southerness. Dum 4A 112
South Erradale. High 1G 155
Southerton. Devn 3D 12
Southery. Norf 1F 65
Southey Green. Essx 2A 54
South Fambridge. Essx 1C 40
South Fawley. W Ber 3B 36
South Feorline. N Ayr 3D 122
South Ferriby. N Lin 2C 94
South Field. E Yor 2D 94
Southfleet. Kent 3H 39
South Garvan. High 1D 141
Southgate. Cdgn 2E 57
Southgate. G Lon 1E 39
Southgate. Norf
nr. Aylsham 3D 78
nr. Fakenham 2A 78
Southgate. Swan 4E 31
South Gluss. Shet 4E 173
South Godstone. Surr 1E 27
South Gorley. Hants 1G 15
South Green. Essx
nr. Billericay 1A 40
nr. Colchester 4D 54
South Green. Kent 4C 40
South Hanningfield. Essx 1B 40
South Harting. W Sus 1F 17
South Hayling. Hants 3F 17
South Hazelrigg. Nmbd 1E 121
South Heath. Buck 5H 51
South Heath. Essx 4E 54
South Heighton. E Sus 5F 27
South Hetton. Dur 5G 115
South Hiendley. W Yor 3D 93
South Hill. Corn 5D 10
South Hill. Som 4H 21
South Hinksey. Oxon 5D 50
South Hole. Devn 4C 18
South Holme. N Yor 2B 100
South Holmwood. Surr 1C 26
South Hornchurch. G Lon 2G 39
South Huish. Devn 4C 8
South Hykeham. Linc 4G 87
South Hylton. Tyne 4G 115
Southill. C Beds 1B 52
Southington. Hants 2D 24
South Kelsey. Linc 1H 87
South Kessock. High 4A 158
South Killingholme. N Lin 3E 95
South Kilvington. N Yor 1G 99
South Kilworth. Leics 2D 62
South Kirkby. W Yor 3E 93
South Kirkton. Abers 3E 153
South Knighton. Devn 5B 12
South Kyme. Linc 1A 76
South Lancing. W Sus 5C 26
South Ledaig. Arg 5D 140
Southleigh. Devn 3F 13
South Leigh. Oxon 5B 50
South Leverton. Notts 2E 87
South Littleton. Worc 1F 49
South Lopham. Norf 2C 66
South Luffenham. Rut 5G 75
South Malling. E Sus 4F 27
South Marston. Swin 3G 35
South Middleton. Nmbd 2D 121
South Milford. N Yor 1E 93
South Milton. Devn 4D 8
South Mimms. Herts 5C 52
Southminster. Essx 1D 40
South Molton. Devn 4H 19
South Moor. Dur 4E 115
Southmoor. Oxon 2B 36
South Moreton. Oxon 3D 36
South Mundham. W Sus 2G 17
South Muskham. Notts 5E 87
South Newbald. E Yor 1C 94
South Newington. Oxon 2C 50
South Newsham. Nmbd 2G 115
South Newton. N Ayr 4H 125
South Newton. Wilts 3F 23
South Normanton. Derbs 5B 86
South Norwood. G Lon 4E 39
South Nutfield. Surr 1E 27
South Ockendon. Thur 2G 39
Southoe. Cambs 4A 64
Southolt. Suff 4D 66
South Ormsby. Linc 3C 88
Southorpe. Pet 5H 75
South Otterington. N Yor 1F 99
South Owersby. Linc 1H 87
Southowram. W Yor 2B 92
South Oxhey. Herts 1C 38
South Perrott. Dors 2H 13
South Petherton. Som 1H 13
South Petherwin. Corn 4D 10
South Pickenham. Norf 5A 78
South Pool. Devn 4D 9
South Poorton. Dors 3A 14
South Port. Arg 1H 133
Southport. Mers 3B 90
Southpunds. Shet 10F 173
South Queensferry. Edin 2E 129
South Radworthy. Devn 3A 20
South Rauceby. Linc 1H 75
South Raynham. Norf 3A 78
Southrepps. Norf 2E 79
South Reston. Linc 2D 88
Southrey. Linc 4A 88
Southrop. Glos 5G 49
Southrope. Hants 2E 25
South Runcton. Norf 5F 77
South Scarle. Notts 4F 87
Southsea. Port 3E 17
South Shields. Tyne 3G 115
South Shore. Bkpl 1B 90
Southside. Orkn 5E 172
South Somercotes. Linc 1D 88
South Stainley. N Yor 3F 99
South Stainmore. Cumb 3B 104
South Stifford. Thur 3G 39
South Stoke. Bath 5C 34
South Stoke. Oxon 3D 36
South Stoke. W Sus 5B 26
South Street. E Sus 4E 27
South Street. Kent
nr. Faversham 5E 41
nr. Whitstable 4F 41
South Tawton. Devn 3G 11
South Thoresby. Linc 3D 88
South Tidworth. Wilts 2H 23
South Town. Devn 4C 12
South Town. Hants 3E 25
Southtown. Norf 5H 79
Southtown. Orkn 8D 172
South View. Shet 7E 173
Southwaite. Cumb 5F 113
South Walsham. Norf 4F 79
South Warnborough. Hants 2F 25
Southwater. W Sus 3C 26
Southwater Street. W Sus 3C 26
Southway. Som 2A 22
South Weald. Essx 1G 39
South Weirs. Hants 2A 16
Southwell. Dors 5B 14
Southwell. Notts 5E 86
South Weston. Oxon 2F 37
South Wheatley. Corn 3C 10
South Wheatley. Notts 2E 87
Southwick. Hants 2E 17
Southwick. Nptn 1H 63
Southwick. Tyne 4G 115
Southwick. W Sus 5D 26
Southwick. Wilts 1D 22
South Widcombe. Bath 1A 22
South Wigston. Leics 1C 62
South Willingham. Linc 2A 88
South Wingfield. Derbs 5A 86
South Witham. Linc 4G 75
Southwold. Suff 3H 67
South Wonston. Hants 3C 24
Southwood. Norf 5F 79
Southwood. Som 3A 22
South Woodham Ferrers. Essx 1C 40
South Wootton. Norf 3F 77
South Wraxall. Wilts 5D 34
South Zeal. Devn 3G 11
Soval Lodge. W Isl 5F 171
Sowerby. N Yor 1G 99
Sowerby. W Yor 2A 92
Sowerby Bridge. W Yor 2A 92
Sowerby Row. Cumb 5E 113
Sower Carr. Lanc 5C 96
Sowley Green. Suff 5G 65
Sowood. W Yor 3A 92
Sowton. Devn 3C 12
Soyal. High 4C 164
Soyland Town. W Yor 2A 92
Spa, The. New M 5H 179
Spacey Houses. N Yor 4F 99
Spa Common. Norf 2E 79
Spalding. Linc 3B 76
Spaldington. E Yor 1A 94
Spaldwick. Cambs 3A 64
Spalford. Notts 4F 87
Spamount. Derr 4E 176
Spanby. Linc 2H 75
Sparham. Norf 4C 78
Sparhamhill. Norf 4C 78
Spark Bridge. Cumb 1C 96
Sparket. Cumb 2F 103
Sparkford. Som 4B 22
Sparkwell. Devn 3B 8
Sparrow Green. Norf 4B 78
Sparrowpit. Derbs 2E 85
Sparrow's Green. E Sus 2H 27
Sparsholt. Hants 3C 24
Sparsholt. Oxon 3B 36
Spartylea. Nmbd 5B 114
Spath. Staf 2E 73
Spaunton. N Yor 1B 100
Spaxton. Som 3F 21
Spean Bridge. High 5E 149
Spear Hill. W Sus 4C 26
Speen. Buck 2G 37
Speen. W Ber 5C 36
Speeton. N Yor 2F 101
Speke. Mers 2G 83
Speldhurst. Kent 1G 27
Spellbrook. Herts 4E 53
Spelsbury. Oxon 3B 50
Spencers Wood. Wok 5F 37
Spennithorne. N Yor 1D 98
Spennymoor. Dur 1F 105
Spernall. Warw 4E 61
Sperrin. Derr 7C 174
Spetchley. Worc 5C 60
Spetisbury. Dors 2E 15
Spexhall. Suff 2F 67
Speybank. High 3C 150
Spey Bay. Mor 2A 160
Speybridge. High 1E 151
Speyview. Mor 4G 159
Spilsby. Linc 4D 88
Spindlestone. Nmbd 1F 121
Spinkhill. Derbs 3B 86
Spinney Hills. Leic 5D 74
Spinningdale. High 5D 164
Spital. Mers 2F 83
Spitalhill. Derbs 1F 73
Spital in the Street. Linc 1G 87
Spithurst. E Sus 4F 27
Spittal. Dum 4A 110
Spittal. E Lot 2A 130
Spittal. High 3D 168
Spittal. Nmbd 4G 131
Spittal. Pemb 2D 43
Spittalfield. Per 4A 144
Spittal of Glenmuick. Abers 5H 151
Spittal of Glenshee. Per 1A 144
Spittal-on-Rule. Bord 2H 119
Spixworth. Norf 4E 79
Splatt. Corn 4C 10
Spofforth. N Yor 4F 99
Spondon. Derb 2B 74
Spon End. W Mid 3H 61
Spooner Row. Norf 1C 66
Sporle. Norf 4H 77
Spott. E Lot 2C 130
Spratton. Nptn 3E 62
Spreakley. Surr 2G 25
Spreyton. Devn 3H 11
Spridlington. Linc 2H 87
Springburn. Glas 3H 127
Springfield. Dum 3E 113
Springfield. Fife 2F 137
Springfield. High 2A 158
Springfield. W Mid 2E 61
Springhill. Staf 5D 73
Spring Hill. W Mid 1C 60
Springholm. Dum 3F 111
Springside. N Ayr 1C 116
Springthorpe. Linc 2F 87
Spring Vale. IOW 3E 16
Spring Valley. IOM 4C 108
Springwell. Tyne 4F 115
Sproatley. E Yor 1E 95
Sproston Green. Ches W 4B 84
Sprotbrough. S Yor 4F 93
Sproughton. Suff 1E 54
Sprouston. Bord 1B 120
Sprowston. Norf 4E 79
Sproxton. Leics 3F 75
Sproxton. N Yor 1A 100
Sprunston. Cumb 5E 113
Spurstow. Ches E 5H 83
Squires Gate. Bkpl 1B 90
Sraid Ruadh. Arg 4A 138
Srannda. W Isl 9C 171
Sron an t-Sithein. High 2C 140
Sronphadruig Lodge. Per 1E 142
Sruth Mor. W Isl 2E 170
Stableford. Shrp 1B 60
Stackhouse. N Yor 3H 97
Stackpole. Pemb 5D 43
Stackpole Elidor. Pemb 5D 43
Stacksford. Norf 1C 66
Stacksteads. Lanc 2G 91
Staddiscombe. Plym 3B 8
Staddlethorpe. E Yor 2B 94
Staddon. Devn 2D 10
Stadhampton. Oxon 2E 36
Stadhlaigearraidh. W Isl 5C 170
Stafainn. High 2D 155
Staffield. Cumb 5G 113
Staffin. High 2D 155
Stafford. Staf 3D 72
Stafford Park. Telf 5B 72
Stagden Cross. Essx 4G 53
Stagsden. Bed 1H 51
Stag's Head. Devn 4G 19
Stainburn. Cumb 2B 102
Stainburn. N Yor 5E 99
Stainby. Linc 3G 75
Staincliffe. W Yor 2C 92
Staincross. S Yor 3D 92
Staindrop. Dur 2E 105
Staines-upon-Thames. Surr 3B 38
Stainfield. Linc
nr. Bourne 3H 75
nr. Lincoln 3A 88
Stainforth. N Yor 3H 97
Stainforth. S Yor 3G 93
Staining. Lanc 1B 90
Stainland. W Yor 3A 92
Stainsacre. N Yor 4G 107

Stainton—Swimbridge Newland

Stainton. Cumb
nr. Carlisle 4E 113
nr. Kendal 1E 97
nr. Penrith 2F 103
Stainton. Dur 3D 104
Stainton. Midd 3B 106
Stainton. N Yor 5E 105
Stainton. S Yor 1C 86
Stainton by Langworth. Linc 3H 87
Staintondale. N Yor 5G 107
Stainton le Vale. Linc 1A 88
Stainton with Adgarley. Cumb 2B 96
Stair. Cumb 2D 102
Stair. E Ayr 2D 116
Stairhaven. Dum 4H 109
Staithes. N Yor 3E 107
Stakeford. Nmbd 1F 115
Stake Pool. Lanc 5D 96
Stakes. Hants 2E 17
Stalbridge. Dors 1C 14
Stalbridge Weston. Dors 1C 14
Stalham. Norf 3F 79
Stalham Green. Norf 3F 79
Stalisfield Green. Kent 5D 40
Stallen. Dors 1B 14
Stallingborough. NE Lin 3F 95
Stalling Busk. N Yor 1B 98
Stallington. Staf 2D 72
Stalmine. Lanc 5C 96
Stalybridge. G Man 1D 84
Stambourne. Essx 2H 53
Stamford. Linc 5H 75
Stamford. Nmbd 3G 121
Stamford Bridge. Ches W 4G 83
Stamford Bridge. E Yor 4B 100
Stamfordham. Nmbd 2D 115
Stamperland. E Ren 4G 127
Stanah. Lanc 5C 96
Stanborough. Herts 4C 52
Stanbridge. C Beds 3H 51
Stanbridge. Dors 2F 15
Stanbury. W Yor 1A 92
Stand. N Lan 3A 128
Standburn. Falk 2C 128
Standeford. Staf 5D 72
Standen. Kent 1C 28
Standen Street. Kent 2C 28
Standerwick. Som 1D 22
Standford. Hants 3G 25
Standford Bridge. Telf 3B 72
Standingstone. Cumb 5D 112
Standish. Glos 5D 48
Standish. G Man 3D 90
Standish Lower Ground. G Man 4D 90
Standlake. Oxon 5B 50
Standon. Hants 4C 24
Standon. Herts 3D 53
Standon. Staf 2C 72
Standon Green End. Herts 4D 52
Stane. N Lan 4B 128
Stanecastle. N Ayr 1C 116
Stanfield. Norf 3B 78
Stanfield. Suff 5G 65
Stanford. C Beds 1B 52
Stanford. Kent 2F 29
Stanford Bishop. Here 5A 60
Stanford Bridge. Worc 4B 60
Stanford Dingley. W Ber 4D 36
Stanford in the Vale. Oxon 2B 36
Stanford-le-Hope. Thur 2A 40
Stanford on Avon. Nptn 3C 62
Stanford on Soar. Notts 3C 74
Stanford on Teme. Worc 4B 60
Stanford Rivers. Essx 5F 53
Stanfree. Derbs 3B 86
Stanghow. Red C 3D 107
Stanground. Pet 1B 64
Stanhoe. Norf 2H 77
Stanhope. Dur 1C 104
Stanhope. Bord 2D 118
Stanion. Nptn 2G 63
Stanley. Derbs 1B 74
Stanley. Dur 4E 115
Stanley. Per 5A 144
Stanley. Shrp 2B 60
Stanley. Staf 5D 84
Stanley. W Yor 2D 92
Stanley Common. Derbs 1B 74
Stanley Crook. Dur 1E 105
Stanley Hill. Here 1B 48
Stanlow. Ches W 3G 83
Stanmer. Brig 5E 27
Stanmore. G Lon 1C 38
Stanmore. Hants 4C 24
Stanmore. W Ber 4C 36
Stannersburn. Nmbd 1A 114
Stanningfield. Suff 5A 66
Stannington. Nmbd 2F 115
Stannington. S Yor 2H 85
Stansbatch. Here 4F 59
Stanshope. Staf 5F 85
Stanstead. Suff 1B 54
Stanstead Abbotts. Herts 4D 53
Stansted. Kent 4H 39
Stansted Airport. Essx 3F 53
Stansted Mountfitchet. Essx 3F 53
Stanthorne. Ches W 4A 84
Stanton. Derbs 4G 73
Stanton. Glos 2F 49
Stanton. Nmbd 5F 121
Stanton. Staf 1F 73
Stanton. Suff 3B 66
Stanton by Bridge. Derbs 3A 74
Stanton-by-Dale. Derbs 2B 74
Stanton Chare. Suff 3B 66
Stanton Drew. Bath 5A 34
Stanton Fitzwarren. Swin 2G 35
Stanton Harcourt. Oxon 5C 50
Stanton Hill. Notts 4B 86
Stanton in Peak. Derbs 4G 85
Stanton Lacy. Shrp 3G 59
Stanton Long. Shrp 1H 59
Stanton-on-the-Wolds. Notts 2D 74
Stanton Prior. Bath 5B 34
Stanton St Bernard. Wilts 5F 35
Stanton St John. Oxon 5D 50
Stanton St Quintin. Wilts 4E 35
Stanton Street. Suff 4B 66
Stanton under Bardon. Leics 4B 74
Stanton upon Hine Heath. Shrp 3H 71
Stanton Wick. Bath 5B 34
Stanwardine in the Fields. Shrp 3G 71
Stanwardine in the Wood. Shrp 3G 71
Stanway. Essx 3C 54
Stanway. Glos 2F 49
Stanwell. Surr 3B 38
Stanwell Green. Suff 3D 66
Stanwell Moor. Surr 3B 38
Stanwick. Nptn 3G 63
Stanydale. Shet 6D 173
Staoinebrig. W Isl 5C 170
Stape. N Yor 5E 107
Stapehill. Dors 2F 15
Stapeley. Ches E 1A 72
Stapenhill. Staf 3G 73
Staple. Kent 5G 41
Staple Cross. Devn 4D 20
Staplecross. E Sus 3B 28
Staplefield. W Sus 3D 27
Staple Fitzpaine. Som 1F 13
Stapleford. Cambs 5D 64
Stapleford. Herts 4D 52
Stapleford. Leics 4F 75
Stapleford. Linc 5F 87
Stapleford. Notts 2B 74
Stapleford. Wilts 3F 23
Stapleford Abbotts. Essx 1G 39
Stapleford Tawney. Essx 1G 39
Staplegrove. Som 4F 21
Staplehay. Som 4F 21
Staple Hill. S Glo 4B 34
Staplehurst. Kent 1B 28
Staplers. IOW 4D 16
Stapleton. Bris 4B 34
Stapleton. Cumb 2G 113
Stapleton. Here 4F 59
Stapleton. Leics 1B 62
Stapleton. N Yor 3F 105
Stapleton. Shrp 5G 71
Stapleton. Som 4H 21
Stapley. Som 1E 13
Staploe. Bed 4A 64
Staplow. Here 1B 48
Star. Fife 3F 137
Star. Pemb 1G 43
Starbeck. N Yor 4F 99
Starbotton. N Yor 2B 98
Starcross. Devn 4C 12
Stareton. Warw 3H 61
Starkholmes. Derbs 5H 85
Starling. G Man 3F 91
Starling's Green. Essx 2E 53
Starston. Norf 2E 67
Start. Devn 4E 9
Startforth. Dur 3D 104
Start Hill. Essx 3F 53
Startley. Wilts 3E 35
Stathe. Som 4G 21
Stathern. Leics 2E 75
Station Town. Dur 1B 106
Staughton Green. Cambs 4A 64
Staughton Highway. Cambs 4A 64
Staunton. Glos
nr. Cheltenham 3C 48
nr. Monmouth 4A 48
Staunton in the Vale. Notts 1F 75
Staunton on Arrow. Here 4F 59
Staunton on Wye. Here 1G 47
Staveley. Cumb 5F 103
Staveley. Derbs 3B 86
Staveley. N Yor 3F 99
Staveley-in-Cartmel. Cumb 1C 96
Staverton. Devn 2D 9
Staverton. Glos 3D 49
Staverton. Nptn 4C 62
Staverton. Wilts 5D 34
Stawell. Som 3G 21
Stawley. Som 4D 20
Staxigoe. High 3F 169
Staxton. N Yor 2E 101
Staylittle. Powy 1A 58
Staynall. Lanc 5C 96
Staythorpe. Notts 5E 87
Stean. N Yor 2C 98
Stearsby. N Yor 2A 100
Steart. Som 2F 21
Stebbing. Essx 3G 53
Stebbing Green. Essx 3G 53
Stedham. W Sus 4G 25
Steel. Nmbd 4C 114
Steel Cross. E Sus 2G 27
Steelend. Fife 4C 136
Steele Road. Bord 5H 119
Steel Heath. Shrp 2H 71
Steen's Bridge. Here 5H 59
Steep. Hants 4F 25
Steep Lane. W Yor 2A 92
Steeple. Dors 4E 15
Steeple. Essx 5C 54
Steeple Ashton. Wilts 1E 23
Steeple Aston. Oxon 3C 50
Steeple Barton. Oxon 3C 50
Steeple Bumpstead. Essx 1G 53
Steeple Claydon. Buck 3E 51
Steeple Gidding. Cambs 2A 64
Steeple Langford. Wilts 3F 23
Steeple Morden. Cambs 1C 52
Steeton. W Yor 5C 98
Stein. High 3B 154
Steinmanhill. Abers 4E 161
Stelling Minnis. Kent 1F 29
Stembridge. Som 4H 21
Stemster. High
nr. Halkirk 2D 169
nr. Westfield 2C 168
Stenalees. Corn 3E 6
Stenhill. Devn 1D 12
Stenhouse. Edin 2F 129
Stenhousemuir. Falk 1B 128
Stenigot. Linc 2B 88
Stenscholl. High 2D 155
Stenso. Orkn 5C 172
Stenson. Derbs 3H 73
Stenson Fields. Derbs 2H 73
Stenton. E Lot 2C 130
Stenwith. Linc 2F 75
Steòrnabhagh. W Isl 4G 171
Stepaside. Pemb 4F 43
Stepford. Dum 1F 111
Stepney. G Lon 2E 39
Steppingley. C Beds 2A 52
Stepps. N Lan 3H 127
Sterndale Moor. Derbs 4F 85
Sternfield. Suff 4F 67
Stert. Wilts 1F 23
Stetchworth. Cambs 5F 65
Stevenage. Herts 3C 52
Stevenston. N Ayr 5D 126
Stevenstone. Devn 1F 11
Steventon. Hants 2D 24
Steventon. Oxon 2C 36
Steventon End. Essx 1F 53
Stevington. Bed 5G 63
Stewartby. Bed 1A 52
Stewarton. E Ayr 5F 127
Stewartstown. M Ulst 2C 178
Stewkley. Buck 3G 51
Stewkley Dean. Buck 3G 51
Stewley. Som 1G 13
Stewton. Linc 2C 88
Steyning. W Sus 4C 26
Steynton. Pemb 4D 42
Stibb. Corn 1C 10
Stibbard. Norf 3B 78
Stibb Cross. Devn 1E 11
Stibb Green. Wilts 5H 35
Stibbington. Cambs 1H 63
Stichill. Bord 1B 120
Sticker. Corn 3D 6
Stickford. Linc 4C 88
Sticklepath. Devn 3G 11
Sticklinch. Som 3A 22
Stickling Green. Essx 2E 53
Stickney. Linc 5C 88
Stiffkey. Norf 1B 78
Stifford's Bridge. Here 1C 48
Stileway. Som 2H 21
Stillingfleet. N Yor 5H 99
Stillington. N Yor 3H 99
Stillington. Stoc T 2A 106
Stilton. Cambs 2A 64
Stinchcombe. Glos 2C 34
Stinsford. Dors 3C 14
Stiperstones. Shrp 5F 71
Stirchley. Telf 5B 72
Stirchley. W Mid 2E 61
Stirling. Abers 4H 161
Stirling. Stir 202 (4G 135)
Stirton. N Yor 4B 98
Stisted. Essx 3A 54
Stitchcombe. Wilts 5H 35
Stithians. Corn 5B 6
Stittenham. High 1A 158
Stivichall. W Mid 3H 61
Stixwould. Linc 4A 88
Stoak. Ches W 3G 83
Stobo. Bord 1D 118
Stobo Castle. Bord 1D 118
Stoborough. Dors 4E 15
Stoborough Green. Dors 4E 15
Stobs Castle. Bord 4H 119
Stobswood. Nmbd 5G 121
Stock. Essx 1A 40
Stockbridge. Hants 3B 24
Stockbridge. W Yor 5C 98
Stockbury. Kent 4C 40
Stockcross. W Ber 5C 36
Stockdalewath. Cumb 5E 113
Stocker's Head. Kent 5D 40
Stockerston. Leics 1F 63
Stock Green. Worc 5D 61
Stocking. Here 2B 48
Stockingford. Warw 1H 61
Stocking Green. Essx 2F 53
Stocking Pelham. Herts 3E 53
Stockland. Devn 2F 13
Stockland Bristol. Som 2F 21
Stockleigh English. Devn 2B 12
Stockleigh Pomeroy. Devn 2B 12
Stockley. Wilts 5F 35
Stocklinch. Som 1G 13
Stockport. G Man 2C 84
Stocks, The. Kent 3D 28
Stocksbridge. S Yor 1G 85
Stocksfield. Nmbd 3D 114
Stockstreet. Essx 3B 54
Stockton. Here 4H 59
Stockton. Norf 1F 67
Stockton. Shrp
nr. Bridgnorth 1B 60
nr. Chirbury 5E 71
Stockton. Telf 4B 72
Stockton. Warw 4B 62
Stockton. Wilts 3E 23
Stockton Brook. Staf 5D 84
Stockton Cross. Here 4H 59
Stockton Heath. Warr 2A 84
Stockton-on-Tees. Stoc T 3B 106
Stockton on Teme. Worc 4B 60
Stockton-on-the-Forest. York 4A 100
Stockwell Heath. Staf 3E 73
Stockwood. Bris 5B 34
Stock Wood. Worc 5E 61
Stodmarsh. Kent 4G 41
Stody. Norf 2C 78
Stoer. High 1E 163
Stoford. Som 1A 14
Stoford. Wilts 3F 23
Stogumber. Som 3D 20
Stogursey. Som 2F 21
Stoke. Devn 4C 18
Stoke. Hants
nr. Andover 1C 24
nr. South Hayling 2F 17
Stoke. Medw 3C 40
Stoke. W Mid 3A 62
Stoke Abbott. Dors 2H 13
Stoke Albany. Nptn 2F 63
Stoke Ash. Suff 3D 66
Stoke Bardolph. Notts 1D 74
Stoke Bliss. Worc 4A 60
Stoke Bruerne. Nptn 1F 51
Stoke by Clare. Suff 1H 53
Stoke-by-Nayland. Suff 2C 54
Stoke Canon. Devn 3C 12
Stoke Charity. Hants 3C 24
Stoke Climsland. Corn 5D 10
Stoke Cross. Here 5A 60
Stoke D'Abernon. Surr 5C 38
Stoke Doyle. Nptn 2H 63
Stoke Dry. Rut 1F 63
Stoke Edith. Here 1B 48
Stoke Farthing. Wilts 4F 23
Stoke Ferry. Norf 5G 77
Stoke Fleming. Devn 4E 9
Stokeford. Dors 4D 14
Stoke Gabriel. Devn 3E 9
Stoke Gifford. S Glo 4B 34
Stoke Golding. Leics 1A 62
Stoke Goldington. Mil 1G 51
Stokeham. Notts 3E 87
Stoke Hammond. Buck 3G 51
Stoke Heath. Shrp 3A 72
Stoke Holy Cross. Norf 5E 79
Stokeinteignhead. Devn 5C 12
Stoke Lacy. Here 1B 48
Stoke Lyne. Oxon 3D 50
Stoke Mandeville. Buck 4G 51
Stokenchurch. Buck 2F 37
Stoke Newington. G Lon 2E 39
Stokenham. Devn 4E 9
Stoke on Tern. Shrp 3A 72
Stoke-on-Trent. Stoke 202 (1C 72)
Stoke Orchard. Glos 3E 49
Stoke Pero. Som 2B 20
Stoke Poges. Buck 2A 38
Stoke Prior. Here 5H 59
Stoke Prior. Worc 4D 60
Stoke Rivers. Devn 3G 19
Stoke Rochford. Linc 3G 75
Stoke Row. Oxon 3E 37
Stoke St Gregory. Som 4G 21
Stoke St Mary. Som 4F 21
Stoke St Michael. Som 2B 22
Stoke St Milborough. Shrp 2H 59
Stokesay. Shrp 2G 59
Stokesby. Norf 4G 79
Stokesley. N Yor 4C 106
Stoke sub Hamdon. Som 1H 13
Stoke Talmage. Oxon 2E 37
Stoke Town. Stoke 202 (1C 72)
Stoke Trister. Som 4C 22
Stoke Wake. Dors 2C 14
Stolford. Som 2F 21
Stondon Massey. Essx 5F 53
Stone. Buck 4F 51
Stone. Glos 2B 34
Stone. Kent 3G 39
Stone. Som 3A 22
Stone. Staf 2D 72
Stone. Worc 3C 60
Stonea. Cambs 1D 64
Stoneacton. Shrp 1H 59
Stone Allerton. Som 1H 21
Ston Easton. Som 1B 22
Stonebridge. N Som 1G 21
Stonebridge. Surr 1C 26
Stone Bridge Corner. Pet 5B 76
Stonebroom. Derbs 5B 86
Stonebyres Holdings. S Lan 5B 128
Stone Chair. W Yor 2B 92
Stone Cross. E Sus 5H 27
Stone Cross. Kent 2G 27
Stone-edge Batch. N Som 4H 33
Stoneferry. Hull 1D 94
Stonefield. Arg 5D 140
Stonefield. S Lan 4H 127
Stonegate. E Sus 3A 28
Stonegate. N Yor 4E 107
Stonegrave. N Yor 2A 100
Stonehall. Worc 1D 49
Stonehaugh. Nmbd 2A 114
Stonehaven. Abers 5F 153
Stone Heath. Staf 2D 72
Stone Hill. Kent 2E 29
Stone House. Cumb 1G 97
Stonehouse. Glos 5D 48
Stonehouse. Nmbd 4H 113
Stonehouse. S Lan 5A 128
Stone in Oxney. Kent 3D 28
Stoneleigh. Warw 3H 61
Stoneley Green. Ches E 5A 84
Stonely. Cambs 4A 64
Stonepits. Worc 5E 61
Stoner Hill. Hants 4F 25
Stonesby. Leics 3F 75
Stonesfield. Oxon 4B 50
Stones Green. Essx 3E 55
Stone Street. Kent 5G 39
Stone Street. Suff
nr. Boxford 2C 54
nr. Halesworth 2F 67
Stonethwaite. Cumb 3D 102
Stoneyburn. W Lot 3C 128
Stoney Cross. Hants 1A 16
Stoneyford. Devn 2D 12
Stoneygate. Leic 5D 74
Stoneyhills. Essx 1D 40
Stoneykirk. Dum 4F 109
Stoney Middleton. Derbs 3G 85
Stoney Stanton. Leics 1B 62
Stoney Stoke. Som 3C 22
Stoney Stratton. Som 3B 22
Stoney Stretton. Shrp 5F 71
Stoneywood. Aber 2F 153
Stonham Aspal. Suff 5D 66
Stonnall. Staf 5E 73
Stonor. Oxon 3F 37
Stonton Wyville. Leics 1E 63
Stonybreck. Shet 1B 172
Stony Cross. Devn 4F 19
Stony Cross. Here
nr. Great Malvern 1C 48
nr. Leominster 4H 59
Stonyford. Lis 2G 179
Stony Houghton. Derbs 4B 86
Stony Stratford. Mil 1F 51
Stoodleigh. Devn
nr. Barnstaple 3G 19
nr. Tiverton 1C 12
Stopham. W Sus 4B 26
Stopsley. Lutn 3B 52
Stoptide. Corn 1D 6
Storeton. Mers 2F 83
Stormontfield. Per 1D 136
Stornoway. W Isl 4G 171
Stornoway Airport. W Isl 4G 171
Storridge. Here 1C 48
Storrington. W Sus 4B 26
Storrs. Cumb 5E 103
Storth. Cumb 1D 97
Storwood. E Yor 5B 100
Stotfield. Mor 1G 159
Stotfold. C Beds 2C 52
Stottesdon. Shrp 2A 60
Stoughton. Leics 5D 74
Stoughton. Surr 5A 38
Stoughton. W Sus 1G 17
Stoul. High 4F 147
Stoulton. Worc 1E 49
Stourbridge. W Mid 2C 60
Stourpaine. Dors 2D 14
Stourport-on-Severn. Worc 3C 60
Stour Provost. Dors 4C 22
Stour Row. Dors 4D 22
Stourton. Staf 2C 60
Stourton. Warw 2A 50
Stourton. W Yor 1D 92
Stourton. Wilts 3C 22
Stourton Caundle. Dors 1C 14
Stove. Orkn 4F 172
Stove. Shet 9F 173
Stoven. Suff 2G 67
Stow. Linc
nr. Billingborough 2H 75
nr. Gainsborough 2F 87
Stow. Bord 5A 130
Stow Bardolph. Norf 5F 77
Stow Bedon. Norf 1B 66
Stowbridge. Norf 5F 77
Stow cum Quy. Cambs 4E 65
Stowe. Glos 5A 48
Stowe. Shrp 3F 59
Stowe. Staf 4F 73
Stowe-by-Chartley. Staf 3E 73
Stowell. Som 4B 22
Stowey. Bath 1A 22
Stowford. Devn
nr. Colaton Raleigh 4D 12
nr. Combe Martin 2G 19
nr. Tavistock 4E 11
Stowlangtoft. Suff 4B 66
Stow Longa. Cambs 3A 64
Stow Maries. Essx 1C 40
Stowmarket. Suff 5C 66
Stow-on-the-Wold. Glos 3G 49
Stowting. Kent 1F 29
Stowupland. Suff 5C 66
Straad. Arg 3B 126
Strabane. Derr 3F 176
Strachan. Abers 4D 152
Stradbroke. Suff 3E 67
Stradishall. Suff 5G 65
Stradsett. Norf 5F 77
Stragglethorpe. Linc 5G 87
Stragglethorpe. Notts 2D 74
Straid. Ant 7K 175
Straid. ME Ant 7G 175
Straid. S Ayr 5A 116
Straight Soley. Wilts 4B 36
Straiton. Midl 3F 129
Straiton. S Ayr 4C 116
Straloch. Per 2H 143
Stramshall. Staf 2E 73
Strang. IOM 4C 108
Strangford. Here 3A 48
Strangford. New M 5K 179
Stranocum. Caus 3G 175
Stranraer. Dum 3F 109
Strata Florida. Cdgn 4G 57
Stratfield Mortimer. W Ber 5E 37
Stratfield Saye. Hants 5E 37
Stratfield Turgis. Hants 1E 25
Stratford. G Lon 2E 39
Stratford. Worc 2D 49
Stratford St Andrew. Suff 4F 67
Stratford St Mary. Suff 2D 54
Stratford sub Castle. Wilts 3G 23
Stratford Tony. Wilts 4F 23
Stratford-upon-Avon. Warw 202 (5G 61)
Strath. High
nr. Gairloch 1G 155
nr. Wick 3E 169
Strathan. High
nr. Fort William 4B 148
nr. Lochinver 1E 163
nr. Tongue 2F 167
Strathan Skerray. High 2G 167
Strathaven. S Lan 5A 128
Strathblane. Stir 2G 127
Strathcanaird. High 3F 163
Strathcarron. High 4B 156
Strathcoil. Arg 5A 140
Strathdon. Abers 2A 152
Strathkinness. Fife 2G 137
Strathmashie House. High 4H 149
Strathmiglo. Fife 2E 136
Strathmore Lodge. High 4D 168
Strathpeffer. High 3G 157
Strathrannoch. High 1F 157
Strathtay. Per 3G 143
Strathvaich Lodge. High 1F 157
Strathwhillan. N Ayr 2E 123
Strathy. High
nr. Invergordon 1A 158
nr. Melvich 2A 168
Strathyre. Stir 2E 135
Stratton. Corn 2C 10
Stratton. Dors 3B 14
Stratton. Glos 5F 49
Stratton Audley. Oxon 3E 50
Stratton-on-the-Fosse. Som 1B 22
Stratton St Margaret. Swin 3G 35
Stratton St Michael. Norf 1E 66
Stratton Strawless. Norf 3E 78
Stravithie. Fife 2H 137
Stream. M Ulst 7D 174
Stream. Som 3D 20
Streat. E Sus 4E 27
Streatham. G Lon 3E 39
Streatley. C Beds 3A 52
Streatley. W Ber 3D 36
Street. Corn 3C 10
Street. Lanc 4E 97
Street. N Yor 4E 107
Street. Som
nr. Chard 2G 13
Street. Som
nr. Glastonbury 3H 21
Street Ash. Som 1F 13
Street Dinas. Shrp 2F 71
Street End. Kent 5F 41
Street End. W Sus 3G 17
Streetgate. Tyne 4F 115
Streethay. Staf 4F 73
Streethouse. W Yor 2D 93
Streetlam. N Yor 5A 106
Street Lane. Derbs 1A 74
Streetly. W Mid 1E 61
Streetly End. Cambs 1G 53
Street on the Fosse. Som 3B 22
Strefford. Shrp 2G 59
Strelley. Notts 1C 74
Strensall. York 3A 100
Strensall Camp. York 4A 100
Stretcholt. Som 2F 21
Strete. Devn 4E 9
Stretford. G Man 1C 84
Stretford. Here 5H 59
Strethall. Essx 2E 53
Stretham. Cambs 3E 65
Stretton. Ches W 5G 83
Stretton. Derbs 4A 86
Stretton. Rut 4G 75
Stretton. Staf
nr. Brewood 4C 72
nr. Burton upon Trent 3G 73
Stretton. Warr 2A 84
Stretton en le Field. Leics 4H 73
Stretton Grandison. Here 1B 48
Stretton Heath. Shrp 4F 71
Stretton-on-Dunsmore. Warw 3B 62
Stretton-on-Fosse. Warw 2H 49
Stretton Sugwas. Here 1H 47
Stretton under Fosse. Warw 2B 62
Stretton Westwood. Shrp 1H 59
Strichen. Abers 3G 161
Strines. G Man 2D 84
Stringston. Som 2E 21
Strixton. Nptn 4G 63
Stroanfreggan. Dum 5F 117
Stroat. Glos 2A 34
Stromeferry. High 5A 156
Stromemore. High 5A 156
Stromness. Orkn 7B 172
Stronachie. Per 3C 136
Stronachlachar. Stir 2D 134
Stronchreggan. High 1E 141
Strone. Arg 1C 126
Strone. High
nr. Drumnadrochit 1H 149
nr. Kingussie 3B 150
Stronenaba. High 5E 148
Stronganess. Shet 1G 173
Stronmilchan. Arg 1A 134
Stronsay Airport. Orkn 5F 172
Strontian. High 2C 140
Strood. Kent 2C 28
Strood. Medw 4B 40
Strood Green. Surr 1D 26
Strood Green. W Sus
nr. Billingshurst 3B 26
nr. Horsham 2C 26
Strothers Dale. Nmbd 4C 114
Stroud. Glos 5D 48
Stroud. Hants 4F 25
Stroud Green. Essx 1C 40
Stroxton. Linc 2G 75
Struan. High 5C 154
Struan. Per 2F 143
Struanmore. High 5C 154
Strubby. Linc 2D 88
Strugg's Hill. Linc 2B 76
Strumpshaw. Norf 5F 79
Struthehill. S Lan 4A 128
Struy. High 5G 157
Stryd. IOA 2B 80
Stryt-issa. Wrex 1E 71
Stuartfield. Abers 4G 161
Stubbington. Hants 2D 16
Stubbins. Lanc 3F 91
Stubble Green. Cumb 5B 102
Stubb's Cross. Kent 2D 28
Stubbs Green. Norf 1F 67
Stubhampton. Dors 1E 15
Stubton. Linc 1F 75
Stubwood. Staf 2E 73
Stuckton. Hants 1G 15
Studham. C Beds 4A 52
Studland. Dors 4F 15
Studley. Warw 4E 61
Studley. Wilts 4E 35
Studley Roger. N Yor 2E 99
Stuntney. Cambs 3E 65
Stunts Green. E Sus 4H 27
Sturbridge. Staf 2C 72
Sturgate. Linc 2F 87
Sturmer. Essx 1G 53
Sturminster Marshall. Dors 2E 15
Sturminster Newton. Dors 1C 14
Sturry. Kent 4F 41
Sturton. N Lin 4C 94
Sturton by Stow. Linc 2F 87
Sturton le Steeple. Notts 2E 87
Stuston. Suff 3D 66
Stutton. N Yor 5G 99
Stutton. Suff 2E 55
Styal. Ches E 2C 84
Stydd. Lanc 1E 91
Styrrup. Notts 1D 86
Suainebost. W Isl 1H 171
Suardail. W Isl 4G 171
Succoth. Abers 5B 160
Succoth. Arg 3B 134
Suckley. Worc 5B 60
Suckley Knowl. Worc 5B 60
Sudborough. Nptn 2G 63
Sudbourne. Suff 5G 67
Sudbrook. Linc 1G 75
Sudbrook. Mon 3A 34
Sudbrooke. Linc 3H 87
Sudbury. Derbs 2F 73
Sudbury. Suff 1B 54
Sudgrove. Glos 5E 49
Suffield. Norf 2E 79
Suffield. N Yor 5G 107
Sugnall. Staf 2B 72
Sugwas Pool. Here 1H 47
Suisnish. High 5E 155
Sulaisiadar. W Isl 4H 171
Sùlaisiadar Mòr. High 4D 155
Sulby. IOM 2C 108
Sulgrave. Nptn 1D 50
Sulham. W Ber 4E 37
Sulhamstead. W Ber 5E 37
Sullington. W Sus 4B 26
Sullom. Shet 4E 173
Sully. V Glam 5E 33
Sumburgh. Shet 10F 173
Sumburgh Airport. Shet 10E 173
Summer Bridge. N Yor 3E 98
Summercourt. Corn 3C 6
Summergangs. Hull 1E 94
Summerhill. Aber 3G 153
Summerhill. Pemb 4F 43
Summer Hill. W Mid 1D 60
Summerhouse. Darl 3F 105
Summersdale. W Sus 2G 17
Summerseat. G Man 3F 91
Summit. G Man 3H 91
Sunbury. Surr 4C 38
Sunderland. Cumb 1C 102
Sunderland. Lanc 4D 96
Sunderland. Tyne 202 (4G 115)
Sunderland Bridge. Dur 1F 105
Sundon Park. Lutn 3A 52
Sundridge. Kent 5F 39
Sunk Island. E Yor 3F 95
Sunningdale. Wind 4A 38
Sunninghill. Wind 4A 38
Sunningwell. Oxon 5C 50
Sunniside. Dur 1E 105
Sunniside. Tyne 4F 115
Sunny Bank. Cumb 5D 102
Sunny Hill. Derb 2H 73
Sunnyhurst. Bkbn 2E 91
Sunnylaw. Stir 4G 135
Sunnymead. Oxon 5D 50
Sunnyside. S Yor 1B 86
Sunnyside. W Sus 2E 27
Sunton. Wilts 1H 23
Surbiton. G Lon 4C 38
Surby. IOM 4B 108
Surfleet. Linc 3B 76
Surfleet Seas End. Linc 3B 76
Surlingham. Norf 5F 79
Surrex. Essx 3B 54
Sustead. Norf 2D 78
Susworth. Linc 4B 94
Sutcombe. Devn 1D 10
Suton. Norf 1C 66
Sutors of Cromarty. High 2C 158
Sutterby. Linc 3C 88
Sutterton. Linc 2B 76
Sutterton Dowdyke. Linc 2B 76
Sutton. Buck 3B 38
Sutton. Cambs 3D 64
Sutton. C Beds 1C 52
Sutton. E Sus 5F 27
Sutton. G Lon 4D 38
Sutton. Kent 1H 29
Sutton. Norf 3F 79
Sutton. Notts 2E 75
Sutton. Oxon 5C 50
Sutton. Pemb 3D 42
Sutton. Pet 1H 63
Sutton. Shrp
nr. Bridgnorth 2B 60
nr. Market Drayton 2A 72
nr. Oswestry 3F 71
nr. Shrewsbury 4H 71
Sutton. Som 3B 22
Sutton. S Yor 3F 93
Sutton. Staf 3B 72
Sutton. Suff 1G 55
Sutton. W Sus 4A 26
Sutton. Worc 4A 60
Sutton Abinger. Surr 1C 26
Sutton at Hone. Kent 3G 39
Sutton Bassett. Nptn 1E 63
Sutton Benger. Wilts 4E 35
Sutton Bingham. Som 1A 14
Sutton Bonington. Notts 3C 74
Sutton Bridge. Linc 3D 76
Sutton Cheney. Leics 5B 74
Sutton Coldfield, Royal. W Mid 1F 61
Sutton Corner. Linc 3D 76
Sutton Courtenay. Oxon 2D 36
Sutton Crosses. Linc 3D 76
Sutton cum Lound. Notts 2D 86
Sutton Gault. Cambs 3D 64
Sutton Grange. N Yor 2E 99
Sutton Green. Surr 5B 38
Sutton Howgrave. N Yor 2F 99
Sutton in Ashfield. Notts 5B 86
Sutton-in-Craven. N Yor 5C 98
Sutton Ings. Hull 1E 94
Sutton in the Elms. Leics 1C 62
Sutton Lane Ends. Ches E 3D 84
Sutton Leach. Mers 1H 83
Sutton Maddock. Shrp 5B 72
Sutton Mallet. Som 3G 21
Sutton Mandeville. Wilts 4E 23
Sutton Montis. Som 4B 22
Sutton on Hull. Hull 1E 94
Sutton on Sea. Linc 2E 89
Sutton-on-the-Forest. N Yor 3H 99
Sutton on the Hill. Derbs 2G 73
Sutton on Trent. Notts 4E 87
Sutton Poyntz. Dors 4C 14
Sutton St Edmund. Linc 4C 76
Sutton St Edmund's Common. Linc 5C 76
Sutton St James. Linc 4C 76
Sutton St Michael. Here 1A 48
Sutton St Nicholas. Here 1A 48
Sutton Scarsdale. Derbs 4B 86
Sutton Scotney. Hants 3C 24
Sutton-under-Brailes. Warw 2B 50
Sutton-under-Whitestonecliffe. N Yor 1G 99
Sutton upon Derwent. E Yor 5B 100
Sutton Valence. Kent 1C 28
Sutton Veny. Wilts 2E 23
Sutton Waldron. Dors 1D 14
Sutton Weaver. Ches W 3H 83
Swaby. Linc 3C 88
Swadlincote. Derbs 4G 73
Swaffham. Norf 5H 77
Swaffham Bulbeck. Cambs 4E 65
Swaffham Prior. Cambs 4E 65
Swafield. Norf 2E 79
Swainby. N Yor 4B 106
Swainshill. Here 1H 47
Swainsthorpe. Norf 5E 79
Swainswick. Bath 5C 34
Swalcliffe. Oxon 2B 50
Swalecliffe. Kent 4F 41
Swallow. Linc 4E 95
Swallow Beck. Linc 4G 87
Swallowcliffe. Wilts 4E 23
Swallowfield. Wok 5F 37
Swallownest. S Yor 2B 86
Swampton. Hants 1C 24
Swanage. Dors 5F 15
Swanbister. Orkn 7C 172
Swanbourne. Buck 3G 51
Swanbridge. V Glam 5E 33
Swan Green. Ches W 3B 84
Swanland. E Yor 2C 94
Swanley. Kent 4G 39
Swanmore. Hants 1D 16
Swannington. Leics 4B 74
Swannington. Norf 4D 78
Swanpool. Linc 4G 87
Swanscombe. Kent 3H 39
Swansea. Swan 203 (3F 31)
Swan Street. Essx 3B 54
Swanton Abbott. Norf 3E 79
Swanton Morley. Norf 4C 78
Swanton Novers. Norf 2C 78
Swanton Street. Kent 5C 40
Swanwick. Derbs 5B 86
Swanwick. Hants 2D 16
Swanwick Green. Ches E 1H 71
Swarby. Linc 1H 75
Swardeston. Norf 5E 78
Swarister. Shet 3G 173
Swarkestone. Derbs 3A 74
Swarland. Nmbd 4F 121
Swarraton. Hants 3D 24
Swartha. W Yor 5C 98
Swarthmoor. Cumb 2B 96
Swaton. Linc 2A 76
Swatragh. M Ulst 6E 174
Swavesey. Cambs 4C 64
Sway. Hants 3A 16
Swayfield. Linc 3G 75
Swaythling. Sotn 1C 16
Sweet Green. Worc 4A 60
Sweetham. Devn 3B 12
Sweetholme. Cumb 3G 103
Sweets. Corn 3B 10
Sweetshouse. Corn 2E 7
Swefling. Suff 4F 67
Swell. Som 4G 21
Swepstone. Leics 4A 74
Swerford. Oxon 2B 50
Swettenham. Ches E 4C 84
Swetton. N Yor 2D 98
Swffryd. Blae 2F 33
Swiftsden. E Sus 3B 28
Swilland. Suff 5D 66
Swillington. W Yor 1D 93
Swimbridge. Devn 4G 19
Swimbridge Newland. Devn 3G 19

Swinbrook—Tosside

Swinbrook. Oxon 4A 50
Swincliffe. N Yor 4E 99
Swincliffe. W Yor 2C 92
Swinderby. Linc 4F 87
Swindon. Glos 3E 49
Swindon. Nmbd 5D 121
Swindon. Staf 1C 60
Swindon. Swin 203 (3G 35)
Swine. E Yor 1E 95
Swinefleet. E Yor 2A 94
Swineford. S Glo 5B 34
Swineshead. Bed 4H 63
Swineshead. Linc 1B 76
Swineshead Bridge. Linc 1B 76
Swiney. High 5E 169
Swinford. Leics 3C 62
Swinford. Oxon 5C 50
Swingate. Notts 1C 74
Swingbrow. Cambs 2C 64
Swingfield Minnis. Kent 1G 29
Swingfield Street. Kent 1G 29
Swingleton Green. Suff 1C 54
Swinhill. S Lan 5A 128
Swinhoe. Nmbd 2G 121
Swinhope. Linc 1B 88
Swinister. Shet 3E 173
Swinithwaite. N Yor 1C 98
Swinmore Common. Here 1B 48
Swinscoe. Staf 1F 73
Swinside Hall. Bord 3B 120
Swinstead. Linc 3H 75
Swinton. G Man 4F 91
Swinton. N Yor
nr. Malton 2B 100
nr. Masham 2E 98
Swinton. Bord 5E 131
Swinton. S Yor 1B 86
Swithland. Leics 4C 74
Swordale. High 2H 157
Swordly. High 2H 167
Sworton Heath. Ches E 2A 84
Swyddffynnon. Cdgn 4F 57
Swynnerton. Staf 2C 72
Swyre. Dors 4A 14
Sycharth. Powy 3E 70
Sychdyn. Flin 4E 83
Sychnant. Powy 3B 58
Sychtyn. Powy 5B 70
Syde. Glos 4E 49
Sydenham. G Lon 3E 39
Sydenham. Oxon 5F 51
Sydenham. Som 3G 21
Sydenham Damerel. Devn 5E 11
Syderstone. Norf 2H 77
Sydling St Nicholas. Dors 3B 14
Sydmonton. Hants 1C 24
Sydney. Ches E 5B 84
Syerston. Notts 1E 75
Syke. G Man 3G 91
Sykehouse. S Yor 3G 93
Sykes. Lanc 4F 97
Syleham. Suff 3E 66
Sylen. Carm 5F 45
Sylfaen. Powy 5D 70
Symbister. Shet 5G 173
Symington. S Ayr 1C 116
Symington. S Lan 1B 118
Symondsbury. Dors 3H 13
Symonds Yat. Here 4A 48
Synod Inn. Cdgn 5D 56
Syre. High 4G 167
Syreford. Glos 3F 49
Syresham. Nptn 1E 51
Syston. Leics 4D 74
Syston. Linc 1G 75
Sytchampton. Worc 4C 60
Sywell. Nptn 4F 63

T

Tabost. W Isl
nr. Cearsiadar 6F 171
nr. Suainebost 1H 171
Tachbrook Mallory. Warw 4H 61
Tackley. Oxon 3C 50
Tacleit. W Isl 4D 171
Tacolneston. Norf 1D 66
Tadcaster. N Yor 5G 99
Taddington. Derbs 3F 85
Taddington. Glos 2F 49
Taddiport. Devn 1E 11
Tadley. Hants 5E 36
Tadlow. Cambs 1C 52
Tadmarton. Oxon 2B 50
Tadwick. Bath 4C 34
Tadworth. Surr 5D 38
Tafarnaubach. Blae 4E 46
Tafarn-y-bwlch. Pemb 1E 43
Tafarn-y-Gelyn. Den 4D 82
Taff's Well. Rhon 3E 33
Tafolwern. Powy 5A 70
Taibach. Neat 3A 32
Tai-bach. Powy 3D 70
Taigh a Ghearraidh. W Isl 1C 170
Taigh Bhuirgh. W Isl 8C 171
Tain. High
nr. Invergordon 5E 165
nr. Thurso 2E 169
Tai-Nant. Wrex 1E 71
Tai'n Lon. Gwyn 5D 80
Tairbeart. W Isl 8D 171
Tairgwaith. Neat 4H 45
Takeley. Essx 3F 53
Takeley Street. Essx 3F 53
Talachddu. Powy 2D 46
Talacre. Flin 2D 82
Talardd. Gwyn 3A 70
Talaton. Devn 3D 12
Talbenny. Pemb 3C 42
Talbot Green. Rhon 3D 32
Taleford. Devn 3D 12
Talerddig. Powy 5B 70
Talgarreg. Cdgn 5D 56
Talgarth. Powy 2E 47
Talisker. High 5C 154
Talke. Staf 5C 84
Talkin. Cumb 4G 113
Talladale. High 1B 156
Talla Linnfoots. Bord 2D 118
Tallaminnock. S Ayr 5C 116
Tallarn Green. Wrex 1G 71
Tallentire. Cumb 1C 102
Talley. Carm 2G 45
Tallington. Linc 5H 75
Talmine. High 2F 167
Talog. Carm 2H 43
Talsarn. Carm 3A 46
Talsarn. Cdgn 5E 57
Talsarnau. Gwyn 2F 69
Talskiddy. Corn 2D 6
Talwrn. IOA 3D 81
Talwrn. Wrex 1E 71
Tal-y-bont. Cdgn 2F 57
Tal-y-Bont. Cnwy 4G 81
Tal-y-bont. Gwyn
nr. Bangor 3F 81
nr. Barmouth 3E 69
Talybont-on-Usk. Powy 3E 46
Tal-y-cafn. Cnwy 3G 81
Tal-y-coed. Mon 4H 47
Tal-y-llyn. Gwyn 5G 69
Talyllyn. Powy 3E 46
Talysarn. Gwyn 5D 81
Tal-y-waenydd. Gwyn 1F 69
Talywain. Torf 5F 47
Tal-y-Wern. Powy 5H 69
Tamerton Foliot. Plym 2A 8
Tamlaght. Ferm 8E 176
Tamlaght O'Crilly. M Ulst 6F 174
Tamnamore. M Ulst 3C 178
Tamworth. Staf 5G 73
Tamworth Green. Linc 1C 76
Tandlehill. Ren 3F 127
Tandragee. Arm 5E 178
Tandridge. Surr 5E 39
Tanerdy. Carm 3E 45
Tanfield. Dur 4E 115
Tanfield Lea. Dur 4E 115
Tangasdal. W Isl 8B 170
Tang Hall. York 4A 100
Tangiers. Pemb 3D 42
Tangley. Hants 1B 24
Tangmere. W Sus 5A 26
Tangwick. Shet 4D 173
Tankerness. Orkn 7E 172
Tankersley. S Yor 1H 85
Tankerton. Kent 4F 41
Tan-lan. Cnwy 4G 81
Tan-lan. Gwyn 1F 69
Tannach. High 4F 169
Tannadice. Ang 3D 145
Tanner's Green. Worc 3E 61
Tannington. Suff 4E 67
Tannochside. N Lan 3A 128
Tan Office Green. Suff 5G 65
Tansley. Derbs 5H 85
Tansley Knoll. Derbs 4H 85
Tansor. Nptn 1H 63
Tantobie. Dur 4E 115
Tanton. N Yor 3C 106
Tanvats. Linc 4A 88
Tanworth-in-Arden. Warw 3F 61
Tan-y-bwlch. Gwyn 1F 69
Tan-y-fron. Cnwy 4B 82
Tanyfron. Wrex 5E 83
Tanygrisiau. Gwyn 1F 69
Tan-y-groes. Cdgn 1C 44
Tan-y-pistyll. Powy 3C 70
Tan-yr-allt. Den 2C 82
Taobh a Chaolais. W Isl 7C 170
Taobh a Deas Loch Aineort. W Isl 6C 170
Taobh a Ghlinne. W Isl 6F 171
Taobh a Tuath Loch Aineort. W Isl 6C 170
Taplow. Buck 2A 38
Tapton. Derbs 3A 86
Tarbert. Arg
on Jura 1E 125
on Kintyre 3G 125
Tarbert. W Isl 8D 171
Tarbet. Arg 3C 134
Tarbet. High
nr. Mallaig 4F 147
nr. Scourie 4B 166
Tarbock Green. Mers 2G 83
Tarbolton. S Ayr 2D 116
Tarbrax. S Lan 4D 128
Tardebigge. Worc 4D 61
Tarfside. Ang 1D 145
Tarland. Abers 3B 152
Tarleton. Lanc 2C 90
Tarlogie. High 5E 165
Tarlscough. Lanc 3C 90
Tarlton. Glos 2E 35
Tarnbrook. Lanc 4E 97
Tarnock. Som 1G 21
Tarns. Cumb 5C 112
Tarporley. Ches W 4H 83
Tarpots. Essx 2B 40
Tarr. Som 3E 20
Tarrant Crawford. Dors 2E 15
Tarrant Gunville. Dors 1E 15
Tarrant Hinton. Dors 1E 15
Tarrant Keyneston. Dors 2E 15
Tarrant Launceston. Dors 2E 15
Tarrant Monkton. Dors 2E 15
Tarrant Rawston. Dors 2E 15
Tarrant Rushton. Dors 2E 15
Tarrel. High 5F 165
Tarring Neville. E Sus 5F 27
Tarrington. Here 1B 48
Tarsappie. Per 1D 136
Tarscabhaig. High 3D 147
Tarskavaig. High 3D 147
Tarves. Abers 5F 161
Tarvie. High 3G 157
Tarvin. Ches W 4G 83
Tasburgh. Norf 1E 66
Tasley. Shrp 1A 60
Tassagh. Arm 6C 178
Taston. Oxon 3B 50
Tatenhill. Staf 3G 73
Tathall End. Mil 1G 51
Tatham. Lanc 3F 97
Tathwell. Linc 2C 88
Tatling End. Buck 2B 38
Tatsfield. Surr 5F 39
Tattenhall. Ches W 5G 83
Tatterford. Norf 3A 78
Tattersett. Norf 2H 77
Tattershall. Linc 5B 88
Tattershall Bridge. Linc 5A 88
Tattershall Thorpe. Linc 5B 88
Tattingstone. Suff 2E 55
Tattingstone White Horse. Suff 2E 55
Tattle Bank. Warw 4F 61
Tatworth. Som 2G 13
Taunton. Som 203 (4F 21)
Taverham. Norf 4D 78
Taverners Green. Essx 4F 53
Tavernspite. Pemb 3F 43
Tavistock. Devn 5E 11
Tavool House. Arg 1B 132
Taw Green. Devn 3G 11
Tawstock. Devn 4F 19
Taxal. Derbs 2E 85
Tayinloan. Arg 5E 125
Taynish. Arg 1F 125
Taynton. Glos 3C 48
Taynton. Oxon 4H 49
Taynuilt. Arg 5E 141
Tayport. Fife 1G 137
Tay Road Bridge. D'dee 1G 137
Tayvallich. Arg 1F 125
Tealby. Linc 1A 88
Tealing. Ang 5D 144
Teams. Tyne 3F 115
Teangue. High 3E 147
Teanna Mhachair. W Isl 2C 170
Tebay. Cumb 4H 103
Tebworth. C Beds 3H 51
Tedburn St Mary. Devn 3B 12
Teddington. Glos 2E 49
Teddington. G Lon 3C 38
Tedsmore. Shrp 3F 71
Tedstone Delamere. Here 5A 60
Tedstone Wafer. Here 5A 60
Teemore. Ferm 7J 177
Teesport. Red C 2C 106
Teesside. Stoc T 2C 106
Teeton. Nptn 3D 62
Teffont Evias. Wilts 3E 23
Teffont Magna. Wilts 3E 23
Tegryn. Pemb 1G 43
Teigh. Rut 4F 75
Teigncombe. Devn 4G 11
Teigngrace. Devn 5B 12
Teignmouth. Devn 5C 12
Telford. Telf 4A 72
Telham. E Sus 4B 28
Tellisford. Som 1D 22
Telscombe. E Sus 5F 27
Telscombe Cliffs. E Sus 5E 27
Tempar. Per 3D 142
Templand. Dum 1B 112
Temple. Corn 5B 10
Temple. Glas 3G 127
Temple. Midl 4G 129
Temple Balsall. W Mid 3G 61
Temple Bar. Carm 4F 45
Temple Bar. Cdgn 5E 57
Temple Cloud. Bath 1B 22
Templecombe. Som 4C 22
Temple Ewell. Kent 1G 29
Temple Grafton. Warw 5F 61
Temple Guiting. Glos 3F 49
Templehall. Fife 4E 137
Temple Hirst. N Yor 2G 93
Temple Normanton. Derbs 4B 86
Templepatrick. Ant 8J 175
Temple Sowerby. Cumb 2H 103
Templeton. Devn 1B 12
Templeton. Pemb 3F 43
Templeton. W Ber 5B 36
Templetown. Dur 5E 115
Tempo. Ferm 8F 176
Tempsford. C Beds 5A 64
Tenandry. Per 2G 143
Tenbury Wells. Worc 4H 59
Tenby. Pemb 4F 43
Tendring. Essx 3E 55
Tendring Green. Essx 3E 55
Tenga. Arg 4G 139
Ten Mile Bank. Norf 1F 65
Tenterden. Kent 2C 28
Terfyn. Cnwy 3B 82
Terhill. Som 3E 21
Terling. Essx 4A 54
Termon Rock. Ferm 2A 178
Ternhill. Shrp 2A 72
Terregles. Dum 2G 111
Terrick. Buck 5G 51
Terrington. N Yor 2A 100
Terrington St Clement. Norf 3E 77
Terrington St John. Norf 4E 77
Terry's Green. Warw 3F 61
Teston. Kent 5B 40
Testwood. Hants 1B 16
Tetbury. Glos 2D 35
Tetbury Upton. Glos 2D 35
Tetchill. Shrp 2F 71
Tetcott. Devn 3D 10
Tetford. Linc 3C 88
Tetney. Linc 4G 95
Tetney Lock. Linc 4G 95
Tetsworth. Oxon 5E 51
Tettenhall. W Mid 5C 72
Teversal. Notts 4B 86
Teversham. Cambs 5D 65
Teviothead. Bord 4G 119
Tewel. Abers 5F 153
Tewin. Herts 4C 52
Tewkesbury. Glos 2D 49
Teynham. Kent 4D 40
Teynham Street. Kent 4D 40
Thackthwaite. Cumb 2F 103
Thakeham. W Sus 4C 26
Thame. Oxon 5F 51
Thames Ditton. Surr 4C 38
Thames Haven. Thur 2B 40
Thamesmead. G Lon 2F 39
Thamesport. Medw 3C 40
Thanington Without. Kent 5F 41
Thankerton. S Lan 1B 118
Tharston. Norf 1D 66
Thatcham. W Ber 5D 36
Thatto Heath. Mers 1H 83
Thaxted. Essx 2G 53
The . . .
Names prefixed with 'The' for example 'The Aird' are indexed under the main name such as 'Aird, The'
Theakston. N Yor 1F 99
Thealby. N Lin 3B 94
Theale. Som 2H 21
Theale. W Ber 4E 37
Thearne. E Yor 1D 94
Theberton. Suff 4G 67
Theddingworth. Leics 2D 62
Theddlethorpe All Saints. Linc 2D 88
Theddlethorpe St Helen. Linc 2D 89
Thelbridge Barton. Devn 1A 12
Thelnetham. Suff 3C 66
Thelveton. Norf 2D 66
Thelwall. Warr 2A 84
Themelthorpe. Norf 3C 78
Thenford. Nptn 1D 50
Therfield. Herts 2D 52
Thetford. Linc 4A 76
Thetford. Norf 2A 66
Thethwaite. Cumb 5E 113
Theydon Bois. Essx 1F 39
Thick Hollins. W Yor 3B 92
Thickwood. Wilts 4D 34
Thimbleby. Linc 4B 88
Thimbleby. N Yor 5B 106
Thingwall. Mers 2E 83
Thirlby. N Yor 1G 99
Thirlestane. Bord 5B 130
Thirn. N Yor 1E 98
Thirsk. N Yor 1G 99
Thirtleby. E Yor 1E 95
Thistleton. Lanc 1C 90
Thistleton. Rut 4G 75
Thistley Green. Suff 3F 65
Thixendale. N Yor 3C 100
Thockrington. Nmbd 2C 114
Tholomas Drove. Cambs 5D 76
Tholthorpe. N Yor 3G 99
Thomas Chapel. Pemb 4F 43
Thomas Close. Cumb 5F 113
Thomastown. Abers 4E 160
Thomastown. Rhon 3D 32
Thompson. Norf 1B 66
Thomshill. Mor 3G 159
Thong. Kent 3A 40
Thongsbridge. W Yor 4B 92
Thoralby. N Yor 1C 98
Thoresby. Notts 3D 86
Thoresway. Linc 1A 88
Thorganby. Linc 1B 88
Thorganby. N Yor 5A 100
Thorgill. N Yor 5E 107
Thorington. Suff 3G 67
Thorington Street. Suff 2D 54
Thorlby. N Yor 4B 98
Thorley. Herts 4E 53
Thorley Street. Herts 4E 53
Thorley Street. IOW 4B 16
Thormanby. N Yor 2G 99
Thorn. Powy 4E 59
Thornaby-on-Tees. Stoc T 3B 106
Thornage. Norf 2C 78
Thornborough. Buck 2F 51
Thornborough. N Yor 2E 99
Thornbury. Devn 2E 11
Thornbury. Here 5A 60
Thornbury. S Glo 2B 34
Thornby. Cumb 4D 112
Thornby. Nptn 3D 62
Thorncliffe. Staf 5E 85
Thorncombe. Dors 2G 13
Thorncombe Street. Surr 1A 26
Thorncote Green. C Beds 1B 52
Thorndon. Suff 4D 66
Thorndon Cross. Devn 3F 11
Thorne. S Yor 3G 93
Thornehillhead. Devn 1E 11
Thorner. W Yor 5F 99
Thorne St Margaret. Som 4D 20
Thorney. Notts 3F 87
Thorney. Pet 5B 76
Thorney. Som 4H 21
Thorney Hill. Hants 3G 15
Thorney Toll. Cambs 5C 76
Thornfalcon. Som 4F 21
Thornford. Dors 1B 14
Thorngrafton. Nmbd 3A 114
Thorngrove. Som 3G 21
Thorngumbald. E Yor 2F 95
Thornham. Norf 1G 77
Thornham Magna. Suff 3D 66
Thornham Parva. Suff 3D 66
Thornhaugh. Pet 5H 75
Thornhill. Cphy 3E 33
Thornhill. Cumb 4B 102
Thornhill. Derbs 2F 85
Thornhill. Dum 5A 118
Thornhill. Sotn 1C 16
Thornhill. Stir 4F 135
Thornhill. W Yor 3C 92
Thornhill Lees. W Yor 3C 92
Thornhills. W Yor 2B 92
Thornholme. E Yor 3F 101
Thornicombe. Dors 2D 14
Thornington. Nmbd 1C 120
Thornley. Dur
nr. Durham 1A 106
nr. Tow Law 1E 105
Thornley Gate. Nmbd 4B 114
Thornliebank. E Ren 3G 127
Thornroan. Abers 5F 161
Thorns. Suff 5G 65
Thornsett. Derbs 2E 85
Thornthwaite. Cumb 2D 102
Thornthwaite. N Yor 4D 98
Thornton. Ang 4C 144
Thornton. Buck 2F 51
Thornton. E Yor 5B 100
Thornton. Fife 4E 137
Thornton. Lanc 5C 96
Thornton. Leics 5B 74
Thornton. Linc 4B 88
Thornton. Mers 4B 90
Thornton. Midd 3B 106
Thornton. Nmbd 5F 131
Thornton. Pemb 4D 42
Thornton. W Yor 1A 92
Thornton Curtis. N Lin 3D 94
Thorntonhall. S Lan 4G 127
Thornton Heath. G Lon 4E 39
Thornton Hough. Mers 2F 83
Thornton-in-Craven. N Yor 5B 98
Thornton in Lonsdale. N Yor 2F 97
Thornton-le-Beans. N Yor 5A 106
Thornton-le-Clay. N Yor 3A 100
Thornton-le-Dale. N Yor 1C 100
Thornton le Moor. Linc 1H 87
Thornton-le-Moor. N Yor 1F 99
Thornton-le-Moors. Ches W 3G 83
Thornton-le-Street. N Yor 1G 99
Thorntonloch. E Lot 2D 130
Thornton Rust. N Yor 1B 98
Thornton Steward. N Yor 1D 98
Thornton Watlass. N Yor 1E 99
Thornwood Common. Essx 5E 53
Thornythwaite. Cumb 2E 103
Thoroton. Notts 1E 75
Thorp Arch. W Yor 5G 99
Thorpe. Derbs 5F 85
Thorpe. E Yor 5D 101
Thorpe. Linc 2D 89
Thorpe. Norf 1G 67
Thorpe. N Yor 3C 98
Thorpe. Notts 1E 75
Thorpe. Surr 4B 38
Thorpe Abbotts. Norf 3D 66
Thorpe Acre. Leics 3C 74
Thorpe Arnold. Leics 3E 75
Thorpe Audlin. W Yor 3E 93
Thorpe Bassett. N Yor 2C 100
Thorpe Bay. S'end 2D 40
Thorpe by Water. Rut 1F 63
Thorpe Common. S Yor 1A 86
Thorpe Common. Suff 2F 55
Thorpe Constantine. Staf 5G 73
Thorpe End. Norf 4E 79
Thorpe Fendike. Linc 4D 88
Thorpe Green. Essx 3E 55
Thorpe Green. Suff 5B 66
Thorpe Hall. N Yor 2H 99
Thorpe Hamlet. Norf 5E 79
Thorpe Hesley. S Yor 1A 86
Thorpe in Balne. S Yor 3F 93
Thorpe in the Fallows. Linc 2G 87
Thorpe Langton. Leics 1E 63
Thorpe Larches. Dur 2A 106
Thorpe Latimer. Linc 1A 76
Thorpe-le-Soken. Essx 3E 55
Thorpe le Street. E Yor 5C 100
Thorpe Malsor. Nptn 3F 63
Thorpe Mandeville. Nptn 1D 50
Thorpe Market. Norf 2E 79
Thorpe Marriott. Norf 4D 78
Thorpe Morieux. Suff 5B 66
Thorpeness. Suff 5G 67
Thorpe on the Hill. Linc 4G 87
Thorpe on the Hill. W Yor 2D 92
Thorpe St Andrew. Norf 5E 79
Thorpe St Peter. Linc 4D 89
Thorpe Salvin. S Yor 2C 86
Thorpe Satchville. Leics 4E 75
Thorpe Thewles. Stoc T 2A 106
Thorpe Tilney. Linc 5A 88
Thorpe Underwood. N Yor 4G 99
Thorpe Waterville. Nptn 2H 63
Thorpe Willoughby. N Yor 1F 93
Thorpland. Norf 5F 77
Thorrington. Essx 3D 54
Thorverton. Devn 2C 12
Thrandeston. Suff 3D 66
Thrapston. Nptn 3G 63
Thrashbush. N Lan 3A 128
Threapland. Cumb 1C 102
Threapland. N Yor 3B 98
Threapwood. Ches W 1G 71
Threapwood. Staf 1E 73
Three Ashes. Here 3A 48
Three Bridges. Linc 2D 88
Three Bridges. W Sus 2D 27
Three Burrows. Corn 4B 6
Three Chimneys. Kent 2C 28
Three Cocks. Powy 2E 47
Three Crosses. Swan 3E 31
Three Cups Corner. E Sus 3H 27
Threehammer Common. Norf 3F 79
Three Holes. Norf 5E 77
Threekingham. Linc 2H 75
Three Leg Cross. E Sus 2A 28
Three Legged Cross. Dors 2F 15
Three Mile Cross. Wok 5F 37
Threemilestone. Corn 4B 6
Three Oaks. E Sus 4C 28
Threlkeld. Cumb 2E 102
Threshfield. N Yor 3B 98
Thrigby. Norf 4G 79
Thringarth. Dur 2C 104
Thringstone. Leics 4B 74
Thrintoft. N Yor 5A 106
Thriplow. Cambs 1E 53
Throckenholt. Linc 5C 76
Throcking. Herts 2D 52
Throckley. Tyne 3E 115
Throckmorton. Worc 1E 49
Throop. Bour 3G 15
Throphill. Nmbd 1E 115
Thropton. Nmbd 4E 121
Throsk. Stir 4A 136
Througham. Glos 5E 49
Throughgate. Dum 1F 111
Throwleigh. Devn 3G 11
Throwley. Kent 5D 40
Throwley Forstal. Kent 5D 40
Throxenby. N Yor 1E 101
Thrumpton. Notts 2C 74
Thrumster. High 4F 169
Thrunton. Nmbd 3E 121
Thrupp. Glos 5D 48
Thrupp. Oxon 4C 50
Thrushelton. Devn 4E 11
Thrushgill. Lanc 3F 97
Thrussington. Leics 4D 74
Thruxton. Hants 2A 24
Thruxton. Here 2H 47
Thrybergh. S Yor 1B 86
Thulston. Derbs 2B 74
Thundergay. N Ayr 5G 125
Thundersley. Essx 2B 40
Thundridge. Herts 4D 52
Thurcaston. Leics 4C 74
Thurcroft. S Yor 2B 86
Thurdon. Corn 1C 10
Thurgarton. Norf 2D 78
Thurgarton. Notts 1D 74
Thurgoland. S Yor 4C 92
Thurlaston. Leics 1C 62
Thurlaston. Warw 3B 62
Thurlbear. Som 4F 21
Thurlby. Linc
nr. Alford 3D 89
nr. Baston 4A 76
nr. Lincoln 4G 87
Thurleigh. Bed 5H 63
Thurlestone. Devn 4C 8
Thurloxton. Som 3F 21
Thurlstone. S Yor 4C 92
Thurlton. Norf 1G 67
Thurmaston. Leics 5D 74
Thurnby. Leics 5D 74
Thurne. Norf 4G 79
Thurnham. Kent 5C 40
Thurning. Norf 3C 78
Thurning. Nptn 2H 63
Thurnscoe. S Yor 4E 93
Thursby. Cumb 4E 113
Thursford. Norf 2B 78
Thursford Green. Norf 2B 78
Thursley. Surr 2A 26
Thurso. High 2D 168
Thurso East. High 2D 168
Thurstaston. Mers 2E 83
Thurston. Suff 4B 66
Thurston End. Suff 5G 65
Thurstonfield. Cumb 4E 112
Thurstonland. W Yor 3B 92
Thurton. Norf 5F 79
Thurvaston. Derbs
nr. Ashbourne 2F 73
nr. Derby 2G 73
Thuxton. Norf 5C 78
Thwaite. Dur 3D 104
Thwaite. N Yor 5B 104
Thwaite. Suff 4D 66
Thwaite Head. Cumb 5E 103
Thwaites. W Yor 5C 98
Thwaite St Mary. Norf 1F 67
Thwing. E Yor 2E 101
Tibbermore. Per 1C 136
Tibberton. Glos 3C 48
Tibberton. Telf 3A 72
Tibberton. Worc 5D 60
Tibenham. Norf 2D 66
Tibshelf. Derbs 4B 86
Tibthorpe. E Yor 4D 100
Ticehurst. E Sus 2A 28
Tichborne. Hants 3D 24
Tickencote. Rut 5G 75
Tickenham. N Som 4H 33
Tickhill. S Yor 1C 86
Ticklerton. Shrp 1G 59
Ticknall. Derbs 3H 73
Tickton. E Yor 5E 101
Tidbury Green. W Mid 3F 61
Tidcombe. Wilts 1A 24
Tiddington. Oxon 5E 51
Tiddington. Warw 5G 61
Tiddleywink. Wilts 4D 34
Tidebrook. E Sus 3H 27
Tideford. Corn 3H 7
Tideford Cross. Corn 2H 7
Tidenham. Glos 2A 34
Tideswell. Derbs 3F 85
Tidmarsh. W Ber 4E 37
Tidmington. Warw 2A 50
Tidpit. Hants 1F 15
Tidworth. Wilts 2H 23
Tidworth Camp. Wilts 2H 23
Tiers Cross. Pemb 3D 42
Tiffield. Nptn 5D 62
Tifty. Abers 4E 161
Tigerton. Ang 2E 145
Tighnabruaich. Arg 2A 126
Tigley. Devn 2D 8
Tilbrook. Cambs 4H 63
Tilbury. Thur 3H 39
Tilbury Green. Essx 1H 53
Tilbury Juxta Clare. Essx 1A 54
Tile Hill. W Mid 3G 61
Tilehurst. Read 4E 37
Tilford. Surr 2G 25
Tilgate Forest Row. W Sus 2D 26
Tillathrowie. Abers 5B 160
Tillers Green. Glos 2B 48
Tillery. Abers 1G 153
Tilley. Shrp 3H 71
Tillicoultry. Clac 4B 136
Tillingham. Essx 5C 54
Tillington. Here 1H 47
Tillington. W Sus 3A 26
Tillington Common. Here 1H 47
Tillybirloch. Abers 3D 152
Tillyfourie. Abers 2D 152
Tilmanstone. Kent 5H 41
Tilney All Saints. Norf 4E 77
Tilney Fen End. Norf 4E 77
Tilney High End. Norf 4E 77
Tilney St Lawrence. Norf 4E 77
Tilshead. Wilts 2F 23
Tilstock. Shrp 2H 71
Tilston. Ches W 5G 83
Tilstone Fearnall. Ches W 4H 83
Tilsworth. C Beds 3H 51
Tilton on the Hill. Leics 5E 75
Tiltups End. Glos 2D 34
Timberland. Linc 5A 88
Timbersbrook. Ches E 4C 84
Timberscombe. Som 2C 20
Timble. N Yor 4D 98
Timperley. G Man 2B 84
Timsbury. Bath 1B 22
Timsbury. Hants 4B 24
Timsgearraidh. W Isl 4C 171
Timworth Green. Suff 4A 66
Tincleton. Dors 3C 14
Tindale. Cumb 4H 113
Tindale Crescent. Dur 2F 105
Tingewick. Buck 2E 51
Tingrith. C Beds 2A 52
Tingwall. Orkn 5D 172
Tinhay. Devn 4D 11
Tinshill. W Yor 1C 92
Tinsley. S Yor 1B 86
Tinsley Green. W Sus 2D 27
Tintagel. Corn 4A 10
Tintern. Mon 5A 48
Tintinhull. Som 1H 13
Tintwistle. Derbs 1E 85
Tinwald. Dum 1B 112
Tinwell. Rut 5H 75
Tippacott. Devn 2A 20
Tipperty. Abers 1G 153
Tipps End. Cambs 1E 65
Tiptoe. Hants 3A 16
Tipton. W Mid 1D 60
Tipton St John. Devn 3D 12
Tiptree. Essx 4B 54
Tiptree Heath. Essx 4B 54
Tirabad. Powy 1B 46
Tircoed Forest Village. Swan 5G 45
Tiree Airport. Arg 4B 138
Tirinie. Per 2F 143
Tirley. Glos 3D 48
Tiroran. Arg 1B 132
Tir-Phil. Cphy 5E 47
Tirril. Cumb 2G 103
Tirryside. High 2C 164
Tir-y-dail. Carm 4G 45
Tisbury. Wilts 4E 23
Tisman's Common. W Sus 2B 26
Tissington. Derbs 5F 85
Titchberry. Devn 4C 18
Titchfield. Hants 2D 16
Titchmarsh. Nptn 3H 63
Titchwell. Norf 1G 77
Tithby. Notts 2D 74
Titley. Here 5F 59
Titlington. Nmbd 3E 121
Titsey. Surr 5F 39
Titson. Corn 2C 10
Tittensor. Staf 2C 72
Tittleshall. Norf 3A 78
Titton. Worc 4C 60
Tiverton. Ches W 4H 83
Tiverton. Devn 1C 12
Tivetshall St Margaret. Norf 2D 66
Tivetshall St Mary. Norf 2D 66
Tivington. Som 2C 20
Tixall. Staf 3D 73
Tixover. Rut 5G 75
Toab. Orkn 7E 172
Toab. Shet 10E 173
Toadmoor. Derbs 5A 86
Tobermore. M Ulst 5E 174
Tobermory. Arg 3G 139
Toberonochy. Arg 3E 133
Tobha Beag. W Isl 5C 170
Tobha-Beag. W Isl 1E 170
Tobha Mor. W Isl 5C 170
Tobhtarol. W Isl 4D 171
Tobson. W Isl 4D 171
Tocabhaig. High 2E 147
Tocher. Abers 5D 160
Tockenham. Wilts 4F 35
Tockenham Wick. Wilts 3F 35
Tockholes. Bkbn 2E 91
Tockington. S Glo 3B 34
Tockwith. N Yor 4G 99
Todber. Dors 4D 22
Todding. Here 3G 59
Toddington. C Beds 3A 52
Toddington. Glos 2F 49
Todenham. Glos 2H 49
Todhills. Cumb 3E 113
Todmorden. W Yor 2H 91
Todwick. S Yor 2B 86
Toft. Cambs 5C 64
Toft. Linc 4H 75
Toft Hill. Dur 2E 105
Toft Monks. Norf 1G 67
Toft next Newton. Linc 2H 87
Toftrees. Norf 3A 78
Tofts. High 2F 169
Toftwood. Norf 4B 78
Togston. Nmbd 4G 121
Tokavaig. High 2E 147
Tokers Green. Oxon 4F 37
Tolastadh a Chaolais. W Isl 4D 171
Tolladine. Worc 5C 60
Tolland. Som 3E 20
Tollard Farnham. Dors 1E 15
Tollard Royal. Wilts 1E 15
Toll Bar. S Yor 4F 93
Toller Fratrum. Dors 3A 14
Toller Porcorum. Dors 3A 14
Tollerton. N Yor 3H 99
Tollerton. Notts 2D 74
Toller Whelme. Dors 2A 14
Tollesbury. Essx 4C 54
Tolleshunt D'Arcy. Essx 4C 54
Tolleshunt Knights. Essx 4C 54
Tolleshunt Major. Essx 4C 54
Tollie. High 3H 157
Tollie Farm. High 1A 156
Tolm. W Isl 4G 171
Tolpuddle. Dors 3C 14
Tolstadh bho Thuath. W Isl 3H 171
Tolworth. G Lon 4C 38
Tomachlaggan. Mor 1F 151
Tomaknock. Per 1A 136
Tomatin. High 1C 150
Tombuidhe. Arg 3H 133
Tomdoun. High 3D 148
Tomich. High
nr. Cannich 1F 149
nr. Invergordon 1B 158
nr. Lairg 3D 164
Tomintoul. Mor 2F 151
Tomnavoulin. Mor 1G 151
Tomsléibhe. Arg 5A 140
Ton. Mon 2G 33
Tonbridge. Kent 1G 27
Tondu. B'end 3B 32
Tonedale. Som 4E 21
Tonfanau. Gwyn 5E 69
Tong. Shrp 5B 72
Tonge. Leics 3B 74
Tong Forge. Shrp 5B 72
Tongham. Surr 2G 25
Tongland. Dum 4D 111
Tong Norton. Shrp 5B 72
Tongue. High 3F 167
Tongue End. Linc 4A 76
Tongwynlais. Card 3E 33
Tonmawr. Neat 2B 32
Tonna. Neat 2A 32
Tonnau. Neat 2A 32
Ton Pentre. Rhon 2C 32
Ton-Teg. Rhon 3D 32
Tonwell. Herts 4D 52
Tonypandy. Rhon 2C 32
Tonyrefail. Rhon 3D 32
Toome. Ant 7F 175
Toot Baldon. Oxon 5D 50
Toot Hill. Essx 5F 53
Toothill. Hants 1B 16
Topcliffe. N Yor 2G 99
Topcliffe. W Yor 2C 92
Topcroft. Norf 1E 67
Topcroft Street. Norf 1E 67
Toppesfield. Essx 2H 53
Toppings. G Man 3F 91
Toprow. Norf 1D 66
Topsham. Devn 4C 12
Torbay. Torb 2F 9
Torbeg. N Ayr 3C 122
Torbothie. N Lan 4B 128
Torbryan. Devn 2E 9
Torcross. Devn 4E 9
Tore. High 3A 158
Torgyle. High 2F 149
Torinturk. Arg 3G 125
Torksey. Linc 3F 87
Torlum. W Isl 3C 170
Torlundy. High 1F 141
Tormarton. S Glo 4C 34
Tormitchell. S Ayr 5B 116
Tormore. High 3E 147
Tormore. N Ayr 2C 122
Tornagrain. High 4B 158
Tornaveen. Abers 3D 152
Torness. High 1H 149
Toronto. Dur 1E 105
Torpenhow. Cumb 1D 102
Torphichen. W Lot 2C 128
Torphins. Abers 3D 152
Torpoint. Corn 3A 8
Torquay. Torb 2F 9
Torr. Devn 3B 8
Torra. Arg 4B 124
Torran. High 4E 155
Torrance. E Dun 2H 127
Torrans. Arg 1B 132
Torranyard. N Ayr 5E 127
Torre. Som 3D 20
Torre. Torb 2F 9
Torridon. High 3B 156
Torrin. High 1D 147
Torrisdale. Arg 5B 125
Torrisdale. High 2G 167
Torrish. High 2G 165
Torrisholme. Lanc 3D 96
Torroble. High 3C 164
Torroy. High 4C 164
Torry. Aber 3G 153
Torryburn. Fife 1D 128
Torthorwald. Dum 2B 112
Tortington. W Sus 5B 26
Tortworth. S Glo 2C 34
Torvaig. High 4D 155
Torver. Cumb 5D 102
Torwood. Falk 1B 128
Torworth. Notts 2D 86
Toscaig. High 5G 155
Toseland. Cambs 4B 64
Tosside. N Yor 4G 97

Tostock—Valley End

Tostock. Suff 4B 66
Totaig. High 3A 154
Totardor. High 5C 154
Tote. High 4D 154
Totegan. High 2A 168
Tothill. Linc 2D 88
Totland. IOW 4B 16
Totley. S Yor 3H 85
Totnell. Dors 2B 14
Totnes. Devn 2E 9
Toton. Notts 2B 74
Totronald. Arg 3C 138
Totscore. High 2C 154
Tottenham. G Lon 1E 39
Tottenhill. Norf 4F 77
Tottenhill Row. Norf 4F 77
Totteridge. G Lon 1D 38
Totternhoe. C Beds 3H 51
Tottington. G Man 3F 91
Totton. Hants 1B 16
Touchen-end. Wind 4G 37
Toulvaddie. High 5F 165
Towans, The. Corn 3C 4
Toward. Arg 3C 126
Towcester. Nptn 1E 51
Towednack. Corn 3B 4
Tower End. Norf 4F 77
Tower Hill. Mers 4C 90
Tower Hill. W Sus 3C 26
Towersey. Oxon 5F 51
Towie. Abers 2B 152
Towiemore. Mor 4A 160
Tow Law. Dur 1E 105
Town, The. IOS 1A 4
Town End. Cambs 1D 64
Town End. Cumb
nr. Ambleside 4F 103
nr. Kirkby Thore 2H 103
nr. Lindale 1D 96
nr. Newby Bridge 1C 96
Town End. Mers 2G 83
Townend. W Dun 2F 127
Townfield. Dur 5C 114
Towngate. Cumb 5G 113
Towngate. Linc 4A 76
Town Green. Lanc 4C 90
Town Head. Cumb
nr. Grasmere 4E 103
nr. Great Asby 3H 103
Townhead. Cumb
nr. Lazonby 1G 103
nr. Maryport 1B 102
nr. Ousby 1H 103
Townhead. Dum 5D 111
Townhead of Greenlaw.
Dum 3E 111
Townhill. Fife 1E 129
Townhill. Swan 3F 31
Townjoy. M Ulst 3D 178
Town Kelloe. Dur 1A 106
Town Littleworth. E Sus 4F 27
Town Row. E Sus 2G 27
Towns End. Hants 1D 24
Townsend. Herts 5B 52
Townshend. Corn 3C 4
Town Street. Suff 2G 65
Town Yetholm. Bord 2C 120
Towthorpe. E Yor 3D 100
Towthorpe. York 4A 100
Towton. N Yor 1E 93
Towyn. Cnwy 3B 82
Toxteth. Mers 2F 83
Toynton All Saints. Linc 4C 88
Toynton Fen Side. Linc 4C 88
Toynton St Peter. Linc 4D 88
Toy's Hill. Kent 5F 39
Trabboch. E Ayr 2D 116
Traboe. Corn 4E 5
Tradespark. High 3C 158
Tradespark. Orkn 7D 172
Trafford Park. G Man 1B 84
Trallong. Powy 3C 46
Y Trallwng. Powy 5E 70
Tranent. E Lot 2H 129
Tranmere. Mers 2F 83
Trantlebeg. High 3A 168
Trantlemore. High 3A 168
Tranwell. Nmbd 1E 115
Trapp. Carm 4G 45
Traquair. Bord 1F 119
Trash Green. W Ber 5E 37
Trawden. Lanc 1H 91
Trawscoed. Powy 2D 46
Trawsfynydd. Gwyn 2G 69
Trawsgoed. Cdgn 3F 57
Treaddow. Here 3A 48
Trealaw. Rhon 2D 32
Treales. Lanc 1C 90
Trearddur. IOA 3B 80
Treaslane. High 3C 154
Treator. Corn 1D 6
Trebanog. Rhon 2D 32
Trebanos. Neat 5H 45
Trebarber. Corn 2C 6
Trebartha. Corn 5C 10
Trebarwith. Corn 4A 10
Trebetherick. Corn 1D 6
Treborough. Som 3D 20
Trebudannon. Corn 2C 6
Trebullett. Corn 5D 10
Treburley. Corn 5D 10
Treburrick. Corn 1C 6
Trebyan. Corn 2E 7
Trecastle. Powy 3B 46
Trecenydd. Cphy 3E 33
Trecott. Devn 2G 11
Trecwn. Pemb 1D 42
Trecynon. Rhon 5C 46
Tredaule. Corn 4C 10
Tredavoe. Corn 4B 4
Tredegar. Blae 5E 47
Trederwen. Powy 4E 71
Tredington. Glos 3E 49
Tredington. Warw 1A 50
Tredinnick. Corn
nr. Bodmin 2F 7
nr. Looe 3G 7
nr. Padstow 1D 6
Tredogan. V Glam 5D 32
Tredomen. Powy 2E 46
Tredunnock. Mon 2G 33
Tredustan. Powy 2E 47
Treen. Corn
nr. Land's End 4A 4
nr. St Ives 3B 4
Treeton. S Yor 2B 86
Trefaldwyn. Powy 1E 58
Trefasser. Pemb 1C 42
Trefdraeth. IOA 3D 80
Trefdraeth. Pemb 1E 43
Trefecca. Powy 2E 47
Trefechan. Mer T 5D 46
Trefeglwys. Powy 1B 58
Trefenter. Cdgn 4F 57
Treffgarne. Pemb 2D 42
Treffynnon. Flin 3D 82
Treffynnon. Pemb 2C 42
Trefil. Blae 4E 46
Trefilan. Cdgn 5E 57
Trefin. Pemb 1C 42
Treflach. Shrp 3E 71
Trefnant. Den 3C 82
Trefonen. Shrp 3E 71
Trefor. Gwyn 1C 68
Trefor. IOA 2C 80
Treforest. Rhon 3D 32
Trefrew. Corn 4B 10
Trefriw. Cnwy 4G 81
Tref-y-Clawdd. Powy 3E 59
Trefynwy. Mon 4A 48
Tregada. Corn 4D 10
Tregadillett. Corn 4C 10
Tregare. Mon 4H 47
Tregarne. Corn 4E 5
Tregaron. Cdgn 5F 57
Tregarth. Gwyn 4F 81
Tregear. Corn 3C 6
Tregeare. Corn 4C 10
Tregeiriog. Wrex 2D 70
Tregele. IOA 1C 80
Tregeseal. Corn 3A 4
Tregiskey. Corn 4E 6
Tregole. Corn 3B 10
Tregolwyn. V Glam 4C 32
Tregonetha. Corn 2D 6
Tregonhawke. Corn 3A 8
Tregony. Corn 4D 6
Tregoodwell. Corn 4B 10
Tregorrick. Corn 3E 6
Tregoss. Corn 2D 6
Tregowris. Corn 4E 5
Tregoyd. Powy 2E 47
Tregrehan Mills. Corn 3E 7
Tre-groes. Cdgn 1E 45
Tregullon. Corn 2E 7
Tregurrian. Corn 2C 6
Tregynon. Powy 1C 58
Trehafod. Rhon 2D 32
Trehan. Corn 3A 8
Treharris. Mer T 2D 32
Treherbert. Rhon 2C 32
Trehunist. Corn 2H 7
Trekenner. Corn 5D 10
Trekenning. Corn 2D 6
Treknow. Corn 4A 10
Trelales. B'end 3B 32
Trelan. Corn 5E 5
Trelash. Corn 3B 10
Trelassick. Corn 3C 6
Trelawnyd. Flin 3C 82
Trelech. Carm 1G 43
Treleddyd-fawr. Pemb 2B 42
Trelewis. Mer T 2E 32
Treligga. Corn 4A 10
Trelights. Corn 1D 6
Trelill. Corn 5A 10
Trelissick. Corn 5C 6
Trellech. Mon 5A 48
Trelleck Grange. Mon 5H 47
Trelogan. Flin 2D 82
Trelystan. Powy 5E 71
Tremadog. Gwyn 1E 69
Tremail. Corn 4B 10
Tremain. Cdgn 1C 44
Tremaine. Corn 4C 10
Tremar. Corn 2G 7
Trematon. Corn 3H 7
Tremeirchion. Den 3C 82
Tremore. Corn 2E 6
Tremorfa. Card 4F 33
Trenance. Corn
nr. Newquay 2C 6
nr. Padstow 1D 6
Trenarren. Corn 4E 7
Trench. Telf 4A 72
Trencreek. Corn 2C 6
Trendeal. Corn 3C 6
Trenear. Corn 5A 6
Treneglos. Corn 4C 10
Trenewan. Corn 3F 7
Trengune. Corn 3B 10
Trent. Dors 1A 14
Trentham. Stoke 1C 72
Trentishoe. Devn 2G 19
Trentlock. Derbs 2B 74
Treoes. V Glam 4C 32
Treorchy. Rhon 2C 32
Treorci. Rhon 2C 32
Tre'r-ddol. Cdgn 1F 57
Tre'r llai. Powy 5E 71
Trerulefoot. Corn 3H 7
Tresaith. Cdgn 5B 56
Trescott. Staf 1C 60
Trescowe. Corn 3C 4
Tresham. Glos 2C 34
Tresigin. V Glam 4C 32
Tresillian. Corn 4C 6
Tresimwn. V Glam 4D 32
Tresinney. Corn 4B 10
Treskillard. Corn 5A 6
Treskinnick Cross. Corn 3C 10
Tresmeer. Corn 4C 10
Tresparrett. Corn 3B 10
Tresparrett Posts. Corn 3B 10
Tressady. High 3D 164
Tressait. Per 2F 143
Tresta. Shet
on Fetlar 2H 173
on Mainland 6E 173
Treswell. Notts 3E 87
Treswithian. Corn 3D 4
Tre Taliesin. Cdgn 1F 57
Trethomas. Cphy 3E 33
Trethosa. Corn 3D 6
Trethurgy. Corn 3E 7
Tretio. Pemb 2B 42
Tretire. Here 3A 48
Tretower. Powy 3E 47
Treuddyn. Flin 5E 83
Trevadlock. Corn 5C 10
Trevalga. Corn 4A 10
Trevalyn. Wrex 5F 83
Trevance. Corn 1D 6
Trevanger. Corn 1D 6
Trevanson. Corn 1D 6
Trevarrack. Corn 3B 4
Trevarren. Corn 2D 6
Trevarrian. Corn 2C 6
Trevarrick. Corn 4D 6
Trevaughan. Carm
nr. Carmarthen 3E 45
nr. Whitland 3F 43
Treveighan. Corn 5A 10
Trevellas. Corn 3B 6
Trevelmond. Corn 2G 7
Treverva. Corn 5B 6
Trevescan. Corn 4A 4
Trevethin. Torf 5F 47
Trevia. Corn 4A 10
Trevigro. Corn 2H 7
Trevilley. Corn 4A 4
Treviscoe. Corn 3D 6
Trevivian. Corn 4B 10
Trevone. Corn 1C 6
Trevor. Wrex 1E 71
Trevor Uchaf. Den 1E 71
Trew. Corn 4D 4
Trewalder. Corn 4A 10
Trewarlett. Corn 4D 10
Trewarmett. Corn 4A 10
Trewassa. Corn 4B 10
Treween. Corn 4C 10
Trewellard. Corn 3A 4
Trewen. Corn 4C 10
Trewennack. Corn 4D 5
Trewern. Powy 4E 71
Trewetha. Corn 5A 10
Trewidland. Corn 3G 7
Trewint. Corn 3B 10
Trewithian. Corn 5C 6
Trewoofe. Corn 4B 4
Trewoon. Corn 3D 6
Treworthal. Corn 5C 6
Trewyddel. Pemb 1B 44
Treyarnon. Corn 1C 6
Treyford. W Sus 1G 17
Triangle. Staf 5E 73
Triangle. W Yor 2A 92
Trickett's Cross. Dors 2F 15
Trillick. Ferm 7F 176
Trimdon. Dur 1A 106
Trimdon Colliery. Dur 1A 106
Trimdon Grange. Dur 1A 106
Trimingham. Norf 2E 79
Trimley Lower Street. Suff 2F 55
Trimley St Martin. Suff 2F 55
Trimley St Mary. Suff 2F 55
Trimpley. Worc 3B 60
Trimsaran. Carm 5E 45
Trimstone. Devn 2F 19
Trinafour. Per 2E 143
Trinant. Cphy 2F 33
Tring. Herts 4H 51
Trinity. Ang 2F 145
Trinity. Edin 2F 129
Trisant. Cdgn 3G 57
Triscombe. Som 3E 21
Trislaig. High 1E 141
Trispen. Corn 3C 6
Tritlington. Nmbd 5G 121
Trochry. Per 4G 143
Troedrhiwdalar. Powy 5B 58
Troedrhiwfuwch. Cphy 5E 47
Troedrhiw-gwair. Blae 5E 47
Troedyraur. Cdgn 1D 44
Troedyrhiw. Mer T 5D 46
Trondavoe. Shet 4E 173
Troon. Corn 5A 6
Troon. S Ayr 1C 116
Troqueer. Dum 2A 112
Troston. Suff 3A 66
Trottiscliffe. Kent 4H 39
Trotton. W Sus 4G 25
Troutbeck. Cumb
nr. Ambleside 4F 103
nr. Penrith 2E 103
Troutbeck Bridge. Cumb 4F 103
Troway. Derbs 3A 86
Trowbridge. Wilts 1D 22
Trowell. Notts 2B 74
Trowle Common. Wilts 1D 22
Trowley Bottom. Herts 4A 52
Trowse Newton. Norf 5E 79
Trudoxhill. Som 2C 22
Trull. Som 4F 21
Trumaisgearraidh. W Isl 1D 170
Trumpan. High 2B 154
Trumpet. Here 2B 48
Trumpington. Cambs 5D 64
Trumps Green. Surr 4A 38
Trunch. Norf 2E 79
Trunnah. Lanc 5C 96
Truro. Corn 4C 6
Trusham. Devn 4B 12
Trusley. Derbs 2G 73
Trusthorpe. Linc 2E 89
Tryfil. IOA 2D 80
Trysull. Staf 1C 60
Tubney. Oxon 2C 36
Tuckenhay. Devn 3E 9
Tuckhill. Shrp 2B 60
Tuckingmill. Corn 4A 6
Tuckton. Bour 3G 15
Tuddenham. Suff 3G 65
Tuddenham St Martin. Suff 1E 55
Tudeley. Kent 1H 27
Tudhoe. Dur 1F 105
Tudhoe Grange. Dur 1F 105
Tudorville. Here 3A 48
Tudweiliog. Gwyn 2B 68
Tuesley. Surr 1A 26
Tufton. Hants 2C 24
Tufton. Pemb 2E 43
Tugby. Leics 5E 75
Tugford. Shrp 2H 59
Tughall. Nmbd 2G 121
Tulchan. Per 1B 136
Tullibardine. Per 2B 136
Tullibody. Clac 4A 136
Tullich. Arg 2H 133
Tullich. High
nr. Lochcarron 4B 156
nr. Tain 1C 158
Tullich. Mor 4H 159
Tullich Muir. High 1B 158
Tulliemet. Per 3G 143
Tulloch. Abers 5F 161
Tulloch. High
nr. Bonar Bridge 4D 164
nr. Fort William 5F 149
nr. Grantown-on-Spey 2D 151
Tulloch. Per 1C 136
Tullochgorm. Arg 4G 133
Tullybeagles Lodge. Per 5H 143
Tullyhogue. M Ulst 2C 178
Tullymurdoch. Per 3B 144
Tullynessle. Abers 2C 152
Tumble. Carm 4F 45
Tumbler's Green. Essx 3B 54
Tumby. Linc 4B 88
Tumby Woodside. Linc 5B 88
Tummel Bridge. Per 3E 143
Tunbridge Wells, Royal.
Kent 2G 27
Tunga. W Isl 4G 171
Tungate. Norf 3E 79
Tunley. Bath 1B 22
Tunstall. E Yor 1G 95
Tunstall. Kent 4C 40
Tunstall. Lanc 2F 97
Tunstall. Norf 5G 79
Tunstall. N Yor 5F 105
Tunstall. Staf 3B 72
Tunstall. Stoke 5C 84
Tunstall. Suff 5F 67
Tunstall. Tyne 4G 115
Tunstead. Derbs 3F 85
Tunstead. Norf 3E 79
Tunstead Milton. Derbs 2E 85
Tunworth. Hants 2E 25
Tupsley. Here 1A 48
Tupton. Derbs 4A 86
Turfholm. S Lan 1H 117
Turfmoor. Devn 2F 13
Turgis Green. Hants 1E 25
Turkdean. Glos 4G 49
Turkey Island. Hants 1D 16
Tur Langton. Leics 1E 62
Turleigh. Wilts 5D 34
Turlin Moor. Pool 3E 15
Turnastone. Here 2G 47
Turnberry. S Ayr 4B 116
Turnchapel. Plym 3A 8
Turnditch. Derbs 1G 73
Turners Hill. W Sus 2E 27
Turners Puddle. Dors 3D 14
Turnford. Herts 5D 52
Turnhouse. Edin 2E 129
Turnworth. Dors 2D 14
Turriff. Abers 4E 161
Tursdale. Dur 1A 106
Turton Bottoms. Bkbn 3F 91
Turtory. Mor 4C 160
Turves Green. W Mid 3E 61
Turvey. Bed 5G 63
Turville. Buck 2F 37
Turville Heath. Buck 2F 37
Turweston. Buck 2E 50
Tushielaw. Bord 3F 119
Tutbury. Staf 3G 73
Tutnall. Worc 3D 61
Tutshill. Glos 2A 34
Tuttington. Norf 3E 79
Tutts Clump. W Ber 4D 36
Tutwell. Corn 5D 11
Tuxford. Notts 3E 87
Twatt. Orkn 5B 172
Twatt. Shet 6E 173
Twechar. E Dun 2A 128
Tweedale. Telf 5B 72
Tweedbank. Bord 1H 119
Tweedmouth. Nmbd 4F 131
Tweedsmuir. Bord 2C 118
Twelveheads. Corn 4B 6
Twemlow Green. Ches E 4B 84
Twenty. Linc 3A 76
Twerton. Bath 5C 34
Twickenham. G Lon 3C 38
Twigworth. Glos 3D 48
Twineham. W Sus 4D 26
Twinhoe. Bath 1C 22
Twinstead. Essx 2B 54
Twinstead Green. Essx 2B 54
Twiss Green. Warr 1A 84
Twiston. Lanc 5H 97
Twitchen. Devn 3A 20
Twitchen. Shrp 3F 59
Two Bridges. Devn 5G 11
Two Bridges. Glos 5B 48
Two Dales. Derbs 4G 85
Two Gates. Staf 5G 73
Two Mile Oak. Devn 2E 9
Twycross. Leics 5H 73
Twyford. Buck 3E 51
Twyford. Derbs 3H 73
Twyford. Dors 1D 14
Twyford. Hants 4C 24
Twyford. Leics 4E 75
Twyford. Norf 3C 78
Twyford. Wok 4F 37
Twyford Common. Here 2A 48
Twynholm. Dum 4D 110
Twyning. Glos 2D 49
Twyning Green. Glos 2E 49
Twynllanan. Carm 3A 46
Twyn-y-Sheriff. Mon 5H 47
Twywell. Nptn 3G 63
Tyberton. Here 2G 47
Tyburn. W Mid 1F 61
Tyby. Norf 3C 78
Tycroes. Carm 4G 45
Tycrwyn. Powy 4D 70
Tyddewi. Pemb 2B 42
Tydd Gote. Linc 4D 76
Tydd St Giles. Cambs 4D 76
Tydd St Mary. Linc 4D 76
Tye. Hants 2F 17
Tye Green. Essx
nr. Bishop's Stortford 3F 53
nr. Braintree 3A 54
nr. Saffron Walden 2F 53
Tyersal. W Yor 1B 92
Ty Issa. Powy 2D 70
Tyldesley. G Man 4E 91
Tyler Hill. Kent 4F 41
Tylers Green. Buck 2G 37
Tyler's Green. Essx 5F 53
Tylorstown. Rhon 2D 32
Tylwch. Powy 2B 58
Y Tymbl. Carm 4F 45
Tynan. Arm 5B 178
Ty-nant. Cnwy 1B 70
Tyndrum. Stir 5H 141
Tyneham. Dors 4D 15
Tynehead. Midl 4G 129
Tynemouth. Tyne 3G 115
Tyneside. Tyne 3F 115
Tyne Tunnel. Tyne 3G 115
Tynewydd. Rhon 2C 32
Tyninghame. E Lot 2C 130
Tynron. Dum 5H 117
Ty'n-y-bryn. Rhon 3D 32
Tyn-y-celyn. Wrex 2D 70
Tyn-y-cwm. Swan 5G 45
Tyn-y-ffridd. Powy 2D 70
Tynygongl. IOA 2E 81
Tynygraig. Cdgn 4F 57
Ty'n-y-groes. Cnwy 3G 81
Ty'n-yr-eithin. Cdgn 4F 57
Tyn-y-rhyd. Powy 4C 70
Tyn-y-wern. Powy 3C 70
Tyrie. Abers 2G 161
Tyringham. Mil 1G 51
Tythecott. Devn 1E 11
Tythegston. B'end 4B 32
Tytherington. Ches E 3D 84
Tytherington. Som 2C 22
Tytherington. S Glo 3B 34
Tytherington. Wilts 2E 23
Tytherleigh. Devn 2G 13
Tywardreath. Corn 3E 7
Tywardreath Highway. Corn 3E 7
Tywyn. Cnwy 3G 81
Tywyn. Gwyn 5E 69

U

Uachdar. W Isl 3D 170
Uags. High 5G 155
Ubbeston Green. Suff 3F 67
Ubley. Bath 1A 22
Uckerby. N Yor 4F 105
Uckfield. E Sus 3F 27
Uckinghall. Worc 2D 48
Uckington. Glos 3E 49
Uckington. Shrp 5H 71
Uddingston. S Lan 3H 127
Uddington. S Lan 1A 118
Udimore. E Sus 4C 28
Udny Green. Abers 1F 153
Udny Station. Abers 1G 153
Udston. S Lan 4H 127
Udstonhead. S Lan 5A 128
Uffcott. Wilts 4G 35
Uffculme. Devn 1D 12
Uffington. Linc 5H 75
Uffington. Oxon 3B 36
Uffington. Shrp 4H 71
Ufford. Pet 5H 75
Ufford. Suff 5E 67
Ufton. Warw 4A 62
Ufton Nervet. W Ber 5E 37
Ugadale. Arg 3B 122
Ugborough. Devn 3C 8
Ugford. Wilts 3F 23
Uggeshall. Suff 2G 67
Ugglebarnby. N Yor 4F 107
Ugley. Essx 3F 53
Ugley Green. Essx 3F 53
Ugthorpe. N Yor 3E 107
Uidh. W Isl 9B 170
Uig. Arg 3C 138
Uig. High
nr. Balgown 2C 154
nr. Dunvegan 3A 154
Uigshader. High 4D 154
Uisken. Arg 2A 132
Ulbster. High 4F 169
Ulcat Row. Cumb 2F 103
Ulceby. Linc 3D 88
Ulceby. N Lin 3E 94
Ulceby Skitter. N Lin 3E 94
Ulcombe. Kent 1C 28
Uldale. Cumb 1D 102
Uley. Glos 2C 34
Ulgham. Nmbd 5G 121
Ullapool. High 4F 163
Ullenhall. Warw 4F 61
Ulleskelf. N Yor 1F 93
Ullesthorpe. Leics 2C 62
Ulley. S Yor 2B 86
Ullingswick. Here 5H 59
Ullinish. High 5C 154
Ullock. Cumb 2B 102
Ulpha. Cumb 5C 102
Ulrome. E Yor 4F 101
Ulsta. Shet 3F 173
Ulting. Essx 5B 54
Ulva House. Arg 5F 139
Ulverston. Cumb 2B 96
Ulwell. Dors 4F 15
Umberleigh. Devn 4G 19
Unapool. High 5C 166
Underbarrow. Cumb 5F 103
Undercliffe. W Yor 1B 92
Underdale. Shrp 4H 71
Underhoull. Shet 1G 173
Underriver. Kent 5G 39
Under Tofts. S Yor 2H 85
Underton. Shrp 1A 60
Underwood. Newp 3G 33
Underwood. Notts 5B 86
Underwood. Plym 3B 8
Undley. Suff 2F 65
Undy. Mon 3H 33
Union Mills. IOM 4C 108
Union Street. E Sus 2B 28
Unstone. Derbs 3A 86
Unstone Green. Derbs 3A 86
Unthank. Cumb
nr. Carlisle 5E 113
nr. Gamblesby 5H 113
nr. Penrith 1F 103
Unthank End. Cumb 1F 103
Upavon. Wilts 1G 23
Up Cerne. Dors 2B 14
Upchurch. Kent 4C 40
Upcott. Devn 2F 11
Upcott. Here 5F 59
Upend. Cambs 5F 65
Up Exe. Devn 2C 12
Upgate. Norf 4D 78
Upgate Street. Norf 1C 66
Uphall. Dors 2A 14
Uphall. W Lot 2D 128
Uphall Station. W Lot 2D 128
Upham. Devn 2B 12
Upham. Hants 4D 24
Uphampton. Here 4F 59
Uphampton. Worc 4C 60
Up Hatherley. Glos 3E 49
Uphill. N Som 1G 21
Up Holland. Lanc 4D 90
Uplawmoor. E Ren 4F 127
Upleadon. Glos 3C 48
Upleatham. Red C 3D 106
Uplees. Kent 4D 40
Uploders. Dors 3A 14
Uplowman. Devn 1D 12
Uplyme. Devn 3G 13
Up Marden. W Sus 1F 17
Upminster. G Lon 2G 39
Up Nately. Hants 1E 25
Upottery. Devn 2F 13
Uppat. High 3F 165
Upper Affcot. Shrp 2G 59
Upper Arley. Worc 2B 60
Upper Armley. W Yor 1C 92
Upper Arncott. Oxon 4E 50
Upper Astrop. Nptn 2D 50
Upper Badcall. High 4B 166
Upper Ballinderry. Lis 3F 179
Upper Bangor. Gwyn 3E 81
Upper Basildon. W Ber 4D 36
Upper Batley. W Yor 2C 92
Upper Beeding. W Sus 4C 26
Upper Benefield. Nptn 2G 63
Upper Bentley. Worc 4D 61
Upper Bighouse. High 3A 168
Upper Boddam. Abers 5D 160
Upper Boddington. Nptn 5B 62
Upper Bogside. Mor 3G 159
Upper Booth. Derbs 2F 85
Upper Borth. Cdgn 2F 57
Upper Boyndlie. Abers 2G 161
Upper Brailes. Warw 1B 50
Upper Breinton. Here 1H 47
Upper Broughton. Notts 3D 74
Upper Brynamman. Carm 4H 45
Upper Bucklebury. W Ber 5D 36
Upper Bullington. Hants 2C 24
Upper Burgate. Hants 1G 15
Upper Caldecote. C Beds 1B 52
Upper Canterton. Hants 1A 16
Upper Catesby. Nptn 5C 62
Upper Chapel. Powy 1D 46
Upper Cheddon. Som 4F 21
Upper Chicksgrove. Wilts 4E 23
Upper Church Village.
Rhon 3D 32
Upper Chute. Wilts 1A 24
Upper Clatford. Hants 2B 24
Upper Coberley. Glos 4E 49
Upper Coedcae. Torf 5F 47
Upper Cound. Shrp 5H 71
Upper Cudworth. S Yor 4D 93
Upper Cumberworth.
W Yor 4C 92
Upper Cuttlehill. Abers 4B 160
Upper Cwmbran. Torf 2F 33
Upper Dallachy. Mor 2A 160
Upper Dean. Bed 4H 63
Upper Denby. W Yor 4C 92
Upper Derraid. High 5E 159
Upper Diabaig. High 2H 155
Upper Dicker. E Sus 5G 27
Upper Dinchope. Shrp 2G 59
Upper Dochcarty. High 2H 157
Upper Dounreay. High 2B 168
Upper Dovercourt. Essx 2F 55
Upper Dunsforth. N Yor 3G 99
Upper Dunsley. Herts 4H 51
Upper Eastern Green.
W Mid 2G 61
Upper Elkstone. Staf 5E 85
Upper Ellastone. Staf 1F 73
Upper End. Derbs 3E 85
Upper Enham. Hants 2B 24
Upper Farmcote. Shrp 1B 60
Upper Farringdon. Hants 3F 25
Upper Framilode. Glos 4C 48
Upper Froyle. Hants 2F 25
Upper Gills. High 1F 169
Upper Glenfintaig. High 5E 149
Upper Godney. Som 2H 21
Upper Gravenhurst.
C Beds 2B 52
Upper Green. Essx 2E 53
Upper Green. W Ber 5B 36
Upper Green. W Yor 2C 92
Upper Grove Common.
Here 3A 48
Upper Hackney. Derbs 4G 85
Upper Hale. Surr 2G 25
Upper Halliford. Surr 4B 38
Upper Halling. Medw 4A 40
Upper Hambleton. Rut 5G 75
Upper Hardres Court. Kent 5F 41
Upper Hardwick. Here 5G 59
Upper Hartfield. E Sus 2F 27
Upper Haugh. S Yor 1B 86
Upper Hayton. Shrp 2H 59
Upper Heath. Shrp 2H 59
Upper Hellesdon. Norf 4E 78
Upper Helmsley. N Yor 4A 100
Upper Hengoed. Shrp 2E 71
Upper Hergest. Here 5E 59
Upper Heyford. Nptn 5D 62
Upper Heyford. Oxon 3C 50
Upper Hill. Here 5G 59
Upper Hindhope. Bord 4B 120
Upper Hopton. W Yor 3B 92
Upper Howsell. Worc 1C 48
Upper Hulme. Staf 4E 85
Upper Inglesham. Swin 2H 35
Upper Kilcott. S Glo 3C 34
Upper Killay. Swan 3E 31
Upper Kirkton. Abers 5E 161
Upper Kirkton. N Ayr 4C 126
Upper Knockando. Mor 4F 159
Upper Knockchoilum.
High 2G 149
Upper Lambourn. W Ber 3B 36
Upperlands. M Ulst 6E 174
Upper Langford. N Som 1H 21
Upper Langwith. Derbs 4C 86
Upper Largo. Fife 3G 137
Upper Latheron. High 5D 169
Upper Layham. Suff 1D 54
Upper Leigh. Staf 2E 73
Upper Lenie. High 1H 149
Upper Lochton. Abers 4D 152
Upper Longdon. Staf 4E 73
Upper Longwood. Shrp 5A 72
Upper Lybster. High 5E 169
Upper Lydbrook. Glos 4B 48
Upper Lye. Here 4F 59
Upper Maes-coed. Here 2G 47
Upper Midway. Derbs 3G 73
Uppermill. G Man 4H 91
Upper Millichope. Shrp 2H 59
Upper Milovaig. High 4A 154
Upper Minety. Wilts 2F 35
Upper Mitton. Worc 3C 60
Upper Nash. Pemb 4E 43
Upper Neepaback. Shet 3G 173
Upper Netchwood. Shrp 1A 60
Upper Nobut. Staf 2E 73
Upper North Dean. Buck 2G 37
Upper Norwood. W Sus 4A 26
Upper Nyland. Dors 4C 22
Upper Oddington. Glos 3H 49
Upper Ollach. High 5E 155
Upper Outwoods. Staf 3G 73
Upper Padley. Derbs 3G 85
Upper Pennington. Hants 3B 16
Upper Poppleton. York 4H 99
Upper Quinton. Warw 1G 49
Upper Rissington. Glos 4H 49
Upper Rochford. Worc 4A 60
Upper Rusko. Dum 3C 110
Upper Sandaig. High 2F 147
Upper Sanday. Orkn 7E 172
Upper Sapey. Here 4A 60
Upper Seagry. Wilts 3E 35
Upper Shelton. C Beds 1H 51
Upper Sheringham. Norf 1D 78
Upper Skelmorlie. N Ayr 3C 126
Upper Slaughter. Glos 3G 49
Upper Sonachan. Arg 1H 133
Upper Soudley. Glos 4B 48
Upper Staploe. Bed 5A 64
Upper Stoke. Norf 5E 79
Upper Stondon. C Beds 2B 52
Upper Stowe. Nptn 5D 62
Upper Street. Hants 1G 15
Upper Street. Norf
nr. Horning 4F 79
nr. Hoveton 4F 79
Upper Street. Suff 2E 55
Upper Strensham. Worc 2E 49
Upper Studley. Wilts 1D 22
Upper Sundon. C Beds 3A 52
Upper Swell. Glos 3G 49
Upper Tankersley. S Yor 1H 85
Upper Tean. Staf 2E 73
Upperthong. W Yor 4B 92
Upperthorpe. N Lin 4A 94
Upper Thurnham. Lanc 4D 96
Upper Tillyrie. Per 3D 136
Upperton. W Sus 3A 26
Upper Tooting. G Lon 3D 39
Upper Town. Derbs
nr. Bonsall 5G 85
nr. Hognaston 5G 85
Uppertown. Derbs 4H 85
Upper Town. Here 1A 48
Uppertown. High 1F 169
Upper Town. N Som 5A 34
Uppertown. Nmbd 2B 114
Uppertown. Orkn 8D 172
Upper Tysoe. Warw 1B 50
Upper Upham. Wilts 4H 35
Upper Upnor. Medw 3B 40
Upper Urquhart. Fife 3D 136
Upper Wardington. Oxon 1C 50
Upper Weald. Mil 2F 51
Upper Weedon. Nptn 5D 62
Upper Wellingham. E Sus 4F 27
Upper Whiston. S Yor 2B 86
Upper Wield. Hants 3E 25
Upper Winchendon. Buck 4F 51
Upperwood. Derbs 5G 85
Upper Woodford. Wilts 3G 23
Upper Wootton. Hants 1D 24
Upper Wraxall. Wilts 4D 34
Upper Wyche. Worc 1C 48
Uppincott. Devn 2B 12
Uppingham. Rut 1F 63
Uppington. Shrp 5A 72
Upsall. N Yor 1G 99
Upsettlington. Bord 5E 131
Upshire. Essx 5E 53
Up Somborne. Hants 3B 24
Upstreet. Kent 4G 41
Up Sydling. Dors 2B 14
Upthorpe. Suff 3B 66
Upton. Buck 4F 51
Upton. Cambs 3A 64
Upton. Ches W 4G 83
Upton. Corn
nr. Bude 2C 10
nr. Liskeard 5C 10
Upton. Cumb 1E 102
Upton. Devn
nr. Honiton 2D 12
nr. Kingsbridge 4D 8
Upton. Dors
nr. Poole 3E 15
nr. Weymouth 4C 14
Upton. E Yor 4F 101
Upton. Hants
nr. Andover 1B 24
nr. Southampton 1B 16
Upton. IOW 3D 16
Upton. Leics 1A 62
Upton. Linc 2F 87
Upton. Mers 2E 83
Upton. Norf 4F 79
Upton. Nptn 4E 62
Upton. Notts
nr. Retford 3E 87
nr. Southwell 5E 87
Upton. Oxon 3D 36
Upton. Pemb 4E 43
Upton. Pet 5A 76
Upton. Slo 3A 38
Upton. Som
nr. Somerton 4H 21
nr. Wiveliscombe 4C 20
Upton. Warw 5F 61
Upton. W Yor 3E 93
Upton. Wilts 3D 22
Upton Bishop. Here 3B 48
Upton Cheyney. S Glo 5B 34
Upton Cressett. Shrp 1A 60
Upton Crews. Here 3B 48
Upton Cross. Corn 5C 10
Upton End. C Beds 2B 52
Upton Grey. Hants 2E 25
Upton Heath. Ches W 4G 83
Upton Hellions. Devn 2B 12
Upton Lovell. Wilts 2E 23
Upton Magna. Shrp 4H 71
Upton Noble. Som 3C 22
Upton Pyne. Devn 3C 12
Upton St Leonards. Glos 4D 48
Upton Scudamore. Wilts 2D 22
Upton Snodsbury. Worc 5D 60
Upton upon Severn. Worc 1D 48
Upton Warren. Worc 4D 60
Upwaltham. W Sus 4A 26
Upware. Cambs 3E 65
Upwell. Norf 5E 77
Upwey. Dors 4B 14
Upwick Green. Herts 3E 53
Upwood. Cambs 2B 64
Urafirth. Shet 4E 173
Uragaig. Arg 4A 132
Urchany. High 4C 158
Urchfont. Wilts 1F 23
Urdimarsh. Here 1A 48
Ure. Shet 4D 173
Ure Bank. N Yor 2F 99
Urgha. W Isl 8D 171
Urlay Nook. Stoc T 3B 106
Urmston. G Man 1B 84
Urquhart. Mor 2G 159
Urra. N Yor 4C 106
Urray. High 3H 157
Usan. Ang 3G 145
Ushaw Moor. Dur 5F 115
Usk. Mon 5G 47
Usselby. Linc 1H 87
Usworth. Tyne 4G 115
Utkinton. Ches W 4H 83
Uton. Devn 3B 12
Utterby. Linc 1C 88
Uttoxeter. Staf 2E 73
Uwchmynydd. Gwyn 3A 68
Uxbridge. G Lon 2B 38
Uyeasound. Shet 1G 173
Uzmaston. Pemb 3D 42

V

Valley. IOA 3B 80
Valley End. Surr 4A 38

Valley Truckle—Weston

Valley Truckle. Corn 4B 10
Valsgarth. Shet 1H 173
Valtos. High 2E 155
Van. Powy 2B 58
Vange. Essx 2B 40
Varteg. Torf 5F 47
Vatsetter. Shet 3G 173
Vatten. High 4B 154
Vaul. Arg 4B 138
Vauld, The. Here 1A 48
Vaynor. Mer T 4D 46
Veensgarth. Shet 7F 173
Velindre. Powy 2E 47
Vellow. Som 3D 20
Velly. Devn 4C 18
Veness. Orkn 5E 172
Venhay. Devn 1A 12
Venn. Devn 4D 8
Venngreen. Devn 1D 11
Vennington. Shrp 5F 71
Venn Ottery. Devn 3D 12
Venn's Green. Here 1A 48
Venny Tedburn. Devn 3B 12
Venterdon. Corn 5D 10
Ventnor. IOW 5D 16
Vernham Dean. Hants 1B 24
Vernham Street. Hants 1B 24
Vernolds Common. Shrp 2G 59
Verwood. Dors 2F 15
Veryan. Corn 5D 6
Veryan Green. Corn 5D 6
Vicarage. Devn 4F 13
Vickerstown. Cumb 3A 96
Victoria. Corn 2D 6
Victoria Bridge. Derr 3F 176
Vidlin. Shet 5F 173
Viewpark. N Lan 3A 128
Vigo. W Mid 5E 73
Vigo Village. Kent 4H 39
Vinehall Street. E Sus 3B 28
Vine's Cross. E Sus 4G 27
Viney Hill. Glos 5B 48
Virginia Water. Surr 4A 38
Virginstow. Devn 3D 11
Vobster. Som 2C 22
Voe. Shet
nr. Hillside 5F 173
nr. Swinister 3E 173
Vole. Som 2G 21
Vowchurch. Here 2G 47
Voxter. Shet 4E 173
Voy. Orkn 6B 172
Vulcan Village. Mers 1H 83

W

Waberthwaite. Cumb 5C 102
Wackerfield. Dur 2E 105
Wacton. Norf 1D 66
Wadbister. Shet 7F 173
Wadborough. Worc 1E 49
Wadbrook. Devn 2G 13
Waddesdon. Buck 4F 51
Waddeton. Devn 3E 9
Waddicar. Mers 1F 83
Waddingham. Linc 1G 87
Waddington. Lanc 5G 97
Waddington. Linc 4G 87
Waddon. Devn 5B 12
Wadebridge. Corn 1D 6
Wadeford. Som 1G 13
Wadenhoe. Nptn 2H 63
Wadesmill. Herts 4D 52
Wadhurst. E Sus 2H 27
Wadshelf. Derbs 3H 85
Wadsley. S Yor 1H 85
Wadsley Bridge. S Yor 1H 85
Wadswick. Wilts 5D 34
Wadwick. Hants 1C 24
Wadworth. S Yor 1C 86
Waen. Den
nr. Llandymog 4D 82
nr. Nantglyn 4B 82
Waen. Powy 1B 58
Waen Fach. Powy 4E 70
Waen Goleugoed. Den 3C 82
Wag. High 1H 165
Wainfleet All Saints. Linc 5D 89
Wainfleet Bank. Linc 5D 89
Wainfleet St Mary. Linc 5D 89
Wainhouse Corner. Corn 3B 10
Wainscott. Medw 3B 40
Wainstalls. W Yor 2A 92
Waitby. Cumb 4A 104
Waithe. Linc 4F 95
Wakefield. W Yor 2D 92
Wakerley. Nptn 1G 63
Wakes Colne. Essx 3B 54
Walberswick. Suff 3G 67
Walberton. W Sus 5A 26
Walbottle. Tyne 3E 115
Walby. Cumb 3F 113
Walcombe. Som 2A 22
Walcot. Linc 2H 75
Walcot. N Lin 2B 94
Walcot. Swin 3G 35
Walcot. Telf 4H 71
Walcot. Warw 5F 61
Walcote. Leics 2C 62
Walcot Green. Norf 2D 66
Walcott. Linc 5A 88
Walcott. Norf 2F 79
Walden. N Yor 1C 98
Walden Head. N Yor 1B 98
Walden Stubbs. N Yor 3F 93
Walderslade. Medw 4B 40
Walderton. W Sus 1F 17
Walditch. Dors 3H 13
Waldley. Derbs 2F 73
Waldridge. Dur 4F 115
Waldringfield. Suff 1F 55
Waldron. E Sus 4G 27
Wales. S Yor 2B 86
Walesby. Linc 1A 88
Walesby. Notts 3D 86
Walford. Here
nr. Leintwardine 3F 59
nr. Ross-on-Wye 3A 48
Walford. Shrp 3G 71
Walford. Staf 2C 72
Walford Heath. Shrp 4G 71
Walgherton. Ches E 1A 72
Walgrave. Nptn 3F 63
Walhampton. Hants 3B 16
Walkden. G Man 4F 91
Walker. Tyne 3F 115
Walkerburn. Bord 1F 119
Walker Fold. Lanc 5F 97
Walkeringham. Notts 1E 87
Walkerith. Linc 1E 87
Walkern. Herts 3C 52
Walker's Green. Here 1A 48
Walkerton. Fife 3E 137
Walkerville. N Yor 5F 105
Walkford. Dors 3H 15
Walkhampton. Devn 2B 8
Walkington. E Yor 1C 94
Walkley. S Yor 2H 85
Walk Mill. Lanc 1G 91
Wall. Corn 3D 4
Wall. Nmbd 3C 114
Wall. Staf 5F 73
Wallaceton. Dum 1F 111
Wallacetown. Shet 6E 173
Wallacetown. S Ayr
nr. Ayr 2C 116
nr. Dailly 4B 116
Wallands Park. E Sus 4F 27
Wallasey. Mers 1E 83
Wallaston Green. Pemb 4D 42
Wallbrook. W Mid 1D 60
Wallcrouch. E Sus 2A 28
Wall End. Cumb 1B 96
Wallend. Medw 3C 40
Wall Heath. W Mid 2C 60
Wallingford. Oxon 3E 36
Wallington. G Lon 4D 39
Wallington. Hants 2D 16
Wallington. Herts 2C 52
Wallis. Pemb 2E 43
Wallisdown. Bour 3F 15
Walliswood. Surr 2C 26
Wall Nook. Dur 5F 115
Walls. Shet 7D 173
Wallsend. Tyne 3G 115
Wallsworth. Glos 3D 48
Wall under Heywood. Shrp 1H 59
Wallyford. E Lot 2G 129
Walmer. Kent 5H 41
Walmer Bridge. Lanc 2C 90
Walmersley. G Man 3G 91
Walmley. W Mid 1F 61
Walnut Grove. Per 1D 136
Walpole. Suff 3F 67
Walpole Cross Keys. Norf 4E 77
Walpole Gate. Norf 4E 77
Walpole Highway. Norf 4E 77
Walpole Marsh. Norf 4D 77
Walpole St Andrew. Norf 4E 77
Walpole St Peter. Norf 4E 77
Walsall. W Mid 1E 61
Walsall Wood. W Mid 5E 73
Walsden. W Yor 2H 91
Walsgrave on Sowe.
W Mid 2A 62
Walsham le Willows. Suff 3C 66
Walshaw. G Man 3F 91
Walshford. N Yor 4G 99
Walsoken. Norf 4D 76
Walston. S Lan 5D 128
Walsworth. Herts 2B 52
Walter's Ash. Buck 2G 37
Walterston. V Glam 4D 32
Walterstone. Here 3G 47
Waltham. Kent 1F 29
Waltham. NE Lin 4F 95
Waltham Abbey. Essx 5D 53
Waltham Chase. Hants 1D 16
Waltham Cross. Herts 5D 52
Waltham on the Wolds.
Leics 3F 75
Waltham St Lawrence.
Wind 4G 37
Waltham's Cross. Essx 2G 53
Walthamstow. G Lon 2E 39
Walton. Cumb 3G 113
Walton. Derbs 4A 86
Walton. Leics 2C 62
Walton. Mers 1F 83
Walton. Mil 2G 51
Walton. Pet 5A 76
Walton. Powy 5E 59
Walton. Som 3H 21
Walton. Staf
nr. Eccleshall 3C 72
nr. Stone 2C 72
Walton. Suff 2F 55
Walton. Telf 4H 71
Walton. Warw 5G 61
Walton. W Yor
nr. Wakefield 3D 92
nr. Wetherby 5G 99
Walton Cardiff. Glos 2E 49
Walton East. Pemb 2E 43
Walton Elm. Dors 1C 14
Walton Highway. Norf 4D 77
Walton in Gordano.
N Som 4H 33
Walton-le-Dale. Lanc 2D 90
Walton-on-Thames. Surr 4C 38
Walton-on-the-Hill. Staf 3D 72
Walton on the Hill. Surr 5D 38
Walton-on-the-Naze. Essx 3F 55
Walton on the Wolds.
Leics 4C 74
Walton-on-Trent. Derbs 4G 73
Walton West. Pemb 3C 42
Walwick. Nmbd 2C 114
Walworth. Darl 3F 105
Walworth Gate. Darl 2F 105
Walwyn's Castle. Pemb 3C 42
Wambrook. Som 2F 13
Wampool. Cumb 4D 112
Wanborough. Surr 1A 26
Wanborough. Swin 3H 35
Wandel. S Lan 2B 118
Wandsworth. G Lon 3D 38
Wangford. Suff
nr. Lakenheath 2G 65
nr. Southwold 3G 67
Wanlip. Leics 4C 74
Wanlockhead. Dum 3A 118
Wannock. E Sus 5G 27
Wansford. E Yor 4E 101
Wansford. Pet 1H 63
Wanshurst Green. Kent 1B 28
Wanstead. G Lon 2F 39
Wanstrow. Som 2C 22
Wanswell. Glos 5B 48
Wantage. Oxon 3C 36
Wapley. S Glo 4C 34
Wappenbury. Warw 4A 62
Wappenham. Nptn 1E 51
Warbleton. E Sus 4H 27
Warblington. Hants 2F 17
Warborough. Oxon 2D 36
Warboys. Cambs 2C 64
Warbreck. Bkpl 1B 90
Warbstow. Corn 3C 10
Warburton. G Man 2B 84
Warcop. Cumb 3A 104
Warden. Kent 3E 40
Warden. Nmbd 3C 114
Ward End. W Mid 2F 61
Ward Green. Suff 4C 66
Ward Green Cross. Lanc 1E 91
Wardhedges. C Beds 2A 52
Wardhouse. Abers 5C 160
Wardington. Oxon 1C 50
Wardle. Ches E 5A 84
Wardle. G Man 3H 91
Wardley. Rut 5F 75
Wardley. W Sus 4G 25
Wardlow. Derbs 3F 85
Wardsend. Ches E 2D 84
Wardy Hill. Cambs 2D 64
Ware. Herts 4D 52
Ware. Kent 4G 41
Wareham. Dors 4E 15
Warehorne. Kent 2D 28
Warenford. Nmbd 2F 121
Waren Mill. Nmbd 1F 121
Warenton. Nmbd 1F 121
Wareside. Herts 4D 53
Waresley. Cambs 5B 64
Waresley. Worc 4C 60
Warfield. Brac 4G 37
Warfleet. Devn 3E 9
Wargate. Linc 2B 76
Wargrave. Wok 4F 37
Warham. Norf 1B 78
Waringsford. Arm 5G 179
Waringstown. Arm 4F 178
Wark. Nmbd
nr. Coldstream 1C 120
nr. Hexham 2B 114
Warkleigh. Devn 4G 19
Warkton. Nptn 3F 63
Warkworth. Nptn 1C 50
Warkworth. Nmbd 4G 121
Warlaby. N Yor 5A 106
Warland. W Yor 2H 91
Warleggan. Corn 2F 7
Warlingham. Surr 5E 39
Warmanbie. Dum 3C 112
Warmfield. W Yor 2D 93
Warmingham. Ches E 4B 84
Warminghurst. W Sus 4C 26
Warmington. Nptn 1H 63
Warmington. Warw 1C 50
Warminster. Wilts 2D 23
Warmley. S Glo 4B 34
Warmsworth. S Yor 4F 93
Warmwell. Dors 4C 14
Warndon. Worc 5C 60
Warners End. Herts 5A 52
Warnford. Hants 4E 24
Warnham. W Sus 2C 26
Warningcamp. W Sus 5B 26
Warninglid. W Sus 3D 26
Warren. Ches E 3C 84
Warren. Pemb 5D 42
Warrenby. Red C 2C 106
Warren Corner. Hants
nr. Aldershot 2G 25
nr. Petersfield 4F 25
Warrenpoint. New M 8F 178
Warren Row. Wind 3G 37
Warren Street. Kent 5D 40
Warrington. Mil 5F 63
Warrington. Warr 2A 84
Warsash. Hants 2C 16
Warse. High 1F 169
Warslow. Staf 5E 85
Warsop. Notts 4C 86
Warsop Vale. Notts 4C 86
Warter. E Yor 4C 100
Warthermarske. N Yor 2E 98
Warthill. N Yor 4A 100
Wartling. E Sus 5A 28
Wartnaby. Leics 3E 74
Warton. Lanc
nr. Carnforth 2D 97
nr. Freckleton 2C 90
Warton. Nmbd 4E 121
Warton. Warw 5G 73
Warwick. Warw 4G 61
Warwick Bridge. Cumb 4F 113
Warwick-on-Eden. Cumb 4F 113
Warwick Wold. Surr 5E 39
Wasbister. Orkn 4C 172
Wasdale Head. Cumb 4C 102
Wash. Derbs 2E 85
Washaway. Corn 2E 7
Washbourne. Devn 3D 9
Washbrook. Suff 1E 54
Wash Common. W Ber 5C 36
Washerwall. Staf 1D 72
Washfield. Devn 1C 12
Washfold. N Yor 4D 104
Washford. Som 2D 20
Washford Pyne. Devn 1B 12
Washingborough. Linc 3H 87
Washington. Tyne 4G 115
Washington. W Sus 4C 26
Washington Village. Tyne 4G 115
Waskerley. Dur 5D 114
Wasperton. Warw 5G 61
Wasp Green. Surr 1E 27
Wasps Nest. Linc 4H 87
Wass. N Yor 2H 99
Watchet. Som 2D 20
Watchfield. Oxon 2H 35
Watchgate. Cumb 5G 103
Watchhill. Cumb 5C 112
Watcombe. Torb 2F 9
Watendlath. Cumb 3D 102
Water. Devn 4A 12
Water. Lanc 2G 91
Waterbeach. Cambs 4D 65
Waterbeach. W Sus 2G 17
Waterbeck. Dum 2D 112
Waterditch. Hants 3G 15
Water End. C Beds 2A 52
Water End. E Yor 1A 94
Water End. Essx 1F 53
Water End. Herts
nr. Hatfield 5C 52
nr. Hemel Hempstead 4A 52
Waterfall. Staf 5E 85
Waterfoot. Caus 4J 175
Waterfoot. E Ren 4G 127
Waterfoot. Lanc 2G 91
Waterford. Herts 4D 52
Water Fryston. W Yor 2E 93
Waterhead. Cumb 4E 103
Waterhead. E Ayr 3E 117
Waterhead. S Ayr 5C 116
Waterheads. Bord 4F 129
Waterhouses. Dur 5E 115
Waterhouses. Staf 5E 85
Wateringbury. Kent 5A 40
Waterlane. Glos 5E 49
Waterlip. Som 2B 22
Waterloo. Cphy 3E 33
Waterloo. Corn 5B 10
Waterloo. Here 1G 47
Waterloo. High 1E 147
Waterloo. Mers 1F 83
Waterloo. Norf 4E 78
Waterloo. N Lan 4B 128
Waterloo. Pemb 4D 42
Waterloo. Per 5H 143
Waterloo. Pool 3F 15
Waterloo. Shrp 2G 71
Waterlooville. Hants 2E 17
Watermead. Buck 4G 51
Watermillock. Cumb 2F 103
Water Newton. Cambs 1A 64
Water Orton. Warw 1F 61
Waterperry. Oxon 5E 51
Waterrow. Som 4D 20
Watersfield. W Sus 4B 26
Waterside. Buck 5H 51
Waterside. Cambs 3F 65
Waterside. Cumb 5D 112
Waterside. E Ayr
nr. Ayr 4D 116
nr. Kilmarnock 5F 127
Waterside. E Dun 2H 127
Waterstein. High 4A 154
Waterstock. Oxon 5E 51
Waterston. Pemb 4D 42
Water Stratford. Buck 2E 51
Waters Upton. Telf 4A 72
Water Yeat. Cumb 1B 96
Watford. Herts 1C 38
Watford. Nptn 4D 62
Wath. Cumb 4H 103
Wath. N Yor
nr. Pateley Bridge 3D 98
nr. Ripon 2F 99
Wath Brow. Cumb 3B 102
Wath upon Dearne. S Yor 4E 93
Watlington. Norf 4F 77
Watlington. Oxon 2E 37
Watten. High 3E 169
Wattisfield. Suff 3C 66
Wattisham. Suff 5C 66
Wattlesborough Heath.
Shrp 4F 71
Watton. Dors 3H 13
Watton. E Yor 4E 101
Watton. Norf 5B 78
Watton at Stone. Herts 4C 52
Wattston. N Lan 2A 128
Wattstown. Rhon 2D 32
Wattsville. Cphy 2F 33
Wauldby. E Yor 2C 94
Waulkmill. Abers 4D 152
Waun. Powy 4E 71
Y Waun. Wrex 2E 71
Waunarlwydd. Swan 3F 31
Waun Fawr. Cdgn 2F 57
Waunfawr. Gwyn 5E 81
Waungilwen. Carm 1H 43
Waun-Lwyd. Blae 5E 47
Waun y Clyn. Carm 5E 45
Wavendon. Mil 2H 51
Waverbridge. Cumb 5D 112
Waverley. Surr 2G 25
Waverton. Ches W 4G 83
Waverton. Cumb 5D 112
Wavertree. Mers 2F 83
Wawne. E Yor 1D 94
Waxham. Norf 3G 79
Waxholme. E Yor 2G 95
Wayford. Som 2H 13
Way Head. Cambs 2D 65
Waytown. Dors 3H 13
Way Village. Devn 1B 12
Wdig. Pemb 1D 42
Wealdstone. G Lon 2C 38
Weardley. W Yor 5E 99
Weare. Som 1H 21
Weare Giffard. Devn 4E 19
Wearhead. Dur 1B 104
Wearne. Som 4H 21
Weasdale. Cumb 4H 103
Weasenham All Saints.
Norf 3H 77
Weasenham St Peter. Norf 3A 78
Weaverham. Ches W 3A 84
Weaverthorpe. N Yor 2D 100
Webheath. Worc 4E 61
Webton. Here 2H 47
Wedderlairs. Abers 5F 161
Weddington. Warw 1A 62
Wedhampton. Wilts 1F 23
Wedmore. Som 2H 21
Wednesbury. W Mid 1D 61
Wednesfield. W Mid 5D 72
Weecar. Notts 4F 87
Weedon. Buck 4G 51
Weedon Bec. Nptn 5D 62
Weedon Lois. Nptn 1E 50
Weeford. Staf 5F 73
Week. Devn
nr. Barnstaple 4F 19
nr. Okehampton 2G 11
nr. South Molton 1H 11
nr. Totnes 2D 9
Week. Som 3C 20
Weekley. Nptn 2F 63
Week Green. Corn 3C 10
Week St Mary. Corn 3C 10
Weel. E Yor 1D 94
Weeley. Essx 3E 55
Weeley Heath. Essx 3E 55
Weem. Per 4F 143
Weeping Cross. Staf 3D 72
Weethly. Warw 5E 61
Weeting. Norf 2G 65
Weeton. E Yor 2G 95
Weeton. Lanc 1B 90
Weeton. N Yor 5E 99
Weetwood Hall. Nmbd 2E 121
Weir. Lanc 2G 91
Welborne. Norf 4C 78
Welbourn. Linc 5G 87
Welburn. N Yor
nr. Kirkbymoorside 1A 100
nr. Malton 3B 100
Welbury. N Yor 4A 106
Welby. Linc 2G 75
Welches Dam. Cambs 2D 64
Welcombe. Devn 1C 10
Weld Bank. Lanc 3D 90
Weldon. Nptn 2G 63
Weldon. Nmbd 5F 121
Welford. Nptn 2D 62
Welford. W Ber 4C 36
Welford-on-Avon. Warw 5F 61
Welham. Leics 1E 63
Welham. Notts 2E 87
Welham Green. Herts 5C 52
Well. Hants 2F 25
Well. Linc 3D 88
Well. N Yor 1E 99
Welland. Worc 1C 48
Wellbank. Ang 5D 144
Well Bottom. Dors 1E 15
Welldale. Dum 3C 112
Wellesbourne. Warw 5G 61
Well Hill. Kent 4F 39
Wellhouse. W Ber 4D 36
Welling. G Lon 3F 39
Wellingborough. Nptn 4F 63
Wellingham. Norf 3A 78
Wellingore. Linc 5G 87
Wellington. Cumb 4B 102
Wellington. Here 1H 47
Wellington. Som 4E 21
Wellington. Telf 4A 72
Wellington Heath. Here 1C 48
Wellow. Bath 1C 22
Wellow. IOW 4B 16
Wellow. Notts 4D 86
Wellpond Green. Herts 3E 53
Wells. Som 2A 22
Wellsborough. Leics 5A 74
Wells Green. Ches E 5A 84
Wells-next-the-Sea. Norf 1B 78
Wellswood. Torb 2F 9
Wellwood. Fife 1D 129
Welney. Norf 1E 65
Welsford. Devn 4C 18
Welshampton. Shrp 2G 71
Welsh End. Shrp 2H 71
Welsh Frankton. Shrp 2F 71
Welsh Hook. Pemb 2D 42
Welsh Newton. Here 4H 47
Welsh Newton Common.
Here 4A 48
Welshpool. Powy 5E 70
Welsh St Donats. V Glam 4D 32
Welton. Bath 1B 22
Welton. Cumb 5E 113
Welton. E Yor 2C 94
Welton. Linc 2H 87
Welton. Nptn 4C 62
Welton Hill. Linc 2H 87
Welton le Marsh. Linc 4D 88
Welton le Wold. Linc 2B 88
Welwick. E Yor 2G 95
Welwyn. Herts 4C 52
Welwyn Garden City.
Herts 4C 52
Wem. Shrp 3H 71
Wembdon. Som 3F 21
Wembley. G Lon 2C 38
Wembury. Devn 4B 8
Wembworthy. Devn 2G 11
Wemyss Bay. Inv 2C 126
Wenallt. Cdgn 3F 57
Wenallt. Gwyn 1B 70
Wendens Ambo. Essx 2F 53
Wendlebury. Oxon 4D 50
Wendling. Norf 4B 78
Wendover. Buck 5G 51
Wendron. Corn 5A 6
Wendy. Cambs 1D 52
Wenfordbridge. Corn 5A 10
Wenhaston. Suff 3G 67
Wennington. Cambs 3B 64
Wennington. G Lon 2G 39
Wennington. Lanc 2F 97
Wensley. Derbs 4G 85
Wensley. N Yor 1C 98
Wentbridge. W Yor 3E 93
Wentnor. Shrp 1F 59
Wentworth. Cambs 3D 65
Wentworth. S Yor 1A 86
Wenvoe. V Glam 4E 32
Weobley. Here 5G 59
Weobley Marsh. Here 5G 59
Wepham. W Sus 5B 26
Wereham. Norf 5F 77
Wergs. W Mid 5C 72
Wern. Gwyn 1E 69
Wern. Powy
nr. Brecon 4E 46
nr. Guilsfield 4E 71
nr. Llangadfan 4B 70
nr. Llanymynech 3E 71
Wernffrwd. Swan 3E 31
Wernyrheolydd. Mon 4G 47
Werrington. Corn 4D 10
Werrington. Pet 5A 76
Werrington. Staf 1D 72
Wervin. Ches W 3G 83
Wesham. Lanc 1C 90
Wessington. Derbs 5A 86
West Aberthaw. V Glam 5D 32
West Acre. Norf 4G 77
West Allerdean. Nmbd 5F 131
West Alvington. Devn 4D 8
West Amesbury. Wilts 2G 23
West Anstey. Devn 4B 20
West Appleton. N Yor 5F 105
West Ardsley. W Yor 2C 92
West Arthurlie. E Ren 4F 127
West Ashby. Linc 3B 88
West Ashling. W Sus 2G 17
West Ashton. Wilts 1D 23
West Auckland. Dur 2E 105
West Ayton. N Yor 1D 101
West Bagborough. Som 3E 21
West Bank. Hal 2H 83
West Barkwith. Linc 2A 88
West Barnby. N Yor 3F 107
West Barns. E Lot 2C 130
West Barsham. Norf 2B 78
West Bay. Dors 3H 13
West Beckham. Norf 2D 78
West Bennan. N Ayr 3D 123
Westbere. Kent 4F 41
West Bergholt. Essx 3C 54
West Bexington. Dors 4A 14
West Bilney. Norf 4G 77
West Blackdene. Dur 1B 104
West Blatchington. Brig 5D 27
Westborough. Linc 1F 75
Westbourne. Bour 3F 15
Westbourne. W Sus 2F 17
West Bowling. W Yor 1B 92
West Brabourne. Kent 1E 29
West Bradford. Lanc 5G 97
West Bradley. Som 3A 22
West Bretton. W Yor 3C 92
West Bridgford. Notts 2C 74
West Briggs. Norf 4F 77
West Bromwich. W Mid 1E 61
Westbrook. Here 1F 47
Westbrook. Kent 3H 41
Westbrook. Wilts 5E 35
West Buckland. Devn
nr. Barnstaple 3G 19
nr. Thurlestone 4C 8
West Buckland. Som 4E 21
West Burnside. Abers 1G 145
West Burrafirth. Shet 6D 173
West Burton. N Yor 1C 98
West Burton. W Sus 4B 26
Westbury. Buck 2E 50
Westbury. Shrp 5F 71
Westbury. Wilts 1D 22
Westbury Leigh. Wilts 1D 22
Westbury-on-Severn. Glos 4C 48
Westbury on Trym. Bris 4A 34
Westbury-sub-Mendip.
Som 2A 22
West Butsfield. Dur 5E 115
West Butterwick. N Lin 4B 94
Westby. Linc 3G 75
West Byfleet. Surr 4B 38
West Caister. Norf 4H 79
West Calder. W Lot 3D 128
West Camel. Som 4A 22
West Carr. N Lin 4H 93
West Chaldon. Dors 4C 14
West Challow. Oxon 3B 36
West Charleton. Devn 4D 8
West Chelborough. Dors 2A 14
West Chevington. Nmbd 5G 121
West Chiltington. W Sus 4B 26
West Chiltington Common.
W Sus 4B 26
West Chinnock. Som 1H 13
West Chisenbury. Wilts 1G 23
West Clandon. Surr 5B 38
West Cliffe. Kent 1H 29
Westcliff-on-Sea. S'end 2C 40
West Clyne. High 3F 165
West Coker. Som 1A 14
Westcombe. Som
nr. Evercreech 3B 22
nr. Somerton 4H 21
West Compton. Dors 3A 14
West Compton. Som 2A 22
West Cornforth. Dur 1A 106
Westcot. Oxon 3B 36
Westcott. Buck 4F 51
Westcott. Devn 2D 12
Westcott. Surr 1C 26
Westcott Barton. Oxon 3C 50
West Cowick. E Yor 2G 93
West Cranmore. Som 2B 22
West Croftmore. High 2D 150
West Cross. Swan 4F 31
West Cullerlie. Abers 3E 153
West Culvennan. Dum 3H 109
West Curry. Corn 3C 10
West Curthwaite. Cumb 5E 113
Westdean. E Sus 5G 27
West Dean. W Sus 1G 17
West Dean. Wilts 4A 24
West Deeping. Linc 5A 76
West Derby. Mers 1F 83
West Dereham. Norf 5F 77
West Down. Devn 2F 19
Westdowns. Corn 4A 10
West Drayton. G Lon 3B 38
West Drayton. Notts 3E 86
West Dunnet. High 1E 169
West Ella. E Yor 2D 94
West End. Bed 5G 63
West End. Cambs 1D 64
West End. Dors 2E 15
West End. E Yor
nr. Kilham 3E 101
nr. Preston 1E 95
nr. South Cove 1C 94
nr. Ulrome 4F 101
West End. G Lon 2D 39
West End. Hants 1C 16
West End. Herts 5C 52
West End. Kent 4F 41
West End. Lanc 3D 96
West End. Linc 1C 76
West End. Norf 4H 79
West End. N Som 5H 33
West End. N Yor 4D 98
West End. S Glo 3C 34
West End. S Lan 5C 128
West End. Surr 4A 38
West End. Wilts 4E 23
West End. Wind 4G 37
West End Green. Hants 5E 37
Westenhanger. Kent 2F 29
Wester Aberchalder. High 2H 149
Wester Balgedie. Per 3D 136
Wester Brae. High 2A 158
Wester Culbeuchly. Abers 2D 160
Westerdale. High 3D 168
Westerdale. N Yor 4D 106
Wester Dechmont. W Lot 2D 128
Wester Fearn. High 5D 164
Westerfield. Suff 1E 55
Wester Galcantray. High 4C 158
Westergate. W Sus 5A 26
Wester Gruinards. High 4C 164
Westerham. Kent 5F 39
Westerleigh. S Glo 4C 34
Westerloch. High 3F 169
Wester Mandally. High 3E 149
Wester Quarff. Shet 8F 173
Wester Rarichie. High 1C 158
Wester Shian. Per 5F 143
Wester Skeld. Shet 7D 173
Westerton. Ang 3F 145
Westerton. Dur 1F 105
Westerton. W Sus 2G 17
Westerwick. Shet 7D 173
West Farleigh. Kent 5B 40
West Farndon. Nptn 5C 62
West Felton. Shrp 3F 71
Westfield. Cumb 2A 102
Westfield. E Sus 4C 28
Westfield. High 2C 168
Westfield. Norf 5B 78
Westfield. N Lan 2A 128
Westfield. W Lot 2C 128
Westfields. Dors 2C 14
Westfields of Rattray. Per 4A 144
West Fleetham. Nmbd 2F 121
Westford. Som 4E 20
West Garforth. W Yor 1D 93
Westgate. Dur 1C 104
Westgate. Norf 1B 78
Westgate. N Lin 4A 94
Westgate on Sea. Kent 3H 41
West Ginge. Oxon 3C 36
West Grafton. Wilts 5H 35
West Green. Hants 1F 25
West Grimstead. Wilts 4H 23
West Grinstead. W Sus 3C 26
West Haddlesey. N Yor 2F 93
West Haddon. Nptn 3D 62
West Hagbourne. Oxon 3D 36
West Hagley. Worc 2D 60
West Hall. Cumb 3G 113
Westhall. Suff 2G 67
West Hallam. Derbs 1B 74
Westhall Terrace. Ang 5D 144
West Halton. N Lin 2C 94
Westham. Dors 5B 14
Westham. E Sus 5H 27
West Ham. G Lon 2E 39
Westham. Som 2H 21
Westhampnett. W Sus 2G 17
West Handley. Derbs 3A 86
West Hanney. Oxon 2C 36
West Hanningfield. Essx 1B 40
West Hardwick. W Yor 3E 93
West Harptree. Bath 1A 22
West Harting. W Sus 4F 25
West Harton. Tyne 3G 115
West Hatch. Som 4F 21
Westhay. Som 2H 21
Westhead. Lanc 4C 90
West Head. Norf 5E 77
West Heath. Hants
nr. Basingstoke 1D 24
nr. Farnborough 1G 25
West Helmsdale. High 2H 165
West Hendred. Oxon 3C 36
West Heogaland. Shet 4D 173
West Heslerton. N Yor 2D 100
West Hewish. N Som 5G 33
Westhide. Here 1A 48
Westhill. Abers 3F 153
West Hill. Devn 3D 12
West Hill. E Yor 3F 101
Westhill. High 4B 158
West Hill. N Som 4H 33
West Hill. W Sus 2E 27
West Hoathly. W Sus 2E 27
West Holme. Dors 4D 15
Westhope. Here 5G 59
Westhope. Shrp 2G 59
West Horndon. Essx 2H 39
Westhorp. Nptn 5C 62
Westhorpe. Linc 2B 76
Westhorpe. Suff 4C 66
West Horrington. Som 2A 22
West Horsley. Surr 5B 38
West Horton. Nmbd 1E 121
West Hougham. Kent 1G 29
Westhoughton. G Man 4E 91
West Houlland. Shet 6D 173
Westhouse. N Yor 2F 97
Westhouses. Derbs 5B 86
West Howe. Bour 3F 15
Westhumble. Surr 5C 38
West Huntspill. Som 2G 21
West Hyde. Herts 1B 38
West Hynish. Arg 5A 138
West Hythe. Kent 2F 29
West Ilsley. W Ber 3C 36
Westing. Shet 1G 173
West Keal. Linc 4C 88
West Kennett. Wilts 5G 35
West Kilbride. N Ayr 5D 126
West Kingsdown. Kent 4G 39
West Kington. Wilts 4D 34
West Kirby. Mers 2E 82
West Knapton. N Yor 2C 100
West Knighton. Dors 4C 14
West Knoyle. Wilts 3D 22
West Kyloe. Nmbd 5G 131
Westlake. Devn 3C 8
West Lambrook. Som 1H 13
West Langdon. Kent 1H 29
West Langwell. High 3D 164
West Lavington. W Sus 4G 25
West Lavington. Wilts 1F 23
West Layton. N Yor 4E 105
West Leake. Notts 3C 74
West Learmouth. Nmbd 1C 120
West Leigh. Devn 2G 11
Westleigh. Devn
nr. Bideford 4E 19
nr. Tiverton 1D 12
Westleigh. G Man 4E 91
West Leith. Herts 4H 51
Westleton. Suff 4G 67
West Lexham. Norf 4H 77
Westley. Shrp 5F 71
Westley. Suff 4H 65
Westley Waterless. Cambs 5F 65
West Lilling. N Yor 3A 100
West Lingo. Fife 3G 137
Westlington. Buck 4F 51
Westlinton. Cumb 3E 113
West Linton. Bord 4E 129
West Littleton. S Glo 4C 34
West Looe. Corn 3G 7
West Lulworth. Dors 4D 14
West Lutton. N Yor 3D 100
West Lydford. Som 3A 22
West Lyng. Som 4G 21
West Lynn. Norf 4F 77
West Mains. Per 2B 136
West Malling. Kent 5A 40
West Malvern. Worc 1C 48
Westmancote. Worc 2E 49
West Marden. W Sus 1F 17
West Markham. Notts 3E 86
Westmarsh. Kent 4G 41
West Marsh. NE Lin 4F 95
West Marton. N Yor 4A 98
West Meon. Hants 4E 25
West Mersea. Essx 4D 54
Westmeston. E Sus 4E 27
Westmill. Herts
nr. Buntingford 3D 52
nr. Hitchin 2B 52
West Milton. Dors 3A 14
Westminster. G Lon 3D 39
West Molesey. Surr 4C 38
West Monkton. Som 4F 21
Westmoor End. Cumb 1B 102
West Moors. Dors 2F 15
West Morden. Dors 3E 15
West Muir. Ang 2E 145
Westmuir. Ang 3C 144
West Murkle. High 2D 168
West Ness. N Yor 2A 100
Westness. Orkn 5C 172
Westnewton. Cumb 5C 112
West Newton. E Yor 1E 95
West Newton. Norf 3F 77
Westnewton. Nmbd 1D 120
West Newton. Som 4F 21
West Norwood. G Lon 3E 39
Westoe. Tyne 3G 115
West Ogwell. Devn 2E 9
Weston. Bath 5C 34
Weston. Ches E
nr. Crewe 5B 84
nr. Macclesfield 3C 84
Weston. Devn
nr. Honiton 2E 13
nr. Sidmouth 4E 13
Weston. Dors
nr. Weymouth 5B 14
nr. Yeovil 2A 14

Weston —Woodfalls

Weston. *Hal* 2H 83
Weston. *Hants* 4F 25
Weston. *Here* 5F 59
Weston. *Herts* 2C 52
Weston. *Linc* 3B 76
Weston. *Nptn* 1D 50
Weston. *Notts* 4E 87
Weston. *Shrp*
nr. Bridgnorth 1H 59
nr. Knighton 3F 59
nr. Wem 3H 71
Weston. *S Lan* 5D 128
Weston. *Staf* 3D 73
Weston. *Suff* 2G 67
Weston. *W Ber* 4B 36
Weston Bampfylde. *Som* 4B 22
Weston Beggard. *Here* 1A 48
Westonbirt. *Glos* 3D 34
Weston by Welland. *Nptn* 1E 63
Weston Colville. *Cambs* 5F 65
Westoncommon. *Shrp* 3G 71
Weston Coyney. *Stoke* 1D 72
Weston Ditch. *Suff* 3F 65
Weston Favell. *Nptn* 4E 63
Weston Green. *Cambs* 5F 65
Weston Green. *Norf* 4D 78
Weston Heath. *Shrp* 4B 72
Weston Hills. *Linc* 4B 76
Weston in Arden. *Warw* 2A 62
Westoning. *C Beds* 2A 52
Weston in Gordano.
N Som 4H 33
Weston Jones. *Staf* 3B 72
Weston Longville. *Norf* 4D 78
Weston Lullingfields. *Shrp* 3G 71
Weston-on-Avon. *Warw* 5F 61
Weston-on-the-Green.
Oxon 4D 50
Weston-on-Trent. *Derbs* 3B 74
Weston Patrick. *Hants* 2E 25
Weston Rhyn. *Shrp* 2E 71
Weston-sub-Edge. *Glos* 1G 49
Weston-super-Mare.
N Som 5G 33
Weston Town. *Som* 2C 22
Weston Turville. *Buck* 4G 51
Weston under Lizard. *Staf* 4C 72
Weston under Penyard.
Here 3B 48
Weston under Wetherley.
Warw 4A 62
Weston Underwood.
Derbs 1G 73
Weston Underwood. *Mil* 5F 63
Westonzoyland. *Som* 3G 21
West Orchard. *Dors* 1D 14
West Overton. *Wilts* 5G 35
Westow. *N Yor* 3B 100
Westown. *Per* 1E 137
West Panson. *Devn* 3D 10
West Park. *Hart* 1B 106
West Parley. *Dors* 3F 15
West Peckham. *Kent* 5H 39
West Pelton. *Dur* 4F 115
West Pennard. *Som* 3A 22
West Pentire. *Corn* 2B 6
West Perry. *Cambs* 4A 64
West Pitcorthie. *Fife* 3H 137
West Plean. *Stir* 1B 128
West Poringland. *Norf* 5E 79
West Porlock. *Som* 2B 20
Westport. *Som* 1G 13
West Putford. *Devn* 1D 10
West Quantoxhead. *Som* 2E 20
Westra. *V Glam* 4E 33
West Rainton. *Dur* 5G 115
West Rasen. *Linc* 2H 87
West Ravendale. *NE Lin* 1B 88
Westray Airport. *Orkn* 2D 172
West Raynham. *Norf* 3A 78
Westrigg. *W Lot* 3C 128
West Rounton. *N Yor* 4B 106
West Row. *Suff* 3F 65
West Rudham. *Norf* 3H 77
West Runton. *Norf* 1D 78
Westruther. *Bord* 4C 130
Westry. *Cambs* 1C 64
West Saltoun. *E Lot* 3A 130
West Sandford. *Devn* 2B 12
West Sandwick. *Shet* 3F 173
West Scrafton. *N Yor* 1C 98
Westside. *Orkn* 5C 172
West Sleekburn. *Nmbd* 1F 115
West Somerton. *Norf* 4G 79
West Stafford. *Dors* 4C 14
West Stockwith. *Notts* 1E 87
West Stoke. *W Sus* 2G 17
West Stonesdale. *N Yor* 4B 104
West Stoughton. *Som* 2H 21
West Stour. *Dors* 4C 22
West Stourmouth. *Kent* 4G 41
West Stow. *Suff* 3H 65
West Stowell. *Wilts* 5G 35
West Strathan. *High* 2F 167
West Stratton. *Hants* 2D 24
West Street. *Kent* 5D 40
West Tanfield. *N Yor* 2E 99
West Taphouse. *Corn* 2F 7
West Tarbert. *Arg* 3G 125
West Thirston. *Nmbd* 4F 121
West Thorney. *W Sus* 2F 17
West Thurrock. *Thur* 3G 39
West Tilbury. *Thur* 3A 40
West Tisted. *Hants* 4E 25
West Tofts. *Norf* 1H 65
West Torrington. *Linc* 2A 88
West Town. *Bath* 5A 34
West Town. *Hants* 3F 17
West Town. *N Som* 5H 33
West Tytherley. *Hants* 4A 24
West Tytherton. *Wilts* 4E 35
West View. *Hart* 1B 106
Westville. *Notts* 1C 74
West Walton. *Norf* 4D 76
Westward. *Cumb* 5D 112
Westward Ho!. *Devn* 4E 19
Westwell. *Kent* 1D 28
Westwell. *Oxon* 5H 49
Westwell Leacon. *Kent* 1D 28
West Wellow. *Hants* 1A 16
West Wemyss. *Fife* 4F 137
Westwick. *Cambs* 4D 64
Westwick. *Dur* 3D 104
Westwick. *Norf* 3E 79
West Wick. *N Som* 5G 33
West Wickham. *Cambs* 1G 53
West Wickham. *G Lon* 4E 39
West Williamston. *Pemb* 4E 43
West Willoughby. *Linc* 1G 75
West Winch. *Norf* 4F 77
West Winterslow. *Wilts* 3H 23
West Wittering. *W Sus* 3F 17
West Witton. *N Yor* 1C 98
Westwood. *Devn* 3D 12
Westwood. *Kent* 4H 41
Westwood. *Pet* 5A 76
Westwood. *S Lan* 4H 127
Westwood. *Wilts* 1D 22
West Woodburn. *Nmbd* 1B 114
West Woodhay. *W Ber* 5B 36
West Woodlands. *Som* 2C 22
West Woodside. *Cumb* 5E 112
Westwoodside. *N Lin* 1E 87
West Worldham. *Hants* 3F 25
West Worlington. *Devn* 1A 12
West Worthing. *W Sus* 5C 26
West Wratting. *Cambs* 5F 65
West Wycombe. *Buck* 2G 37
West Wylam. *Nmbd* 3E 115
West Yatton. *Wilts* 4D 34
West Yell. *Shet* 3F 173
West Youlstone. *Corn* 1C 10
Wetheral. *Cumb* 4F 113
Wetherby. *W Yor* 5G 99
Wetherden. *Suff* 4C 66
Wetheringsett. *Suff* 4D 66
Wethersfield. *Essx* 2H 53
Wethersta. *Shet* 5E 173
Wetherup Street. *Suff* 4D 66
Wetley Rocks. *Staf* 1D 72
Wettenhall. *Ches E* 4A 84
Wetton. *Staf* 5F 85
Wetwang. *E Yor* 4D 100
Wetwood. *Staf* 2B 72
Wexcombe. *Wilts* 1A 24
Wexham Street. *Buck* 2A 38
Weybourne. *Norf* 1D 78
Weybourne. *Surr* 2G 25
Weybread. *Suff* 2E 67
Weybridge. *Surr* 4B 38
Weycroft. *Devn* 3G 13
Weydale. *High* 2D 168
Weyhill. *Hants* 2B 24
Weymouth. *Dors* 204 (5B 14)
Weythel. *Powy* 5E 59
Whaddon. *Buck* 2G 51
Whaddon. *Cambs* 1D 52
Whaddon. *Glos* 4D 48
Whaddon. *Wilts* 4G 23
Whale. *Cumb* 2G 103
Whaley. *Derbs* 3C 86
Whaley Bridge. *Derbs* 2E 85
Whaley Thorns. *Derbs* 3C 86
Whalley. *Lanc* 1F 91
Whalton. *Nmbd* 1E 115
Whaplode. *Linc* 3C 76
Whaplode Drove. *Linc* 4C 76
Whaplode St Catherine.
Linc 3C 76
Wharfe. *N Yor* 3G 97
Wharles. *Lanc* 1C 90
Wharley End. *C Beds* 1H 51
Wharncliffe Side. *S Yor* 1G 85
Wharram-le-Street. *N Yor* 3C 100
Wharton. *Ches W* 4A 84
Wharton. *Here* 5H 59
Whashton. *N Yor* 4E 105
Whasset. *Cumb* 1E 97
Whatcote. *Warw* 1B 50
Whateley. *Warw* 1G 61
Whatfield. *Suff* 1D 54
Whatley. *Som*
nr. Chard 2G 13
nr. Frome 2C 22
Whatlington. *E Sus* 4B 28
Whatmore. *Shrp* 3A 60
Whatstandwell. *Derbs* 5H 85
Whatton. *Notts* 2E 75
Whauphill. *Dum* 5B 110
Whaw. *N Yor* 4C 104
Wheatacre. *Norf* 1G 67
Wheatcroft. *Derbs* 5A 86
Wheathampstead. *Herts* 4B 52
Wheathill. *Shrp* 2A 60
Wheatley. *Devn* 3B 12
Wheatley. *Hants* 2F 25
Wheatley. *Oxon* 5E 50
Wheatley. *S Yor* 4F 93
Wheatley. *W Yor* 2A 92
Wheatley Hill. *Dur* 1A 106
Wheatley Lane. *Lanc* 1G 91
Wheatley Park. *S Yor* 4F 93
Wheaton Aston. *Staf* 4C 72
Wheatstone Park. *Staf* 5C 72
Wheddon Cross. *Som* 3C 20
Wheelerstreet. *Surr* 1A 26
Wheelock. *Ches E* 5B 84
Wheelock Heath. *Ches E* 5B 84
Wheelton. *Lanc* 2E 90
Wheldrake. *York* 5A 100
Whelford. *Glos* 2G 35
Whelpley Hill. *Buck* 5H 51
Whelpo. *Cumb* 1E 102
Whelston. *Flin* 3E 82
Whenby. *N Yor* 3A 100
Whepstead. *Suff* 5H 65
Wherstead. *Suff* 1E 55
Wherwell. *Hants* 2B 24
Wheston. *Derbs* 3F 85
Whetsted. *Kent* 1A 28
Whetstone. *G Lon* 1D 38
Whetstone. *Leics* 1C 62
Whicham. *Cumb* 1A 96
Whichford. *Warw* 2B 50
Whickham. *Tyne* 3F 115
Whiddon. *Devn* 2E 11
Whiddon Down. *Devn* 3G 11
Whigstreet. *Ang* 4D 145
Whilton. *Nptn* 4D 62
Whimble. *Devn* 2D 10
Whimple. *Devn* 3D 12
Whimpwell Green. *Norf* 3F 79
Whinburgh. *Norf* 5C 78
Whin Lane End. *Lanc* 5C 96
Whinney Hill. *Stoc T* 3A 106
Whinnyfold. *Abers* 5H 161
Whippingham. *IOW* 3D 16
Whipsnade. *C Beds* 4A 52
Whipton. *Devn* 3C 12
Whirlow. *S Yor* 2H 85
Whisby. *Linc* 4G 87
Whissendine. *Rut* 4F 75
Whissonsett. *Norf* 3B 78
Whisterfield. *Ches E* 3C 84
Whistley Green. *Wok* 4F 37
Whiston. *Mers* 1G 83
Whiston. *Nptn* 4F 63
Whiston. *S Yor* 1B 86
Whiston. *Staf*
nr. Cheadle 1E 73
nr. Penkridge 4C 72
Whiston Cross. *Shrp* 5B 72
Whiston Eaves. *Staf* 1E 73
Whitacre Heath. *Warw* 1G 61
Whitbeck. *Cumb* 1A 96
Whitbourne. *Here* 5B 60
Whitburn. *Tyne* 3H 115
Whitburn. *W Lot* 3C 128
Whitburn Colliery. *Tyne* 3H 115
Whitby. *Ches W* 3F 83
Whitby. *N Yor* 3F 107
Whitbyheath. *Ches W* 3F 83
Whitchester. *Bord* 4D 130
Whitchurch. *Bath* 5B 34
Whitchurch. *Buck* 3F 51
Whitchurch. *Card* 4E 33
Whitchurch. *Devn* 5E 11
Whitchurch. *Hants* 2C 24
Whitchurch. *Here* 4A 48
Whitchurch. *Pemb* 2B 42
Whitchurch. *Shrp* 1H 71
Whitchurch Canonicorum.
Dors 3G 13
Whitchurch Hill. *Oxon* 4E 37
Whitchurch-on-Thames.
Oxon 4E 37
Whitcombe. *Dors* 4C 14
Whitcot. *Shrp* 1F 59
Whitcott Keysett. *Shrp* 2E 59
Whiteabbey. *Ant* 1H 179
Whiteash Green. *Essx* 2A 54
Whitebog. *High* 2B 158
Whitebridge. *High* 2G 149
Whitebrook. *Mon* 5A 48
Whitecairns. *Abers* 2G 153
Whitechapel. *Lanc* 5E 97
Whitechurch. *Pemb* 1F 43
White Colne. *Essx* 3B 54
White Coppice. *Lanc* 3E 90
White Corries. *High* 3G 141
Whitecraig. *E Lot* 2G 129
Whitecroft. *Glos* 5B 48
White Cross. *Corn* 4D 5
Whitecross. *Corn* 1D 6
Whitecross. *Falk* 2C 128
Whitecross. *New M* 6D 178
White End. *Worc* 2C 48
Whiteface. *High* 5E 164
Whitefarland. *N Ayr* 5G 125
Whitefaulds. *S Ayr* 4B 116
Whitefield. *Dors* 3E 15
Whitefield. *G Man* 4G 91
Whitefield. *Som* 4D 20
Whiteford. *Abers* 1E 152
Whitegate. *Ches W* 4A 84
Whitehall. *Devn* 1E 12
Whitehall. *Hants* 1F 25
Whitehall. *Orkn* 5F 172
Whitehall. *W Sus* 3C 26
Whitehaven. *Cumb* 3A 102
Whitehaven. *Shrp* 3E 71
Whitehead. *ME Ant* 7L 175
Whitehill. *Hants* 3F 25
Whitehill. *N Ayr* 4D 126
Whitehills. *Abers* 2D 160
Whitehills. *Ang* 3D 144
White Horse Common.
Norf 3F 79
Whitehough. *Derbs* 2E 85
Whitehouse. *Abers* 2D 152
Whitehouse. *Arg* 3G 125
Whiteinch. *Glas* 3G 127
Whitekirk. *E Lot* 1B 130
White Kirkley. *Dur* 1D 104
White Lackington. *Dors* 3C 14
Whitelackington. *Som* 1G 13
White Ladies Aston. *Worc* 5D 60
White Lee. *W Yor* 2C 92
Whiteley. *Hants* 2D 16
Whiteley Bank. *IOW* 4D 16
Whiteley Village. *Surr* 4B 38
Whitemans Green. *W Sus* 3E 27
White Mill. *Carm* 3E 45
Whitemire. *Mor* 3D 159
Whitemoor. *Corn* 3D 6
Whitenap. *Hants* 4B 24
Whiteness. *Shet* 7F 173
White Notley. *Essx* 4A 54
Whiteoak Green. *Oxon* 4B 50
Whiteparish. *Wilts* 4H 23
White Pit. *Linc* 3C 88
Whiterashes. *Abers* 1F 153
Whiterock. *Ards* 3K 179
White Rocks. *Here* 3H 47
White Roding. *Essx* 4F 53
Whiterow. *High* 4F 169
Whiterow. *Mor* 3E 159
Whiteshill. *Glos* 5D 48
Whiteside. *Nmbd* 3A 114
Whiteside. *W Lot* 3C 128
Whitesmith. *E Sus* 4G 27
Whitestaunton. *Som* 1F 13
Whitestone. *Abers* 4D 152
Whitestone. *Devn* 3B 12
White Stone. *Here* 1A 48
Whitestones. *Abers* 3F 161
Whitestreet Green. *Suff* 2C 54
Whitewall Corner. *N Yor* 2B 100
White Waltham. *Wind* 4G 37
Whiteway. *Glos* 4E 49
Whitewell. *Lanc* 5F 97
Whitewell Bottom. *Lanc* 2G 91
Whiteworks. *Devn* 5G 11
Whitewreath. *Mor* 3G 159
Whitfield. *D'dee* 5D 144
Whitfield. *Kent* 1H 29
Whitfield. *Nptn* 2E 50
Whitfield. *Nmbd* 4A 114
Whitfield. *S Glo* 2B 34
Whitford. *Devn* 3F 13
Whitford. *Flin* 3D 82
Whitgift. *E Yor* 2B 94
Whitgreave. *Staf* 3C 72
Whithorn. *Dum* 5B 110
Whiting Bay. *N Ayr* 3E 123
Whitkirk. *W Yor* 1D 92
Whitland. *Carm* 3G 43
Whitleigh. *Plym* 3A 8
Whitletts. *S Ayr* 2C 116
Whitley. *N Yor* 2F 93
Whitley. *Wilts* 5D 35
Whitley Bay. *Tyne* 2G 115
Whitley Chapel. *Nmbd* 4C 114
Whitley Heath. *Staf* 3C 72
Whitley Lower. *W Yor* 3C 92
Whitley Thorpe. *N Yor* 2F 93
Whitlock's End. *W Mid* 3F 61
Whitminster. *Glos* 5C 48
Whitmore. *Dors* 2F 15
Whitmore. *Staf* 1C 72
Whitnage. *Devn* 1D 12
Whitnash. *Warw* 4H 61
Whitney. *Here* 1F 47
Whitrigg. *Cumb*
nr. Kirkbride 4D 112
nr. Torpenhow 1D 102
Whitsbury. *Hants* 1G 15
Whitsome. *Bord* 4E 131
Whitson. *Newp* 3G 33
Whitstable. *Kent* 4F 41
Whitstone. *Corn* 3C 10
Whittingham. *Nmbd* 3E 121
Whittingslow. *Shrp* 2G 59
Whittington. *Derbs* 3B 86
Whittington. *Glos* 3F 49
Whittington. *Lanc* 2F 97
Whittington. *Norf* 1G 65
Whittington. *Shrp* 2F 71
Whittington. *Staf*
nr. Kinver 2C 60
nr. Lichfield 5F 73
Whittington. *Warw* 1G 61
Whittington. *Worc* 5C 60
Whittington Barracks. *Staf* 5F 73
Whittlebury. *Nptn* 1E 51
Whittleford. *Warw* 1H 61
Whittle-le-Woods. *Lanc* 2D 90
Whittlesey. *Cambs* 1B 64
Whittlesford. *Cambs* 1E 53
Whittlestone Head. *Bkbn* 3F 91
Whitton. *N Lin* 2C 94
Whitton. *Nmbd* 4E 121
Whitton. *Powy* 4E 59
Whitton. *Bord* 2B 120
Whitton. *Shrp* 3H 59
Whitton. *Stoc T* 2A 106
Whittonditch. *Wilts* 4A 36
Whittonstall. *Nmbd* 4D 114
Whitway. *Hants* 1C 24
Whitwell. *Derbs* 3C 86
Whitwell. *Herts* 3B 52
Whitwell. *IOW* 5D 16
Whitwell. *N Yor* 5F 105
Whitwell. *Rut* 5G 75
Whitwell-on-the-Hill.
N Yor 3B 100
Whitwick. *Leics* 4B 74
Whitwood. *W Yor* 2E 93
Whitworth. *Lanc* 3G 91
Whixall. *Shrp* 2H 71
Whixley. *N Yor* 4G 99
Whoberley. *W Mid* 3H 61
Whorlton. *Dur* 3E 105
Whorlton. *N Yor* 4B 106
Whygate. *Nmbd* 2A 114
Whyle. *Here* 4H 59
Whyteleafe. *Surr* 5E 39
Wibdon. *Glos* 2A 34
Wibtoft. *Warw* 2B 62
Wichenford. *Worc* 4B 60
Wichling. *Kent* 5D 40
Wick. *Bour* 3G 15
Wick. *Devn* 2E 13
Wick. *High* 3F 169
Wick. *Shet*
on Mainland 8F 173
on Unst 1G 173
Wick. *Som*
nr. Bridgwater 2F 21
nr. Burnham-on-Sea 1G 21
nr. Somerton 4H 21
Wick. *S Glo* 4C 34
Wick. *V Glam* 4C 32
Wick. *W Sus* 5B 26
Wick. *Wilts* 4G 23
Wick. *Worc* 1E 49
Wick Airport. *High* 3F 169
Wicken. *Cambs* 3E 65
Wicken. *Nptn* 2F 51
Wicken Bonhunt. *Essx* 2E 53
Wickenby. *Linc* 2H 87
Wicken Green Village.
Norf 2H 77
Wickersley. *S Yor* 1B 86
Wicker Street Green. *Suff* 1C 54
Wickford. *Essx* 1B 40
Wickham. *Hants* 1D 16
Wickham. *W Ber* 4B 36
Wickham Bishops. *Essx* 4B 54
Wickhambreaux. *Kent* 5G 41
Wickhambrook. *Suff* 5G 65
Wickhamford. *Worc* 1F 49
Wickham Green. *Suff* 4C 66
Wickham Heath. *W Ber* 5C 36
Wickham Market. *Suff* 5F 67
Wickhampton. *Norf* 5G 79
Wickham St Paul. *Essx* 2B 54
Wickham Skeith. *Suff* 4C 66
Wickham Street. *Suff* 4C 66
Wick Hill. *Wok* 5F 37
Wicklewood. *Norf* 5C 78
Wickmere. *Norf* 2D 78
Wick St Lawrence. *N Som* 5G 33
Wickwar. *S Glo* 3C 34
Widdington. *Essx* 2F 53
Widdrington. *Nmbd* 5G 121
Widdrington Station.
Nmbd 5G 121
Widecombe in the Moor.
Devn 5H 11
Widegates. *Corn* 3G 7
Widemouth Bay. *Corn* 2C 10
Wide Open. *Tyne* 2F 115
Widewall. *Orkn* 8D 172
Widford. *Essx* 5G 53
Widford. *Herts* 4E 53
Widham. *Wilts* 3F 35
Widmer End. *Buck* 2G 37
Widmerpool. *Notts* 3D 74
Widnes. *Hal* 2H 83
Widworthy. *Devn* 3F 13
Wigan. *G Man* 4D 90
Wigbeth. *Dors* 2F 15
Wigborough. *Som* 1H 13
Wiggaton. *Devn* 3E 12
Wiggenhall St Germans.
Norf 4E 77
Wiggenhall St Mary Magdalen.
Norf 4E 77
Wiggenhall St Mary the Virgin.
Norf 4E 77
Wiggenhall St Peter. *Norf* 4F 77
Wiggens Green. *Essx* 1G 53
Wigginton. *Herts* 4H 51
Wigginton. *Oxon* 2B 50
Wigginton. *Staf* 5G 73
Wigginton. *York* 4H 99
Wigglesworth. *N Yor* 4H 97
Wiggonby. *Cumb* 4D 112
Wiggonholt. *W Sus* 4B 26
Wighill. *N Yor* 5G 99
Wighton. *Norf* 2B 78
Wightwick. *W Mid* 1C 60
Wigley. *Hants* 1B 16
Wigmore. *Here* 4G 59
Wigmore. *Medw* 4B 40
Wigsley. *Notts* 3F 87
Wigsthorpe. *Nptn* 2H 63
Wigston. *Leics* 1D 62
Wigtoft. *Linc* 2B 76
Wigton. *Cumb* 5D 112
Wigtown. *Dum* 4B 110
Wike. *W Yor* 5F 99
Wilbarston. *Nptn* 2F 63
Wilberfoss. *E Yor* 4B 100
Wilburton. *Cambs* 3D 65
Wilby. *Norf* 2C 66
Wilby. *Nptn* 4F 63
Wilby. *Suff* 3E 67
Wilcot. *Wilts* 5G 35
Wilcott. *Shrp* 4F 71
Wilcove. *Corn* 3A 8
Wildboarclough. *Ches E* 4D 85
Wilden. *Bed* 5H 63
Wilden. *Worc* 3C 60
Wildern. *Hants* 1C 16
Wilderspool. *Warr* 2A 84
Wilde Street. *Suff* 3G 65
Wildhern. *Hants* 1B 24
Wildmanbridge. *S Lan* 4B 128
Wildmoor. *Worc* 3D 60
Wildsworth. *Linc* 1F 87
Wildwood. *Staf* 3D 72
Wilford. *Nott* 2C 74
Wilkesley. *Ches E* 1A 72
Wilkhaven. *High* 5G 165
Wilkieston. *W Lot* 3E 129
Wilksby. *Linc* 4B 88
Willand. *Devn* 1D 12
Willaston. *Ches E* 5A 84
Willaston. *Ches W* 3F 83
Willaston. *IOM* 4C 108
Willen. *Mil* 1G 51
Willenhall. *W Mid*
nr. Coventry 3A 62
nr. Wolverhampton 1D 60
Willerby. *E Yor* 1D 94
Willerby. *N Yor* 2E 101
Willersey. *Glos* 2G 49
Willersley. *Here* 1G 47
Willesborough. *Kent* 1E 28
Willesborough Lees. *Kent* 1E 29
Willesden. *G Lon* 2D 38
Willesley. *Wilts* 3D 34
Willett. *Som* 3E 20
Willey. *Shrp* 1A 60
Willey. *Warw* 2B 62
Willey Green. *Surr* 5A 38
Williamscot. *Oxon* 1C 50
Williamsetter. *Shet* 9E 173
Willian. *Herts* 2C 52
Willingale. *Essx* 5F 53
Willingdon. *E Sus* 5G 27
Willingham. *Cambs* 3D 64
Willingham by Stow. *Linc* 2F 87
Willingham Green. *Cambs* 5F 65
Willington. *Bed* 1B 52
Willington. *Derbs* 3G 73
Willington. *Dur* 1E 105
Willington. *Tyne* 3G 115
Willington. *Warw* 2A 50
Willington Corner. *Ches W* 4H 83
Willisham Tye. *Suff* 5C 66
Willitoft. *E Yor* 1H 93
Williton. *Som* 2D 20
Willoughbridge. *Staf* 1B 72
Willoughby. *Linc* 3D 88
Willoughby. *Warw* 4C 62
Willoughby-on-the-Wolds.
Notts 3D 74
Willoughby Waterleys.
Leics 1C 62
Willoughton. *Linc* 1G 87
Willow Green. *Worc* 5B 60
Willows Green. *Essx* 4H 53
Willsbridge. *S Glo* 4B 34
Willslock. *Staf* 2E 73
Wilmcote. *Warw* 5F 61
Wilmington. *Bath* 5B 34
Wilmington. *Devn* 3F 13
Wilmington. *E Sus* 5G 27
Wilmington. *Kent* 3G 39
Wilmslow. *Ches E* 2C 84
Wilnecote. *Staf* 5G 73
Wilney Green. *Norf* 2C 66
Wilpshire. *Lanc* 1E 91
Wilsden. *W Yor* 1A 92
Wilsford. *Linc* 1H 75
Wilsford. *Wilts*
nr. Amesbury 3G 23
nr. Devizes 1F 23
Wilsill. *N Yor* 3D 98
Wilsley Green. *Kent* 2B 28
Wilson. *Here* 3A 48
Wilson. *Leics* 3B 74
Wilsontown. *S Lan* 4C 128
Wilstead. *Bed* 1A 52
Wilsthorpe. *E Yor* 3F 101
Wilsthorpe. *Linc* 4H 75
Wilstone. *Herts* 4H 51
Wilton. *Cumb* 3B 102
Wilton. *N Yor* 1C 100
Wilton. *Red C* 3C 106
Wilton. *Bord* 3H 119
Wilton. *Wilts*
nr. Marlborough 5A 36
nr. Salisbury 3F 23
Wimbish. *Essx* 2F 53
Wimbish Green. *Essx* 2G 53
Wimblebury. *Staf* 4E 73
Wimbledon. *G Lon* 3D 38
Wimblington. *Cambs* 1D 64
Wimboldsley. *Ches W* 4A 84
Wimborne Minster. *Dors* 2F 15
Wimborne St Giles. *Dors* 1F 15
Wimbotsham. *Norf* 5F 77
Wimpole. *Cambs* 1D 52
Wimpstone. *Warw* 1H 49
Wincanton. *Som* 4C 22
Winceby. *Linc* 4C 88
Wincham. *Ches W* 3A 84
Winchburgh. *W Lot* 2D 129
Winchcombe. *Glos* 3F 49
Winchelsea. *E Sus* 4D 28
Winchelsea Beach. *E Sus* 4D 28
Winchester. *Hants* 203 (4C 24)
Winchet Hill. *Kent* 1B 28
Winchfield. *Hants* 1F 25
Winchmore Hill. *Buck* 1A 38
Winchmore Hill. *G Lon* 1E 39
Wincle. *Ches E* 4D 84
Windermere. *Cumb* 5F 103
Winderton. *Warw* 1B 50
Windhill. *High* 4H 157
Windle Hill. *Ches W* 3F 83
Windlesham. *Surr* 4A 38
Windley. *Derbs* 1H 73
Windmill. *Derbs* 3F 85
Windmill Hill. *E Sus* 4H 27
Windmill Hill. *Som* 1G 13
Windrush. *Glos* 4G 49
Windsor. *Wind* 203 (3A 38)
Windsor Green. *Suff* 5A 66
Windyedge. *Abers* 4F 153
Windygates. *Fife* 3F 137
Windyharbour. *Ches E* 3C 84
Windyknowe. *W Lot* 3C 128
Wineham. *W Sus* 3D 26
Winestead. *E Yor* 2G 95
Winfarthing. *Norf* 2D 66
Winford. *IOW* 4D 16
Winford. *N Som* 5A 34
Winforton. *Here* 1F 47
Winfrith Newburgh. *Dors* 4D 14
Wing. *Buck* 3G 51
Wing. *Rut* 5F 75
Wingate. *Dur* 1B 106
Wingates. *G Man* 4E 91
Wingates. *Nmbd* 5F 121
Wingerworth. *Derbs* 4A 86
Wingfield. *C Beds* 3A 52
Wingfield. *Suff* 3E 67
Wingfield. *Wilts* 1D 22
Wingfield Park. *Derbs* 5A 86
Wingham. *Kent* 5G 41
Wingmore. *Kent* 1F 29
Wingrave. *Buck* 4G 51
Winkburn. *Notts* 5E 86
Winkfield. *Brac* 3A 38
Winkfield Row. *Brac* 4G 37
Winkhill. *Staf* 5E 85
Winklebury. *Hants* 1E 24
Winkleigh. *Devn* 2G 11
Winksley. *N Yor* 2E 99
Winkton. *Dors* 3G 15
Winlaton. *Tyne* 3E 115
Winlaton Mill. *Tyne* 3E 115
Winless. *High* 3F 169
Winmarleigh. *Lanc* 5D 96
Winnal Common. *Here* 2H 47
Winnard's Perch. *Corn* 2D 6
Winnersh. *Wok* 4F 37
Winnington. *Ches W* 3A 84
Winnington. *Staf* 2B 72
Winnothdale. *Staf* 1E 73
Winscales. *Cumb* 2B 102
Winscombe. *N Som* 1H 21
Winsford. *Ches W* 4A 84
Winsford. *Som* 3C 20
Winsham. *Devn* 3E 19
Winsham. *Som* 2G 13
Winshill. *Staf* 3G 73
Winsh-wen. *Swan* 3F 31
Winskill. *Cumb* 1G 103
Winslade. *Hants* 2E 25
Winsley. *Wilts* 5D 34
Winslow. *Buck* 3F 51
Winson. *Glos* 5F 49
Winson Green. *W Mid* 2E 61
Winsor. *Hants* 1B 16
Winster. *Cumb* 5F 103
Winster. *Derbs* 4G 85
Winston. *Dur* 3E 105
Winston. *Suff* 4D 66
Winstone. *Glos* 5E 49
Winswell. *Devn* 1E 11
Winterborne Clenston.
Dors 2D 14
Winterborne Herringston.
Dors 4B 14
Winterborne Houghton.
Dors 2D 14
Winterborne Kingston.
Dors 3D 14
Winterborne Monkton.
Dors 4B 14
Winterborne St Martin.
Dors 4B 14
Winterborne Stickland.
Dors 2D 14
Winterborne Whitechurch.
Dors 2D 14
Winterborne Zelston. *Dors* 3D 15
Winterbourne. *S Glo* 3B 34
Winterbourne. *W Ber* 4C 36
Winterbourne Abbas. *Dors* 3B 14
Winterbourne Bassett.
Wilts 4G 35
Winterbourne Dauntsey.
Wilts 3G 23
Winterbourne Earls. *Wilts* 3G 23
Winterbourne Gunner.
Wilts 3G 23
Winterbourne Monkton.
Wilts 4G 35
Winterbourne Steepleton.
Dors 4B 14
Winterbourne Stoke. *Wilts* 2F 23
Winterbrook. *Oxon* 3E 36
Winterburn. *N Yor* 4B 98
Winter Gardens. *Essx* 2B 40
Winterhay Green. *Som* 1G 13
Winteringham. *N Lin* 2C 94
Winterley. *Ches E* 5B 84
Wintersett. *W Yor* 3D 93
Winterton. *N Lin* 3C 94
Winterton-on-Sea. *Norf* 4G 79
Winthorpe. *Linc* 4E 89
Winthorpe. *Notts* 5F 87
Winton. *Bour* 3F 15
Winton. *Cumb* 3A 104
Winton. *E Sus* 5G 27
Wintringham. *N Yor* 2C 100
Winwick. *Cambs* 2A 64
Winwick. *Nptn* 3D 62
Winwick. *Warr* 1A 84
Wirksworth. *Derbs* 5G 85
Wirswall. *Ches E* 1H 71
Wisbech. *Cambs* 4D 76
Wisbech St Mary. *Cambs* 5D 76
Wisborough Green. *W Sus* 3B 26
Wiseton. *Notts* 2E 86
Wishaw. *N Lan* 4A 128
Wishaw. *Warw* 1F 61
Wisley. *Surr* 5B 38
Wispington. *Linc* 3B 88
Wissenden. *Kent* 1D 28
Wissett. *Suff* 3F 67
Wistanstow. *Shrp* 2G 59
Wistanswick. *Shrp* 3A 72
Wistaston. *Ches E* 5A 84
Wiston. *Pemb* 3E 43
Wiston. *S Lan* 1B 118
Wiston. *W Sus* 4C 26
Wistow. *Cambs* 2B 64
Wistow. *N Yor* 1F 93
Wiswell. *Lanc* 1F 91
Witcham. *Cambs* 2D 64
Witchampton. *Dors* 2E 15
Witchford. *Cambs* 3E 65
Witham. *Essx* 4B 54
Witham Friary. *Som* 2C 22
Witham on the Hill. *Linc* 4H 75
Witham St Hughs. *Linc* 4F 87
Withcall. *Linc* 2B 88
Witherenden Hill. *E Sus* 3H 27
Withergate. *Norf* 3E 79
Witheridge. *Devn* 1B 12
Witheridge Hill. *Oxon* 3E 37
Witherley. *Leics* 1H 61
Withermarsh Green. *Suff* 2D 54
Withern. *Linc* 2D 88
Withernsea. *E Yor* 2G 95
Withernwick. *E Yor* 5F 101
Withersdale Street. *Suff* 2E 67
Withersfield. *Suff* 1G 53
Witherslack. *Cumb* 1D 96
Withiel. *Corn* 2D 6
Withiel Florey. *Som* 3C 20
Withington. *Glos* 4F 49
Withington. *G Man* 1C 84
Withington. *Here* 1A 48
Withington. *Shrp* 4H 71
Withington. *Staf* 2E 73
Withington Green. *Ches E* 3C 84
Withington Marsh. *Here* 1A 48
Withleigh. *Devn* 1C 12
Withnell. *Lanc* 2E 91
Withnell Fold. *Lanc* 2E 90
Withybrook. *Warw* 2B 62
Withycombe. *Som* 2D 20
Withycombe Raleigh.
Devn 4D 12
Withyham. *E Sus* 2F 27
Withypool. *Som* 3B 20
Witley. *Surr* 1A 26
Witnesham. *Suff* 5D 66
Witney. *Oxon* 4B 50
Wittering. *Pet* 5H 75
Wittersham. *Kent* 3C 28
Witton. *Norf* 5F 79
Witton. *Worc* 4C 60
Witton Bridge. *Norf* 2F 79
Witton Gilbert. *Dur* 5F 115
Witton-le-Wear. *Dur* 1E 105
Witton Park. *Dur* 1E 105
Wiveliscombe. *Som* 4D 20
Wivelrod. *Hants* 3E 25
Wivelsfield. *E Sus* 3E 27
Wivelsfield Green. *E Sus* 4E 27
Wivenhoe. *Essx* 3D 54
Wiveton. *Norf* 1C 78
Wix. *Essx* 3E 55
Wixford. *Warw* 5E 61
Wixhill. *Shrp* 3H 71
Wixoe. *Suff* 1H 53
Woburn. *C Beds* 2H 51
Woburn Sands. *Mil* 2H 51
Woking. *Surr* 5B 38
Wokingham. *Wok* 5G 37
Wolborough. *Devn* 5B 12
Woldingham. *Surr* 5E 39
Wold Newton. *E Yor* 2E 101
Wold Newton. *NE Lin* 1B 88
Wolferlow. *Here* 4A 60
Wolferton. *Norf* 3F 77
Wolfhill. *Per* 5A 144
Wolf's Castle. *Pemb* 2D 42
Wolfsdale. *Pemb* 2D 42
Wolgarston. *Staf* 4D 72
Wollaston. *Nptn* 4G 63
Wollaston. *Shrp* 4F 71
Wollaston. *W Mid* 2C 60
Wollaton. *Nott* 1C 74
Wollerton. *Shrp* 2A 72
Wollescote. *W Mid* 2D 60
Wolseley Bridge. *Staf* 3E 73
Wolsingham. *Dur* 1D 105
Wolstanton. *Staf* 1C 72
Wolston. *Warw* 3B 62
Wolsty. *Cumb* 4C 112
Wolterton. *Norf* 2D 78
Wolvercote. *Oxon* 5C 50
Wolverhampton.
W Mid 203 (1D 60)
Wolverley. *Shrp* 2G 71
Wolverley. *Worc* 3C 60
Wolverton. *Hants* 1D 24
Wolverton. *Mil* 1G 51
Wolverton. *Warw* 4G 61
Wolverton. *Wilts* 3C 22
Wolverton Common.
Hants 1D 24
Wolvesnewton. *Mon* 2H 33
Wolvey. *Warw* 2B 62
Wolvey Heath. *Warw* 2B 62
Wolviston. *Stoc T* 2B 106
Womaston. *Powy* 4E 59
Wombleton. *N Yor* 1A 100
Wombourne. *Staf* 1C 60
Wombwell. *S Yor* 4D 93
Womenswold. *Kent* 5G 41
Womersley. *N Yor* 3F 93
Wonersh. *Surr* 1B 26
Wonson. *Devn* 4G 11
Wonston. *Dors* 2C 14
Wonston. *Hants* 3C 24
Wooburn. *Buck* 2A 38
Wooburn Green. *Buck* 2A 38
Wood. *Pemb* 2C 42
Woodacott. *Devn* 2D 11
Woodale. *N Yor* 2C 98
Woodall. *S Yor* 2B 86
Woodbank. *Ches W* 3F 83
Woodbastwick. *Norf* 4F 79
Woodbeck. *Notts* 3E 87
Woodborough. *Notts* 1D 74
Woodborough. *Wilts* 1G 23
Woodbridge. *Devn* 3E 13
Woodbridge. *Dors* 1C 14
Woodbridge. *Suff* 1F 55
Wood Burcote. *Nptn* 1E 51
Woodbury. *Devn* 4D 12
Woodbury Salterton. *Devn* 4D 12
Woodchester. *Glos* 5D 48
Woodchurch. *Kent* 2D 28
Woodchurch. *Mers* 2E 83
Woodcock Heath. *Staf* 3E 73
Woodcombe. *Som* 2C 20
Woodcote. *Oxon* 3E 37
Woodcote Green. *Worc* 3D 60
Woodcott. *Hants* 1C 24
Woodcroft. *Glos* 2A 34
Woodcutts. *Dors* 1E 15
Wood Dalling. *Norf* 3C 78
Woodditton. *Cambs* 5F 65
Woodeaton. *Oxon* 4D 50
Wood Eaton. *Staf* 4C 72
Wood End. *Bed* 4H 63
Woodend. *Cumb* 5C 102
Wood End. *Herts* 3D 52
Woodend. *Nptn* 1E 50
Woodend. *Staf* 3F 73
Wood End. *Warw*
nr. Bedworth 2G 61
nr. Dordon 1G 61
nr. Tanworth-in-Arden 3F 61
Woodend. *W Sus* 2G 17
Wood Enderby. *Linc* 4B 88
Woodend Green. *Essx* 3F 53
Woodfalls. *Wilts* 4G 23

INDEX TO SELECTED PLACES OF INTEREST

(1) A strict alphabetical order is used e.g. Benmore Botanic Gdn. follows Ben Macdui but precedes Ben Nevis.

(2) Entries shown without a main map index reference have the name of the appropriate Town Plan and its page number; e.g. Ashmolean Mus. of Art & Archaeology (OX1 2PH) .... **Oxford 200**
The Town Plan title is not given when this is included in the name of the Place of Interest.

(3) Entries in italics are not named on the map but are shown with a symbol only.
Where this occurs the nearest town or village may also be given, unless that name is already included in the name of the Place of Interest.

SAT NAV POSTCODES

Postcodes (in brackets) are included as a navigation aid to assist Sat Nav users and are supplied on this basis. It should be noted that postcodes have been selected by their proximity to the Place of Interest and that they may not form part of the actual postal address. Drivers should follow the Tourist Brown Signs when available.

ABBREVIATIONS USED IN THIS INDEX

Garden : Gdn. Museum : Mus. Park : Pk.
Gardens : Gdns. National : Nat

T

U

V

W

Y

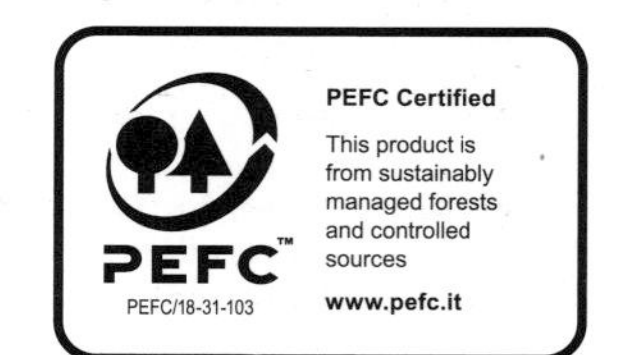

PEFC Certified
This product is from sustainably managed forests and controlled sources
PEFC
PEFC/18-31-103
www.pefc.it

Limited Interchange Motorway Junctions are shown on the mapping pages by red junction indicators [2]

Junction M1

Junction	Direction	Restriction
2	Northbound	No access, exit to A1 only
	Southbound	No exit, access from A1 only
4	Northbound	No exit, access from A41 only
	Southbound	No access, exit to A41 only
6a	Northbound	No exit, access from M25 only
	Southbound	No access, exit to M25 only
17	Northbound	No access, exit to M45 only
	Southbound	No exit, access from M45 only
19	Northbound	Exit to M6 only, access from A14 only
	Southbound	Access from M6 only, exit to A14 only
21a	Northbound	No access, exit to A46 only
	Southbound	No exit, access from A46 only
24a	Northbound	Access from A50 only
	Southbound	Exit to A50 only
35a	Northbound	No access, exit to A616 only
	Southbound	No exit, access from A616 only
43	Northbound	Exit to M621 only
	Southbound	Access from M621 only
48	Eastbound	Exit to A1(M) northbound only
	Westbound	Access from A1(M) southbound only

Junction M2

Junction	Direction	Restriction
1	Eastbound	Access from A2 eastbound only
	Westbound	Exit to A2 westbound only

Junction M3

Junction	Direction	Restriction
8	Eastbound	No exit, access from A303 only
	Westbound	No access, exit to A303 only
10	Northbound	No access from A31
	Southbound	No exit to A31
13	Southbound	No access from A335 to M3 leading to M27 Eastbound

Junction M4

Junction	Direction	Restriction
1	Eastbound	Exit to A4 eastbound only
	Westbound	Access from A4 westbound only
21	Eastbound	No exit to M48
	Westbound	No access from M48
23	Eastbound	No access from M48
	Westbound	No exit to M48
25	Eastbound	No exit
	Westbound	No access
25a	Eastbound	No exit
	Westbound	No access
29	Eastbound	No exit, access from A48(M) only
	Westbound	No access, exit to A48(M) only
38	Westbound	No access, exit to A48 only
39	Eastbound	No access or exit
	Westbound	No access, exit to A48 only
42	Eastbound	No access from A48
	Westbound	No exit to A48

Junction M5

Junction	Direction	Restriction
10	Northbound	No exit, access from A4019 only
	Southbound	No access, exit to A4019 only
11a	Southbound	No exit to A417 westbound
18a	Northbound	No access from M49
	Southbound	No exit to M49

Junction M6

Junction	Direction	Restriction
3a	Eastbound	No exit to M6 Toll
	Westbound	No access from M6 Toll
4	Northbound	No exit to M42 northbound; No access from M42 southbound
	Southbound	No exit to M42; No access from M42 southbound
4a	Northbound	No exit, access from M42 southbound only
	Southbound	No access, exit to M42 only
5	Northbound	No access, exit to A452 only
	Southbound	No exit, access from A452 only
10a	Northbound	No exit, access from M54 only
	Southbound	No access, exit to M54 only
11a	Northbound	No exit to M6 Toll
	Southbound	No access from M6 Toll
20	Northbound	No exit to M56 eastbound
	Southbound	No access from M56 westbound
24	Northbound	No exit, access from A58 only
	Southbound	No access, exit to A58 only
25	Northbound	No access, exit to A49 only
	Southbound	No exit, access from A49 only
30	Northbound	No exit, access from M61 northbound only
	Southbound	No access, exit to M61 southbound only
31a	Northbound	No access, exit to B6242 only
	Southbound	No exit, access to B6242 only
45	Northbound	No access onto A74(M)
	Southbound	No exit from A74(M)

Junction M6 Toll

Junction	Direction	Restriction
T1	Northbound	No exit
T2	Northbound	No access or exit
	Southbound	No access
T5	Northbound	No exit
	Southbound	No access
T7	Northbound	No access from A5
T8	Northbound	No exit to A460 northbound
	Southbound	No exit

Junction M8

Junction	Direction	Restriction
6	Eastbound	No exit, access only
	Westbound	No access, exit only
6a	Eastbound	No access, exit only
	Westbound	No exit, access only
7	Eastbound	No exit, access only
	Westbound	No access, exit only
7a	Eastbound	No access from A725 Northbound only
	Westbound	No access, exit to A725 Southbound only
8	Eastbound	No exit to M73 northbound
	Westbound	No access from M73 southbound
9	Eastbound	No access, exit only
	Westbound	No access, exit only
13	Eastbound	No access from M80 southbound
	Westbound	No exit to M80 northbound
14	Eastbound	No exit, access only
	Westbound	No access, exit only
16	Eastbound	No exit, access only
	Westbound	No access, exit only
17	Eastbound	No exit, access A82 only
	Westbound	No access, exit to A82 only
18	Westbound	No exit, access only
19	Eastbound	No exit to A814 eastbound
	Westbound	No access from A814 westbound
20	Eastbound	No exit, access only
	Westbound	No access, exit only
21	Eastbound	No exit, access only
	Westbound	No access, exit only
22	Eastbound	No exit, access from M77 only
	Westbound	No access, exit to M77 only
23	Eastbound	No exit, access from B768 only
	Westbound	No access, exit to B768 only
25	Eastbound & Westbound	Access from A739 southbound only; Exit to A739 northbound only
25a	Eastbound	Access only
	Westbound	Exit only
28	Eastbound	No exit, access from airport only
	Westbound	No access, exit to airport only

Junction M9

Junction	Direction	Restriction
2	Northbound	No exit, access from B8046 only
	Southbound	No access, exit to B8046 only
3	Northbound	No access, exit to A803 only
	Southbound	No exit, access from A803 only
6	Northbound	No exit, access only
	Southbound	No access, exit to A905 only
8	Northbound	No access, exit to M876 only
	Southbound	No exit, access from M876 only

Junction M11

Junction	Direction	Restriction
4	Northbound	No exit, access from A406 eastbound only
	Southbound	No access, exit to A406 westbound only
5	Northbound	No access, exit to A1168 only
	Southbound	No exit, access from A1168 only
8a	Northbound	No access, exit only
	Southbound	No exit, access only
9	Northbound	No access, exit only
	Southbound	No exit, access only
13	Northbound	No access, exit only
	Southbound	No exit, access only
14	Northbound	No access from A428 eastbound; No exit to A428 westbound
	Southbound	No exit, access from A428 eastbound only

Junction M20

Junction	Direction	Restriction
2	Eastbound	No access, exit to A20 only (access via M26 Junction 2a)
	Westbound	No exit, access only (exit via M26 Jun.2a)
3	Eastbound	No access, exit to A26 only
	Westbound	No exit, access from A26 westbound only
11a	Eastbound	No access from Channel Tunnel
	Westbound	No exit to Channel Tunnel

Junction M23

Junction	Direction	Restriction
7	Northbound	No exit to A23 southbound
	Southbound	No access from A23 northbound

Junction M25

Junction	Direction	Restriction
5	Clockwise	No exit to M26 eastbound
	Anti-clockwise	No access from M26 westbound
Spur to A21	Northbound	No exit to M26 eastbound
	Southbound	No access from M26 westbound
19	Clockwise	No access, exit only
	Anti-clockwise	No exit, access only
21	Clockwise	No exit to M1 southbound
	Anti-clockwise	No access from M1 northbound
31	Northbound	No access, exit only (access via Jun.30)
	Southbound	No exit, access only (exit via Jun.30)

Junction M26

Junction	Direction	Restriction
Junction with M25 (M25 Jun.5)	Eastbound	No access from M25 clockwise or spur from A21 northbound
	Westbound	No exit to M25 anti-clockwise or spur to A21 southbound
Junction with M20 (M20 Jun.3)	Eastbound	No access from M20 westbound
	Westbound	No exit to M20 eastbound

Junction M27

Junction	Direction	Restriction
4	Eastbound & Westbound	No exit to A33 southbound (Southampton); No access from A33 northbound
10	Eastbound	No exit, access from A32 only
	Westbound	No access, exit to A32 only

Junction M40

Junction	Direction	Restriction
3	North-Westbound	No access, exit to A40 only
	South-Eastbound	No exit, access from A40 only
7	N.W bound	No access, exit to M6 only
	S.E bound	No exit, access only
13	N.W bound	No exit, access only
	S.E bound	No access, exit only
14	N.W bound	No access, exit only
	S.E bound	No exit, access only
16	N.W bound	No access, exit only
	S.E bound	No exit, access only

Junction M42

Junction	Direction	Restriction
1	Eastbound	No exit
	Westbound	No access
7	Northbound	No access, exit to M6 only
	Southbound	No exit, access from M6 only
8	Northbound	No exit, access from M6 southbound only
	Southbound	Exit to M6 northbound only; Access from M6 southbound only

M45

Junction	Direction	Restriction
Junction with M1 (M1 Jun.17)	Eastbound	No exit to M1 northbound
	Westbound	No access from M1 southbound
Junction with A45 east of Dunchurch	Eastbound	No access, exit to A45 only
	Westbound	No exit, access from A45 northbound only

M48

Junction	Direction	Restriction
Junction with M4 (M4 Jun.21)	Eastbound	No exit to M4 westbound
	Westbound	No access from M4 eastbound
Junction with M4 (M4 Jun.23)	Eastbound	No access from M4 westbound
	Westbound	No exit to M4 eastbound

Junction M53

Junction	Direction	Restriction
11	Northbound & Southbound	No access from M56 eastbound, no exit to M56 westbound

Junction M56

Junction	Direction	Restriction
1	Eastbound	No exit to M60 N.W bound; No exit to A34 southbound
	S.E bound	No access from A34 northbound
	Westbound	No access from M60
2	Eastbound	No exit, access from A560 only
	Westbound	No access, exit to A560 only
3	Eastbound	No access, exit only
	Westbound	No exit, access only
4	Eastbound	No exit, access only
	Westbound	No access, exit only
7	Westbound	No access, exit only
8	Eastbound	No access or exit
	Westbound	No exit, access from A556 only
9	Eastbound	No access from M6 northbound
	Westbound	No exit to M60 southbound
10a	Northbound	No access, exit only
	Southbound	No exit, access only
15	Eastbound	No exit to M53
	Westbound	No access from M53

Junction M57

Junction	Direction	Restriction
3	Northbound	No access, exit only
	Southbound	No exit, access only
5	Northbound	No exit, access from A580 westbound only
	Southbound	No access, exit to A580 eastbound only

Junction M58

Junction	Direction	Restriction
1	Eastbound	No exit, access from A506 only
	Westbound	No access, exit to A506 only

Junction M60

Junction	Direction	Restriction
2	N.E bound	No access, exit to A560 only
	S.W bound	No exit, access from A560 only
3	Eastbound	No access from A34 southbound
	Westbound	No exit to A34 northbound
4	Eastbound	No exit to M56 S.W bound; No exit to A34 northbound; No access from A34 southbound
	Westbound	No access from A34 southbound; No exit to M56 eastbound
5	N.W bound	No access from or exit to A5103 southbound
	S.E bound	No access from or exit to A5103 northbound
14	Eastbound	No exit to A580; No access from A580 westbound
	Westbound	No access from A580; No exit to A580 eastbound; No access from A580
16	Eastbound	No exit, access from A666 only
	Westbound	No access, exit to A666 only
20	Eastbound	No access from A664
	Westbound	No exit to A664
22	Westbound	No access from A62
25	S.W bound	No access from A560 / A6017
26	N.E bound	No access or exit
27	N.E bound	No exit, access only
	S.W bound	No access, exit only

Junction M61

Junction	Direction	Restriction
2&3	N.W bound	No access from A580 eastbound
	S.E bound	No exit to A580 westbound
Junction with M6 (M6 Jun.30)	N.W bound	No exit to M6 southbound
	S.E bound	No access from M6 northbound

Junction M62

Junction	Direction	Restriction
23	Eastbound	No access, exit to A640 only
	Westbound	No exit, access from A640 only

Junction M65

Junction	Direction	Restriction
9	N.E bound	No access, exit to A679 only
	S.W bound	No exit, access from A679 only
11	N.E bound	No access, exit only
	S.W bound	No exit, access only

Junction M66

Junction	Direction	Restriction
1	Northbound	No access, exit to A56 only
	Southbound	No exit, access from A56 only

Junction M67

Junction	Direction	Restriction
1	Eastbound	Access from A57 eastbound only
	Westbound	Exit to A57 westbound only
1a	Eastbound	No exit, access from A6017 only
	Westbound	No access, exit to A6017 only
2	Eastbound	No exit, access from A57 only
	Westbound	No access, exit to A57 only

Junction M69

Junction	Direction	Restriction
2	N.E bound	No exit, access from B4669 only
	S.W bound	No access, exit to B4669 only

Junction M73

Junction	Direction	Restriction
1	Southbound	No exit to A721 eastbound
2	Northbound	No access from A89 eastbound; No exit to A89 eastbound
	Southbound	No exit to M8 westbound; No access from A89 westbound
3	Northbound	No exit to A80 S.W bound
	Southbound	No access from A80 N.E bound

Junction M74

Junction	Direction	Restriction
1	Eastbound	No access from M8 Westbound
	Westbound	No exit to M8 Westbound
3	Eastbound	No exit
	Westbound	No access
7	Northbound	No exit, access from A72 only
	Southbound	No access, exit to A72 only
9	Northbound	No access or exit
	Southbound	No access, exit to B7078 only
10	Northbound	No exit, access from B7078 only
11	Northbound	No access, exit to B7078 only
	Southbound	No exit, access from B7078 only
12	Northbound	No access, exit to A70 only
	Southbound	No exit, access from A70 only

Junction M77

Junction	Direction	Restriction
Junction with M8 (M8 Jun.22)	Northbound	No exit to M8 westbound
	Southbound	No access from M8 eastbound
4	Northbound	No exit
	Southbound	No access
6	Northbound	No exit to A77
	Southbound	No access from A77
7	Northbound	No access from A77; No exit to A77

Junction M80

Junction	Direction	Restriction
1	Northbound	No access from M8 westbound
	Southbound	No exit to M8 eastbound
4a	Northbound	No access
	Southbound	No exit
6a	Northbound	No exit
	Southbound	No access
8	Northbound	No access from M876
	Southbound	No exit to M876

Junction M90

Junction	Direction	Restriction
1	Northbound	No exit
	Southbound	No Access from A90
2a	Northbound	No access, exit to A92 only
	Southbound	No exit, access from A92 only
7	Northbound	No exit, access from A91 only
	Southbound	No access, exit to A91 only
8	Northbound	No access, exit to A91 only
	Southbound	No exit, access from A91 only
10	Northbound	No access from A912; Exit to A912 northbound only
	Southbound	No exit to A912; Access from A912 southbound only

Junction M180

Junction	Direction	Restriction
1	Eastbound	No access, exit only
	Westbound	No exit, access from A18 only

Junction M606

Junction	Direction	Restriction
2	Northbound	No access, exit only

Junction M621

Junction	Direction	Restriction
2a	Eastbound	No exit, access only
	Westbound	No access, exit only
4	Southbound	No exit
5	Northbound	No access, exit to A61 only
	Southbound	No exit, access from A61 only
6	Northbound	No exit, access only
	Southbound	No access, exit only
7	Eastbound	No access, exit only
	Westbound	No exit, access only

Junction M876

Junction	Direction	Restriction
Junction with M80 (M80 Jun.5)	N.E bound	No access from M80 southbound
	S.W bound	No exit to M80 northbound
Junction with M9 (M9 Jun.8)	N.E bound	No exit to M9 northbound
	S.W bound	No access from M9 southbound

Junction A1(M)

Hertfordshire Section

Junction	Direction	Restriction
2	Northbound	No access, exit only
	Southbound	No exit, access from A1001 only
3	Southbound	No access, exit only
5	Northbound	No access, exit only
	Southbound	No access or exit

Cambridgeshire Section

Junction	Direction	Restriction
14	Northbound	No exit, access only
	Southbound	No access, exit only

Leeds Section

Junction	Direction	Restriction
40	Southbound	Exit to A1 southbound only
43	Northbound	Access from M1 eastbound only
	Southbound	Exit to M1 westbound only

Durham Section

Junction	Direction	Restriction
57	Northbound	No access, exit to A66(M) only
	Southbound	No exit, access from A66(M) only
65	Northbound	Exit to A1 N.W bound and to A194(M) only
	Southbound	Access from A1 S.E bound and from A194(M) only

Junction A3(M)

Junction	Direction	Restriction
4	Northbound	No access, exit only
	Southbound	No exit, access only

A38(M) Aston Expressway

Junction	Direction	Restriction
Junction with Victoria Road, Aston	Northbound	No exit, access only
	Southbound	No access, exit only

Junction A48(M)

Junction	Direction	Restriction
Junction with M4 (M4 Jun.29)	N.E bound	Exit to M4 eastbound only
	S.W bound	Access from M4 westbound only
29a	N.E bound	Access from A48 eastbound only
	S.W bound	Exit to A48 westbound only

A57(M) Mancunian Way

Junction	Direction	Restriction
Junction with A34 Brook Street, Manchester	Eastbound	No access, exit to A34 Brook Street, southbound only
	Westbound	No exit, access only

A58(M) Leeds Inner Ring Road

Junction	Direction	Restriction
Junction with Park Lane / Westgate	Southbound	No access, exit only

A64(M) Leeds Inner Ring Road (continuation of A58(M))

Junction	Direction	Restriction
Junction with A58 Clay Pit Lane	Eastbound	No access
	Westbound	No exit

A66(M)

Junction	Direction	Restriction
Junction with A1(M) (A1(M) Jun.57)	N.E bound	Access from A1(M) northbound only
	S.W bound	Exit to A1(M) southbound only

A167(M) Newcastle Central Motorway

Junction	Direction	Restriction
Junction with Camden Street	Northbound	No exit, access only
	Southbound	No access or exit

A194(M)

Junction	Direction	Restriction
Junction with A1(M) (A1(M) Jun.65) and A1 Gateshead Western By-Pass	Northbound	Access from A1(M) northbound only
	Southbound	Exit to A1(M) only

Northern Ireland

Junction M1

Junction	Direction	Restriction
3	Northbound	No access, exit only
	Southbound	No access, exit only
7	Westbound	No access, exit only

Junction M2

Junction	Direction	Restriction
2	Eastbound	No access to M5 northbound
	Westbound	No exit to M5 southbound

Junction M5

Junction	Direction	Restriction
2	Northbound	No access from M2 eastbound
	Southbound	No exit to M2 westbound

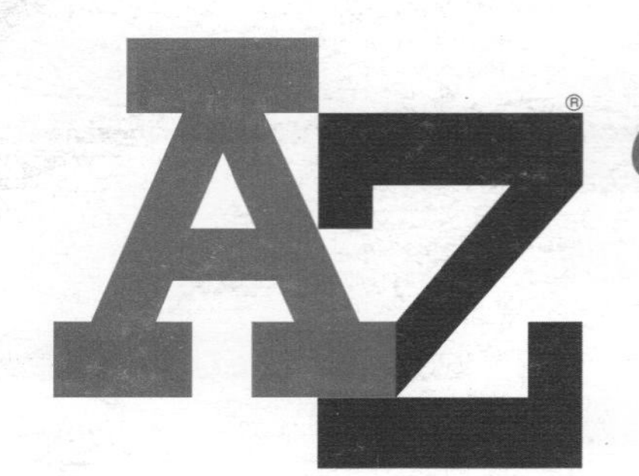

customised **MAP** products

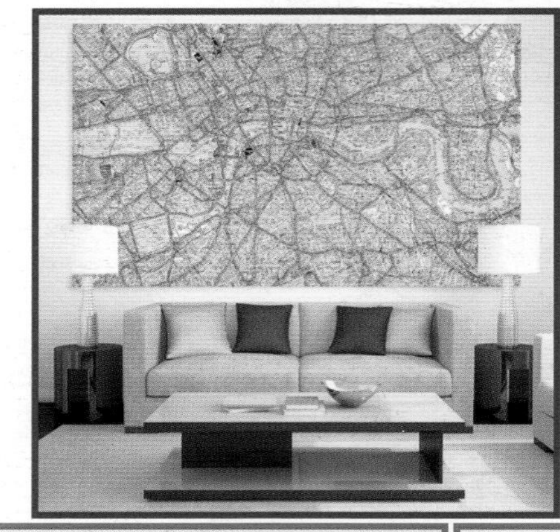

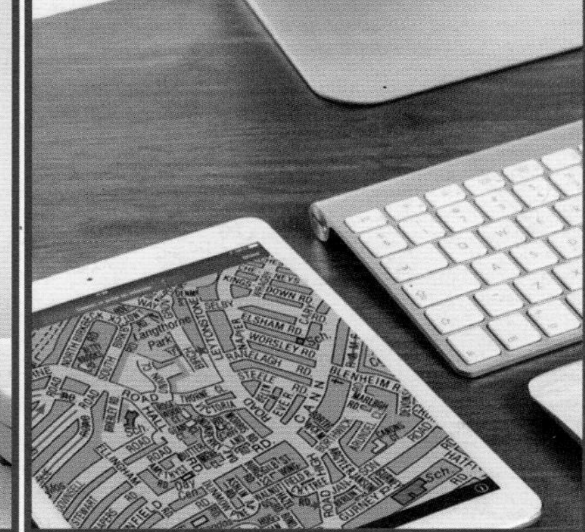

Customised Wall Maps

- Any area and size, designed to your specification. Perfect for display in your office.
- Add logos, company information or have the map in your corporate colours.
- Additional information can be overlaid, such as postcode boundaries or radius rings.
- Choose from a range of mounting types such as Acrylic, Foamex board, wallpaper and many more.

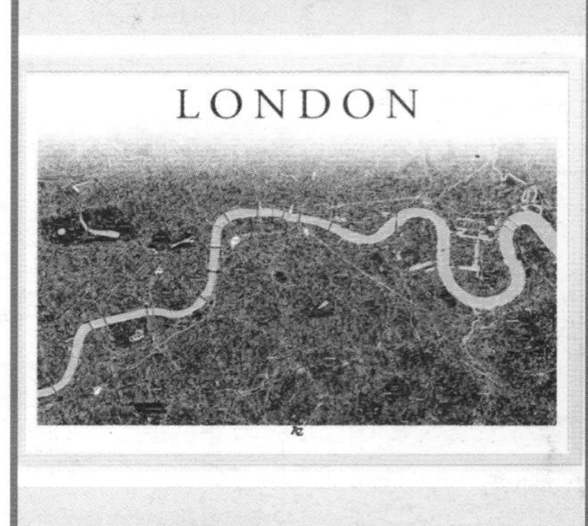

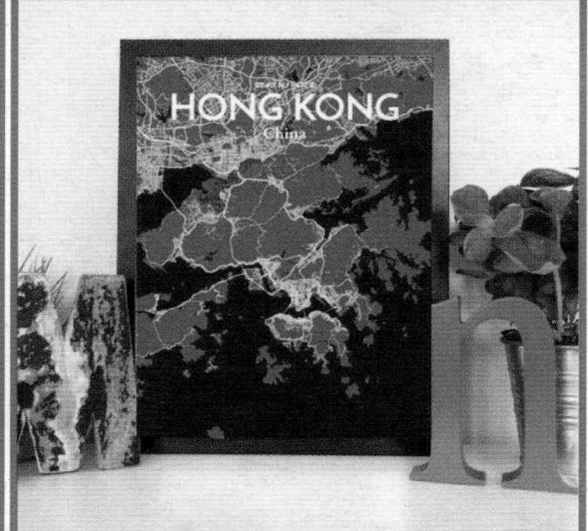

Digital Mapping

- High resolution map data available in a range of scales – road, street and large scale.
- Perfect for use within GIS applications.
- Ideal for large format printing, within brochures or in presentations.
- Mapping can be supplied in full colour, black and white or corporate colours.
- A separate gazetteer of street names and grid references can be supplied to accompany a custom map image.

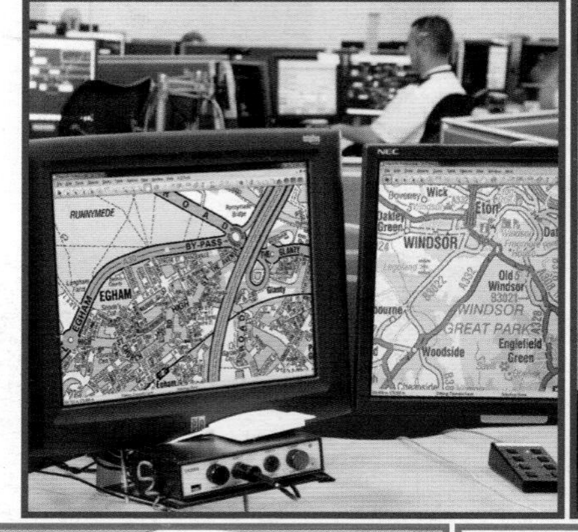

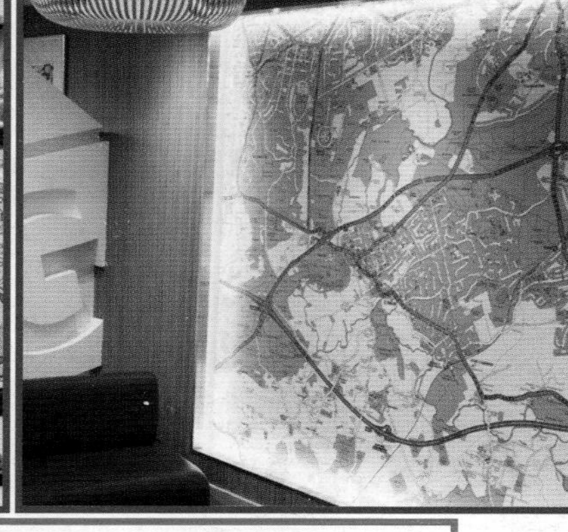

Additional Products

- Posters, which can be framed, covering a range of cities and in a variety of colours.
- Wallpaper: all major cities across the UK are available. Our set size, set area wallpaper makes the perfect feature wall that you won't get bored of.
  For more personalised areas, maybe centred on a location of your choice, please contact us.
- Gifts that are perfect for those special occasions.
- A range of customised gifts.

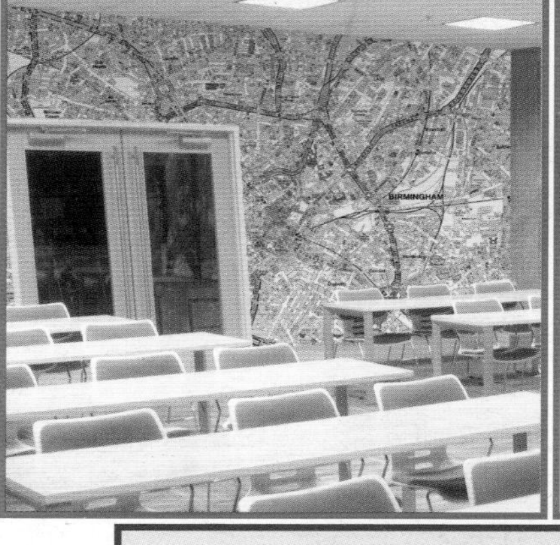

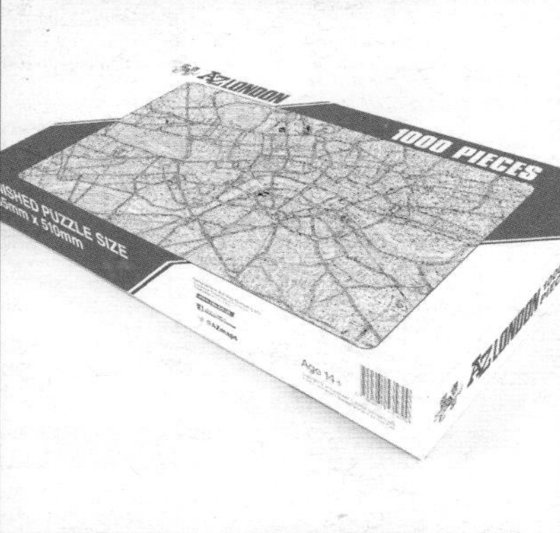

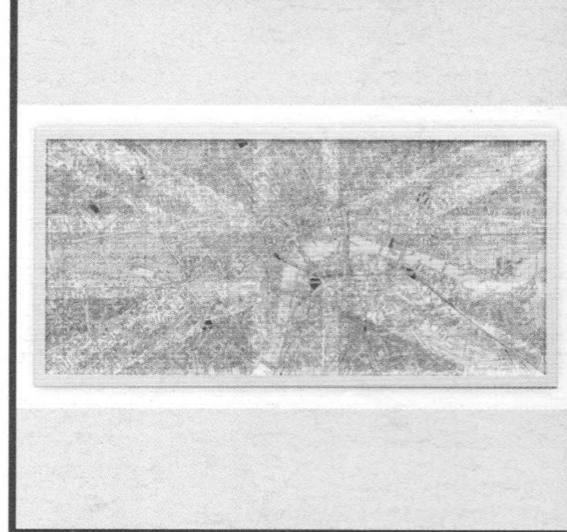

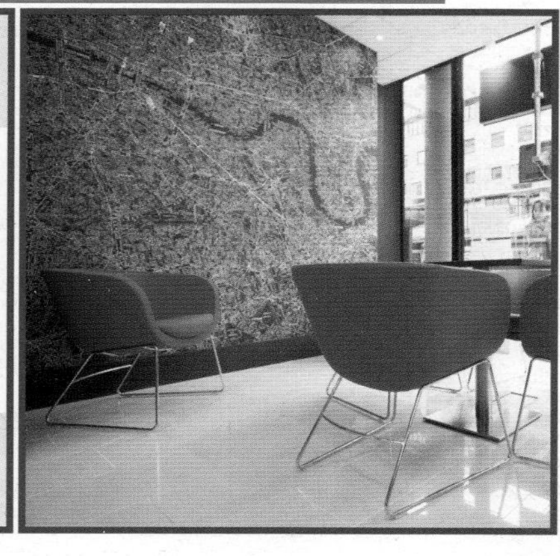

Cartographic Services

Our highly skilled and experienced cartographic services team can modify and interpret geographical data to create products for your business. Working with you on map design and bespoke cartographic projects including advertising material, walking and cycle guides, transport maps, major event publications and information panels.

To discuss your specific map requirements please call us on: 01732 783413 or contact us via our online enquiry form on www.azdigital.co.uk

www./az.co.uk

Control room image based upon a Highways Agency image Licence: CC Attribution 2.0 Generic Licence.